# READER'S DIGEST BOOK OF FACTS

BOOK OF FACTS
was edited and designed by
The Reader's Digest Association Limited
London

First Edition
Copyright © 1985
The Reader's Digest Association Limited
25 Berkeley Square
London W1X6AB

Copyright © 1985
Reader's Digest Association
Far East Limited

Philippines Copyright 1985
Reader's Digest Association
Far East Ltd

Printed in Great Britain

# READER'S DIGEST BOOK OF FACTS

PUBLISHED BY
THE READER'S DIGEST ASSOCIATION LIMITED
London New York Montreal Sydney Cape Town

# CONTENTS

# CONTRIBUTORS

## CONSULTANT EDITOR

Magnus Magnusson
Presenter, BBC TV 'Mastermind' programme

The publishers are grateful for the assistance of Guinness Books in providing access to the information contained in their range of titles.

## WRITERS

Dr Basil Booth, BSc, PhD
Visiting Professor, Iowa State University,
Former UK representative on
UNESCO Volcanic Hazards Committee

Fred Burcombe · Windsor Chorlton · Michael Cross

Professor David Crystal, BA, PhD
Professor of Linguistic Science, University of Reading

Dr A. H. Dickenson
Department of Pharmacology, University College, London

Paul Donovan

Richard Fifield Managing Editor, *New Scientist*

Paul Finch Editor, *Building Design*

Jill Frankham

Dr Paul Freeman, ARCS, DSc, FRES
Former Keeper of Entomology,
British Museum (Natural History)

Ian Gillies, BA (Oxon)
Former BBC 'Brain of Britain' and 'Brain of Brains'

Kelvin Gosnell · Michael Groushko

Jack Hill, BA, BLitt (Oxon)
Lecturer in Literature, University of Essex

Peter Joyce · Dr John Kahn, DPhil

Professor Eric Laithwaite, PhD, DSc, C. Eng, FIEE, FIEEE
Professor of Heavy Electrical Engineering,
Imperial College of Science and Technology, London

David McMillan

Norris McWhirter
Editor and Compiler, *Guinness Book of Records*

Patrick Moore

Dr Venetia Newall, MA, FRGS, FRSA
Hon. Research Fellow in Folklore, University of London,
Editor, *International Folklore Review*

Alan Palmer, MA, MLitt, FRSL · Walt Patterson, MSc

David Pritchard · Dr Ian Ramsay, MD, FRCP

Dr Tessa Richards, MRCP, MRCGP

Ian Ridpath · Patrick Robertson

Theodore Rowland-Entwistle, BA, FRGS, FZS

Nick Russel

Martin Sherwood, BSc, PhD
Former Editor, *Chemistry and Industry*

John Stidworthy, MA
Former Lecturer, British Museum (Natural History)

Dr David Sutton
Department of Botany,
British Museum (Natural History)

Boswell Taylor · Tim Turner · Nigel West

# CONSULTANTS

Dr Peter Adams, BSc, PhD, FGS
Geological Museum, London

Paul Barthaud
Head of Ceramics, Christies

Penny Bateman
Museum of Mankind, London

Dr Ralph Beddard
Faculty of Law,
University of Southampton

Dr Ian Blair
Atomic Energy Research Establishment,
Harwell

Dr Harold Blakemore
Reader in Latin American History,
University of London

Isabel Boucher

Dr D. R. Brooks
History Department,
Queen Mary College,
University of London

Bill Bruce
Meteorological Office, London

A. E. Butcher
Assistant Keeper, Science Museum,
London

James Cameron-Wilson
Deputy Editor, *Film Review*

Vivienne Canter

Fiona Cawsey
Department of Classics, Bedford College,
University of London

Henry Clother
Lecturer in Journalism, City University

William Crampton
Director, The Flag Institute

Dr John Davies
Professor of Social Anthropology,
Kent University

Philip Davies
Lecturer in American Studies,
University of Manchester

Dr C. G. Down, BSc, PhD
Royal School of Mines

Dr Brian Durrans
Deputy Keeper, Museum of Mankind,
London

Dr Martin Dzelzainis
Department of English,
Royal Holloway College,
University of London

Edward England

Dr J. V. Field
Science Museum, London

Dr J. C. Foreman, PhD, MB, BS
School of Medicine, University College,
London

Dr R. Gaita
Department of Philosophy,
King's College,
University of London

Keith Geddes
Deputy Keeper,
Science Museum, London

Dr Catherine Geissler
Department of Nutrition,
Queen Elizabeth College,
University of London

Wilma George
Fellow of Lady Margaret Hall,
Oxford University

Dr G. A. Gledhill
Physics Department, Westfield College,
University of London

Caroline Goodfellow
Bethnal Green Museum of Childhood

Stan Greenberg
Former Sports Editor,
*Guinness Book of Records*

Dr James Harris, MA, PhD, RIBA
School of Architecture,
University of Manchester

J. Henderson
Department of Forestry,
University of Aberdeen

Gordon Higgins
Meteorological Office, London

Clive Holland
Curator,
The Scott Polar Research Institute

Mick Imlah
Editor, *Poetry Review*

Philip Jarrett
Production Editor, *Flight International*

Peter Jones
Lecturer in International Politics,
Reading University

Professor Willem Kleynhans
Department of Political Science,
University of South Africa

Janice Lee
House of Commons Library

Alfred Leutscher, BSc

Dr B. P. Levitt
Department of Chemistry,
Imperial College of Science and
Technology, London

Dr Thomas Long, MA

M. J. Murphy
Lecturer in Population Studies,
London School of Economics

Andrew Nahum
Department of Transport,
Science Museum,
London

D. J. Penn
Imperial War Museum

K. Read

Susanna van Rose, BSc, FGS
Geological Museum, London

Dr Simon Schaffer
Lecturer in History of Science,
Cambridge University

Jacqueline Simpson, MA

Christine Skinner

Mike Stanner
Merseyside Maritime Museum

Miriam Stead
Department of Egyptian Antiquities,
British Museum

Dr David Stickland
Royal Greenwich Observatory

Dr J. Stocks
Royal School of Mines

Dr Oliver Strimpel
Science Museum, London

Martin Suggett
Assistant Keeper,
Physical Sciences Department,
Merseyside County Museums

Gordon Taylor
Royal Greenwich Observatory

Dr W. A. Thomas
Department of Economic and
Business Studies,
Liverpool University

Jonathan Tubb
Department of Western Asiatic
Antiquities,
British Museum

Dr E. R. Valentine
Lecturer in Psychology, Bedford College,
University of London

Dr Alan Williams
Lecturer in Religious Studies,
University of Sussex

Shane Winser
Royal Geographical Society

# FOREWORD

By Magnus Magnusson, Consultant Editor
Presenter, BBC TV Mastermind Programme

*But facts are chiels that winna ding,*
*An' downa be disputed.*

Yes, facts are lads that won't be beat, and cannot be disputed.

That's what Robert Burns, Scotland's national bard, wrote in an ode called *A Dream*, written for the birthday of King George III in 1786.

But facts are not just 'chiels that winna ding'. Facts are also fun. Facts are useful. Facts are the basic building bricks of knowledge – knowledge that is founded upon accurate, reliable information.

In the Reader's Digest *Great Illustrated Dictionary*, the word 'fact' is given four definitions: something known with certainty; something asserted as certain; something that has been objectively verified; and something having real, demonstrable existence.

As far as definitions go, these are impeccable; but I still prefer Robert Burns, because, to Burns, facts were 'chiels' – living things, lads with minds of their own, and determined minds at that. And like all living creatures, they come in all sorts of shapes and sizes and guises: eccentric facts, intriguing facts, entertaining facts, astonishing facts, brazen facts, subtle facts, unexpected facts, dry facts, fat and jolly facts.

In this magnificently readable assemblage of facts, you will find facts about the arts, about people and places, about science and technology, about the Earth and the Universe of which it is part, about the animal kingdom, about plants, about history, about kings and queens, poets and princes.

Did you know that false eyelashes were invented by the film director D. W. Griffith for his 1916 epic *Intolerance*? Did you know that children's teddy bears were named after President Theodore Roosevelt? Did you know that a new-born baby has 300 bones in its body, whereas an adult has only 206? Did you know that the fastest moon in the solar system (Jupiter's tiny 16th moon, discovered only in 1979) travels at more than 113,000km/h (70,000mph)?

All these are facts that 'downa be disputed'. They have been researched, and checked, and re-checked by a team of immensely experienced researchers, editors and contributors, who were always prepared to go back to prime sources rather than just take an alleged 'fact' for granted.

In fact (there I go again!), there is only one fact about this *Book of Facts* which I cannot tell you – the actual number of facts in it! All I know is that each one of its 432 pages is chock-a-block with them.

If you had every single fact in the *Book of Facts* at your fingertips, I'll bet you would come through BBC TV's 'Mastermind' quiz programme with flying colours.

That's a fact. And I should know!

*Magnus Magnusson*

# PEOPLE

# Ancestors of man

## FROM SOUP TO MAN

The emergence of man from the first forms of life in the primordial soup of the oceans, some 3500 million years ago, cannot be traced completely. Few fossils exist from more than 570 million years ago, and in any case early forms of life were soft-bodied and therefore left little or no trace. The first forms of life were undoubtedly single-celled creatures, perhaps not unlike the primitive amoeba of today. From these single-celled creatures, known as protozoans, evolved the multi-celled animals known as metozoans. And from the metozoans developed the chain of species that culminated in man.

## THE SURVIVORS

Man and the other mammals are descended from reptiles that survived a period of huge climatic and geological change some 225 million years ago. This period, which is called the Permo-Triassic catastrophe, lasted for about 85 million years. During it, two-thirds of all marine animal species, three-quarters of all amphibians and four-fifths of all reptiles became extinct. With the competition removed, the reptiles that survived evolved in many directions, but two important groups emerged. They are known as the-codonts and therapsids. The thecodonts evolved into the dinosaurs, which dominated the world for 100 million years. The therapsids – a small group of reptiles which may have been hairy warm-blooded animals – were the forerunners of modern mammals.

After 100 million years of domination most of the dinosaurs vanished about 65 million years ago. Why they vanished is not clear. Continental upheavals may have played a part by changing the environment, but a possible answer is a change in the climate. Cold-blooded reptiles, taking their temperature from the environment, would have been unable to withstand a widespread temperature drop. The mammals – warm-blooded and therefore adaptable to both hot and cold environments – were able to exploit the habitats deserted by the dwindling stocks of reptiles. After millions of years of being subordinate in both numbers and size, probably hiding by day and hunting at night when the reptiles became torpid, the mammals came out into the open and began the huge expansion that has resulted in their present-day supremacy.

## NEW WORLD

No evidence of man's early ancestors has so far been found in either North or South America. Fossil and other remains suggest that the first Americans crossed the Bering Strait (which was then dry land) from Asia between 40,000 and 20,000 years ago. These ancestors of the American Indians were already modern men – *Homo sapiens sapiens*.

## RETURN FROM THE TREES

When Charles Darwin's evolutionary thesis, *The Origin of Species*, was published in 1859, Darwin was pilloried because people thought he was suggesting that man's ancestors might have been tree-dwelling monkeys. In fact, the first mammals, 200 million years ago and long before the apes evolved, lived on the ground. They had developed from reptiles and at first resembled modern, insect-eating animals, such as the hedgehog. It was only later that some of these creatures – the forerunners of the primates – took to the trees because trees provided plenty of food and a degree of safety from predators. Man's earliest primate ancestor probably looked something like the modern, squirrel-like tree-shrew of southern and eastern Asia. Millions of years later, some of the descendants of these tiny creatures once more came down from the trees. The animals that climbed down evolved into man. Those that stayed behind developed, about 40 million years ago, into the monkey family.

## DATING BY VOLCANIC ASH

Volcanoes, as well as destroying life, have also helped to preserve details of the early forms. Three of the most important fossil sites for man's ancestors – the Olduvai Gorge in Tanzania, Lake Turkana in Kenya, and the Lower Omo Valley in Ethiopia – lie in the volcano-studded Great Rift Valley. The best known dating method, known as carbon-14 dating, is wildly inaccurate beyond about 40,000 years and of little use when testing remains millions of years old. But chemical changes that occur in the mineral components of volcanic ash during the heat and pressure of an eruption set in motion a different kind of 'atomic clock': the decay of an isotope of potassium into an isotope of argon. By measuring the isotopes' rate of decay, scientists can date layers of volcanic ash, and thus the human remains that lie buried in or near them.

## IGNORED BECAUSE OF A HOAX

One of the most important finds in the search for man's ancestors was ignored for years because of the Piltdown Man hoax. The Piltdown skull – 'found' in England in 1912 but exposed as a fake only in the 1950s – had purported to show that man's ancestors had large man-like skulls and ape-like jaws. So, in 1924, when Raymond Dart, Professor of Anatomy at Witwatersrand University, found a very different-looking skull at the Taung caves in South Africa, his conclusion that it belonged to an early hominid was dismissed. Only when other bones from the same species – named *Australopithecus africanus* – were discovered did doubts begin to grow about Piltdown Man. Today the species Dart discovered is thought to have lived about 5 million years ago, making it one of the earliest stages in the development of man.

## DRAGON BONE MEDICINE

Nineteenth-century Chinese pharmacists had known for generations that a cave-studded limestone hill outside the village of Zhoukoudian (Choukoutien) near Beijing (Peking) was a rich source of fossil bones, which they ground up to make medicine for their patients. What they did not know was that some of the bones were those of their own ancestors, and about half a million years old. The bones were recognised as human or near-human in 1903, and in the 1920s archaeologists began excavating the site.

In 1927 Davidson Black of the Peking Union Medical College discovered two hominid teeth, and he announced that a new species of primitive man had been discovered: Peking Man. His discovery was confirmed in 1929 with the unearthing of part of a skull. Peking Man is now classified as *Homo erectus*, a man-like species that came immediately before *Homo sapiens* in the evolutionary chain.

## LEMURS, THE LIVING LEGACY

Very few of man's ancestors have survived unchanged down the long corridors of evolution. One that has is the lemur of Madagascar. Developing after the first primates, it is now classified as a prosimian – meaning 'before monkey' – and is one of the common ancestors of both monkeys and men. The prosimians, small insect-eating animals that lived in trees and hunted by night, are known from fossil finds to have flourished from about 60 million to 40 million years ago. They gradually died out in most parts of the world and were replaced by monkeys and apes. In Madagascar, uniquely, they survived in the form of lemurs – thanks to a geological accident which separated the island from Africa at least 30 million years ago and so protected the lemurs from competition.

## NAMED AFTER A CHIMP

A chimpanzee from London Zoo gave its name to a group of ape-like animals that lived 10 – 25 million years ago in Africa. In 1931 the fragmentary remains of a creature thought to be an ancestor of modern chimpanzees were found in Kenya. Arthur Hopwood, of the Natural History Museum in London, suggested that the creature should be given the generic name *Proconsul* – after Consul, one of the chimps then in London Zoo. Several forms of Proconsul fossils have since been found, including, in 1948, a nearly complete skull of a species now known as *Proconsul africanus*. The Proconsul fossil apes are now often included in the genus *Dryopithecus* (from the Greek *drus* meaning 'tree'). The genus is so called because the fossils often occur with oak leaves.

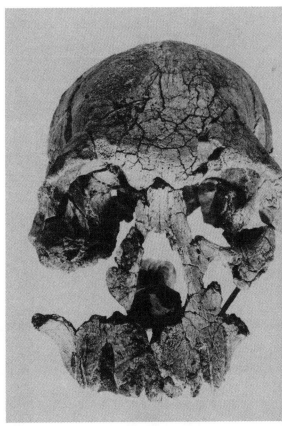

ONE GIANT STEP FOR MANKIND *The world's oldest footprints, one of which is pictured on the left, were made when a group of early man-like creatures walked across a patch of damp volcanic ash near the Olduvai Gorge in Tanzania. The ash later set hard, preserving the prints. Discovered in 1976, they show that man's ancestors were walking upright 3.75 million years ago. By comparison, the world's oldest complete human skull (right), found near Lake Turkana in Kenya, is relatively recent. Known by its museum number as 1470, it is around 2 million years old.*

## OUR RELATIVE, THE STARFISH

Man and other mammals are vertebrates, animals with backbones. And all vertebrates belong to the scientific family called the Chordata, animals with a rod-like structure that supports the body.

The chordates and the echinoderms – creatures such as starfish and sea urchins – diverged into separate evolutionary paths at least 500 million years ago. But scientists believe that both groups descended from a common ancestor – making the starfish one of man's oldest living relatives.

## THE FIRST FIRE

Man and his ancestors, the hominids, have known how to use fire for at least 500,000 years, and man has probably been able to make fire for himself since about 12,000 years ago. The earliest fire was undoubtedly started naturally by lightning, so that the old and widespread religious custom of a 'sacred flame' which was never allowed to go out is likely to be a folk-memory of the days when fire had to be kept alight, because people could not make it for themselves. Peking Man, who lived about 500,000 years ago, seems to have been the first species to make regular use of fire. Charred embers were found with Peking Man's remains in a cave near the Chinese capital in 1929.

## THE LONELY PIONEER

A young 19th-century Dutch anatomist, Eugène Dubois, was the first to establish that early man had lived in Asia as well as Africa. Yet his search for proof was dismissed by orthodox scientists as a waste of time and his finds went unrecognised until after his death.

Dubois went to the island of Sumatra in 1887 to test the theories of Alfred Russel Wallace, a contemporary of Darwin, who had argued that the ancestors of man probably lived in Southeast Asia, home of the highly intelligent orang-utan. At the time the atten-

tion of the academic world was concentrated on finds in Europe, and nobody was prepared to sponsor Dubois on his expedition. So he had to support himself and his family by working as a surgeon for the Dutch East India Army.

Dubois found nothing in Sumatra. But in Java, in 1891, he found the skull of a man-like creature. Later he found a thigh bone as well. It was only after his death in 1940 that the significance of his discoveries came to be recognised. As a result of his work, confirmed by other skulls found in the 1930s and 1940s, scientists now know that the Java Man Dubois found was a specimen of *Homo erectus* (upright man) – a species which is the immediate ancestor of *Homo sapiens* and which lived in Java some time between about 1.5 million and 500,000 years ago.

# THE LONG PATH TO MAN

Of the 4500 million years or so since the Earth's crust formed, man-like creatures have been present for a mere 14 million years – and our own species, *Homo sapiens sapiens*, emerged only 35,000 years ago. The chart below shows the major steps on the evolutionary journey from ape-like primate to man. The drawings are based on fossil

bones, where these exist. But the colour of skin, hair and eyes, and the distribution of hair, are purely speculative. The crucial breakthrough in the evolution of man came when creatures became adapted to standing and walking upright. This freed the hands to develop a distinctively human skill: the ability to use, and make, tools.

RAMAPITHECUS *Fossil remains of this advanced primate, which lived between 14 and 8 million years ago and apparently stood upright, have been found in Africa, the Middle East and Asia. Many scholars regard* Ramapithecus *as man's oldest direct ancestor.*

AUSTRALOPITHECUS *This man-like ape lived in eastern and southern Africa between 5 and 1.5 million years ago. He probably used tools and seems to have walked upright; it was a group of these creatures which left the world's oldest footprints (pictured on page 11).*

HOMO HABILIS *The first true human beings lived in East Africa from about 2 to 1.5 million years ago, overlapping with Australopithecus. Homo habilis (meaning 'Handy Man') is also known as 1470 Man from the museum number of a skull found in Kenya in 1972.*

FLAT FACE
Ramapithecus
had a shorter
muzzle than
other apes, but
its brain size is
unknown.

SMALL BRAIN
*The teeth are
human-like, but
the 500cc brain
was no larger
than a modern
ape's.*

1470 MAN *The
teeth resemble
Australopithecus,
but the brain is
one and a half time
bigger.*

# Prehistoric man

### THE FIRST TECHNOLOGICAL REVOLUTION
The technological revolution of the mid-20th century is not the first. The first took place during the last Ice Age, between 40,000 and 10,000 years ago. Before that period, man had for hundreds of thousands of years made do with the most basic of tool-kits – crude knives, spears and clubs. Then, about 40,000 years ago, an explosion of inventiveness began. Sophisticated tools such as the bow and arrow, chisels,

needles, adzes and spear-throwers (devices which gave extra leverage for throwing spears) began to appear. The great technological leap forward was created by the successors to Neanderthal Man: our own species *Homo sapiens sapiens*.

### THE FIRST METAL-WORKERS
Until recently scholars believed almost universally that the development of metal-working techniques began in Mesopotamia in about 3500 – 3000 BC and

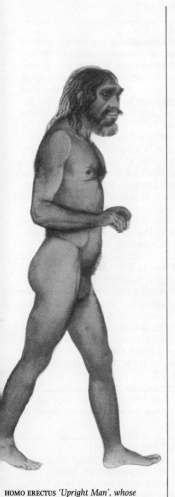

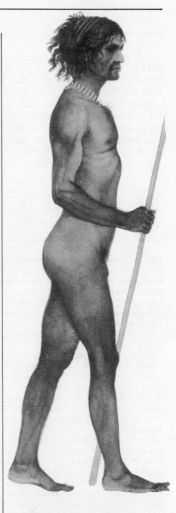

HOMO ERECTUS *'Upright Man', whose remains were first found in Java in 1891, lived in Europe, Asia and Africa between about 1.5 and 0.5 million years ago. He hunted large animals and was the first to use fire for cooking food and for keeping himself warm.*

NEANDERTHAL MAN *This variant of* Homo sapiens *dominated Europe and western Asia between 100,000 and 40,000 years ago, before and during the last Ice Age. But he appears to have been an evolutionary dead end; our own species descended from* Homo erectus.

HOMO SAPIENS SAPIENS *The earliest known remains of our own species, dating from some 35,000 years ago, were found in France, though the species probably developed originally outside Europe. Every human being alive today is a member of this species.*

HEAVY BROW *A thick brow ridge guards a 1000cc brain; by contrast, 1470 Man had a 750cc brain.*

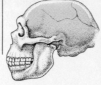

WEAK CHIN *The chin is poorly developed, but the brain, at 1500cc, was larger than modern man's.*

HIGH BROW *The skull of a modern human has space, on average, for a brain of 1400cc.*

spread to the rest of the world from there. However, in 1974 a discovery in Thailand threw doubt on that theory. American and Thai archaeologists working at the village of Ban Chiang in northeast Thailand found graves containing a bronze spearhead, a bronze anklet and bronze bracelets, and the archaeologists believe that the objects date from 3600 BC.

If the date is correct, the find suggests that the Bronze Age was well established in Thailand at that time, several hundred years before it reached a similar stage in Mesopotamia.

### FLOWERS FOR A CAVEMAN'S FUNERAL
A Neanderthal grave found in the 1950s in a large cave near the village of Shanidar in northeastern Iraq contained the body of a man who had been laid to rest 60,000 years ago with bunches of carefully placed flowers: the first time flowers are known to have been used in a funeral ceremony.

Analysis of the pollen grains which are now all that remain of the flowers shows that the cavemen's tributes included cornflowers, hollyhocks, ragwort, grape hyacinths, yarrow and a species of centaurea known as St Barnaby's thistle.

### RITE OF PASSAGE
The ceremonial practice of burying the dead – rather than just leaving them where they fall – is far more ancient than Neanderthal Man's tradition of paying his respects to the dead with flowers. The first known burial took place in a cave at the Chinese village of Zhoukoudian (Choukoutien), just north of Beijing (Peking), about 400,000 years ago. Some scholars see the burial as the first evidence of belief in some form of

afterlife. At a time when human communities were small and scattered, and when scavenging animals would quickly dispose of an abandoned corpse, hygiene cannot, archaeologists believe, have been the reason for burial. So some other factor – a belief in some sort of immortality, perhaps provoked by dreams about the dead person – probably prompted the start of the custom.

### PAINTINGS UNDER STONE
Some prehistoric cave paintings are so old that archaeologists can date them by measuring the thickness of layers of stone that have built up on top of the colours. Flowstone – limestone leached out of the rock by water – builds up on the walls of caves covering portions of the paintings.

It is this substance – which, in thin layers, is semi-transparent – that also forms stalactites on the ceilings of caves and stalagmites on the floors.

The rate at which the layers build up is known and so the minimum age of the paintings can be calculated. Some of the paintings on cave walls in France and Spain are more than 30,000 years old.

### MYSTERY MOUND
Silbury Hill, which lies among the rolling fields of Wiltshire in England, is the largest man-made mound in Europe. According to some of the many legends connected with the flat-topped hill, a life-sized figure of gold, a king in a golden coffin or a man on horseback wearing golden armour is buried there. But excavations have found no evidence that the mound was built as a burial site.

The mound is 40m (130ft) high and covers an area of about 2.2 hectares (5.5 acres). It was built about 4500 years ago in a series of layers covering a group of chalk walls. The chalk walls are arranged like the spokes of a wheel and appear to have been built simply in order to stabilise the mound. Altogether the hill contains about 340,000m³ (12 million cu ft) of turf, earth and chalk rubble. Despite the enormous scale of the achievement and the elaborate design, though, nobody knows why it was built.

### STONEHENGE BEFORE THE DRUIDS
Although Stonehenge is traditionally associated with the Druids, in fact they had no connection with the building of Stonehenge or any other of the Stone Age and Bronze Age structures in Britain. Priests of the Celtic religion, the Druids came to Britain with Celtic invaders in about the 3rd century BC. Stonehenge, on the other hand, was built more than 1000 years before their arrival, in three phases between about 2750 BC and 1300 BC.

The Druids merely used Stonehenge as a temple for sun-worship until their religion was stamped out by the Romans after Britain became a Roman colony in the 1st century AD.

### AUSTRALIA'S FIRST COLONISTS
The ancestors of Australia's Aborigines braved the open sea to colonise Australia at least 30,000 years ago – thousands of years before anyone else is known to have dared to move out of sight of land. At the time, the last Ice Age had locked up vast quantities of water in the polar ice caps, lowering sea levels around the world by more than 90m (300ft).

As a result, Europe (including Britain), Asia, Africa and even the Americas (linked to Asia by a land bridge across the Bering Strait) formed a single vast continent across which early man could, and did, migrate. But Australia (then uninhabited by man and linked to New Guinea) was out on its own, with at least 60km

# HOW CARBON-14 DATING WORKS

Early archaeologists relied on two major techniques for calculating the age of what they found: the principle of stratigraphy – that the remains of earlier generations are covered over by those of their successors; and comparison of styles of, say, pottery to determine whether one influenced and therefore preceded the other. In the 1950s, however, a new technique known as radio-carbon or carbon-14 dating came into use.

Carbon-14 is a radioactive isotope of carbon, which is present in tiny quantities in the atmosphere. Living things such as wood and the bones of living animals absorb this carbon naturally. But when the tree is cut down or the animal dies, the absorption stops and the level of carbon-14 begins to fall as the isotope decays.

**Rate of decay**
Since the level of carbon-14 present in living things is known, and its rate of decay – its half-life – is also known, the age of the object can be worked out by measuring how much carbon-14 is left and comparing it with the original level. Carbon-14 has a half-life of 5700 years, meaning that half of it is converted to non-radioactive carbon in 5700 years, and every 5700 years thereafter half of the remainder is converted. An object with exactly half as much carbon-14 as its living counterpart, therefore, died exactly 5700 years ago.

For many prehistoric objects – bones, for example, or the charred logs of a caveman's campfire – the system is accurate to within a few hundred years. But the margin of error increases with the age of the object, and carbon-14 dating is not at all reliable for anything more than about 40,000 years old. Older fossils are usually dated by means of a similar method known as potassium-argon dating.

(40 miles) of open sea between it and the nearest part of Indonesia (then linked to Asia) – much too far, given northern Australia's flat terrain, for any part of the continent to be visible over the horizon.

Despite the gap, Aborigines are known to have crossed it. The earliest known human remains in Australia are of a woman who was cremated and buried between 25,000 and 30,000 years ago. The remains were found in New South Wales – more than 3200km (2000 miles) from the northern coast – suggesting that the Aborigines had by then already been in the continent for centuries.

The exact date of the Aborigines' first voyage, and the type of boat or raft they used, will probably never be known. The dank tropical coastline on which they probably landed no longer exists. It was drowned by the rising sea at the end of the last Ice Age around 10,000 years ago.

## MAMMOTH EATERS
The cave-dwellers of Predmost in Czechoslovakia were mighty hunters and mammoth eaters. Their rubbish dumps, dating back to between 15,000 and 10,000 BC, have been analysed by modern archaeologists and found to contain the bones of nearly 2000 mammoths, including stacks of neatly sorted tusks and teeth. Mammoths – cold-climate relatives of the elephant, and now extinct – roamed across much of Europe, Asia and North America at a time when the Ice Age had buried most of the northern parts of the continents under vast glaciers.

## THE AGES OF MAN

Scholars divide the long span of prehistory into several ages as a way of describing in shorthand form the dominant features of each set of cultures. The dates they attach to these ages are, however, only approximate. Moreover, since technological developments occurred in different parts of the world at different times, the cut-off dates vary from country to country. The dates shown here are commonly accepted divisions for the prehistory of northwestern Europe.

| | |
|---|---|
| **PALAEOLITHIC AGE** (Old Stone Age) | 300,000 – 8000 BC |
| **MESOLITHIC AGE** (Middle Stone Age) | 8000 – 2700 BC |
| **NEOLITHIC AGE** (New Stone Age) | 2700 – 1900 BC |
| **BRONZE AGE** | 1900 – 500 BC |
| **IRON AGE** | 500 BC – 51 BC (date of publication of Julius Caesar's *Gallic Wars* and beginning of recorded history in northwestern Europe) |

BULL FIGHT *An enraged bison, above, attacks a human figure in a painting created 15,000 years ago. The painting, one of several vivid animal scenes on the walls of a cave at Lascaux in southwest France, was discovered by four boys out walking with their dog on September 12, 1940. The dog disappeared down a hole in the ground and, when the boys went to rescue it, they found a large cavern. They returned the next day with ropes and a light, which revealed what is now regarded as the world's finest collection of prehistoric art.*

STENCIL ART *Scores of hands wave from cave walls in France and Spain. Many of the 35,000-year-old outlines are mutilated – the result of ritual sacrifice, perhaps, or of frostbite in the bitter Ice Age weather.*

15

# Land of the pharaohs

## HAREM FOR A BOY

No other pharaoh of Egypt can compare with Ramesses II for achievement and self-glorification. At the age of ten he was already a captain in the army and had his own harem. By the time he died in 1213 BC, aged over 90, he had ruled for 66 years (longer than Britain's Queen Victoria), fathered 111 sons and 67 daughters, built the exquisite temples of Abu Simbel and added to those at Luxor and Karnak. The great Battle of Kadesh in about 1274, in which he claimed to have subdued the Hittites, is celebrated in a gigantic relief on one of the walls of his mortuary temples on the Nile's west bank at Thebes.

On the obelisk which is now in the Place de la Concorde, Paris, he had his glory described in these words: 'Ramesses, conqueror of all foreign peoples, master of all crown-bearers, Ramesses who fought the millions, bids the whole world subdue itself to his power. . . .' The massive fallen statue of Ramesses at the Ramesseum of Thebes probably inspired English poet Percy Bysshe Shelley's sonnet of faded glory. Called *Ozymandias* (Ozymandias was the Greek rendering of one of the pharaoh's names, User-ma'at-re), the poem ends with the lines:

*'My name is Ozymandias, king of kings;*
*Look on my works, ye Mighty, and despair!*
*Nothing beside remains. Round the decay*
*Of that colossal wreck, boundless and bare,*
*The lone and level sands stretch far away.'*

## RISE AND FALL OF ANCIENT EGYPT

**About 3100 BC** Unification of Upper and Lower Egypt by Menes; invention of hieroglyphic writing.

**About 2650** Imhotep builds the Step Pyramid of Zoser.

**About 2560** Construction of the Giza pyramids and Sphinx.

**2181** End of Old Kingdom; papyrus already in use; civil wars.

**1786** Middle Kingdom collapses in the face of invasions from the east.

**1567** Beginning of New Kingdom as invaders are repulsed.

**About 1450** Egyptian empire extends from Sudan to Syria.

**About 1378** Akhenaten (ruled about 1378–1362), a pharaoh of the 18th dynasty, introduces monotheism, worship of a single god.

**1200–1100** Libyan incursions; decline of the pharaohs' power.

**About 940** Egypt reunited under Libyan kings.

**746** Nubian kings conquer Egypt; Assyria makes incursions and becomes steadily more influential.

**About 620** Psamtik I (ruled about 663–609), a 26th-dynasty pharaoh, breaks with Assyria; Egyptian independence reasserted.

**525** Persian empire absorbs Egypt.

**404** Independence restored.

**341** Persian rule restored.

**332** Alexander the Great conquers Egypt.

**305** Ptolemy I (ruled about 305–285) comes to the throne; library at Alexandria founded.

**285** Ptolemy II (ruled about 285–246) comes to the throne; Pharos lighthouse – one of the seven wonders of the ancient world – built at Alexandria (about 270).

**47** Cleopatra (about 47–30) takes over the throne with the help of Julius Caesar.

**30** Cleopatra commits suicide; Egypt becomes a province of the Roman empire.

## THE SPHINX

The Great Sphinx by the pyramids at Giza, near Cairo, stands 20m (66ft) high, is 73m (240ft) long and was carved from a knoll left from the quarrying of stone for the Great Pyramid – only the paws were carved separately. It dates from the 26th century BC, which makes it the oldest known sphinx in Egypt.

Sphinxes were mythological animals, like the unicorn of northern Europe, and they are found in Mesopotamian and Greek mythology as well as in Egyptian tales. Sphinxes were usually male in Egyptian legends and female in Greek ones. Egyptian sphinxes were often constructed with the body of a lion, the tail of a serpent, a human head and sometimes wings as well, but they could vary: at Karnak, for example, there is an avenue of sphinxes with the heads of rams. Originally, sphinxes were considered by the Egyptians to represent the guardian of the Gates of Sunset, and were erected to protect tombs from intruders. The features of the Great Sphinx are those of the Pharaoh Chephren (Kafre), whose tomb is in one of the three nearby pyramids.

## BIRTH OF THE MUMMY

The word mummy, for the embalmed bodies of Egyptian notables, does not come from Egypt, or even from the Arab world. It is thought to be derived from a Persian word *mummia*, meaning 'bitumen' or 'tar'. Mummies were so named because ancient peoples who came across the age-blackened corpses believed wrongly that the bodies were a source of tar.

## THE HEALING ARTS

Medicine and surgery were both advanced and respected in ancient Egypt – so respected that Pharaoh Atothis is supposed to have written a book on anatomy around 3000 BC. Nine medical treatises have survived. One, the oldest surviving book of surgery in the world, contains details of 48 operations, among them trepanning – boring a hole in the skull to relieve pressure on the brain. Others contain medical advice which is largely based on superstition, but they also list drugs that are still familiar, such as castor oil, wormwood, sodium bicarbonate and arsenic. Egyptian doctors even used adhesive plasters on wounds.

# THREE KINGDOMS OF THE NILE

Egypt before the pharaohs consisted of two countries: Upper Egypt and Lower Egypt. Upper Egypt was the southern part, south of Thebes. Lower Egypt included the Nile delta and the cities of Memphis and Alexandria. The settlement of Egypt seems to have originated in the south, a land of extensive green plains and forests. These turned to desert with a change in climate, and the population gradually moved north up the fertile Nile Valley. Historians divide the history of ancient Egypt into three main periods, or kingdoms. The time between unification of the country in about 3100 BC and the start of the Old Kingdom is known as the Protodynastic Period.

| OLD KINGDOM | 2686–2181 BC |
| --- | --- |
| MIDDLE KINGDOM | 1991–1786 BC |
| NEW KINGDOM | 1567–1085 BC |

The three kingdoms were separated by periods of foreign domination and civil disorder.

## PRESERVING THE DEAD

The first Egyptian mummies date from about 2600 BC, and the practice survived until Muslim Arabs conquered Egypt in AD 641. At its height, around the time of the 21st dynasty of pharaohs (about 1085–945 BC), the most sophisticated techniques of mummification took about 70 days to complete.

The internal organs were first removed through a cut about 100mm (4in) long near the left hip. They were cleaned in wine and spices, and the abdominal cavity was flushed out with cedar oil. The brain was removed by forcing a pointed tool up through the nose and then scraping out the inside of the skull, probably with a small ladle.

Once cleaned, the body and organs were packed in natron – a natural rock salt which was a mixture of washing soda (sodium carbonate) and baking soda (sodium bicarbonate) – to dry them. Then the organs were individually wrapped and replaced in the body, and the cavity was topped up with sawdust, linen, tar or even mud, depending on what was available.

The face and body were restored to a lifelike plumpness by inserting tiny wads of linen under the skin.

Finally each limb, along with the head and torso, was wrapped separately in layers of resin-smeared linen before the body was handed back to the family for burial. This last stage must have taken considerable time. On some mummies that have been unwrapped by modern scholars, the total length of the bandages has been about 2.5km (1.5 miles).

ANIMALS' AFTER-LIFE *Ancient Egyptians preserved the bodies of sacred animals such as cats, ibises and bulls as well as those of humans. This mummified cat dates from about the start of the 1st century AD.*

## TREASURE OF A TEENAGE KING

Almost 2000 fabulous objects, including gold figurines and masks and priceless jewellery, were found when British archaeologist Howard Carter uncovered the tomb of Pharaoh Tutankhamun in November 1922. It was one of the most stunning archaeological finds of all time. Carter, asked what he could see as he peered into the tomb, could only gasp: 'Wonderful things. . . .' Yet Tutankhamun, who died in about 1352 BC at the age of 18 or 19, was only a minor pharaoh. Far more amazing treasures must have been buried with the more important pharaohs. But their larger and more conspicuous tombs were emptied by grave-robbers thousands of years ago.

SEE-THROUGH CLOTHES *Very fine linen – thought to have been as sheer as modern nylon stockings and probably worn by both men and women – was fashionable for centuries in ancient Egypt. This revealingly dressed statue of Selket, a scorpion goddess, was made of gilded wood for the tomb of Tutankhamun in the 14th century BC.*

# Persia: home of the three wise men

## THE FIRST WORLD EMPIRE

The Persian empire reached its greatest extent under Darius I, who seized the throne in 522 BC. It stretched about 4000km (2500 miles) from the River Indus in present-day Pakistan to what is now Benghazi in Libya in the west, and from the Arabian Sea in the south to the Caucasus and Macedonia in the north. This, the first of the so-called 'world empires', covered about 5,000,000km² (almost 2,000,000 square miles), and had a population of 10,000,000.

## THE FIRST SUEZ CANAL

In order to boost trade between Egypt and the Persian Gulf, Darius I ordered the construction of a canal linking the Nile and the Red Sea. In fact, this predecessor of the Suez Canal had been started in around 600 BC by the Egyptian pharaoh Necho, but it was abandoned when only half completed. Darius's workers began completing the canal in about 500 BC and finished the job a few years later, setting up five inscribed stelae – stone slabs – of which four survive.

Darius's canal – which ran along a course similar to the modern Suez Canal, from the Nile Delta through the Bitter Lakes to near the port of Suez – remained in more or less regular use until the 8th century AD. Then part of it was blocked for military reasons – anticipating the similar closures of the Suez Canal in 1956 and 1967 by 12 centuries.

## MEN OF MAGIC

The English word 'magic' comes originally from the Magi, a mysterious Persian priestly clan. A Magus was a person wise in religious matters, and the Magi were probably also scribes and keepers of records. The word magic may have acquired its modern meaning from a branch of the clan which moved to Babylonia and specialised in telling fortunes and working religious 'wonders'. It was three of the Persian Magi, 'wise men from the east', whose journey to visit the infant Christ is described in St Matthew's Gospel.

## CULT OF MYSTERY

One of the main religions in ancient Persia was the cult of Mithras, who was generally portrayed as a man slaying a bull. It was a men-only religion, and several of the ceremonies had parallels with those of Christianity, including baptism with water and the sharing of a sacramental meal. Mithraism later spread to the West and, because of its emphasis on the warrior's virtues of strength and courage, became particularly popular among Roman soldiers.

## GUARDING THE HAREM

The Persian kings had many wives, and even more concubines, kept in a harem guarded by eunuchs. After Cyrus subdued Babylonia in 539 BC, the province had to supply already castrated boys each year to learn their trade as eunuchs. Probably none of the kings had more wives and concubines than Xerxes I, who reigned from 486 to 465 BC and who appears as the amorous King Ahasuerus (the Hebrew version of his name) in the Old Testament book of Esther. It was said that his harem had as many women in it as there were days in the year.

## STORMY CROSSING

When the Persian king, Xerxes I, led an expedition against Greece in 480 BC, he had some of his Egyptian and Phoenician engineers throw two pontoon bridges across the narrow Hellespont Strait to carry his armies over. But a storm wrecked the bridges – and in a fury Xerxes ordered his men to give the Hellespont 300 lashes and to throw a symbolic pair of shackles into the waves. Some accounts say that he also had the waters branded with hot irons to show his displeasure. The engineers were beheaded as well. Their successors, however, kept their heads because the weather improved and the Persians were able to cross safely. At first, the invasion was successful. But after a crushing naval defeat at the Battle of Salamis later that year, Xerxes had to withdraw from Greece.

## LIFE-SAVING REPLY

Cyrus the Great's son, Cambyses, was a hard-drinking man of violent rages. He was also fond of asking people what they thought of him. It was a question that

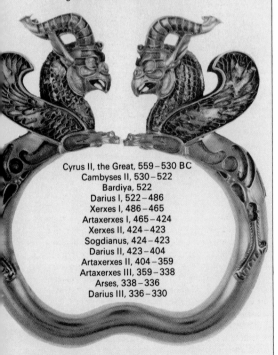

# EMPERORS OF PERSIA

The core of the Persian empire was formed from two kingdoms: the original home of the Persians, known as Fars or Parsa (now in SW Iran); and Media (in NW Iran). The empire began when Cyrus the Great conquered his Median overlord in the 6th century BC. Both the Persians and the Medes were Aryans – the word from which Persia gets its modern name, Iran.

Cyrus II, the Great, 559 – 530 BC
Cambyses II, 530 – 522
Bardiya, 522
Darius I, 522 – 486
Xerxes I, 486 – 465
Artaxerxes I, 465 – 424
Xerxes II, 424 – 423
Sogdianus, 424 – 423
Darius II, 423 – 404
Artaxerxes II, 404 – 359
Artaxerxes III, 359 – 338
Arses, 338 – 336
Darius III, 336 – 330

ROYAL CIRCLE *Golden griffins glare from an armlet that may have been worn by Cyrus the Great. Originally encrusted with stones, the armlet was found in a cache thought to have belonged to a wealthy temple in the former Persian province of Bactria, now part of Afghanistan.*

KING'S HEAD *The Persian empire, toppled by Alexander the Great in 330 BC, was ruled by the Achaemenid dynasty – named after Achaemenes, a 9th-century king of Persia. This marble head depicts one of the Achaemenids, probably either Cyrus the Great, who founded the empire in the 6th century by conquering the neighbouring Medes, or Darius I, who won the throne by murdering the previous king, Bardiya. Darius, the first to style himself 'King of kings', justified his coup by claiming in public notices that Bardiya had been an impostor – an early attempt to rewrite history.*

could cost an undiplomatic vassal his life. But the Greek historian Herodotus, writing in the 5th century BC, reported that at least one courtier, faced with this dangerous question, found a life-saving reply. The courtier is said to have told the king: 'I do not think you are equal to your father; for you do not yet have a son like the son he left behind him in yourself.'

## FLAMES OVER THE PALACE

A hall which could hold 10,000 people was a central feature of Persepolis, the enormous palace complex built by Darius I in what is now southern Iran. Yet the roof of the hall was supported by only 36 pillars. The secret: the roof was made of huge cedar beams from Lebanon, which could support a larger span than was possible with stones. Persepolis – a name

that also came to be applied to the city which grew up around the palace – is a corruption of the Greek name for the palace, *Perseptolis*. The Persians themselves called the palace complex Parsa, after the surrounding province, which was the true Persian homeland. Darius began Persepolis in about 520 BC, and his successors completed it. It remained intact for less than two centuries, however. The wooden-roofed palace was burnt to the ground by the invading troops of Alexander the Great in 331 BC.

## PLEASURE GARDEN

The word 'paradise' comes from an old Persian word for a pleasure garden or a deer park. Not only the king had such gardens: many of the provincial governors, known as satraps, had them too.

# China: behind the Great Wall

## TRESPASSERS WILL BE SHOT

China's first emperor, Qin Shi Huangdi, who died in 210 BC, wanted to make sure that he would not be disturbed in his final resting place. So he had booby traps positioned around his huge burial mound at Mount Li in northwest China. According to the historian Sima Qian, the emperor ordered loaded hair-trigger crossbows to be set up in the passages leading to his tomb and in the undergrowth around the mound.

There was much that needed protecting. Sima Qian also recorded that more than 700,000 men had been conscripted to build the mound and tomb in a project which took 36 years to complete. The imperial treasures buried with the emperor were so valuable that specialist workers who helped to move the riches into the tomb were buried alive to ensure that no details leaked out.

In 1974 a group of astonished peasants sinking a well near Mount Li discovered a number of life-sized terracotta soldiers. These later proved to be part of a buried army of more than 7000 clay figures. Since Emperor Qin Shi Huangdi had been interred, they had maintained their vigil close to the imperial burial mound. Standing in battle formation, complete with life-sized models of chariots and horses, the clay men were wearing armour denoting their different ranks,

GUARD COMMANDER *For more than 2000 years, this stern figure – his rank denoted by his uniform and his 1.95m (6ft 5in) height – commanded an underground army. The army, of more than 7000 life-sized clay soldiers, formed a burial guard for Qin Shi Huangdi, the emperor who had the Great Wall built.*

## CHINESE DYNASTIES

Before the 3rd century BC, China consisted of a number of independent states.

The Chinese empire was founded in 221 BC by Qin Shi Huangdi, who had acquired sufficient strength to defeat his rivals – known as the Warring States – and so establish the first imperial dynasty, Qin.

All the imperial dynasties, and the two major pre-imperial ruling houses, are listed here. Gaps in the sequence of dates mark periods when the country was divided between two or more rulers.

China became a republic under the nationalist leader Sun Zhongshan (Sun Yat-sen) in 1912 after the last of the Manchus was overthrown. It became a Communist state in 1949 under Mao Zedong (Mao Tse-t'ung) after civil war ended in defeat for the nationalists under Jiang Jieshi (Chiang Kai-shek). The nationalists retreated from the mainland, but established an independent state on the island of Formosa (now Taiwan).

Shang, about 1600–1100 BC
Zhou (Chou), about 1100–256
Qin (Ch'in), 221–206
Han, 206 BC-AD 220
Wei, Chin and Northern and Southern, 220–581
Sui, 581–618
Tang, 618–906
Song, 960–1279
Yuan, 1279–1368
Ming, 1368–1644
Manchu (Qing), 1644–1912

GRIN OF DEATH *A toothy smile leers menacingly from the blade of a Shang dynasty axe, found at the entrance to a large tomb in northeastern China. Inside the tomb, built near the end of the Shang period, were the remains of 48 people. Every one had been decapitated.*

and carrying real weapons. Incredibly, after 2000 years in the ground, one of the swords was still sharp enough to split a hair.

## HOW CHINA GOT ITS NAME
China, the world's oldest surviving civilisation, acquired its name in the 3rd century BC. In 221, Cheng, ruler of the small state of Ch'in, from which the country's modern name comes, annexed the last of six rival kingdoms and took the title of Ch'in Shih Huang Ti, meaning 'First August Emperor of Ch'in'.

The Anglicised form of Chinese names has changed since the introduction in 1957 of pinyin, a new system for transliterating Chinese characters into Roman letters. In pinyin Cheng became Zheng, Ch'in became Qin and his title became Qin Shi Huangdi. China itself in pinyin is Zhong Guo.

## FIRST HISTORY BOOK
China's oldest comprehensive written history dates from about 90 BC. Known as the *Shi Ji* ('Historical Records'), it was compiled by Sima Qian, a court astrologer and Grand Scribe, whose father may have begun the work. The *Shi Ji* represents the history of man according to Chinese records from about 1500 to 90 BC. The 130-chapter book became the model for a series of 26 standard histories which continued in unbroken succession down to 1912, when Xuangtong, the last Manchu emperor, abdicated.

## EMPEROR WHO PRESCRIBED DEATH
The price of failure in ancient China could be steep. When the young daughter of the Tang dynasty emperor, Yizong (who reigned from AD 860 to 874), was struck down by fever, 20 leading physicians of China were summoned to the imperial capital, Changan, to minister to her.

Each doctor prescribed a remedy, but none was successful, and the princess died. Consumed with grief and frustration, the emperor had the unfortunate experts beheaded.

## FROM CHINA TO ROME
Ancient China traded with imperial Rome, but the Chinese and the Romans never met. The only link between the two civilisations was the Silk Road, which ran overland around the northern edge of the Hima- layas from China to the eastern Mediterranean coast, with a branch leading south into India. During the 2nd century BC, camel caravans laden with silk, then a Chinese monopoly, began to move regularly along this arduous 11,200km (7000 miles) route. The Chinese themselves did not venture beyond their own frontiers, however.

Instead they transferred their bales of merchandise at a point near the Afghanistan border to other traders, often from Persia or Central Asia. These merchants in turn sold the silk to Syrians and Greeks near the western end of the route, and from there the silk was shipped to Rome.

## BREATH OF LIFE
Treating asthma with ephedrine, a drug derived from the horsetail plant, has been known in the West since the 1920s. But Chinese doctors were using the drug nearly 1700 years earlier. Its use was being advocated by a doctor called Zhang Zhongjing as early as the 2nd century AD.

Zhang, who lived from about AD 152 to 219, wrote a massive compendium of all the medical knowledge then available in China. In addition, he compiled a detailed list of techniques that doctors could use to diagnose a patient's illness.

## TOP MARKS, TOP JOBS
Written examinations were being used to select Chinese civil servants as far back as the 2nd century BC – at a time when government jobs elsewhere in the world were largely filled by the relatives or protégés of those in power.

By the time of the Tang dynasty (AD 618–906), this principle of selecting public officials on the basis of merit had developed into a system of centralised public examinations open to all. A Jesuit missionary, Matteo Ricci, who reached China in 1583, described how the system worked.

Exams lasted several days, he said, and candidates were allowed all day to write their answers. Ricci also reported that the Chinese took enormous trouble to avoid even the possibility of favouritism affecting the examiners' marks. When the exams were over, he said, the completed papers all had to be copied out by another hand in order to conceal the candidate's identity from the examiners.

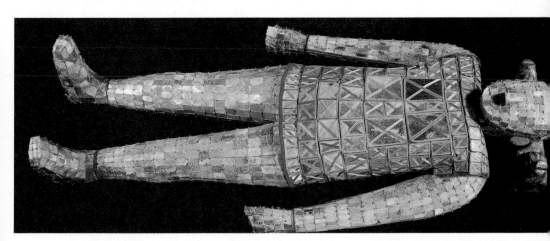

JADE PRINCESS *A burial suit made of 2160 pieces of jade, tied together with gold wire, was intended to preserve forever the body of the Han princess Dou Wan. The princess was the principal wife of Liu Sheng, son of the Han dynasty emperor, Jingdi. She died in about 125 BC, at a time when jade was believed to be an infallible preservative because of its hardness. The prince, who died in about 113 BC, had a suit even more elaborate than his wife's; it contained 2690 polished discs of the highly prized stone. The jade suits were uncovered at Mancheng, about 110km (70 miles) southwest of the capital, Beijing (Peking), in 1968.*

# Mesopotamia: civilisation's cradle

### BABES IN THE WOOD

The life of a Babylonian princess named Sammu-rammat, the most powerful woman in Mesopotamian history, is also the source of a touching children's tale: the Babes in the Wood. As told by the Greek historian Herodotus, Sammu-rammat, who was born in the 9th century BC, married Shamshi-Adad V, king of Assyria. When her husband died in 812 BC, she became regent for her son, helping to establish close political and economic ties between the two neighbouring kingdoms of Babylon and Assyria.

According to a Babylonian myth which grew up later around her life, Sammu-rammat was the child of divine parents who abandoned her, and she was fed by doves until a shepherd found her and took her in. Modern scholars believe that the myth is the direct ancestor of the European fairy tale about the two infants abandoned in a wood.

### FIRST ARCHAEOLOGIST

Nabonidus, king of Babylon from 556 to 539 BC, was one of the world's first archaeologists. Centuries before the modern discipline was invented, he excavated ruined shrines and temples near the city, and restored the great ziggurat (tower) of Ur. He left inscribed cylinders in the foundations for posterity. His daughter, Princess Ennigaldi-Nanna, collected antiques from southern Mesopotamia, which she stored in a temple at Ur – the world's first known museum.

ABRAHAM'S HOME *Ur of the Chaldees, as the Bible calls it, was the home of the Old Testament patriarch Abraham. This mosaic, which appears on a wooden box thought to have been part of a musical instrument, shows a king of Ur at ease with a drink. The box was made in about 2800–2700 BC.*

### COLLAPSIBLE BOATS

Traders in ancient Sumeria, in southern Mesopotamia, devised a simple but ingenious way to make the best use of river transport. Upstream they built boats of hides stretched over light wooden frames. The boats were loaded with whatever cargo was to be shipped, plus a donkey. The boats then floated downstream with the current to their destination.

Once the cargo was unloaded, the boat was dismantled and its frame was sold as well to the timber-poor cities of the south. The crew then loaded the hides on to the donkey and walked back, having saved themselves all the problems of propelling a boat up-river against the current. At the other end they built a new frame, covered it with the old hides and were ready to set off again.

A relief carved on the wall of a palace built at Nineveh in the 7th century BC for the Assyrian king, Sennacherib, shows one of these leather boats carrying stone down the Tigris. Even today, similarly made boats are still used on the Euphrates.

### EARLIEST LIBRARIES

Records of commercial transactions, religious practices, political history, popular legends, government accounts, and mathematical and astronomical discoveries, are by no means isolated survivals from ancient Mesopotamian civilisation. Hundreds of thousands of clay tablets – all covered with the wedge-shaped script known as cuneiform – have survived to the present day, partly because the Sumerians and Babylonians wrote down a great deal, and partly because dry, sun-baked clay is almost imperishable.

Several collections of tablets so numerous that they can only be called libraries have come to light. Excavations at a site called Tell Hariri in northern Syria, begun in 1933, uncovered the archives of the ancient Mesopotamian city of Mari.

The archives contained 23,600 tablets, covering a period of 500 years between 2285 and 1755 BC. Another library, compiled for the Assyrian king Assur-banipal in the 7th century BC, even contained specially commissioned Sumerian and Assyrian grammars and dictionaries, providing scholars with an invaluable key to these ancient languages.

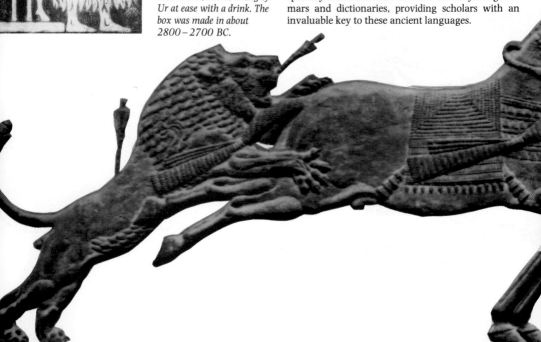

# LAND BETWEEN THE RIVERS

Ancient Mesopotamia's prosperity depended on the rivers Tigris and Euphrates (the name comes from Greek words meaning 'between the rivers'). The rivers irrigated the region, making settled agriculture possible. Farming settlements dating back to about 9000 BC grew by about 3500 into independent, self-governing city-states. Writing, mathematics, astronomy and complex architecture were all developed in Mesopotamia; and the wheel seems to have been first used there.

At times the rulers of individual cities dominated huge territories in the Middle East. The Sumerian city-states, for example, came together under Sargon the Great in the 24th century BC to form the first Mesopotamian empire, setting a pattern of dominance that prevailed in the region for the next 2000 years. Two of the most important cities during this long period were Babylon and Ur.

## BABYLON
Located 90km (55 miles) south of Baghdad on the Euphrates, Babylon was one of the focal points of southern Mesopotamia and capital of the area which has become known as Babylonia. Its first era of magnificence was under Hammurabi in the 18th century BC. The city's fortunes revived under Nebuchadnezzar II, who built the Tower of Babel and the Hanging Gardens in about 600 BC.

## UR
Built on the Euphrates, Ur was founded between 6000 and 5000 BC. It came to prominence as a political, commercial and cultural centre in the 26th century BC, but its political power in southern Mesopotamia was destroyed by the year 2000. Ur remained a major trade centre until it finally fell into ruin in the 4th century BC after the course of the Euphrates changed and river trade by-passed the city.

## OLD ALE
Beer may well have been the most popular drink in Mesopotamia. It was being made from malted barley before 6000 BC and the Sumerians even had a goddess of intoxicating drink called Ninkasi. Clay tablets found in Babylonia record the words of a hymn to her, as well as the words of a drinking song. They also make clear that the Mesopotamians enjoyed variety in their drinking. The tablets list 19 different brews.

## MIDDLE EAST OIL
Mesopotamians were exploiting the Middle East's best-known natural asset – oil – thousands of years before Christ. They probably used natural petroleum, which seeped from the ground in places, as fuel for lamps. They also used the heavier bitumen, or pitch, both for bonding brickwork on buildings and for waterproofing boats. The great city of Ur was discovered in the 19th century under mounds, one of which the Arabs called *Tell al-Mukayyar*, which means 'the mound of pitch'. And the Bible record of the founding of Babylon describes how the builders 'used bricks for stone and bitumen for mortar'.

## THE TOWER OF BABEL
The Book of Genesis tells how the descendants of Noah started to build a tower 'with its top in the heavens'. Some scholars believe that the foundations of the tower – the Tower of Babel – can still be seen on the site of ancient Babylon in southern Iraq.

The tower was not a straight-sided building like a church tower. It was in fact a ziggurat, a stepped pyramid about 90m (300ft) high. It was built during the reign of Nebuchadnezzar II, who ruled Babylon between about 605 and 562 BC. Nebuchadnezzar also built the Hanging Gardens of Babylon, one of the seven wonders of the ancient world. The Babylonians called the tower *Etemenanki*, the 'House of the Foundations of Heaven and Earth'. According to the Greek historian Herodotus, it consisted of eight levels, topped by a temple to the city's paramount god, Marduk. Herodotus reported that in the temple was a bed, which was used for fertility rites. The room might also have been an astrological observatory.

KING'S PREROGATIVE *Only royalty were allowed to kill lions in Assyria. When Assurbanipal (who ruled from 668 to about 627 BC) built a new palace at Nineveh in about 645 BC, he commissioned a series of stone reliefs showing his prowess in the lion hunt to decorate the corridors. Here Assurbanipal spears a charging lion while behind him a wounded lion attacks his spare horse.*

# Japan: people of the rising sun

## CHARACTER REFERENCE

Japan's oldest book, the *Kojiki* (completed in AD 712), describes the nation's history from its mythical origins to about AD 600. The book was written to substantiate the imperial family's claim to be descended from the Shinto sun goddess Amaterasu – the origin of Japan's national symbol, the rising sun.

The book marked a turning point in Japanese culture because it was the first to use Japanese characters (the script known as *kana*). Before the 8th century, Japan made use of Chinese characters because it had no script of its own.

## TEA BREAK

Zen monks introduced the habit of drinking tea from China in the 12th century as a 'cure' for a variety of ailments and also to keep themselves awake while meditating. It later became a stylised ceremony teaching courtesy and tranquillity.

Guests enter the ceremonial room on their knees through a low door and sip green tea from bowls. The precisely defined protocol extends even to the room in which the ceremony takes place. Traditionally the room is square and only about 2.7m (9ft) across.

## THE SHOGUNS

Few Japanese emperors have wielded personal power. Instead a military dictatorship (the shogunate) has ruled in the emperor's name for much of Japan's history. The last of the shogun dynasties was the Tokugawa clan, who for more than 200 years kept Japan in seclusion from the world. The dynasty, whose ruling members are listed here, dominated Japan until 1867, when the emperor Meiji reasserted the power of the throne and abolished the shogunate.

| | |
|---|---|
| Ieyasu, 1603–5 | Ieshige, 1745–61 |
| Hidetada, 1605–23 | Ieharu, 1761–87 |
| Iemitsu, 1623–51 | Ienari, 1787–1838 |
| Ietsuna, 1651–80 | Ieyoshi, 1838–53 |
| Tsunayoshi, 1680–1709 | Iesada, 1853–8 |
| Ienobu, 1709–13 | Iemochi, 1858–66 |
| Ietsugu, 1713–16 | Keiki, 1866–7 |
| Yoshimune, 1716–45 | |

DRESSED FOR COURT *The first Tokugawa chief, Ieyasu – shown in his court clothes – brought internal peace to Japan. He made his base in the port of Edo, which grew into Tokyo.*

## ANCIENT AND MODERN

The 220 sacred wooden buildings at Japan's ancient Shinto shrine at Ise have been pulled down and replaced by identical buildings every 20 years since they were first put up in the 5th century AD. Only unpainted cypress wood is used, and no nails – just dowels and joints. It is thought that the buildings are rebuilt every two decades to symbolise the coming of a new generation. The last rebuilding was in 1973.

## DEATH BEFORE DISHONOUR

Hara-kiri, or ritual suicide, was a custom of the feudal samurai warriors – and, later, of officers in Japan's imperial army – to avoid dishonour or capture by an enemy. Sometimes hara-kiri was committed to show loyalty to a dead or disgraced lord.

The term *hara-kiri* means, literally, 'belly-cutting'. The victim first cut open his own stomach with a short sword or dagger and disembowelled himself. Then he was beheaded by a companion. The ceremony, known formally in Japan as *seppuku*, is still occasionally used as an extreme form of protest. The Japanese novelist and playwright Yukio Mishima committed hara-kiri in 1970 in protest against what he saw as the weakness of post-war Japan.

## GUNSLINGERS

Portuguese traders took guns to Japan in 1543, but 100 years later the government banned them. The traditional sword became the sole weapon of the warrior. And ordinary citizens were forbidden to carry any weapons at all. Only in 1853, when US warships under Commodore Matthew Perry forced Japan to open its ports to foreign traders, were guns allowed into the country again.

## ATISHOO

Paper tissues have been used by the Japanese for more than 300 years. An English traveller in 1637 wrote: 'The Japanese blow their noses with a certain soft and tough kind of paper which they carry about them in small pieces, which, having used, they fling away as a filthy thing.'

## WINDS OF DEATH

Second World War suicide pilots who crashed their bomb-laden planes into enemy ships named themselves *kamikaze* – meaning 'divine wind'. The name was first given to sudden, providential typhoons that helped to destroy the seaborne invading forces of Kublai Khan, the Mongol emperor, in 1274 and again in 1281. The 1281 storm wrecked the enemy fleet after almost two months of fighting, and the stranded invaders were massacred. Not until 1945 did another invading army set foot on Japanese soil.

## ROCKS OF AGES

One of the world's oldest stone gardens was laid out at the Zen temple of Ryoanji in Kyoto in 1490. The garden contains just 15 large stones set apparently at random in a walled area about 21m × 9m (70ft × 30ft) on fine grey-white gravel. The garden is designed to represent nature in the abstract: the stones symbolise islands or mountains; the gravel stands for the sea or trees. The garden contains no plants at all, but the gravel is raked each day.

SAMURAI'S LAST STAND *The 14th-century samurai Kusunoki Masashige killed himself rather than surrender to the enemies of his emperor – and so became a Japanese hero. He committed suicide in 1336 after unsuccessfully defending the capital of the emperor Daigo II against shogun rebels. This print of his last battle was made in 1851.*

## BUSHIDO – THE WAY OF THE WARRIOR

The proud warrior class of the *samurai* (meaning 'those who serve') grew from bands of mercenaries hired by feudal landowners in the 11th century to win them control of Honshu, Japan's main island. These mercenaries lived by the cult of the sword, worshipping athletic prowess and martial skills. They developed a fierce loyalty to their masters and a fearlessness that made them formidable adversaries. They fought in elaborate armour, wielding their most prized possession, a double-edged sabre with which they could cut a man in half.

Later the spartan principles of Zen Buddhism, with its love of nature, softened their fighting zeal. It became fashionable for them to live sparse and frugal lives during the Kamakura era (1192–1333), when the ruling warrior family Minamato moved their seat of power to the eastern city of Kamakura. Confucian thought, with its emphasis on honesty, also influenced the samurai.

### Oriental knights
By the 16th century these principles had become codified into *bushido* (meaning 'the way of the warrior'). First loyalty remained to the samurai lord and to skill with the sword, but the warriors also became an Oriental version of the Christian knights, embracing duty, honour and nobility of spirit. In 1871 the last 400,000 samurai were pensioned off and became *shizoku*, Japanese gentry. Most were absorbed into the civil service and business management. Five years later it became illegal for anyone but the military to wear a sword.

The virtues of the samurai were, however, kept as an ideal for the whole nation to follow, with the emperor as the supreme object of loyalty. This was the key that in times of crisis turned Japanese nationalism into a potent force.

25

# The glory that was India

## RAILROAD INTO HISTORY

Two British railway builders, the brothers John and William Brunton, stumbled unknowingly in the 1850s on the two most ancient cities in the Indian subcontinent: Harappa and Mohenjo Daro. Looking for ballast for the line of the East India Railway in what is now Pakistan, they were led by locals to two earth mounds packed with baked earth bricks.

Unaware of the mounds' importance, the brothers plundered them to make a base of hardcore for their tracks. Near Harappa, William broke up 125,000m³ (164,000 cubic yards) of India's priceless heritage to lay 150km (93 miles) of railway. It was not until the 1920s that archaeologists discovered that the mounds were the remains of a highly developed Indus Valley civilisation dating from 2500 BC.

## DRAIN BRAINS

The town planners of the Indus civilisation built into the city of Mohenjo Daro the world's first known main drainage system – and every house was plumbed into it. Earthenware waste pipes carried sewage from each home into covered channels that ran along the centres of the city's main streets to disposal points away from the city. The drains took waste from kitchens, bathrooms and indoor toilets. The main drains even had movable stone slabs as inspection points.

## FIRST TOWN PLANNERS

The city of Mohenjo Daro, built about 4500 years ago, was no haphazard construction. Its streets were laid  out north-south and east-west in the gridiron fashion used today in many Canadian and US cities. Main streets were about 14m (45ft) wide and side streets about 9m (30ft). The houses were usually 9m (30ft) by 8m (26ft), and most were two storeys high. They had blank walls facing the streets and opened inwards on to courtyards and small alleyways. The walls kept out the heat of the sun and the dust of passing cart traffic.

GODDESS IN CLAY *This terracotta figurine, depicting an ancient Indian mother goddess, was found in the ruins of Mohenjo Daro in the 1920s. It dates from about 2000 BC.*

## UNITED INDIA – A NATION OF DIVISIONS

Between 2000 and 1000 BC settlers from Central Asia arrived in the Punjab and upper Ganges valley. They were lighter-skinned than the local Dravidian people, who originated in the south of India, and became known as Aryans from the Sanskrit word meaning 'noble ones'. The Aryans brought with them an early form of the Hindu religion, and it was probably at this stage that they devised the rudiments of the caste system to maintain their superiority over the Dravidians. From a fairly flexible set of distinctions the caste system has developed in 3000 years into the most complex class system of any society in the world.

Four main castes were formed. They were: the Brahmans, the priest class; the Kshatriyas, who were warriors and rulers; the Vaisyas, who were originally herdsmen and later merchants and farmers; and the Sudras, who served the other three castes and carried out menial tasks. In Hindu teaching, these four classes are said to have been formed from the head (Brahmans), arms (Kshatriyas), trunk (Vaisyas) and feet (Sudras) of the god-creator Brahma.

**Castes within castes**

Over centuries, marriage between the four main castes led to the formation of subdivisions, and these were further subdivided by occupations. By the time India became independent in 1947, there were an estimated 2000 castes within the general framework of the four main classes. The lowest of all was the group known as the Untouchables, or Harijans. They were confined to occupations which were shunned by the higher castes as polluting, such as clearing excrement or handling the dead.

In each caste there were rules of eating, washing and religious conduct, and well-defined laws of contact with other castes. Women, for example, could marry into a caste above that into which they were born, but not below. Today, the government of India is committed to abolishing the caste system. The constitution lays down as a principle of law the equality of all Indians, regardless of caste. And Untouchability has been outlawed altogether.

## FLOOD RIDDLE

The story of life in the twin cities of the Indus civilisation is still being pieced together by scholars and archaeologists. The cities' economy was mostly based on farming and herding, but they also traded and there appears to have been a riverside landing-place at Harappa. They were also potters and toolmakers, working in wood and metal.

The reasons for the sudden collapse of the Indus Valley cities in about 1500 BC are not certain. Military conquest, economic decline or earthquake have all been suggested. The collapse, however, may have been accelerated by a major river flood which washed water and mud over the cities at about that time and drove the inhabitants away.

## MAIDENS IN PERIL

The Lion's Rock at Sigiriya in Sri Lanka, a granite block 180m (600ft) high, was once crowned by a fortified palace built by a Ceylonese king, Kasyapa I, who was killed in AD 495. A man-made path spirals up the rock to its 2 hectare (5 acre) summit.

A small area of plastered rock is still covered with frescoes depicting 21 voluptuous women, known as cloud maidens because clouds usually obscure their lower parts. Poems to these cold, unyielding beauties were scribbled into the plaster between the 8th and 10th centuries AD.

During the Second World War, vibrations from Allied planes taking off near by threatened irreversible damage to the maidens. But the frescoes were saved for posterity by a covering of cotton padding held against the rock face by bamboo scaffolding.

# THE MUGHAL EMPERORS OF INDIA

Indian civilisation goes back to 2500 BC or even earlier. But although some rulers – particularly the Buddhist emperor Ashoka (about 273–232 BC) – came close to dominating the entire subcontinent, it was not until the Middle Ages that all India became a single political unit. The dynasty that established India-wide rule was the Mughal empire – from whose name the English word mogul, for a powerful ruler, is derived. It was founded by Baber, a Muslim descendant of the Central Asian Tartar conqueror Tamerlane (1336–1405), and lasted until India became formally a British colony in 1857. India became independent from British rule in 1947 and has been a republic since 1950.

| | |
|---|---|
| Baber, AD 1526–30 | Farruk-Siar, 1713–19 |
| Humayun, 1530–56 | Mohammed Shah, 1719–48 |
| Akbar the Great, 1556–1605 | Ahmed, 1748–54 |
| Jahangir, 1605–27 | Alamgir, 1754–9 |
| Shah Jahan, 1628–58 | Shah Alam, 1759–1806 |
| Aurangzeb, 1658–1707 | Mohammed Akbar II, 1806–37 |
| Bahadur Shah I, 1707–12 | Bahadur Shah II, 1837–57 |
| Jahandar Shah, 1712–13 | |

## PILLARS OF WISDOM

Lasting exhortations to the people of India to be kind, benevolent and peaceful were carved into huge sandstone pillars and set up throughout the country by the emperor Ashoka (about 273–232 BC). Ashoka – often written as Asoka – was the grandson of Chandragupta (about 321–298 BC) and ruler of the Mauryan dynasty that came to govern much of India from its capital Pataliputra (now Patna) in the northeast of the country. A bloodthirsty campaign to subjugate the state of Kalinga in about 261 BC sickened the victorious Ashoka of war. Full of remorse, he renounced conquest, embraced Buddhism and spent the rest of his life preaching goodness to his people. His pillars – or rock edicts – ordered tree-planting, well-digging, kindness to children and the setting up of hospitals for humans and animals. At the top of each of Ashoka's stone pillars was a stone lion holding the wheel of law, a Buddhist symbol of enlightenment. The same symbol is today part of India's national flag.

BATTLE ROYAL *Fights between trained elephants were a popular spectator sport among the Mughal emperors. Here, Jahangir – the father of Shah Jahan, builder of the Taj Mahal – watches a fight from horseback. The fights ended when one elephant brought the other to the ground, and neither elephant was usually hurt seriously. The* mahouts, *or riders, however, formally took leave of their families before each fight – because they often did not survive.*

# Greece: democracy's birthplace

## RISE AND FALL OF ALEXANDER'S EMPIRE

Alexander the Great created the greatest empire the world had yet seen – and also the shortest lived. He became king of Macedonia in 336 BC at the age of 20, and then subdued the Greek states. Two years later, in 334 BC, he led a large army to conquer Persia. During the next 11 years he conquered an area nearly as large as the United States. His empire extended from Greece and Egypt in the west to beyond the Indus River in the east. When his weary army refused to march further eastwards into India, Alexander retired to Babylon. He died there of a fever in 323 BC, aged 33. The empire he had built in 13 years was broken up as quickly as it had been formed. Within 13 years of his death, the countries Alexander had united were divided again, their territories carved up between his generals.

## CONSULTING THE ORACLE

Delphi was the site of Greece's most important oracle, where the advice of the gods was sought. The answer was given by a *pythia*, a priestess who went into a trance and shouted wildly. Her cries were 'interpreted' by the priests, who gave the answers, often very ambiguous, in doggerel verse.

It is said that Croesus, the king of Lydia in Asia Minor, whose name has become a symbol of wealth, asked the oracle if he should attack the Persian empire. He was told that if he did he would destroy a great empire. Croesus duly attacked in 546 BC and did indeed destroy an empire: his own. Cyrus the Great defeated his army, annexed his kingdom, and took Croesus hostage.

MINOAN LIB *Women in Minoan Crete appear very feminine on this wall-painting from Knossos, dating from about 1500 BC, but they had far greater rights than their contemporaries elsewhere. A woman's dowry remained wholly at her disposal and could not be used by her husband without her permission. Divorce was a right available to women as well as men, and if the husband was shown to be at fault the wife could reclaim any property she had given him during the marriage. Women occupied influential roles in Minoan society, partly because Crete was a maritime nation and the men were away for long stretches at sea.*

## CITY-STATES OF ANCIENT GREECE

Ancient Greece was not a unified nation. Control of the country was divided between a number of independent city-states which often formed shifting alliances with each other or fought to expand or preserve their spheres of influence. These are the major city-states which influenced and sometimes dominated Greek civilisation.

### ARGOS

Founded in prehistoric times. In Homer's poem, the *Iliad*, it was the kingdom of the sailor-warrior Diomedes. Ascendancy challenged by Sparta in 8th – 7th centuries BC. It later periodically sided with Athens against Sparta.

### ATHENS

Founded in prehistoric times. Became the leading city-state in 5th century BC, particularly under the statesman Pericles (about 494 – 429 BC). Defeat by Sparta in 404 BC led to its political decline.

### CORINTH

Founded about 1350 BC. Important industrial and commercial centre in 7th century BC. Alternately supported Athens and Sparta. Looted and destroyed by Romans in 146 BC and rebuilt in 44 BC.

### RHODES

Founded 408 BC. Became the richest city-state through trade. Sided with Rome against the Syrian king Antiochus the Great, who was defeated at Thermopylae in 191 BC. Was later dominated by Rome and its maritime power declined.

### SPARTA

Founded about 1000 BC by Dorian Greeks. Defeated Athens in Peloponnesian War (431 – 404 BC) and became most powerful city-state. It went into decline after its defeat by Thebes in 371 BC.

### THEBES

Founded in prehistoric times. Helped Sparta defeat Athens in 404 BC, then drove the Spartans out of central Greece in 371. Briefly became chief city-state, but in 362 was defeated by a Spartan alliance and destroyed by Alexander the Great in 336 BC.

## END OF THE MINOANS

The Minoan civilisation of Crete, the immediate predecessor of the culture of ancient Greece, came to a sudden and mysterious end in about 1450 BC. Some scholars believe that the Minoans were destroyed by invaders from the Greek mainland. Other scholars, however, think that the disaster was the result of a volcanic explosion on the nearby island of Santorini (formerly Thera), which sent 90m (300ft) high walls of water crashing over Crete. The destruction of the Minoans may have given rise to the legend of the drowned island-continent of Atlantis.

The centre of the Minoan civilisation around the palace of Knossos, which was situated well inland, survived another 75 years. Then, in about 1375 BC, Knossos too was destroyed – by fire.

## A GIFT OF DEMOCRACY

The Greeks gave democracy to the world. The word itself comes from the Greek words *demos*, meaning 'the people', and *kratos*, meaning 'rule'. Greek democracy evolved from the 7th century BC, and it grew out of the mosaic of independent city-states which then covered Greece.

Not all the city-states were democratic. Sparta, for example, was ruled by land-owning aristocrats. But those that were shared more power among more people than any earlier civilisations. The leading democracy was Athens, which overthrew its aristocracy early in the 6th century and under the reformer Solon (about 638 – 559 BC) established a constitution giving supreme power to a citizens' assembly known as the *Ecclesia*. The right to vote at the assembly's meetings in the market-place was by no means universal, however. Only free-born male citizens – about 40,000 people out of a total population of between 300,000 and 400,000 – had the vote. Women, slaves, freed slaves and immigrants were all excluded.

## BORN TO BE SOLDIERS

In the city-state of Sparta the elite male citizens – the Spartiate – were groomed for a life of military service. The Spartan existence began at birth when babies were inspected by the elders, and weak infants were put on a mountainside to die of exposure. From the age of seven, boys were trained in the skills of a soldier. They wore no clothes until they reached the age of 12; then they were allowed one mantle a year. They lived in military barracks up to the age of 30 and moved into clubs until they were 60.

The men were encouraged to marry in order to produce strong and healthy children for the state. But they were not allowed to spend the whole night with their wives. They had to slip out after dinner and then return to the barracks to sleep. Spartan girls also received physical training so that they would give birth to sturdy babies.

All the Spartiate's work – including farming and trading – was done by 'helots': serfs who were owned by the state.

BOUND FOR GLORY *Success in athletics meetings was a passport to fame for the ancient Greeks. Competition was almost always between individuals rather than teams, and a champion could become a hero throughout the Greek world. Statues of him would be made and songs composed about his exploits. Success in the Olympic Games – held every four years between 776 BC and AD 393 at Olympia in the Western Peloponnese – was particularly prestigious. Athens welcomed its Olympic champions with banquets. Some athletes were exempted from paying taxes. Theogenes of Thasos, a wrestler who competed in the Olympic Games for 22 years in the 4th century BC, was so revered that he was declared a descendant of the legendary Heracles (Hercules). The chief events were running, wrestling, boxing, the long jump, throwing the discus, throwing the javelin, and the pankration (a form of all-in wrestling). Many games also included horse and chariot races. This picture of a foot race appears on a jar dating from about 350 BC. Filled with oil from holy olives, the jar was one of the prizes at the Panathenaea, a religious and sporting festival held every year in Athens to celebrate the birth of the goddess Athena. Athletes were traditionally portrayed naked, but many modern scholars believe that they may actually have stripped only for boxing and wrestling.*

29

# The Roman empire

## ETERNAL ROME

At its height in AD 117, the mighty Roman empire was almost as big as Australia, covering an area of around 6,500,000km² (2.5 million square miles). So confident were Romans of the enduring power of their empire that they spoke of their city as *Roma eterna* ('eternal Rome'), and of the Mediterranean as *Mare nostrum* ('our sea').

## WITH THIS RING . . .

Two modern Christian wedding traditions derive from pagan Roman customs. Brides wore wedding rings on the third finger of their left hand because the Romans believed that a nerve led directly from that finger to the heart. And brides were carried over the threshold of their new home to avoid the risk that they might stumble in the doorway or enter left foot first – either was thought to bring bad luck from the gods.

## HIGH-RANKING HORSE

The mad Roman emperor Caligula, who ruled Rome from AD 37 to 41, favoured his stallion, Incitatus, above many men who had proved themselves loyal servants of the state. Incitatus was housed in an ivory stall in a marble stable, with a retinue of slaves to care for him. He wore a jewelled collar, and his blankets were woven of imperial purple – a colour usually reserved for the highest-ranking Romans.

Caligula is thought to have planned to honour Incitatus further by making him a member of the college of priests and then consul, one of the highest offices of state. But Caligula was assassinated in AD 41, and Incitatus was stripped of his privileges.

## WRITING ON THE WALL

The writing and drawing of graffiti is by no means new – it was rife in Roman times. The word graffiti itself is derived from the Latin *graphium*, meaning 'stylus', a pointed instrument for scratching letters on to tablets. Walls in the coastal town of Pompeii, for instance, preserved by ash from the eruption of Vesuvius in AD 79, are still daubed with inscriptions and scribblings of all kinds, from brief election addresses to offers of rewards for the return of stolen property. In addition, there are also obscenities, rude drawings and many complaints from lovers, such as: 'What use to have a Venus, if she is made from marble?'

## LEATHER BIKINI

The wearing of bikinis goes back at least to Roman times. Girls wearing similar two-piece costumes are portrayed on a Roman mosaic which was found in the ruins of a villa near Piazza Armerina in Sicily. The fashion spread as far north as Britain, too. A leather bikini, made by the Romans in the late 1st century AD, was found in a well in London.

BATHING BEAUTY *A painted bikini adorns this statue of Venus from the town of Pompeii. The statue was found in a group of houses which may have been a brothel.*

## NERO THE FIRE-FIGHTER

The story that the emperor Nero (AD 54 – 68) deliberately started the fire which roared through Rome in AD 64 is fiction. When the fire broke out, he was at his villa in Actium, 56km (35 miles) from the city. Far from celebrating the blaze by playing his favourite instrument, the lyre, he raced to the stricken capital to take charge of the fire-fighting – mainly because his new palace was burning down.

The legend appears to have sprung from the resentment that the citizens of Rome felt as a result of Nero's behaviour after the fire. He used the destruction as an excuse to start work on his most ambitious building project – the so-called Golden House – which he intended as a palace fit for a god. Had it been finished, this monumental building would have covered one-third of the entire city.

## FIGHT TO THE DEATH

Public fights between gladiators were among the most popular spectator sports in ancient Rome. The first of these bloody combats was recorded in 264 BC; they continued until they were finally banned by the emperor Honorius (AD 395 – 423) in AD 404. Most battles were fought to the death, and they were held so often that several hundred gladiators were killed in the arena every year. Some of the fighters were volunteers, but most were prisoners of war, slaves, or condemned criminals.

There were several categories of gladiator. The *retiarius* carried a net which he used to entangle his opponent and a trident with which to kill him. The *mirmillo* was armed with a sword, shield and helmet. The *laqueator* was armed with a noose. All were trained in their art in special schools.

## PAGAN FESTIVALS

Roman festivals were a mixture of public holiday and religious ritual. One of the oldest of them was a fertility rite, called the *Lupercalia*, which was celebrated every year on February 15.

The celebrations began with the ritual sacrifice of goats and a dog at the Lupercal, a cave on Rome's chief hill, the Palatine, in which Romulus and Remus, the legendary founders of Rome, were reputedly suckled by a she-wolf.

Two youths, naked except for leather girdles, were smeared with the blood from the sacrifices and then ran around the Palatine hill, carrying thongs cut from the goats' skins. By striking any woman they passed with the thongs, the runners were thought to confer the gift of fertility.

This particular ceremony was known as *februa* ('purification'). It is from this that the name of the month is derived.

## VIRGIN PRIESTESSES

One of the chief rituals in the worship of Vesta, the Roman goddess of the hearth, was keeping a fire burning in her circular temple. This fire was allowed to go out only once a year, on March 1, the Roman New Year's Day.

Tending the fire was the responsibility of six priestesses, the Vestal Virgins. These were girls of noble birth, who were recruited between the ages of six and ten and remained in the service of the goddess for 30 years. During that time they swore to remain chaste, though, at the end of it, they could leave their order to marry if they wished.

Discipline could be severe. For even minor offences a Vestal was liable to be flogged, but if she broke her oath of chastity a worse fate lay in store. She would be taken to an underground room beneath a mound near one of the city gates. There she was given a bed, a lamp and some food. The entrance to the mound was then closed and covered with earth and the unfortunate Vestal was left, in theory, to starve to death. In some cases, however, condemned Vestals were secretly released from their underground tombs, perhaps by their families or lovers.

# EMPERORS OF ROME

The Roman empire was founded in 27 BC by Octavian, the grand-nephew and adopted son of Julius Caesar (100–44 BC) who had become dictator of Rome in 49 BC. Octavian became known as Augustus Caesar on his accession – and the word Caesar is the origin of the German title Kaiser and the Russian title Tsar.

The empire was divided formally into east and west after the death of Theodosius the Great in AD 395. The western empire ended less than 100 years later when the German chieftain Odoacer forced the emperor Romulus Augustulus to abdicate in 476. The eastern half survived under largely Greek rulers as the Byzantine empire until its capital Constantinople (now Istanbul) was conquered by the Turks in 1453.

The list shows the dates of all the Roman emperors between the foundation of the empire and its division. Where dates in the sequence overlap, the title of emperor was shared.

Augustus, 27 BC – AD 14
Tiberius, 14 – 37
Caligula, 37 – 41
Claudius, 41 – 54
Nero, 54 – 68

*Coin from Nero's reign*

Galba, 68 – 69
Otho, 69
Vitellius, 69
Vespasian, 69 – 79
Titus, 79 – 81
Domitian, 81 – 96
Nerva, 96 – 98
Trajan, 98 – 117
Hadrian, 117 – 38

*Coin from Hadrian's reign*

Antoninus Pius, 138 – 61
Marcus Aurelius, 161 – 80
Lucius Verus, 161 – 9
Commodus, 180 – 92
Pertinax, 193
Didius Julianus, 193
Septimus Severus, 193 – 211
Geta, 211 – 12
Caracalla, 198 – 217
Macrinus, 217 – 18
Heliogabalus (Elagabulus), 218 – 22
Severus Alexander, 222 – 35
Maximinus, 235 – 8
Gordianus I Africanus, 238
Gordianus II, 238
Balbinus, 238
Pupienus Maximus, 238
Gordianus III, 238 – 44
Philip the Arab, 244 – 9
Decius, 249 – 51

Hostilian, 251
Trebonianus Gallus, 251 – 3
Aemilian, 253
Valerian, 253 – 9
Gallienus, 259 – 68
Claudius II Gothicus, 268 – 70
Quintillus, 270
Aurelian, 270 – 5
Tacitus, 275 – 6
Florian, 276
Probus, 276 – 82
Carus, 282 – 3
Carinus, 283 – 5
Numerian, 283 – 4
Diocletian, 284 – 305

Maximian, 286 – 305; 307 – 8
Constantius I Chlorus, 305 – 6

SEVERED HEAD *English looters chopped this life-size bronze head of Emperor Claudius I from its body. The looters were probably followers of Boudicca – the queen of the Iceni in East Anglia – who led a revolt against the Romans in AD 6. The head vanished until 1907, when it was found in the River Alde at Rendham in Suffolk.*

Galerius, 305 – 11
Severus, 306 – 7
Maxentius, 306 – 12
Maximinus Daia, 308 – 13
Licinius, 311 – 24
Constantine I the Great, 311 – 3
Constantine II, 337 – 40
Constans, 337 – 50
Constantius II, 337 – 61
Julian the Apostate, 361 – 3
Jovianus, 363 – 4
Valentinian I, 364 – 75
Valens, 364 – 72
Gratian, 375 – 83
Valentinian II, 383 – 92
Theodosius I the Great, 379 – 9
Magnus Maximus, 383 – 7
Eugenius, 392 – 4

*Coin from Constantine the Great's reign*

# South America: land of gold

## SHORT-LIVED EMPIRE

The Inca empire, which grew to control a 4000km (2500 mile) long stretch of the Andes in South America, survived for less than 100 years. Until the reign of Pachacutec Inca Yupanqui (AD 1438–71) the Incas had spent almost 250 years as a small tribal group centred on their capital Cuzco in the Peruvian highlands. Then, after repelling an attack by neighbouring Chanca warriors in 1438, Pachacutec and his successors, Tupa Inca (1471–93) and Huayna Capac (1493–1525), launched a series of campaigns that established Inca rule from present-day southern Colombia through Ecuador and Peru to central Chile, spilling over into Bolivia and Argentina.

The culture gets its name from the word Inca – a shortened form of *Sapa Inca* meaning the 'unique Inca'. The word, which comes from the Quechua term *inka*, meaning 'king', was used as a title by the rulers, who were worshipped as gods. The empire was toppled by a mere 180 men under the Spaniard Francisco Pizarro. Taking advantage of his men's superior firepower, of epidemics introduced by the Spaniards to which the Indians had no immunity, and of divisions among the Incas themselves after a seven-year civil war, Pizarro conquered the whole of the empire within six years of his arrival in 1532.

MUMMIFIED MONARCHS *Inca kings were worshipped even in death. This sketch, from a Spanish chronicle published in about 1610, shows how their mummified bodies were carried out into the main square of the capital, Cuzco, each day. There the corpses were honoured with prayers and the sacrifice of white llamas.*

PIERCING STARE *Funerary masks, placed over the faces of the dead, were a common feature of South American civilisations. This hammered gold mask, painted and decorated with smaller pieces of gold, including two needles jutting menacingly from the eyes, was probably made for a wealthy Chimu nobleman. Found near the Chimu capital of Chan Chan in northwestern Peru, it is thought to date from the early 15th century.*

## ROYAL HABIT

Centuries before cocaine became known in the West, the leaves of the coca plant (*Erythroxylon coca*), from which cocaine is derived, were being chewed by the Incas. Originally reserved for the *Inca* and leading nobles, the habit became general among commoners after the Spanish Conquest. Besides its mood-changing properties, the drug diminishes hunger, increases stamina and counteracts the effects of exertion at high altitudes. It is still widely used by Andean Indians.

## SKULL SURGERY

In the Inca empire, priests doubled as doctors and surgeons and appear to have been able to carry out some sophisticated operations. The remains of some Inca skulls, for instance, show that the priests knew how to perform the operation known as trepanning – cutting a hole in the skull. It is uncertain whether the operation was performed to relieve pressure caused by injury or to release evil spirits, but it seems likely that coca was used as an anaesthetic.

## SAY IT WITH KNOTS

Ignorant of written numbers, the Incas devised an ingenious counting method based on knotted cords, called *quipus*. The system, which is still used by Peruvian peasants, made use of single knots, double knots and slip knots with loops to represent numbers. Different coloured cords identified subjects such as tax and census information, and even historical records.

Official messages were memorised and delivered by relays of runners, or *chasquis*, who could cover 240 km (150 miles) in a single day. In this postal service, established by Pachacutec Inca and made possible by the empire's efficient road network, pairs of *chasquis* were stationed in roadside huts every 3km (1.8 miles). When a runner approached a hut he shouted out his message and a relief *chasqui* took off for the next hut. Complex messages were sent by *quipus*.

## FOOD FROM THE HILLS

Besides flooding Spain with looted wealth – 160 tonnes of gold and 16,000 tonnes of silver by 1650 – the *conquistadores* introduced several new foods to Europe. These included maize, tomatoes, gourds, manioc (cassava), guavas and potatoes. The potato had been cultivated by Andean farmers since at least AD 200. Its English name is derived from the Inca word for the sweet potato, *batata*.

The potato was so important to the Inca diet that they invented a method of freeze-drying to preserve it. Potatoes were left out to freeze for several nights, thawing by day. Softened by repeated freezing and thawing, the vegetables were then squeezed by hand to remove most of their moisture and put out in the sun to dry completely. Finally they reached a stage known as *chuño* in which they could be kept indefinitely. Andean Indians still use this technique.

## THE GOLDEN ROOM

The Inca ruler Atahualpa, backed by thousands of warriors, came face to face with Francisco Pizarro, backed by 180 men and 37 horses, for the first time at Cajamarca in Peru. The encounter was a disaster for the Indians. Pizarro kidnapped Atahualpa, and the demoralised warriors were put to flight by their first experience of firearms and cavalry.

After the kidnap, Atahualpa offered to ransom himself by filling his 7 × 5m (23 × 16ft) cell with gold piled as high as he could reach. He was a tall man and standing on tiptoe could stretch 2.7m (9ft). Atahualpa also offered to fill a smaller room twice over with silver. The Spaniards accepted, but before the ransom had been completely collected they changed their minds, realising that Atahualpa would become the focus of rebellion if he was released. Instead they tried him on several trumped-up charges – accusing him of murdering the former *Inca* Huascar, and plotting to overthrow the Spanish – and sentenced him to death. Atahualpa was garrotted in 1533.

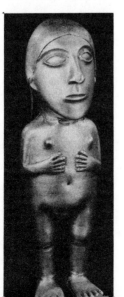

GOLDEN GIRL *The Incas revered gold as 'the sweat of the sun' and silver as 'the tears of the moon'. The Spaniards, however, saw only wealth. This small figurine is one of the very few Inca gold objects to escape being melted down into ingots.*

## INSTANT GALOSHES

Amazonian Indians invented rubber boots many centuries before the Duke of Wellington was born. They dipped their feet and legs in latex, the raw liquid of the rubber trees. The latex formed a tough extra skin, or boot, that protected them from insect bites and thorns.

## MASS MARRIAGES

Marriage by decree was the norm for ordinary people within the Inca empire. Although nobles often had several wives, commoners were limited to one. Furthermore, the state dictated whom and when each commoner could marry. Each year local chiefs assembled all eligible inhabitants (all men over 24, all girls over 18), separating them by sex into lines before calling them up to be paired off.

# PRINCIPAL PRE-COLUMBIAN CIVILISATIONS

The arrival of Europeans in the Americas in the late 15th and early 16th centuries brought to an abrupt end a series of cultures dating back more than 2000 years. These civilisations are known as pre-Columbian from the Italian explorer Christopher Columbus (1451–1506).

### CHAVIN

Earliest highly developed Peruvian culture, existing from about 900 to 200 BC. The Chavins were a farming society composed of several different regional groups. Their capital was the city of Chavin de Huantar in northern Peru.

### NAZCA

Mysterious southern Peruvian culture about which little is known for certain. Thought to have been founded about the time of Christ, but its people had disappeared by the time of the Spanish Conquest. The major evidence for the nature of Nazca culture is a series of enormous figures and designs drawn with lines of pebbles across the coastal desert of southern Peru, which are best seen from the air. The largest design is of a bird; it is about 275m (900ft) long.

### TIAHUANACO

Named after the city of Tiahuanaco, founded in about 800 BC near Lake Titicaca in present-day Bolivia. The city was occupied by a series of five different cultures until about AD 1200. Then it was largely abandoned, for unknown reasons.

### CHIBCHA

Civilisation founded in Colombian highlands and eventually destroyed by Spanish in 16th century. May have inspired the legends of Eldorado.

### MOCHICA

Flourished in northern Peru from about 200 BC to AD 600. Mochica farmers used irrigation systems, built fortifications and developed sophisticated crafts and sculpture.

### CHIMU

Civilisation established on northwest Peruvian coast in about AD 1000. Its capital was the city of Chan Chan, which at its peak had a population of 100,000. Expanded into the Andes under Nancen Pinco after 1370. Conquered in about 1470 by Incas.

### INCA

Last and largest pre-Columbian civilisation in South America. Created vast Andean empire between 1438 and 1532. Destroyed by Spanish *conquistadores* under Francisco Pizarro in 1530s.

# Middle America

## DOUBLE HANDICAP

All the pre-Columbian civilisations of Middle America set up brilliantly organised states and trade systems without two developments considered vital in the Old World. They made no use of the wheel and had no draught animals such as horses or oxen. However, they did have their own form of currency – cacao beans. The absence of practical wheels is all the more remarkable because the principle of the wheel was known in Middle America. Small wheeled clay models of animals – possibly toys or religious offerings – have been found in Mexican tombs dating from around the time of Christ. But although several Middle American peoples, in particular the Mayas, built broad flat roads between their cities, the wheel was never put to any practical use for pottery or transport.

CLAY TOY *The wheel was not put to work in the Americas until the Spanish Conquest. But its principle was known; this clay model was made in Mexico before AD 100.*

## STAR STRUCK

Sky-gazing Mayan priests accurately calculated the 365-day solar year more than 1500 years ago. They broke the year up into 18 months of 20 days each – plus five odd days. Superimposed on the Mayan solar year was a sacred, 260-day calendar used to indicate days of religious ritual. The Mayas had no clocks or telescopes, but they could predict solar and lunar eclipses and calculated the time Venus took to make a complete circuit of the sky to within two hours of the actual figure – 583.92 days.

TEARS AND LAUGHTER
*This Olmec jade of a weeping ld dates from 850 to 150 BC. The smiling figure in terracotta belongs to the Totonac culture. It dates from AD 300 to 800.*

## LONELY EMPIRES OF THE INDIANS

Five sophisticated civilisations flourished in brilliant isolation in Middle America – the term scholars use to describe the area of Central America stretching from Mexico to the northern edge of Nicaragua – over a period of 3500 years. Their first contact with Europe in 1519 was decisive and disastrous. In a few decades their systems were swamped by the invader. It was more than 300 years before archaeologists and scholars began to uncover and discover the richness of the civilisations so carelessly swept aside.

### OLMEC

First of the great ancient Middle American cultures. They dominated the coastal plain along the Gulf of Mexico from about 1200 BC to about 400 BC. They were named *Olmec*, a Nahuatl Indian word meaning 'inhabitant of rubber country', because of the rubber trees that grew there. They began as subsistence farmers, but became brilliant pyramid builders, using clay and earth. Their pyramid at La Venta is 30m (100ft) high. The Olmecs were also great sculptors, carving giant stone heads, some 3m (10ft) tall, and making figurines and animals from jade.

### MAYA

Most enduring of the Middle American civilisations. The Mayas were a recognisable political group as early as 2000 BC in southern Mexico, Guatemala and parts of Belize. Their Golden Age lasted from about AD 250 to AD 900. Their hieroglyphic writing is only partly understood. They were superb astronomers with an accurate calendar and a sophisticated knowledge of mathematics.

### TEOTIHUACAN

City and cultural centre of a trade empire that flourished on Mexico's central plateau from about 300 BC to about AD 750. Archaeological evidence suggests that at its peak (AD 350–600) it had as many as 125,000 inhabitants. Its grid network of streets covered nearly 21km² (8 square miles), making it bigger than imperial Rome. The name Teotihuacan means City of the Gods, and its huge Pyramid of the Sun – which soared, in four great terraces, to a height of 65m (212ft) – is Mexico's most imposing pre-Columbian edifice. The city appears to have been destroyed by Toltecs in about AD 750.

### TOLTEC

A warrior culture based at the city of Tollan (now Tula) 90km (56 miles) north of Mexico City. The Toltecs forged their civilisation from several different ethnic groups. They are believed to have brought about the collapse of Teotihuacan and subsequently ruled central Mexico between AD 900 and 1200. Between 987 and 1185, the Toltecs also ruled the city of Chichén Itzá in the Yucatan peninsula of Mexico.

### AZTEC

An originally nomadic civilisation of warriors from northern Mexico who settled in the island heart of Lake Texcoco and created Tenochtitlan – now Mexico City – in about AD 1200. They conquered central Mexico and imposed worship of their gods, Tezcatlipoca and Huitzilopochtli, on the surrounding agricultural villages. They reached their height under Montezuma II (1502–20), but were conquered by the Spanish under Hernán Cortés in 1519–21.

## WINNER TAKES ALL—FROM THE FANS

Vigorous ball games played in a walled court were a regular part of Mayan and other Middle American religious festivals. Players were apparently not allowed to use their hands, but bounced the solid rubber ball off padded elbows and hips. Injuries seem to have been common, and sometimes fatal. And losing teams were sometimes sacrificed to the gods.

In the Aztec version of the ball game, known as *tlachtli*, the aim was to knock the ball into the opponents' end of the court in much the same way as in modern volleyball. Teams could also win the game outright by knocking the ball through either of two stone rings set on the side walls. Since the rings were often 6m (20ft) off the ground and only just big enough for the ball, goals of this kind were rare. But any player who scored one was allowed to confiscate the clothes and possessions of any spectators he and his friends could catch.

## ROCK OF AGES

The Aztecs believed that there had been four previous creations of the world . . . and that theirs was the fifth and last. They carved this belief into a single stone, the Sun Stone or Calendar Stone, a huge block 3.5m (12ft) across. The stone was dug up in 1790 in the Zocalo, the main square of both ancient Tenochtitlan and the modern capital of Mexico, Mexico City.

In the centre of the stone is carved the sun god, and on the four panels around it are the four previous creations, their once-bright Aztec colours worn away by time. The stone is now in the city's National Museum of Anthropology.

## WELL OF DEATH

Chichén Itzá, last outpost of the Mayan civilisation, was built in the heart of the arid Yucatan peninsula, unlike most of the earlier Mayan cities, which were built in rain forests further south and east. It got its water from two wells, known as *cenotes*, fed by underwater streams. The city folk drank from one well, and used the other as a well of sacrifice. In times of crisis a maiden was hurled at dawn into the 18m (60ft) deep hole in the limestone rock. If she survived in the dark water until midday, priests hauled her out to ask what the gods had told her. The Mayas also threw cherished possessions into the hole. Carved jade, gold, nodules of resin used as incense, copper discs and human skeletons have all been dredged out of it.

## TEMPLES OF BLOOD

Aztecs believed that the sun died every night and needed human blood to give it strength to rise next day. So they sacrificed 15,000 men a year to their fearsome sun god, Huitzilopochtli. Most were prisoners taken in wars which were often started solely to round up sacrificial victims.

## DEATH ROW DELIGHT

A particularly handsome prisoner was chosen each year by the Aztecs as a sacrifice to their chief god, Tezcatlipoca. Tezcatlipoca was the god of matter – and arch-rival of the Aztecs' god of wind and spirit, Quetzalcoatl. For 12 months the prisoner was allowed every luxury. He was taught to play the flute, feasted like a king and paid homage. He spent his last month with four lovely girls. Then he led a great procession to the temple of Tezcatlipoca. Five men held him down over the sacrificial altar and a priest, using a knife of obsidian, a glass-like volcanic stone, cut open his chest and tore out his heart.

## RETURN OF THE WIND GOD

Aztec chiefs fell on their knees in awe and hailed the invading Spaniard Hernán Cortés as a god. By an extraordinary coincidence Cortés had unknowingly fulfilled an ancient Aztec prediction. Priests taught that the wind god Quetzalcoatl, who was both fair and bearded, had been forced into exile across the eastern sea, promising to return in the year One Reed of the Aztec calendar. The bearded Cortés, bent only on conquest and plunder, arrived on the Atlantic coast to begin his invasion of Mexico in 1519 – in Aztec time, the year of One Reed.

TERRACOTTA TRIO *A Mayan woman stares from beneath the arm of a Mayan statuette known as 'The Orator'. On the right is a model of a Zapotec woman in a poncho. All date from about AD 600 to 1000.*

# Key dates in world history

The chart that begins on these pages summarises the most important events in world history since the end of the last Ice Age some 10,000 years ago. From the earliest farming settlements to the present day, it traces on a global scale man's political, social, commercial, scientific and cultural development.

## POLITICS AND WAR 4000–45 BC

### 4000–3000 BC

**3100** AFRICA Egyptian kingdom established under Pharaoh Menes.
**3000** ASIA First city at Troy.

### 3000–2000 BC

**About 2371–2316** ASIA Sargon I of Akkad conquers Sumerians; creates an empire from Syria to SW Persia; and establishes Susa as capital of Persia.
**2300** ASIA Indus river civilisation begins (Mohenjo-Daro, Harappa).
**2230** ASIA End of Akkadian empire. Rise of Sumerian empire (Ur).
**2006** ASIA End of Sumerian empire, fall of Ur to Elamites from SW Persia.
**About 2000** EUROPE First palaces in Crete. Greeks settle in Mycenae, Tiryns.

ETRUSCAN WARRIOR *Skill at metalworking, shown in this bronze figure, 260mm (10in) high, was one of the reasons for the spread of the Etruscan civilisation. It reached its peak in about 550 BC; the figure dates from about 300 BC.*

### 2000–1000 BC

**About 1720** AFRICA Hyksos (Palestinians) invade Egypt and occupy the Nile delta.
**1650–1590** EUROPE Minoan kingdom (Crete) at its height.
**About 1600** ASIA Start of Shang dynasty in China. Fall of Indus valley civilisation in India.
**1567** ASIA/AFRICA 'New Kingdom' of Egypt expels invaders and extends its empire to Nubia and Palestine.
**About 1375** EUROPE Knossos destroyed. Mycenaeans rule Crete.
**About 1250–1150** AFRICA Peoples of the Sea, possibly Mycenaean refugees, attack Egypt; they are defeated (1174) but some settle in Canaan (Philistines).
**About 1200–1150** EUROPE Fall of Mycenaean civilisation in Greece and Crete. Dorians move into Greece.
ASIA Trojan War and fall of Troy.
**1100** ASIA Start of Zhou dynasty in China.

**1010–925** ASIA Kingdom of Israel established under David and Solomon. Divided, after 925, into Israel and Judah.

### 1000–0 BC

**About 814** AFRICA Phoenicians from Tyre found Carthage in Tunisia. Rise of Nubian kingdom of Kush in Sudan.
**753** EUROPE Foundation of Rome by Romulus (legendary).
**745–727** ASIA Tiglath-pileser III of Assyria conquers Babylon, Syria and half Israel.
**722–705** ASIA Sargon II of Assyria continues conquests, extending the Assyrian empire from Lebanon to Iran.
**689** ASIA Babylon destroyed by Sennacherib of Assyria.
**671** AFRICA Assyria briefly conquers Egypt.
**About 650** ASIA Rise of kingdom of Medes in Persia.
**614–612** ASIA Medes allied with Babylon overthrow Assyria and destroy its capital Nineveh.
**About 610** EUROPE Sparta dominates Peloponnese and adopts rigid constitution (Lycurgan laws).
**About 592** EUROPE Solon establishes constitution in Athens.
**587** ASIA Nebuchadnezzar II of Babylon destroys Jerusalem. Many Jews taken captive to Babylon.
**559–530** EUROPE/ASIA Cyrus the Great of Persia establishes Persian empire. Conquers Media (550), Ionian Greek cities, Lydia (547–546) and Babylon (539).
**About 550** EUROPE Etruscans dominate Italy and rule Rome.
**546–511** EUROPE Peisistratus and his sons rule Athens as tyrants.
**538** ASIA Babylonian captivity of Jews ended by Cyrus the Great.
**525** AFRICA Cambyses, king of Persia, conquers Egypt.
**509** EUROPE Tyranny in Athens overthrown, democracy begins. Republic established at Rome, with tribunes introduced as representative of the general citizens (*plebs*) about 500.

To clarify what is an enormously complex story, the key events have been divided in three ways. First, they have been grouped into five broad themes. In order, the themes are: Politics and war; Social and religious history; Exploration and trade; Science, inventions and medicine; and the Arts.

Second, the events have been divided geographically, by continents, so that it is possible to trace easily the developments in any one part of the world, or to make comparisons between different areas. Third, the events have been grouped into periods – sometimes several thousand years long, sometimes as short as a single decade – making it easy to locate any particular period and simplifying comparisons between different fields of human activity.

Additional information about many of the events mentioned here can be found elsewhere in the book. For details, see the index.

**490** EUROPE First Persian invasion of Greece repelled by Athenians at Marathon.
**480–479** EUROPE Xerxes of Persia invades Greece: battles of Thermopylae (Persian victory), Salamis and Plataea (Greek victories). Persians retreat, Ionia freed.
**480** EUROPE Syracuse (Sicily) defeats Carthaginian invasion.
**478** EUROPE Athens forms the Delian League, an anti-Persian alliance which becomes nucleus of Athenian empire (460 onwards).
**461–430** EUROPE Pericles (died 429), leading statesman in Athens.
**449** EUROPE/ASIA Peace treaty between Persia and Greece.
**431–421** EUROPE Peloponnesian War; first stage, primarily between Athens and Sparta, ends in Peace of Nicias.

GIANT-KILLERS *War galleys like this one were part of the Spartan fleet which destroyed the Athenian navy in 413 BC during the second Peloponnesian War.*

**415–404** EUROPE Peloponnesian War, second stage. Athenian expedition against Syracuse (Sicily) fails. Sparta invades and defeats Athens, destroying Athenian navy and the city's walls; Sparta dominates Greece (until 371).

**404** AFRICA Egypt regains independence from Persia.
**403** EUROPE Democracy restored in Athens.
ASIA Warring States epoch begins in China.
**390** EUROPE Rome, head of Latin League, destroyed by Gauls under Brennus.
**371** EUROPE City of Thebes defeats Sparta at Leuctra and leads Greece.
**357** EUROPE Philip II of Macedon begins campaign to rule Greece.
**341** ASIA Persia reconquers Egypt.
**338** EUROPE Philip of Macedon defeats Greeks at Chaeronea, elected leader for war against Persia. Rome heads federation of central Italy.
**336** EUROPE Philip of Macedon murdered at the instigation of his wife; succeeded by Alexander the Great.
**334–330** ASIA Alexander invades Persia and defeats King Darius.
**332–331** ASIA/AFRICA Alexander conquers Egypt and Tyre, founds Alexandria.
**331–326** ASIA Alexander conquers Bactria (Turkestan, N Afghanistan), and invades NW India.
**323** ASIA Alexander dies at Babylon; heirs and generals fight among themselves for 20 years.
**321** ASIA Chandragupta founds Maurya dynasty in N India and expels Greeks.
**305** ASIA/AFRICA Alexander's generals divide empire. Ptolemy I (Egypt) and Seleucus I (Syria) found dynasties with Alexandria and Antioch as capitals. Bactria becomes independent Greek kingdom.
**By 280** EUROPE Rome, having defeated Etruscans and Samnites, dominates all Italy, except Greek cities in the south.

**280–275** EUROPE Pyrrhus, king of Epirus, attacks S Italy and Sicily; but is forced to withdraw despite several victories over Romans. Rome dominates all Italy.
**273** ASIA Ashoka rules two-thirds of the Indian subcontinent. He becomes a Buddhist (261).
**264–241** EUROPE/AFRICA Rome defeats Carthage in first Punic War, and acquires Sicily as its first province.
**From 221** ASIA Qin (Ch'in) dynasty unites China; Great Wall started.
**218–202** EUROPE/AFRICA Second Punic War: Hannibal of Carthage crosses Alps, defeats Romans (notably at Cannae, 216) but finally defeated by Scipio Africanus in modern Algeria.
**206** ASIA Han dynasty begins in China.
**202** EUROPE/AFRICA Carthage disarmed. Spain becomes a Roman province.
**163** ASIA Jews, led by Judas Maccabeus, revolt against Syria and form independent Judaea.
**147–146** EUROPE Rome sacks Corinth, and rules Greece from Macedonia.
AFRICA Third Punic War: Rome destroys Carthage.
**133** EUROPE Reforms of Gracchi brothers (133,123–121) begin a 100-year challenge to Senate power in Rome.
**By 126** ASIA Parthian empire established in Middle East, except Syria and Judaea.
**121** EUROPE Rome completes conquest of S Gaul.
**90–88** EUROPE Social War, in which Italians rebel against Rome. Roman citizenship is extended to all Italy.
**By 87** ASIA Chinese empire includes Korea and N Vietnam.
**By 62** ASIA Pompey completes conquest of Syria and Judaea, which become Roman provinces.
**58–50** EUROPE Julius Caesar conquests rest of Gaul for Rome and invades Britain and Germany (55–54).
**49–45** EUROPE First Roman Civil War; Caesar defeats Pompey and Senate, and becomes dictator. Murdered March 15, 44.

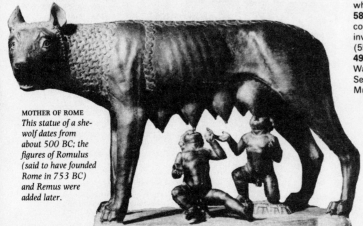

MOTHER OF ROME *This statue of a she-wolf dates from about 500 BC; the figures of Romulus (said to have founded Rome in 753 BC) and Remus were added later.*

# POLITICS AND WAR 44 BC – AD 1492

**44–31** EUROPE Second Roman Civil War; Mark Antony and Caesar's heir, Octavian, defeat Caesar's assassins (led by Brutus and Cassius) and divide Roman empire.
AFRICA Mark Antony, with help of Cleopatra of Egypt, fights Octavian but is defeated at Battle of Actium (31). Egypt becomes Roman province.
**27** EUROPE Octavian (now Augustus) takes control of Roman empire and establishes Julio-Claudian dynasty.

## AD 0–500

**41–54** EUROPE/ASIA/AFRICA Emperor Claudius extends Roman empire to Britain (43), Mauretania (N Africa), Thrace and Lycia (Asia Minor).
**61** EUROPE Boudicca leads revolt in Britain against Rome, but fails.
**66–70** ASIA Jewish revolt against Rome. Siege of Jerusalem (70). Temple destroyed. Masada, scene of final Jewish resistance, falls (73).
**69** EUROPE 'Year of Four Emperors' in Rome; internal conflict ends with Vespasian as first emperor of Flavian dynasty.
**69–96** EUROPE Southern Scotland and Rhineland added to Roman empire, Syria extended eastwards.
**By 100** AFRICA Rise of Axum kingdom in Ethiopia.
**101–6** EUROPE/AFRICA Emperor Trajan adds Dacia (Romania) and Arabia to Roman empire.
**113–17** ASIA Trajan defeats Parthians and annexes their empire.
**117–38** ASIA Emperor Hadrian establishes fixed Roman frontiers. Hadrian's Wall built in Britain (122).
**132–5** ASIA Final Jewish revolt suppressed. Judaea becomes Palestine. Jews banned from Jerusalem and dispersed.
**161–80** EUROPE Barbarian invasions of Roman empire begin from the northeast.
**220** ASIA Han dynasty ends in China, followed by division into three kingdoms.
**224–7** ASIA Artaxerxes I (Ardashir) founds Sassanid dynasty and re-establishes Persian empire.
**306** EUROPE Constantine the Great proclaimed Roman emperor at York, England. He founds Constantinople (now Istanbul) in 330 on the site of Greek Byzantium.
**395** EUROPE Roman empire permanently divided: Rome capital in west, Constantinople in east (Byzantine empire).
**By 400** ASIA Rise of Japanese empire.
**410** EUROPE Alaric leads Visigoths to plunder Rome.

**451–3** EUROPE Attila leads Huns into Italy.
**455** EUROPE Vandals sack Rome.
**476** EUROPE Western Roman empire overthrown by Odoacer, German chief, who becomes first king of Italy.
**486–7** EUROPE Franks (German tribe) under Clovis I control all France.
**493** EUROPE Theodoric (Ostrogoth) becomes king of Italy.

## AD 500–1000

**507** EUROPE Visigoths invade Spain.
**527–65** EUROPE/AFRICA Eastern Roman emperor Justinian reconquers Italy, N Africa, SE Spain.
**589** ASIA Sui dynasty temporarily reunites China. Great Wall rebuilt.
**590–610** EUROPE Pope Gregory I extends secular and spiritual power of papacy.
**622** ASIA Muslims (Arab followers of Muhammad) begin Holy War against non-believers in Medina.
**632** ASIA Muhammad dies. Caliphate is established.
**By 650** ASIA/AFRICA Arabs led by Caliph Omar (634–44) take Syria, Palestine, Persia, Egypt and destroy Persian empire.
**661–80** ASIA/AFRICA Arabs conquer N Africa and extend empire eastwards to Afghanistan and the Indus valley.
**687** EUROPE Venice lagoon settlement elects first Doge.
**711** EUROPE Arabs invade Spain and southern France.
**732** EUROPE Charles Martel (The Hammer), grandfather of Charlemagne, leads Franks to victory over Arabs at the Battle of Poitiers, halting Muslim advance into Europe.

**768–814** EUROPE Charlemagne, king of Franks, conquers N Italy, Germany, NE Spain.
**800 (December 25)** EUROPE Coronation of Charlemagne as emperor by Pope Leo III in Rome.
**810** EUROPE Venice recognised as independent state by both Charlemagne and Byzantines.
**808 onwards** EUROPE Rise of Bulgarian empire.
**878–99** EUROPE Alfred the Great of Wessex defeats Danes, and rules southern England.
**893–927** EUROPE Height of Bulgarian empire under Simeon I.
**By 900** ASIA Khmer empire established in Cambodia (Kampuchea), with capital Angkor.
**911** EUROPE Rollo (Hrolf) the Norseman is granted lordship over Normandy (France).
ASIA Byzantium acknowledges power of Kiev Russian state, after 50 years of intermittent warfare around Black Sea.
**930** EUROPE World's first legislative assembly (the Althing) founded by Norse settlers in Iceland.
**962** EUROPE Otto I the Great, King of the Germans, conquers central Europe and is crowned Holy Roman Emperor.
**973** EUROPE Edgar of Wessex crowned first king of England at Bath.
**987** EUROPE Hugh Capet crowned first king of France at Noyon.
**992** EUROPE Boleslaw I becomes first king of Poland.

## AD 1000–1100

**1001–22** EUROPE Basil II (The Bulgar Slayer) restores eastern Roman empire at Constantinople, defeating Bulgars and Armenians.
**1001** EUROPE Stephen (later Saint) crowned first king of Hungary with 'Holy Crown'.
**1013–42** EUROPE Danes rule England. (King Knut, or Canute, reigns in Scandinavia and England 1017–35.)
**By 1035** EUROPE Rise of Spanish Christian kingdom in Castile under Ferdinand I (1033–65).
**1055** ASIA Seljuk Turks take Baghdad. Sultanate established.
**1066** EUROPE Normans under William I (The Conqueror) invade England, winning the Battle of Hastings (October 14).
**1096–7** EUROPE First Crusade: three armies of Normans and French reach Constantinople, defeat the Turks, on way to free Palestine from Muslims.
**1099** ASIA Crusaders take Jerusalem and found a Latin kingdom there under Godfrey of Bouillon.

WARRIOR AND SCHOLAR *This jewel, which may have been a pointer used for reading manuscripts, was owned by Alfred the Great, who drove the Danes out of southern England in 878.*

## AD 1100-1200

**1143** EUROPE Alfonso I becomes first king of Portugal.
**1146-8** ASIA Second Crusade, led by King Louis VII of France and Emperor Conrad VII, attacks Damascus but achieves little.
**1170** EUROPE State-Church power struggle in England between Henry II and Archbishop Thomas Becket ends in Becket's murder at Canterbury.
**1175 onwards** ASIA Muslim rulers established in central India.
**1187** ASIA Saladin, Sultan of Turkish Syria and Egypt, retakes Jerusalem.
**1189** ASIA Third Crusade, led by Emperor Frederick Barbarossa, Philip Augustus of France and Richard I of England, fails militarily but truce with Saladin allows Christians access to Jerusalem.

## AD 1200-1300

**1204** EUROPE Venice gains control of the Aegean and the Ionian islands.
ASIA Fourth Crusade is diverted to Constantinople, which is sacked by Crusaders; Latin empire set up while Byzantines flee to Nicaea (now Iznik).
**1206-23** ASIA Genghis Khan leads Mongol warriors through China and Persia to defeat the Russians.

KHAN'S CAVALRY
*Tough, small ponies, that needed no fodder because they fed on grass, carried the archers that swept through Asia in the army of the Mongol leader, Genghis Khan.*

**1215** EUROPE King John of England seals Magna Carta, accepting limits on royal powers demanded by barons.
**1218-21** EUROPE Fifth Crusade tries but fails to take Egypt.
**1228-9** ASIA Sixth Crusade led by Emperor Frederick II against pope's wishes, recaptures Holy City. Frederick crowns himself King of Jerusalem.
**1235** AFRICA Rise of Mali empire in West Africa.
**1240-1450** ASIA Mongol Khanates of the 'Golden Horde' rule central and southern Russia.
**1242** EUROPE Prince Alexander Nevsky defeats Teutonic Knights near Pskov in northern Russia.
**1244** ASIA Muslims retake Jerusalem, which remains under Muslim rule until 1917.
**1248** ASIA Seventh Crusade, led by Louis IX (St Louis) of France, fails. Louis captured and ransomed.
**1260-94** ASIA Kublai Khan completes Mongol conquest of China and establishes his capital at Beijing (Peking).
**1261** EUROPE Greek army from Nicaea (Iznik) reconquers Constantinople and overthrows Latin rule, restoring Byzantine empire.
**By 1262** EUROPE Teutonic Knights complete conquests south of the Baltic, Germanising Prussia.
**1270** ASIA Eighth Crusade, led by Louis IX and Edward (later I) of England, attacks Tunis, with little success. Louis dies in Tunis.
**1273** EUROPE Rudolf of Hapsburg elected emperor. Dynasty rules Austria until 1918.
**1276-84** EUROPE Edward I conquers Wales and unites it with England.
**1285-1307** EUROPE Edward I conquers Scotland.
**1290-1326** ASIA Osman I founds Ottoman dynasty in Turkey.

## AD 1300-1400

**1307-32** AFRICA Height of Mali (Mandingo) empire under Sultan Mansa Musa.
**1314** EUROPE Robert Bruce re-establishes Scottish independence by defeating English at Bannockburn.
**1337** EUROPE Anglo-French Hundred Years War begins as Edward III claims French throne. Edward wins naval battle of Sluys (1340), and land battle of Crécy (1346).
**1338-1573** ASIA Ashikaga Shoguns dominate Japan, based on Kyoto.
**1347-1558** EUROPE Calais (France) held by English.
**1354** EUROPE Ottoman Turks establish foothold in Europe at Gallipoli.
**1369-1405** ASIA Timur-i-lenk (Tamerlane) of Samarkand establishes Mongol empire over all central Asia. It disintegrates after his death.
**1389** EUROPE Turkish victory at Kossovo over Serbs, Bulgarians and Albanians gives Ottoman Turks control of the Balkans for 500 years.

## AD 1400-1500

**1415-20** EUROPE Henry V of England defeats French at Agincourt (1415), captures Paris (1420).
**1429** EUROPE Joan of Arc (about 1412-31) leads French to victory at siege of Orléans; is convicted of sorcery and burnt at the stake in Rouen (1431).
**1453** EUROPE French defeat English at Castillon; Hundred Years War ends.
ASIA Fall of Constantinople to Muhammad II (The Conqueror) ends Byzantine empire. Constantinople becomes Ottoman Turks' capital city.
**1455-85** EUROPE Civil War in England between dynasties of York and Lancaster, later called the Wars of the Roses. It ends with death of Richard III (of York) at Battle of Bosworth.
**1479** EUROPE Spain unified by marriage and joint rule of Fernando (Ferdinand) II, king of Aragon, and Isabella, queen of Castile.
**1479-80** EUROPE Turks wrest control of southern Adriatic from the Venetians.
**1492-1529** AFRICA Zenith of the Songhoy empire of the middle Niger region under Askia Mohammed.

# POLITICS AND WAR AD 1519–1821

## AD 1500–1600

**1519–21** N AMERICA Hernan Cortes and Spanish *conquistadores* defeat Aztecs and seize Mexico.
**1526** EUROPE Turks defeat Hungarians at Mohacs and conquer Hungary.
**1526** ASIA India: Baber occupies Delhi and sets up Mughal empire.
**1531–5** N AMERICA Francisco Pizarro and Spanish *conquistadores* defeat Incas and seize Peru.
**1546–55** EUROPE Schmalkaldic War in Germany between Holy Roman Emperor Charles V and Lutheran princes.
**1547** EUROPE Ivan IV (The Terrible), on the throne from 1533, crowned first tsar of Russia in Moscow.
**1562–98** EUROPE 'Wars of Religion' in France, between Protestant Huguenots and Catholic League; Paris Huguenots killed in Massacre of St Bartholomew (1572).
**1571** EUROPE Turkish naval power in Mediterranean destroyed by Christian League under Don John of Austria at Battle of Lepanto.
**1571–1603** AFRICA Idris Alooma rules North African Muslim empire from Kanem.
**1572** EUROPE Dutch revolt against Spanish rule.
**1580** EUROPE Philip II of Spain conquers and absorbs Portugal.
**1582–98** ASIA Toyotomi Hideyoshi completes unification of Japan.
**1588** EUROPE Spanish Armada defeated by English ships, bulk of remaining fleet wrecked by gales.

## AD 1600–1700

**1603** EUROPE Union of English and Scottish crowns.
**1605 (November 5)** EUROPE Gunpowder plot by group of Catholic extremists, which included a former soldier named Guy Fawkes, fails in attempt to blow up English king and Parliament.
**1618** EUROPE Thirty Years War begins with Protestant revolt in Bohemian capital of Prague against Emperor Ferdinand II.
**1636–8** ASIA Shogun Iemitsu forbids Japanese to travel abroad or foreigners to enter Japan. Ban maintained until 1853.
**1640** EUROPE Charles I of England forced to summon Long Parliament which seeks to curb power of English Crown and Church. Disputes lead to Civil War (1642–6).
**1643** EUROPE Victory of French general Prince Louis of Condé (1621–86) over Spain at Rocroi marks start of France's military superiority in W Europe.

**1644** ASIA Manchu dynasty established in China after period of political anarchy.
**1644–5** EUROPE English Parliamentarian leader Oliver Cromwell (1599–1658) beats Royalists at Battles of Marston Moor (1644) and Naseby (1645).
**1648** EUROPE Treaties of Westphalia end Thirty Years War, with gains for France, Sweden, Brandenburg and Holland. Losers are Spain and the Holy Roman Empire.
**1648–53** EUROPE 'La Fronde' – a series of outbreaks of civil unrest in France against Cardinal Mazarin and the growing power of the French throne.
**1649** EUROPE Charles I tried for treason in England and beheaded (January 30).
**1655** N AMERICA Jamaica seized by Britain from Spain.
**1660** EUROPE British monarchy restored under Charles II.
**1664** N AMERICA British expedition captures New Amsterdam from Dutch and renames it New York.
**1667–8** EUROPE 'War of Devolution', in which Louis XIV of France gains part of Flanders from Spain.
**1668** EUROPE Spain restores Portugal's independence.
**1675** EUROPE Frederick William of Brandenburg (The Great Elector) defeats Sweden at Fehrbellin and lays foundation of Brandenburg-Prussia's military power.
**1683** EUROPE Vienna relieved from Turkish siege by army of Polish king, John Sobieski.
**1687** EUROPE Venetians bombard Athens. Gunpowder stored by Turks in Parthenon explodes.
**1688** EUROPE Britain's 'Glorious Revolution'. Parliament invites Prince William of Orange and his wife, Mary (both Protestants and grandchildren of Charles I), to cross from Holland and succeed the Catholic James II (reigned 1685–8) on the throne (1689). Bill of Rights (1689) safeguards parliamentary government.
**1690** EUROPE William III defeats James II's Catholic rebellion in Ireland at Battle of the Boyne (July 11).
**1696** EUROPE Peter I (The Great) becomes sole tsar of Russia, and captures Azov.

## AD 1700–1750

**1700–21** EUROPE Great Northern War in Baltic. Charles XII of Sweden defeats Russia at Battle of Narva (1700) but loses at Poltava (1709).
**1701** EUROPE Brandenburg becomes kingdom of Prussia.

**1701–13** EUROPE War of Spanish Succession: victories of English Duke of Marlborough against France at Blenheim (1704), Ramillies (1706), Oudenarde (1708) and Malplaquet (1709). Peace treaties of Utrecht accept Philip V, grandson of French king, Louis XIV, as king of Spain, provided that French and Spanish thrones are never united. French gain land along the Rhine; English gain colonies in Canada and West Indies.
**1707** EUROPE United Kingdom established by union of English and Scottish parliaments under Queen Anne (1702–14).
**1739** ASIA Nadir Shah of Persia sacks Delhi.
**1740–8** EUROPE War of the Austrian Succession: Britain supports Austria's Maria Theresa against France, Spain and Prussia.
**1745** EUROPE Jacobite rebellion in Scotland in support of Catholic Stuart pretender, Bonnie Prince Charlie. Rebels finally defeated at Battle of Culloden (April 1746).
**1748** EUROPE Peace of Aix-la-Chapelle ends War of Austrian Succession. Austria cedes Silesia to Prussia.
**1749–56** EUROPE Diplomatic revolution reverses earlier alliances: France and Austria combine against Britain and Prussia.

## AD 1750–1800

**1756–63** EUROPE Seven Years War, during which Prussia builds up position in central Europe, and Britain consolidates its colonial grasp of Canada and India.
**1757** ASIA British general Robert Clive wins Battle of Plassey and conquers Bengal.
**1759** N AMERICA British general James Wolfe defeats French at Battle of Quebec.
**1768–74** EUROPE Russo-Turkish War: Russia gains Crimea and northern Black Sea coast.
**1772, 1793, 1795** EUROPE Poland partitioned between Russia, Prussia and Austria.
**1773** N AMERICA Boston Tea Party protest against British taxation (December 16).
**1773–5** EUROPE Peasant revolt in Russia led by Cossack Emelian Pugachev suppressed by Catherine the Great.
**1774** N AMERICA Continental Congress (September) at Philadelphia lists American grievances.
**1775–83** N AMERICA American War of Independence. Americans defeat British troops at Battle of Saratoga (1777) and decisively at Battle of Yorktown (1781).
**1776** N AMERICA American Declaration of Independence (July 4).

**1783** N AMERICA Peace of Versailles recognises America's independence.
**1787** N AMERICA US constitution signed (September). George Washington becomes first President in 1789.
**1789–95** EUROPE French Revolution. Bastille falls (1789). Louis XVI beheaded (1793). Radical Jacobins under Maximilien Robespierre institute a 'reign of terror' in which 35,000 die, mostly on the guillotine (1794). Robespierre guillotined (July 1794).
**1792–7** EUROPE War of the First Coalition against France. French revolutionary armies take over Netherlands, Switzerland, Rhineland, north Italy.
**1794–6** N AMERICA/AFRICA Britain takes over French and Dutch colonies (West and East Indies, southern Africa).
**1796–7** EUROPE First Italian campaign of Napoleon Bonaparte; he defeats Austria at Battle of Rivoli (January 1797).
**1796–1802** N AMERICA Slave revolt of Toussaint l'Ouverture in Haiti forces French colonial troops to withdraw from the island.
**1798–9** EUROPE Bonaparte occupies Egypt, but French fleet is destroyed by Horatio Nelson at Battle of Nile (August 1798).
**1798** EUROPE Irish rebellion suppressed.
**1798–1802** EUROPE War of the Second Coalition – Austria, Russia and Turkey. The allies' early successes – against France – are countered by Bonaparte's victory at the Battle of Marengo (1800).
**1799–1804** EUROPE Bonaparte becomes ruler of France as First Consul (1799); reforms French legal system with new code of law, the Code Napoléon (issued 1804).
**1799** ASIA In India pro-French Sultan of Mysore, Tipu, killed when British take Seringapatam.

# AD 1800–1850

**1800** EUROPE Parliamentary Union of Britain and Ireland. Malta seized by Britain from France.
**1804** EUROPE In Vienna, Franz (Francis) I assumes title Emperor of Austria, leading to the abolition of the Holy Roman Empire in 1806. Napoleon is crowned Emperor of the French in Paris.
N AMERICA Haiti becomes independent – the second country in the New World after the USA to do so – under a former slave, Emperor Dessalines.
**1805–7** EUROPE War of the Third Coalition – Britain, Austria and Russia joined in 1806 by Prussia – against France. British under Horatio Nelson defeat French and Spanish fleets at Battle of Trafalgar, near Gibraltar (October 21, 1805). Napoleon defeats Russia and Austria at Battle of Austerlitz (December 2, 1805).
**1806** EUROPE Prussia decisively defeated by France at twin battles of Jena and Auerstadt.
**1806–14** EUROPE Napoleon's continental empire attempts to blockade Britain.
**1808–14** EUROPE French occupy Spain and Portugal but meet resistance in the Peninsular War.
**1809** EUROPE Austria re-enters war but is defeated by Napoleon at Wagram (July 5–6).
**1809–16** S AMERICA First South American wars for independence from Spain gain some success in Argentina (1810) and in Paraguay (1811), but fail in Mexico and Venezuela.
**1812–15** N AMERICA Anglo-American War, caused mainly by US resentment of British naval harassment, ended by Treaty of Ghent (signed December 1814, effective from February 1815).

**1812** EUROPE Napoleon invades Russia, defeating Russians at Battle of Borodino (September) and occupying Moscow. But the city's destruction by fire forces him into a disastrous winter retreat to Germany.
**1813** EUROPE War of Liberation in Germany culminates in Napoleon's defeat by Fourth Coalition at Leipzig (October 16–19). British Duke of Wellington's Peninsular Army wins Battle of Vitoria (June) and crosses Pyrenees to invade France (October).
**1814** EUROPE Napoleon abdicates (April 6) after allies capture Paris, and is exiled to Elba. Bourbon dynasty (Louis XVIII) restored in France.
**1814–15** EUROPE Congress of Vienna restores old frontiers of France. Russia given mastery over Poland, Austria over northern Italy; Holland and Belgium united. Sweden gains Norway; and 39 states linked in a German confederation dominated by Austria and Prussia. Britain retains colonial gains in West Indies, southern Africa and Ceylon (now Sri Lanka) as well as Malta.
**1815 (March–June)** EUROPE Napoleon returns to Paris and in the Hundred Days seeks to recover his empire. He is defeated at Battle of Waterloo and exiled to St Helena (died 1821).
**1819–23** ASIA Singapore developed as British possession by Sir Stamford Raffles.
**1819–25** S AMERICA Simon Bolivar secures independence from Spain of modern Colombia, Venezuela, Peru and Bolivia (named after him).
**1821** N AMERICA Mexico declares independence from Spain.
**1821–9** EUROPE Greek War of Independence from Turkey. Britain, France and Russia intervene to sink Turko-Egyptian fleet at Navarino (1827).

BASTILLE DAY *On July 14, 1789, French revolutionaries stormed the hated Bastille prison in Paris.*

# POLITICS AND WAR AD 1822–1918

**1822** S AMERICA Brazil becomes independent constitutional empire under Dom Pedro I, son of the Portuguese King João.
**1823** AUSTRALIA Legislative council established in New South Wales, Australia – the first move towards representative government for the penal colony.
**1830–45** AFRICA France occupies Algiers (July 1830) and wages colonial war to conquer Algeria.

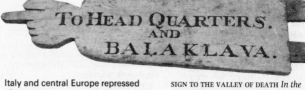

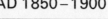

DRAGON SAILOR *During the Opium War (1839–40), the Chinese saw English sailors as monsters snorting tobacco smoke.*

**1836** N AMERICA Texas secedes from Mexico. It joins USA in 1845.
**1838–41** N AMERICA Costa Rica, El Salvador, Guatemala, Honduras, Nicaragua become independent.
**1839–40** ASIA Anglo-Chinese Opium War. Britain gains Hong Kong (1841).
**1840** OCEANIA New Zealand's Maori chiefs accept British rule in return for civic guarantees (Treaty of Waitangi).
**1846–8** N AMERICA Mexican War: USA gains New Mexico and California.
**1848–9** EUROPE Liberal and nationalist revolutions in France,

Italy and central Europe repressed after temporary triumphs for Louis Kossuth (1802–94) in Hungary and Giuseppe Garibaldi (1807–82) in Italy.

---

## AD 1850–1900

**1850–64** ASIA Taiping Rebellion against Manchu rulers in China put down with help of Western and Chinese troops under Charles 'Chinese' Gordon (1833–85).
**1854–6** EUROPE Crimean War: Britain and France join Turkey against Russia and besiege Sebastopol. At Battle of Balaclava, 247 cavalrymen die in Charge of Light Brigade. Peace congress in Paris, ending the war, limits Russian power in Black Sea.
**1857–8** ASIA Indian Mutiny (Bengal Army) suppressed. Britain takes over direct government of India from the East India Company.
**1858–61** ASIA France conquers South Vietnam and colonises Saigon area.
**1860–1** EUROPE Unification of Italy completed under Count Camillo di Cavour and Giuseppe Garibaldi.
**1860** ASIA British and French troops in China burn Summer Palace in Beijing (Peking).
**1861** N AMERICA Confederacy formed by 11 Southern US states. Civil War (1861–5) begins.

GRIM MUTINY *British soldiers recaptured Cawnpore (Kanpur) on July 16, 1857, after Indian rebels had massacred the garrison.*

SIGN TO THE VALLEY OF DEATH *In the Charge of the Light Brigade at Balaclava (October 25, 1854), 247 British cavalrymen out of 600 died.*

**1861** EUROPE Russian tsar, Alexander II (reigned 1855–81), emancipates 10 million male serfs and their families.
**1863–4** EUROPE Polish rebellion against Russia suppressed.
**1863–7** N AMERICA French establish puppet Mexican empire under Maximilian.
**1863** N AMERICA US Union army wins Battle of Gettysburg (July 1–3).
**1864** EUROPE Prussia and Austria, after war against Denmark, share provinces of Schleswig-Holstein.
**1865** N AMERICA American Civil War ends in victory for the North.
**1865–70** S AMERICA Paraguayan War: Argentina, Brazil and Uruguay invade Paraguay.
**1866** EUROPE Seven Weeks War: Prussia victorious over Austria and other German states. Prussia's ally, Italy, gains Venice in the peace settlement.
**1867** EUROPE Otto von Bismarck (1815–98) establishes North German Confederation. Austria grants home rule to Hungary, creating dual monarchy of Austria-Hungary.
N AMERICA Mexican emperor Maximilian shot by republicans after withdrawal of French support.
**1870–1** EUROPE Franco-Prussian War: France becomes a republic.
**1870** EUROPE Italy annexes Rome, which becomes the capital.
**1871** EUROPE Wilhelm (William) I of Prussia proclaimed German emperor (Kaiser), with Otto von Bismarck as chancellor.
**1877** EUROPE Russia attacks Turkey and reaches outskirts of Constantinople.
**1879–83** S AMERICA War of the Pacific: Chile defeats Peru and Bolivia.
**1881–98** AFRICA Imperial rivalry as Britain, Germany, France and Italy carve out colonies in the 'scramble for Africa'.
**1885** AFRICA Congo Free State (later Zaire) set up by Belgium's King Leopold II.
**1885–6** ASIA Burma conquered by British troops.
**1893** OCEANIA New Zealand becomes the first country to give the vote to women.
**1895** ASIA Japan gains Korea and Formosa (now Taiwan) in war with China (1894–5).
**1896** AFRICA Italian invasion of Ethiopia (1895–6) defeated at Adowa.

**1898** AFRICA Britain conquers Sudan at Battle of Omdurman. Fashoda Crisis: Britain and France near to war over control of upper Nile.
OCEANIA USA annexes Hawaii.
N AMERICA/ASIA Spanish-American War ends Spanish rule in Cuba, Philippines and Puerto Rico.
**1899–1902** AFRICA Boer War. Britain defeats Dutch settler republics of Transvaal and Orange Free State.

## AD 1900–1950

**1900** ASIA Boxer Rising in China against foreigners. Order restored by international army (1901).
**1901** AUSTRALIA Unified Commonwealth of Australia set up.
**1904** EUROPE *Entente Cordiale*: Anglo-French settlement of colonial differences.

**1904–5** ASIA Russo-Japanese War gives Japan mastery over Korea and the approaches to Manchuria.
**1905** EUROPE Russian liberal revolution forces tsar to create a parliament (*Duma*). Norway given independence from Sweden.
**1908–9** EUROPE Austria annexes Bosnia-Herzegovina (now part of Yugoslavia).
**1910** AFRICA Union of South Africa established.
**1911** ASIA Chinese nationalist revolution overthrows Manchu dynasty. Emperor Xuang-tong abdicates (1912).
**1911–12** EUROPE/AFRICA Italo-Turkish War. Italy gains Libya.
**1912** EUROPE First Balkan War. Balkan states – Serbia, Greece, Bulgaria and Montenegro – defeat Turkey. Albania is created (1913).
**1913** EUROPE Second Balkan War. Balkan states fight over spoils of first Balkan War, drawing Russia and Austria-Hungary into closer involvement.
**1914** EUROPE Sarajevo Crisis: assassination (June 28) of Archduke Franz Ferdinand, heir to Austrian throne, by Bosnian Serb leads rival alliances into First World War. Germany invades Belgium and Russia (August). Germany defeats Russia at Tannenberg (August 26–30). German advance on Paris repulsed at Battle of the Marne (September 5–19).
**1915** EUROPE Gallipoli: unsuccessful British attempt to defeat Germany's ally, Turkey, by advancing through the Dardanelles.
N AMERICA USA occupies Haiti.
**1915–18** EUROPE Static trench warfare along Western Front from Ypres in Belgium through to Franco-Swiss frontier.
**1916** EUROPE Ireland: Dublin Easter Rebellion suppressed by British troops. Heavy inconclusive battles in France at Verdun (February–December) and Somme (July–November). British navy defeats Germans at Battle of Jutland (May 31–June 1).
**1917** EUROPE Russian Revolution. Liberals force downfall of tsar (February). Bolsheviks led by Vladimir Lenin (1870–1924) establish Soviet government (October) and seek peace with Germany, Austria-Hungary and Turkey. USA declares war on Germany (April). Balfour Declaration (November 2) promises British support for a Jewish national home in Palestine.
**1918** EUROPE Military collapse of Germany's allies: Bulgaria (September 29); Turkey (October 30); Austria-Hungary (November 3). Germany signs armistice (November 11).

"PAWS OFF!"

I WANT YOU FOR U.S. ARMY
NEAREST RECRUITING STATION

HIGH TENSION *The first two decades of the 20th century were torn by war: tensions between Japan and Russia over Korea, noted by Punch in 1901 (above left), broke into war in 1904. In 1917 the USA entered the First World War and Uncle Sam recruited soldiers to fight in Europe.*

43

# POLITICS AND WAR AD 1918–1983

**1918–19** EUROPE New republics formed: Germany, Austria, Hungary, Poland, Finland, Czechoslovakia, Lithuania, Latvia, Estonia. Southern Slavs form Yugoslavia, a kingdom dominated by Serbia.

**1919** EUROPE Paris Peace Conference. Treaties of Versailles, St Germain and Neuilly signed. Germany loses all colonies and much European territory; armed forces severely restricted; obliged to pay reparations to Allies; blamed for starting the war. League of Nations established.

**1920** EUROPE Hungary becomes a kingdom under a regent, Miklos Horthy, but by the Treaty of Trianon is limited to one-third of its historic territories.

**1921** EUROPE Ireland partitioned. Eire becomes independent (1922). Six Ulster counties remain in United Kingdom.

**1922** EUROPE Benito Mussolini (Il Duce) becomes Italy's Fascist prime minister and by 1928 is a dictator. ASIA Turkey proclaimed a republic by Mustafa Kemal (later known as Atatürk).

**1924** EUROPE Death of Lenin (January) leads to power struggle in Russia, won by Joseph Stalin (1879–1953).

**1925** ASIA Pahlavi dynasty secures throne in Iran and reigns until 1979.

**1926** EUROPE General Strike in Britain.

**1928** WORLDWIDE Kellogg-Briand Pact outlawing war signed by 65 governments, including Britain, Germany, Italy, Russia, Japan and the USA.

**1929** EUROPE Lateran Treaties between Mussolini and Papacy create Vatican City state.

**1930** EUROPE French troops, occupying Rhineland since 1918, withdraw from Germany.

**1931** WORLDWIDE Statute of Westminster defines dominion status with the British Commonwealth of Nations. Recognises Canada, Australia, Newfoundland, South Africa and New Zealand as 'autonomous communities'. EUROPE Spanish monarchy overthrown by republicans. ASIA Japanese troops occupy Manchuria in China.

**1932** EUROPE Antonio Salazar (1889–1970) becomes prime minister and dictator of Portugal. ASIA Saudi Arabia established as united kingdom by Ibn Saud.

**1932–5** S AMERICA Chaco War between Bolivia and Paraguay after oil discovered in the desert region. After 100,000 deaths, Paraguay gains three-quarters of the disputed territory.

**1933** EUROPE Adolf Hitler becomes German Chancellor (January 30) and establishes Nazi dictatorship.

**1934–5** ASIA Long March across 10,000km (6000 miles) of China by 100,000 Communists under Mao Zedong (Mao Tse-tung, 1893–1976) to escape besieging army of nationalists under Jiang Jieshi (Chiang Kai-shek, 1887–1975).

**1935–6** AFRICA Abyssinian War: Italy invades and occupies Ethiopia.

**1936** EUROPE Rome-Berlin Axis proclaimed (collaboration of Hitler and Mussolini).

**1936–8** EUROPE Stalinist purge of rivals in Soviet army and Communist party. Hundreds of thousands of Soviet citizens sent to forced labour camps in the Arctic and Siberia.

**1936–9** EUROPE Spanish Civil War: General Francisco Franco overthrows republic and becomes dictator with support from Germany and Italy.

**1937** ASIA Japan attacks China, but war remains undeclared until 1945.

**1938** EUROPE Germany annexes Austria (March). Munich Agreement (September) allows Germany to seize Czechoslovak frontier region of Sudetenland.

**1939** EUROPE Italy annexes Albania (April). Germany invades Poland (September 1), triggering Second World War.

**1939–40** EUROPE Russo-Finnish War: Soviet Union pushes back Finnish frontiers.

**1940** EUROPE Norway and Denmark occupied by Germany (April). Germany overruns Holland, Belgium and France (May 10–June 22). Latvia, Lithuania and Estonia occupied and annexed by USSR (August). Battle of Britain (August–September): Germany fails to gain air superiority.

**1941** EUROPE Germany overruns Yugoslavia and Greece. Germany, Romania and Finland attack Soviet Union (June 22). AFRICA British army liberates Ethiopia from Italians. OCEANIA Surprise Japanese attacks on Pearl Harbor in Hawaii, Malaya and Hong Kong (December 7). USA enters Second World War.

**1942** ASIA Japanese successes in Singapore, Burma and Philippines checked by US victory at Midway Island (June 4).

**1942–3** EUROPE Russians defeat Germans at Stalingrad (now Volgograd). AFRICA British and US troops free North Africa from German and Italian control (October–May). Decisive British victory at El Alamein (1942).

**1943** EUROPE Italian king dismisses Mussolini (July 25). Anglo-American Allies land in southern Italy (September 3).

**1944** EUROPE Russians relieve Leningrad after 900-day siege (January 27). Allies enter Rome (June 4). Allies land in Normandy (D-DAY, June 6) and advance across France. ASIA US troops return to Philippines (October 19).

**1945** WORLDWIDE United Nations charter signed in San Francisco. ASIA British XIV Army completes re-conquest of Burma (July 25). Atomic bombs dropped on Hiroshima and Nagasaki, Japan (August 6 and 9). Japan surrenders, ending Second World War (August 14). EUROPE Yalta Conference (February), Churchill, Roosevelt and Stalin meet to discuss post-war settlement of Eastern Europe and Soviet entry into war against Japan. Soviet and US troops link up at Torgau in Germany. Hitler shoots himself as Russians enter Berlin (April 30). Germany surrenders (May 7). Communist-dominated governments set up in Poland, Romania, Bulgaria, Hungary, Albania and Yugoslavia.

**1945–9** ASIA Indonesian War for independence from Dutch rule.

**1946** EUROPE Italy becomes a republic (June). ASIA Philippines given independence by USA (July).

**1946–9** EUROPE Greek civil war. Communists defeated.

**1946–54** ASIA Indochina War by pro-Communist Vietminh against French colonialists.

PEACE AT LAST *This London* Daily Mirror *cartoon marked Germany's surrender on May 7, 1945. The caption read: 'Here you are – don't lose it again.'*

**1947** ASIA India and Pakistan become independent within British Commonwealth.
**1948** EUROPE Coup in Czechoslovakia perpetuates Communist control of government. Yugoslavia under Marshal Tito breaks clear of Soviet domination. ASIA Independence for Burma and Ceylon (Sri Lanka). State of Israel established (May 14); unsuccessfully attacked by six Arab neighbouring states. AFRICA Afrikaner nationalists win South African election and introduce *apartheid* laws.
**1948–9** EUROPE Russian blockade of West Berlin defeated by Anglo-American Berlin airlift (June to May). ASIA Chinese Communists defeat Nationalists and establish Chinese People's Republic on October 1, 1949.
**1948–60** ASIA Malayan Emergency: British Commonwealth troops suppress Communist guerrillas.
**1949** EUROPE/AMERICA Western powers sign treaty creating North Atlantic Treaty Organisation (NATO). EUROPE Federal Republic of Germany (capital, Bonn) established on September 21. German Democratic Republic (capital, East Berlin) established on October 7. Full sovereignty granted to both Germanies in 1955.

## AD 1950–1984

**1950–3** ASIA Korean War: UN forces repel North Korean Communists.
**1952–4** AFRICA Mau Mau (secret society amongst Kikuyu tribe) terrorist reprisals against Europeans in Kenya.
**1954** ASIA France defeated by Vietminh at Dien Bien Phu.
**1954–62** AFRICA Algerian War. Nationalist guerrillas win bitter fight against French settlers and army leaders.
**1955** EUROPE Warsaw Pact created (May) as military alliance of Eastern European states.
**1955–60** EUROPE Guerrilla attacks on British troops in Cyprus by EOKA terrorist movement in favour of union with Greece, *Enosis*. Settlement (1960) establishes Cyprus as independent republic.
**1956** EUROPE Hungarian national rising (October 23 – November 4), an attempt to make Hungary independent and neutral, put down by Russians. AFRICA Suez crisis after Egyptian President Gamal Nasser nationalises Suez Canal. Anglo-French-Israeli military action to regain control of canal ends after US and UN protests.

**1957** AFRICA Ghana becomes independent within British Commonwealth, starting an acceleration of de-colonisation.
**1958** EUROPE France: Fifth Republic set up under General Charles de Gaulle.
**1959** N AMERICA Fidel Castro seizes power in Cuba.
**1960** ASIA Mrs Sirimavo Bandaranaike, in Sri Lanka, becomes world's first woman prime minister. Communist ideological differences split Soviet Union and China.
**1960–7** AFRICA Belgian grant of independence to Congo (later Zaire) is followed by internal revolts in Katanga and Kasai.
**1961** EUROPE Berlin Wall built (August) to check East Germans escaping to West. ASIA India seizes Goa, ending Portuguese colonial rule. AFRICA South Africa leaves Commonwealth.
**1962** N AMERICA US blockade (October) forces Russia to remove Soviet missiles from Cuba.
**1963** WORLDWIDE Nuclear Test Ban Treaty signed by USA, USSR and Britain. N AMERICA President John F. Kennedy assassinated in Dallas (November 22).
**1965** AFRICA Southern Rhodesia unilaterally declares independence.
**1965–73** ASIA Vietnam War. US troops support South Vietnam against North.
**1966–9** ASIA Cultural revolution in China, launched by Mao Zedong to rekindle revolutionary ideals.
**1967** ASIA Six Day War (June). Israel attacks Egypt, Syria and Jordan.
**1967–70** AFRICA Nigerian Civil War checks secession of Biafra.
**1968** EUROPE Warsaw Pact troops invade Czechoslovakia (August) to crush liberal Communist reforms. N AMERICA Martin Luther King, US civil rights leader, assassinated at Memphis (April 4).
**1969** EUROPE British troops first stationed in Northern Ireland (April) to check sectarian violence. AFRICA Mu'ammar al-Gaddafi establishes a socialist republic in Libya.
**1970–3** S AMERICA Chile governed by elected Communist president, Salvador Allende. Allende killed in right-wing coup (1973).

**1971** ASIA Bangladesh becomes independent from Pakistan.
**1972** WORLDWIDE First Strategic Arms Limitation Treaty signed by USA and USSR.
**1973** ASIA Yom Kippur War: Israel fights off surprise attack by Egypt and Syria. US troops withdrawn from Vietnam.
**1974** EUROPE Cyprus partitioned into Turkish and Greek regions after Turkish invasion.
**1975** WORLDWIDE Helsinki Pact: 35 nations, including Soviet Union, agree to respect national frontiers and human rights. EUROPE Death of General Franco (born 1892) leads to restoration and gradual return of democracy in Spain. ASIA Vietnam unified under Communists. Communists take over Cambodia.

HANOI HOMILY *North Vietnamese posters urged unity against the USA.*

**1975–6** ASIA Civil war in Lebanon leads to Syrian military intervention.
**1979** ASIA/AFRICA Israel and Egypt sign peace treaty. ASIA Iranian monarchy toppled; Ayatollah Khomeini establishes fundamentalist Islamic republic. USSR invades Afghanistan.
**1979–80** AFRICA Rhodesian settlement creates independent Zimbabwe.
**1980** ASIA Iraq-Iran War breaks out over control of Persian Gulf headwaters.
**1982** EUROPE/S AMERICA Argentina invades Falkland Islands (April). Ejected by British troops (June). ASIA Israel occupies parts of Lebanon during renewed civil war.
**1983** AMERICA US troops, with some Caribbean forces, invade Grenada after left-wing coup.

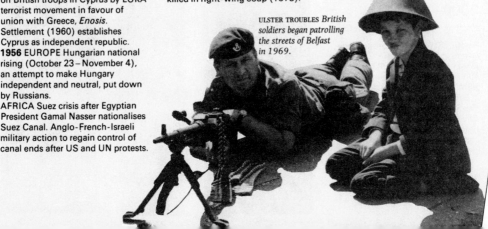

ULSTER TROUBLES *British soldiers began patrolling the streets of Belfast in 1969.*

# SOCIAL AND RELIGIOUS HISTORY 8000 BC – AD 1376

## 8000 – 3000 BC

**8000 – 7000** ASIA First farming settlements at Jericho in Jordan and Hacilar, Turkey.
**7000 – 6000** ASIA First known urban settlement at Çatal Hüyük, Turkey.
**3500 – 3000** ASIA First Sumerian city states at Uruk and Ur, in Iraq.
**3000** EUROPE Stone circles built in Hebrides, Scotland.

NEOLITHIC PIN-UP *This female figure was made in Çatal Hüyük, Turkey, in about 6000 BC.*

## 3000 – 1000 BC

**About 2750** EUROPE Stonehenge started in England.
**2000 onwards** EUROPE Indo-Europeans (Aryans) enter Europe. ASIA Canaanites settle in Lebanon at Byblos and in Syria at Ugarit, now Ras Shamra.
**About 1758** ASIA King Hammurabi, ruler of Babylon, codifies and publishes laws.

**1650 – 1590** EUROPE Mycenaean civilisation begins in Greece. ASIA Aryans move into India.
**1378 – 1362** AFRICA Pharaoh Akhenaten tries to establish monotheism in Egypt.
**About 1300** EUROPE Last stage of Stonehenge built in England.
**1100 – 1000** ASIA/AFRICA Aramaic language (spoken by Christ) becomes common tongue of Middle East.

## 1000 – 500 BC

**About 950** N AMERICA Olmec civilisation flourishing.
**About 900** EUROPE First Iron Age cultures in continental Europe and Britain.
**About 800** ASIA Hindu caste system developed in India.
**About 550** ASIA Lao Zi (born about 604) founds Taoism in China.
**About 530** ASIA Prince Siddartha Gautama (about 563 – 483) founds Buddhism in India and Nepal.
**About 500** ASIA Confucianism developed in China, based on the teachings of Confucius (about 551 – 479).
**About 500** EUROPE Celtic cultures develop in mainland Europe, and later in Britain and Ireland.

## 500 – 0 BC

**325 – 323** EUROPE/ASIA Alexander the Great decrees racial equality within his empire and encourages intermarriage between Greeks, Macedonians and Persians.
**After 221** ASIA Mandarin administrative system of nine ranks of officials set up in China.
**27** EUROPE/ASIA Roman empire organised; beginning of imperial civil service.
**About 7** ASIA Jesus Christ (crucified about AD 30) born in Bethlehem.

## AD 0 – 500

**About 14** WORLDWIDE Estimated world population 256 million.
**About 30 – 60** EUROPE/ASIA Christian communities founded in eastern Mediterranean by disciples of Jesus Christ, and linked by the missionary journeys of Paul of Tarsus in Asia Minor, Greece and to Rome.
**64** EUROPE Great Fire of Rome (July 18). Emperor Nero executes some Christians as scapegoats. Traditional date for killing of St Peter and St Paul by Nero.

MARTYR'S HUMILITY *According to legend, St Peter asked to be crucified upside down because he was not worthy to die in the same way as Christ.*

**79** EUROPE Vesuvius erupts, destroying Roman town of Pompeii.
**By 100** EUROPE/ASIA Mithraic religion spreads in Roman empire. Christian gospels written.
**166** EUROPE/ASIA Plague in Roman empire.
**250** EUROPE/ASIA General persecution of Christians in Roman empire, intensified under Emperor Diocletian (284 – 305).
N AMERICA Beginning of golden age of Mayan civilisation.

VICTIMS OF VESUVIUS *About 2000 people died under the ash that buried Pompeii in AD 79. These plaster figures were made from holes left by bodies in the ash.*

**312** EUROPE Constantine becomes Christian after seeing a flaming cross in the sky before the battle of Milvian Bridge in Italy.
**313** EUROPE/ASIA Constantine legalises Christianity in Roman empire.
**About 350** WORLDWIDE Estimated world population 254 million.
**360–3** EUROPE/ASIA Emperor Julian (The Apostate) restores paganism briefly.
**381** EUROPE/ASIA Emperor Theodosius establishes official Christian Church and bans paganism (391).
**About 400** EUROPE Huns establish empire in central Europe. Saxons settle in Britain.
**About 432** EUROPE St Patrick goes from France to convert Ireland.
**About 490** EUROPE Last Romano-British stand against Anglo-Saxon invaders at Badon Hill. The Britons' unknown leader is later identified with the legendary King Arthur.
**496** EUROPE Clovis I, King of the Franks, becomes Christian.
**By 500** ASIA Buddhism spread in China by Indian missionaries.

# AD 500–1000

**528–34** EUROPE *Codex Justinianus* published, reorganising and restating imperial Roman law.
**529** EUROPE Monasticism spreads in W Europe under the influence of an Italian monk, St Benedict (about 480–547), who founds the first Benedictine monastery of Monte Cassino. Irish monasteries become centres of learning.
**568 onwards** EUROPE Lombards settle in N Italy.
**587** ASIA Japanese Emperor Yomei converted to Buddhism.
**596–7** EUROPE St Augustine sent to England, becomes first Archbishop of Canterbury.
**About 600** WORLDWIDE Estimated world population 237 million.
EUROPE Slavs begin to settle in central Europe.
**600–700** AFRICA Earliest settlement of Zimbabwe.
**612** ASIA Muhammad begins preaching in Mecca.
**622** ASIA Muhammad flees from Mecca to Medina. Islam founded. Islamic calendar is dated from July 16, the start of the lunar year in 622.
**645–784** ASIA Japan assumes characteristics of Chinese culture.
**651–2** ASIA Definitive text of the *Koran*, sacred book of Islam, published under Caliph Uthman (about 574–656), Muhammad's son-in-law.
**700 onwards** EUROPE Feudalism begins in W Europe. Personal service to overlord replaces duty to state.

RAIDING FORCES *The dragon-prowed longboats of the Vikings came to be known and feared along the Atlantic coasts of Europe from 780.*

**780 onwards** EUROPE Vikings from Scandinavia start raids on Britain and the Atlantic seaboard of continental Europe.
**843** EUROPE Danish Vikings invade France and Germany. Frankish kingdom disintegrates.
**862** EUROPE Swedish Vikings enter Russia and found Novgorod, the basis of the Russian state.
**863** EUROPE St Cyril and St Methodius bring Christianity to South Slavs (modern Yugoslavs and Bulgars); St Cyril invents a Greek-based script which becomes the Cyrillic alphabet.
**865** EUROPE Danish army invades England and captures York.
**867–70** EUROPE/ASIA Orthodox schism: Eastern Church separates from Roman Church.
**892** ASIA Baghdad becomes the capital of the Eastern Muslim caliphate.
**898** EUROPE Arpad (about 840–907) leads the Magyar tribe from S Russia to found Hungary.
**About 980** AFRICA Arab towns founded along E African coast.
**988–9** EUROPE Vladimir, Prince of Kiev, converted to Christianity. His Russian subjects join the Eastern Orthodox Church.
**About 1000** WORLDWIDE Estimated world population 280 million.
**By 1000** EUROPE Scandinavians converted to Christianity.
ASIA Turks of Central Asia converted to Islam.
AFRICA African kingdom of Ghana at height.

# AD 1000–1500

**1054** AFRICA Muslims enter W Africa.
**1086** EUROPE Domesday Book compiled in England.
**About 1100–1450** AFRICA Age of Great Zimbabwe in southern Africa.
**1120–30** EUROPE Crusading orders of chivalry founded: Knights Templars (1120); Knights of St John (1130).
**1185** ASIA Feudalism begins in Japan.

**About 1190** ASIA Teutonic Order of Knights founded at Acre.
**About 1200** EUROPE Italian cities organised as independent communes. Rise of craft guilds in towns of W Europe.
AMERICA Collapse of Mayan civilisation in Central America. Rise of Inca civilisation in Peru.
**1212** EUROPE Children's Crusade: French and German children start out for Palestine. Many die or are sold into slavery.
**By 1223** EUROPE Mendicant preaching orders (Franciscan and Dominican friars) established, spreading from Italy across W Europe.
**About 1340** WORLDWIDE Estimated world population 378 million.
**1347–51** EUROPE Bubonic plague (Black Death) sweeps W Europe, killing one person in four.
**1348–55** AFRICA Egypt devastated by plague.

RENT DAY *In the 14th century, peasants began to pay rent in money, but the Black Death created a shortage of labour which delayed the end of feudalism.*

**1376–82** EUROPE Religious reformer John Wyclif (about 1328–84) and the Lollards in England denounce Church abuses.

# SOCIAL AND RELIGIOUS HISTORY AD 1378–1980

**1378–1415** EUROPE Great schism divides Europe as rival popes in Rome and Avignon compete for authority.
**1434–68** AFRICA Ethiopian sovereign Zara Yagub institutes social and religious reforms.
**About 1447** ASIA First Dalai Lama recognised as high priest of Buddhism in Tibet.
**1470–1570** EUROPE Rapid population growth in Europe.

## AD 1500–1600

**1502–1736** ASIA Shi'ism recognised as the only official Islamic faith, under Safavid dynasty in Persia.
**About 1510–33** ASIA Indian mystic Chaitanya (1485–1533) spreads Vaishnava movement (Hindu devotion to the god Vishnu), especially in Bengal.
**1517** EUROPE Martin Luther (1483–1546) begins German Reformation at Wittenberg by posting on a church door 95 theses attacking Catholic practices (October 13).

SATAN'S BAGPIPES *When this anti-Protestant cartoon was drawn in 1521, the Catholic Church saw Martin Luther as an instrument of the Devil.*

**1533–4** EUROPE English Reformation led by Archbishop Thomas Cranmer (1489–1556) after pope's refusal to annul Henry VIII's marriage to Catherine of Aragon.
**1534** EUROPE Society of Jesus (Jesuit order) founded by the Spaniard Ignatius of Loyola.
**1536** EUROPE French theologian John Calvin (1509–64) begins Presbyterian Reformation in Geneva, winning support in France (from Huguenots), Scotland, Holland and England (from Puritans).

DAY OF TRAGEDY *At 9.40 on the morning of All Saints Day in 1755, when most of the population was in church, an earthquake struck Lisbon, killing more than 60,000.*

**1536–40** EUROPE Dissolution of English monasteries re-distributes landed property.
**1545–63** EUROPE Council of Trent reforms Roman Catholic Church.
**About 1550–1600** EUROPE Heavy importation of gold and silver into Spain from Central and South America leads to rapid European inflation.
**1550–1700** EUROPE/N AMERICA Peak period of prosecution for witchcraft, originally in Western Europe and from 1648 onwards in North America.
**1598** EUROPE Henry IV signs Edict of Nantes granting religious freedom to Protestant Huguenots.
**About 1600** WORLDWIDE Estimated world population 498 million.

## AD 1600–1700

**1603–49** EUROPE Movement of serfs restricted in E Europe to boost farm output.
**1642–60** EUROPE Puritan social repression in Britain.

GENEVA DOODLE *Not all Calvin's students concentrated on study. This sketch of the Protestant thinker was made in a lecture.*

**1665–6** EUROPE London devastated by the Plague and Great Fire (September 1666).
**1685** EUROPE Flight of Huguenots from France, after the revocation of the Edict of Nantes by Louis XIV ends religious freedom for Protestants.

## AD 1700–1800

**1701–25** EUROPE Peter the Great (1672–1725) westernises Russia, and founds St Petersburg (now Leningrad) in 1703.
**About 1750** WORLDWIDE Estimated world population 731 million.
**1755** EUROPE Portuguese capital, Lisbon, destroyed by six-minute earthquake (November 1).
**1760** EUROPE Industrial Revolution begins in Britain.
**1785–1815** EUROPE Accelerated rate of enclosures of common land in England by landowners increases movement of peasants to towns.
**1792** EUROPE Denmark bans slave trade.

## AD 1800–1900

**1811–18** EUROPE Recession in Britain leads to machine-breaking by Luddites.
**1824** EUROPE Britain legalises trade unions, the first country to do so.
**1833** WORLDWIDE Slavery abolished throughout British empire.
**1835–47** EUROPE/N AMERICA The railway boom: fevered investment in railways in Britain, France and USA.
**1846–51** EUROPE Irish famine, after potato blight devastates crops in 1845.

**1849** N AMERICA California Gold Rush begins.

GOLD FEVER *A photograph of one of the 80,000 prospectors who headed for California in 1849.*

**1851** AUSTRALIA Gold Rush in Australia begins after gold is discovered at Ballarat, Victoria.
**1861 – 3** EUROPE Limited liability laws in Prussia, Britain and France – limiting shareholders' responsibility for company debts – encourage investment in industrial companies.
**1864** WORLDWIDE Geneva Convention sets up International Red Cross.
**1865** N AMERICA US constitutional amendment outlaws slavery.
**1870** EUROPE Vatican Council recognises Papal infallibility on matters of faith and morals.
**1881 – 2** EUROPE Anti-Jewish laws and violence (*pogroms*) in Russia.
**1883 – 9** EUROPE Bismarck pioneers a state insurance policy in Germany: workers protected against loss of income from sickness (1883), given accident insurance (1884) and pensions (1889).
**1900** WORLDWIDE Estimated world population 1668 million.

# AD 1900 – 1950

**1909 – 13** EUROPE Britain, France, USA and Holland introduce old age and sickness insurance.
**1918 – 28** EUROPE/N AMERICA Rapid social and political emancipation of women in Britain, Germany, USA and Russia.
**1918 – 19** WORLDWIDE Influenza epidemic spreads from India to Europe, causing more deaths than the entire First World War.

VOTES FOR WOMEN *Mrs Pankhurst, leader of the English suffragettes, had to be carried away from a demonstration outside Buckingham Palace in 1914.*

**1920 – 33** N AMERICA Prohibition Era in USA. Evasion of ban on alcoholic liquor is exploited by criminals.
**1924** ASIA Kemal Atatürk (1881 – 1938), founder of modern Turkey, abolishes caliphate, effectively dethroning Islam from its position as state religion, and ends (1925 – 8) Islamic restraints on women.
**1928 – 33** EUROPE/ASIA First Five-Year Plan in USSR develops heavy industry and forcibly collectivises agriculture.
**1929 – 34** N AMERICA World financial depression triggered by Wall Street Crash.
**1933** N AMERICA USA abandons the Gold Standard, followed by other Western nations.
**1935** EUROPE Violent anti-Semitism in Germany.
**1938** N AMERICA USA introduces laws on minimum wages and maximum work hours, and bans child labour.
**1941 – 5** EUROPE Peak of the Holocaust. Systematic extermination of 5 – 6 million Jews in Nazi-controlled Europe.
**1942** EUROPE Beveridge Report in Britain recommends state social insurance 'from the cradle to the grave' – the principle adopted in the postwar Welfare State.
**1945** WORLDWIDE International Monetary Fund set up to help nations in financial difficulties.
**1946** EUROPE Churchill uses the phrase 'Iron Curtain' in a speech in Fulton, Missouri, deploring the ideological restraint imposed by Soviet-type governments on the peoples of Eastern Europe.
**1947** EUROPE European Recovery Programme (Marshall Aid) set up under US patronage.
**1948** EUROPE British National Health Service inaugurated.

**1948** N AMERICA Television Age starts with boom in television sets in USA. It spreads to Europe in early 1950s.
**1949** EUROPE Comecon established in Moscow to maintain common economic policies in Soviet bloc.
**About 1950** WORLDWIDE Estimated world population 2525 million.

# AD 1950 – 1984

**1950 – 60** EUROPE 'Economic miracle' revives prosperity of West Germany.
**1957** EUROPE Treaties of Rome establish European Economic Community (EEC) of France, West Germany, Italy, Belgium, Holland and Luxembourg.
**1958 – 61** ASIA China's Great Leap Forward – a programme of radical agricultural and industrial change.
**1959** N AMERICA USA and Canada open St Lawrence Seaway.
**1960s and 70s** WORLDWIDE Women's liberation movement becomes influential in the wake of the publication of *The Feminine Mystique* (1963) by US feminist Betty Friedan, and *The Female Eunuch* (1970) by Australian lecturer Germaine Greer.
**1967 – 74** AFRICA Drought in Sahel region causes mass starvation and migration.
**1973** EUROPE EEC enlarged with entry of Britain, Ireland and Denmark.
**1978** EUROPE John Paul II (Polish Cardinal Karol Wojtyla) becomes first non-Italian pope since 1522.
**About 1980** WORLDWIDE Estimated world population 4432 million.

# EXPLORATION AND TRADE 7000 BC–AD 1637

## 7000–1000 BC

**7000–6000** EUROPE/ASIA Trade in obsidian from Anatolia to Palestine and Cyprus.
**About 2700** ASIA Egyptian colony set up at Byblos, Lebanon.
**About 2500** EUROPE Trade begins between Aegean Sea and Spain. AFRICA Egyptian trading expeditions explore as far south as Ethiopia in about 2400.
**About 2371–2316** ASIA Akkadians cross Persian Gulf to trade with Indus peoples.
**2065** EUROPE/AFRICA Trade begins in faience and ivory between Egypt and Crete.
**1580** ASIA/AFRICA Canaanites of Byblos and Ugarit trade as middlemen with Egypt, Hittites and Mycenae.
**1100–1000** EUROPE/ASIA/AFRICA Phoenicians (descendants of Canaanites) settle at Tyre, and trade with Britain, Spain, Italy, N Africa. Israel trades with Arabia and Ethiopia.

## 1000–500 BC

**884–859** EUROPE Phoenicians establish trading post at Cadiz, Spain.

*TIMBER TRADE Phoenician sailors load their ship with logs of cedar in a stone relief dating from the 8th century BC.*

**750–700** EUROPE Greeks colonise S Italy and Sicily. Town of Syracuse founded by Corinth (about 734).
**700–500** EUROPE/ASIA Greeks and Phoenicians develop ships with several banks of oars (bireme, trireme, quinquereme).
**About 605** AFRICA Greek trading posts set up in Egypt.
**About 600** EUROPE Phocaeans (Greeks from Asia Minor) colonise S France, found Marseilles and trade with Spain.
**About 535** EUROPE Carthage colonises Sardinia.
ASIA Network of partly paved roads built across Persian empire, with posting stations.
**By 500** EUROPE Carthage dominates S Spain and W Sicily with colonies and trading posts.

## 500–0 BC

**About 480** AFRICA Hanno of Carthage explores W African coast to Sierra Leone.
**437** EUROPE Athens colonises Amphipolis (Thrace) and Athenian leader Pericles (about 494–429) leads expedition to the Black Sea.
**About 310–306** EUROPE Pytheas of Massilia (Marseilles) reputed to have sailed round Britain and found island of Thule (Iceland) to the north.
**166–69** EUROPE Free port of Delos dominates E Mediterranean trade, especially in slaves.
**About 100–66** EUROPE/ASIA/AFRICA Pirates wreck Mediterranean trade.

*TRAVELLERS ON THE SILK ROAD By the start of the Tang dynasty (AD 618), foreign merchants were familiar in China. Two appear in this ceramic model.*

**About 90** ASIA Silk Road from China opened as far west as Parthia (Iran).
**44–31** AFRICA Roman trading posts set up on E African coast.
**About 27** EUROPE/ASIA Discovery of monsoon winds opens direct sea route to India from Aden.

## AD 0–500

**1st century** EUROPE Rome trades with N Germany, Denmark.
**About 61–63** EUROPE/AFRICA Roman expedition to Ethiopia.
**About 66–70** EUROPE Amber route from Danube to Baltic opens.
**67** EUROPE Romans, under Nero, begin work on Corinth Canal in Greece, but abandon the project.
**After 250** EUROPE Decline of Roman trade and travel, except to N Africa.

# AD 500–1000

**606** ASIA First Japanese trade contacts with China.
**796** EUROPE Emperor Charlemagne concludes trade treaty with King Offa of Mercia, England. English woven fabric exported.
**874** EUROPE Norwegians colonise Iceland.
**907** EUROPE Russians trade with Constantinople.
**982–6** EUROPE Norseman Eirik the Red colonises Greenland.
**About 1000** N AMERICA Leif Eiriksson, son of Eirik the Red, establishes settlement in Vinland, the coast of Newfoundland.
**1000** EUROPE Venice dominates Adriatic, and over the next 100 years sets up trading posts throughout E Mediterranean.

# AD 1000–1500

**About 1147** EUROPE Wool trade flourishing between England and Flanders.
**About 1189** EUROPE Cornish tin exported to Rhineland, Flanders and France.
**About 1228** EUROPE German Gothland Society trades between Lübeck, Cologne, Riga, Hamburg and Novgorod in Russia.
**1252–99** EUROPE Trade war between Venice and Genoa for commercial control of Black Sea and the Levant won by Venice.
**1253–5** ASIA Trade mission of William of Rubruck from France to Mongol court at Karakorum opens up Central Asia.
**1255–95** EUROPE/ASIA Increasing Venetian links with Central Asia and China.
**1271–95** EUROPE/ASIA Venetian traveller Marco Polo (1254–1324) crosses Central Asia, visits China, India, Sumatra and Persia.
**About 1337–50** EUROPE Hanseatic League in northern Germany organises trade from Baltic to Flanders, centred on Lübeck and Bruges.
**1418–60** EUROPE/AFRICA Portugal's Prince Henry the Navigator (1394–1460) sponsors expeditions to W Africa and opens school of navigation at Sagres.
**1488** EUROPE Portugal's Bartolomeu Dias (died 1500) rounds Cape of Good Hope, opening a new route to India.
**1492–1502** S AMERICA Four Spanish-backed voyages by the Genoese-born explorer Christopher Columbus (1451–1506) reach Bahamas, Cuba, Hispaniola (Haiti), Trinidad and the mouth of the Orinoco River, and Panama.

**1493** WORLDWIDE Papal edict assigns Africa and Brazil to Portugal, rest of S America to Spain.
**1497–8** N AMERICA Genoese-born explorer John Cabot (1461–98) makes two English-backed voyages in search of a North-West Passage to China and discovers Newfoundland.
**1498 (May)** ASIA Vasco da Gama (about 1469–1524) of Portugal reaches west coast of India at Calicut (also known as Kozhikode) after rounding southern Africa.
**1499–1501** S AMERICA Florentine navigator Amerigo Vespucci (1454–1512) explores coast of S America, and gives his name to the continent.

# AD 1500–1600

**1501** N AMERICA Black slaves brought from Africa to Spain's colony of Santo Domingo in the Caribbean.
**1510** ASIA Portugal sets up trading post in India at Goa.
**1513** N AMERICA Spanish pioneer Vasco Nuñez de Balboa (1475–1519) crosses the isthmus of Panama, becoming the first European to see the Pacific.
**1519–22** WORLDWIDE Ferdinand Magellan (about 1480–1521), a Portuguese in Spanish service, leads first expedition to circumnavigate the world.
**1527–31** N AMERICA Commercial tobacco farming begins in Haiti, the first place to grow a crop on a large scale.
**1535** N AMERICA French navigator Jacques Cartier (1491–1557) sails up the St Lawrence, winters at Quebec and explores the site of present-day Montreal.
**1542** ASIA First Portuguese reach · Japan.
**1545** S AMERICA Spanish find silver deposits at Potosi in modern Bolivia. Convoys of treasure ships begin (1560) carrying bullion to Europe.
**1557** ASIA China grants Portugal a treaty to establish Macao as a trading colony.
**1562–8** AFRICA/N AMERICA John Hawkins (1532–95) begins English slave trade between W Africa and the Caribbean.
**1568** ASIA Nagasaki developed as Portuguese trading centre in Japan.
**1577–80** WORLDWIDE English seaman Francis Drake (about 1545–96) sails around the world, landing in California, the Moluccas and Java.

**1584–5** N AMERICA Sir Walter Raleigh (about 1552–1618) leads English expedition to colonise N American region which he names Virginia, after Elizabeth I, England's 'Virgin Queen'.
**1600** ASIA English East India Company founded.

# AD 1600–1700

**1602** ASIA Dutch East Indies Company set up. It dominated Indonesia by 1641, controlling trade with the islands until 1799.
**1603** N AMERICA French explorer Samuel de Champlain (1567–1635) makes the first of 11 voyages to explore Canada up to the Great Lakes.
**1616–27** AUSTRALIA Dutch vessels explore coast of W Australia.
**1618** ASIA Cossack explorers establish trading post in Siberia at Yeniseysk. They reach Okhotsk on the Pacific coast in 1649.
**1620** N AMERICA Puritan pioneers aboard the *Mayflower* settle in present-day Massachusetts, USA.
**1637** S AMERICA Dutch slave trade with Curaçao established from present-day Ghana.

A QUEEN'S SOUVENIR *When Francis Drake returned from his voyage round the world in 1580, he gave Elizabeth I a coconut. She had this globe made to hold it and presented the trophy to Drake.*

51

# EXPLORATION AND TRADE AD 1642–1979

**1642** OCEANIA Dutch explorer Abel Tasman (about 1603–59) discovers Tasmania, sights New Zealand, and discovers Tonga and Fiji.
**1652** AFRICA Dutch establish trade settlement at Cape Town and colonise hinterland.
**1670** N AMERICA Hudson's Bay Company set up to establish trading stations in Canada.

## AD 1700–1800

**1728** ASIA/N AMERICA Vitus Bering (1681–1741), a Dane in Russian service, passes through straits between Siberia and Alaska into Arctic Ocean.
**1768–71** AUSTRALIA/OCEANIA Captain James Cook (1728–79) explores coasts of New Zealand and New South Wales.
**1772–3** ANTARCTICA Cook discovers Antarctica on his second voyage.
**1776** AMERICA Spanish explorer Juan Bautista de Anza (1735–88) completes exploration of northern California and founds city of San Francisco.
**1784** N AMERICA Russians establish trading post in Alaska.
**1788** AUSTRALIA First convict settlement established by Britain at Botany Bay, Australia.
**1792** EUROPE Denmark becomes the first country to outlaw the slave trade.
**1795–1805** AFRICA Scottish explorer Mungo Park (1771–1806) leads expeditions into the upper Niger in Africa.

MRI SKILL early New Zealanders made carvings to their weapons.

## AD 1800–1900

**1803–6** AMERICA Meriwether Lewis (1774–1809) and William Clark (1770–1838) lead first expedition across the American Rockies.

**1817–18** AUSTRALIA John Oxley begins to explore interior of Australia.
**1819–44** EUROPE Growth of German Free Trade Association (*Zollverein*) under Prussia's leadership.
**1836** AFRICA Dutch Boers start the 'Great Trek' north of the Orange River to escape British interference.
**1840–1** AUSTRALIA British-born pioneer Edward Eyre (1815–1901) crosses the deserts of southern Australia.
**1842** ASIA China opens five 'Treaty Ports' for foreign trade.
**1842–6** N AMERICA Three expeditions under John Frémont (1813–90) map the whole of the American West.
**1845–7** N AMERICA Expedition led by British explorer Sir John Franklin (1786–1847) discovers North-West Passage round Canada, but all 129 members perish.
**1845–7** N AMERICA Mormons open up Utah, USA, in migration from Illinois.

## AD 1850–1900

**1853–6** AFRICA Scottish missionary David Livingstone (1813–73) crosses Africa and explores Zambezi.
**1854** ASIA US Commodore Matthew Perry negotiates treaty with Japan, opening the country to commerce with USA.
**1858–60** ASIA Russians develop Far Eastern territories and found Vladivostok.
**1860–1** AUSTRALIA Robert Burke and William Wills cross Australia from south to north, but die on return journey.
**1869** N AMERICA US Railway crossing of the continent completed.
AFRICA Suez Canal opened.
**1885** N AMERICA Canadian Pacific Railway spans the continent. It is officially opened in 1887.
**1891–1917** EUROPE/ASIA Trans-Siberian Railway built.

FIRE AND ICE *During his last voyage, in 1778, Captain Cook ventured into the Arctic Ocean. His crew added walrus meat to their diet.*

**1893–5** ARCTIC Norwegian explorer Fridtjof Nansen (1861–1930) in the *Fram* penetrates the Arctic.
**1895–8** AFRICA Jean Marchand (1863–1934) leads a French expedition from the Congo to the White Nile.

## AD 1900–1950

**1903–6** AMERICA Norwegian explorer Roald Amundsen (1872–1928) navigates North-West Passage.
**1911** ANTARCTICA Amundsen reaches South Pole (December), a month before British expedition led by Captain Robert Scott (1868–1912).
**1914** AMERICA Panama Canal opened.
**1932–9** WORLDWIDE Spread of international airlines.
**1947–8** WORLDWIDE Liberalisation of international commerce by General Agreement on Tariffs and Trade (GATT).

## AD 1950–1984

**1955–70** EUROPE/S AMERICA/AFRICA Common Markets in Europe, Latin America and E Africa establish protected trade zones.
**1960** WORLDWIDE Organisation of Petroleum Exporting Countries (OPEC) founded to control world oil prices.
**1966** EUROPE North Sea oil discovered.
**1967** AFRICA Suez Canal closed after Six Day War – encouraging development of supertankers. Canal re-opened 1975.
**1973** AFRICA/ASIA Oil embargo by Arab oil-producing countries after Yom Kippur War causes rise in oil prices.
**1979–82** WORLDWIDE British Transglobe expedition becomes first team to circumnavigate the Earth via the Poles.

# SCIENCE, INVENTIONS AND MEDICINE 7000 BC – AD 1476

## 7000 – 2000 BC

**7000 – 6000** ASIA Pottery made in Middle East.
**About 5500** ASIA/AFRICA Copper, gold and silver worked in Mesopotamia and Egypt.
**About 4000 – 3500** ASIA/AFRICA Basket-making begins. Spindle developed for spinning. Wheel and kiln invented. Mud bricks used.
**About 3500 – 3000** ASIA Cuneiform writing developed in Sumeria. Plough and cart invented, bronze cast.
**3100** ASIA/AFRICA Hieroglyphic writing in Egypt. Reed boats in Egypt and Assyria (now Iraq).
**3000** ASIA Cotton cultivated in Indus Valley.
**About 2500** AFRICA Wooden boats used in Egypt. Papyrus writing material and ink made.
**2100 – 2050** EUROPE Linear A writing in Crete.
ASIA Glass made in Mesopotamia.

## 2000 – 1000 BC

**1792 – 1750** ASIA Mathematics and medicine practised in Babylon.
**About 1740** ASIA Horses (ridden and used for draught) and war chariot introduced from Persia to Mesopotamia (and later Egypt).
**1650 – 1590** EUROPE Linear B writing (syllabic, early form of Greek) developed in Crete.
**1372 – 1354** ASIA Iron weapons used by Hittites. Alphabetic script used at Byblos and Ugarit.
**About 1000** ASIA Industrial use of iron in Egypt and Mesopotamia.

## 1000 – 500 BC

**About 800** EUROPE Greek alphabet first used.
**About 750** ASIA Babylonian astronomy developed and eclipses predicted. A calendar established (747).
**About 650** ASIA Coinage invented in Lydia (Asia Minor).
**About 600** EUROPE Etruscans invent the arch. Roman alphabet develops from Greek via Etruscan.
**About 509** EUROPE Pythagoras of Samos (about 582 – 507) establishes community at Croton (S Italy), studying mathematics, astronomy, and reincarnation.

SAILOR'S FRIEND *The Pharos lighthouse, built in about 270 BC, was more than 130m (400ft) high. The light was provided by a wood fire.*

## 500 – 0 BC

**About 400** EUROPE Hippocrates of Kos, physician and founder of scientific medicine, formulates the Hippocratic Oath.
ASIA Crossbow invented in China.
**About 300** AFRICA In Alexandria, Egypt, Euclid (dates unknown) teaches mathematics; spring, screw, pump, lever, cog invented; first use of steam power and water clock.
**About 250** EUROPE Archimedes (287 – 212), Greek mathematician and engineer, states law of lever and invents Archimedes' screw for raising water.
**About 270** AFRICA Pharos, one of the Seven Wonders of the Ancient World, built at Alexandria.
**About 133** EURQPE Romans begin to use concrete.
**About 100** EUROPE Hypocaust (underfloor heating) and public baths introduced in Italy.
**46** EUROPE Caesar reforms the calendar, creating the Julian calendar.

## AD 0 – 500

**Before 21** EUROPE Strabo (about 63 BC – after AD 21), Greek writer, produces the *Geographia*, a compendium of historical and geographical knowledge.
**By 77** EUROPE Pliny the Elder (about 23 – 79) completes *Historia naturalis*, an encyclopedia of natural science.
**About 100** ASIA Paper invented in China.
**By 400** ASIA Decimal system of numbers in use in India, symbol for zero first used.

## AD 500 – 1000

**By 650** ASIA Persians using windmills – not known in W Europe until about 1100.
**786 – 96** EUROPE Palace school flourishes at Aachen (Charlemagne's capital) under English scholar monk Alcuin of York (about 735 – 804).
**About 813** ASIA Observatories set up at Baghdad and Damascus.
**About 850** EUROPE University established at Constantinople.
**878 – 99** EUROPE Alfred the Great (849 – 99) establishes schools for English nobles' sons.
**About 868** ASIA First printed book, *The Diamond Sutra*, published in China using wood blocks.

## AD 1000 – 1500

**1040 – 50** ASIA Printing from movable type invented by Chinese alchemist Bi Sheng.
**About 1164** ASIA Gunpowder in use in China, probably for fireworks.
**About 1250 – 77** EUROPE Friar Roger Bacon (about 1214 – 94), experimental scientist at Oxford, England, invents magnifying glass and has knowledge of gunpowder.
**1438** EUROPE German printer Johann Gutenberg (about 1397 – 1468) invents a mould for casting individual letters in metal. His first printed books appear in 1450s.
**1476** EUROPE William Caxton (about 1421 – 91) sets up printing press at Westminster, England.

# SCIENCE, INVENTIONS AND MEDICINE  AD 1509–1981

## AD 1500–1600

**1509** EUROPE Earliest known pocket watch made at Nuremberg, Germany.
**1527** EUROPE Swiss physician and alchemist Philippus Paracelsus (about 1493–1541) compiles the earliest manual of surgery.
**1543** EUROPE Polish astronomer Nicolaus Copernicus (1473–1543) publishes his theory that the Earth revolves round the Sun.
**1550s** EUROPE First muskets manufactured in Spain.
**1568** EUROPE Flemish geographer Gerhard Kremer (1512–94), also known as Gerardus Mercator, publishes map of the world using the projection that now bears his name.
**About 1590** EUROPE Dutch opticians Hans and Zacharias Janssen invent the first true microscope using a combination of lenses.
**1592** EUROPE Italian astronomer Galileo Galilei (1564–1642) at Padua, invents the first thermometer.

## AD 1600–1700

**1614** EUROPE Scottish theologian John Napier (1550–1617) devises the first logarithms.
**1628** EUROPE British physician William Harvey (1578–1657) discovers circulation of the blood.
**1650** EUROPE Otto von Guericke, Mayor of Magdeburg in present-day East Germany, invents the air pump and (1654) demonstrates the vacuum pump.
**1659–62** EUROPE Anglo-Irish chemist and physicist Robert Boyle (1627–91) perfects his theories on gases and pneumatics.
**1668** EUROPE Isaac Newton (1642–1727) invents the reflecting telescope.
**1687** EUROPE Newton publishes *Philosophiae naturalis principia mathematica*, which includes his laws of motion and gravity.
**1665–1704** EUROPE Newton and German philosopher-mathematician Gottfried von Leibniz (1646–1716) independently develop the system of calculus.

## AD 1700–1800

**1709** EUROPE Abraham Darby (1677–1717) first uses coke in a blast furnace to smelt iron at Coalbrookdale, Shropshire, England.
**1712** EUROPE First practical steam engine invented by Devon blacksmith Thomas Newcomen.
**1733** EUROPE British engineer John Kay invents flying shuttle to speed up cotton weaving.
**1735** EUROPE Swedish botanist Carolus Linnaeus (1707–78) publishes *Systema naturae*, which presents his method of classifying plants and animals.
**About 1740** EUROPE Swedish astronomer Anders Celsius (1701–44) invents Centigrade temperature scale.
**1752** N AMERICA Scientist Benjamin Franklin (1706–90) installs the first lightning conductor on his home in Philadelphia.
**1757** EUROPE Sextant invented by Royal Navy captain, James Campbell.
**1764–9** EUROPE James Hargreaves' spinning jenny and Richard Arkwright's water frame launch first textile factories in northern England.
**1774** EUROPE British scientist Joseph Priestley (1733–1804) discovers oxygen. Swedish chemist Karl Scheele (1742–86) discovers chlorine.
**1777** EUROPE Jame Watt invents first steam engine with separate condenser.
**1781** EUROPE Seventh planet, Uranus, discovered by German-born astronomer William Herschel (1738–1822).
**1783** EUROPE First ascent in hot-air balloon by Montgolfier brothers in Paris.
**1786** EUROPE Experiments in Italy by Alessandro Volta (1745–1827) and Luigi Galvani (1737–98) lead to the first simple electrical battery.
**1793** N AMERICA Inventor Eli Whitney (1765–1825) devises labour-saving cotton gin, boosting US cotton industry.
**1796** EUROPE English physicist Edward Jenner (1749–1823) successfully completes 20 years of experiments in the protective power of vaccination.
**1799** EUROPE Metric system adopted in France.

## AD 1800–1850

**1821–31** EUROPE Development of the electric generator by British scientist Michael Faraday (1791–1867) culminating in discovery of electro-magnetic induction–the basis of electric motors.
**1825** EUROPE Steam locomotive first used on public railway in England.
**1827** EUROPE Law relating current, voltage and resistance formulated by German physicist Georg Ohm (1787–1854).
**1832–44** N AMERICA Inventor Samuel Morse (1791–1872) develops the electric telegraph and sends first message from Baltimore to Washington (May 1844).
**1834** N AMERICA Inventor Cyrus McCormick (1809–84) devises reaping machine, making possible mass harvesting of grain.
**1836** N AMERICA Inventor Samuel Colt (1814–62) patents the revolver.
**1839** N AMERICA Inventor Charles Goodyear (1800–60) discovers how to vulcanise rubber, patenting the process in 1844.
**1846** EUROPE Eighth planet, Neptune, discovered by German astronomer Johann Galle (1812–1910).

## AD 1850–1900

**1859** EUROPE British naturalist Charles Darwin (1809–82) publishes the *Origin of Species*, setting out his theory of evolution. N AMERICA First commercial oil well dug at Titusville, Pennsylvania.
**1862** EUROPE First plastic articles–made from 'Parkesine' invented by British inventor Alexander Parkes–exhibited in London.
**1865–6** EUROPE Antiseptic surgery introduced by Joseph Lister (1827–1912).
**1866** EUROPE Austrian monk Gregor Mendel (1822–84) publishes his findings about the mechanics of heredity.
**1867** EUROPE Swedish chemist Alfred Nobel (1833–96) invents dynamite.

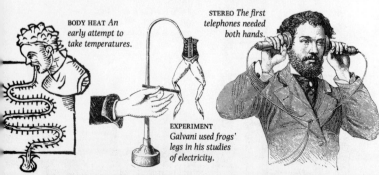

BODY HEAT *An early attempt to take temperatures.*

STEREO *The first telephones needed both hands.*

EXPERIMENT *Galvani used frogs' legs in his studies of electricity.*

CRACKER *A stick of dynamite made in Nobel's factory in 1884.*

SIX-SHOOTER *A Colt revolver from about 1880.*

**1876** N AMERICA Scottish-American scientist Alexander Graham Bell (1847–1922) transmits the first telephone message. Four-stroke internal combustion engine invented by German engineer Nikolaus Otto (1832–91).
**1878–9** EUROPE/N AMERICA Thomas Edison (1847–1931) in USA and Joseph Swan (1828–1914) in Britain produce first successful incandescent electric light.
**1881** EUROPE First power station goes into operation in Godalming, Surrey, England.
**1885** EUROPE French chemist Louis Pasteur (1822–95) successfully vaccinates animals and people against rabies.
**1887** EUROPE Gottlieb Daimler, working with Karl Benz, produces first successful motor car in Stuttgart, Germany.
**1889–93** N AMERICA Thomas Edison perfects motion-picture technique through his Kinetoscope.
**1892** EUROPE German engineer Rudolf Diesel patents first compression-ignition (diesel) engine.
**1895** EUROPE Radio demonstrated by Italian physicist Guglielmo Marconi (1874–1937). German physicist Wilhelm Röntgen (1845–1923) discovers X-rays.
**1898** EUROPE Pierre and Marie Curie discover radium.

## AD 1900–1950

**1900** EUROPE Sigmund Freud (1856–1939) pioneers psycho-analysis with *Interpretation of Dreams*.
**1901** EUROPE/N AMERICA Marconi transmits wireless message across Atlantic.
**1903** N AMERICA Wright brothers make first successful aeroplane flight at Kitty Hawk, North Carolina, USA, December 17.
**1905** EUROPE Albert Einstein (1879–1955) formulates his Special Theory of Relativity, revolutionising physics.
**1906** EUROPE Count Ferdinand von Zeppelin (1838–1917) builds first practical rigid airship. British biochemist Sir Frederick Hopkins (1861–1947) discovers 'accessory food factors', later renamed vitamins.
**1911** EUROPE New Zealand-born physicist Ernest Rutherford (1871–1937) discovers the nucleus of the atom.

EARLY SHUTTLE Enterprise *never went into orbit, but did pave the way for Columbia, first launched on April 12, 1981.*

**1913** EUROPE Danish physicist Niels Bohr (1885–1962) explains the structure of the atom.
**1915** EUROPE First metal aircraft built by Junkers in Germany. Einstein publishes General Theory of Relativity.
**1926** EUROPE Scottish inventor John Logie Baird (1888–1946) projects first television images.
**1928** EUROPE Scottish bacteriologist Alexander Fleming (1881–1955) discovers antibiotic powers of penicillin.
**1930** EUROPE British aviator and engineer Frank Whittle patents jet aircraft engine.
N AMERICA Ninth planet, Pluto, discovered by US astronomer Clyde Tombaugh (1906–   ) at Lowell Observatory, Arizona, USA.
**1935–9** EUROPE British physicist Robert Watson-Watt (1892–1973) develops radar.
**1944** EUROPE German scientist Wernher von Braun (1912–77) produces first long-range rockets (V-2).
**1945** N AMERICA Experimental atom bomb exploded, New Mexico, USA (July 17). First truly electronic computer built at University of Pennsylvania, USA.
**1948** N AMERICA Transistor – invented by American scientists John Bardeen, Walter Brattain and William Shockley – first demonstrated, leading to development of silicon chip for electronics in 1960s.

## AD 1950–1984

**1952** AMERICA US experimental hydrogen bomb exploded, Eniwetok island (November 1).
**1953** EUROPE James Watson, Francis Crick and Maurice Wilkins discover the helical structure and genetic importance of DNA (deoxyribonucleic acid).
**1954** EUROPE First atomic power station begins generating electricity in Obninsk, USSR.
N AMERICA First successful organ transplant, of a kidney, carried out at Harvard Medical School, USA.
**1956** AMERICA Oral contraceptive developed by US researcher Dr Gregory Pincus.
**1957** EUROPE First successful launching of intercontinental ballistic missile announced by Soviet government. *Sputnik*, first Earth satellite, launched into space by Soviet Union (October 4).
**1959** EUROPE First full-sized model of hovercraft, invented by Christopher Cockerell, launched at Cowes, Isle of Wight, England.
**1960** N AMERICA US scientists develop laser beam.
**1960–3** N AMERICA US geologist Harry Hess develops theory of ocean-floor spreading which leads to theory of plate tectonics.
**1961** EUROPE Soviet cosmonaut Yuri Gagarin becomes first man in space aboard *Vostok I* (April 12).
**1962** EUROPE/N AMERICA First communications satellite, *Telstar*, launched by the USA.
**1967** AFRICA First human heart transplant operation carried out in Cape Town, S Africa, by Dr Christiaan Barnard (1923–   ).
**1969** N AMERICA US astronaut Neil Armstrong, in *Apollo 11*, becomes the first man on the Moon (July).
**1971** EUROPE First space station – USSR's *Salyut* – launched. AMERICA First pocket calculators become commercially available in USA. Microprocessor (logic and arithmetic unit of a computer on a single silicon chip) patented by the Intel Corporation, USA.
**1978** EUROPE First test-tube baby born in Oldham, Lancashire, following fertilisation in a laboratory (July).
**1979** WORLDWIDE World Health Organisation announces the eradication of smallpox.
**1981** N AMERICA US space shuttle *Columbia* takes off on maiden flight (April 12) – 20 years to the day after Gagarin's flight. *Solar Challenger*, a solar-powered American aircraft, crosses the English Channel.

# THE ARTS 8000 BC – AD 1497

DEATH MASK *The face, in beaten gold, of a Mycenaean king from about 1500 BC.*

## 8000 – 1000 BC

**8000 – 7000** ASIA Painting on plaster and stone. Plaster features made on skulls in Jericho.
**7000 – 6000** ASIA Shrines, wall paintings and figurines made in the Middle East.
**Before 3000** EUROPE First known stone temples built in Malta.
**3100** AFRICA Royal tombs of Abydos, Upper Egypt, built.
**2800** ASIA Royal cemetery built at Ur, Mesopotamia.
**About 2700** AFRICA Pyramid Age in Egypt begins. Pyramids and Sphinx built at Giza (about 2560).
**About 2600** ASIA 'Priam's treasure' of gold and jewellery made in Troy.
**About 2371 – 2316** ASIA Akkadian statues and bronzes made.
**2100** ASIA First ziggurat built at Ur.
**1792 – 1750** ASIA Babylonian palaces and temples built.
**1650 – 1590** EUROPE Cretan palaces built at Knossos and Phaistos.
**1580 – 1330** AFRICA Egypt's New Kingdom culture builds tombs in Valley of Kings, and temples at Luxor, Karnak and Abu Simbel. Tutankhamun buried 1352.
**About 1250** EUROPE The Lion Gate and tombs built at Mycenae.
**About 1000** AMERICA Olmec pyramids and pavements built at La Venta, Mexico.

## 1000 – 500 BC

**About 900** AFRICA Nok culture makes pottery heads in Central Nigeria.
**884 – 859** ASIA Relief sculptures created at Assyrian palace at Nimrud.
**About 800** EUROPE *Iliad* and *Odyssey*, Greek epic poems traditionally composed by Homer. AFRICA Royal tombs and pyramids built in Nubian kingdom of Kush, Sudan.
**776** EUROPE First Olympic Games at Olympia in Greece.
**722 – 705** ASIA Assyrian kings at Nineveh collect libraries of Akkado-Sumerian inscriptions, including the epic poem Gilgamesh.
**650** EUROPE Archaic Greek sculpture begins.
**About 600** EUROPE Forum and Capitol built in Rome.
**From 600** ASIA Babylon rebuilt with Hanging Gardens and Tower of Babel ziggurat.
**600 – 500** EUROPE Etruscans begin wall painting in tombs.
**About 600 – 400** EUROPE Flourishing of Greek poetry and drama.
**About 520** EUROPE Thespis in Athens transforms performance of chorus into primitive drama by introducing solo actor.

## 500 – 0 BC

**490** EUROPE Classic sculpture and temple building begins in Greece.
**472** EUROPE Earliest surviving Greek play *The Persians* written by Aeschylus (525 – 456).
**458** EUROPE *Oresteia* trilogy, considered the greatest Greek tragedy, written by the playwright Aeschylus.
**448 – 438** EUROPE Parthenon in Athens built by Greek architect Ictinus, with sculptures by Phidias.
**447** EUROPE Herodotus (484 – 425) writes the first history of the western world.
**About 425** EUROPE Sophocles writes tragedy of *Oedipus Rex*.
**About 421** EUROPE Socrates (about 470 – 399) begins teaching as scientific philosopher in Athens.
**About 385** EUROPE Plato (427 – 347) founds his Academy in Athens.
**336** EUROPE Greek philosopher Aristotle (384 – 322) founds his school in Athens.
**About 330** EUROPE Greek philosopher Diogenes (about 400 – 325) founds philosophy of austerity known as Cynicism.
**About 313** EUROPE Greek philosopher Zeno of Citium (about 334 – 262) founds philosophy of Stoicism.
**About 300** AFRICA Museum and library founded at Alexandria, on northern coast of Egypt.
**From 100** ASIA Buddhist art flourishes in India.
**52 – 51** EUROPE Julius Caesar (about 100 – 44) writes *Gallic Wars*.
**29** EUROPE Roman poet Virgil (70 – 19) starts his epic the *Aeneid*, about the founding of Rome.
**From 27** EUROPE Age of Augustan writers: poets Virgil, Horace (65 – 8) and Ovid (43 – AD 18), and historian Livy (59 – AD 17). Forum, palaces and library built on Palatine Hill in Rome.

## AD 0 – 500

**120 – 200** ASIA Baalbeck temples built in Lebanon.
**From 250** AMERICA Mayan pyramids and temples built in Central America.
**From 320** ASIA Classical Indian art begins under Gupta dynasty (about 320 – 550).
**About 400** AFRICA St Augustine of Hippo (354 – 430) writes *Confessions*, a classic of Christian mysticism, in N Africa.
**About 404** ASIA St Jerome completes translation of the Bible into Latin (Vulgate) in Palestine.

# AD 500–1200

**About 530** EUROPE Illuminated manuscripts made in N Europe. Byzantine art flourishes in Constantinople and Ravenna with mosaics and painted frescoes. Church of St Sophia built in Constantinople 532–7.
**About 618** ASIA Art of Tang dynasty in China includes figure painting, lyric poetry.
**645–784** ASIA Japanese classical art imitates Chinese style.
**731** EUROPE English monk the Venerable Bede (around 673–735) completes in Latin his *History of English Church and People*.
**About 800** EUROPE *Beowulf*, Anglo-Saxon epic poem, written by a bard.
**813–33** ASIA Caliph Mamun sets up a centre of learning at Baghdad.
**From 887** EUROPE King Alfred of England (849–99) translates Bede into Anglo-Saxon and encourages start of the *Anglo-Saxon Chronicle*.
**About 900** AMERICA Mayan city of Chichén Itzá rebuilt under Toltecs.
**About 912** EUROPE Córdoba, Spain, becomes Moorish cultural centre under Caliph Abdurrahman III and his successors.
**By 1000** EUROPE Latin love lyrics produced in France and Germany. ASIA Tales of *The Thousand and One Nights* compiled in Arabia.
**About 1000–1200** EUROPE Romanesque architecture flourishes in Italy and France.
**1049–1109** EUROPE Hugh of Semur rebuilds the abbey of Cluny, France – the start of the flowering of ecclesiastical architecture in England and France.
**1063–73** EUROPE St Mark's Basilica, Venice, built in Byzantine style.
**By 1100** EUROPE University of Bologna founded.
**About 1100** AFRICA Timbuktu founded as centre of culture in W Africa.
**From 1100** EUROPE Medieval *Chansons de geste* ('Songs of deeds') written down.
**1144** EUROPE Choir of Benedictine Abbey of St Denis built outside Paris; the first example of Gothic architecture.
**From 1150** ASIA Averröes (1126–98), Spanish-born Arab philosopher and physician, influences Jewish and Christian thought through his commentary on Aristotle.
**1150–1200** EUROPE Oxford University founded.
**About 1170** EUROPE Poets of courtly love, such as Chrétien de Troyes (about 1150–83), write in French. Vernacular literature begins

ROTTEN TEETH *The mason who carved this figure in Wells Cathedral, England, in the 12th century must have known what agony toothache could be.*

to emerge in Europe. University of Paris founded.
**About 1180** EUROPE Giraldus Cambrensis (Gerald of Wales, about 1146–1223) writes history and topography of Ireland and Wales.
**1194–1260** EUROPE Chartres Cathedral, France, extensively rebuilt.

# AD 1200–1300

**1209** EUROPE Cambridge University founded.
**1257–80** EUROPE Allegorical poem *Roman de la Rose* written.
**1267–73** EUROPE St Thomas Aquinas (1225–74), Italian philosopher, writes his *Summa Theologica*, attempting to reconcile Aristotle and Christianity.
**About 1280–1450** ASIA Flourishing of Chinese classical drama.
**From 1300** ASIA Japanese Noh theatre established.

# AD 1300–1400

**1305–8** EUROPE Italian painter Giotto (1267–1337) paints fresco *The Lives of the Virgin and Christ* in Padua, signalling a turn towards naturalism and the beginning of the Renaissance.
**1307** EUROPE Italian poet Dante (1265–1321) begins *The Divine Comedy*.
**1348–53** EUROPE Italian poet Boccaccio (1313–75) publishes the *Decameron*.
**About 1360** EUROPE Italian poet Petrarch (1304–74) publishes *Canzoniere*.
ASIA Ming blue and white porcelain first made in China.
**1385** EUROPE Heidelberg (West Germany) University founded by Elector Rupert I.
**1360–1402** EUROPE Building of the Alcazar, Seville, Spain.
**1362–3** EUROPE English poet William Langland (about 1331–99) writes *Piers Plowman*.
**1387–1400** EUROPE English poet Geoffrey Chaucer (1340–1400) writes *Canterbury Tales*.

# AD 1400–1500

**1401–52** EUROPE Italian sculptor Lorenzo Ghiberti (1378–1455) works on bronze doors for baptistry in Florence.
**1420–36** EUROPE Italian architect Filippo Brunelleschi (1377–1446) builds Dome of Florence Cathedral – start of the main flowering of the Renaissance.
**About 1420** EUROPE Brunelleschi develops system of perspective.
**About 1420–50** EUROPE Guild mystery plays performed at York and Coventry, England.
**From 1430** EUROPE Flemish artist Jan van Eyck (died 1441) perfects oil-painting technique in Flanders.
**1430–5** EUROPE Italian sculptor Donatello (1386–1466) makes *David*, the first monumental nude since the Roman empire.
**1446–1515** EUROPE King's College Chapel, Cambridge, built in English Perpendicular style.
**1480–5** EUROPE Italian painter Sandro Botticelli (about 1445–1510) paints *The Birth of Venus*.
**1485** EUROPE *Le Morte D'Arthur*, a collection of stories about King Arthur, written by the English prose-writer Sir Thomas Malory.
**From 1495** EUROPE Aldine Press in Venice prints the Greek Classics, spreading rebirth of Greek learning.
**1497** EUROPE Leonardo da Vinci (1452–1519) paints *Last Supper*.

LINES BY LEONARDO *One of da Vinci's sketches for the portrait of St James in the* Last Supper.

# THE ARTS 1501–1867

## AD 1500–1600

**1501** EUROPE First printed music published in Venice by Ottaviano dei Petrucci.
**1501–4** EUROPE Michelangelo (1475–1564), sculptor, painter and architect, makes the statue of *David*.
**1502** EUROPE Leonardo da Vinci paints the *Mona Lisa*.
**1505** EUROPE New St Peter's begun in Rome by architect Donato Bramante (1444–1514); completed 1655.
**About 1507** EUROPE Italian painter Giorgione (1475–1510) paints *The Tempest*, one of the earliest Western landscapes.
**From 1508** EUROPE Raphael (1483–1520), painter and architect, decorates the papal apartments in the Vatican with frescoes.
**1508–12** EUROPE Michelangelo paints frescoes in the Sistine Chapel.
**1509** EUROPE Dutch humanist writer Erasmus (1466–1535) writes *In Praise of Folly*, exposing worldliness of medieval Church.
**From 1510** EUROPE Venetian Renaissance at its peak, major painters include Titian (1487–1576), Veronese (1528–88) and Tintoretto (1518–94).
**1516** EUROPE English lawyer Sir Thomas More (1478–1535) publishes his fantasy *Utopia*.

**ORID GRANDEUR**
ini's statue of an
gel was carved in
59, at the height
Italian baroque.

**1532** EUROPE *The Prince*, by Italian political theorist Niccolo Machiavelli (1469–1527), published.
**1534** EUROPE French writer François Rabelais publishes satirical romances *Gargantua*.
**1550** EUROPE Italian painter and writer Giorgio Vasari (1511–74) publishes *Lives of the most excellent Painters, Sculptors and Architects*.
**1552** EUROPE Italian architect Andrea Palladio (1508–80) begins building the Villa Rotonda in Vicenza, Italy.
**1572** EUROPE Luis de Camões (1524–80) writes epic poem *The Lusiads*, in Portugal.
**1580** EUROPE French writer Michel de Montaigne (1533–92), inventor of a new literary form, the essay, publishes his *Essais*.
**About 1590–2** EUROPE William Shakespeare (1564–1616) writes his first plays: *Henry VI* parts 1, 2 and 3 and *Love's Labour's Lost*.
**1590–6** EUROPE English poet Edmund Spenser (1552–99) writes *The Faerie Queene*.
**1597–1625** EUROPE English statesman and philosopher Francis Bacon (1561–1626) composes his *Essays*, the first examples of the form in English.
**1600** EUROPE Oratorio first emerges in Europe as a sacred equivalent of opera.

## AD 1600–1700

**1605** EUROPE Spanish author Miguel de Cervantes (1547–1616) writes *Don Quixote*.
**1607** EUROPE Italian composer Claudio Monteverdi (1567–1643) in *Orfeo* develops opera as an art form.
**About 1613** EUROPE Lope de Vega (1562–1635), first major Spanish dramatist and poet, publishes *The Sheepfold*, the best known of the estimated 1500–2000 plays he wrote.
**From 1630** EUROPE Baroque art flourishes in Rome.
**1637** EUROPE French dramatist Pierre Corneille (1606–84) writes *Le Cid*. French philosopher René Descartes (1596–1650) publishes his *Discours de la Méthode*, an essay setting out the basis of his scientific philosophy. First public opera house, Teatro di San Cassiano, opens in Venice.
N AMERICA Harvard, the first university in North America, founded.
**1640–60** EUROPE French painter Claude perfects his influential style of poetic, classical landscapes.
**1642** EUROPE Dutch painter Rembrandt Van Rijn (1606–69) produces *The Night Watch*.

**1651** EUROPE English philosopher Thomas Hobbes publishes *Leviathan*.
**1667** EUROPE English poet John Milton (1608–74) writes *Paradise Lost*.
**1669** EUROPE *Thoughts on Religion* by Blaise Pascal (1623–62) published in France.
**1660–80** EUROPE Great age of French drama led by Molière (1622–73). Chapel and palace built at Versailles by Jules Hardouin-Mansart (1646–1708), the gardens created by André Le Nôtre (1613–1700).
**1675** EUROPE Sir Christopher Wren (1632–1723) begins new St Paul's Cathedral, London. Dutch-Jewish rationalist philosopher Benedict Spinoza (1632–77) publishes *Ethics*.
**1678–84** EUROPE English prose writer John Bunyan (1628–88) writes *The Pilgrim's Progress*, a precursor of the modern novel.
**1680** EUROPE Comédie Française, French national theatre, established in Paris.
**1690** EUROPE English empiricist philosopher John Locke (1632–1704) publishes *An Essay Concerning Human Understanding*.

## AD 1700–1800

**1710** EUROPE Irish philosopher Bishop George Berkeley (1685–1753) publishes *The Principles of Human Knowledge*.
**1714** EUROPE German philosopher Gottfried Leibniz (1646–1716) publishes *Monadologie*.
**1719** EUROPE English novelist Daniel Defoe (1660–1731) publishes *Robinson Crusoe*.
**1721** EUROPE German composer J. S. Bach (1685–1750) completes *Brandenburg Concertos*.
**1726** EUROPE Jonathan Swift (1667–1745), Irish satirical writer and poet, publishes *Gulliver's Travels*.
**1728** EUROPE First performance of *The Beggar's Opera*, by John Gay (1685–1732), in London.
**1729** EUROPE Bach composes *St Matthew Passion*.
**1734–7** EUROPE Scottish philosopher David Hume (1711–76) writes *Treatise of Human Nature*.
**1735** EUROPE *A Rake's Progress* painted by English artist William Hogarth (1697–1764).
**1742** EUROPE First performance of *Messiah* by German-born composer George Frederick Handel (1685–1759) in Dublin.
**1747** EUROPE English critic and essayist Samuel Johnson (1709–84) starts compiling the first useful English dictionary.
**1749** EUROPE English novelist Henry Fielding (1707–54) publishes *Tom Jones*.

**1751 – 66** EUROPE *L'Encyclopédie* written in France, with contributions by Diderot (1713 – 84), Voltaire (1694 – 1778), Rousseau (1712 – 78) and Montesquieu (1689 – 1755).
**1754** EUROPE English furniture maker Thomas Chippendale (1718 – 79) publishes his book on furniture design, *Gentleman and Cabinet Maker's Director*.
**1759** EUROPE Voltaire publishes satirical novel *Candide*.
**From 1761** EUROPE Austrian composer Franz Joseph Haydn (1732 – 1809) perfects the classical form of the symphony.
**1762** EUROPE Swiss-born philosopher Jean-Jacques Rousseau publishes *On the Social Contract* and *Emile*.
**1774** EUROPE German writer Johann Goethe (1749 – 1832), leading figure of the romantic *Sturm und Drang* (Storm and Stress) movement, publishes *The Sufferings of Young Werther*.
**1781** EUROPE German philosopher Immanuel Kant (1724 – 1804) publishes the *Critique of Pure Reason*.
**1786** EUROPE Austrian composer Wolfgang Amadeus Mozart (1756 – 91) composes the opera *The Marriage of Figaro*, his first major opera.
**1791** EUROPE Scottish writer James Boswell (1740 – 95) publishes his *The Life of Johnson*.
**1798** EUROPE English poet Samuel Taylor Coleridge (1772 – 1834) publishes *Lyrical Ballads* with William Wordsworth (1770 – 1850), which includes his *The Rime of the Ancient Mariner* and Wordsworth's *Tintern Abbey*.

**1818** EUROPE Mary Shelley (1797 – 1851) publishes the Gothic horror romance *Frankenstein*.
**1818 – 30** ASIA Japanese painter and print designer Katsushika Hokusai (1760 – 1849) produces his best work.
**1820** EUROPE French poet Alphonse de Lamartine (1790 – 1869) publishes lyrical poetry in *Méditations Poétiques*. English painter John Constable (1776 – 1837) paints *The Haywain*.
**1823** EUROPE Beethoven's 9th Symphony, the *Choral*, composed.
**1830** EUROPE French composer Hector Berlioz (1803 – 69) starts his *Symphonie Fantastique*. French novelist Stendhal (1783 – 1842) publishes *Le Rouge et le Noir* (The Red and the Black).
**1831** EUROPE French author Victor Hugo (1802 – 85) leads the French Romantic movement with his drama *Hernani*.
**1833** EUROPE Russian poet Alexander Pushkin (1799 – 1837) begins his novel in epic verse *Eugene Onegin*.
**1835** EUROPE French writer Honoré de Balzac produces *Le Père*

## AD 1850 – 1900

**1851** EUROPE Great Exhibition held in London's Crystal Palace designed by English architect Sir Joseph Paxton (1801 – 65).
**1851 – 3** EUROPE Italian composer Giuseppe Verdi (1813 – 1901) writes *Rigoletto, Il Trovatore* and *La Traviata*.
**1854** EUROPE Hungarian composer Franz Liszt (1811 – 86) invents the symphonic poem with *Les Préludes*.
N AMERICA US writer and poet Henry Thoreau (1817 – 62) writes *Walden*.
**1856** EUROPE French novelist Gustave Flaubert (1821 – 80) writes *Madame Bovary*.
**1857** EUROPE French poet Charles Baudelaire (1821 – 67) publishes his verse in *Les Fleurs du Mal* – the beginning of modern poetry.
**1862** EUROPE Russian novelist and playwright Ivan Turgenev (1818 – 83) publishes *Fathers and Sons*.

ALICE AND THE RED QUEEN *Sir John Tenniel illustrated the first edition of Lewis Carroll's* Through the Looking Glass, *published in 1872.*

## AD 1800 – 1850

**1803** EUROPE Beethoven composes his 3rd Symphony, the *Eroica*, heralding Romanticism.
**1807** EUROPE German philosopher Georg Hegel (1770 – 1831) publishes the *Phenomenology of Mind*.
**1808** EUROPE Goethe publishes the first part of *Faust* (second part 1832).
**1811** EUROPE *Sense and Sensibility*, by the English author Jane Austen, published.
**1815 – 23** EUROPE English architect John Nash (1752 – 1835) reconstructs the Brighton Pavilion in Regency style.
**1816** EUROPE Italian opera composer Gioacchino Rossini (1792 – 1868) composes *The Barber of Seville*.
**1817** EUROPE English poet John Keats (1795 – 1821) publishes his first volume of poetry.

*Goriot*. Danish writer Hans Christian Andersen (1805 – 75) publishes his first book of fairy-tales, *Eventyr*.
**1836 – 7** EUROPE English novelist Charles Dickens (1812 – 70) writes *The Pickwick Papers*.
**1843** EUROPE Danish philosopher Søren Kierkegaard (1813 – 55) publishes *Either/Or*, the foundation of existentialism.
**1847** EUROPE *Jane Eyre*, by English novelist Charlotte Brontë (1816 – 55), and *Wuthering Heights*, by her sister Emily (1818 – 48), published.
**1848** EUROPE Pre-Raphaelite Brotherhood of painters founded in London by John Everett Millais (1829 – 1910) and Dante Gabriel Rossetti (1828 – 82).
N AMERICA US author Nathaniel Hawthorne (1804 – 64) publishes his novel *The Scarlet Letter*.

**1863** EUROPE French painter Edouard Manet (1832 – 83) exhibits *Déjeuner sur l'herbe* at the first Salon de Refusés, causing a scandal. English philosopher John Stuart Mill (1806 – 73) publishes *Utilitarianism*.
**1865** EUROPE English writer Lewis Carroll (1832 – 98) publishes *Alice's Adventures in Wonderland*.
**1866** EUROPE Russian author Feodor Dostoevsky (1821 – 81) publishes *Crime and Punishment*.
**1867** EUROPE Karl Marx (1818 – 83) publishes Volume I of *Das Kapital*. Volumes 2 and 3 published posthumously (1885 and 1894).

59

# THE ARTS 1868–1976

**1868–72** EUROPE Russian composer Modest Mussorgsky (1839–81) writes his opera *Boris Godunov* (first performed in 1874).
**1869** EUROPE Russian writer Leo Tolstoy (1828–1910) finishes his epic novel *War and Peace*.
**1870** EUROPE French novelist Jules Verne (1828–1905) pioneers modern science fiction with *Twenty Thousand Leagues under the Sea*.
**1874** EUROPE First exhibition of Impressionist painting in Paris.
**1875** EUROPE French opera composer Georges Bizet (1838–75) writes the opera *Carmen*.
**1876** EUROPE *The Ring* cycle of operas by German composer Richard Wagner (1813–83) first performed at Bayreuth.
**1878** EUROPE Russian composer Peter Illych Tchaikovsky (1840–93) composes his opera *Eugene Onegin*. *The Age of Bronze*, the first major work of the French sculptor Auguste Rodin (1840–1917), exhibited.
**1879** EUROPE Norwegian dramatist Henrik Ibsen (1828–1906) publishes *A Doll's House*.
**1881** N AMERICA US author Henry James (1843–1916) writes *The Portrait of a Lady*.
**1884–6** EUROPE French painter Georges Seurat (1859–91) paints *Sunday afternoon on the island of La Grande Jatte*. Develops the technique known as pointillism.
**1885** N AMERICA US novelist Mark Twain (1835–1900) writes *Huckleberry Finn*. William Jenney, a member of the Chicago School of architects (about 1885–1900) led by Louis Sullivan (1856–1924), completes the first skyscraper, the Home Insurance Building.
**1885–7** EUROPE Cézanne produces a series of paintings of Mont St Victoire.
**1886** EUROPE German philosopher Friedrich Nietzsche (1844–1900) publishes *Beyond Good and Evil*.
**1887** EUROPE French author Emile Zola (1840–1902) writes *La Terre* (The Earth).
**1891** EUROPE English novelist Thomas Hardy (1840–1928) publishes *Tess of the d'Urbervilles*.
**1893** EUROPE Norwegian artist Edvard Munch (1863–1944) paints *The Cry*.
**1895** EUROPE English novelist H. G. Wells (1866–1946) publishes *The Time Machine*. Irish dramatist Oscar Wilde (1854–1900) publishes *The Importance of Being Earnest*.
**1896** EUROPE Italian composer Giacomo Puccini (1858–1924) writes the opera *La Bohème*.
**1898–1904** EUROPE Moscow Art Theatre under Konstantin Stanislavsky (1865–1938) presents plays by Chekhov. Stanislavsky's theories on acting lead to Method acting in the USA.
**1899** EUROPE Finnish composer Jean Sibelius (1865–1957) writes *Finlandia*. Russian dramatist Anton Chekhov (1860–1904) writes *Uncle Vanya*. English composer Edward Elgar (1857–1934) writes the *Enigma Variations*.
**1900** EUROPE Polish-born English novelist Joseph Conrad (1857–1924) writes *Lord Jim*.

# AD 1900–1950

**1902** EUROPE *Voyage to the Moon* by French film-maker Georges Méliès (1861–1938), made.
**1903** EUROPE *The Way of all Flesh*, by English novelist Samuel Butler (1835–1902), published posthumously.
N AMERICA First narrative film, *The Great Train Robbery*, produced in USA.
**1904** EUROPE Scottish dramatist and novelist James Barrie (1860–1937) publishes *Peter Pan*.
**1905** EUROPE *Salomé*, erotic opera by German composer Richard Strauss (1864–1949), produced in Dresden. Fauvist school of painting named.
**1906–21** EUROPE English novelist and dramatist John Galsworthy (1867–1933) writes *The Forsyte Saga*.
**1907** EUROPE *Les Demoiselles d'Avignon*, painted by the Spanish artist Pablo Picasso (1881–1974), begins the Cubist movement.
**1909** EUROPE Russian impresario Sergei Diaghilev (1872–1929) brings Ballets Russes to Paris with Vaslav Nijinsky (1888–1950) as the leading dancer.

BALLET DRESS *The painter Leon Bakst designed many of the costumes for Diaghilev's productions – including, in 1921, his ballet* The Russian Clown.

**1910–13** EUROPE British philosophers Bertrand Russell (1872–1970) and A. N. Whitehead (1861–1947) publish *Principia Mathematica*.
**1913** EUROPE Russian musician Igor Stravinsky (1882–1971) composes *Rite of Spring* for Diaghilev's Ballets Russes. English novelist D. H. Lawrence (1885–1930) publishes *Sons and Lovers*. French novelist Marcel Proust (1871–1922) starts his eight-part novel *A la recherche du temps perdu* (Remembrance of Things Past). Last volume published 1927. Irish author George Bernard Shaw (1856–1950) publishes his play *Pygmalion*.
N AMERICA Armory Show, New York, introduces modern European art to USA.
ASIA English architect Sir Edwin Lutyens (1869–1944) starts designing the Viceroy's House in New Delhi, India.
**1914** N AMERICA Film maker D. W. Griffith (1875–1948) directs *Birth of a Nation*.
**1915** EUROPE Czech novelist Franz Kafka (1883–1924) completes *The Trial* (published 1925). Radical Dadaist movement, rejecting all previously accepted artistic standards, founded in Zurich, Switzerland, by the French poet Tristan Tzara (1896–1963). Surrealism develops from it.
**1918** EUROPE British essayist Lytton Strachey (1880–1932) publishes *Eminent Victorians*, signalling a change in biographical style.
**1919** EUROPE German designer Walter Gropius (1883–1969) founds Bauhaus Centre for architecture and design.
**1921** EUROPE Italian dramatist Luigi Pirandello (1867–1936) publishes *Six Characters in Search of an Author*. Austrian philosopher Ludwig Wittgenstein (1889–1951) publishes *Tractatus Logico-Philosophicus*.
**1922** EUROPE American-born English poet T. S. Eliot (1888–1965) publishes *The Waste Land*. Irish novelist James Joyce (1882–1941) publishes *Ulysses*, banned in Britain and the USA until the 1930s for obscenity.
N AMERICA Jazz trumpeter Louis Armstrong (1900–71) joins 'King' Oliver's band in Chicago.
**1923** EUROPE Austrian composer Arnold Schönberg (1874–1951) composes *Five Piano Pieces* using a new musical language, serialism.
**1924** EUROPE German novelist Thomas Mann (1875–1955) publishes *The Magic Mountain*. Surrealist movement founded, led by painters Marc Chagall (1889– ), Salvador Dali (1904–83) and Max Ernst (1891–1976). English novelist E. M. Forster (1879–1970) publishes *A Passage to India*.

PIONEER FILM-MAKER *Using swift cutting and close-ups, Eisenstein captured a woman's mounting terror in* The Battleship Potemkin.

**1925** EUROPE Russian film director Sergei Eisenstein (1898–1948) makes *The Battleship Potemkin*.
N AMERICA Comedian Charles Chaplin (1889–1977) directs and stars in the film *The Gold Rush*.
**1925** EUROPE German film director Fritz Lang (1890–1976) makes *Metropolis*.
**1927** N AMERICA First commercially successful talking picture *The Jazz Singer* released.
**1928** EUROPE German composer Kurt Weill (1900–50) writes *The Threepenny Opera*.
N AMERICA Film animator Walt Disney (1901–66) makes the first cartoon talkie, *Steamboat Willie*, in which Mickey Mouse makes his debut.
**1929** EUROPE Russian-born choreographer George Balanchine (1904–83) creates the ballet *Le Fils Prodigue* (The Prodigal Son).
N AMERICA US novelist William Faulkner (1897–1962) publishes *The Sound and the Fury*. US novelist Ernest Hemingway (1898–1961) publishes *A Farewell to Arms*.
**From 1930** N AMERICA Jazz, in the form of swing, spreads to large US cities with dance bands.
**1935** EUROPE British publisher

THEATRE OF THE ABSURD *Beckett's play* Waiting for Godot *(1953) proclaimed the futility of man's existence in a meaningless universe.*

Allen Lane (1902–70) founds Penguin paperback books, revolutionising reading habits.
**1936** EUROPE British philosopher A. J. Ayer (1910– ) publishes *Language, Truth and Logic*, the first account of English logical positivism.
**1937** EUROPE Pablo Picasso paints *Guernica*, in anguished reaction to the destruction of the Basque town Guernica by German bombers in the Spanish Civil War.
**1938–9** EUROPE German Marxist dramatist Bertolt Brecht (1898–1956) writes *Mother Courage*.
**1940** N AMERICA US playwright Eugene O'Neill (1888–1953) writes *Long Day's Journey into Night* (produced 1956).
**1941** N AMERICA US film director Orson Welles (1915– ) makes *Citizen Kane*.
**After 1945** N AMERICA Abstract Expressionist movement in painting develops in USA.
**1947** N AMERICA US dramatist Tennessee Williams (1914–83) produces *A Streetcar named Desire*. US dramatist Arthur Miller (1915– ) produces *Death of a Salesman*.
**1949** EUROPE George Orwell (1903–50) publishes *Nineteen Eighty-Four*.
**From 1950** WORLDWIDE Steel and concrete used in building.

---

## AD 1950–1984

---

**1951** N AMERICA The US author J. D. Salinger (1919– ) publishes *The Catcher in the Rye*.
**1953–60** EUROPE Theatre of the Absurd movement; founded by Romanian-born Eugène Ionesco (1912– ) and Irish-born Samuel Beckett (1906– ).

**1954** EUROPE Radio play *Under Milk Wood* by Welsh poet Dylan Thomas (1914–53), first broadcast. English novelist William Golding (1911– ) writes *Lord of the Flies*. ASIA Japanese film director Akira Kurosawa (1910– ) produces *Seven Samurai*.
**1955** EUROPE Italian film director Michelangelo Antonioni (1912– ) makes *L'Aventura*.
N AMERICA *Rock around the Clock*, a song by US singer Bill Haley and his group *The Comets*, boosts popularity of rock and roll music.
**1956** EUROPE English playwright John Osborne (1929– ), one of the 'Angry Young Men', has *Look Back in Anger* produced.
N AMERICA US Singer Elvis Presley (1935–77) dominates rock music after release of *Heartbreak Hotel*. US 'Beat' poet Allen Ginsberg (1926– ) publishes *Howl*, an attack on American social values.
**After 1956** EUROPE/N AMERICA Beginning of the Pop Art movement.
**1957** EUROPE Russian writer Boris Pasternak (1890–1960) publishes *Doctor Zhivago*. Alain Robbe-Grillet (1922– ), founder of French 'anti-novel' in which objects are given more importance than action or motivation, publishes *Jealousy*.
**1958** S AMERICA City of Brasilia, Brazil, begun by architects Oscar Niemeyer (1907– ) and Lucio Costa (1902– ).
**1959** EUROPE Emergence of *Nouvelle Vague* (New Wave) in French Cinema – includes *Breathless* directed by Jean Luc Godard (1930– ).
**1960** EUROPE *The Beatles* pop group formed (break-up 1970).
**1962** EUROPE Russian poet Yevgeni Yevtushenko (1933– ) publishes his poem *Babi Yar*, an attack on Soviet anti-semitism.
N AMERICA US playwright Edward Albee (1928– ) produces *Who's Afraid of Virginia Woolf?*
**1967** S AMERICA Colombian writer Gabriel García Márquez (Nobel Prize winner 1982, born 1928) publishes *One Hundred Years of Solitude*.
**1968** N AMERICA US film director Stanley Kubrick (1928– ) makes *2001: A Space Odyssey*.
**1969** EUROPE British art-historian Kenneth Clark (1903–83) makes 13-part television series on the arts, *Civilisation* (BBC).
**1973** EUROPE Russian novelist Alexander Solzhenitsyn (1918– ) publishes *The Gulag Archipelago*, describing conditions in Soviet labour camps.
**1972–7** EUROPE Pompidou Centre in Paris designed by Renzo Piano and Richard Rogers.
**1976** AUSTRALIA Film director Peter Weir (1944– ) makes *Picnic at Hanging Rock*, marking a renaissance in the Australian film industry.

# Kings and queens

## SLOW COACH TO DEATH

Marie Antoinette and Louis XVI might well have avoided the guillotine during the French Revolution if the queen had not changed their original escape plan. Instead of allowing the king in 1791 to leave Paris separately in a fast coach, as was first agreed, she insisted that the royal family should travel together. A larger and therefore slower coach had to be used. Because of the delay they missed their rendezvous with an armed escort of loyalists, and it was pitch-dark and difficult to find fresh horses by the time they reached the village of Varennes, only 60km (37 miles) from the French border and safety.

As a result a young man named Drouet, who had recognised them, was able to catch up with them and have their escape route blocked by pro-Revolution troops. Drouet had spotted the family when they changed horses at his stables in the village of Sainte Menehoud earlier in the day. The royal family were captured and sent back to Paris under guard. Louis XVI was guillotined in January 1793, followed nine months later by Marie Antoinette.

## PROCREATION

Augustus the Strong, the Elector of Saxony who was elected king of Poland in 1697, is believed to have fathered more than 300 children. Nevertheless, when he died there was no difficulty about choosing his successor: only one of his sons was legitimate.

## SOLDIER KING

King Karl Gustaf of Sweden is the direct descendant of an undistinguished French lawyer who had a practice in the small town of Pau, in southern France, during the 18th century. The lawyer's son, Jean Bernadotte, rose through the ranks of the French army from being a common soldier to the rank of one of Napoleon's marshals. In 1810 he was elected Crown Prince of Sweden, after the Swedes had sent a delegation to Paris to consult Napoleon – then the master of continental Europe – because the existing royal line was on the point of dying out. Jean Bernadotte had earlier impressed them when he was commanding troops in North Germany and Denmark. With Napoleon's blessing, Jean Bernadotte became in 1818 King Karl XIV Johan, founding Sweden's present ruling house.

## LOST AND FOUND

After Charles I met his death on the scaffold in January 1649, his body was interred without ceremony in the vaults of St George's Chapel, Windsor Castle, where it was to lie undisturbed for nearly 200 years.

This had not been the government's or the royal family's intention, however. At the Restoration of the Monarchy in 1660, Charles II was voted £70,000 by Parliament to pay for his father's reburial beneath a magnificent monument in Westminster Abbey. Then, to general consternation, it was announced that the body had mysteriously vanished – but such was the nation's sympathy towards the bereaved king that no one dreamed of asking him to return the money.

There the matter rested until 1813, when workmen in St George's Chapel accidentally broke into the tomb of Henry VIII. There, next to the coffins of Henry and Jane Seymour, was that of Charles I. The Royal Physician, Sir Henry Halford, was summoned and

positively identified the remains as those of the beheaded Charles I. The lid was then closed and the king left to rest. But it seems that Sir Henry had a most unprofessional bent towards souvenir hunting.

He removed the severed vertebra from the king's neck, had it set in gold, and for the next half-century he and his descendants used it as a salt-cellar – until Queen Victoria heard about it, and ordered that the bone should be returned to the royal coffin.

## THE EMPEROR WHO COULDN'T WRITE

Though Charlemagne (about 742 – 814), the creator of the Holy Roman Empire, was a great patron of learning, he never learnt to write properly. He kept writing materials under his pillow, so that he could practise penmanship in his spare time. But, because he tried to learn late in life, his efforts were of little avail. The few surviving examples of his handwriting show a childishly unformed scrawl.

## PRETENDER'S PORTRAIT

In London's National Portrait Gallery hangs a painting believed to be of James Scott (also called Fitzroy and Crofts), Duke of Monmouth and supposed son of Charles II. He was beheaded in 1685 for trying to seize the throne by force of arms, his claim being that Charles had married his mother, Lucy Walter, when exiled in Holland. If this claim were true, then Monmouth and not James II – Charles's younger brother – was the rightful king of England.

In 1685, when Charles II died, Monmouth attempted to seize the throne; but his rising was a disaster. His pitiful army of West Country farmboys was annihilated at Sedgemoor, and he himself was captured after being found hiding in a ditch. Since he had declared himself king, he could hope for no mercy.

There was no trial – an Act of Attainder had been passed against Monmouth that in effect sentenced him to death without judicial proceedings. The execution was carried out two days after he was brought back to London. It is said that just as his corpse was being taken for burial, it was remembered that no portrait of him existed, a state of affairs that could not be permitted for a member of the royal family, however misguided. The head was therefore hastily stitched back into place, the body propped in a chair, and the portrait painted.

## THE BAVARIAN STUART

One of the descendants of the Stuart kings of Britain was a general who fought on the German side during the First World War. After the direct Stuart line failed with the death of Bonnie Prince Charlie in 1788 and his brother Henry in 1807, the mantle of possible successors passed to the descendants of Princess Henrietta, the sister of Charles II and James II. A series of dynastic marriages brought the Stuart claim to Mary Theresa of Este who married King Louis III of Bavaria in 1868. The German general was their son, Crown Prince Rupprecht (Rupert) of Bavaria.

## UNFAITHFUL DEFENDER

Britain's Protestant kings and queens – who are forbidden by law from becoming Roman Catholics, or even marrying them – still bear a title given to them by the Catholic Church. The title is Defender of the Faith – meaning the Catholic faith. It appears on British coins as the abbreviation F.D. or Fid. Def. (standing for the Latin phrase *Fidei Defensor*). Pope Leo X gave the title to Henry VIII in 1521, for writing a treatise against Martin Luther, just 13 years before the king – angered by Rome's opposition to his divorce from Catherine of Aragon – broke away from the papacy and made himself head of the new Church of England. Although the pope granted the honorary title only for Henry's lifetime, British sovereigns hung on to it even after 1701, when the Act of Settlement made it illegal for a monarch to adopt the Catholic faith, and after 1772, when the Royal Marriages Act made it illegal for a monarch to marry a Catholic. They have kept it ever since.

## POISON-PROOF

King Mithridates VI of Pontus in Asia Minor made himself so immune to poison that he was unable to poison himself when he wanted to. The king spent his life taking small doses of poison in order to build up a resistance to it because he was frightened of being assassinated. He was so successful that, when he tried to commit suicide in 63 BC in order to avoid his imminent capture by the Romans, the poison he took had no effect. In the end he gave up, and ordered a slave to kill him with a sword.

## ALL IN A NAME

The present British royal family's surname was chosen by a commoner. Originally the family's name was Saxe-Coburg and Gotha. But in 1917, during the First World War, it was changed as a gesture to anti-German feeling. The name Windsor was thought up by Lord Stamfordham, George V's private secretary.

## ARTIFICIAL SNOW

An Arab king once had a Spanish hillside planted entirely with almond trees – to please his favourite wife. The king, Almotamid, who ruled the region around Seville in the middle of the 11th century AD, when Spain was largely a Moorish colony, ordered the planting near Cordoba because his wife – a Christian slave named Itimad – did not know what snow looked like. In spring, the falling petals of the almond trees turned the slopes white, the closest approximation to snow available in southern Spain's balmy climate.

QUEEN MOTHER *Queen Victoria and Prince Albert play with their three eldest children in a popular print made in 1843. The couple went on to have in all nine children, most of whom married into other royal houses. As a result of these dynastic links, almost all the crowned heads of Europe in the 20th century have been descendants of the English queen. They include: Wilhelm II, the Kaiser of Germany during the First World War; Alexandra, the wife of Nikolai (Nicholas) II, the last Russian tsar; the present monarchs of Spain, Norway, Denmark and Sweden; the former royal families of Greece, Romania and Yugoslavia; and both Elizabeth II of Britain and her husband Prince Philip, along with all their children and grandchildren.*

THE QUEEN AND PRINCE ALBERT AT HOME.

## HARSH JUSTICE

Frederick the Great of Prussia was so badly treated at home that he tried to run away to France at the age of 18. But his father, Friedrich Wilhelm I, caught him and threw him into prison. During his imprisonment in 1730, a friend named Lieutenant Katte, who had helped him in his attempt to escape, was executed in front of him. Frederick fainted at the sight. Frederick was kept under arrest for 15 months before being grudgingly set free. As king, though, he far outshone his harsh father. He stayed on the throne for 46 years from 1740 – nearly twice as long as his father – and doubled his country's territory.

## GOOD KING MACBETH

The real King Macbeth of Scotland was very different from the tragic hero of Shakespeare's play. Far from being an ambitious usurper, as Shakespeare describes him, Macbeth had a claim to the Scottish throne which was at least as good as that of his rival, Duncan. Furthermore, Duncan was killed in open battle in 1040 and not murdered by Macbeth as Shakespeare's play claims. In fact Duncan was a young, ineffectual king – not Shakespeare's venerable and gracious sovereign. And after Macbeth seized the throne by force, he went on to reign in Scotland for 17 prosperous years, from 1040 to 1057.

# EUROPE'S KINGS AND QUEENS/Britain/France/Austria

The lists shown here give the dates of the major royal houses of Europe. Some dates overlap – usually because two or more monarchs ruled different parts of what is now a single country. Sometimes a single monarch ruled more than one country, with a different title in each. The 16th-century Holy Roman Emperor, Charles V, for example, who is known in Germany as Karl V, was also king of Spain as Carlos I. On other occasions, countries were sometimes left without a monarch for a time because of civil wars or periods of republicanism.

## ENGLAND AND GREAT BRITAIN

### Saxons and Danes
Egbert, 827 – 39
Ethelwulf, 839 – 58
Ethelbald, 858 – 60
Ethelbert, 860 – 6
Ethelred I, 866 – 71
Alfred the Great, 871 – 99
Edward the Elder, 899 – 925
Athelstan, 925 – 40
Edmund, 940 – 6
Edred, 946 – 55
Edwy, 955 – 9
Edgar, 959 – 75
Edward the Martyr, 975 – 8
Ethelred II, 978 – 1016
Edmund Ironside, 1016
Canute (Knut) the Dane, 1016 – 35
Harold I, 1035 – 40
Hardicanute, 1040 – 2
Edward the Confessor, 1042 – 66
Harold II, 1066

### Norman
William I, 1066 – 87
William II, 1087 – 1100
Henry I, 1100 – 35
Stephen, 1135 – 54

### Plantagenet
Henry II, 1154 – 89
Richard I, 1189 – 99
John, 1199 – 1216
Henry III, 1216 – 72
Edward I, 1272 – 1307
Edward II, 1307 – 27
Edward III, 1327 – 77
Richard II, 1377 – 99

### Lancaster
Henry IV, 1399 – 1413
Henry V, 1413 – 22
Henry VI, 1422 – 61, 1470 – 1

### York
Edward IV, 1461 – 70, 1471 – 83
Edward V, 1483
Richard III, 1483 – 5

### Tudor
Henry VII, 1485 – 1509
Henry VIII, 1509 – 47
Edward VI, 1547 – 53
Jane (9 days), 1553
Mary I, 1553 – 8
Elizabeth I, 1558 – 1603

### Stuart
James I, 1603 – 25
Charles I, 1625 – 49

### Commonwealth
*Council of State, 1649 – 53*
*Oliver Cromwell (Protector), 1653 – 8*
*Richard Cromwell (Protector), 1658 – 9*

### Stuart Restoration
Charles II, 1660 – 5
James II, 1685 – 8

### Orange
William III, 1689 – 1702 and Mary II, 1689 – 94

### Stuart
Anne, 1702 – 14

### Hanover
George I, 1714 – 27
George II, 1727 – 60
George III, 1760 – 1820
George IV, 1820 – 30
William IV, 1830 – 7
Victoria, 1837 – 1901

BORN TO BE KING *Two poles and a drape become a makeshift tent for the future George III, sketched at play in his nursery in the 1740s.*

### Saxe-Coburg-Gotha
Edward VII, 1901 – 10

### Windsor
George V, 1910 – 36
Edward VIII (325 days), 1936
George VI, 1936 – 52
Elizabeth II, 1952 –

VIRGIN QUEEN *Framed by a starched lace ruff, Elizabeth I – known as the Virgin Queen because she never married – stares impassively from a portrait by the English miniaturist Nicholas Hilliard. Only four British monarchs have reigned for longer than the 45 years Elizabeth spent on the throne: Henry III (56 years); Edward III (50); George III (60); and Victoria (64).*

## GRANDDAD'S ARMY

The Zulu army which defeated the British at the Battle of Isandhlwana in 1879 included a regiment of men in their sixties. They were the oldest troops in a culture which built itself into a nation of warriors under the Zulu king Chaka (who died in 1828) and later his nephew Cetewayo (about 1826–84). The youngest troops were about 13 years old.

The regiments were divided according to age, and each regiment lived in a separate village where the soldiers worked the land in peacetime. The warrior culture did not last long, however. Six months after the Battle of Isandhlwana the Zulus, whose major weapons were spears, were decisively defeated by British guns at Ulundi, now the capital of the black homeland of Kwa Zulu in South Africa.

## SONS OF THE DESERT

Abdul-Aziz, who in 1932 became the first king of what is now Saudi Arabia, had at least 79 children. Abdul-Aziz, also known as Ibn Saud, used his numerous marriages to form alliances with powerful families in his kingdom. At his death in 1953 there were 34 sons surviving, plus uncounted daughters, and today the Saudi royal family has at least 8000 princes and princesses. King Fahd, who came to the throne in 1982, is one of Abdul-Aziz's sons.

## FRANCE

**Carolingian dynasty**
Pépin the Short, 751–68
Charlemagne, 768–814
Carloman, 768–71
Louis I the Pious, 814–40

ROME'S SUCCESSOR *Charlemagne, the Christian king of the Franks, was crowned emperor of the West on Christmas Day AD 800.*

END OF A MONARCHY *An executioner ʼds out the head of Louis XVI, guillotined in 1793 during the French Revolution. His body still lies beside the blade. Louis' wife, Marie Antoinette, followed him to the guillotine later the same year.*

**West Francia**
Charles II the Bald, 843–77
Louis II, 877–9
Louis III, 879–82
Carloman, 879–84
Karl III, Holy Roman Emperor, 884–7
Eudes, 888–98
Charles III the Simple, 893–923
Robert I, 922–3
Raoul, 923–36
Louis IV, 936–54
Lothair, 954–86
Louis V, 986–7

**Capetian kings**
Hugh Capet, 987–96
Robert II, 996–1031
Henri I, 1031–60
Philippe I, 1060–1108
Louis VI, 1108–37
Louis VII, 1137–80
Philippe II (Auguste), 1180–1223
Louis VIII, 1223–6
Louis IX (St Louis), 1226–70
Philippe III, 1270–85
Philippe IV, 1285–1314
Louis X, 1314–16
Jean I, 1316
Philippe V, 1316–22
Charles IV, 1322–8

**House of Valois**
Philippe VI, 1328–50
Jean II, 1350–64
Charles V, 1364–80
Charles VI, 1380–1422
Charles VII, 1422–61
Louis XI, 1461–83
Charles VIII, 1483–98
Louis XII, 1498–1515
François I, 1515–47
Henri II, 1547–59
François II, 1559–60
Charles IX, 1560–74
Henri III, 1574–89

**Bourbon dynasty**
Henri IV, 1589–1610
Louis XIII, 1610–43
Louis XIV the Sun King, 1643–1715
Louis XV, 1715–74
Louis XVI, 1774–92

*First Republic, 1792–1804*

**House of Bonaparte**
Napoleon I, Emperor, 1804–14
Hundred Days, 1815

**Bourbon Restoration**
Louis XVIII, 1814–24
Charles X, 1824–30

**House of Bourbon–Orléans**
Louis Philippe, 1830–48

*Second Republic, 1848–52*

**House of Bonaparte**
Napoleon III, Emperor, 1852–70

HUNTING PARTY *One of the last Hapsburg rulers of Austria, Franz Josef I, poses for the camera with his son Rudolf.*

## AUSTRIA

**Hapsburg dynasty**
Friedrich III, 1453–93
Maximilian I, 1493–1519
Karl I, 1519–21
Ferdinand I, 1521–64
Maximilian II, 1564–76
Rudolf II, 1576–1611
Mathias, 1611–19
Ferdinand II, 1619–37
Ferdinand III, 1637–57
Leopold I, 1657–1705
Joseph I, 1705–11
Karl II, 1711–40
Maria Theresa, 1740–80
Joseph II, 1765–90
Leopold II, 1790–2
Franz I, 1792–1835 (also held title of Franz II of Holy Roman Empire until 1806)
Ferdinand I, 1835–48
Franz Josef I, 1848–1916
Karl I, 1916–18

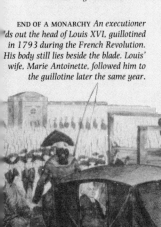

## RISING TIDE

King Canute, the Dane who ruled England from 1016 to 1035, got his feet wet to prove that only God could control the tide. He set his throne on the beach and commanded the tide not to rise in order to show his courtiers how limited – and not how great – his powers were. He allowed the tide to come in round his feet and the waves to lap round his legs. Then he leapt up saying that nobody was worthy of the name king 'save Him whose nod heaven and earth and sea obey under laws eternal'. Afterwards, Canute never wore his crown again. As a mark of respect he placed it instead on a crucifix, above Christ's head.

## THE KING WITH TWO WIVES AT ONCE

When Britain's future king, George IV, married Caroline of Brunswick in 1795 he was already married – and had been for ten years. In 1784 George had fallen in love with Maria Fitzherbert, a Catholic widow. He married her in secret in 1785. The marriage was valid in the eyes of the Catholic Church but not under English law, which bans British monarchs or heirs to the throne from marrying Roman Catholics.

George and Caroline parted after a year when their daughter Princess Charlotte was born, and George went back to Mrs Fitzherbert. Caroline spent most of her time in Italy after the separation, and outraged

# EUROPE'S KINGS AND QUEENS/Holy Roman Empire/Prussia/

## HOLY ROMAN EMPIRE

**Carolingian dynasty**
Charlemagne, 800–14
Louis (Ludwig I) the
  Pious, 814–40
Lothair I, 840–55
Ludwig II the German,
  850–75
Karl II the Bald, 875–7
Karl III the Fat, 877–87
Arnulf, 887–98
Ludwig III the Child,
  899–911

**Franconian house**
Konrad I, 911–18

**Saxon house**
Heinrich I the Fowler,
  919–36
Otto I the Great, 936–73
Otto II, 973–83
Otto III, 983–1002
Heinrich II the Saint,
  1002–24

**Franconian (Salian)
house**
Konrad II, 1024–39
Heinrich III, 1039–56
Heinrich IV, 1056–1105
Heinrich V, 1105–25

**Saxony-Supplinburg
house**
Lothair II, 1125–37

**Hohenstaufen house**
Konrad III, 1138–52
Friedrich I Barbarossa,
  1152–90
Heinrich VI, 1190–7
Philipp of Swabia,
  1198–1208

**Saxon house**
Otto IV of Brunswick,
  1198–1215

**Hohenstaufen house**
Friedrich II, 1215–50
Konrad IV, 1250–4

*Great Interregnum,
1254–73*

**Rulers of various
houses**
Rudolf I of Hapsburg,
  1273–91
Adolf of Nassau, 1292–8
Albrecht I of Austria,
  1298–1308
Heinrich VII of
  Luxembourg, 1308–13
Ludwig IV of Bavaria,
  1314–47
Karl IV of Luxembourg,
  1347–78
Wenzel of Bohemia,
  1378–1400
Rupprecht of Palatinate,
  1400–10
Sigismund of
  Luxembourg, 1410–37

**Hapsburg dynasty**
Albrecht II, 1438–9
Friedrich III, 1440–93
Maximilian I, 1493–1519
Karl (Charles) V, 1519–56
Ferdinand I, 1558–64
Maximilian II, 1564–76
Rudolf II, 1576–1612
Matthias, 1612–19
Ferdinand II, 1619–37
Ferdinand III, 1637–57

KAISER AT THE HELM *Wilhelm II steers the ship of state in a print popular in Germany before the First World War.*

Leopold I, 1658–1705
Josef I, 1705–11
Karl VI, 1711–40
Karl VII, 1742–5
Franz I, 1745–65
Josef II, 1765–90
Leopold II, 1790–2
Franz II, 1792–1806

## PRUSSIA

**Hohenzollern dynasty**
Friedrich I, 1701–13
Friedrich Wilhelm I,
  1713–40
Friedrich II (Frederick the
  Great), 1740–85
Friedrich Wilhelm II,
  1786–97

Friedrich Wilhelm III,
  1797–1840
Friedrich Wilhelm IV,
  1840–61
Wilhelm I, 1861–71
  (ruled as Kaiser of
  Germany, 1871–88)
Friedrich III (Kaiser), 1888
Wilhelm II (Kaiser),
  1888–1918

## SPAIN

**Houses of Aragon and
Castile**
Fernando (Ferdinand) II of
  Aragon and Isabella I of
  Castile, 1479–1504
Fernando II and Joanna
  the Mad, 1504–6
Fernando II, 1506–16

**Spanish Hapsburgs**
Carlos I (as Holy Roman
  Emperor, Charles V),
  1516–56
Felipe (Philip) II,
  1556–98
Felipe III, 1598–1621
Felipe IV, 1621–65
Carlos II, 1665–1700

**Spanish Bourbons**
Felipe V, 1700–46
Fernando VI, 1746–59
Carlos III, 1759–88
Carlos IV, 1788–1808
Fernando VII, 1808

**House of Bonaparte**
Joseph, 1808–13

DEFENDER OF THE FAITH *Philip V of Spain slays the dragon of heresy in an 18th-century painting of himself and his family. Beside him is the figure of Blind Faith. In the centre is El Escorial, the combined palace and monastery built near Madrid for his great-great-great-grandfather, Philip II.*

George by her intimacy with her chamberlain, Bartolomo Bergami. So when she returned to England to claim her rights as queen after George's father died in 1820, George would have none of it.

He ordered her not to attend his coronation in Westminster Abbey in 1821 and when she turned up anyway, he had her forcibly prevented from entering. The humiliated queen fell ill, and died suddenly a month after the coronation.

KNAVE OF HEARTS *Bartolomo Bergami pays extravagant court to George IV's wife, Caroline, while slipping a secret note to her lady-in-waiting. Their affair, caricatured in this 19th-century print, outraged the king.*

# Spain/Greece/Italy/Russia/Sweden

**1st Bourbon Restoration**
Fernando VII, 1813–33
Isabel II, 1833–68

**House of Savoy**
Amadeo I, 1870–3

*1st Spanish Republic, 1873–4*

**2nd Bourbon Restoration**
Alfonso XII, 1874–85
Maria Cristina, 1885–6
Alfonso XIII, 1886–1931

*2nd Spanish Republic, 1931–9*

*Fascist dictatorship Francisco Franco, 1939–75*

**3rd Bourbon Restoration**
Juan Carlos I, 1975–

## GREECE

**House of Wittelsbach**
Otto I, 1832–62

**House of Oldenberg**
George I, 1863–1913
Constantine I, 1913–17
Alexander I, 1917–20
Constantine I, 1920–2
George II, 1922–4

*1st Greek Republic, 1924–35*

George II, 1935–47
Paul I, 1947–64
Constantine II, 1964–74

## ITALY

**House of Savoy**
Vittorio Emanuele II 1861–78
Umberto I, 1878–1900
Vittorio Emanuele III, 1900–46
Umberto II, 1946

## RUSSIA

**Grand Princes of Vladimir**
Vsevolod III, 1176–1212
Yuri II, 1212–16
Konstantin, 1216–19
Yuri II, 1219–38
Yaroslav II, 1238–46
Andrei II, 1246–52

**Princes of Novgorod and Grand Princes of Vladimir**
Aleksandr Nevski, 1238–63
Yaroslav III, 1263–72
Vasili, 1272–6
Dmitri, 1276–94
Andrei III, 1294–1304
Mikhail II, 1304–19
Yuri III, 1319–24
Dmitri II, 1324–7
Aleksandr II, 1327–8

**Grand Princes of Moscow**
Ivan I, 1328–41
Simeon, 1341–53
Ivan II, 1353–9
Dmitri Donskoi, 1359–89
Vasili I, 1389–1425
Vasili II, 1425–62
Ivan III the Great, 1462–1505
Vasili III, 1505–33

**Tsars of Russia**
Ivan IV the Terrible, 1533–84
Fedor I, 1584–98
Irina, 1598
Boris Godunov, 1598–1605
Fedor II, 1605
Dmitri I, 1605–6
Vasili IV, 1606–10

**Romanov dynasty**
Mikhail, 1613–45
Aleksei, 1645–76
Fedor III, 1676–82
Ivan V and Peter I the Great, 1682–96
Peter I the Great, 1696–1725
Ekaterina I, 1725–7
Peter II, 1727–30
Anna, 1730–40

Ivan VI, 1740–1
Elizaveta, 1741–62
Peter III, 1762
Ekaterina II (Catherine the Great), 1762–96
Pavel (Paul), 1796–1801
Aleksandr I, 1801–25
Nikolai I, 1825–55
Aleksandr II, 1855–81
Aleksandr III, 1881–94
Nikolai II, 1894–1917

## SWEDEN

**House of Vasa**
Gustaf I, 1523–60
Eric XIV, 1560–8
Johan III, 1568–92
Sigismund, 1592–9
Karl IX, 1599–1611
Gustaf II Adolf, 1611–32
Christina, 1632–54

**House of Zweibrucken**
Karl X Gustaf, 1654–60
Karl XI, 1660–97

Karl XII, 1697–1718
Ulrika Eleonora, 1718–20

**House of Hesse**
Fredrik I, 1720–51

**House of Holstein-Gottorp**
Adolf Fredrik, 1751–71
Gustaf III, 1771–92
Gustaf IV Adolf, 1792–1809
Karl XIII, 1809–18

**House of Bernadotte**
Karl XIV Johan, 1818–44
Oskar I, 1844–59
Karl XV, 1859–72
Oskar II, 1872–1907
Gustaf V, 1907–50
Gustaf VI Adolf, 1950–73
Karl XVI Gustaf, 1973–

LAST OF THE TSARS *Nikolai II and his wife Alexandra glitter with gems in a 1903 print. On July 16, 1918, they and their children were shot dead by Bolsheviks in a grimy cellar.*

ASCENT OF WASHINGTON *George Washington, the first US President, is carried to heaven by angels in a painting created soon after his death in December 1799. The painting, on glass, was made in China for the US market. Washington's stern expression was only partly a matter of personality. He also suffered because the false teeth he wore did not fit properly.*

# US Presidents

## WHO CAN BE PRESIDENT?

The US constitution stipulates that, to be eligible for the Presidency, a candidate must be a natural-born citizen, must have lived in the United States for a minimum of 14 years and must be at least 35 years old. The requirement to be natural-born was waived at first, because before the War of Independence all Americans were British subjects.

Candidates had merely to be US citizens at the time the constitution was adopted in 1788; Martin Van Buren, the eighth President, was the first not to have been born a British subject.

But there are no other legal qualifications or restrictions for the post, so there is nothing in US law to prevent a lunatic, a bankrupt or a convicted criminal from becoming President.

## MONOPOLY OF POWER

Most Presidents have been Protestants. All have been white and so far no woman has held the post. Until John F. Kennedy was elected in 1960, no Roman Catholic had been President. Although Alfred E. Smith, a Catholic, was nominated as the Democratic Presidential candidate in 1928, he lost the election to the Quaker, Herbert Hoover.

American women have had the vote since 1920, but no woman has ever been within sight of the top political office – First Ladies have only been Presidents' wives. The major parties have not, so far, even got around to nominating a woman to run for the Presidency.

## YOUNG AND OLD

John F. Kennedy was the youngest man to be elected President, at the age of 43. But he was not the youngest President. Theodore Roosevelt was only 42 when he moved from the Vice-Presidency after the assassination of William McKinley in 1901. The oldest man to become President was Ronald Reagan, who was 69 when he first took office in 1981.

## FAMILY TIES

John Quincy Adams, the sixth President, was the son of John Adams, the second President. And Benjamin Harrison, who took office in 1889, was the grandson of William Henry Harrison, who was President in 1841. The two Roosevelts who have been Presidents – Theodore and Franklin – were related only as distant cousins.

## ON THE ROCKS

President Hoover became so unpopular during the Great Depression – for which he was chiefly blamed – that the Hoover Dam on the Colorado River, built in the early 1930s, had its name changed to Boulder Dam in 1933.

The name was changed back by Congress in 1947 – after the passage of time and Hoover's work for famine relief during and after the Second World War had helped to restore his reputation.

## PRESIDENT WHO WAS NEVER ELECTED

Gerald Ford, who was President for three years, never won a national election. He was promoted to the Vice-Presidency by Richard Nixon in 1973 after the elected Vice-President, Spiro Agnew, resigned to avoid being brought to trial over bribery charges. Ford took over as President eight months later when Richard Nixon resigned over the Watergate scandal.

## I CANNOT TELL A LIE

The story of young George Washington nobly confessing to chopping down his father's cherry tree was almost certainly an invention. The fable seems to have been created by an American clergyman and notorious romanticiser, Mason Locke Weems, who wrote a biography of the first President with the avowed intention of extolling his virtues.

The story was first published in the book's fifth edition, which was issued in 1806, when Washington had been dead for seven years.

## KILLED IN OFFICE

Four of America's 39 Presidents have died at the hands of assassins. Abraham Lincoln was shot in a Washington theatre in 1865 by John Wilkes Booth, an actor who had supported the defeated South during the Civil War. James Garfield was shot only four months after his inauguration in 1881 by Charles Guiteau, a disappointed office-seeker. William McKinley was shot by an anarchist, Leon Czolgosz, in 1901. John F. Kennedy was shot in 1963 by Lee Harvey Oswald, a former US Marine.

LAST WALTZ *This image-boosting melody, entitled* Log Cabin March, *was written for William Henry Harrison's Presidential campaign in 1840, and may have helped him win. In fact, however, Harrison was brought up in a palatial home in Virginia and the closest he came to the shack shown here was a sturdy five-roomed cabin that he lived in briefly around the end of the 18th century. Ironically, Harrison's campaign music turned out to be his swan song. Conscious of his image as a rugged soldier, he insisted at his Presidential inauguration on standing hatless and coatless in a cold drizzle. He caught a chill and died exactly a month later on April 4, 1841 – making his term of office the shortest of any President.*

## GENERAL WHO TURNED LINCOLN DOWN

Robert E. Lee, the general who became commander in chief of the Southern Confederate forces towards the end of the Civil War, was originally offered command of the Union army of the North. Lee turned down the offer, made by President Abraham Lincoln, on April 18, 1861 – the day after his home state of Virginia seceded from the Union at the start of the war. Although he opposed secession, he could not bring himself to fight against his own state.

Two days later he resigned from the Union army, and on April 23 he took command of Virginia's military and naval forces.

## BARGAIN BUY

When President Thomas Jefferson began negotiations to buy Louisiana from France (which had itself only just acquired the territory from Spain), he envisaged at the most buying an area round the mouth of the Mississippi River and paying up to $10 million for it. In the end, however, the French, preoccupied with the threat of war in Europe, were so eager to sell that in 1803 Jefferson was able, for a mere $15 million, to buy almost all the land between the Mississippi and the Rocky Mountains. The territory covered more than 2,000,000km² (more than 700,000 square miles), doubling at a stroke the area of the USA.

# PRESIDENTS OF THE UNITED STATES/Washington – Pierce

## MAJOR EVENTS AND ACHIEVEMENTS

### GEORGE WASHINGTON
**1st President/1789–97**
Born 1732 at Wakefield, Virginia; died 1799. Chosen as President after leading Continental Army of the infant United States to victory against the British in the War of Independence (1775–83). Established a stable government, based on a strong currency. Against fierce opposition, maintained US neutrality when war broke out between Britain and Revolutionary France (1793). Failed in his struggle against the rise of party politics.

### JOHN ADAMS
**2nd President/1797–1801**
**(Federalist)**
Born in 1735 at Quincy, Massachusetts; died 1826. Despite attacks by French privateers on American shipping, resisted pressure from his own party for all-out war. Clamour against the Alien and Sedition Acts (1798), under which critics of the government could be jailed, led to collapse of his Federalist party.

### THOMAS JEFFERSON
**3rd President/1801–9**
**(Democratic-Republican)**
Born 1743 at Shadwell, Virginia; died 1826. Doubled area of US by purchase of Louisiana Territory from France (1803) for $15 million. Sponsored Lewis and Clark Expedition (1804–5) that blazed a pioneer trail across America to the Pacific Northwest. His 'Jeffersonian

Democracy' emphasised freedom of choice for the individual, and was to have far-reaching effects on American political thinking.

### JAMES MADISON
**4th President/1809–17**
**(Democratic-Republican)**
Born 1751 at Port Conway, Virginia; died 1836. Led USA into War of 1812 against Britain, which began as protest against British blockade of American ships trading with France. Was forced to flee when British troops captured and burnt the city of Washington in 1814. War was ended, with no gains for either side, by Treaty of Ghent (December 1814). Two weeks later, General Andrew Jackson (later President) – unaware that a peace treaty had been signed – led US troops to victory over a larger British army at the Battle of New Orleans (January 1815).

### JAMES MONROE
**5th President/1817–25**
**(Democratic-Republican)**
Born 1758 at Westmoreland County, Virginia; died 1831. Presided over the acquisition of Florida from Spain for $5 million in 1819. Expounded the Monroe

Doctrine (1823), the principle that Europe should not intervene in the affairs of independent countries in the New World. North-South dissension over the use of slavery was ended temporarily by the Missouri Compromise (1820), by which Missouri was admitted to the Union as a slave state but slavery was to be prohibited in all future states.

### JOHN QUINCY ADAMS
**6th President/1825–9**
**(Non-partisan)**
Born 1767 at Quincy, Massachusetts; died 1848. Alienated politicians by advocating a professional civil service free of patronage and, without either wide popular support or a political party, was able to achieve little. Later, as a Congressman (1831–48), he was an effective campaigner against pro-slavery measures.

### ANDREW JACKSON
**7th President/1829–37**
**(Democratic)**
Born 1768 at Waxhaw Settlement, South Carolina; died 1845. Strengthened the role of the Presidency with the help of a

ON TO VICTORY *On Christmas night 1776, George Washington led his troops across the ice-strewn Delaware river into New Jersey. On Boxing Day, he surprised and defeated a British force at Trenton – one of the first major American victories in the War of Independence.*

## INVISIBLE NAME

The 'S' in Harry S Truman did not stand for a name. He was christened Harry S because both his grandfathers had names beginning with the letter – Anderson Shippe Truman and his maternal grandfather, Solomon Young – and each would have been offended if Harry had been given the other's name.

## DEATH IN THE FAMILY

Abraham Lincoln was not the first member of his family to die violently. Years before the President was born, his grandfather, also named Abraham, was shot dead by an Indian at his Kentucky farm. The raider was about to carry off Thomas Lincoln, the future father of the President, when he was shot in his turn by Thomas's elder brother, Mordecai.

## THE GREY HOUSE

The White House, the President's official home, was originally grey, the colour of the pale Virginia sandstone used to build it. During the War of 1812 between Britain and the United States, which went on until 1814, British troops captured the city of Washington in August 1814 and put the mansion to the torch. When it was rebuilt after the war, the walls were painted white to hide the smoke stains.

---

Kitchen Cabinet of close advisers, and extended the practice of rewarding party supporters with government posts. The practice came to be known as the spoils system.

## MARTIN VAN BUREN
### 8th President/1837–41
### (Democratic)

Born 1782 at Kinderhook, New York; died 1862. Lost popular support by opposing use of federal money to alleviate distress during financial panic of 1837, caused by the collapse of the western land boom and general distrust of paper currency. Resisted extension of slavery and opposed annexation of Texas because he felt it would provoke war with Mexico.

## WILLIAM HENRY HARRISON
### 9th President/1841
### (Whig)

Born 1773 at Charles City County, Virginia; died 1841. As governor of the Indiana Territory (1800–12), led troops to victory at the Battle of Tippecanoe (1811) against the Shawnee Indians, and settled the territory's claims to 12,140km² (4680 square miles) of Indian land. Died of pneumonia a month after inauguration – the first President to die in office.

## JOHN TYLER
### 10th President/1841–5
### (Whig)

Born 1790 at Charles City County, Virginia; died 1862. Earned the enmity of his party by vetoing Whig bills to re-establish the national bank (dismantled by President Andrew Jackson in favour of state banks). Successfully supported the annexation of Texas as a new state. His Secretary of State, Daniel Webster, settled a serious dispute over the Canadian boundary of Maine by negotiating the Webster-Ashburton Treaty with Britain.

## JAMES KNOX POLK
### 11th President/1845–9
### (Democratic)

Born 1795 at Mecklenburg County, North Carolina; died 1849. Believed that the USA had a 'manifest destiny' to spread across the continent. The phrase was coined by newspaper editor John O'Sullivan in 1845 to justify the annexation of Texas and the occupation of Oregon. Tried to buy California and New Mexico from Mexico, and war followed (1846–8) when his offer was rejected. Under the Treaty of Guadalupe Hidalgo, ending the war, Mexico accepted $15 million in return for territory that became the states of California, Nevada, Utah and parts of Wyoming, New Mexico, Arizona and Colorado. By the Oregon Treaty of 1846, Polk also established the 49th parallel as the US-Canadian border.

## ZACHARY TAYLOR
### 12th President/1849–50
### (Whig)

Born 1784 at Orange County, Virginia; died 1850. Although a slave-owner and conservative, he became a strong supporter of the anti-slavery views of the Whigs, and championed in 1850 the admission to statehood of California, an anti-slavery state. Died of cholera on July 9, 1850.

## MILLARD FILLMORE
### 13th President/1850–3
### (Whig)

Born 1800 at Locke, New York; died 1874. Sought to preserve the Union by conciliating the South over slavery, but succeeded only in alienating both sides. Approved the dispatch of Commodore Matthew Perry to open Japanese ports to US trade.

## FRANKLIN PIERCE
### 14th President/1853–7
### (Democratic)

Born 1804 at Hillsboro, New Hampshire; died 1869. Backed the $10 million Gadsden Purchase (1854) of the southern parts of Arizona and New Mexico from Mexico. Tried to conciliate the South over slavery. But guerrilla warfare broke out between opposing factions in Kansas in 1855–6, heightening national tensions.

RAISING THE FLAG *A 19th-century etching records the announcement in 1845 of Texas's admission to the Union as the 28th state. It is now the second largest state after Alaska.*

### KENTUCKY HOMES

Abraham Lincoln and Jefferson Davis, rival Presidents during the Civil War, were both born in Kentucky. Their homes were a mere 160km (100 miles) apart – almost neighbours by frontier reckoning – and only eight months separated their dates of birth.

### THE 20-YEAR CYCLE OF FATE

Seven of the eight Presidents who have died in office – either through illness or assassination – were elected at precisely 20-year intervals.

The seven were: William Harrison (elected 1840), Lincoln (1860), Garfield (1880), McKinley (elected to a second term in 1900), Harding (1920), Franklin Roosevelt (elected to a third term in 1940) and John F. Kennedy (1960).

The eighth was Zachary Taylor, who was elected in 1848 and died in office in 1850.

### UNBEATABLE

Franklin Roosevelt, who won four Presidential elections and spent 12 years in the White House – longer than any other President – is unlikely to have his record beaten.

Since 1951 a constitutional amendment has barred Presidential candidates from being elected to more than two four-year terms.

## PRESIDENTS OF THE UNITED STATES/Buchanan – Taft

### JAMES BUCHANAN
**15th President/1857 – 61**
**(Democratic)**
Born 1791 at Cove Gap, Pennsylvania; died 1868. Proposed preservation of a 'sacred balance' between North and South in an attempt to defuse the slavery crisis. Disapproved of slavery, yet recommended admission of Kansas as a slave state. Deplored talk of secession yet took no steps to prevent it by garrisoning federal forts in the South. In the last months of his term, South Carolina and six other states – Mississippi, Florida, Alabama, Georgia, Louisiana and Texas – seceded to form the Confederate States of America with Jefferson Davis as President.

### ABRAHAM LINCOLN
**16th President/1861 – 5**
**(Republican)**
Born 1809 at Hardin County, Kentucky; died 1865. Four more states – Virginia, Arkansas, North Carolina and Tennessee – joined the Confederacy on Lincoln's inauguration on March 4, 1861, and June 8. The Civil War began with a successful attack by Confederate troops on the federal Fort Sumter at Charleston, South Carolina, on April 12, 1861. Lincoln called for 75,000 volunteers to fight the rebels and ordered a blockade of Southern ports. Lincoln issued the Emancipation Proclamation in 1862, proclaiming freedom for slaves in Confederate-controlled states, but fighting was indecisive until the Union army defeated a Confederate invasion of Pennsylvania under General Robert E. Lee at the Battle of Gettysburg (July 1 – 3, 1863). Lee surrendered to the Northern general, Ulysses S. Grant, at Appomattox in Virginia on April 9, 1865, ending the Civil War. Lincoln was assassinated in a Washington theatre five days later.

### ANDREW JOHNSON
**17th President/1865 – 9**
**(Democratic)**
Born 1808 at Raleigh, North Carolina; died 1875. Angered Republicans – who had formed an alliance with pro-war Democrats during the Civil War – by his conciliatory policies towards the defeated South. Johnson's sacking of Secretary of War Edwin Stanton in defiance of the Tenure of Office Act (1867) led to his impeachment. But the Senate failed by one vote to reach the two-thirds majority needed to convict him. In 1867, Johnson bought Alaska from Russia for $7.2 million.

### ULYSSES SIMPSON GRANT
**18th President/1869 – 77**
**(Republican)**
Born 1822 at Point Pleasant, Ohio; died 1885. Harsh post-war Reconstruction policy, with federal troops occupying the South, gave economic supremacy to Northern bankers and industrialists. Speculators and politicians went south to exploit the defeated Southerners, often carrying only a single bag, which was usually made of a carpet-like material. They became known by the contemptuous term 'carpetbaggers'. First transcontinental railway completed (1869). Constitution amended to give former male slaves and blacks – but not women – the

HIGH COMMAND *President Lincoln with his Civil War commanders at Antietam, the site of the Northern victory in 1862.*

## TEDDY AND THE BEAR

Children's teddy bears get their name from President Theodore 'Teddy' Roosevelt, who always disliked his nickname. On a hunting trip in Mississippi in 1902 Roosevelt refused to shoot a bear cub. The *Washington Post* newspaper publicised the incident in a cartoon, and an enterprising Boston shopkeeper, Morris Michtom, cashed in on the publicity by making toy bears and christening them 'Teddy's bears'.

HUNTER WHO WOULDN'T SHOOT *The Washington Post cartoon which led to the invention of teddy bears – named after President 'Teddy' Roosevelt.*

---

vote (1870). General George Custer's troops massacred by Sioux Indians at Battle of Little Bighorn in Montana (1876).

### RUTHERFORD BIRCHARD HAYES
**19th President/1877–81 (Republican)**
Born 1822 at Delaware, Ohio; died 1893. Withdrew last federal troops from the South (1877), ending Reconstruction. Banned sale of firearms to Indians in an attempt to halt Indian wars in the West.

### JAMES ABRAM GARFIELD
**20th President/1881 (Republican)**
Born 1831 at Orange Township, Ohio; died 1881. Shot on July 2, 1881, by Charles Guiteau, just under four months after his inauguration on March 4. Died on September 19.

### CHESTER ALAN ARTHUR
**21st President/1881–5 (Republican)**
Born 1829 at Fairfield, Vermont; died 1886. Supported the Civil Service Reform Act (1883), designed to limit the spoils system under which government posts were distributed among political supporters.

### GROVER CLEVELAND
**22nd and 24th President 1885–9, 1893–7 (Democratic)**
Born 1837 at Caldwell, New Jersey; died 1908. Established an Interstate Commerce Commission to bring national railways and, later, interstate trade under federal control. In September 1886, the Apache Indian War in the southwestern USA ended with the capture of the Apache chief Geronimo. The only President to serve two separate terms, he lost the 1888 election, but won again in 1892. Economic slump in 1893 led to the collapse of more than 15,000 businesses.

### BENJAMIN HARRISON
**23rd President/1889–93 (Republican)**
Born 1833 at North Bend, Ohio; died 1901. Supported Sherman Antitrust Act of 1890, which outlawed industrial monopolies and led to a series of 'trust-busting' court cases. On December 29, 1890, federal troops massacred 300 Sioux Indians at Wounded Knee, South Dakota, ending the last Indian war in the West.

ALL ABOARD *A gaudy poster announces the opening of the first transcontinental US railway line on May 10, 1869. The railway, with its attractions billed here, rapidly became the main route to the Pacific, replacing the earlier wagon trains and long sea voyages, and opening up the West to a flood of new settlers.*

### WILLIAM McKINLEY
**25th President/1897–1901 (Republican)**
Born 1843 at Niles, Ohio; died 1901. Declared war on Spain in April 1898 after influential US newspapers blamed Spain for a mysterious explosion which sank the US battleship *Maine* in Havana harbour. Spanish repression of a Cuban rebellion in 1895 had earlier led to substantial US property losses on the island. After US victory four months later, Cuba was placed under US military rule. Spain ceded Puerto Rico and the island of Guam to the USA and sold the Philippines to the USA for $20 million. McKinley also annexed Hawaii and, through the Gold Standard Act of 1900, established gold as the backing for US currency. McKinley was shot by an anarchist assassin on September 6, 1901, and died on September 14.

### THEODORE ROOSEVELT
**26th President/1901–9 (Republican)**
Born 1858 at New York City; died 1919. Strengthened government controls over big business by attacking monopolies through the courts. In foreign affairs, his slogan was: 'Speak softly and carry a big stick.' After Colombia refused permission for the USA to build a canal across Panama (then a Colombian province), Roosevelt backed a Panamanian rebellion, then in 1904 bought the Canal Zone for $10 million from the new regime. For his initiative in arranging negotiations to end the Russo-Japanese War, Roosevelt became in 1906 the first American to be awarded the Nobel Peace Prize.

### WILLIAM HOWARD TAFT
**27th President/1909–13 (Republican)**
Born 1857 at Cincinnati, Ohio; died 1930. Endorsed a constitutional amendment in 1913 authorising a federal income tax. Admitted Arizona and New Mexico to the Union, bringing the number of states to 48.

# PRESIDENTS OF THE UNITED STATES/Wilson – Reagan

### WOODROW WILSON
**28th President/1913 – 21
(Democratic)**
Born 1856 at Staunton, Virginia;
died 1924. Centralised American
banking system through the Federal
Reserve Act (1913). Supported laws
limiting the use of child labour and
restricting hours of work, and
backed a constitutional amendment
giving women the vote. Sought to
maintain US neutrality in the First
World War, but after Germany
refused to end submarine attacks on
transatlantic shipping, declared war
on April 6, 1917. Approved the
purchase of the Virgin Islands from
Denmark for $25 million (1917).
Unsuccessfully opposed
introduction of Prohibition in 1920.

### WARREN GAMALIEL HARDING
**29th President/1921 – 3
(Republican)**
Born 1865 at Blooming Grove,
Ohio; died 1923. Post-war recession
led to high unemployment.
Immigration was restricted through
a quota system for the first time.
After Harding's death on August 2,
1923, Senate investigations revealed
widespread government corruption.
The most damaging of these
scandals involved the leasing of
naval oil reserve lands – including an
area in Wyoming called the Teapot
Dome – to a private oil company.
The Secretary of the Interior, Albert
Fall – who had been appointed by
Harding – was later jailed for
accepting bribes totalling $350,000
to approve the leases.

### CALVIN COOLIDGE
**30th President/1923 – 9
(Republican)**
Born 1872 at Plymouth, Vermont;
died 1933. Aggressively pro-
business, Coolidge encouraged tax
cuts and economy in government.
Was unable, though, to control the
speakeasies that flourished in the
cities in defiance of Prohibition, or
to stop the gang wars over their
control. In 1929, American Samoa
became a US territory.

### HERBERT CLARK HOOVER
**31st President/1929 – 33
(Republican)**
Born 1874 at West Branch, Iowa;
died 1964. Great Depression
triggered by stock market crash on
October 24, 1929. By 1931, more
than 37,000 businesses had shut
down and 2 million people were out
of work. Hoover set up government-
funded banks to funnel loans to
businessmen and farmers in an effort
to revive the economy, but the
measures proved ineffective.

### FRANKLIN DELANO ROOSEVELT
**32nd President/1933 – 45
(Democratic)**
Born 1882 in New York City; died
1945. Launched a series of
emergency measures – the New
Deal – to revive the economy by
massive government spending and
to reorganise agriculture and
industry under government controls.
Led USA into the Second World
War after surprise Japanese attack
on Pearl Harbor, Hawaii (December
7, 1941). Planned formation of the
United Nations to ensure lasting
peace after the war, but died of a
cerebral haemorrhage on April 12,
1945 – less than a month before
Germany surrendered to the Allies.

### HARRY S TRUMAN
**33rd President/1945 – 53
(Democratic)**
Born 1884 at Lamar, Missouri; died
1972. Authorised the dropping of
atom bombs on Hiroshima and
Nagasaki. Led US attempts to
contain communism in the Cold War
triggered by Russian imposition of
communist regimes after the Second
World War. Established the Marshall
Plan to help post-war recovery in
Europe and founded the North
Atlantic Treaty Organisation
(NATO) as an anti-communist
military alliance. Sent US troops to
Korea. Anti-communist witch-hunts
in the USA were encouraged by
Senator Joseph McCarthy after a
speech (February 1950) alleging
communist infiltration of the State
Department.

### DWIGHT DAVID EISENHOWER
**34th President/1953 – 61
(Republican)**
Born 1890 at Denison, Texas; died
1969. Was Allied Commander-in-
chief from 1943 to end of Second
World War, and derived much of his
political appeal from his popularity
as a war hero. Settled the Korean
war with an armistice signed in July
1953. Sponsored the formation of
the Southeast Asian Treaty
Organisation (1954) and sent
military advisers to train South
Vietnamese army (1955).
McCarthy's dominance ended by
Senate vote of censure (December
1954). Efforts to ease Cold War
tension with Moscow collapsed in
May 1960 when an American U-2

THE SINKING OF THE 'LUSITANIA' *Nearly
1200 people, including 128 US citizens, died
when the British liner* Lusitania *was sunk by
a German submarine on May 7, 1915.
Anger over the attack helped generate support
for the USA's entry into the First World War
two years later.*

spy plane was shot down over the Soviet Union. A year later, Eisenhower broke off diplomatic relations with Cuba after the establishment of a communist regime under Fidel Castro. Alaska and Hawaii admitted to Union (1959).

## JOHN FITZGERALD KENNEDY
**35th President/1961–3 (Democratic)**
Born 1917 at Brookline, Massachusetts; died 1963. Approved unsuccessful Bay of Pigs invasion of Cuba (April 1961). Provided armed helicopters and crews to fight communists in South Vietnam, extending US involvement. In October 1962, ordered air and naval blockade of Cuba, forcing Soviet Union to withdraw nuclear missiles based on the island. Later set up the first 'hot-line' – a teleprinter link between the Pentagon and the Russian Ministry of Defence – and in October 1963 signed a nuclear test-ban treaty with Britain and the Soviet Union. Was assassinated on November 22, 1963.

## LYNDON BAINES JOHNSON
**36th President/1963–9 Democratic**
Born 1908 at Stonewall, Texas; died 1973. Pushed through much of Kennedy's 'New Frontier' programme of laws designed to ease poverty and establish black civil rights. Later, in his own social reform programme – the 'Great Society' – he cut taxes, enforced black voting rights and set up the Medicare plan giving medical insurance to pensioners. Authorised US troops to take part in ground combat in South Vietnam (1965) and approved the bombing of North Vietnam. Black civil rights leader Martin Luther King was shot dead in Tennessee (April 1968), sparking racial riots in more than 100 cities. Senator Robert Kennedy, brother of President Kennedy, was shot dead in Los Angeles (June 1968).

## RICHARD MILHOUS NIXON
**37th President/1969–74 (Republican)**
Born 1913 at Yorba Linda, California. Improved relations with communist powers. Supported China's admission to United Nations (1971). First US President to visit China and Russia while in office (1972). Pioneered SALT treaties on arms limitations with USSR (1972). Public opinion led him to end direct US participation in Vietnam War (1973), the longest and costliest war in the nation's history. He was forced to resign by the Watergate

scandal (1974), following attempts to cover up crimes committed by aides during his 1972 re-election campaign.

## GERALD RUDOLPH FORD
**38th President/1974–7 (Republican)**
Born 1913 at Omaha, Nebraska. Granted free pardon to President Nixon a month after taking office 'for all offences' committed during his administration. Inflation – largely caused by Arab oil prices – triggered a recession which put 8.5 million people out of work in 1975. Signed the Helsinki Pact (1975) with the USSR, recognising European border changes imposed by the Soviet Union after the Second World War in return for a guarantee of human rights for nations of Eastern Europe.

## JAMES EARL CARTER
**39th President/1977–81 (Democratic)**
Born 1924 at Plains, Georgia. Pardoned Vietnam War draft-

dodgers (1977). Negotiated treaty with Panama (1978), agreeing to give up control of the Canal Zone. Lost popularity because of high inflation and unemployment, and because of his inability to rescue more than 50 Americans captured by Iranian militants at US embassy in Teheran on November 4, 1979, and held prisoner for more than a year.

## RONALD WILSON REAGAN
**40th President/1981– (Republican)**
Born 1911 at Tampico, Illinois. Cut taxes and government spending, reducing inflation from 13 per cent in 1981 to about 5 per cent in 1982. But the cut in federal tax revenues, caused by the economic slump, led to a 1982 budget deficit of $100,000 million – the highest in US history. By late 1983, however, the economy was showing signs of recovery. Abroad, Reagan took a harder line with the Soviet Union and increased spending on defence.

HEADLINES
*Eisenhower's 1952 election victory, as seen by a newspaper in Abilene, Kansas, where he spent his youth; the 1963 assassination of President Kennedy and the 1974 resignation of President Nixon.*

# Prime Ministers of Britain

## THE PM WHO WASN'T

Robert Walpole, Britain's first Prime Minister, formally held the post only of First Lord of the Treasury. He became George I's chief minister because the German-born king had little knowledge of or interest in British affairs, and since he spoke no English he could not follow Cabinet discussions. Since Walpole spoke no German, either, the two were able to communicate with each other only in Latin.

Before Walpole's appointment, British monarchs had themselves been the 'prime' ministers, choosing and directing the government as they saw fit. But since Walpole the influence of the monarch has gradually waned, and from the time of Queen Victoria the Prime Minister has generally been the leader of the largest party in the House of Commons.

## YOU . . . PRIME MINISTER!

The title of Britain's top political office was originally a term of abuse. It was used to describe the chief minister of a despotic monarch, and carried overtones that the politician was merely a lackey of the Crown. Robert Walpole, George Grenville and Lord North all denied hotly that they were prime ministers.

The title was given official recognition only in 1937, when the Salaries of the Ministers of the Crown Act made provision for paying 'the First Lord of the Treasury and Prime Minister' – the two offices that have, since the late 18th century, usually been held by the Prime Minister. Despite the recognition, however, the brass plate outside the front door of the Prime Minister's Downing Street residence in London still bears only the title of First Lord of the Treasury.

## RELUCTANT PREMIERS

Lord Grenville, who was Prime Minister from 1806 to 1807, and the Duke of Devonshire (1756–7) both hated the job. When Lord Grenville followed his cousin, William Pitt the Younger, into the post, he wrote to his brother that he was not 'competent to the management of men. I never was so naturally, and toil and anxiety more and more unfit me for it'. When he resigned the premiership he wrote again to his brother: 'The deed is done and I am again a free man.'

The Duke of Devonshire agreed to take on the job for George II only on condition that he could resign if he 'disliked the employment'. He did. He resigned in July 1757 after only seven months in office.

## NICKNAME THAT STUCK

The name Tory – now used for members of the Conservative Party – was once an insult. It comes from the Irish word *toiridhe*, meaning a 'pursuer'. It was used to describe Irish robbers who preyed on travellers. From about 1680 it was applied sneeringly to the supporters of royal power – because they were thought to be chasing royal favours – and thus to politicians who supported traditional policies. In the USA, the term Tory was used to describe people who supported the British during the American War of Independence.

## DUKE OF LONDON

Winston Churchill turned his back on an offer of the highest rank in England's peerage for the sake of his son. When Churchill retired from the premiership in April 1955 he was offered a dukedom – rather than

Politicians are often more fiercely critical of each other than any outsider. These are some of the most memorable put-downs that have been aimed at Prime Ministers. Most were aimed by Prime Ministers as well.

● 'It is fitting that we should have buried the Unknown Prime Minister by the side of the Unknown Soldier' (Asquith on Bonar Law).

● 'A sophistical rhetorician, inebriated with the exuberance of his own verbosity' (Disraeli on Gladstone).

● 'An arch-mediocrity, presiding over a Cabinet of mediocrities' (Disraeli on Lord Liverpool).

● 'He is a self-made man, and worships his creator' (MP John Bright on Disraeli).

● 'His smile was like the silver plate on a coffin' (MP Daniel O'Connell on Peel).

● 'He saw foreign policy through the wrong end of a municipal drainpipe' (Lloyd George on Chamberlain).

● 'He couldn't see a belt without hitting below it' (Prime Minister's wife Margot Asquith on Lloyd George).

● 'A sheep in sheep's clothing' (attributed to Churchill on Attlee).

● 'Churchill on top of the wave has in him the stuff of which tyrants are made' (newspaper tycoon Lord Beaverbrook on Churchill).

● 'If Harold Wilson ever went to school without any boots, it was because he was too big for them' (Macmillan on Wilson).

the usual earldom – in recognition of his unique wartime services. He toyed with the idea of becoming Duke of London, but decided to decline the offer, mainly at the request of his son Randolph who hoped to make a career in the House of Commons. At that time Randolph would not have been able to disclaim the peerage when he succeeded to the title, and so would have been confined to the House of Lords.

## DEATH AT POINT-BLANK RANGE

Only one British Prime Minister has been assassinated: Spencer Perceval, who was shot at point-blank range in the lobby of the House of Commons on May 11, 1812. The assassin was John Bellingham, a bankrupt merchant who believed that the British government owed him compensation because the British ambassador had refused to intervene when he was arrested and imprisoned while trading in Russia. Perceval died almost immediately, and Bellingham was tried, convicted and hanged within a week.

## NUMBER 10

The official residence of British Prime Ministers – Number 10 Downing Street – was built in about 1680 by Sir George Downing, a diplomat, spy and turncoat whom the diarist Samuel Pepys called 'a perfidious rogue'. Downing supported Oliver Cromwell after the English Civil War (1642–9). But after the Restoration of the Monarchy in 1660, Downing entered Charles II's service and betrayed some of his former associates to execution. In 1738 George II offered Number 10 to Robert Walpole, Britain's first Prime Minister, as a present. Walpole declined it as a personal gift, but accepted it as an official residence for the holder of the premiership. Not all Prime Ministers have lived there, and not all its occupants have liked it. Asquith's wife Margot found it 'an inconvenient house with three poor staircases'. And Churchill called it 'shaky and lightly built'.

## THE PLAYING FIELDS OF PREMIERSHIP
No fewer than 37 of Britain's 49 Prime Ministers went to public school. Of that total, almost half – 18 Prime Ministers – went to Eton, and another seven went to Harrow. After school, 38 Prime Ministers went on to study at Oxbridge – 24 at Oxford and 14 at Cambridge.

## SNAP DECISION
Britain acquired effective control of the Suez Canal thanks to an Arab potentate's poverty and a Jewish Prime Minister's risky gamble. In November 1875 the Khedive of Egypt, who was in financial difficulties, was planning to raise cash by mortgaging in Paris more than 40 per cent of the shares in the Suez Canal Company. Hearing of the deal, Britain's Jewish Prime Minister, Benjamin Disraeli, quickly arranged a personal loan of £4 million from the Rothschild family of bankers and bought the shares outright . . . without waiting for Parliament's approval.

Had the purchase not won political backing, Disraeli could have been ruined by the repayments on the enormous sum he had borrowed. In the event, though, Parliament ratified the deal, took over the loan and the shares, and made Britain mistress of the world's most important maritime shortcut. By the time the canal was nationalised by President Gamal Abdel Nasser of Egypt in 1956, Disraeli's snap investment had paid for itself many times over.

## BOB'S YOUR UNCLE
The expression 'Bob's your uncle' is said to have come from the political partnership of Robert Gascoyne-Cecil, 3rd Marquess of Salisbury (1830–1903), and his nephew Arthur Balfour. Salisbury, who was Prime Minister for a total of 14 years, appointed Balfour to various posts, such as Secretary for Ireland, First Lord of the Treasury and Leader of the House of Commons. Balfour thus obtained the reputation of having only to ask for an appointment and it would be granted – because 'Bob's your uncle'.

## OFF WITH THEIR HEADS
The last people sentenced to be hanged and quartered for high treason in Britain were five of the ten men known as the Cato Street conspirators. In 1820 the group plotted to seize London after assassinating the Prime Minister Lord Liverpool and the Cabinet. But the plot was betrayed, and most of the group were arrested in a loft in Cato Street, London. The leader, Arthur Thistlewood, escaped until the following day.

Five of the conspirators were sentenced to be transported to Australia as convicts. But Thistlewood and four others were sentenced to a relatively merciful form of the old high treason punishment of hanging, drawing and quartering. They were not to be cut

SPHERE OF INFLUENCE *Pitt the Younger and Napoleon carve up the globe in a cartoon satirising the nationalistic ambitions of both men. The cartoon was published in 1805 by the English caricaturist James Gillray. At the time, Bonaparte and France were masters of most of continental Europe; Britain under Pitt was the world's foremost maritime power.*

down and disembowelled ('drawn') while still alive. Instead, the court ordered, they were to be hanged until they were dead, and only then beheaded and quartered. The crowd watching the executions outside Newgate Prison at first jeered at the prisoners, but it became so outraged by the beheadings that the quartering was dispensed with.

## OFFICE RECORDS

Britain's youngest Prime Minister was William Pitt the Younger, who took office at the age of 24. The oldest was William Gladstone, who began his fourth term of office at 83. The longest-ruling was Robert Walpole, who held office without a break for almost 21 years – from April 3, 1721, to February 2, 1742. The shortest-ruling was George Canning. He became premier on April 10, 1827, and died of pneumonia less than four months later, on August 8.

## PISTOLS FOR FOUR

Two Prime Ministers have fought duels, one of them while in office. When the Duke of Wellington changed his mind about giving Catholics the vote and passed the Catholic Relief Bill in 1829 to enfranchise them, Lord Winchilsea accused him of double-dealing. This charge infuriated Wellington and he challenged Winchilsea to a duel, which they fought in Battersea Park, London. Wellington is said to have aimed at his

# PRIME MINISTERS OF BRITAIN/Walpole – Grenville

## MAJOR EVENTS AND ACHIEVEMENTS

### SIR ROBERT WALPOLE
**1st Prime Minister/1721 – 42**
**(Whig)**
Born 1676; died 1745. Restored confidence after the stock market panic which followed the South Sea Bubble – the collapse of the South Sea Company in 1720. Started a fund to help to pay off the national debt. Resigned after the government was accused of rigging a by-election in Chippenham, Wiltshire.

### EARL OF WILMINGTON
**2nd Prime Minister/1742 – 3**
**(Whig)**
Born around 1673; died 1743. Passed the Place Act (1742), an anti-corruption measure to limit the number of offices MPs could hold, and led Britain as Austria's ally during the War of the Austrian Succession (1740 – 8).

### HENRY PELHAM
**3rd Prime Minister/1743 – 54**
**(Whig)**
Born 1696; died 1754. Formed a coalition government which included the Tory William Pitt and the Whig Henry Fox. Agreed Treaty of Aix-la-Chapelle with France (1748), ending the War of the Austrian Succession. Passed Reform of the Calendar Act (1751), which replaced the inaccurate Julian calendar with the modern Gregorian calendar. He died in office on March 6, 1754.

### DUKE OF NEWCASTLE
**4th Prime Minister/1754 – 6;**
**1757 – 62**
**(Whig)**
Born 1693; died 1768. Became Prime Minister on the death of his brother, Henry Pelham. But disagreements with ministers and British setbacks at the start of the Seven Years' War (1756 – 63) led to his resignation in 1756. His second administration was largely dominated by William Pitt the Elder, the Secretary of State, who directed the Seven Years' War.

### DUKE OF DEVONSHIRE
**5th Prime Minister/1756 – 7**
**(Whig)**
Born 1720; died 1764. Passed the Militia Act (1757) which provided troops for the Seven Years' War against France, Austria, Spain and Russia. Sanctioned the execution of Admiral John Byng for failing to save Minorca from the French. Resigned in July 1757.

COLOSSUS OF LONDON *This 1740 engraving shows Sir Robert Walpole straddling the world like the gigantic statue known as the Colossus of Rhodes. Walpole held office continuously for almost 21 years – longer than any other Prime Minister.*

opponent's legs, but missed. Winchilsea then fired into the air and apologised to the duke.

In 1809 George Canning, the Foreign Secretary who was to become Prime Minister, fought a duel on Putney Heath in London with Lord Castlereagh, the War Minister. Castlereagh was outraged because Canning had demanded his sacking in private while behaving to his face as though all was well. After the duel, in which Canning was slightly wounded by a pistol shot in the leg, both ministers resigned office.

DUEL AT DAWN *The Duke of Wellington, pistol lowered, waits for his opponent, Lord Winchilsea, to fire. Winchilsea eventually fired into the air – then apologised.*

## EARL OF BUTE
### 6th Prime Minister/1762–3 (Tory)
Born 1713; died 1792. Allied himself with George III to end Whig supremacy in Parliament and restore power to the throne. Signed Treaty of Paris (1763) which brought the Seven Years' War to an end. Under the treaty, Britain gained Canada and all French territory east of the Mississippi. Spain also ceded Florida to Britain in exchange for Cuba.

## GEORGE GRENVILLE
### 7th Prime Minister/1763–5 (Whig)
Born 1712; died 1770. Re-established the authority of Parliament despite opposition from George III. Passed Stamp Act (1765) which imposed taxation on American colonies.

## MARQUESS OF ROCKINGHAM
### 8th Prime Minister/1765–6; 1782 (Whig)
Born 1730; died 1782. Established trade with Russia, and cut unpopular taxes on cider. During his second term of office he secured legislative independence for Ireland. Banned government contractors from being MPs, and abolished many government sinecures.

## EARL OF CHATHAM
### 9th Prime Minister/1766–8 (Whig)
Born 1708; died 1778. Often called William Pitt the Elder, he became known as the Great Commoner for his foreign policy successes, guiding Britain to victory in colonial wars against the French in India and Canada.

## DUKE OF GRAFTON
### 10th Prime Minister/1768–70 (Whig)
Born 1735; died 1811. Became premier after serving as First Lord of the Treasury under Chatham. Unsuccessfully opposed taxation of the American colonies.

## LORD NORTH
### 11th Prime Minister/1770–82 (Tory)
Born 1732; died 1792. Favoured a negotiated settlement with the American colonies during the quarrel over taxation. But was forced into war by the king.

## EARL OF SHELBURNE
### 12th Prime Minister/1782–3 (Whig)
Born 1737; died 1805. Made peace with United States, recognising American independence (1783). Signed Treaty of Versailles (1783), bringing peace with America's allies, France and Spain.

## DUKE OF PORTLAND
### 13th Prime Minister/1783; 1807–9 (Tory)
Born 1738; died 1809. His first ministry ended after the House of Lords rejected the India Bill, a measure designed to bring the

BOSTON MASSACRE *Five men were killed when British troops fired on a rioting crowd in Boston on March 5, 1770, stoking American resentment against British rule. Lord North later came to be blamed for the loss of the colonies despite his opposition to Britain's tough policies.*

administration of India by the East India Company under greater government control. His second was blighted by failing health and faction fights between his ministers.

## WILLIAM PITT
### 14th Prime Minister/ 1783–1801; 1804–6 (Tory)
Born 1759; died 1806. Known as Pitt the Younger to distinguish him from his father, the Earl of Chatham. Introduced the India Act (1784) limiting the autonomy of the East India Company, the Canada Act (1791) dividing Canada into French-speaking and English-speaking areas, and the Act of Union (1800) uniting the parliaments of Dublin and Westminster. Set up a new fund (1787) to reduce the national debt. Introduced income tax in 1799 as a temporary measure to help pay for the War with Revolutionary France which had broken out in 1793. The top rate was 2 shillings in the pound: 10 per cent. Resigned in 1801 when the king refused to accept the Catholic Emancipation Bill, giving Catholics the right to vote and sit in Parliament. Was brought back to office to cope with the threat of Napoleonic invasion in the aftermath of the French Revolution.

## HENRY ADDINGTON
### 15th Prime Minister/1801–4 (Tory)
Born 1757; died 1844. Opposed Catholic emancipation. Signed Treaty of Amiens (March 1802), ending war with France. But war erupted again in 1803.

## LORD GRENVILLE
### 16th Prime Minister/1806–7 (Whig)
Born 1759; died 1834. Formed 'Ministry of All the Talents' composed of the best men from all political parties. Pushed through Abolition of Slavery Act (1807). Resigned when the king refused again to accept Catholic emancipation.

# PRIME MINISTERS OF BRITAIN/Perceval – Balfour

## SPENCER PERCEVAL
### 17th Prime Minister/1809 – 12
### (Tory)
Born 1762; died 1812. Was supported by George III but not by politicians, many of whom refused to serve under him. Opposed Catholic emancipation and pressure for parliamentary reform aimed at giving more people the vote. Was assassinated in the House of Commons lobby by an aggrieved merchant, John Bellingham, who blamed the government for his bankruptcy (see *Death at point-blank range*, page 76).

## LORD LIVERPOOL
### 18th Prime Minister/1812 – 27
### (Tory)
Born 1770; died 1828. Abolished income tax (1816). Imposed steep duties on imported wheat in Corn Laws (1815), pleasing farmers but provoking protests over the resulting high price of bread. The laws helped to trigger the first organised strike – by Lancashire cotton spinners in 1818 – and the Peterloo Massacre (1819), when cavalry was ordered to charge a crowd of 80,000 protesters in Manchester. In the fighting that followed, 11 people were killed and hundreds injured. In the wake of the violence, the government passed the Six Acts (1819), designed to regulate political dissent. In 1824 Liverpool repealed the Combination Acts, which had outlawed trade unions.

## GEORGE CANNING
### 19th Prime Minister/1827
### (Tory)
Born 1770; died 1827. Supported Catholic emancipation but opposed parliamentary reform. Died of pneumonia only 100 days after taking office.

LONDON'S FINEST *Britain's first uniformed police force was set up in London in 1829 by Sir Robert Peel. Constables – then top-hatted, now helmeted – became known as Peelers and are still called bobbies after the Prime Minister.*

## VISCOUNT GODERICH
### 20th Prime Minister/1827 – 8
### (Tory)
Born 1782; died 1859. Resigned after four months.

## DUKE OF WELLINGTON
### 21st Prime Minister/1828 – 30
### (Tory)
Born 1769; died 1852. Turned to politics after leading British troops to victory over Napoleon. As Prime Minister, passed Catholic Relief Act (1829), granting Catholics right to vote and sit in Parliament. But opposed parliamentary reform, believing that full democracy would pave the way for mob rule.

## EARL GREY
### 22nd Prime Minister/1830 – 4
### (Whig)
Born 1764; died 1845. Introduced the Parliamentary Reform Act (June 7, 1832), enlarging the franchise and abolishing 'rotten boroughs' – former towns which had lost most of their population but still existed as parliamentary constituencies with the right to elect MPs. Also supported the first Factory Act (1833), banning children under nine from working in factories, and limiting the working hours of children under 13 to 48 hours a week. Abolished slavery in British colonies.

## VISCOUNT MELBOURNE
### 23rd Prime Minister/1834; 1835 – 41
### (Whig)
Born 1779; died 1848. Resisted pressure for further parliamentary reform and opposed repeal of the Corn Laws. During his second term, Queen Victoria came to the throne (1837) and he became her trusted adviser and tutor in statecraft.

## SIR ROBERT PEEL
### 24th Prime Minister/1834 – 5; 1841 – 6
### (Tory)
Born 1788; died 1850. Became Prime Minister after a successful career as Home Secretary during which he created the Metropolitan Police Force in 1829. As soon as he took office he called an election, during which he made the speech now known as the 'Tamworth Manifesto' to his constituents at Tamworth, Staffordshire. In the speech he promised that his government would be 'conservative', accepting moderate reforms while respecting established institutions. The speech helped him to victory in the election and began the transformation of the Tory Party into the modern Conservative Party. During the term of his second administration he pursued a free-trade policy, reduced or abolished tariffs and introduced a new income

tax of 7d in the pound: 3 per cent. In 1842 he pushed through the Mines Act forbidding the employment of women and children in mines. And in 1844 he sponsored a new Factory Act limiting further the working hours of women and children; introduced the Railway Act requiring the railways to provide daily services at fares of 1d (less than ½p) a mile; and supported the Bank Charter Act, which regulated the number of banknotes printed and gold stocks held by the Bank of England. In 1846 he repealed the 1815 Corn Laws – which had blocked the import of cheap foreign wheat – after potato blight caused famine in Ireland. Nearly a million people died during the famine and another million emigrated to the USA.

## LORD JOHN RUSSELL
### 25th Prime Minister/1846 – 52; 1865 – 6
### (Whig)
Born 1792; died 1878. Introduced measures to help Ireland in the aftermath of the 1845 potato famine. Passed a third Factory Act (1847) limiting the working hours of women to ten hours a day.

## EARL OF DERBY
### 26th Prime Minister/1852; 1858 – 9; 1866 – 8
### (Conservative)
Born 1799; died 1869. In the wake of the Indian Mutiny (1857 – 8), he introduced the India Act (1858) which transferred the government of India from the East India Company to the Crown. Pushed through the second Reform Bill (1867), giving the vote to urban labourers.

PEARL OF THE EAST *Disraeli, dressed as the wizard in the children's story of Aladdin (below), offers Queen Victoria the crown of India in an 1876 cartoon.*

"NEW CROWNS FOR OLD ON
(ALADDIN *adapted*)

## EARL OF ABERDEEN
### 27th Prime Minister/1852–5
### (Tory)

Born 1784; died 1860. Led Britain into the Crimean War against Russia in 1854. But ten months later, after criticism of his handling of the unpopular war, his government was brought down by a vote of no confidence.

## VISCOUNT PALMERSTON
### 28th Prime Minister/1855–8; 1859–65
### (Liberal)

Born 1784; died 1865. As Foreign Secretary, helped Belgium to independence from the Netherlands (1830) – installing Leopold, Queen Victoria's uncle, as first king – and made a trade agreement with China (1841) which gave Britain control of Hong Kong. As Prime Minister, ended the Crimean War and signed the Treaty of Paris (1856), under which Russia agreed not to keep warships in the Black Sea. Suppressed the Indian Mutiny (1857–8) and maintained British neutrality in the American Civil War (1861–5).

## BENJAMIN DISRAELI
### 29th Prime Minister/1868; 1874–80
### (Conservative)

Born 1804; died 1881. With Peel, was founder of modern Conservatism, combining domestic reform with development of the British empire. Was defeated by the Liberals at the general election in December 1868 after only ten months in office. During his second term he introduced: the Trade Union Acts (1875) which allowed peaceful picketing; the Artisans Dwelling Act (1875) to provide housing for the poor; the Climbing Boys Act (1875) which strengthened previous Acts abolishing the employment of children as chimney-sweeps; the Public Health Act (1875) which improved mains water supplies and refuse collection; the Education Act (1876) which made schooling compulsory for children between the ages of four and ten; and the Merchant Shipping Act (1876) which established the Plimsoll Line as the loading limit for ships. His purchase of shares from the Khedive of Egypt in 1875 led to Britain acquiring effective control of the Suez Canal, and in 1876 he proclaimed Queen Victoria Empress of India.

## WILLIAM EWART GLADSTONE
### 30th Prime Minister/1868–74; 1880–5; 1886; 1892–4
### (Liberal)

Born 1809; died 1898. A supporter of Home Rule for Ireland, he disestablished the Irish Church (1869) and supported the Land Act (1870) to protect Irish peasants from wealthy landlords. He also introduced: the Education Act (1870) establishing school boards to supply education where no parish schools existed; the Trade Union Act (1871) giving trade unions legal status; the Ballot Act (1872) making voting secret; and the Licensing Act (1872) regulating the opening hours of public houses. During his second administration Lord Frederick Cavendish, Viceroy of Ireland, was assassinated in Dublin (1882), and General Gordon was killed at Khartoum in the Sudan (1885). In 1884 he supported the third Reform Act extending the vote to agricultural workers. He resigned from his third administration after his Home Rule for Ireland Bill was defeated.

## MARQUESS OF SALISBURY
### 31st Prime Minister/1885–6; 1886–92; 1895–1902
### (Conservative)

Born 1830; died 1903. Introduced the Local Government Act (1888), giving the counties greater control of their own affairs, and established free education in elementary schools. Led Britain into the Boer War in South Africa in 1899. The war ended in 1902 with British victory over the Boer republics of the Transvaal and the Orange Free State. In European affairs, he pursued a policy of 'splendid isolation', refusing to align Britain with any of the continental powers.

## EARL OF ROSEBERY
### 32nd Prime Minister/1894–5
### (Liberal)

Born 1847; died 1929. With the House of Lords hostile to all Liberal legislation, Rosebery was able to achieve little. He resigned when his War Minister, Henry Campbell-Bannerman, was censured by the Commons over his handling of army supplies during the war in South Africa.

## ARTHUR BALFOUR
### 33rd Prime Minister/1902–5
### (Conservative)

Born 1848; died 1930. Introduced a new Education Act (1902) which made local authorities responsible for financing elementary schools through property taxes. As Foreign

GATEWAY TO INDIA *An 1875 cartoon from the magazine* Punch *(left) shows Disraeli and the Sphinx winking at each other conspiratorially after Disraeli bought effective control of Egypt's Suez Canal. The deal gave Britain mastery of the most important sea route to India.*

SPARRING PARTNERS *Gladstone (right) and Disraeli, shown in this* Punch *sketch after agreeing on a Budget amendment in 1860, dominated politics for more than 20 years – mostly as opponents.*

Secretary in 1917, was responsible for the Balfour Declaration, promising British support for the creation of a national home for Jews in Palestine.

## SIR HENRY CAMPBELL-BANNERMAN
**34th Prime Minister/1905–8
(Liberal)**
Born 1836; died 1908. Introduced the Trades Disputes Act (1906) which gave trade unions immunity from legal damages, and restored self-government to the Boer republics of the Transvaal (1906) and the Orange Free State (1907).

## HERBERT HENRY ASQUITH
**35th Prime Minister/1908–16
(Liberal)**
Born 1852; died 1928. Began the creation of the Welfare State in 1908 by providing old age pensions of 5 shillings a week for people over 70 whose incomes did not exceed 10 shillings a week. Pushed through the Parliament Act (1911), under which the House of Lords lost its power to reject money Bills and had its power to delay other Bills limited to three years. The Act also reduced the maximum term of any Parliament from seven to five years. In 1912 he supported the National Insurance Act which compelled manual workers between the ages of 16 and 70 to insure against sickness and unemployment. Led Britain into the First World War (1914–18). Formed coalition with Conservatives (1915). But military failures brought pressure for his removal. Resigned in 1916.

## DAVID LLOYD GEORGE
**36th Prime Minister/1916–22
(Liberal)**
Born 1863; died 1945. Formed the Imperial War Cabinet to co-ordinate the British empire war effort (1917), introduced the convoy system (1917) to protect merchant shipping from German submarines, and played a major part in establishing unified command of Allied armies in France (1918). Sponsored the Representation of the People Act (1918) which gave the vote to women over the age of 30 who were either householders or the wives of householders. In 1919 signed the Treaty of Versailles, which imposed severe terms on Germany after the end of the First World War and established the League of Nations. Also signed an agreement giving independence to Southern Ireland (now Eire).

## ANDREW BONAR LAW
**37th Prime Minister/1922–3
(Conservative)**
Born 1858; died 1923. Ill-health forced him to resign in May 1923, seven months after taking office.

## STANLEY BALDWIN
**38th Prime Minister/1923;
1924–9; 1935–7
(Conservative)**
Born 1867; died 1947. Sponsored the Franchise Act (1928) extending votes to women over 21. During the General Strike in 1926, he organised volunteers to maintain all essential services, and refused to negotiate until the strike was called off; it was after nine days. His government later passed the Trades Disputes and Trade Union Act (1927), making general strikes illegal.

## JAMES RAMSAY MACDONALD
**39th Prime Minister/1924;
1929–35
(Labour)**
Born 1866; died 1937. Led, with Liberal Party support, Britain's first Labour government. His government lost the 1924 election after the Foreign Office issued – four days before polling – the text of the 'Zinoviev letter', a letter purporting to be from Grigori Zinoviev, chairman of the Communist International (Comintern), to the British Communist Party and advocating armed revolution. The letter was shown later to have probably been a forgery by Russian exiles in Berlin. For the Liberals, the election was disastrous: the number of Liberal MPs plunged from 159 to 40. During his second term of office, unemployment rose from 1 million to 2.5 million by 1931 and the government could not afford to pay unemployment benefit.

## ARTHUR NEVILLE CHAMBERLAIN
**40th Prime Minister/1937–40
(Conservative)**
Born 1869; died 1940. Followed a policy of appeasement of Hitler and in September 1938 signed the Munich agreement approving the transfer of German-speaking border areas of Czechoslovakia to Germany Claimed that the agreement was 'symbolic of the desire of our two peoples never to go to war with one another again'. War was declared by Britain on September 3, 1939, after German troops occupied the Czech capital of Prague and invaded Poland. In 1940 Norway fell to the Germans, after a British force failed to save it. Chamberlain attempted to form a National Government of both major parties but Labour leaders refused to serve under him.

## SIR WINSTON CHURCHILL
**41st Prime Minister/1940–5;
1951–5
(Conservative)**
Born 1874; died 1965. As Prime Minister of a coalition government, Churchill led Britain through the Second World War. In May 1945,

after the defeat of Germany, he became head of a 'caretaker' Conservative government which agreed to the use by the USA of atomic weapons against Japan. During his second term of office he denationalised the iron and steel industry (1952) and road transport (1953). Withdrew British troops from Egypt (1954).

## CLEMENT ATTLEE
**42nd Prime Minister/1945–51
(Labour)**
Born 1883; died 1967. Set up the National Health Service (1946). Nationalised the Bank of England and the civil aviation and coal industries (1946), the transport and electricity industries (1947), the gas industry (1949) and the steel industry (1950). Repealed the 1927 Trades Disputes and Trade Union Act (1946), and began a building programme which included the establishment of new towns (1946). Abroad, he helped India, Pakistan, Ceylon and Burma to independence (1947 and 1948), supported the Western airlift during the Russian blockade of Berlin (1948–9) and backed the formation of the North Atlantic Treaty Organisation (1949). He resigned when Labour lost the general election in October 1951 despite polling 13,948,883 votes – the largest number ever gained by one party in Britain.

## SIR ANTHONY EDEN
**43rd Prime Minister/1955–7
(Conservative)**
Born 1897; died 1977. After Egypt nationalised the Suez Canal in July 1956 (Britain had been principal shareholder in the company that controlled the canal), Eden ordered the bombing of the Egyptian forces and sent in troops to Port Said at the canal's northern end. But the troops were withdrawn under pressure from the USA and the United Nations without re-establishing British control of the canal.

## HAROLD MACMILLAN
**44th Prime Minister/1957–63
(Conservative)**
Born 1894. Presided over an economic boom during the late 1950s. In a speech in July 1957, he declared: 'Let us be frank about it, most of our people have never had it so good.' But balance of payments difficulties and unemployment rising to nearly 1 million people brought the boom years to an end in 1961. Abroad, he sensed that 'the wind of change was blowing throughout the continent' (of Africa), and he oversaw the transition to independence of 12 former British colonies: Gold Coast (now Ghana), Malaya (now part of Malaysia), Cyprus, Nigeria, Sierra Leone, Tanganyika (now part of Tanzania),

HIGH FLIER *Macmillan was given the nickname Supermac for his political skill. He was made an earl in 1984.*

Jamaica, Trinidad and Tobago, Uganda, Western Samoa, Kenya and Singapore. In July 1963 he negotiated the Nuclear Test-Ban Treaty with the USA and the Soviet Union. But his attempt to take Britain into the Common Market was vetoed by France's president, General Charles de Gaulle, in the same year; and his popular support was undermined by the discovery of a Russian spy in the Foreign Office, John Vassall, and the resignation of his War Minister, John Profumo, over a call-girl scandal.

### SIR ALEC DOUGLAS-HOME
**45th Prime Minister/1963–4 (Conservative)**
Born 1903. Renounced his title as 14th Earl of Home in order to sit in the House of Commons – the first peer to become Prime Minister since 1902. He was made a life peer in 1974, taking the title Lord Home of the Hirsel.

### HAROLD WILSON
**46th Prime Minister/1964–70; 1974–6 (Labour)**
Born 1916. Imposed a surcharge on imports, other than raw materials, to help close the balance of payments

gap (1964). Abolished the death penalty (1965), rejected Rhodesia's unilateral declaration of independence (1965), devalued the pound (1967) and set up the Metrication Board (1969) to organise Britain's conversion to the metric system. In 1969, in the wake of sectarian violence in Northern Ireland, he sent in British troops to help keep the peace. In 1975 Britain held its first referendum, in which the majority voted in favour of remaining in the Common Market. Resigned in April 1976.

### EDWARD HEATH
**47th Prime Minister/1970–4 (Conservative)**
Born 1916. Took Britain into the European Economic Community (Common Market) in January 1973, and two years before that introduced the Industrial Relations Act designed to promote better relations between workers and employers and to curb the power of the trade unions. But his policies led to confrontations with the unions. In the wake of fuel shortages caused by the Arab oil embargo and an overtime ban by coal-miners, he imposed a three-day week for industry. During a prolonged pay dispute with the miners' union, he called a general election in February 1974, hoping to win popular support for his stand. Lost the Tory leadership after losing the election and losing a second general election in October 1974.

### JAMES CALLAGHAN
**48th Prime Minister/1976–9 (Labour)**
Born 1912. Formed the Lib-Lab pact with the Liberal Party in 1977 to protect his slender majority in the House of Commons. Defied in July 1978 the Trades Union Congress by declaring a 5 per cent guideline limit for wage rises. The unions

responded with a series of strikes in the 'Winter of Discontent'. In early 1979, there were strikes by petrol delivery men, lorry drivers, train drivers, car workers and by local government and hospital workers. In two referenda in March 1979, voters turned down proposals to give greater local autonomy to Wales and Scotland – and the Scottish National Party's 11 MPs withdrew their support from the government. His ministry was brought down by a vote of no confidence, which it lost by only one vote on March 28 – the first time that a government had been defeated on such a vote since 1924. Was followed as Labour leader in 1980 by Michael Foot, and in 1983 by Neil Kinnock.

### MARGARET THATCHER
**49th Prime Minister/1979– (Conservative)**
Born 1925. Britain's first woman Prime Minister. Cut the standard rate of income tax from 33 to 30 per cent and the highest rate from 83 to 60 per cent (1979), but raised indirect taxation in the form of Value-Added Tax from 8 to 15 per cent. Supported negotiations which ended the rebel regime in Rhodesia and led to the creation on April 18, 1980, of the independent state of Zimbabwe. Took as her main aim the control of inflation, which, during her administration, dropped from a peak of 18 per cent at the end of 1980 to 4 per cent in 1983, but only at the cost of mounting unemployment. Two million people were out of work by August 1980, and more than 3 million by mid-1983. Sent British troops to the Falkland Islands in April 1982 after Argentina invaded on April 2. Argentine forces on the islands surrendered on June 14. In June 1983 she was returned to power with a majority of 144 seats in the House of Commons.

FIVE IN ONE *Five Prime Ministers appear in this detail from* Statesmen of World War I, *a canvas painted by Sir James Guthrie in the 1920s and now in the National Portrait Gallery, London. Perhaps prophetically, the artist made the central and most brightly lit figure Sir Winston Churchill, who was a Cabinet Minister for part of the First World War but did not become the head of government until 1940, at the height of the Second World War.*

Balfour

Bonar Law

Asquith

Lloyd George

Churchill

# Prime Ministers of Australia

## NATIONAL MEETING PLACE

For 26 years, from 1901 to 1927, the Australian Parliament was based in temporary quarters in Melbourne while politicians argued about where to build a national capital. Each state backed its own cause until politicians finally agreed in 1911 to create a new federal territory – not part of any state – midway between Sydney and Melbourne. The new capital built there was named Canberra from the Aboriginal word *canberry*, meaning 'meeting place'.

## MING DYNASTY

Australia has had its own Ming dynasty. Prime Minister Sir Robert Menzies, who served for a total of 18 years, longer than any other Australian Prime Minis-

---

# MAJOR EVENTS AND ACHIEVEMENTS

**SIR EDMUND BARTON**
**1st Prime Minister/1901–3**
**(Protectionist)**
Born 1849; died 1920. Established, with his successor Alfred Deakin, the structure of the new federal administration. In 1902, he backed votes for women, and introduced the first tariffs, designed to protect industry against cheap imports.

**ALFRED DEAKIN**
**2nd, 5th and 7th Prime Minister/1903–4; 1905–8; 1909–10**
**(Protectionist)**
Born 1856; died 1919. Tried to introduce in 1904 the Industrial Conciliation and Arbitration Bill, which aimed to settle industrial disputes in the courts rather than through strikes. Resigned when Labor carried an amendment bringing government employees under the jurisdiction of the Bill. Introduced pensions for invalids and the elderly (1908) and established the White Australia policy to block immigration from Asia. Raised protectionist tariffs in 1908. In the 'Fusion government' of 1909, he combined with his former opponent Joseph Cook (leader of the conservative Free Traders) in the newly formed Liberal Party.

**JOHN CHRISTIAN WATSON**
**3rd Prime Minister/1904**
**(Labor)**
Born 1867; died 1941. The world's first Labour Prime Minister, he resigned after less than four months in office when his proposal to secure preference for trade unionists in the Industrial Conciliation and Arbitration Bill was defeated by a combined lobby of Free Traders and Protectionists.

**SIR GEORGE HOUSTON REID**
**4th Prime Minister/1904–5**
**(Free Trader)**
Born 1845; died 1918. Headed a government in coalition with the Protectionists. Pushed through the Industrial Conciliation and Arbitration Bill.

**ANDREW FISHER**
**6th, 8th and 10th Prime Minister/1908–9; 1910–13; 1914–15**
**(Labor)**
Born 1862; died 1928. Established the Commonwealth Bank (1911) as a government bank. Introduced maternity allowances (1912), and backed the formation of a national navy and the construction of a transcontinental railway. Introduced a land tax to break up large estates. At the outbreak of the First World War, he pledged that Australia would assist Britain 'to the last man and the last shilling'.

**SIR JOSEPH COOK**
**9th Prime Minister/1913–14**
**(Liberal)**
Born 1867; died 1947. Elected Prime Minister with a one-seat majority in the House of Representatives, but much of his legislation was blocked by a predominantly Labor Senate.

**WILLIAM (BILLY) MORRIS HUGHES**
**11th Prime Minister/1915–23**
**(National Labor)**
Born 1862; died 1952. Led Australia through most of the First World War.

A supporter of conscription, he was expelled in 1916 by the Labor Party, which opposed conscription. But he remained Prime Minister as head of a new party, the National Labor Party, which merged with the Liberal Party in 1917 to form a Nationalist coalition government. Hughes secured for Australia a mandate over German New Guinea in the Treaty of Versailles (1919).

**STANLEY MELBOURNE BRUCE**
**12th Prime Minister/1923–9**
**(Nationalist)**
Born 1883; died 1967. Promoted economic growth under the slogan 'Men, Money, Markets'. Set up the Council for Scientific and Industrial Research (1926). Introduced an insurance scheme designed to help the unemployed. In 1927 the federal government moved to the new capital, Canberra. His economic policies produced industrial expansion, but left Australia with subsidies on most industries other than wool, and high tariffs, high prices and a huge national debt.

**JAMES HENRY SCULLIN**
**13th Prime Minister/1929–32**
**(Labor)**
Born 1876; died 1953. Became Prime Minister just as the full force of the Depression hit Australia. Unemployment reached a peak of more than 25 per cent. Scullin adopted in 1932 the Premiers' Plan – worked out with the leaders of the states – which cut government spending and lowered wages in an attempt to encourage economic recovery.

**JOSEPH ALOYSIUS LYONS**
**14th Prime Minister/1932–9**
**(United Australia)**
Born 1879; died 1939. Took advantage of worldwide economic recovery and gradually brought the nation out of the Depression. Governed in coalition with the Country Party after the 1934 election. Responding to tension in Europe and Japanese aggression in China, Lyons expanded the armed forces and set up an independent Australian air force.

*SECOND CHOICE Sir Edmund Barton, first Prime Minister of Australia, was appointed only after the governor-general, Lord Hopetoun, was forced to abandon his first choice, Sir William Lyne.*

ter, became known as 'Ming the Merciless' – after the villain in the Flash Gordon comic strips and films – and his stay in the Prime Minister's official residence in Canberra was nicknamed the Ming dynasty.

## THE WRONG CHOICE

The first choice by the governor-general of Australia, Lord Hopetoun, for Prime Minister of the newly formed Commonwealth of Australia in 1901 was a man who had opposed the setting up of the federation. He was Sir William Lyne (1844–1913), Premier of the oldest colony, New South Wales.

In the event, however, Lyne failed to form a government. Leading politicians refused to serve in his Cabinet, and Lyne had no alternative but to recommend that Sir Edmund Barton, who had supported federation, should be made Australia's first Prime Minister.

## PARTY LINES

Political conservatives in Australia are usually supporters of the Liberal Party; and liberals mostly support the Labor Party. The Liberal Party is the result of a merger in 1909 between rival groups: the Protectionists, who favoured high tariffs to protect industry against cheap imports; and the Free Traders, who opposed them.

The Australian Labor Party, founded before 1901, adopted the US-style spelling of 'Labor' in 1918.

---

### SIR EARLE CHRISTMAS PAGE
**15th Prime Minister/1939 (Country)**
Born 1880; died 1961. Became caretaker Prime Minister for 19 days only when Lyons died.

### SIR ROBERT GORDON MENZIES
**16th and 21st Prime Minister/ 1939–41; 1949–66 (United Australia and Liberal)**
Born 1894; died 1978. Menzies – Australia's longest-serving Prime Minister – introduced an extensive immigration scheme, improved state-funded medical benefits, and gave state aid to independent schools. Created strong defence links with the United States by signing in 1951 the ANZUS pact – a military alliance of Australia, New Zealand and the USA – and by active participation in the Southeast Asia Treaty Organisation, set up as a defensive alliance in 1955 but disbanded in 1977. Supported Britain during the Suez crisis (1956) and in the Malaysia-Indonesia conflict of the early 1960s, and backed the USA in the Vietnam War.

### SIR ARTHUR WILLIAM FADDEN
**17th Prime Minister/1941 (Country)**
Born 1895; died 1973. Became Prime Minister when Menzies resigned, but he resigned five weeks later when his Budget was defeated.

### JOHN JOSEPH CURTIN
**18th Prime Minister/1941–5 (Labor)**
Born 1885; died 1945. During the Second World War, he fell out with Britain over his decision in 1942 to withdraw Australian troops from the Middle East. Encouraged the development of a welfare state.

### FRANCIS (FRANK) MICHAEL FORDE
**19th Prime Minister/1945 (Labor)**
Born 1890; died 1983. Took over for one week only after Curtin died in office.

### JOSEPH BENEDICT (BEN) CHIFLEY
**20th Prime Minister/1945–9 (Labor)**
Born 1885; died 1951. Set up a mass migration scheme, which included assisted passages for settlers. Introduced pensions for widows, and unemployment, sickness and hospital benefits. Established the Snowy Mountains Hydro-Electricity Authority, nationalised the national airline, Qantas, and Australia's overseas communications. Lost support within his own party when he used troops to break a coal strike in 1949. Supported the Indonesians in their fight for independence against the Dutch.

### HAROLD EDWARD HOLT
**22nd Prime Minister/1966–7 Liberal**
Born 1908; died 1967. Gave the USA military support in Vietnam. Disappeared while swimming in Port Phillip Bay near Melbourne.

### SIR JOHN McEWEN
**23rd Prime Minister/1967–8 (Country Party)**
Born 1900; died 1980. Took over as caretaker Prime Minister for 23 days after Holt's death.

### SIR JOHN GREY GORTON
**24th Prime Minister/1968–71 (Liberal)**
Born 1911. The first senator to be elected Prime Minister. Introduced legislation to improve educational and employment opportunities for Aborigines. Refused to increase Australia's commitment in Vietnam.

### SIR WILLIAM (BILL) McMAHON
**25th Prime Minister/1971–2 (Liberal)**
Born 1908. Came to office when Gorton was overthrown.

### EDWARD GOUGH WHITLAM
**26th Prime Minister/1972–5 (Labor)**
Born 1916. Led the first Labor government since 1949. Withdrew Australian troops from Vietnam.

Revalued the Australian dollar, imposed import controls and reduced tariffs. Expanded government spending and increased social services and other benefits. In 1974, faced with the blockage by the Opposition-dominated Senate of the Supply Bill – which provided the government with money – he called a snap election. But he failed to win control of the upper House. A similar challenge by the Senate the following year led to Whitlam's dismissal by the governor-general, Sir John Kerr.

### JOHN MALCOLM FRASER
**27th Prime Minister/1975–83 (Liberal)**
Born 1930. Was installed as caretaker Prime Minister after Whitlam's dismissal. In the election that followed, his Liberal-Country Party coalition gained a record majority in the House of Representatives, winning 91 of the 127 seats. Dismantled much of the public health service. Negotiated friendship treaty with Japan which provided for the strengthening of trade and commercial ties. Preferential trade tariffs for British goods were dropped (1979). Ended traditional arrangements encouraging immigration, including assisted passages (1981).

### ROBERT JAMES LEE HAWKE
**28th Prime Minister/1983– (Labor)**
Born 1929. A former president of Australia's national trade union organisation, the Australian Council of Trade Unions, he became an MP in 1980 – and party leader in February 1983, four weeks before the election. Floated the Australian dollar – ending the fixed exchange-rate policies of earlier Prime Ministers – and reintroduced a national health scheme. Passed Sex Discrimination Act. Made arms control a priority in foreign policy and appointed an Ambassador for Disarmament. Established a working party with the ACTU to consider options for taxation relief, directed at helping lower and middle income groups.

# Prime Ministers of Canada

## PREMIERS WHO PAID RENT

The first Prime Minister to move into the official residence of Canadian leaders – 24 Sussex Drive in Ottawa – did so only on condition that he paid rent for it. The high-minded tenant was Louis St Laurent, who moved in in 1950. His successors kept up the custom until Pierre Trudeau abandoned it in 1971.

## SAVED BY DEFEAT

W. L. Mackenzie King, who was Canada's Prime Minister three times, was a fervent believer in the supernatural. In 1930 his fortune-teller predicted that if King called an election that year he would emerge from it stronger than ever. King called the election – and lost to R. B. Bennett. But the fortune-teller

## MAJOR EVENTS AND ACHIEVEMENTS

### SIR JOHN A. MACDONALD
**1st Prime Minister/1867 – 73; 1878 – 91**
**(Conservative)**
Born 1815; died 1891. Played a leading role in the unification of Britain's Canadian colonies as a confederation in 1867. Negotiated the purchase (1868 – 9) of the Northwest Territories from the Hudson's Bay Company for £300,000. Put down the Red River Rebellion (1869 – 70), during which an alliance of Indians and Métis (people descended from French and Scottish fur traders who had intermarried with the Indians) rebelled against federal government attempts to take over the region west of Ontario. In December 1869 the rebels, led by a Métis named Louis Riel (1844 – 85), captured Fort Garry (now Winnipeg), headquarters of the Hudson's Bay Company. They forced the federal government in July 1870 to create the new province of Manitoba, with equal rights for French and English. But after Riel's government court-martialled and executed an English-speaking Canadian who opposed the Métis, federal troops were sent from Ontario and recaptured Fort Garry in August 1870. Riel had already fled, eventually into exile in the USA. Convicted of treason after returning to Canada in 1884 to lead a second, unsuccessful Métis rebellion in Saskatchewan, he was hanged on November 16, 1885. In 1871, Macdonald negotiated the entry of British Columbia into the confederation, on terms which included a federal promise to build a transcontinental railway within ten years. But he lost power in the 1873 election over the Pacific Scandal, in which a syndicate was awarded the contract to build the railway in

PACIFIC SCANDAL *A cartoon published in the wake of a scandal over a railway contract shows an unrepentant Sir John A. Macdonald (right) saying to Opposition leader Alexander Mackenzie: 'I admit I took the money, and bribed the electors with it. Is there anything wrong with that?'*

return for political campaign contributions. The railway line was finally completed by the Canadian Pacific Railway Company on November 7, 1885.

### ALEXANDER MACKENZIE
**2nd Prime Minister/1873 – 8**
**(Liberal)**
Born 1822; died 1892. Introduced legislation that led to the creation of the North West Mounted Police, forerunner of the Mounties, the Royal Canadian Mounted Police. Supported the building of the Canadian Pacific Railway. Defeated in the 1878 election by the Conservative platform of tariff protection to combat the economic depression of the late 1870s.

### SIR JOHN J. C. ABBOTT
**3rd Prime Minister/1891 – 2**
**(Conservative)**
Born 1821; died 1893. Canada's first native-born leader. Was pressed into service as a caretaker premier when Macdonald died in office because, as he said, he was 'not particularly obnoxious to anybody'.

### SIR JOHN S. D. THOMPSON
**4th Prime Minister/1892 – 4**
**(Conservative)**
Born 1844; died 1894. Served as Supreme Court judge and premier of

Nova Scotia. As federal Justice Minister he revised and codified Canada's criminal law. As Prime Minister, he negotiated international copyright and shipping agreements.

### SIR MACKENZIE BOWELL
**5th Prime Minister/1894 – 6**
**(Conservative)**
Born 1823; died 1917. At one time the Grand Master of the Orange Order, an organisation hostile to French Canadians and Catholics, he became Prime Minister after Thompson's sudden death. The abolition in 1890 of French schools in Manitoba had provoked continuing resentment in French-speaking Quebec. Bowell's vacillation over the issue led to seven resignations in his Cabinet and his own resignation in 1896.

### SIR CHARLES TUPPER
**6th Prime Minister/1896**
**(Conservative)**
Born 1821; died 1915. Flamboyant veteran statesman who had fought for confederation alongside Macdonald. Took office in May 1896, and introduced a Bill to protect separate French schools in Manitoba. But the Bill was unpopular with English-speaking Canadians, and led to electoral defeat one month later.

### SIR WILFRID LAURIER
**7th Prime Minister/1896 – 1911**
**(Liberal)**
Born 1841; died 1919. During his term, Canada entered a period of prosperity known as the 'Sunshine Years'. The economy flourished, and – thanks to an aggressive policy designed to encourage immigration – the population boomed. A huge gold rush followed the discovery in 1896 of gold nuggets along the Klondike Creek, a tributary of the Yukon River. Laurier is credited as the founder of Canadian independence. Under him, British troops were withdrawn from Canada, the militia came under Canadian command, the Navy was founded (1910) and Canada won the right to negotiate its own trade treaties. In 1905 the area between

turned out to be right. By losing the election, King avoided being blamed for the Depression of the early 1930s. In 1935 he led his Liberal Party back to power – and held power for another 13 years.

## KNIGHT FLIGHTS

Canada's first Prime Minister, Sir John A. Macdonald, was a sharp-tongued wit, a shrewd politician and an enthusiastic drinker. In a political career that spanned 47 years, including 18 as Canada's leader, he fired off a hail of barbed aphorisms, observations and jibes.

The teetotal Liberal Party leader, George Brown, once criticised Macdonald in Parliament for drunkenness. The Prime Minister was unflustered. The honourable members, he retorted, 'would rather have John A. drunk than George Brown sober'.

## BENNETT BUGGIES

During the early 1930s, when 1.5 million Canadians were out of work and the western plains were a dustbowl, many farmers hitched horses to their cars because they could not afford to license or run them. The strange vehicles came to be called 'Bennett buggies' after R. B. Bennett, who was Prime Minister during the worst years of the Depression.

An abandoned farm was similarly dubbed a 'Bennett barnyard', and hoboes brewed 'Bennett coffee' with scavenged wheat or barley.

---

Manitoba and the Rocky Mountains was divided into two new provinces: Saskatchewan and Alberta.

### SIR ROBERT BORDEN
**8th Prime Minister/1911–20 (Conservative)**
Born 1854; died 1937. Insisted that Canada should have a say in the conduct of the First World War, and that Canadian troops should be a distinct force in the British army. Helped to negotiate the terms of the Treaty of Versailles (1919), and insisted that Canada should sign the agreement separately, thus effectively achieving international recognition of Canada's autonomy. Supported the Women's Franchise Act (1918), giving women equal voting rights in federal elections.

### ARTHUR MEIGHEN
**9th Prime Minister/1920–1; 1926 (Conservative)**
Born 1874; died 1960. Persuaded Britain (1921) not to renew the 1902 Anglo-Japanese Alliance – as a result of which Japan had sided against Germany during the First World War – on the grounds that Japan was becoming a rival to US interests in the Pacific. His success left Japan without any allies until it signed the Tripartite Pact with Germany and Italy in 1940 – the year before the Japanese attack on Pearl Harbor. At home he advocated a protective tariff system to shelter Canada from US economic power.

### WILLIAM LYON MACKENZIE KING
**10th Prime Minister/1921–6; 1926–30; 1935–48 (Liberal)**
Born 1874; died 1950. Led Canada throughout the Second World War. Signed in 1941 a pact of US-Canadian co-operation to aid Britain's war effort. Expanded the Department of External Affairs (which had been established in 1909) and posted diplomats in all Commonwealth countries, making it possible for Canada to follow a truly Canadian foreign policy for the first time.

### RICHARD BEDFORD BENNETT
**11th Prime Minister/1930–5 (Conservative)**
Born 1870; died 1947. Oversaw Canada's transition to formal independence under the Statute of Westminster, passed by the British Parliament in 1931. Introduced legislation on minimum wages, maximum hours of work, pensions, price controls, and unemployment and health insurance. Created the Canadian Wheat Board, the Bank of Canada, and the forerunners of the Canadian Broadcasting Corporation and Air Canada.

### LOUIS ST LAURENT
**12th Prime Minister/1948–57 (Liberal)**
Born 1882; died 1973. Brought Newfoundland into the Canadian confederation in 1949. Backed the building in 1954–9 of the 3700km long (2300 miles) St Lawrence Seaway to link the Atlantic with the Great Lakes, and supported the building of the Trans-Canada Highway. Established the Canada Council to support the arts. Helped to make the Canadian Supreme Court Canada's final court of appeal, ending Canada's judicial links with Britain.

### JOHN GEORGE DIEFENBAKER
**13th Prime Minister/1957–63 (Conservative)**
Born 1895; died 1979. Introduced the Bill of Rights and set up federal agencies to help both western and Atlantic provinces. Initiated grain sales to Communist China and maintained trade and diplomatic links with Cuba after the 1962 crisis in which the USA forced Russia to withdraw nuclear missiles stationed on the island.

### LESTER BOWLES PEARSON
**14th Prime Minister/1963–8 (Liberal)**
Born 1897; died 1972. Served in 1952 as both president of the United Nations General Assembly and chairman of the North Atlantic Treaty Organisation council. Won the Nobel Peace Prize in 1957 for his work in organising the UN Emergency Force during the Suez crisis of 1956. His administration introduced: Medicare (a national health insurance plan); the Canada Pension Plan; and an official Canadian flag and national anthem. It also oversaw the country's centennial in 1967.

### PIERRE ELLIOTT TRUDEAU
**15th Prime Minister/1968–79; 1980–4 (Liberal)**
Born 1919. Backed policies designed to establish the equality of Canada's two official languages (French and English) in the federal civil service. Invoked the War Measures Act in 1970 to maintain order during a series of kidnappings in Quebec by extremist supporters of Quebec separatism. Extended the offshore fishing limit from 12 to 200 miles (19km to 320km), and introduced the metric system. In 1980 Trudeau led federalist forces to victory when predominantly French-speaking Quebec held a referendum on whether the province should break away from the confederation under a formula known as 'sovereignty-association'.

### JOE CLARK
**16th Prime Minister/1979–80 (Conservative)**
Born 1939. After six months in power, his minority government was toppled by opposition to its first Budget, and was defeated at the polls in February 1980.

### JOHN TURNER
**17th Prime Minister/1984 (Liberal)**
Born 1929. Chosen at a leadership convention in June 1984 to replace Pierre Trudeau. He had earlier served as Minister of Finance and as Justice Minister.

### BRIAN MULRONEY
**18th Prime Minister/1984– (Progressive Conservative)**
Born 1939. In an election in September 1984, he won the largest majority in Canadian parliamentary history – 211 seats out of 282 in the federal House of Commons.

# Prime Ministers of New Zealand

**FROM BALLROOM TO BEEHIVE**
For ten years the New Zealand Parliament debated measures and passed laws in the elegant surroundings of a ballroom. Their previous home, Parliament House in Wellington, burnt down in 1907. Lord Plunket, the governor (the title changed to governor-general in 1917), moved out of his nearby residence, Govern-

ment House, so that Parliament could use the building. Debates were held in the ballroom there.

When the new Parliament House was finally ready in 1917, the governor's house was not handed back. It continued to be used as offices for another 52 years until it was torn down in 1969 to make room for a high-rise block of government offices nicknamed the Beehive. The Beehive was opened by the Queen in

## MAJOR EVENTS AND ACHIEVEMENTS

**RICHARD JOHN SEDDON**
**1st Prime Minister 1893–1906**
**(Liberal)**
Born in 1845; died 1906. Supported the Industrial Conciliation and Arbitration Act (1894) which made it compulsory for industrial disputes – including strikes – to be settled by arbitration. Purchased Maori land and provided loans to settlers to encourage the expansion of agriculture, particularly dairy farming and meat production. Extended the vote to women (1893), making New Zealand the first country in the world to do so. Introduced old age pensions (1898), free secondary education (1902). Established a state coalmining industry (1901), a state fire insurance scheme (1903), and a state house-building industry (1905). Sent troops to support the British Army in the Anglo-Boer War (1899–1902), and introduced a preferential tariff for British imports (1903). Annexed the Cook Islands in 1901.

**SIR WILLIAM HALL-JONES**
**2nd Prime Minister 1906**
**(Liberal)**
Born 1851; died 1936. Served as caretaker Prime Minister for six weeks after Seddon's death.

**SIR JOSEPH GEORGE WARD**
**3rd Prime Minister 1906–12;**
**1928–30**
**(Liberal and National)**
Born 1856; died 1930. New Zealand was officially given self-governing status as a Dominion during Ward's first ministry. He increased New Zealand's contribution to the British navy. At home he established the National Provident Fund with the object of providing a superannuation scheme for the general public, introduced widows' pensions (1911), and passed the Defence Act (1910) which made military service in the Territorial Army compulsory.

**SIR THOMAS MACKENZIE**
**4th Prime Minister 1912**
**(National)**
Born 1854; died 1930. Served as Prime Minister for only 14 weeks before his government was defeated.

**WILLIAM FERGUSON MASSEY**
**5th Prime Minister/1912–15;**
**1915–19; 1919–25**
**(Reform)**
Born 1856; died 1925. Passed a law allowing tenant farmers who had perpetual leases to buy their freeholds on favourable terms (1913). Transferred most civil service appointments to a non-political public service commissioner, ending political patronage. Broke a dockers' strike by calling in farmers to load ships. Supported Britain during First World War, forming a patriotic coalition with the Liberals 1915–19. Rising prices led to industrial unrest during his last ministry.

**SIR FRANCIS HENRY DILLON BELL**
**6th Prime Minister/1925**
**(Reform)**
Born 1851; died 1936. The first Prime Minister to have been born in New Zealand, those before him were all born in the United Kingdom with the exception of Sir Joseph Ward who was born in Australia. He served for only 16 days, after Massey's death in office.

**JOSEPH GORDON COATES**
**7th Prime Minister/1925–8**
**(Reform)**
Born 1878; died 1943. Faced with the deepening Depression, he devalued the New Zealand pound against sterling, protected farmers against foreclosure on their mortgages, and set up a national credit agency, the Mortgage Corporation. But unemployment soared in 1926 (earlier there had been no significant unemployment in the country), and the overseas market for meat and wool crumbled.

**GEORGE WILLIAM FORBES**
**8th Prime Minister/1930–1;**
**1931–5**
**(United)**
Born 1869; died 1947. Introduced mortgage relief legislation in 1931 as part of his response to the Depression. But overseas prices for wool, meat and dairy products dropped, unemployment continued to rise and tax revenues fell, making public works impossible. Formed a coalition with the Reform Party (1931–5) but recovery from the Depression continued to be slow.

**MICHAEL JOSEPH SAVAGE**
**9th Prime Minister/1935–40**
**(Labour)**
Born 1872; died 1940. Won 55 out of 80 seats in the House of

SOCIAL REFORMER *Richard Seddon, New Zealand's first Prime Minister, made his country one of the most socially advanced in the world. Under his administration in 1893, New Zealand became the first nation to give women the vote. Old age pensions followed five years later in 1898.*

1977 although it was still unfinished. The Prime Minister, Sir Robert Muldoon, finally moved in with his Cabinet in 1979.

## OFFICE RECORDS

New Zealand's oldest Prime Minister was Sir Walter Nash who held office from the age of 75 to 78 until his defeat in 1960.

Richard Seddon, the first Prime Minister, served for the longest consecutive term (13 years between 1893 and 1906) as well as being the longest-serving Prime Minister.

Sir Francis Dillon Bell had the shortest term in office – only 16 days in 1925.

## SILENT MAJORITY

New Zealand's Reform Party, established in 1912, managed to remain in power for 16 years from 1912 to 1928 without ever winning an overall majority of the popular vote. In 1935 it merged with the United Party (a successor of the Liberal Party) to form the present-day National Party.

Like Australia, New Zealand today has a two-party system – that is, there are only two political groupings in the country that can muster sufficient support to form a government. The National Party is traditionally conservative and the Labour Party, which first came to power in 1935, is traditionally liberal.

---

Representatives to become New Zealand's first Labour Prime Minister. Introduced a guaranteed-price policy for dairy products and began a programme of public works and house building. Unemployment fell from 11.5 per cent of the workforce in 1935 to 2.9 per cent in 1937. Brought in a state-funded social security scheme in 1938, which gave benefits to invalids, widows, families, the sick, the old and the unemployed, and provided free medical treatment. At the outbreak of the Second World War in 1939, he pledged to Britain: 'Where she goes, we go; where she stands, we stand.'

### PETER FRASER
**10th Prime Minister/1940–9 (Labour)**
Born 1884; died 1950. Led country during the main part of Second World War. Imposed price controls, wage restraints and heavy taxation during and after the war. Played a major role in the foundation of the United Nations (1945).

### SIR SIDNEY GEORGE HOLLAND
**11th Prime Minister/1949–57 (National)**
Born 1893; died 1961. Abolished the upper house in the New Zealand Parliament, the Legislative Council (1950). Relaxed controls over prices and land sales. Increased his party's majority in a snap election (1951) called after a waterfront strike which he broke by using troops.

### SIR KEITH HOLYOAKE
**12th Prime Minister/1957; 1960–72 (National)**
Born 1904. Signed the New Zealand Australian Free Trade Agreement (1965), abolishing all tariffs

*RADICAL CONSERVATIVE Sir Sidney Holland, leader in the 1940s and '50s of the conservative National Party, took in 1950 the radical step of abolishing the Legislative Council, the upper house of the nation's Parliament – making New Zealand one of the few Western countries with a single-chamber legislature.*

between the two countries. Negotiated with Britain over the supply of dairy products when Britain joined the European Economic Community (1971). Holyoake was also a close supporter of the USA's Vietnam policy and sent troops there. He was appointed governor-general for three years in 1977 – the first politician to hold the office.

### SIR WALTER NASH
**13th Prime Minister/1957–60 (Labour)**
Born 1882; died 1968. Abolished conscription and introduced equal pay for men and women working for the government. Tightened wage restraints and price controls.

### JOHN ROSS MARSHALL
**14th Prime Minister/1972 (National)**
Born 1912. Took over when Holyoake resigned the party leadership but was defeated in an election ten months later.

### NORMAN ERIC KIRK
**15th Prime Minister/1972–4 (Labour)**
Born 1923; died 1974. Withdrew New Zealand troops from Vietnam and gave diplomatic recognition to Communist China. Passed legislation to combat sex discrimination in employment and introduced the Accident Compensation Act (1972) which provides state compensation for injury to all accident victims – replacing the need for some forms of insurance and ending the need for lengthy and expensive civil court actions to establish liability.

### WALLACE EDWARD ROWLING
**16th Prime Minister/1974–5 (Labour)**
Born 1927. Faced with dropping world prices for dairy products, meat and wool, and rising transport costs, he devalued the New Zealand dollar by 15 per cent and borrowed heavily abroad. Abolished official wage restraints.

### SIR ROBERT MULDOON
**17th Prime Minister/1975–84 (National)**
Born 1921. Signed the Closer Economic Relations Agreement (1983) between New Zealand and Australia which aimed to remove duties and other trade restrictions on goods manufactured in either country. But unemployment remained high although inflation dropped from 15.3 per cent in 1982 to 3.6 per cent in 1983. The population dropped as New Zealanders left the country, mostly for Australia. In 1980, 34,417 more people left than arrived, a net emigration of 1 per cent.

### DAVID LANGE
**18th Prime Minister/1984– (Labour)**
Born 1943. Won a landslide victory in July 1984 through his attacks on his predecessor's economic policies and his plan to ban nuclear vessels from New Zealand waters.

# Prime Ministers of South Africa

## GRAPES OF WRATH

Daniel Malan, the founder of apartheid, South Africa's policy of racial segregation, was an uncompromising clergyman long before he became a politician.

Between 1905 and 1915, he was a minister in the Dutch Reformed Church – and on one Sunday he launched a thunderous attack from the pulpit on the evils of alcohol, making an impassioned plea for temperance, if not outright prohibition, of the demon drink.

The sermon was not well received. The church was in the grape-growing Cape district of Montagu, and most of the congregation were wealthy wine farmers. Malan was moved soon afterwards to the town of Graaff-Reinet, whose economy was based on sheep.

## MAJOR EVENTS AND ACHIEVEMENTS

### LOUIS BOTHA
**1st Prime Minister/1910 – 19 (South African Party)**
Born 1862; died 1919. Commanded Boer forces during the Anglo-Boer War (1899 – 1902). Was elected Prime Minister when the Union of South Africa was created in 1910 from the areas of Natal, the Cape, the Transvaal and the Orange Free State. Founded the South African Party in 1911. But his policy of reconciliation of Boers and Britons caused resentment among some of his Afrikaner (Boer) followers. In 1913 he pushed through the Natives' Land Act, which limited the right of Africans to own land and thus forced many to become labourers for white farmers and industrialists. During the First World War he led South Africa's successful invasion of German South West Africa (1915). He died in office.

### JAN CHRISTIAAN SMUTS
**2nd Prime Minister/1919 – 24; 1939 – 48 (South African Party/United)**
Born 1870; died 1950. Fought against Britain during the Anglo-Boer War but afterwards supported the creation of the Union of South Africa within the British empire. Joined Botha's Cabinet (1910), and fought alongside him in German South West Africa (1915). Was appointed to the British War Cabinet, and helped to found Britain's Royal Air Force and the League of Nations, forerunner of the UN. Was reinstated as premier when Parliament voted in favour of South Africa's participation in the Second World War.

### JAMES BARRY MUNNIK HERTZOG
**3rd Prime Minister/1924 – 39 (National)**
Born 1866; died 1942. Fought as a Boer general during the Anglo-Boer War. Was a member of Botha's first Cabinet but was sacked by Botha because of his anti-British views. Formed in 1914 the largely Afrikaner National Party which won the election of 1924 in a pact with the Labour Party. In 1934, he merged his party with Smuts's South African Party to form the United Party. The merger led to a split in the National Party. In 1939 he tried to reunite the Nationalists as a separate party after Parliament voted against his motion that South Africa should remain neutral in the Second World War. The attempt failed, but the party he had founded became the forerunner of the National Party that won the election in 1948 – and has been in power ever since.

### DANIEL FRANÇOIS MALAN
**4th Prime Minister/1948 – 54 (National)**
Born 1874; died 1959. Established the first exclusively Afrikaner government. He founded the policy of racial segregation which came to be known as *apartheid*, an Afrikaans word meaning 'separatism'. A vigorous champion of Afrikaner interests and of the use of the Afrikaans language, he prepared the way for South Africa to become an independent republic.

### JOHANNES GERHARDUS STRIJDOM
**5th Prime Minister/1954 – 58 (National)**
Born 1893; died 1958. An ardent Afrikaner nationalist, republican and advocate of white supremacy, his energetic campaigning in the Transvaal and his powerful rhetoric in Parliament earned him the nickname of 'Lion of the North'. When the Senate – South Africa's Upper House – failed to give him the two-thirds majority he needed to push through constitutional changes necessary for his apartheid legislation, he radically increased the number of Senate seats (1955) and nominated government supporters to them to ensure passage of his Bills. The following year a separate electoral roll was created for coloureds (people of mixed African and European descent), a major step in the creation of an exclusively white electorate. Strijdom died in office on August 24, 1958.

### HENDRIK FRENSCH VERWOERD
**6th Prime Minister/1958 – 66 (National)**
Born 1901; died 1966. Further entrenched apartheid by elaborate legislation which enforced segregation and provided for the resettlement of black Africans away from the major cities. Introduced the Promotion of Bantu Self-Government Act (1959) to create African tribal 'homeland' areas, also known as Bantustans. The Act also abolished the last African

MAN OF WAR *Louis Botha, Boer general and South Africa's first premier, led his country's forces against German South West Africa in 1915. Since then, the territory – also known as Namibia – has been under effective South African control despite UN opposition.*

## PEACE OFFERING FROM A WARRIOR

The Cullinan diamond, pieces of which are now the largest stones in the British Crown Jewels, was given to Edward VII by a man who fought against Britain throughout the Anglo-Boer War (1899–1902). The man was General Louis Botha, who became South Africa's first Prime Minister in 1910. He was premier of the Transvaal when he persuaded his government to buy the 3025-carat stone in 1907 and offered it to the king 'as an expression of . . . loyalty and affection'.

The diamond – found in January 1905 when a mine manager's walking stick accidentally knocked it out of a tunnel wall – was named after Sir Thomas Culli-

nan, who had discovered the mine, near Pretoria, in 1902. It was later cut into nine large stones and 96 smaller ones, all flawless. The largest, the 530-carat Star of Africa, was set in the royal sceptre. Another, the 317-carat Cullinan II, is now the most valuable stone in the imperial state crown. The two stones, which are kept in the Tower of London, are the world's largest cut diamonds.

## HIGH ACHIEVER

Jan Smuts, South Africa's second Prime Minister, did not go to school until he was 12 years old. But by the time he left five years later he was top of his class. He went on to graduate in 1891 from the University of the Cape of Good Hope (now the University of Cape Town) in science and literature simultaneously, gaining first-class degrees in both.

He then won a third first-class degree in law at Cambridge University, England. He became later a fellow of the Royal Society, Britain's most prestigious scientific association. He wrote a philosophical work, entitled *Holism and Evolution*, and he rose to become a field-marshal in the British army.

Smuts was also the first South African politician to achieve world prominence as a statesman. He was one of Prime Minister David Lloyd George's closest advisers in the First World War and similarly advised Winston Churchill between 1940 and 1945.

representation in Parliament (three elected whites). His uncompromising racial policies – particularly the Pass Laws, which regulate where an African may live or work – provoked demonstrations, and led to protests both locally and abroad. At an anti-Pass Law demonstration at Sharpeville near Johannesburg in 1960, police fired on the protesters, killing about 70 people and wounding hundreds more. In 1961, after a referendum by white voters, South Africa withdrew from the Commonwealth and became a republic. He was assassinated in Parliament in 1966.

### BALTHAZAR JOHANNES (JOHN) VORSTER
**7th Prime Minister/1966–78**
**(National)**
Born 1915; died 1983. Softened some aspects of apartheid – particularly in sport – and tried to improve relations with neighbouring black African states. Abolished in 1968 the last four seats in Parliament which had been reserved for representatives of coloureds. Endorsed the Prohibition of Political Interference Act (1968), which outlawed multiracial political parties, and the Bantu Homelands Citizenship Act (1970), which prepared the way for every African to become nominally a citizen of one of the tribal homelands, rather than a citizen of South Africa. Oversaw the transition to full independence of the first two tribal homelands – Transkei (1976) and Bophuthatswana (1977) – but neither state has won international recognition. Supported tough police action when riots broke out in the black city of Soweto (short for South West Township) near Johannesburg in 1976, over government proposals that education for blacks should be in Afrikaans, not English. But dropped the plans in the wake of the riots. Retired on grounds of ill-health in 1978 but a month later was elected President. He resigned in 1979 after he was implicated in a scandal over the use of government funds to buy sympathetic overseas coverage of South African politics.

### PIETER WILLEM BOTHA
**8th Prime Minister/1978–**
**(National)**
Born 1916. Has softened some of the government's discriminatory policies, notably in sport, and has continued a policy of trade and political links with black African states. But he has remained committed to consolidating and continuing the black homelands policies of previous Nationalist governments. A referendum in 1983 among whites supported his plans for a constitution which would give limited Parliamentary representation to Indians and coloureds, but not to blacks. Under the new constitution, which went into effect in September 1984, his title became State President.

## SECOND TIME UNLUCKY

Dr Hendrik Verwoerd, whose apartheid legislation led to widespread protests by black South Africans – including a demonstration at Sharpeville in 1960, in which about 70 protesters were shot dead by police – was stabbed to death in Parliament in 1966 by a white man. The assassin was a Mozambique-born Portuguese named Dimitri Tsafendas, who was working in the Cape Town Parliament as a messenger.

Six years earlier, Verwoerd had survived another attempt on his life, again by a white man. A wealthy Transvaal farmer named David Pratt shot him twice in the head with a small-calibre revolver just after Verwoerd had opened the Rand Easter Show in Johannesburg. Verwoerd recovered after surgeons removed the bullets.

Both attackers escaped the gallows because they were judged to be insane. Pratt committed suicide in a mental institution in 1961. But in late 1984, Tsafendas was still being held in prison in Pretoria.

## PREMIERS' CAMPUS

Seven of South Africa's eight Prime Ministers have links with what is now the Afrikaans University of Stellenbosch near Cape Town. The university, founded in 1918, had earlier been one of South Africa's most prestigious schools. Six premiers – Smuts, Hertzog, Malan, Strijdom, Verwoerd and Vorster – studied there. And the present Prime Minister, Pieter Botha, is the university's chancellor. The 'missing' premier was South Africa's first, Louis Botha.

## DETAINED WITHOUT TRIAL

John Vorster, who as Prime Minister in the 1960s and 1970s backed the detention without trial of political dissidents, was himself imprisoned without trial for two years. He was arrested in 1942 under wartime regulations because of his activities as a leader of the anti-British, extreme right-wing organisation known as Ossewa-Brandwag (literally 'ox-wagon sentinel'). He was kept in police cells for three months, then sent to an internment camp where he passed his time lecturing in law, and studying German, genetics and sociology. He was released in 1944.

# Men at the top

## HIEDLER, HUTTLER, HITLER

Adolf Hitler, Nazi Führer of Germany from 1933 to 1945, was never known as Adolf Schicklgrüber – despite the popular belief that he was.

Hitler's father, Alois, was the illegitimate son of a servant girl called Maria Schicklgrüber. Five years after the birth of Alois, she married one Johann Georg Hiedler, but he took no steps to legitimise the boy, who used his mother's name until he was nearly 40. Then his step-father's brother, Johann Huttler, persuaded the local priest to amend the parish register to show that Hiedler acknowledged his paternity of Alois, though Huttler himself may well have been his father. From then on, Alois called himself Hitler.

The variations in the spelling of the family name seem to have been due simply to the illiteracy that was then common in rural communities. The amendment took place 12 years before Adolf's birth. The name Schicklgrüber had long been forgotten until his political opponents tried to discredit him by revealing his father's illegitimacy.

## THE RED PRIEST

The mother of Joseph Stalin (1879–1953), dictator of Soviet Russia from 1927 until his death, intended her son to become a priest, not a revolutionary. In 1894, when the young Stalin was 14, he was awarded a scholarship to study at the theological academy in Tiflis, the capital city of his native province of Georgia. In 1899, however, he left the academy.

According to his own account he was expelled for preaching Marxism, but, according to his mother, he left for reasons of health. At the time, Stalin was known by his original name of Joseph Vissarionovich Dzhugashvili. It was only later, after he became a revolutionary leader, that he adopted as an image-building alias the name by which he is known to history: Stalin, or 'man of steel'.

## PICKLED HERO

The British admiral Horatio Lord Nelson (1758–1805), who joined the navy at the age of 12 and was made a captain at 20, made his last sea voyage in a barrel. Mortally wounded in his hour of triumph at the Battle of Trafalgar in 1805, he died aboard his flagship *Victory*. His body was brought back to England for burial pickled in brandy to stop it decomposing on the long journey home.

## SERGEANT-MAJOR GANDHI

Mohandas Gandhi (1869–1948), advocate of non-violence and leader of India's struggle for independence from Britain, served twice with British forces and was awarded a British decoration.

On the outbreak of the Anglo-Boer War in South Africa in 1899, Gandhi was living in Natal. For a mixture of motives, but primarily because of his belief that winning civil rights could come about only by taking on responsibilities, he raised an Indian Ambulance Corps of more than 1000 men. At the end of the war, he and 37 others were awarded the War Medal. In 1906 he tried to persuade the British authorities to accept Indian recruits to help put down a Zulu uprising. The government, however, would accept them only as stretcher-bearers, commanded by Gandhi as sergeant-major. Gandhi's pro-British stance contin-

ued after he left South Africa. On the outbreak of the First World War in 1914, while based in England, he again helped to raise a Field Ambulance Corps from among Indians studying in the country. Ill-health forced his return to India and there, in 1917, he took part in a recruiting drive for the Indian Army at the request of the British administration.

## TURNING POINT

The Austrian archduke Franz Ferdinand might well have escaped assassination in Sarajevo in 1914, and the First World War might not have broken out then – if his chauffeur had been told of a change of plan. At the beginning of the archduke's visit to the capital of Bosnia, then under Austrian rule, a bomb was thrown at his car. But it fell into the road and injured the occupants of the car behind. Panicked by the failure, six other would-be assassins – all members of the bomb-thrower's group – left their posts along the route.

Later, after an official reception in the city hall, the archduke announced that he wanted to go to the hospital to see the injured men. Nobody passed on the message to the chauffeurs, though, so the leading car turned to follow the route originally planned to a museum – and Franz Ferdinand's driver followed suit.

Realising the mistake, the governor of Bosnia, who was riding with the archduke, told the chauffeur to turn the car round. The driver stopped and began to reverse – precisely opposite the spot where one of the remaining conspirators, Gavrilo Princip, was standing on the pavement. With his target only a few metres away in an almost motionless open car, Princip could hardly miss. He shot both the archduke and his wife, and was about to shoot himself when he was seized by bystanders. Because Princip was only 19 he escaped the death penalty, but he survived only four years before dying in 1918 of tuberculosis in an Austrian prison.

## PHONEY HERO

Senator Joseph McCarthy (1908–57), the scourge of alleged Red traitors in the United States in the early 1950s, exaggerated his war record to further his political career. He had been a ground intelligence officer with a Marine dive-bomber squadron in the Pacific during the Second World War, but his campaign literature described him as 'Tail Gunner Joe' and showed him wearing a flying helmet and standing by a bomber's machine guns. McCarthy did fly some operational missions as a gunner and photographer, but the number he claimed to have flown multiplied over the years – from 14 in 1944 to 32 in 1951. His commanding officer put McCarthy's total at only 11.

McCarthy also boasted that he had 'ten pounds of shrapnel' in his leg. Yet the only injury he received during the war was when he was on his way by ship to the Pacific in 1943. During a 'Crossing the Line' ceremony as the ship crossed the Equator, McCarthy broke a bone in his foot – falling off a ladder.

## MAO ON THE MARCH

Mao Zedong (1893–1976), ruler of Communist China from 1949 until his death, rose to power largely through his leadership of the Long March during the 1930s. In this, some 100,000 Chinese communists, with their wives and families, marched and fought the staggering distance of 10,000km (6000 miles) from the southeastern part of China to the northern province of Shaanxi to escape from the Nationalist forces of Jiang Jieshi (Chiang Kai-shek).

The march began in October 1934 and ended in October 1935. Along the way, between 70,000 and 80,000 of the marchers died – including Mao's younger brother and his two small children.

## THE WHITE RAJAHS
For over a century, Sarawak, on the island of Borneo, was ruled as a virtually independent state by a family of English white rajahs. The founder of the dynasty was James Brooke, an ex-employee of the East India Company. While sailing along the Borneo coast, Brooke helped the Sultan of Brunei to suppress a revolt and, as a reward, the grateful sultan made him Rajah of Sarawak in 1841.

The country prospered under Brooke's rule and that of his successor, his nephew, Sir Charles Brooke. Though Sir Charles placed Sarawak under British protection in 1888, the country retained its independence until the Japanese invaded it during the Second World War. After the defeat of Japan, the third and last of the white rajahs, Sir Charles Vyner Brooke, relinquished all his rights to Britain in 1946. In 1963, Sarawak became a part of the newly independent state of Malaysia.

## TAMERLANE THE TERRIBLE
The 14th-century Tartar warlord Tamerlane (1336–1405), who built an empire stretching from China to Turkey, had an insatiable appetite for death. In 1387, after a rebellious mob in Isfahan (in present-day Iran) had massacred 3000 of his occupying troops, Tamerlane ordered his commanders to collect a sickening ransom in human heads. By the time the army moved on, 70,000 heads were heaped in grisly pyramids outside the city walls.

The city of Sivas in Turkey fell victim to a lethal trick. Tamerlane is said to have promised the city elders that not a drop of the defenders' blood would be shed if the city surrendered. He kept his promise to the

letter: 4000 Armenian soldiers who had led the city's resistance were buried alive; Christians were strangled or tied up and tossed in a moat to drown; and children were herded into a field to be trampled to death by Tamerlane's Mongol cavalry.

Despite his love of war, Tamerlane did not die on the battlefield. He died in bed, possibly from the effects of a wild drinking party.

## DEATH BY VIOLENCE
Five of Britain's Archbishops of Canterbury have died violently. They were: the Saxon prelate Aelfheah (killed by Danes in 1012); Thomas Becket (murdered in 1170); Simon of Sudbury (beheaded by a mob in 1381); Thomas Cranmer (burnt at the stake in 1556); and William Laud (beheaded in 1645).

## WHAT KILLED NAPOLEON?
By the time Napoleon died on the island of St Helena in 1821 at the age of 52 he was a very sick man. But the nature of the illness that killed him has never been established for certain. Some doctors have argued that he died of cancer, others that he was poisoned by one of his retainers. Still others have argued that his death was hastened accidentally by toxic vapours from wallpaper dyed with arsenic in his house on St Helena.

In 1982, however, a US specialist, Dr Robert Greenblatt, came up with a new diagnosis: suggesting that, far from being a sick *man*, the former emperor of France was becoming a sick *woman*. Dr Greenblatt, who specialises in the study of hormones, says that Napoleon was suffering from a glandular disease called the Zollinger-Ellison syndrome. The disease, he says, explains why one of the doctors who examined the emperor's body after his death observed: 'His type of plumpness was not masculine; he had beautiful arms, rounded breasts, white soft skin (and) no hair.'

The disease, which was not understood at the time, left another clue, according to Dr Greenblatt. Napoleon was an ardent lover during his marriage to his first wife, Josephine. But he himself admitted that he had little interest in love-making after he married his second wife, Marie Louise, in 1810.

HICCUPS OF FATE *Napoleon (1769–1821) tried to poison himself once, in April 1814 after surrendering to the Allies. But the phial he used was two years old and had lost its potency. It merely gave him a violent attack of hiccups, which made him vomit and saved his life. Without the hiccups, the 1815 Battle of Waterloo would probably never have taken place.*

ARSENIC AND OLD PAPER *Napoleon spent the last six years of his life in exile, at Longwood House (above) on the South Atlantic island of St Helena. The house's drawing room was decorated with wallpaper patterned with green and brown rosettes (detail, left). An English chemist tested a scrap of the paper in 1982 and found that the green shades (the lighter parts of the rosette) had been dyed with a commonly used pigment containing arsenic.*

## DOWN WITH ME

A 19th-century Mexican president led a rebellion against himself. He was Ignacio Comonfort (1812–63), a politically moderate general who came to power after a revolution in 1855. The liberal party he led was committed to putting into effect a radical new constitution which aimed to sweep aside legal restraints on the Press and political activity, demolish the political power of the army and nationalise the vast wealth of the Catholic Church in Mexico. The trouble was that there was by no means universal support for the new constitution: riots by protesters were commonplace, several factions had taken up arms against the government, and even some of Comonfort's own ministers urged that the constitution was unworkable.

Comonfort, who had always been a moderate among the liberals anyway, dithered amid the chaos for two years. Then, when many of the liberals' opponents united in open rebellion under a conservative general named Felix Zuloaga, Comonfort acted. On December 17, 1857, he abandoned his attempts to govern under the constitution he had sworn to uphold, left the presidential palace and joined the rebels to topple his own government.

The rebellion was a disaster. Although the conservatives captured Mexico City, the liberals – under one of Comonfort's ministers, Benito Juarez – simply set up a rival government in Veracruz. And in 1861 Juarez, victorious in the civil war, became Mexico's president.

Comonfort himself rapidly lost the support of the conservatives and fled to the USA in January 1858. He returned to Mexico in the early 1860s to join another unsuccessful fight – against invading French troops – and was killed in battle in 1863.

## FUNERAL FOR A LEG

A Mexican president once held a funeral for his own leg. The president, Antonio de Santa Anna, was the general who in 1836 led Mexican troops to victory over Texan rebels at the siege of the Alamo. American frontiersmen James Bowie – after whom the Bowie knife was named – and Davy Crockett died in the siege. Santa Anna's leg was amputated below the knee after he was wounded during a battle with French troops in December 1838. Santa Anna kept the leg at his hacienda near Veracruz for four years, during which he rose to become effectively dictator of Mexico and the centre of an adoring political cult.

On September 26, 1842, his supporters solemnly paraded the leg through the streets of Mexico City to the accompaniment of bands and orchestras, then laid it to rest in a national shrine known as the Pantheon of Saint Paula. Two years later, however, the leg was stolen during the riots that surrounded Santa Anna's fall from power. Santa Anna died in 1876 at the age of 62 – poor, blind and ignored. The fate of his leg remains unknown.

## WHITE CHIEF OF THE ZULUS

Africa's powerful Zulu tribe once had an Englishman for a chief. His name was John Dunn and he grew up as an orphan in the 19th-century British colony of Natal, South Africa. Dunn was making a living as a big game hunter when, in the 1850s, he met the Zulu king, Cetewayo. Cetewayo was so impressed by Dunn that he appointed him a royal adviser. By the end of the Anglo-Zulu War in 1872, Dunn had become a power behind the Zulu throne, and after the Zulus' defeat, he was made ruler of the largest of the states into which the British partitioned Zululand.

By the time Dunn died in 1895 he had 50 wives and 117 children, and had accumulated so many dependants that the colonial government set aside a special 4000 hectare (10,000 acre) reserve for them near the Tugela River in Natal.

## IF AT FIRST . . .

The band of aristocrats who plotted the murder of Grigori Rasputin (about 1871–1916) in St Petersburg (now Leningrad) took on more than they bargained for when it came to carrying out their scheme.

According to Prince Yussopov, the leader of the conspirators, the dissolute Siberian mystic, who virtually ruled Russia through his dominance of Tsar Nicholas II and his wife, was lured to a cellar in the prince's house late in the winter of 1916 by the promise of an evening of debauchery. There, he was first offered cakes and wine containing potassium cyanide. Rasputin may not have eaten a cake – he is reported to have disliked sweet things – but, to Yussopov's dismay, even the wine Rasputin drank had no apparent ill-effects. Drawing a revolver, the prince then shot Rasputin near the heart. Rasputin fell, but when Yussopov approached the apparently lifeless corpse, the monk attacked him and then crawled up the stairs of the cellar on his hands and knees in an attempt to reach the safety of the street. Another of the conspirators shot him in the shoulders and head, while Yussopov set about his body with a rubber club. Convinced that, this time, they must have succeeded, the conspirators bound and weighted Rasputin's body and threw it in the River Neva.

Despite all this, Rasputin appears not to have died instantly. After the recovery of his corpse from the river, a post-mortem examination revealed water in his lungs, indicating that he was still breathing at the time he was thrown in. In addition, there were deep marks on his wrists, showing that, having regained consciousness through the shock of the freezing water, he had struggled to break his bonds.

Alexei Kosygin of Russia

Charles de Gaulle of France

Hayato Ikeda of Japan

Adolf Hitler of Germany

Francesco Nitti of Italy

Niceto Alcala Zamora of Spain

# HEADS OF GOVERNMENT

## PRESIDENTS OF FRANCE

1906 Clement Armand Fallieres
1913 Raymond Poincaré
1920 Paul Deschanel
1920 Alexandre Millerand
1924 Gaston Doumergue
1931 Paul Doumer
1932 Albert Lebrun
1940–4 France occupied
1944–7 Provisional government
1947 Vincent Auriol
1954 René Coty
1959 General Charles de Gaulle
1969 Alain Poher (interim)
1969 Georges Pompidou
1974 Alain Poher (interim)
1974 Valéry Giscard d'Estaing
1981 François Mitterand

## CHANCELLORS OF GERMANY

### Empire
1900 Bernhardt, Prince von Bülow
1909 Theobald von
    Bethmann-Hollweg
1917 Dr Georg Michaelis
1917 Count Georg von Herling
1918 Prince Maximilian of Baden
1918 Friedrich Ebert

### Republic
1919 Philipp Scheidemann
1919 Gustav Adolf Bauer
1920 Hermann Müller
1920 Konstantin Fehrenbach
1921 Karl Joseph Wirth
1922 Wilhelm Carl Josef Cuno
1923 Dr Gustav Stresemann
1923 Wilhelm Marx
1925 Dr Hans Luther
1926 Wilhelm Marx
1928 Hermann Müller
1930 Dr Heinrich Brüning
1932 Franz von Papen
1932 General Kurt von Schleicher
1933 Adolf Hitler
1945 Admiral Karl Dönitz

### Federal Republic (West Germany)
1949 Konrad Adenauer
1963 Professor Ludwig Erhard
1966 Dr Kurt Georg Kiesinger
1969 Dr Willy Brandt
1974 Walter Scheel
1974 Helmut Schmidt
1982 Helmut Kohl

## RUSSIA

### Provisional government
1917 Prince Georgy
    Yevgenyevich Lvov
1917 Aleksandr Fyodorovich
    Kerensky

### Soviet Socialist Republic
1917 Yakov Sverdlov
1919 Mikhail Kalinin

### Union of Soviet Socialist Republics
1922 Vladimir Ilyich Lenin
1924 Grigori Zinoviev,
    Lev Kamenev and
    Joseph Stalin
1927 Joseph Stalin
1953 Georgy Malenkov

1955 Marshal Nikolai Bulganin
1958 Nikita Khrushchev
1964 Alexei Kosygin and
    Leonid Brezhnev
1982 Yuri Andropov
1984 Konstantin Chernenko

## CHINA

### Republic
1912 Sun Zhongshan (Sun Yat-
    sen)
1912 Yüan Shikai (General Yüan
    Shih-k'ai)
1916 Li Yüanhong (Li Yüan-hung)
1917–28 China divided into
    Northern and
    Southern regimes
1928 Jiang Jieshi (Chiang Kai-
    shek)

### Communist
1949 Mao Zedong (Mao Tse-t'ung)
1976 Hua Guofeng (Hua Kuo-feng)
1978 Ye Jianying (Ye Chien-ying)

## PRIME MINISTERS OF IRELAND

1922 Arthur Griffith
1922 Michael Collins
1922 William Thomas Cosgrave
1932 Eamon de Valera
1948 John Costello
1951 Eamon de Valera
1954 John Costello
1957 Eamon de Valera
1959 Sean Lemass
1966 Jack Lynch
1973 Liam Cosgrave
1977 Jack Lynch
1979 Charles Haughey
1981 Dr Garret Fitzgerald
1982 Charles Haughey
1982 Dr Garret Fitzgerald

## SPAIN

### Prime Ministers
1923 General Miguel Primo de Rivera
1930 General Damaso Berenguer
1931 Admiral Juan Batista Aznar
1931 Niceto Alcala Zamora
1931 Manuel Azaña
1933 Alejandro Lerroux
1933 Diego Martinez Barrio
1933 Alejandro Lerroux
1934 Ricardo Samper

1934 Alejandro Lerroux
1935 Joaquin Chapaprieta
1935 Manuel Portela Valladares
1936 Manuel Azaña
1936 Augusto Barcia
1936 Santiago Casares Quiroga
1936 Diego Martinez Barrio
1936 José Giral

**1936–9 Spanish Civil War**
1939–73 Generalissimo Francisco
    Franco
1973 Admiral Luis Carrero Blanco
1973 Carlos Arias Novarro
1976 Adolfo Suarez Gonzalez
1981 Leopoldo Calva-Sotelo

## JAPAN

### Prime Ministers
1945 Prince Naruhiko Higashikuni
1945 Baron Kijuro Shidehara
1946 Tetsu Katayama
1946 Shigeru Yoshida
1947 Tetsu Katayama
1947 Hitoshi Ashida
1948 Shigeru Yoshida
1955 Ichiro Hatoyama
1956 Tanzan Ishibashi
1957 Nobusuke Kishi
1960 Hayato Ikeda
1964 Eisaku Sato
1972 Kakeui Tanaka
1974 Takeo Miki
1976 Takeo Fukuda
1980 Zenko Susuki
1982 Yashuhiro Nakasone

## PRIME MINISTERS OF ITALY

### Kingdom
1919 Francesco Nitti
1920 Giovanni Giolitti
1921 Ivanoe Bonomi
1922 Luigi Facta
1922 Benito Mussolini
1943 Marshal Pietro Badoglio
1944 Ivanoe Bonomi
1945 Ferruccio Parri
1945 Alcide de Gasperi

### Republic
1946 Alcide de Gasperi
1953 Giuseppe Pella
1954 Amintore Fanfani
1954 Mario Scelba
1955 Antonio Segni
1957 Adone Zoli
1958 Amintore Fanfani
1959 Antonio Segni
1960 Fernando Tambroni
1963 Amintore Fanfani
1963 Giovanni Leone
1963 Aldo Moro
1968 Giovanni Leone
1970 Mariano Rumor
1970 Emilio Colombo
1972 Giulio Andreotti
1973 Mariano Rumor
1974 Aldo Moro
1976 Giulio Andreotti
1979 Francesco Cossiga
1980 Arnaldo Forlani
1981 Giovanni Spadolini
1982 Amintore Fanfani
1982 Giovanni Spadolini
1982 Amintore Fanfani
1983 Bettino Craxi

Michael Collins
of Ireland

Mao Zedong
of China

# Laws and lawyers

## THE FIRST LAWS
Rules and laws – and the conventions or customs from which they are descended – have been a part of human life ever since man first began to live in large and settled groups. But little is known of them in detail until well after the invention of writing in about 3500 BC. The earliest known legal text was written by Ur-Nammu, a king of the Mesopotamian city of Ur, in about 2100 BC. It dealt largely with compensation for bodily injuries, and with the penalties for witchcraft and runaway slaves.

## LAW OF BABYLON
One of the most detailed ancient legal codes was drawn up in about 1758 BC by Hammurabi, a king of Babylon. The entire code, consisting of 282 paragraphs, was carved into a great stone pillar, which was set up in a temple to the Babylonian god Marduk, so that it could be read by every citizen.

The pillar, lost for centuries after the fall of Babylon in the 16th century BC, was rediscovered by a French archaeologist in 1901 amid the ruins of the Persian city of Susa – with Hammurabi's words still legible on its surface. It is now in the Louvre Museum in Paris.

The laws laid down by Hammurabi were more extensive than any that had gone before. They covered crime, divorce and marriage, the rights of slave-owners and slaves, the settlement of debts, inheritance and property contracts, and even set out regulations about taxes and the prices of goods.

Punishments under the code were often harsh. Not only murderers but also thieves and false accusers faced the death penalty. And a child who hit his father could expect to lose the hand that struck the blow. The eye-for-an-eye principle was sometimes carried to extremes. If a house-owner's son was killed as the result of negligence in construction, for example, the life of the builder's son – not of the guilty builder himself – could be forfeit.

Nevertheless the code represented an advance on earlier tribal customs because it meant that the penalty should not be worse than the crime: that no more than an eye could be forfeit for an eye.

It outlawed private blood feuds and banned the tradition by which a man could kidnap and keep the woman he wanted for his bride. In addition, the new laws took account of the circumstances of the offender as well as of the offence. So a lower-ranking citizen who lost a civil case would be fined less than an aristocrat in the same position – though he would also be awarded less if he won.

## NAPOLEON'S LAW
The laws of much of continental Europe, particularly France, of Quebec in Canada and of much of Latin America – along with the civil laws of Louisiana in the United States – owe their modern shape largely to the work of a man who never even studied the law. Napoleon Bonaparte, the Corsican soldier who became emperor of France after the French Revolution, established in 1800 five commissions to refine and organise the disparate legal systems of France. The result, enacted in 1804, was the *Code Napoléon*.

Some of its original 2281 articles were drafted by Napoleon himself – and all were affected by his thinking, even though he was completely self-taught in

legal matters. The code was a triumphant attempt to create a legal system which treated all citizens as equal, without regard to their rank or previous privileges. It was also so clearly written that it could be read and understood by ordinary people at a time when only Latin scholars could make sense of the earlier laws handed down since Roman times.

The code was adopted intact in most of the areas of Europe that Napoleon dominated and spread from there across the Atlantic. Many of its principles are still in force today.

## BIRTH OF THE JURY
Juries first came into being in Norman Britain because of the Church. In early medieval Europe, trials were usually decided by ordeals, in which it was believed that God intervened, revealing the wrongdoer and upholding the righteous. In the ordeal by water, for instance, a priest admonished the water not to accept a liar. The person whose oath was being tested was then thrown in. If he floated, his oath was deemed to have been perjured. If he was telling the truth he might drown, but his innocence was clear.

In 1215, however, the Catholic Church decided that trial by ordeal was superstition and priests were forbidden to take part. As a result, a new method of trial was needed and the jury system emerged.

At first, the jury was made up of local people who could be expected to know the defendant. The jury was convened only to 'say the truth' on the basis of its knowledge of local affairs. The word verdict reflects this early function: the Latin word from which it is derived, *veredictum*, means 'truly said'. It was not until centuries later that the jury assumed its modern role of deciding facts on the sole basis of what it heard in court. Today the jury system has spread to numerous other countries, particularly the USA. Every year more than 100,000 jury trials are held in US courts – 90 per cent of the world total.

## GOOD MEN AND TRUE
G. K. Chesterton (1874 – 1936), the English author who created the detective stories featuring a Roman Catholic priest named Father Brown, was also a powerful champion of the virtues of traditional common sense. After serving as a juror himself, he wrote an essay in which he summed up the value of the jury system in this way.

'Our civilisation has decided, and very justly decided, that determining the guilt or innocence of men is a thing too important to be trusted to trained men. It wishes for light upon that awful matter, it asks men who know no more law than I know, but who can feel the things that I felt in the jurybox.

'When it wants a library catalogued, or the solar system discovered, or any trifle of that kind, it uses up its specialists. But when it wishes anything done which is really serious, it collects 12 of the ordinary men standing round. The same thing was done, if I remember right, by the Founder of Christianity.'

## A CRY FOR JUSTICE
Residents of the Channel Islands still have a legal right to call for help on a nobleman who died more than 1000 years ago. The nobleman was Rollo, the first Duke of Normandy, who died in 932. Householders can invoke the right by falling on their knees in the

presence of witnesses, shouting 'Haro, haro, haro, à l'aide mon prince; on me fait tort' (Haro, haro, haro, help, my lord; I am being wronged), and then reciting the Lord's Prayer in French. The Clameur de Haro, as the law is known, was used as recently as April 1950 to stop the local water board from digging up the road outside the home of a Guernsey resident. Once the cry has been made, the work in dispute must be stopped for 12 months so that the issue can be settled in court. If work is not stopped, the offender can be imprisoned for 24 hours in a castle dungeon – as can a citizen who raises the cry wrongfully.

## CALLING IT QUITS

Every year the solicitor to the City of London attempts to cut a bundle of faggots with a blunt billhook, then does cut it with a sharp axe. The reason for this solemn ceremony, which is called 'Quit Rent', dates back to 1211 when the City Corporation rented from the Crown a farm near Bridgnorth in Shropshire. The rent, which has remained unchanged for more than 700 years, is the blunt billhook and the sharp axe. Having tested the two implements, the solicitor hands them over to a Crown official called the Queen's Remembrancer – and the City is 'quitted of' (regarded as having paid) its rent for another year.

## 'LET THE BODY BE BROUGHT . . .'

Habeas Corpus, the law which in Britain, the USA and many other English-speaking countries guarantees that nobody can be held in prison without trial, was passed because of a wild party. The party was held in 1621 at the London home of a notoriously rowdy lady called Alice Robinson. When a constable called to complain about the noise, Alice allegedly swore at him so violently that he arrested her, and a local Justice of the Peace committed her to the Clerkenwell House of Correction.

When Alice was finally brought to trial at the Old Bailey, her story of her treatment in prison caused an outcry. She had been put on a punishment diet of black bread and water, forced to sleep on the bare earth, stripped and given 50 lashes: treatment that was barbaric even by the harsh standards of the time. What made it worse was that she was pregnant.

Public anger was so great that she was acquitted, the constable who had arrested her without a warrant was sent to Newgate Prison, and the JP was severely reprimanded. In addition, her case, along with other similar cases, led directly to the passing of the Habeas Corpus Act in 1679. The Act is still on the statute books today and a version of it is still used in the USA. Indeed, the founders of the USA regarded the law as such an important guarantee of liberty that Article 1 of the US constitution declares that it shall not be suspended except in cases of 'rebellion or invasion'.

Habeas Corpus is part of a Latin phrase – Habeas corpus ad subjiciendum – which means 'Let the body be brought before the judge'. In effect, a writ of Habeas Corpus is an order in the name of the Sovereign (or, in the USA, of the People) to produce an imprisoned person in court at once.

WIG AND PEN *A bewigged and pompous judge props up two dozing colleagues in a satirical engraving by the English artist William Hogarth (1697–1764). Judges and lawyers in Britain have been wearing wigs for at least 300 years. Originally, the wigs were made of human hair; today, however, they are made of horsehair. Barristers also wear gowns in court. Junior barristers wear gowns made of alpaca wool; senior barristers, known formally as Queen's Counsel, are more commonly called 'silks' because their gowns are made of silk. The gown of every barrister has a small pouch sewn into the left shoulder – a reminder of the time when barristers were not allowed to solicit fees and instead solicitors would quietly slip golden guineas into the pouch. Another legacy from the past is Britain's Privy Council, which was set up after the Norman Conquest in 1066 to advise the monarch. Today the council's Judicial Committee acts as a final court of appeal for ten independent nations, all former British colonies: Australia; the Bahamas; Fiji; Hong Kong; Jamaica; Kiribati; New Zealand; Singapore; Trinidad and Tobago; and Tuvalu.*

## TRIAL BY COMBAT

The ancient medieval right of a man to challenge his accuser to personal combat remained valid under British law until less than 200 years ago. It had been almost forgotten until, in 1817, a man called Thornton was accused of murdering a woman named Mary Ashford. Thornton claimed the right to decide his guilt or innocence in battle with his accuser, the dead girl's brother – and the law courts were forced to uphold his claim. Because Mary Ashford's brother refused the challenge, Thornton got off scot-free. Parliament changed the law a year later.

MIGHT IS RIGHT *Two axe-swinging men hack at each other in a trial by combat sketched in England in 1249. The right to fight an accuser was abolished only in 1818 as 'a mode of trial unfit to be used'.*

## WAYWARD WILLS

● Charles Vance Millar, a Canadian lawyer and financier who died a bachelor in 1926, bequeathed the bulk of his fortune to whichever Toronto woman gave birth to the largest number of children in the ten years after his death. Four women eventually tied in the 'Stork Derby' that followed the publication of his will. Each had nine children, and they shared between them $750,000. A fifth woman who had ten children was ruled out because five were illegitimate.

● One of the world's shortest wills was left by an Englishman named Mr Dickens. It was contested in 1906, but upheld by the courts, and read simply: 'All for mother.'

● John Nicholson, a London stationer whose will was dated April 28, 1717, was so obsessed by his name that he left most of his money to support poor people who carried it. He left £100 a year to be divided between any poor couple who wanted to marry – providing both their names were Nicholson. He left another £100 to poor boys and girls named Nicholson who wanted to learn a trade. And he chose as his executors and trustees the Lord Bishop of Carlisle, his son, and three other men – all of whom were called Nicholson.

● A long-suffering parson in Ontario, Canada, left $3000 to his daughter – on condition she gave up singing.

● A hen-pecked London publican who died at the end of the 19th century left his property to his wife – on condition that every year, on the anniversary of his death, she walked barefoot to the local market, held up a lighted candle and read out a full confession of her nagging ways. The theme of the confession was that if her tongue had been shorter, her husband's days would probably have been longer. If she failed to keep the appointment, she was to receive no more than £20 a year – just enough to live on.

## THE MAN THEY COULDN'T HANG

The idea that if a condemned man survived three attempts to hang him, his sentence was automatically commuted to life imprisonment is no mere story. John Lee, for instance, a 19-year-old footman who was found guilty of murdering his spinster employer, was condemned to death in 1885 and survived three attempts by the hangman, John Berry, to execute him at Exeter Gaol in Devon.

The wooden gallows had warped in the rain and three times the trapdoor refused to open when Lee was placed on it – although it worked perfectly when he was moved down to the ground. So Lee was sentenced to life imprisonment and spent 22 years in prison. He was released in 1907 and later emigrated to the United States. He married there and died of natural causes in 1933 at the age of 67.

## SILENT WITNESS

A slander case in Thailand was once settled by a witness who said nothing at all. The case, recounted in the memoirs of Justice Gerald Sparrow, a 20th-century British barrister who served as a judge in Bangkok, involved two rival Chinese merchants: Swee Ho and Pu Lin.

Pu Lin had stated sneeringly at a party that Swee Ho's new wife, Li Bua, was merely a decoration to show how rich her husband was. Swee Ho, he said, could no longer 'please the ladies'.

Swee Ho sued Pu Lin for slander in the British consular court, claiming that Li Bua was his wife in every sense – and he won his case, along with substantial damages, without a word of evidence being taken. Swee Ho's lawyer simply put the blushing Li Bua in the witness box. She had long, gold-painted fingernails and she was quite obviously pregnant.

## DEADLINES

One of the most bizarre methods of executing a condemned criminal was inflicted in ancient Rome on people found guilty of murdering their fathers. Their punishment was to be put in a sack with a cock, a viper and a dog, then drowned along with the three animals. In ancient Greece, the custom of allowing a condemned man to end his own life by poison was extended only to full citizens. The philosopher Socrates died in this way. Condemned slaves were beaten to death instead.

In medieval Europe, some methods of execution were deliberately drawn out to inflict the maximum suffering. Some felons were tied to a heavy wheel, then rolled around the streets until they were crushed to death. Others were strangled – slowly. One of the most terrible punishments was hanging, drawing and quartering. The victim was hanged, cut down and disembowelled while still alive, then finally beheaded and his body cut into four quarters. It remained a legal method of execution in Britain until 1814.

The first country to abolish capital punishment was Austria in 1787. Russia abolished it for every crime except treason on the orders of Tsar Nicholas I in 1826, but it was re-introduced after the Communist revolution in 1917. In Britain, the death penalty was abolished for murder in 1965, but it can still be imposed for treason.

## KILLER TORTOISE

In July 1981, a tortoise was sentenced to death for murder. Tribal elders in the eastern Kenyan village of Kyuasini formally condemned the tortoise because they suspected it of causing the deaths of six people, apparently through magic. However, because none of the frightened villagers was prepared to risk the tortoise's wrath by carrying out the execution, it was chained to a tree instead. The tortoise was later freed after the government promised an official inquiry into the deaths.

# INTERNATIONAL COURTS

Since the creation of the United Nations in 1945 and the European Economic Community in 1958, four major international courts have been set up.

## INTERNATIONAL COURT OF JUSTICE

Often known as the World Court; composed of 15 judges, all of different nationalities and all elected by the UN General Assembly and the Security Council; sits in 's-Gravenhage (The Hague) in Holland; deals with cases involving disputes between states and the interpretation of international treaties.

## EUROPEAN COURT OF JUSTICE

Composed of ten judges, all of different nationalities and appointed by the ten member governments of the EEC; sits in Luxembourg; interprets EEC law at the request of national courts and deals with cases brought by states or individuals against EEC institutions, or by EEC institutions against member states, but cannot impose fines or prison sentences to enforce its decisions.

## EUROPEAN COURT OF HUMAN RIGHTS

Composed of 21 judges – one for each of the 21 nations in the Council of Europe – appointed by the council's Parliamentary Assembly; sits in Strasbourg, France; hears cases involving alleged breaches of the 1950 European Convention for the Protection of Human Rights and Fundamental Freedoms.

## INTER-AMERICAN COURT OF HUMAN RIGHTS

Composed of seven judges elected by the General Assembly of the Organisation of American States; sits in San José, Costa Rica; hears cases involving the interpretation of the 1969 American Convention on Human Rights.

# HOW LAWS ARE MADE

## UNITED STATES

The US Congress – the law-making arm of the federal government – consists of two Houses: the House of Representatives and the Senate. Any Congressman in either House, or the President, may initiate new legislation.

The Bill is first introduced in the House of Representatives, then referred to one of the standing committees, which organises hearings on it and may approve, amend or shelve the draft. If the committee passes the Bill, it is considered by the House of Representatives as a whole. If passed again, it goes to the Senate for a similar sequence of committee hearings and general debate.

In cases of disagreement, the House of Representatives and the Senate confer together. Once passed by the Senate as a whole, the Bill has to be examined by two more standing committees – the Committee on House Administration and the Senate Committee on Rules and Administration – and is then signed by the Speaker of the House and by the President of the Senate. Finally it must be signed by the President, who has the right to veto it. If the President does veto the Bill, it can still become law – but only if it is passed by a two-thirds majority in both Houses of Congress.

## BRITAIN

New legislation in Britain usually starts in the House of Commons and then goes on to the House of Lords. In each House the Bill is considered in three stages, called readings. The first reading is purely formal to introduce the Bill. The second reading is usually the occasion for debate. After the second reading, the Bill is examined in detail by a committee.

The Bill is then brought back to the House for the report stage when it can be amended. Finally, it has its third reading and, if passed, goes to the other House. Amendments made to a Bill by the House of Lords have to be considered by the Commons. If the House of Commons does not agree, the Bill is altered and sent back to the Lords. In the event of persistent disagreement between the two Houses, the will of the Commons prevails.

Finally the Bill goes to the reigning monarch for the Royal Assent. Nowadays the Royal Assent is merely a formality. In theory, the Queen could still refuse her consent. But the last monarch to use this power was Queen Anne, who vetoed the unpopular Scottish Militia Bill in 1707.

## SOVIET UNION

New legislation is initiated by the Presidium of the Communist Party's Central Committee. It is then considered by either the Presidium of the Supreme Soviet or the Presidium of the Council of Ministers. Once approved by either body, the legislation has the force of law, though it may also be formally approved by the Supreme Soviet.

ORDER! ORDER! *The Speaker, or chairman, bangs his gavel while Congressmen chat, shout or read the paper in this mocking, and English, view of the US House of Representatives in 1861.*

# Great explorers

## THE LONG SHORTCUT

To the end of his life the Italian explorer Christopher Columbus clung to his belief that by sailing westwards he had found, not a new continent, but merely a short sea-route to Asia. Like other geographers, he underestimated the size of the Earth and overestimated the east-west extent of Asia. A globe made at the time of Columbus's first voyage in 1492 showed the distance from the Azores westwards to Japan as no greater than the length of the Mediterranean. Thus when Columbus reached the Bahamas he thought he had arrived at the Indies (the collective name then used for India, Southeast Asia and Indonesia), which is why the Caribbean islands are called the West Indies. During his second voyage, in 1494, all the members of his crews had to swear that the coast of Cuba, along which they were voyaging, was 'the mainland at the beginning of the Indies'. The penalties for breaking the oath later depended on rank: offenders paid a fine, had their tongue cut out, or received 100 lashes.

## QUARREL THAT ENDED IN TRAGEDY

A row about the source of the Nile may have cost the life of the Victorian explorer John Hanning Speke. He died on the morning of the day when he was to debate the question with his fellow-explorer and, latterly, arch-rival, Sir Richard Burton. Burton and Speke had twice gone to East Africa together. On the second expedition, when Burton became too ill to travel,

Speke went off on his own in July 1858 and found the lake he named Victoria. This he believed, correctly, to be a main source of the Nile, but Burton disagreed. The controversy rumbled on until 1864 when Speke agreed to the public debate. He is known not to have been looking forward to it, because he was less articulate than Burton. On the morning of the confrontation, Speke went out partridge-shooting – and was later found dead from shotgun wounds. Whether it was an accident or suicide is uncertain.

## THE FAITHFUL FOLLOWERS

Ten Africans gave their lives to get the body of the Scottish missionary and explorer David Livingstone back to Britain after his death in 1873. When he died at the village of Chitambo in what is now Zambia, the 60 Africans of his party determined to take the body to the coast near Zanzibar so that it could be returned home for burial. They removed and buried the heart and other internal organs, embalmed the body with raw salt, and dried it in the sun. The gruelling journey, which covered 1600km (1000 miles), took from May 1873 to February 1874 and ten men died during it. But the survivors' only reward was their normal wages, paid by the British consul in Zanzibar, and a

DR LIVINGSTONE, I PRESUME *The Anglo-American journalist Henry Stanley (left) steps forward to utter his famous greeting to the Scottish missionary David Livingstone after finding him at a village beside Lake Tanganyika on November 10, 1871. This engraving of the encounter, drawn with Stanley's guidance, was published in 1872.*

commemorative medal struck by the Royal Geographical Society which probably very few of them received. Only the two Africans – Chuma and Susi – who led the journey gained real benefit, because they were brought to Britain to help fill gaps in Livingstone's journals. The fame they gained in Europe made them sought-after guides when they returned to Africa.

### THE SHIP THAT CHANGED ITS NAME
The *Golden Hind*, the flagship in which the English explorer Sir Francis Drake sailed round the world in 1577–80, started the voyage with a different name. It was originally named the *Pelican*. The renaming happened after Drake suppressed a threatened mutiny and had the ringleader, Thomas Doughty, beheaded. The execution created a political problem for Drake because Doughty had been secretary to Sir Christopher Hatton, a major shareholder in the expedition and a man who was high in Queen Elizabeth's favour. Drake solved the problem by an astute gesture of flattery. The crest on Hatton's coat of arms was 'a hind statant or', which means a standing golden female deer without antlers. And by the time Drake's ships entered the Strait of Magellan a few days after Doughty's execution, the *Pelican* had become the *Golden Hind* in Hatton's honour.

### SURVIVOR WHO WENT NATIVE
John King, the first white man to cross the Australian continent and survive, did so only because of the generosity of Aborigines. King was a member of the Burke and Wills expedition which set out from Melbourne in 1860. After the expedition established a supply camp at Cooper's Creek in South Australia, four men went on northwards and reached the tidal marshes at the edge of the Gulf of Carpentaria. They were Robert Burke, William Wills, King and a man named Charles Gray. But the party ran out of supplies on their return journey and Gray died of starvation before they reached Cooper's Creek.

The three exhausted survivors were horrified to discover at the camp a message saying that the support party had given up waiting and gone back south that same morning. Even though the support party had left a cache of supplies, the three men were so weak and ill that they could not get far without help. Aborigines had helped the explorers on their outward trip by giving them fish. However, Burke, crazed by hunger, lost his head when they approached

again and ordered King to fire over their heads to drive them away. Burke and Wills later died of starvation. But King used his rifle to shoot birds for Aborigines and so win their help. A relief party found him, emaciated but alive, six months later.

### DOGS VERSUS PONIES
The British explorer Captain Robert Scott made a fatal decision during the preparations for his journey to the South Pole. He chose the pony as the principal means of haulage, although he had a few dogs as well. The Manchurian ponies were specially purchased in Siberia by one of the team members. Scott insisted on the ponies being white, because he believed they were more hardy than brown ponies. But since few Manchurian ponies are white, the dealers were able to demand and get inflated prices for them.

Preliminary trips across the Antarctic ice painfully exposed the vulnerability of the ponies. Scott, however, refused to alter his plans. As a dog-lover, he also refused to kill and eat dogs. On the drive to the Pole, the ponies were killed one by one to provide meat for both men and dogs. And after the dogs were taken back to the base camp, sledges pulled by men in harness became the only way of shifting equipment and stores. The Norwegian explorer Roald Amundsen, meanwhile, relying on his experienced dog teams, reached the Pole in December 1911, 34 days ahead of the British expedition. Scott and his three companions all died on the return journey.

LAST WORDS *Captain Scott and the last of his companions died of cold and hunger in Antarctica just 18km (11 miles) from a supply base and safety. This is the last page of his diary, discovered later beside his frozen body.*

### PRISON DIARY
Marco Polo's account of his years of travel in Asia, *The Description of the World*, was written when he was a prisoner of war. After his return from the East he served in the Venetian forces fighting Genoa. He was captured in 1298 and imprisoned in a Genoese jail. There he and another prisoner, Rusticiano of Pisa, an experienced writer, collaborated on the book. It was widely read, and was given the nickname *Il Milione*, meaning 'The Million', probably because of the innumerable tall stories it was thought to contain.

### DOUBLE FIRST
A few days before Robert Peary announced he had reached the North Pole in 1909, another American, Dr Frederick Cook, claimed he had done so a year earlier, and many believed Cook and doubted Peary. Peary's critics doubted that Peary could have made the journey as quickly as he claimed. Peary insisted that he had covered 1300km (800 miles) at an average speed of 54km (34 miles) a day, and that at times he had travelled at least 74km (46 miles) in a day – figures which British explorer Wally Herbert, who led the first crossing of the Arctic ice cap in 1968–9, has described as incredible. Some critics also pointed out that the only non-Eskimo witness of his

dash to the Pole was his Negro servant. In addition, Peary's book on the expedition contained many discrepancies because it was ghost-written, and Peary undermined his own credibility by refusing to admit that he had been helped with the writing.

Later, however, Cook's own account was questioned. His claim to have climbed Mount McKinley was shown to be false, and later imprisonment for a financial fraud did nothing to improve his reputation.

Nevertheless, the case for or against Peary or Cook is not proven, and almost certainly never will be. The reason: the North Pole is merely a point on a constantly shifting ice pack. So nothing is left there to substantiate either man's claim.

## WESTWARD HO

Huge Chinese fleets were travelling westward into the Indian Ocean on diplomatic and trading missions more than 60 years before the Portuguese explorer Vasco da Gama became the first European sailor to round Africa in 1498. Chinese records show that between 1405 and 1433 a navigator called Zheng He (Cheng Ho) made seven voyages into the South China Sea and on to the coasts of India and East Africa. On his fourth expedition Zheng took a fleet of 63 ships and 27,000 men, including 180 doctors, as far as the Persian Gulf. His largest vessels, well over 1500 tonnes, were more than 180m (600ft) long.

## EXPLORER WHO BOUGHT A WIFE

Samuel Baker, the Victorian explorer who discovered Lake Albert and the Murchison Falls on the Nile, made a most unusual purchase: he bought himself a wife. She was a Hungarian girl whom Baker, a widower, rescued from Turkish slavery at a slave auction. They spent six years in Africa together, and married on their return to England. Baker's tales of his wife's courage made her a popular heroine at home, but although Baker was knighted, Queen Victoria refused to receive his wife because of their earlier liaison.

## VOYAGE OF DISASTERS

The Portuguese explorer Ferdinand Magellan's expedition, the first to go round the globe, was a disaster as well as a triumph. Of the five Spanish ships and about 270 men who sailed in 1519, only one ship and fewer than 20 men completed the voyage three years later. One ship had been wrecked and one turned back before they even rounded Cape Horn and entered the Pacific Ocean.

Another was burnt and scuttled in the Pacific because so many men had died on the voyage that only two ships could be manned. These two ships separated, and one was captured by the Portuguese. Even Magellan himself did not survive the voyage. He was killed by natives in the Philippines and it was the last surviving Spanish captain, Sebastian del Cano, who brought the last ship, the *Victoria*, home to Spain.

## FIRST EXPLORERS BY AIR

In 1897, three Swedes set off from Spitsbergen, an island in the Arctic Ocean, to fly a balloon to the North Pole. They were never seen again. The explorers had hoped to control the balloon's course by keeping low and dragging trail ropes along the ground, which would reduce their speed to less than that of the wind. Sails could then be used to steer. But soon after the balloon was launched it almost came down in the sea, and part of the trail ropes and a quantity of sand ballast were lost. Relieved of the weight the balloon disappeared into the clouds. The full story emerged only in 1930 when some of the expedition's remains were found by sealers. What seems to have happened

is that the balloon became so coated with ice that it was forced down well short of the Pole. The marooned explorers spent nearly two months struggling to get back over the moving ice, but finally died on White Island – only a few kilometres from the spot where they had taken off.

## GREEN AND CHILLY LAND

The frigid island of Greenland was given its name as a sales ploy. The island, most of which lies under a permanent ice cap, was discovered by the Norseman Eirik (Eric) the Red who sailed from Iceland in AD 982. He said that he chose the name to make it sound more attractive to potential settlers. The strategy

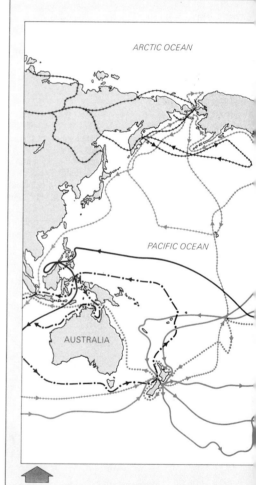

# GOLDEN AGE OF DISCOVERY

*ARCTIC OCEAN*

*PACIFIC OCEAN*

*AUSTRALIA*

**World Exploration 1492–1780**
Europeans were not the first to explore unfamiliar parts of the world – Polynesians spread across the Pacific and Aborigines colonised Australia centuries earlier. But they were the first to draw together knowledge of the globe as a whole. The map shows the routes of the major explorers. The dates of their voyages are shown in the key below.

| | |
|---|---|
| ·········· | *Christopher Columbus 1492–3* |
| – – – – | *Vasco da Gama 1497–9* |
| ——— | *Ferdinand Magellan 1519–22* |
| –––––– | *William Barentz 1594–7* |
| ·········· | *Jacques Cartier 1534–6* |
| –·–·–· | *Abel Tasman 1642–4* |
| ·········· | *Robert La Salle 1679–82* |
| +++++++ | *Vitus Bering 1728–9, 1741* |
| ·········· | *James Cook 1st journey 1768–71* |
| ——— | *James Cook 2nd journey 1772–5* |
| +++++++ | *James Cook 3rd journey 1776–80* |

worked, too. In 986 about 25 small ship-loads of emigrants followed him from Iceland to Greenland, founding a Norse colony that lasted for 500 years.

## MUTINY ON THE *DISCOVERY*

Mutiny cost the British explorer Henry Hudson his life. He and his young son (thought to have been about 12 years old), along with seven other men, died after they were set adrift in an open boat in the Canadian bay which now bears his name. In November 1610 while seeking a North-West Passage to the Orient, his ship *Discovery* became trapped in the ice in James Bay, on the south of Hudson Bay. Food became short, and Hudson was accused of distributing it unfairly. When the ice began to break up, the crew mutinied and Hudson and the others were put over the side in June 1611.

None of the occupants of the boat was ever seen again. Of the 13 mutineers, four were killed in a fight with Eskimos, one died of scurvy, and eight managed to get back to England. Despite the mutiny, the sailors appear to have escaped punishment, probably because their experience made them too valuable to future exploration. Only four of the mutineers were finally brought to trial – five years later – and, though most of the trial records have been lost, it is thought that they were able to save themselves from the gallows by throwing the blame on to the five dead men.

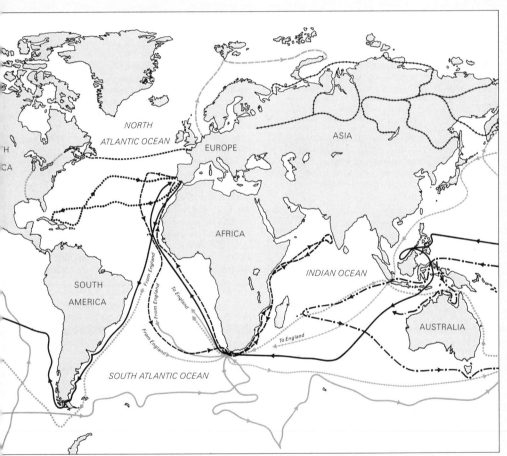

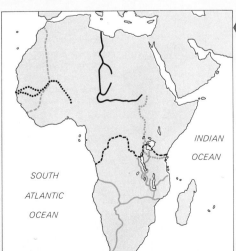

### Opening up Africa

Africa was the last but one continent to be crossed; Antarctica remained largely unexplored until the 20th century. The dark continent's interior began to be opened up by the travels of Mungo Park. In his wake came others, triggering a scramble for colonies by European powers in the 19th century. The routes of the pioneers are shown on the map; the dates appear below.

| | |
|---|---|
| ············· | *Mungo Park 1795–7, 1805–6* |
| – – – – | *Rene Caillie 1827–8* |
| —————— | *David Livingstone 1849–73* |
| ············ | *John Speke 1857–9* |
| ———— | *Gustav Nachtigal 1869–74* |
| – – – – – | *Henry Stanley 1874–7* |

103

# The world's richest people

## THE HISTORY OF CASH

Without money, people have to give away some goods in exchange for any they receive. This system, known as barter, was the earliest form of trade. It still has its uses today. A certain amount of barter is sometimes written into East-West trade agreements because Soviet bloc countries are often short of the 'hard' currencies which the West recognises as being of value. Nevertheless, barter is extremely limiting. Some goods perish easily and are difficult to transport. And if someone requires, say, eggs, and has only sacks of corn, then he has to find a person with eggs who wants corn. In addition, large objects are often not divisible. A cart seller, faced with a buyer's offer of 12 sacks of corn, may not need so much grain. But he has nothing to give but a whole cart.

Because of these difficulties, general items such as beads, salt or cattle have often become convenient means of exchange – in other words, money.

By around 2000 BC metal, which was attractive and durable, had become a means of exchange in the Middle East. By the 7th century BC bronze was being cast in China into miniature knives or spades, each assigned the value of the real equivalent.

The forerunners of modern coins first appeared in Lydia, in what is now eastern Turkey, between 690 and 650 BC. They were crudely cast slugs of electrum, a natural alloy of gold and silver found locally. Their value depended on their weight.

### Paper money

The use of paper money is believed to have started in China between the 7th and 9th centuries AD, to overcome shortages of coins. In Europe in medieval times, letters of credit – effectively personal banknotes – were exchanged between businessmen who knew and trusted each other. Later, a practice grew in which goldsmiths gave receipts for gold left in their charge, and these receipts were exchanged as money. During the 18th and 19th centuries, first private bankers, then central banks, took over this role. They issued notes, each of which was a 'promise to pay': words that still appear on many banknotes. Until 1931 – when many countries, including Britain, went off the Gold Standard – the holders of banknotes were usually entitled, in theory, to demand from the issuing bank that the notes should be redeemed in gold. Since then, however, notes have resumed the status of primitive beads – a means of exchange which has value only because the paper is trusted.

This process has been taken a step further by the use of cheques and credit cards. Both are essentially 'promises to pay', backed by the person signing the cheque or guaranteed, within limits, by a bank or credit-card company. More recently still, in much of the developed world, electronic accounting has begun to replace notes and coins altogether. Instead, the transaction takes place only on a computer screen – with not a trace of metal or paper.

### CASH FLOW

Many of the great personal fortunes of the past 100 years have flowed from holes in the ground: oil wells. Once the steam engine had been adapted to drive a drill and a method of cleaning, or 'refining', oil had been developed in the mid-19th century, the way was open for oil products to become an indispensable fuel for modern industry. For those who foresaw this, and had the chance to invest in the new oil business, there were vast riches to be gained.

It was oil which gave American tycoon John D. Rockefeller the opportunity to acquire probably the biggest personal fortune of modern times. At present-day values, it would be worth around £31,000 million. Rockefeller (1839–1937) began his business life at 16 as a book-keeper. By the age of 19 he had saved enough to help start a small company, and he then entered the oil business, backing Samuel Andrews, the inventor of an oil-refining process. In 1870 Rockefeller helped found Standard Oil, which swallowed smaller firms, and by 1879 controlled 90 per cent of US oil refineries, making Rockefeller master of 75 per cent of the world's oil production. His huge combine survived until 1911 when the US Supreme Court ordered it to be broken up because of its overwhelming commercial power.

Arab oil sheikhs are now often thought to be the wealthiest people in the world, but they are usually rulers of states rather than gatherers of purely personal riches. Sheikh Zayid ibn Sultan an-Nuhayan of the United Arab Emirates is said to be entitled to £6000 million a year – more than £16 million a day – from oil royalties which have not been made over officially to the state. He is not thought, however, to draw anything approaching that amount, and so the remainder of the money is kept by the state.

### HALF A BILLION IN A DAY

The eccentric American recluse Howard Hughes (1905–76) once made half a billion dollars in one day. He received a single banker's draft for $546,549,771 in 1966 in return for his 75 per cent holding in Trans World Airlines.

### WEALTH OF THE STARS

Big fortunes can be made by the stars of pop music, films and sport, and Paul McCartney is said to have earned £25 million in a year in 1979/80, mostly from royalties for songs written and recorded while he was with the Beatles.

US actor Marlon Brando is said to have collected a

CROESUS'S GOLD *The fabulously wealthy King Croesus of Lydia, in present-day Turkey, issued the first coins with fixed values. This 8g (0.3oz) gold coin, bearing the imprint of a lion and a bull, was issued by Croesus in about 550 BC. It was worth ten silver coins.*

PRICE CUTTING *This stylised iron hunting knife, some 720mm (2ft 4in) long and so heavy it was carried by a strap, was used by Zaire's Bakutu tribe.*

DEAR LADIES I central Africa, U-shaped copp kougas could a male slave. A female slave ca three, a wife te

# WHY MONEY IS VALUED

Money by itself is not wealth. It is simply a means by which people can exchange goods that do have value. While a pile of banknotes is being kept in an attic by a miser and never exchanged for anything, it is worth less than a heap of old rags. Money is a promise, a piece of trust which is passed from hand to hand and can be easily stored without perishing. It has value only if the trust lasts.

To be trusted, money, it seems, must be of limited supply. If there is too much, people trust it less. They then want more and more of it in return for goods. It can become practically worthless, as in times of chronic inflation. If there is too little, then people cannot expand their activities because they cannot find the 'credit' in the form of loans to keep themselves going while they develop new ventures. This can lead to economic depression, or recession, which means not enough things going on, not enough money in people's pockets to cause 'demand' for goods, and not enough jobs.

### Queues and quotas
The problem of achieving the delicate balance between too little and too much money has bedevilled 20th-century governments all over the world. Some communist countries have tried to find a way round the problem by fixing prices artificially and planning their economies, allocating quotas of goods to state factories. But shortages and queues, reminiscent of wartime rationing, often result.

fee of $3.7 million, plus $15 million in royalties, for a mere 12 days' work in the 1978 film *Superman* – a rate of more than $1,500,000 a day.

By comparison, sport is not so well paid, although Czech tennis star Ivan Lendl earned $2,028,850 during 1982 to place himself among the highest-earning sports celebrities.

## RICH AND POOR
The Persian Gulf oil states, such as the United Arab Emirates and Kuwait, are the world's richest nations in terms of the average income per person. The richest of all is the United Arab Emirates with an income of £21,000 a year for every man, woman and child in the country. The poorest is Bhutan – a Himalayan nation whose citizens have an average income of little more than £50 a year.

Using a different measure – the average wage paid to those in work – the countries of the industrialised West and Japan emerge as the world's wealthiest. The average wage in the United States in 1981 was £8438 a year, in Norway it was £8317 and in Britain £5782. By comparison, using available statistics, the equivalent in Kenya in 1978 was £79 a year, and in Bangladesh in 1977 it was £88 a year.

## BIG SPENDER
On inheriting more than $1 million in cash and oil wells, one of the fastest fortune-losers in modern times deserted his wife, moved into a smart New York hotel and began offering champagne and oysters to all comers. In one year of riotous living in 1864, John Washington Steel, known as Coal-Oil Johnny, got through his entire inheritance. Then, sober and bankrupt, he went back to his wife, moved west to Nebraska and found a job as a railway goodsyard supervisor. He died – solvent again, but not rich – in 1920.

## NOT WORTH THE PAPER
● In Germany after the First World War the government printed money frantically as the mark's value plunged. Wheelbarrow loads of paper notes were needed to buy bread and common household goods. In 1921, the German rate of exchange was 81 marks to one American dollar. By July 1923, a dollar was worth a million German marks.
● In Indonesia in the 1960s, prices were rising at 1000 per cent a year. But even if inflation stays at only 1 per cent a year, prices will double in about 60 years; at 10 per cent, they double in $7\frac{1}{2}$ years.
● The world's worst inflation happened in Hungary in 1946. Hungary, like many other countries, had gone off the Gold Standard in 1931. By June 1946, one 1931 gold pengö was worth 130 million million million paper pengös, and prices in the Hungarian capital, Budapest, were being raised as often as ten times a day. The pengö was later replaced as a unit of currency by the present forint and, by 1980, inflation was down to a modest 4 per cent a year.

## THE FIRST INCOME TAX
Taxes have been collected since ancient times. The earliest – recorded in Mesopotamia and Egypt – were taxes on imported goods (the equivalent of Customs duties) and on houses and land. Income tax, however, is a relatively recent invention. It was first introduced in Britain in 1799 by Prime Minister William Pitt – with a top rate of just 10 per cent – to help pay for the Napoleonic Wars. Progressive income tax – increasing in proportion as earnings rise – was developed in Prussia in 1853 and has been used in Britain since 1907, in the United States since 1914 and in France since 1917.

## DIAL M FOR MONEY
Guests at the country home of one of the 20th century's richest men, J. Paul Getty, had to pay for any telephone calls they made. Getty (1892–1976) had coin-operated telephones installed in the bedrooms of his 16th-century Tudor mansion, Sutton Place, in Surrey, England. The American financier and art collector was estimated to be worth about $3000 million by the time of his death.

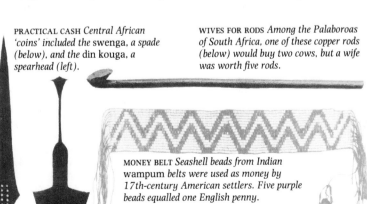

PRACTICAL CASH *Central African 'coins' included the swenga, a spade (below), and the din kouga, a spearhead (left).*

WIVES FOR RODS *Among the Palaboroas of South Africa, one of these copper rods (below) would buy two cows, but a wife was worth five rods.*

SHELLING OUT *Shells have been widely used as currency in the Pacific and Africa. These shell-like seed husks, strung on a cord, were used by the Olemba people of southern Africa.*

MONEY BELT *Seashell beads from Indian* wampum *belts were used as money by 17th-century American settlers. Five purple beads equalled one English penny.*

# Languages 1: the beginnings

## HOW WRITING DEVELOPED

Pictures form the basis of all the earliest known examples of writing. The symbols used are simplified pictures of the objects or people referred to, such as 'sun' or 'king'. But other symbols were also needed to express more abstract ideas such as 'love' or 'happy', and since these could not be drawn directly, early writers borrowed and adapted symbols from those already in use, usually with additional marks to help to distinguish between them. The early deciphered scripts – among them the cuneiform script of Mesopotamia, and early Chinese and Egyptian hieroglyphics – all developed symbols for abstract concepts in this way. The word cuneiform is from the Latin *cuneus*, meaning 'wedge', and cuneiform script is so called because of its wedge-shaped outlines, made by scribing on wet clay with reeds. 'Hieroglyphics' is from Greek words meaning 'sacred writings (or carvings)'.

These pictorial scripts later gave way to writing in which the symbols came to stand for the words themselves, rather than the things the words represented. And the pictorial element disappeared or became marginal. Symbols of this kind are called logograms and include the modern English symbols &, =, + and %, as well as all the numerals.

### Symbols for syllables

Next, symbols were used to stand for the sound of a word or the various syllables in it. Such systems are called syllabaries and came into use alongside or as an alternative to logograms in many cultures. The first syllabaries were developed in the Middle East in about 2000 BC. Chinese characters – descended from a form of picture writing first devised in about 1500 BC – still combine symbols for words and symbols for syllables, and are often called logo-syllabic for this reason. Japanese script, however, which developed from Chinese in about AD 800, is wholly syllabic. The Japanese script, known as *kana*, is still in use.

The last major step in the development of writing was from the syllabary to the alphabet. Syllabaries were an advance over picture writing and logograms in that they broke down a language into simpler units and vastly reduced the number of symbols in use. Alphabets took this process of simplification further – breaking down the language into individual sounds. Alphabets seem to have been invented only in the West, beginning with the early consonantal alphabets of the eastern Mediterranean in about 1700 BC, and followed by Greek – which added separate symbols for vowels as well as consonants.

MESSAGE IN STONE *Primitive languages used pictures – sometimes stylised – to convey ideas. This Central American carving, or 'glyph', is the symbol for grass.*

### THE FIRST SPEAKERS

Using plaster casts of the remains of ancient man, anthropologists have tried to estimate when man's skull and vocal tract became suitable for speech. Even Neanderthal Man, who lived between about 100,000 and 40,000 years ago, may well not have been able to produce the range of sounds found in known languages. Our own species, *Homo sapiens sapiens*, first appeared about 35,000 years ago; and this has led some anthropologists to conclude that speech developed some time between then and about 20,000 years ago. Unfortunately, these conclusions tell us nothing about the origins of language. Between the dawn of modern man and the earliest reconstructed spoken languages is a gap of at least 20,000 years.

Most European languages, as well as many of those of southwest Asia and India, belong to a single linguistic family: Indo-European. Together they form the largest group of spoken languages – more than 80 in all. No written evidence of the parent language has been found, but scholars have reconstructed parts of it by comparing the languages of the group as a whole, and have called the parent tongue Proto-Indo-European. Opinions differ on where Proto-Indo-European was first spoken. Some scholars believe that it was the language of farming peoples in an area of northeastern Europe around 4000 BC. Others assert that it was spoken by nomadic tribes who ranged across southeastern Europe and southern parts of Russia.

### WHERE WRITING BEGAN

The earliest known examples of writing are forms of picture writing, found on clay tablets in parts of the Middle East and southeastern Europe. The pictures – such as a foot, which represented the idea of walking – were drawn on the clay when it was soft. The tablets were then baked in the sun, and many of them have been found in what are now Iraq and Iran. The tablets – the earliest of which date from around 3500 BC – mostly record land sales, business deals and tax accounts. Symbols from this period have also been found on clay tablets in Romania.

In addition, archaeologists have found even more ancient tokens at sites in the Zagros Mountains of Iran. The tokens are marked with symbols which appear to represent numbers and specific objects such as animals and garments. The tokens date from about 8500 BC – some 5000 years before the accepted date for the invention of writing. But scholars are divided on whether the symbols are a form of artistic decoration, or whether they qualify as the beginnings of a written language.

### CHILDREN WHO INVENTED A LANGUAGE

In 1880, thousands of immigrants from Europe and Asia were brought to Hawaii to work in the island's new sugar industry. The result was linguistic chaos, because the immigrants – mostly Chinese, Japanese, Korean, Spanish and Portuguese – could understand neither the largely English-speaking owners of the sugar plantations nor the native Hawaiians.

At first, a crude pidgin English emerged as each group struggled to make sense to the others. But by about 1910 – in other words, within a single generation – a remarkably sophisticated language had developed. Now known as Hawaiian Creole, the language

# NEW LETTERS FOR OLD

All the alphabets in use around the world today can be traced back to a North Semitic alphabet which emerged in about 1700 BC at the eastern end of the Mediterranean. From this alphabet developed Hebrew, Arabic and Phoenician. The Phoenician alphabet was adopted and adapted by the Greeks, who introduced it into Europe in modified form around 1000 BC. The Greeks standardised the direction of the written lines to read from left to right and added some symbols for vowels. The Greek alphabet in turn gave rise to both the Roman alphabet now used for all modern Western European languages (including English) and the Cyrillic alphabet. Cyrillic – devised by two Greek missionaries, St Cyril and St Methodius, in the 9th century AD, and named after St Cyril – is now used in Eastern Europe and the Soviet Union. The North Semitic alphabet also gave rise to the Aramaic alphabet, which spread eastwards to develop into Asian alphabets such as Hindi.

TAKE A LETTER *The same letter can appear very different in different alphabets. Yet all the forms can be traced back to a common ancestor. The word alphabet itself comes from the first two Greek letters: alpha and beta.*

## BABIES THAT SUFFERED FOR SCIENCE

More than 2500 years ago, two babies were kept in isolation for at least two years in a cruel experiment aimed at tracking down the world's first language. The experiment was carried out by an Egyptian pharaoh, Psamtik I, who ruled from about 663 to 609 BC. He believed that, without anyone to copy, children would instinctively talk the world's 'original language'. So he put two newborn babies of poor parents into solitary confinement.

A shepherd was given the job of looking after the babies, but Psamtik insisted that nobody should speak in their presence. When, after two years, the shepherd reported that the children had begun to repeat a sound like *bekos* – the Phrygian word for 'bread' – Psamtik concluded that Phrygian was the oldest language. But he overlooked the fact that *bekos* sounds very much like the bleating of sheep – something the children had often heard. So the experiment proved nothing.

LEFT, RIGHT, RIGHT, LEFT *The first scripts known to have been written in regular lines are two Minoan scripts from Crete dating from about 2000 BC. Known for this reason as Linear A and Linear B, they are thought to have been written in lines arranged like the furrows in a ploughed field, so that the words ran alternately from left to right and right to left. The Western habit of writing consistently from left to right down the page became established only in about 1000 BC. Elsewhere, other patterns dominated. The Mayas of Central America, for example, wrote numbers in columns read from bottom to top; in the detail pictured above from a Mayan manuscript, the numbers appear as groups of dots and dashes between pictorial symbols. In each group, each dot stands for 1, and each dash for 5. Arabs still write from right to left, and Arabic newspapers have their front page where the back page would be in Europe or North America. In traditional Chinese, words are arranged in columns rather than lines. The columns are read from top to bottom and right to left.*

included ready-made words from all the original languages in the islands' mix, but its rules of grammar bore very little resemblance to any of them.

Hawaiian Creole's astonishingly rapid evolution was studied in detail by Derek Bickerton, a professor of linguistics at the University of Hawaii. And he came to the conclusion in his book, *Roots of Language*, that Hawaiian Creole had been invented entirely by children at play. Only the children could have done it, Professor Bickerton argues, because there was no time for their parents to have learnt the new language and passed it on. Indeed, he points out, their parents did not understand Hawaiian Creole when it first appeared. They had to learn it from their offspring.

## THE MYSTERY OF THE RUNES

The runic alphabet is one of the oldest in northern Europe, with most early examples dating from around the 3rd century AD. Long associated with magic and witchcraft, runes have been found in about 4000 inscriptions and a few manuscripts, mainly in Britain, Scandinavia and Iceland. Nobody knows for certain where the alphabet came from, but some scholars believe that it was derived from the Etruscan alphabet, used in southern Europe after about 800 BC, and that it was brought north by the Goths during their invasion of the Roman empire.

## WOLF CHILDREN

Children left in the wild or otherwise deprived of human contact do not learn how to speak spontaneously, linguistic experts believe. There are now more than 50 recorded cases of 'wolf children' – mostly in India – who have been found living among animals. All were mentally retarded and unable to speak.

A report on a similar case in the United States was published in 1977. It concerned a young girl known as 'Genie', who had been locked up in her home for 14 years – and who had since made some very limited progress in speaking.

# Languages 2: the way we talk

## BABY'S FIRST WORDS

Babies begin to recognise elements of speech sounds very shortly after birth, and to imitate the patterns of speech well before they begin to form intelligible words. At the age of one month they begin to distinguish between certain features of the spoken language that will later represent vowels and consonants. In English, for example, the presence or absence of the vocal cord vibration which distinguishes *pin* and *bin*, *to* and *do*, is picked up at this early age.

From around four months, babies can gauge the mood of an adult from his tone of voice. And at six months the sounds they make begin to mimic the rhythm and intonation of adult speech. Soon afterwards it is possible to tell English, French and Chinese children apart simply on the basis of tape recordings of their unintelligible babblings.

## PLAY LANGUAGES

Children all over the world devise their own 'secret' play languages, mostly just for fun. But some scholars argue that these play languages also have a serious role: in introducing changes into the languages of adults. Two British researchers, Iona and Peter Opie, even suggested in a book published in 1959 that some developments in language down the generations were due to innovations first created by children at play. Records of these children's languages go back only to the 19th century, because experts did not begin to study them until then. But play languages are thought to have a far longer history. Three used in Britain are: back slang, pig Latin and eggy-peggy speech.

Back slang takes its name from the way words are said backwards, as in 'Tup taht koob yawa' (for 'Put that book away'). The colloquial British word 'yob', for example, is back slang for 'boy'. A commoner version of back slang takes the final sound and moves it to the front of the word, adding an occasional consonant for ease of pronunciation, as in 'Teput tetha keboo yawa'. In pig Latin, the first consonants are placed at the end of the word and 'ay' or 'e' added, as in 'Utpay atthay ookbay wayay'. Eggy-peggy or 'aygo-paygo' speech is produced by inserting an extra syllable as in 'Pegut thegat begook egaway'.

## RHYMING SLANG

Rhyming slang – the traditional language of Cockney Londoners – can be traced back to the 17th century, though it became widely known only in the 19th century. It probably began as a kind of thieves' jargon in the East End of London, though rhymes of this kind are also known in other parts of Britain and similar features have been found in other languages among groups such as criminals and gypsy clans, where the desire to preserve secrecy is strong.

More than 1000 examples of English rhyming slang have been recorded, though not all are still in use. Among them are *Hampstead Heath* (teeth), *Barnet Fair* (hair), *bottle and glass* (class), *bird-lime* (time in prison), *saucepan lid* (kid, meaning child or to fool), *china plate* (mate), *Scapa Flow* (go), *jam-jar* (car), *tit for tat* (hat), *lean and lurch* (church), *Cain and Abel* (table), *frog and toad* (road), *apples and pears* (stairs), *plates of meat* (feet), *whistle and flute* (suit), *half-inch* (pinch, in the sense of steal), *butcher's hook* (look) and *loaf of bread* (head – whence comes 'use your loaf'). In each case

## WHO SPEAKS WHAT

There are some 4500 million people in the world, speaking between them around 9000 languages and dialects. The 12 most widespread languages are the mother tongues of 2500 million people.

The largest number, 1000 million, speak Chinese, but since this consists of several mutually unintelligible dialects it is perhaps incorrect to think of it as one language. The Mandarin dialect, however, is already spoken by more than 500 million Chinese and will probably become even more widespread now that it is being taught in schools throughout the country.

English is the next most widely spoken language. It is the mother tongue of 350 million people, and is used by another 1150 million people – in all about one-third of the world's population. Below it in the world league table are: Hindi (145 million); Russian (130 million); Spanish (125 million); German (120 million); Japanese (116 million); and Arabic and Bengali, each with 100 million.

## GRIMM'S LAW

Grimm's law is one of several linguistic laws that explain the different forms taken by words in languages with a common origin. It takes its name from the pioneering German scholar Jacob Grimm (1785–1863), who showed, for example, that many *p* sounds in Latin and Greek had become *f* sounds in English and German. Thus the Latin word *pater* had become *father* in English and *Vater* (pronounced 'fahter') in German. And the Latin word *pisces* became *fish* in English and *Fisch* in German. Grimm – who with his brother Wilhelm was also the author of *Grimm's Fairy Tales* – charted the transformation of whole groups of vowels and consonants in several Indo-European languages. He was also the first to prove that such changes take a regular form and are not, as had previously been thought, random processes affecting only certain words.

only the first, non-rhyming half of each phrase is usually used – *Barnet*, say, or *bottle* – so that to a stranger the conversation is incomprehensible.

English rhyming slang expressions have also sometimes been exported. Australians still call a bar, or pub, a *rubbedy*, from the expression 'rub-a-dub-dub'.

## HOW MANY WORDS

Precise estimates of the number of words in any language are almost impossible. New words are constantly being added to living languages, and old words are changing their meaning. The Merriam-Webster *Third New International Dictionary* – one of the largest English dictionaries – has half a million entries. But even this massive number is thought by linguistic scholars to represent barely half the total of words in the English language. There are hundreds of local and international dialects in English for which no entries exist, and new words are constantly appearing in such fields as literature and science. Even highly educated people are likely to know less than 10 per cent of the words in the total vocabulary. And they are likely to make regular use in speech or writing of less than 10 per cent of that fraction – usually fewer than 10,000 words in all.

## THE IMPOSSIBLE TYPEWRITER

The Japanese, whose genius for machines has put them in the forefront of the industrial world, have not yet mastered the humble typewriter. The reason is that even the everyday language requires more than 2000 characters – far more than would fit on to a conventional keyboard.

Written Japanese is a combination of three writing systems: *kanji*, which are borrowed Chinese ideograms (characters which symbolise the idea of a word rather than its sound); and two systems of *kana*, which are phonograms (characters which represent spoken sounds). Large dictionaries can contain more than 10,000 *kanji* symbols, but after the Second World War the government revised the language, creating a simplified vocabulary of about 1800 *kanji* symbols for everyday use. The two *kana* systems, *hiragana* and *katakana*, date from the 9th century and each contains 112 symbols.

A Western typewriter can cope with an entire language, including numbers and punctuation, with fewer than 50 keys. In comparison, a Japanese typewriter is a cumbersome machine with a limited vocabulary. It consists of a single key and 2000 symbols held in a matrix. The typist moves the matrix each time to get the appropriate *kanji* or *kana* character opposite the key. A second set of 2000 symbols is also available for more complex subjects. If one of these additional symbols is required, the character is selected and placed in an empty space in the matrix. Because of this slow and expensive procedure, Japanese executives and secretaries still write most of their correspondence by hand.

## DIVIDED BY A COMMON LANGUAGE

Dialects in China vary so widely that they can be mutually unintelligible – as different from each other as French, Italian and Spanish. But they share the same written language, which is understood by literate Chinese in all parts of the world, whatever dialect they speak. As a result, a Cantonese-speaking businessman in Hong Kong could not discuss a project by phone with a Mandarin-speaking businessman from Beijing (Peking), but he could do so by letter. And Chinese films shown to Chinese audiences often have Chinese sub-titles to help the audience understand what is said. Chinese dialects fall into six main groups: Mandarin (in the north); Wu; Min; Kan; Hsiang; and Cantonese (in the south). The Mandarin dialect of the Beijing area is now taught in schools all over China as the standard language, although it will be some time before everyone speaks it.

## TAKE A LETTER, JULIUS

The Roman general Julius Caesar knew how to do shorthand. He used a system which was invented by a scholar named Marcus Tullius Tiro in 63 BC. Tiro devised the system to record the speeches of the orator

TOWER OF CONFUSION *According to the Bible, the world's huge variety of languages began at the Tower of Babel, shown here in a painting by the 16th-century Flemish artist, Pieter Bruegel the Younger. Some 9000 languages and dialects are now in use, and new ones are still being discovered in remote areas. Another 1000 languages, such as ancient Egyptian, are known but no longer used.*

Cicero. Tiro's system is the first known complete shorthand, and it remained in use for 1000 years.

Several new shorthand systems were devised in the 17th century but modern shorthand is a product of the 19th and early 20th centuries. Pitman's shorthand – still widely used in Britain and Europe – was devised by Sir Isaac Pitman in 1837, and the commonest American system, Gregg's shorthand, was created in 1888 by J. R. Gregg. Both make use of straight lines, curves, dots and dashes, though Pitman's also uses different thicknesses of stroke, to distinguish between phonetically similar letters. The symbol for 'p' for instance – an oblique line – is a lighter version of the symbol for 'b'. Several other systems, among them Speedwriting, which was invented in the 1920s by an American named Emma Dearborn, consist of abbreviations of the Roman alphabet. The Pitman system holds the world records for shorthand of 300 words a minute over five minutes, and 350 words a minute over two minutes. Both records were set by an American, Nathan Behrin, in New York in 1922.

## STRINE

Just as American English has developed its own distinctive accent and vocabulary, so Australian English has diverged from the language spoken in Britain. In particular, Australians have developed a vivid set of verbal images: words and phrases often known collectively as Strine, from a comic version of the Australian pronunciation of the word 'Australian'. Among the phrases are colourful descriptions of people: 'lower than a snake's belly', 'so mean he wouldn't shout in a shark attack', 'as busy as a one-armed bill-poster in a high wind' and 'mad as a cut snake'.

There are now over 5000 words or expressions distinctive to the Australian continent. Some, such as *kangaroo*, *boomerang* and *bush telegraph* are well known outside Australia as well. Others, less well known, include *lolly* for 'sweet' and *station* for 'stock farm'. There is also a lively collection of Australian slang words, such as *sheila* for 'girl', *crook* for 'ill' or 'angry', *drongo* for 'fool', *ocker* for 'an uncultured person' and *wowser* for 'killjoy'.

## UPSIDE-DOWN DOWN UNDER

Boys undergoing initiation rites among the Warlpiri tribe of Australian Aborigines learn to speak a special upside-down language. Called *Tjiliwirri* – meaning 'funny' or 'clown' – it expresses every idea as its opposite. Instead of saying, for example, 'You are tall', a boy speaking *Tjiliwirri* would say 'I am short'. And instead of saying 'Give me water', he would say 'I withhold water from you'.

## DON'T CALL ME MOTHER

Among Australian Aborigines, many tribes have a special language which is reserved for speaking to in-laws. In Djirbal, for example, spoken in parts of northeast Queensland, the basic language is known as Guwal, but when a man wants to talk to his mother-in-law he speaks a special language called Dyalnguy. In Guugu-Yimidhirr, spoken farther north, the men use a special language for their brothers-in-law and fathers-in-law. Some tribes treat all their in-laws in this way. Aboriginal words for members of the family are also quite different from those used in Western languages. In some tribes, the word for 'father' is also used for the father's brothers and cousins, or a wife may also call her husband's brothers 'husband'.

# WORDS FROM ABROAD

English belongs to the Germanic branch of the Indo-European family of languages. It began about 1500 years ago as Anglo-Saxon, the language of the Angles, Saxons and Jutes, who invaded Britain from the Continent at that time. But dozens of other languages from all over the world have also contributed to its rich vocabulary as a result of invasion, trade and scholarship.

These are some of the languages that English has drawn on, and some of the words they have given it:

**Anglo-Saxon** Answer, folk, freedom, go, kill, life, love, night, old, stone, thing, what, when, where, who, year.

**Norse** Anger, awe, clumsy, crooked, enthral, fog, husband, law, ransack, root, skill, snare, they, wrong.

**Norman French** Abbot, baron, beauty, Bible, court, crown, dress, feast, joy, justice, liberty, market, marriage, navy, parliament, peace, people, pleasure, power, prayer, reign, soldier, treasure, verdict, war.

**Modern French** Ballet, cafe, camouflage, elite, espionage, garage, menu, police, regime, soup, theatre.

**Latin** Accommodate, bacillus, circus, exit, focus, invention, manufacture, penicillin, persecute, refrigerator, status, tradition, vacuum.

**Greek** Agnostic, alphabet, character, clinic, cycle, electron, epidemic, idea, irony, museum, neurology, parallel, polystyrene, rhythm, telegraph, theory.

**Italian** Arcade, concerto, replica, vendetta.

**Dutch** Brandy, decoy, landscape, schooner.

**Caribbean languages** Canoe, hammock, hurricane, maize, mosquito, tobacco.

**Aztec** Chocolate, tomato.

**Chinese** Ketchup, kowtow, tea, typhoon.

**Japanese** Judo, karate, kimono, tsunami, tycoon.

**Malay** Amok, bamboo, caddy (box), sago.

**Turkish** Caviar, coffee, kiosk, tulip, yoghurt.

**Arabic** Alcohol, algebra, amber, assassin, cipher, crimson, cotton, ghoul, mattress, sofa, zero.

**Indian languages** Bangle, bazaar, bungalow, chintz, jungle, khaki, pepper, pyjamas, shawl, teak, thug, verandah.

**Persian** Azure, candy, caravan, checkmate, divan, lemon, taffeta.

**African languages** Banana, banjo, chimpanzee, cola, mumbo-jumbo, raffia, tango, tote (to carry), voodoo, yam, zombie.

*Crossed wrists mean odds on*

*Patting the shoulder means 33:1*

*Hands on the head mean 9:4*

TALKING HANDS *British bookmakers use a special sign language called 'tic-tac' to keep in touch with fluctuating betting odds among their rivals around the racecourse.*

## THUS SPAKE THE TRADER

Pidgin languages are simplified forms of language, invented by people with mutually unintelligible tongues to form a bridge between them. Well over 100 pidgins are in use today – all versions of Portuguese, Spanish, French, Dutch, Italian or English. Spoken mostly in colonies or former colonies, where there might be hundreds of local languages, pidgins began as trading languages. The word pidgin is thought by some scholars to derive from a pidgin rendering of the English word 'business', in which the first syllable has been stretched into two and the final 'ess' sound has been lost. Many pidgins have served traders, sailors and local merchants for more than 500 years. In some countries, such as Papua New Guinea, pidgins have become an official national language – and road signs, newspapers, even Parliamentary debates, all make use of pidgin.

More than 60 varieties of pidgin English still flourish, and some are very widely spoken. Tok Pisin (meaning 'talk pidgin'), the pidgin of Papua New Guinea, is spoken by at least 1 million people. And 2 million people speak Cameroon Pidgin.

## WORDS BELONG HAMLET

Numerous works of literature have been translated into pidgin languages. Translated into the pidgin English of the Solomon Islanders, Shakespeare's most famous speech appears in these words:

'Which way this time? Me killem die finish body b'long me

Or me no do 'im? Me no savvy.

Might 'e better 'long you-me catchem this fella string for throw 'im this fella arrow,

Altogether b'long number one bad fella, name b'long him fortune? Me no savvy.

Might 'e better 'long you-me. For fightem 'long altogether where him 'e makem you-me sorry too much,

Bimeby him fall down die finish? Me no savvy.'

In English the same lines – from the prince's soliloquy on suicide in *Hamlet* (Act 3, Scene 2) – are:

'To be, or not to be: that is the question;

Whether 'tis nobler in the mind to suffer

The slings and arrows of outrageous fortune,

Or to take arms against a sea of troubles,

And by opposing end them?'

## THE SOUNDS OF LANGUAGE

The number of different sounds varies enormously from language to language. In speech, English generally has about 20 vowel sounds, but some languages have far more, or far fewer. The largest numbers of vowel sounds are in the languages of Southeast Asia. Bru, a Vietnamese language, has 40 vowel sounds; and Sedang, also spoken in Vietnam, has 55. However, many languages, including some from the Caucasus mountains of southern Russia such as Abhaz and Adygh, have only one type of vowel – usually a kind of open 'a', as in the English word 'are'.

Spoken consonants, too, show a wide range. English accents usually have 24; but many of the languages spoken in the Caucasus have more than 70, and one – Ubykh – has 80. By contrast, several languages make do with fewer than ten consonants – among them Mohawk, an American Indian language, which has only seven.

## LETTER FROM KAMPUCHEA

Alphabets – in which each symbol stands for a single sound – are a far more economical method of representing a language than syllabaries or pictographic scripts – in which the symbols stand for complete syllables or words. But even within alphabets, some are shorter than others. The world's longest alphabet is Cambodian; it has 74 letters – nearly three times as many as English. The shortest alphabet is Rotokas, from the Solomon Islands; it has only 11 letters.

## CLICKS OF THE TONGUE

The disapproving clicking noise which is written as 'tut-tut' in English is used as a consonant in several African languages. Some southern African languages have as many as 15 different click consonants, including the sound made with the sides of the tongue to urge on a horse. Zulu, the most widespread language with clicks, has 3 million speakers, but Bushman, Hottentot and Xhosa all use clicks as well.

Other sounds quite foreign to Indo-European languages also serve as consonants. One of these, resembling the 'glug-glug' sound that children make to imitate a bath emptying, is used in several West African languages.

## WHISTLE FOR IT

The Mazateco Indians of Mexico can hold a complete conversation – just by whistling. Mazateco 'whistled speech', which is used only by the men of the tribe, is based on the tones and rhythms of the spoken language. By varying the speed, pitch and intensity of the whistles, the men can deal with a wide range of subjects. For example, a trader can strike a bargain with a customer, spelling out in whistles exact details of quantity and price, without either side speaking a word. A similar language of whistles, called *silbo*, is used on the Canary Island of La Gomera. The sounds carry so well across the valleys that a speaker can be understood up to 8km (5 miles) away.

## ODD MAN OUT

Basque is unique among the languages of Europe because it has no known relatives. It is spoken by more than 500,000 people in the French and Spanish Pyrenees, but bears no relationship to any other European language.

Scholars, baffled by Basque's linguistic independence, have developed a number of theories to explain it. Some experts see it as the last example of the language spoken in southwestern Europe before the Roman invasion. Some see a relationship between Basque and an extinct Iberian language found on inscriptions along the Mediterranean coasts. Others link it with the languages of North Africa, or with those of the Caucasus region in southern Russia. No theory, however, has yet won universal support.

Right hand on the nose means 2:1

Clenched fists shaken mean 50:1

Arms raised in a circle mean 11:10

Number one, or the first horse on the race card

# Wit and wisdom

## A DWARFISH WHOLE

Epigrams were originally inscriptions – the word comes from the Greek *epi*, meaning 'upon', and *graphein*, meaning 'to write'. In ancient Greece an inscription was normally carved in stone, and because stone carving is laborious, inscriptions tended to be short.

The Greek origin is preserved in two English words: epigraph, used for a short and serious observation, as on a monument; and epigram, meaning a short, witty expression of a point of view. The English poet Samuel Taylor Coleridge (1772 – 1834) defined the epigram with another epigram:

'*What is an Epigram? A dwarfish whole,*
*Its body brevity, and wit its soul.*'

## VERSE OR PROSE?

Classic epigrams were always meant to be in verse, but prose has long been an acceptable alternative. The poet Alexander Pope (1688 – 1744) was entirely at ease in epigrammatic verse, as:

'*Words are like leaves; and where they most abound,*
*Much fruit of sense beneath is rarely found.*'

In prose, however, he could express similar sentiments in an even more scathing manner. 'It is with narrow-souled people as with narrow-necked bottles,' he wrote. 'The less they have in them, the more noise they make in pouring out.'

## WIT AND WISECRACKING

The American critic Dorothy Parker (1893 – 1967), who observed that 'wit has truth in it; wisecracking is simply calisthenics with words', was expert at both sorts of humour.

She once demolished a performance by the actress Katherine Hepburn with the jibe: 'She ran the whole gamut of emotions from A to B.' But she also wrote the thoughtfully humorous lines:

'*Four be the things I am wiser to know:*
*Idleness, sorrow, a friend and a foe.*
*Four be the things I'd be better without:*
*Love, curiosity, freckles and doubt.*'

## DOCTOR'S VISIT

Britain's Dr Samuel Johnson (1709 – 84), creator of the first modern dictionary, was once asked by a novice writer to give his opinion on a piece the young man had written. 'Sir,' Johnson is said to have replied, 'this piece is both original and good. Unfortunately, the parts that are original are not good, and the parts that are good are not original.'

## REQUEST STOP

George Bernard Shaw was at one time even more celebrated as a music critic than as a playwright. One night, it is said, he was eating in a restaurant whose orchestra was inferior, to say the least, and the conductor asked him what he would like the orchestra to play next. 'Dominoes,' said Shaw.

## HIGH SOCIETY

The essence of the retort (from the Latin *re*, meaning 'back', and *torquere*, meaning 'to turn or twist') is to use the first speaker's words to deflate him or her. Few people can have been so effectively put down as the 1930s actress Jean Harlow who, triumphant as a Hollywood sex goddess, met the immensely patrician Margot, Lady Asquith, wife of the British Prime Minister Herbert Asquith.

Harlow insisted on addressing Lady Asquith by her first name, which might have been a sufficient social offence, but made it worse by pronouncing the 't' on the end of Margot. Lady Asquith, tiring of this ignorant impertinence, set Jean Harlow straight: 'My dear, the 't' is silent – as in Harlow.'

## ANIMAL CRACKS

Mark Twain (1835 – 1910), American wit and prolific author, took a dim view of most of his fellow men – and was blunt in expressing it. On human gullibility, for instance, he declared: 'One of the most striking differences between a cat and a lie is that a cat has only nine lives.' And on mankind's capacity for gratitude, he said: 'If you pick up a starving dog and make him prosperous he will not bite you. This is the principal difference between a dog and a man.'

## THE QUIET AMERICAN

Calvin Coolidge, President of the United States from 1923 to 1929, was remarkably uncommunicative. One story told about him has it that a friend missed a sermon on sin that Coolidge had sat through. The friend asked Coolidge what the preacher had said about sin and Coolidge replied: 'He said he was against it.' Perhaps in church he had merely been bored, but he appeared to be wittier when, at a public dinner, a woman told him that she had bet some friends that she could make him speak at least three words to her in the course of the evening. All he said to her was: 'You lose.'

Dorothy Parker, as so often, had the last word. It is reported that when she was told Coolidge was dead, she merely asked: 'How can they tell?'

## BITCHINESS REWARDED

Clare Booth Luce, the American diplomat, was in the habit of speaking her mind and not fearing the consequences. But she came to grief when, it is reported, she stood aside and gestured Dorothy Parker to precede her through a door, saying: 'Age before beauty.' Parker swept on, saying only: 'Pearls before swine.'

## CHINESE BURN

A British Labour MP was succinctly squashed in the early 1930s by a Chinese delegate to the League of Nations, C. T. Wang, at a banquet in Nanjing. The two men found themselves sitting close to one another and the MP, not knowing what to say, opened up with: 'Likee soupee?' Mr Wang did not dignify this remark with a reply, and at the end of the dinner made an address to the gathering in impeccable, erudite, elegant English. He then turned to the MP and asked politely: 'Likee speechee?'

## BULLDOG HUMOUR

Winston Churchill's scathing gruffness would have seemed rudeness in many a lesser man, but some stories about Churchill are so funny that the insults they contain have to be overlooked. Nancy Astor, for example, the society hostess and MP, was feeling particularly ill-disposed towards Churchill one day and is supposed to have said: 'Winston, if I were married to you, I'd put poison in your coffee.'

To which Churchill retorted: 'Nancy, if you were

my wife, I'd drink it.' Bessie Braddock, a formidable and outspoken Labour MP, is reported to have rebuked Churchill for intoxication. 'Winston, you're drunk,' she said, and must have regretted it immediately, for his reply was: 'Bessie, you're ugly. And tomorrow morning I shall be sober.'

Churchill crossed swords with the playwright George Bernard Shaw as well. The story goes that Shaw sent Churchill two tickets for the first night of one of his plays with a note saying: 'Bring a friend – if you have one.' Churchill returned the tickets saying he would not be able to attend, but would be grateful for tickets for the second night – 'if there is one'.

## IN THE BAG
Horatio Bottomley, the British journalist and Member of Parliament jailed for fraud in 1922, preserved his wit even in prison. A passing prison visitor, noticing him stitching mailbags, said: 'Ah, Bottomley, sewing?'
'No, sir,' said Bottomley, 'reaping.'

# FAMOUS LAST WORDS

The last words of a dying person are sometimes a matter for argument among scholars. Incoherence, the chance presence or absence of witnesses, and family sentiment can all interfere with an accurate record. The sayings quoted here are widely accepted by historians.

**Ludwig Van Beethoven,** German composer who suffered progressive impairment of his hearing for the last 29 years of his life; died in 1827: 'I shall hear in heaven.'

**Leonardo da Vinci,** Italian artist and inventor; died in 1519: 'I have offended God and mankind because my work did not reach the quality it should have.'

**Douglas Fairbanks Senior,** American film star; died in 1939: 'I've never felt better.'

**Henry Fox,** Lord Holland, British politician; died in 1774: 'If Mr Selwyn (a rival politician) calls again, show him up. If I am alive I shall be delighted to see him, and if I am dead he would like to see me.'

**Ned Kelly,** Australian outlaw and gang-leader, who was hanged in 1880: 'Such is life.'

**Hugh Latimer,** Bishop of Worcester and English Protestant reformer, burnt at the stake in 1555 with the Bishop of Rochester, Nicholas Ridley, on the orders of the Catholic Queen Mary: 'Be of good comfort, Mr Ridley, and play the man. We shall this day light such a candle by God's grace in England, as I trust shall never be put out.'

**Niccolò Machiavelli,** Florentine diplomat and political philosopher; died in 1527: 'I desire to go to hell and not to heaven. In the former place I shall enjoy the company of popes, kings and princes, while in the latter are only beggars, monks and apostles.'

**Karl Marx,** German philosopher who died in 1883, to his housekeeper after she asked if he had a last message for the world: 'Go on, get out! Last words are for fools who haven't said enough.'

**William Somerset Maugham,** British author; died in 1965: 'Dying is a very dull, dreary affair. And my advice to you is to have nothing whatever to do with it.'

**Sir Thomas More,** English Catholic statesman who was beheaded in 1535 on the orders of Henry VIII: 'See me safe up (on to the scaffold); for my coming down, let me shift for myself.'

**Sir Isaac Newton,** British scientist; died in 1727: 'I don't know what I may seem to the world. But as to myself I seem to have been only like a boy playing on the seashore and diverting myself in now and then finding a smoother pebble or prettier shell than ordinary, whilst the great ocean of truth lay all undiscovered before me.'

**Lawrence Oates,** British explorer; walked to his death in 1912 in an attempt to save his starving companions during Scott's expedition to the Pole: 'I am just going outside and I may be some time.'

**Cecil Rhodes,** S African tycoon and statesman; died in 1902: 'So little done, so much to do.'

**General John Sedgwick,** Union commander in the American Civil War, shot at the Battle of Spotsylvania Court House in 1864 while looking over a parapet at the enemy lines: 'They couldn't hit an elephant at this dist . . .'

DEATH IN VICTORY *The British admiral Horatio Nelson died at the Battle of Trafalgar in 1805. His last words were not 'Kiss me, Hardy', as is often supposed, but: 'Now I am satisfied. Thank God, I have done my duty.'*

## THE EVER-OPEN MOUTH

Politicians apparently live by talking – as the American politician Adlai Stevenson put it: 'A politician is a statesman who approaches every question with an open mouth.' It is therefore not surprising that some of the wittiest epigrams come from politicians. Adlai Stevenson himself came up with: 'Man does not live by words alone, despite the fact that sometimes he has to eat them.'

A Biblical turn of phrase was also favoured by Jeremy Thorpe, former leader of the British Liberal Party, when he summed up British Prime Minister Harold Macmillan's dismissal of several close colleagues in his Cabinet reshuffle of 1962: 'Greater love hath no man than this, than to lay down his friends for his life.'

## THE ANGELIC ELECTION

Sir Robert Menzies, twice Premier of Australia, was addressing an election meeting. A heckler, so the story goes, shouted: 'I wouldn't vote for you if you were the Archangel Gabriel.' Menzies shouted back: 'If I were the Archangel Gabriel, madam, you would scarcely be in my constituency.'

## THE EPIGRAMS OF OSCAR

The Irish playwright Oscar Wilde (1854–1900) is perhaps the most quoted of wits for his brilliant epigrams. On the generation gap, for example, he wrote: 'Children begin by loving their parents; after a time they judge them; rarely, if ever, do they forgive them.' On a novel: 'The good ended happily, and the bad unhappily. That is what Fiction means.' On experience: 'Experience is the name everyone gives to their mistakes.'

On gossip: 'There is only one thing in the world worse than being talked about, and that is not being talked about.' On hunting: 'The English country gentleman galloping after a fox – the unspeakable in full pursuit of the uneatable.'

And on the cynic: 'A man who knows the price of everything and the value of nothing.'

THAT'S MY LINE *A contemporary cartoon shows Oscar Wilde in the languid pose of the aesthete. Today, he is best remembered for apt and witty epigrams. The American Dorothy Parker – herself an incisive wit – paid tribute to his unsurpassed mastery of this form in a rhyme:* 'If, with the literate, I am/Impelled to try an epigram,/I never seek to take the credit;/We all assume that Oscar said it.' *Wilde, however, was himself once upstaged by the American painter James Whistler. It happened when he was heard to declare admiringly of another's witty remark: 'I wish I'd said that.' Instantly Whistler responded: 'You will, Oscar, you will.'*

# CARVED IN STONE

Epitaphs – brief inscriptions usually carved on tombs or gravestones – are often memorable and even humorous. These are some striking examples.

Sir Christopher Wren, the architect of St Paul's Cathedral in London, has his epitaph carved in Latin over the interior of the cathedral's north door: *Si monumentum requiris circumspice* (If his monument you seek, look around).

At Reading in Berkshire, England:
'Here lies the body of William Gordon
He'd a mouth almighty and teeth accordin';
Stranger tread lightly on this sod
For if he gapes you're gone, by God.'

In Tombstone, Arizona, USA, on the grave of a Wells Fargo agent:
'Here lies
Lester Moore
four slugs
from a 44
no less
no more.'

On a tombstone in Edinburgh, Scotland:
'Erected to the memory of
John MacFarlane, Drowned in the Water of Leith
By a few affectionate friends.'

On a grave in Nantucket, Massachusetts, USA:
'Under the sod, under the trees
Lies the body of Jonathan Pease
He is not here
But only his pod:
He shelled out his peas
And went to God.'

On a Staffordshire tombstone in England:
'Here lies father and mother and sister and I
We all died within the space of one short year;
They all be buried at Wimble, except I,
And I be buried here.'

On a grave in Lillington churchyard, near Leamington Spa, Warwickshire, England:
'Poorly lived,
And poorly died,
Poorly buried,
And no one cried.'

On a grave in Stoke-on-Trent, England:
'All who come my grave to see
Avoid damp beds and think of me.'

On a tombstone in Devon, England:
'Here lie I by the chancel door,
They put me here because I was poor.'
The further in, the more you pay,
But here lie I as snug as they.'

*From a Cornish tombstone dated 1869*

# World religions

## STRANGLED AT THE STAKE

One of the world's most familiar Bible translations was made and printed by the English religious scholar and reformer William Tyndale in the first half of the 16th century. His versions of the Old and New Testaments were largely taken over by the Authorised Version – also known as the King James Bible – which was first published in 1611 and is still in use today. Tyndale wrote in ordinary, everyday English – language, he said, that every ploughboy would be able to understand. But his efforts outraged the orthodox churchmen of his day. They felt that Tyndale was usurping the Church's role as guardian and sole interpreter of the Scriptures. Only scholars could read the Latin and Greek translations then in existence; and almost all scholars were priests. To escape perse- cution, Tyndale was forced, in 1524, to flee to the Continent. The following year his New Testament translation was published in Germany, and copies of it were smuggled into England – much to the annoy- ance of Henry VIII, who accused Tyndale, a Prot- estant, of spreading sedition.

Tyndale later moved to Holland, where he published English versions of parts of the Old Testament and revised versions of the New Testament. But in 1535 he was arrested by the authorities in Antwerp and accused of heresy. He was taken to the state prison for the Low Countries at Vilvorde and brought to trial the following year. After being found 'guilty', he was strangled at the stake and his body burnt. To the end, his greatest regret was that his work had been banned in his homeland. And his last words were: 'Lord, open the King of England's eyes!'

## HOW THE GREAT RELIGIONS BEGAN

### BUDDHISM

Founded about 2500 years ago by Prince Siddhartha Gautama, who lived from about 563 to 483 BC in northeast India. He was known as Buddha, a Sanskrit title meaning 'the Awakened One'. Its main writings are contained in a number of sacred books called the Pali Canon (Pali is the Indian language in which they are written), and in a vast collection of Sanskrit, Tibetan and Chinese sacred texts. There are now some 256 million believers, mainly in Southeast Asia and the Far East.

### CHRISTIANITY

Founded about 2000 years ago by Jesus Christ, who lived from about 7 BC to AD 30. Its writings are contained in the Bible. There are now about 1200 million believers in the world – including some 806 million Roman Catholics, 343 million Protestants and 74 million members of the Eastern Orthodox Church.

### CONFUCIANISM

Founded about 2500 years ago by the philosopher Kong Zi ('The Master Kung'), known by the Latin name Confucius, who lived from about 551 to 479 BC. His teachings are contained in what are now called the Analects, from the Greek word *analekta* meaning 'a collection of facts and sayings'. There are now about 275 million believers, mainly in China and Taiwan.

### HINDUISM

Hinduism is the European name for the *Sanatana Dharma*, 'the Eternal Law'. The earliest Hindu text – the Rig Veda – dates from before 1000 BC. But the best-known texts are the Upanishads, Brahmanas and Puranas, collectively called the Veda, or 'Knowledge'. The most popular text is the *Bhagavad Gita*. There are now about 500 million believers in India and in Indian communities throughout the world.

### ISLAM

Founded about 1400 years ago by the prophet Muhammad, who lived from about AD 570 to 632. Its holy scripture is the Koran, written by Arab scholars in about AD 651. Tradition has it that Muhammad himself was unable to read or write. There are now about 1100 million believers throughout the world.

### JUDAISM

Founded about 4000 years ago by the Hebrew chieftain Abraham, who taught his people to worship one God – Jehovah, or Yahweh. Its chief writings are contained in the Torah – which reveals the will of God as stated in the first five books of the Old Testament, the Pentateuch – and the Talmud, which contains the Jewish religious and civil laws. There are now about 14 million Jews in the world, of which some 6 million live in the USA, 3 million in Israel and 500,000 in Britain.

### SHINTO

Dates from antiquity as a Japanese folk religion. It has no holy book and its ethical principles are derived from Confucianism and Buddhism. From the early 6th century AD the emperor of Japan was regarded as the religion's god, but the idea of divinity was officially renounced in 1946 by Emperor Hirohito, who instead became the constitutional monarch. There are now more than 98 million believers in Japan.

### SIKHISM

Founded in India in about AD 1500 by Guru Nanak, who lived from 1469 to 1539 and was the first of the ten 'gurus', or teachers, of the Sikhs. Its main writings are contained in the Adi Granth, a Punjabi phrase meaning 'The Original (or First) Book', compiled by the fifth guru, Arjun, in 1604. There are now about 14 million believers throughout the world.

### TAOISM

Founded in prehistoric times and described about 2600 years ago by the philosopher Lao Zi, who lived in about 600 BC. He believed in a life of contemplation and passivity. Tao is the Chinese word for 'path' or 'way', and refers to the path of contentment and withdrawal which Lao Zi declared should be chosen above the path of self- seeking and worldly ambition. Lao Zi's beliefs and sayings are contained in the *Tao-Te Ching* ('The Classic of the Way and its Virtue'). There are now about 30 million believers throughout the world.

### ZOROASTRIANISM

Founded more than 3000 years ago in Persia by the prophet Zoroaster or Zarathustra. His philosophical and moral teachings – concerning the endless war between the forces of good and evil – are preserved in his *Gathas*, or 'hymns', written in Avestan, a sister language to Sanskrit. Zoroastrianism was once the faith of the Persian empire, but today it is the smallest major religion in the world, with some 130,000 believers, mainly in northeast India and Iran.

## MARTYRS OF THE PAPACY

When Pope John Paul II – the first non-Italian pope since the Dutch-born Adrian VI (1522 – 3) – was shot and wounded by a Turkish gunman in Rome in 1981, the Christian world was outraged. But he was by no means the first pope to become the target of violence. Of the 266 churchmen who have so far held office as the head of the Roman Catholic Church, 33 have died by violence.

The earliest martyr was St Peter, regarded by Catholics as the first pope, who is believed to have been crucified upside down in about AD 64 during the reign of the Roman emperor Nero.

The first to be assassinated (rather than executed on a government's orders) was John VIII, who was killed in December 882.

Despite the pomp that often surrounds the Vatican, the pope – the word comes from the Greek *pappas*, meaning 'father' – has long had a formal reminder of humility. Since the reign of Gregory I (590 – 604), every pope has called himself the 'Servant of the servants of God'.

## THE ROOTS OF RELIGION

Judaism is the oldest of the world's three Western religions. Christianity and Islam have both sprung from it. Christianity takes from Judaism the idea of one all-powerful Creator and God, and the concept of how he has revealed himself in human history. Churches followed synagogues as centres of prayer and worship. Psalm-singing, incense and the Eucharist – the sharing of a consecrated meal – all have their basis in Jewish ceremonies. The names of Abraham and Moses, familiar in the Christian Bible, also appear often in the sacred book of Islam, the Koran, as Ibrahim and Musa. Muslims accept, too, that Jesus was a prophet of God, though not that he was the Son of God. And Islam's weekly sabbath and its regular fasting both parallel Jewish beliefs.

# PATRON SAINTS OF WORKING PEOPLE

Since the beginnings of Christianity certain saints have come to be adopted as the patrons of specific groups of people, and the process has continued into the 20th century. This list shows the names of some of the saints who have become associated with particular occupations.

Accountants, St Matthew
Actors, St Genesius
Advertisers, St Bernadino of Siena
Altar boys, St John Berchmans
Anaesthetists, St René Goupil
Archers, St Sebastian
Architects, St Thomas the Apostle, St Barbara
Artists, St Luke, St Catherine of Bologna
Astronomers, St Dominic
Athletes, St Sebastian
Authors, St Francis de Sales
Aviators, Our Lady of Loreto, St Thérèse of Lisieux, St Joseph of Cupertino
Bakers, St Elizabeth of Hungary, St Nicholas
Bankers, St Matthew
Barbers, St Cosmas and St Damian, St Louis
Blacksmiths, St Dunstan
Bookkeepers, St Matthew
Booksellers, St John of God
Brewers, St Augustine of Hippo, St Luke
Bricklayers, St Stephen
Builders, St Vincent Ferrer
Butchers, St Antony of Egypt, St Luke
Cabinetmakers, St Anne
Carpenters, St Joseph
Comedians, St Vitus
Cooks, St Lawrence, St Martha
Dairy workers, St Brigid
Dentists, St Apollonia
Doctors, St Pantaleon, St Cosmas and St Damian, St Luke, St Raphael
Editors, St John Bosco
Engineers, St Ferdinand III
Farmers, St George, St Isidore the Farmer
Firemen, St Florian
Fishermen, St Andrew

Florists, St Dorothy, St Thérèse of Lisieux
Gardeners, St Dorothy, St Adelard, St Tryphon, St Fiacre, St Phocas
Glassworkers, St Luke
Gravediggers, St Anthony
Grocers, St Michael
Housewives, St Anne
Hunters, St Hubert, St Eustachius
Infantrymen, St Maurice
Innkeepers, St Amand
Jewellers, St Eligius
Journalists, St Francis de Sales
Jurists, St Catherine of Alexandria, St John of Capistrano
Labourers, St Isidore, St James, St John Bosco
Lawyers, St Ivo, St Genesius, St Thomas More
Librarians, St Jerome
Maids, St Zita
Merchants, St Francis of Assisi, St Nicholas of Myra
Messengers, St Gabriel
Metalworkers, St Eligius
Miners, St Barbara
Mountaineers, St Bernard of Montjoux
Musicians, St Gregory the Great, St Cecilia, St Dunstan
Nurses, St Camillus de Lellis, St John of God, St Agatha, St Raphael
Orators, St John Chrysostom

Painters, St Luke
Paratroopers, St Michael
Pawnbrokers, St Nicholas of Myra
Pharmacists, St Cosmas and St Damian, St James the Greater
Philosophers, St Justin
Plasterers, St Bartholomew
Poets, St David, St Cecilia
Policemen, St Michael
Postal workers, St Gabriel
Priests, St Jean-Baptiste Vianney
Printers, St John of God, St Augustine of Hippo, St Genesius
Public relations, St Bernardino of Siena
Radio workers, St Gabriel
Sailors, St Cuthbert, St Brendan, St Eulalia, St Christopher, St Peter Gonzales, St Erasmus
Scholars, St Brigid
Scientists, St Albert the Great
Sculptors, St Claude
Secretaries, St Genesius
Servants, St Martha, St Zita
Shoemakers, St Crispin, St Crispinian
Shorthand typists, St Genesius, St Cassian
Singers, St Gregory, St Cecilia
Skaters, St Lidwina
Skiers, St Bernard
Social workers, St Louise de Marillac
Soldiers, St Hadrian, St George, St Ignatius, St Sebastian, St Joan of Arc, St Martin of Tours
Students, St Thomas Aquinas, St Catherine of Alexandria
Tailors, St Homobonus
Tax collectors, St Matthew
Taxi drivers, St Fiacre
Teachers, St Gregory the Great, St Catherine of Alexandria, St John Baptist de la Salle
Theologians, St John the Evangelist, St Augustine, St Alphonsus Liguori
Travellers, St Anthony of Padua, St Christopher, St Nicholas of Myra, St Raphael
TV workers, St Gabriel
Undertakers, St Dismas, St Joseph of Arimathea
Writers, St John the Evangelist, St Francis de Sales

*Gospel author St John the Evangelist; patron of writers and theologians.*

THE FACE OF CHRIST *Because the early Church disapproved of idols, there is no contemporary record of Christ's physical appearance. The earliest representations, showing him as a beardless youth, date only from the 3rd century. And the traditional vision of a bearded Christ, as in this 12th-century English carving, began only in the 4th century. Christ's life and teachings, however, were set down very quickly in the New Testament, all of which was written within about 70 years of his death in AD 30. The earliest document was St Paul's letter to the Romans, written in about AD 58. Then, in succession, came St Mark's Gospel, St Matthew's (written for Jewish readers) and St Luke's (written for Gentiles). The last, St John's, was written in about AD 100.*

## WILL OF GOD

Devout Jews obey no fewer than 613 commandments, including the ten of the Christian faith. The commandments are derived from the Pentateuch – the first five books of the Old Testament – which is for Jews the most important religious text. Together, the commandments provide a moral framework for life. Among the rules are several restrictions on food. Like Islam, Judaism prohibits the eating of pork because the pig – a scavenger – is held to be unclean. But in addition a *kosher* or 'clean' kitchen in an orthodox Jewish home should contain no shellfish; nor should a Jew prepare meat and dairy products in the kitchen at the same time, or serve them at the same meal.

## THE TONGUE OF THE PROPHET

Arabs today still use the language of the prophet Muhammad – more than 1300 years after his death. Modern written Arabic – and the spoken language of educated Arabs – is not significantly different from Classical Arabic, the language on which the Koran is based; and the Koran was written soon after Muhammad died. Modern colloquial Arabic, however, has diverged from the written language. It appears in numerous dialects which are as different from each other as German and English. So although Muhammad would be able to converse with educated Arabs throughout the Arab world, he would not be understood by or understand the ordinary people.

## THE MONKS WHO NEVER SPOKE

Until the 1960s Trappist monks spent their lives in perpetual silence. But the Second Vatican Council of 1962–9 relaxed this rule and the monks are now allowed to talk during the day. They are still not allowed to talk in the cloisters, however, nor are they permitted to talk at night, except in emergencies. In some monasteries they still sleep in common dormitories on straw mattresses – sometimes home-made – and rise at 3.15am. They are allowed to eat meat only after an illness, but can eat eggs whenever they want to. They have fish twice a week.

The Trappists' proper name is the Cistercians of the Strict Observance. Until 1892 they were based in La Trappe, the abbey from which they get their common name, near Soligny-la-Trappe in northwest France. Today there are about 4000 Trappist monks in more than 60 monasteries scattered throughout the world. They can be recognised by their habit – white with a black 'scapular', a short cloak covering the shoulders.

## ADAM AND . . .

Adam, the first man, is mentioned by name 30 times in the Authorised Version of the Bible. Part of the reason is that the word in Hebrew is not a name; it simply means 'man'. Eve's name, by contrast, appears only four times.

## PILGRIMAGE TO MECCA

Every Muslim is supposed to make the pilgrimage to Muhammad's birthplace, the holy city of Mecca in Saudi Arabia, at least once in his lifetime. A Muslim who completes the pilgrimage – known as the *hajj* – gains the right to add the title 'hajji' to the end of his name. For many Muslims the *hajj* means a journey of thousands of kilometres and the spending of their life savings.

Once they reach the outskirts of Mecca, the pilgrims change into a two-piece white robe. In addition, the women are veiled from head to toe, so that all appear alike and equal in the presence of God.

The sacred Black Stone of the Kaaba shrine must be touched or kissed, and pilgrims can buy pieces of the cloth that covers the stone. The Black Stone, which is set in the wall of the shrine, is thought to be a meteorite dating from prehistoric times. In fact, Mecca was a place of worship centuries before Muhammad was born. Muslims believe that the shrine was built by Abraham and Ishmael in Biblical times as a place in which to worship God.

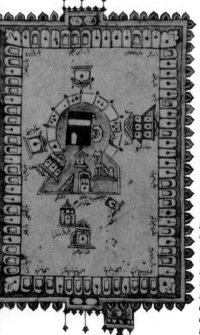

HOLY MAP *Islamic tradition forbids Muslims to portray living creatures. Instead their art has to take other themes, such as texts from the Koran, or, as in this 17th-century tile, a plan of the Kaaba mosque in Mecca.*

## THE HOLY FAST

The Muslim month of Ramadan – the holy month in which the Koran was revealed to Muhammad – is a time of fasting and atonement. During this period no Muslim may drink, eat or smoke between sunrise and sunset. Only the sick and those travelling abroad are exempt. But even they must perform or complete their fast at a later date.

Ramadan, the ninth month of the Muslim year, begins at different times each year because the Muslim calendar is based on the moon. Its practice of self-denial resembles the 40 days of Lent, marking Christ's fasting in the wilderness, and the Jewish Day of Atonement, Yom Kippur, when fasting is ordained.

## THE SIGNIFICANCE OF SEVEN

The number seven appears to have a special significance in religions throughout the world. But it is particularly important in religions of Semitic origin – Judaism, Christianity and Islam – which reckon time in periods of seven days.

The seven deadly sins of Christianity were first compiled by Pope Gregory I around the year 600. They are: Pride, Covetousness, Lust, Envy, Gluttony, Anger and Sloth. Gregory also compiled a less well-known list of the Seven Virtues: Faith, Hope, Charity, Justice, Prudence, Temperance and Fortitude.

The number's religious significance seems to stem from pre-Christian times when it was regarded as a 'sacred' or mystical number. In the 6th century BC, for instance, the followers of the Greek philosopher Pythagoras believed three and four to be lucky numbers – and thought that by adding them together they became even more potent.

## SPEAKING FROM THE THRONE

The Roman Catholic doctrine of papal infallibility – the inability of the pope to err on matters of faith – dates only from the 19th century. It was declared to be dogma only in 1870 by the First Vatican Council and it can act retrospectively. Under this doctrine the pope is deemed to be infallible when speaking *ex cathedra*, meaning 'from his throne'.

Even so, it is not entirely clear how many times the pope has spoken with 'infallibility', and the subject is debated and disputed by Catholics throughout the world. Some maintain that Pope Paul VI's encyclical on birth control in 1968, *Humanae Vitae* (Of Human Life), is an example of papal infallibility. But most Catholic theologians have denied this.

There are two cases, however, which are not disputed. They concern the divinity of the Virgin Mary and are: the doctrine of Immaculate Conception, proclaimed by Pope Pius IX in 1854; and the Assumption (the doctrine that she ascended bodily to heaven), proclaimed by Pope Pius XII in 1950.

## CENTURIES OF PERSECUTION

The Nazis were by no means the first people to persecute the Jews. Jews were expelled from England in 1290 by Edward I and not allowed back until Oliver Cromwell ended the ban in 1650. Jewish communities in southern Italy were almost wiped out between 1290 and 1293. Jews were expelled from France in 1306 by Philip IV. And they were falsely accused – among other things – of poisoning wells and causing the Black Death which killed some 75 million people in Europe and Asia between 1347 and 1351.

In medieval Spain – where Jews were squeezed between the twin zeals of Christianity and Islam – attacks on their communities reached a peak in 1391 and thousands were driven abroad. A century later, in 1492, Spain forced another exodus by giving Jews the choice of being converted to Christianity or deported. Martin Luther, the 16th-century founder of the Protestant Reformation, began by showing tolerance towards Jews. But he later denounced them in violent outbursts. And in the following century Jews were attacked in Germany, Poland and the Ukraine.

In most instances the Jews were unpopular because of their money-lending activities – despite the fact that these activities were largely forced on them by Christian laws forbidding Christians to charge interest on loans and banning Jews from owning land.

## THE SIGN OF THE FISH
Today's born-again Christians often display a sketch of a fish to show their faith. This is not just because the Bible calls the Apostles fishers of men. It is because the letters of the Greek word for fish, *ichthus*, stand for the Greek phrase *Iesous Christos Theou Uios Soter* (Jesus Christ, Son of God, Saviour). The symbol appears in Christian art from the 2nd century AD as a symbol of Christ and the newly baptised.

## THE FORTUNES OF SAINTHOOD
St George, the patron saint of England since the 14th century, was demoted in May 1969 by order of the Vatican. His feast day of April 23 was ruled to be no longer a compulsory Day of Devotion, though it remains an optional one. St Nicholas, better known as Santa Claus, was similarly downgraded. However, they were spared the fate of more than 30 other saints, whose individual feast days were removed from the official Liturgical Calendar of the Roman Catholic Church and replaced by a joint feast day for all of them on New Year's Day. The demoted saints include: St Christopher, patron saint of travellers; St Barbara, patron saint of gunpowder; and St Catherine of Alexandria, who gave her name to the spinning firework, the Catherine wheel.

After a 15-year investigation into their backgrounds, these saints were demoted because of doubts about their ever having existed. However, several saints were added to the Liturgical Calendar in their place – including Sir Thomas More, the 16th-century English Chancellor who was beheaded for refusing to recognise Henry VIII as head of the Church of England.

## THE BIBLE SAID IT FIRST
Some of the English language's most familiar sayings and words come from the Bible – and from the Old Testament in particular. For instance, the word 'scapegoat' was coined by the 16th-century English scholar William Tyndale in his translation of the Old Testament. It comes from Leviticus 16 and refers to a goat which was ritually laden with the sins of the community. Other familiar sayings derived from the Old Testament include: Can the Ethiopian change his skin, or *the leopard his spots?* (Jeremiah 13 verse 23). *Pride goeth* before destruction, and an haughty spirit

*before a fall* (Proverbs 16 verse 18). Come not near to me; for I am *holier than thou* (Isaiah 65 verse 5). And after the earthquake a fire; but the Lord was not in the fire: and after the fire *a still small voice* (I Kings 19 verse 12). He kept him as *the apple of his eye* (Deuteronomy 32 verse 10). And Moses sent them to *spy out the land* of Canaan (Numbers 13 verse 17).

## SWEEPING AWAY THE INSECTS
The religious sect of Jainism, which has some 205 million members in India, developed in the 6th century BC when its disciples broke away from conventional Hinduism. Jains believe that the worst act a person can commit is to take any form of life. Therefore they are not allowed to be butchers or soldiers. The eating of meat and fish is forbidden – and particularly devout Jains do not eat eggs.

Jain priests also gently sweep the paths before them so that they do not step on and kill any insects. The 20th-century Indian leader Gandhi – who was a

PREACHING POSTURE *A stone statue carved in Pakistan in the 2nd century BC shows Buddha in a traditional preaching posture; fingers interlaced and legs crossed in the lotus position. The spot in the middle of his forehead symbolises the so-called 'third eye' of enlightenment. Unlike the adherents of most major religions, Buddhists do not believe in an all-powerful God, nor do they accept the existence of the human soul.*

Hindu – came from an area on the west coast of India steeped in Jainism. He adopted the Jain principle of *ahimsa* – non-violence – and gave it political as well as social significance.

Strict Jains take the principle of non-violence to such extremes that they will risk their own lives rather than harm anything. In the mid-1970s, many Jain householders in the west coast city of Mangalore in India refused to let government health workers spray their homes with DDT as protection against mosquitoes. They preferred to take the chance of catching malaria and other insect-borne diseases rather than countenance the death of the insects.

PEACE TO ALL *Devout Jains, like the 15th-century monk Kalaka shown here, abhor violence in any form, and will avoid harming even insects.*

## HOW HINDUS GOT THEIR NAME

The name Hindu comes originally from the Sanskrit word *sindhu*, meaning 'river'. Persian settlers who moved in about 1500 BC into the main river valley in what is now Pakistan derived the Persian word *Hind* from Sanskrit. In time the land beyond the river became known as Hind (from which India gets its name), and the people who lived there became known as Hindus. The same word was also the source of the modern name for the river along which the Persians settled. It became known as the Indus.

## DARK AS A CLOUD

The modern religious sect of Hari Krishna – whose shaven-headed disciples can be seen on city streets throughout the world – takes its name from the Hindu god Krishna. The name Krishna means 'dark as a cloud', and the deity is always depicted with blue or black skin. Hari is another name for the god Vishnu, whose eighth incarnation on earth was as Krishna.

By tradition, Krishna was raised by foster parents near Agra in northern India. He grew up to be an amorous, fun-loving young man and he is supposed on one occasion to have stolen the clothes of some milkmaids as they bathed naked in a river. He became renowned for his romantic adventures and is usually depicted playing a flute and surrounded by adoring and beautiful maidens.

His weak spot was his heel, and he was fatally wounded in the back of the foot by a hunter who mistook him for a deer. This parallel with the fate of the Greek hero Achilles is probably the result of the Greek influence in India after the invasion of Alexander the Great in 326 BC.

## MEN OF THE LION

One of the world's youngest religions is Sikhism, which stems from the beginning of the 16th century. It aims to unite Muslim and Hindu thinking, and believes that the one reality is God – although he may be known by various names. The Sikhs later clashed with the Mughal emperors, who ruled much of India from the early 16th to the mid-18th centuries and who persecuted those who were not Muslims like themselves. In 1699 the Sikh leader Govind Singh organised a fighting group in which the men took the name of Singh, meaning 'lion'.

Since then every orthodox male Sikh has taken the same name, and has followed five symbolic rules of appearance which help to establish Sikh identity. These rules are known as the Five Ks because the central words all begin with that letter in Punjabi. The rules are: to keep his hair (*kesh*) uncut – hence the Sikh turban to keep it tidy (though the turban itself is not required by the five rules); to keep a comb (*kangha*) in his hair; to wear shorts (*kaccha*) under his trousers; to wear a steel bangle (*kara*); and to carry a short dagger (*kirpan*).

The uncut but tidy hair, and the comb, symbolise the Sikh's liking for moderation and compromise. The shorts and steel bangle represent his moral restraint and chastity. And the dagger – today, usually a tiny and purely ornamental blade attached to the comb – stands for his readiness to take up arms in the defence of the faith.

## SONG OF THE LORD

Hinduism's most important sacred text is the *Bhagavad Gita*, or 'Song of the Lord' – a poem of about 700 verses. It is just one section of the *Mahabharata* ('Great Epic of the Bharata Dynasty'), a work of 100,000 Sanskrit couplets, which is the longest poem ever written. It was composed between 200 BC and AD 200.

## TOWERS OF SILENCE

Hindus and Buddhists traditionally burn the bodies of their dead on funeral pyres – and Muslims bury their dead. For Eastern followers of the ancient Persian religion of Zoroastrianism, however, neither method is permissible because both fire and earth are regarded as holy – and they cannot be 'polluted' by such 'unclean' acts. So Zoroastrians place their corpses on platforms known as Towers of Silence. The circular towers are built on high ground and the bodies are exposed to the air – allowing them to be quickly devoured by vultures.

## BENEATH THE BANYAN TREE

Buddhism was not founded by a person called Buddha. The word itself means merely 'the Awakened One'. It was the title given to Siddhartha Gautama, a Hindu of noble birth. He was brought up in the foothills of the Himalayas on what is now the India-Nepal border. According to legend he led a life of luxury as a young man and in about 530 BC – when he was married with a baby son – he left his family and wandered in search of spiritual enlightenment.

He found it six years later after meditating for a day and a night beneath a banyan or fig tree beside a tributary of the River Ganges. From then on he devoted his time to the teaching of his new religion – Buddhism. But sacred though he is, Gautama is only *a* Buddha, not *the* Buddha. Buddhists believe that there were other Buddhas before him – who also received enlightenment beneath the banyan tree – and that there is another Buddha still to come, who will continue his work.

## CONFUCIUS'S GOLDEN RULE

Confucius, the Chinese philosopher and social reformer who lived between about 551 and 479 BC, was the first person to advocate what has come to be called the Golden Rule of ethics: 'Do to others as you would be done by.' This was the key to the philosophy named after him, which was a moral and ethical code as well as a religion.

His real name was Kong Zi ('The Master Kung'), and the Latin form of his name was bestowed by Jesuit missionaries centuries after his death. Confucius worked as a minor civil servant and teacher and he stressed the virtues of truthfulness, loyalty, learning – and moderation in eating and drinking. He believed in the modest, regular life, and urged his followers not to be extremists. He considered war to be one of the greatest evils and urged people to negotiate and make compromises rather than fight.

About a week before he died he told a disciple of a prophetic dream he had experienced. He had learnt, he said, that 'the great mountain must crumble; the strong beam must break; the wise man must wither away like a plant'. If by 'wise man' he meant himself, his prophecy took more than 2000 years to come true.

In 1907 he became officially one of the main gods of China – on a par with other deities of heaven and earth. But as a defender of traditional values he has been regarded as a conservative, and his teachings officially discouraged since the communists came to power in 1949. Indeed, the former leader of Red China, Mao Zedong (Mao Tse-t'ung), stated that from the age of eight he had hated Confucius.

## YIN AND YANG

Disciples of Taoism – the Chinese mystical religion which advocates a life of passivity – believe that each individual's personality is a mixture of two opposite sets of qualities: Yin and Yang. Yin is feminine, mother, soft, wet, dark; Yang is masculine, father, strong, dry, light. The contrasts of Yin and Yang – and their coming together as one – are thought to be responsible for all that happens in the world.

The principle of Yin and Yang is depicted by a circle divided into halves, one dark the other light – and each half is shaped like a raindrop with a long tail. The symbol decorates many Chinese buildings, banners, pieces of crockery and ornaments.

## THE GODS OF A HINDU

In every devout Hindu home there is a shrine with images of one or more of the thousands of gods worshipped. The two major gods are Shiva and Vishnu, and most of the great Hindu temples belong to the Shaiva cult which worships Shiva, or the Vaishnava cult which worships Vishnu.

Shiva is a god of violence whose frenzied dancing – sometimes shown as taking place within a circle of fire on the body of a dwarf demon – symbolises the eternal cycle of creation and destruction. He is portrayed with a blue neck caused by his holding in his throat poisonous scum thrown up, according to Hindu mythology, when the oceans were churned and threatened to destroy mankind.

Shiva's consort – the fierce, blood-drinking goddess Kali – is worshipped as a leading divinity by most orthodox Hindus.

Vishnu, the preserver, is a kindly god who protects those who worship him, restores health and banishes bad luck. He is said to come to earth periodically as an *avatar* – an incarnation in various forms – to help mankind at times of crisis. His consort is Lakshmi, the goddess of good fortune. Another major god is Brahma, the creator, whose consort Sarasvati is the patroness of arts and learning.

### Limbs of power

Among other gods who are widely worshipped are two of Shiva's sons: Ganesh and Karttikeya. Ganesh, the elephant god, is the bringer of good fortune. Karttikeya, a god of war, is usually depicted with six heads and 12 arms – a sign of his power. Other popular gods include: Sitala, to whom mothers traditionally pray to protect their children from disease; Rama, the personification of reason, virtue and chivalry; Hanuman, the monkey god who is revered as a guardian spirit; and Krishna, the 8th *avatar* of Vishnu, who is depicted with blue or black skin and who is honoured for his skills as a warrior and lover.

WAY OF LIFE *The contemplative Chinese philosophy of Taoism – whose central figure, Lao Zi, is shown here with his disciples – holds that man can overcome all difficulties by following the natural path of life, in much the same way that water effortlessly finds its own course. Lao Zi is believed to have written Taoism's central book, the* Tao-Te Ching *('The Classic of the Way and its Virtue') in the 6th century BC.*

# Philosophers and philosophy

## WHO SAID WHAT

**Aristotle** (384–322 BC) 'Man is by nature a political animal.'

**Jeremy Bentham** (1748–1832) 'The greatest happiness of the greatest number is the foundation of morals and legislation.'

**Cicero** (106–43 BC) 'The good of the people is the chief law.'

**René Descartes** (1596–1650) 'Cogito ergo sum' (I think, therefore I am).

**Friedrich Engels** (1820–95) 'The state is not "abolished", it withers away.'

**Georg Hegel** (1770–1831) 'What experience and history teach is this – that people and governments have never learned anything from history, or acted on principles deduced from it.'

**Thomas Hobbes** (1588–1679) 'The life of man (in a state of nature) is solitary, poor, nasty, brutish, and short.'

**Immanuel Kant** (1724–1804) 'Happiness is not an ideal of reason but of imagination.'

**John Locke** (1632–1704) 'No man's knowledge here can go beyond his experience.'

**Karl Marx** (1818–83) 'A spectre is haunting Europe – the spectre of Communism.'
'The workers have nothing to lose but their chains. They have a world to gain. Workers of the world unite!'
'Religion is the opium of the people.'
'The class struggle necessarily leads to the dictatorship of the proletariat.'

**John Stuart Mill** (1806–73) 'Liberty consists in doing what one desires.'

**Friedrich Nietzsche** (1844–1900) 'I teach you the Superman. Man is something to be surpassed.'

**Blaise Pascal** (1623–62) 'Man is only a reed, the weakest thing in nature, but he is a thinking reed.'

**Jean-Jacques Rousseau** (1712–78) 'Man is born free, and everywhere he is in chains.'

**Bertrand Russell** (1872–1970) 'It is undesirable to believe a proposition when there is no ground whatever for supposing it true.'

**Seneca** (about 4 BC–AD 65) 'Even while they teach, men learn.'

**Socrates** (about 470–399 BC) 'The unexamined life is not worth living.'

**Henry David Thoreau** (1817–62) 'It takes two to speak the truth – one to speak, the other to hear.'

**Voltaire** (1694–1778) 'If God did not exist, it would be necessary to invent Him.'
'I disapprove of what you say, but I will defend to the death your right to say it.'

## PHILOSOPHER WHO PUT NOTHING ON PAPER

Although the Athenian thinker Socrates (about 470–399 BC) is regarded as the father of Western philosophy, he never committed his ideas to paper. Our only knowledge of him comes from the writings of his Greek contemporaries – Aristophanes, Xenophon and particularly his pupil, Plato.

Socrates appears as the main character in Plato's *Dialogues*. Most scholars believe, however, that in the book Plato was not reporting Socrates' views, merely using him as a mouthpiece for his own.

Condemned to death for impiety and corrupting the youth of Athens, Socrates continued to discuss philosophy with his friends and pupils in jail. He refused to take advantage of their offers to help him escape, electing instead to drink the lethal hemlock handed to him by his executioners.

## THINKER WITHOUT CREDENTIALS

David Hume (1711–76), the Scottish thinker now recognised as one of the founders of empiricism – the doctrine that experience, not reason or God, is the supreme touchstone of truth – was never able to teach philosophy because he lacked the proper academic credentials. Unable to secure the chair of philosophy at either Edinburgh or Glasgow universities, Hume worked as a general's secretary on a military expedition to Brittany and on a diplomatic mission to Turin, and as keeper of the Advocates Library in Edinburgh.

His major works, such as the *Treatise of Human*

*Nature* and *An Enquiry concerning the Human Understanding*, were largely ignored during his lifetime, but later had an important influence on thinkers such as the Englishman Jeremy Bentham and the German Immanuel Kant (1724–1804).

## LASTING LEGACY

One of the major influences on Western philosophy has been the Greek philosopher Aristotle (384–322 BC). Personal tutor to Alexander the Great and later his protégé, Aristotle established a philosophical school, called the Lyceum, outside Athens in 336 BC. This wide-ranging research centre bequeathed to the world numerous academic disciplines, including logic, ethics, physics, rhetoric, metaphysics, economics and psychology.

## TYCOON'S SON WHO TURNED GARDENER

Despite a wealthy background, the Austrian philosopher Ludwig Wittgenstein (1889–1951) preferred to live a simple existence. The son of a steel tycoon, Wittgenstein gave away the fortune he inherited and

divided his time between an active academic life and working as a schoolmaster, gardener and hospital porter. His book *Tractatus Logico-Philosophicus*, published in 1921, took as its basic axiom that 'all philosophy is a critique of language', and attempted to construct a language system which was as precise and logical as mathematics. Although Wittgenstein became a teacher of philosophy at Cambridge University from 1929 to 1947, he never abandoned his taste for the simple life. He made a habit of wearing open-necked shirts – at a time when most teachers and students wore ties – and furnished his college rooms with nothing more luxurious than deck chairs.

## SEEING IS BELIEVING

The Irish philosopher Bishop George Berkeley (1685–1753) offered a startling theory to prove the existence of God. Stating that no material objects existed unless they were perceived by the senses, Berkeley claimed that objects continued to exist when they were not being observed by man only because they were being continuously observed by God. Berkeley's beliefs were lampooned two centuries later in a pair of limericks by the English theologian Ronald Knox (1888–1957):

> There was a young man who said: 'God
> Must think it exceedingly odd
> If he finds that this tree
> Continues to be
> When there's no one about in the Quad.'

To which the reply was:

> 'Dear Sir, Your astonishment's odd
> I am always about in the Quad;
> And that's why the tree
> Will continue to be,
> Since observed by Yours faithfully, GOD.'

Despite the criticism, Berkeley's reputation as a major thinker spread across the Atlantic. The US town of Berkeley, home of part of the giant University of California, is named after him.

## DESTITUTE ECONOMIST

Karl Marx (1818–83), who revolutionised thinking about money more than anyone else who has ever lived, was hopeless at acquiring it himself. Shortly after arriving in London as a political exile from Europe in 1849, Marx and his family were evicted from their rooms in Chelsea for non-payment of rent, losing most of their possessions in the process.

From 1851 to 1856 the Marx family rented rooms in Soho, living in such poverty that two of their children died. Although Marx worked as a journalist

A DOG'S LIFE *A Roman sculpture of the 1st century AD records the meeting of Alexander the Great with the Greek philosopher Diogenes (about 400–325 BC). Diogenes – who lived for a time in an earthenware tub (not, as is often claimed, in a barrel) in the grounds of an Athenian temple – is said to have been asked if there was anything he wanted. He replied: 'Yes, get out of my sunlight!' Impressed by such directness, the conqueror is said to have remarked to him: 'Were I not Alexander, I would wish to be Diogenes.' Diogenes, who dressed like a beggar, lived so austerely that he was nicknamed 'the dog'. As a result, his disciples came to be known sneeringly as Cynics, from the Greek* kunikos, *meaning 'dog-like' – an insult they accepted proudly, saying they were watchdogs of morality. On his death, Diogenes asked to be buried like a dog: thrown into a ditch and covered with rubbish. Instead he was given a splendid funeral at Corinth – and, in memory of his nickname, his tomb was topped with a carving of a dog.*

for the *New York Daily Tribune*, he was unable to earn enough to feed his family. They were saved from starvation only by the generosity of Marx's friend Friedrich Engels, who gave Marx part of his income.

After inheriting £120 from his wife's mother in 1856, Marx moved his family to a house in Kentish Town, North London, where he wrote most of the basic material for *Das Kapital*, the first volume of which was published in 1867.

## DEATH WISH
Jeremy Bentham (1748–1832), the English Utilitarian philosopher, had very decided views on what should happen to bodies after death. He even wrote a book on the subject – *Auto-Icon, or the Uses of the Dead to the Living* – in which he suggested that 'if all bodies were embalmed every man might be his own statue'.

Bentham, who had been one of the founders of University College, London, bequeathed his body to the college so that it could be used for medical research. Interpreting Bentham's will in the widest possible sense, the college authorities dressed the carefully preserved corpse in a suit of Bentham's best clothes and placed it in a glass case. Thus for many years the deceased Bentham presided over meetings of the college committee – and was always described in the minutes as 'present, but not voting'.

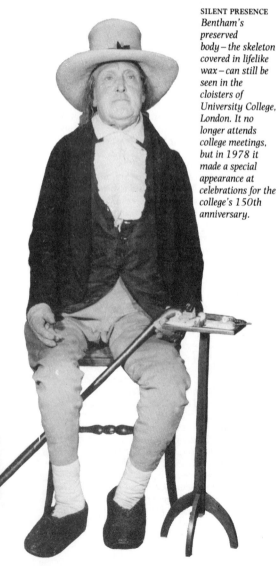

SILENT PRESENCE
*Bentham's preserved body – the skeleton covered in lifelike wax – can still be seen in the cloisters of University College, London. It no longer attends college meetings, but in 1978 it made a special appearance at celebrations for the college's 150th anniversary.*

## HOTHOUSE EDUCATION
The 19th century's most influential English liberal thinker, John Stuart Mill (1806–73), never went to school. Instead he was given a highly intensive education at home by his father, James – an economist, historian and disciple of Jeremy Bentham, whose Utilitarian ideas John Stuart Mill later embraced.

Mill started learning Greek at the age of three, Latin, algebra and geometry when he was eight and logic at the age of 12. By the time he was 14, Mill had digested most of the Greek and Roman classics in their original languages. Although Mill's hothouse education helped him to become one of Britain's leading scholars, it seems to have exacted a heavy psychological price as well: Mill suffered a nervous breakdown when he was 20 years old.

## ALL THINGS IN MODERATION
The Athenian philosopher Epicurus (341–270 BC) – from whose name is derived the word 'epicure', meaning a high-living gourmet – was actually an advocate of moderation. Epicurus felt that pleasure was preferable to pain, but warned that over-gratification of physical desire led to greater pain than pleasure. Temperance, courage and justice were, he said, the qualities that promoted an enjoyable life.

His philosophy, known as hedonism, acquired its modern sense of wallowing in idle pleasure when a distorted form of it was adopted by wealthy pleasure-seekers in France in the 17th and 18th centuries and used to justify their self-indulgent lifestyle.

## PIONEER DOCTOR
The Greek physician and philosopher Hippocrates (460–380 BC) – often regarded by scholars as the father of modern medicine and the man after whom the doctors' Hippocratic Oath is named – knew less about the workings of the human body than most 20th-century schoolchildren. He believed that veins carried air, not blood, and claimed that illness was caused by vapours secreted by undigested food from unsuitable diets. The vapours seeped into the body, he thought, producing disease. Hippocrates' modern reputation stems from his then radical but now widely accepted view that medical treatment had to take account of the patient's body as a whole, not just the affected part. The same illness, he asserted, might require different treatments depending on the age, condition and lifestyle of the patient.

## DEMOLISHED BY A NOVEL
The darkly comic novel *Candide*, by the French writer Voltaire, helped to demolish the elaborate philosophy of a German thinker, Gottfried Wilhelm von Leibniz.

Leibniz (1646–1716) developed his complicated theories in an attempt to reconcile the existence of God with the presence of evil. He concluded in his *Théodicé*, published in 1710, that since the universe had been created by God, it was 'the best of all possible worlds', and that all was for the best in it.

But his system foundered on the twin rocks of *Candide* and the Lisbon earthquake of 1755, in which about 60,000 people were killed. *Candide*, published in 1759, scathingly caricatured the disciples of Leibniz in the ludicrously optimistic character of Dr Pangloss. Leibniz's conclusions were also undermined by the reaction to the quake which struck the Portuguese capital on the morning of November 1, 1755. Most scholars found it difficult to reconcile Leibniz's devout views with the scale of the disaster – and the fact that many of the victims died in the rubble of the churches in which they had been celebrating All Saints Day.

**VICTORIAN BESTSELLER**
Charles Darwin's evolutionary masterpiece, known as *The Origin of Species*, was a bestseller. Despite its length and technical nature – its full title read *On the Origin of Species, by means of Natural Selection, or the Preservation of Favoured Races in the Struggle for Life* – it sold out on publication day in 1859, and by 1872 had run through six more editions.

*DOWN FROM THE FAMILY TREE A terrified flunkey announces the arrival of a gorilla in a 19th-century* Punch *cartoon lampooning Darwin's theories.*

# MAJOR SCHOOLS OF THOUGHT

**ARISTOTELIANISM**
A philosophy originated by the Greek thinker Aristotle (384 – 322 BC), who stressed that virtue was a mean or middle way between opposing extremes. He classified everything in a 'ladder of nature', with inanimate matter at the bottom and man at the top.

**CYNICISM**
Originated by the Greek philosopher Diogenes (about 400 – 325 BC), who advocated a simple, self-sufficient life as the best way of achieving happiness. His scorn for mankind gave rise to the present meaning of cynicism.

**DIALECTIC**
Method of discovering the truth by proceeding from an assertion, or thesis, to a denial, or antithesis, and reconciling the two through a synthesis, which becomes in its turn a new thesis. For instance, mankind is basically good (thesis); mankind is basically bad (antithesis); man is both good and bad (synthesis). The dialectical system was devised by the German philosopher Georg Hegel (1770 – 1831) and later used by Karl Marx (1818 – 83) to develop his theory of Dialectical Materialism.

**EMPIRICISM**
Seventeenth-century British philosophy that all knowledge is derived from sensory experience, by observing and experimenting. Proponents included Francis Bacon (1561 – 1626), John Locke (1632 – 1704) and David Hume (1711 – 76).

**EPICUREANISM**
Philosophy originated by the Athenian thinker Epicurus (341 – 270 BC), who argued that good was pleasure and that evil was pain. But he also stressed the importance of virtue and moderation in all things.

**EXISTENTIALISM**
Philosophical doctrine which emphasises the freedom of human beings to make choices – and to assume responsibility for the consequences – in a world in which there are no absolute values outside man himself. Proponents include the Dane Sören Kierkegaard (1813 – 55), the German Martin Heidegger (1889 – 1976), and the Frenchmen Jean-Paul Sartre (1905 – 80) and Albert Camus (1913 – 60).

**HUMANISM**
Renaissance philosophy, revived in the 20th century, which rejects belief in all forms of the supernatural.

**IDEALISM**
Doctrine that matter is an illusion and that the only reality is that which exists mentally. Proponents included the German philosopher Georg Hegel (1770 – 1831) and the Irish philosopher Bishop George Berkeley (1685 – 1753).

**LOGICAL POSITIVISM**
School of 20th-century thinking which tried to base knowledge on sense-experience – that is, observations – governed by scientific principles. Alternatively

called the Vienna Circle, after its city of origin. Leaders included the German Moritz Schlick (1882 – 1936) and the Austrian mathematician Kurt Gödel (1906 – 78).

**MARXISM**
Nineteenth-century philosophy, sometimes called Dialectical Materialism, which interprets history as a struggle between opposing economic forces. According to its originator, the German thinker Karl Marx (1818 – 83), the ultimate result of this struggle is the emergence of a classless society: Communism. The German philosopher Friedrich Engels (1820 – 95) helped to develop the philosophy

**PRAGMATISM**
Nineteenth-century American doctrine that the meaning or value of an idea lies only in its practical consequence: what its leading proponent Charles Pierce (1839 – 1914) called 'its bearing upon the conduct of life'. Other proponents included William James (1842 – 1910) and John Dewey (1859 – 1952).

**PREDESTINATION**
Doctrine that the events of everyone's life are determined beforehand by God, and that free will is an illusion. It was introduced by St Augustine (354 – 430) to the early Christian Church.

**RATIONALISM**
Seventeenth-century European philosophy that reason is the only true source of knowledge. The opposite of empiricism. Main proponents included the Dutch thinker Benedict Spinoza (1632 – 77) and the German philosopher Gottfried von Leibniz (1646 – 1716).

**SCEPTICISM**
Greek doctrine that everything is open to doubt. Later adopted by the French philosopher René Descartes (1596 – 1650) who – as a starting point – doubted everything except the workings of his own mind.

**STOICISM**
Philosophy that virtue – not honour, or family or possessions – is the only worthy aim in life, and that a virtuous man can achieve happiness however adverse his circumstances. Proponents included the Greek thinker Zeno of Citium (about 334 – 262 BC) and the Roman statesman Seneca (about 4 BC – AD 65).

**TRANSCENDENTALISM**
Nineteenth-century doctrine that philosophy must extend beyond the limits of experience. Proponents included the American writer and naturalist Henry David Thoreau (1817 – 62) and the American essayist and poet Ralph Waldo Emerson (1803 – 82).

**UTILITARIANISM**
The belief that good consists in creating the greatest happiness for the greatest number of people. Main proponents included the British philosophers Jeremy Bentham (1748 – 1832), James Mill (1773 – 1836), John Stuart Mill (1806 – 73) and Henry Sidgwick (1838 – 1900).

# Spies and spying

## OPENING THE MAILS

Alexander the Great (356 – 323 BC), the Macedonian who conquered much of Asia in his twenties, is credited with inventing a spying technique that is still widely used today. During his campaigns in the Middle East and Asia between 334 and 326 BC, Alexander gauged his officers' loyalty by encouraging them to write letters home. He then intercepted the mail to discover and eliminate potential malcontents.

## FIFTH COLUMN

One of the earliest known spying coups occurred in 539 BC when the Persian leader Cyrus the Great (ruled 559 – 530 BC) recruited secretly a force of dissident Babylonian priests to help him defeat Belshazzar, the ruler of Babylon. Although the nature of the priests' help is not known, Babylonian documents show that Cyrus's soldiers were able to enter the city without having to fight their way in.

## TUDOR SPYMASTER

Sir Francis Drake, the English naval commander who played bowls during the approach of the Spanish Armada in 1588, could afford to be nonchalant because the English already knew of the enemy invasion plans. The English intelligence was provided by a secret service organisation created by Sir Francis Walsingham. Sir Francis, one of Elizabeth I's leading advisers, recruited agents in England and sent them to operate as 'deep cover' spies in enemy territory. One spy, Anthony Standen, styled himself as a courtier named Pompeo Pellegrini and penetrated the entourage of the Marquis de Santa Cruz, Grand Admiral of the Spanish fleet. By intercepting letters between Santa Cruz and Philip II of Spain, Standen was able to warn his master of the preparations for the Armada in 1587 – months before it sailed to defeat.

## CAUGHT BY ACCIDENT

Between 1945 and 1972, Britain's security services captured only one Soviet spy without American help – and even that was by accident. In April 1952 an MI5 surveillance expert was on his way home for lunch when, as he got off a bus in Kingston, London, he spotted a Soviet diplomat talking to a young man. The unknown man was trailed and found to be a 24-year-old radio operator named William Marshall, who worked for Britain's Diplomatic Wireless Service, handling secret radio transmissions to and from British embassies around the world. Three months later, Marshall was caught red-handed selling secrets to the Russian diplomat and was jailed for five years.

## CRACKING THE ENIGMA

Fifteen thousand people kept the secret of one of Britain's most important intelligence advantages during the Second World War. The 15,000 were employed by the British Secret Intelligence Service, MI6, at Bletchley Park, a Bedfordshire country estate, monitoring and decoding Germany's most secret communications. At the heart of their achievement was the German Enigma code machine and . . . a simple weather report.

Each morning at dawn, a German double agent prepared – with the help of the British Security Service, MI5 – a routine weather report. The report was trans-mitted to German Abwehr chiefs in Hamburg, then coded on the Enigma machine and sent on to Berlin.

The codes used on the Enigma were regarded by the Germans as unbreakable and, as an extra safeguard, the codes were altered each day. In fact all the precautions were useless. By monitoring the coded signal to Berlin and comparing it with the original weather report, the Bletchley code-breakers were able to work out the Enigma code for the day within a few hours of dawn. The rest of the day's messages could then be deciphered almost as soon as they were transmitted.

## SAVAGE PENALTY

Jail is one of the lesser risks a spy runs. In the late 1950s Colonel Peter Popov, an officer in Russia's military intelligence service, the GRU, was discovered to be a double agent working for the West. His penalty – later leaked and officially recorded as a dreadful warning to Western intelligence agencies – was savage. He was tossed live into a furnace in front of an audience of his GRU colleagues in 1959.

## FROM RUSSIA WITH DEATH

SMERSH, the Soviet spy organisation made familiar by James Bond's creator, Ian Fleming, is a real KGB department. Named after its motto, *Smert Shpionen* ('Death to Spies'), SMERSH has the job of eliminating enemies of the Soviet Union who live abroad. Its most important victim was Leon Trotsky, the former Bolshevik leader in the 1917 Revolution, who was murdered in Mexico in 1940.

## THE SQUAD THAT FOXED A SATELLITE

During the battle for the Falklands in 1982, Britain's Royal Air Force claimed that pinpoint bombing of Port Stanley's only runway had effectively closed the airport to Argentina's air force. This view was supported by sophisticated aerial photographs taken by US satellites which showed what appeared to be several deep bomb craters. After the fighting ended, however, it was discovered that a handful of Argentine soldiers, equipped only with buckets and spades, had fooled the most advanced military equipment simply by constructing convincing-looking crater walls of loose earth under cover of darkness. The bogus craters were left in view during the day for the satellites to photograph, then cleared away after dark. By this simple and cheap expedient the Argentine forces were able to fly in supplies and reinforcements every night, right up to the final surrender.

## A SPY NAMED CICERO

A British ambassador's early morning bath led to one of the most notorious espionage episodes of the Second World War. For it was while Sir Hughe Knatchbull-Hugessen – His Majesty's ambassador in Ankara, the capital of neutral Turkey – was soaking in his tub that his Turkish valet, Elyesa Bazna, made a wax impression of the key to the top-secret documents box which stood on the desk in Sir Hughe's study. It was October 1943 – a time when Turkey was debating whether to join in the fight against Hitler – and by the end of the month Bazna had copied 52 documents, which he sold to Nazi officials in Ankara.

The Germans gave Bazna the code name of Cicero, after the Roman orator and statesman (106 – 43 BC) noted for his great eloquence. Bazna continued his

# INTELLIGENCE AGENCIES AROUND THE WORLD

**CIA (United States)** Founded in 1947 by President Harry Truman. Known to staff as 'the company'. Headquarters at Langley, Virginia, just outside Washington DC. Second centre at Maclean, Virginia. Estimated to employ 25,000 staff, mostly analysts openly engaged on routine work. Covert work is by a smaller nucleus employed in the Plans Division which runs CIA sections – called 'stations' – in US embassies. CIA stands for Central Intelligence Agency.

**MI6 (Britain)** Founded in 1909 and known to staff as 'the firm'. Also called the British Secret Intelligence Service. Based in Westminster Bridge Road, London, and responsible for gathering intelligence outside Britain. MI stands for Military Intelligence.

**MI5 (Britain)** Also founded in 1909 and originally called the Special Intelligence Bureau. Known to staff as 'the office'. Based at Curzon Street in London and responsible for internal security and counter-intelligence in Britain.

**KGB (Soviet Union)** Known as 'the centre'. The Soviet Committee of State Security (KGB) was founded in 1953, the latest in a line of Russian intelligence organisations stretching back to the 16th century. Based in Moscow with headquarters at Dzerzhinsky Square. Employs an estimated 200,000 staff – including 70,000 censors – and is thought to have recruited more than 750,000 non-Russian agents abroad. Eighty per cent of Soviet embassy staff around the world are thought to be KGB agents. Responsible for internal security and, with its military counterpart, the GRU, for overseas espionage.

**SDECE (France)** The *Service de Documentation Exterieure et Contre-Espionage* (SDECE) was created in 1958. Headquarters in eastern Paris at Boulevard Mortier. The building is known to staff as *'la piscine'* because of a nearby public swimming pool. Responsible for gathering overseas intelligence. Estimated to employ 4000 people.

**MOSSAD (Israel)** Founded in 1950. Based in Tel Aviv, its headquarters is moved to new premises at irregular but frequent intervals for security reasons. Estimated to employ about 1200 people, it is responsible for overseas espionage. The name Mossad is an abbreviation for Hebrew words meaning Institution for Intelligence and Special Assignments.

## HOW THE CIA BEGAN

America's Central Intelligence Agency owes its existence to the British. Before the Second World War, the USA had no centralised intelligence organisation. However, in 1940, as a result of British pressure, President Franklin Roosevelt authorised the creation of the Office of Strategic Services (OSS) to co-ordinate the nation's spying activities. The OSS was officially disbanded after the war, but many of its personnel remained in government service and provided the nucleus for the CIA when it was established by President Harry Truman in 1947.

## MATA HARI: THE SPY WHO WASN'T

Mata Hari, who was executed by firing squad in France in October 1917, is probably the most famous spy of all time. She is renowned for her beauty, her numerous military lovers, her provocative Oriental dancing, and, above all, her espionage. Yet in fact she was not attractive, Oriental, talented or even a spy. Mata Hari was the stage name adopted by a plump, middle-aged Dutch divorcée named Mrs Margaretha MacLeod who had left her alcoholic Scottish husband in the East Indies (now Indonesia) and opted to become a dancer in Europe.

The evidence of her alleged espionage on behalf of the German Kaiser is based merely on her being mistaken for a known German agent, Clara Benedix, by the British in November 1916. In that month Mrs MacLeod was arrested in Falmouth, Cornwall, on board the SS *Hollandia* while she was on her way to Holland. The police released her when they realised the mistake. Later, she was arrested in France and charged with having been in contact with German intelligence officers in Madrid – and at her trial in Paris her lurid lifestyle was used to damning effect. It was only in 1963, when the secret files relating to her case were released, that the legend was reassessed.

INNOCENT VICTIM *Most historians now accept that, far from being a spy, Mata Hari (photographed here at the height of her dancing career) was simply an innocent scapegoat – shot because the French government wanted to cover up its military ineptitude by manufacturing an all-powerful ring of German agents.*

work as a spy until April 1944, by which time Turkey had decided not to enter the war. He had amassed some £300,000 from his activities – and hid the money under the floorboards of his bedroom in the British embassy. He then handed in his notice to Sir Hughe and dropped out of sight, taking his fortune with him. At the end of the Second World War Bazna resurfaced in Istanbul with the idea of building a luxury hotel for tourists. It was then he discovered that he, too, had been betrayed. The money the Germans had given him turned out to be worthless forgeries. The man who had sold so many secrets had finally been 'sold' himself.

## OF MOLES AND MEN

The word 'mole' for a long-term agent who burrows into a rival intelligence agency was devised by an author. British thriller writer and former MI6 officer John Le Carré (real name David Cornwell) coined the term in 1974 in his spy novel *Tinker, Tailor, Soldier, Spy* – and the word was later adopted by real spies.

# Fashion – the pursuit of beauty

## LOOKING LIKE A MILLION

The costliest dress ever made was priced at £1 million – a high-waisted and embroidered white muslin evening gown decorated with 516 diamonds. An armoured car took it from the makers, Schiaparelli, to a fashion show at the Ritz, Paris, in 1977. Shoes extravagant enough to match it could not be found, so the model wore it barefoot. The dress was eventually bought for an Arab princess whose identity has not been revealed; and, according to the makers, she still has it.

## FEATHER-FOOTED

Feather-light shoes created by New York designer Yanturni in the 1920s took up to three years to make, and he refused even to make a start on a pair without a $1000 deposit. He made plaster casts of clients' feet and moulded the shoes around the contours.

Yanturni made 300 pairs for the Spanish-American hostess Rita de Acosta Lydig. Some were made with 12th-century velvet, some of lace appliqué, others of brocade or gold and silver metal tissue. Mrs Lydig collected violins so that Yanturni could use the delicate wood to make his shoe-trees. Designer Cecil Beaton once claimed that a Yanturni shoe, complete with its tree, weighed no more than an ostrich feather.

## THE TROUSER REVOLUTION

Only at the start of the 19th century did fashion-conscious men begin wearing trousers in preference to knee-breeches. Tsar Alexander I of Russia regarded trousers as subversive, probably because they were worn by extremists of the French Revolution. In 1807, Alexander ordered his troops to stop all carriages – and any man inside wearing trousers had them instantly cut off at the knee.

## FRAGRANT THOUGHT

French actress Leslie Caron, while a small girl, had the idea of boiling her underclothes in a tub of perfume to give them lasting fragrance. It worked a treat. Leslie, however, had no need to bother about the economic impracticability of her idea. The tubful of scent cost her nothing – her family owned the perfume house of Caron.

## COSMETICS THROUGH THE AGES

**7500 BC** Egyptian shepherds and hunters in the Nile valley used oil crushed from castor beans to protect their skin from the sun.

**3500** Women in Egypt and Mesopotamia used henna dyes to colour their feet and hands. Eye shadow called kohl, made from lead ore, antimony and malachite, was believed to drive away danger.

**1370** Queen Nefertiti of Egypt painted her fingernails and toenails ruby red – a colour forbidden to all but royalty.

**750** Greek women dyed their hair black and whitened their skins with lead powder.

**150** Romans, new masters of the Mediterranean, painted gold from saffron around their eyes and used wood ash to blacken their eyelids.

**50** Cleopatra, Queen of Egypt, rouged her cheeks with red ochre; she also painted her upper eyelids blue-black and lower lids green.

**AD 10** Ovid, the Roman poet, wrote the first book on cosmetics. He recommended a face pack of barley-bean flour, egg and mashed narcissus bulbs to promote smooth skin.

**65** The Roman emperor Nero and his wife, Poppaea, used lead and chalk to whiten their faces, rouged their cheeks and put kohl around their eyes.

**200** The Greek physician Galen mixed water, beeswax and olive oil into a cream. When rubbed on the face, the water evaporated, cooling the skin. Modern cold cream is virtually the same mixture.

**1580** Queen Elizabeth dyed her hair red, plucked her eyebrows and whitened her face. She was the first English queen to see herself in a clear glass mirror. She banned mirrors from court as she aged.

**1660** In Restoration England, women painted their faces and decorated them with black patches shaped as stars, crescents and suns. The fashion grew from a trick used by the Duchess of Newcastle to cover her blotches.

**1700** Powder rooms were created for fashionable British men and women. They applied powder to their hair, wigs and faces. Smooth skin was the rage. In bed, women put oiled cloths on their foreheads and wore gloves to prevent wrinkles.

**1840** Make-up went out of fashion in Britain. The Victorian ideal demanded peaches-and-cream skin and a small, pink mouth.

**1886** David McConnell went knocking on doors in the USA to sell anthologies of Shakespeare . . . and accidentally launched the cosmetics industry. His gimmick was a giveaway bottle of perfume, but McConnell found that customers preferred it to the bard. McConnell began making cosmetics and shrewdly used housewives as a sales force. Fifty-three years later he changed the name of his Californian Perfume Company to Avon, after the home-town river of the English playwright.

**1916** Liquid nail polish was introduced in the USA, followed by mass-produced, bright red lipstick.

**1920** The cinema age was launched in Hollywood and the studio make-up teams created the celluloid beauties every Western girl set out to copy. Arched eyebrows, cupid-bow lips and bright colours were the rage.

PALE AND INTERESTING
*Suntans are a 20th-century notion of beauty. This 19th-century advertisement extols the virtues of a skin-whitening cream which 'never fails to remove Freckles (and) Sunburn'.*

EXQUISITE BEAUTY TO THE FACE, NECK, ARMS AND HANDS.

BRIDAL BOUQUET BLOOM. Beautifies the Complexion.

## COVER GIRL

A Dutch model named Wilhelminia still holds the world record for appearances on the covers of the world's top fashion magazines – 250 covers between 1960 and 1967, when she retired. That is nearly twice the combined total amassed by the runners-up, British models Jean Shrimpton and Twiggy. Despite the exposure, Wilhelminia's name remained almost unknown to the general public.

## SILENT MODEL

The first model girls, a century ago, were hardly seen, never heard, and chosen purely as clothes-horses. They had no social status or respectability, and were even not picked for their looks in case they drew attention from the creations they were showing off.

In 1920, Paul Poiret, a Parisian couturier, took his models on tour, all kitted alike in semi-military uniforms with belts, buckles, epaulettes and peaked caps. Lunching at the Carlton Hotel in London with fashion writer Alison Settle, Poiret was startled when she turned to address a silent model beside her. 'No, mademoiselle, do not speak to the girls,' he warned Miss Settle. 'They are not there.'

## THE BARE-LEGGED LOOK

Victorian women considered even the merest glimpse of female leg indecent – much more so if the leg was unclad. Right up to present times, no fashion-conscious woman would go stockingless – despite a virtual ban on them by the British government during the Second World War because of material shortages. Even when supplies of wartime cotton and rayon stockings ran out, many women used specially prepared leg make-up.

The first real attempt to abandon stockings was made during the First World War by actress Gaby Deslys, mistress of King Manuel of Portugal. She shocked women and amused men by declaring that she would not wear stockings again until Germany surrendered to the Allies. In the 1920s Hollywood *femme fatale* Pola Negri went bare-legged, and actress Joan Crawford discarded stockings for evening wear in 1926.

In 1934, after a long debate, the fashion weekly *Sketch* concluded that 'going bare-legged is inartistic and tends to spoil the softness of the skin'. The British government's official disapproval of stockings came in 1942, when the Board of Trade warned that if women did not stop wearing them in summer, there would be none by winter.

As late as the 1960s, matrons in Melbourne, Australia, disapproved when model Jean Shrimpton appeared as guest of honour at Flemington racecourse hatless, gloveless – and stockingless. Then in 1983 the Princess of Wales attended a Government House party in Canberra with her elegant legs covered only by a golden suntan: the bare-legged look had finally won the royal seal of approval. Nobody could argue with that.

A LA MODE *A 19th-century engraving shows the extravagant costumes worn at Versailles, the court of France's Sun King, Louis XIV (1643 – 1715). The fashions set there were eagerly imitated all over Europe. The coat became part of everyday wear in this way, having developed from the military dress sometimes worn by the king. Louis promoted French fashions – sometimes by force. When his troops occupied Strasbourg – then an independent city – in 1681, its citizens were ordered to adopt French styles within four months.*

## MOUSTACHE BAN

Faded photographs of moustachioed Victorian males show only one side of 19th-century Britain's love-hate relationship with the hairy upper lip. A wealthy Englishman named Henry Budd died in 1862 leaving one London estate, Pepper Park, to his son Edward and another estate, Twickenham Park, to his second son William – on condition that they did *not* wear moustaches. Seven years later a British upholsterer left £10 to each employee 'if no moustaches'. In 1904, Regent Street drapers in London stopped employing assistants who wore moustaches (or parted their hair in the middle). The Bank of England, by contrast, neatly and scrupulously avoided interfering with staffs' private lives: moustaches were merely forbidden 'during working hours'.

## MEET MR BEETON

Mrs Isabella Beeton and her encyclopaedic *Book of Household Management* are justifiably famous. But her unsung husband, Samuel Orchard Beeton, has had an even more lasting influence on women: he invented the fashion magazine.

In 1852, four years before he married, 21-year-old Samuel published *The Englishwoman's Domestic Magazine*. With each issue, he gave away a paper dress pattern, starting, in Volume I, with 'A Lady's Jacket and Vest'. There was then no ready-to-wear fashion trade. Mr Beeton's giveaway patterns and practical instructions in his magazine established home dressmaking, and gave fashion to the nation's housewives for just the price of the material – and, of course, the magazine itself.

## FALSE EYELASHES

False eyelashes were invented by the American film director D. W. Griffith, when making his 1916 epic *Intolerance*. He wanted actress Seena Owen to have lashes that brushed her cheeks, to make her eyes shine larger than life.

A wigmaker wove human hair through fine gauze, which was then gummed to her eyelids. *Intolerance* was critically acclaimed but flopped financially, leaving Griffith with huge debts which he might have been able to settle easily – had he only thought to patent the eyelashes.

## WASP WAIST

For around 100 years, women laced themselves into ever-tighter corsets in pursuit of the 19th-century ideal of the hour-glass figure. Wasp waists as tiny as 400mm (16in), 375mm (15in) and even 325mm (13in) were claimed.

Photographs of the French dancer Polaire suggest that her claim to a 425mm (17in) waist was genuine, but anything less may be anatomically impossible. An English museum curator, Doris Langley Moore, measured the waists of 200 Victorian and Edwardian dresses in Bath's Museum of Costume: all were more

# HATS AROUND THE WORLD

### Bowler
English landowner William Coke ordered the first bowler hat to protect his head from low branches while shooting on his Norfolk estate. On December 17, 1849, he tested it in the St James's shop of the London hatters, Lock's, by stamping on it twice. It was undamaged and Coke bought it for 12 shillings. The hat was named after Thomas Bowler, who made it to Lock's orders; however, Lock's still call it a coke, after the man who first ordered it. The bowler was adopted by British office workers and was their standard wear until its use declined in the 1950s. In the USA, the same design is known as a derby, because Lord Derby was the first person to popularise it there.

### Fez
A tasselled, red felt hat, shaped like a flat-topped cone, the fez became a symbol of Middle Eastern Muslims. In Turkey, it was banned by Mustafa Kemal, otherwise known as Ataturk, father of the Turkish revolution, who swept aside the ruling sultans in 1922 and thereafter Westernised the nation.

### Trilby
Actors playing Bohemian characters in the 1894 stage production of George du Maurier's novel *Trilby* wore soft felt hats with wide brims and a dented crown. This style of hat became known as the trilby, after the name of the novel's heroine, Trilby O'Ferral, a singer swept to fame under the hypnotic influence of a magician named Svengali.

### Topper
Londoners mobbed James Heatherington when he first wore his tall, shiny 'topper' hat in the city in 1797. Women fainted in the crush, one boy had an arm broken, and Mr Heatherington was arrested. He was fined £50 – an enormous sum then – for causing a breach of the peace. But his top hat later became obligatory headgear for racegoers at Royal Ascot, at society weddings, and for ambassadors presenting their credentials to the British monarch at the Court of St James's.

ample, suggesting that the extravagant claims made were exaggerated.

For a modern comparison, the actress Twiggy, who was a legend of slenderness during her 1960s modelling career, had a 550mm (22in) waist.

## POKE BONNET

Nothing evokes a more appealing image of demure 19th-century femininity than the 'poke bonnet'. Yet it was originally meant to conceal the face rather than add allure to it. It was devised by an aristocrat named Baroness Oldenburg in 1818 to hide her unfortunate looks – the bonnet's side flaps curled around and all but covered her face.

Intrigued by the bonnet, pretty women of the day began decorating it with ribbons and flowers, and turning back its sides to give coy and provocative glimpses of their faces.

A straw version, common in the 1880s, was adapted by Quaker women and, later, by the English-

PUTTING ON THE AGONY
*A 19th-century cartoon hints at the discomfort involved in achieving a minuscule waistline.*

woman Catherine Booth for the new battalions of Salvation Army women – not because of its simple charm, but because the stiffened straw offered protection against stones and missiles hurled at the courageous girl pioneers.

## FASHIONABLE BEGINNINGS

**Tweed** Two simple mistakes gave this Scottish fabric its lasting name. A Scots weaver offered London merchant James Locke some twilled – diagonally ribbed – cloth in 1832. But in his letter, he spelled twilled in its Scottish form of 'tweeled'. Locke misread 'tweeled' as 'tweed' – and the name stuck.

**Worsted** Also known as wusted, worsett, wirsed and wossat, the woollen fabric, worsted, made from twisted yarn, originated in the English village of Worstead, Norfolk. No one knows exactly when it was first made, but by the 14th century worsted was frequently figuring in household accounts, wills and lawsuits as a material for garments or furnishing fabrics. The cloth is now manufactured in places far from Norfolk – including the USA and Australia.

**Tawdry** The term 'tawdry', meaning cheap and gaudy, once meant something very different. Tawdry is an abbreviation of St Audrey, whose name was given to St Audrey's Lace, a silk ribbon worn around the neck in the Middle Ages. The saint died in AD 679 of a throat tumour, which she blamed on the vanity of wearing pretty necklaces. Stallholders at medieval fairs offered cheap, bright substitutes to country girls who could not afford real silk, and they called it 'tawdry'.

**Poplin** Poplin was originally a corded fabric in which a silk warp was mixed with a worsted weft. It was first made in France in the mid-17th century at Avignon – a *papalino*, or papal city – and that is the origin of its name. The silk has long since gone, and poplin is now generally a mixture of worsted and cotton.

**Mae West** The name was given to an automatically inflatable lifejacket issued to RAF aircrew in the Second World War. When inflated, it rose in two great curves on the wearer's chest, irresistibly reminiscent of the exuberant charms of the US comedienne.

**Jeans** The hard-wearing work trousers, thought to have been invented by a sailmaker named Levi Strauss in San Francisco in 1850, get their name from 'gene (or jene) fustian' – a heavy, twilled cotton cloth first made in Genoa, Italy. Denim comes from the French phrase *serge de Nîmes* (serge of Nîmes).

**Tuxedo** Man-about-town Griswold Lorillard shocked his fellow members at the Tuxedo Park Country Club, New York, when he appeared at the 1886 Autumn Ball wearing a short black coat with shiny satin lapels instead of the conventional white tie and tail coat. Lorillard explained that his 'dinner jacket' was a more formal version of the British smoking jacket; and the club's name came to be used, particularly in the USA, for the style Lorillard had launched there.

*Blocked by a stile*

*Getting dressed*

*At the ball*

*Romantic leanings*

CUPID AND THE CRINOLINE *A series of cartoons published in 1835 pokes fun at the hazards of the crinoline. This fashion for billowing skirts, formed by vast quantities of material draped over wicker or steel frames hung from the waist, emerged in France in the mid-19th century. By the late 1850s, crinolines had become so enormous that two ladies could not enter a room at the same time, or sit on the same sofa – and presented male suitors with an almost impassable barrier. At the height of the fashion, a single dress could use up 1km (1100yds) of lace and gauzy tulle. Yet despite this extravagant design, white crinolines were often worn only once and then discarded, because their freshness was thought to have been lost. Underneath the whole elaborate structure, ankle-length, lacy pantaloons protected ladies' legs from indecent exposure in a high wind.*

# Mythology and legends

ATLAS  In Greek legend, Atlas was a Titan, an early Greek god, and was condemned – after the Titans were defeated by the classical gods of Olympus under Zeus – to carry the heavens on his shoulders. Later, when he refused hospitality to the Greek hero Perseus, Perseus turned him to stone by showing him the head of the Gorgon Medusa. His body became the Atlas Mountains of northwest Africa. Medieval map collections were often bound together with the image of Atlas as the frontispiece, giving rise to the modern use of his name.

CASSANDRA  The name Cassandra is often applied to anyone who predicts a future of gloom and doom. Originally, though, Cassandra was gloomy not because of any bleak prophecy, but because nobody would believe her no matter what she forecast or however accurate she proved to be. The original Cassandra, daughter of Priam, king of Troy, was given the gift of prophecy by Apollo, on condition that she would accept him as her lover. When Cassandra withheld her side of the bargain, Apollo was unable to retract his gift. But he ordained that her predictions would always be ignored.

HALCYONE  The phrase 'halcyon days' for any period of peace and tranquillity comes from the Greek legend of Halcyone, the daughter of Aeolus, god of the winds. When her husband Ceyx was drowned, Halcyone threw herself into the sea in despair. But the gods took pity on the couple and changed them into kingfishers, still sometimes called halcyons. Zeus also forbade the winds to blow for a week on either side of the winter solstice – midwinter day – when the birds breed, so creating the 'halcyon days' of calm.

> *The English word for cleanliness, hygiene, comes from the name of a Greek goddess. She was Hygieia, goddess of health and the daughter of Asclepius (Roman Aesculapius), the god of healing.*

HERMES  Son and messenger of the supreme Greek god Zeus, Hermes (the Roman Mercury) in his winged cap and sandals was among the busiest of the gods. When not carrying tidings or leading the dead to Hades, he was god of roads, of fraud and cunning, commerce – and luck. The serpent-entwined staff of

SNAKES ALIVE *The Gorgon Medusa, depicted here on a clay tablet dating from the 7th century BC, was one of three sisters made hideous by the gods for their misdeeds. Her face, surrounded by a mass of writhing serpents instead of hair, was so awful that, according to Greek mythology, anyone who looked upon it was turned instantly to stone. Medusa was finally killed and beheaded by the legendary Greek hero Perseus. He avoided looking at her directly during the battle by using his polished shield as a mirror. Medusa's blood gave birth to the winged horse Pegasus, her son by the Greek sea god Poseidon.*

Hermes is still the emblem of the medical profession. The staff is known as the Caduceus. To the ancient Greeks, a snake's ability to slough its skin was a symbol of renewal and fresh vigour, and hence of the healing power of medicine.

**HERACLES** Greatest and strongest of the Greek demigods, Heracles (known to the Romans as Hercules) was the son of Zeus by a mortal woman and was hated by Zeus's wife, Hera. He began his life of heroic violence by strangling two serpents while still in his cot. In manhood, driven mad by Hera, he murdered his wife and children and, as penance, spent 12 years in the service of his rival Eurystheus. Hoping to destroy Heracles, Eurystheus set him 12 supposedly impossible tasks, but the hero completed them all.

The Twelve Labours of Heracles were: one, strangling a lion that terrorised Nemea; two, striking off the many heads of the poisonous water snake Hydra of Lerna; three and four, delivering alive to Eurystheus the terrifying Erymanthian boar and the Arcadian stag sacred to Artemis; five, killing the savage man-eating birds of Lake Stymphalis; six, cleaning in one day the stables of Augeas, king of Elis, which contained 3000 oxen and had not been cleaned for 30 years (he did this by diverting two rivers); seven, capturing and bearing on his shoulders to Mycenae the white Cretan bull, sire of the Minotaur; eight, capturing the man-eating mares of Diomedes (a Thracian king and son of the war god Ares) and feeding them with the flesh of Diomedes; nine, fetching for Eurystheus's daughter the girdle of the Amazon queen, Hippolyte; ten, killing the three-bodied monster, Geryon – along with his giant herdsman Eurytion and the two-headed dog Orthrus – in order to capture Geryon's oxen; eleven, freeing Prometheus and temporarily bearing the weight of the world in place of Atlas, who went to fetch for him the golden apples of the Hesperides; and twelve, descending to the underworld to bring the three-headed dog Cerberus to its master, Hades.

His servitude ended, Heracles took part in the voyage of Jason and the Argonauts to find the Golden Fleece. He was reconciled with Hera only after his death when, in recognition of his exploits, he was made a god.

> *The endless chatter of Echo, a mountain nymph, foiled the jealous goddess Hera's attempts to catch her husband Zeus making love to other women. The enraged Hera punished Echo by leaving her only the power to repeat the last words spoken to her. Echo's unrequited love for Narcissus – who loved only his own image – caused her to fade away until only her voice was left.*

**TANTALUS** Eternal tantalising torment was the lot of Tantalus, mythical Greek king of Phrygia. He cut up his son Pelops and presented the flesh to the gods at a banquet to test their all-powerful knowledge. The gods duly detected the outrage, restored Pelops to life, and condemned Tantalus to an eternity of suffering in Tartarus, the lower depths of the underworld, which were reserved for those who defied the gods. Racked by endless hunger and thirst, Tantalus was forced to stand up to his neck in water surrounded by luscious

## THE GODS OF GREECE AND ROME

As well as absorbing Greece into the Roman empire in the 2nd century BC, the Romans adopted and adapted many of the Greek myths, linking the legends and deities of Greece with their own gallery of gods.

| GREEK | ROMAN | |
|---|---|---|
| Aphrodite | Venus | Goddess of love and beauty |
| Apollo, Phoebus | Apollo, Phoebus | Greek god of sun, god of music, poetry and prophecy |
| Ares | Mars | God of war |
| Artemis | Diana | Virgin huntress, goddess of the moon |
| Asclepius | Aesculapius | God of medicine |
| Athena (Pallas) | Minerva | Goddess of wisdom and art |
| Cronus | Saturn | Father of the supreme god: Zeus or Jupiter |
| Demeter | Ceres | Goddess of the harvest |
| Dionysus | Bacchus | God of wine and fertility |
| Eros | Cupid | God of love |
| Hades, Pluto | Dis | God of the underworld |
| Hephaestus | Vulcan | God of fire |
| Hera | Juno | Queen of heaven, wife of Zeus/Jupiter, goddess of women and marriage |
| Hermes | Mercury | Messenger of the gods, god of roads, cunning, commerce, wealth and luck |
| Hestia | Vesta | Goddess of the hearth |
| Hymen | Hymen | God of marriage |
| Irene | Pax | Goddess of peace |
| Pan | Faunus | God of flocks and shepherds |
| Persephone | Proserpina | Goddess of corn and the spring, goddess of the dead |
| Poseidon | Neptune | God of the sea |
| Zeus | Jupiter, Jove | Supreme ruler of gods and men, king of heaven and overseer of justice and destiny |

# Mythology and legends

fruit trees. But every time he stooped to drink, the water level dropped, and every time he stretched up for a fruit, the trees drew away – perpetually just out of reach.

HYACINTHUS The hyacinth flower is said to have sprung from the blood of Hyacinthus, a golden youth loved by the sun god Apollo and Zephyrus. Because the youth preferred Apollo, Zephyrus, the god of the west wind, had him killed by a quoit flung by Apollo. Marks on the petals were thought by Greeks to resemble the letters α (alpha) and ι (iota), standing for Hyacinthus's dying cry: 'Ai, ai' (Alas, alas).

PANDORA According to Greek myth, Pandora was the first woman. She was sent to the rebellious Titans on earth by Zeus as a punishment for mankind. She was given a box to take with her, with instructions not to open it. Because she was curious she disobeyed, opened the box and all the evils of the world flew out. Only Hope was left. Pandora's box has since become a symbol for any action whose consequences are dangerously unpredictable.

PSYCHE Psychology, the science of the mind, gets its name from Psyche, a beautiful girl in Greek mythology who was desired by Eros, the god of love. He forbade her to look at him because he was a god and, when she disobeyed by lighting a lamp in the dark, he abandoned her. Eventually she was reunited with Eros and joined the immortals, where she was revered as the personification of the human soul.

TITANS Before Mount Olympus became the home of the gods, the ancient Greeks believed the Titans had ruled a golden age on the earth. The 12 Titans were

## GODS THE EGYPTIANS WORSHIPPED

Ancient Egyptians bound together the folk tales and legends of several civilisations that had lived in the Nile valley before Egypt was unified in about 3100 BC, weaving from them a complex network of myths around their chief god: Ra, or Re.

Originally, ancient Egyptians believed, the earth arose as a hill from the featureless ocean Nun. Darkness was dispersed by the sun god Ra, alighting as a phoenix on the hill. His offspring were Shu, the god of air, and Tefnut, goddess of water. Shu and Tefnut in turn had twins – the earth god Geb and the sky goddess Nut – who remained locked in incestuous embrace until Shu parted them to create heaven and earth.

Each day Nut, who was depicted as a cow, gave birth to the sun anew. Each dawn, the sun rose as Khepri, a giant scarab beetle, and crossed the sky as Ra in a barque crewed by other gods. Each night, it sank below the horizon as an old man, then crossed the underworld to begin the cycle again.

Other major Egyptian gods and goddesses included:

### AMON
Supreme god of Thebes, later identified with Ra.

### ANUBIS
Jackal-headed god of embalming, son of Nephthys and Osiris. He supervised the weighing of souls at judgment.

### HATHOR
Goddess of joy, music and marriage, daughter of Ra. As the Eye of Ra, she was responsible for subduing rebellious mortals. She was later identified with other goddesses of love, including Aphrodite.

### HORUS
Originally a falcon-headed god of the sky and son of Nut. He was later regarded as son of Isis and Osiris, and grew up to defeat his evil uncle Set.

### ISIS
Fertility goddess, daughter of Nut and sister and wife of Osiris. She was founder of marriage and teacher with Osiris of agriculture, spinning and weaving.

### NEPHTHYS
Funerary goddess and sister of Isis, she befriended dead mortals at judgment.

### OSIRIS
Corn god, son of Nut and Geb. He married his sister Isis while still in the womb, became king on earth and abolished cannibalism. Murdered by his brother Set, he was restored to life by Isis and became supreme judge of the dead and ruler of the underworld. He was usually shown as a mummified pharaoh, sometimes green with vegetation, bearing a shepherd's crook and flail.

### PTAH
High god of Memphis, said by his devotees to be creator of all other gods. Magician and patron of craft and the arts. Later, when Osiris's cult became prominent, Ptah became a judge of the dead, and was represented as a mummy.

### SET
Son of Nut and Geb, and brother of Osiris. In early myths he was Ra's chief defender; later he became the personification of evil, murdering Osiris and persecuting Horus. Also regarded as lord of Upper Egypt. His eventual destruction by Horus, lord of Lower Egypt, symbolised the unification of the country. Usually depicted with red hair, he personified the desert and its sterility.

### THOTH
Magician and inventor of speech and hieroglyphics, Thoth was often identified with the moon. Later became vizier for Osiris and teacher of the arts of civilisation. He was represented as an ibis or a dog-headed baboon.

GODDESS WHO WADED IN BLOOD Hathor was Egypt's sky goddess and protector of women. In early mythology she was ordered by her father, Ra, to destroy mankind and was depicted wading in blood. Mankind was saved, according to the myth, because Hathor was tricked into drinking a mixture of beer and red ochre resembling blood, and so became drunk before she could complete the slaughter.

*To kill a cat in ancient Egypt brought immediate death. To the Egyptians, cats were sacred to Bast, the cat-headed goddess of pleasure, and cat funerals were so numerous that the animals' cemeteries are still used by modern Egyptians as a source of rich fertiliser.*

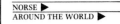

the offspring of Uranus, god of the heavens, and Gaea, the goddess of earth. Cronus, the youngest of the 12, became their leader when he overthrew his father. Cronus, the god of time, was later overthrown in his turn by his son, Zeus.

*The planet Jupiter – the largest in the solar system – gets its name from Rome's supreme god, Jupiter. His name, and that of his Greek counterpart, Zeus, comes from an ancient Indo-European word for the sky – suggesting that they were both descended from a primitive weather god.*

**NARCISSUS** Narcissists – people who are obsessed with their looks – are named after Narcissus, a handsome youth in Greek mythology. Narcissus refused all offers of love, including that of the nymph Echo. He was punished by Aphrodite, the goddess of love, for his indifference by being made to fall in love with his own reflection in a forest pool. Unable to possess the image, he pined away and was changed into the flower that bears his name. The modern psychological term narcissism was coined by the Austrian psychiatrist and pioneer of psychoanalysis, Sigmund Freud (1856–1939).

**THESEUS** The mythical Greek hero Theseus, who killed the bull-headed Minotaur, escaped from the monster's labyrinth on Crete afterwards with the help of a ball of thread which he had paid out behind him as he went into the underground maze. When the legend was told in medieval England – where the word for a ball of thread was 'clew' – a guide to the solution of any problem became known as a 'clew' or 'clue'.

**WEIGHED AGAINST A FEATHER** *An Egyptian papyrus dating from about 1300 BC shows Anubis, the jackal-headed god of embalming (bottom centre), weighing a heart, symbolising the conscience of a dead person, against a feather, the symbol of truth. The heart is that of a senior administrator called Ani, shown on the left in white robes with his wife. Above, a jury of 12 gods sits in judgment. To the right of Anubis stands Thoth, scribe of the gods, noting down the results; and behind Thoth crouches the monster Amemit, waiting to devour Ani's soul if it is found wanting.*

**LUCKY BEETLE** Dung beetles, or scarabs, were venerated by ancient Egyptians as lucky. The insect was revered because its habit of rolling a ball of dung to its nest seemed to symbolise the sun god, Ra, rolling the ball of the sun across the heavens. Crocodiles, too, were sacred and the Nile crocodile god, Sebek, was worshipped at his own city – named, appropriately, Crocodilopolis.

**MUMMY WHO JUDGED THE DEAD** Ptah was a judge of the dead in ancient Egyptian mythology and was usually depicted as a mummy. Ptah, whose cult was centred on the city of Memphis, was thought to have saved the Egyptians in a war against the Assyrians by raising an army of rats which chewed through the enemy's bow strings and shield thongs, leaving the Assyrians weaponless and defenceless.

# Mythology and legends

HORSE SENSE According to Norse legend, Sleipnir – Odin's eight-legged steed – was born soon after the gods had built Asgard. A giant turned up and offered to build a great wall around the stronghold in the space of a single winter with no other help than that of his stallion, Svadilfari. If he completed the work by the first day of summer, he was to be given the fertility goddess, Freya, and the sun and the moon as payment. Otherwise he would get nothing.

With the help of his horse, the giant made swift progress, and to the alarm of the gods the work was almost completed with three days left. Only the gates remained to be fitted. Loki, the god of mischief, therefore turned himself into a mare and lured the stallion away from his work. The giant failed to fulfil his contract and he was slain by Thor, the god of thunder. Several months later, however, Loki gave birth to a grey colt with eight legs: Sleipnir.

ONE-EYED KING *Odin, the supreme Norse god – shown here on his eight-legged steed Sleipnir – is said to have sacrificed an eye in return for wisdom.*

---

*The Vikings had a colourful explanation for the Northern Lights, which blaze from time to time in the skies of the far north. They believed that the lights were caused by the flashing armour and spears of Odin's handmaidens, the Valkyries, riding out to collect warriors slain in battle to take them to Odin's palace of Valhalla.*

---

MEAD OF INSPIRATION One of the legends about the Vikings' supreme god Odin tells how he brought poetic inspiration to mankind by stealing a magic potion of mead made from the blood of the wisest of all creatures in Norse myth, the giant Kvasir. A giant called Suttung hid the mead in three casks inside a mountain under the care of his daughter, Gunnlöd.

Odin crawled into the mountain in the shape of a snake and seduced Gunnlöd for three nights. As a reward he was allowed three drinks of the mead. Odin emptied all three casks, then changed into the shape of an eagle and flew off towards Asgard, the home of the gods – hotly pursued by Suttung.

The gods had placed a line of vats on the walls of Asgard, and Odin managed to regurgitate the precious mead into these vessels before Suttung could catch him. Some of the mead splashed from the vats and fell outside the walls of Asgard; and this less heady brew inspired mortal versifiers and writers of doggerel.

BEWARE THE MISTLETOE In many ancient religions the mistletoe was regarded as a sacred plant. The Druids believed that a sprig of mistletoe, fastened above a doorway, would ward off evil and enhance the hospitality – and fertility – of the household. Hence the Christmas custom of kissing under the mistletoe.

But to the Norsemen the mistletoe was a baleful plant, because it caused the death of Baldur, the shining god of youth. Odin, his father, who knew the future, sought to prevent Baldur's predestined fate. The gods collected pledges from all objects that they would not harm Baldur. But the gods did not ask the mistletoe, thinking it too feeble.

Since Baldur was now apparently impervious to injury, he entertained the other gods by letting them try to hurt him. One day, when the gods were at this sport, Loki, the god of mischief, noticed that Baldur's blind brother, Hödur, was taking no part in it. So Loki cut a sprig of mistletoe in the shape of a javelin, gave it to Hödur, and directed his aim at Baldur. The mistletoe pierced Baldur to the heart, killing him.

---

*Baldur's death was the signal for the Battle of Ragnarök – the Norse equivalent of Armageddon – to begin. The gods were overwhelmed by the giants and monsters of evil. The whole universe was consumed in a holocaust of destruction. But after Ragnarök, Baldur rose from the grave to a new and revitalised world of men and of one god – Baldur. It was a poetic foreshadowing of the conversion to Christianity which was eventually to mellow the warrior ferocity of the Viking peoples.*

---

## BIRTH OF THE NORSE GODS

The main sources for Norse mythology are two medieval books, both called Edda: the Poetic Edda; and the Prose Edda. The meaning of the word Edda is not known. The Poetic Edda is a collection of ancient mythological lays, now found only in a single manuscript, the *Codex Regius*, which was copied in Iceland in the 1270s.

The Prose Edda was written around 1220 by the Icelandic scholar and historian Snorri Sturluson, as a handbook for aspiring poets. According to the Edda, the universe emerged out of a Great Void. The first living being to emerge was a giant called Ymir, ancestor of the evil race of Frost Giants. From the blocks of salty ice around Ymir's head, a primeval cow licked into shape another being called Búri, the ancestor of the gods. Búri married a giantess who was born in Ymir's left armpit, and their offspring were the first three gods: Odin and his two brothers.

### How the first man was made

Together the three of them set upon Ymir and slew him, fashioning the world from his carcass. The first men and women were whittled out of two pieces of driftwood by Odin and his brothers, and were given a home in Midgard (sometimes written as Midgarth), a name meaning the Middle Enclave. In the heart of Midgard, the gods built their own fortified home, Asgard, on a high crag which was connected to earth by the shining rainbow-bridge of Bifrost.

Belief in the Norse gods continues to the present day. In Iceland there is a small cult of the Norse gods, called Ásatrú (Belief in the Gods). Its members conduct marriages and funerals according to ancient Norse rites, and the ceremonies are recognised as legal by the state.

CRUSADING SAINT *A Spanish picture painted in about 1400 shows St George, patron saint of England, killing a dragon. The story is pure fiction, a medieval adaptation of the Greek legend about the hero Perseus rescuing Andromeda from a monster. If he existed at all, St George seems to have been a Christian soldier martyred for his faith at Lydda in Palestine in about AD 300. He was a little-known figure until he was adopted as a soldier-saint by medieval Crusaders. At the height of his cult in the later Middle Ages, he was adopted as patron of Venice, Genoa, Portugal and Catalonia as well as England. But in 1969 the Roman Catholic Liturgical Calendar was revised, and St George was demoted to the ranks of lesser saints.*

MAN WHO MET A ZOMBIE Belief in zombies, the 'living dead' of the black magic religion known as voodoo, may be based on fact. In 1983 a Canadian scientist from Harvard University, Wade Davis, reported that he had actually met one. The zombie was a Haitian known as Louis Ozias, who said that he had been certified dead at a US-run hospital on the Caribbean island, buried – then dug up and made to work as a slave on a remote sugar plantation for two years. He had escaped only after his master died.

Davis believes that Ozias and other zombies are victims not of magic but of powerful natural drugs known to voodoo initiates. The drugs, administered as a series of complex and highly dangerous 'cocktails', have the effect first of putting the victim into a state of suspended animation so that he – or she – appears temporarily dead, then of putting him into a trance-like stupor. Davis identifies three types of drug known to be used in the cocktails, which are capable, he believes, of inducing the zombie effects.

One type, derived from puffer fish and known as tetrodotoxin, is known to be capable of inducing paralysis and other symptoms which are part of the zombie legend. Curiously, the symptoms match very closely those reported in Japan by victims of puffer poisoning. Puffer fish are eaten as a delicacy in Japan, where they are known as *fugu* – and there are numerous cases on record of victims being pronounced dead and then reviving. In one case, reported in 1880, a gambler poisoned after eating *fugu* recovered in a mortuary store seven days after being declared dead. According to Davis, tetrodotoxin is an exceptionally potent anaesthetic, 160,000 times stronger than cocaine.

The second group of drugs is derived from a New World species of toad, *Bufo marinus*, and is known to boost physical strength – matching voodoo legends which say that a new zombie has to be tied up and beaten to subdue him. The third group, derived from *Datura* plants, is known to have powerful hallucinogenic properties – capable of inducing the dazed trance-like state which is traditionally characteristic of zombies.

CATHERINE'S WHEEL The Vatican downgraded the feast day of St Catherine of Alexandria in 1969 because it is doubtful whether she ever existed. Her legend says that she was a virgin of noble birth, martyred at Alexandria in the 4th century for protesting to the Roman emperor Maxentius about his persecution of Christians. She was tortured on a spiked wheel, which broke when she was bound to it, and the pieces flew in all directions injuring bystanders. The episode gave rise to her emblem, the Catherine wheel, which is also a rotating firework. Eventually she was beheaded and milk is said to have flowed from her severed head. According to the legend, angels transported her body to Mount Sinai and it was there that her cult began in the 9th century. The legend appealed to the imagination of medieval artists and her cult flourished among the Crusaders.

THE ALLIGATORS OF NEW YORK Many American children still believe that the sewers of New York City are infested with giant drug-crazed alligators. The 20th-century legend maintains that holidaymakers, returning from the Florida swamps, brought baby alligators home as souvenirs. When they grew larger, their owners panicked and flushed them down the lavatory. Deep in the New York sewers, they flourished on a diet of rats and sewage, grew to enormous size and bred prolifically. Starved of natural light, these giant alligators turned white and went blind. They supplemented their diet by devouring drugs supposedly growing in the sewers after being flushed down lavatories during police raids. The exact origin of this peculiar legend is unknown, although a *New York Times* story from February 1935 actually describes the capture of a 2m (7ft) long alligator in an uptown sewer. The story reports that the alligator was killed by its 'rescuers' when it turned on them.

THE EASTER HARE Children's stories in many European countries tell how Easter eggs are brought not by a chicken but by a hare. Hares – or, more recently, rabbits – have represented fertility in many cultures because they breed so quickly. In traditional Christian art, the hare represents lust – and paintings of the Virgin Mary sometimes show a hare at her feet to signify that she has triumphed over the temptations of the flesh. It was natural to link such a potent symbol of new life to the spring festival of Easter.

DISAPPEARING TRICK The legend of the Vanishing Hitchhiker is told as a true story in many parts of the world. According to the legend, a young girl is given a lift and mysteriously disappears during the journey. The baffled driver calls at the address she gave him only to discover from her parents that she died some years ago at the very spot where he picked her up. He goes to look at her nearby grave and finds the sweater that he had lent her during the car journey draped over the tombstone. This modern ghost story dates from the turn of the 20th century. With variations, it is told all over Britain, Ireland, China, Turkey, Europe and the United States. In Hawaii, a rickshaw replaces the car.

*Ethiopians, who believe that they are God's chosen people, have a special creation legend to justify their confidence. According to the legend, God moulded the first men from clay. He put the first batch in the oven but left them too long. They came out burnt and black, so he threw them away to the south of Africa. He took the second batch out too soon and they were pasty white, so he threw them away to the north, where they became Arabs and Europeans. The third batch came out just right and he put them in Ethiopia.*

WHO'LL COME A-WALTZING? The Australian tramp who sang *Waltzing Matilda* may have been thinking of his bundle of belongings rather than his lady-love. *Waltzing Matilda* is well-known as Australia's unofficial national anthem, but its origins are obscure. The most romantic explanation, from East Gippsland, Victoria, has been handed down as a folktale. Matilda, the first woman 'swaggie' (tramp), wandered through the bush with her husband Joe. When she died, Joe said sadly to his bundle of possessions: 'You'll be Matilda to me now, and we'll waltz along together till the end.'

Less romantically, *Waltzing Matilda* probably came to Australia with German-speaking settlers in the late 19th century. In southern Germany a tramp is a *Bruder* (Brother), and when he takes to the road, he is said to be 'on the waltz'. A greatcoat, rolled up like an Australian tramp's bundle, was known as a 'Mathilda' in the old Austrian army.

THE REAL FATHER CHRISTMAS The original Santa Claus lived nowhere near the North Pole. If he existed at all, he lived in the Mediterranean. Santa Claus is a corruption of the Dutch name Sinte Klaas, for St Nicholas, who seems to have been a 4th-century bishop of Myra in Turkey. St Nicholas was the patron of children and unmarried girls. Tradition says that he gave bags of gold to three daughters from a noble, but poor, family as their dowries, thus saving them from a life of prostitution. As the legend developed in the Netherlands, the three bags of gold were replaced by a bulging sack of presents which Santa Claus distributed to children on December 6, St Nicholas's feast day. Dutch settlers took this custom to North America, where it fused with north European legends about a winter spirit who gave gifts to good children and punished the bad.

WITCHES' SABBATH Walpurgis Night, when German witches traditionally ride to meet their master the Devil, is named after an English abbess who was a formidable opponent of witchcraft. St Walpurgis, or Walburga, was the niece of St Boniface, who helped to introduce Christianity into Germany. She founded several religious houses in Germany during the 8th century and became known as a protectress against witchcraft. Her name is linked with the witches' sabbath on April 30 only because her feast day falls on May 1. The night of April 30 was simply the eve of Walpurgis Day.

In Roman times May was associated with the spirits of the dead, and this may be one of the reasons why the month, and particularly May Day, became a time for practising witchcraft. Another reason is that witches were thought to be particularly active at turning points of the year – for instance, when cattle were taken to summer pasture early in May. On Walpurgis Night (German *Walpurgisnacht*), villagers in Germany used to light fires, to drive any passing witches away from their homes and their cattle.

*One of the most persistent modern legends concerns the New York blackout of November 9, 1965. As a result of a power failure, the lights went out all over the city; and, nine months later, so the story goes, up leapt the New York birthrate. In fact, nothing of the sort happened. Any rise in the birthrate would have shown up between July 27 and August 14, 1966. But demographers have found that the number of births in New York for that period was slightly below the average – 13.9 per cent of all births for the year, against a five-year average of 14 per cent for the same period in 1960 – 5.*

SACRIFICIAL FIRE Grief-stricken Indian widows used to sacrifice themselves on their husbands' funeral pyres to commemorate an episode in Hindu mythology. The episode concerned Sati – a name meaning 'chaste wife' – who was a wife of Shiva, one of the principal Hindu deities, and daughter of a sage named Daksha. When her husband and father quarrelled, she killed herself in sorrow by walking into a fire. Suttee, the custom named after Sati of burning a Hindu woman on her husband's funeral pyre, dates from the 4th century BC, and by the 6th century AD it was obligatory for devout Hindus. The widows, or satis, who immolated themselves in this way were promised 35 million years in Svarga (the Hindu paradise). The satis also became important female saints and were believed to possess miraculous healing powers. The practice of suttee was outlawed in British India by the governor general, Lord William Bentinck, in 1829.

## ANNIVERSARY GIFTS

Particular wedding anniversaries have come to be associated in the Western world with particular types of gift. The choice of gift varies slightly in different countries. This list is one of the most common.

| | |
|---|---|
| 1st Cotton | 25th Silver |
| 2nd Paper | 30th Pearl |
| 3rd Leather | 35th Coral |
| 4th Fruit, flowers | 40th Ruby |
| 5th Wooden | 45th Sapphire |
| 6th Sugar | 50th Golden |
| 7th Wool, copper | 55th Emerald |
| 8th Bronze, pottery | 60th Diamond |
| 9th Pottery, willow | 70th Platinum |
| 10th Tin | |
| 11th Steel | |
| 12th Silk, linen | |
| 13th Lace | |
| 14th Ivory | |
| 15th Crystal | |
| 20th China | |

## BIRTHSTONES AND FLOWERS

The origins of birthstones and of the flowers associated with each month of the year go back at least to the Middle Ages, when astrologers and magicians taught complicated systems of 'correspondences' involving such things as jewels, plants, planets and the signs of the zodiac. The combinations vary in different parts of the world. This list is widely used in Britain and North America.

| | |
|---|---|
| **January** | **July** |
| Garnet | Ruby |
| Carnation or snowdrop | Larkspur or water lily |
| **February** | **August** |
| Amethyst | Peridot or sardonyx |
| Violet or primrose | Gladiolus or poppy |
| **March** | **September** |
| Aquamarine or bloodstone | Sapphire |
| Jonquil or violet | Morning glory or aster |
| **April** | **October** |
| Diamond | Opal or tourmaline |
| Daisy or sweet pea | Calendula or cosmos |
| **May** | **November** |
| Emerald | Topaz |
| Hawthorn or lily of the valley | Chrysanthemum |
| **June** | **December** |
| Pearl, alexandrite or moonstone | Turquoise or zircon |
| Rose or honeysuckle | Narcissus, holly or poinsettia |

# Customs and festivals

## FEASTING WITH THE DEAD
Macabre graveside picnics take place in Mexico on the Day of the Dead when, according to Indian folklore, the dead return to life. Marigolds, tequila – a fiery national drink – and food are offered to the dead by families who afterwards feast in the cemeteries on their gifts. The food always follows the theme of death, and revellers eat chocolate hearses and coffins, sugar skulls, skeletons and funeral wreaths and fancy breads

patterned with skulls and crossbones. The occasion is widely celebrated as a national holiday every November 2, All Souls' Day in the Roman Catholic Liturgical Calendar, when prayers are traditionally offered for souls in purgatory.

SWEET HEAD
*Mexicans eat skulls made out of sugar in cemetery picnics on the Day of the Dead.*

## THE MONARCH'S MONEY
Every Maundy Thursday – the day before Good Friday – the reigning British monarch personally distributes money to the poor in Westminster Abbey, London. Purses containing silver pennies, two-pennies, three-pennies and four-pennies, specially minted for the occasion, are given to poor people – one for each year that the sovereign has lived. The recipients, chosen from a different area each year, are people who have given a lifetime of voluntary service to their church or community. The custom commemorates the washing of the Apostles' feet by Christ.

Until 1689, when William III and Mary II took the throne, the reigning monarch personally washed the feet of the poor in Britain – but thereafter money was given instead. The money – known as Maundy money – is legal tender in Britain but is worth much more than its face value.

## EASTER SOAKING
Hungarian men splash their girlfriends with water until they are rewarded with coloured Easter eggs on Water Drench Monday, as Easter Monday is sometimes called there. In big cities the old-fashioned water drenching ritual has been replaced by a ceremony in which a few drops of perfume or eau-de-cologne are sprinkled over women by their boyfriends. The ceremony is meant to bring a good harvest and ensure good health.

## HOLY SMOKE
Every year Chinese families burn one of their own gods. This fiery ritual takes place before the Chinese New Year (held between late January and early February) as part of the Festival of the Kitchen God, Tsao Chun. Wishing to court Tsao Chun's favour, so that

he will speak well of them to the other gods, families offer cakes and sweets to his picture, smear his mouth with syrup and dip him into wine to make him tipsy and amiable. Afterwards they burn his picture in the belief that the god will ascend to heaven in the smoke. Tsao Chun is believed to return to the household on New Year's Day when a new picture is hung on the kitchen wall.

## HORSE RACING, ITALIAN STYLE
Every summer jockeys dressed in medieval costume honour the Virgin Mary by racing bareback around the main square of Siena, Italy. Jockeys ride for individual city wards after having their mounts blessed in church, and the winner of the race is presented with a silk banner depicting the Virgin. The contest – known as the Palio – was started by the Papal States in the 13th century and is held every July 2 and August 16. Each jockey is given a whip before the start and, under the rules, he is allowed to use it not only on his own mount but on other horses as well – and on their riders.

## MOON'S BIRTHDAY
In China there is no man in the moon. Instead there is a toad in the moon, as well as moon rabbits and a goddess, all of which appear as decorations on moon cakes, baked to celebrate the moon's birthday on the 15th day of the 8th moon (September). These cakes – which are traditionally circular to symbolise the full moon – are exchanged between friends while children receive toy pagodas made from clay. The birthday marks the end of the harvest, when debts are meant to be settled.

## BEANS MEAN SPRING
Shouting 'Good luck in! Evil spirits out!', Japanese families throw beans around their homes every February 3. Each person throws one bean for every year of his life. The origin of the custom is unknown, but in many cultures beans are thought to possess magical properties – perhaps because they resemble human kidneys and testicles, symbols of renewal and fertility. The festival, known as Setsubun, or Bean Throwing Night, celebrates the end of winter and the beginning of spring, and is also observed in shrines and temples.

## FLYING THE CARP
Giant kites depicting red and black carp are flown every May 5 by Japanese families in honour of their young sons. This ancient festival, known as Tango-No-Sekku, meaning 'Boys' Festival', is intended to encourage the development of manly qualities in small

boys. Carp were chosen as symbols of strength and virility because the fish battles its way up fast-flowing rivers to mate and breed.

## LIVING DOLL
Dolls are honoured in Japan as a way of encouraging the development of feminine qualities in young girls. During the Festival of Hinamatsuri, meaning 'Girls' Festival', dolls are arranged in a special alcove, known as the *Tokonoma*, in family living rooms. The dolls often represent a medieval emperor, empress and retinue of courtiers. Along with family guests, the dolls are offered fruit and vegetables on miniature dishes by young girls dressed in their finest kimonos. The ceremony takes place every March 3.

## QUEENS OF THE LIGHT
Every December Swedish girls dispel midwinter gloom by placing small electric candles in their hair to honour St Lucia, the patron saint of light. Long white dresses, scarlet sashes and evergreen garlands complete their costumes, and communities throughout Sweden elect their own St Lucias, or Queens of the Light. Candles are also burnt in homes, shops and offices during the day and special saffron buns – shaped like cats for luck – are eaten.

## GIVING THANKS
Turkey, cranberry sauce and pumpkin pie are the traditional menu for dinner on Thanksgiving, which takes place annually in the United States on the fourth Thursday in November. The custom originated in 1621 when the Pilgrim Fathers invited neighbouring Indians, who had helped the fledgling colony survive, to a celebratory feast for their successful harvest. In 1863 President Abraham Lincoln declared the tradition a national holiday, and today it is marked by spectacular parades and special church Thanksgiving services. The holiday is also observed in Canada.

## CHIVALROUS INDIANS
Indian men pledge their lives and swear loyalty to their women in return for a bracelet made of cotton, silk, a coloured material, or gold thread. The Hindu custom originated in ancient times when a Rajput princess is believed to have sought help by sending part of her silk bracelet to a Muslim emperor in Delhi. After providing assistance the emperor kept her bracelet as a token of loyalty between them. The deed is celebrated in the Rakhi Festival, which takes place in the Indian month of Sravana in July and August.

## TRAMPLED . . . A FEAT OF FLOWERS
Every Easter, Andean farmers and villagers transform the small market town of Tarma, northeast of the Peruvian capital, Lima. In a double ceremony – first on Good Friday and again on Easter Sunday – every square millimetre of the town centre streets is covered with thousands upon thousands of glowing flower petals painstakingly arranged in exquisite designs.

Preparations start the day before Good Friday when village womenfolk pluck the petals from flowers

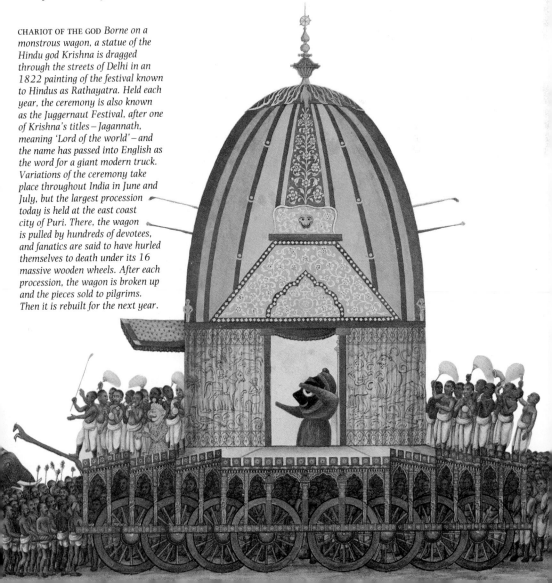

CHARIOT OF THE GOD *Borne on a monstrous wagon, a statue of the Hindu god Krishna is dragged through the streets of Delhi in an 1822 painting of the festival known to Hindus as Rathayatra. Held each year, the ceremony is also known as the Juggernaut Festival, after one of Krishna's titles – Jagannath, meaning 'Lord of the world' – and the name has passed into English as the word for a giant modern truck. Variations of the ceremony take place throughout India in June and July, but the largest procession today is held at the east coast city of Puri. There, the wagon is pulled by hundreds of devotees, and fanatics are said to have hurled themselves to death under its 16 massive wooden wheels. After each procession, the wagon is broken up and the pieces sold to pilgrims. Then it is rebuilt for the next year.*

harvested locally and separate them by colour into sacks. As dusk falls, designers from each village crouch in the street, copying on to the dusty tarmac with chalk the outlines of llamas, bulls, Andean pipers, geometrical patterns reminiscent of Persian carpets, or even whimsical cartoons of familiar Western characters such as Donald Duck.

The villagers then spend all night filling in the designs with petals, so that by dawn the streets are a continuous series of flower carpets, each about 10m (33ft) long and each containing – in petals – the name of the group or village that created it.

Soon after dawn on Good Friday, the doors of the Catholic church swing open and a statue of the Virgin Mary is carried out on a litter twice as high as a man. A priest walks in front, blessing each village as he reaches – and crosses – its carpet, and behind him the statue sways upon the shoulders of some 30 shuffling men. And as the procession passes, the designs, many of which were still being frantically completed only minutes before, are trampled into a litter of scuffed confetti blowing in the gutters. Nothing remains – except that on the following day, Easter Saturday, the villagers begin the whole procedure again, often with wholly new designs.

## THE RACE THAT IS FIXED

Since the 12th century the people of Gubbio in northern Italy have staged a 'rigged' race to commemorate St Ubaldo, who is believed to have saved the town from invasion then. Every May statues of St Ubaldo, St George and St Anthony are paraded through the town atop 9m (30ft) poles during the Festival of Candles. Afterwards the statues are raced up the nearby 820m (2690ft) Monte Ingino to the Church of St Ubaldo. However, because the track is too narrow to allow overtaking, the result of the race has not varied since its origin. The statues always reach the church in the same order – St Ubaldo, St George and then St Anthony.

## BLESSING THE ANIMALS

Animals attend church services on St Anthony's Day in Mexico. This popular saint, who is regarded as a healer of men and animals, is asked to protect pets, which are decorated with flowers and ribbons for the occasion. In rural areas, peasants also bring bags of insects and worms to be blessed in church, in the hope that this will prevent these creatures from damaging crops. The saint, whose feast day is on January 17, lived in Egypt between AD 251 and 356 and founded the first Christian monastery there.

## GREEN POWER

Christians in parts of central Europe believe that green plants and green food acquire special healing powers on Green Thursday, the name given locally to Maundy Thursday, the Thursday before Easter. The origins of the belief are obscure. It may have developed because excommunicated sinners, wearing sprigs of green as a sign of joy, were readmitted to the early Christian Church on this day.

## THE LIVING GODDESS

Hindus in Nepal worship a living goddess – a young girl. Known as Kumari Devi, a title meaning 'Living Goddess', she is chosen from the Buddhist goldsmith's caste when she is three years old and must be without any physical blemish. She assumes divinity after proving her bravery by remaining alone for a while in a darkened room filled with skeletons and gruesome objects. Thereafter she spends much of her time reciting prayers to Hindu gods until puberty when she

ceases to be divine, and is replaced by a new goddess. During her term of office, Kumari Devi is supported by the state and lives with her family and friends in a temple in Kathmandu's Durbar Square. She is allowed out once a year. Worshippers, including the King of Nepal, visit her temple and place their heads between her knees for luck. The period of divinity carries a heavy penalty for the girls, however. Nepalese men, possibly daunted by the thought of marrying a goddess, even a former goddess, often avoid them later in life. In addition, Nepalese folklore predicts an early death for the goddess's husband.

## RITE OF SPRING

Children in parts of Czechoslovakia burn a straw effigy before Easter to mark the passing of winter. The effigy is of a figure of death called Smrt, and is decorated with coloured rags and strands of eggshells. The straw figure is carried into the fields and either burnt or thrown into a river. After Smrt's destruction, the children carry flower garlands home to symbolise the arrival of spring.

## CHEAP RENT

A small tricolour flag is used to pay the rent on one of the properties of the British monarch. Every June 18, on Waterloo Day, the current Duke of Wellington formally presents the Queen with the flag at a special dinner held in the Waterloo Chamber at Windsor Castle. The flag is the rent due for the lease of the Strathfield Saye estate, granted to the first duke after his victory over Napoleon at the Battle of Waterloo in 1815. The rent has never gone up.

## GIFTS FROM THE GODS

Followers of some of the world's youngest and most bizarre religions believe that modern technology originates from supernatural sources. Cargo cults, as these religions are called, sprang up among many primitive and isolated New Guinea and Melanesian tribes after they came into contact with white culture from the late 19th century onwards. Devotees believe that aeroplanes, for instance, are messengers from the gods or from the spirits of their dead ancestors. Tribesmen pray to the gods for gifts such as radios, tinned foods and refrigerators. Sometimes they even destroy or abandon everything they own, and build storehouses to hold the gifts and gadgets they hope soon to receive.

## LOOK, NO HANDS

Bulgarian children help their parents prepare for Lent by trying to eat food dangled on strings from the ceiling, without using their hands. Lumps of cheese, hard-boiled eggs and Turkish delight are hung as titbits for children as families use up their dairy products – forbidden during Lent by the Orthodox Christian Church. The festival, called Cheese Week, takes place immediately before Lent. Cheese Week is also celebrated in Greece. Orthodox Russians call the festival Butter Week, using up their butter and eggs in special rye-flour pancakes known as *bliny*.

## GORGING BEFORE FASTING

A 1000-egg omelette is eaten on the Friday before Lent at Ponti in Italy. This feast is one of many similar traditions which are observed in Christian countries before Lent, a period of abstinence lasting for 40 days (excluding Sundays) to commemorate Christ's time in the wilderness.

Lent formally begins on Ash Wednesday. Since Christians were traditionally forbidden meat and dairy produce during Lent, they used up these foods beforehand. Eggs and butter are often eaten on Shrove

Tuesday, popularly called Pancake Day in Britain, and on Mardi Gras, meaning 'Fat Tuesday', in France. In Germany the ritual is called Fastnacht or 'Eve of the Fast'. Italy and many other Catholic countries call this feast a carnival, a word derived from the Latin phrase *carnem levare*, meaning 'to remove the meat'.

In such countries the carnival has developed into a boisterous festival, marked by noisy parades, dancing, fireworks, masquerades and feasting, that sometimes lasts for up to a fortnight. The most spectacular carnivals are at Rio de Janeiro in Brazil and at New Orleans in the United States.

## SPRING CLEANING

Greeks smash jugs against their front doors, crying 'Away with fleas and mice!', while their children bang on tins and shout 'Away February, welcome March!' every March 1. According to superstition, only if the ritual is observed on this specific day will homes be rid of fleas and mice for the remainder of the year. Spring cleaning traditionally occurs in Britain and many other countries at about the same time.

## SURPRISE PACKAGE

Swedish men sometimes give themselves as presents to their girlfriends at Christmas. Concealed in huge gift-wrapped boxes, they have themselves delivered to their girlfriends' homes. Alternatively, presents known as *julklapp* are sometimes elaborately disguised so that they seem much bigger than they really are. This is done by placing a small present in progressively larger boxes, each covered with paper and tightly tied with string – rather like Chinese boxes.

## EIGHT-DAY WONDER

One of the most famous Jewish emblems is the seven-stemmed candelabrum (known as the *menorah* in Hebrew), which commemorates the seven lamps of Solomon's Temple. But once a year Jews use a larger, nine-stemmed *menorah* to commemorate a victory. In 165 BC the Jewish leader Judas Maccabeus defeated the Syrian king Antiochus Epiphanes and occupied Jerusalem. When the Jews entered the temple they discovered that there was only enough oil left to keep the lamps lit for one day. Miraculously, however, the oil lasted for eight days, until more oil could be bought. The episode is celebrated in the eight-day Festival of Lights, called *Chanukkah* in Hebrew, which begins in December. On the first evening of the festival a single branch of the *menorah* is lit. Each subsequent evening a further branch is lit until by the end of the festival all the branches are alight. The ninth branch of the *menorah* is a pilot light which is kept burning throughout the festival. Special pancakes, called *latkes*, are also eaten and children play with a top bearing four Hebrew letters standing for the words 'a great miracle happened here'.

LAMP OF FAITH *Aaron, the elder brother of Moses and first high priest of the Jews, fills the seven-branched lamp known to Jews as the* menorah *in a detail from a Hebrew manuscript dating from the late 13th century.*

## JUNE WEDDINGS

The popularity of June weddings is an age-old tradition. It was the ancient Romans' favourite time because they believed that Juno, the goddess of marriage, would bring prosperity and happiness to all who wed in her month. The custom also has practical advantages. Marriage in June meant that the bride was likely to bear her first child in early spring, allowing her time to recover before the next harvest. As an old Scottish proverb put it: 'He's a fool that marries at Yule, For when the corn's to shear, the bairn's to bear.'

## SECRET BRIDES

Brides have traditionally gone to great trouble to conceal their identity from evil spirits. In ancient Sparta, brides disguised themselves as men and cut their hair short to confuse malevolent spirits. The bridal veil may also have first been adopted to hide the bride from evil spirits who might cast a spell on the bride and groom and ruin their marriage. Even brides-maids may have been first introduced as a way of protecting the bride. For if she surrounded herself with girls of her own age in similar dress, it was hoped that the spirits would be confused and only the groom would recognise her.

## DUCKING THE ELEPHANT

Hindus celebrate the birthday of their elephant god, Ganesh, by parading his statue through the streets and then ducking it in a river or lake. Ganesh is depicted as a red fat man with a pot belly, four arms and an elephant head with a single tusk, and he usually rides on a rat. Regarded as the remover of obstacles, he is particularly popular with merchants, who often invoke his favour at the start of a new business enterprise. Many banks display his image outside their premises, and if ever they go bankrupt they turn his face to the wall.

# CALENDAR OF FESTIVALS

Many festivals around the world are based on the lunar calendar, so that – like Easter – they fall on different dates each year. In this list, specific dates are given only for festivals which always fall on the same day. The entries also identify places or groups associated with each event.

## JANUARY

**January – February**
Kitchen God Festival
China
**January – February**
Yuan Tan (Chinese New Year)
China
**January 1**
New Year's Day
Gregorian Calendar
**January 1**
First Footing
Scotland and Northern England
**January 6**
Epiphany
Christian
**January 6 – 7**
Christmas Eve and Christmas Day
Eastern Orthodox (Julian Calendar)

## FEBRUARY

**February – March:**
**week before Lent**
Butter and Cheese Week
Eastern Orthodox
**February – March: day**
**before Ash Wednesday**
Shrove Tuesday
Christian
**February – March**
Carnival
Catholic countries
**February – March**
Ash Wednesday (1st day of Lent)
Christian
**February – March**
Purim (Feast of Lots)
Jewish
**February – March**
Holi (Festival of Fire)
Hindu
**February – April**
Lent
Christian
**February 2**
Candlemas Day
Christian
**February 3**
Setsubun
(Bean Throwing Night)
Japan
**February 14**
St Valentine's Day
Christian

## MARCH

**March – April**
Pesach (Passover)
Jewish
**March – May**
Easter
Christian
**March 3**
Hinamatsuri
(Girls' Festival)
Japan
**March 17**
St Patrick's Day
Ireland
USA
**March 21**
Noruz (New Year's Day)
Iran
**March 25**
Feast of Annunciation
Christian

## APRIL

**April – May**
Baisakhi (New Year Festival)
Hindu
**April – May**
Wesak
Southeast Asia
Buddhist

## MAY

**May – June**
Pentecost (Feast of Weeks)
Jewish
**May – June: 50 days**
**after Easter**
Pentecost/Whit Sunday
Christian
**May – June: Sunday**
**after Pentecost**
Trinity Sunday
Christian
**May – June: Thursday**
**after Trinity Sunday**
Corpus Christi
Roman Catholic

GOING A-MAYING *An English sketch published in 1826 shows May Day revellers in Norfolk celebrating the start of summer.*

**May 1**
May Day
Worldwide
**May 5**
Tango-No-Sekku (Boys' Festival)
Japan

## JUNE

**June – July**
Juggernaut Festivals
India

## JULY

**July 2 (and August 16)**
Palio
Italy
**July 4**
Independence Day
USA
**July 14**
Bastille Day
France

## AUGUST

**August – September**
Birthday of Krishna
Hindu
**August 15**
The Assumption of the Virgin Mary
Roman Catholic

## SEPTEMBER

**September**
Chinese Moon Festival
China
**September – October**
Rosh Hashanah (New Year)
Jewish
**September – October**
Yom Kippur (Day of Atonement)
Jewish

**September – October**
Succoth (Harvest Festival)
Jewish

## OCTOBER

**October – November**
Diwali (Harvest Festival)
Hindu
**October 31**
Halloween
N Europe, USA

## NOVEMBER

**November – December:**
**Sunday nearest to St**
**Andrew's Day**
Advent Sunday
Christian
**November 2**
Day of the Dead
Mexico
**November 5**
Guy Fawkes Day
England
**November 11**
Remembrance Day
Canada
**November: 2nd Sunday**
Remembrance Sunday
Britain
**November: 4th**
**Thursday**
Thanksgiving, USA
**November 30**
St Andrew's Day, Scotland

## DECEMBER

**December**
Chanukkah (Festival of Lights)
Jewish
**December**
Winter Solstice Feast
China
**December 13**
St Lucia's Day, Sweden
**December 16 – 24**
Posadas (Nativity)
Mexico
**December 24**
Christmas Eve
Christian
**December 25**
Christmas Day
Christian
**December 26**
Boxing Day, Britain
**December 31**
New Year's Eve
Gregorian calendar

## ANY MONTH

Ramadan, ninth month of the Muslim year. It can fall in any month because the Muslim calendar, which is lunar, does not keep in step with the seasons.

# PLACES

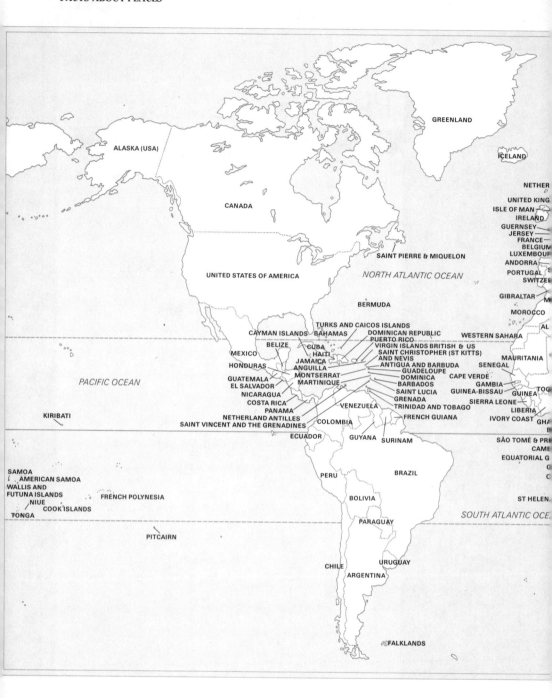

# Nations of the world

## COUNTRY WHERE NO ONE IS BORN

The world's smallest independent state is the Vatican City, with a population of about 1000 – and a nil birthrate. Its area is 0.44km² (0.17 square miles). The country with the largest area is the USSR. It covers 22,402,200km² (8,649,500 square miles).

The country with the largest population is the People's Republic of China, which in 1982 had nearly 1032 million inhabitants – almost one in four of the world's people.

## THE INCREDIBLE SHRINKING COUNTRY

Two disastrous wars and one near-war have cost Bolivia more than half the territory to which it laid claim when it became independent in 1825. In the 1879 – 83 War of the Pacific, Chile annexed Bolivia's Pacific seacoast, along with the port of Antofagasta and the mineral-rich Atacama Desert. In 1903, when war with neighbouring Brazil was narrowly avoided, Bolivia was forced to cede the rubber-producing Acre territory to Brazil. Finally, after the 1932 – 5 Chaco

War with Paraguay, Bolivia lost three-quarters of the southern Chaco region which it claimed. It also abandoned hope of an outlet of its own to the Atlantic along the Paraguay river, at a point where the river is navigable for large vessels. Despite having no coastline, Bolivia still has a navy of some 4000 men. They are confined, however, to the calm waters of Lake Titicaca high in the Andes and to stretches of some rivers on the fringes of the Amazon basin.

## THE NEED FOR AN HEIR

If Monaco's ruling House of Grimaldi should ever be without an heir (male or female), the country will cease to be a sovereign state. Instead, under a 1918 treaty between France and Monaco, the principality will become a self-governing French protectorate.

## VENICE – SOUTH AMERICAN STYLE

While sailing along the Caribbean coast of South America in 1499, the Spanish explorer Alonso de Ojedo saw Indian houses built on stilts over the water. The area reminded him of Venice and so he named it 'Little Venice', which in Spanish is Venezuela.

## COASTLINE OF ISLANDS

Indonesia consists entirely of islands – somewhere between 3000 and 3500 of them, though the number has never been precisely calculated. As a result, it has the world's second longest coastline at 54,716km (33,978 miles), but is only the fifteenth largest nation. The nation with the longest coastline is Canada, which is five times larger than Indonesia.

147

## THE FRENCH FOR FALKLANDS

Islas Malvinas, the Argentine name for the Falkland Islands, is not of Spanish origin but of French. Many of the sailors who went there early in the 18th century to fish and hunt seals were from St Malo in Brittany – so the French called the islands Iles Malouines, after the townsfolk. In Spanish this became Islas Malvinas. The name 'Falklands' came from an English sailor, Captain John Strong, who in 1690 named the sound between the two main islands Falkland Sound after Viscount Falkland, then the Treasurer of the British Navy.

## CHANGING HANDS

In the 17th and 18th centuries the West Indian island of Tobago changed hands a record 31 times as one country after another sought to use it as a Caribbean naval base. The keenest rivals were the British, Spanish, French and Dutch – and they were even chal-

# NATIONS A – Z/Afghanistan-Bolivia

This list contains basic information about all the independent nations of the world, and about the major dependent territories. Details of national capitals can be found on pages 170 – 7, and of national flags on pages 178 – 81.

**AFGHANISTAN**
Area 647,497km² (249,995 square miles).
Population 15,900,000 (1980).
Climate Continental; average temperature in Kabul ranges from −8 to 2°C (18 – 36°F) in January to 16 – 33°C (61 – 91°F) in July.
Government Socialist republic; under Soviet occupation.
Language Pushtu, Dari (Persian).
Religion Muslim.
Currency Afghàni (Af) = 100 puls.

**ALBANIA**
Area 28,748km² (11,100 square miles).
Population 2,595,000 (1979).
Climate Mediterranean; average temperature in Tirana ranges from 2 – 12°C (36 – 54°F) in January to 17 – 31°C (63 – 88°F) in July.
Government Socialist republic.
Language Albanian.
Religion Largely Muslim; also Greek Orthodox and Roman Catholic. Officially atheist.
Currency Lek (Lk) = 100 quintars.
National anthem *The flag that united us in the struggle*.

**ALGERIA**
Area 2,381,741km² (919,590 square miles).
Population 19,536,000 (1982).
Climate Mediterranean on the coast, hot and dry in the south. Average temperature in Algiers ranges from 9 – 15°C (48 – 59°F) in January to 22 – 29°C (72 – 84°F) in August.
Government Socialist republic.
Language 80% Arabic; also Berber and French.
Religion Muslim.
Currency Algerian dinar (AD) = 100 centimes.
National anthem *A vow to God*.

**ANDORRA**
Area 464km² (179 square miles).
Population 40,000 (1982).
Climate Winters are harsh, summers cool and usually sunny and dry. Average temperature in Les Escaldes ranges from −1 to 6°C (30 – 43°F) in January to 12 – 26°C (54 – 79°F) in July.
Government Principality.
Language Catalan; also Spanish and French.
Religion Mainly Roman Catholic.
Currency French franc and Spanish peseta.
National anthem *The great Charlemagne my father*.

**ANGOLA**
Area 1,246,700km² (481,351 square miles).
Population 6,900,000 (1981 estimate).
Climate Tropical; average temperature in Luanda ranges from 18°C (64°F) to 30°C (86°F).
Government One-party socialist republic.
Language Portuguese, African languages.
Religion Mainly tribal.
Currency Kwanza (Kw) = 100 lwei.

**ANGUILLA**
Area 91km² (35 square miles).
Population 6500 (1980 estimate).
Climate Subtropical; average temperature ranges from 24°C (75°F) to 27°C (81°F).
Government UK dependency with internal self-government.
Language English.
Religion Christian.
Currency East Caribbean dollar (EC$) = 100 cents.
National anthem *God Save the Queen*.

**ANTIGUA AND BARBUDA**
Area 441km² (170 square miles).
Population 100,000 (1980).
Climate Tropical; average temperature ranges from 22°C (72°F) to 30°C (86°F).
Government Constitutional monarchy.
Language English.
Religion Christian.
Currency East Caribbean dollar (EC$) = 100 cents.

**ARGENTINA**
Area 2,791,810km² (1,077,639 square miles).
Population 27,863,000 (1980).
Climate Subtropical in the north to subarctic in the south. Average temperature in Buenos Aires ranges from −5 to 14°C (23 – 57°F) in June to 17 – 29°C (63 – 84°F) in January.
Government Federal republic.
Language Spanish.
Religion Mainly Roman Catholic.
Currency Argentine peso (Arg$) = 100 centavos.
National anthem *Hear, O mortals! the sacred cry*.

**AUSTRALIA**
Area 7,686,848km² (2,967,892 square miles).
Population 15,379,000 (1983).
Climate Generally hot and dry. Average temperature in Canberra ranges from 1 – 11°C (34 – 52°F) in July to 13 – 28°C (55 – 82°F) in January.
Government Federal parliamentary monarchy.
Language English.
Religion 31% Church of England, 27% Catholic, 29% other Christian.
Currency Australian dollar (A$) = 100 cents.
National anthem *Advance Australia fair*.
National emblem Wattle (Australian acacia).

**AUSTRIA**
Area 83,855km² (32,368 square miles).
Population 7,555,000 (1981).
Climate Temperate continental. Average temperature in Vienna ranges from −4 to 1°C (25 – 34°F) in January to 15 – 25°C (59 – 77°F) in July.
Government Democratic federal republic.
Language 99% German; also Slovene, Croat, Hungarian, Czech.
Religion 88% Roman Catholic, 6% Protestant.
Currency Schilling (Sch) = 100 groschen.
National anthem *Land of mountains, land of rivers*.

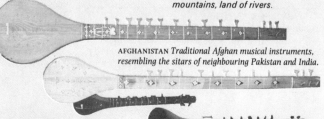

AFGHANISTAN *Traditional Afghan musical instruments, resembling the sitars of neighbouring Pakistan and India.*

lenged by settlers from minor powers such as Latvia (now part of Russia). Tobago was eventually ceded to Britain in 1814 and was joined with Trinidad in 1899 as a British Crown Colony. The two islands became independent in 1962.

## LAKE LAKE LAND

When Nyasaland adopted the name Malawi on its independence in 1964, it partially removed from the map of Africa a reminder of a misunderstanding which arose 105 years earlier. Nyasaland was originally named after Lake Nyasa – a name bestowed by the Scottish explorer David Livingstone. Livingstone reached the lake in 1859 and asked local people what it was called. He was told *nyasa* and he therefore called the water Lake Nyasa. However, *nyasa* was not the name, simply a word meaning 'mass of waters'. So Lake Nyasa meant, in effect, 'Lake lake'.

In 1964 Malawi's new government renamed the lake Lake Malawi, a name derived from Maravi, a

### BAHAMAS
**Area** 13,935km² (5380 square miles).
**Population** 210,000 (1980).
**Climate** Mild and subtropical; average temperature in Nassau ranges from 18–25°C (64–77°F) in February to 24–32°C (75–90°F) in August.
**Government** Parliamentary monarchy.
**Language** English.
**Religion** Mainly Anglican, Roman Catholic and Baptist.
**Currency** Bahamian dollar (Ba$) = 100 cents.
**National anthem** *March on Bahamaland*.

### BAHRAIN
**Area** 598km² (230 square miles).
**Population** 359,000 (1981).
**Climate** Very dry; very hot summers with high humidity. Average temperature ranges from 14–20°C (57–68°F) in January to 29–38°C (84–100°F) in August.
**Government** Sheikdom.
**Language** Arabic, English.
**Religion** Muslim.
**Currency** Bahrain dinar (BD) = 1000 fils.

### BANGLADESH
**Area** 143,998km² (55,598 square miles).
**Population** 87,051,000 (1981).
**Climate** Tropical; monsoon from June to September. Dry season between January and March. Average temperature in Chittagong ranges from 13–26°C (55–79°F) in January to 25–31°C (77–88°F) in June.
**Government** Republic.

**Language** 85% Bengali, English.
**Religion** 85% Muslim.
**Currency** Taka (Tk) = 100 poisha.
**National anthem** *My Bengal of gold, I love you.*
**National emblem** Water lily.

### BARBADOS
**Area** 431km² (166 square miles).
**Population** 251,000 (1982).
**Climate** Subtropical; average temperature in Bridgetown ranges from 21–28°C (70–82°F) in February to 23–31°C (73–88°F) in June to September.
**Government** Parliamentary monarchy.
**Language** English.
**Religion** Mainly Anglican.
**Currency** Barbados dollar (Bds$) = 100 cents.
**National anthem** *In plenty and in time of need.*
**National emblem** Head of a trident.

### BELGIUM
**Area** 30,519km² (11,783 square miles).
**Population** 9,855,000 (1982).
**Climate** Temperate; average temperature in Brussels ranges from −1 to 4°C (30–39°F) in January to 12–23°C (54–73°F) in July.
**Government** Parliamentary monarchy.
**Language** Flemish and Walloon (French).
**Religion** 90% Roman Catholic.
**Currency** Belgian franc (BFr) = 100 centimes.
**National anthem** *The Brabançonne.*
**National emblem** Lion.

### BELIZE (formerly British Honduras)
**Area** 22,965km² (8867 square miles).
**Population** 158,000 (1983 estimate).
**Climate** Subtropical; average temperature in Belize City ranges from 19–27°C (66–81°F) in January to 24–31°C (75–88°F) in August.
**Government** Parliamentary monarchy.
**Language** English and Spanish; also Creole and local languages.
**Religion** Christian.
**Currency** Belizean dollar (Bz$) = 100 cents.
**National anthem** *Land of the free.*

### BENIN (formerly Dahomey)
**Area** 112,622km² (43,483 square miles).
**Population** 3,520,000 (1981 estimate).
**Climate** Tropical; average temperature in Cotonou ranges from 23°C (73°F) to 28°C (82°F).
**Government** Socialist republic.
**Language** French, tribal.
**Religion** 65% tribal, also Christian and Muslim.
**Currency** African Financial Community franc (CFAFr) = 100 centimes.

### BERMUDA
**Area** 53km² (21 square miles).
**Population** 54,000 (1980 estimate).
**Climate** Subtropical; average temperature ranges from 8°C (46°F) to 21°C (70°F).
**Government** UK dependency with internal self-government.
**Language** English.
**Religion** Christian.
**Currency** Bermuda dollar (Bda$) = 100 cents.
**National anthem** *God save the Queen.*

### BHUTAN
**Area** 47,000km² (18,000 square miles).
**Population** 1,300,000 (1980 estimate).
**Climate** Temperate; average temperature in Thimphu ranges from 4°C (39°F) in January to 17°C (63°F) in July.
**Government** Constitutional monarchy.
**Language** Dzongkha (Tibetan/ Burmese), Nepali, English.
**Religion** 75% Mahayana Buddhist, 25% Hindu.
**Currency** Ngultrum (N) = 100 chetrum.

### BOLIVIA
**Area** 1,098,581km² (424,062 square miles).
**Population** 5,300,000 (1980 estimate).
**Climate** Tropical; cooler at altitude. Temperature in La Paz varies little from the annual average of 10°C (50°F). Very dry.
**Government** Republic.
**Language** Spanish; also local languages.
**Religion** Roman Catholic.
**Currency** Bolivian pesa (B$) = 100 centavos.
**National anthem** *People of Bolivia, happy destiny.*

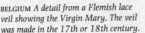

BELGIUM *A detail from a Flemish lace veil showing the Virgin Mary. The veil was made in the 17th or 18th century.*

kingdom said to have ruled from the Zambezi river to the eastern part of Mombasa in the 16th and 17th centuries. But other countries bordering the lake still call it Lake Nyasa.

## THE INTERNATIONAL ANTHEM

The tune of *God Save the Queen* (or King) is based upon a keyboard piece written in 1619 by the English composer Dr John Bull. But despite its origin it has been used as a national anthem by various other countries besides Britain. Germany's national anthem between 1870 and 1922, *Heil Dir im Siegerkranz* ('Hail to the Conqueror's Crown'), was sung to the same tune. So was the Swiss song *Rufst du, mein Vaterland* ('Hail to You, my Fatherland'), which often did duty as an anthem until 1961, when Switzerland officially adopted a new anthem.

In the United States, immediately after the Declaration of Independence in 1776, the old British anthem was often used with new words – such as 'God save

# NATIONS A – Z/Botswana-Cuba

## BOTSWANA (formerly Bechuanaland)
**Area** 581,730km² (224,605 square miles).
**Population** 800,000 (1980).
**Climate** Subtropical and dry; average temperature in Francistown ranges from 5–22°C (41–72°F) in June to 18–33°C (64–91°F) in December/January.
**Government** Republic.
**Language** Setswana, English.
**Religion** Christian, tribal.
**Currency** Pula (P) = 100 thebe.

## BRAZIL
**Area** 8,511,965km² (3,286,470 square miles).
**Population** 119,024,600 (1980).
**Climate** Mainly tropical and subtropical. Average temperature at Rio de Janeiro ranges from 17–24°C (63–75°F) in July to 23–29°C (73–84°F) in February.
**Government** Republic.
**Language** Portuguese.
**Religion** Roman Catholic.
**Currency** Cruzeiro (Cr) = 100 centavos.
**National anthem** *The peaceful banks of the River Ipiranga.*

## BRUNEI
**Area** 5765km² (2226 square miles).
**Population** 220,000 (1980).
**Climate** Tropical; generally very humid and wet. Average temperature ranges from 24°C (75°F) to 30°C (86°F).
**Government** Sultanate.
**Language** Mostly Malay, Chinese, English.
**Religion** Muslim, Confucianist, Buddhist, Taoist.
**Currency** Brunei dollar (Br$) = 100 sen (cents).

## BULGARIA
**Area** 110,912km² (42,823 square miles).
**Population** 8,929,000 (1982).
**Climate** Continental in the mountains and the north, Mediterranean in the south-facing valleys. Average temperature in Sofia ranges from −4 to 2°C (25–36°F) in January to 16–27°C (61–81°F) in July.
**Government** Communist republic.
**Language** Bulgarian.
**Religion** Mainly atheist; 30% Greek Orthodox.
**Currency** Lev (Lv) = 100 stótinki.
**National anthem** *Dear Fatherland.*

## BURMA
**Area** 676,552km² (261,217 square miles).
**Population** 35,680,000 (1982/3).
**Climate** Tropical; monsoon from May to September. Average temperature in Rangoon ranges from 18–32°C (64–90°F) in January to 24–36°C (75–97°F) in April.
**Government** Socialist republic.
**Language** Burmese; also tribal.
**Religion** Mainly Buddhist.
**Currency** Kyat (Kt) = 100 pyas.
**National anthem** *We shall love evermore Burma.*

## BURUNDI
**Area** 27,834km² (10,747 square miles).
**Population** 4,500,000 (1980).
**Climate** Tropical; average temperature in Bujumbura 24°C (75°F).
**Government** Republic.
**Language** French, Kirundi.
**Religion** Tribal, Roman Catholic, also Muslim.
**Currency** Burundi franc (BuFr) = 100 centimes.

## CAMEROON
**Area** 475,442km² (183,569 square miles).
**Population** 8,500,000 (1980).
**Climate** Tropical; average temperature in Yaoundé ranges from 18°C (64°F) to 29°C (84°F).
**Government** One-party republic.
**Language** French, English, tribal.
**Religion** Tribal, Roman Catholic, Muslim.
**Currency** African Financial Community franc (CFAFr) = 100 centimes.
**National anthem** *O Cameroon, cradle of our ancestors.*

## CANADA
**Area** 9,976,139km² (3,851,787 square miles).
**Population** 24,848,000 (1983).
**Climate** Arctic, continental and marine; average temperature in Ottawa ranges from −15 to −6°C (5–21°F) in January to 15–26°C (59–79°F) in July.
**Government** Federal parliamentary monarchy.
**Language** English and French.
**Religion** Mainly Christian.
**Currency** Canadian dollar (C$) = 100 cents.
**National anthem** *O Canada.*
**National emblem** Maple leaf.

## CAPE VERDE
**Area** 4,033km² (1,557 square miles).
**Population** 300,000 (1980).
**Climate** Tropical maritime; average temperature at Praia ranges from 19–25°C (66–77°F) in February/March to 24–29°C (75–84°F) in October.
**Government** One-party republic.
**Language** Portuguese.
**Religion** Roman Catholic.
**Currency** Cape Verde escudo (CVEsc) = 100 centavos.

## CAYMAN ISLANDS
**Area** 260km² (100 square miles).
**Population** 18,000 (1979).
**Climate** Subtropical; average temperature in George Town ranges from 18–24°C (64–75°F) in January/February to 24–30°C (75–86°F) in July/August.
**Government** UK dependency.
**Language** English.
**Religion** Mainly Protestant.
**Currency** Cayman Islands dollar (CI$) = 100 cents.
**National anthem** *Beloved isle Cayman.*

## CENTRAL AFRICAN REPUBLIC
**Area** 622,984km² (240,534 square miles).
**Population** 2,200,000 (1980 estimate).
**Climate** Tropical; average temperature in Bangui ranges from 21–29°C (70–84°F) in July/August to 21–34°C (70–93°F) in February.
**Government** Republic.
**Language** Sango, French.
**Religion** Mainly tribal; Christian, Muslim.
**Currency** African Financial Community franc (CFAFr) = 100 centimes.

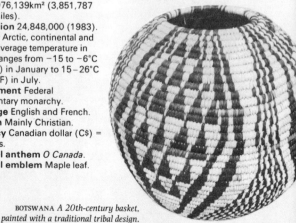

BOTSWANA *A 20th-century basket, painted with a traditional tribal design.*

George Washington' and 'God save the Thirteen States'. Another version, which began 'My country, 'tis of thee', was written in 1831 – and shared the honours with *The Star-Spangled Banner* as the US national song until 1931, when Congress officially chose the second song as the American anthem.

Other nations to use the tune of *God Save the Queen* for their anthems were Denmark, Sweden, Russia and several German states. But the only other independent country still to do so is Liechtenstein.

## THE KINGDOM THAT VANISHED

In 1771 the kingdom of Poland was larger in area than any other European country except Russia, and had a bigger population than any other European country except France. But within 25 years it had vanished from the map. In 1772 Russia, Prussia and Austria between them annexed about one-fifth of Poland. Twenty years later Russia took over half what remained, and all three powers shared in a final

### CHAD
**Area** 1,284,000km² (496,000 square miles).
**Population** 4,500,000 (1980).
**Climate** Tropical; average temperature in N'djamena ranges from 14 – 33°C (57 – 91°F) in December to 23 – 42°C (73 – 108°F) in April.
**Government** Republic.
**Language** French, Arabic, tribal.
**Religion** 52% Muslim, 43% tribal.
**Currency** African Financial Community franc (CFAFr) = 100 centimes.

### CHILE
**Area** 756,945km² (292,258 square miles).
**Population** 11,199,000 (1980).
**Climate** Varies from desert in the north to subarctic in the south. Average temperature in Santiago ranges from 3 – 14°C (37 – 57°F) to 12 – 29°C (54 – 84°F) in January.
**Government** Republic.
**Language** Spanish.
**Religion** Mainly Roman Catholic.
**Currency** Chilean peso (Ch$).
**National anthem** *Pure Chile, your sky is blue.*
**National emblems** Condor and huemul (small American deer).

### CHINA
**Area** 9,596,961km² (3,705,387 square miles).
**Population** 1,031,883,000 (1982).
**Climate** Temperate and humid in the southeast and central south, dry in the north and northeast. Average temperature in Beijing ranges from 1 – 8°C (34 – 46°F) in January to 22 – 31°C (72 – 88°F) in July/August.
**Government** Communist republic.
**Language** Chinese (including Mandarin and other dialects), Tibetan, Korean.
**Religion** Confucianist, Buddhist, Taoist, Muslim and others.
**Currency** Yuan (Y) = 100 fen.
**National anthem** *March on, brave people of our nation.*

### COLOMBIA
**Area** 1,138,914km² (439,735 square miles).
**Population** 28,500,000 (1982).
**Climate** Tropical; temperate on the plateaux. Average temperature in Bogota ranges from 10 – 18°C (50 – 64°F) in July to 9 – 20°C (48 – 68°F) in February.
**Government** Republic.
**Language** Spanish.
**Religion** Roman Catholic.
**Currency** Colombian peso (Col$) = 100 centavos.
**National anthem** *O unfading glory.*

### COMOROS
**Area** 2171km² (838 square miles).
**Population** 300,000 (1980).
**Climate** Tropical; average temperature in Moroni ranges from 19 – 27°C (66 – 81°F) in August to 24 – 31°C (75 – 88°F) in March.
**Government** Federal republic.
**Language** Swahili, Arabic, French.
**Religion** Muslim.
**Currency** African Financial Community franc (CFAFr) = 100 centimes.

### CONGO
**Area** 342,000km² (132,000 square miles).
**Population** 1,576,000 (1980).
**Climate** Tropical; average temperature in Brazzaville ranges from 17 – 28°C (63 – 82°F) in July to 22 – 33°C (72 – 91°F) in April.
**Government** One-party republic.
**Language** French, tribal.
**Religion** 50% tribal, 48% Christian.
**Currency** African Financial Community franc = 100 centimes.

### COOK ISLANDS
**Area** 234km² (90 square miles).
**Population** 18,200 (1979).
**Climate** Tropical; average

temperature in Rarotonga ranges from 18 – 25°C (64 – 77°F) in July to 23 – 29°C (73 – 84°F) in January.
**Government** Self-governing state in free association with New Zealand.
**Language** English, Polynesian.
**Currency** New Zealand dollar and Cook Islands dollar (CI$) = 100 cents.

### COSTA RICA
**Area** 50,700km² (19,600 square miles).
**Population** 2,190,000.
**Climate** Tropical; temperate on plateaux. Average temperature in San José ranges from 14 – 24°C (57 – 75°F) in December/January to 17 – 27°C (63 – 81°F) in May.
**Government** Republic.
**Language** Spanish.
**Religion** Roman Catholic.
**Currency** Costa Rican colón (CR¢) = 100 céntimos.
**National anthem** *Noble motherland, your beautiful flag.*

### CUBA
**Area** 110,922km² (42,827 square miles).
**Population** 9,706,000 (1981).
**Climate** Subtropical; average annual temperature ranges from 19°C (66°F) to 35°C (95°F).
**Government** Socialist republic.
**Language** Spanish.
**Religion** Roman Catholic.
**Currency** Cuban peso (Cub$) = 100 centavos.
**National anthem** *The Hymn of Bayamo.*

CONGO *A Bembe tribal mask, representing an old woman.*

CHINA *Sandalwood struts scent this delicate fan.*

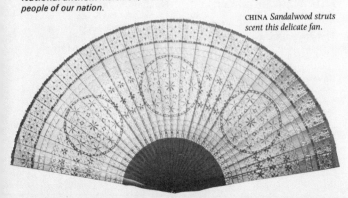

carve-up in 1795. It was not until 1918, in the aftermath of the First World War, that an independent Poland surfaced again.

into as many as five states whenever it chose. So far, though, the Lone Star State has remained intact: the second largest US state after Alaska.

## FIVE STATES IN ONE
The number of states in the USA could increase at any time from 50 to 54. The reason is that Texas could still exercise an option granted after it broke away from Mexico and became, in 1845, part of the USA. Congress decreed that the new state could divide itself

## SIX REPUBLICS, ONE NATION
Yugoslavia is one country with two alphabets, three religions, four principal languages, five main nationalities, and six republics. The alphabets are the Roman (used in English) and the Cyrillic (the alphabet used in Russia). The religions are Roman Catholicism, the

# NATIONS A – Z/Cyprus-West Germany

## CYPRUS
**Area** 9,251km² (3,572 square miles). **Population** 650,000 (1983 estimate). **Climate** Mediterranean; average temperature in Nicosia ranges from 5–15°C (41–59°F) in January to 21–37°C (70–99°F) in July. **Government** Republic. Since the 1974 invasion by Turkey the island has been effectively divided into North (Turkish sector) and South (Greek sector). **Language** Greek, Turkish, English. **Religion** 77% Greek Orthodox. **Currency** Cyprus pound (C£) = 1000 mils. **National anthem** *Hymn to Liberty*.

## CZECHOSLOVAKIA
**Area** 127,869km² (49,370 square miles). **Population** 15,280,000 (1980). **Climate** Continental; hot summers and cold winters. Average temperature in Prague ranges from −4 to 1°C (25–34°F) in January to 14–23°C (57–73°F) in July. **Government** Socialist republic. **Language** Czech and Slovak. **Religion** Mainly Roman Catholic. **Currency** Koruna, or crown (Krcs) = 100 haleru. **National anthem** *Where is my home?*

## DENMARK
**Area** 43,080km² (16,633 square miles). **Population** 5,123,989 (1981). **Climate** Maritime; average temperature in Copenhagen ranges from −3 to 2°C (27–36°F) in February to 14–22°C (57–72°F) in July. **Language** Danish. **Religion** Lutheran. **Currency** Danish krone (DKr) = 100 øre. **National anthem** *King Christian stood by the lofty mast.* **Royal anthem** *This is a lovely land.*

## DJIBOUTI
**Area** 22,300km² (18,000 square miles). **Population** 450,000 (1983). **Climate** Very hot and dry; average temperature in Djibouti City ranges from 23–29°C (73–84°F) in January to 31–41°C (88–106°F) in July. **Government** Republic. **Language** French, Arabic. **Religion** Muslim. **Currency** Djibouti franc (DjFr) = 100 centimes.

## DOMINICA
**Area** 751km² (290 square miles). **Population** 83,000 (1980). **Climate** Subtropical; average temperature ranges from 20–29°C (68–84°F) December to March, to 23–32°C (73–90°F) February to May. **Government** Republic. **Language** French patois, English. **Religion** Christian. **Currency** East Caribbean dollar (EC$) = 100 cents. **National anthem** *Isle of beauty, isle of splendour.* **National emblem** Sisserou parrot.

## DOMINICAN REPUBLIC
**Area** 48,442km² (18,703 square miles). **Population** 5,648,000 (1981). **Climate** Subtropical and maritime tropical; average temperature in Santo Domingo ranges from 19–29°C (66–84°F) in January to 23–31°C (73–88°F) in August. **Government** Republic. **Language** Spanish. **Religion** Roman Catholic. **Currency** Dominican Republic peso (DR$) = 100 centavos. **National anthem** *People of Quisqueya, we bravely raise our voices in song.*

## ECUADOR
**Area** 283,561km² (109,483 square miles). **Population** 8,000,000 (1980). **Climate** Tropical; cooler at altitude. Average temperature in Quito ranges from 8°C (46°F) to 21°C (70°F). **Government** Republic. **Language** Spanish, local languages. **Religion** Roman Catholic. **Currency** Sucre (Su) = 100 centavos. **National anthem** *Long live the country.*

## EGYPT
**Area** 1,002,000km² (387,000 square miles). **Population** 46,000,000 (1983). **Climate** Hot and dry; average temperature in Cairo ranges from 8–18°C (46–64°F) in January to 21–36°C (70–97°F) in July. **Government** Republic. **Language** Arabic. **Religion** Mainly Muslim. **Currency** Egyptian pound (E£) = 100 piastres = 1000 milliemes.

## EL SALVADOR
**Area** 21,041km² (8124 square miles). **Population** 5,124,000 (1981 estimate). **Climate** Subtropical, cool in the highlands; average temperature in San Salvador ranges from 16°C (61°F) to 33°C (91°F). **Government** Republic. **Language** Spanish. **Religion** Roman Catholic. **Currency** El Salvador colón (ES¢) = 100 centavos. **National anthem** *Let us proudly salute our fatherland.*

## EQUATORIAL GUINEA
**Area** 28,051km² (10,830 square miles). **Population** 400,000 (1980 estimate). **Climate** Tropical; average temperature in Malabo ranges from 21°C (70°F) to 32°C (90°F). **Government** Republic. **Language** Spanish, also African languages. **Religion** Roman Catholic. **Currency** Ekuele (E) = 100 céntimos.

## ETHIOPIA
**Area** 1,223,500km² (472,393 square miles). **Population** 32,774,000 (1982). **Climate** Temperate on plateau; hot on lowlands. Average temperature in Addis Ababa ranges from 5°C (41°F) to 25°C (77°F). **Government** Socialist republic. **Language** Amharic. **Religion** Ethiopian Orthodox (Coptic), Muslim. **Currency** Birr (Br) = 100 cents. **National anthem** *Ethiopia, Ethiopia.*

## FALKLANDS
**Area** 16,300km² (6300 square miles), including Sandwich Island group and South Georgia. **Population** 1810 (1980). **Climate** Generally cool and windy; average temperature in Stanley ranges from −1 to 4°C (30–39°F) in July to 6–13°C (43–55°F) in January. **Government** UK dependent territory. **Language** English. **Religion** Christian. **Currency** Falkland Islands pound (Fl£) = 100 new pence.

Eastern Orthodox Church and Islam. The four languages are Serb, Croat, Slovene and Macedonian – although the first two are often grouped together as Serbo-Croat. The five nationalities are Serbs, Croats, Slovenes, Macedonians and Montenegrins. The republics are Slovenia, Croatia, Bosnia-Herzegovina, Serbia, Montenegro and Macedonia. In addition, Yugoslavia has a common border with seven other countries: Italy, Austria, Hungary, Romania, Bulgaria, Greece and Albania.

## NEAR NEIGHBOURS
Although the United States and the Soviet Union are divided by a wide gulf politically, they are, at their closest point, only 4km (2.5 miles) apart. This is the distance between two islands in the Bering Strait: Big Diomede, which is Russian; and Little Diomede, which is American. The two islands are also, however, a whole day apart – because the International Date Line runs between them.

### FIJI
**Area** 18,333km² (7078 square miles).
**Population** 634,000 (1980).
**Climate** Tropical; average temperatures range from 20°C (68°F) in August to 30°C (86°F) in March.
**Government** Constitutional monarchy.
**Language** English, Fiji, Hindi.
**Religion** Christian, Hindu.
**Currency** Fiji dollar (F$) = 100 cents.
**National anthem** *God bless Fiji.*

### FINLAND
**Area** 337,009km² (130,119 square miles).
**Population** 4,844,000 (1982).
**Climate** Temperate, with cold winters. Average temperature in Helsinki ranges from −9 to −4°C (16 – 25°F) in February to 12 – 22°C (54 – 72°F) in July.
**Government** Republic.
**Language** Finnish and Swedish.
**Religion** Lutheran.
**Currency** Markka (FMk) = 100 penni.
**National anthem** *Our land.*

### FRANCE
**Area** 547,026km² (211,207 square miles).
**Population** 54,335,000 (1982).
**Climate** Temperate, with dry, hot summers on the Mediterranean coast. Average temperature in Paris ranges from 1 – 6°C (34 – 43°F) in January to 14 – 25°C (57 – 77°F) in July.

**Government** Republic.
**Language** French.
**Religion** Roman Catholic.
**Currency** Franc (Fr) = 100 centimes.
**National anthem** *The Marseillaise.*

### FRENCH GUIANA
**Area** 91,000km² (35,000 square miles).
**Population** 73,000 (1982).
**Climate** Hot and humid; average temperature in Cayenne ranges from 23°C (73°F) to 33°C (91°F).
**Government** External French department.
**Language** French.
**Religion** Roman Catholic.
**Currency** French franc (Fr) = 100 centimes.

### FRENCH POLYNESIA
**Area** 4000km² (1500 square miles).
**Population** 155,000 (1980 estimate).
**Climate** Tropical; average temperature in Papeete ranges from 20°C (68°F) to 32°C (90°F).
**Government** French overseas territory.
**Language** French, also Polynesian languages.
**Religion** Christian.
**Currency** French Pacific Community franc (CFPFr) = 100 centimes.

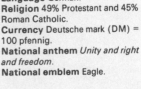

DENMARK *This piece of Copenhagen porcelain, showing a couple with their two dogs, was made in about 1870.*

### GABON
**Area** 267,667km² (103,347 square miles).
**Population** 600,000 (1980 estimate).
**Climate** Tropical; average temperature in Libreville ranges from 20°C (68°F) to 32°C (90°F).
**Government** Republic.
**Language** French; also African languages.
**Religion** Christian, tribal.
**Currency** African Financial Community franc (CFAFr) = 100 centimes.

### GAMBIA
**Area** 11,295km² (4361 square miles).
**Population** 603,000 (1980).
**Climate** Tropical; average temperature ranges from 16°C (61°F) November to April, to 38°C (100°F) May to September.
**Government** Republic.
**Language** English, African languages.
**Religion** 80% Muslim, tribal, Christian.
**Currency** Dalasi (Di) = 100 bututs.

### GERMANY, EAST (GERMAN DEMOCRATIC REPUBLIC)
**Area** 108,333km² (41,827 square miles).
**Population** 16,732,000 (1981).
**Climate** Continental, temperate; average temperature in Potsdam ranges from 1°C (34°F) in January to 18°C (64°F) in July.
**Government** Communist republic.
**Language** German.
**Religion** Mainly Protestant.
**Currency** Mark (DDR mark or 'Ostmark') = 100 pfennig.

### GERMANY, WEST (GERMAN FEDERAL REPUBLIC)
**Area** 248,577km² (95,976 square miles).
**Population** 61,561,000 (1980).
**Climate** Continental, temperate; average temperature in Frankfurt ranges from −1 to 3°C (30 – 37°F) in January to 14 – 25°C (57 – 77°F) in July.
**Government** Federal republic.
**Language** German.
**Religion** 49% Protestant and 45% Roman Catholic.
**Currency** Deutsche mark (DM) = 100 pfennig.
**National anthem** *Unity and right and freedom.*
**National emblem** Eagle.

# NATIONS A – Z/Ghana-Ivory Coast

## GHANA
**Area** 238,500km² (92,100 square miles).
**Population** 11,680,000 (1981 estimate).
**Climate** Tropical; average temperature in Accra ranges from 22°C (72°F) to 31°C (88°F).
**Government** Republic.
**Language** English, African languages.
**Religion** Tribal, Christian, Muslim.
**Currency** Cedi (₡) = 100 pesewas.
**National anthem** *God bless our homeland Ghana.*

## GIBRALTAR
**Area** 5.8km² (2.2 square miles).
**Population** 30,000 (1982).
**Climate** Temperate; average temperature ranges from 8–16°C (46–61°F) in February to 20–29°C (68–84°F) in August.
**Government** UK dependency.
**Language** English, also Spanish.
**Religion** 77% Roman Catholic.
**Currency** Gibraltar pound (Gib£) = 100 new pence = £1 sterling.
**National emblem** Castle and key.

## GREECE
**Area** 131,944km² (50,944 square miles).
**Population** 9,600,000 (1980 estimate).
**Climate** Mediterranean; average temperature in Athens ranges from 8–16°C (46–61°F) in February to 23–33°C (73–91°F) in July.
**Government** Republic.
**Language** Greek.
**Religion** Greek Orthodox.
**Currency** Drachma (Dr) = 100 lepta.
**National anthem** *Hymn to freedom.*

## GREENLAND
**Area** 2,175,600km² (840,000 square miles).
**Population** 51,000 (1981).
**Climate** Very cold; average temperature in Godthåb ranges from −12to−7°C (10–19°F) in January to 3–11°C (37–52°F) in July.
**Government** Part of the Kingdom of Denmark, with home rule.
**Language** Danish, also Eskimo.
**Religion** Mainly Lutheran.
**Currency** Danish krone (DKr) = 100 øre.

## GRENADA
**Area** 344km² (133 square miles).
**Population** 110,000 (1980).
**Climate** Subtropical; average temperature in St George's ranges from 23°C (73°F) to 31°C (88°F).
**Government** Parliamentary monarchy.
**Language** English.
**Religion** Christian.
**Currency** East Caribbean dollar (EC$) = 100 cents.

## GUADELOUPE
**Area** 1779km² (687 square miles).
**Population** 328,000 (1982).

**Climate** Subtropical; average temperature in Point-à-Pitre ranges from 17–24°C (63–75°F) in February to 21–28°C (70–82°F) in August/September.
**Government** Overseas French department.
**Language** French.
**Religion** Mainly Roman Catholic.
**Currency** French franc (Fr) = 100 centimes.
**National anthem** *The Marseillaise.*

## GUAM
**Area** 549km² (212 square miles).
**Population** 106,000 (1980).
**Climate** Tropical; average temperature all year round in Sumay ranges from 23°C (73°F) to 31°C (88°F).
**Government** US 'unincorporated' territory, self-governing.
**Language** English, Chamorro.
**Religion** 96% Roman Catholic.
**Currency** US dollar ($) = 100 cents.
**National song** *Stand ye Guamians.*

## GUATEMALA
**Area** 108,889km² (42,042 square miles).
**Population** 7,195,000 (1981).
**Climate** Subtropical, temperate on highlands. Average temperature in Guatemala City ranges from 12–23°C (54–73°F) in January to 16–29°C (61–84°F) in May.
**Government** Republic.
**Language** Spanish; also local languages.
**Religion** Roman Catholic.
**Currency** Quetzal (Q) = 100 centavos.
**National anthem** *Guatemala, blest land.*

## GUERNSEY and dependencies
**Area** 78.4km² (30.3 square miles).
**Population** 56,000 (1980 estimate).
**Climate** Temperate.
**Government** UK dependency with internal self-government.
**Language** English, French.
**Religion** Christian.
**Currency** UK pound and Guernsey pound (G£) = 100 new pence.

## GUINEA
**Area** 245,857km² (94,925 square miles).
**Population** 5,000,000 (1980 estimate).
**Climate** Tropical; average temperature in Conakry ranges from 22°C (72°F) to 32°C (90°F).
**Government** One-party republic.
**Language** French, local languages.
**Religion** Muslim, tribal.
**Currency** Syli (Sy) = 100 cauris.

## GUINEA-BISSAU (formerly Portuguese Guinea)
**Area** 36,125km² (13,948 square miles).
**Population** 777,000 (1979).
**Climate** Tropical; average temperature in Bolama ranges from

19°C (66°F) to 32°C (90°F).
**Government** One-party republic.
**Language** Portuguese; also Creole.
**Religion** Muslim, tribal, Christian.
**Currency** Guinea-Bissau peso (GBP) = 100 centavos.

## GUYANA (formerly British Guiana)
**Area** 214,969km² (82,999 square miles).
**Population** 793,000 (1980).
**Climate** Tropical; average temperature in Georgetown ranges from 23°C (73°F) to 31°C (88°F).
**Government** Republic.
**Language** English; also Creole, Hindi, Urdu and local languages.
**Religion** Christian, Hindu, Muslim.
**Currency** Guyanese dollar (G$) = 100 cents.
**National anthem** *Dear land of Guyana.*
**National emblem** Canje pheasant.

## HAITI
**Area** 27,750km² (10,714 square miles).
**Population** 5,800,000 (1980 estimate).
**Climate** Tropical; average temperature in Port-au-Prince ranges from 20°C (68°F) to 34°C (93°F).
**Government** Republic.
**Language** French, Creole.
**Religion** Roman Catholic; also Voodoo.
**Currency** Gourde (Gde) = 100 centimes.
**National anthem** *The Dessalinienne.*

## HONDURAS
**Area** 112,088km² (43,277 square miles).
**Population** 4,000,000 (1983 estimate).
**Climate** Tropical; average temperature in Tegucigalpa ranges from 6–25°C (43–77°F) in December/January to 11–31°C (52–88°F) in July/August. Wet season May to October.
**Government** Republic.
**Language** Spanish, also English.
**Religion** Roman Catholic.
**Currency** Lempira (La) = 100 centavos.
**National anthem** *Your standard serves.*

## HONG KONG
**Area** 1065km² (411 square miles).
**Population** 5,233,000 (1982 estimate).
**Climate** Subtropical; monsoon from May to September. Average temperature ranges from 16°C (61°F) in February to 29°C (84°F) in July/August.
**Government** British dependent territory.
**Language** English and Chinese.
**Religion** Mainly Buddhist and Taoist.
**Currency** Hong Kong dollar (HK$) = 100 cents.
**National flower** Bauhinia (orchid tree).

## HUNGARY
**Area** 93,030km² (35,919 square miles).
**Population** 10,700,000 (1980).
**Climate** Continental; average temperature in Budapest ranges from −4 to 1°C (25 − 34°F) in January to 16 − 28°C (61 − 82°F) in July.
**Government** Socialist republic.
**Language** Magyar (Hungarian).
**Religion** 50% Roman Catholic, 25% Protestant.
**Currency** Forint (F) = 100 fillér.
**National anthem** *God bless the Hungarians with good cheer and prosperity.*

## ICELAND
**Area** 103,000km² (39,800 square miles).
**Population** 235,000 (1982).
**Climate** Temperate; warmed by the Gulf Stream. Average temperature in Reykjavik ranges from −2 to 2°C (28 − 36°F) in January to 9 − 14°C (48 − 57°F) in July.
**Government** Republic.
**Language** Icelandic.
**Religion** Lutheran.
**Currency** Icelandic new króna (1 Kr) = 100 aurar (singular: eyrir).
**National anthem** *Iceland's thousand years.*

## INDIA
**Area** 3,287,782km² (1,269,084 square miles).
**Population** 685,185,000 (1981).
**Climate** Tropical; monsoon from June to September. Average temperature in New Delhi ranges from 7 − 21°C (45 − 70°F) in January to 26 − 41°C (79 − 106°F) in May.
**Government** Parliamentary republic, union of states.
**Language** Hindi and English, also other languages and dialects.
**Religion** 83% Hindu, also Muslims, Christians, Sikhs, Buddhists, Jains and others.
**Currency** Indian rupee (IR) = 100 paise.
**National anthem** *Thou art the ruler of minds.*

## INDONESIA
**Area** 1,904,569km² (735,354 square miles).
**Population** 150,000,000 (1983).
**Climate** Equatorial; average year-round temperature in Jakarta ranges from 23°C (73°F) to 33°C (91°F).
**Government** Republic.
**Language** Bahasa Indonesia; also other languages and dialects.
**Religion** 91% Muslim; also Roman Catholic, Protestant and Hindu.
**Currency** Rupiah (Rp) = 100 sen.
**National anthem** *Indonesia the Great.*

## IRAN
**Area** 1,648,000km² (636,000 square miles).
**Population** 38,500,000 (1980 estimate).
**Climate** Continental; average temperature in Tehran ranges from −3 to 7°C (27 − 45°F) in January to 22 − 37°C (72 − 99°F) in July.
**Government** Islamic republic.
**Language** Farsi (Persian).
**Religion** Muslim.
**Currency** Rial (RI) = 100 dinars.

## IRAQ
**Area** 434,924km² (167,924 square miles).
**Population** 13,300,000 (1980).
**Climate** Very hot summers, cool winters. Average temperature in Baghdad ranges from 4 − 16°C (39 − 61°F) in January to 24 − 50°C (75 − 122°F) in July/August.
**Government** Socialist republic.
**Language** Arabic; also Kurdish, Turkish and Assyrian.
**Religion** Muslim.
**Currency** Iraqi dinar (ID) = 20 dirhams = 1000 fils.
**National anthem** *Land of two rivers.*

## IRELAND, REPUBLIC OF
**Area** 70,283km² (27,136 square miles).
**Population** 3,443,000 (1981).
**Climate** Temperate; warmed by the Gulf Stream. Average temperature ranges from 4 − 7°C (39 − 45°F) in January/February to 14 − 16°C (57 − 61°F) in July/August.
**Government** Parliamentary republic.
**Language** English and Irish.
**Religion** Roman Catholic.
**Currency** Irish punt (pound) (I£) = 100 pighne (new pence).
**National anthem** *The soldier's song.*
**National emblem** Harp.

## ISRAEL
**Area** 20,700km² (7992 square miles).
**Population** 3,978,000 (1981).
**Climate** Subtropical; average temperature in Jerusalem ranges from 5 − 13°C (41 − 55°F) in January to 18 − 31°C (64 − 88°F) in August.
**Government** Republic.
**Language** Hebrew and Arabic.
**Religion** Jewish.
**Currency** Shekel (Sk).
**National anthem** *The Hope.*
**National emblem** Candelabrum.

## ITALY
**Area** 301,255km² (116,303 square miles).
**Population** 56,742,000 (1983).
**Climate** Mediterranean; average temperature in Rome ranges from 4 − 11°C (39 − 52°F) in January to 20 − 30°C (68 − 86°F) in July.
**Government** Republic.
**Language** Italian.
**Religion** Roman Catholic.
**Currency** Lira (L).
**National anthem** *Brothers of Italy.*

## IVORY COAST
**Area** 322,463km² (124,503 square miles).
**Population** 8,000,000 (1980).
**Climate** Tropical; average temperature in Abidjan ranges from 22°C (72°F) to 32°C (90°F).
**Government** One-party republic.
**Language** French; tribal.
**Religion** 65% tribal, 23% Muslim.
**Currency** African Financial Community franc (CFAFr) = 100 centimes.
**National anthem** *The Abidjanaise.*
**National emblem** Elephant.

IRAN *A Persian plate made in the 9th or 10th century.*

ITALY *Gleaming with gold leaf, this 16th-century glass goblet, which stands about 125mm (5in) high, was probably made in Venice.*

# NATIONS A – Z/Jamaica-Isle of Man

**JAMAICA**
**Area** 10,991km² (4244 square miles).
**Population** 2,188,000 (1980).
**Climate** Tropical at sea level, temperate in mountain areas. Average year-round temperature in Kingston ranges from 19°C (66°F) to 32°C (90°F).
**Government** Parliamentary monarchy.
**Language** English, Spanish.
**Religion** Roman Catholic, Protestant.
**Currency** Jamaican dollar (J$) = 100 cents.

**JAPAN**
**Area** 372,313km² (143,750 square miles).
**Population** 117,884,000 (1981 estimate).
**Climate** Monsoon climate modified by the influence of the sea. Average temperature in Tokyo ranges from −2 to 8°C (28–46°F) in January to 22–30°C (72–86°F) in August.
**Government** Parliamentary monarchy.
**Language** Japanese.
**Religion** The majority adhere to both Shintoism and Buddhism.
**Currency** Yen (¥).
**National anthem** *The reign of our Emperor.*

**JERSEY**
**Area** 116km² (45 square miles).
**Population** 76,100 (1980).
**Climate** Temperate.
**Government** UK dependency with internal self-government.
**Language** English, French.
**Religion** Christian.
**Currency** UK pound and Jersey pound (J£) = 100 new pence.

**JORDAN**
**Area** 96,000km² (37,740 square miles).
**Population** 3,050,000 (1981).
**Climate** Hot and dry, cool in winter. Average temperature in Amman ranges from 4–12°C (39–54°F) in January to 18–32°C (64–90°F) in August.
**Government** Constitutional monarchy.
**Language** Arabic.
**Religion** Muslim.
**Currency** Jordan dinar (JD) = 1000 fils.
**National anthem** *Long live the King.*

**KAMPUCHEA** (formerly Cambodia)
**Area** 181,035km² (69,898 square miles).
**Population** 5,756,141 (1981).
**Climate** Tropical; monsoon from April to October. Average annual temperature in Phnom Penh 27°C (81°F).
**Government** Communist republic.
**Language** Khmer.
**Religion** Buddhist.
**Currency** Riel (KRL) = 100 sen.

**KENYA**
**Area** 582,646km² (24,960 square miles).
**Population** 15,320,000 (1979).
**Climate** Tropical; temperate inland. Average temperature in Nairobi ranges from 11°C (52°F) to 26°C (79°F).
**Government** One-party republic.
**Language** Swahili and English; also other African languages.
**Religion** 50% Christian, 35% tribal, Muslim.
**Currency** Kenya shilling (KSh) = 100 cents.
**National anthem** *O God of all creation.*

**KIRIBATI** (formerly the Gilbert, Phoenix and Line Islands and Banaba)
**Area** 823km² (318 square miles).
**Population** 60,000 (1982 estimate).
**Climate** Tropical; average temperature in Tarawa ranges from 25°C (77°F) to 32°C (90°F).
**Government** Republic.
**Language** English, I-Kiribati.
**Religion** Christian.
**Currency** Australian dollar (A$) = 100 cents.
**National anthem** *Stand up Gilbertese.*

**KOREA, NORTH**
**Area** 120,538km² (46,540 square miles).
**Population** 17,900,000 (1980 estimate).
**Climate** Continental; average temperature in Wonsan ranges from −8 to −1°C (18–30°F) in January to 20–27°C (68–81°F) in August.
**Government** Communist republic.
**Language** Korean.
**Religion** Buddhist, Confucianist, Shamanist, Chundo kyo (Ch'ŏndogyo).
**Currency** North Korean won (NKW) = 100 jun.
**National anthem** *The song of General Kim Il Sung.*

**KOREA, SOUTH**
**Area** 98,484km² (38,025 square miles).
**Population** 40,000,000 (1983 estimate).
**Climate** Continental; average temperature in Seoul ranges from −9 to 0°C (16–32°F) in August to 22–31°C (72–88°F) in August.
**Government** One-party republic.
**Language** Korean.
**Religion** Buddhist, Christian, Confucianist, Chundo Kyo (Ch'ŏndogyo).
**Currency** South Korean won (SKW) = 100 chon (jun).
**National anthem** *Rose of Sharon, thousand miles of range and river land.*

**KUWAIT**
**Area** 17,818km² (6880 square miles).
**Population** 1,357,952 (1980).

**Climate** Hot and dry; average temperature in Kuwait City ranges from 8–18°C (46–64°F) in winter to 29–45°C (84–113°F) in summer.
**Government** Parliamentary emirate.
**Language** Arabic, English.
**Religion** Muslim.
**Currency** Kuwaiti dinar (KD) = 1000 fils.

**LAOS**
**Area** 236,800km² (91,400 square miles).
**Population** 3,725,000 (1982).
**Climate** Tropical; monsoon May to October. Average temperature in Vientiene ranges from 14–28°C (57–82°F) in January to 23–34°C (73–93°F) in April.
**Government** Communist republic.
**Language** Lao.
**Religion** Mainly Buddhist.
**Currency** Kip (Kp) = 100 att.
**National anthem** *For all time the Lao people have glorified their Fatherland.*

**LEBANON**
**Area** 10,452km² (4036 square miles).
**Population** 3,750,000 (1983 estimate).
**Climate** Subtropical; cool in highlands. Average temperature in Beirut ranges from 11–17°C (52–63°F) in January to 23–32°C (73–90°F) in August.
**Government** Republic.
**Language** Arabic.
**Religion** 50% Christian, 50% Muslim.
**Currency** Lebanese pound (L£) = 100 piastres.
**National anthem** *We are all for the motherland.*
**National emblem** Cedar tree.

**LESOTHO** (formerly Basutoland)
**Area** 30,355km² (11,720 square miles).
**Population** 1,300,000 (1980 estimate).
**Climate** Continental; average temperature in Maseru ranges from −3 to 17°C (27–63°F) in July to 15–33°C (59–91°F) in January.
**Government** Parliamentary monarchy.
**Language** Sesotho, English.
**Religion** 70% Christian.
**Currency** Loti (Lo) = 100 lisente.

**LIBERIA**
**Area** 111,369km² (43,000 square miles).
**Population** 2,000,000 (1982 estimate).
**Climate** Tropical; average temperature in Monrovia ranges from 22°C (72°F) to 31°C (88°F).
**Government** Republic.
**Language** English, tribal.
**Religion** Tribal, Christian, Muslim.
**Currency** Liberian (L$) and US dollars = 100 cents.
**National anthem** *All hail, Liberia, hail.*

## LIBYA
**Area** 1,759,540km² (679,358 square miles).
**Population** 3,000,000 (1980 estimate).
**Climate** Hot and dry, especially in the south; average temperature in Tripoli ranges from 8 – 16°C (46 – 61°F) in January to 22 – 30°C (72 – 86°F) in August.
**Government** Republic.
**Language** Arabic.
**Religion** Muslim.
**Currency** Libyan dinar (LD) = 1000 millemes.

## LIECHTENSTEIN
**Area** 160km² (62 square miles).
**Population** 25,000 (1980).
**Climate** Temperate.
**Government** Principality.
**Language** German.
**Religion** 82% Roman Catholic, 7% Protestant.
**Currency** Swiss franc or franken (SFr) = 100 centimes or rappen.
**National anthem** *Above the young Rhine river Liechtenstein is perched.*

## LUXEMBOURG
**Area** 2586km² (998 square miles).
**Population** 364,000 (1981).
**Climate** Temperate; average temperature in Luxembourg City ranges from −10 to 9°C (14 – 48°F) in January to 7 – 31°C (45 – 88°F) in July.
**Government** Parliamentary monarchy.
**Language** Letzeburgesh (a spoken language, but not a written one); French and German as well.
**Religion** Roman Catholic.
**Currency** Luxembourg franc (LFr) = 100 centimes.
**National anthem** *Our Fatherland.*
**National emblem** Lion with crown.

## MACAU (Macao)
**Area** 16km² (6 square miles).
**Population** 300,000 (1980 estimate).
**Climate** Subtropical.
**Government** Territory under Portuguese administration.
**Language** Chinese and Portuguese.
**Religion** Buddhist and Roman Catholic.
**Currency** Pataca (Pat) = 100 avos.

## MADAGASCAR
**Area** 587,041km² (226,657 square miles).
**Population** 8,700,000 (1980 estimate).
**Climate** Tropical; average temperature in Antananarivo, the capital, ranges from 9 – 20°C (48 – 68°F) in July to 16 – 27°C (61 – 81°F) in December.
**Government** Republic.
**Language** French and Malagasay; also local dialects.
**Religion** 51% tribal, 38% Christian, 5% Muslim.
**Currency** Madagascar franc (MgFr) = 100 centimes.

## MALAWI (formerly Nyasaland)
**Area** 118,484km² (45,747 square miles).
**Population** 5,951,000 (1980).
**Climate** Tropical; cooler in the highlands. Average temperature ranges from 7 – 23°C (45 – 73°F) in November to April, to 17 – 29°C (63 – 84°F) May to October.
**Government** One-party republic.
**Language** Chichewa, English.
**Religion** Christian, tribal.
**Currency** Malawi kwacha (MK) = 100 tambala.

## MALAYSIA
**Area** 330,434km² (127,580 square miles).
**Population** 14,200,000 (1982).
**Climate** Tropical; average temperature in Kuala Lumpur ranges from 22°C (72°F) to 33°C (91°F). Monsoon from October to February in the east and May to September in the west.
**Government** Parliamentary monarchy.
**Language** Malay; also Chinese, English and others.
**Religion** 50% Muslim, 26% Buddhist.
**Currency** Ringgit or dollar (Ma$) = 100 sen or cents.
**National anthem** *My country.*

## MALDIVES
**Area** 298km² (115 square miles).
**Population** 154,000 (1980).
**Climate** Tropical; average temperature ranges from 25°C (77°F) to 29°C (84°F). Monsoon from June to August.
**Government** Republic.
**Language** Divehi, English.
**Religion** Mainly Muslim.
**Currency** Maldivian rupee (MvR) = 100 laris.

## MALI
**Area** 1,240,000km² (479,000 square miles).
**Population** 6,830,000 (1981 estimate).
**Climate** Hot and dry; average temperature at Bamako ranges from 16 – 33°C (61 – 91°F) in January to 24 – 39°C (75 – 102°F) in April.
**Government** One-party republic.
**Language** French, local languages.
**Religion** 65% Muslim, 30% tribal.
**Currency** Mali franc (MFr) = 100 centimes.

## MALTA
**Area** 316km² (122 square miles).
**Population** 320,000 (1983).
**Climate** Mediterranean; average temperature in Valletta ranges from 10 – 14°C (50 – 57°F) in January to 23 – 29°C (73 – 84°F) in August.
**Government** Republic.
**Language** Maltese, English.
**Religion** Roman Catholic.
**Currency** Maltese lira (LM) = 100 cents = 1000 mils.
**National anthem** *To this beautiful land, the mother that gave us our name.*

## MAN, ISLE OF
**Area** 588km² (227 square miles).
**Population** 64,000 (1980 estimate).
**Climate** Temperate.
**Government** UK dependency with internal self-government.
**Language** English; also Manx.
**Religion** Mainly Church of England.
**Currency** UK pound and Isle of Man pound (IoM£) = 100 new pence.

MALAYSIA *Shadow puppets, manipulated by thin rods, are usually made of cow hide.*

# NATIONS A – Z/Marshall Islands-Norway

**MARSHALL ISLANDS** (part of the US Trust Territory of the Pacific Islands)
**Area** 181km² (70 square miles).
**Population** 27,000 (1977 estimate).
**Climate** Tropical.
**Government** Republic.
**Language** English and Malayo-Polynesian languages.
**Religion** Christian.

## MARTINIQUE
**Area** 1102km² (425 square miles).
**Population** 329,000 (1982).
**Climate** Subtropical; average temperature at Fort-de-France ranges from 21°C (70°F) to 31°C (88°F).
**Government** French overseas department.
**Language** French, Creole.
**Religion** Roman Catholic.
**Currency** French franc (Fr) = 100 centimes.

## MAURITANIA
**Area** 1,030,700km² (398,000 square miles).
**Population** 1,680,000 (1981 estimate).
**Climate** Hot and dry; average temperature in Nouakchott ranges from 13–28°C (55–82°F) in December to 24–34°C (75–93°F) in September.
**Government** One-party republic.
**Language** Arabic, French.
**Religion** Muslim.
**Currency** Ouguiya (U) = 5 khoums.

MOROCCO
*Tall brass water jars and coffee pots – resembling Russian samovars – are common in Morocco.*

## MAURITIUS
**Area** 2045km² (790 square miles).
**Population** 957,000 (1980 estimate).
**Climate** Subtropical; average temperature ranges from 7–25°C (45–77°F) June to October, to 24–31°C (75–88°F) November to April.
**Government** Constitutional monarchy.
**Language** English, French, Creole.
**Religion** Hindu, Roman Catholic, Muslim.
**Currency** Mauritius rupee (MR) = 100 cents.

## MAYOTTE
**Area** 376km² (145 square miles).
**Population** 47,000 (1978).
**Climate** Tropical.
**Government** French *collectivité particulière*.
**Language** French; also local dialects.
**Religion** Mainly Christian; also Muslim.
**Currency** French franc (Fr) = 100 centimes.
**National anthem** *The Marseillaise*.

## MEXICO
**Area** 1,978,800km² (764,015 square miles).
**Population** 68,000,000 (1981 estimate).
**Climate** Tropical and temperate depending on altitude. Average temperature in Mexico City ranges from 6–19°C (43–66°F) in January to 12–26°C (54–79°F) in May.
**Government** Federal republic.
**Language** Spanish; also local languages.
**Religion** Roman Catholic.
**Currency** Mexican peso (Mex$) = 100 centavos.
**National anthem** *Mexicans, at the call of battle*.

## MICRONESIA, FEDERATED STATES OF
**Area** 701km² (271 square miles).
**Population** 69,000 (1979 estimate).
**Climate** Tropical.
**Government** Federation in 'free association' with the USA.
**Language** English; also Malayo-Polynesian languages.
**Religion** Christian.

## MONACO
**Area** 1.9km² (0.73 square miles).
**Population** 27,000 (1982).
**Climate** Mediterranean; average temperature in Monaco ranges from 8–12°C (46–54°F) in January to 22–26°C (72–79°F) in August.
**Government** Principality.
**Language** French.
**Religion** Roman Catholic.
**Currency** French franc (Fr) = 100 centimes. Monégasque franc (MnFr) also in circulation = 100 centimes.
**National anthem** *The march of Monaco*.

## MONGOLIA
**Area** 1,565,000km² (604,000 square miles).
**Population** 1,685,000 (1981).
**Climate** Dry and cold; average temperature in Ulan Bator ranges from −32 to −19°C (−26 to −2°F) in January to 11–22°C (52–72°F) in July.
**Government** Communist republic.
**Language** Mongolian.
**Religion** Buddhist.
**Currency** Tugric or Tögrög (Tug) = 100 möngö.
**National emblem** The Soyombo (ideogram for freedom and independence).

## MONTSERRAT
**Area** 102km² (39 square miles).
**Population** 12,000 (1980).
**Climate** Tropical but windy; average temperature ranges from 23°C (73°F) to 30°C (86°F).
**Government** UK dependency.
**Language** English.
**Religion** Christian.
**Currency** East Caribbean dollar (EC$) = 100 cents.
**National anthem** *God save the Queen*.

## MOROCCO
**Area** 659,970km² (254,814 square miles), but southern boundaries not defined.
**Population** 21,000,000 (1980 estimate).
**Climate** Warm; average temperature in Rabat ranges from 8–17°C (46–63°F) in January to 18–28°C (64–82°F) in August.
**Government** Monarchy.
**Language** Arabic; also Spanish, French.
**Religion** Muslim.
**Currency** Dirham (Dh) = 100 centimes.

## MOZAMBIQUE
**Area** 801,590km² (309,494 square miles).
**Population** 12,100,000 (1980).
**Climate** Tropical; average temperature in Maputo, the capital, ranges from 13–24°C (55–75°F) in July to 22–31°C (72–88°F) in February.
**Government** One-party republic.
**Language** Portuguese; African languages and dialects.
**Religion** 70% tribal; also Muslim and Christian.
**Currency** Metical (Mt) = 100 centavos.
**National anthem** *Long live Frelimo, guide of the Mozambican people*.

## NAMIBIA (formerly South-West Africa)
**Area** 824,292km² (318,259 square miles).
**Population** 1,000,000 (1980 estimate).
**Climate** Very dry; average temperature in Windhoek ranges from 6–20°C (43–68°F) in July to

17–29°C (63–84°F) in January.
**Government** Disputed territory administered by South Africa.
**Language** Afrikaans, German, English, African languages.
**Religion** 50% Christian.
**Currency** South African rand (R) = 100 cents.

## NAURU
**Area** 21km² (8 square miles).
**Population** 7300 (1977).
**Climate** Tropical; average temperature ranges from 23°C (73°F) to 32°C (90°F). Monsoon from November to February.
**Government** Republic.
**Language** Nauruan, English.
**Religion** Christian.
**Currency** Australian dollar (A$) = 100 cents.

## NEPAL
**Area** 140,797km² (54,362 square miles).
**Population** 14,000,000 (1980 estimate).
**Climate** Temperate; average temperature in Kathmandu ranges from 2–23°C (36–73°F) in January to 20–29°C (68–84°F) in July.
**Government** Constitutional monarchy.
**Language** Nepali; also other local languages.
**Religion** 90% Hindu; also Buddhist.
**Currency** Nepalese rupee (NR) = 100 paisa (pice).
**National anthem** *May glory crown our illustrious sovereign.*

## NETHERLANDS
**Area** 41,160km² (15,892 square miles).
**Population** 14,300,000 (1982).
**Climate** Temperate, maritime; average temperature ranges from −1 to 4°C (30–39°F) in January to 13–22°C (55–72°F) in July.
**Government** Parliamentary monarchy.
**Language** Dutch.
**Religion** Roman Catholic, Dutch Reformed.
**Currency** Guilder or florin (Gld, Fl) = 100 cents.
**National anthem** *Wilhelmus.*
**National emblem** Lion.

## NETHERLANDS ANTILLES
**Area** 996km² (384 square miles).
**Population** 232,000 (1981).
**Climate** Subtropical; average temperature in Willemstad ranges from 23°C (73°F) to 32°C (90°F).
**Government** Netherlands territory, with plans for independence.
**Language** Dutch; also Spanish, English and Papiamentoe.
**Religion** Christian (80% Roman Catholic).
**Currency** Netherlands Antillian guilder or florin (NAGld; NAFI) = 100 cents.
**National anthems** *Wilhelmus. Bonairiano Hymn.*

## NEW CALEDONIA
**Area** 19,058km² (7358 square miles).
**Population** 154,000 (1980 estimate).
**Climate** Subtropical; average temperature all year round in Nouméa ranges from 16°C (61°F) to 30°C (86°F).
**Government** French overseas territory.
**Language** French; also many languages and dialects.
**Religion** 65% Roman Catholic.
**Currency** French Pacific Community franc (CFPFr) = 100 centimes.
**National anthem** *The Marseillaise.*

## NEW ZEALAND
**Area** 268,808km² (103,787 square miles).
**Population** 3,192,000 (1983 estimate).
**Climate** Temperate; average temperature in Wellington ranges from 6–12°C (43–54°F) in July to 13–21°C (55–70°F) in January.
**Government** Parliamentary monarchy.
**Language** English.
**Religion** Mainly Protestant.
**Currency** New Zealand dollar (NZ$) = 100 cents.
**National anthems** *God defend New Zealand. God save the Queen.*
**National emblems** Southern cross, fern, kiwi.

## NICARAGUA
**Area** 118,358km² (45,698 square miles).
**Population** 2,733,000 (1980).
**Climate** Tropical; average temperature throughout the year in Managua ranges from 20°C (68°F) to 34°C (93°F).
**Government** Republic.
**Language** Spanish.
**Religion** Roman Catholic.
**Currency** Còrdova (C$) = 100 centavos.
**National anthem** *Hail to you, Nicaragua.*

## NIGER
**Area** 1,267,000km² (489,000 square miles).
**Population** 5,619,000 (1981).
**Climate** Hot and dry; average temperature in Niamey ranges from 14–34°C (57–93°F) in January to 27–41°C (81–106°F) in May.
**Government** Republic with military government.
**Language** French and local languages, especially Hausa.
**Religion** Mainly Muslim.

## NEW CALEDONIA

**Currency** French Atlantic Community franc (CFAFr) = 100 centimes.

## NIGERIA
**Area** 923,768km² (356,667 square miles).
**Population** 85,000,000 (1983 estimate).
**Climate** Tropical; average temperature ranges from 23°C (73°F) to 32°C (90°F).
**Government** Federal republic.
**Language** English, Hausa, Ibo, Yoruba.
**Religion** Muslim, Christian.
**Currency** Naira (₦) = 100 kobo.
**National anthem** *Arise O Compatriot.*

## NIUE
**Area** 260km² (100 square miles).
**Population** 3200 (1981).
**Climate** Subtropical; average temperature in Niue ranges from 19°C (66°F) to 31°C (88°F).
**Government** Self-governing state in free association with NZ.
**Language** Niue (Polynesian) dialect.
**Religion** Mainly Ekalesia Niue.
**Currency** New Zealand dollar (NZ$) = 100 cents.
**National anthem** *Our Lord in heaven.*
**National emblem** War club and javelin.

## NORFOLK ISLAND
**Area** 36km² (14 square miles).
**Population** 1800 (1982 estimate).
**Climate** Subtropical; average temperature ranges from 13°C (55°F) to 25°C (77°F).
**Government** Australian external territory.
**Language** English and 'Norfolk' (Old English/Tahitian).
**Currency** Australian dollar (A$) = 100 cents.

## NORWAY
**Area** 386,975km² (149,411 square miles).
**Population** 4,106,000 (1982).
**Climate** Temperate; cold in the north. Average temperature in Oslo ranges from −7 to −2°C (19–28°F) in January to 13–22°C (55–72°F) in July.
**Government** Parliamentary monarchy.
**Language** Norwegian.
**Religion** Lutheran.
**Currency** Norwegian krone (NKr) = 100 øre.
**National anthem** *Yes, we love this country.*
**National emblem** Lion.

*NETHERLANDS Carved wooden clogs are now more often sold as ornaments than as footwear.*

# NATIONS A – Z/Oman-Saudi Arabia

## OMAN
**Area** 300,000km² (120,000 square miles).
**Population** 1,500,000 (1983 estimate).
**Climate** Hot summer, mild winter. Average temperature in Muscat ranges from 16 – 32°C (61 – 90°F) in winter to 49°C (120°F) in summer.
**Government** Sultanate.
**Language** Arabic, English.
**Religion** Muslim.
**Currency** Omani rial (OR) = 1000 baiza.
**National anthem** *May God keep his majesty the Sultan*.

## PAKISTAN
**Area** 803,943km² (310,403 square miles).
**Population** 83,400,000 (1980/1).
**Climate** Subtropical; monsoon from June to October. Average temperature in Karachi ranges from 13 – 25°C (55 – 77°F) in January to 28 – 34°C (82 – 93°F) in June.
**Government** Republic.
**Language** Urdu; also English and Punjabi.
**Religion** 97% Muslim.
**Currency** Pakistan rupee (PR) = 100 paisa.
**National anthem** *May the pure land live happily*.
**National emblem** Jasmine.

## PALAU (formerly Belau, part of the US Trust Territory of the Pacific Islands)
**Area** 465km² (179 square miles).
**Population** 13,500 (1977).
**Climate** Tropical.
**Government** Republic in 'free association' with the USA.
**Language** English, Malayo-Polynesian languages.
**Religion** Christian.

## PANAMA
**Area** 77,082km² (29,761 square miles).
**Population** 1,825,000 (1980).
**Climate** Tropical; average temperature in Balboa Heights ranges from 22°C (72°F) to 32°C (90°F).
**Government** Republic.
**Language** Spanish.
**Religion** Roman Catholic.
**Currency** Balboa (Ba) = 100 centésimos.
**National anthem** *Let us at last achieve victory*.

## PAPUA NEW GUINEA
**Area** 461,691km² (178,260 square miles).
**Population** 3,082,000 (1980 estimate).
**Climate** Tropical; average temperature in Port Moresby ranges from 23°C (73°F) to 32°C (90°F).
**Government** Parliamentary monarchy.
**Language** English, Tok Pisin (Pidgin English), and more than 700 languages and dialects.

**Religion** Christian.
**Currency** Kina (Ka) = 100 toea.
**National emblem** Bird of paradise.

## PARAGUAY
**Area** 406,752km² (157,047 square miles).
**Population** 3,026,000 (1982).
**Climate** Subtropical; average temperature in Asunción ranges from 12 – 22°C (54 – 72°F) in January to 22 – 35°C (72 – 95°F) in July.
**Government** Republic.
**Language** Spanish and Guaraní.
**Religion** Roman Catholic.
**Currency** Guaraní (₲) = 100 centimos.

## PERU
**Area** 1,285,216km² (496,225 square miles).
**Population** 17,780,000 (1980 estimate).
**Climate** Temperate, cooler at altitude; average temperature in Lima ranges from 13 – 19°C (55 – 66°F) in August to 19 – 28°C (66 – 82°F) in February.
**Government** Republic.
**Language** Spanish and Quechua (both official).
**Religion** Roman Catholic.
**Currency** Sol (S) = 100 centavos.
**National anthem** *We are free, we will always be free*.

## PHILIPPINES
**Area** 300,000km² (116,000 square miles).
**Population** 52,000,000 (1980).
**Climate** Tropical; average temperature all year round in Manila ranges from 21°C (70°F) to 34°C (93°F).
**Government** Republic.
**Language** Pilipino (Tagalog); also English, Spanish and local dialects.
**Religion** 85% Roman Catholic.
**Currency** Philippine peso (PP) = 100 centavos.
**National anthem** *Beloved country*.

## PITCAIRN
**Area** 5km² (2 square miles).
**Population** 70 (1970).
**Climate** Subtropical.
**Government** UK dependency.
**Language** English and English/Tahitian dialect.
**Religion** Christian.
**Currency** New Zealand dollar (NZ$) = 100 cents.

## POLAND
**Area** 321,683km² (120,727 square miles).
**Population** 36,399,000 (1982 estimate).
**Climate** Temperate; average temperature in Warsaw ranges from −5 to 0°C (23 – 32°F) in January to 15 – 24°C (59 – 75°F) in July.
**Government** People's socialist republic.
**Language** Polish.
**Religion** Roman Catholic.
**Currency** Zloty (Zl) = 100 groszy.

**National anthem** *Poland has not yet perished*.
**National emblem** Eagle.

## PORTUGAL
**Area** 92,082km² (35,553 square miles).
**Population** 9,966,000 (1980).
**Climate** Hot, dry summers, warm, moist winters; average temperature in Lisbon ranges from 8 – 14°C (46 – 57°F) in January to 17 – 28°C (63 – 82°F) in August.
**Government** Republic.
**Language** Portuguese.
**Religion** Roman Catholic.
**Currency** Escudo (Esc) = 100 centavos.
**National anthem** *The Portuguese*.

## PUERTO RICO
**Area** 8897km² (3435 square miles).
**Population** 3,197,000 (1980).
**Climate** Subtropical; average temperature throughout the year in San Juan ranges from 21°C (70°F) to 29°C (84°F).
**Government** US commonwealth with internal self-government.
**Language** Spanish, English.
**Religion** Roman Catholic.
**Currency** US dollar ($) = 100 cents.

## QATAR
**Area** 11,437km² (4416 square miles).
**Population** 240,000.
**Climate** Hot, mild in winter. Summer temperature rises to 40°C (104°F).
**Government** Independent emirate.
**Language** Arabic, English.
**Religion** Muslim.
**Currency** Qatar riyal (QR) = 100 dirhams.

## REUNION
**Area** 2510km² (969 square miles).
**Population** 515,814 (1982).
**Climate** Subtropical, warm and humid; average temperature in Hell-Bourg ranges from 8 – 19°C (46 – 66°F) in August to 15 – 24°C (59 – 75°F) in February.
**Government** French overseas department.
**Language** French.
**Religion** Roman Catholic.
**Currency** French franc (Fr) = 100 centimes.
**National anthem** *The Marseillaise*.

## ROMANIA
**Area** 237,500km² (91,700 square miles).
**Population** 22,300,000 (1981).
**Climate** Continental; average temperature in Bucharest ranges from −2°C (28°F) in winter to 21°C (70°F) in summer.
**Government** Socialist republic.
**Language** Romanian.
**Religion** Mainly Romanian Orthodox.
**Currency** Leu (plural: lei) = 100 bani.
**National anthem** *Three colours*.

## RWANDA
**Area** 26,338km² (10,169 square miles).
**Population** 5,100,000 (1980 estimate).
**Climate** Tropical; average annual temperature in Kigali 19°C (66°F).
**Government** Republic.
**Language** Kinyarwanda, French.
**Religion** Tribal, Roman Catholic, Muslim.
**Currency** Rwanda franc (RwFr) = 100 centimes.

## SAHARA, WESTERN
**Area** 266,000km² (103,000 square miles).
**Population** 95,000 (1980 estimate).
**Climate** Hot and dry; average temperature in Dakhla ranges from 13°C (55°F) to 27°C (81°F).
**Government** Territory disputed between Morocco and Saharan independence movement.
**Language** Arabic, Hassaniyah, Spanish.
**Religion** Muslim, Roman Catholic.
**Currency** Moroccan dirham (Dh) = 100 centimes.

## SAINT CHRISTOPHER (ST KITTS) AND NEVIS
**Area** 261km² (101 square miles).
**Population** 50,000 (1979).
**Climate** Subtropical; average temperature in La Guérite (St Kitts) ranges from 22°C (72°F) to 30°C (86°F).
**Government** Constitutional monarchy.
**Language** English.
**Religion** Christian.
**Currency** East Caribbean dollar (EC$) = 100 cents.

## ST HELENA and dependencies
**Area** St Helena, 122km² (47 square miles). Ascension, 88km² (34 square miles). Tristan da Cunha, 104km² (40 square miles).
**Population** St Helena, 5216 (1977). Ascension, 1022 (1980). Tristan da Cunha, 323 (1980).
**Climate** St Helena: mild with little variation. Ascension: tropical but dry. Tristan da Cunha: temperate and oceanic with rapid weather changes.
**Government** UK dependency. Governor on St Helena; Ascension and Tristan da Cunha have administrators.
**Language** English.
**Religion** Christian.
**Currency** UK pound (£) = 100 new pence.

## SAINT LUCIA
**Area** 616km² (238 square miles).
**Population** 120,000 (1980).
**Climate** Subtropical; average temperature 26°C (79°F). Dry season January to April.
**Government** Parliamentary monarchy.
**Language** English, French patois.
**Religion** Mainly Roman Catholic.
**Currency** East Caribbean dollar (EC$) = 100 cents.
**National anthem** *Sons and daughters of St Lucia.*

## SAINT PIERRE & MIQUELON
**Area** 242km² (93 square miles).
**Population** 6000 (1982).
**Climate** Temperate; average temperature in St Pierre ranges from −8 to −1°C (18–30°F) in February to 10–17°C (50–63°F) in August.
**Government** French overseas department.
**Language** French.
**Religion** Roman Catholic.
**Currency** French franc (Fr) = 100 centimes.
**National anthem** *The Marseillaise.*

## SAINT VINCENT AND THE GRENADINES
**Area** 388km² (150 square miles).
**Population** 107,000 (1980).
**Climate** Subtropical; average temperature ranges from 18°C (64°F) to 32°C (90°F). Dry season January to May.
**Government** Constitutional monarchy.
**Language** English.
**Religion** Christian.
**Currency** East Caribbean dollar (EC$) = 100 cents.

## SAMOA
**Area** 2849km² (1100 square miles).
**Population** 157,000 (1981).
**Climate** Tropical; average temperature in Apia ranges from 23°C (73°F) to 30°C (86°F).
**Government** Parliamentary monarchy.
**Language** English, Samoan.
**Religion** Christian.
**Currency** Western Samoan tala (WS$) = 100 sene.
**National anthem** *The banner of freedom.*

## SAMOA, AMERICAŃ
**Area** 197km² (76 square miles).
**Population** 31,000 (1978 estimate).
**Climate** Tropical.
**Government** Unincorporated US territory.
**Language** English, Samoan.
**Religion** Christian.
**Currency** US dollar ($) = 100 cents.
**National song** *Amerika Samoa.*

## SAN MARINO
**Area** 61km² (24 square miles).
**Population** 21,700 (1982 estimate).
**Climate** Mediterranean.
**Government** Republic.
**Language** Italian.
**Religion** Roman Catholic.
**Currency** San Marino lira (SML) circulates at par with Italian and Vatican lira.
**National emblem** Feathers.

## SÃO TOMÉ & PRINCIPE
**Area** 964km² (372 square miles).
**Population** 87,000 (1981 estimate).
**Climate** Warm and humid; average temperature in São Tomé ranges from 21°C (70°F) to 31°C (88°F).
**Government** Republic.
**Language** Portuguese and local languages.
**Religion** Roman Catholic.
**Currency** Dobra (Db) = 100 céntimos.

## SAUDI ARABIA
**Area** 2,150,000km² (830,000 square miles).
**Population** 8,367,000 (1980 estimate).
**Climate** Hot and dry; average temperature in Riyadh ranges from 8–21°C (46–70°F) in January to 26–42°C (79–108°F) in July.
**Government** Monarchy.
**Language** Arabic.
**Religion** Muslim.
**Currency** Saudi rial (SAR) = 20 quirsh = 100 halalas.
**National anthem** *Long live our beloved king.*

PORTUGAL *A traditional port boat on the River Douro. The boat is steered from the high platform.*

# NATIONS A–Z/Senegal-Turkey

## SENEGAL
**Area** 196,192km² (75,750 square miles).
**Population** 6,000,000 (1983 estimate).
**Climate** Tropical; average temperature in Dakar ranges from 18–26°C (64–79°F) in January to 24–32°C (75–90°F) in September and October.
**Government** Republic.
**Language** French; also native languages.
**Religion** Mainly Muslim.
**Currency** African Financial Community franc (CFAFr) = 100 centimes.
**National anthem** *Hope*.
**National emblem** Baobab tree.

## SEYCHELLES
**Area** 280km² (108 square miles).
**Population** 66,000 (1980).
**Climate** Tropical; average temperature 24°C (75°F).
**Government** One-party republic.
**Language** Creole, English, French.
**Religion** 90% Roman Catholic, 8% Anglican.
**Currency** Seychelles rupee (SR) = 100 cents.

## SIERRA LEONE
**Area** 71,740km² (27,700 square miles).
**Population** 3,500,000 (1980 estimate).
**Climate** Tropical; average temperature in Freetown ranges from 23°C (73°F) to 31°C (88°F).
**Government** Republic.
**Language** English and local languages.
**Religion** Muslim and Christian.
**Currency** Leone (Le) = 100 cents.
**National anthem** *High we exalt thee*.
**National emblem** Lion.

SYRIA *This inlaid chair is typical of the furniture still made in Damascus.*

## SINGAPORE
**Area** 618km² (239 square miles).
**Population** 2,443,300 (1981).
**Climate** Equatorial; average daily temperature 27°C (81°F).
**Government** Republic.
**Language** Chinese, Malay, English, Tamil.
**Religion** Multi-religious.
**Currency** Singapore dollar (S$) = 100 cents.
**National anthem** *Let Singapore flourish*.

## SOLOMON ISLANDS
**Area** 27,560km² (10,641 square miles).
**Population** 250,000 (1983 estimate).
**Climate** Equatorial; average temperature in Honiara 27°C (81°F).
**Government** Constitutional monarchy.
**Language** Pidgin English, English, 87 vernacular languages.
**Religion** Mainly Christian.
**Currency** Solomon Islands dollar (SI$) = 100 cents.
**National anthem** *God save our Solomon Islands*.

## SOMALIA
**Area** 637,657km² (246,200 square miles).
**Population** 3,600,000 (1980 estimate).
**Climate** Hot and dry; average temperature in Mogadishu ranges from 23°C (73°F) to 32°C (90°F).
**Government** One-party republic.
**Language** Somali, Arabic, English, Italian.
**Religion** Muslim.
**Currency** Somali shilling (SoSh) = 100 cents.

## SOUTH AFRICA
**Area** 1,221,037km² (471,442 square miles); includes Black States of Bophuthatswana, Ciskei, Transkei and Venda.
**Population** 28,480,000 (1979 estimate); includes Black States.
**Climate** Temperate; average temperature in Cape Town ranges from 9–17°C (48–63°F) in July to 16–27°C (61–81°F) in February.
**Government** Republic.
**Language** Afrikaans, English, and African languages.
**Religion** Christian, Hindu, Muslim, tribal.
**Currency** Rand (R) = 100 cents.
**National anthem** *The call of South Africa*.

## SPAIN
**Area** 504,750km² (194,884 square miles).
**Population** 37,682,355 (1981).
**Climate** Mediterranean in the southern and eastern coastlands, temperate elsewhere. Average temperature in Madrid ranges from 1–8°C (34–46°F) in January to 17–31°C (63–88°F) in July.
**Government** Parliamentary monarchy.

**Language** Spanish (Castilian), Catalan, Galician, Basque.
**Religion** Roman Catholic.
**Currency** Peseta (Pa) = 100 céntimos.
**National flower** Carnation.

## SRI LANKA
**Area** 65,863km² (25,430 square miles).
**Population** 14,850,000 (1981).
**Climate** Tropical; average temperature ranges from 26–28°C (79–82°F) in the low country and from 14–24°C (57–75°F) in the high country.
**Government** Republic.
**Language** Sinhala, Tamil, English.
**Religion** 67% Buddhist, Hindu, Christian, Islam.
**Currency** Sri Lanka rupee (SLR) = 100 cents.
**National anthem** *Sri Lanka Motherlan*
**National emblem** Lion.

## SUDAN
**Area** 2,505,800km² (967,500 square miles).
**Population** 19,302,000 (1982 estimate).
**Climate** Tropical; average temperature in Khartoum ranges from 15–32°C (59–90°F) in January to 26–41°C (79–106°F) in June.
**Government** One-party republic.
**Language** Arabic, also local languages, especially Nubian.
**Religion** 70% Muslim.
**Currency** Sudanese pound (S£) = 100 piastres = 1000 millièmes.
**National anthem** *We are the soldiers of God*.
**National emblem** Secretary bird.

## SURINAM
**Area** 163,265km² (63,037 square miles).
**Population** 352,000 (1980).
**Climate** Tropical; average temperature in Paramaribo ranges from 23°C (73°F) to 33°C (91°F).
**Government** Republic.
**Language** Dutch, English, Spanish, Hindi, Javanese, Chinese, and local languages and dialects.
**Religion** Hindu, Muslim, Christian.
**Currency** Surinam guilder or florin (SGld SFl) = 100 cents.

## SWAZILAND
**Area** 17,363km² (6,705 square miles).
**Population** 555,000 (1976).
**Climate** Subtropical; average temperature in Mbabane ranges from 6–19°C (43–66°F) in June to 15–25°C (59–77°F) in January/ February.
**Government** Parliamentary monarchy.
**Language** English and Swazi.
**Religion** 60% Christian, tribal.
**Currency** Lilangeni (plural emalangeni; Li or Ei) = 100 cents.
**National anthem** *Creator of benevolence*.
**National emblem** Lion and elephant.

## SWEDEN
**Area** 486,661km² (187,900 square miles).
**Population** 8,323,000 (1981).
**Climate** Short, hot summers and long, cold winters. Average temperature in Stockholm ranges from −5 to −1°C (23–30°F) in February to 14–22°C (57–72°F) in July.
**Government** Parliamentary monarchy.
**Language** Swedish.
**Religion** Lutheran.
**Currency** Swedish krona (SKr) = 100 öre.
**National anthem** *Thou ancient, thou freeborn.*

## SWITZERLAND
**Area** 41,288km² (15,941 square miles).
**Population** 6,384,000 (1982).
**Climate** Warm summers, cold winters; average temperature in Zurich ranges from −3 to 2°C (27–36°F) in January to 13–24°C (55–75°F) in July.
**Government** Federal republic.
**Language** German, French, Italian, Romansch.
**Religion** 48% Roman Catholic, 44% Protestant.
**Currency** Swiss franc or franken (SFr) = 100 centimes or rappen.
**National anthem** *On our mountains, when the sun.*

## SYRIA
**Area** 185,180km² (71,500 square miles).
**Population** 9,500,000 (1983 estimate).
**Climate** Mediterranean on the coast, very hot and dry inland. Average temperature in Damascus ranges from 0–12°C (32–54°F) in January to 20–45°C (68–113°F) in August.
**Government** Socialist republic.
**Language** Arabic.
**Religion** Muslim.
**Currency** Syrian pound (Sy£) = 100 piastres.
**National anthem** *We salute you guardian of the homeland.*
**National emblem** Eagle.

## TAIWAN
**Area** 35,989km² (13,895 square miles).
**Population** 17,800,000 (1980 estimate).
**Climate** Subtropical; average temperature in Taipei ranges from 12–18°C (54–64°F) in February to 24–33°C (75–91°F) in July.
**Government** Republic.
**Language** Chinese and dialects.
**Religion** Confucianist, Buddhist, Taoist.
**Currency** New Taiwan dollar (NT$) = 100 cents.

## TANZANIA (formerly Tanganyika, Zanzibar and Pemba)
**Area** 939,389km² (362,700 square miles).
**Population** 17,552,000 (1978).
**Climate** Tropical; average temperature in Dar-es-Salaam ranges from 19°C (66°F) to 31°C (88°F).
**Government** One-party republic.
**Language** Swahili and English.
**Religion** Tribal, Christian, Muslim.
**Currency** Tanzanian shilling (TSh) = 100 cents.

## THAILAND
**Area** 514,000km² (198,500 square miles).
**Population** 48,847,000 (1982).
**Climate** Tropical; monsoon from May to October. Average temperature in Bangkok ranges from 20–35°C (68–95°F).
**Government** Parliamentary monarchy.
**Language** Thai.
**Religion** 95% Buddhist.
**Currency** Baht (Bt) = 100 satangs.

## TOGO
**Area** 56,785km² (21,925 square miles).
**Population** 2,787,000 (1981 estimate).
**Climate** Tropical; average temperature in Lomé 27°C (81°F).
**Government** One-party republic.
**Language** French, local languages.
**Religion** Christian, Muslim, tribal.
**Currency** African Financial Community franc (CFAFr) = 100 centimes.

## TONGA (Friendly Islands)
**Area** 699km² (270 square miles).
**Population** 95,800 (1983).
**Climate** Subtropical; average annual temperature in Nuku'alofa 24°C (75°F).
**Government** Constitutional monarchy.
**Language** Tongan, English.
**Religion** Christian.

**Currency** Tongan pa'anga (T$) = 100 seniti.
**National anthem** *O Almighty God above.*

## TRINIDAD AND TOBAGO
**Area** 4828km² (1864 square miles).
**Population** 1,060,000 (1980).
**Climate** Tropical; average temperature ranges from 22°C (72°F) to 31°C (88°F).
**Government** Republic.
**Language** English.
**Religion** 37% Roman Catholic, 25% Hindu, 18% Anglican.
**Currency** Trinidad and Tobago dollar (TT$) = 100 cents.
**National anthem** *Forged from the love of liberty.*
**National emblem** Hummingbird.

## TUNISIA
**Area** 163,610km² (63,170 square miles).
**Population** 6,360,000 (1980).
**Climate** Temperate on the coast, very dry inland. Average temperature in Tunis ranges from 6–14°C (43–57°F) in January to 21–33°C (70–91°F) in August.
**Government** Republic.
**Language** Arabic, French.
**Religion** Muslim.
**Currency** Tunisian dinar (TD) = 1000 millimes.

## TURKEY
**Area** 780,576km² (301,380 square miles).
**Population** 45,218,000 (1980).
**Climate** Mediterranean on the coast, continental inland. Average temperature in Ankara ranges from −4 to 4°C (25–39°F) in January to 15–31°C (59–88°F) in August.
**Government** Republic.
**Language** Turkish; also Kurdish and Arabic.
**Religion** 98% Muslim.
**Currency** Turkish lira (TL) = 100 kurus or piastres.
**National anthem** *March of independence.*
**National emblem** Crescent and star.

TURKEY *Islamic quotations surround the intricate central design of a 19th-century Turkish carpet.*

# NATIONS A – Z/Turks and Caicos Islands-Zimbabwe

## TURKS AND CAICOS ISLANDS
**Area** 430km² (166 square miles).
**Population** 7400 (1979).
**Climate** Equable; average temperature ranges from 16°C (61°F) to 32°C (90°F).
**Government** UK dependency.
**Language** English.
**Religion** Christian.
**Currency** US dollar ($) = 100 cents.
**National anthem** *God save the Queen.*

## TUVALU (formerly Ellice Islands)
**Area** 26km² (10 square miles).
**Population** 8000 (1980).
**Climate** Tropical with little seasonal variation; average temperature 30°C (86°F).
**Government** Constitutional monarchy.
**Language** Tuvaluan, English.
**Religion** Christian, Baha'i.
**Currency** Australian dollar (A$) = 1000 cents. Tuvaluan coins.

## UGANDA
**Area** 236,036km² (91,133 square miles).
**Population** 13,201,000 (1980).
**Climate** Tropical; temperature ranges from 15°C (59°F) to 26°C (79°F). Cooler in mountain areas.
**Government** Republic.
**Language** English, Luganda, Lwo, Ateso, Swahili.
**Religion** Christian, Muslim.
**Currency** Ugandan shilling (USh) = 100 cents.

## UNION OF SOVIET SOCIALIST REPUBLICS
**Area** 22,402,200km² (8,649,500 square miles).
**Population** 267,700,000 (1982 estimate).
**Climate** Continental, arctic in the north. Average temperature in Moscow ranges from −16 to −9°C (3–16°F) in January to 13–23°C (55–73°F) in July.
**Government** Socialist federation of republics.
**Language** Russian, Ukrainian, Belorussian and others.
**Religion** Christian, Muslim. No state religion.
**Currency** Rouble (Rub) = 100 kopecks.
**National anthem** *Unbreakable union of freeborn republics.*
**National emblem** Hammer and sickle.

## UNITED ARAB EMIRATES
**Area** 83,600km² (32,300 square miles).
**Population** 1,040,000 (1980).
**Climate** Hot, mild in winter; average temperature in Sharjah ranges from 12–23°C (54–73°F) in January to 28–38°C (82–100°F) in August.
**Government** Federation of emirates.
**Language** Arabic.
**Religion** Muslim.
**Currency** UAE dirham (UAEDh) = 10 dinar = 1000 fils.

## UNITED KINGDOM
**Area** 244,046km² (94,226 square miles).
**Population** 55,676,000 (1981).
**Climate** Temperate; average temperature in London ranges from 2–6°C (36–43°F) in January to 13–22°C (55–72°F) in July.
**Government** Parliamentary monarchy.
**Language** English.
**Religion** Christian.
**Currency** Pound (£) = 100 new pence.
**National anthem** *God save the Queen.*

## UNITED STATES OF AMERICA
**Area** 9,363,123km² (3,615,102 square miles).
**Population** 226,505,000 (1980).
**Climate** Temperate, subtropical in the south. Mainly hot summers, cold winters in the north. Average temperature in Washington ranges from −3 to 6°C (27–43°F) in January to 20–31°C (68–88°F) in July.
**Government** Republic; federation of 50 states.
**Language** English; there is now a sizeable minority whose native language is Spanish.
**Religion** 33% Protestant, 23% Roman Catholic, 3% Jewish.
**Currency** Dollar ($) = 100 cents.
**National anthem** *The Star-Spangled Banner.*
**National emblem** Bald eagle.

USA *An Algonquin Indian chief is thought to have given this deer-hide cloak to a settler in Virginia in about 1608.*

USSR *This north Russian walrus-bone comb dates from the 17th century.*

## UPPER VOLTA
**Area** 274,200km² (105,870 square miles).
**Population** 6,908,000 (1981).
**Climate** Tropical, very dry, especially in the north. Average temperature in Ouagadougou ranges from 16–33°C (61–91°F) in January to 26–39°C (79–102°F) in April.
**Government** Republic with military government.
**Language** French, also local languages.
**Religion** 50% tribal.
**Currency** African Financial Community franc (CFAFr) = 100 centimes.
**National anthem** *Unity, work, justice.*

## URUGUAY
**Area** 176,215km² (68,037 square miles).
**Population** 2,900,000.
**Climate** Temperate; average temperature in Montevideo ranges from 6–14°C (43–57°F) in January to 17–28°C (63–82°F) in July.
**Government** Republic.
**Language** Spanish.
**Religion** Roman Catholic.
**Currency** Uruguayan new peso (UrugN$) = 100 centésimos.
**National anthem** *People of the East, the country or the grave.*

## VANUATU (formerly New Hebrides)
**Area** 12,189km² (4706 square miles).
**Population** 128,000 (1982 estimate).
**Climate** Tropical; average temperature in Vila throughout the year ranges from 19°C (66°F) to 31°C (88°F).
**Government** Republic.
**Language** Bislama (Pidgin), English, French, and other Melanesian languages and dialects.
**Religion** Christian.
**Currency** Vatu (VT).

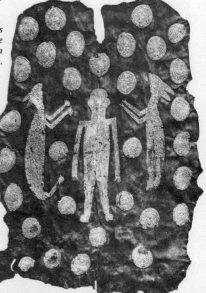

## VATICAN
**Area** 0.44km² (0.17 square miles).
**Population** 1000.
**Climate** Mediterranean.
**Government** Ecclesiastical state, seat of the Holy See.
**Language** Italian.
**Religion** Roman Catholic.
**Currency** Vatican City lira (VL) at par with the Italian lira, also in use.

## VENEZUELA
**Area** 916,490km² (353,857 square miles).
**Population** 13,900,000 (1980 estimate).
**Climate** Tropical; average temperature ranges from 25–28°C (77–82°F) at sea level to 15–18°C (59–64°F) in the mountains.
**Government** Republic.
**Language** Spanish.
**Religion** Roman Catholic.
**Currency** Bolívar (B) = 100 céntimos.
**National anthem** *Glory to the brave nation.*

## VIETNAM
**Area** 329,556km² (127,242 square miles).
**Population** 52,299,000 (1980 estimate).
**Climate** Tropical; temperatures vary with seasons in the north but hardly at all in the south. Average temperature in Hanoi ranges from 17°C (63°F) in January to 29°C (84°F) in June.
**Government** Socialist republic.
**Language** Vietnamese.
**Religion** Mainly Buddhist.
**Currency** Dong (D) = 10 hao = 100 xu.
**National anthem** *Marching to the front.*

## VIRGIN ISLANDS, BRITISH
**Area** 153km² (59 square miles).
**Population** 12,500 (1979 estimate).
**Climate** Subtropical; average temperature ranges from 17–28°C (63–82°F) in winter to 26–31°C (79–88°F) in summer.
**Government** UK dependency.
**Language** English.
**Religion** Christian.
**Currency** US dollar ($) = 100 cents.

## VIRGIN ISLANDS, US
**Area** 344km² (133 square miles).
**Population** 95,000 (1980).
**Climate** Subtropical; average temperature in St Croix and St Thomas ranges from 21°C (70°F) to 32°C (90°F).
**Government** Unincorporated US territory.
**Language** English.
**Religion** Mainly Christian.
**Currency** US dollar ($) = 100 cents.
**National song** *Virgin Islands march.*

## WALLIS AND FUTUNA ISLANDS
**Area** 274km² (106 square miles).
**Population** 9000 (1980 estimate).
**Climate** Tropical.
**Government** French overseas territory.
**Language** French, also Polynesian languages.
**Religion** Roman Catholic.
**Currency** French Pacific Community franc (CFP Fr) = 100 centimes.
**National anthem** *The Marseillaise.*

## YEMEN ARAB REPUBLIC
**Area** 195,000km² (75,300 square miles).
**Population** 7,702,000 (1980).
**Climate** Hot and humid on the coast, semi-desert inland.
**Government** Republic.
**Language** Arabic.
**Religion** Muslim.
**Currency** Yemen rial (YR) = 100 fils.
**National anthem** *Under the shadow of the flag of the revolution I declared my republic.*

## YEMEN, SOUTH
**Area** 287,683km² (111,074 square miles).
**Population** 2,000,000 (1980 estimate).
**Climate** Hot and dry; average temperature in Khormaksar ranges from 22°C (72°F) to 37°C (99°F).
**Government** Socialist republic.
**Language** Arabic.
**Religion** Muslim.
**Currency** South Yemeni dinar (YD) = 1000 fils.

## YUGOSLAVIA
**Area** 255,804km² (98,766 square miles).
**Population** 22,418,000 (1981).
**Climate** Mediterranean on coast, temperate inland. Average temperature in Belgrade ranges from −3 to 3°C (27–37°F) in January to 17–28°C (63–82°F) in July.
**Government** Socialist republic.
**Language** Serbo–Croatian, Slovene, Macedonian.
**Religion** 41% Serbian Orthodox, 32% Roman Catholic, 12% Muslim.
**Currency** Yugoslavian dinar (YuD) = 100 para.
**National anthem** *Fellow Slavs, the spirit of your ancient breed still triumphs.*

## ZAIRE
**Area** 2,345,409km² (905,562 square miles).
**Population** 29,300,000 (1980 estimate).
**Climate** Tropical; average temperature in Kinshasa ranges from 18°C (64°F) to 32°C (90°F).
**Government** One-party republic.
**Language** French, African languages.
**Religion** Christian, tribal.
**Currency** Zaïre (Z) = 100 makuta = 10,000 sengi.

## ZAMBIA (formerly Northern Rhodesia)
**Area** 752,614km² (290,584 square miles).
**Population** 5,500,000 (1979).
**Climate** Tropical, cool on plateaux. Average temperature in Lusaka ranges from 9–23°C (48–73°F) in July to 18–31°C (64–88°F) in October.
**Government** One-party republic.
**Language** English, local languages.
**Religion** Christian, traditional.
**Currency** Kwacha (K) = 100 ngwee.
**National anthem** *Stand and sing of Zambia, proud and free.*

## ZIMBABWE (formerly Rhodesia)
**Area** 390,580km² (150,800 square miles).
**Population** 7,539,000 (1982 estimate).
**Climate** Subtropical; average temperature in Harare ranges from 7–21°C (45–70°F) in June/July to 16–27°C (61–81°F) in November.
**Government** Republic.
**Language** English, local languages.
**Religion** Tribal, Christian.
**Currency** Zimbabwe dollar (Z$) = 100 cents.
**National anthem** *God bless Africa.*
**National emblem** Zimbabwe bird.

ZAIRE *This carved and polished wooden head is in fact a cup. It stands 200mm (8in) high and was made by a craftsman of the Kuba tribe, who live near the Kasai river, east of the nation's capital, Kinshasa.*

# International organisations

## SAVED FROM EXTINCTION
Since its foundation in 1961 the World Wildlife Fund has helped to save from extinction some 30 animal species – including tigers, polar bears and African elephants. The fund, which works closely with an international team of scientists, raises money to provide sanctuaries for threatened species. But there are still about 1000 different kinds of animals – among them the Japanese crested ibis, the Californian condor, the American crocodile, the blue whale and the Javan tiger – in danger of dying out. Some 25,000 flowering plants are also threatened with extinction.

So far the fund – with headquarters in Gland, Switzerland, and branches in almost 30 countries – has raised more than £40 million to finance over 6000 life-saving projects in 135 countries.

## PAVING THE WAY FOR PEACE
Amnesty International – the worldwide organisation for the defence of human rights – is one of the few institutions to have won a Nobel Peace Prize. Most winners have been individual people. The only institutions to have won the prize more than once are the United Nations High Commission for Refugees, in 1954 and 1981, and the Red Cross, in 1917, 1944 and 1963. Amnesty's prize was awarded in 1977 for the organisation's help in paving the way 'for freedom, for justice, and thereby also for peace in the world'.

Amnesty International was founded in 1961 by a British lawyer, Peter Benenson, and is financially independent and without any political ties or affiliations. The organisation – which handles 5000–6000 individual cases a year – campaigns for: the release of all prisoners of conscience, provided they have not used or advocated violence; fair and prompt trials for all political prisoners; and the abolition of torture and capital punishment. It estimates that around the world there may be as many as 500,000 prisoners of conscience, and many more who have been killed unjustly by governments.

## THE $8.5 MILLION GIFT
The United Nations – most of whose members are poor Third World countries – meets on a site donated by one of the world's richest men. The gift came from the multi-millionaire philanthropist and industrialist John D. Rockefeller Junior, son of the founder of the giant American oil company, Standard Oil. Rockefeller bought the 7 hectare (18 acre) tract of land beside New York's East River for $8.5 million in 1946. He then gave it to the UN as a site for its headquarters building, which was opened in 1952. The land is now officially international territory, and a team of guides takes about a million visitors around the headquarters each year.

## THE MAN WHO STARTED THE RED CROSS
In the summer of 1859 a young Swiss businessman named Henri Dunant, travelling through northern Italy, became an eye-witness at the Battle of Solferino during the Franco-Austrian War. He was so appalled by the bloodshed and slaughter – altogether some 30,000 soldiers were killed or wounded as France tried to free Italy from Austrian domination – that he stayed on to organise local relief work.

The following year Dunant, who became a full-time philanthropist, published a booklet, *A Memory of*

## INTERNATIONAL ALLIANCES

**Arab League**
Founded March 22, 1945. Headquarters in Tunis, Tunisia. Promotes co-operation among Arab nations.

**Association of South-East Asian Nations (ASEAN)**
Founded August 9, 1967. Promotes economic growth in the region.

**Commonwealth, The**
Founded April 27, 1949. Secretariat in London. Includes most countries and dependencies formerly in British empire, plus a number of fully independent nations.

**Colombo Plan**
Founded July 1, 1951. Headquarters in Colombo, Sri Lanka. Aids economic development of southern Asia.

**Council for Mutual Economic Assistance (COMECON)**
Founded January 25, 1949. Headquarters in Moscow. Economic organisation of communist-bloc nations. Promotes trade and economic growth.

**Council of Europe**
Founded August 3, 1949. Headquarters in Strasbourg, France. Promotes unity, social and economic progress among members. But, unlike the EEC, it does not concern itself with international commerce.

**European Economic Community (EEC, or Common Market)**
Founded January 1, 1958. Headquarters in Brussels, Belgium. Promotes economic unity among member states – most of the nations of Western Europe – and has trade agreements throughout the world.

**European Free Trade Association (EFTA)**
Founded May 3, 1960. Headquarters in Geneva. Promotes free trade among members, none of which is a member of the EEC.

United Nations

International Red Cross

Amnesty International

The Commonwealth

*Solferino*, in which he called for the formation of a permanent relief society for those wounded in war. Four years later, in 1864, Dunant formed the International Red Cross in his home town of Geneva, and in 1901 he became the co-winner of the first Nobel Peace Prize.

Today the Red Cross has about 200 million members in 131 countries, and its work has expanded to help relieve the suffering caused by political upheavals and natural disasters as well as war.

The international symbol of the Red Cross – a red cross on a white background – is the reverse of the flag of Switzerland, birthplace of the society. In most Islamic countries, however, the organisation displays a red crescent instead of the cross. And the Russian Red Cross uses the cross and crescent combined.

## WHEN INTERPOL WORKED FOR THE NAZIS

Adolf Hitler was so impressed by the efficiency of Interpol – the International Criminal Police Organisation – that he made it part of the Gestapo, the Nazi secret police. This followed the German occupation of Austria in 1938, when Interpol had its headquarters in Vienna. The organisation's records were transferred to Berlin, where Gestapo officials used the files to keep track of wanted criminals – and, in some cases, to capture them and persuade them to work for the German cause. Interpol was founded in 1923 at a special criminal police congress held in Vienna and attended by delegates from some 20 countries. In 1946, after the end of the Second World War, the organisation was reformed and a new headquarters was set up in Paris. It now has more than 120 member countries – including, however, only one communist nation, Yugoslavia.

## POWER OF THE VETO

The Security Council of the United Nations has five permanent members: Britain, the United States, France, China and the Soviet Union. Each has the power to block any motion put before the council – even if all the other members support it. The council can also veto any proposed new member nation of the UN. Only when a new nation has been accepted by the council can its membership be approved by a vote of the UN General Assembly. Since the Security Council is the executive arm of the UN, this means that the UN cannot order any action to be taken – though it can make recommendations to governments – unless it wins the support or acquiescence of the five nuclear powers. A 'no' vote by any one of them is enough to overrule the wishes of the other 158 member nations.

All UN proceedings are recorded in the organisation's six official languages: English, French, Russian, Chinese, Spanish and Arabic. And in all, the UN employs about 620 translators and interpreters to keep pace with its output of words.

## THREE VOTES IN ONE

The Soviet Union can always rely on three votes in the United Nations General Assembly because two Soviet republics have seats as though they were fully independent sovereign states.

At the Dumbarton Oaks Conference in Washington DC in 1944 – which led to the establishment of the United Nations – Russia demanded separate representation for all of the Soviet Union's republics. At the time there were 16 of them, each with its own ministries of defence and foreign affairs. But at the Yalta Conference held in the Crimea in the following year, the Russians climbed down. The conference – which was attended by the Russian dictator Joseph Stalin, US President Franklin D. Roosevelt and the British premier Winston Churchill – mainly discussed the unconditional surrender of Germany. But the Allied leaders also agreed on a compromise over Soviet representation: that UN seats should be given to the Ukrainian and Byelorussian Soviet Socialist Republics, as well as to the Soviet Union as a whole.

---

**North Atlantic Treaty Organisation (NATO)**
Founded April 4, 1949. Headquarters in Brussels. Guarantees mutual defence among members, all of which are Western-bloc nations.

**Organisation for Economic Co-operation and Development (OECD)**
Founded September 30, 1961. Headquarters in Paris. Promotes economic co-operation among members. Members are all Western-bloc nations with the exception of Yugoslavia.

**Organisation of African Unity (OAU)**
Founded May 25, 1963. Headquarters in Addis Ababa, Ethiopia. Promotes unity and development among more than 40 African member states.

**Organisation of American States (OAS)**
Founded December 31, 1951. Headquarters in Washington. Promotes co-operation and defence among its members, nearly 30 nations in North and South America.

**Organisation of Petroleum Exporting Countries (OPEC)**
Founded November 14, 1960. Headquarters in Vienna. Aims to control production and pricing of crude oil.

**United Nations (UN)**
Founded October 24, 1945. Headquarters in New York. In 1984 had 159 members. There are still some states that are not members – including North and South Korea, Taiwan, Switzerland, Monaco, Tonga and the Vatican City. Includes International Monetary Fund (IMF) and World Health Organisation (WHO). Promotes international co-operation, peace and security.

**Warsaw Pact**
Founded June 5, 1955. Headquarters in Moscow. Military alliance – the communist equivalent of NATO.

---

*Arab League*

*World Wildlife Fund*

WWF

*European Economic Community*

*Interpol*

# Great cities

## YOU MEAN KRUNG THEP?

Krung Thep has been the correct name for the capital of Thailand for more than 130 years, but foreigners persist in calling it Bangkok. The city has changed its name four times since its foundation in 1767, a few years after the destruction of the Thai kingdom's old capital, Ayutthaya.

The first site was at Thonburi, just down the Menam river from Ayutthaya. But in 1782 King Rama I began building a new capital on the opposite bank at Bangkok, then a small village. In 1787, two years after completion, the city was named Rattanakosin. Finally, during the reign of Rama III, from 1824 to 1851, the name was altered to Krungthep Maha Nakorn, Amarn Rattanakosindra, Mahindrayudhya, Mahadilokpop Noparatana Rajdhani Mahasathan, Amorn Piman Avatarn Satit, Sakkatultiya Vishnukarn Prasit. Or Krung Thep for short.

The full name translates as: 'The City of Gods, the Great City, the Residence of the Emerald Buddha, the Impregnable City (of Ayutthaya) of God Indra, the grand capital of the world endowed with nine precious gems, the happy city, abounding in an enormous Royal Palace which resembles the heavenly abode where reigns the reincarnated god, a city given by Indra and built by Vishnukarn.'

## INSIDE THE HUNDRED GATES

Some of the most conservative Orthodox Jews living in the Mea Shearim (Hundred Gates) quarter of Jerusalem do not recognise the state of Israel, because it is secular rather than religious. So they refuse to pay taxes or send their children to state schools, and the women refuse to do military service.

Mea Shearim was founded in 1875 outside the Old City by Orthodox Jews from Eastern and Central Europe. It has a variety of synagogues, theological institutions, and religious schools. Strict rules govern modesty of dress, and only Yiddish is spoken. Hebrew, the language of prayer, is deemed too sacred for ordinary speech.

## ABOUT FACE

Jerusalem, not Mecca, was the place towards which the founder of Islam, Muhammad, and his followers first turned to pray. Muhammad revered the Old Testament and claimed to be the successor of Abraham and Moses, so it was natural for him to face the holy city of Jerusalem. But Jews formed an important group in Mecca, where Muhammad was born, and they refused to accept his claim that Abraham was a

Muslim and that he (Muhammad) was the prophet foretold by Moses.

Finally he broke with them and began to pray facing Mecca, believing – as do all Muslims – that the Kaaba, the city's sacred shrine, was built by Abraham.

## SILENT – THE BIGGEST CANNON

A portrait of Russia's Tsar Fedor Ivanovich (1584–98), son of Ivan the Terrible, decorates the largest calibre cannon ever made. The 40 tonne gun stands in the Kremlin, the 28 hectare (69 acre) complex of palaces, cathedrals and churches which dominates Moscow. The cannon's bronze barrel is 3.18m (10ft 5in) long, with a bore of 920mm (36in). It has never been fired.

## SILENT – THE BIGGEST BELL

The Kremlin also houses the heaviest bell in the world – weighing 196 tonnes and standing 5.87m (19ft 3in) high. It is known as the Tsar Kolokol and was cast in 1735, but cracked two years later in a fire. The bell remains on a platform at the foot of the 80m (263ft) tall bell tower for which it was originally intended. It has never been rung. The original Kremlin – the word means 'town fortress' – was built of wood early in the 10th century. Its walls were rebuilt in red brick during the 15th century and it has been altered, repaired and added to since then.

## CAPITAL CHOICE

Four cities were bitter rivals for the honour of becoming Canada's capital: Quebec, Montreal, Kingston and Toronto. Each made clear that any three of them would stoutly oppose the choice of the fourth – so in 1858 Queen Victoria was asked to arbitrate. She compromised by choosing a fifth – Ottawa.

Toronto was more than 100 years old; Quebec, Montreal and Kingston were founded in the 17th century. Ottawa, which was barely three decades old, had been a city for only four years.

## KITTED BY MICHELANGELO

The Vatican City's Swiss Guard still wears a uniform designed by the Italian artist Michelangelo early in the 16th century. The Guard was formed in 1506, when Pope Julius II made a contract with the Swiss Confederacy ensuring that no other country could recruit in Switzerland, or employ Swiss mercenaries, without papal permission.

The original force, 6000 strong, was raised to defend the Church and its worldly possessions. Now there are just 100 men, who form the papal guard within the Vatican City.

NEW YORK, NEW YORK *A forest of concrete thrusts upwards from Manhattan, one of the world's most crowded islands. In the top right of the picture, the Empire State building juts above the rest. In the bottom left, a helicopter touches down on the roof of an airline terminal. Peter Minuit of the Dutch West India Company bought the island from local Indians in 1626 for cloth, beads and trinkets worth just $24. Minuit – first governor of New Amsterdam, now New York – thought he was buying 89km² (34 square miles) of land. The island turned out to be only 57km² (22 square miles), but his real estate deal remains among the most one-sided transactions in history.*

## COOK'S COTTAGE – MAYBE

'Captain Cook's cottage' – now in Melbourne's Fitzroy gardens in Australia – was originally built in Yorkshire, England. The English explorer and navigator Captain James Cook landed at Botany Bay in 1770. But the cottage got to Melbourne only in 1934, when it was shipped to Australia from England.

Originally, the cottage stood at Great Ayton, in North Yorkshire. It was built by Cook's father in 1775. But by then the son was 27 and had been at sea for about ten years – so it is unlikely that he ever actually lived in the cottage, although he may well have slept there when visiting his parents.

## SINKING CITY
Mexico City is built on top of an underground reservoir. As wells draw out more and more water for the city's expanding population of more than 15 million people, the entire city is slowly sinking at the rate of 150–200mm (6–8in) per year.

## CIRCUS COLLAR
Piccadilly in London gets its name from ornamental collars called 'piccadills', which used to be made in the area by a 17th-century tailor named Robert Baker. Baker built himself a grand house, Piccadilly Hall, with the fortune he made, and the name spread to the whole neighbourhood.

## NAMED AFTER A GAME
The grandest street in London's West End, Pall Mall, is built on the site of a long green where Charles I played 'paille maille', a fashionable game that was the forerunner of croquet. After Charles II was restored to the throne in 1660, he replaced the old pall-mall green with a new one running parallel to it – and the new green later became the site of The Mall, which links Buckingham Palace and Trafalgar Square.

## THE 853km BOOKSHELF
The world's largest library, in Washington DC, was re-established after British troops fired the American capital in 1814, and burnt every book in the original

# CAPITAL CITIES OF THE WORLD/Afghanistan – Cuba

The capitals of all the nations of the world – and of the major dependent territories – are listed here, together with the dates of each capital's foundation and the origin of its name, where known.

**AFGHANISTAN, Kabul**
Founded on River Kabul more than 3000 years ago. Made capital in 1774. The name is the Persian for 'warehouse'.

**ALBANIA, Tirana (Tiranë)**
Founded early 17th century by Turkish general, Suleiman. Thought to be named after his home city of Tehran. Made capital in 1920.

**ALGERIA, Algiers (Alger)**
Founded on four islands by Phoenicians in about 2000 BC. Islands joined to mainland in 1525. City named after the Arabic phrase *al-jazair*, meaning 'the islands'.

**ANDORRA, Andorra la Vella**
Founded probably at the time of the 8th-century emperor, Charlemagne. The name may be connected with the Basque word *andurrial*, meaning 'heath'.

**ANGOLA, Luanda**
Founded in 1576 by Portuguese settlers. Made capital in 1627.

**ANGUILLA, The Valley**
Island named by Christopher Columbus in 1493 from Spanish word *anguila* – meaning 'eel' – probably because of its long thin shape.

**ANTIGUA AND BARBUDA, St John's**
Island of Antigua named by Christopher Columbus in 1493, after a church in Seville, Spain, called *Santa Maria la Antigua* (St Mary the Ancient).

**ARGENTINA, Buenos Aires**
Founded in 1535 by Spanish settlers, with the full name of *Ciudad de la Santissima Trinidad y Puerto de Nuestra Señora la Virgen Maria de los buenos aires* (City of the Most Holy Trinity, and Port of Our Lady the Virgin Mary of good winds). The name was chosen because the city

ANCESTRAL HALL *Brussels' soaring city hall, built between 1402 and 1480, still dominates the main square of the Belgian capital. The spire is 96m (315ft) high.*

was founded on Trinity Sunday and because the Virgin Mary was a patron saint of sailors (who needed favourable winds for their ships). By the 19th century the name had been shortened to the last two words.

**AUSTRALIA, Canberra**
Founded as a purpose-built capital – replacing the former capital of Melbourne – in 1913. Its name comes from an Aboriginal word *canberry*, meaning 'meeting-place'.

**AUSTRIA, Vienna (Wien)**
Founded by Celts as a fortified settlement astride the River Wien during the 1st millennium BC.

**BAHAMAS, Nassau**
Founded on the site of a pirate haven in 1729 with the name of Charlestown, after Charles II. Was renamed Nassau when William III, of the Dutch House of Orange-Nassau, came to the British throne.

**BAHRAIN, Manama (Al Manamah)**
The island kingdom gets its name from the Arabic word *bahr*, meaning 'sea'.

**BANGLADESH, Dacca (Dhaka)**
Founded 1st century AD. Named after Durga, goddess of fertility and wife of the Hindu deity Shiva.

**BARBADOS, Bridgetown**
Founded in 1628 by British settlers.

**BELGIUM, Brussels (Brussel or Bruxelles)**
Developed AD 580 on marshy island in River Senne. Its name comes from the Flemish words *brock*, meaning 'marsh', and *sali*, meaning 'building'.

**BELIZE, Belmopan**
Capital city originally Belize, on the Caribbean coast, and named after the River Belize. In 1970, because of a severe hurricane in 1961, the capital was moved inland to Belmopan on the River Mopan.

**BENIN, Porto Novo**
Founded in 15th or 16th century by Portuguese slave-traders. Its name is Portuguese for 'new-port'.

**BERMUDA, Hamilton**
Founded in 1790. Became capital in 1815.

**BHUTAN, Thimphu**
Himalayan kingdom named after the Sanskrit words *Bhyot* (Tibet) and *anta* (end), because it lies on the frontier of Tibet.

**BOLIVIA, La Paz**
Founded in 1548 by Spanish *conquistadores*. Originally called *Pueblo Nuevo de Nuestra Señora de la Paz*, meaning 'New Town of Our Lady of Peace'.

**BOTSWANA, Gaborone**
Capital since 1966. Country named after the Tswana group of Bantu tribes.

**BRAZIL, Brasília**
Laid out in 1957. Became capital in 1960. Named, like the country, from the Latin word *brasilium*, the name for a red dye-wood imported to Rome

library. US President Thomas Jefferson, author of the Declaration of Independence, donated 6487 of his own books to start the present Library of Congress.

The huge library now contains more than 20 million books, 10 million prints and photographs, and 4 million atlases and maps. They are housed in three buildings, with 26 hectares (64 acres) of floor space and 853km (530 miles) of shelving. The library is open to the public.

## VOLCANO BROLLIES
People tend to carry umbrellas even in fine weather in the Japanese seaport of Kagoshima, on the island of Kyushu. They use the umbrellas for protection against showers of fine ash that descend on the city, blown

over from the nearby volcano of Sakurajima. The volcano itself was a small island until 1914, when a tremendous eruption spewed forth enough lava and ash to link it with the main island.

## PILES OF STRENGTH
Exactly 13,659 piles were driven into firm clay to form the foundations of the Dutch capital, Amsterdam. The city takes its name from the Amstel river – it means 'dam or dyke on the Amstel'. The river was dammed in 1240 and the city was first mentioned in a charter of 1275.

Its canals were built to drain and reclaim precious, low-lying land – unlike those of Venice, which were built simply to ease travel around the city.

---

from the Orient. Rich supplies of a similar wood were found in Brazil by European settlers, and the country became known as *terra de brasil*, meaning 'land of red dye-wood'.

**BRUNEI, Bandar Seri Begawan**
The name of the sultanate comes from the Malay *berunai*, meaning 'plant'.

**BULGARIA, Sofia (Sofija)**
Founded by Romans in 2nd century AD on site of a Thracian settlement. It was named *Sofia* – the Greek word for 'wisdom' – in the 14th century, possibly after the 6th-century church of St Sofia in the city. Became capital in 1879.

**BURMA, Rangoon**
Developed as a port by 18th-century Burmese ruler, King Alaungpaya. Became capital in 1755. Name may be derived from the Burmese word *yangun*, meaning 'peaceful'. Name may also be linked with Dagon, the god whose golden-spired Shwe Dagon pagoda dominates the city.

**BURUNDI, Bujumbura**
Country thought to be named after the Barundi people.

**CAMEROON, Yaoundé**
Founded in 1888. Country named from Portuguese *camerões*, meaning 'prawns', because Portuguese explorers found plentiful supplies along the coast.

**CANADA, Ottawa**
Grew up in 1820s around riverside headquarters of British Royal Engineers. Became capital in mid-19th century (see **CAPITAL CHOICE**, page 169). It gets its name from an Algonquian Indian word *adawe*, probably meaning 'big river'.

**CAPE VERDE, Praia**
Islands named *Cabo Verde*, meaning 'green cape', by the Portuguese.

**CAYMAN ISLANDS, Georgetown**
Islands colonised by British in 1670, and named after the cayman alligators common in the region.

**CENTRAL AFRICAN REPUBLIC, Bangui**
Named after Ubangi river, on whose banks it lies.

**CHAD, N'djaména**
Founded in 1900 by French, with the name of Fort-Lamy. It was renamed in 1973.

**CHILE, Santiago**
Founded in 1541 by Spanish *conquistadores*. Named after the Spanish name for St James, *San Iago*.

**CHINA, Beijing (Peking)**
Founded about 3000 years ago on the site of a former Chinese capital, Ch'i. Its name comes from the Chinese

words *bei* and *kin*, meaning 'northern capital'.

**COLOMBIA, Bogotá**
Founded 1538 by Spanish explorers as *Santa Fé de Bogota*. Named after a Chibcha Indian chief, Bagotta, who once ruled the area.

**COMOROS, Moroni**
Islands associated with moon worship. Their name derives from the Arabic *Jebel-el-Komr*, a translation of the original Greek name *ore seleniae*, meaning 'moon mountains'. *Komr* is Arabic for 'moon'.

**CONGO, Brazzaville**
Founded about 1880 by French explorer Pierre Savorgnan de Brazza, after whom it is named.

**COOK ISLANDS, Avarua**
Islands named in honour of Captain James Cook who discovered some of them in 1773.

**COSTA RICA, San José**
Founded 1736 by Spanish settlers. Name comes from the Spanish for 'St Joseph'. Made capital 1823.

**CUBA, Havana (Habana)**
Founded 1519 by Spanish explorer Diego Velásquez. Originally called *San Cristobal de la Habana* in honour of Christopher Columbus. Cristobal is the Spanish equivalent of Christopher.

CUBAN HAVEN *Crosses punctuate the skyline of Havana in an 18th-century sketch – a reminder of Cuba's colonisation in 1511 by Catholic Spain. Spain was forced out by the USA in 1898, and in 1959 the island became a communist republic under Fidel Castro.*

## BRIDGE OF NO RETURN

The Bridge of Sighs, most famous of the 400 bridges in Venice, Italy, connects the Doge's Palace to the old state prisons and the place of execution. It was built in 1600 and is believed to have got its name from the sighs of the condemned. The designer was Antonio da Ponte, who also designed the city's Rialto bridge.

## MAO'S WESTERN BASE

China's Communist Party was founded in the nation's most westernised city – Shanghai. The founders, including Mao Zedong (Mao Tse-t'ung), met there in 1921 in a house that is now preserved as a shrine. Foreign companies, which moved into the city after an International Settlement was established in 1863, were ousted after the communist takeover in 1949. But Shanghai, with about 11 million inhabitants, is still China's main industrial centre and its largest city.

## MURDER CAPITAL

Cape Town, the city at the southern tip of Africa, has a higher murder rate than Chicago, Detroit or any other of the North American cities traditionally associated with violent crime. In 1981 a total of 645 murders were committed in the Cape Town metropolitan area, giving it a rate of 43 killings for every 100,000 inhabitants. The US city with the worst record has been Miami, whose 1980 homicide rate was 32.7 per 100,000 inhabitants, followed by Hous-

# CAPITAL CITIES OF THE WORLD/Cyprus – Iceland

**CYPRUS, Nicosia**
Founded before 7th century BC. Named after Nike, Greek goddess of victory.

**CZECHOSLOVAKIA, Prague (Praha)**
Began as settlement in 9th century AD. There are many possible derivations of the name, including the Czech *praziti*, meaning a 'place where wood has been burnt', and *praha*, meaning 'threshold'.

**DENMARK, Copenhagen (København)**
Founded 12th century. Named from Danish *kiopman*, meaning 'merchant' (from Old Norse *kaupmanna*, meaning 'of the merchants'), and *havn*, meaning 'harbour'.

**DJIBOUTI, Djibouti**
Founded as a port by the French about 1888. Made capital 1892.

**DOMINICA, Roseau**
Island named by Columbus who discovered it on Sunday (in Latin *dominica*), November 3, 1493.

**DOMINICAN REPUBLIC, Santo Domingo**
Founded on a Sunday in 1496 by Christopher Columbus's brother, Bartolomé. Named *Santo Domingo* ('Holy Sunday') in 1697. Made capital in 1844.

**ECUADOR, Quito**
Named by Spanish explorers in 1533 after the local Indian Quitu tribe. Until 1830 the whole country was called Quito.

**EGYPT, Cairo (Al-Qāhira)**
Founded in 969 AD by the Fatimids, members of a Muslim dynasty. Originally named *al-Kahira*, 'the Triumphant One'. This refers to the planet Mars (*Kahir*), which was in the ascendant when the foundation stones were laid.

**EL SALVADOR, San Salvador**
Founded 1524 by Spanish settlers. City's name is Spanish for 'Holy Saviour', possibly because the city was founded on August 6, the Feast of Transfiguration.

**EQUATORIAL GUINEA, Malabo**
Country's name probably comes from the Berber word *aguinau*, meaning 'black-skinned people'.

**ETHIOPIA, Addis Ababa (Addis Abeba)**
Site chosen in 1887 by Emperor Menelek II. Name comes from the Amharic *addis*, meaning 'new', and *abeba*, meaning 'flower'.

**FALKLAND ISLANDS, Port Stanley**
Founded 1833. Named, in 1842, after Lord Stanley, then Britain's Colonial Secretary.

**FIJI, Suva**
Founded 1849. Made capital 1882.

**FINLAND, Helsinki**
Founded 1550 by Swedes. Originally named by them *Helsingfors* from the name of the tribe *Helsingi* and the Swedish word *fors*, meaning 'waterfall'. Helsinki is the Finnish version of the Swedish name.

**FRANCE, Paris**
Founded about 5th century BC by the *Parisii*, a Gallic tribe, after whom it is named.

**FRENCH GUIANA, Cayenne**
Founded by the French in 1643, on Cayenne Island. The city gave its name to Cayenne pepper, which grows on the island.

**FRENCH POLYNESIA, Papeete**
Name of group of islands comes from the Greek *polys*, meaning 'many', and *nesos*, meaning 'island'.

**GABON, Libreville**
Founded 1848 for liberated slaves. The French name means 'free town'.

**GAMBIA, Banjul**
According to tradition, the city's name arose when Portuguese settlers, who discovered the country in the 15th century, asked what the place was called. The question was thought to be 'What are you doing?' and the natives replied *'Bangjulo'*, meaning 'Making rope-mats'.

**GERMANY, EAST, East Berlin**
Two 13th-century villages – Kolln and Berlin – on the Stree river were united under the name Berlin. East Berlin made capital in 1949.

**GERMANY, WEST, Bonn**
Founded as a Roman garrison in the 1st century AD. Made capital 1949.

**GHANA, Accra**
Founded 17th century by English and Dutch. Name probably comes from *Akan ukran*, meaning 'black ant', the name given to Nigerian tribes who came to settle in the region in the 16th century.

**GIBRALTAR, Gibraltar**
Name comes from the Arabic *Jebel-al-Tarik*, meaning 'mountain of Tarik'. Named after the Arab general, Tarik ibn Zaid, who captured Gibraltar in AD 711.

**GREECE, Athens (Athínai)**
Traditionally named after the goddess Athena, protector of Greek cities. But the name may be from a pre-Greek word meaning 'hill', from the language

CANNON OVER CAIRO *The Egyptian capital sprawls below the Citadel, the fortress built by the 12th-century ruler Saladin. On the horizon are the pyramids of Giza.*

ton (27.6), Las Vegas (23.4), Los Angeles-Long Beach (23.3), New Orleans (22.3) and New York (21). Detroit recorded only 16.1 and Chicago a modest 14.5. Nationally the murder rate in the USA averaged out at 10.2 per 100,000 people – less than a third of the South African average of 32.

---

## DOOMED SHIP

One of Sweden's most popular tourist attractions is a ship that sank within hours of leaving the quayside on her maiden voyage. The ship, the *Wasa*, set sail in August 1628 – despite being known to be dangerously unstable. While still in the shelter of Stockholm harbour a squall caught her and she tipped over and sank. The ship was the newest addition to the royal fleet and one of the largest: her overall length was about 60m (200ft) and she carried 64 bronze guns.

A Swedish admiral, Klas Fleming, had earlier conducted a stability test during which 30 men ran together from one side of the ship to the other. The test had to be stopped after only three crossings because the *Wasa* was in danger of capsizing, but for some reason the admiral took no action.

The most successful early salvage attempt was made in the 1660s by the Swede Albrecht von Treileben, who used an early diving bell and managed to bring up most of the guns. However, not until 1961 was the entire hull raised to the surface – 333 years after it went down. The restored ship is now in the *Wasa* museum in Stockholm.

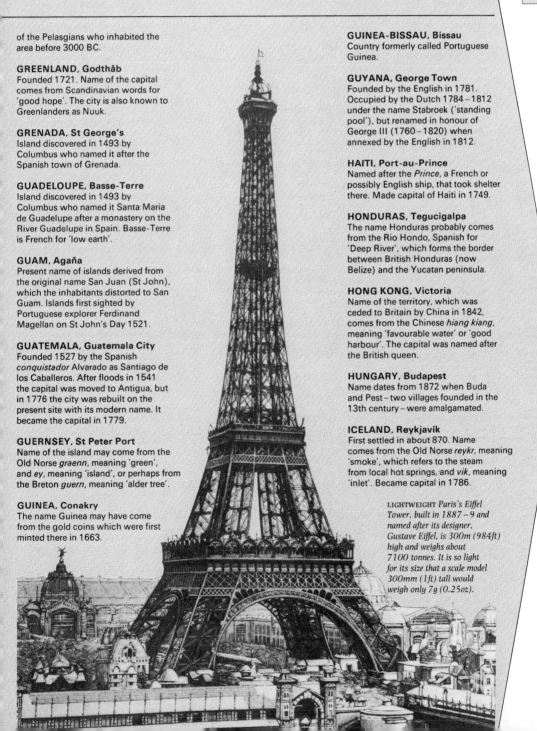

of the Pelasgians who inhabited the area before 3000 BC.

### GREENLAND, Godthåb
Founded 1721. Name of the capital comes from Scandinavian words for 'good hope'. The city is also known to Greenlanders as Nuuk.

### GRENADA, St George's
Island discovered in 1493 by Columbus who named it after the Spanish town of Grenada.

### GUADELOUPE, Basse-Terre
Island discovered in 1493 by Columbus who named it Santa Maria de Guadelupe after a monastery on the River Guadelupe in Spain. Basse-Terre is French for 'low earth'.

### GUAM, Agaña
Present name of islands derived from the original name San Juan (St John), which the inhabitants distorted to San Guam. Islands first sighted by Portuguese explorer Ferdinand Magellan on St John's Day 1521.

### GUATEMALA, Guatemala City
Founded 1527 by the Spanish *conquistador* Alvarado as Santiago de los Caballeros. After floods in 1541 the capital was moved to Antigua, but in 1776 the city was rebuilt on the present site with its modern name. It became the capital in 1779.

### GUERNSEY, St Peter Port
Name of the island may come from the Old Norse *graenn*, meaning 'green', and *ey*, meaning 'island', or perhaps from the Breton *guern*, meaning 'alder tree'.

### GUINEA, Conakry
The name Guinea may have come from the gold coins which were first minted there in 1663.

### GUINEA-BISSAU, Bissau
Country formerly called Portuguese Guinea.

### GUYANA, George Town
Founded by the English in 1781. Occupied by the Dutch 1784–1812 under the name Stabroek ('standing pool'), but renamed in honour of George III (1760–1820) when annexed by the English in 1812.

### HAITI, Port-au-Prince
Named after the *Prince*, a French or possibly English ship, that took shelter there. Made capital of Haiti in 1749.

### HONDURAS, Tegucigalpa
The name Honduras probably comes from the Rio Hondo, Spanish for 'Deep River', which forms the border between British Honduras (now Belize) and the Yucatan peninsula.

### HONG KONG, Victoria
Name of the territory, which was ceded to Britain by China in 1842, comes from the Chinese *hiang kiang*, meaning 'favourable water' or 'good harbour'. The capital was named after the British queen.

### HUNGARY, Budapest
Name dates from 1872 when Buda and Pest – two villages founded in the 13th century – were amalgamated.

### ICELAND, Reykjavík
First settled in about 870. Name comes from the Old Norse *reykr*, meaning 'smoke', which refers to the steam from local hot springs, and *vik*, meaning 'inlet'. Became capital in 1786.

LIGHTWEIGHT *Paris's Eiffel Tower, built in 1887–9 and named after its designer, Gustave Eiffel, is 300m (984ft) high and weighs about 7100 tonnes. It is so light for its size that a scale model 300mm (1ft) tall would weigh only 7g (0.25oz).*

# CAPITAL CITIES OF THE WORLD/India – Poland

**INDIA, New Delhi**
Founded 1912 to replace Calcutta as capital of British India. Adjacent to 'Old' Delhi, which dates from the 15th century BC. Delhi was the name of an ancient capital in Hindu legends.

**INDONESIA, Jakarta**
Founded 1619 by Dutch and became headquarters of the Dutch East India Company. Made capital 1949. Name may come from the Sanskrit *Jaya-kerta*, meaning 'place of victory', or from the Persian *kert*, meaning 'place'.

**IRAN, Tehran**
Made capital about 1795. Name may mean 'plain'.

**IRAQ, Baghdad**
Built by the Islamic leader Mansur in the 8th century AD on the site of an earlier settlement. Name is probably Persian for 'God's gift'.

**IRELAND, Dublin**
Founded 9th century AD by Norsemen. Named from the Gaelic *dubh linn*, meaning 'black pool'.

**ISRAEL, Jerusalem**
In existence by 14th century BC. Name may come from Old Hebrew words *ieru* and *shalom*, meaning 'city of peace'.

**ITALY, Rome (Roma)**
Traditionally founded in 753 BC by Romulus, after whom it was named. But the name may come from Ruma, the ancient name for the River Tiber.

**IVORY COAST, Abidjan**
Country a trading centre for elephant tusks since 15th century.

**JAMAICA, Kingston**
Founded 1692 by British and named in honour of William III.

**JAPAN, Tokyo**
Founded about 1456. Its name is Japanese for 'eastern capital'.

**JERSEY, St Helier**
Name of the island may come from the Old Friesian word *gers*, meaning 'grass', and the Scandinavian word *ey*, meaning 'island', or from Geirr, a Viking who seized the island.

**JORDAN, Amman**
Capital of the Biblical Ammonites. Named after the ancient Egyptian god Ammon.

**KAMPUCHEA, Phnom Penh**
Traditionally founded in the 14th century. City's name comes from Khmer words meaning 'mountain of abundance'.

**KENYA, Nairobi**
Founded 1899 as headquarters of Mombasa – Uganda railway. Name comes from the Swahili word for 'swamp'.

**KIRIBATI, Tarawa**
Made capital of Gilbert and Ellice Islands (now independent states of Kiribati and Tuvalu) after the Second World War. Remained as capital of Kiribati after independence in 1979.

**KOREA, NORTH, Pyongyang**
Site of a Chinese colony in 2nd century BC. In Korean, *p'hyon* means 'plain'.

**KOREA, SOUTH, Seoul (Sŏul)**
Name comes from the Korean word *sieur*, meaning 'capital'. Made capital August 15, 1948.

**KUWAIT, Kuwait**
Arabic name is *Al Kuwait*, meaning 'the enclosed'. This may refer to a Portuguese fort built there in the 16th century.

**LAOS, Vientiane**
Country named after the Lao people. The 's' was added by Portuguese settlers.

**LEBANON, Beirut (Bayrūt)**
Site of an ancient Phoenician settlement. Name comes from the Greek word *berytos*, meaning 'well' or 'spring'.

**LESOTHO, Maseru**
Founded 1869 by Moshesh, a Basuto chief.

**LIBERIA, Monrovia**
Founded 1822 by American Colonisation Society for freed slaves. Named after the then US President, James Monroe (1758 – 1831).

**LIBYA, Tripoli**
Name comes from the Greek word *tripolis*, meaning 'three towns'. Name refers to the ancient cities of Osa, Sabratha and Leptis.

**LIECHTENSTEIN, Vaduz**
Came into possession of the Liechtenstein family in 1712.

**LUXEMBOURG, Luxembourg**
Name comes from Old Saxon words *lytel* and *burh*, meaning 'little town'. The duchy was named after the town.

**MACAU, Macau City**
Peninsula settled by the Portuguese in 1557.

**MADAGASCAR, Antananarivo**
Name of island derives from Malagasy, the name of the island's major language. The country was known as the Malagasy Republic between 1960 and 1975.

**MALAWI, Lilongwe**
Became capital, replacing Zomba, in 1975.

**MALAYSIA, Kuala Lumpur**
Founded 1857 as a tin-mining camp. Name is Malay for 'estuary mud'.

**MALDIVES, Malé**
Name of islands may come from Sanskrit words *malai*, meaning 'mountain', and *dwipa*, meaning 'island'.

**MALI, Bamako**
Country's name, first used by Africans in 11th – 15th centuries, may come from the Mandingo word *mali*, meaning 'hippopotamus'.

**MALTA, Valletta**
Founded 1565. Made capital 1570. Named after Jean de la Valette, Grand Master of the Knights of Malta.

**MAN, ISLE OF, Douglas**
The name Douglas comes from the Gaelic *dubh glaise*, meaning 'black brook'. The city replaced Castletown as the island's capital in 1869.

**MARTINIQUE, Fort-de-France**
Island discovered by Columbus on June 15, 1502, and named because June 15 was St Martin's Day.

**MAURITANIA, Nouakchott**
Name of country comes from the Greek word *mauros*, meaning 'black', describing the inhabitants.

**MAURITIUS, Port Louis**
Founded in 1736 by the French, and probably named in honour of the French king, Louis XV.

**MEXICO, Mexico City (Ciudad de Mexico)**
Founded by Spanish on an island in a lake – the site of the 14th-century Aztec capital now known as Tenochtitlan. Named, like the country, after an earlier name for the city, *Metz-xih-co*, meaning 'in the centre (literally navel) of the waters of the moon'.

**MICRONESIA, FEDERATED STATES OF, Kolonia**
Islands formerly part of US trust territory of the Pacific Islands. Named from the Greek *mikros*, 'small', and *nesos*, 'island'.

**MONACO, Monaco**
Probably founded by the Phoenicians. Name comes from Greek word *monoikos*, meaning 'hermit' or 'monk'. The rock on which it stands bore a temple to the god Hercules the Hermit in 7th – 6th centuries BC.

**MONGOLIA, Ulan Bator (Ulaanbaatar)**
Founded in 17th century. Originally named Urga, but renamed in 1924 in honour of Sukhe Baator (1893 – 1923) who founded the modern republic of Mongolia. Name means 'red warrior'.

**MONTSERRAT, Plymouth**
Island discovered by Christopher Columbus in 1493. He named it after the craggy Montserrat in Catalonia in Spain, which he thought it resembled.

**MOROCCO, Rabat**
Founded 1306 on the site of a camp established in 12th century. Name may be from Arabic, meaning 'place of faith' or 'small town'.

**MOZAMBIQUE, Maputo**
Name changed from Lourenço Marques in 1976.

**NAMIBIA, Windhoek**
Name comes from Dutch words meaning 'windy cape', because of prevailing southeast winds.

**NAURU, Yaren**
Island formerly called Pleasant Island. Discovered in 1798 by British whaling captain John Fearn.

**NEPAL, Katmandu (Kathmandu)**
Founded AD 723. Name may mean 'border place', or the city may be named after the ancient temple of Kastamandap, whose name means 'wooden temple'.

**NETHERLANDS, Amsterdam**
Started as 13th-century fishing village. Named after dam built about 1240 at mouth of Amstel river.

**NETHERLANDS ANTILLES, Willemstad**
Founded 1634; became a centre for oil refining after 1918.

**NEW CALEDONIA, Nouméa**
Island discovered by Captain Cook in 1774. He named it from the Roman name for Scotland.

**NEW ZEALAND, Wellington**
Founded 1840. The city is named after the Duke of Wellington (1769–1852), the victor at the Battle of Waterloo in 1815.

**NICARAGUA, Managua**
Made capital in 1857. Country discovered by Spanish explorer Gil Gonzalez who named it after the region's Indian chief.

**NIGER, Niamey**
Made capital 1926. Country, like Nigeria, is named after the River Niger that flows through it, from the Tuareg word *n'eghirren*, meaning 'flowing water'.

**NIGERIA, Lagos/Abuja**
Lagos named by the Portuguese from the lagoon surrounding the island on which it was built. *Lagos* is Portuguese for 'lake'. The Nigerian government planned to make a new city, Abuja, the capital in the 1980s.

**NIUE, Alofi**
Island discovered by Captain Cook in 1774.

**NORFOLK ISLAND, Kingston**
Island discovered by Captain Cook in 1774. Named after 9th Duke of Norfolk. Kingston is short for King's Town.

**NORWAY, Oslo**
Founded in 1050 by King Harald III at the head of Oslo Fjord. The city became the capital in 1299. Its name may come from Norwegian word *os*, meaning 'mouth', combined with the name of the River Lo.

**OMAN, Muscat (Masqat)**
Founded before 6th century BC when taken over by Persians.

**PAKISTAN, Islamabad**
Built in the early 1960s, it became the capital in 1967. Name is an Iranian phrase meaning 'city of Islam'.

**PALAU, Koror**
Territorial centre under the Japanese before 1944. Devastated in the Second World War.

**PANAMA, Panama City**
Original city – founded in 1519 – was destroyed by the Welsh pirate Henry Morgan in 1671. It was later rebuilt on a new site about 11km (7 miles) to the west.

**PAPUA NEW GUINEA, Port Moresby**
Harbour where city now stands discovered by British explorer John Moresby (1830–1922) in 1873. City is named after him.

**PARAGUAY, Asunción**
Spanish explorers built a fort here on the Feast of the Assumption (August 15), 1536, giving it the full name *Nuestra Señora de la Asunción*, meaning 'Our Lady of the Assumption'.

**PERU, Lima**
Founded 1535 by Spanish explorer Francisco Pizarro. He named it *Ciudad de los Reyes*, meaning 'city of the kings', but its present name comes from the River Rimac on which it stands.

**PHILIPPINES, Manila**
Founded 1571. Name probably comes from the Tagalog language – the principal language in the Philippines – and means 'place where there is indigo', from *may*, meaning 'to be', and *nila*, meaning 'indigo'.

**PITCAIRN, Adamstown**
Island discovered in 1767 by the British explorer Philip Carteret. He named it after the midshipman who sighted it.

**POLAND, Warsaw (Warszawa)**
Site first settled 11th century. City founded about 1300. Name traditionally comes from Czech founding family called Warsew, but

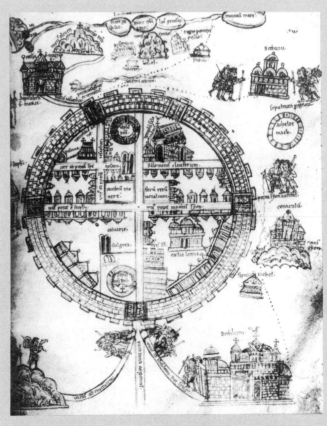

JERUSALEM *A detail from a 12th-century map shows Calvary (just below and to the left of the central crossroads) and Bethlehem (bottom right beyond the walls).*

# CAPITAL CITIES OF THE WORLD/Portugal – Zimbabwe

possibly from the Polish word *var*, meaning 'castle'. A castle was built in the area in the 9th century.

**PORTUGAL, Lisbon (Lisboa)**
The original settlement on the site was colonised by Phoenicians and Carthaginians. The city's modern name is probably Phoenician; it may come from the word *ippo*, meaning 'fortress', or *alisubbo*, meaning 'joyful bay'.

**PUERTO RICO, San Juan**
Founded 1521 by Spanish explorer Juan Ponce de Léon. Named after *San Juan*, Spanish for St John.

**QATAR, Doha**
Arabic name, *ad-Dawhah*, comes from a Persian Gulf Arabic word meaning 'bay'.

**RÉUNION, Saint-Denis**
Island discovered by Magellan in 1513. Given its present name in 1793, during the French Revolution, to celebrate the union of the revolutionaries from Marseilles with the National Guard on August 10, 1792.

**ROMANIA, Bucharest (Bucureşti)**
Traditionally founded in 15th century by shepherd named Bucur.

**RWANDA, Kigali**
Name of country comes from that of the inhabitants.

**SAHARA, WESTERN, Aaiún**
Name of the country – which was governed by Spain until February 1976 – comes from the Arabic word *sahr*, meaning 'desert'.

**ST HELENA, Jamestown**
Island discovered in 1502 by the Portuguese explorer João da Nova. Named after St Helena (about 250 – 330) who reputedly discovered Christ's cross.

**ST KITTS-NEVIS, Basseterre**
Founded 1643. Island discovered by Christopher Columbus in 1493 and probably named by him after his patron saint. Full name of island is St Christopher-Nevis. Kit is an English familiar name for Christopher. Capital's name is French for 'low ground' or 'low earth'.

**ST LUCIA, Castries**
Island discovered by Columbus on the feast day (December 13) of St Lucy in 1502, and named after her.

**ST PIERRE AND MIQUELON, St Pierre**
Islands first named Eleven Thousand Virgins because discovered by the Portuguese explorer Joãs Alvarez Faguendez in 1520 on the feast day of St Ursula and the 11,000 virgin martyrs, October 21. Renamed by 1536.

**ST VINCENT AND THE GRENADINES, Kingstown**
Island probably named by Columbus who is thought to have discovered it on January 22 (St Vincent's Day), 1498, and named it after the saint.

**SAMOA, Apia**
Island named after the *Moa*, extinct members of the ostrich family. Name may have come from the New Zealand Maoris, or been given by the islanders.

**SAN MARINO, San Marino**
Traditionally founded in the 4th century by St Marinus of Dalmatia, a stonecutter, after whom it is named.

**SÃO TOMÉ AND PRINCIPE, São Tomé**
Island discovered by the Portuguese in 1471. *São Tomé* is Portuguese for St Thomas.

**SAUDI ARABIA, Riyadh**
Became the centre of Sheik Ibn Saud's conquest of Arabia during the period 1902 – 24. Was designated capital of the newly proclaimed Saudi Arabia in 1932.

**SENEGAL, Dakar**
Built in 1857 on volcanic rocks. Name probably comes from African (Wolof language) word meaning 'waterless'.

**SEYCHELLES, Victoria**
Founded 19th century by British. Named after Queen Victoria.

**SIERRA LEONE, Freetown**
Founded 1787 by British as settlement for freed slaves, and named for that reason.

**SINGAPORE, Singapore**
Malay city of importance in 13th century. Name comes from Sanskrit words *singa*, meaning 'lion', and *pura*, meaning 'town'.

**SOLOMON ISLANDS, Honiara**
Islands named by Spanish explorer Alvaro de Mendaña. When he discovered the islands he thought they were the Biblical land of Ophir from which gold was brought to King Solomon (1 Kings 9 v.28), because of the gold ornaments worn by the islanders.

**SOMALIA, Mogadishu (Mogadiscio)**
Name of country may come from a Cushite word meaning 'dark' or 'black', and referring to the colour of the inhabitants.

**SOUTH AFRICA, Pretoria**
Founded 1855. Named after Andries Pretorius (1799 – 1853), a Boer leader.

**SPAIN, Madrid**
Moorish fortress captured by Alfonso VI of Spain in 1083. Made capital in 1561. Name may be an adaptation of the Arabic name *Medshrid*, which

comes from *materia*, meaning 'timber'. The area was abundant in wood when Arabs were in occupation.

**SRI LANKA, Colombo**
Founded 8th century AD by Arab traders. City's name probably comes from old Sinhalese word for 'port', *kolamba*.

**SUDAN, Khartoum**
Founded 1823 as Egyptian army camp. Name comes from the Arabic *Ras-al-hartum*, meaning 'end of the elephant's trunk', referring to the city's position on trunk-shaped land at confluence of Blue and White Niles.

**SURINAM, Paramaribo**
Founded by French in 1640 on site of an Indian village. Name comes from Indian words *para*, meaning 'water' or 'sea', and *maribo*, meaning 'inhabitants'.

**SWAZILAND, Mbabane**
Country named after a Bantu nation, the Swazis. Swazi was a former chief whose name meant 'the rod'.

**SWEDEN, Stockholm**
Traditionally founded by a Swedish baron, Birger Jarl, in about 1250, but the settlement probably existed before then. Name may come from Swedish words *stäk*, meaning 'bay' (or *stock*, meaning 'pole'), and *holm*, meaning 'island'.

**SWITZERLAND, Bern**
Founded 1191 by Zäringen family. Made capital 1848. According to legend a count, unable to think of a name for the city he had founded, met a bear out hunting and so decided on 'Bear Town' (*Bär* is German for 'bear').

**SYRIA, Damascus (Dimashq)**
City's name dates back at least 3000 years. It may mean 'place of industry'.

**TAIWAN, Taipei**
Founded 1708. Name of island comes from Chinese words meaning 'terraced shore', referring to the appearance of the coastline.

**TANZANIA, Dodoma**
Country's name formed by combining elements of the names Tanganyika and Zanzibar when the two countries were united in 1964. Dodoma became the official capital in 1983, replacing the former capital of Dar-es-Salaam.

**THAILAND, Bangkok (Krung Thep)**
Became capital 1782. The name Bangkok probably comes from the Bengali word *bangaung*, meaning 'forest village' or 'olive groves'.

**TOGO, Lomé**
Country named after Lake Togo.

**TONGA, Nuku'alofa**
Native name for islands is *Tonga* or *Tongatabu*, meaning 'holy'.

## TRINIDAD AND TOBAGO, Port-of-Spain
Tobago named by Christopher Columbus in 1498 from Haitian word *tambaku*, meaning 'pipe' – possibly because he was struck by the native habit of smoking tobacco in pipes. Trinidad also named by Columbus in 1498, perhaps from Trinity Sunday, or from three island peaks visible at sea.

## TUNISIA, Tunis
City known in pre-Phoenician times. Country named after city which became capital in 9th century AD.

## TURKEY, Ankara
Became capital of modern Turkey in 1923. Name may come from Indo-European root *ank*, meaning 'hook' (as in anchor).

## TUVALU, Fongafale
Island of Funafuti, on which chief town stands, discovered in 1819.

## UGANDA, Kampala
Capital's name may come from a Bantu word meaning 'antelope' or 'basket'.

## UNION OF SOVIET SOCIALIST REPUBLICS, Moscow (Moskva)
Named after River Moskva on which it stands. Founded by the 12th century.

## UNITED ARAB EMIRATES, Abu Dhabi
State is the union of seven emirates formed in 1971–2. Formerly known as the Trucial States.

## UNITED KINGDOM, London
Founded 1st century BC by Romans. Its Roman name *Londinium* possibly derives from the name of a tribe or person.

## UNITED STATES OF AMERICA, Washington
Laid out 1791. Named after George Washington (1732–99), first President of the USA.

MOSCOW BOATMEN *The Kremlin palace towers above the Moskva river in a woodcut of the Russian capital carved in the 1830s.*

## UPPER VOLTA, Ouagadougou
Seat of the Mossi dynasty from the 15th century until 1896, when the French established a protectorate in the region.

## URUGUAY, Montevideo
Probably named by Portuguese explorer Ferdinand Magellan in 1520. Settled in 1726 by Spanish. Name may mean 'I saw the mountain' (from Portuguese *monte-vide-eu*).

## VANUATU, Vila
Islands, formerly called New Hebrides, discovered in 1606 by the Portuguese explorer Pedro de Queiros.

## VATICAN CITY, Vatican City
Papal residence since 5th century AD. City named after *Mons Vaticanus*, the Roman hill on which it stands, and the hill's name may come from the Latin *Vaticinia*, meaning a 'place of divination', perhaps because it was the site of a pre-Christian shrine.

## VENEZUELA, Caracas
Founded by Spanish explorers in 1567. Named after the Caracus, a local Indian tribe. Its original name was *Santiago de Caracus*, 'St James of the Caracus'.

## VIETNAM, Hanoi
Founded about AD 43 by the Chinese. City's name comes from the Chinese for 'inside (the loop) of a river'.

## VIRGIN ISLANDS (British), Road Town
Islands discovered by Christopher Columbus in 1493 and said to have been named after the feast day of St Ursula and the virgin martyrs (October 21), the day when Columbus first sighted them.

## VIRGIN ISLANDS (US), Charlotte Amalie
Islands bought from Denmark in 1917 for US$25 million.

## WALLIS AND FUTUNA ISLANDS, Mata-Utu
Futuna island group discovered by Dutch in 1617. Wallis island group – the site of the capital – occupied in 1842 by France, which established a protectorate over both groups in 1887.

## YEMEN ARAB REPUBLIC, Sana
Believed to have been founded about 1st century AD. Yemen named after Arabic word for 'oath'.

## YEMEN, SOUTH, Aden ('Adan)
Port believed to have been founded in Biblical times as trade centre.

## YUGOSLAVIA, Belgrade (Beograd)
Grew up around 4th-century AD Celtic fort. City's name means 'white fortress'.

## ZAIRE, Kinshasa
Formerly Leopoldville, named after Leopold II of Belgium. Became capital of Belgian colony of Congo in 1920s and of independent state in 1960. Renamed in 1966.

## ZAMBIA, Lusaka
Country named after Zambezi river, which rises in the northeast of the republic. Until 1964, Zambia was known as Northern Rhodesia.

## ZIMBABWE, Harare
City founded in 1890 with the name of Fort Salisbury (later Salisbury) after the British Prime Minister Lord Salisbury. Name changed to Harare in 1982.

# Flags of the world

## THE CHANGING FLAG

The USA's Stars and Stripes flag was introduced in 1777, and it has been changed 26 times as new states have joined the Union – sometimes singly and sometimes in groups. The flag that in 1814 inspired lawyer Francis Scott Key to compose the words of *The Starspangled banner* (now the US national anthem) had 15 stripes and 15 stars, because at that time a stripe as well as a star was added for each new state. But since 1818, only the number of stars has been increased – to its present total of 50 – and the number of stripes has reverted to 13, one for each of the original states.

## BATTLE-STAINED

The simple red-and-white Austrian flag is derived from the original arms of Austria. According to legend, these were granted to the Crusader, Leopold V, Duke of Babenberg, at the Battle of Ptolemais in 1191 by the Holy Roman Emperor, Henry VI. The battle,

## NATIONAL FLAGS/Afghanistan – Iraq

Flags have been flown as rallying signs or as distinguishing marks for at least 3000 years. The Chinese emperor Zhou, who founded the Zhou (Chou) dynasty in about 1100 BC, used to have a white flag carried before him on horseback to announce his presence. In the West, objects raised on staffs were used to identify particular groups, but the first proper flags were Roman. Known as *vexillae*, these emblem-bearing cloths were carried by Roman soldiers to distinguish one legion from another.

In the modern world, the flags of individual countries have become powerful patriotic symbols, the focus of nationalistic sentiments; and each new independent state

designs for itself a unique flag as an expression of national pride. Often, too, flags carry reminders of historical links.

The national flags of Australia, New Zealand, Fiji, South Africa and Tuvalu, for instance, all contain the Union Jack. And in Africa, almost a quarter of the countries use the colours red, green and yellow – known as the Pan-African colours – in their flags.

The colours are those of Ethiopia, the continent's oldest independent country. The first modern African state to adopt them was Ghana, when it gained its independence from British rule in 1957.

ghanistan

Albania

Algeria

Andorra

Angola

ntigua and Barbuda

Argentina

Australia

Austria

Bahamas

hrain

Bangladesh

Barbados

Belgium

Belize

enin

Bhutan

Bolivia

Bophuthatswana

Botswana

azil

Brunei

Bulgaria

Burma

Burundi

meroon

Canada

Cape Verde

Central African Republic

Chad

ile

China, People's Republic of

Ciskei

Colombia

Comoros

between the Crusaders and the Muslim Saracens, resulted in the recapture of the strategic Holy Land town of Acre from the Saracen leader Saladin. Leopold is said to have fought so fiercely in the battle that his white tunic was completely covered in blood except for a band protected by his belt – and his tunic became the model for the flag. In fact, however, the Austrian arms almost certainly come from those of an extinct family of Lower Austrian counts called Poigen-Hohenburg-Wildbergs.

### TRIPLE ALLIANCE
The British flag – the Union Flag, known popularly as the Union Jack – records two major constitutional changes. The first Union Flag – combining the red-on-white English cross of St George with the white-on-blue Scottish cross of St Andrew – was introduced in 1606 after England and Scotland were united under James VI of Scotland and I of England. The modern flag appeared when Ireland was joined to the United Kingdom in 1800. The new flag included the diagonal red-on-white Cross of St Patrick. This cross probably came from the arms of the powerful and largely pro-English Fitzgerald family, and was used to complete the slightly asymmetrical modern design.

### TWO IN ONE
The flag of Paraguay is the only national flag which is not the same on both sides. One side features red, white and blue stripes with the national arms on the white stripe. The other has the same stripes – but with the treasury seal on the white one.

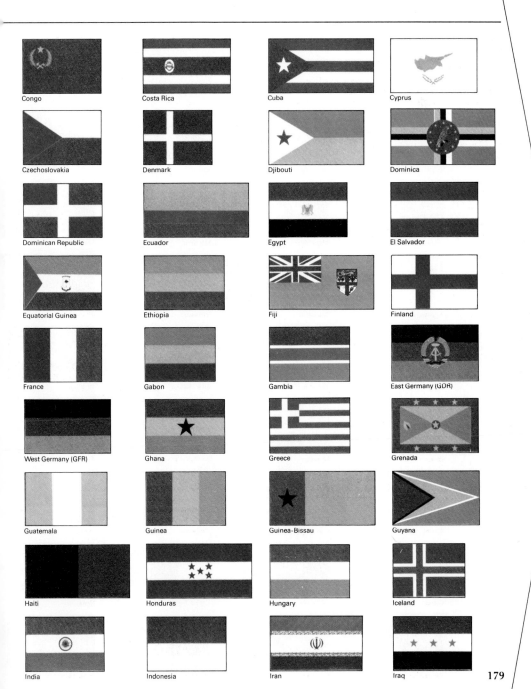

Congo

Costa Rica

Cuba

Cyprus

Czechoslovakia

Denmark

Djibouti

Dominica

Dominican Republic

Ecuador

Egypt

El Salvador

Equatorial Guinea

Ethiopia

Fiji

Finland

France

Gabon

Gambia

East Germany (GDR)

West Germany (GFR)

Ghana

Greece

Grenada

Guatemala

Guinea

Guinea-Bissau

Guyana

Haiti

Honduras

Hungary

Iceland

India

Indonesia

Iran

Iraq

# NATIONAL FLAGS/ Ireland – Zimbabwe

and, Republic of    Israel    Italy    Ivory Coast    Jamaica

an    Jordan    Kampuchea    Kenya    Kiribati

th Korea    South Korea    Kuwait    Laos    Lebanon

otho    Liberia    Libya    Liechtenstein    Luxemboug

lagascar    Malawi    Malaysia    Maldives    Mali

ta    Northern Marianas    Mauritania    Mauritius    Mexico

ronesia, Federated States of    Monaco    Mongolia    Morocco    Mozambique

ru    Nepal    Netherlands    New Zealand    Nicaragua

er    Nigeria    Norway    Oman    Pakistan

u (formerly Belau)    Panama    Papua New Guinea    Paraguay    Peru

ppines    Poland    Portugal    Qatar    Romania

anda    St Kitts Nevis    St Lucia    St Vincent and the Grenadines    Samoa (Western)

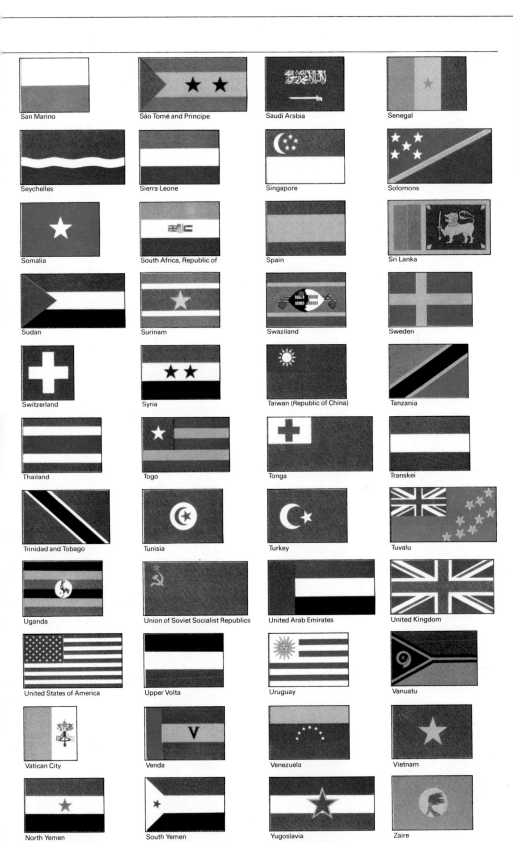

San Marino

Sào Tomé and Principe

Saudi Arabia

Senegal

Seychelles

Sierra Leone

Singapore

Solomons

Somalia

South Africa, Republic of

Spain

Sri Lanka

Sudan

Surinam

Swaziland

Sweden

Switzerland

Syria

Taiwan (Republic of China)

Tanzania

Thailand

Togo

Tonga

Transkei

Trinidad and Tobago

Tunisia

Turkey

Tuvalu

Uganda

Union of Soviet Socialist Republics

United Arab Emirates

United Kingdom

United States of America

Upper Volta

Uruguay

Vanuatu

Vatican City

Venda

Venezuela

Vietnam

North Yemen

South Yemen

Yugoslavia

Zaire

Zambia

Zimbabwe

United Nations Organisation

# Great spectacles: sites of splendour

## PRINCIPAL MOUNTAINS OF THE WORLD

Inaccessibility, changing depths of ice on the peaks of high mountains and instrument errors caused by the gravitational pull of the mountains themselves all combine to make accurate height measurements difficult. These figures are, however, widely accepted.

| Name and location | Height in metres (feet) |
| --- | --- |
| Everest, Nepal-Tibet | 8848 (29,028) |
| K2 (Godwin Austen), Kashmir-China | 8611 (28,250) |
| Kangchenjunga, Nepal-Sikkim | 8600 (28,215) |
| Lhotse, Nepal | 8501 (27,890) |
| Makalu, Nepal-Tibet | 8475 (27,805) |
| Dhaulagiri, Nepal | 8172 (26,810) |
| Nanga Parbat, Pakistan | 8126 (26,660) |
| Annapurna, Nepal | 8078 (26,504) |
| Gasherbrum, Pakistan | 8068 (26,470) |
| Xixabangma Feng (Gosainthan), Tibet | 8013 (26,291) |
| Nanda Devi, India | 7817 (25,645) |
| Rakaposhi, Pakistan | 7787 (25,550) |
| Kamet, India-Tibet | 7756 (25,447) |
| Namcha Barwa, Tibet | 7756 (25,447) |
| Gurla Mandhata, Tibet | 7728 (25,355) |
| Muztag, Tibet | 7723 (25,338) |
| Kongur Shan, China | 7719 (25,325) |
| Tirich Mir, Pakistan | 7690 (25,230) |
| Gongga Shan (Minya Konka), China | 7556 (24,790) |
| Muztagata, China | 7546 (24,757) |
| Kommunisma, USSR | 7495 (24,590) |
| Pobedy, USSR-China | 7439 (24,407) |
| Chomolhari, Bhutan-Tibet | 7313 (23,993) |
| Lenina, USSR | 7134 (23,406) |
| Aconcagua, Argentina | 6960 (22,834) |
| Bonete, Argentina | 6870 (22,541) |
| Tupungato, Chile | 6800 (22,310) |
| Huascaran, Peru | 6768 (22,205) |
| Llullaillaco, Argentina-Chile | 6723 (22,057) |
| Kangrinboqe Feng (Kailas), Tibet | 6714 (22,028) |
| Yerupaja, Peru | 6632 (21,758) |
| Sajama, Bolivia | 6542 (21,463) |
| Illampu, Bolivia | 6485 (21,276) |
| Coropuna, Peru | 6425 (21,079) |
| Illimani, Bolivia | 6402 (21,004) |
| Chimborazo, Ecuador | 6310 (20,701) |

MOUNTAIN HIGH *An early watercolour of Everest, painted soon after an 1852 British survey put its height at 8840m (29,002ft). Its official height has since been raised to 8848m (29,028ft).*

### THE GIANT 'TREE STUMP'

The Devil's Tower (pictured on the right) erupts like a monstrous tree stump above the Belle Fourche river in the plains country northwest of Sundance, Wyoming, in the United States. This flat-topped freak mountain is 265m (869ft) high, and its summit is 85m (279ft) across. Geologists estimate that its history began about 50 million years ago, when a mass of molten rock thrust up through sedimentary rocks laid down on the bed of an ancient inland sea millions of years before. The molten rock cracked as it cooled, forming a mass of innumerable columns. Over succeeding millennia, the softer sedimentary rocks were eroded away by the weather and the Belle Fourche river, leaving the spectacular mountain of today.

### RIDDLE OF THE CANYON

Scientists have yet to unlock the secrets of the Grand Canyon through which the Colorado river runs in the western US state of Arizona. The canyon is more than 350km (217 miles) long, some 6 to 20km (4 to 13 miles) wide, and up to 1615m (5300ft) deep. More than 2 million million cubic metres (2.6 million million cubic yards) of rock were swept away in its making, but nobody has yet worked out where this vast quantity of debris went.

Until recently most scientists believed that the canyon formed during the world's last major period of mountain building. They thought that the river established its course, and then maintained it by eroding its bed at the same rate as the land rose during subsequent earth movements. However, these movements ended more than 50 million years ago, and no river deposits dating back more than 50 million years have been found downstream from the canyon.

In fact, there is evidence that, while the river above the canyon was established in its present course 30 to 40 million years ago, the river course below the canyon was formed less than 9 million years ago. Before then, the river must have followed another route to the sea: a route that has still to be found.

Curiously, the river now only just reaches the sea. So much water is taken out of it by a series of canals and ten major dams for irrigation and drinking water that by the time it reaches the Gulf of California it is a mere trickle, no deeper than a child's paddling pool and only about 3m (10ft) wide. At times it dries out completely before reaching the sea.

### PREHISTORIC PINES

Trees more than 4000 years old, some of the most ancient living things on Earth, were discovered in the White Mountains of eastern California, USA, during the 1960s. The oldest is a bristlecone pine dating back 4600 years. By studying the tree rings of such pines and matching their pattern against the rings of even older dead trees, scientists have been able to produce a reliable chronological sequence going back more than 6000 years. So much so, that dates in this period fixed earlier by the carbon-14 method of radioactive dating have had to be drastically revised.

### FOREST OF STONE

Thousands of conifer trees were turned to stone to form a petrified forest in the US state of Arizona. Some 175 million years ago, the desert plateau on which

CLOSE ENCOUNTERS *An Indian legend claims that the great score marks down the flanks of the 265m (869ft) high Devil's Tower – in the US state of Wyoming – were gouged by a giant bear trying to reach seven maidens stranded on top. In a more modern fantasy, the summit of the US peak became the landing site of an alien spaceship in the 1977 Hollywood science-fiction film* Close Encounters of the Third Kind.

the forest now stands was part of a swampy flood plain. Huge trees, up to about 60m (195ft) tall, flourished in the warm, moist climate. When they died they fell, and were covered by thick layers of mud and sand, which eventually hardened into shales and sandstones. Ground water containing silica – the min-

eral of which sand is made – seeped into the trunks, gradually replacing each cell with an exact copy in silica. As a result each solid stone trunk still has the precise shape and grain of the wood which patterned it. Millions of years later, earth movements lifted the rocks with the fossilised trunks. Then erosion did its

work, gradually stripping away the layers, leaving the more resistant trunks high and dry. And, with the passage of time, the dead forest will 'grow', as erosion eats into yet lower rock layers.

## HIGH WATER
The first steamship to cross Lake Titicaca – the highest navigable lake in the world, 3810m (12,500ft) up in the Andes – was carried up to the lake in pieces. She was the *Yavari*, 165 tonnes, built in Scotland in 1862 and taken in pieces around Cape Horn to Chile. After being transported by rail into Peru, the parts were loaded on to mules for the arduous climb to Puno, by the lakeside.

The ship was reassembled by Peruvian Indians working under a Scottish engineer, and went into service in 1874 as a ferry, crossing the lake from Puno in Peru to the Bolivian shore near La Paz, 80km (50 miles) away. She is now used as a floating warehouse by the Peruvian navy. The main passenger ferry is now the *Ollanta*, which was built in Hull, England, in 1931, then dismantled and reassembled at the lake.

Titicaca is also the largest lake in South America, 190km (118 miles) long, covering an area of 9065km² (3500 square miles) and with a maximum depth of 275m (903ft). Venezuela's Lake Maracaibo is larger than Titicaca, but it is not strictly a lake, just an almost land-locked bay of the Caribbean Sea.

## THE DEAD SEA LIVES
Fish cannot live in the super-salty waters of the Dead Sea, but some salt-loving micro-organisms thrive there. One of these is *Halobacterium halobium*. It produces a purple pigment, which, like the chlorophyll of green plants, enables living cells to photosynthesise – to absorb sunlight and use this energy to convert water and carbon dioxide to energy-giving carbohydrates such as glucose. Another salt-loving micro-organism found there is the alga *Dunaliella*, from which petroleum can be made.

So the sea is not dead – and neither is it a sea. It is a salt lake occupying a northern extension of the great East African Rift Valley on the Israel-Jordan border. Its shore, 396m (1299ft) below the mean sea level of the eastern Mediterranean, is the lowest place on the Earth's land surface. Summer temperatures along its shores frequently exceed 40°C (104°F). The Dead Sea is the world's saltiest body of water, some seven to eight times more salty than seawater. Nearly a third of it consists of dissolved salt and other minerals, such as potash, magnesium compounds and bromides, which are extracted in vast quantities for the chemical and fertiliser industries.

The extraction industry is based at Sedom, in the region of the Biblical Sodom, near which Lot's wife is said to have been turned into a pillar of salt.

## STONE MOUNTAIN
Dome-shaped Stone Mountain, 25km (16 miles) northeast of Atlanta, in the southern US state of Georgia, is the largest mass of exposed granite in the world. It is some 2.5km (1.5 miles) across, and rises more than 250m (800ft) above the surrounding plain. It is also the South's answer to Mt Rushmore National Memorial in South Dakota, which carries the faces of four presidents – George Washington, Thomas Jefferson, Abraham Lincoln and Theodore Roosevelt. Stone Mountain features the mounted figures, each about 27m (90ft) high, of three Confederate heroes of the Civil War: Jefferson Davis (president of the Confederacy), General Robert E. Lee (commander in chief), and General Thomas 'Stonewall' Jackson.

## THE TRUTH ABOUT TAMERLANE
The bones of the great Tartar conqueror Tamerlane (1336–1405) rest in a magnificent mausoleum in Samarkand, in the Soviet republic of Uzbekistan. His tomb, topped by an enormous slab of jade, was opened in 1941 by Russian archaeologists, who were able to confirm the truth behind his name: Tamerlane is a corruption of Timur-i-Lenk, meaning 'Timur the Lame'. His skeleton revealed that he had tuberculosis in his right thigh and shin, and both his right knee joint and right arm were immobilised.

Modern Samarkand was built after the Russian Revolution in 1917, but the city was already old when Alexander the Great destroyed it in 329 BC. The Arabs took it in AD 712 and made it a cultural centre, but it was destroyed again by the Mongol emperor Genghis Khan in 1220.

The city flourished anew under Tamerlane, who made it the capital of his Central Asian empire. Later it was ruled by the Chinese and the emirs of Bukhara before falling to the Russians in 1868.

SUNSET SPECTACLE *Ayers Rock at sunset glows like a burning coal. Australian Aborigines, who call the rock Uluru, revere it as sacred. One blood-streaked cave was used until earlier this century for initiation rites: Pitjandjara Aborigines opened veins in their arms there as a sign of approaching manhood. The rock was given its European name in 1873 by the explorer William Gosse. He named it after Sir Henry Ayers, premier of South Australia.*

## SACRED HEART

Ayers Rock, close to the geographical centre of Australia, is a sacred place to the country's Aborigines. The native Pitjandjara people believe that each of its features represents an important person or event in their history, and some of the rock's caves contain Aborigine paintings and engravings representing human figures and epic journeys made by distant ancestors. One pothole, they believe, is the spot where a spear fell during the battle between rival clans of Aborigines. And a cave entrance is the mouth of a woman weeping for her lost son.

The rock, 348m (1143ft) tall and 9km (5.5 miles) round, sits alone on a desert plain, a remnant of a vast sandstone formation which once covered the entire region. It changes colour dramatically at sunset, finally glowing deep red – a spectacle that draws more than 50,000 visitors a year.

Ayers Rock is not the world's largest monolith. It is surpassed by Mt Augustus in Western Australia, which is about twice its size.

## BRIGHT BLUE

The Blue Grotto on the island of Capri in the Bay of Naples, Italy, has been a popular tourist attraction for more than 150 years. But it became popular only as a result of some quick-thinking sales promotion. In 1826 a landslide suddenly blocked the *Grotta Oscura* (Hidden Grotto), then the current favourite, so a local hotel keeper had the bright idea of offering the *Grotta Azzura* (Blue Grotto) as a substitute. The Blue Grotto can be reached only by boat, and must be seen on a calm, sunny day. Sunlight is refracted as it enters the grotto from an opening half below the sea, bathing the cave in a silvery blue light.

## OUT OF SPACE

Despite its enormous size, Meteor Crater – 32km (20 miles) west of Winslow, in the US state of Arizona – was discovered only as recently as 1891. It is also called Coon Butte, or Barringer Crater after the man who found it, Daniel Moreau Barringer, a mining

## PRINCIPAL OCEANS AND SEAS OF THE WORLD

| Name | Area in thousands of km² (thousands of square miles) | Greatest depth in metres (feet) |
|---|---|---|
| Pacific Ocean | 165,384 (63,855) | 11,033 (36,198) |
| Atlantic Ocean | 82,217 (31,744) | 9200 (30,184) |
| Indian Ocean | 73,481 (28,371) | 8047 (26,400) |
| Arctic Ocean | 14,056 (5427) | 5450 (17,880) |
| Mediterranean | 2505 (967) | 4846 (15,900) |
| South China Sea | 2318 (895) | 5514 (18,090) |
| Bering Sea | 2269 (876) | 5121 (16,800) |
| Caribbean Sea | 1943 (750) | 7680 (25,197) |
| Gulf of Mexico | 1544 (596) | 4377 (14,360) |
| Sea of Okhotsk | 1528 (590) | 3475 (11,400) |
| East China Sea | 1248 (482) | 2999 (9840) |
| Hudson Bay | 1233 (476) | 259 (850) |
| Sea of Japan | 1008 (389) | 4000 (13,123) |
| North Sea | 575 (222) | 661 (2170) |
| Black Sea | 461 (178) | 2243 (7360) |
| Red Sea | 438 (169) | 2246 (7370) |
| Baltic Sea | 422 (163) | 439 (1440) |

ISLAND IN THE STORM *Angry South Atlantic waves heave and froth around St Helena, the island where Napoleon died.*

engineer and geologist. The crater is almost circular, 1265m (4150ft) across, and about 175m (575ft) deep. Its rim stands 40–48m (130–155ft) above the surrounding plain. Most people decided it was an extinct volcano, but Barringer was convinced it had been caused by a huge meteorite, and was proved correct. It is now recognised as the world's largest known meteorite crater.

The crater is thought to have been blasted out by an iron-nickel meteorite weighing about 2 million tonnes that fell to Earth in about 25,000 BC.

## FARMERS IN 6700 BC

Fourteen different crops were being grown 8500 years ago by some of the world's earliest farmers: the inhabitants of a settlement at Çatal Hüyük in southern Turkey. Wheat, barley, peas, lentils and vetch were among the plants they cultivated.

Scientists have discovered that the farmers, who also kept sheep and goats, lived in timber-framed houses with mud-brick walls, plastered and decorated with red paint. They also built shrines and buried their dead under their sleeping platforms. The site was occupied from about 6700 BC onwards. *Hüyük* is the Turkish equivalent of the Arabic *tel*, meaning 'an ancient mound'. And though the site is no longer inhabited, much of the town's layout, which dates back to 6700 BC, has been uncovered again by archaeologists. Residents are known, for instance, to have moved around their city over the roofs because there were no streets. Each house was built up against its neighbours, so that the whole city was like a series of huge honeycombs, each cluster of homes separated by irregular courtyards.

Because of this arrangement, there were no front doors. The only way into each mud-brick home was by a ladder through a hole in the roof.

The farmers of Çatal Hüyük were also among the world's first potters. Clay pots have been found there dating from before 5000 BC. The pots were not thrown on a wheel, for potters' wheels were not invented until about 3500 BC. Instead they were moulded by hand. Some scientists believe that the first pots may have been created by accident. They speculate that soft clay was pushed into woven baskets to make them waterproof and that accidental burning of these baskets left hard shells of baked clay.

# PRINCIPAL RIVERS OF THE WORLD

| Name and location | Approximate length in kilometres (miles) |
| --- | --- |
| Nile, Africa | 6695 (4160) |
| Amazon, South America | 6440 (4000) |
| Mississippi-Missouri, USA | 6210 (3860) |
| Irtysh-Ob, USSR | 5570 (3460) |
| Chang Jiang (Yangtze), China | 5520 (3430) |
| Huang He (Yellow), China | 4670 (2900) |
| Zaire (Congo), Africa | 4670 (2900) |
| Amur, Asia | 4510 (2800) |
| Lena, USSR | 4270 (2650) |
| Mackenzie-Peace, Canada | 4240 (2635) |
| Mekong, Asia | 4180 (2600) |
| Niger, Africa | 4170 (2590) |
| Yenisey, USSR | 4130 (2570) |
| Parana, South America | 3940 (2450) |
| Murray-Darling, Australia | 3720 (2310) |
| Volga, USSR | 3690 (2290) |
| Madeira, South America | 3315 (2060) |
| Purus, South America | 3220 (2000) |
| Yukon, USA-Canada | 3185 (1979) |
| St Lawrence, Canada | 3060 (1900) |
| Rio Grande, USA-Mexico | 3030 (1885) |
| Orinoco, South America | 2900 (1800) |
| São Francisco, South America | 2900 (1800) |
| Salween, Burma-China | 2900 (1800) |
| Danube, Europe | 2850 (1770) |
| Indus, Asia | 2740 (1700) |
| Brahmaputra, Asia | 2700 (1680) |

DEEP AND WIDE *The Orinoco 600km (370 miles) inland.*

## 200,000-YEAR-OLD ESCALATOR

Powered by the inexorable movements of the Earth's crust, a giant escalator has been climbing out of the sea for at least 200,000 years – and it is still moving. The staircase, on the Huon Coast of northeastern Papua New Guinea, is formed by a series of huge grass-covered coral terraces, some up to 100km (60 miles) wide.

In places the escalator has risen to 700m (2300ft) above sea level and new coral steps are already breaking through the waves offshore as the land goes on rising. Old coral reefs and lagoons form the staircase's treads, while the risers are made up of outer reef slopes and ancient cliffs that were once under water. In all, there are 20 major steps in the staircase and innumerable minor ones. The older, higher steps have been severely eroded by rain over the centuries, but the younger, lower steps are more clearly defined.

The movement – of about 3mm (0.12in) a year, or around 1 m (3.3ft) every 350 years – is caused by a collision between two of the continent-bearing rock plates that make up the Earth's crust. The edge of the Indo-Australian plate, on which Papua New Guinea and Australia stand, is being lifted as the Pacific plate slides beneath it at the rate of 110mm (4.3in) a year.

## SILVER THREAD TO THE ATLANTIC

The source of the Amazon, the world's mightiest river, is a silver thread of a mountain brook about 5200m (17,000ft) high in the snowbound peaks of the Peruvian Andes. From the roof of the South American continent, a mere 190km (120 miles) from the Pacific Ocean, the Amazon flows east. Swollen by innumerable torrents and streams, it plunges off the Andes, through gorges and ravines, and flows ever wider, deeper and slower through its vast basin until it finally disgorges into the Atlantic, some 6440km (4000 miles) away.

The length of the Amazon has never been precisely calculated; but in the world league table it takes second place to the Nile, which is approximately 6695km (4160 miles) long. But in all other respects the statistical superlatives belong to the Amazon.

For instance, so powerful is the Amazon's outflow that it pushes a fan of yellow-brown silt 160km (100 miles) out to sea. The river also has more tributaries than any other – 1100 of them. And several of the tributaries, such as the Negro, the Xingu, the Tapajos,

ROSE-RED CITY *The 19th-century English poet and clergyman John Burgon extolled Petra, in southern Jordan, as 'a rose-red city, half as old as time'. Concealed within a ring of hills in the desert, the city can be reached only on foot or, more commonly, on horseback through a dark and narrow gorge known as the Siq. Inside, magnificent façades of temples, tombs and other buildings are carved into the sandstone cliffs. One of the most spectacular of these buildings is the Khazneh Firaoun, or Pharaoh's Treasury, which is 28m (92ft) wide and some 30m (100ft) high. It stands opposite the inner mouth of the Siq (below). A large urn near the top (left) was once thought to contain a pharaoh's gold treasure – and was scarred by rifle bullets fired in the hope of smashing it open. The urn is now known, however, to be solid. The city flourished between the 2nd century BC and the 3rd century AD as an oasis on the caravan route between the Mediterranean and the Persian Gulf. It declined when a new route was built via Syria.*

the Madeira and the Trombetas, are more than 1600km (1000 miles) long. It drains a basin of approximately 6.5 million square kilometres (2.5 million square miles), drawing water from both hemispheres and six countries: Brazil, Bolivia, Peru, Ecuador, Colombia and Venezuela. The mouth of the river is 320km (200 miles) wide and from it flows one-fifth of all the river water in the world.

## LABOUR OF LOVE
Twenty thousand men laboured for nearly 20 years to bring the Taj Mahal at Agra, in India, to its final shining glory of perfection beside the Yamuna river. The building, a mausoleum of pure white marble, was built by the Mughal emperor Shah Jahan to house the body of his beloved second wife, Mumtaz Mahal (known as 'the Exalted of the Palace').

She bore him 14 children, dying in childbirth in 1630 at the age of 39.

Originally Shah Jahan, who ruled India from 1628 to 1658, had planned to build a matching mausoleum in black marble on the opposite bank of the river to house his own body. But the project never got off the ground. Instead he was buried beside his wife in the shrine he had built for her.

## OVER THE WALL
The Great Wall of China first came into being in about 215 BC when the first Chinese emperor, Qin Shi Huangdi, used convict labourers to link up long stretches of much older ramparts. The world's largest man-made structure, the wall is about 7m (23ft) high, and a stone roadway about 5.5m (18ft) across – the width of a modern two-way road – runs along the top. The wall was rebuilt many times, and the present one is largely the work of the Ming emperors, who ruled from AD 1368 to 1644. But though it stretches for 2240km (1400 miles), it is not visible from the Moon, 385,000km (239,000 miles) from Earth, as is often asserted. It is not even visible from a fraction of that distance. The theory that it could be seen from space was finally exploded in 1969 by the US astronaut Alan Bean. He reported that even when his spacecraft was only a few thousand kilometres from Earth, no man-made object was visible.

## THE LOST GLORY OF ANGKOR
The ancient Khmer empire reached its peak of wealth and power in the 12th century, and it was the ruler Suryavarman II (1113–50) who directed the construction of its crowning glory: the temple-tomb of Angkor Wat. But the vast, extravagantly carved structure was destined to lie hidden for centuries in the dense jungle of what is now central Kampuchea before being rediscovered by the French naturalist Albert Henri Mouhot in 1860.

It was built outside the walls of Angkor Thom, the Khmer capital set in the fertile plain of the Mekong

ANGKOR'S GOD-KING *The rulers of the Khmer empire in Kampuchea were revered as gods. This giant face, one of scores carved on the towers of a temple complex at the centre of the Khmer capital, Angkor Thom, is a portrait of Jayavarman VII, who ruled from AD 1181 to about 1215. The city, laid out on a precise gridiron plan aligned with the points of the compass, stands near the temple-tomb of Angkor Wat. The god-kings were not denied all earthly pleasures, however. According to Zhou Daguan, a Chinese diplomat who visited the capital in 1296, tradition required them to make love every night with a sacred nine-headed serpent. Fortunately, Zhou Daguan added, the serpent always appeared in the form of a young girl.*

river. The capital eventually grew to become a huge complex of temples, palaces, lakes and canals covering some 1040km² (400 square miles).

Angkor Wat is crowned by five lofty towers: one at each corner and a central pinnacle soaring to 65m (213ft). It is surrounded by a moat exactly 190m (623ft) wide at every point, some way from its outer walls, which are 1550 × 1400m (5085 × 4592ft).

The Khmers – a Hindu people – built their wealth on rice. They skilfully cultivated three crops a year by irrigation from a precisely engineered system of lakes and canals. Their civilisation flourished from the 9th century until 1431, when the Thais looted Angkor Thom. When the Thais returned later they found the city abandoned; its 1 million inhabitants had vanished into the jungle.

## NOWHERE NEAR
Cape Three Points, on the Gulf of Guinea near Tokoradi in Ghana, West Africa, is known as 'The Land Nearest Nowhere'. It is the nearest land to a spot (in the sea) where zero latitude meets zero longitude at zero altitude.

# PRINCIPAL LAKES OF THE WORLD

| Name and location | Area in km² (square miles) |
|---|---|
| Caspian Sea (salt), USSR-Iran | 393,898 (152,084) |
| Superior, USA-Canada | 82,103 (31,692) |
| Victoria, Africa | 69,485 (26,828) |
| Aral (salt), USSR | 68,682 (26,518) |
| Huron, USA-Canada | 59,570 (22,994) |
| Michigan, USA-Canada | 57,757 (22,294) |
| Tanganyika, Africa | 32,893 (12,700) |
| Baykal, USSR | 31,492 (12,159) |
| Great Bear, Canada | 31,328 (12,093) |
| Great Slave, Canada | 28,570 (11,028) |
| Erie, USA-Canada | 25,667 (9907) |
| Winnipeg, Canada | 24,390 (9415) |
| Malawi (Nyasa), Malawi-Mozambique-Tanzania | 23,310 (9000) |
| Maracaibo (salt), Venezuela | 21,487 (8296) |
| Ontario, USA-Canada | 19,011 (7338) |
| Balkhash, USSR | 18,260 (7050) |
| Ladoga, USSR | 18,130 (7000) |
| Chad, Africa | 15,540 (6000) |
| Onega, USSR | 9842 (3800) |
| Eyre (salt), Australia | 9324 (3600) |
| Turkana (salt), Kenya-Ethiopia | 9065 (3500) |
| Titicaca, Peru-Bolivia | 9065 (3500) |
| Athabasca, Canada | 7936 (3063) |
| Nicaragua, Nicaragua | 7697 (2972) |

RUSSIAN GIANT *In volume, Lake Baykal is the world's largest body of fresh water. It holds as much as all five of North America's Great Lakes combined. It is also the world's deepest lake – up to 1940m (6365ft) deep in places.*

## WELL OF HORROR

Human beings, including children, were hurled down an enormous natural well near the Mayan city of Chichen Itza in Yucatan, Mexico, to placate a rain god. The Well of Sacrifice, as it is called, was sacred to the god Chac, and precious objects of gold, jade and copper were also thrown down. A rich hoard of these artefacts has been recovered from the depths.

Chichen Itza itself dominated the final flowering of the Mayan civilisation, from AD 987 to 1185, after it was occupied by the fierce Toltec tribe. Then it was gradually destroyed, probably by internal strife, and abandoned in the 15th century, about 100 years before the Spaniards arrived in Yucatan.

One of the city's best-preserved buildings is a pyramid topped by a temple and known as El Castillo (The Castle). The four-sided pyramid – which is 24m (78ft) high – contains a total of 365 steps: the number of days in a year.

## CASCADING TO NOTHING

The November-to-March rainy season swells the River Iguacu (or Iguassu) in South America so much that water sometimes pours over its spectacular Iguacu Falls at the rate of 12.7 million litres (2.8 million gallons) a second – enough to fill about six and a half Olympic-size swimming pools every second. But in some years rainfall is so light that the river slows to a trickle – even drying up occasionally, as it did for a month in 1978. There are 275 individual cascades in the falls, close to the Brazil-Argentina border. They plunge 80m (about 260ft) down a crescent-shaped precipice that is 4km (2.5 miles) wide.

## FALLING BACK

During the past 10,000 years the Niagara Falls, on the US-Canadian border, have been moving upstream at an average rate of about 90m (295ft) a century.

But geologists estimate that it will take another 25,000 years at least before the Niagara river cuts its way back to its source: Lake Erie, some 28km (17 miles) away. When it finally breaks through the wall of the lake, the lake will drain away . . . and the falls will disappear.

## DIVERTING SPECTACLE

Victoria Falls, on the Zambia-Zimbabwe border in Africa, will eventually be left high and dry. The falls began thousands of years ago when the Zambezi river found a vertical crack in the region's rocks at right angles to its course. The river gradually deepened and widened the crack to form the chasm – more than 100m (330ft) deep and 2km (1.25 miles) long – into which it now plunges.

But the present falls are doomed. The water – flowing at 7.7 million litres (about 1.7 million gallons) a second – constantly cuts back the lip of the

falls, and each time the lip meets a new crack, another slot-like chasm is formed. The present falls are the eighth to have formed in the last half million years. And the river has already started gouging out a new crack, known as the Devil's Cataract, into which all of it will one day plunge.

## FALLEN ANGEL

American adventurer Jimmy Angel was credited with discovering the highest waterfall in the world after he spotted it from the air in 1935 while prospecting for gold in the Guiana Highlands of South America. Two years later he returned to the area in a single-engine plane and crashed while trying to land on the plateau above the falls.

He survived the crash and the waterfall is now named Salto Angel (Angel Fall) after him.

But Angel was not the first non-Indian to see the spectacular cascade on the River Churún. The waterfall, plunging 979m (3212ft) down the side of Auyán Tepuí (Devil's Mountain), had also been reported by a Spanish explorer, Ernesto Sanchez La Cruz, in 1910.

## DEADLY GLOW

An eerie blue glow lights a grotto in the Waitomo Caves, a series of caverns into which the Waitomo Stream disappears some 200km (125 miles) south of Auckland, New Zealand. It emanates from thousands of gnat larvae which live on the grotto walls and

## PRINCIPAL WATERFALLS OF THE WORLD

| Name and location | Total height in metres (feet) |
|---|---|
| Angel, Venezuela | 979 (3212) |
| Yosemite, California, USA | 739 (2425) |
| Southern Mardalsfossen, Norway | 655 (2149) |
| Tugela, South Africa | 614 (2014) |
| Cuquenán, Venezuela | 610 (2000) |
| Sutherland, New Zealand | 580 (1904) |
| Ribbon, California, USA | 491 (1612) |
| Great Kamarang, Guyana | 488 (1600) |
| Northern Mardalsfossen, Norway | 468 (1535) |
| Della, British Columbia, Canada | 440 (1443) |
| Gavarnie, France | 422 (1385) |
| Skjeggedal, Norway | 420 (1378) |
| Glass, Brazil | 404 (1325) |

HIGH JUMP *Yosemite Falls, in the USA, leaps 739m (2425ft) – more than twice the height of the Eiffel Tower.*

ISLAND RIDDLE *Ever since Easter Island (left), a lonely speck of land in the southeastern Pacific, was sighted and named by the Dutch explorer Jacob Roggeven on Easter Day 1722, scholars have argued about the 1000 or more giant statues which are scattered across it. Many weigh 20 tonnes and the largest, some 9.5m (32ft) tall, tips the scales at 90 tonnes. Most scholars agree that the statues once stood upright on stone huas (temple platforms); that they are images of chiefs or spiritual leaders of Polynesians who reached the island from the west about 2000 years ago; and that they were carved before 1650, when civil strife rent the island's society. However, some scientists believe that the Polynesians came from the east, and the Norwegian anthropologist-explorer Thor Heyerdahl in 1947 proved this a possibility when he sailed the raft Kon Tiki from Peru to the Tuamoto archipelago, west of Easter Island.*

*Nine years later, Heyerdahl visited Easter Island and conducted two experiments. In one, six natives using only stone tools left by the earlier masons roughed out the front of a statue on a quarry side in three days. They estimated that it would take them a year to complete and polish a free-standing figure. In the other test, a dozen islanders raised a statue upright on to its hua by building a platform under the stomach of the prone figure while levering it up with two 5m (16ft) tree trunks. Wood would have been available to the early statue makers for the treeless island was once largely forested. And the Polynesians told Heyerdahl and his American associate William Mulloy that the figures were transported on Y-shaped wooden sledges pulled by teams of men. None of this proves that the statues were carved, carried and raised upright in this way, but it seems a good possibility that they were.*

191

ceiling, and the larvae use the light to trap the midges on which they feed.

The midges, breeding on the edge of the water in the grotto, find the glow irresistible and fly up towards the light. But the glowing grubs dangle sticky threads from the ceiling to trap them. Once the grub has caught a victim, it hauls up the line like an angler, and sucks the body dry. Tourists have been able to visit Glowworm Grotto, as the cave is known, but the disturbance caused by their presence, combined with silting, is threatening the delicately balanced underground environment.

## LEAN YEARS
The Leaning Tower of Pisa, northern Italy, was built as a bell tower for the nearby cathedral. Its top is about 5m (17ft) out of true because the tower's foundations are inadequate – only 3m (10ft) deep, though the tower is 54.5m (179ft) high and weighs 14,453 tonnes.

The tower started to settle sideways almost as soon as building began in 1173, and it was not completed for nearly 200 years. The top tier was built out of line with the rest in a vain attempt to correct the tilt. In 1983 a temporary metal cage was erected around the marble tower, as part of a three-year programme to strengthen its structure and foundations.

## MEN-ONLY MOUNTAIN
No woman or female animal has knowingly been allowed to set foot on Mt Athos on a rocky peninsula in Macedonian Greece, since a special decree was issued in AD 1060. And this despite the fact that the mountain is dedicated to a woman. Athos is the holy mountain of the Eastern Orthodox Church, dedicated to the Virgin Mary.

Indeed, some religious scholars believe that Mary herself visited the mountain and so, ironically, no other female was considered fit to set foot on it.

About 1400 monks live in 20 monasteries and 14 other monastic places, on the 2033m (6670ft) high mountain, and form a self-governing religious community. The first monastery on Mt Athos was founded in AD 963.

## SUPERHIGHWAY IN THE SKY
Stretches of the Great Royal Road, a 4800km (3000 mile) superhighway built by the Incas, are still visible along the Andes of South America. It was constructed between about 1200 and the coming of the Spanish in the 16th century.

The road was about 7m (23ft) wide, and was marked on each side by a low stone wall. Like Roman roads, it always followed the shortest practicable distance between two points, usually staying on the ridges of hills rather than winding through the valleys.

## BETHLEHEM AS IT WAS
The Church of the Nativity at Bethlehem has been a place of pilgrimage at least since the Middle Ages. Accounts of one visit by pilgrims have survived in documents dating from 1458.

The pilgrims stayed overnight with Franciscan friars, attending Mass in the 6th-century church above the underground stable where Christ is thought to have been born. The stable – now an ornate crypt – was originally a hollowed-out cave.

One of the medieval visitors particularly noted the marble manger and its 'extraordinary whiteness'. The church, now in the Israeli-occupied West Bank, still attracts thousands of visitors annually. And the marble-faced manger – originally a trough cut into the wall of the cave, where Christ is said to have been laid after his birth – is still in place.

## PEOPLE'S PALACE
During the 18th century, ordinary people could roam at will through the splendours of Versailles, the great palace built by the Sun King, Louis XIV, in the previous century. Even the king's bedchamber was on view. Indeed, when the royal births took place, dozens of spectators – nobles and commoners – had the right to be present throughout so that there could be no suspicion about the heir's identity.

Work on the palace, which is 18km (11 miles) from Paris, began in 1661 and for the rest of that century and most of the 18th it was both the French court and the seat of government.

The aristocracy were compelled to move there – partly so that the king could keep an eye on them – and so were the principal ministries. The gardens had 1400 fountains, using so much water that they could play for only three hours at a time. The 73m (240ft) long Hall of Mirrors was lit by 3000 candles. In 1919 the Treaty of Versailles between the Allies and Germany was signed in the hall, formally ending the First World War.

## PRINCIPAL ACTIVE VOLCANOES OF THE WORLD

| Name and location | Height in metres (feet) |
|---|---|
| Cotopaxi, Ecuador | 5896 (19,344) |
| Kluchevskaya, USSR | 4750 (15,584) |
| Mt Wrangell, Alaska | 4270 (14,000) |
| Mauna Loa, Hawaii | 4170 (13,680) |
| Cameroon, Cameroon | 4070 (13,350) |
| Erebus, Antarctica | 3720 (12,200) |
| Nyiragongo, Zaire | 3520 (11,560) |
| Iliamna, Aleutian Range, USA | 3350 (11,000) |
| Etna, Sicily | 3340 (10,958) |
| Baker, Cascade Range, USA | 3285 (10,778) |
| Chillan, Chile | 3200 (10,500) |
| Nyamuragira, Zaire | 3090 (10,150) |
| Villarica, Chile | 2842 (9325) |
| Ruapehu, New Zealand | 2797 (9175) |
| Paricutin, Mexico | 2770 (9100) |
| Asama, Japan | 2540 (8340) |
| Mt St Helens, USA | 2530 (8300) |
| Ngauruhoe, New Zealand | 2291 (7515) |
| Hecla, Iceland | 1491 (4892) |
| Vesuvius, Italy | 1277 (4190) |
| Kilauea, Hawaii | 1247 (4090) |
| Stromboli, Italy | 925 (3034) |

BLAST-OFF *A contemporary sketch records an eruption which created a new crater on Vesuvius in 1829. The eruption which entombed Pompeii took place in AD 79.*

# PRINCIPAL ISLANDS OF THE WORLD

| Name and location | Area in km² (square miles) |
|---|---|
| Greenland | 2,175,000 (840,000) |
| New Guinea, Pacific Ocean | 789,900 (305,000) |
| Borneo, Pacific Ocean | 751,000 (290,000) |
| Madagascar, Indian Ocean | 587,041 (226,657) |
| Baffin Land, Canada | 507,451 (195,876) |
| Sumatra, Indonesia | 422,200 (163,000) |
| Honshu, Japan | 230,092 (88,839) |
| Britain | 229,849 (88,745) |
| Victoria, Canada | 217,290 (83,874) |
| Ellesmere, Canada | 196,236 (75,747) |
| Sulawesi, Indonesia | 178,700 (69,000) |
| South Island, New Zealand | 150,460 (58,093) |
| Java, Indonesia | 126,400 (48,800) |
| North Island, New Zealand | 114,687 (44,281) |
| Cuba | 110,922 (42,827) |
| Newfoundland, Canada | 108,860 (42,020) |
| Luzon, Philippines | 104,400 (40,400) |
| Iceland | 103,000 (40,000) |

CONE ISLAND *The snow-tipped 2518m (8261ft) summit of Mt Egmont – one of numerous volcanic peaks in New Zealand – looms over the west coast of the North Island.*

ROOM SERVICE *The Spanish king Philip II (1556 – 98) had a balcony built near his bedroom in the Escorial palace (above) so that he could attend Mass without getting up. The balcony, beside the altar of the palace chapel, was added because he suffered from gout and found walking difficult. The palace, built near Madrid between 1563 and 1584, became the hub of the Spanish empire. Philip's rule, however, was over-centralised. Petitions could remain unanswered for years. 'If death came from the Escorial,' a provincial governor once complained, 'we should all live to a very great age.'*

STARS OF INDIA *This huge bowl, set in the ground at Jaipur, about 240km (150 miles) from the Indian capital of New Delhi, is an astronomical observatory. The black markings on the bowl are slots. Astronomers in an underground room beneath the bowl took sightings through the slots, and noted on the edges of the slots the positions of the stars as they moved into view. The observatory, built in 1728 by an Indian prince named Jai Singh II, includes 12 massive stone instruments – each lined up on a different sign of the zodiac. It also contains a huge sundial, about 27m (90ft) tall, which is known as the Samrat Yantra ('The emperor of instruments').*

## PRINCIPAL CAVES OF THE WORLD

| Name and location | Depth in metres (feet) |
| --- | --- |
| Atea Kananda, Papua New Guinea | 1500 (4920) estimated |
| Gouffre Jean Bernard, France | 1490 (4888) |
| Sima de Las Puertas de Illamina, Spain | 1338 (4390) |
| Gouffre de la Pierre-Saint-Martin, France | 1332 (4370) |
| Snezhnaya, USSR | 1280 (4200) |
| Sistema Huautla, Mexico | 1240 (4068) |
| Mammuthöhle, Austria | 1175 (3855) |
| Sumidero de Cellagua, Spain | 970 (3182) |
| Antro di Corchia, Italy | 950 (3117) |
| Kievskaya, USSR | 950 (3117) |
| Kacherlschacht, Austria | 913 (2995) |
| Reseau de Siebenhengste, Switzerland | 860 (2821) |
| Sotano de San Agustin, Mexico | 859 (2818) |
| Hollochgrotten, Switzerland | 827 (2713) |
| Anou Boussouil, Algeria | 800 (2625) |
| Jaskini Snieznej, Poland | 783 (2569) |
| Brezno pri Gamsovi Glavici, Yugoslavia | 765 (2510) |
| Ghar Parau, Iran | 751 (2464) |
| Kef Toghobeit, Morocco | 700 (2296) |
| Harwood's Hole, New Zealand | 357 (1171) |
| Ogof Ffynnon Ddu, Wales | 308 (1010) |

WELSH POOL *A rock column rises from an underground lake in Britain's deepest cave: Ogof Ffynnon Ddu in Wales.*

## THE GREATER PYRAMID

A massive pyramid that is believed to be the biggest monument ever built was raised by the fierce Toltec people at Cholula de Rivadabia in central Mexico. It stands 54m (177ft) high, less than half the height of Egypt's Great Pyramid of Cheops, but its volume is estimated to be 3.3 million cubic metres (4.3 million cubic yards), compared with the 2.5 million cubic metres (3.3 million cubic yards) of the Egyptian struc-

ture. The pyramid, known as the Quetzalcoatl, was built between AD 900 and 1200 and covers 18 hectares (45 acres) – 3½ times the area of the Great Pyramid. When the Spaniards found it in the 16th century, they built a church on the top.

## THE EARLIEST WALLED CITY

The Old Testament Book of Joshua tells how the Israelites marched seven times around Jericho before a blast from their sacred trumpets brought the walls tumbling down, and they sacked the city. Modern archaeology has revealed that Jericho is the oldest known walled city on Earth – incredibly ancient even when the Israelites descended upon it some time between 1400 and 1250 BC. Walls 9000 years old have been discovered, though no remains of any city walls dating from the time of Joshua have been found. They may have eroded to dust centuries ago.

An excavation-riddled mound, measuring 256 × 160m (839 × 524ft) and 18m (60ft) high, is all that remains of old Jericho. It lies alongside modern Jericho just north of the Dead Sea. But within it archaeologists have unearthed a succession of cities, each built upon the ruins of the previous one. The oldest walls were found about 15m (50ft) below the surface.

## OVER THE LINE

Ecuador is Spanish for equator, and in 1936 the nation set up a granite column marking where the imaginary line of the Equator passes near a village 24km (15 miles) from the capital, Quito. Unfortu-

nately, the column was in the wrong place. It was a few hundred metres off the line, but tourists seldom minded – they were too intrigued by the notion of invariably equal days and nights, or too busy stepping in a moment from one hemisphere to the other. The monument was finally demolished in the early 1980s and a new one was built in the right place.

### RUSTLESS RIDDLE
Metallurgists still do not know why a tall iron pillar at Meharauli, near the Indian capital of Delhi, has never rusted – despite an estimated 1500 years of exposure to the weather.

The pillar is a solid shaft of pure wrought iron with an ornamental top, about 7m (23ft) high, 400mm (16in) across and weighing about 6 tonnes. Incised on the side is a six-line poem celebrating the deeds of Chandragupta II (AD 375–415), who ruled over much of northern India.

### SKELETON REEF
The skeletons of countless billions of tiny sea creatures called coral polyps form the Great Barrier Reef, stretching 2000km (1250 miles) along the northeast coast of Australia. The reef – the largest structure ever made by any living creature, including man – is a complex chain of coral reefs and islands, rather than a single great wall, but there are only two major gaps – Trinity Opening and Grafton Passage, both just north of Cairns. In 1983 the first man to row across the Pacific Ocean, Britain's Peter Bird, failed to get through the reef and was rescued just before his boat sank. The distance between the reef and the coast varies between 8km (5 miles) near the northern end and 187km (116 miles) at the southern. It covers an area about the size of England and Scotland, stretching almost as far as Papua New Guinea, and has taken 12 to 15 million years to form.

### THE BIG HOLE
Diamond miners wielding picks and shovels dug the largest excavation made by man – the Big Hole at Kimberley, in South Africa. In the course of 44 years, from 1871 until the mine closed in 1915, they removed nearly 23 million tonnes of clay and rock – and 14.5 million carats (about 2.7 tonnes) of diamonds. The great mineshaft is nearly 500m (1640ft) across and 400m (1312ft) deep – though shafts from its base go down to about 1200m (nearly 4000ft). It is now an open-air museum.

### IN THE BEGINNING
The oldest man-made structures still standing are Stonehenge-like temples. The megalithic buildings are at Mgarr and Skorba on Malta, and at Ggantija on the nearby island of Gozo. All date from about 3250 BC.

### TRIPLE-DECKER BRIDGE
The best-preserved Roman buildings in France are in and around Nîmes in southern France. They include one of the most remarkable engineering feats of ancient times – the 564m (1850ft) long Pont du Gard,

195

an aqueduct designed to carry both water and pedestrians across the River Gard, 19km (12 miles) northeast of the town.

The enormous aqueduct was built in AD 19, the topmost of its three tiers soaring 48m (160ft) above the river to carry the water. The 36 small arches of this tier stand upon an 11-arched middle tier, all supported by the six great arches of the lowest tier, which carries the road.

## BRAKE ON PROGRESS

When the driver of a San Francisco cable car wants to go, he puts the main brake on – and releases it when he wants to stop. This is because the car is pulled by a cable that moves at a constant 14.5km/h (9mph) inside a groove in the road. The main brake operates by gripping the cable, so that the car moves with it. Releasing the brake frees the car from the cable and a second set of brakes, on the wheels, brings the car to a halt. The system was invented by a London-born wire-rope maker and engineer, Andrew Hallidie, and his cable cars have been clanking up and down San Francisco's steep hills since 1873. The system is now preserved as a landmark in the Californian city.

## MUSICAL CHAIRS

Sydney's dazzling Opera House, opened in 1973 after 16 years' work, cost A$102 million – 14 times the original estimate. But its 2690-seat main hall is used only for concerts – opera and ballet are staged in the smaller 1547-seat Opera Theatre. There is no car park for the buildings, either. One was planned under the adjoining botanical gardens, but Australian conservationists objected that it would disturb three old trees in a protected area, and building workers backed them with a strike threat. As a result, theatregoers have to park about 1.6km (1 mile) away, and ride to the Opera House on buses.

# SEVEN WONDERS OF THE ANCIENT WORLD

The Greek author Antipater of Sidon, who lived in the 2nd century BC, was one of several writers to list the greatest monuments and buildings known to the Classical world. He settled on seven because that was considered a magic number by the Greeks.

**The Egyptian pyramids**
Built more than 4000 years ago, they are the oldest of the ancient wonders and the only ones still surviving. They served as tombs for the Egyptian pharaohs, whose mummified bodies were surrounded by treasures and personal belongings.

**The Colossus of Rhodes**
A bronze statue of the sun god Helios standing 32m (105ft) high at the mouth of Rhodes harbour. According to legend, the Colossus straddled the harbour and vessels sailed between its legs. It was built on the Greek island in about 305–292 BC and was destroyed in 224 BC by an earthquake.

**The Hanging Gardens of Babylon**
Built in the 6th century BC by Nebuchadnezzar II, they consisted of a series of terraces on which flowers and trees were grown. The gardens stretched along the banks of the Euphrates and were watered by irrigation channels.

**The Mausoleum at Halicarnassus, Asia Minor**
The tomb of Mausolus, a ruler of the city in the 4th century BC. It was built by his widow and was destroyed by an earthquake before the 15th century.

**The Pharos of Alexandria**
The world's first known lighthouse, it stood 122m (400ft) high and had a spiral ramp leading to the beacon. It was built on the island of Pharos, at the entrance to Alexandria harbour in Egypt, in about 270 BC. By the 15th century it had fallen into ruin.

**The Statue of Zeus at Olympia**
An imposing figure – 9m (30ft) high – of the supreme Greek god with the body made of wood and covered with gold and ivory. It was designed in the 5th century BC by the Athenian sculptor Phidias and was destroyed by fire in AD 475.

**The Temple of Artemis at Ephesus, Asia Minor**
Built of marble in the 6th century BC in honour of the Greek virgin goddess of the hunt and the moon, it was rebuilt in the 4th century BC and finally destroyed by invading Goths in the 3rd century AD. Fragments of the temple are in the British Museum, in London.

# SEVEN WONDERS OF THE MODERN WORLD

No formal list exists of the wonders of the modern world. These seven, all of which can still be seen today, were selected by *Reader's Digest* editors.

**The Taj Mahal**
Built 1630–48 by the emperor Shah Jahan as a mausoleum for his wife Mumtaz Mahal. The tomb, made of white marble and inlaid with other stones, is in Agra, north India. Shah Jahan is also buried there.

**The Great Wall of China**
Built originally to keep out nomadic invaders from the north, most of the present wall was constructed during the Ming dynasty (1368–1644). Altogether, the wall winds for 2240km (1400 miles) across northern China and has an average height of 7m (23 ft).

**The Easter Island statues**
Colossal, elongated heads – up to 9.5m (32ft) high – carved from volcanic rock. The South Pacific island on which they stand was discovered on Easter Day 1722 by the Dutch explorer Jacob Roggeven – and the statues were probably made by the ancestors of the island's Polynesian inhabitants.

**The Eiffel Tower**
Built for the 1889 Paris Exhibition by the French bridge engineer Alexandre Gustave Eiffel. Made of wrought iron, it stands 300m (984ft) high on the left bank of the River Seine. Its revolutionary lattice-work earned Eiffel the title 'magician of iron'.

**The Mayan city of Tikal, Central America**
Tikal, the ceremonial centre of the Mayan empire, dates from about 300 BC and was rediscovered in 1848 by a team of Guatemalan explorers. Situated in northern Guatemala, its temples and buildings include the imposing Pyramid of the Great Jaguar and the Palace of the Nobles.

**The space shuttle**
The US space shuttle *Columbia* was first launched from Cape Canaveral, Florida, in 1981. With a crew of two or three astronauts, it is designed to carry satellites into space, to retrieve and repair them, and to build large stations in space.

**Chartres Cathedral**
The Gothic cathedral, dating from the 12th and 13th centuries, stands on a hill overlooking the French market town. Among its glories are its stained-glass windows (173 in all), which produce a unique 'Chartres-blue' light.

# Temples and churches

## A CHIP OF THE MOON
A tiny slice of moon rock is sealed in the stained-glass window dedicated to scientists and technicians in Washington Cathedral, USA. The rock was brought to the Earth by Apollo astronauts in 1969.

## SACRED MIRROR
The holiest of all Shinto objects is a mirror said to have been looked into by Amaterasu, the sun goddess, soon after the world was created. Millions of pilgrims visit the mirror each year at Ise, the most revered Shinto shrine in Japan. In the past the Japanese imperial family claimed descent from Amaterasu, which is why

Japan is known as the Land of the Rising Sun. Emperor Hirohito formally renounced the dynasty's claim to divinity after the Second World War.

## CLIFF OF TEMPLES
Cave temples are among the earliest forms of religious architecture. Buddhist monks cut 29 such temples out of a riverside cliff-face at Ajanta in central India between 200 BC and AD 700. The builders used no scaffolding. They simply began their work at the top by finding a small cave or digging a tunnel into the cliff. Then their method was to cut away the floor, carving the walls as they went, following the formations in the sandstone.

THE GLORY OF CHARTRES *Stained-glass pictures of angels, doves, kings and prophets encircle the central image of the Virgin Mary and Christ in the north rose window of Chartres Cathedral in France. The cathedral's most precious relic is a veil said to have been worn by the Virgin Mary, which was given to the cathedral in AD 876 by Charles the Bald, grandson of the first Holy Roman Emperor, Charlemagne. There have been in all six cathedrals on the site. The first was put to the torch by a French duke in 743, the second was burnt down by Danes in 858, and three others were destroyed by fires in 962, 1020 and 1194. The present cathedral, a vaulting masterpiece of medieval architecture lit by the glow from its enormous and predominantly blue stained-glass windows, was begun in 1194. The main structure was completed in just 26 years, and the windows and sculptures were in place by the time the cathedral was consecrated in 1260.*

## SLUMBERING GIANT

Few modern cathedrals have taken as long to build as that of St John the Divine in New York, USA. Work began in 1892 but stopped during the Second World War when money ran out. The twin towers and the interior of the Protestant Episcopal church were left half-built for nearly 40 years. Building began again only in 1979, by which time New Yorkers had nick-named it 'St John the Unfinished'. The cathedral began to be used for services in 1899, at a time when only the crypt had been built.

In 1984, the cathedral's western towers, the tran-septs and part of the roof were still unfinished and estimates of how long the remaining work would take ranged from 20 to 100 years. It is, however, already the world's biggest cathedral: 183m (601ft) from end to end of the nave, long enough to hold two American football fields; and 38m (124ft) from floor to vaulted ceiling, as high as a 12-storey building.

## ST PETER'S THE GREAT

The world's largest church is St Peter's Basilica in the Vatican City, Rome. It is 186m (611ft) long, and at its peak is 140m (458ft) high. The original 4th-century building began to collapse in the 15th century. Rebuilding began in 1506 and ended with the completion of St Peter's Square – its colonnades designed by the Italian architect Gianlorenzo Bernini – at the end of the 17th century.

## PLUNDERED SHRINE

Little remains of the Canterbury Cathedral where Thomas Becket – the Archbishop of Canterbury who quarrelled with Henry II on a number of religious matters – was murdered by the English monarch's knights on December 29, 1170. The great Norman building was destroyed by fire four years later, and a virtually new cathedral rose in its place. In it, a splendid golden shrine was built for Becket's body, and for three centuries the shrine was visited by thousands of pilgrims. One such pilgrimage was the setting for *The Canterbury Tales*, a collection of narrative poems by the English writer Geoffrey Chaucer (1340–1400).

In 1534, however, Henry VIII made himself supreme head of the Church of England. He destroyed the shrine, burnt the murdered archbishop's remains . . . and took the gold.

## MOUNTAIN OF FAITH

An ancient Buddhist mountain temple, Borobudur in Java, has been saved from the ravages of the ages by one of man's most modern inventions, the computer. Borobudur is a vast series of stone terraces built on the sides of a natural earth mound. Circle after circle of small pinnacles climb to a central shrine, or *stupa* (a Sanskrit word meaning 'the crown of the head'), at the top of the hill.

The temple was built by migrant Indian Buddhists in the second half of the 8th century AD. They used thousands of tonnes of stone quarried from a nearby river bed. On Borobudur's rising terraces are 504 carved shrines of seated Buddhas, and bas-reliefs cut into the stone recount Buddhist legends.

Over centuries, rainwater drew destructive salts from the soil into the stone temple. Algae, fungi and lichen began eating away at the terraces. In addition, the rain began to wash away the soil beneath the stones, undermining the terraces.

In a ten-year plan, organised by the United Nations and the Indonesian government and completed in 1983, more than a million stones were removed from the temple, cleaned with chemicals and then replaced. At the same time the earth beneath was shored up with new foundations, and drains were installed to carry rainwater away from the temple. A computer was used to index every slab, to ensure that each could be slotted back into its rightful place.

## PRECIOUS UMBRELLA

A gilded and jewelled umbrella erected in 1871 crowns the 6th-century Shwe Dagon pagoda in Burma. The eight-spoked umbrella – which symbolises the eight-fold path of Buddhism – was presented by King Min-don, founder of Malaya. The pagoda, on a hill overlooking the Burmese capital, Rangoon, is a solid brick spire, 99m (326ft) high.

It contains relics of the Buddha. The spire is covered with 8688 thin sheets of gold, each about 300mm square (1sq ft). At modern prices each of the golden sheets is worth about £5000.

## SACRED STONE

One of Islam's most sacred monuments, the Dome of the Rock, stands in the heart of Jerusalem above a huge stone claimed as sacred by Jews, Christians and Muslims. Jews and Christians believe that the limestone rock – 18 × 15m (60 × 50ft) – was the altar on which Abraham was prepared to sacrifice his son, Isaac. Jews also venerate it as the site of Solomon's Temple. Muslims believe that Muhammad ascended to heaven from the rock and point to an indentation in its surface as his footprint. The original dome was built by Arabs between AD 684 and 691, on the site of an old Jewish temple.

## ROUND TRIP

Some of the bells that once hung in the basilica of Santiago de Compostela in northwest Spain – still visited by Catholic pilgrims from all over the world – spent more than 200 years in a mosque. The bells were plundered from the Apostol Basilica in Santiago after Arabs captured the city in AD 997. The Arabs forced Christian prisoners to carry the bells more than 800km (500 miles) across the country to the great mosque of Cordoba. There the bells were set upside down and used as lamps. In 1236, after the Spanish recaptured Cordoba, King Ferdinand III made Moorish prisoners carry the bells all the way back. Since then, the bells have vanished from the church and from history, and their fate is unknown. The church does, however, still contain the world's largest censer. In use, the censer, which is about 1.2m (4ft) high, swings across the nave on a large rope from the roof. Eight men are required to keep it swinging.

## TOWN THAT STOLE A CHURCH

In 1897, the tiny railway hamlet of Donald in western Canada was condemned to death. The Canadian Pacific Railway – the hamlet's only employer – decided to move its local headquarters 130km (80 miles) to Revelstoke to take advantage of a more profitable freight route across the Rocky Mountains.

The church from Donald was supposed to go to Revelstoke, too. But many of Donald's residents had already moved to another town named Windermere in anticipation of the closure. And they were furious at the idea. So they stole the church. Dismantling it, they smuggled it by rail and river ferry to their new home. The church reached Windermere safely, all except its bell. That was stolen along the way by a second group of Anglicans from the village of Golden.

Today, two churches still bear witness to the thefts. Windermere's church is called St Peter's the Stolen, and Golden's is known as St Paul's of the Stolen Bell.

## BIBLE BLOOMERS

A number of editions of the Bible have contained unusual translations or printing errors. Some have even acquired special names as a result. In 1560 the 'Breeches Bible' was published in Geneva. It got its name because Genesis 3:7 read: 'Adam and Eve sewed fig tree leaves together and made themselves breeches.' Traditionally, their clothes were 'aprons'.

● The 'Cider Bible', in the medieval library of Hereford Cathedral, England, is a manuscript copy made in about 1400 of Wycliffe's Bible – but with one small change. The admonition in St Luke about strong drink was amended by the copyist to read: 'He shall drink ne wine ne cider' – an apt alteration in an English county renowned for its cider.

● In the 'Adulterer's Bible', which appeared in 1632, the word 'not' in the seventh commandment was left out so that it read: 'Thou shalt commit adultery.' Its London printers, Robert Barker and Martin Lucas, were fined £300 for the oversight.

● Another 17th-century English printer was fined £3000 for substituting 'a' for 'no' in Psalm 14 so that it read: 'The fool hath said in his heart there is a God.'

● The 'Bathroom Bible', a modern version originally published by a US firm in 1971, is so called because I Samuel 24:3 reads: 'Saul went into a cave to go to the bathroom.' The Authorised Version of 1611 keeps to the Hebraic euphemism at this point and has: 'Saul went in to cover his feet.'

DOME OF FAITH *Sanchi in central India, the site of a group of three enormous stupas, or shrines, is one of the holiest places in the world for Buddhists. This stone carving, which appears on a gateway to the largest of the three, shows the main stupa and the gateway surrounded by a crowd of human and mythical worshippers. The stupas were built on the orders of the Buddhist emperor Ashoka, who ruled much of India between about 273 and 232 BC – some 200 years after the death of Siddartha Gautama, the Himalayan prince who founded Buddhism.*

# STONES THAT SPEAK THE FAITH

The world's great religions have moulded not only thought and behaviour, but bricks and stone, too. Each has generated a traditional style of building to reflect its central beliefs and often its history.

### BUDDHIST
The typical Buddhist building is a stupa, a circular mound of earth usually covered with bricks and plaster. Relics were often buried in the mound. Most stupas are topped by a small spire, a stylised umbrella or parasol. Parasols were a royal symbol, and they were used on stupas to signify Buddha's universal dominion. In Korea, China and Japan, the stupa was adapted into the pagoda. Buddhism's holiest places are: the temple of Borobudur, Java; and the stupas of Sanchi and Bharhut, both in Madhya Pradesh, India.

### CHRISTIAN
Most Christian churches are built in the shape of a cross, symbolising the crucifixion. The altar is usually at the east end of the nave, towards Jerusalem. Not all follow this pattern, however. Many early churches – including the church of San Clemente in Rome – have their altars at the western end, and some Nonconformist churches are square or circular. Christianity's holiest places are the Church of the Holy Sepulchre, Jerusalem – the presumed site of Christ's crucifixion – and the grave of St Peter, beneath the altar of St Peter's Basilica, Vatican City, Rome.

### HINDU
Extravagant decoration and an enormous variety of styles mark Hindu architecture, reflecting the thousands of gods worshipped. Temple walls, such as those at Khajuraho in northern India, are often richly carved with figures from Hindu legend. Hinduism's holiest places are the River Ganges and the holy city of Varanasi (Benares) on its banks.

### JEWISH
A synagogue can be anything from a room in a private house to a grand hall, reflecting the need for discretion during long periods of persecution. The word comes from the Greek *sunagoge*, meaning 'assembly'. The only requirements for a synagogue are two candelabra, an Ark, or alcove, to hold the Scriptures, and a platform to read them from. Judaism's holiest places are: Mount Sinai, in the Sinai peninsula, Egypt, where God is said to have delivered the ten commandments on stone tablets to Moses while the Jews were in the wilderness; and the Wailing, or Western, Wall in Jerusalem – believed to be part of the Temple of Solomon.

### MUSLIM
The earliest mosques (from the Arabic word *masjid*, meaning 'place of worship') were often open rectangular courtyards surrounded by covered colonnades, featureless from the outside. Later, the central sanctuaries were usually covered by domes and surrounded by one or more high minarets from which the *muezzin* or crier could call the faithful to prayer five times a day. Every mosque has a niche called the *mihrab* built into the wall facing Mecca to indicate the direction for worshippers to face when praying. Most also have a fountain or well in the courtyard for ritual cleansing. Decorations are limited to abstract designs or inscriptions from the Koran. The *Haddith*, the Islamic Traditions, forbid the representation of living human figures in art to avoid image worship. Islam's holiest place is the Kaaba shrine in the Great Mosque at Mecca, Saudi Arabia, which is believed to be a replica of God's house in Heaven, built on Earth by Abraham and Ishmael.

LIFE IN THE TREE-TOPS  In tropical rain forests most of the animals feed and make their homes in the tree-tops. Many monkeys and rodents use their tails to help them climb. Other mammals and reptiles have developed wing-like skin flaps and broadly webbed toes to help them glide from tree to tree, so there are 'flying' species of frogs, lizards, snakes and squirrels.

By contrast, some tropical forest birds – such as hornbills, parrots and touracos – spend much of their lives walking along the branches of trees rather than flying. Plants, too, have adapted to life in the tree-tops: lianas, bromeliads and orchids all grow high in trees and are scarce on the ground.

---

*The Southeast Asian jungle tree* Adinandra dumosa *takes two or three years to reach flowering size – and then bears flowers and fruit almost continuously for the next 100 years or more, making it one of the world's longest-flowering plants.*

---

AN INFINITE VARIETY  The unique profusion and diversity of plant and animal life in the world's rain forests defies classification or enumeration.

Constant heat and humidity turn rain forests into natural greenhouses where summer's abundance lasts all year round. In Amazonia alone, the rivers teem with 40 per cent of all the world's species of freshwater fish. Birdlife is even richer, with more than half the world's total of 8600 species thriving in the great green sanctuary – 319 different sorts of hummingbird alone have been recorded. Entomologists cannot even guess at the number of species of insects that live in rain forests. Estimates range upwards from a million species, but of these, perhaps no more than a quarter have been catalogued.

RAZOR TEETH  The most famed, and the most feared, fish of the Amazon are the piranhas. Voracious carnivores, with immensely strong jaws and razor-sharp teeth – and occasionally as much as 300mm (1ft) long – piranhas attack their prey in ferocious packs of a hundred or more.

---

*Amazonia boasts the largest rodent in the world: the web-footed capybara. It is on record that a shoal of piranhas reduced a 45kg (100lb) capybara to a skeleton in less than 60 seconds.*

---

INSECTS THAT KILL TREES  Attempts to establish forestry plantations in tropical rain forests have often failed disastrously as pests and diseases of epidemic proportions have swept through the plants. The Ford motor company's efforts after 1928, for instance, to grow rubber at its testing ground at Fordlandia in Amazonia were thwarted by a leaf blight called *Dothidella ulei*, which infects wild trees.

Other plantations in rain forests around the world have been wiped out by insects which feed on the living timber, destroying its commercial value before it can be harvested.

In the wild, most rain forest trees grow anything up to 400m (440yds) apart from others of their own kind, so that although any given area may be crowded with hundreds of different species, it usually has only a handful of specimens of any one type. The trees are

kept apart, scientists believe, by the very pests that prey on them. Detailed analyses of tree distribution have shown that most specimens are just far enough away from neighbours of their own kind to be beyond the flying range of the pests or disease-carriers which attack them.

THE WEEPING TREE  The Amazonian Indians have been responsible for discoveries of global importance. It is to them, for instance, that the world owes rubber. Columbus was the first European to record that the Indians made balls out of a black vegetable gum. The Indians called the gum and its source *cahuchu*, meaning 'the tree that weeps'.

The word passed into European languages as *caoutchouc*. The English alternative, rubber, may have been coined by the 18th-century English scientist Joseph Priestley (1733 – 1804) who observed that caoutchouc rubbed out pencil marks.

# Rain forests

MONOPOLY BUSTER Rubber became vital for the world's wheeled transport after the US inventor Charles Goodyear (1800–60) discovered in 1839 a new way of hardening it called vulcanisation. And since raw rubber was a Brazilian monopoly at first, Amazonian merchants made fortunes. It was an English botanist, Sir Henry Wickham, who broke the Brazilian stranglehold. In 1876 he chartered a ship to take 70,000 rubber-tree seeds from Brazil to England.

He was allowed to take the seeds out of the country by Brazilian customs officials because he pretended that the seeds were simply botanical specimens for the royal plant collection at Kew Gardens. In fact, once the seeds had been successfully grown in hothouses at Kew, seedlings were sent out to Ceylon (now Sri Lanka) and Malaya where vast, efficiently managed plantations were established. The 'wild' rubber of Amazonia could not compete in price with cultivated products and the Brazilian market crashed.

MAJOR RAIN FORESTS *The largest of the world's rain forests (above) is Amazonia, in S America. It covers about 6.5 million km² (2.5 million square miles) – an area larger than Western Europe. The world's largest forest of any kind is not a rain forest, but coniferous. It covers an area of 11 million km² (4.5 million square miles) in Siberia in the north of the Soviet Union.*

## THE TROPICAL FOREST'S MANY LAYERS

In a small area of tropical rain forest in South America, covering only 2.6km² (1 square mile), 117 different species of trees, lianas, and flowering plants have been discovered, competing in a delicately balanced, multi-layered system. Its uppermost level (1) is the widely spaced tops of the tallest trees – such as the silk-cotton *(Ceiba)* – which tower 41m (135ft) or more into the sky.

Below these is a second layer (2) of tree-tops, 18–24m (60–80ft) high, forming a continuous canopy. Beneath that again is a middle layer of trees (3) standing up to 12m (40ft) with long narrow crowns to make the most of the light. These are shade-loving trees, such as mauritia, orbygnia and euterpe; many are covered with orchids, ferns, bromeliads and cacti.

So densely packed are these upper layers that they block out the light almost completely from the lowest levels – a sparser layer of dwarf trees, struggling saplings, palms and shrubs (4) and a ground layer of ferns and non-woody herbs (5).

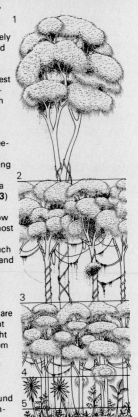

LIVING CURTAIN *A stream writhes through jungle near the Amazon's northern headwaters. Along its banks, sunlight stimulates a chaotic growth of plants, which form a thick curtain across the forest's dark and less cluttered heart.*

# The world's last wildernesses

MOUNTAIN RANGES *The world's longest mountain chain is the Andes, which stretches 7200km (4500 miles). It is followed by the Rockies (6000km; 3750 miles), the Himalayas (3800km; 2400 miles) and Australia's Great Dividing Range (3600km; 2250 miles).*

UP-AND-DOWN MOUNTAIN Officially Everest, the world's highest mountain, is 8848m (29,028ft) high, but its summit seems to bob up and down. Theodolites were first used to measure it in 1852, but a mass such as Everest generates its own gravitational pull, so the British surveyors could not be sure that their spirit levels were true – nor, therefore, that their theodolites were level and so giving a correct reading.

They made six measurements and took the average: exactly 29,000ft. This sounded too neat a figure, so they settled for 29,002ft. Indian and Chinese surveyors have made more recent measurements and they put the height at 8849m (29,030ft). Changing depths of ice on the peak also alter the mountain's actual height. As Nick Estcourt, a member of the 1975 British expedition, put it: 'If Everest is bobbing up and down, we must hope to catch it on a low day.'

## LIFE ON THE SLOPES

Mountainsides are microcosms of the natural world because the effects of altitude mirror the effects of latitude, but in much shorter distances. A mountain near the Equator can be tropical at its base and arctic at its summit, with other climatic zones represented on the slopes between. And though the species at each level vary in different parts of the world, the patterns of mountainside living are similar everywhere.

In middle-latitude foothills, for example, deciduous and evergreen trees grow and ferns and flowers flourish. Birds and plant-eating animals, including rabbits, deer and squirrels, thrive.

### Alpine zone

Higher up, the air becomes thinner and there is more sunlight and wind. Temperatures drop about 2°C (3.6°F) for every 300m (1000ft). Gradually the softer world of the foothills gives way to the alpine zone, where conifer trees dominate. It is a zone of predators. Bears, wolves, martens and lynxes are found alongside elk and red deer. Woodpeckers, crossbills and nutcrackers feed on insects and seeds in the firs.

Above the treeline, only the toughest flora and fauna survive the thin air, sparse growth and chill winds. Mosses, saxifrage and crowberry cling to the rocks. Marmots, mountain goats and chamois pick the scanty grazing. The sky here is the eagle's domain. The highest-living mammal is a member of the rabbit family: the collared pika. It survives at 6100m (20,000ft) on Everest. Tiny flies, spiders and springtails are also found at that height. The highest-living bird is probably the Alpine chough, which has been found feeding at 8000m (26,250ft).

### Merging boundaries

On a mountain there is no sudden cut-off where one zone ends and another begins. They merge together at their edges. Nor are the zones found at standard heights throughout the world. They fluctuate according to how far the mountains are from the Equator. In the European Alps, for instance, the alpine zone begins at about 2135m (7000ft). In the Himalayas, on the other hand, the same zone begins more than 900m higher, at about 3050m (10,000ft).

A PASSAGE TO INDIA *The Kali Gandaki river snakes its way from the plains of Tibet towards India through the deepest valley in the world. At the valley's deepest point, shown here, the river flows 5.5km (3.5 miles) below the 8172m (26,810ft) high peak of Dhaulagiri (on the right).*

*The Himalayas present a huge hurdle for migrating birds from Central Asia. At Dehra Dun, India, geese have been seen flapping steadily over the peaks at an estimated 8830m (28,970ft). Not all birds survive the crossing. Steppe eagles have been found frozen dead on Everest's South Col at 8000m (26,246ft).*

OLD MEN OF THE MOUNTAINS Genetics probably play the largest part in longevity, but there is evidence that people can live longer at high altitudes than at sea level. At Vilcabamba, a Peruvian village about 2750m (9000ft) up in the Andes, birth certificates show nine people out of 819 aged more than 100. In the United States the average is three per 100,000.

Mountain people, medical researchers have found, are less likely than lowlanders to suffer from leukaemia, hypertension, arteriosclerosis, heart attacks and high blood pressure. On the other hand, they get more tuberculosis, bronchitis and pneumonia.

CLIMBING COURTIER The first man known to have climbed a mountain for no reason other than that it was there was Antoine de Ville in 1492. Charles VIII of France ordered de Ville, his chamberlain, to take a party to the top of Mont Aiguille, a 2097m (6880ft) peak near Grenoble. De Ville is said to have been so impressed with the view and his achievement that he stayed up there for six days. The first serious Alpine climb was made by a geologist named Jacques Balmat and a physician, Michel Paccard. They climbed Europe's highest mountain, Mont Blanc, in 1786.

# The world's last wildernesses

SEVEN-YEAR HITCH Mountaineers wanting to climb Everest–named after Sir George Everest (1790–1866), a British Surveyor-General in India–have to book their turn up to seven years in advance. Only two expeditions are allowed to take place at the same time, and each has to use a different route. In addition, Himalayan weather conditions mean that there are only three periods a year when a climb is practicable: in April and May before the monsoon rains; in October just after the monsoon; and in December and January during the winter.

Since Sir Edmund Hillary and the Sherpa, Tenzing Norgay, first climbed Everest in 1953, more than 130 mountaineers have made it to the top, including five without oxygen and four women. But by the early 1980s about 50 climbers had died on the mountain.

LIVERISH BEAR Black bears do not actually hibernate in their mountain habitats. They doze away the winter in a state of lethargy, rousing from time to time, but not eating. In autumn, after fattening themselves up, they eat indigestible roots and pine needles which form a plug in their intestines. They cannot eat until the plug is passed in spring–which may account for their short tempers at that time of year.

*The very slightest vibration can trigger a disastrous avalanche. In spring, when the risk is greatest, Swiss mountain villagers traditionally ban yodelling and forbid their children to shout or even sing.*

BAREFOOT IN THE SNOW At high altitudes humans adjust to the lower level of oxygen in the air by producing more red blood corpuscles which contain haemoglobin, the substance that absorbs oxygen into the blood stream. Most native mountain-dwellers have also developed other physical advantages to cope with the thin air and lower temperatures. The Quechua Indians of the Andes in South America, many of whom live at heights of around 3650m (12,000ft), have short, squat bodies that minimise heat loss, and bigger hearts and lungs than normal to enable them to carry 20 per cent more blood. In addition, their hands and feet have extra blood vessels which speed circulation so effectively that the Indians can walk barefoot on ice and snow without getting frostbite.

SKYSCRAPER BLOOMS The world's tallest flower spikes–4.5 to 6m (15 to 20ft) high–bloom on an Andean plant. *Puya raimondii*, which has a sturdy trunk with a globe-shaped rosette of spiky leaves, may take up to 150 years to reach its full height of 10.7m (35ft). Then it throws out its spike of blooms, as many as 800 on a single stalk.

EMPTY QUARTER *From the air, the dunes of Saudi Arabia's Rub al Khali ('The Empty Quarter')–part of the Arabian Desert–resemble the ripples of beach sand. But some of these dunes are up to 200m (660ft) high, and they can be more than 100km (60 miles) long. Dunes in fact cover only 10 to 15 per cent of the world's deserts. Much larger areas–known in the Sahara as hammada–have been worn down to bare rock. Others–known as regs or, in Australia, as gibber plains–are covered with pebbles and gravel from which the sand has been blown away.*

CURED BY A CAR-JACK During a sandstorm, the friction generated by billions of sand particles hitting each other can raise the air's electric potential to some 80 volts per square metre–high enough to cause nausea and splitting headaches. This phenomenon was first recorded by a German geographer named van der Esch, who explored large areas of the eastern Sahara before the Second World War. He suffered agonising headaches during sandstorms until he managed to discharge his body's electric potential by trailing a conductor–a car-jack–on the ground.

DEAD BEFORE NIGHTFALL If an adult were put without clothes, food or water in a shadeless part of the Sahara on a hot day, he would be dead before nightfall. By noon he would have sweated away from 2 to 3½ litres (4–6 pints) of water to keep his body temperature down. By the late afternoon he would have lost a total of 7 to 9 litres (1.5–2 gallons). Water

would then be lost from his blood – which would thicken and flow more slowly, causing his body temperature to rise. Before sunset, his temperature would have risen to about 46°C (115°F), producing fever, delirium and eventually death. Even if he drank 5.5 litres (10 pints) of water a day, he would last for no more than five days. To survive indefinitely in hot and exposed desert conditions, the average adult requires at least 6.5 litres (1.5 gallons) of water each day.

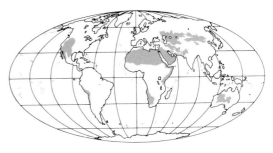

*Of the 250,000 or so flowering plants on Earth, only a handful can exist without water in liquid form. One of them, the hairnet plant of California's Death Valley, obtains moisture from mist. The water vapour is absorbed by the plant's roots, which grow up out of the ground and surround the plant like a net.*

HOT SPOTS *The world's hot deserts, shown here, can be freezingly cold at night because there are no clouds to retain the day's heat. In winter, temperatures in the Sahara can plummet to −4°C (24°F) after dark. The world's hottest place is Al Aziziyah in the Libyan Sahara; on September 13, 1922, shade temperatures there reached a record 58°C (136.4°F).*

# The world's last wildernesses

BEETLE THAT DRINKS FOG  A southern African beetle stays alive in the rainless wilderness of the Namib Desert by drinking fog. About one day in five, thick sea mists roll inland from the desolate Skeleton Coast of Namibia, creating a 'fog zone' that sustains a surprising variety of plant and animal life, including *Onymacris unguicularis*.

This flightless black beetle spends most of its time underground in the sand dunes where temperatures remain more or less constant. When thirsty, though, it emerges, climbs to the crest of a dune, faces the breeze in a prayer-like stance and allows fog to condense on its body. Droplets then trickle down narrow grooves on its shell, and into its mouth.

SHIPS OF THE DESERT  Contrary to popular belief, the camel does not store water in its hump. The hump is a food reserve composed mainly of fat. Although water is produced when the fat is broken down, the oxygen used in the process causes an additional loss of water through the lungs. This more or less cancels the amount of water gained from the hump. The main advantage of the hump is that the camel's fat is concentrated in a single place – allowing the camel to lose heat freely from the rest of its body.

Another way in which camels conserve water is by retaining the urea which most mammals excrete in their urine. The urea is built up into proteins by bacteria in the camel's stomach.

In addition, camels avoid sweating by allowing their body temperature to vary over a greater range than that of any other mammal. Camels do not begin to sweat until their body temperature reaches 46°C (115°F) – a temperature that would produce a high fever in a human. After a lengthy period without water, camels will drink up to 180 litres (40 gallons) at a time. They swell visibly in the process, and dilute their blood and tissue fluids to an extent that would kill most other mammals. Part of the explanation for the camel's prodigious drinking ability may be the unusual shape of its blood corpuscles. They are oval rather than round. When it drinks, its blood as well as its tissues can absorb large amounts of water because the oval corpuscles can swell into spheres without any danger of the cell walls bursting.

EMERGENCY RATIONS  Spadefoot toads sometimes breed in temporary desert pools without sufficient food supplies for the tadpoles to develop. The toads then supply their offspring with emergency rations: other tadpoles. First the female lays a large number of small eggs that develop into small tadpoles. The microflora and fauna in the water are usually too sparse to sustain these tadpoles through their change into toads. But before the tadpoles die, the female lays about ten large eggs which hatch into large tadpoles. These feed on the smaller tadpoles and grow so rapidly that they reach maturity – and gain the ability to survive on land – before the pool dries up.

*The largest iceberg so far recorded was sighted in the southern Pacific Ocean in 1956. It covered an area of about 31,000km² (12,000 square miles) – making it slightly larger than Belgium.*

## WORLD'S MAJOR DESERTS

Scientists define deserts as areas which have less than 250mm (10in) of rain a year. They include not only the hot deserts listed below, but also cold deserts such as Greenland, Antarctica and northern Russia. A third type, known as an edaphic desert, is one where, despite an adequate rainfall, the soil is too poor to support plants. Edaphic deserts occur on some volcanic islands, in parts of Iceland and on the Colorado plateau in the USA. Cold deserts cover 16 per cent of the world's land surface. Hot and edaphic deserts account for a further 18 per cent: a total of 34 per cent, or just over a third of the world's land.

The driest spot on Earth is the Atacama Desert in South America. Parts went without rain for 400 years from 1570 to 1971.

| Name and location | Area in km² (square miles) |
|---|---|
| Sahara, N Africa | 8,400,000 (3,250,000) |
| Australian | 1,550,000 (600,000) |
| Arabian, SW Asia | 1,300,000 (500,000) |
| Gobi, Central Asia | 1,040,000 (400,000) |
| Kalahari, southern Africa | 520,000 (200,000) |
| Turkestan, Central Asia | 450,000 (175,000) |
| Takla Makan, China | 320,000 (125,000) |
| Sonoran, USA and Mexico | 310,000 (120,000) |
| Namib, SW Africa | 310,000 (120,000) |
| Thar, NW India and Pakistan | 260,000 (100,000) |
| Somali, Somalia | 260,000 (100,000) |
| Atacama, N Chile | 180,000 (70,000) |
| Dasht-e-Lut, E Iran | 52,000 (20,000) |
| Mojave, California, USA | 35,000 (13,500) |
| Sechura, NW Peru | 26,000 (10,000) |

LANDS OF ICE  About one-tenth of the Earth's surface is permanently covered with ice, most of it in Antarctica in the south and Greenland in the north. If it all melted, the sea would rise by about 60m (200ft), submerging many of the world's largest cities, including London, Tokyo and New York.

During the last Ice Age, which ended about 10,000 years ago, there was three times as much ice, locking up 90 per cent of the world's fresh water. Average sea level was about 100m (330ft) lower, leaving 8 per cent more dry land. America and Eurasia were linked and so were Ireland, Britain and France. And Venice, the lagoon city of the Adriatic, was 160km (100 miles) from the sea.

*The world's longest glacier is the Lambert Glacier in Antarctica, which is at least 402km (250 miles) long. The fastest-flowing major glacier, the Qarajaq Glacier in Greenland, moves from 4m (13ft) to 20m (65ft) a day.*

SEABIRD SAUSAGE  The world's most northerly people, the Polar Eskimos, live in a land of permanent ice in Thule, northwest Greenland, fewer than 1600km (1000 miles) from the North Pole. They augment their high-protein diet of walrus, fish and seal with a piquant Arctic delicacy: a type of sausage. They net little auks – small seabirds that nest in the coastal cliffs – then stuff them, feathers, legs, beaks and all, into a seal skin still lined with blubber. The sausage is then sewn up and buried under a rock pile. Six months later – usually at Christmas time – the sausage is dug up and eaten. It has a taste like oily Camembert cheese.

HUNTERS IN THE ICE  Most polar seals retreat to open water during the winter, but two types have learnt to survive on and under the ice all year round: the Weddell seal of the Antarctic, and the ringed seal of the Arctic. Both hunt fish in the rich polar waters beneath the frozen seas. The seals bore a series of up to ten breathing holes through the ice, which is often 3m (10ft) thick, returning to any one of them to breathe between dives. The seals can stay submerged

ICE FIELDS *More than 75 per cent of the world's fresh water is locked up in permanent ice fields. In total, the fields cover about 15,000,000km² (5,800,000 square miles) – or some 10 per cent of the world's land surface. If all of this ice melted, many of the world's major cities would be flooded by the rising sea.*

ICE-COLD IN ANTARCTICA *A razor-sharp pinnacle of wind-scoured ice – forced upwards by the pressure of surrounding floes – thrusts 8m (25ft) into the air above pack ice off the coast of Antarctica.*

# The world's last wildernesses

## THREE WAYS ISLANDS ARE FORMED

**CORAL** Millions and millions of chalky skeletons, deposited by tiny animals that live only in shallow tropical waters, lock together to form huge coral reefs. Coral islands, such as the Maldives in the Indian Ocean and the islands of Australia's Great Barrier Reef, are the tips of reefs built during periods of warm climate, when the polar ice caps were smaller and sea levels higher. Dead reefs now deep under the sea grew during the Ice Ages, when sea levels were lower.

**MOUNTAIN** Many islands, such as the Hebrides off the northwest coast of Scotland, are really the tops of submerged mountains. The mountains became surrounded by water when rising temperatures ended the last Ice Age about 10,000 years ago, lifting sea levels by about 100m (330ft).

**VOLCANIC** At weak points in the Earth's crust, erupting volcanoes form islands like Surtsey, off Iceland, and Hawaii, in the Pacific, by forcing millions of tonnes of molten rock and ash from deep in the Earth up through the sea. Once cooled, the new land is colonised by plants and animals.

BIRTH OF A VOLCANIC ISLAND *Molten rock and ash, forced up from the seabed, form a cone-shaped island, scored with deep gullies and surrounded by vapour from the vent.*

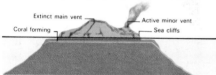

EROSION *Waves eat into the island, eroding cliffs and forming a platform on which, in warm seas, coral grows. The main vent is now extinct, but a lesser one is still active.*

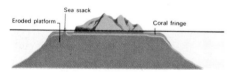

MATURITY *Rock crumbles, forming soil. Plants and animals colonise the cooled island. Erosion continues to extend the platform, leaving an occasional offshore stack.*

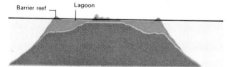

SINKING *The island sinks, leaving only the tip of the original cone still visible. It is surrounded by a lagoon and, in tropical waters, may be protected by a coral barrier reef.*

for up to ten minutes and swim at 32km/h (20mph) down to depths of about 90m (300ft).

The Weddell seal has no land-based predators, but the ringed seal is hunted by Eskimos and polar bears. The bear waits at a breathing hole until a seal comes up for air, then pounces. The bear may also stop up any other breathing holes in the vicinity to increase its chances of a catch.

*The most remote island on Earth is Bouvet Island, an uninhabited Norwegian dependency in the southern Atlantic Ocean at 54°26'S, 3°24'E. It is 1700km (1050 miles) from the nearest land – another uninhabited island off eastern Antarctica.*

LAND OF THE LONELY The world's loneliest people live on the British dependency of Tristan da Cunha. Their nearest neighbours are 2120km (1320 miles) away on St Helena, where Napoleon died in exile after Waterloo. After a volcanic eruption in 1961, the Tristan islanders were all evacuated to Britain. Most went back two years later, however, after the danger had passed. Life in Britain, they found, was too hectic for them.

BAROMETER OF THE PAST Weather conditions hundreds of years ago can be plotted by scientists studying coral islands and the reefs that surround them. Marine biologists know that layers of darker-coloured corals form when conditions are unfavourable – as a result of cold periods, say, or pollution.

By analysing these layers in 3m (10ft) cores of coral from Florida, USA, covering 360 years of growth, scientists have been able to identify years when there were cold fronts and storms, air pollution, and even – in recent years – radioactive fallout from nuclear weapons tests.

THE LITTLE ISLANDERS Colonies of animals cut off on islands by rising sea levels tend to evolve into smaller species than their continental cousins. Increased competition for food in a confined space and fewer predators tend to favour smaller individuals.

Dwarf island species that exist today include the key deer of the Florida islands, the sika deer of Japan and the dwarf buffalo of the Celebes. In the past 2 million years, miniature elephants and hippopotamuses, now extinct, also evolved on Mediterranean islands and tiny mammoths lived on the Channel Islands off southern California.

BACK TO NATURE In 1883, the Indonesian island volcano of Krakatoa exploded, blowing 25km³ (5 cubic miles) of the island into the air. A sterile carpet of ash and pumice rained down on the island, obliterating all life forms. Just nine months later, a solitary spider was found spinning its web among the desolation for non-existent prey. But the island was recolonised with astonishing speed. After three years, 11 species of fern and 15 flowering plants were growing on Krakatoa. After ten years there was enough vegetation to hide the scars of the explosion, and in 1908, naturalists counted 263 living species, including 16 birds, two reptiles and four land snails. Forty years after the eruption, Krakatoa was covered once again in lush forest, supporting 1200 species of animals, including pythons, bats and rats.

# SCIENCE & TECHNOLOGY

# Marvels of the human body

## MALE OR FEMALE?

Male and female embryos are outwardly identical until eight to ten weeks after conception. What happens then depends on whether the chromosomes inherited from the embryo's parents are female – a pattern scientists define as XX – or male, in which case the pattern is XY. The embryo always inherits an X chromosome from its mother, but its father can contribute either another X or a Y chromosome. So it is the father that determines the baby's sex.

Depending on the pattern of chromosomes, either primitive testes (testicles) or ovaries are produced. If testes develop, they secrete a chemical to suppress the so-called Müllerian ducts. These would otherwise develop into the female reproductive organs – the Fallopian tubes, uterus and vagina. The testes also produce a hormone called testosterone. This stimulates another set of ducts – the Wolffian ducts – to develop into the internal male genital organs and also brings about the development of the external organs.

## VICTIMS OF INHERITANCE

Chromosomes determine not only sex, but also physical strength and character. If the balance between the chromosomes is abnormal, the baby can develop mixed characteristics. Tests have shown, for instance, that some Soviet women athletes possess an abnormal

## FACTS AND FIGURES ABOUT THE ASTONISHING BODY

● Doubling a child's height on his second birthday gives a close estimate of his final adult height. A boy of two is 49.5 per cent of his adult height; a girl of two is 52.8 per cent of her adult height.

● Each finger and toenail takes about six months to grow from its base to the tip.

● During pregnancy a woman's blood volume can increase by up to 50 per cent to a total of 6.75 litres (12 pints) as a reserve against possible loss of blood during delivery.

● The brain accounts for about 3 per cent of body weight. But it uses 20 per cent of all the oxygen we breathe, 20 per cent of the calories in the food we eat, and about 15 per cent of the body's blood supply.

● The adult human body contains approximately 650 muscles, over 100 joints, 100,000km (60,000 miles) of blood vessels and 13,000 million nerve cells. An adult has 206 bones – nearly half of them in the hands and feet. A baby has 300 bones at birth, but 94 fuse together during childhood.

● Human bone is as strong as granite in supporting weight. A block the size of a matchbox can support 9 tonnes – four times as much as concrete.

● A man's testicles manufacture 10 million new sperm cells a day – enough in six months to populate the entire world.

● The heart beats more than 2000 million times during the average human life span, and in that time will pump around 500 million litres (110 million gallons) of blood. Even during sleep, the fist-sized heart of an adult pumps about 340 litres (75 gallons) an hour – enough to fill an average car's petrol tank every seven minutes. It generates enough muscle power every day to lift an average-sized car about 15m (50ft).

● The average pulse rate is 70 – 72 beats per minute at rest for adult males and 78 – 82 for adult females. The rate can increase to as much as 200 per minute during violent exercise.

● The lungs contain a total of 300,000 million capillaries – tiny blood vessels – which would stretch 2400km (1500 miles) if laid end to end.

● The body of the average adult contains 45 litres (79 pints) of water – about 65 per cent of his weight.

● The stomach's digestive acids are strong enough to dissolve zinc. But the cells in the stomach lining are renewed so quickly – 500,000 cells are replaced every minute and the entire lining every three days – that the acids do not have time to dissolve the lining.

● Each kidney contains some 1 million individual filters, and between them the two kidneys filter an average of about 1.3 litres (2.2 pints) of blood in a minute. The waste products are expelled as urine at the rate of about 1.4 litres (2.5 pints) a day.

● The body's entire blood supply – about 4.5 litres (8 pints) – washes through the lungs about once a minute. Human red blood corpuscles are created by bone marrow at the rate of about 1.2 million corpuscles per second. Each lives for 100 – 120 days. In a lifetime the marrow creates about half a tonne of red corpuscles.

● The body's largest organ is the skin. In an adult man it covers about 1.9m² (20sq ft); a woman has about 1.6m² (17sq ft). The skin is constantly flaking away and being completely replaced by new tissue about once every 50 days. On average, each person sheds about 18kg (40lb) of skin during his lifetime.

● The smallest human muscle is in the ear; it is a little over 1mm (0.05in) long. The ear also contains one of the few parts of the body which has no blood vessels. Cells in part of the inner ear, where sound vibrations are converted to nerve impulses, are fed by a constant bath of fluid instead of blood – otherwise the sensitive nerves would be deafened by the sound of the body's own pulse.

● You grow by about 8mm (0.3in) every night when you are asleep, but shrink to your former height the following day. During the day, the cartilage discs in the spine are squeezed like sponges by gravity while you stand or sit. But at night, when you lie down to sleep, the pressure is relieved and the discs swell again. For the same reason, astronauts can be temporarily 50mm (2in) taller after a long spaceflight.

● Besides water, the body contains an assortment of other substances. On average, it has enough lime to whitewash a small shed, the equivalent in carbon of a 12.7kg (28lb) bag of coke, enough phosphorus to make 2200 match heads, about a spoonful of sulphur, enough iron to make a 25mm (1in) nail – and about 30g (1oz) of other metals.

● The focusing muscles of the eye move about 100,000 times a day. To give the leg muscles the same exercise would involve walking 80km (50 miles) a day.

● The retina inside the eye covers about 650mm² (1sq in) and contains 137 million light-sensitive cells: 130 million rod cells for black-and-white vision; and 7 million cone cells for colour vision.

● The average person in the West eats 50 tonnes of food and drinks 50,000 litres (11,000 gallons) of liquid during his life.

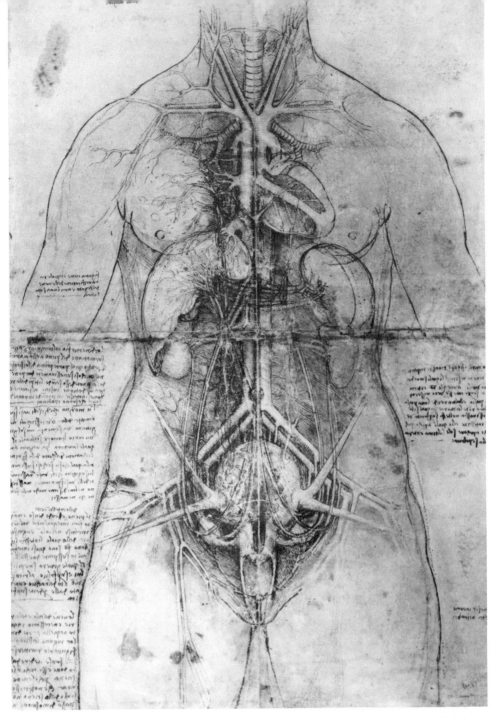

ARTIST'S IMPRESSION *The Italian artist Leonardo da Vinci (1452–1519) learnt about the workings of the body by dissecting more than 30 corpses. This sketch by him – though in parts inaccurate – shows the basic anatomy of a woman. Leonardo also created moulds of organs such as the heart, lungs and womb by injecting molten wax into them.*

XXY chromosomal pattern – in other words, they have inherited an extra male (Y) chromosome. This helps to give them added physical strength. Men with an extra Y chromosome (giving them an XYY pattern) tend to be taller and more aggressive than the average; research in the USA has shown that men with this abnormal chromosomal pattern are also more likely to turn to crime.

### THE RISING SON
It is a fallacy that people's height depends solely on their genetic make-up. What they eat makes a difference, too. Western food, for instance, has transformed Japanese patterns of growth. In 1900, the average height of 12-year-old Japanese children was 1.34m (4ft 5in). The influence of the West brought about a dramatic change, firstly in the children of Japanese immigrants to the USA, who ate more proteins, particularly in the form of meat. By 1957, these children were far taller than their homeland counterparts. By the 1970s, however, the Japanese in Japan had caught up with those living in the USA. Japanese men and women now average 1.69m (5ft 7in) and 1.56m (5ft 1in) in height respectively, only slightly shorter than Britons and Americans.

### THE RACE FOR LIFE
The single sperm to penetrate and fertilise the female egg in the womb is the winner of a race in which up to 500 million competitors leave the starting line. In

211

a single ejaculation, a man can produce this many sperm, swimming in a teaspoonful of semen. But only a few thousand survive to reach the target area near the Fallopian tubes, where fertilisation takes place. The distance from the start – in the coiled tubules in the testicles where the semen is created – to the finish is some 7.5m (24ft 7in).

Once the winner has fertilised the egg, the egg's wall becomes impermeable to other sperm. The losers can survive within the female body for three to five days, until they die naturally or are destroyed by the body's cleansing mechanisms.

## THE HAIR FACTS

On average, both men and women have a total of about 5 million hairs on their bodies. Fair-haired people have slightly more than the average, redheads slightly fewer. The only areas that are totally hairless are the lips, the palms of the hands, the soles of the feet, the sides of the toes and fingers, and the upper part of the ends of the fingers and toes.

Though dead from the roots up, the 100,000 or so hairs on the head grow at a rate of approximately 10mm (0.4in) per month, with a slight increase in speed in summer. Cutting does not speed up or slow down the process. Thickness varies – redheads have thicker hair than brunettes and blondes. On average,

most people lose and replace up to 100 hairs a day, though hairs can remain in place for up to six years.

It is a fallacy that normal-coloured hair can turn white overnight as the result of a sudden shock. What happens in such cases is that the shock causes the coloured hair to fall out, leaving behind white hair which may have been concealed in it.

## TRANSPLANTS AND THE PIG

As far as transplant surgery is concerned, man's best friend is the pig. Pig heart valves, for instance, can be used as replacements for human ones, while, in emergencies, pig skin has been grafted to deal with severe burns. Because pig tissues are the nearest in chemical composition to those of man, they are not so readily rejected by the defence systems of the recipients' bodies as tissues from other animals. The only organ which can be transplanted without the risk of rejection is the cornea of the human eye. This is because the cornea does not contain blood vessels, which might otherwise carry white blood cells to the site of the transplant to attack the foreign tissue.

## HIGH AND LOW

There is no such thing as a constant, normal body temperature. During the day, it can vary by as much as 1.1°C (2°F) either side of the accepted standard of

# PHYSICAL RECORDS

● The world's tallest man was Robert Wadlow (1918–40) of the United States, who reached a height of 2.72m (8ft 11in). The world's tallest woman was Zeng Jinlian (1964–82) of China. She was 2.46m (8ft 1in) tall.

● The world's shortest male was an American, Calvin Phillips (1791–1812), whose final height was 670mm (26.4in). The shortest woman was Pauline Musters (1876–95) of Holland, who was only 590mm (23.2in) tall.

● The heaviest man is an American, Jon Minnoch, who was born in 1941. In 1978 he weighed an estimated 635kg (1400lb or 100 stone). The world's heaviest woman was also an American, Mrs Pearl Washington. She died at the age of 46 in 1972 weighing an estimated 399kg (880lb or nearly 63 stone).

● The world's oldest authenticated person is Shigechiyo Izumi of Japan, who was born on June 29, 1865. In 1984 he celebrated his 119th birthday. He attributes his longevity to refusal to worry about life.

# PATTERNS OF HEREDITY

Genetic scientists have established that some physical characteristics, known as dominant, are more likely to be passed on to children. Characteristics that are less likely to be passed on are known as recessive.

| Dominant | Recessive |
| --- | --- |
| Curly hair | Straight hair |
| Dark hair | Light hair |
| Non-red hair | Red hair |
| Normal skin pigmentation | Albinism |
| Brown eyes | Blue or grey eyes |
| Near or far sightedness | Normal vision |
| Broad lips | Thin lips |
| Large eyes | Small eyes |
| Short stature | Tall stature |
| Nervous temperament | Calm temperament |
| A or B blood group | O blood group |
| Rhesus positive blood | Rhesus negative blood |

37°C (98.6°F), dropping in the middle of the night and rising during the late afternoon or early evening. The rise and fall is not necessarily an indication of illness; it can be brought about by exercise, eating, and by the body's own metabolic process of converting food into energy. Women's temperatures also vary during the menstrual cycle. They are higher in the second half of the cycle than in the first.

Temperature also varies depending on where it is taken. Armpit temperatures are on average 0.5°C (1°F) lower than mouth temperatures, while rectal temperatures are higher by the same amount.

## WHAT HAPPENS WHEN WE GET HICCUPS

Hiccups occur when the diaphragm and the muscles between the ribs suddenly contract. This causes a sharp, uncontrollable, inhalation of air, which is unable to reach the lungs because the muscle spasm has closed the windpipe.

Hiccups usually occur repeatedly in short spasms lasting a few minutes. Traditional remedies include drinking cold water from the wrong side of a glass and holding the breath to increase the amount of carbon dioxide in the lungs, so triggering the breathing reflex which opens the windpipe.

The longest attack of hiccups on record has been affecting an American, Charles Osborne, since 1922.

It began while he was slaughtering a hog and was still going on – more than 430 million hiccups later – in 1984.

## WHAT HAPPENS WHEN WE BLUSH

The ability to blush is not present from birth – it is a reflex action which develops between the ages of two and four. It can also be controlled consciously.

Blushing is commoner among girls than boys. In response to feelings of shame or self-consciousness, the brain sends nerve signals which release a powerful chemical called a peptide. The chemical dilates the small blood vessels in the skin of the face, neck and upper chest. It is the dilation which causes the blush.

## WHAT HAPPENS WHEN WE SNEEZE

Sneezing is the body's reflex response to the irritation of the nerve endings in the nose by foreign particles or gases. Just as with coughing, a nervous reflex causes a deep breath to be taken.

The glottis, near the top of the windpipe, closes off the larynx, so that the pressure in the lungs builds up as breathing out starts. The glottis then opens, allowing an explosive rush of air to pass through the nose, blowing out particles and mucus at a speed which can be more than 160km/h (100mph). The longest fit of sneezing recorded is that of an English teenager named

# THE LIFE THAT LIVES ON US

LITTLE HELPERS *Ball-like cells (left) in the large bowel – shown here 3850 times normal size – support a forest of microscopic life. The strings and the sausage shapes are both harmless types of intestinal bacteria.*

Man is never alone, for he shares his body with hundreds of millions of organisms – most of which are bacteria. More than 600 million individual bacteria live on the skin alone. More than a dozen types of bacteria make their homes on the skin, in the saliva of the mouth and in the lower part of the digestive system. In addition, several fungi, a virus and a type of mite share the body of even a healthy person. The bacteria in the bowel do no harm as long as they stay where they are, and they actually prevent other, disease-causing bacteria (which may be swallowed accidentally) from multiplying. Some bacteria also manufacture vitamin B12 – normally found only in meat – from plant sources. The vitamin helps in the formation of blood cells.

● Four main groups of bacteria live on human skin and can be found almost anywhere on the body. They are known to scientists as: corynebacteria (including *Corynebacterium acnes*, which causes acne); micrococci; streptococci; and coliform bacteria.

● Other harmless bacteria live in moist areas such as the armpits and the groin. They include: coagulase negative staphylococci; gram positive cocci; and diphtheroids. The skin of the armpits can harbour up to 800 bacteria per square millimetre (516,000 per sq in), while drier areas such as the forearm have only about 20 bacteria per square millimetre (13,000 per sq in).

● Saliva contains at least six types of bacteria, some of which can cause dental plaque, tooth decay and gum disease. They are: streptococci; corynebacteria; fusobacteria; *Neisseriae*; bacilli; and spirochaetes.

● The large bowel is also rich in bacteria. Among them are: coliform bacteria (especially *Escherichia coli*); *Bacteroides*; lactobacilli; clostridia; and streptococci. In the bowel, they are harmless. But if they escape to other parts of the body – as a result of an ulcer, say, or a burst appendix – they

can cause peritonitis (an inflammation of the abdominal cavity), blood poisoning and urinary infections.

● Three main types of yeast commonly live on the skin. *Malassezia furfur* is found mainly on the chest and back. *Candida albicans* is found mainly between the toes; but it is also found in the mouth, where it can cause thrush, an infection especially common in babies. *Trichospora beigelii* lives mainly on the scalp. Skin also harbours two other types of fungus (yeasts are themselves fungi) – *Trichophyton* and *Microsporum*. They can cause ringworm and athlete's foot.

● The mite *Democlex folliculorum*, related to the spider family, lives in hair follicles (the cavities containing hair roots) and in the sebaceous (fatty) glands on most adults' faces.

● One strain of the virus *Herpes simplex* lives inside the nerve fibres of 90 per cent of adults – the only virus to do so. It is usually dormant, but when the host's health is low it can sometimes erupt on the lips as cold sores. The sores can also be brought on by over-exposure to the sun. This strain cannot cause the disease known as genital herpes.

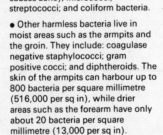

DENTAL FLOSS *Fluffy bacilli (above) – magnified here 17,000 times – can, with other bacteria, create plaque, the dark film which sometimes develops on teeth.*

SPAGHETTI JUNCTION *Magnified 490 times, threads of the fungus* Trichophyton *grow like tangled straws. The 'ground' behind is skin.*

213

Donna Griffiths. It began in January 1981 when she was 12 years old. She was still sneezing – about 20 times a day on average – in 1984.

## WHAT HAPPENS WHEN WE COUGH
When we cough, we release an explosive charge of air at a speed of up to about 96km/h (60mph). The explosion – which works in much the same way as a sneeze – is triggered by the presence of a foreign object, or accumulated mucus, in the main airways to the lungs, and is designed to dislodge whatever caused the initial irritation.

## REPAIRING THE DAMAGE
Without the protection provided by the body's natural defences, we might bleed to death from even minor cuts. In normal circumstances, the blood clots to seal a wound within about two hours of the injury.

The first line of defence is provided by the platelets, small cells in the blood which clump together to build up a temporary plug at the site of the injury. They also release into the area of the wound a chemical called serotonin, which constricts the damaged vessels, reducing the flow of blood. In addition, the damaged blood-vessel walls themselves release a second chemical called thromboplastin. Thromboplastin enables strands of a protein called fibrin to form a sticky mesh which traps red cells, so creating a more permanent clot which hardens into a protective scab.

## THE MIGHTY SNORE
The sound of a snore (up to 69 decibels) can be almost as loud as the noise of a pneumatic drill (70 – 90 decibels). It is caused by the vibration of the soft, mobile back part of the palate, the roof of the mouth, and the arch which sweeps down from this behind the tonsils. In most cases, the nose is partly blocked; so sufferers tend to breathe through their mouths.

Although snoring is more likely to occur if the sufferer is sleeping on his back, this is not always the case. The best way to stop someone snoring is to change his position in bed.

## OUTER PROTECTION
Skin is far more than just a protective covering. Five-sixths of the heat produced by the body is lost through the pores of the skin through sweating, conduction, convection and radiation – processes that are keyed by nerve signals to the sweat glands and to small blood vessels just under the skin. If these pores become blocked so that heat and moisture cannot escape, the result is death. The process only works one way, however. Externally, the skin – aided by an oily substance from the sebaceous glands – is waterproof.

The skin also reacts in two ways to the sun's ultraviolet rays. It contains a substance called ergosterol, which reacts with the rays to produce vitamin D. At the same time, the skin protects itself from the burning effects of excessive ultraviolet radiation by producing a protective dark pigment called melanin – the cause of a suntan.

## THE AMAZING INTESTINE
If the small intestine, where digestion takes place, were removed from the body it would be 6.7m (22ft) long; if all its internal corrugations were opened out flat, the space it would take up would amount to some 300m² (360sq yds). In the body, however, it is shortened like a concertina to a mere 2.4m (8ft).

The main business of the small intestine is the absorption of carbohydrate, fat and protein from food which has first been broken down into molecules by the action of chemicals called enzymes. The absorption can take place in a surprisingly small working part of the intestine, despite the organ's vast potential area. If, for instance, part of the intestine has to be surgically removed as a result of disease, the remaining intestine can function almost as well without it.

## TONSILS ON GUARD
Until the 1970s, some 200,000 children in Britain alone were having their tonsils removed each year. However, except in a small minority of cases, there is no medical evidence that there is any benefit to be derived from the operation. Quite the reverse, in fact, since any surgical operation carries some risk of death, however small – but nobody has ever been known to die because of inflamed tonsils. Both tonsils and adenoids are part of the body's natural defences against disease, standing guard over the entrance to the respiratory and digestive tubes. Some of the cells contained in their tissues produce antibodies designed to deal with invading bacteria, viruses, parasites and allergy-causing substances; other cells are capable of swallowing invading organisms.

## THE LIFE-GIVING LUNGS
The lungs are not simply inflatable bags – they are complex structures, containing between them 300 million air sacs in which oxygen can be absorbed by the blood. The area these sacs would cover if spread out flat is about 100m² (120sq yds) – roughly comparable in size to half of a doubles tennis court.

Because of their extreme elasticity, the lungs are 100 times easier to blow up than a child's balloon. Only about 14 per cent of the air in the lungs is actually changed with each breath.

## SUNTANS IN THE SHADE
It is possible to get a tan or sunburn even on a cloudy day – because about 80 per cent of the ultraviolet rays from the sun get through cloud.

## WHEN OXYGEN CAN BE POISONOUS
If pure oxygen is breathed at more than $2\frac{1}{2}$ times atmospheric pressure, it can act as a poison. This is why deep-sea divers usually breathe not pure oxygen but compressed air (in which oxygen forms only about 20 per cent of the total), or a mixture of air and an inert gas such as helium (which causes the Donald Duck voice of divers working at great depths). Signs of oxygen poisoning include twitching lips, nausea, vomiting, vertigo and fainting; these may lead to convulsions, similar to an epileptic fit, and to death.

At atmospheric pressure, pure oxygen can harm only new-born babies, when it may cause a type of blindness called retrolental fibroplasia. Because of this danger – which once affected numerous babies – pure oxygen is no longer used in incubators without special monitoring equipment.

## SUPER-STRENGTH HORMONE
The hormone adrenalin, produced naturally in the body under stress, has the power to increase a person's strength far beyond its usual limits. A remarkable demonstration of its effects took place in the US city of Tampa, Florida, on April 24, 1960. Mrs Maxwell Rogers, who weighs a mere 55.8kg (8st 11lb), was at home with her teenage son when a car jack collapsed, pinning him under the family's station wagon. Hysterical with fear, she rescued him by lifting one end of the 1.6 tonne (3600lb) car unaided.

So massive was the effort that she cracked some back vertebrae. But for a few seconds, the surge of hormone triggered by her panic had helped to make her at least as strong as an Olympic weightlifter.

# Marvels of the human mind

## MIND CONTROL

Meditation, yoga and other mind-control techniques, which have been practised in the East since about 1000 BC, can have a measurable effect on the body, scientists have found. They can even affect the body in ways that are ordinarily beyond the reach of conscious control. Researchers in Britain in the mid-

## FACTS AND FIGURES ON THE ASTONISHING MIND

● The weight of the average human brain triples between birth and adulthood – reaching a final weight of about 1.4kg (3lb) for men and 1.3kg (2.9lb) for women. By the age of 50, though, it shrinks slightly, losing about 30g (a little more than an ounce).

● There is no correlation between brain size and intelligence. A man's brain is usually slightly larger than a woman's, but in both sexes the brain makes up a similar proportion of total body weight.

● Two writers hold opposite records for brain size. The brain of the Russian author Ivan Turgenev (1818–83) weighed 2.012kg (4.44lb). The brain of the French writer Anatole France (1844–1924) weighed little more than half that figure, 1.017kg (2.24lb).

● The brain is divided into two hemispheres, each a mirror image of the other. The right hemisphere controls the muscles of and receives information from the left half of the body; the left hemisphere monitors and controls the right half of the body.

● In right-handed people – the majority – the left side of the brain is concerned with such skills as reading, writing and talking. The right hemisphere deals with artistic activity and the workings of the imagination. In left-handed people the functions of the two hemispheres may be reversed.

● The average brain contains about 10,000 million neurons – microscopic nerve cells. Each cell has a slender projection called an axon which links it to other parts of the central nervous system. Some axons stretch the length of the spinal cord – making them more than a metre (3.3ft) long and the longest cells in the body. Each neuron is also linked to neighbouring neurons by up to 50,000 connections known as dendrites.

● New information reaching the brain from the senses is stored, analysed and acted upon by means of electrochemical impulses passing from neuron to neuron through the dendrite connections. Quite how complex information is coded into these impulses, or how it is translated back again, is imperfectly understood. But it is known that the brain remains active to some degree round the clock, and that each day it triggers hundreds of millions of impulses – more connections than all the world's telephone systems put together.

● The thumb is so important to human dexterity that a larger proportion of the brain is devoted to controlling it than to controlling the whole of the chest and abdomen.

● Nerve impulses to and from the brain travel as fast as some racing cars. The fastest impulses recorded, in experiments carried out in 1966, travelled at nearly 290km/h (180mph). Nerve impulses move slightly more slowly in elderly people: at up to about 240km/h (150mph).

1970s taught yoga relaxation techniques to half of a group of people who suffered from high blood pressure. The trained group were later able to lower their blood pressure by an average of 16 per cent, simply through using the techniques. Normally, blood pressure – like the heart's pulse rate – is controlled unconsciously by the body's nervous system.

In the early 1980s, British researchers discovered that similar results could be achieved with biofeedback. In this technique, the patients were hooked up to machines that displayed their blood pressure visibly, and they were encouraged to concentrate on trying to reduce the reading by mental effort alone.

## IT FEELS NO PAIN

Pain from any injury or illness is always perceived by the brain. Yet, curiously, the brain itself is immune to pain; it contains none of the specialised receptor cells that sense pain in other parts of the body. Surgical operations on the brain sometimes have to be carried out while the patient is conscious, so that the surgeon can enlist the patient's help to pick his way through the brain's complex tissue. Once the discomfort of the initial incision through the skull and the brain's

MAPPING THE BRAIN *Scientists can analyse which parts of the brain are most involved in different activities by mapping the varying rates of blood flow. The pictures here, showing flow patterns in the left side of the brain, were put together by a computer from scans of several people. In each, the darker tinted areas show greater than average activity. Areas of peak flow show up as white.*

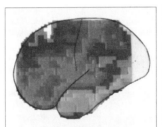
RESTING WITH EYES CLOSED

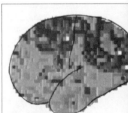
LOOKING AT A MOVING OBJECT

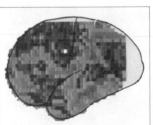
READING SILENTLY

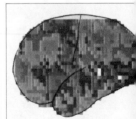
READING ALOUD

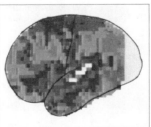
LISTENING TO MUSIC

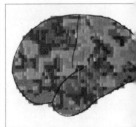
LISTENING TO WORDS

coverings has been deadened by a local anaesthetic, the patient feels no pain.

The technique has been used, for example, to locate areas of the brain responsible for epileptic fits. Weak electric shocks are applied to different parts of the brain until the patient reports feeling the first symptoms of a fit. The area which produces the symptoms is then surgically removed or destroyed.

## HOW TO IMPROVE YOUR MEMORY

Only a very few people have 'eidetic', or photographic, memories in which they can 'see' the information they want in their mind's eye. Nevertheless, there are simple devices which can help anyone to remember things – and many of these techniques also rely on turning information into pictures.

People's names, for instance, become easier to remember if they can be turned into visual cues, no matter how ludicrous the result. Visualise someone called Hooper as playing with a hula hoop, a Smith as a blacksmith, and more complex names as combinations of images: a Macdonald as a kilted duck, say.

Numbers can be remembered in the same way, by hanging them on visual pegs. One such list of pegs creates an easily memorised sequence of rhyming images for the numbers one to ten: bun, shoe, tree, door, hive, sticks, heaven, gate, line and hen. Then, to remember 4391, visualise a door in a tree, and through it a line leading to a cream bun.

## DREAM MEANINGS

Although the details of dreams tend to be highly individual, varying from person to person, their overall themes and patterns are remarkably consistent. These are the commonest themes and how psychologists usually interpret them:

**Falling** may indicate a fear of lost status – for example, failing an examination or losing a job.

**Flying**, if accompanied by a general mood of elation, can be an expression of confidence, a feeling of being on top of the world.

**Nudity** can reveal a feeling of vulnerability in life. The more embarrassing the circumstances – being naked in a street, say – the more acute the feeling.

**Examinations** which have questions that seem unanswerable suggest a testing situation in real life, in work or at home. **Losing money or valuables** may demonstrate a concern for lost values in life; finding them can symbolise confidence.

PHARAOH'S DREAM
*Seers in Mesopotamia were studying dreams at least 5000 years ago. This 13th-century manuscript painting illustrates the Bible story about the pharaoh who dreamed of seven fat and seven lean cattle. Joseph interpreted it to mean that Egypt would have seven years of plenty followed by seven years of famine.*

# DREAMS AND SLEEP

The biological purposes of sleeping and dreaming are as yet imperfectly understood. People deprived of sleep or of the chance to dream for long periods usually become disorientated, lack concentration and can suffer from hallucinations. A few people, however, are able to do without sleep – and thus without dreams – indefinitely without any ill effects.

Most researchers believe that dreamless sleep is largely a period of physical rest. Blood pressure, body temperature, body heartbeat all drop and some body tissues – the skin and the internal linings of the stomach and lungs, for instance – regenerate more rapidly than at other times.

Dreaming sleep is thought to be primarily a period of mental restoration during which the mind may sort and store new information acquired during the day.

During a typical eight-hour night, most people spend about two hours dreaming, split up into four periods of around 30 minutes each. The first dreaming period usually begins about 60–90 minutes after falling asleep, the second about 60–90 minutes later and so on through the night.

Dreaming sleep is often known as REM sleep – standing for rapid eye movement – because during it the eyes move around visibly behind the closed eyelids as if scanning a picture. It is also called paradoxical sleep because, although the brain is as active as it is in very light sleep, the sleeper's muscles are relaxed, and his responsiveness to external stimuli (noise or a pinprick, say) is as low as in very deep sleep. Curiously, humans are not the only animals to exhibit rapid eye movements during sleep. Other warm-blooded mammals, and birds, do it too, though for shorter periods – suggesting that these animals also dream.

COVERED IN CONFUSION *A French illustration published in 1867 shows what psychoanalyst Sigmund Freud later called a typical dream: being naked among clothed strangers.*

## CALCULATING STRESS

Dr Thomas Holmes, a professor of psychiatry at the University of Washington, USA, has found that four out of every five people whose lives change dramatically in the course of a year can expect a major illness within the next two years.

He has helped to devise a rating scale (shown below) to assess the 'stress risk'.

Research showed that 80 per cent of those scoring 300 or more, and 53 per cent of those with 150–300 ratings, became clinically depressed, had heart attacks or suffered other serious illnesses. By contrast, two out of three of the people who scored less than 100 avoided these disorders.

The stress risk is calculated by adding up the points for each fundamental change in the patient's life during the past year.

Death of spouse 100; Divorce 73; Marital separation 65; Jail term 63; Death of a close family member 63;

Personal injury or illness 53; Marriage 50; Being fired at work 47; Marital reconciliation 45; Retirement 45.

Change in health of a family member 44; Pregnancy 40; Sex difficulties 39; Gain of a new member in the family 39; Business readjustment 39; Change in financial state 38.

Death of close friend 37; Change to a different line of work 38; Change in number of arguments with spouse 35; Large mortgage 31; Foreclosure of mortgage or loan 30; Change of personal responsibility at work 29.

Son or daughter leaving home 29; Trouble with in-laws 29; Outstanding personal achievement 28; Wife begins or finishes work 26; Beginning or ending school 26; Change in living conditions 20; Moving home 20.

Change in schools 20; Change in recreation 19; Change in social activity 18; Small mortgage or loan 17; Change in sleeping habits 16; Change in number of family get-togethers 15; Change in eating habits 15; Vacation 13; Minor violations of the law 11.

## BUILT-IN PAINKILLERS

Sportsmen who play on despite injury, and soldiers who fight on despite wounds, may not be demonstrating unusual courage. They may simply not notice the pain until the game or the battle is over.

Medical researchers believe that part of the reason may be that the brain creates its own painkillers, known as endorphins and enkephalins, which are capable of blocking the sensation of pain without having any of the undesirable side-effects associated with manufactured drugs.

Extreme physical effort and stress both trigger the brain to produce more of the painkillers – hence the players' and the soldiers' immunity.

# PIONEERS OF PSYCHOLOGY

The discipline of psychology is little more than a century old. These are some of the people who have played a major part in its development. They are arranged in chronological order.

**WILHELM WUNDT (1832–1920)**
German psychologist, founder of the first laboratory of experimental psychology at Leipzig in 1879. Gave psychology the status of a science by carrying out experiments on people rather than putting forward philosophical theories about the mind, as his predecessors had done.

**WILLIAM JAMES (1842–1910)**
American philosopher and psychologist who argued that emotions were caused by physical changes in the body: we feel sorry because we cry, happy because we laugh and afraid because we tremble, not the other way around.

**IVAN PAVLOV (1849–1936)**
Russian physiologist whose experiments with dogs in the early 1900s led to discovery of the conditioned reflex. Pavlov trained dogs to salivate at the sound of a bell by ringing the bell immediately before giving them food. Eventually the dogs became conditioned to salivate at the sound alone. Some psychologists believe that similar conditioning processes are the basis of all learning in animals and humans.

**SIGMUND FREUD (1856–1939)**
Austrian doctor, founder of psychoanalysis. Believed that the human personality had three parts: the *id*, the unconscious and most primitive part, which aims to satisfy instinctive and biological, primarily sexual, drives; the *ego*, the ordinary social self which deals with the external world; and the *super-ego*, which incorporates parental and social standards of morality and acts, in part, as the individual's conscience.

**ALFRED BINET (1857–1911)**
French psychologist who developed in 1905 the first reliable intelligence test. A modified version, devised at Stanford University, USA, and known as the Stanford-Binet Intelligence Scale, is still used today to measure IQ (intelligence quotient).

**ALFRED ADLER (1870–1937)**
Austrian psychiatrist who broke away from Freud in 1911 and founded what is now called the school of individual psychology. Developed the concept of the inferiority complex – strong feelings of inadequacy and insecurity stemming from real or imagined deficiencies. Believed that mankind's main driving force was the desire for power.

**CARL GUSTAV JUNG (1875–1961)**
Swiss psychologist who broke with Freudianism in 1912. Believed that human behaviour was largely determined by a general 'life urge', not primarily sexual in nature, and that the deepest level of the personality was the 'collective unconscious' – an inherited part of the unconscious mind found in all members of a race or species.

MIND MASTER *A portrait of Freud by the Surrealist painter Salvador Dali.*

Developed new classifications of personality types, including the 'introvert' (who tends to withdraw into himself) and the 'extrovert' (who is outgoing).

**JOHN WATSON (1878–1958)**
American psychologist, founder of the school of behaviourism, which holds that people's behaviour and reactions to given situations – rather than their mental states – are the proper subject of psychological study, since behaviour is all that can be objectively measured and assessed in others.

**SIR FREDERIC BARTLETT (1886–1969)**
English psychologist who applied methods of experimental psychology to industrial and other problems. In his book *Remembering* (1932), he showed that a person tends to remember things which fit into his existing system of knowledge.

**WOLFGANG KÖHLER (1887–1967)**
German psychologist and leader of the Gestalt school of psychology which argues that behaviour and experience must be treated as a whole rather than as a collection of specific behaviour patterns or responses to stimuli. In learning, he introduced the idea of insight, suggesting that problems were often solved in a flash of insight rather than by trial and error.

**B. F. SKINNER (1904– )**
American psychologist who discovered practical applications for behaviourism in the form of techniques known as behavioural therapy and programmed learning. Both work by providing rewards for good behaviour or correct answers to questions – a device known as reinforcement – and punishment (which may merely be the absence of reward) for bad behaviour or incorrect answers.

# The fight against disease

## MODESTY AND THE STETHOSCOPE

The first stethoscope – the instrument which has become the trademark of doctors around the world – was constructed because a young doctor was shy. It was devised in a matter of moments by the early 19th-century French physician René Laennec. One day in 1816, Laennec was consulted by a young woman, whose symptoms suggested that she might be suffering from heart disease. Laennec's modesty prevented him from following the usual practice of placing his ear next to her naked chest to listen to the heartbeat. So he rolled up a newspaper and used that instead. Realising that the tube magnified the sounds, he went on to construct a 300mm (1 ft) long cylinder of wood – the first true stethoscope.

## THE FIRST ANAESTHETICS

The use of anaesthetics to relieve pain in surgery was pioneered by US dentists. The first man to use nitrous oxide as an anaesthetic successfully was Horace Wells (1815 – 48), a Connecticut dentist, who used the gas to pioneer the painless extraction of teeth in 1844. Two years later, William Morton (1819 – 68), a Boston dentist and pupil of Wells, constructed the first anaesthetic machine.

Morton's simple device consisted of a glass globe housing an ether-soaked sponge; the patient inhaled the vapour through one of two outlets.

Morton's invention was put to the test on October 16, 1846, in the surgical amphitheatre of the Massachusetts General Hospital, Boston. A 20-year-old man was successfully anaesthetised so that a tumour on his jaw could be removed painlessly.

News of the success spread quickly and, within a year, surgeons around the world were using the new technique. Morton, however, did not reap the benefits of his discovery. When his greed led him to try to patent the invention, medical and public opinion turned against him and he died, rejected, in poverty.

## ROYAL EXAMPLE

Even after the introduction of anaesthetics into other forms of surgery, some people resisted their use in childbirth because of the Biblical commandment in the Book of Genesis: 'In sorrow shalt thou bring forth children.' It took the combination of a Scottish surgeon and a queen to overcome this obstacle.

The surgeon was James Simpson (1811 – 70), the Professor of Midwifery at Edinburgh University, who was the first man to use chloroform to relieve the pain of childbirth. Simpson was dissatisfied with ether not only because it irritated the eyes, had an unpleasant smell, sometimes caused vomiting and was highly inflammable, but because there was no certainty that its use was absolutely safe. In October 1847, however, David Waldie, a friend of Simpson's from their student days, suggested to him that it might be worth trying pure chloroform. On November 4, 1847, Simpson experimented with the drug on himself and two of his friends. Five days later, he used it to deliver a baby.

The drug was administered simply by sprinkling some of it on a handkerchief, which was placed over the patient's mouth and nose so that she could inhale the vapours. Delighted by the painless delivery, the mother christened her child Anaesthesia.

Even after this success, it took the seal of royal approval to win the technique complete acceptance. In 1853, Queen Victoria was given chloroform during the birth of her eighth child, Prince Leopold. She found the experience 'soothing, quieting and delightful beyond all measure', and after that her subjects were quick to copy the royal example.

## X MARKED A MYSTERY

Wilhelm Konrad Röntgen (1845 – 1923), the discoverer of X-rays, came across them by chance. Indeed, he initially regarded his research as merely of academic significance and actually resented the immediate interest the public took in his findings.

In November 1895, Röntgen, a professor of physics at Wurzburg University in Bavaria, was studying cathode rays when he noticed that the rays were causing a sheet of paper coated with a chemical called barium platinocyanide to glow, even though there was a sheet of cardboard between the source of the rays and the affected paper. The effect continued even when Röntgen took the paper into the next room. Puzzled by this, he embarked immediately on a programme of experiments to find out more about the mysterious rays and, a month later, put forward his discoveries in a paper 'On a New Kind of Rays', which he read to the Wurzburg Physico-Medical Society on December 28, 1895. He christened the new rays 'X-rays' simply because of their mysterious nature.

The medical and surgical value of X-rays was soon appreciated and Röntgen won worldwide fame as a result. In 1901 he was awarded a Nobel prize for his work. However, public opinion turned against him when his discovery was wrongly attributed to an assistant. Disillusioned, Röntgen retired from his professorship and finally died a lonely and forgotten man.

## MAGIC MOULD

One of the key discoveries in modern medicine came about by accident. In the autumn of 1928, Alexander Fleming (1881 – 1955), a Scottish scientist, returned to his laboratory in St Mary's Hospital, London, after a four-week holiday. On his work bench, he noticed that, during his absence, the lid of a culture plate containing staphylococcus bacteria – the cause of a

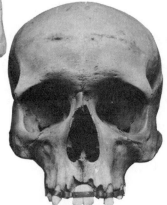

SKULL GAP *Doctors in Jericho bored four holes in this skull (left) in about 2000 BC. All the holes show signs of healing, proving that the patient survived the surgery.*

FALSE TEETH *A carved ox tooth served as two front teeth for this Etruscan, who died in about 700 BC.*

number of diseases from boils to pneumonia – had snapped off and the plate was contaminated by a number of yeasts and moulds.

What immediately interested Fleming was that one of the moulds – *Penicillium notatum* – had killed the staphylococcus in the area of the plate it had infiltrated. On further investigation, he narrowed down the reasons for its success to the presence of an active ingredient which he named penicillin after the mould. In 1940 Howard Florey and E. B. Chain managed to isolate penicillin in their Oxford laboratory, demonstrate its anti-bacterial action and show that it could be safely administered by mouth, injection, or applied directly to wounds as a powder. All three men were awarded the Nobel prize in 1945.

Fleming himself was the first to recognise that chance had played a vital role in his discovery. He later wrote: 'There are thousands of different moulds and there are thousands of different bacteria and that chance put that mould in the right place at the right time was like winning the Irish Sweep.'

### BLOOD CONFUSION
The Incas of South America were carrying out blood transfusions 400 or 500 years before the technique was successfully achieved in Europe. Most South American Indians are of the same blood group – O Rhesus positive – so that reactions because of incompatibility were unlikely, and this may have accounted for the Incas' success.

In Europe, attempts at transfusions were made by an Italian physicist, Giovanni Colle, from 1628. But most of his patients died because they received blood from the wrong group, and the practice was forbidden by the Church and government in Italy, France and England in the late 1600s – though some researchers still continued their experiments.

Blood transfusions became practicable and safe in 1900, after Karl Landsteiner, a Viennese pathologist, discovered blood groups, and matching of the correct blood between donor and patient became possible.

### TISSUE TREATMENT
The ancient Hindus practised plastic surgery before AD 1000. They worked with steel surgical instruments, and used alcohol to dull the senses. One reason for the development of this skill was because of the common punishment for adultery – cutting off the nose. Surgeons repaired the damage with tissues cut from either the cheek or forehead, rebuilding the nose around the stump. During the operation the patient breathed through reeds placed in the nostrils.

Plastic surgery became common in Western medicine only during the First World War.

### THE LONG BATTLE AGAINST THE 'WHITE DEATH'
For centuries, tuberculosis was one of the most feared of all infections. This disorder, also known as consumption, usually attacks the lungs and at one time it played a part in one in five of the world's deaths. Its characteristic lesions – named tubercles in the 17th century – have been identified in Neolithic skeletons in Europe and in Egyptian mummies of 3700 BC.

Despite all their efforts, doctors remained powerless in the face of tuberculosis until Robert Koch (1843–1910), a self-trained Prussian bacteriologist, identified the rod-like tubercle bacillus in 1882.

The next advance came in 1922, when an effective vaccine – originally developed by two French scientists, Léon Calmette and Camille Guérin, in 1906 – was first given to children. The vaccine was named BCG (Bacille-Calmette-Guérin) and is still in use today.

The final part of the puzzle – a treatment that could cure the disease, not merely prevent it – was solved in 1944 with the discovery of streptomycin, the first effective anti-tuberculous drug. The drug was discovered by Selman Waksman (1888–1973), a Russian-born scientist working in the USA.

### THE LONELY LEPER
Lepers were shunned and feared for centuries – largely needlessly. Doctors now know that leprosy is a disease of low infectivity, meaning that it can be transmitted only by close contact over a prolonged period of time.

# THE HIPPOCRATIC OATH

Medical ethics around the world are often measured against the Hippocratic oath, thought to have been written by the Greek physician Hippocrates (about 460–370 BC). In some medical schools and universities, graduating doctors are still obliged to swear to a form of the oath. This is what the original oath says:

'I swear by Apollo the healer, invoking all the gods and goddesses to be my witnesses, that I will fulfil this oath and this written covenant to the best of my ability and judgment.

'I will look upon him who shall have taught me this art even as one of my own parents. I will share my substance with him, and I will supply his necessities if he be in need. I will regard his offspring even as my own brethren, and I will teach them this art, if they would learn it, without fee or covenant. I will impart this art by precept, by lecture and by every mode of teaching, not only to my own sons but to the sons of him who has taught me and to disciples bound by covenant and oath, according to the law of medicine.

'The regimen I adopt shall be for the benefit of the patients according to my ability and judgment, and not for their hurt or for any wrong. I will give no deadly drug to any, though it be asked of me, nor will I counsel such, and especially I will not aid a woman to procure abortion. Whatsoever house I enter, there will I go for the benefit of the sick, refraining from all wrongdoing or corruption, and especially from any act of seduction, of male or female, of bond or free. Whatsoever things I see or hear concerning the life of men, in my attendance on the sick or even apart therefrom, which ought not to be noised abroad, I will keep silence thereon, counting such things to be as sacred secrets. Pure and holy will I keep my life and my art.'

PORTRAIT OF A DOCTOR *A Byzantine artist's impression of the 5th-century BC Greek doctor Hippocrates.*

Known to the ancient Hebrews, Greeks and Romans, leprosy spread to northern Europe in the 6th century AD. As early as AD 583, the Church prohibited the free movement of lepers and charged its priests to segregate all cases of leprosy from their flocks. The unfortunate victim was forced to wear a burial shroud and to lie in a coffin placed before his local church's altar. The priest scattered earth over him and then declared him to be legally dead. From that moment onwards, the leper was an outcast, obliged to beg for alms to support himself. He had to carry a pointing stick – to point out anything he wanted to buy – carry a bell to warn of his approach, and wear gloves and special fur shoes to protect barefooted travellers journeying behind him.

The bacteria which causes leprosy, *Mycobacterium leprae*, was discovered in 1874 by Armauer Hansen, a Norwegian doctor, but drugs which are effective against most forms of the disease have been developed only since the 1940s.

## RECURRING NIGHTMARE
When bubonic plague – the Black Death – struck Europe in 1347, it was regarded as the greatest single disaster ever to befall mankind. Towns and cities were wiped off the map. About 30 million people – more than a quarter of the population – died in Europe, another 45 million in Asia. Waves of plague followed at intervals over the centuries. One such epidemic swept Europe in 1664–5. The last major outbreak was as late as 1910, when, in eastern Siberia, 60,000 people died in just seven months.

It was not until 1893 that a Japanese scientist, Shibasaburo Kitasato, finally showed that the plague was a bacterial disease carried by infected rat fleas – and enabled an effective vaccine to be developed.

## LEGACY FROM THE BLACK DEATH
The modern word quarantine comes from a preventative measure taken in Italy in the 1370s in an attempt to prevent a renewed outbreak of the dreaded Black Death sweeping the city. In 1374, Venice appointed three medical officers whose duties were to inspect all ships entering the port and exclude any they suspected of harbouring the plague. Three years later, the nearby Dalmatian republic of Ragusa (in present-day Yugoslavia) compelled all suspected sailors, together with their cargoes, to be held in isolation on a neighbouring island for *quaranta giorni* (40 days), to make sure that they were not carrying the disease. The word quarantine comes from the Italian for 40. The time limit was fixed at 40 days because it was believed that all such diseases, like the Biblical Flood, were limited to that period.

## BIRTH OF THE CAESAR
The Romans are thought to have invented the childbirth operation known as Caesarean section. According to legend, the name was given to the operation because Julius Caesar was delivered by its means. More probably, however, it is derived from the Latin *caedere* (to cut).

## INFECTION DETECTION
For centuries, women feared childbirth – not because of the risks of the birth itself, but because of the danger of death after it from a form of blood poisoning known as puerperal sepsis. It took the zeal of one man, the Hungarian obstetrician Ignaz Semmelweis (1818–65), to introduce the simple hygienic techniques that saved the lives of thousands of women.

In 1844, Semmelweis joined the maternity department of the Vienna General Hospital and was immediately appalled by the death toll in the main ward, where mothers were attended by medical students. However, he also noticed that, in another ward, where midwives were responsible for the patients, the death rate was far lower. What, he asked, was the reason for the difference?

Semmelweis refused to accept the official explanation that the deaths were caused by 'hospital miasma' or bad air. He concluded that the reason for the difference was that the medical students were treating their patients straight from the dissecting rooms and therefore were carrying disease to their pregnant patients. The midwives, on the other hand, were not involved in autopsies.

In May 1847, defying the heated opposition of his colleagues, Semmelweis asked his students to wash their hands in chlorinated lime water and to scrub their fingernails before entering their ward.

The results were dramatic. Before this, the death rate had stood at a staggering 12.4 per cent. Within two months, it had fallen to 1.27 per cent. Semmel-

PLASTIC SURGERY *Doctors in India were using tissue from the forehead to rebuild noses in AD 1000.*

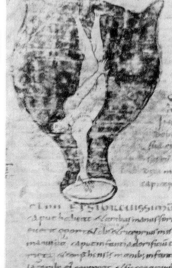

READY FOR BIRTH *Soranus, a Greek doctor of the 1st century AD, made a careful study of childbirth. This illustration – showing a foetus in the womb – is from a 13th-century edition of one of his works.*

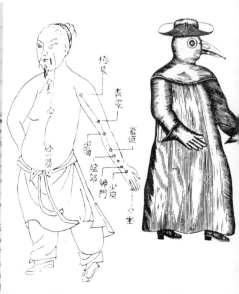

PAINS AND NEEDLES *A Chinese acupuncture chart published in 1679 marks where needles are inserted to treat heart diseases.*

DEATH MASK *17th-century plague doctors wore masks fitted with spice-filled beaks to protect themselves from infection.*

weis's fellow doctors, however, could not forgive him for being right. He found himself blocked at every turn, and in 1850 he left the hospital to return to Budapest to carry on his work. In 1865, he died in a lunatic asylum – probably from a form of the same blood poisoning that he had sacrificed his career in the Austrian capital to treat.

## HOLES IN THE HEAD

Cutting a hole in the skull – trepanning, or trephining – was practised in prehistoric times, using sharp flint or bronze instruments. At Bannes-Channdes in France, a burial site dating from 2500 BC was found to contain 60 trepanned skulls. In Peru, trepanned skulls from between the 5th century BC and the 5th century AD have been found. Amongst the earliest of all trepanned skulls is a Neolithic one found in Germany, dating from about 5000 BC.

The operation may have been used to relieve skull fractures and tumours, but it was probably more often an attempt to allow the 'escape' of an illness from the body – a practice employed by later primitive societies.

The modern trepanning method – cutting a hole in the skull of a live person with a cylindrical, or crown, saw, usually as a prelude to a brain operation – was recorded as a surgical technique in the 15th century in a medical book, Lanfranc's *Chirurgica*.

## THE ELUSIVE HORMONE

For centuries, diabetes, in which the body is unable to use the sugar it absorbs because the pancreas fails to produce enough of the key hormone insulin, was a lethal disease – even though the condition had been described by the Greek physician Aretaeus as long ago as the 2nd century AD. On average, anybody falling ill with diabetes had a future life expectancy of less than five years; most eventually fell into a coma which led to death. In 1922, however, Frederick Grant Banting and Charles Best, two Toronto-based surgeons, made a revolutionary discovery.

Both men were aware of the research carried out by the British physiologist Edward Sharpey Schafer, in which he theorised that the islets of Langerhans – so called after their discoverer, the German pathologist Paul Langerhans – produced a substance which controlled the body's ability to use the carbohydrates it absorbed. In 1916, Schafer named this substance insulin, but, as yet, it existed in theory, not in fact.

Banting and Best resolved to track down this elusive hormone. In 1921, they finally succeeded in isolating a watery extract, which they called isletin, from the islets of Langerhans. They then injected a dog in diabetic coma with the extract; within two hours, its blood sugar level had halved and it was on the road to recovery. In January 1922, they injected their first human patient.

Mass production of the new wonder drug, now known as insulin, was quick to start. Today, though more than one in a hundred people suffer from diabetes, most lead perfectly normal lives.

## SPRAY THAT SAVED

The introduction of effective anaesthetics in the 19th century meant that surgeons were able to perform more complex operations than ever before. But, paradoxically, this advance was accompanied by a substantial drawback – a dramatic rise in the number of post-operative complications. Wounds rarely healed cleanly and more than half the patients died of blood poisoning. The Scottish obstetrician James Simpson, one of the pioneers of anaesthesia, wrote: 'A man laid on the operating table in one of our surgical hospitals is exposed to more chances of death than the English soldier on the field of Waterloo.' It took the genius of a Quaker surgeon to transform this situation. The surgeon's name was Joseph Lister (1827–1912), and his revolutionary innovation was the use of chemicals to prevent surgical infection.

Lister was deeply influenced by the work of the French scientist Louis Pasteur and his germ theory, and argued that the risk of infection would be reduced if chemical antiseptics were used to protect wounds against the germs in the atmosphere. He began experimenting to prove his point in the 1860s – his first successful experiments were in 1865 – using carbolic acid in the form of a spray during operations and on his surgical dressings. The experiments proved dramatically successful, reducing mortality by one-third. Later, he also developed the principle of asepsis – sterilisation of the surgeon's instruments and hands before an operation.

## FOOD PERIL

Unexplained attacks of migraine, eczema, stomach pain, diarrhoea, nausea and vomiting could all be cured, some doctors believe, by a simple change of

---

# VACCINE VICTORIES

**1796** Edward Jenner, Gloucestershire doctor, makes the first successful smallpox vaccination.

**1880** French bacteriologist Louis Pasteur prepares the first anti-cholera vaccine, followed by vaccines against anthrax (1881) and rabies (1885).

**1891** Anti-toxins produced to treat diphtheria and tetanus by Emil Adolf von Belming and Shibasaburo Kitasato, working in Prussian scientist Robert Koch's laboratory in Berlin.

**1922** Tuberculosis vaccine – originally developed by Léon Calmette and Camille Guérin in 1906 at the Pasteur Institute, Paris, for use in cattle – successfully tested on French schoolchildren.

**1954** Polio vaccine developed in Pittsburgh, USA, by American physician Jonas E. Salk.

**1960** Measles vaccine developed by American virologist John F. Enders.

**1962** Rubella (German measles) vaccine developed to protect pregnant women by American physician Thomas H. Weller.

BREAKTHROUGH *Dr Jenner inoculates eight-year-old James Phipps against smallpox.*

diet. According to a report published in 1983 about the results of tests carried out at Britain's Great Ormond Street Hospital and Institute of Child Health, many of these disorders can be caused by allergies.

To prove the point, the researchers took a sample of 88 children, all of whom suffered from frequent severe migraine attacks, and put them on a special diet for three to four weeks. The diet consisted of lamb or chicken, rice or potato, a single type of fruit and one vegetable, together with water and vitamin supplements. Other foodstuffs were then reintroduced one at a time at the rate of one per week, so that, if the migraines returned, another foodstuff could be substituted. Of the 88 patients, an amazing 78 recovered completely and four more were greatly improved. At the same time, the researchers noted that other associated ailments, such as abdominal pain, behavioural disorders, fits, asthma and eczema also disappeared.

The suspected foods were then disguised by mixing them with a savoury or sweet base so that the children had no idea if they were eating the suspected food or not. In this further series of tests, 70 of the 88 children became ill again when the suspected foods – these included tea, eggs, milk, rye and artificial food colourings – were reintroduced into their diets.

## A PLACE FOR THE LEECH

Modern research has shown that the humble leech – a mainstay of medicine from ancient times to the 19th century in the treatment of almost every disease from whooping cough to madness – has an important role to play in plastic surgery. These blood-sucking worms are capable of absorbing three to four times their own weight in blood. They also produce a natural anticoagulant that stops the blood clotting.

When plastic surgeons transfer or graft new skin onto a damaged area, the tissues usually become severely bruised and congested with blood. Applying leeches to reduce the swelling is considered by many doctors to be the safest way of dealing with the problem. The technique was pioneered at the Pellegrin hospital in Bordeaux, France. Today, more than 100 hospitals in Europe and North America routinely use leeches for this purpose.

## WHY YOU ARE SEASICK

Sea or air sickness is nothing to do with eating or drinking. It is the body's nervous response to the information transmitted to the brain by the eyes and

EARPIECE *A French doctor, René Laennec, invented the stethoscope in 1816. This three-piece wooden cylinder was one of the first he made.*

ANAESTHETIC *By the 1860s, chloroform was being widely used to ease the pain of childbirth.*

the organs of touch and balance. Though some people have or develop a natural resistance to the conditions, many do not. Horatio Lord Nelson, Britain's greatest admiral, was often seasick.

Research to find a cure began during the Second World War, so that fighting troops could be transported by ship and landing craft and disembarked fit for immediate action. Yet, even today, no drug is fully effective. Most of the drugs used act by sedating the sufferer, not by treating the symptoms or dealing with the causes themselves.

## THE KILLERS

Heart disease, cancer and strokes kill more people around the world each year than any other illnesses. Heart disease is by far the biggest killer in the Western world. In the USA, for example, 360 out of every 100,000 people in the country die of heart disease each year. In Britain, the figure is 458 per 100,000; in Australia it is 292. By comparison, lung cancer kills a relatively small proportion of the population each year: 49 per 100,000 in the USA, 32 per 100,000 in Australia and 72 per 100,000 in Britain.

In the Third World, diseases such as pneumonia, enteritis and diarrhoeal disorders are often bigger killers than heart disease. In Ecuador, for instance, enteritis and other diarrhoeal disorders kill 106 people per 100,000 each year; heart disease kills only two-thirds as many. Moreover, in some of the world's poorest countries, at least one baby in two dies in the first five years of life, often from common childhood infections such as measles or from 'perinatal' disorders – those associated with birth.

## GERM OF AN IDEA

The science of preventive medicine – actually preventing disease, rather than merely coping with its effects – started with the work of a 19th-century French chemist, whose original interest lay in wine and vinegar rather than human beings. In the 1860s, Louis Pasteur (1822–95) was commissioned by France's wine-growers to establish why their products were going off in the vats, becoming sour and unsaleable. Through his researches, he discovered that the unwanted changes were due to the invasion of the vats by invisible, airborne microbes. He called the microbes germs.

Pasteur went on to prove that germs were also the cause of human disease. He argued that the then-popular scientific belief that diseases were spontaneously generated within individual sufferers was totally incorrect. Diseases, he said, were caused by airborne germs and bacteria invading the body and multiplying there. This huge step forward marked the foundation of the science of bacteriology and was a milestone in man's understanding of the nature of infectious diseases.

The germ theory itself, however, was not new. Girolamo Fracastoro, an Italian professor of philosophy, had put forward the first scientific statement of its principles in 1546 in his book *On Contagion and Contagions*. But 16th-century medicine was not advanced enough to prove the theory or make practical use of it.

Pasteur, on the other hand, was able to track down and study germs and bacteria and so develop effective vaccines against them. His two most notable discoveries were vaccines against anthrax (1881) and rabies (1885). His rabies vaccine was the subject of one of his most dramatic demonstrations. In 1885, he saved the life of a nine-year-old German boy, Joseph Meister, with a course of 14 injections after the boy had been badly mauled by a rabid dog.

## INDIAN MEDICINE MEN

The first effective treatment for malaria was not devised by doctors, but by Peruvian Indians. It was popularised in Europe in the 1640s by Jesuit monks, who brought the secret of the cure back from South America. The Indians had found that an extract of the bark of the cinchona tree was extremely effective in dealing with the deadly fever. When samples of the bark were distributed in Europe by the Jesuits, its powers were quickly demonstrated.

Two factors, however, stood in the way of the miracle bark's success. Despite the evidence, many physicians at first remained sceptical. In addition, the use of the bark was resisted in Protestant countries because of its Jesuit associations. When Oliver Cromwell, Lord Protector of England, contracted malaria in 1658, for instance, he refused to take any 'Jesuits' bark' because of this prejudice – and died the same year as a result.

It was not until 1820 that the active ingredient of the bark was isolated and named quinine. The actual cause of the disease remained a mystery until 1897, when a British doctor in India, Sir Ronald Ross, showed that it was transmitted to humans by the bites of the female *Anopheles* mosquito.

## THE STORY OF ASPIRIN

No home medicine cupboard is complete without a packet of Aspirin. The drug – properly known as acetylsalicylic acid, Aspirin being the trade name invented for it in the 1890s by the Bayer Drug Company of Germany – is one of the most widely used in the world. More than 45,000 million Aspirin tablets are swallowed every year in the USA, and another 7000 million in Britain. The world as a whole gulps down about 123,000 million Aspirins a year – an average of around two pills a month for every man, woman and child on the planet.

The drug's origins go back to 1758, when an English clergyman, Edward Stone, noticed that the bark of the willow tree had a peculiarly bitter flavour, very similar to that of 'Peruvian bark'. Peruvian bark, obtained from the South American cinchona tree, contained quinine and had been used since the 1640s to bring down fevers and to treat malaria. When Stone obtained some pulverised willow bark and tested its properties, he found that it was also extremely effective in reducing high temperatures and dealing with rheumatic aches and pains. In 1763, Stone presented his findings to the British Royal Society, but, though he could show what effects the crushed willow had, he could not say what part of the bark caused them. This had to wait until 1826, when two Italian chemists, Brugnatelli and Fontana, found that the active chemical in the bark was salicin, the central ingredient of the modern pill.

## DOCTOR IN THE DAIRY

Measures to deal with the threat of smallpox were devised by the Chinese as early as AD 590, when they introduced the first protective vaccinations against the disease. With variations, this practice, known as variolation, spread throughout the East. It was introduced into England in 1720 by Lady Mary Wortley Montagu, who brought the idea from Turkey where her husband was British ambassador.

The technique involved inoculating a person with pus taken from victims of a mild form of the disease. The idea was that, by being infected with the mild form, the patient would acquire immunity to the severe form. But there was a major drawback: the patient could also become infected with the lethal severe form as a result of the treatment.

A much safer method was discovered in the late 18th century. It was the work of Edward Jenner (1749 – 1823), a British country doctor, who, after years of patient research, performed the first successful anti-smallpox vaccination in 1796. Basing his theory on a chance remark by a dairy maid – 'I cannot take the smallpox, since I have had the cowpox' (a similar but mild disease contracted from cows) – he vaccinated a young boy, James Phipps, with an extract taken from a cowpox pustule on the infected hand of a dairy maid named Sarah Nelmes. Six weeks later, he inoculated Phipps with a mild form of smallpox. No trace of infection developed.

Jenner's vaccination technique – named from the Latin word *vacca*, meaning 'cow' – was eventually adopted all over the world. And in 1980, the World Health Organisation officially declared the world free of smallpox – the first time that man has ever eliminated a major disease.

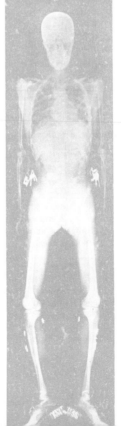

ASPIRIN *The first bottles of Aspirin (below) went on sale in 1899.*

X-RAYS *The first X-ray picture of a human body. Metal keys and suspenders show up as white.*

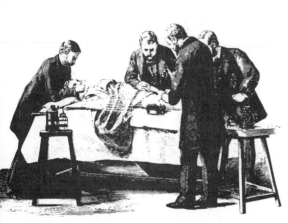

ANTISEPTIC SPRAY *The surgeon Joseph Lister began using carbolic acid to cut down surgical infections in the 1860s. In this engraving, published in 1882, a Lister spray gun pumps a fine mist of the antiseptic acid over surgeons and patient during an operation.*

223

# Food and drink

## ACID DIGESTION

The process of digestion begins as soon as food goes into the mouth. Enzymes in the saliva start to break up the food even before it is swallowed. The major digestive organ, though, is the stomach, whose lining contains about 35 million tiny glands. Between them, these stomach glands produce some 2.5 litres (4 pints) of gastric juices every day – mostly in the form of hydrochloric acid.

## TASTING, TASTING

The human tongue is capable of distinguishing only four basic tastes. The tongue's surface is covered by thousands of nerve endings – taste buds – divided into four groups: those on the tip sense sweetness; those at the back sense bitterness; those at the sides sense saltiness and sourness. In addition, other taste buds are scattered around the inside of the mouth. The primary tasters of sour and bitter, for instance, are in the roof of the mouth.

All the more complex tastes are made up of combinations of the basic four. Young adults have about 8000 taste buds, but the nerve endings start to die after the age of 45, so that elderly people normally have only about 6500. Much of what we perceive as flavour in food is in fact a combination of taste and smell, which is why food seems to lose its flavour when the nose is blocked during a cold.

## WHEN A TONIC IS HARMFUL

Gin and tonic taken on an empty stomach can damage concentration and judgment, not only because of the alcohol, but also because of the tonic. The reason is that the sugar in the tonic stimulates the pancreas to produce insulin which soaks up the excess sugar and stores it. As the remaining sugar is used up to provide energy, the level of sugar in the blood falls.

In ordinary circumstances, this drop triggers other hormones to release the stored sugar or create more. But the alcohol in the gin blocks the triggering process, so that the blood sugar level continues to fall. And since the brain is powered solely by sugar in the form of glucose, mental performance can be seriously affected for several hours.

## POPEYE'S MISTAKE

The idea that spinach promotes strength – one made popular by the cartoon character Popeye the Sailor – is based on a mistake. The misconception arose in 1870, when a misplaced decimal point in a set of published food tables made spinach appear to contain ten times as much iron as other vegetables. In fact, it has much the same. Furthermore, the iron in any vegetable is less valuable than a similar quantity of iron in meat, because the body is less efficient at absorbing iron from vegetables. Only between 2 and 10 per cent of the iron in vegetables is absorbed, compared with 10 to 30 per cent of the iron in meat.

## WHY CHINESE FOOD IS SO FILLING

The bloated feeling and the thirst that may sometimes follow a meal in a Chinese restaurant seem to be caused by nothing more exotic than salt. At one time doctors believed that the feelings were caused by the addition of monosodium glutamate, a preservative and taste-enhancer which is traditionally used in Chinese food. Now, however, many doctors believe that the feelings are caused by the high salt content of Chinese meals. The feelings persist until the body gets rid of the salt overload several hours later.

## GOURMET MEAL FOR BABIES

Avocado pears – often regarded simply as a delicacy for adults – are so easily digestible that even babies can eat them. The fruits are extremely nutritious, too. An avocado contains twice as much protein as the same volume of breast milk, more than three times as much fat, nearly ten times as much carbohydrate, three times as much vitamin A and vitamin B (thiamin), almost three times as much vitamin C, and more than twice as many calories.

## HOOKED ON ASPARAGUS

Asparagus has remarkable properties beyond the taste for which gardeners grow it. It can be used to catch fish. According to an eminent American scientist, Homer Smith, tinned asparagus was made part of the emergency rations given during the Second World War to American pilots in the Pacific who were working for the US spy organisation, the Office of Strategic Services.

The idea was that pilots who were shot down or marooned on remote islands should eat the asparagus and then urinate into the sea. Asparagus contains mercaptans, powerful chemical attractants, and the chemicals would pass into the urine, spread through the water and draw fish to the area – making it easier for the pilot to catch them for food. As a bonus, asparagus is also an excellent source of vitamin A, which is necessary for good night vision.

## CLEAN LIVING

Devout Mormons – who abstain from alcohol, cigarettes, tea and coffee – get cancer far less often than other people. Doctors who have studied the patterns of disease in Utah – home to more than one in three of the USA's 2.1 million Mormons – have found that American men as a whole are almost three times more likely to get lung cancer than Mormon men. There is

## WHY VITAMINS ARE VALUABLE

Vitamins are chemical substances present naturally in most foods and, in synthetic form, in vitamin pills. Both forms are equally nutritious since the vitamins in each case are chemically identical. The body needs only tiny quantities of them – ranging from about 30mg (30 thousandths of a gram) a day of vitamin C, for instance, down to 1 microgram (one millionth of a gram) of vitamin B12. They play no direct part in producing body tissues or energy, but they are essential for the body to function efficiently, just as oil is essential for the running of a car.

Vitamin deficiencies can lead to illness and, in extreme cases, death. The killer diseases scurvy and beri-beri are caused by deficiencies of the vitamins C and B1 respectively. Deficiency of vitamin A can cause night blindness, and rickets (a childhood disease of the bones) is due to a deficiency of vitamin D. Anyone who eats a variety of foods, however, is very unlikely to run into problems.

a similar reduction in cancer of the throat among Mormons. And cancer of the large bowel is about 40 per cent less common.

## FOOD: FACTS AND FALLACIES

● An apple a day does not keep the doctor away. A medium-sized apple supplies only 10mg (0.0004oz) of vitamin C; an orange has five times as much. Apart from 12g (0.4oz) of sugar (45 calories), apples have little other than about 2g (0.07oz) of dietary fibre.

● Brown bread *is* better for your health than white – particularly if it is wholemeal. Wholemeal bread contains much more iron, vitamins and dietary fibre than white bread. Ordinary brown breads are between the two.

● White eggs are just as nutritious as brown ones. The colour of the shell is a characteristic of the breed of chicken. It has nothing to do with nutritive value.

● Margarine is just as fattening as butter. In Britain and in many other countries, margarine must by law contain no more than 16 per cent water, the same as butter. So all margarines contain 84 per cent fat – just as butter does. Margarine is also no less nutritious than butter. It has as much vitamin A added as there is in butter, and it has more vitamin D.

● Carrots can help to make you see better in the dark. People whose eyesight is normal but who are short of vitamin A cannot see in dim light – an ailment known as night blindness. Carrots will cure this condition because they are rich in carotene, which forms vitamin A in the body. Carrots will not, however, help if the inability to see at night is due to some other cause.

● Honey, often thought to be particularly health-giving, has no exceptional value. It consists only of fructose (fruit sugar), glucose (grape sugar) and water. Vitamins are present in such small amounts that they make no worthwhile contribution to the diet.

● The belief that brown sugar is better for health than white has no scientific foundation. White sugar is 99.9 per cent pure sucrose. Brown sugar is 98 per cent sucrose and 1 per cent water, leaving room for only minute traces of mineral salts and protein. The difference is therefore negligible.

## EATING FOR TWO

The idea that pregnant women need to eat for two is a fallacy. Mothers-to-be do need extra nourishment, but over the whole nine months of pregnancy, the total needed is only about 80,000 calories – roughly the equivalent of one month's normal food intake. So the saying could be rephrased more accurately as: a pregnant woman should eat for one and one-ninth. British research published in 1983 also suggests that food may be absorbed more efficiently than usual during pregnancy, so that the mother-to-be's normal diet may provide the extra calories without her actually needing to eat more.

Some women also develop bizarre cravings for particular foods during pregnancy, even eating coal and soil. It was once thought that they were trying to make up for deficiencies in their diet, but there is little scientific evidence for this. Cravings of this kind were common 50 years ago, but are rare today.

## MILK FOR THE MONGOLS

Dried milk was used as long ago as the 13th century – by the cavalry of the Mongol emperor, Genghis Khan (about 1162–1227). The Mongol soldiers dried mare's milk to a powder in the sun to preserve it. Then, at the beginning of each day's journey, they put some of the powder in a water bottle hung on the saddle. The horse's jogging acted like a whisk, turning the mixture into a thin porridge by nightfall.

## LIND'S 'LIMEYS'

The slang expression 'limey' – now used for anyone British – was coined in the early 19th century to describe British sailors. The word came from the Royal Navy's practice of issuing a compulsory daily ration of lemon or lime juice to its men to prevent scurvy, a disease caused by a lack of vitamin C.

Scurvy had been a major health hazard for sailors ever since the start of long-distance voyages of exploration in the 15th century. On some voyages, three out of four sailors died of it. Yet little was done to check the disease until a Scottish naval surgeon, James Lind, embarked on a programme of research to devise an effective counter-measure. He began his work in 1747, when he sailed as ship's surgeon on HMS *Salisbury* and found that 80 out of the 350-strong crew were suffering from scurvy. He took 12 of these, dividing them into six pairs, and, for a week, got five of the pairs to drink one of five potions each day: cider; an elixir of acidic vitriol; vinegar; seawater; or a mixture of garlic, mustard seed, balsam of fern, myrrh and barley water. The sixth pair ate a lemon and two oranges. Within six days, the sailors taking the lemon and oranges were so much better that they could help to nurse the remaining ten.

Lind published his findings in his *Treatise of the Scurvy* in 1753. But his prescription was ignored for 42 years because of naval prejudice. Not until 1795 – a year after his death – did the British Admiralty make citrus juice an official part of naval diet.

FACTS ABOUT SCIENCE & TECHNOLOGY

COOK'S LIST *A 1768 cargo manifest for the British explorer James Cook includes sauerkraut and malt. Both were thought, wrongly, to help prevent scurvy.*

## ESKIMO HEALTH

Eskimos eat more fat than any other people in the world, but heart diseases, which are often caused by a fatty diet, are rare among them.

The reason is that the fats the Eskimos eat in their traditional diet of fish and seal blubber are of a type known to doctors as unsaturated – which are liquid at room temperature. Most vegetable fats are of the same type. The fats that can lead to heart disease – because they build up in the walls of arteries, restricting the flow of blood and putting extra strain on the heart – are known as saturated fats. They are solid at room temperature. Animal meat and eggs are particularly rich in saturated fats.

## PINTA POWER
Half a litre (0.9 pints) of milk a day provides, on average, one-sixth of a person's daily energy requirements, all the calcium, a third of the protein, about a quarter of the vitamin A, a fifth of the vitamin B1 and half the vitamin B2. However, there is no evidence that milk is indispensable – even for children –

providing the rest of the diet is well-balanced. Many nutritionists have warned about the dangers of cholesterol, the white, waxy substance contained in milk and other foods, which can build up in the arteries and lead to heart disease. But half a litre of milk contains only about 0.05g (0.002oz) of cholesterol – less than a quarter as much as one boiled egg. And such a small amount – even added to the cholesterol which the body itself manufactures – is unlikely to cause anyone any harm.

## COLD COMFORT
Large doses of vitamin C – the vitamin found in oranges and many other fruits – are no help in warding off colds. The belief that they were came from a

# COUNTING CALORIES

Calories are a measure of heat. In physics, one calorie is the heat required to raise one cubic centimetre of water by one degree Centigrade. The calorie unit used by dieticians is technically a kilocalorie – 1000 calories – but it is usually shortened to calorie for convenience. The body uses the calories in food to provide energy including heat. About two-thirds of a person's normal food intake is used up in

maintaining body temperature, the normal tone of muscles and in keeping the heart and other organs functioning healthily. An adult weighing 64kg (10 stones) uses up about 1600 calories a day in this way – even if he spends all day in bed. The harder people work and the more they move about, the more calories they burn up. A coal miner, for instance, uses about 4000

| Food | Energy (calories) | Protein (grams) | Fat (grams) | Carbohydrate (grams) | Water (grams) | Fibre (grams) | Vitamin (good sources of) | | |
|---|---|---|---|---|---|---|---|---|---|
| **Dairy products** | | | | | | | | | |
| Milk | 65 | 3.3 | 4 | 5 | 88 | — | A | B2 | Nia |
| Butter | 740 | — | 82 | — | 15 | — | A | | |
| Cream, single | 210 | 2 | 21 | 3 | 72 | — | A | | |
| Cheese, cheddar type | 300 | 23 | 23 | — | 37 | — | A | B2 | Nia |
| Cheese, Danish blue | 350 | 23 | 29 | — | 40 | — | A | B2 | Nia |
| Cheese, Stilton | 460 | 26 | 40 | — | 28 | — | A | B2 | Nia |
| Cheese, cottage | 100 | 14 | 4 | 1 | 80 | — | | | Nia |
| Cheese, processed | 310 | 22 | 25 | — | 44 | — | A | B2 | Nia |
| Ice cream, dairy | 170 | 4 | 7 | 25 | 64 | — | B1 | B2 | Nia |
| Yoghurt, natural | 50 | 5 | 1 | 6 | 86 | — | B1 | B2 | Nia |
| Yoghurt, flavoured | 80 | 5 | 1 | 14 | 79 | — | B1 | B2 | Nia |
| Margarine | 730 | — | 81 | — | 16 | — | A | | |
| Low fat spread | 370 | — | 40 | — | 57 | — | A | | |
| **Meat and fish** | | | | | | | | | |
| Bacon, gammon—boiled | 270 | 25 | 19 | — | 54 | — | B1 | | Nia |
| Bacon, streaky—fried | 500 | 23 | 45 | — | 28 | — | B1 | | Nia |
| Eggs | 150 | 12 | 11 | tr | 75 | — | A | B1 | B2 | Nia |
| Beef, brisket—boiled | 330 | 28 | 24 | — | 48 | — | | B2 | Nia |
| Beef, minced—stewed | 230 | 23 | 15 | — | 59 | — | | B2 | Nia |
| Beef, rump steak—fried | 250 | 29 | 15 | — | 56 | — | B1 | B2 | Nia |
| Corned beef | 220 | 27 | 12 | — | 58 | — | | B2 | Nia |
| Lamb cutlets—grilled | 370 | 23 | 31 | — | 45 | — | B1 | B2 | Nia |
| Pork chop—grilled | 330 | 29 | 24 | — | 36 | — | B1 | B2 | Nia |
| Veal cutlet—fried | 215 | 31 | 8 | — | 55 | — | | | |
| Chicken—roast | 150 | 25 | 5 | — | 68 | — | B1 | B2 | Nia |
| Calf's liver—fried | 250 | 27 | 13 | — | 53 | — | A | B1 | B2 | Nia |
| Sausages, beef—fried | 270 | 13 | 18 | 15 | 48 | — | | | Nia |
| Sausages, pork—fried | 320 | 14 | 25 | 11 | 45 | — | | B2 | Nia |
| Ham | 120 | 18 | 5 | — | 73 | — | B1 | B2 | Nia |
| White fish, e.g. cod | | | | | | | | | |
| White fish—fried in batter | 200 | 20 | 10 | 8 | 60 | — | B1 | | Nia |
| White fish—steamed | 80 | 19 | 1 | — | 79 | — | B1 | | Nia |
| Fatty fish, e.g. herring | | | | | | | | | |
| Fatty fish—fried | 230 | 23 | 15 | 1.5 | 58 | — | | B2 | Nia |
| Sardines—in oil | 220 | 24 | 14 | — | 58 | — | | B2 | Nia |
| Sardines—in tomato sauce | 180 | 18 | 12 | — | 65 | — | | B2 | Nia |
| **Vegetables and fruit** | | | | | | | | | |
| Beans, French—boiled | 20 | 2 | — | 3 | 90 | 3 | A | | |
| Beans, baked—canned | 60 | 5 | — | 10 | 73 | 7 | B1 | | |
| Brussels sprouts | 20 | 3 | — | 2 | 88 | 4 | A | B1 | B2 | C |

Nobel prizewinner, the US chemist Dr Linus Pauling. But trials at the Common Cold Research Centre in Salisbury, England, have shown that volunteers given large doses of vitamin C got colds just as often as those who were given no vitamin C at all.

## CAFFEINE CUPPA
A teaspoon of tea leaves contains more of the stimulant drug caffeine than a teaspoon of ground coffee. But tea has a less marked effect on the body because it is more diluted in use. As a result, a cup of tea contains only about 60 per cent as much caffeine as a cup of coffee. Caffeine, which is also found in cocoa and in cola drinks, can in large doses cause anxiety, irritability, restlessness and heart palpitations.

BAKER'S LEGACY *This crusty loaf of bread was baked 1900 years ago. It was found in a bakery oven in Pompeii – preserved by ash from the eruption of Vesuvius in AD 79.*

calories a day, an office worker about 2500, a modern housewife about 2200. As long as what you eat and what you use are in balance, your weight will remain constant. People who eat more food than they use put on weight – about 450g (1lb) of fat for every 3500 excess calories. The figures given in this chart are based on 100g (3.5oz) portions. This is an average helping, but in some cases, such as butter or bran, it is unlikely that anyone would eat 100g at a sitting. All figures have been rounded off, so the total of all the nutrients including the water may be more than 100g. A food is listed as a good source of vitamins if it provides a reasonable proportion of daily needs. 'Nia' stands for niacin, one of the B vitamins. 'Tr' indicates a trace of the nutrient – too little to be of value.

| Food | Energy (calories) | Protein (grams) | Fat (grams) | Carbohydrate (grams) | Water (grams) | Fibre (grams) | Vitamin (good sources of) | | |
|---|---|---|---|---|---|---|---|---|---|
| Cabbage—boiled | 10 | 1 | — | 1 | 96 | 2.5 | A | | C |
| Carrots—boiled | 20 | 0.6 | — | 4 | 91 | 3 | A | | |
| Cauliflower | 10 | 1.5 | — | 1 | 93 | 2 | | | C |
| Cucumber—raw | 10 | 0.6 | — | 2 | 96 | 0.4 | | | C |
| Peas—boiled | 50 | 5 | — | 8 | 80 | 12 | A | B1 B2 | Nia C |
| Potatoes—boiled | 80 | 1 | — | 20 | 77 | 1 | | B1 | |
| Potatoes—roast | 160 | 3 | 5 | 27 | 64 | 1 | | B1 | |
| Potatoes—chipped | 250 | 4 | 11 | 37 | 47 | 1 | | B1 | |
| Tomatoes | 15 | 1 | — | 3 | 93 | 1.5 | A | | C |
| Apples | 45 | 0.3 | — | 12 | 84 | 2 | | | |
| Bananas | 80 | 1 | tr | 20 | 70 | 3 | | | C |
| Cherries | 50 | 0.6 | — | 12 | 81 | 2 | | | |
| Grapes | 60 | 0.6 | — | 15 | 80 | 1 | | | |
| Oranges | 35 | 1 | — | 9 | 86 | 2 | | | C |
| Pears | 40 | tr | — | 11 | 83 | 2 | | | |
| Plums | 40 | 0.6 | — | 10 | 84 | 2 | A | | |
| Almonds | 570 | 17 | 54 | 4 | 5 | 14 | | B1 B2 | Nia |
| Chestnuts | 620 | 2 | 3 | 37 | 52 | 7 | | B1 B2 | |
| Peanuts—roasted | 570 | 24 | 49 | 9 | 4 | 8 | | B1 B2 | Nia |
| Peanut butter | 620 | 23 | 54 | 13 | 1 | 8 | | B1 B2 | Nia |
| **Drinks** | | | | | | | | | |
| Beer | 30 | 0.3 | — | 2 | | — | | | |
| Strong ale | 70 | 0.7 | — | 6 | | — | | B2 | Nia |
| Wine | 70 | tr | — | tr | | — | | | |
| Spirits | 220 | — | — | — | | — | | | |
| Tea—black | — | — | — | — | | — | | | |
| Coffee—black | — | — | — | — | | — | | | Nia |
| Sugar—teaspoon | 24 | — | — | — | | — | | | |
| Soup—chicken noodle | 20 | 1 | 0.3 | 4 | | tr | | | |
| Soup—cream of tomato | 55 | 1 | 3 | 6 | | tr | | | |
| **Food from cereals** | | | | | | | | | |
| Bread, wholemeal | 215 | 9 | 3 | 42 | 40 | 8.5 | | B1 | Nia |
| Bread, white | 230 | 8 | 2 | 50 | 39 | 2.7 | | B1 | Nia |
| Rice, white—boiled | 120 | 2 | — | 30 | 70 | 0.8 | | | |
| Spaghetti—without sauce | 120 | 4 | — | 26 | 72 | unknown | | | |
| Cornflakes—with milk | 205 | 6.5 | 4 | 34.7 | | 1.2 | A | B1 B2 | Nia D |
| Chocolate biscuits | 520 | 6 | 28 | 67 | 2 | 3.1 | | B2 | Nia |
| Water biscuits | 440 | 11 | 13 | 76 | 5 | 3.0 | | B1 | Nia |
| Sponge cake—with fat | 460 | 6 | 27 | 53 | 15 | 1.0 | | | Nia |
| Porridge—cooked | 45 | 1.5 | 1 | 8 | 90 | 0.8 | | | |
| Bran—wheat | 200 | 14 | 6 | 23 | 8 | 44 | | B1 B2 | Nia |

# Chemistry – the study of matter

## CARBON, THE KEY TO LIFE

If life has formed anywhere else in the Universe, it is almost certain to be based on molecules of carbon, just as it is on Earth. For the compounds of carbon outnumber tenfold the compounds of all the other elements put together.

Carbon atoms can join together to form stable molecules almost regardless of the number of carbon atoms involved. As a result, a virtually endless variety of molecular 'backbones' can be constructed from carbon. Giant molecules, such as those which make up natural proteins and man-made plastics, are based on it. Very few other elements can form such large molecules and those that can, such as sulphur, are more restricted in the range of other elements with which they will combine.

Each carbon atom can link with up to four other atoms, including other carbon atoms. So the number of possible compounds which can be made from carbon escalates rapidly as the number of carbon atoms in a molecule increases.

Propane, used as bottled gas, has the chemical formula $CH_3CH_2CH_3$, showing that each molecule contains three carbon and eight hydrogen atoms. Butane ($C_4H_{10}$), a similar gas, has four carbon atoms. The four atoms can be arranged in a single chain, or with the fourth carbon forming a branch in the middle. These different structural forms give rise to two compounds – known as isomers, from Greek words meaning 'the same parts' – which have slightly different properties. The straight-chain form is normal butane, and the other is named *isobutane*.

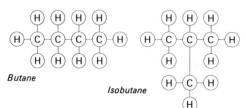

Butane

Isobutane

As the number of carbon atoms in a molecule increases, more and more isomeric forms of the same molecule become possible. By the time a molecule has 40 carbon atoms – as in some waxes found in crude oil – the theoretically possible number of isomers has risen to 62.5 million million, creating a vast field of compounds whose properties are still being explored.

## CAESAR'S LAST GASP

Atoms and molecules are almost unimaginably tiny. There are, for instance, at least as many molecules in a single teaspoon of water as there are teaspoons of water in the entire Atlantic Ocean.

There are so many molecules of air in a single breath that, even when all the molecules have been dispersed evenly throughout the Earth's atmosphere, there will still be one or two taken into the lungs with every subsequent breath.

Every time you breathe in, therefore, you inhale one or two of the same molecules that you inhaled with the first breath you took as a baby. And each breath also contains some molecules from the last gasp of Julius Caesar, Napoleon and every other person in history.

## THE ALCHEMISTS

When modern chemistry began to develop in the late Middle Ages in Europe, much of its knowledge came from the alchemists of the Arab world, who had preserved and developed scientific scholarship during the Dark Ages. Indeed, the word chemistry itself comes from the mystical science of alchemy, from the Arabic *al-kimia*, which may be derived from an Arab name for Egypt, *Khemia*. Other chemical terms, such as alkali and alcohol, are also derived from Arabic words. The prefix *al-* is simply the Arabic word for 'the'.

## EXPLODING APRON

Christian Schönbein, a German chemist, founded the modern explosives industry in 1845 in his wife's kitchen. While working there, he accidentally spilt a mixture of nitric and sulphuric acid onto a cotton apron. He hung the apron up to dry, but as soon as it dried out it exploded. Schönbein (1799–1868) had discovered nitrocellulose – the explosive which, in the form of guncotton, was in use by 1890 to fire artillery shells farther and faster than had ever been possible with gunpowder.

## FOUR ELEMENTS OF ARISTOTLE

For nearly 2000 years, scholars believed that everything was made up of combinations of just four elements: air, earth, fire and water. The belief, established by the Greek philosopher Aristotle (384–322 BC), survived until the 17th century when scientists began to insist on direct observation and experiment, rather than abstract philosophy, as the only reliable way to acquire new knowledge.

In chemistry, one of the first challengers of Aristotle was the Englishman Robert Boyle (1627–91), who in 1661 published *The Skeptical Chymist*. In it he defined for the first time the modern idea of an element as a substance which cannot be broken down into simpler ones. Boyle also discovered the physical law now named after him. Boyle's law states that at a constant temperature, the volume of a gas varies inversely with its pressure – so that if a quantity of gas is compressed into a third of its original volume, its pressure will triple.

VACUUM FLASK *Robert Boyle used a pump like this in his experiments on gas pressure. Turning the handle dragged down a piston, sucking air out of the glass sphere.*

## DREAM THAT LED TO DISCOVERY

The structure of benzene – the parent of a family of hydrocarbons found in coal tar and known as aromatic compounds because of their pleasant smell – was discovered by a German chemist as the result of a dream. The chemist, Friedrich Kekulé (1829 – 96), was working as a professor at Ghent in Belgium when he had the dream in 1862.

Kekulé knew that the atoms in any molecule are linked by chemical hooks, known as valency bonds. Carbon has four such hooks, hydrogen one. So one carbon atom can link with four hydrogen atoms to form methane. Kekulé also knew that atoms could be joined by double or even triple bonds. In the gas ethylene ($C_2H_4$), for instance, two carbon atoms are joined by a double bond with each other and by single bonds with four hydrogen atoms.

In benzene, however, six carbons are linked with six hydrogens. Try as he might, Kekulé could not work out how the atoms could be linked in a chain without leaving some hooks unattached – a chemical impossibility. Then he had the dream, in which he saw a snake suddenly wriggle into a circle and swallow its tail.

*Methane*

*Ethylene*

*Benzene*

The dream gave him the clue he needed: that the carbon atoms in benzene were arranged not in a chain but in a ring. His discovery opened up a whole new field of chemistry, the ring compounds, which became the basis of the prosperous German dye industry and led to the discovery of toluene, from which the explosive TNT (trinitrotoluene) is derived.

## THE FIRST FIZZY DRINK

Joseph Priestley, who shares the credit for the discovery of oxygen with the Swedish chemist Karl Wilhelm Scheele, also invented the fizzy drink. While living in Leeds, England, in the 1770s, he had a brewery for a neighbour – and it provided him with abundant carbon dioxide for his experiments with gases.

In 1772 he published directions for 'impregnating water with fixed air (carbon dioxide), in order to communicate to it the peculiar spirits and virtues of Pyrmont water' – named after a fashionable German mineral spring near Hamelin. Priestley hoped that his carbonated water might be effective against scurvy. It was not, but the fizzy drink caught on.

## ACID TESTS

Litmus – a dye derived from lichen which turns pink if dipped into acid and blue in an alkali – is only one of numerous natural pigments which change colour depending on acidity. Red cabbage, for instance, turns bright red only when vinegar, which contains acetic acid, is added to the water in which it is cooked. If the acidity is removed – by neutralising it with an alkali such as bicarbonate of soda – the red dye in the cabbage turns blue-green.

Flowers are sensitive to acidity, too. Hydrangeas, for example, tend to be pink in alkaline soil and blue in acid soil – the reverse of litmus.

## CLERIC WHO DIDN'T BELIEVE

Oxygen is now known to be essential for all burning. But the English clergyman Joseph Priestley (1733 – 1804), who discovered the gas in 1774, died without ever being convinced of its importance. He preferred the phlogiston theory, which held that burning objects gave off a substance called phlogiston.

The phlogiston theory began to be discredited soon after the discovery of oxygen, when Antoine Lavoisier (1743 – 94) established in the late 1770s that oxygen was present in the atmosphere. Lavoisier, a French chemist, was the first person to explain combustion correctly and was the man who gave oxygen its modern name. Joseph Priestley had called it 'dephlogisticated air'. By establishing the importance of oxygen, Lavoisier paved the way for modern chemistry and is often regarded as its founder. A treatise he published in 1787, *Methods of Chemical Nomenclature*, also pioneered the modern custom of naming chemical compounds after the elements they contain. But he did not live to see the effect of his ideas. Denounced for his work as a government tax collector – one of several posts he held – he was guillotined during the French Revolution at the age of 51.

PARTNERS IN SCIENCE
*Lavoisier's wife worked closely with him on his experiments, taking notes and learning English so that she could keep track of British discoveries.*

LAVOISIER'S LAB *By heating mercury in the retort and seeing that the water level in the bell jar (far right) rose, Lavoisier showed that a burning object absorbed gas (oxygen) from the air. It did not give off anything, as Priestley had believed.*

SOLAR FURNACE *A lens and dish used by Priestley in his study of the process of burning.*

## ASH THAT MAKES FIRE

Catalysts – substances which help chemical reactions to take place, but which are not themselves used up in the process – are used widely in industry and in living organisms. Enzymes, for instance, are natural catalysts which speed up by many thousands of times the ability of an animal's body to digest food.

Cigarette ash can also be a catalyst. If a lighted match is held to a sugar cube (on a dish for safety), the sugar will bubble and char but not burn. If cigarette ash is dropped on the sugar, however, minute traces of elements in the ash act as catalysts, speeding up the reaction and causing the sugar to catch fire.

## FIRST OF THE SYNTHETIC DYES

Mauveine, the first synthetic dye, was discovered by accident by an 18-year-old English research assistant. William Henry Perkin made the dye from coal tar in his home laboratory during a vacation from his job in London in 1856. He had been trying to make an

# THE PERIODIC TABLE

Everything in the Universe, living or non-living, is made up of combinations of a few basic substances: the chemical elements. Each element consists solely of atoms of the same type. Of the 106 known elements, 92 are found in nature. The remaining 14 – known as transuranium elements – have been created by nuclear bombardment in laboratories since 1934. Atoms differ from one another in the number of protons and neutrons in the nucleus, and in the number of electrons surrounding the nucleus. The number of electrons is, however, always equal to the number of protons. The number of protons is known as the element's atomic number. Hydrogen, with just one proton and one electron, is the simplest of all elements and has the atomic number 1. The most complex element in nature, uranium, has the atomic number 92. Its atom contains 92 protons, 92 electrons and usually 146 neutrons.

The Periodic Table, in which the elements are arranged in numerical order in such a way that those with similar properties appear in columns together, was first devised by a Russian chemist, Dmitri Mendeleev (1834–1907), in 1869. A modern table is shown below. Each square

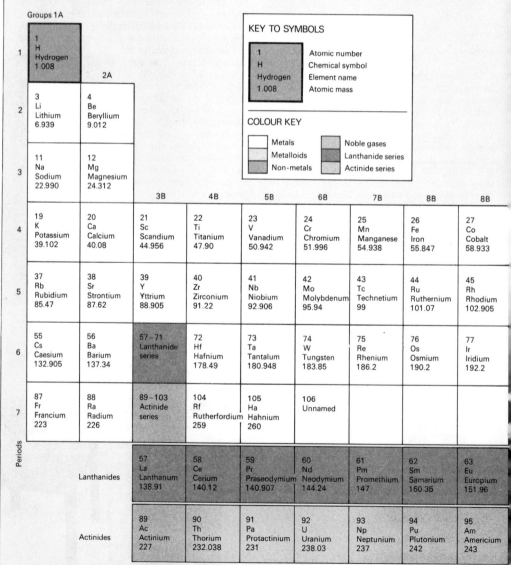

artificial form of quinine, a compound which occurs naturally in cinchona bark and which has been important in the treatment of malaria.

Perkin's discovery was the basis for a new synthetic dye industry which rapidly put out of business growers of natural dyestuffs, such as indigo and root madder. More than 7000 synthetic dyes are now in daily use.

## MAN WHO PREDICTED ELEMENTS

Dmitri Mendeleev, the Russian chemist who published the first Periodic Table of the elements in 1869, deliberately left gaps in the table for three elements which had not yet been discovered, but which he predicted did exist.

So accurate was his table in the way it grouped and arranged the elements according to their atomic structure and chemical properties that Mendeleev was even able to spell out in detail the nature of the missing elements years before they were isolated. Mendeleev's gaps were eventually filled by the elements now known as gallium (discovered in 1875), scandium (1879) and germanium (1886).

represents an element, identified by its atomic number, chemical symbol, name and atomic mass. The atomic mass is not usually a whole number because most elements are a mixture of isotopes – atoms with the same number of protons but different numbers of neutrons – and the figure reflects the isotopes' relative abundance. Uranium, for instance, is a mixture of 15 known isotopes. The three commonest are uranium-238 (which has 146 neutrons), uranium-235 (143 neutrons) and uranium-234 (142 neutrons). All the isotopes of any element share the same chemical properties, but may differ in other ways – such as their degree of radioactivity.

Each column in the table contains elements with similar properties. Group 1A, for example – lithium, sodium and so on – consists of soft metals which react with water to release hydrogen and form alkaline solutions. Moving from left to right across the table, the elements become less metallic, eventually becoming typical non-metals such as carbon, sulphur and chlorine. The two rows shown separately at the foot of the table represent elements which interrupt the sequence and fit in by a different analysis of their atomic structure.

| 8B | 1B | 2B | 3A | 4A | 5A | 6A | 7A | 0 |
|---|---|---|---|---|---|---|---|---|
| | | | | | | | | 2<br>He<br>Helium<br>4.003 |
| | | | 5<br>B<br>Boron<br>10.811 | 6<br>C<br>Carbon<br>12.011 | 7<br>N<br>Nitrogen<br>14.007 | 8<br>O<br>Oxygen<br>15.999 | 9<br>F<br>Fluorine<br>18.998 | 10<br>Ne<br>Neon<br>20.183 |
| | | | 13<br>Al<br>Aluminium<br>26.982 | 14<br>Si<br>Silicon<br>28.086 | 15<br>P<br>Phosphorus<br>30.974 | 16<br>S<br>Sulphur<br>32.064 | 17<br>Cl<br>Chlorine<br>35.453 | 18<br>Ar<br>Argon<br>39.948 |
| 28<br>Ni<br>Nickel<br>58.71 | 29<br>Cu<br>Copper<br>63.54 | 30<br>Zn<br>Zinc<br>65.37 | 31<br>Ga<br>Gallium<br>69.72 | 32<br>Ge<br>Germanium<br>72.59 | 33<br>As<br>Arsenic<br>74.922 | 34<br>Se<br>Selenium<br>78.96 | 35<br>Br<br>Bromine<br>79.909 | 36<br>Kr<br>Krypton<br>83.80 |
| 46<br>Pd<br>Palladium<br>106.4 | 47<br>Ag<br>Silver<br>107.870 | 48<br>Cd<br>Cadmium<br>112.40 | 49<br>In<br>Indium<br>114.82 | 50<br>Sn<br>Tin<br>118.69 | 51<br>Sb<br>Antimony<br>121.75 | 52<br>Te<br>Tellurium<br>127.60 | 53<br>I<br>Iodine<br>126.904 | 54<br>Xe<br>Xenon<br>131.30 |
| 78<br>Pt<br>Platinum<br>195.09 | 79<br>Au<br>Gold<br>196.967 | 80<br>Hg<br>Mercury<br>200.59 | 81<br>Tl<br>Thallium<br>204.37 | 82<br>Pb<br>Lead<br>207.19 | 83<br>Bi<br>Bismuth<br>208.980 | 84<br>Po<br>Polonium<br>209 | 85<br>At<br>Astatine<br>210 | 86<br>Rn<br>Radon<br>222 |
| | | | | | | | | |
| 64<br>Gd<br>Gadolinium<br>157.25 | 65<br>Tb<br>Terbium<br>158.924 | 66<br>Dy<br>Dysprosium<br>162.50 | 67<br>Ho<br>Holmium<br>164.930 | 68<br>Er<br>Erbium<br>167.26 | 69<br>Tm<br>Thulium<br>168.934 | 70<br>Yb<br>Ytterbium<br>173.04 | 71<br>Lu<br>Lutetium<br>174.97 | |
| 96<br>Cm<br>Curium<br>247 | 97<br>Bk<br>Berkelium<br>247 | 98<br>Cf<br>Californium<br>251 | 99<br>Es<br>Einsteinium<br>254 | 100<br>Fm<br>Fermium<br>257 | 101<br>Md<br>Mendelevium<br>256 | 102<br>No<br>Nobelium<br>256 | 103<br>Lw<br>Lawrencium<br>257 | |

# Physics – the science of energy

## THE MAN WHO SHOUTED 'EUREKA'

Little is known for certain about the Greek physicist and mathematician Archimedes except his dates, 287–212 BC, and his home, Syracuse in Sicily. But the extraordinary story of his greatest discovery has survived for more than 2000 years. It was first recorded in a book on architecture published in about 30 BC by the Roman architect and author Vitruvius.

The discovery is said to have resulted from a request by King Hieron II of Syracuse for Archimedes to find out whether a goldsmith had cheated him over a new gold crown. The king suspected that the smith had made the crown out of a mixture of gold and less valuable silver.

Archimedes reasoned that an alloy would be bulkier than the same weight of pure gold, because silver is less dense than gold. But it was difficult to measure the volume of the crown. Inspiration came when he was taking a bath and slopped water over the side as he got into the tub. He realised that anything put into a tub of water would displace exactly its own volume of water. So by comparing the water level before and after he put the crown in, he would have his answer. Elated by his breakthrough, Archimedes is said to have leapt naked from the bath and rushed through the streets of Syracuse, shouting: 'Eureka' (meaning 'I have found it').

Back at home, Archimedes found that the suspect crown did displace more water than a gold block of the same weight – proving that the crown was bulkier, and that the king had indeed been cheated. What happened to the goldsmith after the king heard the news is not recorded.

## CONVERSATIONS WITH A DOG

James Clerk Maxwell (1831–79), the Scottish theoretical physicist who described the existence of electromagnetic waves 20 years before they were discovered, used to hold imaginary scientific conversations with his dog, Tobi. Maxwell said that he often worked out his ideas in this way – even during noisy parties.

Maxwell published his theory that light was merely one form of the much wider spectrum of electromagnetic radiation in 1865. Not until the late 1880s did a German physicist, Heinrich Hertz (1857–94), confirm it by producing the invisible waves which now carry radio transmissions around the world.

## THE BRILLIANT PAUPER

The Heaviside layer – a band in the upper atmosphere which, by acting as a giant radio mirror, allows radio hams around the world to bounce signals to each other – is named after a man who cared little for human contact, or for wealth.

The scientist was Britain's Oliver Heaviside (1850–1925), who spent much of his life as a hermit in Devon. Even at the age of 71, when he had won public recognition for his scientific achievements, he was still so poor that he could not always afford to pay his gas bill. As a result, the gas company cut off his supply, and Heaviside spent 15 months in 1921 and 1922 without any light or heat in his home.

His habits were eccentric, too. He often started work at about 10pm and went through until dawn. And he would startle his few visitors by dressing bizarrely. Once – after Heaviside had accidentally burnt his face

with a gas flame – a visitor recalled: 'We found him with a large blanket over his head, held in place by a rope tied round his neck. He peered at us with one eye through a chink in the drapery.'

Despite his unorthodox lifestyle, Heaviside is now widely recognised as a scientific thinker who was far ahead of his time. He described the existence of the Heaviside layer in 1902, 22 years before its presence was verified. And in 1912, when the electron and the nucleus were the only known components of the atom, Heaviside wrote: 'As the universe is boundless one way towards the great, so it is equally boundless the other way towards the small. From the atom to the electron is a great step. But it is not finality.'

Scientists have since discovered more than 100 sub-atomic particles, and the hunt for still smaller particles, known as quarks, continues even today.

## EDISON'S BLACK MARKS

Thomas Alva Edison, the American who invented the forerunner of the record player, the first practical electric light, the microphone and 'talkie' cinema films, had only three months of formal schooling in his life – in 1855 when he was just eight years old. And even that ended with him running away after a teacher said that his brain was 'addled'.

Edison recalled later of his time at the Michigan school run by a strap-swinging clergyman, the Reverend G. B. Engle: 'I used never to be able to get along. I used to feel that the teachers did not sympathise with me and that my father thought I was stupid.'

Despite the rebuff, Edison went on to become one of the greatest practical scientists in history. By the time he died in 1931, he held almost 1300 patents: about one patent for every three weeks of his life.

## ELECTRICAL HAT-TRICK

The dynamo, the transformer and the direct-current motor now used to drive battery-powered machines were all invented in a single year by one man. The year was 1831 and the man a 39-year-old British scientist, Michael Faraday (1791–1867).

## AMPERE'S OVERSIGHTS

André Ampère, the French physicist after whom the unit of electrical current (the ampere or amp) is named, had observed the voltage-altering effect now used in modern transformers in 1821 – ten years before Michael Faraday demonstrated it. But he had dismissed the effect as unimportant, and ignored it.

Ampère (1775–1836) also overlooked another chance, in 1832: the chance to develop a modern electrical generator. Faraday demonstrated the principle, in the form of a dynamo, in 1831 and a year later a Frenchman named Hippolyte Pixii built an improved model. Like Faraday's dynamo, Pixii's machine generated 'alternating' current – a current in which the positive and negative terminals are constantly reversed.

Pixii took his device to Ampère, who declared at once that people would not want current that flowed

TUG OF AIR *In the Magdeburg hemisphere experiment in 1657, German physicist Otto von Guericke (1602–86) pitted horses against a vacuum created by pumping air from between two fitted copper hemispheres. It took 16 horses to separate them.*

# NEWTON'S LAWS OF MOTION

The three laws of motion devised by English physicist Sir Isaac Newton (1642–1727) explain the basic principles which govern the movements of all objects, on the Earth and in space. First published in 1687, they opened the way for the inventions and calculations that, nearly three centuries later, took man to the Moon.

The laws are:

1. A body continues in a state of rest, or of motion at constant speed in a straight line, except when this state is changed by forces acting on it.
2. Force is equal to mass multiplied by acceleration. (In other words, a given force on a given mass will produce a given acceleration. On twice the mass, it will produce half the acceleration. If the force on a given mass is doubled, however, the acceleration will double too.)
3. To every action, there is an equal and opposite reaction.

# THE FOUR LAWS OF THERMODYNAMICS

The classical laws of thermodynamics, which deal with the ways in which energy such as heat can be passed from one body of matter to another, were devised by several scientists during the late 19th and early 20th centuries.

The final law to be worked out was given the name of the zeroth law (bearing the number zero) because, although it was added as an afterthought, it belongs logically in front of the other three, which had by then already been given numbers. The four laws can be summarised as:

0. No heat will flow between any two bodies that are at the same temperature (regardless of what the bodies are made of).
1. Energy can neither be created nor destroyed. So a body can gain or lose heat (or any other form of energy) only by taking it from or passing it to its environment (or to another body).
2. Heat will not pass spontaneously from a cold body to a hotter one.
3. It is impossible to cool a body right down to the temperature of absolute zero ($-273.16°C$), the lowest possible temperature in the Universe, because to do so would require the presence of a still colder body.

All four laws are connected with the idea known as entropy, which is a measure of how much useful work can be extracted from a given system. Energy can be extracted from a system only by increasing its degree of entropy.

A hot-water bottle, for instance, filled with boiling water and placed in a cold bed, passes heat to the bed, losing its own heat in the process. But once bottle and bed are at the same lukewarm temperature, no more useful work can be extracted from the bottle. The dissipated heat cannot be recaptured.

Since the same principle is at work in the Universe as a whole, scientists believe that the energy the Universe contains will also, eventually, be dissipated evenly and irrecoverably throughout space. This stage of maximum and universal entropy is known as the 'heat death' of the Universe.

---

first in one direction and then the other. Instead, he showed Pixii how to make a 'commutator' – a switch which would convert the device's output to direct current, the kind delivered by batteries.

Pixii accepted Ampère's advice and for 50 years little use was made of alternating current. But Ampère turned out to be wrong. Mains electricity around the world is now supplied in the form of alternating current – all generated by machines descended from Pixii's and Faraday's originals.

## HOW BRUSHES GOT THE BRUSH-OFF

The 'commutator' devised by André Ampère to convert alternating current to direct current had a major drawback: brushes. In order to cancel out the constantly reversing current generated by a dynamo, electrical contacts had to rub, or 'brush', against the spinning core, just as they do in the traditional generator which recharges the direct-current battery in a car. The constant rubbing meant that the contacts wore out quickly and had to be replaced. Similarly, motors which were powered by direct current had to be fitted with brushes.

The man who eventually discovered how to do away with the inefficient brushes was Nikola Tesla (1856–1943). Tesla was born in Croatia (now part of Yugoslavia) but emigrated to the USA in 1884 and became a US citizen.

A compulsive worker, Tesla never married and refused to have friends because they kept him from his studies. In the early part of his life, rather than accept the distractions of a regular job, he would dig roads from time to time to earn money, then retreat to his laboratory once more to continue his hunt for a brushless motor. Finally, in 1888, he made the breakthrough he wanted, with an alternating-current motor that he declared would 'dominate the world of electric drives'.

It did. About 95 per cent of the power of all the world's electric motors – from washing machines and kitchen mixers to giant industrial motors – now run on the lines of Tesla's design. Tesla patented his design in 1888 and later sold the rights to the US Westinghouse company for US$1 million. But he ploughed the money back into his work and by the mid-1890s none of it was left.

## NAME OF FEAR

A 20th-century German physicist had a morbid fear of a name – the name, ironically, of one of the world's greatest physicists, Sir Isaac Newton. The German, Professor Philipp Lenard (1862–1947), was born more than a century after the British scientist died. Yet he could not stand to speak Newton's name, or even to see or hear it. In lectures at the universities of Heidelberg and Kiel, where he worked, Lenard would turn his back if Newton's name had to be mentioned. A student would then write it on the blackboard and it would have to be rubbed out again before Lenard could continue. Lenard's phobia was linked with a passionate dislike of Britain in general and of British scientists in particular. In one of his books, published in 1914, he accused all British scientists of plagiarising the successes of German physicists.

Lenard himself became a pioneering researcher in the study of cathode rays and the structure of the atom. And in 1905 he won the Nobel prize for physics.

# Nuclear physics

## ACCIDENTAL DISCOVERY

Uranium's radioactive properties were discovered accidentally, not by design. In 1896, inspired by the discovery of X-rays, the French scientist Henri Becquerel, an expert on fluorescence – the ability of some substances to give off visible rays – was trying to discover whether other substances gave off invisible rays (radiation) after exposure to sunlight. In the course of these researches, Becquerel left a sample of pitchblende, a mineral containing uranium, in a drawer on top of an envelope containing an unexposed photographic plate. When he developed this plate, it was fogged. Becquerel quickly realised that radiation from the mineral was responsible for this and hence that the substance was 'radioactive'.

## DAWNING OF THE ATOM AGE

**1896** French physicist Henri Becquerel (1852–1908) discovers radioactivity.

**1897** Physicists Pierre and Marie Curie (1859–1906 and 1867–1934) discover radium.

**1897** British physicist Sir Joseph Thomson (1856–1940) discovers the electron.

**1905** Swiss-German physicist and mathematician Albert Einstein (1879–1955) publishes his Special Theory of Relativity, showing that mass can be converted to energy.

**1911** New Zealand physicist Ernest, Lord Rutherford (1871–1937) discovers the atomic nucleus.

**1913** Danish physicist Niels Bohr (1885–1962) describes the structure of the atom.

**1919** Rutherford splits the atom, by bombarding a nitrogen nucleus with alpha particles.

**1932** American chemist Harold Urey (1893–1981) discovers heavy hydrogen (deuterium).

**1932** English physicist Sir James Chadwick (1891–1974) discovers the neutron.

**1932** US physicist Carl Anderson (1905– ) discovers the positron, an electron with a positive charge.

**1932** Britain's Sir John Cockcroft (1897–1967) and Ireland's Ernest Walton (1903– ) split lithium artificially into two alpha particles with a particle accelerator.

**1938** Austria's Lise Meitner (1878–1968), Germany's Otto Hahn (1879–1968) and Fritz Strassmann (1902– ) discover nuclear fission.

**1940** Austrian-born Otto Frisch (1904– ) and German-born Rudolf Peierls (1907– ) calculate critical mass of uranium-235, and write memorandum for British government about a 'super-bomb' – the atom bomb.

**1941** US chemist Glenn Seaborg (1912– ) isolates plutonium – the key element in a nuclear bomb.

**1942** Italian-born physicist Enrico Fermi (1901–54) builds the first nuclear reactor in Chicago.

**1945** First nuclear explosion, at Alamogordo, USA.

**1946** US bomb tests at Bikini atoll in South Pacific.

**1949** First Soviet nuclear test.

**1951** First nuclear electricity generated from Experimental Breeder Reactor in Idaho, USA.

**1952** First British nuclear test in the Monte Bello Islands off the northwest coast of Australia.

**1953** Foundation of the European Centre for Nuclear Research (CERN) near Geneva.

**1956** Start-up of Calder Hall in Britain, the world's first commercial-scale nuclear power station.

**1960** First French nuclear bomb test in the Algerian desert.

**1964** First Chinese nuclear bomb test near Lop Nor, Xinjiang (Sinkiang).

**1964** Discovery of the omega-minus elementary particle, predicted by theory, at Brookhaven, USA.

**1974** First Indian nuclear explosion near Pokharan, in the Rajasthan desert.

**1983** Discovery of the W elementary particle, predicted by theory, at the European Centre for Nuclear Research in Switzerland.

CHICAGO PILE *A contemporary sketch of the world's first nuclear reactor. Built in a squash court beneath a Chicago football stadium, it ran for a few minutes on December 2, 1942 – and proved that nuclear power was feasible.*

## SAVED BY A DRAUGHT

The life of the Polish physicist and Nobel prizewinner Marie Curie (1867–1934) was probably saved by the draughty conditions in the loft in Paris where she was struggling with her French husband, Pierre, to isolate the element radium. The draughts prevented her from inhaling lethal quantities of radioactive dust.

The mysterious element was successfully isolated in 1898, together with polonium, which Marie named after her native Poland. She continued to investigate the properties of radioactive materials until she died in 1934 – of leukaemia caused by the radiation from the elements she was studying. Pierre died in 1906 in a traffic accident, run over by a cart in a Paris street.

## BREAKING DOWN THE ATOM

The New Zealand-born physicist Ernest Rutherford (1871–1937) was the first man to show that the atom was not the smallest unit of matter. He proved this by building a simple instrument in his laboratory in Manchester, England, in the early 1900s which allowed him to observe the flashes produced by what he termed alpha particles – one form of the radiation produced by radioactive decay.

By counting the flashes, Rutherford found that the particles could be deflected almost straight backwards by a thin gold sheet in their path. This was almost as surprising to him as a bullet bouncing back from a piece of tissue paper would be to a soldier.

In 1911, Rutherford concluded that all atoms must have a central positively charged nucleus. It was these nuclei that were massive enough to repel the positively charged alpha particles hitting the gold sheet, just as two like magnetic poles will repel each other. The nucleus, he also concluded, was surrounded by negatively charged electrons, circling the nucleus in the way that planets orbit the Sun. Before this, scientists had seen the atom as a soft plum pudding, with the electrons scattered through it like raisins.

## INFINITE SPACE

An atom is almost entirely empty space, since more than 99.9 per cent of its mass is contained in its infinitesimal core – the nucleus. The word nucleus itself comes from a Latin word meaning 'little nut'. If an atom were the size of a football, its nucleus would still be invisible to the naked eye. If the nucleus were magnified to the size of a tennis ball, its nearest electron would be nearly 1km (half a mile) away.

## RADIATION BLOCKS

Radioactive elements decay in different ways, giving off particles or combinations of particles with very different properties. Some elements emit alpha particles, each particle containing two protons and two neutrons. Some give off beta particles – fast-moving electrons with either a negative or a positive electrical charge. Some emit gamma radiation – high-energy versions of X-rays – or neutrons. Still others give off neutrinos – particles which have no electrical charge and virtually no mass.

The material required to block any of these types of radiation varies hugely. A sheet of paper is enough to stop an alpha particle. A sheet of tinfoil will stop beta particles. Gamma rays and neutrons, however, can penetrate more than 2m (7ft) of concrete. And neutrinos can pass right through the Earth easily.

## HARNESSING THE ATOM

Nuclear energy is the most concentrated source of energy known to man. If all the energy in a single kilogram of uranium-235 – a lump the size of a tennis

ATOM TRACKS *Like the vapour trails of jets, white lines of water droplets mark the paths of unseen atomic particles in a laboratory cloud chamber. These tracks, photographed in 1932, record the splitting of nitrogen nuclei – the first splitting of the atom – by physicist Ernest Rutherford.*

DEATH CLOUD *A vast mushroom cloud rises over the Japanese city of Nagasaki. The atomic blast, pictured here within seconds of the detonation on August 9, 1945, killed or wounded about 75,000 people and levelled a third of the city. Yet by modern standards, the bomb was small: 20 kilotons, or one-fiftieth of a megaton.*

235

ball – could be released in a chain reaction, it would give off as much heat as a million one-bar electric fires operating continuously for more than 2500 years.

A grapefruit-sized piece of plutonium – which is made from uranium-238 – is enough to make an atomic bomb as powerful as the plutonium bomb which levelled the Japanese city of Nagasaki in 1945.

Yet, contrary to popular belief, a nuclear reactor cannot explode. In a bomb, the chain reaction is deliberately designed to get out of control and so its energy is released in a tiny fraction of a second, with devastating effect. In a reactor, the fuel is not concentrated enough to produce such an explosive chain reaction, even if all the safety controls fail.

In addition, if the fuel becomes overheated, it expands, making the chain reaction less efficient and effectively acting as an automatic regulator. Though the heat may damage the nuclear reactor and radioactive material may escape as a result, it cannot trigger an atomic explosion.

## THE WORLD'S MOST EXPENSIVE WATER
The so-called heavy water, used in many nuclear reactors to slow down fast neutrons and make chain reactions more effective, is the world's most expensive water. It costs more than £200 per litre (£900 per gallon) to produce. The main differences between it and ordinary water are that it is about 10 per cent denser and is poisonous.

The variation in density stems from a difference in the hydrogen both types of water contain. The nucleus of ordinary hydrogen contains just one proton. One atom of hydrogen in every 5000, however, also has a neutron in its nucleus, making it twice as massive. This type is called 'heavy hydrogen' or deuterium. It is expensive because it has to be separated out from ordinary water by a laborious process of repeated extractions and purification.

## NOW YOU SEE IT . . .
It is impossible to record the movement of nuclear particles accurately. Whenever a scientist tries to observe a nuclear particle, he or she is always one step behind what the particle is actually doing.

Everyday objects are visible because light beams bounce off them into the observer's eye. The objects remain unaffected. Nuclear particles, however, are so small that a ray of light is enough to knock them off course or out of position. This means that though a scientist can 'see' where a particle was at the moment the ray hit it, he has no way of knowing where it is afterwards, or how it is moving.

The difficulty was summed up in 1927 by the German physicist Werner Karl Heisenberg (1901–76). Heisenberg's Uncertainty Principle asserts that it is impossible to know simultaneously where a particle is and how it is moving. The more accurately its position is measured, the less accurately its momentum can be known, and vice versa.

## NUCLEAR COURT
A disused squash court under Stagg Field football stadium at the University of Chicago was chosen as the site of the world's first man-made nuclear reactor in 1942. The reason was security. It was thought that the reactor would attract less attention there than in a new building. The reactor itself was built by a team of scientists under the Italian physicist Enrico Fermi (1901–54). It was operated only for a few minutes to show that a nuclear chain reaction was possible.

'Chicago Pile No. 1', as it came to be called, consisted of a honeycomb of 57 layers of machined graphite bricks. The bricks were drilled with

holes – 22,000 in all – into which balls of uranium metal and compressed uranium oxide were inserted. The total amounts involved were approximately 36 tonnes of uranium and more than 340 tonnes of graphite. Because of the all-pervading graphite dust during construction, the pile was built inside an airtight square balloon, which was deflated only when the pile was completed.

The pile started up on December 2, 1942. The process was relatively simple. Control rods made of cadmium, a neutron-absorbing material, were slowly withdrawn, until there were enough free neutrons for the chain reaction to become self-sustaining.

## SCRAM FOR SAFETY
The main emergency safety device in Chicago Pile No.1 was a shutdown control rod hanging from a rope – and a scientist with an axe. If the chain reaction looked like becoming uncontrollable, the scientist was supposed to chop through the rope and let the cadmium control rod drop into the pile. Ever since, the emergency shutdown of a reactor has been called a 'scram', standing for 'Safety Control Rod Axe Man'.

## THE MULTI-MEGATON BLAST
The most powerful man-made explosion ever detonated was a 58-megaton hydrogen bomb test set off in the atmosphere at the Soviet test site on the Arctic island of Novaya Zemlya in October 1961. The explosion was the equivalent of 59 million tonnes (58 million tons) of TNT – nearly 3000 times more powerful than the atomic bomb which devastated the Japanese city of Hiroshima in August 1945.

## THE STRAIGHTEST LINE
The Stanford linear accelerator in the United States, which came into operation in May 1966, boosts electrons along a 3km (2 mile) track so straight that its supports are of different heights to compensate for the curvature of the Earth.

The accelerator is capable of boosting electrons to more than 99.9 per cent of the speed of light.

## RADIOACTIVE PEOPLE
Every human is naturally radioactive. This is because potassium, an essential constituent of body tissues and fluids, contains a tiny amount of the radioactive isotope potassium-40. Our bodies also contain radioactive carbon-14, which is produced in the atmosphere by the action of cosmic rays and absorbed by living organisms.

## NATURAL REACTOR
The world's longest recorded nuclear chain reaction – successive splitting of uranium nuclei, as in a nuclear reactor – started spontaneously in Oklo, in the African country of Gabon, some 1800 million years ago and continued for at least 100,000 years. The reaction occurred because of the concentrated uranium deposits there.

Evidence of its existence came to light in 1972. French scientists noticed that the concentration of the fissile isotope uranium-235 in ore from the Oklo mine was as low as 0.29 per cent, compared with 0.72 per cent in natural uranium – suggesting that the uranium's natural rate of decay into other isotopes and other elements had been speeded up by a spontaneous nuclear reaction.

Such a chain reaction would be impossible today because the ever-decreasing concentration of uranium-235 in natural ores is too low. A percentage of at least 1 per cent is necessary to trigger a spontaneous reaction.

# Weapons and warfare

## GREEK FIRE

The first people to use a form of napalm – the highly inflammable petroleum jelly used in flamethrowers and bombs – were the Byzantine Greeks. The chief ingredient of 'Greek fire', a naphtha compound called naphthenate palmitate, is also the main constituent of napalm, which takes its name from the compound (*naphthenate palm*itate).

Greek fire was used in two ways: as a missile hurled from a catapult, or as a flamethrower. It burned spontaneously when it came in contact with water and so was a favourite weapon on Byzantine war vessels. Greek fire may have changed the course of history. Thanks to the fireballs, the Byzantine rulers of Constantinople (present-day Istanbul) were able in AD 716 – 18 to destroy the wooden fleets of Muslim Arabs who were besieging the city – and so blocked the spread of Islam into eastern Europe.

The exact formula for making Greek fire was a closely guarded secret which has not survived. But it probably involved various combinations of naphtha, sulphur, petroleum, bitumen, turpentine, charcoal, quicklime and saltpetre.

## TAKE SEVEN PARTS OF SALTPETRE . . .

The first European recipe for gunpowder – seven parts of saltpetre to five parts of charcoal and five parts of sulphur – is attributed to the 13th-century English monk and scientist Roger Bacon. No one knows who invented the explosive, although the Chinese were using it in the 10th century for signals and fireworks.

## ARROWS TO ATOMS: THE HISTORY OF WEAPONS

**BC**
**500,000** Sharpened poles, the first spears, used in Europe.

**250,000** Stones shaped into axes in Africa, Asia and Europe.

**45,000** Spears with stone heads used in Europe.

**30,000** Bow and arrow invented in Africa.

**3000** First metal swords and shields (bronze) made in Mesopotamia and southeastern Europe. War chariot, the first fighting vehicle, invented.

**2000** First known armour, of bronze scales, made in Mesopotamia.

**About 700** Galleys – warships powered by oars – invented by Phoenicians and Egyptians.

**500** Catapults and giant crossbows used by Greeks and Carthaginians.

**By 200** Hand-held crossbow in use in China.

**AD**
**300** Stirrups used in China.

**950** Gunpowder used by Chinese for fireworks and signalling devices.

**1250–1300** Bronze and iron cannon probably used by Chinese; first European record of cannon dates from 1326.

**1495** First known muzzle-loading rifles made for Holy Roman emperor, Maximilian I.

**1585** Floating mines used by the Dutch at siege of Antwerp.

**By 1650** Bayonets first used in Europe by French.

**1800** Submarine, *Nautilus*, demonstrated by American inventor Robert Fulton.

**1833** Breech-loading bolt-action rifle designed by Prussian inventor Johann Dreyse.

**1849** Aerial bombs dropped from unmanned balloons by Austrian army on Venice.

**1860** HMS *Warrior*, first ironclad warship, launched in England.

**1862** Hand-cranked, multi-barrelled Gatling gun, invented by Richard Gatling, an American. A five-barrelled model could fire 700 rounds a minute.

**1867** Dynamite invented by Swedish chemist Alfred Nobel.

**1875** Gelignite invented by Alfred Nobel.

**1884** Fully automatic machine gun invented by American-English engineer Hiram Maxim.

**1906** HMS *Dreadnought*, first steel-armoured, turbine-propelled battleship, launched at Portsmouth, England.

**1911** Aerial bombs – cans of nitroglycerine – dropped by Italians from aeroplanes on Ain Zara, Libya.

**1915** Fighter aircraft – wooden-framed biplanes – used by Germany and Britain. First modern flamethrowers used by German army.

**1916** First tanks built in England and used in action on the Somme in northern France.

**1939** First turbojet, the Heinkel He178, tested in Germany.

**1942** First jet fighter, Messerschmitt Me262, flown.

**1942** V-1 flying bomb launched in Germany.

**1944** Germany's V-2 (A-4) rocket first used against newly liberated Paris.

**1945** First atomic bomb – a 20-kiloton device – dropped by USA on Hiroshima, Japan.

**1952** First hydrogen bomb – a 10-megaton device – detonated by USA in West Pacific Ocean.

**1957** First intercontinental ballistic missile (ICBM), the *SS-6 (Sapwood)*, launched by Russia. The missile, which had a range of 9600km (6000 miles), was used to launch the first Sputnik.

**1969** First Harrier vertical take-off 'jump jets' enter service with Britain's Royal Air Force.

**1970** Exocet ship-to-ship missile developed in France.

**1977** Neutron bomb, which kills people but leaves buildings intact, developed in USA.

**1983** First Trident missiles installed in USA; ground-launched cruise missiles installed in Europe.

**1984** Anti-satellite missile developed in USA.

AXEMAN *Most medieval soldiers, like this barefoot Englishman of about 1300, were crudely armed.*

By 1300 the Arabs were propelling arrows from guns by means of it. And in 1326 the Council of Florence in Italy made the earliest known European reference to guns and gunpowder in a document ordering a consignment of iron bullets.

## TWENTY-NINE-YEAR SIEGE

The longest siege known in history is one recorded by the 5th-century BC Greek historian, Herodotus. Towards the end of the 7th century BC the Egyptians kept up an assault on the town of Azotus (now Ashdod), in Israel, for 29 years before it surrendered.

## THE CASTLE THAT SETTLED A DEBT

In 1365 France's Duke of Burgundy paid for the loan of some cannon – with a castle. The duke had borrowed the cannon from the town of Chartres to use in his assault on the nearby castle of Camrolles. The cannon soon destroyed the castle walls – and the fall of Camrolles marked the end of traditional medieval fortifications. The duke then presented the battered castle to the townspeople of Chartres to discharge his debt to them.

The first documented use of cannon in Europe took place 19 years earlier when in 1346 Edward III of England defeated the French at the Battle of Crécy, in northwest France. But his victory had less to do with the new weapon than with the superiority of the English longbowmen.

## CANNONS CAST ON THE SPOT

For a thousand years the triple walls of Constantinople presented an impregnable defence against invaders. Each wall was some 9m (30ft) high and about 5m (16ft) thick. But in 1453, in the space of just 55 days, the Turks captured the Byzantine city with the use of some 70 pieces of artillery. Twelve of the bronze cannon used weighed 19 tonnes each. They were cast on the spot and pulled into position by a team of 140 oxen and 200 men. Each piece was 5m (16ft) long, with a 650mm (26in) calibre and could fire a 360kg (800lb) shot 1.6km (1 mile). The maximum rate of fire, however, was extremely slow: a mere seven rounds a day.

None of the original Constantinople cannon survives. But an identical example, cast in the Dardanelles 12 years later and last used in 1807 – when it holed the British frigate *Active*, though it did not sink her – is kept in the Tower of London.

## EXPLOSIVES FOR PEACE

Alfred Nobel, the Swedish chemist and inventor of dynamite (1867) and gelignite (1875), believed that his explosives would bring peace to the world. An ardent pacifist – and founder of the Nobel Peace Prize – he thought his inventions would form the basis of strong national defence systems and so act as deterrents against warlike countries.

## BAREFOOT IN THE STIRRUP

The introduction of the metal stirrup in Europe in the late 8th century or early 9th century AD revolutionised the nature of warfare. Together with the saddle, known in Europe since the 4th century BC, the stirrup gave horsemen greater stability, and allowed them to use their spears underarm, so that they could put their whole weight behind a thrust without getting pushed off the horse. Before, cavalrymen had been limited to a weaker overarm stabbing technique.

The stirrup was first used by barefooted Hindu warriors in the late 2nd century BC. It took the form of a loop which fitted around the rider's big toe. In the 4th century AD it was adapted by the Chinese, who fitted it around a booted foot, the form in which it appears today. Military historians have compared the impact on warfare of the stirrup with that of the tank.

## SEEING IN THE DARK

A regular diet of carrots so improved the eyesight of Britain's night-fighter pilots in the Second World War that they were able to sight and shoot down bomber after German bomber. That, at least, was the story put out by the British Air Ministry – and the one which was widely believed by German intelligence. There is a grain of truth in it. Carrots do contain a substance called carotene, which is converted by the body into vitamin A. And vitamin A, in turn, aids the formation of visual purple, a pigment in the eyes which is essential for good vision in poor light. But other foods, including milk, butter and green vegetables, also contain vitamin A. So extra carrots make no difference to anyone who already has a balanced diet. The wartime story, however, served to cover the truth about why British fighter pilots were so successful.

The real reason for their success was the chain of radar masts along the south and east coasts of England. The 106m (350ft) high masts could detect a German bomber up to 160km (100 miles) away, giving the Royal Air Force plenty of time to get its night-fighters into the air and onto the attack.

Ironically, radar had first been successfully demonstrated in 1934 by Rudolf Kuhnold, head of the German Navy's Signal Research Division. But five years later, at the outbreak of the war, Germany still had not produced an effective radar system – and Britain had.

## HEAVYWEIGHT, LIGHTWEIGHT

A modern fighter pilot wears more layers of clothing than a medieval knight. A knight, whose suit of armour weighed about 27kg (60lb), usually wore two layers of clothing underneath it: a shirt and leggings, and a padded doublet. But a fighter pilot may wear as many as five layers: a heavy-duty cotton or nylon one-piece flying suit, on top of an inflatable rubber G-suit, on top of a fleece-lined jump suit, on top of cotton combination underwear. Over all that may come a rubber 'total immersion suit', with watertight seals at neck, wrists and ankles.

Despite the extra layers, the pilot's clothing is less than half the weight of the medieval knight's. Its total weight, including flying helmet and boots, is only about 12kg (26lb).

## NAZI STRONGHOLD THAT NEVER WAS

In the closing weeks of the Second World War the Allied drive to Berlin was interrupted by a piece of startling news, put out by Joseph Goebbels, the German propaganda minister: that the Nazis had built a huge 'National Redoubt' on the Alpine border of Austria and Bavaria. The report was a hoax. But as intelligence chiefs warned in March 1945 when the news was passed to General Dwight Eisenhower, the Allied supreme commander, details of the fortress, if true, were too alarming not to be taken seriously.

Under Hitler's personal command, so the story went, armaments were being manufactured in bomb-proof factories, food and equipment stored in vast caverns, and a whole underground army trained to liberate Germany from the occupying forces. As a result of the hoax, some Allied divisions were diverted to a wasteful advance on the non-existent Redoubt, slowing the Berlin offensive and contributing to the fact that Soviet troops were the first to enter the German capital.

'Not until after the campaign ended,' wrote Allied

commander General Omar Bradley later, 'were we to learn that this Redoubt existed largely in the imagination of a few fanatical Nazis . . . I am astonished that we believed it as innocently as we did. But while it persisted, this legend of the Redoubt was too ominous a threat to ignore.'

## THE FOUR-PLANE ARMADA

In the mid-1950s, the USA spent millions of dollars building a force of high-altitude supersonic interceptor fighters – to counter a threat that did not exist. The mistake arose when American observers at Moscow's annual May Day military parade in 1954 saw what they thought was a huge fleet of long-range nuclear bombers flying over Red Square.

The Russians did have the bombers – a type known as MYA-4 Bisons – but there was no massed fleet. Instead the same four Bisons simply roared over the square, then circled out of sight and reappeared in a new formation over and over again.

As a result of the deception, the Americans wrongly assumed that the Russians did not possess nuclear missile delivery systems, and that they were concentrating their nuclear weaponry instead on manned bombers. The Russian propaganda ploy was not uncovered for more than three years. Then American U-2 spyplanes revealed in the late 1950s that the real Russian nuclear strength lay in missiles, triggering the development in the West of the Polaris and Minuteman missile systems.

## SCALPING: THE WHITE MAN'S CUSTOM

The Red Indians of North America did not invent scalping. Indeed, some historians believe that the custom was actually introduced by the white man. Cutting off all or part of the scalp of an enemy as proof of victory was first recorded by the ancient Greek historian Herodotus. Writing in the 5th century BC, he attributed the custom to the Scythians – a warlike people of southern Russia.

The custom may have been practised by a few eastern Indian tribes in North America before the arrival of Europeans, though not all historians accept even this. What is certain, however, is that the practice was spread west across the continent by the colonial governments of France and Britain. Officials of both governments encouraged their settlers to kill others by offering a cash reward – a bounty – for each death. The only 'proof' required was a scalp. By the early 18th century, in what is now the USA and Canada, the French were paying for British scalps, the British were paying for French scalps, and each was paying for scalps of the other's Indian allies.

Scalps were usually cut from the dead. But prisoners could be scalped alive and then killed. And sometimes victims, once they had been scalped, were allowed to return home alive as a dreadful warning or challenge to their fellows.

## FINAL CHARGE

The last full-scale cavalry charge took place during the Second World War. In November 1941, a division of Mongolian cavalry thundered across no-man's-land towards a German infantry division dug in near Muscino, a village not far from the Russian capital of Moscow. The attack was a disaster. About 2000 Russians died in the charge – and not a single German.

## INTERNATIONAL BOOMERANG

The boomerang – the V-shaped, hardwood weapon and missile – is not exclusive to Australian Aborigines, who can kill game up to 150m (500ft) away with it. Forms of boomerang were also used by the Hopi Indians of Arizona, by various northeast African tribes and by hunters in ancient Egypt.

SHARP SHOOTER *Four British Rapier anti-aircraft missiles jut menacingly from their battlefield launcher. Since the first flying bombs were developed by Germany during the Second World War, guided missiles have become progressively more sophisticated. In 1984, the USA announced that it had developed an anti-satellite missile which could intercept and destroy targets in space.*

# Mathematics – the numbers game

## EDWARD'S ACRE

Before the reign of England's Edward I, an acre was the amount of land a yoke of oxen could plough in a day; the word comes from the Latin *ager*, meaning 'field'. But since the performance of oxen could vary widely, Edward fixed the acre at an area 40 rods long by 4 rods wide – each rod being 16.5ft (5m) long – and the measurement has survived unchanged.

## FIRST FOOT

As the term implies, a foot was originally the length of a man's foot from heel to big toe. The Romans divided it into 12 *unciae* – the word from which are derived both the inch and the ounce (because the ounce was once a twelfth of a pound). The 12-inch foot was not universally accepted, though. In the 17th century, the Dutch foot was divided into only 11 inches.

The English king, Henry I, established the yard early in the 12th century as the distance from the tip of his nose to the tip of his outstretched thumb. Edward I redefined it as 3 feet (0.9m) in 1305.

## POWER OF SUGGESTION

On the face of it, an attempt to predict someone else's choice of a number between 5 and 10 would be wrong five times out of six. But it is possible to improve the odds. Write the number 7 on a piece of paper and conceal it. Then ask someone to answer rapidly the following questions: 'Five times five? Six times six? Name a colour? Name a number between 5 and 10?' Answering the final question, most people will come up with 7, the number you wrote down. Why the trick works is not clear. It may be that the mind is drawn unconsciously to numbers in the centre of a given range, and that the first two questions help to create a mental sequence: 5,6 . . . 7. The request for a colour merely diverts the subject's attention away from numbers so that he does not spot, and therefore avoid, the next number in the sequence.

## NOAH'S MARK

The cubit, the unit that Noah used to build his ark, was – like most early measures – based on the human body. It was the length from the elbow (*cubitum* is the Latin word for 'elbow') to the tip of the middle finger. Its precise length varied. The Egyptians made it equal to about 530mm (21in); in Biblical times, it was closer to 560mm (22in); but by the time of the Roman empire, it had shrunk to about 460mm (18in).

## FROM FURROW TO FURLONG

The word now largely used only on a racecourse has its origin in the plodding of oxen. The furlong comes from the phrase a 'furrow long', meaning the length of a furrow in a standard square field of 10 acres. By the 9th century, it was regarded as the equivalent of a Roman *stadium* – a unit which was one-eighth of a Roman mile – and so came to be defined as one-eighth of a statute mile, or 220yds (201m).

## MILES AND MILES

The Romans were the first to invent the mile. For them, it meant a thousand paces (*mille* being the Latin for 'one thousand'), in which each pace was two steps or 5ft (1.5m) long – making a total of 5000ft (1524m). In medieval times the furlong was the main unit of length in common use, and so the length of the mile was adjusted to make it equal to 8 furlongs: 1760yds or 5280ft (1.6km). The new length was fixed in England by Act of Parliament in the 16th century – creating the statute mile

The nautical mile – still used by ships and planes – is a much later unit, invented so as to make it easier for navigators to work out from their position how far they have travelled, or vice versa. Each nautical mile along the Equator – 6082.66ft (1853.99m) – represents one-sixtieth of a degree of longitude. So a ship that sails 300 nautical miles along the Equator in a day will be exactly 5 degrees away from her previous position. However, because the Earth is not a perfect

---

# HOW NUMBERS DEVELOPED

The numeral system that is almost universal today was probably invented by the Hindus. It simplified calculations by making the value of a number depend on its position as well as the number itself. In the number 444, the single figure 4 represents 400, 40 and 4, and the whole number is the sum of these values. By contrast, the Romans used symbols whose values were the same whatever their position.

Systems of the modern kind, known as place-value systems, can be based on numbers other than ten. The Babylonians based their system on 60. Modern computers use the binary system, based on 2.

The Hindu system, which included a zero, was adopted by the Arabs and may have reached Europe as early as the 10th century, though it took some time to replace Roman numerals. The man credited with popularising Arab notation is the Italian mathematician Leonardo Fibonacci (about 1170–1240), who advocated its use in his *Book of the Abacus*, published in 1202.

The decimal point is thought to have been a European invention. Its original inventor is not known, but its use was first popularised by a Flemish mathematician named Simon Stevin (1548–1620) in a book called *De Thiende* (*The Tenth*), published in 1585. Until the development of decimals, numbers smaller than 1 had had to be expressed as fractions.

| | 1 | 2 | 3 | 4 | 5 | 6 | 7 | 8 | 9 | 10 | 0 |
|---|---|---|---|---|---|---|---|---|---|---|---|
| Babylonian | 𒁹 | 𒐀 | 𒐁 | 𒐂 | 𒐃 | 𒐄 | 𒐅 | 𒐆 | 𒐇 | ◄ | |
| Egyptian | ı | ıı | ııı | ıııı | ııı ıı | ııı ııı | ıııı ııı | ıııı ıııı | ıııı ıııı ı | ∩ | |
| Greek | A | B | Γ | Δ | E | F | Z | H | Θ | I | |
| Roman | I | II | III | IV | V | VI | VII | VIII | IX | X | |
| Ancient Chinese | 一 | 二 | 三 | 四 | 五 | 六 | 七 | 八 | 九 | 十 | |
| Maya | • | •• | ••• | •••• | — | • | •• | ••• | •••• | = | ≋ |
| Hindu | १ | २ | ३ | ४ | ५ | ६ | ७ | ८ | ९° | ० | |
| Arabic/European 15th century | 1 | 2 | 3 | 2 | 4 | 6 | ʌ | 8 | 9 | 10 | o |
| Modern Arabic/European | 1 | 2 | 3 | 4 | 5 | 6 | 7 | 8 | 9 | 10 | 0 |
| Digits designed for computer printing | 1 | 2 | 3 | 4 | 5 | 6 | 7 | 8 | 9 | 10 | 0 |

# COMMON FORMULAE

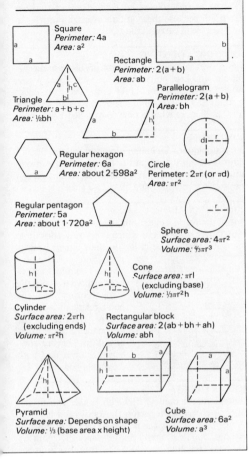

**Square**
Perimeter: 4a
Area: a²

**Rectangle**
Perimeter: 2(a + b)
Area: ab

**Triangle**
Perimeter: a + b + c
Area: ½bh

**Parallelogram**
Perimeter: 2(a + b)
Area: bh

**Regular hexagon**
Perimeter: 6a
Area: about 2·598a²

**Circle**
Perimeter: 2πr (or πd)
Area: πr²

**Regular pentagon**
Perimeter: 5a
Area: about 1·720a²

**Sphere**
Surface area: 4πr²
Volume: ⅓πr³

**Cone**
Surface area: πrl
(excluding base)
Volume: ⅓πr²h

**Cylinder**
Surface area: 2πrh
(excluding ends)
Volume: πr²h

**Rectangular block**
Surface area: 2(ab + bh + ah)
Volume: abh

**Pyramid**
Surface area: Depends on shape
Volume: ⅓ (base area x height)

**Cube**
Surface area: 6a²
Volume: a³

---

defined as being ten times larger or smaller than their neighbours. Since then, the metre has been redefined three times with ever greater precision. The definition now accepted internationally was adopted in October 1983. It defines the metre in terms of time: the distance travelled by a beam of light in a vacuum in a period lasting one 299,792,458th of a second.

## THE SUM THAT'S ALWAYS THE SAME
Take any three-figure number in which the first figure is larger than the last, say 725. Reverse it, making 527, and subtract the smaller from the larger, making 198. Now add the result to the same number reversed, 891. The answer is 1089 – and will be 1089 whatever number you start with. Even if the result of the subtraction is two figures rather than three – 221 minus 122, for instance, comes to 99 – simply put a zero on the front before reversing it, to make the sum 099 plus 990 . . . and the answer again is 1089.

## THE THEOREM PYTHAGORAS DID NOT INVENT
The theorem named after the Greek philosopher and mathematician Pythagoras (about 582 – 507 BC) was not discovered by him. The theorem – which states that in any right-angled triangle the sum of the squares on the two shorter sides equals the square on the hypotenuse, or longest side – was used by ancient Egyptian surveyors, and was known to the Babylonians (though probably not rigorously proved by them) at least 1000 years earlier.

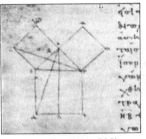

GREEK (ABOUT AD 800)

LATIN (ABOUT 1120)

ARABIC (ABOUT 1250)

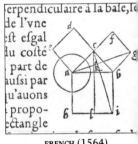

FRENCH (1564)

perpendiculaire à la bale, le
de l'vne
ft efgal
du colté
part de
aufli par
u'auons
propo-
ctangle

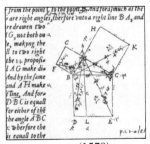

ENGLISH (1570)

CHINESE (1607)

WORLD FIGURES *By the 17th century Pythagoras's theorem was known all over the world. The picture at top left is from a copy of the works of the Greek mathematician Euclid; the others are translations of the same text.*

---

sphere, the correlation is not precise in all parts of the world and an average figure is usually used. The United States uses an 'international nautical mile', a unit of 6076.1033ft (1851.99m); Britain uses the 'Admiralty measured mile' of 6080ft (1853.18m).

The maritime measurement of speed in knots – one knot being equal to one nautical mile per hour – comes from the days when sailors used a knotted rope to determine their speed at sea. A float was tied to the end of the rope, which was knotted at regular intervals, and tossed overboard. As the float bobbed past the sailor holding the rope, an hourglass was turned over and the rope was paid out freely while the sand ran through. When the sand stopped flowing, the boat's speed was calculated simply by counting the number of knots that had been paid out.

## THE REVOLUTIONARY METRE
The metric system – invented by 12 French scientists during the French Revolution, partly to standardise the bewildering variety of local measurements then in use and partly in conscious reaction against the iron hand of tradition – was the first to be based on logic rather than accidents of physique. The scientists, who were appointed by the French National Assembly in 1791, based the system on the circumference of the Earth measured on a line through Paris and both the Poles. To give themselves a convenient-sized unit, they divided the line by 40,000,000 and called the result a metre (from the Greek word *metron*, meaning 'measure'). All the other units of length – from kilometres to millimetres and beyond – were then simply

## PERFECT PROPORTION: THE GOLDEN MEAN

Some of the world's most beautiful buildings, including the Parthenon in Athens, and many paintings derive much of their appeal from mathematics rather than art. In particular they make use of rectangular shapes based on a proportion of height to width known as the Golden Ratio or Golden Mean. Each rectangle has its sides in the proportion of 1 to 1.618033989. Like the number pi ($\pi$), which expresses the mathematical relationship between the diameter of a circle and its circumference, this Golden Ratio number – often denoted by the Greek letter phi ($\varphi$) – is a never-ending decimal. It also has some remarkable properties.

If a Golden Ratio rectangle is divided into a square and a rectangle, the smaller rectangle repeats the same proportion. If the smaller rectangle is divided again, the same is true of the yet smaller rectangle, and so on. If corresponding points on the rectangles are joined in the way pictured below, the result is what mathematicians call a logarithmic spiral – exactly the same spiral as the shell of a snail.

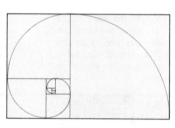

Uniquely, too, the Golden Ratio is the only number which can be squared by adding 1 to it ($\varphi^2 = \varphi + 1$), and the only number which can be turned into its own 'reciprocal' – $1/\varphi$ – just by subtracting 1 ($1/\varphi = \varphi - 1$).

## FIBONACCI'S MAGICAL NUMBERS

The arithmetical sequence now known as the Fibonacci series was invented in 1225 by the Italian mathematician Leonardo Fibonacci (about 1170–1240) to solve a puzzle about the breeding rate of rabbits. Each number in the series – which begins 1,1,2,3,5, 8,13,21,34 – is, after the first two figures, merely the sum of the previous two numbers. Yet this simple sequence has remarkable links with other parts of mathematics and with the world of nature.

If, for instance, you examine any plant that sends out individual leaves from a single stem, find two leaves directly above each other and then count one of the pair plus all the intervening leaves, the total will always be a Fibonacci number. Similarly, if you count the clockwise spirals of seeds on the head of a sunflower, and the anti-clockwise spirals on the same flower, the figures will always be not only Fibonacci numbers but consecutive Fibonacci numbers. The largest such numbers recorded are 144 and 233.

Perhaps even more curious is the ratio of successive terms in the Fibonacci series. The numbers 144 and 233, for instance, are in the ratio of 1 to 1.61805, and 233 and the following Fibonacci number 377 are in the ratio 1 to 1.6180257. Successive ratios in the series converge ever more closely on the number 1.618033989 . . . which is the Golden Ratio known to mathematicians since at least 300 BC.

## COUNTING THE COUNTLESS

The British astronomer Sir Arthur Eddington (1882–1944) once estimated that the total number of fundamental particles in the entire Universe came to only $10^{89}$ – the number 1 followed by 89 noughts. Mathematicians have, however, devised names for even larger numbers than this. The number $10^{100}$, for example, was named a googol by the 20th-century US mathematician Edward Kasner at the suggestion of his 13-year-old son. The largest named number is

$10^{googol}$ – or the figure 1 with $10^{100}$ noughts after it. It is known as a googolplex, but it could never be written out in full because there are not enough particles in the Universe to carry all the zeros.

## COUNTING, COUNTING

If a person counted at the rate of 100 numbers a minute, and kept on counting for eight hours a day, five days a week, it would take a little over four weeks to count to 1 million – and just over 80 years to reach 1000 million, or what is now often called 1 billion.

## NUMBERLESS

The Nambiquara, an Indian people who live in Brazil's Mato Grosso province on the fringes of the Amazon jungle, use no system of numbers at all. The closest they get is a verb meaning 'to be two alike'.

## CHINESE SQUARE

One of the world's oldest magic squares – a pattern of consecutive numbers in which every row adds up to the same total – is described in the Chinese book of

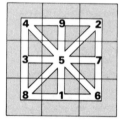

divination called the *I Ching*. Thought to have been written in about the 12th century BC, the book refers to a magic square (pictured on the left) made up of the numbers 1 to 9. Every row, every column and both diagonals add up to 15.

## DOUBLE FIGURES

A simple mathematical trick can enable you to discover any number a person thinks of – and find out his age as well. Ask the person to pick a number of any size, double it, add 5 and multiply the result by 50. Next, tell him to add 1735 (this key number changes every year; for 1986 the number rises to 1736, and so on for each subsequent year), and then to subtract the year in which he was born. Ask him to tell you the final answer. The last two figures in the answer will tell you the person's age this year. The others will be the number he first thought of.

## PRINTER'S PI

The Greek mathematician Archimedes (287–212 BC) was the first to succeed in calculating the ratio between the diameter of a circle and its circumference: the number now known as pi ($\pi$). He did it by drawing two polygons, many-sided figures, just inside and just outside the circle and then calculating the length of the polygons' perimeters. By this means, he established that $\pi$ – so named because it was the first letter of the Greek word *perimetros*, meaning 'perimeter' or 'circumference' – was approximately 22/7.

Later mathematicians, using polygons with more and more sides so that they followed ever more closely the shape of the circle, gradually improved on Archimedes' figure. But the process was agonisingly cumbersome. In 1610, for instance, a Dutchman named Ludolph van Ceulen completed a calculation of $\pi$ based on a polygon with more than a million million million sides. The mathematics occupied him for much of his life, yet it established the value of $\pi$ only to 35 decimal places.

In 1961, by contrast, a computer was able to calculate and print out its value to 100,000 places in just eight hours, and in 1981 a computer in Japan took only a little over five days to calculate its value to 2 million places. For ordinary purposes, the value of $\pi$ is usually approximated to 3.14159 or 3.142.

# MEASURE FOR MEASURE

The table shows how to convert imperial measurements to their metric equivalents, and vice versa. As well as giving precise equivalents, it also shows rough approximations.

## Imperial units

### Length

| | | Precise equivalent | Approximate equivalent |
|---|---|---|---|
| | 1 inch | 25.4mm | 25mm |
| 12in | 1 foot | 304.8mm | 300mm |
| 3ft | 1 yard | 0.9144m | 1m |
| 1760yd | 1 mile | 1.6093km | 1.5km |

### Area

| | | | |
|---|---|---|---|
| | 1 square inch | 645mm² | 650mm² |
| 144sq in | 1 square foot | 0.0929m² | 0.1m² |
| 9sq ft | 1 square yard | 0.836m² | 1m² |
| 4840sq yd | 1 acre | 0.405 hectares | 0.5ha |
| 640 acres | 1 square mile | 259 hectares | 250ha |

### Volume (solid and liquid)

| | | | |
|---|---|---|---|
| | 1 cubic inch | 16,387.1mm³ | 15,000mm³ |
| 1728cu in | 1 cubic foot | 0.028m³ | 0.03m³ |
| 27cu ft | 1 cubic yard | 0.765m³ | 1m³ |
| 20 fluid oz | 1 pint | 0.57 litre | 0.5 litre |
| 2 pints | 1 quart | 1.14 litres | 1 litre |
| 4 quarts | 1 gallon | 4.55 litres | 4.5 litres |

### Weight

| | | | |
|---|---|---|---|
| | 1 ounce | 28.3495g | 30g |
| 16oz | 1 pound | 0.4536kg | 0.5kg |
| 14lb | 1 stone | 6.35kg | 6kg |
| 8 stones | 1 hundredweight | 50.8kg | 50kg |
| 20cwt | 1 ton | 1.016 tonnes | 1 tonne |

## Metric units

### Length

| | | Precise equivalent | Approximate equivalent |
|---|---|---|---|
| | 1 millimetre | 0.03937in | 0.05in |
| 10mm | 1 centimetre | 0.39in | 0.5in |
| 1000mm | 1 metre | 39.37in | 3ft 3in |
| 1000m | 1 kilometre | 0.62 mile | 0.5 miles |

### Area

| | | | |
|---|---|---|---|
| | 1 square millimetre | 0.0016sq in | 0.001sq in |
| 100mm² | 1 square centimetre | 0.155sq in | 0.2sq in |
| 10,000mm² | 1 square decimetre | 15.50sq in | 15sq in |
| 10,000cm² | 1 square metre | 10.76sq ft | 10sq ft |
| 10,000m² | 1 hectare | 2.47 acres | 2 acres |
| 100 hectares | 1 square kilometre | 0.386sq miles | 0.5sq miles |

### Volume (solid and liquid)

| | | | |
|---|---|---|---|
| 1000mm³ | 1 cubic centimetre | 0.061cu in | 0.05cu in |
| 1000cm³ (cc) | 1 cubic decimetre | 61.024cu in | 60cu in |
| 1000dm³ | 1 cubic metre | 35.31cu ft | 35cu ft |
| | | 1.308cu yd | 1cu yd |
| 1000cm³ (cc) | 1 litre | 1.76 pints | 1.5 pints |
| 100 litres | 1 hectolitre | 22 gallons | 20 gallons |

### Weight

| | | | |
|---|---|---|---|
| | 1 gram | 0.035oz | 0.05oz |
| 1000g | 1 kilogram | 2.2046lb | 2lb |
| 1000kg | 1 tonne | 0.9842 ton | 1 ton |

## How to convert units of measurement

### Imperial to metric

| To convert | into | multiply by |
|---|---|---|
| **Length** | | |
| inches | millimetres | 25·4 |
| inches | centimetres | 2·54 |
| feet | metres | 0·3048 |
| yards | metres | 0·9144 |
| miles | kilometres | 1·6093 |
| **Area** | | |
| square inches | square millimetres | 645·16 |
| square feet | square metres | 0·093 |
| square yards | square metres | 0·836 |
| acres | hectares | 0·405 |
| square miles | square kilometres | 2·58999 |
| **Volume** | | |
| cubic inches | cubic millimetres | 16,387 |
| cubic feet | cubic metres | 0·0283 |
| cubic yards | cubic metres | 0·7646 |
| fluid ounces | millilitres | 28·41 |
| pints | litres | 0·568 |
| gallons | litres | 4·55 |
| **Weight** | | |
| ounces | grams | 28·35 |
| pounds | kilograms | 0·45359 |
| tons | tonnes | 1·016 |

### Metric to imperial

| To convert | into | multiply by |
|---|---|---|
| **Length** | | |
| millimetres | inches | 0·0394 |
| centimetres | inches | 0·3937 |
| metres | feet | 3·2808 |
| metres | yards | 1·0936 |
| kilometres | miles | 0·6214 |
| **Area** | | |
| square millimetres | square inches | 0·00155 |
| square metres | square feet | 10·764 |
| square metres | square yards | 1·196 |
| hectares | acres | 2·471 |
| square kilometres | square miles | 0·386 |
| **Volume** | | |
| cubic millimetres | cubic inches | 0·000061 |
| cubic metres | cubic feet | 35·315 |
| cubic metres | cubic yards | 1·308 |
| litres | pints | 1·760 |
| litres | gallons | 0·220 |
| **Weight** | | |
| grams | ounces | 0·0352 |
| kilograms | pounds | 2·2046 |
| tonnes | tons | 0·984 |

## Temperature – degrees Celsius (centigrade) and degrees Fahrenheit

*Exact conversion* $F° = (C° \times 1.8) + 32$   $C° = (F° - 32) \div 1.8$     *Approximate conversion* $F° = (C° \times 2) + 30$   $C° = (F° - 30) \div 2$

## WHAT METRIC PREFIXES MEAN

Prefixes – syllables added to the front of a unit to signify multiples or fractions of it – simplify the use of large and small quantities. Their most familiar use is in the metric system of measurements. One thousand metres, for example, is simply one kilometre, and a thousandth of a metre is a millimetre. The prefix symbols shown here are used with the abbreviation for the basic unit, so kilometre is shortened to km and millimetre to mm.

| Prefix | Symbol | Meaning | Factor by which unit is multiplied | |
|---|---|---|---|---|
| tera | T | one million million | $10^{12}$ | = 1,000,000,000,000 |
| giga | G | one thousand million | $10^{9}$ | = 1,000,000,000 |
| mega | M | one million | $10^{6}$ | = 1,000,000 |
| kilo | k | one thousand | $10^{3}$ | = 1000 |
| hecto | h | one hundred | $10^{2}$ | = 100 |
| deka | da | ten | $10$ | = 10 |
| deci | d | one-tenth | $10^{-1}$ | = 0.1 |
| centi | c | one-hundredth | $10^{-2}$ | = 0.01 |
| milli | m | one-thousandth | $10^{-3}$ | = 0.001 |
| micro | μ | one-millionth | $10^{-6}$ | = 0.000,001 |
| nano | n | one-thousand millionth | $10^{-9}$ | = 0.000,000,001 |
| pico | p | one-million millionth | $10^{-12}$ | = 0.000,000,000,001 |

# Computers – marvels in miniature

## 5000 YEARS OF COMPUTING

The abacus is the earliest form of mechanical computer. Invented more than 5000 years ago, probably in China, it consists of a wooden frame with beads strung on wires which represent units, tens, hundreds and so on. Calculations are made by moving the beads up and down.

It is still used in the Far East and in the Soviet Union, and a skilled operator can make calculations at least as quickly as on a pocket calculator. As recently as 1983, more than 2 million of them were being produced each year in Japan, where they are known as sorobans.

## ACE IN THE HOLE

The punched cards used in computing were developed by French weavers in 1801.

In that year Joseph Jacquard invented a loom for the manufacture of elaborate patterned fabrics. The pattern was coded on a loop of cards with holes punched in them. The holes allowed needles to pass through and lift corresponding threads of the warp. The Englishman Charles Babbage adopted a similar system of punched cards for his computer in 1834.

## THE FIRST DIGITAL COMPUTER

Charles Babbage (1792 – 1871), an English scientist and mathematician, drew up the first plans for a programmable digital computer in 1834 – but never saw it completed. His Analytical Engine, a development of an advanced adding machine he had invented 20 years earlier, was to have been programmed by punched cards, make calculations with the aid of a memory store, print out the answers and operate at the then remarkable speed of one addition per second.

The British government invested £17,000 in the engine and Babbage raised a further £6000 to make it, but the manufacturing precision required to produce the engine's thousands of parts was beyond the capabilities of Victorian engineers.

Government support was withdrawn in 1842 after the Astronomer Royal, George Airy, said the project was worthless. Babbage, however, struggled on unsuccessfully – in the hope of completing the machine – until his death almost 30 years later.

## COUNTING IN TWOS

Human beings count in tens (the decimal system) because we have ten digits on our hands. A computer, however, thinks in terms of just two possibilities: either an electric current is passing a point in its circuitry or it is not. The computer therefore counts in twos (the binary system).

The binary system uses only two symbols, 1 and 0, standing for current and no current. Moving a symbol one place to the left has the effect of doubling its value. Thus the value of 1 as it is doubled becomes 2, 4, 8, 16, 32, 64, 128 and so on. The value of 0 always remains zero. Using the binary system, the notation for the numbers one to ten is: 1, 10, 11, 100, 101, 110, 111, 1000, 1001, 1010.

## OUTLAWS WHO HELPED A CENSUS

Efforts to trap 19th-century train robbers in the Wild West helped to inspire the first electric computer. Outlaws often posed as passengers on US trains and to help identify them, researchers proposed recording the physical characteristics of each passenger on tickets. When a ticket was purchased, holes could be punched next to the appropriate characteristics, such as moustache and hair colour. Then, if a robbery took place, the idea was that the ticket records could be matched against passengers who remained on the train after the theft – and missing passengers could be described.

The idea was never widely adopted, but an American statistician, Herman Hollerith, realised that the

---

## MILESTONES OF COMPUTER DEVELOPMENT

**1622** English mathematician William Oughtred invents the slide rule.

**1642** Blaise Pascal, French mathematician and philosopher, invents the first adding machine.

**1834** Charles Babbage, English scientist, draws up the first plans for a programmable digital computer.

**1890** US statistician Herman Hollerith invents a tabulating machine used for the 1890 US census.

**1930** US scientist Vannevar Bush develops a large electro-mechanical calculator – the first large analogue computer.

**1942** First electronic digital calculator constructed at Iowa State University by Professor John Atanasoff and Clifford Berry.

**1945** ENIAC (Electronic Numerical Integrator and Calculator), the first fully electronic computer, built at the University of Pennsylvania, USA.

**1946** John von Neumann at the Institute of Advanced Study, Princeton, USA, builds a computer which stores information and uses binary numbers.

**1948** First successful stored program computer operated at Manchester University, England.

**1950** The first mass-produced computer, Univac 1 (standing for Universal Automatic Computer), built by the Eckert and Mauchly Computer Company in Philadelphia, USA.

**1953** IBM introduces its first commercial computer – the 701 – which uses valves.

**1954** British catering company J. Lyons installs the first electronic business computer, developed at Cambridge University, to handle its payroll.

**1960** Transistors used in commercial computers, replacing valves, by the Digital Equipment Corporation in the USA.

**1965** Silicon chip introduced in the USA.

**1971** Pocket calculators introduced. The American Intel Corporation patents the microprocessor – an entire computer processor on a single silicon chip.

**1979** Bubble memory – a tiny magnetised area in a material such as garnet – introduced. It can hold the equivalent of a 40-page book in 215mm² (0.3sq in).

method could be adapted for processing census information and, for the 1890 US census, he produced a tabulating machine.

Census information was recorded on punched cards which were 'read' by feelers. The feelers could detect a hole and then generate a corresponding electrical signal. The previous census, in 1880, had taken 18 weeks to complete. Hollerith's machine cut that to six weeks – despite an increase in the population from 50 to 60 million.

In 1896 Hollerith founded the Tabulating Machine Company which, 28 years later, became the basis of what is now the world's largest computer firm, IBM (International Business Machines).

## COMPUTERS THAT PROGRAM THEMSELVES

Despite the proliferation of special computer languages, such as BASIC, COBOL and so on, all computers can essentially understand only two symbols: 1 and 0. But to save programs having to use this cumbersome binary notation, computers usually have built into them a translation program, or 'compiler', which can take a coded language, almost like a real language, and convert it into binary notation.

The most common coded language at present in use is BASIC – or to give it its full name Beginners All Purpose Symbolic Instruction Code. Other languages include: COBOL (Common Business Orientated Language), which is used for general and commercial purposes; FORTRAN (Formula Translation), for scientific use; and ALGOL (Algebraical Orientated Language), which is designed for scientists, engineers and mathematicians.

## THE ONE-MINUTE BOOK

In the early 1980s electronic printers could reach speeds of 450 lines a second and, at that rate, type out a 225-page book in one minute.

## WHIZZ KIDS

Computer experts are getting younger and younger. A British teenager named Eugene Evans was earning £40,000 a year in 1983 when he became, at the age of 17, the head programmer for Imagine, a computer games company in Liverpool, England. And by some standards Eugene was considered an old hand at the game. It is not unusual to find ten-year-olds writing their own programs.

## FIVE GATES OF WISDOM

Since individual circuit elements in computers can only ever be on or off, a method of combining the output from the elements is needed to perform logical calculations. This is achieved by using gates – simple pieces of circuitry which have two input wires and one output wire. An electrical pulse is sent along the output wire only when a particular pattern of pulses is received on the input wires. The five types of gate are named in line with the output that is produced:
● An OR gate produces an output if it receives a pulse on either input wire.
● A NOR gate produces an output only when it does not receive a pulse.
● An AND gate produces an output only if pulses are sent through both input wires at the same time.
● A NAND ('not and') gate supplies an output unless it receives a pulse on both input wires.
● NOT gates, or inverters, have only one input and, as the name implies, the output is always the opposite of the input.
More complex logical steps are dealt with by arranging the gates in sequence or in parallel combinations.

## MEMORIES ARE MADE OF THIS

Computer memories are defined by the number of 'bytes' of information they can store. Each byte is a combination of binary numbers – usually eight of them – and stands for an ordinary number or letter. In one method, for instance, the series 01000001 is the byte standing for the letter A.

Each of the binary numbers – always either a 1 or 0, corresponding to the presence or absence of electric current in a section of circuitry – is known as a bit, from the phrase 'binary digit'.

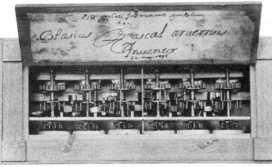

WHEELS WITHIN WHEELS *Blaise Pascal (1623–62), the French philosopher and mathematician, was 19 years old when he invented this adding machine in 1642. A train of cogwheels enabled numbers to be carried automatically, and allowed subtractions to be performed as well.*

TOO HARD TO BUILD *Charles Babbage, who designed the first programmable computer in 1834, never saw it built, because Victorian engineers could not make the parts with sufficient precision. This model (right) was built from his drawings in the late 19th century, years after his death.*

More than 64,000 bytes can be stored on a single fingernail-sized silicon chip, and a memory of this size is often described as a 64K memory. The K stands for kilo-bytes. Technically a kilo-byte is 1024 bytes (equivalent to $2^{10}$, or, in binary notation, the figure 1 followed by ten zeros), so that a 64K memory can actually hold 65,536 bytes. For most practical purposes, though, a kilo-byte is regarded as 1000 bytes.

Mass storage systems are also available which can hold up to 472,000 million bytes – equivalent to 472,000 'mega-bytes'. This is enough to hold a 100-letter record for every person in the world, or to store as many words as there are on 27 million pages of a daily newspaper. The size of even a large memory does not have to be enormous, however. Some disc storage systems which are 'read' by laser beams can store on a disc the size of an ordinary long-playing record up to 12,500 million bytes of information – more than enough for the entire 30 volumes of the *Encyclopaedia Britannica*.

## KEYBOARD CRIMINALS

The main problem with computer crime is that while it is easy to prove that money has been stolen, it is much more difficult to discover who typed the instructions into the computer to carry out the theft.

By assuming that for every known computer crime, five more go undetected or unreported, US researchers in 1974 estimated that computer criminals were netting $300 million a year in America and Western Europe. More recent estimates in the early 1980s put

the figure as high as $3000 million a year in the USA alone, although reported crimes there account for only $100 million.

## THE SILICON CHIP

In its pure form silicon is an insulator, but when it is fractionally impure it will allow a feeble current to pass and so becomes a semi-conductor: the basis of a silicon chip. Silicon, processed to 99.9999999 per cent purity, is drawn into cylindrical bars about 100mm (4in) thick. The bars are then sliced into discs 0.5mm (0.02in) thick. Each disc contains enough material for up to 250 chips.

Miniaturised circuits are photographically printed and etched onto the disc, and layers of substances such as phosphorus, boron, and aluminium are then deposited on the surface to form transistors, resistors, capacitors and diodes: the electronic circuitry which controls and guides the current.

## ELECTRONIC BRAINS

Present-day computers are not electronic brains. They cannot think, nor are they creative. But the day of the true electronic brain is on the way. In the early 1950s researchers in America began work on programs to make computers simulate the behaviour patterns of humans in their approach to problems.

This means that the computer has to work on a trial-and-error basis, which results in the computer developing its own programs.

In the early 1980s Doug Lenat, an American researcher at Stanford University, left his computer working every night to see what it could come up with. By 1983 it had discovered a new way of designing miniature electronic circuits. It had also decided that it was a person and not a machine.

## HOW A PROGRAM WORKS

Without a program to tell it what to do and how to do it, a computer is unable to function. If, for example, you wanted to know how many times the word 'the' appears in this paragraph, or in the whole book, it would not be enough merely to put the text into a computer and then ask it how many times the word appears. For the computer to accomplish the calculation it has to be told what to do in simple steps. The instructions might be:

1. Scan the text until a space followed by 'T' or 't' is found.
2. If the next letter is not 'h', go back to step 1.
3. If the letter is 'h', is the next letter 'e'?
4. If not, go back to step 1. If it is, go to step 5.
5. If 'e' is followed by a space, add 1 to the total.
6. Go back to step 1.

A full computer program for this operation would need to be broken down into even more simple steps, but a series of such programs could enable a computer to analyse any amount of text in great detail.

## COMPUTER PROGRESS

The earliest and largest of the digital machines in the 1940s was the ENIAC (Electronic Numeral Integrator and Calculator). It was built at the University of Pennsylvania and used by the US Army to calculate firing angles for new artillery weapons, taking into account range, the type of shell and weather conditions. ENIAC contained 18,000 valves, occupied several rooms, consumed enough power to drive a locomotive, and could perform 5000 additions a second.

Today a microprocessor, the silicon chip at the heart of a microcomputer, can cost as little as £5, can fit on a child's fingernail, consumes the same power as an electric light bulb and can perform 400,000

HERMAN'S HARDWARE *A magazine cover of 1890 traces the first processing of census information by tabulating machines – the first electric computers. Invented by US statistician Herman Hollerith, the machines cut the time needed for the job by two-thirds – and helped Hollerith to found a business which in 1924 became the heart of IBM, the world's largest computer firm.*

operations a second. And development is still going on at such a rate that computers are often out of date within two years of going on sale.

## SUPERCOMPUTERS

The race is on to develop a new generation of super-computers for the 1990s. In 1983, there were only about 60 supercomputers in the world and they were mainly used for defence work, oil reservoir modelling and designing other computers. The fastest was capable of 1300 million computations per second. The new supercomputers – which are being developed largely in Japan and the USA – will be capable of more than 10,000 million calculations per second.

The speed at which computers can work is astonishing, even when compared with the human brain. The brain contains about 10,000 million nerve cells, each one capable of working 100 times a second. But inside a microprocessor speeds are measured in nanoseconds. A nanosecond is one thousand-millionth of a second. For comparison, a nanosecond is to a second what a second is to 31.7 years.

By the end of the 1980s, however, even nanoseconds will be considered slow. It is expected that speeds will then be measured in picoseconds – and a picosecond is one-thousandth of a nanosecond.

## COMPUTERS THAT TALK

Computers can now be used to read to blind people – by using synthetic speech. Raymond Kurzweil, an American student at the Massachusetts Institute of Technology, designed in 1982 a machine using a mini-computer which will read almost any typeface and convert print into speech, using digitally stored sounds.

It is capable of learning the characteristics of an unfamiliar typeface and is claimed to make fewer mistakes than a human reader, pausing as required by punctuation.

## ELECTRONIC GUINEA PIGS

US scientists are developing electronic animals – to take the place of real ones in laboratory experiments. Computer models of rats, rabbits, dogs and other animals sacrificed every year in scientific laboratories are being devised to allow chemists to test the effect of new drugs without harming real creatures, and to allow medical students to practise surgery.

One program, invented at the University of Pennsylvania, enabled student vets to carry out simulated dissections simply by punching keys on a computer terminal. The model even included the sound of heartbeats and nerve impulses to add realism to the electronic surgery.

The electronic guinea pigs will not, scientists believe, remove completely the need for experiments on real animals. But they could save the lives of many of the 60 million animals now used in scientific research each year in the United States alone.

## DON'T BLAME THE COMPUTER

Computers, contrary to popular belief, cannot make mistakes – except in rare circumstances when they break down. The reason is that they do not think and cannot question any of the data they are provided with. All they can do is apply their programs of instructions to the data and supply the answers.

The answer will always be right if the information and the program fed into the computer are correct. If either is wrong, the answer will be wrong. The computer has no way of knowing this – nor how many times it is blamed for errors which have in fact been made by its human controllers.

## PROGRAM IN A POCKET

Until the 1980s, most computer programs were stored on tapes or discs. But in 1983, an American researcher named Jerome Dexler devised a pocket-sized program device no larger than a credit card. In the device, programs are recorded on cards in the form of minute black holes, each one 5/1000mm in diameter, on a silvery surface.

Each card can carry 16 million bits of information which can be read by a laser scanner when the card is inserted into a specially equipped computer. The cards can be produced more cheaply than an equivalent silicon chip and are easier to carry than other forms of program, such as cassette tape.

SILICON CHIP *The rectangular chip – shown actual size and enlarged – can handle the payroll computing system for a sizable company. Its complex circuitry, which consists of five major subcircuits, was miniaturised photographically before being etched onto the chip.*

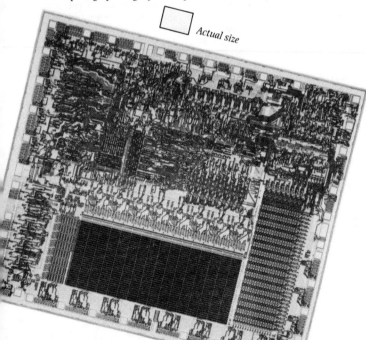

Actual size

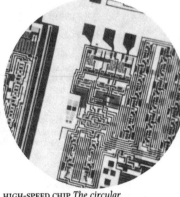

HIGH-SPEED CHIP *The circular picture shows part of an advanced type of chip in which the silicon is laid on sapphire, a technique which increases the speed of operation many times over. The three black components, top centre, are each about 0.3mm across – just twice the thickness of a hair.*

# Business and trade

## AS BIG AS BELGIUM

The giant Exxon oil corporation of New York heads the league table of the world's largest companies, generating more wealth than most of the world's nations. Its annual sales in the early 1980s were more than £60,000 million – almost as much as the total gross domestic product of Belgium. Its after-tax profit in that time was more than £3000 million a year.

Measured by turnover, 270 of the world's top 450 companies are American. Taking assets, rather than sales, as the yardstick, the world's largest company has been Bell Systems (American Telephone and Telegraph). In 1983 its property and plant (mostly telephones) were valued at £106,800 million, and with more than a million workers on its payroll, it was also the world's largest private employer.

At the end of 1983, however, it was broken up into eight separate corporations as the result of an antitrust court case in the USA.

The world's largest public employer is the state-owned rail system of the Soviet Union. It has a staff of some 2 million people.

## BUDGET-BREAKERS

The shell-roofed Sydney Opera House in Australia and the elegant, nose-dipping Concorde supersonic airliner are front-runners for the dubious accolade of the highest over-topping of an original budget.

In January 1957 the opera house, designed by the Danish architect, Jörn Utzon, was expected to cost A\$7.2 million. When it was completed in 1973, ten years later than scheduled and with only half the projected seating capacity, it had cost A\$102 million – 14 times more than anticipated. In addition, its annual running costs had soared to A\$6 million, not far off the original budget for the entire building. Ninety per cent of the money for the project was raised by lotteries.

The Concorde, paid for by French and British taxpayers, was forecast in 1962 to cost between £150 and £170 million for a production run of 16 jets. By 1978, when the last of the 16 came off the production line at the British Aircraft Corporation's Bristol works, the cost had soared to more than 13 times as much: a total of £2000 million, or nearly £182 million for *each* of the 11 Concordes now in service.

## THE FIRST COMPANY

Which is the world's oldest company depends largely on definition; the legal concept was not formalised until the 19th century. Nevertheless, the merchant venturers' companies of the golden age of exploration have a claim to the distinction. Among them were pioneering outfits such as the Russian or Muscovy Company, founded in England in 1553 as 'The Mystery and Company of Merchant Adventurers for the Discovery of Regions, Dominions and Places Unknown'. Its first governor was the Venetian explorer Sebastian Cabot, whose father John Cabot discovered Newfoundland in 1498.

In Europe, the Bayerische Staatsbrauerei (Bavarian State Brewery) began near Munich in 1040, while the firm of Urquell of Pilsen, founded in 1295 in what is now Czechoslovakia, lives on in the word Pilsen, or just Pils, for any strong lager.

Perhaps the most curious claim to the title of the world's oldest company is made by the Faversham Oyster Fishery Company of Kent. An Act of the British Parliament passed in 1930 referred to the fishery's existence 'since time immemorial' – which under a definition still used in English law means before 1189. But the exact foundation date is not known.

---

## ECONOMIC 'LAWS'

The study of economics, founded as a separate academic discipline in the 18th century, is an inexact science – largely because complex patterns of human behaviour have to be reduced to gross simplifications to enable economists to analyse them. Nevertheless, some general observations are known as laws.

**Law of Diminishing Returns** That if one factor of production – staff, say – is continually increased while the others remain constant, eventually the point is reached where each new unit of increase brings a smaller addition to production than the previous one. In a car cruising in top gear, for instance, each additional litre of petrol used produces a smaller and smaller increase in speed, so that a car cruising at 100km/h uses more than twice as much petrol as a car travelling at 50km/h. Also known as the Law of Variable Proportions.

**Gresham's Law** That 'bad money drives out good'. Or, that debasing the metal content of coinage lowers the value of money, since owners of unadulterated coins tend to hoard them or melt them down to purchase a greater number of debased coins. Attributed, with no foundation, to Elizabeth I's financial adviser, Sir Thomas Gresham. Probably first stated by the Polish astronomer Nicolaus Copernicus.

**Iron Law of Wages** That if wages rise above subsistence level, they produce a higher birthrate and expanded population, which in turn forces wages down to subsistence level again. Given wide currency by British economist David Ricardo, but of French origin. Not now accepted, since in the 20th century wealthy nations have in practice tended to have lower birthrates than poor nations.

**Parkinson's Law** That work expands to fill the time available to do it. Or, that the amount of work done varies inversely to the number of people employed. Humorously (but still seriously) published by the British economist Cyril Northcote Parkinson in 1958.

**Peter Principle** That in any organisation every employee rises to his level of incompetence. All valuable work is therefore done by people who have not yet reached that level. Another satirical law, published by a Canadian-born author, Professor Lawrence J. Peter, in 1969.

**Say's Law** That every rise in the supply of goods produces an increase in demand for them. Stated by the French economist Jean-Baptiste Say in 1803. True only of barter economies, but generally believed until the Great Depression.

**Law of Supply and Demand** That competition between consumers and producers brings the supply of goods and the demand for them into balance. Cardinal 'law' of free-market economic theory. Overproduction lowers prices, increasing demand; overconsumption raises prices, decreasing demand.

---

# MAJOR ECONOMISTS

**1723–90 Adam Smith** Scottish economist, chief founder of classical economics. Based theories on the premise that if every man pursued his own self-interest, a guiding 'invisible hand' ensured that the general result was in the best interest of society. Argued for free-market competition, free trade between nations and freedom of commerce and industry from government intervention – a view known as *laissez-faire*, meaning 'let (people) do (as they choose)'. First economist to advocate the division of labour, each worker specialising in making one part of a complex product in factory production.

**1772–1823 David Ricardo** English economist. Developed the labour theory of value: that the value of any product is roughly equal to the value of the labour which has gone into producing it.

**1818–83 Karl Marx** German economist. Theoretical founder, with Friedrich Engels, of Communism. Interpreted history as being chiefly determined by economic forces and the struggle between social classes. Invented the notion of 'surplus value' – that although the value of a product depends on the amount of labour embodied in it, only part of the value is paid to the labourer. The 'surplus' is retained by the owner or employer in the form of profit, dividends or rent, and hoarded as capital.

**1883–1946 John Maynard Keynes** English economist. Most famous of the Cambridge school of economists, who between the two world wars attacked classical economics. Argued that unemployment was reduced, not by cutting wages, but by increasing purchasing power to stimulate demand. Advocated heavy state investment in public works to provide jobs and increase purchasing power.

**1908– John Kenneth Galbraith** Canadian-born US economist. Believes that obsession with growth – in national income, consumer expenditure, jobs and capital investment – leads to the production of waste: goods and services which people do not genuinely need. Attacked such waste in his book, *The Affluent Society*, published in 1958, and advocates government intervention to control it.

**1911–77 Ernst Schumacher** German-born British economist. Coined the slogan: 'Small is beautiful.' Argued against the 20th-century tendency towards bigger enterprises on the grounds that economies of scale – the savings generated by merging smaller firms – were eventually counter-productive, reducing efficiency and profits.

**1912– Milton Friedman** American economist. Chief member of the Chicago school of economists. Anti-Keynesian. Advocates tight control of the money supply – the doctrine known as monetarism – on the grounds that government spending in excess of income produces inflation and leads to higher levels of unemployment.

## WAGES AND TAXES
American and Canadian workers are the highest paid in the world, earning three times as much as Greek workers, the lowest paid among industrial nations outside the Communist bloc. Straight comparisons of hourly wages can be misleading, though, since the real value of earnings depends on a number of factors, including the cost of living.

Taking these into account, however, US wages are still out in front. The cost of living in the USA in 1982 was 12 per cent lower than in Britain, and a New Yorker on the equivalent of £13,000 a year with a wife and two children was paying about 20 per cent of his wages in taxes of one sort or another. A Londoner in the same circumstances was paying about 33 per cent.

The Swedish government takes an even bigger bite out of salaries. In 1982, the cost of living in Sweden was 20 per cent higher than in Britain, and a highly paid Swedish businessman earning, say, £130,000 was taking home only 20 per cent of his salary after deductions, compared with 45 per cent for a Briton on the same salary.

## WHERE TAXES GO
Among the leading industrial nations, Sweden has the highest public spending bill in relation to the country's total wealth. Its outlay on defence, health, education, the civil service and the rest of the public sector amounted in the early 1980s to about 60 per cent of the country's gross national product.

The equivalent figure for Britain was just under 45 per cent and for the USA – whose gross national product of about $3 million million is the world's highest – it was about 33 per cent. For Spain, one of the West's most frugal spenders, it was 29 per cent.

## SIGN OF THE THREE BALLS
The traditional symbol of pawnbrokers – three golden balls – is thought to be derived from the coat of arms of the Medici family, who ruled the Italian city of Florence between the 15th and 16th centuries. The symbol was spread by the Lombards – Italian bankers, goldsmiths and moneylenders who set up businesses in medieval London.

TREE OF MONEY *There are nearly 140 stock exchanges in the world and the two largest – in London and New York – both had humble births. London's stock dealers first did their trading in raffish 18th-century coffee-houses like the one depicted in this 1781 engraving. Dealers in New York began in 1792 to trade underneath a tree outside number 68, Wall Street. The street, near the southern tip of Manhattan, was once the northernmost limit of New York. It gets its name from a boundary stockade, or wall, built in 1653 by Dutch colonists to protect the settlement against attacks by English colonists and Indians. The origins of stock exchanges go back to medieval France, where 13th-century stockbrokers traded 'bills of exchange' – IOUs issued by companies in return for loans. At about the same time, Belgian merchants in Bruges began to gather outside the house of the mercantile family Van der Buerse. A corruption of their name gave Paris's stock exchange its title, the Bourse.*

# Communications – linking the world

## BEACONS IN SPACE

In the 11th century BC, the Greeks used a line of dozens of hill-top bonfires to send news of the fall of Troy to Argos in Greece, 800km (500 miles) away, in just a few hours.

Today, just three communications satellites are enough to link any two places in the world at the speed of light. The space beacons are parked in what are called geostationary orbits 35,900km (22,300 miles) up, where their speed keeps them in step with the Earth as it spins around.

The first such globe-spanning satellites were the Intelsat 2 series, launched from Cape Canaveral in Florida, USA, in the late 1960s. The first of the series was launched in October 1966.

## WIRES THAT TRAPPED A KILLER

The world's first public telegraph line, installed in Britain in May 1843, helped to catch a murderer. Used largely to control train movements, the line was set up along a 30km (18.5 mile) stretch of railway track from London to West Drayton, Middlesex.

The system, invented by two Englishmen, William Cooke and Professor Charles Wheatstone, had five wires connected to five needles. Electric currents sent down any two of the wires simultaneously deflected the corresponding needles to identify individual letters. In 1845, a murder suspect named John Tawell was spotted boarding a train at Slough. It was too late to stop the train, but news of the sighting was telegraphed ahead to London and Tawell was arrested near Paddington Station. He was later tried, convicted and hanged.

## THE CRIPPEN FACTOR

When the Italian Guglielmo Marconi (1874–1937) invented wireless telegraphy in 1895, only ship owners and navies were quick to catch on to the advantages of the new system over the established network of wires and submarine cables. A crime helped to change public opinion. In 1910, Captain Henry Kendal of the SS *Montrose*, bound for Quebec from Liverpool, thought he recognised a wanted British murderer, Dr Hawley Harvey Crippen, and his mistress, Ethel LeNeve, among the passengers.

He telegraphed his suspicions to England. Chief Inspector Walter Dew of Scotland Yard caught a faster boat to Canada and arrested Crippen and LeNeve when they landed. Crippen was subsequently hanged for the murder of his wife.

## TERSE CODE

The lead type used by printers helped the American Samuel Morse (1791–1872) in about 1838 to design the Morse code. He used the numbers of each letter in a printer's tray of type as a guide to how frequently the letters were used in English. Then he assigned the shortest signals to the commonest letters. So E has the shortest code – a single dot – and J, Q and Y, which are rarely used, have the longest codes: combinations of three dashes and a dot.

## PUZZLED GENIUS

The Scottish-born American inventor of the telephone, Alexander Graham Bell (1847–1922), claimed that he never really understood the principles of electricity – crucial to the device which, on March 10, 1876, first successfully transmitted human speech. Even in his later years, when the telephone had become widely used, he said he still did not understand how someone speaking in Washington could be heard by someone in Paris.

## RING AHOY!

The American inventor Thomas Alva Edison (1847–1931) patented almost 1300 inventions, but his most significant contribution to modern life may have been when he suggested how to use the telephone. He advised people to answer the telephone

SMART NUMBER *This phone of the 1890s was custom-built for the wealthy Rothschild family. To call the operator, the user had to wind the handle. Public as well as private telephone systems spread rapidly round the world. Berlin had a city network in 1877 – only a year after Bell's invention.*

SIGNAL SUCCESS *Intelsat VI, shown here in an artist's representation, is due to be launched by the International Telecommunications Organisation in late 1986. Once in orbit, the satellite will be able to relay 30,000 telephone calls and several television programmes all at the same time. The first satellite to relay telephone calls was Telstar, launched in July 1962. It could carry only 12 calls at a time.*

with a simple 'Hello'. One telephone company in the late 1870s had recommended shouting 'Ahoy! Ahoy!' into the mouthpiece.

## MISSED OPPORTUNITY
A Canadian businessman missed a chance to share in the industry founded on the most valuable patent ever granted – number 174,465: Bell's original US patent for the telephone. A Toronto-based publisher, George Brown, was offered exclusive Canadian and British Empire rights to the telephone in the late 1870s – for just $150. Brown turned the offer down; he did not think the rights were worth it. In 1983, the firm that was built on the patent, Bell Systems (American Telephone and Telegraph), was the world's largest in terms of assets and staff. It had assets of £106,800 million, and 1 million employees.

## 'GIRL-LESS' TELEPHONE
An undertaker in Kansas City invented the automatic telephone exchange because he suspected that telephone operators were being paid by rival undertakers not to connect his calls. Almon Brown Strowger set about inventing a 'girl-less, cuss-less, out-of-order-less, wait-less telephone', and in 1889 patented an automatic switchboard whereby callers selected the number by pressing a combination of three buttons. The first automatic exchange was set up in La Porte, Indiana, in 1892. Bell, the largest telephone company in the USA, adopted the new system – by then modified to use a dial instead of buttons – in 1919.

## HELLO . . . HELLO
The time delay in many international telephone conversations is caused by the vast distances the signals have to travel. Even at the speed of light – 300,000km per second (186,000 miles per second) – the signals take about one-eighth of a second to reach a geostationary satellite, and a similar time to bounce back.

In a two-way telephone conversation using two satellites (between Britain and Australia, for instance) the delay can be more than a second – long enough for a speaker to start talking again in the belief that the original remark has gone unheard.

## SIGNALS UNDER THE SEA
Submarine communications cables have been in use since 1851, when the first underwater telegraph cable was laid on the bed of the English Channel between Dover and Calais. Before long it was severed by a fisherman's anchor. Eight years later a cable 3743km (2326 miles) long was laid under the Atlantic between Ireland and Newfoundland. Half the cable was towed out from each side and it was spliced in mid-ocean. That connection lasted only a month.

The first one-piece transatlantic cable was laid by the *Great Eastern*, a giant steamship designed by the British engineer Isambard Kingdom Brunel, in 1866, and the first undersea telephone cable between England and France in 1891. Not until 1956 was the first transatlantic telephone cable laid, when a reliable 'repeater' was developed to amplify the signals over long distances. The cable contained 102 repeaters and carried just 36 conversations at a time.

## NO REFUGE
The telephone has spread to all parts of the world since its invention in 1876, but for more than 100 years a sure refuge for anyone seeking to escape its persistent ringing was an aeroplane. Not any more. In 1983, ten airlines flying across North America fitted their planes with experimental public telephones for use by passengers in mid-flight.

# COMMON CODES

Alphabetical codes are used to transmit messages when other methods are impracticable. Semaphore has a long history in military signalling. Finger-spelling is used by the deaf and dumb. Morse was invented in about 1838. Braille, used in books for the blind, was devised by Louis Braille (1809–52), a blind Frenchman. Phonetic alphabets are used to clarify individual letters in radio messages.

| | Semaphore | Finger-spelling | Morse | Braille | Phonetic |
|---|---|---|---|---|---|
| A | | | ·— | | Alpha |
| B | | | —··· | | Bravo |
| C | | | —·—· | | Charlie |
| D | | | —·· | | Delta |
| E | | | · | | Echo |
| F | | | ··—· | | Foxtrot |
| G | | | ——· | | Golf |
| H | | | ···· | | Hotel |
| I | | | ·· | | India |
| J | | | ·——— | | Juliet |
| K | | | —·— | | Kilo |
| L | | | ·—·· | | Lima |
| M | | | —— | | Mike |
| N | | | —· | | November |
| O | | | ——— | | Oscar |
| P | | | ·——· | | Papa |
| Q | | | ——·— | | Quebec |
| R | | | ·—· | | Romeo |
| S | | | ··· | | Sierra |
| T | | | — | | Tango |
| U | | | ··— | | Uniform |
| V | | | ···— | | Victor |
| W | | | ·—— | | Whisky |
| X | | | —··— | | X-ray |
| Y | | | —·—— | | Yankee |
| Z | | | ——·· | | Zulu |

# Engineering 1: tunnels and mines

## FROM PALACE TO TEMPLE

The earliest successful underwater passage was built before 2000 BC at Babylon, in Mesopotamia. The Euphrates river was diverted during the dry season so that engineers could build a brick-lined channel 900m (2950ft) long in the riverbed to connect the royal palace with a temple on the opposite bank. Once the channel was completed, it was roofed and sealed with waterproof bitumen, and the river was returned to its normal course. The method, known as 'cut and cover', is still used.

## A THOUSAND UNDERGROUND SHRINES

Carthaginians, Greeks, Egyptians and Romans all built elaborate catacombs in which to inter their dead; but few were as complex as the Indian temples built during the 1st century BC. A thousand underground shrines and 10km (6 miles) of tunnel carved out of rock with hand chisels have been found at Ellora, in Bombay province.

## CARRYING THE WATER

The Romans used tunnels extensively for the aqueducts they built to carry water to their towns and cities. The Appian aqueduct, which supplied Rome, ran as a tunnel for 25km (15 miles).

The longest tunnel of any kind in the world today serves the same purpose. It is the New York City/West Delaware water supply tunnel, which is 169km (105 miles) long.

## BIRTHDAY GREETING

Isambard Kingdom Brunel, the 19th-century English engineer, gave himself a unique birthday greeting when he designed the Box railway tunnel in Gloucestershire in the late 1840s. By altering the alignment of the tunnel entrance slightly from its agreed specifications, he ensured that on April 9 each year the rising sun flooded the tunnel with light. That day was Brunel's birthday.

## INSPIRED BY A MOLLUSC

In 1818, after observing the action of the wood-boring mollusc *Teredo navalis*, the French-born engineer Marc Isambard Brunel (father of Isambard Kingdom Brunel) designed the first successful machine for tunnelling beneath riverbeds. The mollusc, scourge of wooden-hulled ships, bores into timbers, gnawing the wood with its powerful jaws and supporting the bore hole with its hard tubular shell.

So Brunel built a box-shaped iron casing, or shield, which could be pushed through soft ground by means of screw jacks. The men dug through shuttered openings in the face of the shield, while the tunnel was lined with bricks behind them.

THE BIGGEST HOLE *The 'Big Hole' at Kimberley, South Africa, is the world's deepest open-cast mine. During the 44 years the mine was open between 1871 and 1915, some 23 million tonnes of earth were removed from it – mostly by labourers with picks and shovels. The hole – which is 1.6km (1 mile) around and a total of about 1200m (4000ft) deep – also produced 14.5 million carats of diamonds.*

The machine drove the world's first underwater tunnel beneath the River Thames from Wapping to Rotherhithe in London. The tunnel was opened in 1842 and 22 years later was being used as a railway tunnel – as it still is today.

## POP GOES THE WORKER
Builders of underwater tunnels in the second half of the 19th century often worked in pressurised chambers called caissons. The air inside the caissons was pressurised in order to keep back water while the tunnel was dug. Similar chambers were used to dig the foundations for bridges.

In 1905 a tunneller working in a caisson under the East River in New York had a lucky escape when the side of the pressure chamber collapsed. The enormous pressure fired him 1.5m (5ft) through the silt of the riverbed, like a cork from a champagne bottle. He shot to the surface and was rescued – shaken but not seriously hurt – by the crew of a passing tug.

## TUNNELLING THROUGH THE ALPS
Four railway tunnels cut through the Alps reduced the travelling time involved in negotiating the largest land barrier in Europe by up to 70 per cent. The Frejus, St Gotthard, Simplon and Lötschberg railway tunnels were completed in the late 19th and early 20th centuries.

During the construction of the Frejus tunnel (1857 – 71), pneumatic power – now commonplace in industry – was used for the first time to drive tools. Altogether, some 400 workmen died while working on the tunnels. At the Simplon tunnel alone there were 5000 casualties – including 133 people permanently disabled.

## THE TUNNEL THAT NOBODY WOULD BUILD
In the 19th century a French eccentric called Thomé de Gamond spent about 40 years and his personal fortune in trying to promote a tunnel beneath the English Channel. His ambition was to span the 32km (20 miles) that separated France from England. But neither of the two governments concerned was sympathetic to his scheme; they thought that the cost would be too great, and that, politically and economically, it was best to keep the two countries apart.

Gamond's main supporter was his daughter Elizabeth, who manned the rowing boat from which he descended to the seabed for rock samples. After all his money had gone, she taught music and gave him her earnings so that he could continue his life's work. But the tunnel remained a dream, and Gamond died penniless and humiliated in 1876.

Since then there have been two main attempts to build a Channel tunnel – one in the 1880s and the other in the mid-1970s. Both failed for lack of government support.

## LUCKY ACCIDENT
A cleaner in an electric lamp factory in Berlin, Germany, in the First World War accidentally created the material used for modern drilling bits – tungsten carbide. At the time there was a shortage of the industrial diamonds used to make light filaments, and the factory's scientists were trying to produce a material to replace the diamonds. They were about to give up when the cleaner spilled some iron filings on the engineers' work. As a result, the new material hardened and formed the metallic compound now called tungsten carbide.

At first, the tungsten was used only for making light filaments. But during the Second World War tungsten formed the tips on armour-piercing shells, and since 1945 it has been used as drill bits for boring through rock, in preference to the much more expensive bits made from diamonds.

## LIFE SENTENCE, DEATH SENTENCE
In ancient Egypt, prisoners of war, criminals and entire families who had displeased the authorities were sentenced to work underground in gold mines for the rest of their lives. Two thousand years later, Charles IX of Sweden (1604 – 11) ordered the overseers in his silver mines to torture and execute Polish prisoners of war who were sent underground and then refused to work there. If the overseers failed in this, they themselves were executed.

## DEEPEST HOLE ON EARTH
The world's deepest borehole is an exploratory geological drilling in the Kola Peninsula, in northern Russia. In 1984 it was more than four-fifths of the way to its target depth of 15,000m (49,000ft).

## COOLING OFF
A refrigerating plant with the cooling capacity of 2500 tonnes of ice is installed in the world's deepest mine: the Western Deep Levels gold mine at Carletonville, South Africa. Without the cooling plant, the temperature at the lowest levels 3777m (12,390ft) down would be as high as 55°C (131°F).

# MINING TECHNIQUES

Today, three main mining techniques are in use: open-cast; drift; and deep underground mining. A fourth technique, known as alluvial mining, is still used by amateur prospectors around the world, but it is not used commercially.

**Alluvial mining** In the 19th century, alluvial mining methods – known since the time of the ancient Egyptians – were used by prospectors to find minerals, particularly precious metals and gems, washed down ancient river courses and settled in pockets in the bedrock. The prospector's basic equipment consisted of a shovel and a sieve or pan into which the mineral-rich gravel was scooped. The miners who thronged to California, the Klondike and Australia in the gold rushes mostly used alluvial techniques. But alluvial mining has been replaced by the science of geochemistry, which traces deposits back to their source by analysing samples of soil, stream sediments and plant material.

**Open-cast mining** Used to gather mineral deposits where they lie close to the surface. Excavators remove coverings of soil or clay, and the ore-bearing rock is then broken up by blasting, and removed. Because the ore is 'open' – on the surface – giant excavating machinery can be used, making the mining process quick and relatively cheap.

**Drift mining** An intermediate technique used for deposits fairly near the surface, but not so near as to make open-cast mining economic. Large shafts, or 'drifts', are driven into the ground – often a hillside – more or less horizontally. This enables conveyor belts and trucks to move ore directly from the working face to the surface.

**Deep underground mining** Used to reach seams hundreds of metres below the surface. It is the most expensive technique because long vertical shafts and tunnels have to be driven to reach the ore, the ore has to be moved a considerable distance to reach the surface, and the size of the tunnels restricts the use of large excavating machinery.

# Engineering 2: bridges and dams

## IMPORTANCE OF THE ARCH

The use of the arch by the Greeks and the Romans as a building technique was as important to bridge-building as the silicon chip has been to electronics. Before the arch, most bridges, like other buildings, made do with the post-and-lintel system of vertical pillars supporting horizontal beams.

Only wood could be used for the longer spans, but it was a fire risk and eventually rotted. The arch was first used by man in mud-brick constructions in about 4000 BC. At Mohenjo Daro in Pakistan between 3000 and 2000 BC, arches were used to span small drains and culverts. And in about 1400 BC, the Egyptians built what was then the largest known arch span, in a grain store at Thebes. The span was 4m (13ft) wide.

## HANGING ON

Stone Age man is thought to have been using simple suspension bridges some 10,000 years ago – crossing streams by means of two creepers tied to trees on each bank. He stood on one creeper and held the other.

## LONDON BRIDGE IS STAYING UP

There has been a bridge on the site of London Bridge at least since before the middle of the 10th century AD. The Romans, who occupied Britain in the 1st century AD, may also have put a bridge across the Thames at the same site, but no evidence of it remains. The first known bridge was a wooden structure, and it was replaced by a 19-arch stone bridge which was completed in 1209. The new bridge, built by an engineer called Peter of Colechurch, was London's only fixed crossing of the Thames for more than 500 years. It was joined by Westminster Bridge in 1750.

London Bridge became much more than a roadway. It was crowded with houses, shops, taverns, chapels and a fort. The children's song, *London Bridge is falling down*, which dates from the 18th century, refers to the frequent collapse or demolition of these often ramshackle buildings – not to the bridge itself.

Peter of Colechurch's bridge was finally pulled down and replaced by a five-arch design in 1831. It was this bridge, known as Rennie's Bridge after its designer John Rennie, which was sold to the US resort of Lake Havasu in Arizona for £1,025,000 and rebuilt there in the 1970s. Its successor, the present bridge, which has only three arches, opened in March 1973.

## DISASTER ON THE HIGH GIRDERS

Thomas Bouch, the 19th-century British designer who built the first Tay railway bridge in Scotland, was knighted for his engineering achievements at the same ceremony in June 1879 as Henry Bessemer, who invented the Bessemer steel-making process in 1856.

Six months after the ceremony, on the night of December 28, Bouch's bridge collapsed in a storm, killing 75 people. The bridge, which was largely made of wrought iron, was so buffeted by gusting winds that its 13 central girders were blown 49m (160ft) into the river below, taking a train with them. A subsequent government inquiry blamed the disaster on faulty design and construction. Had the Tay Bridge been made of Bessemer's steel, modern engineers believe, it could have survived the storm. But steel bridges were illegal in Britain at the time because steel was regarded as an experimental metal.

## WHEEL OF FORTUNE

The family of a Dutch water engineer still earns an income from a water wheel that does not exist. In 1580, the engineer, Pieter Morice, was granted a licence allowing him to set up a water wheel under an arch of London Bridge to provide power for pumping fresh water to neighbouring houses. At the time, the bridge was an ideal site because its 19 arches so constricted the river's flow that there was a difference of up to 1.5m (5ft) between the water levels on either

---

## BRIDGE DESIGN

The earliest type of bridge was a beam bridge: logs or slabs of stone laid flat across a stream. Box-girder bridges, made of metal, are a modern form. In a cantilever bridge, the supporting beam is in at least two parts joined by a hinge – a design which reduces the strain at the centre of the span. In an arch bridge, the weight of the roadway is carried by an arch to the foundations on each bank – in some modern designs, the arch is partly above the roadway. A suspension bridge is essentially an inverted arch, with the roadway hung from a curving cable.

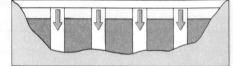

BEAM BRIDGE *Straight slabs or girders carry the roadway in a beam bridge. The spans have to be relatively short, and the load (shown by the arrows) is carried by the piers.*

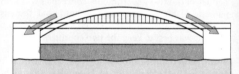

ARCH BRIDGE *The 503m (1650ft) long arch bridge across Sydney harbour is the world's widest long-span bridge. It carries two rail tracks, eight car lanes and a footpath.*

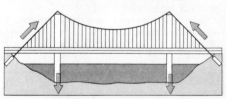

SUSPENSION BRIDGE *The world's longest bridges are now all suspension bridges. In this design, the bulk of the load is carried on cables anchored to the banks.*

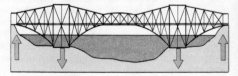

CANTILEVER BRIDGE *The central span pushes down through the piers and pulls up at each end. The longest cantilever – the Quebec Bridge in Canada – is 987m (3239ft) long.*

side. When the bridge was replaced in the 19th century, there was no longer a suitable arch for Morice's heirs to operate the water wheel. Since the licence had been granted for 500 years, Morice's descendants were awarded compensation. They still get £3750 a year from the Thames Water Authority.

## A BRIDGE THAT WENT TOO FAR

Many 19th-century engineers believed that the way to longer suspension bridges was to keep the structure light so that longer spans could be hung from the same cables.

The collapse of the Tacoma Narrows Bridge in the US state of Washington in 1940 proved that, within limits, the reverse was true. Four months after the slender and spectacular bridge opened to carry traffic on a single 850m (2800ft) span across Puget Sound, it fell down. Although it had been designed to be safe in winds of up to 190km/h (120mph), it was destroyed by a wind of only 67km/h (42mph). The bridge deck was so light that it began to heave up and down in the wind, making wavy movements up to 9m (30ft) deep.

After three hours, the deck started to twist back and forth through 90 degrees until some of the suspending cables broke and sent first the middle and then the whole of the span plunging into the water.

## HUMBER HIGHWAY

The new Humber Bridge in northern England – currently the world's longest suspension bridge – has a deck with a curved underside, like an upside-down aeroplane wing, so that the stronger the wind the more firmly it holds itself in place. In addition, the cables that hold the roadway are set at an angle rather than vertically in order to damp down vibrations at low wind speeds. The bridge's central span is 1410m (4626ft) long and the towers are so far apart that they are 36mm (1.4in) out of parallel to allow for the curvature of the Earth.

Work on an even larger bridge began in 1978 in Japan. The Akashi-Kaikyo Bridge, due to be completed in 1988, will be a double-decker, carrying a roadway on one level and a railway on the other. Its main span will stretch for 1780m (5840ft) – more than a mile.

## THE DAM-BUILDERS

The earliest dams in the world were modest affairs, built to create a reservoir for irrigation or for drinking water in times of drought. The earliest known dams, made of earth faced with stone, were built in about 3200 BC at Jawa in the north of present-day Jordan.

## SEEDS OF SUCCESS

One of the pioneers of reinforced concrete – without which it would be impossible to build modern dams or bridges – was a French commercial gardener. Joseph Monier wanted to make larger flowerpots than were possible with clay, so in 1849 he had the idea of making them from wire netting covered in concrete. He soon realised that the principle could be extended to other sorts of construction, and patented the idea of casting concrete round criss-crossing iron bars. The

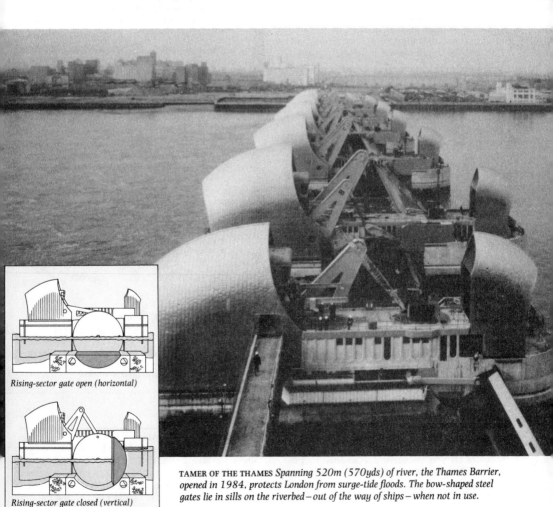

*Rising-sector gate open (horizontal)*

*Rising-sector gate closed (vertical)*

TAMER OF THE THAMES *Spanning 520m (570yds) of river, the Thames Barrier, opened in 1984, protects London from surge-tide floods. The bow-shaped steel gates lie in sills on the riverbed – out of the way of ships – when not in use.*

combination created a material that was stronger than either alone – and the cement covering also prevented the iron bars from rusting.

## A DAM THAT DID NOT LAST . . .

Ancient Egypt depended on the Nile to irrigate its crops. But although the Egyptians built an elaborate network of irrigation canals, they built only one dam. Constructed between 2950 and 2750 BC, it contained about 100,000 tonnes of earth faced with masonry and sprawled for 106m (348ft) across a valley called Wadi el-Garawi, to the south of Cairo. At its base, it was 84m (276ft) thick.

The dam was used to trap rainwater for nearby quarries. But despite its size, it lasted only a few years before being breached by the weight of water behind it. All that remain are the stubs of the wall on either side of the valley.

## . . . AND TWO THAT DID

Two irrigation dams built by Roman engineers in the 2nd century AD in Merida, Spain, are still in use. The only major maintenance work they have needed in the past 1800 years has been the renewal of their stone facings, carried out in the 1930s.

## BREACH OF THE LAW

Dams were so important to the ancient Babylonians of Mesopotamia that in the early 18th century BC, Hammurabi, a king of Babylon, passed a stern law warning citizens of their responsibility for dam maintenance. Anyone, he decreed, who allowed a dam to be breached should be sold into slavery and the proceeds handed over to farmers whose crops had suffered because of the breach. If the sale did not raise enough, the culprit's family were also to be sold.

## THE NAVIGATORS

The colloquial term 'navvy' for a construction worker comes from the word navigator, used to describe the men who dug the bulk of Britain's canals between about 1780 and 1850.

The gangs of hired labourers acquired a fearsome reputation. Newspapers of the period reported that villages and towns along a new canal's route were often terrorised by men on mass drinking sprees. In some areas, terrified townspeople sent their daughters away until work on a nearby canal was finished.

## RECORD-BREAKER

For more than 3000 years, the Great Pyramid of Cheops in Egypt was the world's largest building, with a total volume of more than 2,500,000m³ (3.3 million cubic yards). It was topped only after the 10th century AD by a Mexican pyramid, now known as the Quetzalcoatl, which has a volume of about 3,300,000m³ (4.3 million cubic yards). Then, in 1942, both records were overtaken by the Grand Coulee Dam in the United States. The concrete dam, which blocks the Columbia river and holds back a reservoir 240km (150 miles) long, is 167m (550ft) high – only about 20m (65ft) taller than the Great Pyramid. But its volume is more than three times greater, at 8,100,000m³ (10.6 million cubic yards).

Since the Grand Coulee Dam was built, newer dams have become still larger and higher. An earth-fill dam at New Cornelia Tailings, in the US state of Arizona, is more than 20 times larger, with a total volume of 209,500,000m³ (274 million cubic yards). The Grand Dixence Dam in Switzerland, completed in 1961, is nearly twice as high, at 285m (935ft). Even that has been dwarfed by a Russian dam built in the 1980s across the Vakhsh river; it is 325m (1066ft) high.

# MOVING A BOAT UPHILL

Before canal locks were invented, boats could be moved past obstacles such as hills or rapids only by being portaged – physically carried.

The Vikings, for instance, are known to have portaged their longships on rollers across more than 15km (10 miles) of land to get from the Baltic to the North Sea and bypass the dangerous waters of the Skagerrak. The Kiel Canal, first built as the Eider Canal in 1784, now follows much the same route.

### Flash locks

The first types of lock were stanches or flash locks, which were used to reduce gradients on rivers and raise the water level in shallow stretches. They were usually single barriers built across gaps in weirs. To pass through, the barrier was opened and a boat either rode through on the surge or 'flash' of water, or was hauled through against it.

The Chinese installed two of these flash locks about 75m (250ft) apart on the Grand Canal in AD 984, and some scholars argue that they represent the first true lock, known as a pound lock. But there is no evidence that the gates were used in sequence in the way that the much safer pound lock is.

### Pound locks

Pound locks consist of two sets of gates set close together so that they enclose, or 'impound', a short stretch of water. They made it possible to build canals up steeper and higher slopes. Boats passing upstream enter the pound through the lower gates, which are then closed. Valves, sometimes called paddles or sluices, are opened in the upper gates, allowing the water in the lock to rise. When the level in the lock matches the level upstream, the upper gates are opened and the boat sails on. Boats travelling downstream go through the reverse procedure.

### Inclined planes

To supplement particularly busy locks, inclined planes were sometimes built beside them. In one type, boats were floated on to movable docks, then the docks, which ran on rails, were winched up or down the slope and lowered into the water again. Such a lock was built at Foxton on Britain's Grand Union Canal between 1896 and 1900, but it was abandoned in 1911. Few inclined planes remain in use.

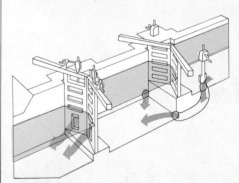

HOW A POUND LOCK WORKS *Valves in or beside the gates at each end of a pound lock allow the water level inside to be raised or lowered to match the level outside.*

## DROWNED WATERFALL

The world's largest waterfall has been drowned by a dam. The lake created by the dam is so big and so deep that the site of the falls – 190km (118 miles) upstream from the dam – is now just an underwater cliff. The drowned waterfall is the Guaira Falls, on the Parana

River between Paraguay and Brazil. The falls had a maximum height of 114m (374ft), far less than several other waterfalls. But the amount of water flowing over them was more than double the flow over the Niagara Falls, 12 times the flow over the Victoria Falls – and enough to fill the entire dome of London's St Paul's Cathedral in little more than half a second.

The dam that has drowned the falls is the Itaipu Dam, completed in November 1982. The installation of giant turbines to generate electricity is still going on. By 1988, the dam is scheduled to have 18 turbines able to produce between them 12,600 million watts of electricity, so making Itaipu the world's largest power station.

## THE GRANDEST CANAL
The first canals were built in about 4000 BC to improve navigation on the sluggish rivers of Mesopotamia. The longest canal in the ancient world, however, was built in China. Called the Grand Canal, it was begun in the 6th century BC as a series of short sections linking stretches of navigable rivers. By AD 1327 it had grown into a waterway 1781km (1107 miles) long, stretching from the Chinese capital, Beijing (Peking), to Hangzhou (Hangchow). When work was at its height during the early 7th century AD, the workforce is estimated to have been 5 million.

The Grand Canal is still in use, but has been overtaken in length by Russia's Volga–Baltic Canal, opened in 1965. This incorporates 2977km (1850 miles) of artificial waterway and links the Black Sea to the Baltic via Leningrad.

## LEONARDO'S LOCK
Modern 'mitre' lock gates owe their design to the man who painted the *Mona Lisa*: the Italian artist and engineer Leonardo da Vinci. He invented them while he was the ducal engineer of Milan in the late 15th century. The first mitre gates were built to his design on the Naviglio Interno, a canal near the city, and were completed in 1497.

Most earlier lock gates opened and closed vertically. They were difficult to seal and the framework from which they hung set a limit on the height of boats that could use the canal. Da Vinci's design arranged the gates in pairs which swung on hinges at the sides of the canal like double doors. Their mitred edges met in a V pointing upstream, so that when they were shut the weight of water made a watertight seal.

## THE MISSING ARCH
Although the Romans mastered the principle of the arch for bridges at least 200 years before the birth of Christ, they did not think of applying it to dams until the 6th century AD. Modern dams derive much of their strength from their shape, which curves against the weight of the water behind them like an arch laid on its side, the crown of the curve jutting upstream into the lake. The first dam known to have used the principle was the Daras Dam. It was built on the Persian frontier for the Byzantine emperor Justinian, between 527 and 565, and was described by the Byzantine historian Procopius in AD 560.

## ALL AT SEA
Among the guests officially invited to a display held in 1914 to mark the completion of the Panama Canal was a representative of a non-existent organisation ... the Swiss Navy. The invitation was presented to the Foreign Office of the land-locked republic by the US ambassador to Switzerland, a Georgian named Pleasant A. Stovall. It was later withdrawn on the orders of the embarrassed US State Department.

## THE FIELD-BUSTER
Although it improves the irrigation of thousands of hectares of land, Egypt's Aswan High Dam – 111m (364ft) high, nearly 4km (2.5 miles) long, and built across the Nile in the 1960s with Russian money and expertise – is turning fields hundreds of kilometres away into desert. For centuries, farmers in the lower Nile delta near the Mediterranean have depended on the fertile silt washed down the river valley in the annual floods. But now that the river has been bottled up in Lake Nasser, the floods and the silt have stopped – and the desert is creeping in.

DESERT LAKE *Lake Nasser covers 5180km² (2000 square miles) of Egypt and the Sudan.*

# Transport

PARK . . . AND DIE! The first paved roads were processional ways leading to the great temples and festival sites in the cities of the Babylonians and Assyrians, and along them were carried idols of the gods of these early Mesopotamian civilisations. The Assyrians were the first to make road-building state business. Rules of the road were strict. King Sennacherib, who ruled Assyria in the early 7th century BC, decreed that anyone putting up a building or parking a chariot alongside the processional way in his capital, Nineveh, should face death by impaling.

---

*The word 'coach' derives from the Hungarian town of Kocs, where, in about AD 1500, a comparatively smooth-riding, horse-drawn vehicle was designed.*
  *The carriage was slung between the axles on leather straps, and the front wheels were smaller than the rear ones to make steering easier.*

---

ALL ROADS LEAD TO ROME  Road-building was one of the great triumphs of the Roman empire. By the time the empire fell in the 4th century AD, the network covered more than 80,000km (50,000 miles) throughout Europe and the Middle East.

Not until railways were built in the 19th century was the Roman system surpassed. At the height of the empire it took six days to travel from London to Rome. By coach on the same route 1700 years later, British Prime Minister Sir Robert Peel took exactly the same length of time.

---

*Gunpowder was used to fuel the first working internal combustion engine, which was made in the 17th century by the Dutch mathematician Christiaan Huygens (1629 – 95). He is better known for inventing, in about 1656, the first working pendulum clock.*

---

QUICK START  It was the development of the electric starter that finally made petrol the fuel choice for the motor car. A British Arnold car had the first fitted electric starter in 1896.

By 1912, the American company Cadillac had introduced the system into production models. Until then, 40 per cent of cars were steam-powered, 38 per cent used electric batteries, and only 22 per cent used petrol. The electric starter meant that petrol-driven cars would start up at once – unlike steam, which had to be built up. And petrol-driven cars could be refuelled more quickly and easily than electric cars.

---

*Mockers hurled insults at the early riders of penny-farthings. In 1876, a British coachman on the London – St Albans run was fined for whipping a cyclist who was overtaking him. The guard on the coach was also fined . . . for hurling an iron ball on the end of a rope into the bicycle's spokes, felling the rider.*

---

RING-A-DING-DING  The bicycle won its right to the roads of Britain in 1888. Parliament passed an Act classifying it as 'a carriage'. Under the law, every bike

## THE CHANGING SHAPE OF THE CAR

**1885** The first petrol-driven car took to the road, looking like a motorised tricycle and steered with a tiller. The machine, designed by the German Karl Benz, produced less than 1hp.

**1886** The first true 'horseless carriage' was the German Gottlieb Daimler's converted phaeton fitted with a petrol engine. A later model, built in 1889, could run twice as fast as Benz's pioneer. It also had a clutch and gears, setting the pattern for the car of the future.

**1891** Two French toolmakers, René Panhard and Emile Levassor, were the first engineers to put the engine at the front of a car. It gave better balance and the weight on the front wheels made it easier to steer.

**1891 – 2** Early Peugeots, which were rear-engined, were light, weighing only around 400kg (900lb). Unusually, they had no radiators. Instead the water used to cool the engine was cooled itself by being circulated around the metal frame.

**1896** British engineer Frederick Lanchester introduced a car with a system of epicyclic gears which could be pre-selected – the forerunner of modern automatic transmissions.

**1901** A new Daimler model was introduced, which combined into one machine for the first time all the vital features of the modern motor car: a powerful four-cylinder engine; a pressed-steel chassis; a honeycomb radiator; and a recognisably modern gear stick moving in a 'gate'. The model was named Mercedes, after the daughter of an Austrian, Emil Jellinek, who was the Daimler representative in Nice, France.

**1908** Henry Ford's Model T – the 'Tin Lizzie' – was the first everyman's car. It not only took motoring to the masses, but was also the pioneer of mass production and one of the foundations of the USA's prosperity.

**1922** The bull-nosed Morris, introduced as the Morris Oxford, launched the family car in Britain. In the 1920s, this popular range could be bought for as little as £170 – at £25 down and £2 per week. In the same year, the Austin Seven was the first of the family runabouts. It had all the big car characteristics contained in a small design. Top speed was 72 – 80km/h (45 – 50mph) and petrol consumption was 14km to a litre (40mpg).

**1936** The Volkswagen Beetle, launched in the late 1930s in Germany (Volkswagen is the German for 'people's car'), has since clocked up world-wide sales of more than 40 million. In the early 1980s, the Beetle was still being made in South America.

**1948** The Rover Car Company in England brought out the revolutionary go-anywhere Land Rover. This was a peacetime version of the American Willys Jeep – short for GP, standing for general purpose. The Jeep was the versatile four-wheel-drive vehicle that did all the army's donkey work in the Second World War.

**1959** The Morris and Austin Mini was introduced. It became hugely popular. It was small enough to squeeze through city traffic, easy to park, cheap to run, yet big enough for four adults. Soon other big-car makers followed with their own mini-models.

**1983** Austin Rover in Britain introduced the Maestro – the first car with a 'talking dashboard'. The synthesised voice, designed to alert the driver to engine problems, was the latest in a line of electronic systems added to cars since the 1960s to make them easier and safer to drive.

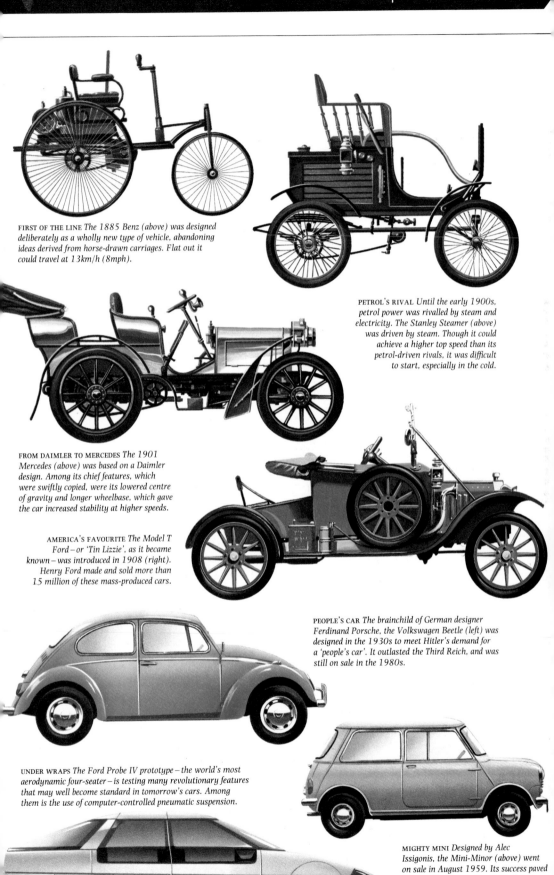

**FIRST OF THE LINE** *The 1885 Benz (above) was designed deliberately as a wholly new type of vehicle, abandoning ideas derived from horse-drawn carriages. Flat out it could travel at 13km/h (8mph).*

**PETROL'S RIVAL** *Until the early 1900s, petrol power was rivalled by steam and electricity. The Stanley Steamer (above) was driven by steam. Though it could achieve a higher top speed than its petrol-driven rivals, it was difficult to start, especially in the cold.*

**FROM DAIMLER TO MERCEDES** *The 1901 Mercedes (above) was based on a Daimler design. Among its chief features, which were swiftly copied, were its lowered centre of gravity and longer wheelbase, which gave the car increased stability at higher speeds.*

**AMERICA'S FAVOURITE** *The Model T Ford – or 'Tin Lizzie', as it became known – was introduced in 1908 (right). Henry Ford made and sold more than 15 million of these mass-produced cars.*

**PEOPLE'S CAR** *The brainchild of German designer Ferdinand Porsche, the Volkswagen Beetle (left) was designed in the 1930s to meet Hitler's demand for a 'people's car'. It outlasted the Third Reich, and was still on sale in the 1980s.*

**UNDER WRAPS** *The Ford Probe IV prototype – the world's most aerodynamic four-seater – is testing many revolutionary features that may well become standard in tomorrow's cars. Among them is the use of computer-controlled pneumatic suspension.*

**MIGHTY MINI** *Designed by Alec Issigonis, the Mini-Minor (above) went on sale in August 1959. Its success paved the way for a generation of small cars.*

# Transport

had to be fitted with a bell, which had to be rung non-stop while the machine was in motion. The law was abolished in 1930.

STEAMING TO DISASTER  A huge, steam-powered gun carriage invented by a French artillery officer, Nicholas Joseph Cugnot, was the world's first mechanically propelled road vehicle. But the three-wheeled monster did not last long. On its first run in 1769, it steamed for 20 minutes, at a speed of 3.6km/h (2.25 mph) . . . then caused the world's first motor vehicle accident by crashing into a wall in Paris.

> *A three-wheeled vehicle powered by dogs was invented in the 1880s by a Monsieur Huret of France. Inside the two huge rear wheels were treadmills driven by the animals. An outcry by animal-lovers led to the idea being scrapped.*

WORLD-BEATER  A round-the-world car race was staged by the French newspaper *Le Matin* in 1908, with the aim of boosting the French car industry – but no French car finished. First home over the 21,725km (13,500 miles) westward course from New York to Paris was a German Protos, which took 165 days but suffered a 15-day penalty for travelling part of the way by train. The winner was an American Thomas in 170 days.

BORN IN A GARDEN SHED  The American Henry Ford, founder of the Ford Motor Company, made his first car in the garden shed at his home in Michigan in 1896. Twelve years later he began producing the Model T in Detroit. Cheap, reliable and mass-produced, the Model T turned the car from novelty to necessity and put the USA on the road. In 27 years of production 15 million were sold. The car was named Model T after Ford had made eight earlier cars, known as models A, B, C, F, K, N, R and S.

> *Henry Ford did not invent the assembly line method of manufacture. He simply made assembly lines move. Static lines had been in use for years.*
> *Ford first used the moving assembly line idea in 1913 to speed production of magnetos – the dynamos that produced the ignition sparks – for the Model T. By the end of 1914, he had installed a chain-driven conveyor to handle chassis construction in the same way, cutting assembly time from 12 hours per chassis to 1½ hours.*

PUNCTURED: THE FIRST TYRE  An inflatable tyre with a rubber inner tube was invented by a Scottish engineer, Robert Thomson, in 1845. Made of canvas with leather treads around the inner tube, it gave a comfortable ride, but there were so many manufacturing and fitting problems that Thomson dropped the idea. In 1888, a Belfast veterinary surgeon, John Dunlop, invented a pneumatic tyre with rubber treads for his ten-year-old son's tricycle. The following year he helped to form a company – which grew into the Dunlop Rubber Company – to produce his invention.

> *A limousine built in 1968 for the official use of the President of the United States cost $500,000. The car, a Lincoln Continental Executive, weighs 5 tonnes, including 2 tonnes of steel plate, and can travel at 80km/h (50mph), even with all its tyres shot away.*

DEATH ON THE ROAD  Two people died in motoring accidents in the United States in 1899. Seventy years later, there were more than 60,000 fatalities in a single year – more deaths than the USA suffered in the entire Vietnam War.

Already this century, more than 25 million people have been killed on the world's roads. By AD 2000,

## THE STORY OF THE ROAD

Some ceremonial routes in the ancient cities of Mesopotamia, paved with stone 4000 years ago, were the first man-made roads. Later, Roman roads formed the most extensive network in Europe and the Middle East, and Roman techniques were still being copied by Napoleonic engineers as late as the 18th century. Only with the introduction of tar, asphalt and concrete in the 19th and 20th centuries have road-building techniques improved significantly on Roman methods.

**ROMAN** The roads the Roman legions tramped across Europe were simple, but lasting, in construction. The road was founded on tightly packed earth covered with pebbles set in mortar. This was overlaid with a hard filling, cambered so that the water would run off each side. Some roads were paved on top with stone slabs.

**MACADAM** In this 19th-century technique, a convex foundation of tightly packed earth formed the base of the road. It was covered with two 100mm (4in) courses of carefully graded stones. These were overlaid with pebbles, which were ground to a fine dust by the wheels of horse-drawn coaches.

**MODERN** The motorways of the 20th century are built on a firm, thick base of pebbly material, with a layer of concrete laid over the top. Above this is a layer of tar or rolled asphalt. The top surface is smoothed off with rolled asphalt, though sometimes concrete slabs have been used.

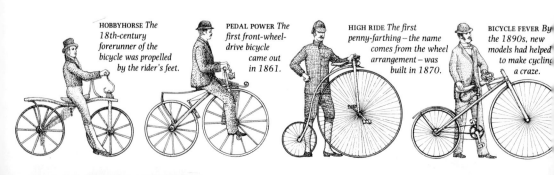

HOBBYHORSE *The 18th-century forerunner of the bicycle was propelled by the rider's feet.*

PEDAL POWER *The first front-wheel-drive bicycle came out in 1861.*

HIGH RIDE *The first penny-farthing – the name comes from the wheel arrangement – was built in 1870.*

BICYCLE FEVER *By the 1890s, new models had helped to make cycling a craze.*

the car will have claimed more victims than both this century's World Wars put together – and those cost an estimated 45 – 50 million lives.

PUTTING IN THE TAR  Tarmac, the most widely used road surface in the world, gets its name from a Scottish engineer who had nothing to do with its invention. The engineer, John Loudon McAdam (1756 – 1836), invented a road-building technique called macadamising in the early 19th century. His technique was for a dry stone surface made of a layer of small stones over a bed of larger tightly packed rocks. Fine gravel or crushed slag was used to fill in the gaps. No tar was involved, however.

The idea for binding the surface together with tar was devised only in 1854, 18 years after McAdam's death, by a Nottingham surveyor named E. P. Hooley. Hooley noticed that a barrel of tar which had been accidentally spilt over some slag formed a smooth, hard-wearing surface. It was Hooley who named the new surface tarmacadam, in McAdam's honour, and the name was later shortened to tarmac.

POTTERY ENGINE  In 1983, Japanese engineers claimed a breakthrough in making a workable engine out of pottery. The pottery engine, developed by researchers at the Asahi Glass Company, is made from carbon silicon and nitrogen silicon ceramics that are almost as strong as steel, but conduct much less heat. Researchers hope that the use of ceramics will allow engines to run safely at much higher temperatures. This would increase their efficiency, cut pollution and allow the use of almost any fuel to power them.

DANGER SIGNALS  The world's first traffic lights were installed near the House of Commons in London in December 1868 – and seriously injured a policeman who was working them. The red and green gas lights were set in a revolving lantern, perched on top of a cast-iron pillar some 7m (23ft) high. One night in January 1869 the gas exploded, blowing gravel into the eye of the constable operating the lever which changed the lights and extended and lowered the signal arms. Despite the accident, the lights were used at night for the convenience of Members of Parliament until 1872, when they were taken down. It was not until 1926 that traffic lights reappeared in London.

SILENT SPIRIT  In 1958, David Ogilvy, the Scottish founder of the US advertising agency Ogilvy and Mather, devised one of the motor industry's most memorable selling lines: 'At 60mph the loudest noise in this new Rolls-Royce comes from the electric clock.' When he showed the slogan to the company's chief engineer, however, the engineer was not impressed by its pithiness. He simply shook his head sadly, Ogilvy recalled later, and said: 'It's time we did something about that damned clock.'

In 1980, the company did. Its new Silver Spirit model was fitted with a soundless digital clock.

LADY'S MOUNT *Women cyclists wore 'bloomers', a split skirt devised by the American Amelia Bloomer.*

## MAJOR INTERNATIONAL REGISTRATION MARKS

| | | | |
|---|---|---|---|
| A | Austria | LB | Liberia |
| ADN | South Yemen | LS | Lesotho |
| AFG | Afghanistan | M | Malta |
| AL | Albania | MA | Morocco |
| AND | Andorra | MEX | Mexico |
| AUS | Australia | MS | Mauritius |
| B | Belgium | MW | Malawi |
| BD | Bangladesh | N | Norway |
| BDS | Barbados | NL | Netherlands |
| BG | Bulgaria | NZ | New Zealand |
| BH | Belize | P | Portugal |
| BR | Brazil | PA | Panama |
| BRN | Bahrain | PAK | Pakistan |
| BRU | Brunei | PE | Peru |
| BS | Bahamas | PL | Poland |
| BUR | Burma | PNG | Papua New Guinea |
| C | Cuba | | |
| CDN | Canada | PY | Paraguay |
| CH | Switzerland | RO | Romania |
| CI | Ivory Coast | RA | Argentina |
| CL | Sri Lanka | RB | Botswana |
| CO | Colombia | RC | Taiwan |
| CR | Costa Rica | RCA | Central African Republic |
| CS | Czechoslovakia | | |
| CY | Cyprus | RCB | Congo |
| D | West Germany | RCH | Chile |
| DDR | East Germany | RI | Indonesia |
| DK | Denmark | RIM | Mauritania |
| DY | Benin | RL | Lebanon |
| DZ | Algeria | RM | Madagascar |
| E | Spain | RMM | Mali |
| EAK | Kenya | RN | Niger |
| EAT | Tanzania | ROK | South Korea |
| EAU | Uganda | ROU | Uruguay |
| EC | Ecuador | RP | Philippines |
| ES | El Salvador | RSM | San Marino |
| ET | Egypt | RU | Burundi |
| F | France | RWA | Ruanda |
| FJI | Fiji | S | Sweden |
| FR | Faroe Islands | SD | Swaziland |
| GB | Britain | SF | Finland |
| GBA | Alderney | SGP | Singapore |
| GBG | Guernsey | SME | Surinam |
| GBJ | Jersey | SN | Senegal |
| GBM | Isle of Man | SU | Soviet Union |
| GBZ | Gibraltar | SY | Seychelles |
| GCA | Guatemala | SYR | Syria |
| GH | Ghana | T | Thailand |
| GR | Greece | TN | Tunisia |
| GUY | Guyana | TR | Turkey |
| H | Hungary | TT | Trinidad and Tobago |
| HK | Hong Kong | | |
| HKJ | Jordan | USA | United States |
| I | Italy | V | Vatican City |
| IL | Israel | VN | Vietnam |
| IND | India | WAG | Gambia |
| IR | Iran | WAL | Sierra Leone |
| IRL | Ireland | WAN | Nigeria |
| IRQ | Iraq | WG | Grenada |
| IS | Iceland | WL | St Lucia |
| J | Japan | WV | St Vincent |
| JA | Jamaica | YU | Yugoslavia |
| K | Kampuchea | YV | Venezuela |
| L | Luxembourg | ZA | South Africa |
| LAO | Laos | ZRE | Zaire |
| LAR | Libya | ZW | Zimbabwe |

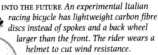

INTO THE FUTURE *An experimental Italian racing bicycle has lightweight carbon fibre discs instead of spokes and a back wheel larger than the front. The rider wears a helmet to cut wind resistance.*

# Transport

**THE FIRST RAILWAY DEATH** The inaugural run of the world's first railway passenger service, in Britain in 1830, also caused the first railway death. Ironically the victim was one of the railway lobby's staunchest supporters. Sir William Huskisson, a former President of the Board of Trade, was a guest of George Stephenson (1781–1848), who, with his son Robert, had invented the *Rocket* locomotive. The *Rocket* was then the fastest engine in the world, having set a speed record of 47km/h (29mph) in 1829.

Wanting to enlist support for the development of railways, the Stephensons had arranged for eight trains to carry various dignitaries, including the Prime Minister, the Duke of Wellington, between Liverpool and Manchester as a publicity exercise. When the first train stopped in a passing place to give the Prime Minister a better view of the other trains in action, several people got off.

Huskisson, who was standing on the main line, misjudged the speed of an approaching train and was run over. During the frantic dash to get the fatally injured Huskisson to hospital, the *Rocket* broke its own record, reaching a speed of 58km/h (36mph).

**WHY STEPHENSON LIED** In 1825, the British railway pioneer George Stephenson deliberately lied to a parliamentary inquiry. He told the committee of MPs that trains would never travel faster than 19km/h (12mph), even though he knew that they could already reach speeds more than twice as great.

Stephenson deceived the MPs in order to allay public fears of the new mode of travel. Political opponents had claimed that it could seriously damage passengers' health. Trains travelling at more than 19km/h, they had insisted, would cause mental disorders and would expose passengers to the risk of being suffocated because the speed would suck all the air from their lungs.

**IN THE GROOVE** The idea of using wheels on rails is much older than trains. As early as 3000 BC the ancient Greeks began using grooves about 150mm (6in) deep and 900–1500mm (3–5ft) apart to move heavy loads on wagons.

European mines began to use hand-propelled trucks on wooden rails from about the 15th century. The first documented railway of this kind was noted in Germany in 1430. The first all-iron rails were laid at Bath in England in 1761, although iron plates had been used to cover wooden rails since the 1690s.

---

*The longest stretch of straight rail track in the world crosses part of Australia's Nullarbor Plain just north of the Great Australian Bight. The arrow-straight section is 478km (297 miles) long.*

---

**THE FIRST TUBES** The trains used on the world's first underground railway, which opened between Paddington and the City of London in 1863, were powered by steam – not electricity. The original tunnels still form part of London Transport's Metropolitan Line. Using a 'cut-and-cover' technique, which involved excavating a trench and then constructing a brick tunnel inside, the line was built to relieve traffic congestion on the roads. Smoke and steam from the engines escaped through ventilators and open-roofed sections. Electric trains began to replace steam only in

## TIMETABLE OF WORLD RAILWAY HISTORY

**1761** First iron rails laid at Bath, England.

**1782** Scotsman James Watt invents a steam engine able to turn wheels.

**1803** Richard Trevithick, a Cornish engineer, constructs the first steam locomotive.

**1814** Englishman George Stephenson builds his first steam locomotive, *Blücher*.

**1825** Stephenson's Stockton and Darlington Railway, the first regularly operated steam railway, opens, carrying freight from a colliery to a river port.

**1829** Robert Stephenson's *Rocket* locomotive sets a new speed record of 47km/h (29mph) at Rainhill Trials, held near Liverpool.

**1830** World's first regular passenger service started between Liverpool and Manchester. Widespread railroad construction begins in Britain, and spreads in the following years to Europe and North America.

**1857** Steel rails first used in Britain.

**1863** First underground railway opened in London.

**1863** Scotsman Robert Fairlie invents an engine with pivoted driving bogies, allowing trains to negotiate tighter bends.

**1865** Pullman sleeping car introduced in the USA.

**1869** Coast-to-coast railway, linking the Atlantic to the Pacific seaboards, completed in the USA.

**1877** Vacuum brakes invented in the United States.

**1879** First electric railway demonstrated at the Berlin Trades Fair.

**1883** First public electric railway opened at Brighton in England.

**1890** First electric underground railway opened in London.

**1891** Construction begins on the 9313km (5787 miles) Trans-Siberian Railway – the longest in the world – between Moscow and Vladivostok in Russia. Construction completed in 1904.

**1925** First diesel locomotive service introduced in Canada.

**1964** 'Bullet train' service between Tokyo and Osaka in Japan opened; trains average speeds of 163km/h (101mph).

**1976** Britain introduces diesel High Speed Trains (HST), capable of reaching 230km/h (143mph).

**1981** Advanced Passenger Train (APT) developed in Britain. Prototypes of the train have a cruising speed of 200km/h (125mph) and a top speed of 250km/h (156mph). Automatic tilting suspension aims to allow the train to take corners at high speed.

**1983** French high-speed train, the TGV (standing for *Train Grande Vitesse*), sets new world speed record for passenger trains, completing the Lyons-Paris run at an average speed of 213km/h (132mph).

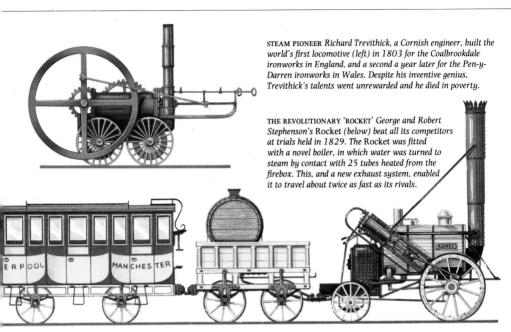

STEAM PIONEER *Richard Trevithick, a Cornish engineer, built the world's first locomotive (left) in 1803 for the Coalbrookdale ironworks in England, and a second a year later for the Pen-y-Darren ironworks in Wales. Despite his inventive genius, Trevithick's talents went unrewarded and he died in poverty.*

THE REVOLUTIONARY 'ROCKET' *George and Robert Stephenson's Rocket (below) beat all its competitors at trials held in 1829. The Rocket was fitted with a novel boiler, in which water was turned to steam by contact with 25 tubes heated from the firebox. This, and a new exhaust system, enabled it to travel about twice as fast as its rivals.*

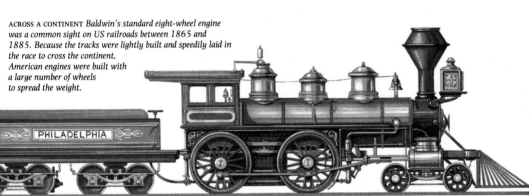

ACROSS A CONTINENT *Baldwin's standard eight-wheel engine was a common sight on US railroads between 1865 and 1885. Because the tracks were lightly built and speedily laid in the race to cross the continent, American engines were built with a large number of wheels to spread the weight.*

PHILADELPHIA

L N E R 4472

IN SEARCH OF A RECORD *Improved design, with the gradual awareness of the importance of streamlining, went hand in hand with faster and faster speeds. In Britain, the crack expresses of the leading railway companies, such as the* Flying Scotsman *linking London and Edinburgh, vied with each other to cut their journey times and beat their rivals on other lines.*

TGV

WORLD BEATER *France's electric-powered TGV train is the fastest in regular service in the world. In 1983 it covered the 425km (264 miles) between Lyons and Paris in exactly 2 hours – an average speed of 213km/h (132mph). Its peak speed is 270km/h (168mph).*

# Transport

the 1890s, when a new line, between 14 and 18m (45 and 60ft) below ground level, was opened. The line ran beneath the River Thames to link the City and the Elephant and Castle. Electric power was used on the new line because of the difficulty of ventilating such a deep tunnel adequately.

---

*A man with a wooden leg, known as 'Bumper Harris', was employed to ride up and down Britain's first moving staircase, which was installed on the London Underground at Earls Court in 1911. The aim was to give the public confidence in the new mode of travel.*

*The world's longest escalator is on Leningrad's underground rail network in Russia; it carries passengers a vertical distance of nearly 60m (195ft).*

---

GETTING THE TRAINS TO RUN ON TIME  The introduction of railways changed the timekeeping habits of a nation. Before the railway age British time was kept on a local basis, so that time throughout the country could differ by as much as 15 minutes. Even within London there was a variation of two minutes between the eastern and western ends of the city.

The system meant, however, that the railway companies could not issue accurate timetables. By 1850 the railways nationwide had adopted London Time, but that merely added to the confusion. Some towns in the mid-19th century even installed clocks with two minute hands: one for local time; the other for railway time.

Pressure for change grew after a court case in Dorset on November 24, 1858. At 10.06am on that day by Dorset clocks, a Dorchester judge found against a man involved in a land battle because he was late for the 10am hearing. Two minutes later, the man arrived and claimed he was on time – by the station clock in his home town of Carlisle in Cumbria.

The case had to be retried, and in 1880 Parliament ended the confusion by ordering the whole country to set its clocks to Greenwich Mean Time.

---

*Wild West souvenir-hunters disconnected North America's first transcontinental railway almost as soon as it was completed. When the Union Pacific and Central Pacific railways met at Promontory, Utah, in 1869, after six years of construction, the occasion was celebrated by linking the last section of track with two golden spikes.*

*However, fearing that the spikes would be stolen, the builders quickly removed them after the ceremony, replacing them with conventional steel spikes. This substitution failed to deter the souvenir-hunters, and within a few days 12 spikes, six ties and two pairs of rails had disappeared from the spot.*

---

STATION ON THE ROOF OF THE WORLD  The world's highest standard-gauge passenger railway runs between Lima and Huancayo in the Peruvian Andes. A metre-gauge line in Bolivia reaches slightly higher, but it is largely a freight line, and carries few passengers. The highest station along the Peruvian route is at Ticlio, 4680m (15,350ft) above sea level. Elsewhere the track runs at up to 4817m (15,806ft) above sea level.

In around four hours, the train climbs from Lima at sea level to Ticlio. The change in altitude is so rapid that some passengers find it difficult to breathe in the thin air, and attendants join the train near the highest point to administer oxygen to those feeling faint.

The track is laid on gradients that reach 1 in 25, and on steep slopes where there is no room for the line to curve back and forth across the mountainside, it is laid out in zigzag sections known as switchbacks. At the end of each section is a short siding, so that the train alternately steams forwards and reverses across the slope as it climbs.

---

*When the construction of the Moscow Metro – the Russian capital's underground rail system – fell behind schedule in the 1930s, 80,000 extra labourers were drafted to help the project catch up, under the supervision of the future Russian leader, Nikita Khrushchev. Most of the drafted 'volunteers' were not paid.*

*The system's 22-station core, on which work started in 1931, was opened by the Soviet leader Joseph Stalin on May 15, 1935. It is now the world's busiest underground system, with up to 6.5 million passengers a day. The longest system is London's, with 418km (260 miles) of routes, but New York's has the most stations: 458 to London's 277.*

---

SLIP-UP FOR A QUEEN  But for the bad phrasing of a question, the transatlantic British liner *Queen Mary* – now a floating hotel in California – would have been known by another name. Shortly before the ship's launch in 1934 Sir Thomas Royden, one of the directors of Cunard, met George V, intending to get his permission to name the ship *Queen Victoria*.

Royden asked if the vessel could be christened 'after the greatest queen this country has ever known'. The king replied: 'That is the greatest compliment ever paid to my wife. I'll ask her.' Naturally, Queen Mary assented, which meant that Cunard had to conceal its original plan.

PHARAOH'S ROYAL SHIP  The 4600-year-old royal ship of the Egyptian pharaoh Cheops is the oldest surviving vessel in the world. Originally buried in separate pieces near the Great Pyramid of Cheops at Giza, the ship has now been reassembled and is housed in a special museum near the pyramid.

Tonnes of silica gel, which is distributed in bags throughout the 48m (158ft) long hull, help to preserve the ship. The gel absorbs moisture given off by the hull during the heat of the day. At night the process is reversed, ensuring that the ship's ancient timbers are kept at a constant level of humidity.

CHINESE EXPERTISE  The hinged sternpost rudder on a boat, the magnetic compass, multiple masts and watertight compartments were all invented by the Chinese long before they were widely taken up in the West. The rudder, which started to replace the steering oar in Europe during the 13th century AD, had been

# MAYDAY, MAYDAY

The internationally recognised distress signal Mayday (from the French phrase *M'aidez*, meaning 'Help me') is used only when a ship is in grave and imminent danger and requires immediate assistance. A ship urgently needing help but not in imminent danger uses the signal Pan Pan (from the French *panne*, meaning 'breakdown'). Pan Pan is also the correct signal for man overboard.

Under the International Convention for the Safety of Life at Sea, there are a number of other recognised ways of calling for help. A ship's captain who sees any of these distress signals is legally obliged to respond to them.

● Gun or other explosive signal fired at intervals of about a minute.
● Continuous sounding of a fog signal, such as a foghorn.
● Rockets or shells throwing red stars fired one at a time at short intervals.
● Morse Code SOS (three dots, three dashes, three dots) transmitted by any means available.
● International Code flags NC (flag N above flag C).
● A square flag with above or below it anything resembling a ball.
● Flames on a vessel (for example, burning tar, oily rags).
● Red parachute flare or red hand flare.
● Orange-coloured smoke.
● Slowly raising and lowering outstretched arms.

An additional sign – a piece of orange canvas with a black-square and circle – can be used to attract the attention of aircraft. The British Navy's Red Ensign flown upside down has been used as a distress signal, but it is not internationally recognised under the convention.

**WRECKED . . . 3000 YEARS AGO** A Turkish sponge boat captain's casual remark about an underwater wreck led to the discovery in 1960 of one of the world's oldest shipwrecks – a Bronze Age cargo vessel that sank in about 1200 BC.

The captain had mentioned to American journalist and diver Peter Throckmorton in 1958 that he intended to dynamite the wreck to sell its cargo of bronze for scrap. Throckmorton, intrigued by the reference to bronze, persuaded the captain to delay his plan, then used the time to pinpoint the wreck – 27m (90ft) down, off Cape Gelidonya in southwest Turkey. He persuaded the University of Pennsylvania to sponsor an expedition.

George Bass, the 27-year-old American appointed to lead the expedition, was a classical archaeologist. So he took the unusual step, then, of learning to dive, and went on to pioneer the first properly disciplined underwater excavation.

Curiously, the wreck's discovery helped to improve the translation of the *Odyssey*, Homer's epic poem, which is set in the 13th century BC – about the time the wreck went down. In one section, the poet tells how Odysseus 'spread out a lot of brushwood' on his ship. Baffled translators had interpreted this to mean

**BLIGH'S SECOND MUTINY** *William Bligh, the notorious commander of the* Bounty, *was the victim of two mutinies, not one. The first, the mutiny on the* Bounty, *took place in 1789. Bligh and 18 men loyal to him were placed in the ship's launch (above) and cast adrift in the Pacific. The mutineers, under Fletcher Christian, sailed on and eventually settled on Pitcairn Island, where their descendants still live. Bligh survived the ordeal triumphantly. After 43 days in the 7m (23ft) open boat, Bligh reached safety at Timor, then part of the Dutch East Indies, and 6700km (4100 miles) from where he had been cast adrift. Only one man died during the voyage. The second mutiny happened in 1808, three years after Bligh became governor of New South Wales in Australia. He was deposed in the uprising known as the Rum Rebellion when he tried to stamp out abuses in the rum traffic, and was imprisoned by the mutineers for two years. He survived that ordeal, too. In 1811, he returned to England for good. He was promoted to vice admiral in 1814, three years before his death.*

known in China since the 1st century BC. Multiple masts were in common use in China by the 3rd century AD, and the compass by the 11th century AD. And watertight compartments, which prevent extensive flooding when a vessel is holed, were being fitted in Chinese ships by the end of the 13th century, 600 years before they were adopted in Europe.

NAVIGATING WITH KNOTS By the 8th century AD Arab seamen using the Red Sea and Indian Ocean had perfected a simple instrument for measuring latitude – their distance north or south of the Equator. Called the *kamal*, from the Arabic for 'guide', it was accurate to within about 50km (30 miles). The device consisted of a hand-sized rectangular board, with a knotted cord attached to its centre. Each knot represented the known latitude of a port.

With the appropriate knot in his teeth, the navigator held the *kamal* out in front of his eyes until it filled the space between Pole Star and horizon, with the board's bottom edge resting on the horizon. The height of the Pole Star is the same at any given latitude; it is almost directly overhead at the North Pole, and just on the horizon at the Equator.

So when the star appeared above the top edge of the *kamal*, it meant that the boat was too far north and had to sail south to reach the required port. When the star was below the top of the *kamal*, the boat altered course and sailed north.

# Transport

## LANDMARKS IN MARITIME HISTORY

**40,000 BC** Aborigines reach Australia aboard first sea-going craft.

**8000 – 7000** Reed boats developed in Mesopotamia and Egypt. Dug-out canoes used in northwest Europe.

**4000-3000** Square-rigged sailing ships used on Nile, Egypt.

**2500-1500** Egyptian reed ships reach Crete and Somalia.

**1200** Phoenicians develop keeled sailing ships, with planked hulls. The keels formed the ships' backbones, to which the frames were attached.

**100 – 0** Rudder invented in China.

**AD 200 – 300** Fore-and-aft sailing rig invented by Arab sailors, allowing boat to sail across the direction of the wind as well as with it.

**By 200** Chinese using sails on several masts.

**800 – 900** Square-rigged Viking longships carry first raiders and colonists across the North Sea to the British Isles, the Faroes and Iceland.

**By 1090** Chinese using magnetic compass.

**By 1300** Chinese using watertight bulkheads.

**1400 – 1500** Three-masted ship developed in western Europe, making possible major European voyages of discovery.

**1620** Submarine invented by Dutch engineer Cornelius Drebbel.

**1776** Buoyancy tanks invented for hand-powered submarine, the *Turtle*, by US engineer David Bushnell.

**1783** Marquis Jouffroy d'Abbans, of France, builds first paddle-driven steam boat.

**1802** Stern paddle-wheel tugboat *Charlotte Dundas*, first successful power-driven vessel, launched by Scottish engineer William Symington.

**1836** Englishman Francis Pettit Smith patents screw propeller. Swedish engineer John Ericsson patents a screw propeller in the USA six weeks later.

**1838** British engineer Isambard Kingdom Brunel's *Great Western*, first steamship built specially for transatlantic service, sails from Bristol to New York in 15 days.

**1845** Brunel's *Great Britain*, first transatlantic screw-driven iron ship, makes maiden voyage to New York.

**1845** US ship *Rainbow*, first true clipper ship, launched.

**1863** France's *Plongeur*, first mechanically driven submarine, uses engine powered by compressed air.

**1866** British clippers *Taeping*, *Serica* and *Ariel* bring new tea crop 25,700km (16,000 miles) from China to London in 99 days.

**1908** Gyroscope compass produced by German scientist Herman Anschutz-Kaempfe. Once set to point north, the gyro-compass remains stable, despite a ship's pitching and rolling.

**1955** USS *Nautilus*, first nuclear-powered submarine, built.

**1955** Hovercraft patented by British designer Christopher Cockerell.

**1959** Russian ice-breaker *Lenin*, first nuclear-powered surface ship, commissioned.

**1980** Japan launches 1600 tonne tanker *Shin-Aitoku-Maru*, first sail-assisted commercial ship for half a century.

**1983** Hinged ship invented by German engineer Ortwin Fries. Ship designed to bend into V-shape and suck up oil spillages into its twin hulls.

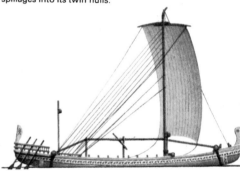

IN ANCIENT EGYPT *Wooden sailing ships, with a single mast set well forward and carrying a single rectangular or 'square' sail, were sailing on the Nile as long ago as 4000 BC. This arrangement meant that the ship could sail only before the wind – that is, with a following wind.*

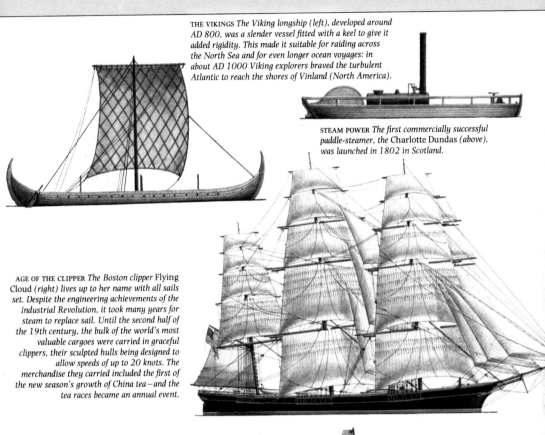

THE VIKINGS *The Viking longship (left), developed around AD 800, was a slender vessel fitted with a keel to give it added rigidity. This made it suitable for raiding across the North Sea and for even longer ocean voyages: in about AD 1000 Viking explorers braved the turbulent Atlantic to reach the shores of Vinland (North America).*

STEAM POWER *The first commercially successful paddle-steamer, the* Charlotte Dundas *(above), was launched in 1802 in Scotland.*

AGE OF THE CLIPPER *The Boston clipper* Flying Cloud *(right) lives up to her name with all sails set. Despite the engineering achievements of the Industrial Revolution, it took many years for steam to replace sail. Until the second half of the 19th century, the bulk of the world's most valuable cargoes were carried in graceful clippers, their sculpted hulls being designed to allow speeds of up to 20 knots. The merchandise they carried included the first of the new season's growth of China tea – and the tea races became an annual event.*

QUEEN OF THE OCEAN *The* Normandie *(left) was one of the most luxurious liners of the 1930s. She was the French challenger for the coveted Blue Riband, a notional award for the fastest transatlantic round trip. Interned after the fall of France in 1940, she was destroyed by fire in New York harbour in 1942.*

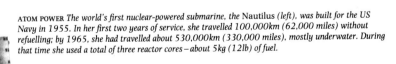

ATOM POWER *The world's first nuclear-powered submarine, the* Nautilus *(left), was built for the US Navy in 1955. In her first two years of service, she travelled 100,000km (62,000 miles) without refuelling; by 1965, she had travelled about 530,000km (330,000 miles), mostly underwater. During that time she used a total of three reactor cores – about 5kg (12lb) of fuel.*

HOVER REVOLUTION *British designer Christopher Cockerell patented his revolutionary amphibious hovercraft in 1955. The first craft 'sailed' in 1959. It rides on a cushion of air, the air being retained by a flexible skirt.*

that he built a wattle fence around the gunwales to keep out high seas and spray. But it now seems clear – from the evidence found in the wreck – that brushwood was actually laid out in the bottom of boats to protect their thin hulls from damage caused by shifting cargo, just as Homer's words had implied.

BLOODY PUNISHMENT European navies in the days of sail were notorious for their savage penalties. Keel-hauling – dragging a man under the ship's bottom – had been in use for about 300 years when it was phased out early in the 18th century. Keel-hauling involved trussing the offender to a line and dropping him from one yardarm into the sea; he was then dragged under the keel and hoisted to the opposite yardarm. Many drowned in the process.

Flogging with the cat o' nine tails – a rope or wooden handle with nine knotted cords each about 450mm (18in) long – is first mentioned in 1702. Captains in Britain's Royal Navy were officially not allowed to order more than a dozen strokes without special written permission, but the regulation was usually ignored. Use of the 'cat' was finally suspended in the Royal Navy in 1879.

---

*The letters SOS were adopted as an international distress signal in 1912 because the Morse code for them – three dots, three dashes and three dots – was easy to remember. The first ship to send the new call sign was the White Star liner* Titanic, *which struck an iceberg and sank on her maiden voyage to New York in April of that year. The letters did not stand for anything. 'Save Our Souls' was a catch-phrase devised later.*

---

LIGHT THAT FAILED Lighthouses have been used as an aid to navigation for more than 2000 years. But the modern lighthouse started with the efforts of a British engineer, Henry Winstanley, to erect a structure on the dangerous Eddystone Rock, which juts from the English Channel 22.5km (14 miles) from Plymouth, Devon. It was a daunting task – at high tide only one rock was exposed, its surface just big enough for the base of the lighthouse. Winstanley's stone and wooden structure, 24m (80ft) high, took two years to build. It came into operation in November 1698, burning a candelabra of 60 candles. Two years later the tower was raised to a height of 36.5m (120ft).

The present Eddystone lighthouse was built in 1882.

NOBLE FAILURE *Henry Winstanley's Eddystone light shone for only five years before it was swept away in a storm in November 1703 with its inventor inside.*

---

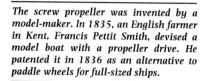

*The screw propeller was invented by a model-maker. In 1835, an English farmer in Kent, Francis Pettit Smith, devised a model boat with a propeller drive. He patented it in 1836 as an alternative to paddle wheels for full-sized ships.*

---

PADDLE VERSUS SCREW A bizarre tug of war to decide which was more efficient – paddle wheels or screw propellers – was staged in 1845 by the British Admiralty. The contest took place between two 800 tonne frigates: HMS *Alecto*, which had paddle wheels, and HMS *Rattler*, which had a propeller. With the ships secured stern-to-stern and both going full ahead, *Rattler* won the contest easily.

TURBINE DASH It took an unofficial appearance at the Spithead Naval Review of 1897 – held as part of Queen Victoria's diamond jubilee celebrations – to win acceptance for *Turbinia*, the world's first turbine vessel, designed and built by Sir Charles Parsons (1854–1931), a British marine engineer. The 45 tonne *Turbinia* cut through the anchored fleet at the unprecedented speed of 34.5 knots (about 64km/h or 40mph). Naval chiefs were so impressed that they commissioned the turbine-driven destroyer *Viper*, which was in service three years later.

---

*Rum was introduced into Britain's Royal Navy in 1687, when Samuel Pepys, the diarist, was Secretary of the Navy. It was abolished in 1970, after the Admiralty finally decided that the issue was not compatible with modern standards of efficiency. Grog – rum which was diluted with water – was first issued by Admiral Edward Vernon in 1740, at a time when the daily ration for each sailor was 0.6 litres (1 pint) of neat spirit. It acquired its name from the admiral himself, who was called 'Old Grogram' because he wore a cloak made of a coarse fabric known as grogram (grosgrain).*

---

BIRKENHEAD DRILL The sailors' code of 'women and children first' originated with the wreck of a British troopship, the *Birkenhead*, on February 26, 1852. The 1900 tonne *Birkenhead*, one of the world's first ironclads, sailed for South Africa from Cork, in

---

## PORT AND STARBOARD

Looking towards the bow (front) of a ship, port is the left-hand side, starboard the right-hand side. When under way at night, all vessels are obliged to display a red sidelight to port, a green one to starboard and a white masthead light.

Starboard is so called because the right-hand side of a boat was the side where the steering oar, or 'steer-board', was set in the days before central, stern-post rudders were used.

Port is so named because ships in harbour always tied up on that side so that the steering oar would not be crushed against the quay. The same terms are now used in exactly the same way by air pilots.

BIRD MAN *Man has always been fascinated by the idea of flight. According to legend, the Greek inventor Daedalus built wings of wax to escape from imprisonment on Crete.*

Ireland, in January 1852, laden with reinforcements – including 476 soldiers – for the fighting against marauding Xhosa tribesmen. Also on board were 20 women and children.

Following what was probably a navigational error, the ship foundered on a rocky promontory near Cape Agulhas, Africa's southernmost point. Of the eight lifeboats, only three proved seaworthy and these were boarded by the civilians. With the ship fast breaking up, the master, Captain Robert Salmond, ordered the assembled redcoats: 'Save yourselves. All those who can swim, jump overboard and make for the boats.'

But the soldiers' commander, Lieutenant Colonel Alexander Seton, quickly countermanded the instruction – he saw only too clearly that the lifeboats would be swamped in the scramble for safety. 'Stand fast, I beg you,' he shouted to his platoons. 'Do not rush the boats carrying the women and children.'

Seton drew his sword, ready to cut down the first man who disobeyed, but the threat was unnecessary. The soldiers remained steady, in strict order, even while the ship broke in two and the funnel and mainmast crashed to the deck. Of those on board, 455 lost their lives, including Seton and Salmond.

---

*The first man to sail solo around the world could not swim. He was a Nova Scotia-born US sea captain named Joshua Slocum. In his 11m (35ft) sloop, Spray, he set out from Boston in 1895 at the age of 51 and returned three years later. He financed the journey by giving lectures at the ports along his route. Slocum set out on a new voyage aboard the same boat at the age of 65. He left from the US state of Rhode Island in November 1909 – and neither he nor Spray were ever seen again.*

---

LITTLE MONSTERS The largest modern supertankers, known as Ultra Large Crude Carriers (ULCCs), are not as heavy as they seem. They are usually described in terms of their deadweight, which is a measure not of the weight of the ships themselves, but of how much cargo they can carry. Empty, the ships usually weigh only a fraction of the deadweight tonnage.

The world's largest ship in the early 1980s was the oil tanker *Seawise Giant*, completed in Japan in 1981 for a Liberian company. The ship itself, which is almost half a kilometre (a quarter of a mile) long – long enough to hold five football pitches end to end – weighs just under 80,000 tonnes, not much more than the 69,000 tonnes of the liner *Queen Elizabeth II*. But its deadweight is nearly 565,000 tonnes. Fully loaded with crude oil, therefore, it weighs a total of around 645,000 tonnes.

In heavy seas, ships of this size can flex by more than a metre (3ft) from stem to stern. And they can take more than 6km (4 miles) to stop.

WHO KILLED THE RED BARON? Nobody knows for certain who shot down Baron Manfred Freiherr von Richthofen, who with 80 kills was the most successful air ace of the First World War. On April 21, 1918, his red Fokker triplane was pursuing a Sopwith Camel close to the ground when he was himself attacked by another Camel flown by Captain A. Roy Brown, a Canadian serving in the newly formed Royal Air Force. Some Australian machine-gunners on the ground fired at Richthofen – who was nicknamed the Red Baron – as Brown attacked. Richthofen's guns are said to have jammed, and he tried to break off the fight, but he was hit. The Fokker landed intact, and von Richthofen's body was found with a bullet wound in the chest. Brown was credited with the victory, but it remains uncertain who fired the fatal shot.

A VIEW OF MONS. GARNERIN'S BALLOON AND PARACHU

HIGH JUMP *By the late 18th century, hot-air balloons had made flight practical, if sometimes perilous. André Garnerin gave the first public demonstration of how to escape from one by parachute in Paris in 1797.*

# Transport

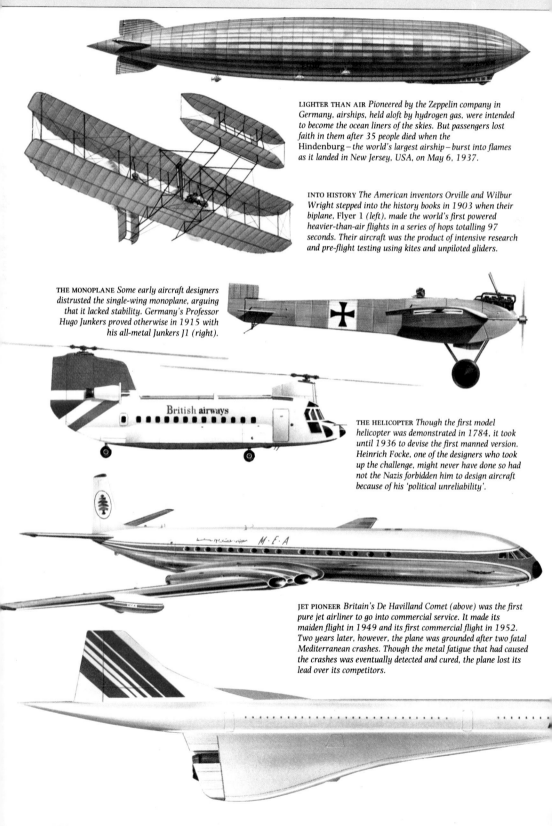

**LIGHTER THAN AIR** *Pioneered by the Zeppelin company in Germany, airships, held aloft by hydrogen gas, were intended to become the ocean liners of the skies. But passengers lost faith in them after 35 people died when the Hindenburg – the world's largest airship – burst into flames as it landed in New Jersey, USA, on May 6, 1937.*

**INTO HISTORY** *The American inventors Orville and Wilbur Wright stepped into the history books in 1903 when their biplane, Flyer 1 (left), made the world's first powered heavier-than-air flights in a series of hops totalling 97 seconds. Their aircraft was the product of intensive research and pre-flight testing using kites and unpiloted gliders.*

**THE MONOPLANE** *Some early aircraft designers distrusted the single-wing monoplane, arguing that it lacked stability. Germany's Professor Hugo Junkers proved otherwise in 1915 with his all-metal Junkers J1 (right).*

**THE HELICOPTER** *Though the first model helicopter was demonstrated in 1784, it took until 1936 to devise the first manned version. Heinrich Focke, one of the designers who took up the challenge, might never have done so had not the Nazis forbidden him to design aircraft because of his 'political unreliability'.*

**JET PIONEER** *Britain's De Havilland Comet (above) was the first pure jet airliner to go into commercial service. It made its maiden flight in 1949 and its first commercial flight in 1952. Two years later, however, the plane was grounded after two fatal Mediterranean crashes. Though the metal fatigue that had caused the crashes was eventually detected and cured, the plane lost its lead over its competitors.*

**1783** A Frenchman, Sebastien Lenormand, was the first person to use a parachute when he jumped from the tower of Montpelier Observatory, France. The first public exhibition jumps were given in Paris in October 1797 when André Jacques Garnerin – a former balloon inspector in the French army – jumped from a balloon. Although he suffered from air-sickness, he made his descents from heights of up to 680m (2230ft).

The parachutes of the late 1790s were rib-supported canvas umbrellas about 60m (195ft) across. In the 1880s the modern, limp canopy type was invented in the USA – and the first exhibition jumps with rip-cord parachutes took place there in 1908.

**1852** The world's first airship flight took place in Versailles, France, in September, when a steam engineer, Henri Giffard, steered his one-man craft for 28km (17 miles). But the airship did not become a practical reality until the petrol engine, and lightweight aluminium for the structure, were introduced in the 1880s. These were used by a former German Army officer, Count Ferdinand von Zeppelin, in his first dirigible, completed in 1900.

The prototype Zeppelin was driven by two 14hp Daimler engines and contained about 11,000m³ (400,000cu ft) of hydrogen in 17 gas-tight bags. The first commercial Zeppelin service started in 1910 and the airships made bombing raids over Britain in the First World War. In the 1930s airship travel became fashionable as the German craft – known as 'flying hotels' – wafted passengers across the Atlantic. The longest scheduled flights were from Frankfurt to Rio de Janeiro. The Zeppelin flights to South America took five days as against five weeks by ship.

**1903** On December 17, the American aviation pioneers Wilbur and Orville Wright made the world's first powered, controlled and sustained flights in their 12hp biplane

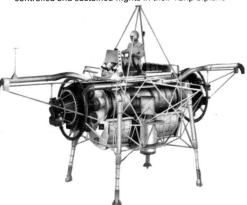

STRAIGHT UP *The Rolls-Royce Thrust Measuring Rig, nicknamed the 'Flying Bedstead' (above), became the world's first vertical take-off (VTO) jet in 1954. It is the direct ancestor of modern VTO aircraft, such as Britain's Harrier 'jump jet'.*

FASTER THAN SOUND *The Anglo-French Concorde, with its streamlined fuselage and pointed nose, was the world's first supersonic airliner to go into passenger service, bringing New York within three hours of London. A rival project in the USA was abandoned because of cost.*

*Flyer I*. Orville was the first to take to the air over coastal sand dunes near Kitty Hawk, North Carolina. The fourth and final flight – with Wilbur as pilot – lasted 59 seconds and covered 260m (852ft).

**1909** The first aeroplane sea crossing – across the English Channel – took place on July 25, when the Frenchman Louis Blériot took off in his 25hp Blériot XI monoplane. The 37km (23 miles) trip from Calais to Dover took $36\frac{1}{2}$ minutes at an average speed of about 60km/h (40mph).

**1911** The first single-shell (or monocoque) fuselage was introduced in the wooden Deperdussin racing plane from France. Another milestone in aviation history was the appearance in 1915 of the Junkers J1 monoplane, made by a German company in Sweden. It was an all-metal aircraft with cantilevered wings which were internally braced and needed no external wires or struts.

**1919** In June the first non-stop transatlantic crossing – from Newfoundland to western Ireland – was made by the British aviators John Alcock and Arthur Whitten Brown. Their Vickers Vimy twin-engined biplane took 16 hours 27 minutes to make the flight.

**1927** The first solo flight across the Atlantic occurred in May when the 25-year-old US airmail pilot Charles Lindbergh flew non-stop from New York to Paris. His single-engined monoplane, *Spirit of St Louis*, covered the 5790km (3600 miles) in 33 hours 32 minutes at an average speed of 173km/h (107.4mph).

**1937** Lindbergh flew in an unpressurised plane, which meant that he could not fly above bad weather. Ten years passed before the first fully pressurised aircraft, the experimental American Lockheed XC-35, was introduced in 1937. The first pressurised airliner to go into commercial service was the Boeing 307 Stratoliner, which made its maiden flight on December 31, 1938.

**1947** The invention of the jet engine in the late 1930s meant that planes would eventually be able to fly at more than the speed of sound – almost 1225km/h (761mph). The first plane to do this was the rocket-powered American Bell X-1 in 1947. Two years later the first jet airliner to go into production – the British de Havilland Comet – took to the air. It went into service in 1952.

**1954** The first successful vertical take-off (VTO) jet aircraft was the Rolls-Royce Thrust Measuring Rig, nicknamed the 'Flying Bedstead', which made its first trial flights in Britain in 1953. Britain's Harrier 'jump jet' fighter was in the mid-1980s the world's most advanced VTO aircraft. In 1969 a Harrier took off from central London and landed in the centre of New York 6 hours, 11 minutes and 57 seconds later.

**1969** The Anglo-French Concorde made its first flight. It entered service seven years later in 1976. It carries comparatively few passengers – up to 100 – at speeds of more than 1600km/h (1000mph), crossing the Atlantic in less than three hours. The plane's long, pointed nose 'droops' on landing so that the pilot can see ahead.

**1970** The era of the jumbo jet began with the introduction by the American Boeing company of its wide-bodied 747, which can carry up to 490 passengers. Part of the 747's height – more than 19m (63ft), as tall as a six-storey office block – consists of an upper deck in the nose. The 747 is currently the largest civil airliner in service in the world. But Boeing already has plans for a 1000-seat, double-decker 'super-jumbo' which will cross the Pacific non-stop.

# Transport

HOW THE WRIGHTS WERE WRONGED   Although the first true flights – by the American Wright brothers in December 1903 – had been publicly recognised by 1908, for many years the prestigious Smithsonian Institution in Washington DC labelled another plane, Samuel Langley's *Aerodrome*, as 'The first aeroplane capable of sustained free flight with a man'.

The *Aerodrome* had twice been launched by catapult from a houseboat on the Potomac river, in October and December 1903. But on both occasions it plunged into the water because it lacked power and was structurally weak.

Because of the Smithsonian's disdain, the Wright *Flyer 1* spent 20 years in exile in the Science Museum in London from 1928. Finally, in 1943, the Smithsonian acknowledged that the Wrights' plane had flown successfully before Langley's, and *Flyer 1* was returned to the USA in 1948.

---

*The first living creatures to be transported by air were a sheep, a cock and a duck. The French Montgolfier brothers – whose hot-air balloon made the first manned flight in November 1783 – sent the animals up from Versailles under a balloon in September the same year to see if they would be harmed by the rarefied air. They survived unharmed except that one wing of the cock was damaged, probably by a kick from the sheep.*

---

WITHOUT A PARACHUTE   In the First World War, no Allied pilot was ever equipped with a parachute, though by 1918 German pilots were regularly saving their lives with them. The reason was that a parachute which the user opened had not been invented, and the type then used was stowed separately from the pilot and hauled from the aircraft by the pilot's weight as he jumped. In certain circumstances – if, say, the aeroplane was in a spin – the line or the parachute might foul some part of the structure. So, rather than have a parachute that could not always be relied on, the Allied authorities preferred to have none.

THE WINDMILL PLANE   In 1925 the Spanish inventor Juan de la Cierva demonstrated a new 'wonder' flying machine – the autogyro. It had a free-wheeling overhead rotor, which was designed to provide extra lift and so eliminate a then serious problem of planes stalling on take-off.

Ironically, Cierva was killed in December 1936 by the very fault his invention had tried to eliminate. An airliner in which he was a passenger stalled and crashed while taking off from Croydon in England.

TROUBLE IN THE AIR   Helicopters were not perfected until decades after the orthodox aeroplane because designers faced two apparently insurmountable problems. First, the spinning rotor that lifted a helicopter tended to make the body of the machine spin faster and faster in the opposite direction. Second, as soon as a helicopter moved forwards, the rotating blades moving in the direction of the flight generated more lift than those moving towards the rear. This was because the speed of the 'advancing' blades was added to the speed of the aircraft itself. And the effect was to make the helicopter roll over.

The two problems were finally solved by two independent inventors: one a Spaniard who never built a helicopter; the other a refugee from the Russian Revolution of 1917. The Spaniard, Juan de la Cierva, whose main interest was in autogyros, invented in 1922 a flapping hinge that allowed the angle of the rotor blades to vary as they were spinning, and so equalise the amount of lift. In the 1940s the Russian Igor Sikorsky – then living in the USA – perfected the use of a small, vertically mounted tail rotor to counter the plane's tendency to spin in the opposite direction to its main rotor.

---

*As a child, Charles Lindbergh – the American aviator who in May 1927 made the first solo flight across the Atlantic – had a morbid terror of heights.*

---

FATHERS OF THE JET   Ideas for applying some form of jet propulsion to aircraft date back to the 19th century. But it was not until the late 1930s that the first practical jet engines were developed. The first jet to be given a bench-run, in March 1937, was the centrifugal-compressor engine developed by the German Hans von Ohain and backed by the Heinkel Aircraft Company. It was followed the next month by the first runs of the centrifugal engine developed by the English engineer and pilot Sir Frank Whittle.

Ohain's engine first flew on August 27, 1939, in the Heinkel He178, but the Whittle W1 engine did not fly until May 1941, when it powered the Gloster Whittle E28/39. By then, Junkers in Germany and Dr A. A. Griffith in England had evolved the more complicated axial-compressor jet engine. Britain adopted the Whittle engine and installed it in the Gloster Meteor fighter, but the Germans chose the axial unit and fitted it in the Messerschmitt Me262. Both aircraft entered combat service in 1944.

Although the Whittle type of engine was dominant in the post-war years, it did not have the thrust potential of the axial type – which is now used to power modern jet aircraft.

# ANIMALS & PLANTS

# The origins of life

## LIVING BUILDING BRICKS

All living things, plant and animal, stem from a single cell. Most cells are too small to see, a mere few thousandths of a millimetre across. A few single-celled organisms, however, such as the freshwater protozoan *Spirostomum*, can be up to 3mm (0.12in) long.

Each cell consists of a thin membrane holding a liquid called cytoplasm which contains fats, proteins, acids and carbohydrates. In the centre of the cytoplasm is a nucleus. The nucleus holds the genetic code which determines how an organism develops. Plants and animals grow by the division of their cells. The form the completed organism takes is decided by chemical messages contained in DNA, short for deoxyribonucleic acid. DNA is a mixture of sugars and phosphates which form a spiral ladder of molecules inside the cell nucleus.

Each time a cell divides, the ladder splits in two down the middle. Half the ladder joins each new nucleus. Each half-rung projecting from the spiral is then able to link up only with the same chemical partner in the newly formed cell as it had in the original cell. As a result, the ladder is 'repaired' exactly as it was before, and the genetic code it contained is faithfully copied in each new generation of cells.

## CRACKING THE CODE

The secret of the DNA code of life was finally unravelled at Cambridge University, England, in 1953 by an American, James Watson, then 25, and a 37-year-old English biologist, Francis Crick. They knew that DNA consisted of a chain of sugars and phosphates held together by four compounds known as nucleotides. Each nucleotide contained a different organic base. There were two large bases, guanine and adenine; and two small, thymine and cytosine. But how did the bases fit together?

Cycling from the station to the college one day after a trip to London, Watson decided to experiment with a two-link structure. He and Crick made cut-out models of the shapes of the four molecule bases, and began trying to fit them.

Watson recorded their moment of triumph: 'Suddenly I became aware that an adenine-thymine pair . . . was identical in shape to a guanine-cytosine pair.' The bases linked in pairs, each pair forming a single rung in the DNA ladder, and each base determined what its partner could be. The two sides of the spiral ladder fell into place. They had found the genetic key.

## HIGH-SPEED COPIER

A DNA molecule is an awesomely complex and extremely fast copier. It may consist of hundreds of thousands of coils containing millions of nucleotide 'rungs'. When a cell divides, the molecule has to untwist and all the new nucleotides necessary have to be assembled in the right order and be joined together by enzymes. Yet all this has to be done – in a bacterium, for example – in the time it takes a cell to divide: less than 20 minutes. The helix must uncoil at the rate of several hundred turns a second – a speed which would tear apart any car engine – and the new chain must be assembled at the rate of several thousand nucleotides a second.

## DIVIDE AND MULTIPLY

The enormous diversity of plant and animal life became possible only after the development of sexual reproduction. The first organisms to use this method were green algae, plant masses formed by groupings of primitive cells, which began about 1000 million years ago to reproduce by fusing with each other.

Until then all reproduction had been simply by cell division, the process now known as cloning. Each organism was identical to its parent. Sexual reproduction, however, enabled a greater variety of organisms to evolve, because the new life could take different combinations of characteristics from the parents.

---

## HOW A CELL BECOMES AN ANIMAL

Biologists believe that the whole history of evolution is re-created in the embryo of an animal as it forms in its mother's womb. At first, the fertilised egg is a single cell like the simplest and earliest forms of life on Earth. But within hours, it begins to divide and multiply: into 2,4,8,16 cells and so on. For some time, all the cells produced by this process of division are very similar. Each cell has the capacity to become any one of the specialist cells in the adult creature.

Then this cluster of undifferentiated cells gradually forms into a hollow ball containing two distinct layers, the inner endoderm and the outer ectoderm. A little later, a third layer, the mesoderm, develops between them. Once these changes take place, no cell can give rise to 'daughter' cells of the other two types.

### Growing specialisation

As the embryo continues to develop and grow, its cells gradually become more and more specialised. The ectoderm cells become skin or nervous tissue, for instance. Endoderm cells can become parts of the digestive system or lungs. Mesoderm cells may develop into muscle and bone. At the same time, the embryo retraces the long evolutionary climb from simple to complex.

A four-week-old human embryo, for example, has slits in the region of the neck which are like the gills of a fish. At six weeks, when the embryo is 12mm (0.5in) long, the shape is still that of a marine animal, but the slits, known as branchial arches, have begun forming into the upper and lower jaws. At seven weeks, the developing child has the attributes of a primate. It has a clearly visible tail and the arms are longer and stronger than the legs – proportions that will be reversed in the born human.

### Human characteristics

By nine weeks after conception, the embryo has human characteristics. The eyes have become part of the front of the face, and the ears and jaws are prominent. The tail has vanished into the growing buttocks and there is the first sign of genital organs.

After 12 weeks, the ears have risen to eye level, the eyelids have shut and nails have begun to form. The limbs are jointed, but the head is still disproportionately large. In the next four weeks, the face will become recognisably different from that of other embryo babies of the same age.

After 28 weeks, all the main characteristics have formed, but the baby is red and wrinkled with the appearance of a dried-up old person. In the next ten weeks it fills out, the lungs develop and it will be ready, after an average 266 days, to enter the world.

## THE SCATTERING SEED

The first plants to colonise the land about 420 million years ago were flowerless mosses, horsetails and ferns. With no sex organs, they reproduced by throwing out spores – minute organisms that carried the genetic blueprint for the plant. Spores can germinate centuries after they have been cast off, but their survival rate is low because they carry no food store.

Ferns began bearing seeds about 345 million years ago. Unlike a spore, a seed has a built-in food store, making its survival chances much greater. The most primitive seed-bearing plants still found on Earth are the cycads, plants which resemble palm trees. They have grown on Earth for some 160 million years.

## HALF AND HALF

There are 46 chromosomes in the living cell of a human being and these chromosomes carry the genetic information that decides how a person will grow – whether he or she will be dark or fair, short or tall, blue-eyed or brown. But the sex cells, the female egg and the male sperm, each have only 23 chromosomes. They fuse at conception to make a cell containing 46 chromosomes, half from each partner, and it is this mixing of two sets of characteristics that creates the diversity of human life.

Other living things which reproduce sexually also have chromosomes, but the numbers vary widely from species to species. A garden pea, for instance, has 14 chromosomes, a potato 48 and a crayfish 200.

## MAN-MADE LIFE

In 1953, an American scientist, Stanley Miller, attempted to reproduce the atmosphere and weather conditions of Earth at the very dawn of life. He passed an electric charge through a mixture of hydrogen, methane and ammonia gases for 20 hours in an enclosed water bath. In the process, he formed some organic compounds, including amino acids, the basic building material of living cells. In 1979 at the University of Texas, researchers Allen J. Bard and Harald Reiche produced amino acids by exposing to sunlight a solution of ammonia, methane and water containing particles of platinum and titanium oxide.

These experiments in man-made life suggest that life began as the result of the Sun's rays and violent electrical storms acting on the gases present in the young Earth's atmosphere.

## MINI-METHUSELAHS

Stunted bristlecone pines in the arid White Mountains of California – the world's oldest trees – cling to a tenuous life and still grow very slowly in the occasional rainfall after 4600 years of life. But they are not the oldest living things on Earth.

In sandstone rocks in a dry valley of Antarctica, American scientists have found tiny lichens – primitive partnerships of plant and fungus – which they have calculated to be at least 10,000 years old.

## HOW A SEED BECOMES A PLANT

A seed cast by the wind, fallen from its parent or planted by man, sinks into the earth and germinates when air and water seep through its outer coat.

An embryo root, called the radicle, bursts out of the seed and begins to grow downwards into the soil seeking moisture and nutrients. One or two seed leaves, called cotyledons, emerge from the seed pod and begin providing food for the baby plant. A shoot called a plumule, which will eventually push its way into the air, grows upwards from the seed pod.

A stem, called the hypocotyl, carries the plumule out into the daylight, bringing with it, in most plants, the seed leaves. As the stem grows upwards, new leaves open out from it. Below ground, the root spreads, pushing minute hairs through the soil to collect water and minerals. Finally, the seed leaves die and fall away as new leaves take over their role.

FACTS ABOUT
ANIMALS & PLANTS

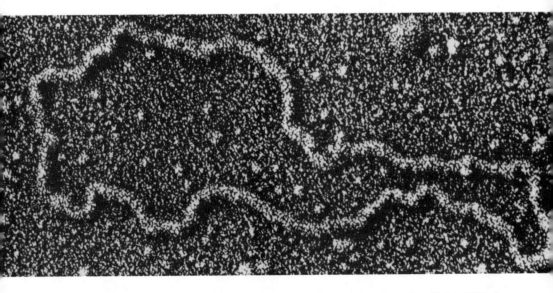

PIONEER GENES *This rope-like molecule of DNA, here magnified more than 170,000 times, was the subject in 1973 of the first successful attempt at genetic engineering. The rope consists of two spiral strands twisted together and joined like the rungs of a ladder – a double helix. Scientists from Stanford University in the USA severed the loop (taken from* Escherichia coli *bacteria found in the human gut) and spliced it to another piece of DNA from the same species. They introduced the new genetic combination into a living cell, and encouraged the cell to multiply. The new cells had properties derived from both the original pieces of DNA – proving that the splice had worked.*

# How plants are classified

## THE PLANT KINGDOM

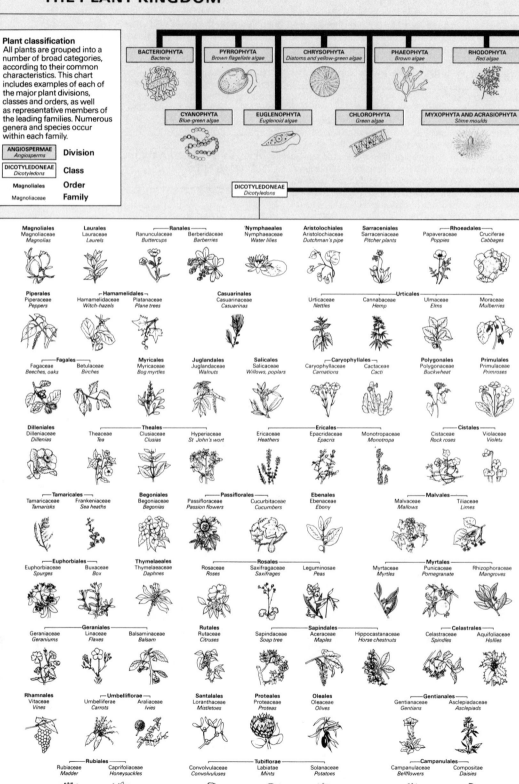

**Plant classification**
All plants are grouped into a number of broad categories, according to their common characteristics. This chart includes examples of each of the major plant divisions, classes and orders, as well as representative members of the leading families. Numerous genera and species occur within each family.

| | |
|---|---|
| **ANGIOSPERMAE** *Angiosperms* | **Division** |
| **DICOTYLEDONEAE** *Dicotyledons* | **Class** |
| **Magnoliales** | **Order** |
| Magnoliaceae | **Family** |

**BACTERIOPHYTA** *Bacteria*

**PYRROPHYTA** *Brown flagellate algae*

**CHRYSOPHYTA** *Diatoms and yellow-green algae*

**PHAEOPHYTA** *Brown algae*

**RHODOPHYTA** *Red algae*

**CYANOPHYTA** *Blue-green algae*

**EUGLENOPHYTA** *Euglenoid algae*

**CHLOROPHYTA** *Green algae*

**MYXOPHYTA AND ACRASIOPHYTA** *Slime moulds*

**DICOTYLEDONEAE** *Dicotyledons*

**Magnoliales** Magnoliaceae *Magnolias*

**Laurales** Lauraceae *Laurels*

**Ranales** Ranunculaceae *Buttercups* — Berberidaceae *Barberries*

**Nymphaeales** Nymphaeaceae *Water lilies*

**Aristolochiales** Aristolochiaceae *Dutchman's pipe*

**Sarraceniales** Sarraceniaceae *Pitcher plants*

**Rhoeadales** Papaveraceae *Poppies* — Cruciferae *Cabbages*

**Piperales** Piperaceae *Peppers*

**Hamamelidales** Hamamelidaceae *Witch-hazels* — Platanaceae *Plane trees*

**Casuarinales** Casuarinaceae *Casuarinas*

**Urticales** Urticaceae *Nettles* — Cannabaceae *Hemp* — Ulmaceae *Elms* — Moraceae *Mulberries*

**Fagales** Fagaceae *Beeches, oaks* — Betulaceae *Birches*

**Myricales** Myricaceae *Bog myrtles*

**Juglandales** Juglandaceae *Walnuts*

**Salicales** Salicaceae *Willows, poplars*

**Caryophyllales** Caryophyllaceae *Carnations* — Cactaceae *Cacti*

**Polygonales** Polygonaceae *Buckwheat*

**Primulales** Primulaceae *Primroses*

**Dilleniales** Dilleniaceae *Dillenias*

**Theales** Theaceae *Tea* — Clusiaceae *Clusias* — Hyperiaceae *St John's wort*

**Ericales** Ericaceae *Heathers* — Epacridaceae *Epacris* — Monotropaceae *Monotropa*

**Cistales** Cistaceae *Rock roses* — Violaceae *Violets*

**Tamaricales** Tamaricaceae *Tamarisks* — Frankeniaceae *Sea heaths*

**Begoniales** Begoniaceae *Begonias*

**Passiflorales** Passifloraceae *Passion flowers* — Cucurbitaceae *Cucumbers*

**Ebenales** Ebenaceae *Ebony*

**Malvales** Malvaceae *Mallows* — Tiliaceae *Limes*

**Euphorbiales** Euphorbiaceae *Spurges* — Buxaceae *Box*

**Thymelaeales** Thymelaeaceae *Daphnes*

**Rosales** Rosaceae *Roses* — Saxifragaceae *Saxifrages* — Leguminosae *Peas*

**Myrtales** Myrtaceae *Myrtles* — Punicaceae *Pomegranate* — Rhizophoraceae *Mangroves*

**Geraniales** Geraniaceae *Geraniums* — Linaceae *Flaxes* — Balsaminaceae *Balsam*

**Rutales** Rutaceae *Citruses*

**Sapindales** Sapindaceae *Soap tree* — Aceraceae *Maples* — Hippocastanaceae *Horse chestnuts*

**Celastrales** Celastraceae *Spindles* — Aquifoliaceae *Hollies*

**Rhamnales** Vitaceae *Vines*

**Umbelliflorae** Umbelliferae *Carrots* — Araliaceae *Ivies*

**Santalales** Loranthaceae *Mistletoes*

**Proteales** Proteaceae *Proteas*

**Oleales** Oleaceae *Olives*

**Gentianales** Gentianaceae *Gentians* — Asclepiadaceae *Asclepiads*

**Rubiales** Rubiaceae *Madder* — Caprifoliaceae *Honeysuckles*

**Tubiflorae** Convolvulaceae *Convolvuluses* — Labiatae *Mints* — Solanaceae *Potatoes*

**Campanulales** Campanulaceae *Bellflowers* — Compositae *Daisies*

The basic classification unit for plants, as for animals, is the species. This chart shows how botanists group related species into larger units: the genus, family, order, class and division. The chart includes fungi, but some scientists classify the 80,000 or so species of fungus as a separate kingdom, alongside plants and animals. Other organisms which are neither plant nor animal are grouped into two further kingdoms: Protista, primitive organisms such as the amoeba; and Procaryota, organisms such as viruses.

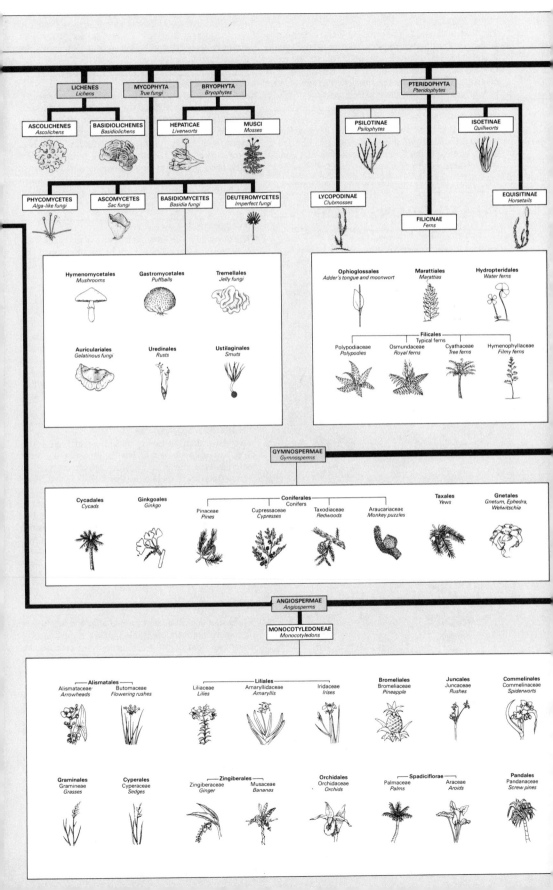

# Flowering plants and fungi

## FIRST AND LAST
The first land plants appeared at least 400 million years ago. They had forked stems but no proper leaves, flowers or seeds. A few closely similar plants still exist: the whisk ferns, which are native to tropical and subtropical regions; and the *Tmesipteris* group of ferns in New Zealand, Australia and Polynesia.

## TIME CAPSULE
The oldest known living seed came from a North American arctic lupin. It was found in 1954 buried in frozen silt near Miller Creek in central Yukon, Canada, by a mining engineer named Schmidt. It had been

there for 10,000 years. Yet, when scientists planted it, a plant grew which was identical to the modern plant. Modern seed banks keep stocks of seeds in similarly cold, dry conditions so that rare plants are assured of a future.

## BUILT-IN GREENHOUSE
The window plant, *Fenestraria*, makes a private greenhouse to protect itself from the harsh sun of the deserts of southern Africa. Most of the plant grows underground, and only a small transparent window is exposed above the surface. The window, which is composed of translucent cells, has two layers. An outer layer blocks the most damaging ultraviolet rays of the sun, and an inner layer cuts down and diffuses the light to a safe level for the green photosynthetic tissue deep within the plant body.

## PATTERN FOR A PALACE
The Crystal Palace – a vast structure of glass and iron, built in Hyde Park, London, to house the Great Exhibition of 1851 – was inspired by the pattern of a water lily. The designer, Sir Joseph Paxton, had been head gardener to the Duke of Devonshire at Chatsworth, and had successfully grown – for the first time in Europe – the giant South American water lily, *Victoria amazonica*. The plant's leaves are up to 2m (7ft) across, and the arrangement of the ribs gives them such strength that they can support a child. Paxton studied the pattern of the ribs and, years later, used a closely similar pattern of ribs and struts to support the roof of his iron and glass palace. The building, which was moved to south London after the exhibition, was destroyed by a fire in 1936.

## UNDERGROUND BLOOMS
Two Australian species of orchid spend their entire lives buried in the earth. The only part which ever emerges is a cluster of capsules which are pushed above the surface to disperse the dust-like seeds. Both species feed on decaying plant material in the soil, breaking it down with the aid of fungi. The first of the two orchids, *Rhizanthella gardneri*, was discovered in 1928 by a Mr J. Trott, who ploughed it up by accident on a farm in Corrigin, Western Australia. The second, *Cryptanthemis slateri*, was discovered by a Mr E. Slater in 1931 at Alum Mountain in New South Wales. Very little is known about either species because very few specimens have ever been found.

## CORPSE FLOWER
*Rafflesia*, a parasitic plant named after the founder of Singapore, Sir Stamford Raffles, grows in the forests of Southeast Asia and has the largest and perhaps the smelliest flower in the world. The bud, which looks like a wrinkled brown cabbage, opens into a huge purplish or reddish-brown flower 300–900mm (1–3ft) across. The bloom weighs up to 7kg (15lb), and is covered with irregular warts. Looking and smelling like a hunk of blood-encrusted and decaying carrion, the flower is visited by vast swarms of flies which pollinate the flower while crawling over it.

## RIDDLE OF THE COCONUTS
The largest seeds in the plant kingdom are also the most mysterious. The seeds – which belong to the double coconut or coco de mer, *Lodoicea maldi-*

## POLLEN: GRAINS OF LIFE

Pollen is the name given to the minute grains, borne by the male stamens of a flower, which fertilise the female egg cells to create the seed of a new plant. Although all pollen may look the same to the naked eye – tiny and usually yellow particles – each type has its own distinctive characteristics.

Insect-pollinated plants such as apple and blue succory (chicory) have rough and often sticky grains which cling to insects; and the flowers are usually bright and scented to attract insects.

Wind-pollinated plants, such as pine, have smooth grains, and the flowers are much less conspicuous.

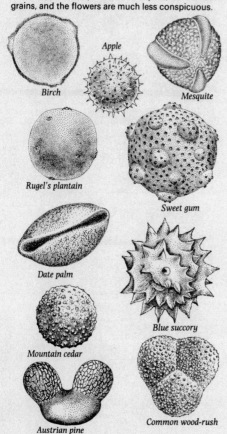

Apple

Birch

Mesquite

Rugel's plantain

Sweet gum

Date palm

Blue succory

Mountain cedar

Common wood-rush

Austrian pine

# HOW SEEDS ARE DISPERSED

Plants have evolved ingenious ways of scattering their seeds so that young plants grow far enough away from the parents to prevent competition between them. Many seeds are carried by wind, animals or water. Some plants have tasty fruits which are eaten by animals who then deposit the seeds in their droppings. Others have explosive pods to scatter their seeds. Many plants are astonishingly lavish in the production of seeds. Orchids hold the record with up to 20,000 in a single capsule. Sizes of seeds vary from those of orchids, which are about 0.25mm (0.01in) long and so light that a million of them weigh only a third of a gram (0.01oz), to the giant double coconut of the Seychelles, which weighs up to 20kg (44lb).

WIND-BORNE SEEDS *A dandelion seed has a fluffy parachute. Clematis – including the wild species, traveller's joy – has a feathery tail. Sycamore has a papery, oval wing.*

SPREAD BY ANIMALS *Birds rub sticky mistletoe into tree bark. Blackberry seeds are contained in edible fruits. The hooked seeds of wood avens cling to animal fur.*

SHAKEN AND STIRRED *A poppy capsule sprinkles seeds like a salt shaker. Water lilies have floating fruit. The cranesbill's capsule splits, throwing out seeds.*

vica – take up to ten years to develop, before they are ready to grow into a new palm tree. They look like two coconuts joined together, and can weigh up to 20kg (44lb) each.

In the wild they grow almost invariably on hilltops on remote islands in the Seychelles. What baffles scientists is how the seeds got there. Since the seeds are so heavy, the trees might be expected to spread downhill as each generation of seeds falls from its parents. But how could the seeds travel uphill to colonise a new peak? No native animal or bird would be capable of carrying them, and since they sink in water, they cannot have been carried up by the sea.

## TRAPPER IN WAITING

The Venus's flytrap, *Dionea muscipula*, which grows in nitrogen-poor bogs in the eastern United States, has developed a natural gin trap to collect the nitrogen it needs. Its leaves, which are hinged along the spine, are colourful and sweetly scented to attract insects. As soon as an insect touches down, sensitive hairs on the leaf trigger off a sudden expansion of cells in the hinge base, causing the halves of the leaf to spring shut. Curved spines along the edge of the leaves form a cage around the insect. The plant then floods the trap with digestive juices to dissolve the insect's body and extract the nitrogen it contains.

## RISE OF THE ROSE

More than 8000 varieties of rose have been developed for garden cultivation – yet all of them are descended from a mere handful of wild species. Roses have been cultivated for almost 5000 years and were known to the Persians, Greeks and Romans, but until the end of the 18th century only four or five species were grown. They included the dog rose, musk rose, Phoenician rose and the red Provins rose, which became the emblem of the Lancastrians during the 15th-century Wars of the Roses in Britain. The white rose of York was probably a form of dog rose.

Modern varieties such as hybrid tea roses (single-flowered) and floribundas (cluster-flowered) began to be bred only around 1900, after the European species were crossed with cultivated oriental species imported from China.

## MINIATURE BLOOM

The floating *Wolffia* species – members of the duckweed family – are among the world's smallest flowering plants. *Wolffia arrhiza*, which occurs on freshwater ponds and lakes in most continents, is a rootless green blob as little as 0.5mm (0.02in) across.

## PLANTS IN MEDICINE

Many plant species produce drugs which are invaluable in modern medicine. The foxglove is the source of the drug digitalis, which is used to treat heart disease.

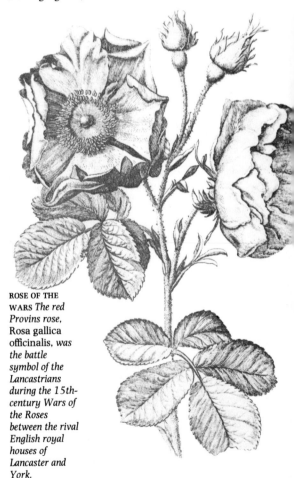

ROSE OF THE WARS *The red Provins rose,* Rosa gallica officinalis, *was the battle symbol of the Lancastrians during the 15th-century Wars of the Roses between the rival English royal houses of Lancaster and York.*

But it was used in home medicine long before the medical profession recognised its value and began extracting the drug in the late 18th century.

Deadly nightshade, *Atropa belladonna*, yields atropine, a drug used to dilate the pupils so that an optician, say, can more easily see the retina at the back of the eye. Opium, morphine and heroin, which are powerful painkillers, come from a type of poppy, *Papaver somniferum*. And the ergot fungus, *Claviceps purpurea*, yields lysergic acid, from which many drugs are produced to treat psychiatric disorders.

## RISING FROM THE ASHES
South Africa's national flower, the protea, can survive a forest fire. Indeed, it cannot survive without one. When the seeds of the sugarbush, *Protea repens*, for example, have been fertilised, tough bracts close round the flowerhead containing the seeds, creating a protective shell that can last for up to 20 years.

The bracts – containing asbestos-like fibres which are fireproof – will not open again until they have been scorched by fire, and they begin to open only when the fire has passed. The fluffy seeds, which have been protected by the bracts, then emerge unscathed – and the wind blows them away to ground newly cleared and fertilised by the fire.

## ARGENTINA'S SUCCESSFUL INVASION
More than 175 South African protea species – over half the number in the region – face eventual extinction because of an invasion by South American ants. In order to propagate, these beautiful plants need the services of the indigenous African ant, which collects the seeds, takes them underground and feeds on the elaiosome, a sweet and oily growth carried on the capsule. The ants then leave the seeds underground, effectively planting them.

The Argentine ant – which probably arrived at the turn of the century in forage imported for the British armies fighting in the Anglo-Boer war – has, however, been supplanting the local ant at an increasing rate. Argentine ants also have a taste for the elaiosome, but they eat it on the surface of the ground. So fewer and fewer seeds get buried. Moreover, the more aggressive South American ants destroy any of their African relatives they chance to meet, thus compounding the risk to the flowers.

## SUSPENDED ANIMATION
The bird's-nest clubmoss, *Selaginella lepidophylla*, which is found in North America, can survive for several months without any water. In a drought it rolls up to form a tight ball so as to minimise the area exposed to drying winds and sun; and it turns pale as water is lost from the cells. The plant remains in this state of suspended animation until it is dampened. Then, within about 15 minutes as the water is absorbed, the plant unfurls and becomes green again.

## AND MOTHER CAME TOO
Seeds normally leave their parent plant behind when they are dispersed to a new site. But the rose of Jericho, *Anastatica hierochuntica*, is different. In this plant, which grows in desert regions from Iran to Morocco, the parent travels with the offspring – though the parent dies before it starts the journey.

The fruit containing the seeds ripens at the onset of the dry season. As the drought continues, the dying branches curl protectively around the fruit and the roots wither until desert winds blow the plant away. The branches open to release the seeds only when the rains come – by which time the plant may be tens of kilometres from its original site.

## NON-STOP LEAVES
The leaves on most plants grow to a maximum size and then stop. But the leaves of *Welwitschia mirabilis* never stop growing. The plant, which grows in the Namib Desert of southern Africa, consists of a single woody stump and just one pair of leaves, and it takes about 100 years to reach full size.

Throughout that period, the leaves grow constantly. But since the desert winds fray the leaves at their ends almost as fast as they grow, the leaves never get longer than about 2m (7ft). The fraying has a beneficial effect, since the resulting fringes act like nets, collecting droplets of water from the sea mists which roll across the Namib and keeping the plant alive through droughts that can last for years.

## BALLOON TRAVELLERS
So efficient are pines in their reproductive methods that it is quite possible for a pine tree in Scotland to be pollinated by another in Norway, on the other side of the North Sea. Pine pollen is able to travel such huge distances on the wind because each pollen grain is buoyed up by two microscopic balloons.

## WATER-BOTTLE HOME
The Pima Indians, who made their home in the arid regions of the southwestern USA before Europeans arrived, never needed to make water bottles for their journeys across the desert. They simply filled up natural water bottles made by the massive, candelabra-like saguaro cactus.

Left to its own devices, the cactus does not produce the bottles. But when the desert-dwelling gila woodpecker hollows out a nest for itself in the fibrous flesh, the cactus responds by lining the hole with a tough corky layer of tissue, which remains long after the cactus has died and rotted.

## TOP OF THE POPS
The *Sphagnum* mosses of peat bogs use a battery of natural airguns to disperse the dust-like spores which are their offspring. In the last stages of ripening, the spore capsules shrink to about a quarter of their original size, compressing the air inside, and become shaped like tiny gun barrels, each with its own airtight cap. Each barrel is only about 2mm (0.1in) long. Eventually the cap breaks away and the trapped air escapes with an audible 'pop', firing the packet of spores inside as much as 2m (7ft).

## THE TERRIBLE PALM
Rattans are the longest, though not the tallest, plants in the world. The tallest are the giant redwoods of California. They grow up to 110m (more than 360ft). But the rattan palm, which winds its way snake-like through trees in the tropics, can be far longer. One Malaysian specimen measured 169m (555ft).

The palm climbs up to the highest part of the canopy of its native rainforest using cruel, backward-pointing barbs on whip-like extensions of its long leaves. Once a barb has dug into something it is like a fish-hook, extremely difficult to remove. The barbs have earned one South American species the local name of *Jacitara*, meaning 'The Terrible'.

## JAPANESE LANTERNS
Like fireflies and some fish, there are plants that glow in the dark. The fungus *Mycaena lux-coeli*, for instance, which grows on the Japanese island of Hachijo, can be seen in the dark from 15m (50ft) away, gleaming like a diminutive lantern. A bay near Parguera on Puerto Rico is called Phosphorescent Bay because of

the glow from millions of tiny marine plants called *Pyrodinium* – a type of plankton.

All plants and fungi which have this ability seem to make use of a biological clock, for they produce the enzymes responsible for the phosphorescence only at night. Luminous animals are thought to glow in order to attract mates or warn off predators, but scientists have not yet decided why the same ability should be of any value to plants.

## SNAP AND CRACKLE
The stinkhorn fungus *Dictyophora*, of tropical Brazil, is one of the fastest-growing organisms in the world. The stem pushes out of the ground at 5mm (0.2in) a minute, and grows to full size in just 20 minutes. The power behind the growth is water. When the fungus is ready to grow, chemical changes in its cells allow them to absorb water rapidly. As a result, the growth is so fast that it is possible to hear the fungus crackling as the water swells and tears its tissues.

During the growth, a delicate, net-like veil forms around the fungus – the origin of its other common name, 'the lady of the white veil'. As soon as the fungus reaches full size, it starts to decompose at the tip. Flies are attracted by the strong odour of decaying flesh and they crawl over the surface, collecting spores on their feet, and so ensuring that the fungus's off-spring are carried to new homes.

## THE PLANT THAT MOVES
The slime mould usually lives on rotting wood and feeds on bacteria and rotting vegetation. When it is ready to reproduce, thousands of individual neighbouring mould cells coalesce to form a single organism about 50mm (2in) across.

The new organism, which resembles a slug or a patch of slimy mud, has a property not possessed by any of the original mould cells. It can move. During its few hours of life, the organism moves as far as about 300mm (12in) on a layer of slime, often towards light, in an attempt to find the most favourable home for the next generation.

Then a stalk starts to sprout, lifting some of the cells from the mass. Spores form on the stalk and are dispersed by the wind to develop into colonies of new, and stationary, mould cells. Once the spores have gone, the mobile parent, its function completed, dies.

## THE FUNGUS THAT REFRESHES
Alcoholic drinks would never have been invented without a fungus. The fungus is a family of yeasts called *Ascomycetes*. These yeasts are solely responsible for fermenting all alcoholic drinks, feeding on sugar and turning it into alcohol and carbon dioxide – the gas that bubbles from fermenting liquid. Members of the same fungus family also cause bread to rise, create the veins in blue cheese, and produce antibiotics such as penicillin and streptomycin.

## HIDDEN DEPTHS
Mushrooms are far bigger than they look. The fruiting body – the part that is picked and eaten – represents only about 10 per cent of the fungus. The rest, hidden underground, is a network of tiny strands called hyphae, which spread through the earth to feed on plant debris. Some species of mushroom derive nutrition from the roots of trees, and help the tree in return to soak up vital minerals from the soil. The truffle, for example, often grows alongside the roots of hazel and beech trees. It is so well adapted to its underground life that even the fruiting body – which is collected as a prized delicacy – remains below the surface of the soil and can be found only by its smell.

# LIKE FATHER, UNLIKE SON

Almost every member of the plant kingdom has a very different pattern of reproduction from that of animals. Most adult animals look like their parents. But plants, while not necessarily looking like their parents at all, always resemble their grandparents.

In flowering plants and conifers, this difference between parent and offspring is obscured because part of the offspring generation remains hidden within the flowerhead of the parent plant; the hidden offspring then gives rise to a second generation which does resemble the original plant.

### Alternation of generations
In ferns, however, both forms are easily visible. The familiar woodland fern plant has two sets of genetic codes – 'chromosomes' – in its cells. Scientists call this form diploid, from the Greek *diplous*, meaning 'double'. But its offspring – which is produced from spores – looks quite different: it is a tiny green plant, roughly heart-shaped and about 10mm (0.4in) long.

This plant has only one set of chromosomes in its cells, and is known as haploid, from the Greek word *haplous*, meaning 'single'. The haploid plant produces both female egg cells and male sperm cells, and when fertilisation takes place between them the product is a new diploid fern.

Scientists call this two-stage pattern of reproduction, which is common to all plants except fungi and some algae, the 'alternation of generations'.

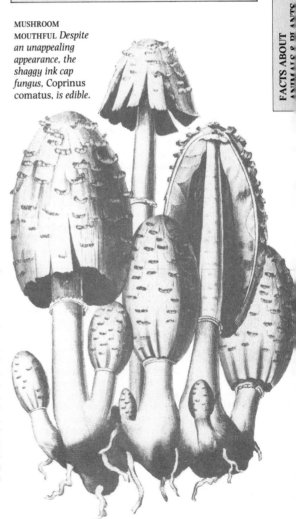

MUSHROOM MOUTHFUL *Despite an unappealing appearance, the shaggy ink cap fungus,* Coprinus comatus, *is edible.*

# Trees – the green giants

## HOPE FOR THE ELM

The elm tree's habit of sending up suckers from its roots has contributed to the spread of Dutch elm disease, which has devastated the species in North America, Europe and Asia. But the same habit may also save the elm.

Dutch elm disease is a fungus carried by bark beetles (*Scolytidae*). In a wood, several trees may be connected underground, all of them starting out as suckers from one tree. When any one of the trees is infected the disease travels throughout the root system killing one tree after the other.

But though the trees die, root buds, which produce the suckers, survive underground, enabling the trees to push out new suckers years after their death. The bark on the new suckers is too thin for the bark beetle to eat or bore into, and the new suckers appear to be able to hold the fungus at bay.

## TALKING TREES

Trees do appear to be able to communicate – at least with others of their kind. Evidence for this startling claim comes from a study carried out in 1982 by two American biologists, Dr Gordon Orians and Dr David Rhoades, of the University of Washington. They placed swarms of predatory caterpillars and web-worms on the branches of willows and alders in a deliberate experiment to find out how trees defend themselves against attack.

Within hours of the assault, the scientists found, the chemical composition of the leaves began to change. Quantities of chemicals known as terpenes and tannins were produced, making the leaves less palatable. At the same time the protein content of the leaves changed, making the protein indigestible. The result was that the insects starved and began dying from protein deficiency.

The scientists' most remarkable discovery, however, was that nearby trees which were not themselves under attack began to produce the same chemical defences – suggesting that the trees were somehow passing information to each other. The trees were far enough apart to have no physical contact between their branches, and there were no underground connections between their root systems. A separate US study of sugar maple trees came up with the same findings, and some biologists now suspect that this ability may be common to many species of plant.

How news of the attacks was transmitted is not known for certain, but scientists believe that as well as defending themselves, the trees may also release scented airborne chemicals known as pheromones which alert their neighbours.

## GIANTS OF THE FOREST

Trees, not whales, are the largest organisms alive on the Earth today. The largest of all is a giant redwood, *Sequoiadendron giganteum*, in California, USA. It is 85m (280ft) tall. Giant redwoods, which are native to the western USA and are sometimes also known as wellingtonias, can have trunks 11m (36ft) thick and can weigh over 2000 tonnes – more than ten times as much as the largest known blue whale.

Trees are also enormously strong. It is not uncommon to find tropical forest giants carrying a tangle of epiphytic plants (plants which grow on the tree but do not feed off it), vines and creepers whose total weight is more than twice that of the tree.

The world's tallest tree – though not the largest – is another Californian redwood species, *Sequoia sempervirens*. The tallest specimen is in Redwood Creek Grove, California. Known, appropriately, as 'Tallest Tree', its tip – which is slowly dying back – reaches 110.3m (362ft).

## DEATH IN BLOOM

The largest display of any flowering plant is produced by a tree – the talipot palm, *Corypha umbraculifera* – found in Sri Lanka and other tropical countries. The palm, which lives for 40 to 70 years, flowers only once in its lifetime. But its blossoming is unforgettable: a spectacular branched head up to 6m (20ft) tall and 9–13m (30–42ft) across. After the display, the palm bears up to 60 million fruits, each about 25mm (1in) across. The fruits – which contain the seeds – take about a year to ripen. Then, its reproduction assured, the palm dies.

## INSTANT TIMBER

The world's fastest-growing tree is a tropical member of the pea family, *Albizzia falcata*. One tree grew 10.74m (35.2ft) in 13 months in Sabah, Malaysia. Another, also planted in Sabah, reached 30.5m (100ft) in only five years four months. The tropical gum tree *Eucalyptus deglupta* also grows very fast. One specimen reached 45.72m (150ft) in only 15 years.

Although some species of bamboo can grow faster than this, bamboo is not classified by botanists as a tree, but as a type of woody grass. Unlike trees and flowering plants, which grow from the tip, bamboos and other grasses grow from the base, pushing out of the ground like toothpaste from a tube. It is for this reason that trees and flowering plants usually die if they are cut down, but grasses can survive close grazing and regular mowing indefinitely.

## HYDRAULIC MARVELS

Trees are the most effective pumps in the world. Silently and without any moving parts, a medium-sized oak tree can raise as much as 630 litres (140 gallons) a day to supply its needs. And even a sapling no higher than a man may lift 45 litres (10 gallons) – enough to fill a car's petrol tank.

A man-made suction pump can raise water up a pipe to a maximum height of only about 10m (33ft). Beyond that height, the weight of the water is sufficient to counteract the force of atmospheric pressure and the column breaks, leaving a vacuum. But a tree's natural pump can lift water more than ten times as high without difficulty.

A tree's pump is powered by the sun. As molecules of water are evaporated from the leaves, others move up the sapwood of the tree to take their place in a process known as osmosis. The tubes up which the water moves are so tiny that the wood acts more like blotting paper than a group of pipes, overcoming the height limit of a vacuum pump.

## NOT QUITE AS DEAD AS THE DODO

A tree once kept alive by the dodo is flourishing again – thanks to turkeys. Stanley Temple, an American biologist working on the Indian Ocean Island of Mauritius in the late 1970s, noticed that the fertile

# HOW A TREE GROWS

Almost all the wood that makes up a tree is dead. Even on a large mature tree, all the growth comes from a few tiny areas – the tips of the shoots and roots, and a thin layer of cells known as the cambium. The cells on the tips allow shoots and roots to grow upwards, outwards and downwards. The cambium layer is responsible for the thickening of the trunk, branches and roots.

The main cambium tissue forms two types of food-carrying cells: phloem tissue on its outer side to carry sugars from the leaves around the tree; and xylem tissue, or sapwood, on its inner side to carry soil water from roots to leaves. A subsidiary layer of cambium tissue produces corky bark.

Each spring the cambium produces large, thin-walled cells to carry water and nutrients needed for the peak growth period. Each summer it produces denser, thick-walled cells. Together, the cells produce a regular pattern of light (spring) and dark (summer) rings in the trunk, which form a diary of the tree's life. Each pair of rings represents a year's growth, and the thickness of the rings from year to year gives a precise record of the tree's health. In years of drought, for instance, growth is slower and the rings thinner.

As xylem cells age, they become impregnated with lignin, a chemical related to cellulose. Eventually they become dense heartwood, the dead core of a tree which provides its structural strength. As phloem cells age, they become part of the bark. The cortex in the outer layers contains additional storage cells and strengthening fibres.

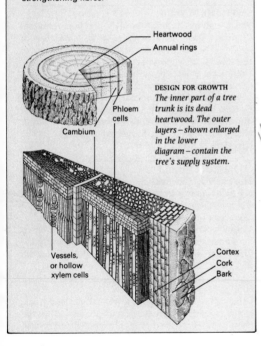

Heartwood
Annual rings

**DESIGN FOR GROWTH**
*The inner part of a tree trunk is its dead heartwood. The outer layers – shown enlarged in the lower diagram – contain the tree's supply system.*

Phloem cells

Cambium

Vessels, or hollow xylem cells

Cortex
Cork
Bark

the metabolic mill, and planted them. For the first time in three centuries *Calvaria major* germinated, and produced thriving young offspring.

## DYING GLORY

The shedding of leaves each autumn is a vital part of the survival technique adopted by deciduous trees to survive winter. In winter much of the water in the soil turns to snow and ice, preventing trees from drawing it up into their tissues. Since the leaves need, and lose, more water than other parts of a tree, they have to go so that the tree can retain a reserve of moisture elsewhere. If the leaves did not fall, the tree would die of drought. An area of trees in leaf of about 90m² (100 square yards) needs some 20 tonnes of water a day to thrive. The same area of trees without leaves needs only a fraction of this quantity.

Coniferous evergreen trees such as pines can survive the winter without shedding their greenery because their narrow needles have a much smaller surface area and so lose less water through evaporation. In addition, the leaves of evergreen trees are often covered with a glossy layer which acts like a sheet of plastic, preventing moisture from escaping.

## HARD AND SOFT

The difference between hardwood and softwood has nothing to do with the density of the timber. Hardwood comes from broad-leaved deciduous trees – those which lose their leaves in winter. Balsa, for instance, is classified as a hardwood because it comes from a broad-leaved tree, even though the wood is very soft. Softwood comes from coniferous trees such as pines and cedars. Yew, similarly, is classified as a softwood even though the wood is strong and very durable.

FACTS ABOUT ANIMALS & PLANTS

seeds of *Calvaria major*, a species of tree indigenous to the island, were not germinating. In fact, none had apparently germinated for 300 years, the age of the youngest specimens of the tree still growing.

Impressed by the coincidence between this date and the known time of the dodo's final extinction, and noting that some large, tough *Calvaria* seeds had been found in the gizzards of semi-fossilised dodos, he concluded that the strong digestive system of the long-gone bird had been an essential part of the tree's propagation process. In an attempt to reproduce the dodo's effects, he fed some of the seeds to domestic turkeys, collected them when they had been through

**PINE GLORY**
*Like other conifers, pines carry their seeds in cones. This is the maritime pine (Pinus pinaster), a Mediterranean species.*

# Crops and agriculture

## FARMING BY THE SEA

Stone Age fishermen may have been the first farmers. The reason: farmers need to live in permanent settlements while their crops grow – unlike hunters, who need to be able to wander in search of game. So Middle Eastern fishermen, who were among the first to build permanent settlements on the edges of lakes or the sea, may well have been the first to grow crops as well.

## BREAD'S FAMILY TREE

Modern wheat hybrids have an ancestry going back to the chance crossing in western Asia of wild einkorn with a related wild grass more than 10,000 years ago. The cross produced wild emmer which, under cultivation, gave rise to emmer, durum and other mutant forms. Wild emmer also crossed with a second wild grass to produce spelt. Bread wheat, which has been cultivated for about 4500 years, is descended from a cross between emmer and the second wild grass. It probably developed first in what is now eastern Turkey and western Iran as a spontaneous hybrid in fields of cultivated emmer where the wild grass was growing as a weed. Modern hybrids are often complex crosses of bread wheat (used for its food quality) with durum and spelt (used for their resistance to disease).

In the future, scientists may be able to manipulate the genetic structure of wheat plants directly to create varieties that can extract nitrogen from the air, like peas and beans, and so can grow well without the need for expensive fertilisers.

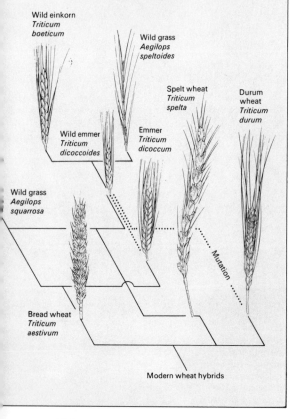

Wild einkorn
*Triticum boeticum*

Wild grass
*Aegilops speltoides*

Spelt wheat
*Triticum spelta*

Durum wheat
*Triticum durum*

Wild emmer
*Triticum dicoccoides*

Emmer
*Triticum dicoccum*

Wild grass
*Aegilops squarrosa*

Mutation

Bread wheat
*Triticum aestivum*

Modern wheat hybrids

Some of the ancient world's most sophisticated inland farmers lived in what is now southern Turkey. At the settlement of Çatal Hüyük, which dates from about 6700 BC, modern archaeologists have found traces of no fewer than 14 different crops – including wheat, barley, peas, lentils and vetch.

## HARVEST TIME

People were harvesting wheat in its wild forms long before they learnt to grow it. Wheat was first cultivated in the Middle East around 8000 BC, but archaeologists have found in the same region crude sickles, used to harvest the wild forerunners of the cereal, dating from about 10,000 BC.

## THAI FOR FIRST PLACE

Agriculture may have originated in present-day Thailand, rather than the Middle East as archaeologists have long believed. Remains of crop plants, including peas, beans, cucumbers and peppers, were found in a cave in northeast Thailand in the early 1970s and have been dated by carbon-14 tests to about 9700 BC – several centuries earlier than the first known farming in the Middle East.

## SPEED THE PLOUGH

The plough has been the farmer's most important tool for nearly 5000 years. Invented in the Middle East in about 3000 BC, it enabled early farmers to turn over the topsoil, burying weeds and thus giving crops a chance to grow without competition. Originally a crude instrument consisting of a forked branch with one prong sharpened to cut through the soil, the plough later acquired a specially shaped wooden frame and was fitted with bronze, and then iron, blades. Oxen were first harnessed to ploughs by the Egyptians in about 1500 BC.

## CIVILISING CEREALS

The world's great civilisations have all been based on the cultivation of cereals. For without an abundant and reliable source of food, villages cannot grow into cities, nor cities into empires. The civilisations of Mesopotamia, Egypt, Greece and Rome were all based on wheat. Rice was the staple food in ancient India, China and Japan, and maize provided the basis for the Inca, Aztec and Mayan empires in the Americas.

## DEADLY FOOD

Cassava, one of the tropical world's staple food crops, contains an extremely dangerous poison. Unless the plant's raw roots are thoroughly washed and cooked they yield prussic acid, which is fatal to humans even in small quantities. The starchy cassava, *Manihot esculenta*, is used to make tapioca.

## CHEWING-GUM TREES

Chewing gum is derived from the latex of the chicle tree, *Manilkara zapota*. A native of Central America, the chicle grows wild and each tree may be several kilometres from its nearest neighbour. Local Indians, known as *chicleros*, harvest the milky latex by cutting chevron-shaped incisions in the bark and letting the juice ooze out. The latex is collected and boiled to provide the gum base for chewing gum. Since the late 1940s chicle latex has been partly replaced by synthetics in gum manufacture.

## MILK TREE
Venezuelans collect milk from a herd that never moves. The South American milk tree, *Brosimum utile*, belongs to the fig family and produces a sap which looks, tastes and is used just like cow's milk.

## PIGEONS WHO BROKE A MONOPOLY
A lucrative Dutch spice monopoly was broken by pigeons. Until the late 18th century, nutmeg trees grew only on the Dutch-owned Indonesian islands of Banda and Amboina (Ambon) – because earlier traders had deliberately destroyed nutmeg trees elsewhere to maintain control of the supply. As a result, Dutch merchants were able to demand artificially high prices for the spice which is derived from the tree's seeds. By 1900, though, island-hopping pigeons which fed on the seeds had carried them to neighbouring islands that were not under Dutch control. Once the new trees grew, the Dutch monopoly was ended and prices tumbled. The nutmeg tree, *Myristica fragrans*, actually produces two spices. Its hard nut-like seeds yield nutmeg, used to flavour cakes and milk dishes; and a red fleshy structure surrounding the seed produces mace, used in chutneys and pickles.

## PLANTS' REVENGE
Two modern garden insecticides – used to protect vegetable crops and flowers from predatory insects – are both derived from plants. Derris is produced from the root of a Southeast Asian pea, *Derris elliptica*, and pyrethrum comes from a type of daisy, *Chrysanthemum cinerariaefolium*. These plant-derived pesticides are regarded by botanists as safer than earlier man-made insecticides such as DDT because they are much less poisonous to mammals, including man, and do not accumulate in animal tissues.

## UNDERGROUND NUTS
The peanut – a relative of the garden pea – buries its own seeds and so ensures the survival of the next generation. After fertilisation, the pods branch downwards from the peanut's flower and force their way into the soil, allowing the peanut, which is the plant's seed, to ripen underground. In this way the seeds are protected from predators. Contact with the moister soil beneath the surface also enables the seeds to soak up more efficiently the water they need to germinate. Most plants, by contrast, grow upwards, towards the light, and release their seeds above ground.

# CROPS AROUND THE WORLD: HOW THEY BEGAN

**Barley** First grown in Egypt in about 4000 BC. Modern varieties are descended from the strain *Hordeum spontaneum*. Now grown mostly in Europe, North America and Australia as fodder for cattle and as a source of malt, used in distilling and brewing.

**Beans** Family of plants now very widely grown, and thought to have been first cultivated in about 6000 BC. String, kidney and lima beans originated in Central and South America. Mung and soya beans were first cultivated in Asia, broad beans in Europe.

**Maize** First cultivated in Mexico in about 5000 BC. Introduced to Europe from the Americas by Christopher Columbus in the late 15th century. Modern varieties are descended from the original cultivated plant which was crossed with a 15th-century hybrid called teosinte.

**Millet** First cultivated in China in about 2700 BC. Now grown mostly for cattle fodder in the USA and USSR, but because of its resistance to drought conditions is also used as food in tropical Africa.

**Oats** Probably originated as a weed growing with other cereals such as wheat or barley, and was domesticated about 2500 years ago in Asia and Europe. The most widely cultivated form is *Avena sativa*, derived from a western Asian wild grass, *Avena fatua*. Predominantly used as cattle food, but also used in breakfast cereals and to make porridge.

**Potato** First known to have been cultivated in the Peruvian and Bolivian Andes in about AD 200. Introduced to Europe by the Spaniards in the late 16th century. More than 150 varieties are now grown.

**Rice** First known to have been cultivated in India in about 3000 BC, later spreading to China, Japan and Southeast Asia, now the main producers. About 25 varieties are grown, all descended from an original wild species, *Oryza sativa*.

**Rye** Originated as a weed growing among other cereals. First cultivated in southwest Asia in about 1000 BC and is now used as flour in rye bread or as food for cattle.

**Sorghum** Probably originated in Africa in about 3000 BC. It is now grown for human and animal consumption in Africa, India, China and the USA.

**Wheat** Probably the earliest domesticated cereal, developing from chance hybridisations of wild grasses more than 10,000 years ago. It was grown by the early civilisations in the Mediterranean and the Middle East, and was being baked into bread in Mesopotamia as early as 8000 BC.

CROP OF AGES
*Sorghum, now grown around the world, probably grew first in Africa some 5000 years ago.*

# Fruit and vegetables

## BREADFRUIT AND THE *BOUNTY*

The mutiny on the *Bounty* happened during a vegetable delivery. In 1789 Captain William Bligh set sail from Tahiti on board the *Bounty* with a cargo of breadfruit plants for the West Indies. The aim was to introduce them as a new crop to provide cheap food for slaves on the islands.

The mutiny interrupted the voyage and the breadfruit plants did not reach their destination then. But four years later Bligh completed the mission aboard another ship. Ironically, the breadfruit was not welcomed in the Caribbean. The slaves and native islanders preferred their traditional fruit – a type of banana known as a plantain.

## WHY BANANAS DON'T GROW ON TREES

Banana trees are not trees at all. Although banana plants resemble small palm trees, they are in fact giant herbaceous plants – that is, they die back in winter. The plant's 'trunk' is not wood; instead it is formed from tightly wrapped leaf-bases. Banana varieties which have been developed for eating as fruit (there are other types, known as plantains, which are eaten as cooked vegetables) have lost the ability to reproduce. They have no viable seeds, so the stock of plants has to be renewed from cuttings: clones which are genetically identical to the parent. All that remain of the seeds are the small, soft black specks in the core of a banana. By contrast, the seeds of wild bananas are the size of peas and extremely hard.

Fibres from the leaves of other relatives of the banana yield Manila hemp, which is used to make water-resistant ropes for the fishing industry, twine, hammocks, hats and table-mats.

## EDIBLE FLOWERS

Western gardeners and cooks regularly ignore one of the tastiest parts of marrow and courgette plants: the flowers. Male flowers, those without the basal swelling that grows into the vegetable, can be cooked with a little butter or coated in batter and lightly fried.

The leaves also make a useful herb for cooking and the seeds, which yield an edible oil, can be roasted, salted and eaten.

The marrow family, which includes courgettes, squashes, gourds and pumpkins, are largely varieties of a single and originally Mexican species, *Cucurbita pepo*, which has been cultivated by man for at least 5500 years.

## TUBER TRAGEDY

The Irish potato famine of the late 1840s happened because of the way potatoes are grown in cultivation. New crops are raised by planting potatoes, not seeds, so that each new generation of potato plants is a clone, genetically identical to the previous year's plants. Because all the plants are identical, if one plant is susceptible to a disease, all the plants can fall to it. The cause of the famine was a fungus disease, potato blight, which swept over Ireland and wiped out the entire potato harvest for four consecutive years between 1847 and 1850.

Had the crops been grown from seeds and thus had a variety of genetic patterns, the disease would not have had such a devastating effect. In the event, more than a million people starved to death, and hundreds

of thousands fled to the USA. Before the famine, the population of Ireland was more than 6.5 million. By 1851, the year after the famine ended, it had dropped to 5.1 million. It has never recovered. In the early 1980s, the population of Eire and Ulster combined was still only 4.9 million.

Ironically, the Irish population had grown vastly in the previous two centuries, partly as a result of the introduction from South America of the potato – a cheap, easily grown and popular staple crop. Blight-resistant strains were later imported from South America. Today Britain, one of the world's potato-eating champions, eats about 15,250 tonnes of potatoes a day – enough to give everyone in the country a 290g (10oz) helping.

## WHY CHILLIES ARE HOT

Even the most fiery chilli pepper gets all its heat from no more than 0.1 per cent of the fruit. The burning taste comes from a chemical called capsicin, of which only a trace is needed to cause an unwary diner to grab for water.

Chillies are the berries of a species of the potato family, *Capsicum annuum*. The species includes both the small hot types, such as the red tabasco pepper, and the large red and green sweet peppers. Hot peppers dried and crushed yield cayenne pepper. Sweet peppers are used to make paprika.

The species is native to the Americas, but the largest crops by far are now grown in India.

## CHANGE FOR THE BETTER

Many crops perform much better in new homes than in their own. The coffee plant, for instance, *Coffea arabica*, is native to Ethiopia (hence the reference to Arabs in its name). But most coffee now comes from Central or South America. Cocoa (*Theobroma cacao*) originated in South and Central America, but Ghana is now the world's main exporter. Citrus fruits, native to Southeast Asia, and soya beans from northern Asia, now grow best in the United States. One of the major reasons for the better performance of the expatriate plant is that the migrant is free, even if only temporarily, from the pests and diseases which evolved alongside it in its original home.

## JACK THE GIANT FRUIT

The jackfruit tree of southern Asia, *Artocarpus heterophyllus*, bears massive fruits weighing up to 50kg (110lb) – the world's largest tree fruits. Up to 250 fruits are produced by a single tree each year, and the sweet pulp is eaten fresh or preserved in syrup, particularly in India and Sri Lanka.

## SCRUB UP WITH A MARROW

The cylindrical bathroom sponges known as loofahs can be eaten when young. They are the fruit of a tropical relative of the marrow, *Luffa cylindrica*, and have nothing to do with the sea. Young cooked fruits taste something like marrow.

To make bathroom loofahs, the ripe fruits are immersed in running water until the outer wall disintegrates, and the fibrous remains are then cleaned and bleached. Loofahs have also been used as filters in steam and diesel engines, in mats, shoe soles and gloves, and as padding in the steel helmets used before the Second World War by the US Army.

# THE APPEAL OF F1 HYBRIDS

Most fruits and vegetables grown around the world by modern farmers and gardeners are hybrids – varieties created, often artificially, from interbreeding two or more separate strains. Over generations of selective breeding and cross-fertilising, hybrid plants can be tailored to have almost any set of characteristics. They may have consistently larger fruit, for instance, faster growth or greater resistance to pests and diseases.

### Perils of inbreeding

Farmers and gardeners also make use, however, of another property which is peculiar to the earliest generations of a new hybrid. Plants which have been bred selectively for generations so that they always grow true to type tend to lose their vigour. They grow feebly because of inbreeding. But if two true-breeding varieties are crossed, the first resulting generation – known as Filial 1, or F1 for short – has the dominant qualities of its parents, plus vastly increased vigour. As a result, F1 seeds can produce more abundant crops than either of their parent varieties.

The generation descended from the F1 has almost as much vigour as the F1, but less uniformity, because about one plant in four will display what are called recessive characteristics, derived from the original varieties but submerged in the F1 generation. These second-generation plants – known as F2 hybrids – are also widely grown because no laboriously controlled cross-pollination is needed, and so the seeds are cheaper to produce.

Later generations than the F2 can be grown as well, but they are usually sold only as mixtures because the genetic structure is by then so scrambled that few of the resulting plants grow true to type.

### A monk's experiments

The genetic principles used by modern plant breeders to create all hybrids, including F1 and F2 strains, were discovered by an Austrian monk named Gregor Mendel (1822 – 84). He published his results, largely based on experiments with garden peas, in 1866, but his discoveries were ignored until other researchers confirmed them in 1900, 16 years after his death. Mendel found that all genetic characteristics, in animals as well as plants, are carried in pairs. He also found that where two opposed characteristics – such as tallness and shortness – are carried by the same plant, one of the factors will consistently dominate. It is this consistency which explains why plants grown from F1 seeds are so uniform.

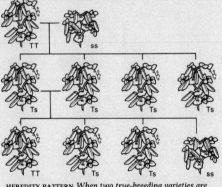

HEREDITY PATTERN *When two true-breeding varieties are crossed – one carrying a pair of dominant genes (tallness, say) and the other its recessive opposite (shortness) – all of the resulting F1 seeds grow into tall plants because each carries the dominant gene. When F1 plants are crossed with each other, however, only three of the four possible genetic combinations contain the dominant tallness gene. The fourth has only the recessive genes and so grows into a short plant.*

## QUEEN OF THE GREENS

Cabbages, broccoli, cauliflowers, brussels sprouts, kohl-rabi and kale, are all varieties of a single Mediterranean species, *Brassica oleracea*. Over thousands of years, man has developed the different vegetables by selecting from originally wild plants and their cultivated progeny those with the densest flower-heads (for cauliflowers and broccoli), those with the best rosettes of winter leaves (for cabbages), those with the largest buds (for brussels sprouts) and those with the thickest stems (for kohl-rabi).

## FALSE FRUIT

The strawberry is technically not a fruit at all. In botanical terms, fruits are seed-bearing structures which grow from a flower's ovaries, and a strawberry is merely the swollen base of the strawberry flower. The plant's true fruits are the small, hard, nut-like pips embedded around the outside of the flesh. The seeds are contained in the pips. Strawberries came originally from the Americas. Garden varieties were first bred in 18th-century France from spontaneous hybrids between a North American species, *Fragaria virginiana*, and a Chilean species *F. chiloensis*.

## NOSE FOR FLAVOUR

The durian, a Southeast Asian fruit from a plant known to botanists as *Durio zibethinus*, is rated by many gourmets as the world's most delicious food. There is just one problem. It smells awful. Critics groping for a description of its qualities have labelled it 'onion-flavoured custard'. Whatever the views of humans, some animals love it. The wild plants are a favourite food of elephants and orang-utans.

TASTE TEST *Gourmets rate the durian of Southeast Asia as the world's most delicious fruit – despite its pungent smell. Critics call it 'onion-flavoured custard'.*

# How animals are classified

## THE ANIMAL KINGDOM

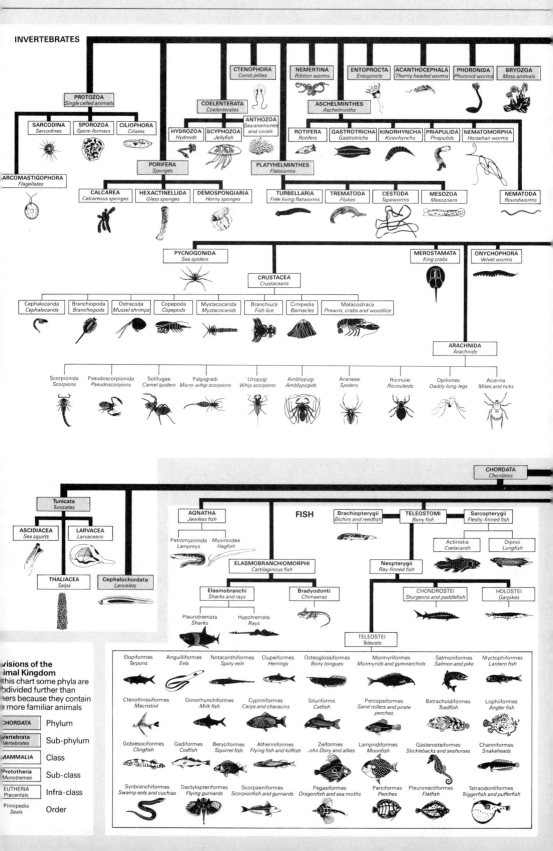

INVERTEBRATES

CTENOPHORA — *Comb jellies*
NEMERTINA — *Ribbon worms*
ENTOPROCTA — *Entoprocts*
ACANTHOCEPHALA — *Thorny headed worms*
PHORONIDA — *Phoronid worms*
BRYOZOA — *Moss animals*

PROTOZOA — *Single celled animals*
COELENTERATA — *Coelenterates*
ANTHOZOA — *Sea anemones and corals*
ASCHELMINTHES — *Aschelminths*

SARCODINA — *Sarcodines*
SPOROZOA — *Spore-formers*
CILIOPHORA — *Ciliates*
HYDROZOA — *Hydroids*
SCYPHOZOA — *Jellyfish*
ROTIFERA — *Rotifers*
GASTROTRICHA — *Gastrotrichs*
KINORHYNCHA — *Kinorhynchs*
PRIAPULIDA — *Priapulids*
NEMATOMORPHA — *Horsehair worms*

SARCOMASTIGOPHORA — *Flagellates*
PORIFERA — *Sponges*
PLATYHELMINTHES — *Flatworms*

CALCAREA — *Calcareous sponges*
HEXACTINELLIDA — *Glass sponges*
DEMOSPONGIARIA — *Horny sponges*
TURBELLARIA — *Free living flatworms*
TREMATODA — *Flukes*
CESTODA — *Tapeworms*
MESOZOA — *Mesozoans*
NEMATODA — *Roundworms*

PYCNOGONIDA — *Sea spiders*
MEROSTAMATA — *King crabs*
ONYCHOPHORA — *Velvet worms*

CRUSTACEA — *Crustaceans*

Cephalocarida — *Cephalocarids*
Branchiopoda — *Branchiopods*
Ostracoda — *Mussel shrimps*
Copepoda — *Copepods*
Mystacocarida — *Mystacocarids*
Branchiura — *Fish lice*
Cirripedia — *Barnacles*
Malacostraca — *Prawns, crabs and woodlice*

ARACHNIDA — *Arachnids*

Scorpionida — *Scorpions*
Pseudoscorpionida — *Pseudoscorpions*
Solifugae — *Camel spiders*
Palpigradi — *Micro-whip scorpions*
Uropygi — *Whip scorpions*
Amblypygi — *Amblypygids*
Araneae — *Spiders*
Ricinulei — *Ricinuleids*
Opiliones — *Daddy long-legs*
Acarina — *Mites and ticks*

CHORDATA — *Chordates*

Tunicata — *Tunicates*
AGNATHA — *Jawless fish*
FISH
Brachiopterygii — *Bichirs and reedfish*
TELEOSTOMI — *Bony fish*
Sarcopterygii — *Fleshy-finned fish*

ASCIDIACEA — *Sea squirts*
LARVACEA — *Larvaceans*
Petromyzonida — *Lampreys*
Myxinoidea — *Hagfish*
Actinistia — *Coelacanth*
Dipnoi — *Lungfish*

ELASMOBRANCHIOMORPHI — *Cartilaginous fish*
Neopterygii — *Ray-finned fish*

THALIACEA — *Salps*
Cephalochordata — *Lancelets*
Elasmobranchi — *Sharks and rays*
Bradyodonti — *Chimaeras*
CHONDROSTEI — *Sturgeons and paddlefish*
HOLOSTEI — *Garpikes*

Pleurotremata — *Sharks*
Hypotremata — *Rays*

TELEOSTEI — *Teleosts*

visions of the
imal Kingdom
this chart some phyla are
bdivided further than
ers because they contain
e more familiar animals

| | |
|---|---|
| CHORDATA *Chordates* | Phylum |
| Vertebrata *Vertebrates* | Sub-phylum |
| MAMMALIA *Mammals* | Class |
| Prototheria *Monotremes* | Sub-class |
| EUTHERIA *Placentals* | Infra-class |
| Pinnipedia *Seals* | Order |

Elopiformes — *Tarpons*
Anguilliformes — *Eels*
Notacanthiformes — *Spiny eels*
Clupeiformes — *Herrings*
Osteoglossiformes — *Bony tongues*
Mormyriformes — *Mormyrids and gymnarchids*
Salmoniformes — *Salmon and pike*
Myctophiformes — *Lantern fish*

Ctenothrissiformes — *Macristiid*
Gonorhynchiformes — *Milk fish*
Cypriniformes — *Carps and characins*
Siluriforms — *Catfish*
Percopsiformes — *Sand rollers and pirate perches*
Batrachoidiformes — *Toadfish*
Lophiiformes — *Angler fish*

Gobiesociformes — *Clingfish*
Gadiformes — *Codfish*
Beryciformes — *Squirrel fish*
Atheriniformes — *Flying fish and killfish*
Zeiformes — *John Dory and allies*
Lampridiformes — *Moonfish*
Gasterosteiformes — *Sticklebacks and seahorses*
Channiformes — *Snakeheads*

Synbranchiformes — *Swamp eels and cuchias*
Dactylopteriformes — *Flying gurnards*
Scorpaeniformes — *Scorpionfish and gurnards*
Pegasiformes — *Dragonfish and sea moths*
Perciformes — *Perches*
Pleuronectiformes — *Flatfish*
Tetraodontiformes — *Triggerfish and pufferfish*

Nature recognises only one way of grouping animals. It is the species: animals which can interbreed in the wild and produce fertile offspring. To show how animals are related through evolution, however, zoologists classify them further – into genera, families, orders, classes and phyla. The modern system of identifying each animal by a two-part Latin name made up of the genus and species was devised by a Swedish naturalist, Karl von Linné (1707–78) – known by his own Latin name: Carolus Linnaeus.

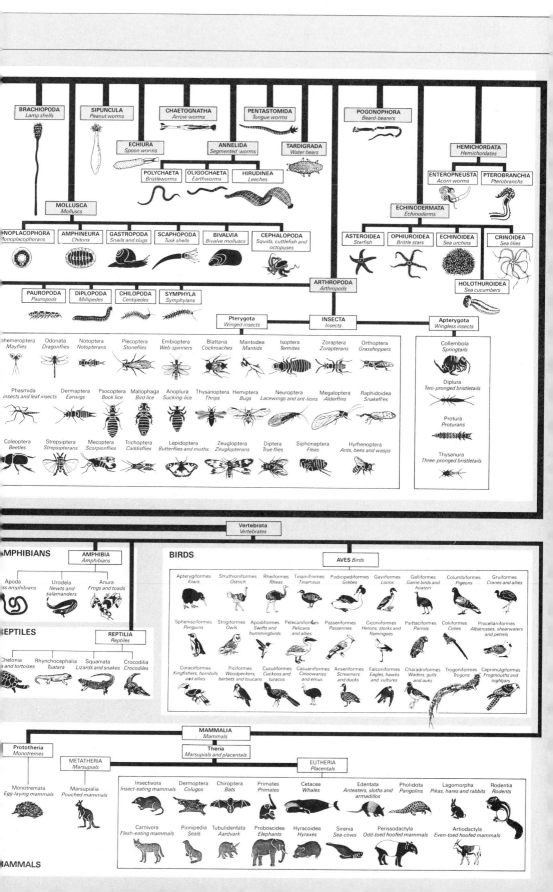

# Animals without backbones

### SECOND-HAND STING

Sea slugs have no shell to protect their soft rippling bodies and no natural defences. So they eat weapons. The sea slug *Glaucus*, for instance, eats the sting cells of the *Porpita* jellyfish but does not digest them. Instead the cells are passed intact to the slug's skin, ready for use against a predator.

Another slug eats the stinging buds of anemones, to which it is immune. The buds are swallowed intact. Then the sea slug's body guides them through the intestinal wall to the back, where they nestle under the skin. If triggered, the stings shoot out at an enemy or attacker.

### DEADLY MEDLEY

The Portuguese man-of-war is not one animal but many, all living in lethal four-part harmony. This bobbing, slimy horror, a type of jellyfish, whose paralysing tentacles can kill human beings, consists of four different types of animal, totalling perhaps 1000 individuals. Each type has its own specialised job – floating, catching food, digestion or reproduction. Yet all work together so well that none could live on its own. Between them, these primitive individuals form the crew of a killing machine with a poison almost as powerful as a cobra's.

For small fish, contact with the man-of-war's trailing tentacles, which can be 18m (60ft) long, means instant oblivion. For humans a bad sting means severe pain, a rapid drop in blood pressure, shock and sometimes death. Luckier victims will carry for days the angry red weals which the tentacles leave. There is no known antidote for the stings, but ordinary vinegar seems to neutralise some of the poison's effects.

### TREE-CLIMBING CRABS

A giant relative of the hermit crab finds food not in the water but in the trees. The robber crab, *Birgus latro*, lives on the islands of the southwest Pacific and Indian Oceans. When young it lodges in an empty shell like the hermit crab, but a mature robber crab can be as long as 450mm (18in).

Its enormously powerful pincers and long walking legs enable it to climb coconut palms as efficiently as a lumberjack with crampons. Once at the top, the crab snips off young coconuts and then returns to the ground to eat them.

### GIANTS OF THE DEEP

The world's largest invertebrates – animals without backbones – are squids of the genus *Architeuthis*. Nobody knows how large these monsters may grow in their home in the ocean abyss, but occasional specimens come to the surface. One measured in New Zealand in 1887 was 17m (57ft) long, including nearly 15m (50ft) of tentacles. Another washed up in New Zealand in 1933 was 21m (70ft) long.

A squid of this size weighs well over a tonne and has an eye 400mm (16in) across, the largest eye in the animal kingdom.

It is possible that squids exist which are many times larger than these. The suckers of a 15m (50ft) squid leave round scars on a sperm whale – the traditional enemy of squids – that are 100mm (4in) across. But sperm whales have been found with scars 450mm (18in) across – more than four times as large.

## MOLLUSCS

Molluscs, which have no close relatives and form a separate grouping – known as a phylum – in the animal kingdom, have soft bodies supported by a shell. The most advanced molluscs are octopuses and cuttlefish, in which the shell is enclosed by the body, like a primitive skeleton.

OCTOPUS *A hard internal structure, like the chalky cuttlebone of a cuttlefish, supports the body.*

MUSSEL *Mussels are bivalve molluscs, so called because their shell has two similar halves, or valves.*

CHITON *The coat-of-mail shell, or chiton, is protected by a set of eight overlapping plates.*

SNAIL *Land and sea snails are known to scientists as gastropods, from Greek words meaning 'belly-footed'.*

## CRUSTACEANS

Like insects and spiders, crustaceans – most of which live in the sea – are classified as arthropods: animals with jointed limbs. Crustaceans have segmented bodies, and each segment usually has a pair of appendages, such as legs or claws.

LOBSTER *Lobsters have the crustacean's typical segmented form.*

BRINE SHRIMP *The shrimp swims upside down, using its rows of appendages like oars.*

FISH LOUSE *The louse's swimming legs project from beneath a large round carapace.*

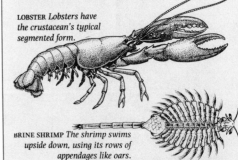

BARNACLE *Hard plates enclose the barnacle's body. They spread to allow its feathery legs to emerge for feeding.*

## FLOATING KILLER

The sting of the box jellyfish or sea wasp, a kind of jellyfish with a dome-shaped bell only 250mm (10in) high, contains one of the world's most potent poisons. It can cause a victim to develop a fierce temperature, go blind, gasp for breath and die, all in the space of a few minutes. In the past 100 years, at least 65 people have died from sea-wasp stings while swimming off Queensland, Australia. An antidote to the poison does exist, but the poison acts so quickly that the victim has little chance of getting treatment in time.

## BIRD-EATING SPIDERS

Spiders large enough to tackle birds – and win – live in holes and under fallen trees on the forest floors of South America, Asia and Africa. Some species found in South America have a body as much as 75mm (3in) across – the size of a man's palm – and a leg span of 200mm (8in). Often called bird-eating spiders, they have been known to catch small birds, but the bulk of their diet consists of small mammals and insects. Like other spiders, the giants do not chew their food. Instead they inject digestive juices into the prey and then suck out the fluids from the body.

## SHELL SHOCK

The Indian and Pacific Oceans, home of many of the world's most poisonous sea creatures, house one of the most beautiful killers in the cone shell snail, a relative of the harmless whelk. Its shell is so highly prized by collectors that a single good specimen can fetch up to £400.

But the animal that lives inside this marvel owns a horrifying, and loaded, living syringe – a trunk-like tube that it can whip against the body of an attacker. In the tip of the trunk are minute needle teeth through which it injects a paralysing fluid. At least ten people have died from its effects, generally within a few hours of the pinprick sting.

## WORM ANAESTHETIC

Leeches, which are related to earthworms, have their own built-in anaesthetic so that they can feed in peace. The leech clamps itself to its victims with suckers at each end of its body. At the centre of the front sucker is the mouth. The leech makes a Y-shaped wound with three sharp-toothed jaws, and then sucks the blood.

Anaesthetic in the saliva numbs the wound so that the victim does not feel his attacker and brush it off. Leeches also secrete a substance that causes the blood vessels to dilate and so increase blood flow, and an anti-coagulant substance to prevent the blood from clotting.

## COURTING DANGER

Because scorpions are not immune to their own poison, even mating is a risky business for them. As a result, the desert hunters, which normally live alone, have evolved a cautious courtship ritual.

The male seizes the female's pincers in his own and the pair then shuffle backwards and forwards, sometimes with their stinging tails carefully entwined to keep them away from their bodies. The male deposits a packet of sperm on the ground and pushes and pulls the female until she is over the packet and can take up the sperm to fertilise the eggs.

After the dance, the pair go their separate ways. The fertilised eggs develop and hatch within the mother's body, the young then clamber out and stay on her back for about two weeks until they are old enough to fend for themselves.

## SHE WHO MUST BE AVOIDED

Hazardous though the mating of scorpions may be, the partners are at least of equal size. In most species of spider, the male is many times smaller than his mate, and runs a real risk of being eaten. Before courting, the male spider spins a tiny pad of web into which he deposits sperm from his abdomen. He then sucks the sperm into a specialised leg known as the pedipalp. To mate successfully he must approach the female close enough to plunge the pedipalp into the genital opening on the front of the female's abdomen.

In one spider species, *Pisaura listeri*, the male hands the female a gift of a fly wrapped in silk as he approaches. Only when the female has her mouth full does he dart in to mate.

## SHARP-SHOOTING SHRIMP

High in the coral reefs of tropical waters lurks a tiny bandit, the 50mm (2in) long pistol shrimp. The pincers on its large right claw form the shape of a matching peg and hole.

When a small fish wanders into the ambush spot, the shrimp scuttles out, aims this 'pistol', and snaps the peg into the hole. The resulting shockwave in the water stuns the fish for a few seconds – and gives the shrimp time to close in for the kill.

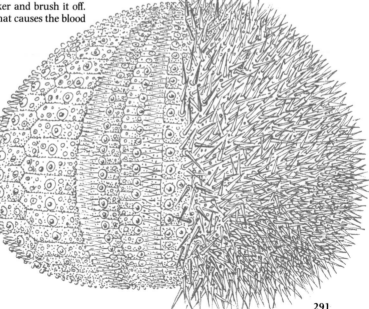

LIVING PINCUSHION *The common sea urchin*, Echinus esculentus, *is one of about 800 species of these spiky, ball-shaped creatures. They are related to the starfish. This cut-away drawing shows the patterned shell which encloses the body, but which is normally hidden by the jutting spines. Sea urchins, which are eaten as a delicacy in many parts of the world, feed through a mouth at the base of the shell: their only vulnerable point.*

## LIFELONG HEADSTAND

Barnacles spend their entire adult lives standing on their heads. The larvae of these crustaceans, which live on coastal rocks around the world, are free-swimming. But when a larva finds a suitable rocky surface, it glues itself to the rock by means of a gland on its head. The barnacle then changes shape, secreting shell plates around its body to protect it for its immobile adult life. When the tide covers it, the barnacle opens the shell plates, and feathery appendages emerge to kick food particles towards the mouth.

Some parasitic barnacles undergo even stranger transformations than their non-parasitic relatives. *Sacculina* barnacles make their homes inside crabs. The larva settles head-first on a crab and throws off its body and legs. It then produces a dart-shaped organ which it thrusts into the crab's body and through which it injects itself as a formless mass of cells.

Settling by the crab's intestine, the larva sends out branches through its host, hindering the crab's development. Finally, the barnacle becomes adult as little more than a bag of sex organs below the crab's abdomen. It has both male and female sexual organs and reproduces itself by shedding sperm and eggs into the surrounding water.

## REWARDS OF RESISTANCE

Pearls, treasured throughout the world as jewellery, are the product of a fight against an invader. Molluscs with double shells, such as clams, oysters and mussels, lay down pearl as the inner layer of their shells. The mother-of-pearl, as it is called, consists largely of thin layers of calcium carbonate, the chemical of which chalk is composed.

When some foreign matter, often a parasitic larva, gets into the body, the mollusc forms a small sac around the foreign body, isolating it, and then builds layer upon layer of calcium carbonate around the sac, imprisoning the invader for ever and creating a pearl. Cultivated pearls are produced by inserting an artificial irritant, usually a bead of mother-of-pearl, into the body of an oyster.

Natural pearls are rare. Only one oyster in a thousand contains one. The freshwater pearl mussel, once widely cultivated in Europe, might take six years to build up a pearl and only one in 3000 mussels examined is likely to contain one. However, with luck the rewards can be considerable: the largest pearl ever found – the Pearl of Laotze – weighs 6.37kg (14lb 1oz) and is 240mm (9.5in) long. It was found in the Philippines, inside a giant clam.

## WORMS, WORMS EVERYWHERE

The world's 10,000 species of roundworm have learnt to make their homes almost anywhere: in the earth, in fresh water, in the sea, even in the bodies of other animals and plants. They are so abundant that a mere handful of garden soil will contain about 1000.

Many roundworms are small or microscopic, but some grow to 900mm (3ft). Some are also phenomenal breeders. Females of one species – the 350mm (14in) long intestinal parasite known as *Ascaris lumbricoides* – can lay 200,000 eggs a day.

## THE LONG AND THE SHORT OF IT

The world's longest insect is the giant stick insect, *Pharnacia serratipes*, of Indonesia. Females of the species can be up to 330mm (13in long). The world's bulkiest insect is the South American hercules beetle, *Dynastes hercules*, the male of which has a total length of 160mm (6in) and a width of 50mm (2in). By contrast, some of the tiny species of *Alaptus*, fairy flies

which develop as parasites inside the eggs of other insects, are only 0.2mm (0.01in) long when fully grown.

## OLDEST INHABITANT

The longest-existing species inhabiting the Earth is a deep sea snail, *Neopilina galatheae*. It was found living at a depth of 3475m (11,400ft) off Costa Rica in 1952 – and fossil remains show that it has not changed at all in 500 million years.

## LONGEST REACH

The Arctic jellyfish of the northwest Atlantic has the longest reach of any animal. One of these creatures, washed up on a Massachusetts beach in about 1865, had a body 2.3m (7.5ft) across and tentacles 36m (120ft) long, giving it a total possible span of more than 74m (240ft).

## LONGEST WORMS

Ribbon worms – named for their flat, ribbon-shaped body – far exceed any other kind of worm in length. The bootlace worm, *Lineus longissimus*, a type of ribbon worm which lives around British coasts, commonly grows to 5m (16.5ft). Some, however, have topped 30m (100ft), and a specimen washed ashore in Scotland in 1864 measured more than 55m (180ft) – the longest worm and the longest animal ever found.

## GARDENING UNDERGROUND

The workers of the South American leaf-cutter ants tend their own food-producing gardens in their underground nests – which measure as much as 10m (33ft) across and contain some 500,000 ants. First of all the workers collect pieces of leaves and carry them flag-like to the nest. They then tear the pieces up and on this compost they grow a crop of fungus which is eaten by the ants.

## DOUBLE-HEADED DECEIVERS

Some insects appear to have a head at both ends of their bodies. A number of hairstreak butterflies, for example, have protuberances on their hind wings that look like frontal antennae when the insect rests with its wings folded. As soon as the butterfly lands, it turns rapidly so that its head is facing the way it has just come. The quick change of direction and the false head deceive predators. Birds rely on knowing which is the head end so that, when they pounce, they can anticipate and allow for the victim's movement. But the hairstreak moves off in the direction its true head is facing – which is usually the opposite direction from that expected.

## SILKEN THREADS

Most moth and butterfly caterpillars make silk. They produce it from salivary glands and use it to construct supporting threads and cocoons which protect them while they undergo the transformation from larva to adult. In most species, the silk is usually produced in short lengths which are glued and woven together in the cocoon and the threads are too short to be commercially useful.

But the mulberry silkworm, *Bombyx mori*, spins single threads up to 1.2km (3900ft) long – a talent which has made the caterpillar so valuable to man that it no longer exists in the wild.

The silk is retrieved by softening the cocoon in hot water – incidentally killing the pupa inside – then unwinding the thread. The discovery of how to rear silkworms on mulberry trees was made 2000 years ago in China.

# HOW INSECTS FLY

Aeroplanes, like most birds, derive their ability to fly largely from the specialised shape of their wings: a rounded leading edge, flattened underneath and bulging on top, tapering away to a slender trailing edge. The wings of insects, however, do not have this typical aerofoil shape. Instead they are roughly the same thickness throughout.

As a result, insect wings are used in the air in much the same way that oars are used in water. They push downwards to help the insect to climb, backwards to move it forwards, and scull horizontally when the insect hovers.

Many insects also use what scientists call a 'clap-fling' mechanism – in which the wings are clapped together at the end of each beat, then flung apart at high speed – to hurl turbulent rings of high-pressure air below and behind them. The action helps to thrust the insect up and forwards.

Some insects, like the larger butterflies and moths, are capable of gliding, twisting their wings slightly to ride the air currents. Most insects, however, and particularly the smaller ones, rely on the sheer speed of their wingbeats to keep them up.

# HOW FAST THEY FLY

Larger insects, such as dragonflies, have relatively slow wingbeats but are fast fliers. Tiny insects, such as mosquitoes, beat their wings extremely fast, but fly fairly slowly. The buzzing sound made by insects is caused by their wing movements and by air turbulence. The faster the wings vibrate, the higher is the pitch of the buzz. The table below shows how many complete up-and-down wingbeats each insect carries out each second in flight, and shows how fast it usually flies.

| | Wingbeats per second | Flight speed (km/h) |
|---|---|---|
| White butterfly | 8–12 | 7–14 |
| Damselfly | 16 | 3–7 |
| Dragonfly | 25–40 | 25–55 |
| Cockchafer beetle | 50 | 11 |
| Hawk moth | 50–90 | 18–50 |
| Hoverfly | 120 | 11–14 |
| Bumblebee | 130 | 11 |
| Housefly | 200 | 7 |
| Honeybee | 225 | 7–11 |
| Mosquito | 600 | 1–2 |
| Midge | 1000 | 1–2 |

## WHY CLEAN AIR IS KILLING A MOTH

A new type of peppered moth, *Biston betularia*, has evolved in order to survive in a changing, man-made environment. The moth is normally coloured a pale, speckled grey. This camouflages it against lichen on the tree trunks where it rests by day. But in about 1860, a black variety – a natural mutation – appeared in industrial areas. The newcomer had a great advantage over the grey moths because the dark colour blended in with the soot-covered trees – and so the black moths were less easily spotted by predators. By 1900, in industrial areas, the black form of the peppered moth far outnumbered the pale form.

The black form is still the dominant type in industrial areas today, but researchers who have been studying it since the 1950s have discovered that its numbers are dwindling. The reason: modern clean-air regulations have cut down the amount of grime in the atmosphere and on trees – and are tipping the biological balance back towards the pale moth.

## MANNA FROM BUGS

The manna eaten by the Israelites on their flight through the Sinai desert from Egypt may have been the sticky honeydew which comes from the mealy bug, *Trabutina mannipara*. The bug, which feeds on the evergreen tamarisk in the deserts of the Middle East, passes the honeydew through its intestines. The honeydew then falls to the ground as shining scales and is eaten today by the nomadic tribes of the desert.

## COLD LIGHT

The light which is chemically produced by tropical *Photinus* fireflies is the most efficient light known. Up to 90 per cent of the energy it uses is turned into light. By contrast, only 5.5 per cent of the energy used to power a household lightbulb emerges as light; the rest is wasted as heat. The glow of a firefly contains only 1/80,000 of the heat that would be produced by a candle flame of equal brilliance. Tropical fireflies are, in fact, beetles, and they provide spectacular night-time displays in which thousands of males flash their light in unison from trees. The flickering beams of light – which are used to attract females – can be seen hundreds of metres away.

## SPRAY-GUN

The bombardier beetle *Brachinus crepitans* of southern Britain, drives off attackers by spraying them with a hot, caustic liquid. The beetle keeps the basic elements of the liquid – hydrogen peroxide and chemicals called

ATTACK AND DEFENCE *Among honeybees, as among other bees, wasps and ants, only females (like the worker bee shown here) have stings. The male drones are harmless. The peacock butterfly (pictured on the right) relies on eyespots on its wings for defence. When suddenly displayed, the spots confuse and frighten off insect-hunting birds.*

hydroquinones – in a gland in its abdomen. When threatened, it passes the liquid into a heat-resistant combustion chamber with a spout-shaped opening. At the same time it releases enzymes which make the liquid explode, producing water, caustic quinones, oxygen and heat. The explosion fires the liquid through the opening at a temperature of about 100°C (212°F) – the boiling point of water.

The beetle itself, which can swivel its rear end in almost any direction to aim the spray at its attacker, remains unhurt by either the heat or the corrosive power of the liquid. Up to 20 of the burning sprays can be fired in quick succession – each giving a gun-like 'pop'. The sprays have a range of about 50mm (2in) – four times the beetle's length.

### BORN TO SLAVERY
The British blood-red ant, *Formica sanguinea*, finds additional slave workers by raiding the nests of negro ants, *Formica fusca*. After killing any worker ants that resist, the blood-red ants carry off dormant pupae – ants which are changing from larvae to adults inside cocoons – to their own nests. There the newly born negro ants become the slaves of their captors. The blood-red ants already have their own workers and are only partly dependent on such slave labour. But the European Amazon ant, *Polyergus rufescens*, is totally dependent upon negro ant slaves, which excavate the Amazons' nests and take care of their young.

### ANT THAT EATS ITSELF
The queen of the black garden ant, *Lasius niger*, feeds partly on its own wing muscles. After mating in mid-air in the summer, the queen returns to earth and bites off its wings for food. Meanwhile, the males – having fulfilled their sexual role – fall to the ground and crawl away to die. The queen finds a crevice for a new nest, where she lives on her fat reserves and on the nutrients contained in the now useless wing muscles. The queen begins to lay eggs in the following spring, and at first the eggs hatch only into larvae which develop into wingless female workers. The workers feed the queen while she lays more eggs – until in the summer winged queens and winged males are born, beginning the cycle all over again.

### LONG JUMP
The human flea, *Pulex irritans*, has a long jump of about 330mm (13in) and a high jump of about 200mm (8in) – or 130 times its own height. This is the equivalent of a human being jumping to a height of about 260m (850ft) – enough to reach the roof of a 70-storey building. The flea achieves this athletic feat by flexing an elastic pad beside its hind legs, and then suddenly releasing it – propelling itself into the air like an arrow with a built-in bow. Each time a flea jumps, it is subjected to a g-force 200 times stronger than normal, a strain that would kill most humans.

### PIGGYBACK PARASITE
The human warble fly, *Dermatobia hominis*, of North and South America does not, despite its name, attack humans directly. Instead it seizes day-flying mosquitoes and flies and attaches its eggs to their bodies. Then it releases them. When the mosquito or fly later lands on a human to bite and feed, the warmth of the victim's body causes the *Dermatobia* egg to hatch. The newly emerged larva bores beneath the victim's skin to feed and grow. A boil forms at the site.

Only when the larva is fully grown does it leave the human victim's body – dropping off to pupate in the soil, become an adult and begin in its turn the hunt for a free ride for its eggs.

# HOW INSECTS EAT

The first primitive insects had biting mouth-parts like those of modern ants, beetles, grasshoppers, cockroaches and praying mantises. But many other types of insects have changed their feeding habits in the course of evolution to include sucking or licking as well as chewing.

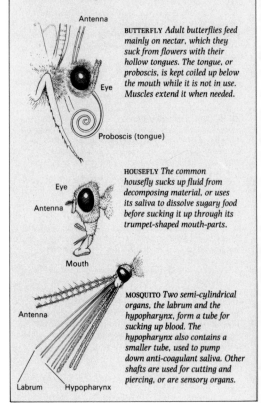

BUTTERFLY *Adult butterflies feed mainly on nectar, which they suck from flowers with their hollow tongues. The tongue, or proboscis, is kept coiled up below the mouth while it is not in use. Muscles extend it when needed.*

Antenna
Eye
Proboscis (tongue)

HOUSEFLY *The common housefly sucks up fluid from decomposing material, or uses its saliva to dissolve sugary food before sucking it up through its trumpet-shaped mouth-parts.*

Eye
Antenna
Mouth

MOSQUITO *Two semi-cylindrical organs, the labrum and the hypopharynx, form a tube for sucking up blood. The hypopharynx also contains a smaller tube, used to pump down anti-coagulant saliva. Other shafts are used for cutting and piercing, or are sensory organs.*

Antenna
Labrum
Hypopharynx

### BLOODSHOT
Some conspicuous slow-moving insects – among them the oil beetle, the bloody-nosed beetle, *Timarcha tenebricosa*, and the common ladybird – bleed not when they have been hurt, but in order to prevent injury. When they are alarmed they release drops of a red, bitter-tasting liquid from their mouths and from pores at their joints. The caustic flavour repels attackers before the insect is seriously harmed.

### THE FLIGHT OF THE HONEYBEE
A queen honeybee lays and fertilises up to 600,000 eggs during her three to five-year reign. She does so after mating only on her single mating flight – with four or five males, or 'drones', in succession. She keeps the collected sperm in an internal reservoir and goes on laying until she is succeeded by one of her royal daughters. The deposed queen then flies off with half the workers and starts a new hive elsewhere. Fertilised eggs produce female bees – queens or workers – and unfertilised eggs produce males. But how the queen is able to control which of the eggs she lays is fertilised – and thus the proportion of workers and drones in the hive – is not known.

### A PLAGUE OF LOCUSTS
Throughout the ages swarms of locusts – a type of grasshopper – have devastated plants and crops as they migrate up to thousands of miles through the

tropics in search of food. A typical swarm can be more than 50km (30 miles) long, 8km (5 miles) wide and contain an estimated 500,000 million insects. Such a swarm – which appears as a vast black cloud, often obliterating the sun – weighs about 80,000 tonnes and can eat each day the weight of food that is needed by 20 million people. The migrations seem to be triggered by sudden population explosions in the desert areas where the insects breed.

### LIFE SPANS
The shortest-lived insects are mayflies, Ephemeroptera, which often live for only four to five hours – or, at most, a few days.

The insect with the longest life is the queen termite, which usually lives for 15 – 20 years. Most insects have an active adult life of a few weeks.

### INSECTS BY THE MILLION
An acre of average pastureland contains an estimated 360 million insects, of which springtails – wingless, leaping insects – are the most common. Although just fewer than 1 million species of insect have so far been classified, the actual total could be as much as five times that number. At least three-quarters of the known animal species in the world today are insects – and there are more than a million insects for every man, woman and child. Together, the world's insect population weighs about 12 times as much as the human one.

### LARVA THAT LIVES IN OIL
The larva of the Californian petroleum fly, *Psilopa petrolei*, lives in pools of crude oil which seep from the ground in oilfields. The larva's skin and intestinal lining are specially adapted to withstand the oil – which permanently fills its gut and surrounds its body, and which would kill most other forms of life. It feeds solely on other insects which become trapped in the oil. The larva, which lives submerged in the oil, rises to the surface of the oil when it is fully grown in order to undergo the metamorphosis to adult form. When the transformation is complete, the fly takes to the air. But it remains in the area of the oilfield, laying its eggs in the pools to start the cycle again.

### SURFACE SKIMMERS
Some rove beetles skim effortlessly over water, pulled by the water's own surface tension in front of them. They lower the surface tension at the rear of their bodies through a glandular secretion at the ends of their abdomens. This allows them to use the surface tension at the front as a driving force. Much the same principle drives the camphor-powered boats that were once popular as children's toys.

### EARLY WORM CATCHES THE FLY
Most caterpillars are sluggish creatures which feed on plants. But a group of about 20 known species found only on the Hawaiian islands have become hunters of flies. The caterpillars, known as inchworms, ambush the flies when they land, lunging out with six tiny claws in as little as one-twelfth of a second.

The caterpillars lie in wait among forest leaves. Their five pairs of eyes are rudimentary. So, to detect their prey, they rely on sensitive hairs along their back. When a fly brushes against the hairs, the caterpillar strikes – devouring the fly, wings, legs and all.

The caterpillars, which grow to about 25mm (1in) long, are called inchworms because they move with a curious looping step – drawing the tail up to the head, then stretching out again – so that they seem to be measuring the surface as they crawl along.

## INSECT LIFE CYCLES

There are two distinct types of insect life cycle. Beetles and moths, for instance, undergo a complete transformation from a grub or caterpillar (the active, larval or immature stage), through a passive stage – known as the pupal or chrysalis stage – to the very different shape of the adult, known as the imago. In other insects, such as the dragonfly, the immature insect more closely resembles the shape of the adult and is called a nymph. The nymph moults several times, its wing pads enlarging on each occasion until it reaches adult size.

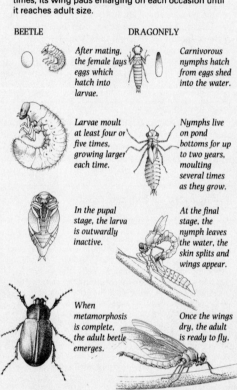

BEETLE — DRAGONFLY

After mating, the female lays eggs which hatch into larvae.

Carnivorous nymphs hatch from eggs shed into the water.

Larvae moult at least four or five times, growing larger each time.

Nymphs live on pond bottoms for up to two years, moulting several times as they grow.

In the pupal stage, the larva is outwardly inactive.

At the final stage, the nymph leaves the water, the skin splits and wings appear.

When metamorphosis is complete, the adult beetle emerges.

Once the wings dry, the adult is ready to fly.

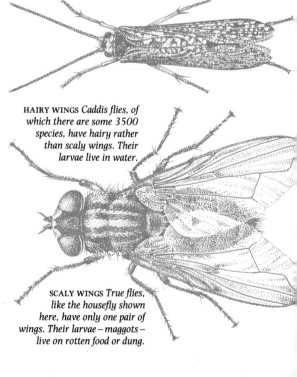

HAIRY WINGS *Caddis flies, of which there are some 3500 species, have hairy rather than scaly wings. Their larvae live in water.*

SCALY WINGS *True flies, like the housefly shown here, have only one pair of wings. Their larvae – maggots – live on rotten food or dung.*

FACTS ABOUT ANIMALS & PLANTS

# Fish – streamlined by evolution

## MAN-EATER

The great white shark, which grows to 6m (20ft) or more, is probably the most dangerous of all sharks. Also known as the white pointer, it is most aggressive when hungry and its teeth, which reach 50mm (2in) in length, can tear off a human limb with one bite. Another ten or so shark species, including the mako, or blue pointer, the tiger and some types of hammerhead shark, are known to attack man, but 90 per cent of shark species are thought to be harmless.

Some bizarre objects have been found in shark stomachs. One dissected grey shark contained the hindquarters of a pig, the front half of a dog, 135kg (300lb) of horsemeat and eight legs of mutton.

## FISH OUT OF WATER

The mudskipper, a small fish that inhabits coastal mangroves and mudflats in tropical Africa, spends much of its time out of water. Using its pectoral fins, which are flexed in the middle rather like legs, it walks

## HOW FISH BREATHE

The gills that a fish uses to breathe under water are more efficient than the lungs used by air-breathing animals. Up to 80 per cent of the oxygen that passes over the gills is absorbed into the fish's blood – four to five times as much as is absorbed from the air by most mammals. The gills – a series of membranes which allow air, but not water, to pass through – are arranged so that the blood in capillaries immediately under the membrane runs in the opposite direction to the water passing over them. As a result, oxygen-rich water starting its passage over the gills meets blood with a fairly high oxygen concentration. Water that has almost finished passing over the gills, and given up most of its oxygen, encounters blood coming into the gills that is deficient in oxygen. Because of the two-way flow, the blood at any point always has less oxygen than the water directly opposite it, so that oxygen is absorbed into the blood across the whole width of the gills.

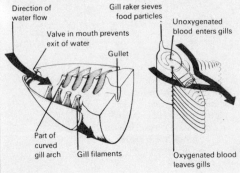

Direction of water flow
Gill raker sieves food particles
Valve in mouth prevents exit of water
Unoxygenated blood enters gills
Gullet
Part of curved gill arch
Gill filaments
Oxygenated blood leaves gills

FLOW OF LIFE *A fish's gills – thin-skinned, blood-filled filaments – are arranged rather like the heat-losing fins on a car engine, and are supported by rigid gill arches. Blood is carried to and from the filaments (shown enlarged on the right) by veins running through the arches.*

or hops for short bursts of a few minutes in search of food. The fish has no lungs to enable it to breathe in air. Instead it keeps its gill chamber full of oxygenated water, occasionally gulping water from pools to replenish its supply. It also absorbs oxygen through the throat and roof of the mouth. The mudskipper's eyes are right on top of its head and can be swivelled in all directions. To keep them moist and working, the fish 'blinks' by pulling the eyes down and wiping them on the moist cheeks.

An African catfish known as the clariid can live out of water for several days, thanks to a lung-like organ which supplements its gills. The fish uses this ability to move home in the dry season, wriggling overland between stretches of water. But how it knows which way to go is still a mystery to scientists.

## AQUATIC ARCHER

The Southeast Asian archer fish shoots down its prey with a jet of water. Firing from beneath the water's surface, it can hit insects about 1m (3.3ft) above the surface by squirting water up a tube formed between the palate and the tongue.

## THE FOUR-EYED FISH

Tropical America is the home of a fish with four eyes. The four-eyed fish swims at the surface of the water searching for its insect food. An eye projects above the level of the top of the head on each side, and each eye is divided into two by a horizontal bar that coincides with the water level. The upper part is adapted for vision in air and the lower part for vision in water. The lens of the eye is shaped so that it can focus in both air and water simultaneously on two distinct retinal areas. So the fish sees four images, enabling it to home in unerringly on its prey.

## CHANCE IN A MILLION

Because most fish breed by shedding their eggs and sperm directly into water, fertilisation is a risky business. A medium-sized female cod may lay more than 6 million eggs at each breeding session – sometimes laying several hundred thousand in a day – but on average only one or two will grow into adults. Most fertilised fish eggs or young fish are eaten by other creatures. This is particularly true for sea fish which lay their eggs in plankton, where they are eaten in vast quantities by whales and other browsing animals.

To compensate for this high casualty rate, most fish species lay large numbers of eggs. Female turbots have been found with up to 9 million eggs in their ovaries, and a ling fish, a large relative of the cod, once yielded 28 million eggs.

## SHELLFISH NURSERY

The bitterling, a small European member of the carp family, uses a mussel as a living nursery. During the breeding season the female bitterling grows a long tube from its genital opening.

Using the tube, she inserts her eggs within the shells of a freshwater mussel so that they develop inside the mussel's gill chamber. The male then releases sperm into the water near the opening through which the mussel breathes. The sperm is drawn in with the water and the eggs are fertilised inside the shellfish.

After hatching, the larvae may remain in the mussel for a month, existing on the remains of their egg yolk before emerging to start life outside. The mussel, far from being harmed by its host-mother role, benefits from the relationship. Its parasitic larvae attach themselves to the young bitterlings' gills, and are carried away when the larvae leave.

## FISH WITH A ROVING EYE

Some adult flatfish, including sole, plaice and halibut, have both eyes on one side of the head. Although they start life with symmetrical heads, one eye moves over the top of the head to the other side as they grow. The two-eyed side (usually the right) develops a strong camouflage colouring, which in some species can change to suit different backgrounds, while the other side remains white.

The reason for the lop-sided growth is that flatfish spend most of their adult lives lying on their sides on the sea bottom, sometimes burying themselves in sand so that only their eyes protrude while they lie in wait for their next meal.

## AIRBORNE FISH

Flying fish do not actually fly. They glide. Propelled by their tails, they leap into the air at speeds of up to 32km/h (20mph) and use their wide pectoral fins as wings. They usually glide close to the ocean's surface where a flick of their tail against the water can produce extra impetus. But flying fish have been known to soar up to 6m (20ft) into the air and to stay aloft for up to 400m (1300ft).

## THE MOTHER WHO IS DAD

Seahorses are one of the few species in the animal world where the male gives birth to the young. The male has a special brood-pouch on its abdomen into which the female lays her eggs.

The eggs are not only fertilised in the pouch. They hatch and develop there until the young begin to resemble a miniature version of their parents. The male then goes into labour and gives birth, jettisoning the young seahorses in a series of convulsive contractions which can last for several hours.

## LIVING JAVELINS

Throughout the world's tropical waters there is an extraordinary breed of living spears. Called needlefish, these nocturnal surface-feeders can be 1.5m (5ft) long, yet weigh only about 4kg (10lb) because they are so slender. When disturbed or frightened, they can swim fast enough to leap out of the water. Their aim in doing this, it seems, is not to attack; it is probably an evasive tactic.

But a panicky needlefish can be a terrifying experience for any human being unlucky enough to get in its way. One sailor, Captain William Gray, of Miami Seaquarium, in Florida, USA, was pinned to his boat when a needlefish ran him through the leg.

Most other victims have been people fishing at night with lights. Many naturalists believe needlefish can be attracted or frightened by light. But divers and swimmers have never been known to be hurt by one. This is because, in the water, needlefish can dart around any obstacles.

## LIVING LIGHTS

Life in the deepest parts of the oceans has taken extraordinary twists to cope with eternal darkness, cold, and pressures hundreds of times greater than at the surface.

More than half the inhabitants of the lowest depths are luminous, both as a mating signal and to attract prey. Others act as hosts to colonies of glowing bacteria which light up parts of their bodies from within. The Indian Ocean fish *Photoblepharon* has a large spot under each eye which is full of blood vessels, and packed with these bacteria. Each headlight has a 'curtain' too – a black fold of skin which the fish can raise to shut off the light when danger threatens.

The bathysphere fish, so called because pale blue, glowing spots on its sides resemble the portholes of a diving bell, has lights in its teeth to invite prey – for many fish seem to be attracted to light. But the hatchet fish has greenish-white lights which look like a row of teeth, and may help to deter would-be enemies while it feeds on plankton.

## MOUTHS WITHOUT BODIES

Some deep-sea fish have developed huge mouths to help them make the most of any food that comes their way. In the abyss, food is scarce, for there are no plants to start the food chain. Instead, tiny shrimps eat the scraps and waste that come slowly down from the surface waters; and they in turn provide food for bigger hunters. Some of these hunters, like the swallower and gulper fish, are little more than tooth-filled mouths attached to elastic stomachs so that they can eat fish several times their own size.

Gulpers may grow to a length of 1.8m (6ft); but most of this is simply a whip-like tail. The rest is gaping mouth.

## ANGLING FOR FOOD

Down below 600m (2000ft) lives the bizarre angler fish. A long fin like a fishing rod grows from its head, and the angler can bend this forward so that the tip hangs just in front of its mouth. On the end is the bait, a worm-like luminous growth that wriggles convincingly. When fish try to take the bait, the angler strikes,

SKELETON KEY *Most fish, like the John Dory shown on the right, have a skeleton made entirely of bone. The 915mm (3ft) long thornback ray, pictured below, has a more primitive skeleton made of cartilage reinforced with bony plates.*

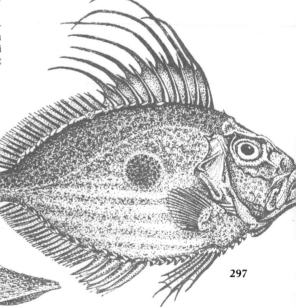

swallowing the catch whole. The angler's method of reproduction is even odder. In the black, sparsely populated depths, it is difficult to locate a mate. So when a pair do meet, the 150mm (6in) long male – which may weigh half a million times less than the 1m (3.3ft) long female – makes certain that they will not lose each other. He sinks his teeth into the female's body and hangs on, sometimes for the rest of his life. In some types of angler fish, the male's mouth and jaw gradually fuse to the female's body. His eyes fade, his internal organs stop working, even his circulatory system hooks up with his mate's so that he is fed by her blood. Effectively, he dies as an individual and becomes merely a part of her body.

His only function then is to fertilise the eggs the female spawns before they float away to begin life.

## PREHISTORIC RELIC

After it disappeared from the fossil record 70 million years ago, the coelacanth was thought by scientists to be extinct. But in 1938 a 1.5m (5ft) coelacanth was caught off the South African coast and since 1952 nearly 100 specimens have been caught near the Comoro Islands off Madagascar.

This primitive fish has a simple heart and its kidneys are positioned away from the backbone, unlike those of other animals with backbones. Female coelacanths have also been found with eggs the size of tennis balls inside them, but it is unknown whether they hatch inside or outside the mother.

## LITTLE AND LARGE

Fish vary enormously in size. The smallest is the dwarf pygmy goby, a freshwater fish found in the Philippines, which can be less than 8mm (0.3in) long. At the other extreme is the whale shark, which can be more than 18m (60ft) long. It weighs about 5000 million times as much as the goby, but despite its immense size the whale shark is a placid animal that feeds on plankton. Whales themselves are not fish, but mammals – the same group of animals as man.

## A MOUTHFUL OF BABIES

Many fish of the cichlid family, such as the Mozambique mouthbrooder, carry their eggs in their mouths after they are laid and fertilised. There the eggs are protected from predators and supplied with a constant stream of oxygen-rich water. After hatching, the young fish remain in the mouth until they have absorbed their egg yolk, before venturing out to feed for short periods. They remain close to the parent's mouth, where they return at night or if threatened.

Brooding may last up to five weeks, and during this time the parent eats nothing at all in order to avoid swallowing its offspring by accident. Usually the female broods, but in some species of cichlid, which are found throughout tropical Africa, Asia and America, the male broods.

The brooding instinct is also exploited by some cichlid species to encourage fertilisation. In these species the male's anal fin is marked with an egg-shaped and egg-coloured spot. When the female tries to catch the decoy egg, she gulps in some sperm from the male and so fertilises the real eggs in her mouth.

## LIVE-IN GUESTS

Some pearlfish seek shelter inside sea cucumbers, backing into the sausage-like animal via its anus. After finding the cucumber's opening, the pearlfish inserts its tail and then wriggles its whole body inside. Several pearlfish, named after their pigment-dotted transparent bodies, may share the same cucumber. The fish get shelter from the arrangement, and food, since they sometimes eat the sea cucumber's internal organs. But though the sea cucumber is not normally killed in the process, because it has the ability to regenerate these organs, it seems to derive no benefit from its live-in guests.

## A FISH'S HOME IS ITS NEST

Some fish are born in nests. Members of the labyrinth fish family, such as the air-breathing fighting fish, build nests from mucus-coated air bubbles. The bubbles are blown by the male and used to form a raft.

The eggs are laid in the water, then caught by the adults in their mouths and spat into the underside of the raft. After the eggs hatch, the young stay on the raft for a time under the protective eye of the father.

Another nest-builder, the male three-spined stickleback, collects pieces of aquatic plants and glues them together with a cement secreted from its kidneys. He assembles the plant mass in a small pit under the water and then creates a burrow inside before luring in a female for egg-laying.

## PERILOUS BEAUTY

Lionfish are among the most beautiful fish in the seas. But among the fragile finery of their plumage lurk weapons: 18 venom-tipped spines. Usually, lionfish swim lazily around coral reefs, but when frightened they stand their ground and swing round to point the spines at the enemy.

Humans who have got in the way have been lucky to escape with their lives. In one case, in 1960, a 38-year-old man got two of the delicate spines in his fingers while skin-diving off the Pacific Marshall Islands. The pain knocked him out and his blood pressure dropped dangerously. But for emergency medical aid, say doctors, he would have died.

## KILLING BY PAIN

Some experts rate the stonefish as the most dangerous fish of all. Squat, warty and slime-covered, this grotesque creature is found round the coasts of the Pacific and Indian oceans from the Red Sea to northern Australia. Wherever they are known, stonefish are greatly feared, for their stone-coloured lumpy bodies make them almost impossible to spot against the rock and coral where they live.

Even disturbances in the water only a few centimetres away will not make a stonefish move. Instead it remains motionless, with its venomous spines raised until it is too late – for its victim.

Stonefish use their spines only for protection, though. When feeding they wait until a fish wanders too close, then they lunge in a blur of speed.

Every human being who has been stung by a stonefish and has lived to tell the tale emphasises one thing – maddening, excruciating pain that can last as long as 12 hours. The pain becomes so intense that the victim froths at the mouth and may bite convulsively even at people who come to help.

Australian doctors who have dealt with cases of stonefish poisoning report that it generally takes three or four strong men to get a stonefish's victim to shore without his drowning in the grip of the agony. And most of those who die are victims of drowning: the pain is so unbearable that they double up in the water, and can think of nothing else.

Once ashore, the simplest antidote to the poison is to apply heat, generally in the form of near-scalding water. An anti-venom has also been developed by marine researchers. But early medical help is vital. Swimmers who get treatment fast can expect to walk again in a month or two. Less fortunate victims can die within six hours.

# Amphibians and reptiles

### TOO CLUMSY TO LIVE ON LAND

The largest amphibian is the giant salamander, *Andrias japonicus*, which grows to a length of 1.8m (6ft). Ungainly on land, it is mainly found in mountain streams, where it feeds on snails, crabs and sometimes fish. It leads an inactive life and surfaces to breathe at irregular intervals. It may also be the longest lived amphibian – one is on record as living for 55 years. Some Japanese consider its cooked flesh a delicacy.

### GOLIATH OF A FROG

The world's largest frog is the Goliath frog of West Africa, *Rana goliath*. It can weigh 3.2kg (7lb) and has an overall length of 915mm (3ft), but only one-third of its length is taken up by its head and torso. The rest is taken up by its 610mm (2ft) long hind legs. Despite their size, the frog's legs are not favoured by gourmets.

### SMALL FROG, BIG EGG

The shortest amphibian and the smallest frog is the Cuban *Sminthillus limbatus*. Fully grown, it is only 13mm (0.5in) long. It is so tiny that it does not lay a large number of small eggs, but produces a single, comparatively large egg at a time.

### GROWING UP SMALLER

Instead of becoming bigger as it grows up, the 'paradoxical' frog, *Pseudis paradoxa*, becomes smaller. It lives in tropical South America and the tadpole grows to as much as 250mm (10in) in length. But when the tadpole turns into a frog, a considerable shrinkage occurs. As with other frogs, the tail is absorbed into the body. And when the process is complete the adult is never more than 75mm (3in) long.

### WHEN THE RAIN COMES

On the very rare occasions when it rains in the deserts of central Australia, the water-holding frog, *Cyclorana platycephalus*, emerges from its underground den and absorbs so much water – as much as 50 per cent of its own weight – that it resembles a small balloon. This enables it to stay alive during long droughts. Rainstorms also encourage the frogs to feed voraciously on insects, and to mate. The eggs are laid in short-lasting pools and hatch quickly, starting the tadpoles on a race against the sun for survival: to win, the tadpoles have to grow into young frogs and so become able to breathe air before their pond dries up. Within a few weeks – far more rapidly than most other species of frog – the tadpoles grow into little froglets.

As the rainwater dries up, the adult frogs and their young burrow underground and make a small living chamber for themselves. Once inside, they secrete a membrane-like envelope around their skins – complete with breathing hole – to stop any of the body-stored water from escaping. The frogs then wait, without moving, possibly for as long as five or six years, until the rain comes again.

### DISAPPEARING VERTICALLY

The spadefoot toad, *Pelobates fuscus*, is named after the 'spade' (a flat, sharp-edged bone) on each of its hind feet. By using each spade in turn, it can dig so rapidly

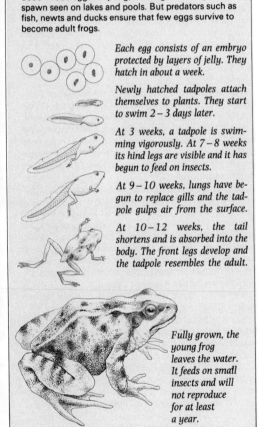

## LIFE CYCLE OF A FROG

The development of the common frog, *Rana temporaria*, is typical of most frogs. Each female lays 3000 – 4000 eggs in spring, creating the clumps of spawn seen on lakes and pools. But predators such as fish, newts and ducks ensure that few eggs survive to become adult frogs.

*Each egg consists of an embryo protected by layers of jelly. They hatch in about a week.*

*Newly hatched tadpoles attach themselves to plants. They start to swim 2 – 3 days later.*

*At 3 weeks, a tadpole is swimming vigorously. At 7 – 8 weeks its hind legs are visible and it has begun to feed on insects.*

*At 9 – 10 weeks, lungs have begun to replace gills and the tadpole gulps air from the surface.*

*At 10 – 12 weeks, the tail shortens and is absorbed into the body. The front legs develop and the tadpole resembles the adult.*

*Fully grown, the young frog leaves the water. It feeds on small insects and will not reproduce for at least a year.*

FIRST ASHORE *Amphibians are the most primitive class of vertebrates – animals with backbones – on land. They were the first group to adapt to life out of water. Yet most of them, like this African clawed toad, still need water, at least for breeding.*

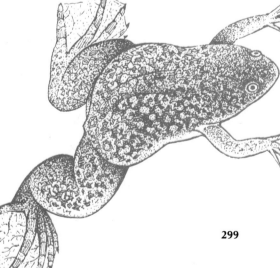

through the dry, sandy soil in the arid areas where it lives that it appears to sink vertically into the ground. The spadefoot and its relatives are found in Europe, Asia, North Africa and the USA.

The spadefoot toad spends most of its life in an underground burrow to avoid excessive loss of water. Even so, it loses 50 per cent of its body weight during prolonged dry periods.

When it rains the animals surface to top up their water supply. As well as drinking, some species can absorb extra water through the undersides of their bodies. The bellies of these species have a thin skin covered with blood vessels, so that the frog's blood-stream and body tissues can soak up water directly.

## USING THEIR HEAD
Some Mexican tree frogs use their heads to survive – literally. The frogs, known as helmet frogs, have bony crests or bumps on the top of their skulls and use them as doors on their homes. The frogs ensure their survival during droughts by moving into the trunks of trees or into holes in bromeliads – plants of the pine-apple family that often grow high up in trees.

Once inside the hole, the frog plugs the entrance with its head and sits out the drought. The helmet loses little water, and the seal ensures that the chamber – and the frog – remain comfortably moist.

## NATURAL-BORN JUMPERS
Frogs are superb jumpers and the small North American frog *Acris gryllus* can jump up to 1.8m (6ft) – 36 times its own 50mm (2in) length. If a human could match this feat, the world's long-jump record would be around 66m (215ft) – more than seven times longer than it actually is. Another frog species, Europe's *Rana dalmatina*, can also jump up to 1.8m (6ft), or 24 times its own length. And even the common North American bullfrog can jump up to ten times its own body-length.

For jumping, frogs use their long back legs which can be folded into three sections and suddenly extended by powerful muscles to provide the impetus. The short front legs act as shock absorbers on landing.

## SECRET OF STAYING YOUNG
As long as it lives in water, the axolotl salamander of Mexico keeps its youthful appearance for life – retaining its feathery external gills and larval tadpole-like shape. It can even breed in this form.

But if the lake in which it lives dries up for any reason, the axolotl, known to scientists as *Ambystoma mexicanum*, can change into an adult form of salamander with lungs in place of gills. It normally grows to be about 200mm (8in) long.

## CARING FOR THE YOUNG
Most amphibians lay up to 4000 eggs a year in water and then abandon them – resulting in huge losses of eggs and young. Indeed, only a tiny fraction of the young survives to breeding age. Some amphibians, however, make special arrangements for the care of their eggs and young. These more protective species tend to produce fewer eggs.

For instance, some tropical tree frogs make foam nests for their eggs. The male and female mate under a branch or leaf overhanging the water. As the eggs are laid, the slime surrounding them is beaten into a thick froth by the frogs' hind legs (some species even stick leaves to the outside of the frothy slime). The inner part of the foam then breaks down into a little protected pond for the developing tadpoles. Eventually the tadpoles drop from the foam nest into the water below to complete their development.

Some South American tree frogs dig a nest pit in the bank of a pond or stream, so that water seeps into the pit. This creates a natural incubator in which the young can be kept warm. At the same time, the incubator protects the young from predators – such as fish or crocodiles – that might lurk in larger, more open areas of water.

Other tree frogs in the tropical South American forests lay their eggs in pockets of water that collect at the leaf-bases of bromeliads high in trees. So the young frogs have a safe nursery and often spend most of their lives in the bromeliad – coming to earth only when they are fully grown.

## GUARDIANS OF THE EGGS
Some species of frogs and toads have special ways of looking after their eggs. In the case of the midwife toad, for instance, the male – not the female – cares for the babies. He gathers up the strings of eggs after they are laid and winds them round his hind legs. He periodically dips his legs in a pool or stream to dampen the eggs, and so keep them alive. He returns to the water for the hatching of the young, which takes place after about three weeks.

In the marsupial frog, the female has a pouch under the skin of her back in which the eggs are carried. The tadpoles usually leave the pouch as soon as they hatch out. But some stay there until they have developed into little frogs.

The Surinam toad, *Pipa pipa*, lives permanently in water – and the female hatches anything up to 60 eggs on her back after they have been fertilised by the male. The eggs stick to the skin, which then grows up around them, so that each egg is contained in its own protective pocket. The young develop in these home-grown cradles until they emerge about 12 weeks later as miniature adults.

## GROWING UP IN FATHER'S THROAT
The eggs of the Darwin's frog of South America, *Rhinoderma darwinii*, are laid in moist ground and the male parent sits on guard until there is a sign of life inside them. The father then swallows from 5 to 15 of the eggs and keeps them in the croaking sac in his throat. The eggs remain in this protected environment until the young are hatched.

The father then lets the froglets hop out of his mouth and they go off to lead their own lives.

The frog is named after Charles Darwin, the 19th-century British naturalist, who was the first scientist to describe it.

## GROWING UP INSIDE THE MOTHER
Some female amphibians have solved the problem of protecting eggs and young by carrying them inside their bodies. The alpine salamander, for example,

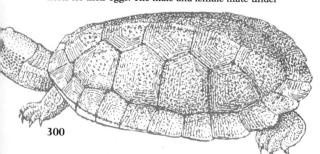

TURTLE *Tortoises and turtles, like this 300mm (12in) long Central American river species, have existed almost unchanged for some 200 million years.*

passes through all the stages from egg to tiny adult inside its mother's body. These animals live in low temperatures, and it takes two to three years before the litter, of just two salamanders, is born. The young are able to live on land and breathe air immediately. Fire salamanders also grow in their mothers' bodies, but they are born in water and have gills.

A few frogs also produce live young with a built-in food supply. The larvae of these species are nourished while they are growing from an egg yolk which is born with them. In the African toad, *Nectophrynoides vivipara*, the embryos take their nourishment direct from the mother. They feed on secretions from the inside walls of the oviduct – the tube through which the eggs leave the ovary – before being born as tiny replicas of the adult.

### POISON FROM THE SKIN
A deadly venom obtained from the skin glands of the arrow-poison frogs of South America is still used by Indian hunters to kill small mammals and birds. The frogs, of the genus *Dendrobates*, are roasted over a fire and the venom which exudes from their skin is coated over the tips of the hunters' arrows. The frogs secrete the venom to protect themselves from predators such as lizards and snakes. And their brightly coloured skins – brilliant mosaics of red, yellow, orange and blue – serve to remind predators of the danger.

The skin of all amphibians is liberally scattered with glands. Most of these glands produce mucus to keep the animal's skin moist – but many of the others can secrete foul-tasting or poisonous substances, like the arrow-poison frog. The majority of the glands are too small to be noticed. But some of them are large and obvious, such as the bulging parotid glands behind the eyes of the common European toad.

### BREATHING THROUGH THE SKIN
Most amphibians breathe with gills in water when they are larvae, and in air with lungs when they are adult. But there are also land-living, cave-dwelling and tree-climbing species which do not breathe through either lungs or gills. Instead they breathe through their moist skins. For instance, frogs of the genus *Telmatobius* – which live under water in the high Andes – can absorb enough oxygen from the cold water through their skins alone. They have no lungs or gills. Some *Telmatobius* species which live on the muddy bottoms of deep lakes have evolved a specially baggy skin to improve their ability to breathe in the oxygen-poor water.

The hairy frog of the Cameroons also seems to make use of its skin to help it breathe. During the mating season, the males grow thin, hair-like pieces of skin on their flanks and hind legs. Scientists believe that the extra skin surface helps the frogs to absorb more oxygen during this period of peak activity.

### TENTACLES FOR EYES
Among the least-known amphibians are about 170 species known as apodans which live in the tropics. They are rarely seen and very difficult to study because most of them burrow underground. Many of the

apodan species are almost completely blind. They seem to feel their way by means of a thin tentacle which protrudes from a pit on each side of the face.

Unlike other amphibians, apodans, which resemble earthworms, have small reptile-like scales embedded in the skin. They also have no legs, shoulders or hip bones. Most of them are only a few millimetres long when fully grown. But one species, *Caecilia thompsoni*, can grow to be more than 1.2m (4ft) long.

## THE CROCODILE FAMILY

Crocodiles, which may be the closest living relatives of the dinosaurs, feed in water, but crawl onto land to sunbathe and breed. Biologists classify them as part of the order known as *Crocodilia*, which includes alligators, caymans and gavials.

GAVIAL *A long slender snout distinguishes gavials. Found in India and Burma, they feed on river fish and grow to about 5m (16ft).*

CROCODILE *The fourth tooth on each side of the lower jaw protrudes on all true crocodiles. This is a Siamese species.*

CAYMAN *These broad-snouted reptiles, up to about 4.5m (15ft) long, are native to South America.*

ALLIGATOR *As with caymans, the fourth tooth on each side of an alligator's lower jaw fits into a socket on the upper jaw.*

SNAKE *Although the grass snake*, Natrix natrix, *can grow up to 1.8m (6ft) long in parts of Africa and Asia, it is harmless. A smaller sub-species,* Natrix natrix helvetica, *is common in Britain and Europe.*

LIZARD *This 380mm (15in) long spiny South African lizard lies flat when disturbed to guard its more vulnerable underside.*

# Birds – the conquest of the sky

## FLYING GIANTS

The largest flying creatures in history were the ptero-dactyls, a group of reptiles that lived more than 70 million years ago alongside the dinosaurs. Unlike birds, these reptiles had wings made of leathery skin, not feathers, and some had awesome wingspans.

The 70 million-year-old *Pteranodon*, for instance, had a wingspan of as much as 7m (23ft). But it lacked strong wing muscles and seems to have glided, rather than flown, in search of its prey. In the 1970s frag-ments of an even larger pterodactyl, with a probable wingspan of 15m (49ft), were found in Texas.

## THE EARLIEST BIRD

Biologists have long hunted for the missing link between man and ape. But one such link in nature was found in fossil form by German quarrymen work-ing near the village of Solnhöfen, Bavaria, in 1861. The link, which proved that birds evolved from rep-tiles, was a species now known as *Archaeopteryx* (meaning 'ancient bird'). It lived about 150 million years ago.

*Archaeopteryx* had feathers and a wishbone, typical of true birds. But its significance as the earliest bird was not recognised at first. Its reptilian fea-tures – teeth, a long tail and claws on its wings – were so strong that one fossilised skeleton languished among the small dinosaurs in a museum in Eichstadt, West Germany, for 20 years because the faint impres-sions of its feathers in the rock were overlooked.

## BORN TO FLY

The bones of modern birds are so completely adapted to the need to conserve weight in flight that a bird's feathers usually weigh more than its entire skeleton. The bones are hollow, braced by internal struts and honeycombed with air sacs. The sacs are connected to the lungs so that during flight air flows through them, speeding the supply of oxygen to body tissues. Even the beak is modified to save weight. Instead of being made of heavy bone, like human jaws, it is made of lightweight horn. And it contains no teeth.

The resulting design is so light that a golden eagle – which can have a wingspan of up to 2.3m (7.5ft) – weighs a total of less than 4kg (8.8lb).

WEIGHT-SAVING *The bones of a bird are honeycombed for strength and lightness.*

## FASTEST AND RAREST

The world's fastest-moving animal is the peregrine falcon, which can swoop on its prey at speeds of up to 350km/h (217mph).

One of the world's rarest birds is the dusky seaside sparrow: only five are known to exist – they are in captivity in Florida, USA – and all are male. Scientists hope to re-create the species by cross-breeding the birds with females of a closely related species.

The world's rarest bird in the wild is uncertain because in many places no reliable count has been made. But one of the rarest must be a Hawaiian honeyeater known as Bishop's ooaa, *Moho bishopi*. A single specimen was sighted in 1982 – the first glimpse of the species for 78 years.

## LARGEST EGG

The largest egg among living birds is laid by the ostrich. However, although the egg weighs 1.4kg (3lb), it is small by comparison with its parent, totall-ing only 1.4 per cent of the ostrich's average 100kg (220lb) weight. Generally, smaller birds lay propor-tionately larger eggs. The egg of the tiny goldcrest, for instance, is 14 per cent of the bird's bodyweight. Proportionately, the largest egg of all is laid by the kiwi, the flightless bird of New Zealand. Its single egg may be 125mm (5in) long and can weigh 0.5kg (1.1lb) – 20 per cent of the mother's weight.

## COMPOST INCUBATOR

Most birds use body heat to incubate their eggs, but the mallee fowl, one of the brush turkey family found in Australia and on many Pacific islands, keeps its eggs warm by burying them in a compost heap of rotting vegetation.

The male bird tends the eggs, testing the incubator's temperature with its bill and adding or removing a covering of sand so that the inside of the mound remains almost constantly at 33°C (91°F). The eggs, which are laid one by one over a period of up to six months, hatch singly, but the care lavished on the eggs is not extended to the chicks. Once hatched, the chicks are ignored by their parents and forced to fend for themselves immediately.

## UNDERGROUND BATBIRD

The oilbird of tropical South America rests and nests in underground caverns that are sometimes more than a kilometre from the open air. Because of the absence of natural light at this depth, it has evolved an echo-location system of navigation similar to the one used by bats. During flight, it emits a series of clicks, finding its way in the blackness of the caves by listening to the echoes. So sophisticated is the system that the bird can distinguish its own echoes even over the clicks, squawks and screeches of other birds.

The oilbird feeds chiefly at night on oil palm nuts, which are also used to make commercial oil. This nut gives the oilbird its oily flesh, which is melted down by Indians for use as a cooking and lighting oil. The oilbird is also remarkable because it appears to use its nose to find food, unlike other birds which generally have a poor sense of smell.

## THE FINCH THAT THINKS IT'S A WOODPECKER

On the Galapagos Islands in the Pacific lives a group of bird species, all of which are believed to be descended from a single South American ancestor. They are named Darwin's finches after the English naturalist Charles Darwin, because their different responses to the island environment helped to suggest to Darwin his theory of evolution.

Each species has adapted itself to a different diet, developing beaks to suit its particular food. One finch has adopted the role of woodpecker, evolving a power-ful beak to chip through bark and get at insects. However, unlike the woodpecker, it lacks an elongated barbed tongue with which to spear its prey.

To compensate for this disadvantage the finch has developed a special trick of its own. It breaks off a spine from a nearby cactus and uses this as a probe to winkle out the insects.

# NESTING PATTERNS

The ways in which birds shelter their young from the weather and predators are almost as varied as the birds themselves. The most elaborate nests are built by weaver birds.

Social weavers build the largest nests. Up to 300 pairs weave individual nesting chambers under a single massive woven roof. By contrast, emperor penguins – which breed in Antarctica, far from any vegetation – make no nests at all.

SOLITARY CONFINEMENT *The male hornbill seals its mate behind a mud wall during incubation, to deter predators. The male feeds her and later the chicks through a hole. When the chicks are older, she breaks out to help in the feeding.*

KNOT NEST *The Baya weaver bird, one of several weaver species, sews, ties and weaves its nest onto a branch, fashioning an entrance tunnel at the bottom. Each species builds its own distinctive style from grass and leaves.*

NIGHT STARVATION *Emperor penguins breed in the cold and dark of the Antarctic winter. The male incubates the egg on its feet for 64 days, during which it is unable to feed or even move. It keeps the egg warm under a flap of skin below its belly. The female returns after the egg hatches.*

## IN THE PINK

Flamingos, the large, long-legged wading birds that inhabit African lakes, owe their distinctive pink colouring to their diet. All flamingos have some pink in their plumage and one, the rosy flamingo, is entirely pink. The colour is derived from carotenoid pigments – also present in carrots – which are contained in the microscopic plants and animals flamingos eat. Without this natural food, the birds seem to feel literally off-colour. Their pink plumage fades and their breeding behaviour can be affected.

## WHY SEABIRDS HAVE RUNNY NOSES

Seabirds face a special food hazard, because of their lifestyle. The hazard is salt, which in large doses is poisonous, leading to dehydration and an overload on the kidneys. Yet seabirds inevitably absorb large quantities of salty water while feeding. The excess is disposed of by special salt glands in the head. The glands discharge a highly concentrated salt solution into the nostrils, from where it drips back into the sea. So efficient is this built-in desalination plant that seabirds never need to drink fresh water. They extract all they need from seawater.

## LIGHT MEAL

Fishermen and anglers who use lights to attract their catch at night have a flying counterpart: the skimmer, which is thought to use minute marine creatures in the same way. The skimmer usually hunts in coastal waters during the evening and on bright nights, flying just above the water with the tip of its lower beak – which is much longer than the upper beak – skimming the surface to catch insects, shrimps and small fish.

As it forages backwards and forwards, it often leaves a phosphorescent wake of disturbed micro-organisms, and marine biologists believe that this light may help attract more fish within range. After catching its prey, the skimmer's beak snaps shut and the knife-like edges hold the food, which is swallowed in flight. Because it flies so close to the water, the skimmer has developed a carefully controlled method of flight. Unlike most birds, its wings never dip below the horizontal, so no noisy splashes alert the fish in its path.

## LOCKING UP FOR THE NIGHT

The perching birds, which make up the majority of bird species, use a lock to stay on their perches. Tendons pass from the muscle at the back of the bird's leg, down round the back of its ankle, to the inside of the toes. When a bird settles its weight on a branch the legs bend, tightening the tendons so that its toes automatically grip the perch. Even when the bird falls asleep, it is in no danger of slipping from the branch. As soon as it straightens its legs or jumps from the perch, however, the tendon relaxes and the grip of the toes is released.

PROUD PERCHER *Fierce and possessive, a great eagle owl grasps its prey against a branch. The bird is found in Europe, Asia and Africa.*

# Mammals – man's family

## BABY IN WAITING
The female red kangaroo of Australia, *Macropus rufus*, has an extraordinary internal production line, which enables it to produce babies (known as 'joeys') – or to stop producing them – depending on whether the outside conditions are suitable. It can speed up the development of a foetus if an existing baby dies. Or it can reverse the development, reabsorbing the foetus, if drought makes the baby's survival unlikely.

Like other marsupials, the female red kangaroo produces tiny young. The baby, born when it is less than 25mm (1in) long, crawls to its mother's pouch, attaches itself to a teat, and remains there for about six months, feeding on milk and growing. Meanwhile, the female mates again, usually within a few days of the birth. At about 200 days old the young joey emerges from the pouch but keeps returning for shelter, before leaving permanently at about 230 days old. For some while after this, though, it continues to put its head back in the pouch to feed on milk.

During this whole time another baby remains in a state of suspended animation inside the mother. A fertilised egg has begun its development but waits at the 'blastocyst' stage – as a minute sphere of cells – until the way is clear for its further development. This may happen in one of two ways. When the first joey starts to leave the pouch, the embryo restarts its development and is born about the time the joey leaves permanently.

Alternatively, if the joey in the pouch dies through accident or through malnutrition in time of drought, the embryo begins developing at once; it is then born some 35 days later, replacing the dead joey.

BIRTH OF A JOEY *A baby kangaroo – only about 20mm (0.75in) long at birth (left) – climbs through the mother's fur to her pouch (centre), then attaches itself to a teat for about six months (right) to complete its development.*

## DOUBLE MILK
The red kangaroo can produce two different kinds of milk at the same time from adjacent teats. While a tiny joey is attached to one of the teats, the other is available to feed a joey which has left the pouch. The elder of the two is given milk with a higher proportion of protein (33 per cent higher) and a much higher proportion of fats (400 per cent higher).

## MAJOR MINER
The Russian mole rat, *Spalax microphthalmus*, is one of the world's champion burrowers. In its search for the underground bulbs, roots and tubers on which it feeds, it excavates long tunnels, punctuated by mounds of earth above ground. Below ground these tunnels contain resting chambers, food storage chambers and latrines. Special chambers are constructed for breeding. Scientists excavated one tunnel system in the USSR and measured its length at 360m (1180ft). It was calculated that this system – a rela-

tively short one – represented two months' work. The longest-known burrow had 114 interconnected mounds, and the two neighbouring mounds on one end of the chain were 170m (560ft) apart. The rat, which is blind, carves out its tunnels with its teeth, not its claws, ramming its blunt head into the soil to loosen it as the tunnel lengthens.

## USELESS TEETH
The numbat, *Myrmecobius fasciatus*, has 52 permanent teeth – more than any other land mammal. Yet it needs none of them. Its diet consists largely of termites and ants, which it swallows whole. The numbat, a marsupial found in western Australia, gathers its prey with its long thin tongue, which can be extended 100mm (4in) or more from the mouth. It spends much of its time in search of food, eating up to 20,000 small termites a day. The numbat's teeth, which are small and widely separated, are thought to be an evolutionary legacy from an ancestor that needed teeth to catch and cut up tougher insect prey.

## ONE OF A KIND
A species of hedgehog-like mammal known as a tenrec is probably the world's rarest land creature. The species, *Dasogale fontoynonti*, is known only from a single specimen which was found in eastern Madagascar and whose body is now preserved in a museum in Paris. Nobody knows whether any others still exist in the wild.

## MIDGET WITH A GIANT HUNGER
The Etruscan shrew, *Suncus etruscus*, from the Mediterranean and Africa, is one of the world's smallest mammals. Fully grown, it weighs only 2g (0.07oz) – just fractionally more than the weight of a British halfpenny coin – and its maximum length, including tail, is about 80mm (3.2in). But, like other shrews, it has a giant-sized appetite. Because they are so tiny, shrews have a large surface area compared to their body volume and lose heat very fast. To make up for this, they eat almost continuously and cannot survive for more than a few hours without food. In the absence of suitable prey, they will even eat each other, including their own young. Some eat up to three times their own body weight in a day.

The smallest of all mammals is a rare type of bat, *Craseonycteris thonglongyai*, which is found only in Thailand. Although an adult has a wingspan of about 160mm (6.3in) – twice the length of the Etruscan shrew – it weighs less: about 1.75g (0.06oz).

## THE DAM-BUILDERS
North American beavers are prodigious dam-builders. Their biggest dams can be 660m (2000ft) long and contain hundreds of tonnes of timber. Even a fairly average dam is more than 20m (65ft) long. Beavers build their homes in the ponds behind the dams, and the homes – known as lodges – can themselves be huge structures up to 1.8m (6ft) high and 6.5m (20ft) across. The pond protects the lodge from predators and also floods the surrounding area, allowing the beavers to gather more food in safety from the drowned forest. The animal's front teeth are so powerful that a group of beavers can fell a tree half a metre (20in) thick in just 15 minutes. Each dam and lodge is made by a colony of beavers working together. But

their structures do not seem to be the product of intelligent cooperation, rather the cumulative result of the instincts of the colony's members. For example, the trigger which starts beavers building a dam is the sound of running water, and construction stops when the water is no longer heard.

## BUILT-IN CHOPSTICKS

The aye-aye, a rare lemur from Madagascar, has on its front paws middle fingers which are so thin and elongated that they resemble chopsticks. Indeed, the aye-aye uses them to eat with, dipping them one at a time into the pulp of fruits, lifting the finger to its mouth and sucking off the juice. It drinks water the same way. The aye-aye's main food is wood-boring insects. It finds them by listening at the bark of trees with its big ears, then gnawing away the bark until it can insert its chopstick finger and extract the prey.

## QUADS TO ORDER

The female of the nine-banded armadillo, *Dasypus novemcinctus*, regularly bears litters of identical quads. Unlike other mammals, in which the babies in a single litter are usually from different eggs, in the nine-banded armadillo all come from the same egg. The egg splits during development and produces identical quadruplets, so that the whole litter is invariably of the same sex. The advantages of this arrangement, if any, are not clear. But it serves the armadillo well enough for it to be a relatively common species across a region from the southern USA to southern Brazil.

## SLOW-MOTION LIVING

Sloths are the slowest of mammals. They spend almost their entire lives upside-down in the trees of South American forests, feeding on leaves and fruit. Their limbs are well adapted as climbing hooks, but they have a top speed of only about 1.5km/h (1mph). Their bodies work slowly and they have a lower and more variable body temperature than other mammals – from 24 to 33°C (75-91°F) in the two-toed sloth. Even their fur is adapted for an upside-down existence – it grows from the belly towards the back, instead of the other way round as in most mammals.

The sloth's apparently slothful way of life is the product of a perfect adaptation to its environment. Its characteristic posture – immobile, hanging upside-down from a branch – guards it from the attention of predators; and its thick, coarse coat, naturally brown or greyish white, is camouflaged green by the presence of microscopic green algae.

The US naturalist William Beebe (1877 – 1962) once followed a sloth through the forest for a week, and discovered that it spent 11 hours feeding, 18 hours moving very slowly about, 10 hours resting – and 129 hours sleeping.

## THE BIG SLEEP

The North American woodchuck spends as much as eight months each year asleep. All its activity is packed into a short summer. The mechanisms used in its hibernation are typical of most true hibernators. As the days shorten, the woodchuck eats far more than normal and this extra food is converted to fat, in particular a nutrient-rich reserve known to biologists as 'brown fat'.

When this fat has built up to a critical level (about one-seventh of the woodchuck's body weight) the animal retreats into its burrow and becomes torpid, allowing its body temperature to drop with that of the surroundings until it may be within a few degrees of freezing point. The brain temperature is still kept up, however, and the temperature sensors still work. If

there is a danger of freezing, some brown fat can be used to raise the temperature rapidly. Then, when spring arrives, the brown fat reserves are used to bring the body temperature back to normal.

## TEETH OF LIFE

An elephant's tusks are specialised front teeth. Yet it can do without them. More important than tusks to the elephant's survival are its 24 molar teeth, used for grinding up food. Unlike the permanent teeth of most mammals, which all develop at about the same time, the elephant's molars appear in succession. When the animal is young, the first two teeth on each side of the upper and lower jaw are in use, but successive teeth grow and move forward from the rear, coming into use as the previous ones are worn down and lost.

By the time an elephant is 45 years old the last four teeth are in full use and the rest of the teeth have gone. These last teeth are massive. They weigh about 4kg (9lb) apiece, are 300mm (12in) long, and have big ridges to help grind the food. But an elephant may eat a quarter of a tonne of tough plant food a day, wearing away even these teeth eventually, so that by the time an elephant is 65 or 70 it faces starvation through a simple inability to chew.

## FERTILITY SYMBOL

The speed at which rabbits breed has become a universal symbol of fertility. Females can start to breed at the age of four months – although in Britain they are usually a year old – and can produce a litter of up to nine young after a gestation period of only 31 days.

They can become pregnant again almost directly after giving birth, and can produce up to six litters a year during spring and summer. Biologists have calculated that if a pair of rabbits bred to their maximum capacity and if there were no losses among the offspring, they could produce a family of more than 33 million animals within three years. Given this poten-

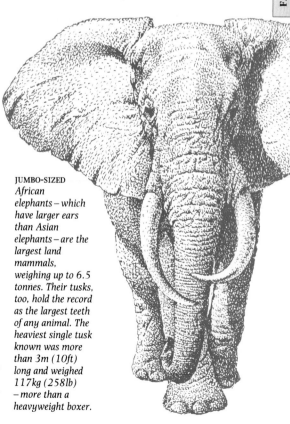

JUMBO-SIZED *African elephants – which have larger ears than Asian elephants – are the largest land mammals, weighing up to 6.5 tonnes. Their tusks, too, hold the record as the largest teeth of any animal. The heaviest single tusk known was more than 3m (10ft) long and weighed 117kg (258lb) – more than a heavyweight boxer.*

tial, the rabbit has been surprisingly rare for much of its history. For one thing, up to 90 per cent of the young are killed by predators.

Rabbits are not native to Britain, but were probably introduced from France in the 12th century and prized for their meat and fur. They were looked after in special enclosed areas, or warrens, by a warrener. Not until the 18th century did escaped rabbits create a significant wild population, and they were not common animals in Britain until the mid-19th century. From then on, the rabbit remained a pest species until 1954, when the North American rabbit disease myxomatosis was introduced to Britain. Four years earlier, the disease had been introduced to Australia to end a plague of rabbits. In Britain, it killed up to 99 per cent of the population. Now in some areas rabbits are common again, but cyclical outbreaks of the disease keep them in check.

## THE LONG MARCH
The barren ground caribou of Canada make the longest migrations of any land mammal. The herds move to the high tundra of the Arctic for the summer, where the young are born, and return south in the autumn to the northern edge of the forest region – a round trip of up to 2250km (1400 miles). The animals migrate in giant herds of up to 20,000 individuals. The trek enables the caribou to feed on the richest available pastures at each season of the year, and so helps to support larger herds than would otherwise be possible.

## EVOLUTIONARY U-TURN
The ancestors of whales were once land animals. Scientific examination of whale skeletons indicates that they have a vestigial pelvis or hipbone, proving that whales once possessed legs. The ancestors of whales, like the ancestors of all animals, came originally from the sea. But whales began returning to the sea about 70 million years ago, steadily losing the physical characteristics of land mammals as they spent more time in the water.

Their front legs changed into flippers, their rear legs disappeared, their bodies acquired a thick insulating layer of blubber and their nostrils moved from the snout to the top of the head to become a blowhole. It is not known why whales returned to the sea, but it may have been because food was more plentiful there or because enemies were fewer.

## TALKING UNDERWATER
Although dolphins have no vocal cords, they can communicate with one another, navigate and hunt for prey by making distinctive underwater sounds. By forcing air past valves and flaps located immediately below their blowhole, dolphins can emit at least 32 different sounds, including whistles, groans, barks, clicks and squeals. Besides using whistles to 'talk' to other members of their school, dolphins navigate and hunt by using an echo-location technique in much the same way as bats.

Whales, too, are able to converse with each other by making whistles and chirps. The male humpback whale, for example, produces a long and complex song that may last for 30 minutes. These sounds are sometimes extremely loud: blue whales have emitted whistles that reach 188 decibels – louder than a jet plane. The moans of fin whales can be picked up by other whales hundreds of kilometres away.

## TAIL FIRST
Whales and dolphins are born tail first. Unlike land mammals, which are able to breathe as soon as the head is born, whales are born under water and this backwards form of delivery is necessary to prevent them from drowning during the time it takes to be born. Like all mammals, whales have no gills; instead they breathe air.

Immediately after birth, the calf is helped to the ocean's surface by its mother – and sometimes by other attendant whales – to take its first breath of air. Baby whales are enormous. At birth a blue whale may be 7.5m (25ft) long and 2 tonnes in weight – nearly as heavy as some adult elephants. Each day, the calves suck up to 600 litres (132 gallons) of milk, which contains about 50 per cent fat, and can double their weight in a week, growing faster than any other mammal. Blue whales grow by about 40mm (1.5in) and 90kg (200lb) daily, and after seven months can weigh 23 tonnes.

## THE DOLPHIN'S ENEMY
Dolphins and sharks both live in all the seas of the world. Both are superbly adapted for life, and speed, in water. Both live on fish. There is just one big difference: sharks sometimes also eat dolphins. Dolphins never eat sharks.

For millions of years, sharks have occasionally preyed on solitary dolphins that have become separated from their school. But in a group, dolphins can outwit, terrify and even kill their more powerful enemy. Dolphins at sea have been spotted chasing a shark, closing in on it from different directions to force it well away from the school. In some aquariums dolphins have been known to kill sharks – by butting them to death with their pointed 'beaks'.

In one case, in the United States, a group of dolphins that had been peacefully sharing a large tank with a shark ganged up on it when one of the females was about to give birth. Why the group took action is not known. But it seems possible that the group decided that having a shark about when there was likely to be blood in the water from the imminent birth was just too big a risk. In any case, the dolphins coolly lined up at the far end of the pool from the shark, then raced through the water one at a time, each smashing its beak into the shark's side. After only a few minutes of this battering-ram punishment, the shark was dead. From the outside it appeared to be unharmed. But its internal organs had been pounded to pulp.

In another case, also in the United States, a group of dolphins are thought to have thrown a shark out of their tank. Its body was found out of the water the next day – nearly 9m (30ft) from the edge of the pool.

## WHALE OF A BRAIN
Sperm whales have the heaviest brain of any animal. It can weigh more than 9kg (20lb), six times larger than an average human brain. Fully grown, sperm whales can weigh 50 tonnes and grow up to 20m (66ft) in length, making them the largest of the toothed whales and the world's biggest carnivores.

The whale's head, which can be one-third the length of its entire body, contains up to 2300 litres (500 gallons) of pure oil, which, until the development

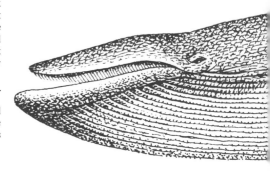

of refined mineral oils, was the finest lubricant known. Early hunters wrongly believed the fluid to be the animal's sperm, hence its name.

## THE BIGGEST MEETING
The greatest gathering of a single species of mammal takes place annually on the Pribilof Islands, an island group in the Bering Sea off southwest Alaska. Each year an estimated 1.5 million Alaskan fur seals assemble there to breed, producing some 500,000 pups.

## WHY SEALS CRY
Seals on land often look miserable, with tears trickling down their cheeks. In fact the tears have nothing to do with their emotional state. As with some other aquatic creatures, the tears produced naturally by seals to lubricate the eyes normally drift off into the surrounding water. There is no need for the duct running from eyes to nose that is found in land mammals, including man. In seals it has disappeared, so when a seal is on land there is nowhere for the tears to go, except down the face.

## UGLY MERMAID
The mermaid legend may have originated with a group of mammals collectively known to science as Sirenians (sirens). Commonly referred to as sea cows, these creatures – which include the dugong and the manatee – are about the same size as a human being and, from a distance, somewhat resemble a woman with the tail of a fish.

Female sea cows have prominent breasts on the front of their body near the forelimbs, and a flattened tail which is sometimes forked. Close up, however, the resemblance to a mermaid vanishes. A sea cow has a chubby, rounded face with small eyes, a cleft upper lip and a bristly moustache.

## TOOTHLESS GIANTS
Although baleen whales include the world's largest creature, the blue whale, they feed on some of the marine world's smallest organisms. Baleen whales are named after the bone-like baleen plates, also called whalebone and once used as the stays in women's corsets. The plates hang from their upper gums and the whales are unable to hunt larger prey because, except during their embryonic stage, they lack teeth. Instead the baleen plates, which are between 1 and 3m long (3.3 – 10ft), and up to 300mm (12in) wide, are used to filter microscopic plankton and other food, such as krill (a small shrimp), from the sea.

The whale feeds by swimming with its mouth open, trapping its food on the frayed insides of the baleen plates, and using its huge tongue to help swallow the catch. Baleen whales strain several tonnes of plankton and krill from the sea each day and the blue whale eats up to 4 tonnes of krill daily. The largest blue whale known was landed on the South Atlantic island of South Georgia in the early 20th century. It was 33.58m (110ft 2in) long.

# MARSUPIAL AND PLACENTAL MAMMALS

The two main groups of present-day mammals are the marsupials, or Metatheria, and the placentals, or Eutheria – the group which includes man. Marsupial females have a pouch in which their young develop. In placentals, the young develop inside the mother. Marsupials now live only in Australia, New Guinea and the Americas. Despite the biological differences, many pouched animals fill the same ecological niches as their placental relatives, and often resemble them.

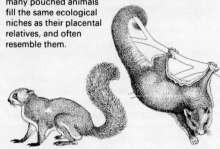

TREE-DWELLERS *Marsupial phalangers (right) glide between trees by using membranes stretched between arms and legs. They resemble flying squirrels (left).*

TUNNELLERS *The southern marsupial mole (right) has a leathery pad on its nose and it digs with clawed forefeet – like the Cape golden mole (left) of Africa.*

SCAVENGERS *Marsupial Tasmanian devils (right) and the Eurasian wolverine (left) have powerful teeth and claws. Both feed largely on carrion.*

HUNTERS *The slope-backed marsupial wolf (right) looks much like an Old World wolf (left). Both are adapted to striking down prey and tearing flesh.*

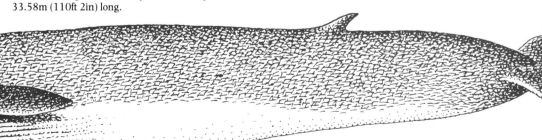

PEACEFUL MONSTERS *Baleen whales – browsers which feed on plankton – are the world's largest animals. The group includes the blue whale, and the fin whale (above).*

# Farm animals and pets

## MAN'S FIRST FRIEND

The dog is man's oldest as well as his best friend. The ancient Egyptians used dogs for hunting 8000 years ago, and Stone Age Man may have had hunting dogs before 10,000 BC. The ancestors of the dog were probably the lighter-built southern Asian races of the wolf, but other wolf races may have contributed.

About 5000 years ago man began to develop breeds of dogs in order to encourage different qualities. Later, the short-legged dachshund was bred for hunting badgers, and the sheepdog was bred for its herding abilities.

All dogs – from a Mexican chihuahua weighing less than lkg (2.2lb) to a huge St Bernard of more than 90kg (198lb) – are members of the same species. In biological terms, this means that any dog can potentially breed with any other dog – although differences in size can make this unlikely in some cases. And despite the long domestication there is no genetic barrier between dogs and wolves, either.

## GIVE A DOG A NAME

● The German Shepherd Dog was originally brought to Britain by soldiers returning from the First World War, who had admired the dogs' courage and devotion when they carried front-line messages for the Germans. But, because of anti-German feeling, the dogs could not be known by their correct name. So they were named Alsatians from the region of their origin, Alsace-Lorraine – the frontier area between France and Germany – where they were used as sheepdogs. The English version of the breed's correct name was officially restored in Britain by the Kennel Club in July 1977, but in some other countries the dogs are still known as Alsatians.

● Doberman dogs get their name from a German tax collector. Aware of the unpopularity of his job, Ludwig Dobermann, of Apolda in Thuringia, developed in the 1880s an especially fierce breed to help him on his rounds. Today Dobermans are widely used as guard dogs.

● Chihuahuas are named after the state of Chihuahua in Mexico. They are believed to have been the sacred dogs of the Aztecs, and were sometimes eaten by the Indians in religious ceremonies.

● Labradors do not come from the Canadian region of Labrador. In fact they come from the neighbouring province of Newfoundland, where they helped fishermen to land their nets. They were introduced to Europe by Canadian fishermen in the 1830s.

● The cocker spaniel originated in 14th-century Spain. The first half of its name comes from its use by hunters to flush out woodcock, the second half from the name of its home country.

● The first Pekingese in Europe were five dogs brought from China after they had been taken by the British from the women's apartments in Peking's Summer Palace during the Boxer Rebellion (1898–1900). Before this, the breed had been monopolised by the Chinese royal family, and theft of a Peke had carried the death penalty.

● The King Charles spaniel is not a British breed. It was being kept as a pet in Japan as early as 2000 BC. It acquired its common English name (in the USA it is often known as the English toy spaniel) after it became fashionable at the 17th-century court of Charles I.

## THE FIRST GUIDE DOG

The idea of using dogs as substitute eyes for the blind grew out of a chance incident at a German hospital during the First World War. A doctor walking in the grounds with a blinded soldier was called away and left his pet German Shepherd (Alsatian) to look after his patient. Impressed by its response, he experimented with training dogs specifically to help the blind.

A wealthy American, Dorothy Eustis, who was then training German Shepherd Dogs in Switzerland for the army and police, heard of the doctor's work. In 1928 she set up a guide-dog centre at Vevey, and three years later lent a trainer to start a trial scheme in Britain. From its success grew The Guide Dogs for the Blind Association, founded in Britain in 1934. Since then, the idea has spread around the world.

## CALL ME MOTHER

All the pet hamsters in the world are descended from a single female wild golden hamster found with a litter of 12 young in Syria in 1930. The species had been named in 1839 when a single animal was found, again in Syria near the city of Aleppo, but it had not been seen by scientists for nearly a century. Selective breeding has now produced several colour varieties.

## AT HOME ON THE RANGE

The word 'maverick' – now used to indicate a rogue animal or a person who does not conform – comes from the name of a Texas lawyer and rancher, Samuel Maverick (1803–70), who did not bother to brand his cattle.

## PIG IN THE MIDDLE

In 1859, the United States and Britain almost went to war over a pig. The pig belonged to an Englishman, Charles Griffin, who lived on San Juan Island just off the Pacific coast of Canada near Vancouver. It kept straying onto the potato patch of his American neighbour, Lyman Cutler. Cutler shot the pig. Griffin complained to his government – and troops from both sides rushed in.

The pig's aimless foraging had highlighted an ambiguity in the 1846 treaty which had established the US-Canadian frontier. At the western end, the treaty fixed the border along the 49th parallel of latitude to 'the middle of the channel' separating Vancouver Island from the mainland. There the border turned south. But the channel is itself divided into several smaller straits by a cluster of islands – and the two sides could not agree on which channel was

PRZEWALSKI'S HORSE *All modern horses are thought to be descended from this wild species which is now found only in Asia.*

DINGO *A forerunner of the domestic dog, the dingo was taken to Australia by Aborigines some 8000 years ago.*

JUNGLE FOWL
*The wild red jungle fowl of Malaya and India is the bird from which domestic chickens were bred.*

meant. The 'Pig War' dragged on for 13 years. No shots were exchanged, but troops remained stationed at opposite ends of the island. The dispute was settled by arbitration when the German Kaiser, Wilhelm I, awarded the islands to the USA in 1872.

## PIGGY PADDLE
In the Tokelau Islands of the South Pacific, pigs have learnt to find their own food in the sea. They wade and swim through the shallow reef waters, ducking under the surface to catch sea slugs and shellfish.

## WITH A GUAU GUAU HERE . . .
Animals do, it seems, speak different languages – at least as far as their countries are concerned. Sheep do not 'baa' in Germany; they say *mäh* (pronounced as a drawn-out 'may'). And in Spain they say *bee* (pronounced 'bay'). Norwegian dogs say *vov vov*, not 'bow wow' or 'woof woof'. French dogs say *whou whou*, and Spanish ones *guau guau*. In France, ducks say *coin coin*, not 'quack quack', and turkeys say *glou glou*, not 'gobble gobble'. In Italy hens say *ko-ko-day*, not 'cluck-cluck', and the roosters greet the dawn by shrieking, not 'cock-a-doodle-doo', but *chicchirichi* (pronounced 'kee-kee-ree-kee').

## TABBIES AND THE CASBAH
Tabby cats are thought to get their name from Attab, a district in Baghdad, now the capital of Iraq. There, according to an Arab observer writing in the 12th century, 'are made the stuffs called *Attabiya*, which are silks and cottons of divers colours'. Brought to the western world in its abbreviated form, the word was originally applied to striped silk taffetas, and the association with striped cats followed.

## COWS AS BIG AS ELEPHANTS
Visitors to farms of the future may feel like Gulliver in the land of the giants. US scientists at Ohio University are working on a project that could result in enormous livestock. By juggling with the genetic structures of animals – adding and subtracting genes, including genes from other species – they hope to create new breeds which will make traditional farm animals look Lilliputian. So far they have bred what is probably the world's largest mouse.

Known only by its laboratory number, 178, it is two and half times larger than a normal mouse, but eats no more. The leader of the project, Professor Thomas Wagner, predicted in early 1984 that in two years it would be possible to use the same techniques on larger animals, so that scientists could breed cows weighing 4.5 tonnes – only slightly smaller than an elephant – and pigs the size of hippos.

## THE FIRST ROUND-UPS

Dates when animals were first domesticated or put into the service of man are not known with any precision. These dates are, however, widely accepted by historians and biologists.

| | |
|---|---|
| Dog By 10,000 BC | Donkey 3000 BC |
| Goat 8000 BC | Cat 2000 BC |
| Cattle 5500 BC | Chicken 2000 BC |
| Sheep 5000 BC | Duck 1500 BC |
| Pig 3000 BC | Goose 1500 BC |
| Horse 3000 BC | Rabbit AD 1000 |

AUROCHS *The ancestor of European cattle is thought to be the aurochs. Although the last known wild one was seen in Poland in 1627, a German biologist, Professor Heinz Heck, re-created the animal in 1932 by crossing domesticated breeds, including Friesian and Highland cattle.*

## TOP DOGS

The popularity of dog breeds varies from country to country and time to time. No world league table exists, but in terms of ownership these were the most popular pedigree breeds in Britain in the early 1980s.

1  German Shepherd Dog (Alsatian)
2  Labrador retriever
3  Yorkshire terrier
4  Golden retriever
5  King Charles spaniel
6  Cocker spaniel
7  English springer spaniel
8  Doberman
9  Rough collie
10  Boxer
11  Staffordshire bull terrier
12  Shetland sheepdog
13  West Highland white terrier
14  Toy poodle
15  Old English sheepdog
16  Irish setter
17  Rottweiler
18  Cairn terrier
19  Pekingese
20  Great Dane

WILD BOAR *Farm pigs are descended from the wild boar, which was crossed with Far Eastern breeds around the end of the 18th century.*

SOAY SHEEP *The Soay, on the Hebridean island of St Kilda, is one of the world's few remaining wild sheep.*

WILD GOAT *Bezoar goats, first domesticated in the Middle East, are related to farm or garden goats.*

# Animal behaviour

GUARD DUTY Caterpillars of the imperial blue butterfly of Australia have their own special escort – a band of black ants. Each morning, as the caterpillars leave their nests on black wattle trees to feed on leaves, the ants join them. The ants use their huge jaws to drive off any would-be predators while the caterpillars feed, and as payment for their guard duty they suck a sugary secretion from the caterpillars' backs. The ants – which nest underground and climb up the trees each day to join the caterpillars – even watch over the insects in their pupa stage, when there are no sweet 'wages' to pay for their work.

---

*The small fish Nomeus spends its life among the dangerous tentacles of the Portuguese man-of-war, and apparently shares the food caught by its lethal host. Nomeus remains safe as long as it is uninjured. But a wound triggers off the predatory instincts of its host – which then eats the little lodger.*

---

BODY BAIT One species of assassin bug, *Salyavata variegata*, uses the bodies of dead termites as bait to capture fresh victims. It captures its first termite by camouflaging itself with pieces of carton – the basic material of a termite nest – then snatching a termite that wanders too close.

Once it has sucked the body dry, it dangles the carcass in an entrance hole. Termite workers instinctively try to clear the body away, but when a worker grasps the body, the bug hauls the body and the worker from the nest. The diligent worker then becomes the bug's next meal and its body the bait for the next victim.

---

*Among the coral reefs of the Indian and Pacific oceans, fish of all kinds make use of the services of cleaner fish, which relieve them of parasites and damaged skin. One such cleaner – there are more than 40 species – is the 100mm (4in) long striped sea swallow, a kind of wrasse. Its clients include large predators such as moray eels, but they do not eat the cleaner and are quiet under its attentions, even allowing it into their mouths.*

---

HOME GUARD Birds use stinging insects as an unwitting army to protect their nests. Some seed-eating African weaver birds build their nests above the homes of fierce papernest wasps. The rufous woodpecker of India and Southeast Asia tunnels into the football-size nests of stinging tree ants, and lays its eggs there. Though woodpeckers are ant-eaters, and the aggressive tree ants will attack any intruder near their nest, the two animals call a truce at the woodpecker's breeding time. The woodpecker benefits from the protection provided for its nest by the ants, and the ants gain by not being eaten by the woodpecker during the rearing season.

MOBILE BODYGUARD The hermit crab often carries a sea anemone on its shell as a bodyguard. The sea anemone's stinging tentacles deter predators, and in return the anemone gains mobility and thus a wider feeding range, as well as scraps of the crab's food.

---

## TYPES OF TOGETHERNESS

Biologists divide partnerships between living organisms into four main categories: symbiotic, parasitic, commensal and epizoic.

**Symbiotic** A word meaning literally 'living together'. Symbiosis is normally used to mean a close and mutually beneficial relationship between two different organisms. Lichens, for example, are a symbiosis of two organisms – a fungus and one of the primitive plants known as algae.

**Parasitic** A close and one-sided relationship in which an organism battens onto and lives off its host, harming it in the process. Flatworms, for example, thrive in the blood vessels of their human hosts.

**Commensal** A close and one-sided relationship in which one organism gains benefit, but not at any cost to its partner. The cattle egret, for example, lives off parasites on the back of cattle and other grazing animals.

**Epizoic** A close relationship in which one partner lives on the skin of another – or is carried or towed about by it. The remora 'sucker' fish, for example, attaches itself to a larger fish by means of a suction disc on its head.

---

Hermit crabs use abandoned mollusc shells as body protection, and move to larger ones when they outgrow them. But they do not leave their bodyguards behind. When about to move, the crab gives the anemone a warning tap so that it relaxes its hold on the shell, then the crab lifts the anemone with its claw to the new shell.

THE BADGER'S SCOUT The ratel or honey-badger of tropical Africa has a flying partner – a small bird which guides the ratel to its favourite food, honey. The bird – the honeyguide, *Indicator indicator* – gives a special call when it has found a bees' nest and attracts the attention of a nearby honey-badger. Then it leads the badger to the nest. The badger, whose tough skin is impervious to stings, breaks in, using its sharp claws, and eats its fill of honey. Meanwhile, the bird picks through the debris of the nest for its favourite food: larvae and insects. The bird, which is unable to break into a bees' nest itself, thus gets food it could not otherwise reach, and the ratel is drawn to food which it might not notice.

FROM HOST TO HOST Most parasites live off only one host – but there is one group of parasites which needs two hosts in order to survive. They are the threadlike flatworms that spread the wasting disease of bilharzia through much of Africa and parts of Asia and South America. Of the four species of bilharzia worm, two, *Schistosoma haematobium* and *Schistosoma mansoni*, depend almost entirely on man himself as the definitive host.

The worm's life cycle is highly complicated. Microscopically small newly hatched worms, born in rivers and pools, have just 24 hours to find their first host: the egg of a minute but hardy freshwater snail.

If the worms fail to find a snail host within 24 hours, they die. If they succeed, they develop inside the snail and eventually return to the water as barely visible young worms. These, in turn, have 72 hours at most to find a human host.

The young worms can penetrate the skin of a swimmer or paddler at any point, travel through the veins to the heart and thence through the lungs to the liver. There they grow into fully fledged worms 10–25mm (0.4–1in) long. Once adult, the worms migrate to the gut and bladder where they can remain for anything up to 25 years. Their eggs are discharged into rivers and pools in the urine and faeces, and so the cycle continues.

More than 200 million people in over 70 countries suffer from bilharzia, whose symptoms include listlessness, diarrhoea and blood in the urine and bowels.

LOBSTERS IN LINE  Each autumn off the Bimini Islands, in the Bahamas, thousands of spiny lobsters migrate from reefs to deeper water. During this journey, they often form a marching column of up to 50 lobsters to cross open areas.

Each hooks one pair of its front legs around the tail of the animal in front, or flicks its antennae to maintain contact. In this way, each lobster's vulnerable belly and tail are protected by the armoured legs and antennae of the one behind, while the column scuttles across the seabed as fast as a man can swim.

SENTRY TO A SHRIMP  The 150mm (6in) goby fish, *Cryptocentrus coeruleopunctatus*, acts as a sentry for a tiny shrimp with which it shares a burrow on the seabed. Whenever the entrance to their burrow becomes littered with rubble, the shrimp – known as the snapping shrimp – emerges to clear the rubble, using its claws like a mechanical digger. While it is at work, the goby stands guard – with one of its antennae touching the shrimp. The moment the goby discerns

danger, it wriggles its body and the shrimp, alerted by the movement of its companion's antenna, shoots back to the safety of the burrow – immediately followed by the goby.

HOME SHARP HOME  Several Central American species of ants have evolved a remarkable living arrangement – with a tree. The ants make their homes in the sharp fleshy spines of swollen thorn acacias. They burrow into the base of the trees' thorns, eating the pulp and hollowing out a nest at the same time. Once established, the ants – species of the genus *Pseudomyrmex* – feed on special protein-rich nodules which grow on the tips of the acacias' leaves.

Far from being harmed by the ants' eating habits, the trees thrive because the ants protect them from all other predators, such as other insects, birds and small animals. As soon as any attacker lands on one of the trees, the patrolling ants close in, biting and stinging, until it is driven away.

FOSTER-CHILD OF THE BUFFALO  South Africa's giant Kruger National Park is the home of an elephant that thinks it is a buffalo. In the early 1970s, five baby elephants which had been the subject of a veterinary experiment were released in the park, close to a herd of buffalo. Later, game rangers reported that one of them had joined the herd, and that it had adopted buffalo habits.

In 1980, a park visitor saw the ten-year-old elephant and its 'family' of 20 buffalo trumpeting and bellowing to drive eight lions away from a waterhole.

In the mid-1980s, the elephant still seemed to be completely at home with the buffalo. So much so that, as one park ranger, Ted Whitfield, put it: 'I've seen him drinking when a herd of elephant arrives. The buffalo make off, and so does he.'

BARBED RETREAT *The clown fish protects itself from predators by taking refuge among an anemone's stinging tentacles. The fish, which is about 50mm (2in) long, secretes a coat of mucus which counteracts the poisonous discharge from the anemone's stinging cells. The anemone seems to benefit because the clown fish acts as a lure to attract unprotected species, and the fish benefits by eating up leftover scraps of the anemone's food.*

# Animal behaviour

SHOCKING TAIL South America's electric eels have enough power in their tails to light up to a dozen household bulbs – or kill a man on contact. The eels can release a shock of about 500 volts at 2 amps – as much power as is used by a single-bar electric fire. The biggest discharge on record is 650 volts. The surge of current is generated chemically from thousands of linked battery cells – modified muscle tissues which fill four-fifths of the eel's 1.8m (6ft) length. The charge can be released in a fraction of a second, but it takes the best part of an hour for the eel to recharge its batteries for another shock.

Despite its name, the electric eel is not an eel at all. It is a type of freshwater fish related to carp and minnows. The fish uses its extraordinary ability to protect itself from predators and to stun prey. Adult eels also use weak 'radar' pulses from their battery cells as an aid to navigation since they live in murky swamps and backwaters.

*The Southeast Asian spider* Cyclosa mulmeinensis *makes dummies of itself. It parcels parts of its prey in silk until they are the same size as itself, then plants them in strategic spots on its web. Spider-hunting birds are quite likely to select a decoy, instead of the spider.*

HOLDING .THE RING The musk oxen of Canada, Alaska and Greenland defend themselves from wolf attacks by forming a defensive ring. Females and the young gather in the centre of the circle and the males form a wall around them, with their horns pointing outwards. Any wolf that ventures too close risks being caught by the horns and tossed over the male's back into the circle, where it will be trampled to death by the females.

CARBON-COPIERS Many animals protect themselves by imitating others. They usually do it in one of two ways.

In Batesian mimicry, named after the 19th-century British naturalist Henry Bates, harmless or edible animals imitate the appearance of poisonous or inedible ones to cash in on their defences. The harmless wasp beetle, for example, flaunts the bright warning colours of the wasp and even apes its flight patterns to fool beetle-eating predators.

In Müllerian mimicry, named after Fritz Müller, a 19th-century German zoologist, poisonous or inedible species imitate each other – a habit also known as economy of coloration. The mechanism cuts down the number of different warning patterns that predators need to remember, and so reduces the numbers eaten by accident.

BLUFFING IT OUT Many animals have found that the next best thing to being fierce is looking fierce. When alarmed, the Australian frilled lizard, which is 1m (3.3ft) long, raises a frill which normally lies flat along the neck. The frill stands out in a disc up to 610mm (2ft) across. The lizard adds to its alarming increase in apparent size by opening its mouth to reveal a bright yellow interior, and hisses loudly. In the face of all this, a potential predator can hardly be blamed for not realising that the lizard is harmless.

STICKY END Tropical termites use a natural quickset glue to defend their nests from marauding ants. Termite soldiers belonging to the genus *Nasutitermes* are able to fire jets of the glue from an aperture on their heads across a range of several centimetres. The glue rapidly becomes tacky, immobilising the assailants, while its smell attracts other soldiers to the nest's defence. Soldier termites of the genus *Coptotermes* also produce this glue, but they are unable to discharge it at a distance. As a result, both the termite and the ant become entangled. Nevertheless, even if the defender dies, its suicidal mechanism helps to preserve the rest of the nest.

*The sea cucumber, or bêche-de-mer, of the Pacific can disembowel itself to escape capture. When frightened, it contracts its dingy sausage-like body violently and expels a tangled mess of its own internal organs. But far from dying in the process, it leaves the organs as a meal for its attacker and slithers away to grow a new set within a few weeks.*

*The sea cucumber, which can grow to more than 610mm (2ft) long, can also eject sticky white threads like an untidy web of spaghetti to entangle small fish and shrimps that disturb it.*

EVASIVE ACTION Moths use a dramatic free-fall tactic to evade pursuing bats. Bats detect their prey by means of a sophisticated echo-location system, bouncing sounds off objects in their path. But because the moth can pick up the bat's high-pitched squeaks from 30m (100ft) away, it has an edge over its faster

## HOW LONG THEY LIVE

Most animals die through violence, disease or accident, not through old age. As a result, the maximum lifespans of animals in the wild are not known with any certainty. Most scientists believe that marine animals are generally capable of living longer than land animals because their bodies, permanently cradled and supported by water, are not worn down or worn out so quickly by the effects of gravity. In addition, many cold-blooded animals, such as reptiles, seem to have no fixed adult size, so that they go on growing until they die. Theoretically, some scientists believe, such animals should, if completely protected, live for ever.

In practice, however, few organisms except bacteria live much longer than man. These are the longest recorded lifespans, in years, for a variety of animals.

| | |
|---|---|
| 152 Marion's tortoise | 50 Lobster |
| 100 Deep-sea clam | 40 Cow |
| 90 Killer whale | 35 Domestic pigeon |
| 90 Blue whale | 34 Domestic cat |
| 90 Fin whale | 29 Dog (Labrador) |
| 80 Freshwater oyster | 28 Budgerigar |
| 70 Cockatoo | 20 Sheep |
| 70 Condor | 18 Goat |
| 70 Indian elephant | 18 Rabbit |
| 62 Ostrich | 10 Golden hamster |
| 62 Horse | 6 House mouse |
| 50 Chimpanzee | 0.2 Housefly |
| 50 Termite | |

adversary, which has a detection range of only about 6m (20ft). When a moth intercepts signals from a bat, it takes evasive action by suddenly dropping to the ground in mid-flight.

The manoeuvre does not always work, though, because the bats can sometimes track the moths as they fall and catch them before they reach the ground. As a result, some moth species have devised new tricks to restore their advantage in the dogfight. They resort to aerobatics in an attempt to shake off the bat. Some tiger moth species have even developed a jamming device – an ultrasonic sound which throws the bats off course.

LEAPING FOR LIFE  Antelopes and gazelles usually rely on their speed to escape from predators such as lions, cheetahs and hyenas, but African impalas and springbok have an even quicker form of evasive action: it is called pronking. The animal arches its

back and leaps repeatedly 3m (10ft) straight up in the air. The repeated jumps can disconcert a predator about to spring, giving its intended target a chance to bound away.

BATTLESHIP ON LEGS  Some species of millipedes have developed a deadly form of chemical warfare to protect themselves against predators: they release clouds of lethal hydrogen cyanide gas through minute vents like gunports along the sides of their bodies.

Laboratory study of the millipedes, which are slow-moving and feed only on plants, shows that they are capable of controlling the broadside so that the gas spurts only from the vents nearest an attacker. At least one African species, *Apheloria corrugata*, can also fire broadsides from both sides at once – if it is handled, say, or attacked by an army of ants. Then it crawls ponderously away, leaving behind a cloud of the poisonous gas.

MASTERS OF DISGUISE *In insects, the whole shape of the body has sometimes adapted to the need to hide. This Costa Rican bush cricket has even developed a two-tone colour scheme so that it resembles a decaying leaf. Stick insects, similarly, resemble twigs, and some South American moths look, at rest, just like bird droppings.*

THE EYES HAVE IT *The North American owl butterfly,* Taenaris phorcas, *frightens attackers away by exposing a pair of startling eyes on its wings. The owl-like false eyes even include a glint of light to complete the illusion.*

WARNING SIGNS *Poisonous animals often have brightly coloured bodies – like the South American arrow-poison frog pictured on the left – to remind predators to keep clear. The world's most poisonous creature is the golden arrow-poison frog of Colombia. An adult contains enough poison to kill 2200 people.*

313

# Animal behaviour

EYE OF THE SQUID  The eyes of squids and octopuses – cephalopods – are similar to man's, and in some ways superior. A cross-section of an octopus eye reveals a cornea, lens, iris and retina, just as in a human eye. But the eye also has two features not possessed by the human eye. Cephalopods can distinguish polarised light, and they have no blind spot because the optic nerve linking eye and brain starts behind the retina rather than in front of it as in the human eye. In addition, some cephalopods have twice as many light-sensitive cells as man in the part of the eye where vision is sharpest, which probably means that they can perceive finer detail than humans – a valuable advantage in the hazy depths of the sea.

HEAT-SEEKING SNAKES  Pit vipers, the family of snakes which includes the North American rattlesnake, can 'see' infrared radiation – the heat radiation, invisible to humans, which is given off by any living creature. Two pits – which give the family its name – lie between the eye and nostril on either side of the snake's face. Each pit contains some 15,000 heat-sensitive cells which enable the snake to tell the direction and distance of a small animal several metres away even in complete darkness – just from the heat of its body. Pythons have a similar but less sophisticated detection mechanism in pits around the lips.

THE NOSE KNOWS  Although most dogs have poor eyesight, they possess a superb sense of smell. Dachshunds have about 125 million smell-sensitive cells in their noses, compared with a human's meagre 5 million. An Alsatian, or German Shepherd Dog, has 220 million smell cells. The extra cells have the effect of multiplying its sense of smell so that its nose is about a million times more sensitive than a human's. A bloodhound's sense of smell is on a par with a German Shepherd Dog's.

Experiments carried out in 1885 with a skilled tracker dog, by British biologist George Romanes, showed that only one scent foxed it: the scent of identical twins. It could distinguish their scents from anyone else's. But it could not distinguish the scents from one another.

Dogs also have superb hearing. They can detect high-pitched sound frequencies of up to 40,000 vibrations a second, as against man's 20,000.

HOW THE BEE SEES *The flowers of fleabane,* Pulicaria dysenterica, *appear yellow to humans (left), but blue to bees, which are sensitive to ultraviolet light (right). Many flowers have special ultraviolet markings which act like beacons, pointing the way to nectar and pollen.*

*Some insects are apparently able to see light through their skin. Experiments with the caterpillars of moths and butterflies show that, even with their eyes covered, they are still sensitive to light.*

COLOUR VISION  Contrary to popular belief, animals are not all colour-blind. Many species, including dogs, horses and sheep, can distinguish some colours – though not as well as humans – while the primates, especially chimpanzees and rhesus monkeys, have colour vision equal to that of humans.

Another popular belief – that bulls dislike the colour red – is probably also wrong. Experiments seem to show that it is the movement of the matador's cape,

## SIGHT LINES

Many creatures see the world very differently from the way humans do, because their eyes have adapted to suit their particular way of life.

**Buzzard** Soaring birds of prey, such as hawks and buzzards, need especially keen eyesight to pick out small animals on the ground. In the fovea, the most sensitive part of the eye's retina, a buzzard has about 1 million light-sensitive cells per square millimetre – five times as many as a human. As a result, the images it sees are much sharper.

**Cat** Although a cat has poorly developed colour vision, seeing the world largely in black, white and grey, it can see far better in the dark, thanks to a crystalline layer in the retina which enables it to absorb 50 per cent more light than human eyes. By day, the cat's irises contract into slits to keep out excessive light.

**Bee** Sensitivity to ultraviolet light, invisible to humans, enables bees to spot special honey-guide markings on many flower petals which point the way to nectar and pollen. The same sensitivity allows bees to 'see' the sun, even on a cloudy day, so that they can find their way back to the hive. On the other hand, bees cannot see red, perceiving it as blue.

**Spider** Most spiders have eight simple eyes, known as *ocelli,* arranged around the top of the head so that they can see in all directions at once. In species such as the jumping spider, which stalks its prey rather than simply waiting for it, two of the eyes at the front are better developed than the rest, allowing the spider to gauge distances accurately for its final pounce.

**Sandpiper** Many foraging birds, such as chickens and shore birds, have eyes set on the side of their head, so that each eye sees a different scene. The resulting wide field of vision allows them to spot danger from almost any direction, but limits their ability to judge distances. Shore birds such as sandpipers compensate for this lack of stereoscopic vision by bobbing their heads up and down and sideways to view an object from several angles against its background.

**Butterfly** Like other adult insects, butterflies have compound eyes, made up of numerous separate eyes – up to 28,000 in a dragonfly but as few as nine in some ant species. Each mini-eye is equipped with its own minute lens, so that insects see objects as a mosaic of overlapping points of light, rather like a badly tuned television picture. Compound eyes are unable to focus sharply, but they are good at spotting movement.

# Super senses

not its colour, that excites them. But a relative of the bull, an Indian buffalo called the zebu, has been found to have some colour vision, so the expression 'like a red rag to a bull' may not be totally meaningless.

SILENT AS DEATH  Some owls, such as the barn owl, can find and catch their prey even in complete darkness, thanks to their remarkable sense of hearing. Many temperate-zone owls can hear sounds ten times softer than a human ear can pick up.

The tufts on the top of many owls' heads are not their ears; they are only for display. In fact, the ears are on the side of the head just behind the flattened face feathers. In some species – the long-eared owl, for example – the right ear is half as large again as the left and set higher on the head. This arrangement is thought to help the owl to zero in on prey by sound alone. The victim gets little warning of the owl's approach because the bird's wings are fringed with soft feathers, making its flight almost silent.

*In the eyes of most creatures the lens focuses light from objects onto a layer of light-sensitive cells called the retina. Images are transmitted to the brain, which forms a mental picture. But a shrimp-like creature,* Copilia quadrata, *in the Mediterranean has eyes which work on a different principle. The animal has one lens in the front of its head, but no retina. Behind the lens is a single light-sensitive spot which darts about, building up an image as a system of dots, rather like a television set. The 'receiving equipment' for these images is in the creature's waist.*

SUNGLASSES FOR A BIRD  Sea birds such as gulls, terns and skuas have built-in sunglasses. The retinas of these birds contain minute droplets of reddish oil which act in much the same way as holding a sheet of red translucent plastic in front of the eyes. The droplets' effect is to screen out much of the blue light before it reaches the light-sensitive cells in the retina, and so to cut down the glare from the sea and sky.

THESE FEET ARE MADE FOR TASTING  Although taste is usually associated with the mouth, blowflies can detect sugars through their feet. The flies' feet are covered with special sweet-sensitive taste buds, enabling them to detect traces of sugar millions of times more efficiently than the human tongue.

*Unlike most birds, which hunt by sight or hearing, the flightless New Zealand kiwi uses smell to find its food. The kiwi has its nostrils at the tip of its 150mm (6in) beak, the only bird that does. It uses them to sniff out food at night, plunging its beak deep into rotten wood or the ground to find worms and grubs.*

THE VIRGIN AND THE GYPSY MOTH  Male gypsy moths are attracted by the scent of female moths as far as 11km (7 miles) away. At this distance there is little more than one molecule of scent in a cubic metre. The males detect the scent through feathery antennae, and by comparing the strength of the scent reaching

each antenna, they can home in on the source. In turn, the female moths have scent-producing glands at the end of the abdomen – and virgin moths send out a particularly alluring smell. Indeed, the smell is so potent that males can be attracted to an empty box which has once held a virgin.

PRECISION DRILLING  The ichneumon fly can hear and smell through its feet. The female of the species *Rhyssa persuasoria* runs up and down tree trunks, hunting the sound and scent of wood wasp larvae as they chew their way through the timber beneath the bark. When it finds one, the fly drills into the tree with its 40mm (1.5in) 'ovipositor' – or egg-laying duct. Then it lays an egg on the tunnelling larva, which later serves as food for the fly's offspring.

EYES FRONT . . . AND BACK *The South African wolf spider has a total of eight eyes, allowing it to see in all directions at once. Two of the front eyes – the larger ones here – are better developed than the rest, allowing the spider to judge the range accurately when it pounces on prey.*

# Animal behaviour

SILENT SERENADE  The huge left pincer of the tropical fiddler crab may look terrifying to an enemy – but its only job is to attract a mate; it is not even used for feeding. At breeding time, the colourful male crab pumps the giant claw back and forth in a sawing motion similar to that of a violinist.

This silent serenade mesmerises the plain female crab, which has no big claw. She then sidles into the male's burrow to mate.

TOUCH-ME-NOT LOVERS  In spring, breeding newts dive into a pond for a whirling courtship dance in which they mate, often without touching one another. The male, his colours brightened and with a prominent new crest along his back and tail, dances around the female, luring her to the bottom of the pond. There, the male deposits his sperm on the pond bed, and the female squats on it to fertilise her eggs.

FAN DANCER  The strutting peacock with its spectacular train, or tail display, is one of the most colourful of courting males. When seeking a mate, the bird, a native of southern India and Sri Lanka, lifts and opens its train to form a fan often spanning 1.5m (5ft).

It then calls in a loud, rasping shriek to draw the attention of the demurely plumaged females to its spectacular display of feathers.

REMOTE-CONTROL MATING  Two nights of mass courtship make up the breeding season of the palolo worms, little marine bristleworms that live in Pacific coral reefs. Yet the mating takes place without the worms themselves being present. On two nights of the last quarter of the October/November moon, the rear end of each worm, called an epitoke, becomes detached from the body and surges to the surface with millions of other epitokes.

At sunrise the epitokes release sperms and eggs into the sea to unite. The worms themselves remain in their coral homes throughout.

A similar palolo worm native to the Caribbean swarms in the same way during the first and third quarters of the July moon.

---

*The madness of March hares, chasing, leaping and boxing each other in the spring, is not as silly as it looks. It is all part of the animals' courtship game, with the show-off males trying to impress the females.*

---

PERFECT TIMING  Fireflies flash their lights to one another in precise and split-second codes to attract a mate of the same species. The male black firefly of the United States flashes every 5.7 seconds when flying. When he gets within 3 – 4m (10 – 14ft) of a female on the ground, she flashes back exactly 2.1 seconds after him. In another family, the male gives two flashes 1.5 seconds apart and the female responds one second later. Some males flash orange when in flight and green on the ground.

FALLING FOR EACH OTHER  There can be no more unusual courtship than the acrobatic, mid-air love dance of the great grey slug of Western Europe. A pair of these astonishing hermaphrodites will circle each other on a tree branch or a wall for up to 90 minutes, forming as they move a mass of sticky mucus. Sud-

denly, they launch themselves into space and hang, locked together and suspended by the sticky rope they have made.

There they will mate, each fertilising the other, in a slow process that can take from seven to 24 hours. Then one will climb back up the rope; the other will drop to the ground.

---

*The male mole cricket sends out his mating call in hi-fi stereo through home-made speakers. He burrows out an underground nest with a twin-tunnel entrance. Then he sits underground at the junction of the tunnels and, by rubbing his forewings together, emits a trilling song that is amplified by the tunnel shape and attracts passing females.*

---

ALL TOGETHER, BOYS!  Contrary to the children's rhyme, the frog rarely does a-wooing go. Instead, the male normally sits down with other males in a stream or pond, blows up his cheeks, and croaks. The sound guides female frogs to the trysting spot. Many frogs call in chorus, and some species even appear to have a chorus master who leads the croaking.

HONEYMOON SUITE  The bowerbird of Australia and New Guinea does not call out for a mate. Instead the male lures the female with an elaborate and distinctive work of art: a bower of love. These hut-like structures are erected in small clearings. Coloured with a mixture of plant juices and saliva, they are decorated with flowers or berries, shells or bones, and sometimes even surrounded with gardens of moss, twigs and stones.

Each species of bird builds its own particular pattern of bower. Some bowers have thousands of twigs and hundreds of decorations. Many take days to build.

After mating, most bowerbird species abandon their honeymoon suites. The hens fly off to build new nests in the trees, where they lay their eggs.

---

*The female praying mantis is such a ruthless huntress that she often eats her smaller partner immediately after mating. Sometimes she even begins her meal while they are still copulating.*

---

MASTER WEAVERS  Weaver birds do not learn about nest-building from their parents. The knowledge is part of their genetic blueprint. In southern Africa, the lesser masked weaver's nest is a complex protective structure of twisted and knotted vegetation, ball-shaped and suspended from the end of a branch or a twig. Its construction is something of an architectural phenomenon: the male bird gathers strands of grass and, by threading, pulling and twisting, knits them into a tough, tightly knotted, enclosed basket, almost impervious to predators.

To find out how much of this ability was instinctive, a team of scientists reared five generations of the weavers in captivity, denying nesting materials to all but the fifth generation. The results of the experiment were reported in France in 1974. The great-great-grandchildren of the original birds were given the necessary grass and twigs and, despite never having seen a weaver's nest nor having had any contact with any bird who had, they built a perfect home.

THE GENTLEMAN WAS A LADY  One of the most unusual of all male-female relationships exists among the brightly coloured cleaner wrasse, *Labroides dimidiatus*, of Australia's Great Barrier Reef. The pugnacious 100mm (4in) male fish vigorously defends his territory – and his harem of up to 16 females – against other male cleaners. But this is not easy, since in addition to patrolling his borders he must keep his females in line. One of these females usually dominates the others, and the male is particularly aggressive towards her, since she threatens to assume his dominance – and even his gender.

Only hours after his death, in fact, she begins to take on his role. She/he now presides over the harem and assumes characteristic male behaviour. Within a month, the dominant female actually becomes a fully functional male. In turn, the death of this new male will result in the next dominant female taking over the male role – and so on – in a never-ending feminine quest to reach the top of the hierarchy.

FLIGHT OF THE CUCKOO  The young of the shining bronze cuckoo, abandoned by their parents and with no adult bird to guide them, set out each March on a 6400km (4000 miles) migration from their breeding grounds in New Zealand. They accurately follow the path of the parent flock over 2000km (1250 miles) of

## SONG AND DANCE ROUTINES

Spectacular displays by animals and birds in their springtime courtship rituals are basically identification parades to ensure that each species mates only with its own kind. The songs and dances of the mating season help each to pick the right partner. Most birds and animals go into season as spring's longer days and extra sunshine trigger hormones which start ovulation in the female and sperm production in the male. Alerted to one another by mating calls, males and females then go into recognition rituals that can sometimes take days to complete.

Strong elements of aggression are involved. A male may make instinctive threatening gestures when a female, summoned by his call, enters his territory, and he is placated only by a correct defensive response. Many animals cannot mate until they have been stimulated by the correct sequence of call, colour and movement. A female rock dove, for instance, does not ovulate until she has seen her mate's courtship ritual. By this elaborate, inborn behaviour, nature makes it probable that the female of the species will not waste her brief, often only once-a-year, period of fertility by mating with the wrong partner.

FACTS ABOUT
ANIMALS & PLANTS

LEAPING FOR LOVE *Crested cranes go through an elaborate dance as a prelude to mating. The ritual starts with the birds stretching out their wings and strutting around each other. Often the performance reaches a climax with an ecstatic leap in the air. One species, the sandhill crane of North America, may jump as high as 6m (20ft).*

# Animal behaviour

open sea to Australia, then turn north to Papua New Guinea and the Bismarck Archipelago. One mistake could be fatal . . . the birds cannot swim.

THE LAW-BREAKER  The tiny, ruby-throated hummingbird apparently defies the laws of physics to propel its tiny body – a mere 3.5g (0.1oz) in weight – on a non-stop 800km (500 miles) flight from North America across the Gulf of Mexico to South America each autumn.

Metabolic tests suggest that the bird is simply too small to store enough energy for the task. But it does, and it flies back again in the spring.

---

*The minute animals that form the plankton in the upper reaches of the ocean waters migrate not horizontally, but vertically. They rise near the surface at night, then sink back down into deeper water by day. No reason has been found for the movement.*

---

THE SUN-SEEKER  The sun-loving Arctic tern makes the longest known migration . . . from the top of the world to the bottom and back. It lives its whole life where the day is longest, breeding in the almost unbroken daylight of the Arctic summer, then flying south with the sun to feed in the near endless day of the Antarctic summer. Each year its flying round trip covers about 35,000km (22,000 miles).

Flocks from Canada, Greenland and Iceland migrate along set routes down Europe and the African coast or along the Pacific coast of the Americas. They travel fast, too. One tern, ringed in Northumberland, England, on June 25, 1982, was caught 17,600km (11,000 miles) away in Melbourne, Australia, just 115 days later – having averaged almost 160km (100 miles) a day.

A DATE FOR THE BIRDS  Each year the short-tailed shearwaters which breed on islands in the Bass Strait between Australia and Tasmania make a five-month, 32,000km (20,000 miles) round tour of the Pacific coasts, visiting Japan, Alaska, Canada and Fiji. Unfailingly, they arrive back in the Bass Strait in the last few days of September.

They go off at once to feed, returning within a day or two of November 20 to begin breeding. Then, in mid-April the whole flock, young and old, sets out on its annual trip once more.

---

*Using their own wing power, many species of butterflies can travel up to 1000km (600 miles) without a refuelling stop. Some have even been known to fly right across the Atlantic Ocean from North America to Europe, backed by the driving force of the prevailing westerly winds.*

---

MASS TRANSFORMATION  The origin of the swarming brown locusts, which devastate all the vegetation in their path, was a mystery for centuries. Then, in 1921, British scientist Sir Boris Uvarov discovered that the pest was nothing more than an altered version of a green grasshopper, common in Africa and Asia. The insect changes its colour and character when population explosions cause overcrowding. The transformed insects then migrate in a swarm to find another home. In 1958, one plague of locusts in Somalia was so large that it covered 1000km² (390 square miles).

JOURNEY TO THE UNKNOWN  Each autumn monarch butterflies, born in the warm summers on North America's eastern coast, fly off on a 3200km (2000 miles) journey into the past. With no guide, and no apparent means of finding their way, they go south, precisely to the spot where their grandparents – not their parents – wintered 12 months before.

Somehow, an inborn migratory instinct is handed down through generations which never make the journey. In summer, the monarch lives for about six weeks, so three or four generations span the northern warm season. Only the grandchildren or great-grand-

children survive to migrate as the autumn cold closes in. The butterflies' main winter quarters, 3000m (10,000ft) up in the Mexican mountains, was discovered only in 1975. There, monarchs crowd in their millions into 15 separate sites, none larger than 4 hectares (10 acres). In spring, they head north again to another summer of frenzied breeding.

MUNCHERS ON THE MARCH  Like restless nomads, the voracious soldier ants of the Americas march across land in almost perpetual migration. Workers carry eggs, larvae and food, flanked by soldier guards, which also protect the queen. At night the whole army bivouacs in a huge ball formed of their own bodies, with the queen, eggs and young in the centre. For up to three weeks the ants may stay in one camp, sending out each day foragers which will pick clean the surroundings, eating up plants, vermin, spiders, even household pets or animals that get in their way. Then the ants will send out scouts to find a new site – and the whole army goes on the march again.

DYING FOR A MEAL  The panic migrations of the lemmings, small vole-like animals of northern Norway, are triggered by a hiccup in the food chain. In years of abundance, the female will have up to four litters of eight young in a season instead of the usual two litters of five. The resultant population explosion turns the food glut into a shortage.

Huge groups of lemmings then dash off in search of food such as roots and grasses. Most of them die on the journey. Heedless of danger, they plunge over cliffs into rivers, and some of them even dive into the sea in their uncontrolled drive to find food.

## WHY ANIMALS MIGRATE

Food and climate are the great driving forces of migration. Swallows and martins, breeding under the eaves in the European spring, must be back in North Africa before the winter frosts which would kill both them and the insects they feed on. Many whales feed in the rich polar seas and swim to the warmer waters of the tropics to breed. Elk, moose and caribou wander in huge circles seeking sparse forage.

For most migrating animals to stay put would mean to die. But some move without apparent reason: the Arctic tern for instance. Some scientists have speculated that the migratory patterns of some sea creatures may have been established as foraging expeditions when the continents were closer together – and that the enormous distances now travelled by salmon and eels, for example, may have grown imperceptibly from one generation to the next as the oceans widened.

## HOW THEY DO IT

It is still not certain how most animals, particularly birds, find their way on long migrations. Experiments have shown that many birds use the sun to navigate, making automatic allowances for its movement across the sky. The pecten, a frond-like projection from the retina of a bird's eye, is believed to be the sextant that guides them through a clear sky . . . but overcast weather does not stop them reaching their destinations.

In 1977, Charles Walcott, a biologist at New York State University, discovered deposits of magnetic iron oxide in the skulls of pigeons and other migratory birds. It seems that this is used as a built-in compass to give the bird a picture of the Earth's magnetic field, by which it can navigate.

But how some first-year birds find their way unaided to ancestral migratory quarters is still a mystery, probably locked up in the genetic code.

FACTS ABOUT ANIMALS & PLANTS

MASSED MONARCHS *Huddled for warmth, monarch butterflies cling to a tree after one of their mysterious migrations. Millions congregate each winter in a few remote sites – so many that their weight bends tree branches to form a domed blanket, protecting them from frosts which could otherwise be fatal.*

# Animal behaviour

HOW SAVING SHELLFISH KILLED THE SEA COW  In the 18th century, American, Russian and Canadian hunters on the Pacific coast of North America reduced the sea otter population almost to extinction in order both to collect the otters' valuable pelts and to preserve stocks of shellfish, the otters' staple diet.

Because of the hunting, though, there was an increase in the number of sea urchins, on which the otter also fed. As a result, urchins destroyed large areas of kelp (seaweed) off the western North American coast. This in turn devastated the habitat of many animal species – including the Steller's sea cow, which relied on the kelp for food.

The adoption of a campaign to eliminate sea urchins and the introduction of legal protection for the sea otter in 1972 has started the regeneration of the kelp beds and the sea otter. But the change has come too late for the Steller's sea cow. The last of the species was seen in 1770.

THE SUN NEVER SETS . . . ON KITTY  The 19th-century British biologist Thomas Huxley – grandfather of Brave New World author Aldous Huxley – once calculated, only half in jest, that the British empire owed its power to the love of elderly spinsters for pet cats. His argument – which extended one used in all seriousness by Charles Darwin, the founder of the theory of evolution, and which illustrates the complex interconnections between different forms of life – went like this.

Because elderly spinsters liked cats, they often kept them as pets. Pet cats kept down the numbers of field mice around towns and villages, preventing them from eating bees, the only insects which can pollinate red clover. As a result, red clover grew abundantly in the pastures around farming villages and provided British cattle with a highly nutritious diet. The plentiful supply of high-quality beef kept British sailors strong and healthy, thus improving the fighting quality of the Royal Navy – which guarded and extended the British empire around the world.

*In spring, many algae breed rapidly as a result of warmer temperatures, abundant food and little competition. This occurs in all parts of the world. But the population increase can be catastrophic if it involves certain types of dinoflagellates, because these organisms are poisonous to animals. Like some Biblical plague, they can turn the water into a blood-coloured soup, with as many as 6000 dinoflagellates in a single drop. Fish and other animals who swim through the red tide die an agonising death in their millions as the poison swamps their body's defences and paralyses their nervous system.*

A PLAGUE OF RABBITS  Homesick settlers in Australia took a small shipment of rabbits from Britain in the mid-19th century – and triggered one of the world's most devastating ecological disasters. Two dozen of the rabbits were released on a livestock farm near Geelong in Victoria in 1859. Within three years, they had outgrown the ranch and for the next two decades they spread out across the southern part of the continent, advancing at the rate of 110km (70 miles) a year. By the end of the century, the population had reached plague proportions. Native shrubs and grasses which had provided lush forage for sheep – then the mainstay of the Australian economy – were wiped out on a huge scale.

Thousands of square kilometres of pastureland were turned into dustbowls, contributing to the extinction of some other browsing species, such as Australia's jumping mice and rabbit-bandicoots. In all, about 5 per cent of the marsupial species of Australia and Tasmania were wiped out.

Ranchers who tried to halt the rabbits' advance were swamped. Some tried to set up fences to keep them away. But the rabbits came in such numbers that, as one rancher put it, 'the whole ground seemed to move'. When the rabbits reached a fence, those behind simply clambered on top of the ones in front, smothering them but creating within minutes a ramp of bodies that enabled the rest to swarm over the top of the fence.

The plague was halted only in 1950 when a North American disease, myxomatosis, was introduced. And as the rabbits died, the grasses returned.

## THE CHAINS OF LIFE

All life on Earth is bound together in complex associations between what is eaten and what eats it – between the hunter and the hunted. Scientists call these associations food chains or food webs. All food webs start with plants, the primary food producers which use the sun's energy to convert chemicals into food. Plants are eaten by primary consumers: plant-eating animals such as cattle. They are in turn eaten by secondary consumers: meat-eaters such as lions and man. At each level waste material, such as dung and the remains of dead organisms, is broken down by bacteria and fungi, and returned to the soil to be absorbed by plants again.

The extermination of a single species in any web can drastically affect all the others. When myxomatosis was introduced into England in 1954 to kill rabbits, for instance, weeds previously eaten by rabbits spread rapidly and mice and beetle populations dropped sharply because foxes began to eat more of them in the absence of rabbits.

### Food, meat and energy

At each link in a food chain, most of the energy contained in the food is used to keep the eater alive and active. Only a small proportion is converted to extra meat for the next predator in the chain. Some animals, such as the pig, convert as much as 20 per cent of their food to meat, but most convert only about 10 per cent. So, for a man to gain 1kg (2.2lb) in body weight, he would need to eat 10kg (22lb) of food such as, say, fish. To gain that much weight, the fish would have to eat 100kg (220lb) of animal plankton, which in turn would need to eat a tonne of plant plankton, the primary producers.

The only way to make this more efficient – and thus to make a given area of the Earth support more people – is to shorten the food chain by cutting out some of the intermediate links. If fish, say, ate plant plankton directly and animal plankton were left out of the food chain, a given quantity of plant plankton could support about ten times as many fish – and thus ten times as many people – as at present. Man can eat plant foods himself, but most are very low in vital protein. One exception, however, is soya beans, half of whose weight is protein – making them one of the richest protein sources of any food.

# THE ARTS & ENTERTAINMENT

# Architecture

## BEND OF HUMILITY

Many Gothic cathedrals, including Notre Dame in Paris, have a slight kink in their main axis so that the nave does not exactly line up with the centre of the altar. According to some scholars, medieval cathedral architects built the kink in deliberately as a humble expression of man's imperfections, and as a reminder to worshippers that God alone was perfect. Other researchers, however, believe that the kinks may simply be the result of mistakes by builders.

## GHOST TRAP

Sarah Winchester, 19th-century heiress of the USA's Winchester rifle company, built an enormous house – as a ghost trap. Doors opened onto blank walls and staircases led nowhere. All were designed to confuse the ghosts that she believed were haunting her. Her obsession began after the deaths of her husband – the son of the company's founder, Oliver Winchester – in 1881, and of her month-old baby daughter, Annie. Sarah visited a spiritualist with the aim of trying to make contact with her lost family – and was told that she was being haunted by the ghosts of countless rifle victims.

In 1884 she began to extend her mansion in San José, California, adding a wild profusion of rooms, doors, windows and staircases in the belief that the ghosts would get lost in the building's maze. By the time she died, in 1922, the house had spread over 2.5 hectares (6 acres) and contained a total of some 160 rooms, 2000 doors and 10,000 windows.

## PALE REFLECTIONS

To modern eyes, ancient Greek temples derive much of their grandeur from their simple lines, their disciplined elegance and the white austerity of their stones. But that was not the way the Greeks built them.

Scholars now know that originally the temples were almost gaudy. Brilliant paints – blues, reds and yellows – were splashed on many of the stones, turning columns, friezes, roofs and sculptures into a riot of colour. There was nothing restrained about the use of the colour. Since the pigments were expensive, their lavish use was simply an ostentatious display of wealth. The temples' present whiteness is the result of time – and the bleaching, paint-flaking power of the Mediterranean sun.

## BEAUTY AND THE TARTAR BEAST

The exquisite dome that crowns the Taj Mahal in India owes its shape to one of the most blood-soaked leaders in history. In 1401 Tamerlane, a 14th-century Tartar warlord who was responsible for hundreds of thousands of deaths, burnt the great mosque in Damascus, Syria, to the ground. Inside it at the time, according to a contemporary historian, were 30,000 women, children, priests and refugees.

Far from wishing to forget this act of carnage, he had the unique bulging dome of the mosque copied at Samarkand for his own magnificent tomb, the Gur Amir, parts of which still stand.

From there the style spread northwards (where it eventually became the onion shape characteristic of the domes on Russian churches as well as on the palace of the Kremlin) and southwards across the Himalayas. It caught on in India after one of Tamer-lane's descendants, Baber, overthrew the Sultan of Delhi in 1526 and founded the Mughal empire. It was one of Baber's dynasty, Shah Jahan, who built the Taj Mahal. The shape of the glittering white dome, completed in 1648, derives directly from the mosque that Shah Jahan's ancestor had reduced to a blackened heap nearly 250 years before.

## REACH FOR THE SKY

On a clear day a visitor to the observation platform at the top of the Empire State Building in New York can see up to 130km (80 miles) away. For 40 years the 102-storey Empire State was the tallest building in the world at 381m (1250ft). It was surpassed in 1971 by the twin-tower World Trade Centre, also in New York, which is 415m (1362ft) tall.

Today the tallest building in the world is the Sears Tower in Chicago (built in 1973 – 4), which has 110 storeys and rises 443m (1454ft).

Thirty people have leapt to their deaths from the Empire State Building since it opened in 1931. But extraordinarily, at least two would-be suicides have survived. On December 22, 1977, a 26-year-old man named Thomas Helms jumped from the observatory on the 86th floor. But because he did not jump far enough outwards from the building, he fell only about 6m (20ft) onto a 1m (3.3ft) wide ledge on the 85th floor. Although he was knocked unconscious for half an hour by the fall, he was not seriously hurt.

On December 2, 1979, 29-year-old Elvita Adams jumped from the same level. She seems to have jumped further outwards, but was saved by a strong gust of wind which blew her onto the same ledge. She escaped with a broken hip.

## GOING UP

Modern cities owe their characteristic skyline, bristling with skyscrapers, to the invention of the lift. In 1854, at the Crystal Palace Exposition in New York, Elisha Otis, a mechanic, demonstrated his new invention – a safe lift. Otis had himself hauled up with some freight and as a stunned crowd watched the lift rope was cut. Otis and the freight remained motionless – protected by an automatic locking system. Not until three years later was the first passenger lift installed in a five-storey Broadway china shop.

From then on, tall blocks sprouted where, before, people's reluctance to climb stairs had restricted most buildings to fewer than six storeys. Modern lifts, which work fast enough to make passengers' ears pop with the changing air pressure, can reach the top of even the tallest building in less than a minute. The world's fastest passenger lift is in Tokyo. Installed in a 60-storey block in 1978, it operates at speeds of up to 36km/h (22mph).

## SUPER HANGAR

The most capacious building in the world is the Vehicle Assembly Building at Cape Canaveral in Florida. Built between 1963 and 1965 for the construction of Apollo spacecraft and Saturn V moon rockets, it encloses a volume of 3,666,500m³ (129,482,000 cubic feet). St Peter's in Rome would fit inside with plenty of room to spare. The steel-frame building is 160m (525ft) high, 218m (716ft) long and 158m (518ft) wide. The four doors are the largest in the world; each is 140m (460ft) high.

MICHELANGELO'S DOME *The great dome of St Peter's in Rome, spanning 42m (137ft), was largely designed by the Italian artist Michelangelo. The base is prevented from splaying outwards under the dome's weight by an encircling iron chain. This revolutionary idea, which did away with the need for massive buttressing, was first used by the architect Filippo Brunelleschi (1377–1446) on the dome of Florence Cathedral. Brunelleschi won a competition in 1417 to design the dome by a trick. Rather than reveal his plans in advance, he persuaded the judges to decide by asking the competitors to stand an egg on its end on smooth marble. After the others failed, Brunelleschi, in an early example of lateral thinking, neatly smashed one end, then stood the egg upright easily.*

## PILLARS OF FOLLY

Sir Christopher Wren (1632–1723), the man who designed the vast dome of St Paul's Cathedral in London, was once ordered to modify a much smaller roof. In 1689, when Wren designed the interior of Windsor Guildhall, he built a ceiling supported by pillars. But after the city fathers inspected the finished work, they decided that the ceiling would not stay up as it was – and ordered Wren to add more pillars.

Wren did not believe that the ceiling needed any extra support, so he put up four sham pillars that serve no structural purpose at all. They do not even reach the ceiling. The illusion fooled the city fathers, though. The phoney pillars still stand – and Wren's 300-year-old ceiling shows no signs of falling down.

# ARCHITECTURE DOWN THE AGES

Western architecture traces its descent from the major public buildings of ancient Greece. Some earlier structures were built with an eye for proportion and striking decoration, but they had little impact on the evolution of building design.

The chart shows the significant periods of Western architectural development, identifies the distinctive features and types of building, and lists some major surviving examples, along with the dates they were built. Each period had its own particular building needs, levels of building knowledge and skill, and range of available material and labour. These factors led to particular 'styles' of architecture such as Norman, Gothic or Baroque. But buildings designed in the styles of a particular period can be found in places far away from the source of the style. Such buildings are often interpretations or revivals of earlier architectural forms and have been given special local names such as Venetian Gothic.

**GREEK (750–30 BC)** Main types of building: temples; stoas, or covered colonnades; theatres and amphitheatres. Temples were built in marble and limestone, replacing earlier timber temples but retaining the column-and-beam construction of the wooden originals. Temples had painted decoration and low-pitched wooden roofs. Columns were decorated with ornamental capitals – the part at the top of the column – in one of three designs known as 'orders'. The simplest order – Doric – consisted of columns with plain, moulded capitals and no base. Ionic capitals were decorated with a pair of scrolls (known as volutes). Corinthian capitals were decorated with an inverted bell-shaped arrangement of acanthus leaves.
***Examples*** Parthenon, Athens (447–432 BC); Erectheum, Athens (421–405 BC); Theatre, Epidaurus (350 BC).

*Doric*   *Ionic*   *Corinthian*

**ROMAN (100 BC–AD 365)** Widescale building programme included temples, baths, basilicas, theatres, amphitheatres, bridges, aqueducts and triumphal arches. Brick, stone and concrete replaced marble and limestone. Romans developed the arch, and devised two other classical styles for columns, adding to the three used in ancient Greece: the Tuscan order was a plain style derived from the Greek Doric order; and the Composite order combined Ionic scrolls with Corinthian leaves.
***Examples*** Pont du Gard, Nîmes, France (AD 14); Colosseum, Rome (AD 70–82); Baths of Caracalla, Rome (AD 211–17).

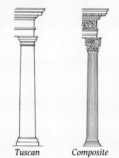

*Tuscan*   *Composite*

**BYZANTINE (330–1453)** Combination of Roman and Eastern influences characterised chiefly by the dome. Exterior surfaces were plastered. Interior surfaces were flat, but brightly coloured and elaborately decorated with marble, mosaic, or frescoes.
***Examples*** San Vitale, Ravenna, Italy (526–47); Hagia Sophia, Istanbul, Turkey (532–7); St Mark's, Venice, Italy (1063–85).

*San Vitale*

**ROMANESQUE (about 850–about 1200)** Roman semicircular vaults and arches were reintroduced in stone to build churches and defensive keeps. Massive piers and thick walls were used. Ornament was sparse and geometrical. Also known as Norman architecture from early examples in Normandy.
***Examples*** Tower of London Keep (1086–97); Durham Cathedral nave, England (1093–1130); Worms Cathedral, West Germany (11th and 12th centuries); St Sernin Cathedral, France (1080–96).

*Worms Cathedral*

**GOTHIC (about 1150–about 1550)** Pointed arch and ribbed vault replaced semicircular Romanesque forms. Strong vertical lines, most noticeable in churches. Pillars were more slender. 'Flying buttresses' were used to support walls of high naves on the outside. Windows were large and divided into panels by slim stonework tracery.

In England the Gothic period is divided into three stages:
**Early English (1189–1307)**
Pointed arches, slim lancet windows, simple tracery.
**Decorated (1307–77)**
Elaborate, geometrical tracery and carving, S-shaped 'ogee' curve often used in windows and doors.
**Perpendicular (1377–1485)**
Characterised by large windows broken into more rectangular, round-topped panels.
***Examples*** Notre Dame, Paris (1163–1250); Lincoln Cathedral, England (1192–1235); Reims Cathedral, France (1211–90); Doge's Palace, Venice (1309–1424); Milan Cathedral, Italy (about 1385–1485); Westminster Hall, London (1397–9); King's College Chapel, Cambridge, England (1446–1515).

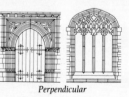

*Early English*

*Decorated*

*Perpendicular*

**RENAISSANCE (about 1420–about 1900)** Revival and adaptation of Greek and Roman designs. Gothic vaulting and spires were replaced by domes, columns and 'pilasters' – rectangular columns usually embedded in a wall.
***Examples*** St Peter's, Rome (1506–1626); Château de Chambord, France (1519–47); Escorial, Madrid (1559–84); Longleat House, England (1567–80).

*Window (left) and column detail (above) on the Château de Chambord.*

**BAROQUE (about 1600–about 1800)** Buildings designed with flowing curves and extravagantly decorated with plasterwork, sculptures, gilt, paint and marble. Style known as rococo is similar to baroque but generally lighter and less formal; rococo decoration often includes a shell motif.
*Examples* Versailles, France (1661–1756); St Paul's Cathedral, London (1675–1710); Vierzehnheiligen Church, Bavaria, West Germany (1744–72).

*A shell motif tops a detail from a rococo panel at Versailles.*

*St Paul's Cathedral*

## PERIOD OF REVIVALS
**Neo-Classical (about 1775–about 1900)** Revival of Greek and Roman styles of architecture. Generally solid and severe with restrained decoration. In England, this period includes Georgian architecture.
*Examples* Petit Trianon, Versailles, France (1762–8); United States Capitol, Washington (1793–1867); British Museum, London (1823–47); St George's Hall, Liverpool, England (1839–54); Houses of Parliament, Melbourne, Australia (1856–80).

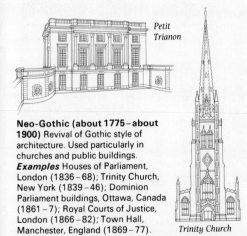

*Petit Trianon*

**Neo-Gothic (about 1775–about 1900)** Revival of Gothic style of architecture. Used particularly in churches and public buildings.
*Examples* Houses of Parliament, London (1836–68); Trinity Church, New York (1839–46); Dominion Parliament buildings, Ottawa, Canada (1861–7); Royal Courts of Justice, London (1866–82); Town Hall, Manchester, England (1869–77).

*Trinity Church*

## INDUSTRIAL REVOLUTION (about 1850–about 1914)
Multi-storey factories and huge glass-covered areas such as markets, railway stations and greenhouses. Progressive use of wrought iron, cast iron, steel and reinforced concrete.
*Examples* Palm House, Kew Gardens, London (1844–8); St Pancras Station, London (1868–74); Carson, Pirie and Scott Store, Chicago, USA (1899–1904).

*Palm House, Kew Gardens*

**ART NOUVEAU (about 1875–about 1914)** Slender proportions and long undulating lines. Designs often asymmetrical. Decorative shapes and ornamental motifs derived from natural forms, such as flowers, flames and waves, and from geometrical patterns.
*Examples* Sagrada Familia Cathedral, Barcelona, Spain (begun 1883); Samaritaine Store, Paris (1905); School of Art, Glasgow, Scotland (1907–9).

*Sagrada Familia Cathedral*

**ART DECO (1920s and 1930s)** Bold geometrical style with unfunctional decoration inspired by tribal art and Egyptian motifs. Man-made materials such as glass, plastic and steel used.
*Examples* Chrysler Building, New York (1928–32); Broadcasting House, London (1932).

*Chrysler Building*

## MODERN ARCHITECTURE (1918–present day)
Design stems from needs, site, economics and new technology rather than stylistic revivals. Early modern buildings were usually rectangular with simple walls and windows. Steel and concrete frameworks and cores replaced load-bearing walls, allowing large areas of glass, often in horizontal bands, and open-plan interiors. A developed and refined version of this 'International Style' makes up much of modern architecture.
*Examples* Bauhaus Building, Dessau, East Germany (1925–8); Daily Express Building, London (1931); Falling Water, Pennsylvania, USA (1936); Unité d'Habitation, Marseilles (1947–52); Seagram Building, New York (1956–8).

*Bauhaus*

## POST-MODERNISM (about 1957–present day)
Reaction to the anonymous simplicity of much modern architecture. Use of variety of structural and decorative features intended to give a new richness and personality to buildings, whilst avoiding revivalism.
*Examples* Piazza d'Italia (which includes a lake in the shape of Italy), New Orleans, USA (1978); TVAM Building, Camden Lock, London (1981–2); AT and T Building, New York (1978–82).

*AT and T Building*

# Painting and sculpture

## MAJOR PAINTING STYLES

**Gothic** Christian art form which flourished between the 12th and 16th centuries. The stylised figures were usually shown clad in flowing drapery.

**Renaissance** Style adopted in Europe in the 15th and 16th centuries, and modelled on classical Greek and Roman styles.

**Baroque** Extravagant and highly decorative style. It was popular mainly in Catholic European countries from 1600 to 1720.

**Rococo** Florid 18th-century style of decoration using light colours, scrollwork and irregular curves.

**Pre-Raphaelite** Highly symbolic style adopted by group of mid-19th-century London artists – including Dante Gabriel Rossetti – who were inspired by the brightly coloured pictures produced in Italy before the time of the artist Raphael (1483 – 1520).

**Romanticism** Sensational or sentimental style, often using a mythological theme. Romanticism reached its peak in France in about 1830.

**Impressionism** Late 19th-century style used largely by French painters – including Claude Monet, Camille Pissarro, Auguste Renoir and Edgar Degas – who concentrated on the effects of light and pure colour.

**Post-impressionism** Turn-of-the-century style which aimed to show the spiritual significance of objects. Its main exponent was the Frenchman Paul Cézanne (1839 – 1906).

**Expressionism** 20th-century style of artists – including the Norwegian Edvard Munch (1863 – 1944) – who expressed their emotional themes through distorted shapes and violent colours.

**Fauvism** Style of painting featuring distorted shapes, violent colours and disregard of perspective. The French painter Henri Matisse (1869 – 1954) was the leader of the school – whose members were known as Les Fauves, meaning 'The wild beasts'.

**Cubism** Geometrical style of drawing invented by the French painter Georges Braque (1882 – 1963) and the Spaniard Pablo Picasso (1881 – 1973). It emphasised the mind's perception of an object, rather than attempting to reproduce actual appearance.

**Abstract art** Non-representational styles of the 20th century. There are two major categories: 'pure' abstract art as in the geometrical works of the Dutch painter Piet Mondrian; and highly subjective treatments of recognisable objects, such as the Cubist canvases of Braque and the sculpture of Henry Moore.

**Realism** Works that show scenes as they really are – and which often have a social or political message.

**Surrealism** French movement dating from the 1920s, which uses dream-like effects to explore the subconscious mind. Major exponents include Salvador Dali (1904 – ) and René Magritte (1898 – 1967).

**Action painting** Modern technique of splashing, throwing and pouring paint on canvas – and allowing it to form its own shapes. It was invented by the US painter Jackson Pollock (1912 – 56).

**Pop art** Style which emerged in the late 1950s and early 1960s. It made use of comic strip cartoons, advertisements and images of film stars (for instance, Marilyn Monroe), often enormously enlarged and garishly painted. Its main exponents included David Hockney (1937 – ), Eduardo Paolozzi (1924 – ), Andy Warhol (1930 – ) and Roy Lichtenstein (1923 – ).

### TREASURE OF THE GOLDEN HOUSE

A vast treasure palace which Nero built in the centre of Rome after the great fire of AD 64 inspired an artistic style 1500 years later in Italy. The palace – called the Golden House because its façade was reputedly clad in gold – was designed by Nero's court painter Famulus. But after Nero's fall from power and his suicide in AD 68, much of the palace was demolished and built over. Little survived except for some forgotten underground rooms.

When these buried rooms were rediscovered in the late 15th century, their florid style of decoration – using a combination of human and animal forms, flowers, foliage and shells – came to be called 'grotesque', from the Italian *grotta* or 'cave'. The style influenced a number of Italian artists – including Raphael – who were let down into the rubble-strewn apartments by rope. Raphael, like his fellow painters, left his own mark on the Golden House. He scratched his signature on one of the ceilings.

### DESTITUTE IN HAARLEM

Despite receiving many well-paid commissions, the Dutch painter Frans Hals was rarely out of financial trouble. When his first wife died in 1615 she was buried in a pauper's grave, and Hals was twice taken

PORTRAITS OF THE ARTIST *In almost 100 ruthlessly honest self-portraits, the Dutch painter Rembrandt van Rijn (1606 – 69) created a pictorial chronicle of his life – from early success to lonely and bitter old age. The three portraits here show him at the age of 23 (above), in fancy dress about five years later (centre). and as a disillusioned man of nearly 60 (right).*

to court for failing to maintain his children. He was also sued for not paying local tradesmen. In 1617 he married an illiterate young woman, Elisabeth Reyniers, who gave birth to a daughter nine days later. She subsequently had eight more children, and added to her husband's problems by being brought before Dutch magistrates several times for brawling.

In his last years Hals – who died in 1666 – was destitute and the city council of Haarlem gave him money for bread and fuel. However, he spent most of his annual allowance on alcohol and was said to have been drunk every night. Despite his troubles, he created in 1624 one of the world's most famous portraits of cheerfulness: *The Laughing Cavalier*.

### THE DOME THAT IS NOT THERE
Andrea Pozzo's most remarkable artistic achievement – a spectacular but 'non-existent' dome – arose from a financial crisis during the building of the church of St Ignazio in Rome. The church is dedicated to the founder of the Jesuits – of which Pozzo was a lay brother – and it was meant to have the biggest dome in Rome after that of St Peter's. The building was completed but for the dome when money ran out, and in 1691 Pozzo – who was famed for his illusionist work – was called in.

A master of perspective, he painted a dome on the flat ceiling of the church. Seen from the church's entrance and nave, the dome appeared to be real and unsuspecting visitors stopped to admire it.

Pozzo's dome was meant originally to be only a temporary measure until money was raised to build a real dome. But the dome that did not exist became

more famous than many that do. And so it remained. Pozzo's illusory dome can still be seen today, together with his impressive fresco the *Triumph of St Ignazio* which covers the nave.

Pozzo's other major achievement was his influential textbook, *Perspective for Painters and Architects*, published between 1693 and 1700. It was translated into several languages including English, and the 18th-century portrait painter Sir Joshua Reynolds said that it inspired him to become an artist. In 1737, 26 years after Pozzo's death, the Jesuits even translated the book into Chinese.

### SEVENTY PICTURES IN SEVENTY DAYS
Although his canvases now fetch prices of more than £100,000 each, the 19th-century Dutch painter Vincent van Gogh made little money out of painting during his lifetime. But this did not affect his prolific output. In one 15-month period in Arles, in southeast France, from 1888 to 1889, he produced over 200 pictures. And, in a feverish burst of creativity, he painted a picture a day in the last 70 days of his life.

The son of a pastor, he was by turn a missionary in a Belgian coalmining district, a tramp and then a painter of genius whose work was unwanted. Van Gogh's frustration and anger turned to insanity. After one particularly violent quarrel with his friend and fellow artist Paul Gauguin, during which he threatened Gauguin with a razor, he cut off his own right ear and sent it to a cousin with whom he was in love. In 1889 he became a voluntary inmate of the asylum of St Remy near Arles. His mental condition seemed to improve and in May 1890 he went to live

FAMILY TRAGEDY *In 1634 – about the time this portrait was painted – Rembrandt married Saskia van Uylenburch and set up home with her in Amsterdam. The marriage was a happy one. But three of their children died in infancy, and in 1642, the year Rembrandt painted his masterpiece, The Night Watch, Saskia died soon after their fourth child was born.*

DOGGED BY DISASTER *After Saskia's death, nothing went right for Rembrandt. A love affair with his son's nurse ended in the courts in 1649. In 1657, his house and furniture were seized when he was made bankrupt. His second common-law wife died in 1663, about three years before this last, sad portrait, and his only son, Titus, died in 1668. Rembrandt died a year later.*

under medical supervision near his brother Theo at Auvers-sur-Oise, an artist's colony north of Paris. But in July 1890 he became overwhelmed by depression and shot himself.

Six months later, Theo – who had financially supported Vincent for most of his creative life – became deeply depressed and died of what his doctor called 'overstrain and sorrow'. He left behind the 750 letters which Vincent had written to him, detailing the painter's artistic philosophy and aims and giving a vivid account of his mental turmoil.

### SUICIDE BID IN THE JUNGLE

In 1882 Paul Gauguin gave up his prosperous position as a Paris stockbroker to become a full-time professional painter. He broke with his family and spent the rest of his life travelling – first to Brittany, then to Martinique and Panama, and later to Arles, in southeast France, where he stayed with Vincent van Gogh. Seeking what he called 'the natural life', he made two visits to the South Pacific – and used the Polynesians and the islands for some of his finest paintings.

However, his canvases did not sell and on New Year's Eve 1897 – starving and ill – he went into the jungle in Tahiti and swallowed a large dose of arsenic. But his suicide attempt failed. After a short sleep, he agonisingly vomited most of the powder. The next morning he dragged himself back to the coast.

Gauguin remained in the South Seas and was in continual conflict with the civil and religious authorities because of his bohemian ways and his siding with the natives. His last years were dominated by sickness and poverty, and on his death in the Marquesas Islands in 1903 the island's French bishop wrote: 'The only noteworthy event here has been the sudden death of a contemptible individual named Gauguin, a reputed artist but an enemy of God and everything that is decent!' In 1980, one of Gauguin's oil paintings, *The Guitar Player*, painted in Tahiti in 1892, was sold at Sotheby's in London for £380,000.

### GENIUS IN A WHEELCHAIR

In 1912 the French Impressionist painter Pierre Auguste Renoir had to choose between walking again and painting. At the time he had been crippled by rheumatoid arthritis for six years and was confined to a wheelchair in his home in the South of France. He consulted an eminent physician who put him on a special diet to build up his strength. Four weeks later the 71-year-old painter was lifted from his chair and managed to struggle a few painful steps. Then, still standing, he turned to the doctor and said: 'I give up. It takes all my will-power and I would have none of it left for painting. And if I have to choose between walking and painting, I'd much rather paint.' He then sat down and never walked again.

But he did carry on painting. And with a brush tied to his misshapen hands he produced at least two masterpieces: *The Judgment of Paris* and *The Women with Hats*. He even took up sculpture, which he achieved by guiding an assistant's hands over the clay with a stick and telling him what to add and remove. By his death in 1919, Renoir had masterminded two of Europe's best-known and most acclaimed sculptures: his large *Venus* and *Woman Suckling her Baby*.

### THE LITTLE CRIPPLE

The Brazilian sculptor and architect Antonio Lisboa carried on working after he had lost the use of his arms and hands. After contracting an unknown but crippling disease in his mid-thirties, he worked with his hammer and chisel strapped to his arms. He was nicknamed *Aleijadinho*, meaning 'Little Cripple', and a granite form of rococo architecture is now called *Aleijadinho* after him. He was born in about 1738 and produced his masterpiece – 12 large stone figures known as *The Prophets* – between 1800 and 1805. The statues still stand today in the open air in the Brazilian town of Congonhas do Campo.

### STATUE THAT BECAME A GIBBET

The equestrian statue of the Roman emperor Marcus Aurelius – the largest bronze Roman sculpture in existence – was once used as a gibbet. Pope John XIII used it in AD 965 to hang a rebellious city prefect by his hair. It is the only Roman bronze equestrian work to survive from more than 20 that were still standing

BEWARE OF THE LEFT BANK Henri de Toulouse-Lautrec, famed for his vivid posters of Paris night life (below and below right) was left permanently stunted after breaking his legs as a child.

NAUGHTY NINETIES By the end of the 1890s, Lautrec was a broken man. He died in 1901 at the age of 37 – killed by acute alcoholism and syphilis.

# PAINTING TERMS: WHAT THEY MEAN

**Aquatint** Form of etching in which varying degrees of tone are produced by dipping the plate repeatedly into acid, covering different parts of the plate with varnish before each dipping.

**Cartoon** Full-size preparatory drawing for a painting.

**Chiaroscuro** Strong contrasts of light and shade in a painting.

**Diptych** Two-panelled hinged altarpiece.

**Engraving** Drawing by means of lines cut on blocks or plates of metal or wood. The lines retain the ink which is spread over the surface before printing. Paintings are traditionally reproduced in this way. Other engraving methods include drypoint, lino-cut, woodcut and etching.

**Etching** Form of engraving in which a resin-coated copper plate is drawn on with a needle and then dipped in acid. The acid eats into the metal through the lines in the resin; thereafter the printing process is the same as in line engraving.

**Gouache** Opaque watercolour paint, in which the colours are mixed with a white base.

**Impasto** Thickly applied oil paint.

**Intaglio** Gem with carving sunk into the surface, as in a signet ring.

**Lithograph** Picture reproduced from a design marked out with an oily crayon on a flat stone. When the design is printed, the stone is dampened. The greasy lines absorb ink and the wet areas repel it.

**Mezzotint** Engraving process, popular during the 18th century, in which the plate is first scored with a network of dots. The dots are later smoothed out to give a variety of tonal effects.

**Mural** Decorative painting applied directly to a wall.

**Plastic** In a painting, conveying a sculptured effect through the modelling and lines of the figures.

**Still life** Study of an arrangement of inanimate objects, such as fruit or flowers.

**Tempera** Powdered paint mixed or 'tempered' with egg yolk and thinned with water. It was widely used until the invention of oil paints in the 15th century.

**Triptych** Three-panelled hinged altarpiece.

---

as late as the 4th century. The 5m (16ft) high statue was mistakenly thought to be of Constantine, the first Roman emperor to be baptised (although only on his deathbed), and because of that belief it was revered throughout the Middle Ages.

In 1347 the tribune Cola di Rienzo, to celebrate a festival, temporarily converted the horse into a fountain, with wine flowing from one nostril and water from the other. In 1539 Michelangelo designed a plinth for the statue in Campidoglio Square in Rome. He is said to have been so impressed by the horse's lifelike beauty that he commanded it to walk.

The statue was originally covered with gold. And, according to legend, if the gold ever reappears the end of the world is at hand – and the Last Judgment will be announced by a voice coming from the horse's head.

---

## WRONG WAY UP

In 1961 the Museum of Modern Art in New York put on display *Le Bateau* (The Boat), a canvas by the French Fauvist painter Henri Matisse (1869 – 1954).

The painting, measuring 1420mm (56in) by 1120mm (44in), was hung upside down – and the mistake was not discovered for 47 days.

---

## SAINT OF BUMPS

Maestro Mateo, the 12th-century Spanish sculptor and creator of the vast cathedral doorway at Santiago de Compostela in northwestern Spain, is known as the Saint of Bumps because of a superstition about a statue of himself. The statue kneels at the foot of the triple-arched doorway's central shaft, and pilgrims visiting the cathedral still bang their heads against the figure in the belief that some of the sculptor's genius will be transmitted to them.

The cathedral, considered to be one of the finest surviving examples of Romanesque architecture, was built between 1078 and about 1211 on the site of what was believed to be a tomb containing the relics of St James.

---

## THE LIVING VENUS

Most portrait sculptures of living people are dignified, modest works. Napoleon's sister, however, posed for a revealing exception: a sculpture now called *Venus*. The statue, a classically elegant semi-nude, was modelled on Pauline Borghese, sister of the French emperor. Venetian sculptor Antonio Canova (1757 – 1822) had been called to Paris to create a vast statue of Napoleon and in 1804 was commissioned to sculpt his sister as well. The young princess was very conscious of the beauty of her bosom and wore startlingly low-cut clothes to show it off. It is alleged that Canova's dedication to realism and Pauline's vanity led to his taking detailed measurements and even casts of her breasts. When asked how she could possibly have posed naked, the princess is said to have replied: 'The studio was heated.' The completed sculpture of Pauline reclining gracefully is now in a museum at the Villa Borghese in Rome.

---

## PARIS'S STATUE OF LIBERTY

The Statue of Liberty – officially called 'Liberty Enlightening the World' – which dominates the approaches to New York Harbour, is a scaled-up copy of an identical statue which still stands on the banks of the River Seine in Paris.

The Paris original, carved by the sculptor Frédéric Auguste Bartholdi (1834 – 1904), is 2.7m (9ft) tall. The New York version, constructed of copper sheets over an iron and steel framework, was engineered by Gustave Eiffel, the builder of the Eiffel Tower, and is 46m (152ft) tall. It stands on a granite and concrete pedestal of about the same height, so that the whole statue measures 93m (305ft) from ground level to the tip of the torch flame.

The statue, a gift from France to commemorate the birth of the United States, was officially handed over on the USA's Independence Day (July 4) 1884 and reassembled in New York two years later.

---

## MATCHBOX COLLECTION

The Swiss sculptor Alberto Giacometti (1901 – 66) was so obsessed with refining the human form to its bare essentials that he often kept chipping away at his sculptures until there was nothing left of them. He worked mainly in France, but between 1942 and 1946 he sought refuge from the Second World War in neutral Switzerland. When he returned to Paris, he took back with him the entire production of those four hard-working years – in six matchboxes. Giacometti's distinctive 'thin man' bronze figures gradually became famous, however, and his work is now represented in major collections throughout the world.

SLIMLI
Standi
Woma
*sculpted*
*Giacom.*
*in 1958*

# Music and drama

## COMPOSERS ROYAL

Many of the royal patrons of music have also been performers, and a few wrote music themselves. Among the most notable were Henry VIII of England, who wrote two masses (now lost), and several surviving short pieces – including an arrangement of a song for three voices, *Passtyme with good cumpanye*. He is also reputed to have written the music for *Greensleeves*.

Henry V, the victor of Agincourt, composed church music under the name of 'Roy Henry'. Frederick the Great of Prussia was a skilled flautist, who wrote numerous flute sonatas and concertos. In the 19th century, Albert, Queen Victoria's Prince Consort, was an accomplished organist and composer of church music. At Victoria's two jubilees, anthems of his were sung in Westminster Abbey.

## RIOT AT THE BALLET

The normally sedate world of classical music and dance became the setting for a full-blown riot at the world premiere of the ballet *The Rite of Spring*, with music by the Russian-born composer Igor Stravinsky. The ballet, organised by the Russian impresario Sergei Diaghilev (1872–1929), was performed on May 29, 1913, to mark the opening of the new Théâtre des Champs-Élysées in Paris.

The protests at the so-called barbarism of the music, and also at the erotic nature of the dancing, began in the gallery and quickly spread to all parts of the house. Protests by Stravinsky's supporters followed, and fighting broke out. One critic of the time described the score as 'the most dissonant and the most discordant composition yet written'. But today the music no longer sounds so controversial and has taken its place in the orchestral repertoire.

## EARLY STARTERS

One of music's most outstanding prodigies was the English composer William Crotch, who at the age of two years and three months could play the national anthem on a home-made organ. The son of a Norwich carpenter, he gave his first public organ recital in his home town shortly before he was three. The following year – 1779 – he gave daily organ recitals in London.

Crotch was hailed as 'the English Mozart', because Mozart was another of music's early starters. Mozart was composing short piano pieces by the age of six and was only 12 when he wrote his first opera, *Bastien and Bastienne*, about a pair of pastoral lovers.

Mozart had an astonishing musical memory, too. At the age of 14 he heard Gregorio Allegri's *Miserere* – a setting of Psalm 50 – performed in the Sistine Chapel in Rome, and after that one hearing wrote down the full score from memory.

HEIGHT OF FASHION *Russian-born designer Leon Bakst (1866–1924) stunned Paris with the sets and costumes he created for Sergei Diaghilev's ballet company in the early 1900s. From left to right are the costumes for the world premieres of* La Péri, The Firebird *and* Le Dieu Bleu. *Of these, only* The Firebird, *with its colourful music by Igor Stravinsky, is still regularly performed today. Though* Le Dieu Bleu *was based on a story by Jean Cocteau, France's leading young writer, it flopped on its first performance in 1911.*

## HOW DID MOZART DIE?

On a rainy day in December 1791 Wolfgang Amadeus Mozart – Europe's most renowned composer – was given a pauper's burial in an unmarked mass grave in St Mark's cemetery, Vienna. Only a few of his close friends attended the ceremony and today no one knows exactly where his bones lie. Three months earlier Mozart's last opera, *The Magic Flute*, had been a huge popular success following its Viennese premiere – but he did not live long enough to enjoy its financial rewards.

For some time before he died, Mozart is said to have been tormented by premonitions of death. He declared that his last work – his *Requiem*, which was completed after his death by his former pupil Franz Sussmäyr – had been commissioned by a mysterious man in a black cloak. He regarded this as an omen that he was soon about to die. Scholars subsequently discovered that the mysterious cloaked figure was, in fact, a messenger from an Austrian nobleman who wanted to commission the *Requiem* secretly in the hope that the work would be taken for his own. There

Title role in
La Péri

is also an air of mystery over the cause of Mozart's death. Some say that he died of a high fever; others ascribe his premature death – he was only 35 – to a combination of kidney disease and overwork.

However, in 1825 the Italian composer Antonio Salieri – who was a rival of Mozart's in Vienna – stated on his deathbed that he had poisoned Mozart. A mediocre musician, he was jealous of Mozart's genius, but there is no proof that he murdered him. It is thought that his confession was a desperate bid to gain some kind of lasting fame – which he knew that his own compositions would not provide.

## DISTANT ADMIRER

In 1877 the Russian composer Peter Ilyich Tchaikovsky received a letter from a wealthy, middle-aged widow with 11 children, Nadezhda von Meck. She wrote to tell him how much she admired his music and offered to pay him a generous annual allowance on one condition – that they never met. She did not want to run the risk of meeting her idol in the flesh and possibly being disillusioned – and this suited Tchaikovsky who, although married, was ill-at-ease in female company.

For the next 14 years – until Madame von Meck became gravely ill with tuberculosis – the couple frequently corresponded, but kept their vow not to meet. However, they sometimes attended the same concerts in Moscow, when they would surreptitiously observe each other. On one occasion they came face to face and Tchaikovsky politely doffed his hat to his patroness. She turned scarlet with embarrassment and became speechless.

This made Tchaikovsky equally flustered and they both hurried off in different directions.

## DEADLY BEAT

The Italian-born composer Jean Baptiste Lully died as the result of a self-inflicted injury sustained while conducting. In 1687 he was directing a *Te Deum* (a Latin hymn of thanksgiving to God) in Paris when he accidentally struck himself on his foot with the heavy, long staff which he was beating on the floor to indicate the tempo. An abscess developed, rapidly followed by gangrene, and Lully – director of music at the court of Louis XIV – died of blood poisoning at the age of 54.

The baton – the lightweight stick used by modern conductors to mark tempo – was introduced at a London concert in 1820 by the German conductor and composer Louis Spohr.

## THERE AND BACH

In the autumn of 1705 the 20-year-old Johann Sebastian Bach, then the church organist at Arnstadt in Thuringia, was given four weeks' leave to visit Lübeck to hear the great Danish-born organist and composer Dietrich Buxtehude. Because Bach was short of money, he walked the 350km (220 miles) between

*Title role costume for* The Firebird

*Costume for a young rajah in* Le Dieu Bleu

the two German towns. On arriving at Lübeck he found that the 68-year-old Buxtehude was ready to retire. Bach was offered his job as organist – on one condition. He had to marry Buxtehude's 30-year-old daughter. Bach turned it down, just as another young composer, George Handel, had done two years earlier. Bach walked back to Thuringia and arrived 12 weeks late – which earned him a severe reprimand from the church authorities.

## OPERA IN THE CASTLE
The music of Richard Wagner so impressed the 18-year-old Ludwig II, king of Bavaria from 1864, that he built an elaborate castle – Neuschwanstein – in which to stage the composer's then little-performed operas. He also put Wagner on his payroll, and gave him the money to start the annual Bayreuth Festival, which is still held today. Only Wagner's works are performed at the festival.

Ludwig was always eccentric, and he ended his days under restraint as a madman. He committed suicide in 1886, three years after Wagner's death.

## THE ORPHANS AND THE RED PRIEST
The Pio Ospedale della Pieta in Venice – a music school for orphaned or illegitimate girls – was the working place in the early 18th century of the priest and master violinist Antonio Vivaldi. In 1723 his contract as music master specified that he had to write two concertos a month, and if he was away he had to send them on to the orphanage, carriage paid. Altogether, Vivaldi – known as *il prete rosso*, 'the red priest', because of the colour of his hair – wrote more than 450 concertos, including the set called *The Four Seasons* for violin and orchestra.

## BRITANNIA RULES AGAIN . . .
Since its first performance in 1899, the 'secret' of Sir Edward Elgar's *Enigma Variations* has intrigued music-lovers. Elgar said that its main musical theme was counterbalanced with another taken from a well-known British song – 'so well-known that it is strange no one has discovered it'. The variations were musical portraits of Elgar's closest friends, and he told

# THE MEANINGS OF MUSICAL TERMS

**Absolute pitch (perfect pitch)** Ability to identify from memory a musical sound, note or key, or to sing any given tone without the aid of an instrument or tuning-fork.

**Adagio** Slow tempo; a composition or movement written to be played at this pace – literally 'at ease'.

**Allegretto** Short, lively piece of music played not quite as fast as allegro.

**Allegro** Lively and fast, literally 'merry'.

**Alto** Male form of female contralto voice, now usually applied to boys; an abbreviation for contralto.

**Andante** Played at a moderate or 'walking' pace or tempo.

**Aria** Solo song usually in operas, oratorios and cantatas.

**Baritone** Middle range male voice, between tenor and bass.

**Baroque** Heavy, ornamental music of the 17th century and first half of the 18th century.

**Bass** Lowest male singing voice; the lowest note of a chord or the lowest vocal or instrumental part of a composition.

**Cadenza** Short, brilliant passage at the end of a concerto movement or aria; although usually prepared beforehand by the composer or performer, it is intended to have an air of spontaneity.

**Canon** Composition in which a voice or instrument is imitated by another (or several others) starting later and overlapping it.

**Cantata** Extended choral work with or without soloists and generally with orchestral accompaniment.

**Castrato** Male singer who has been castrated to allow his voice to develop powerfully in the soprano or contralto range.

**Chord** Combination of two or more notes.

**Coloratura** Florid, virtuoso singing using runs, trills and rapid scale changes; **coloratura soprano**, female singer with a light voice trained in such a style.

**Concerto** Work for solo instrument or instruments, with orchestra, usually in three movements.

**Contralto** Lowest female singing voice.

**Crescendo** Gradually becoming louder.

**Diminuendo** Gradually becoming softer.

**Étude** Study or solo instrumental piece aimed at improving a student's technique. Some composers, notably Chopin, also wrote études for public performance.

**Falsetto** Artificial form of singing in which males reach notes above the normal range of their voices; sometimes used to imitate women's voices or for comic effect.

**Fortissimo** Very loud.

**Fugue** Vocal or instrumental composition in which the instruments or voices enter in close succession and repeat or imitate each other.

**Intermezzo** Instrumental piece played between the acts or scenes of an opera or other dramatic work; short concert piece, usually for piano.

**Larghetto** Slow and dignified tempo slightly faster than largo.

**Largo** Very slow – literally 'broad'.

**Lento** Slow.

**Lieder** Term used to describe German songs for solo voice and piano. It comes from the German word *Lied*, meaning 'song'.

**Madrigal** Composition for two or more unaccompanied voices.

**Mezzo** Middle, or medium; **mezzo piano**, 'quite soft'; **mezzo forte**, 'quite loud'; **mezzo soprano**, female voice midway between soprano and contralto.

**Nocturne** 'Night piece', or melancholic, reflective work for one or more instruments.

**Obbligato** Obligatory part played by a specific instrument – such as 'song with violin obbligato'.

**Opera** Drama generally sung throughout with orchestral accompaniment; **grand opera**, very dramatic and emotional large-scale work; **opera buffa**, comic opera; **opera seria**, serious opera (including grand opera).

**Operetta** Light opera with songs interspersed with spoken dialogue.

**Opus** Work (usually abbreviated as op). For instance, *op 2* is the second work published by a composer – but not necessarily the second one he has actually written.

one of them, Dora Penny: 'With your name you should know it.' When asked if he would reveal the secret, he answered: 'Never!'

From this, and from clues in the music, some musicologists believe that the hidden theme is part of *Rule Britannia* – which was composed in 1740 by Thomas Arne for a musical pageant about King Alfred. The notes of the theme are the notes sung to the words '(Britons) never, never, never. . . .' And the figure of Britannia appeared on the old English penny coin.

## DREAM OF THE DEVIL

The Italian violinist Giuseppe Tartini (1692 – 1770), threatened with arrest for eloping with a 15-year-old girl, Elisabetta Premazone, sought shelter with the Franciscan friars at Assisi. One night in the monastery he dreamt he had sold his soul to the Devil, who in return played a violin sonata of incredible beauty.

Tartini later tried to recapture the sonata he had heard in his dream. The result, *The Devil's Trill* sonata, was, he felt, only a shadow of the dream music. But violinists ever since have felt that the sonata – with its

intricate trill in the last of its four movements – deserves its name, if only because it is fiendishly difficult to play.

## PIGTAIL PRANK

One day in November 1749 a 17-year-old choirboy in St Stephen's Cathedral in Vienna took out his scissors and snipped off the pigtail of the boy in front of him. This prank led to his instant dismissal from the choir school. In the years of hardship that followed, the former star pupil scraped a living by playing the violin in the streets of Vienna.

But his musical genius as a composer gradually asserted itself, and in 1755 he published the first batch of his 84 string quartets. By the end of his long and prolific career (he died in 1809 aged 77) he had written 104 symphonies, numerous piano sonatas and chamber works and two popular oratorios, *The Creation* and *The Seasons*. Had the boy stayed with the choir he might have had a very different musical career – and the world might not have so much of Joseph Haydn's music to enjoy.

---

**Oratorio** Religious musical composition for soloists, chorus and orchestra.

**Overture** Orchestral music generally composed as the introduction to an opera, oratorio or play.

**Pitch** Relative highness or lowness of a note; **concert pitch**, the pitch to which orchestral instruments are tuned – 440 vibrations per second for the A above middle C. It is also called international pitch.

**Pizzicato** Notes plucked with the fingers on the strings of a bowed instrument.

**Presto** Fast.

**Prima donna** Main female singer in an opera.

**Rallentando** Slowing down.

**Recitative** Speech-like singing frequently used in operas, oratorios and cantatas.

**Rhapsody** Romantic, lyrical work usually in one movement.

**Ritornello** Recurring passage or section.

**Rococo** Term used to describe light, decorative music written between 1710 and 1755.

**Rondo** Composition in which one particular section or passage recurs intermittently.

**Rubato** Performed at slightly faster or slower tempos than those marked – so allowing more expressiveness.

**Serenade** Light music to be played outdoors in the evening; music played or sung by a lover outside his sweetheart's window.

**Sinfonia** Symphony; **sinfonia concertante**, term used mainly in the time of Haydn and Mozart for a concerto for two or more instruments.

**Sinfonietta** Short symphony.

**Sonata** Work in three or four movements for one or two instruments – such as a violin or cello with a large part for a piano.

**Sonatina** Short sonata.

**Soprano** Highest female singing voice; also used for boy singers, who are often called trebles.

**Suite** Light instrumental piece in several loosely connected movements.

**Symphony** Large-scale orchestral work usually in four movements – although some shorter symphonies are in one movement; passage in vocal work for instruments alone.

**Tempo** Time or speed.

**Tenor** Highest common male singing voice; **counter-tenor**, higher than tenor but using artificial falsetto.

**Toccata** Keyboard composition which displays the performer's virtuosity, particularly on the organ.

MASTER OF SONG *Franz Schubert, composer of some of the world's finest lieder, accompanies a singer at a musical evening.*

# GROWTH OF THE SYMPHONY ORCHESTRA

The average modern symphony orchestra has from 90 to 120 players. But at the beginning of the 18th century orchestras were much smaller – in about 1715, for instance, Handel composed his *Water Music* suite for what was then a typical orchestra of two oboes, two horns, bassoon, harpsichord and strings. To do justice to the larger-scale music of the Romantics such as Berlioz, the orchestra had to grow. By the beginning of the 19th century it numbered between 40 and 50 players, and by the end of the century it had doubled in size again.

The modern orchestra has balanced sections of strings, brass, woodwind and percussion. The strings section consists of some 30 violins, usually split into groups of 16 and 14, about 12 violas, ten cellos and eight double basses.

The brass section includes four french horns, three trumpets, three trombones and a bass tuba. The percussion section has a variety of instruments including drums, cymbals, triangle, chimes, gongs, tambourines, castanets, rattles and xylophone. The woodwind section normally has two clarinets, two oboes, two flutes, two bassoons and sometimes cor anglais, piccolo and double bassoon. In addition, some works call for a harp or a piano, which are specially provided.

**Percussion instruments**
All percussion instruments are played by being hit or struck with a beater or the hand.

SNARE DRUM *Wires across the drum's bottom give a rattling effect.*

BASS DRUM *The largest of the drum family, it can be operated by foot.*

**Brass instruments**
Valves and the player's lips help to control the pitch of the notes.

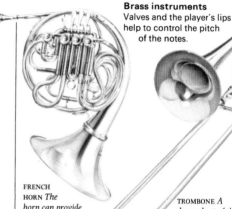

FRENCH HORN *The horn can provide accompaniment or carry the melody.*

TROMBONE *A descendant of the medieval sackbut, the trombone is the bass core of the brass section. The player alters the pitch by moving the slide.*

## FAST WORKERS

George Frederick Handel composed his oratorio *Messiah* in just 24 days, from August 22 to September 14, 1741. He wrote it for a festival in Dublin in aid of various charities including 'poor and distressed prisoners for debt' – and all other performances in his lifetime were in aid of charities of Handel's choice.

Handel was rivalled by at least two equally rapid composers, not of oratorios but of comic operas: Gioacchino Rossini, who in 1816 wrote *The Barber of Seville* in 19 working days; and his fellow Italian Gaetano Donizetti, who composed *The Elixir of Love* in 1832 in ten working days. Rossini put his speed of composition down to laziness, saying that he could not be bothered to write music for longer.

An even more urgent case of fast work occurred in Prague in 1787 – two days before Mozart's opera *Don Giovanni* was to receive its first performance. The manager of the Czech opera house realised to his horror that there was no overture to start the opera and in desperation he asked the composer what could be done about it. 'Don't worry,' replied Mozart airily. 'I have it all in my head!' He spent the intervening time writing the overture, had it copied as quickly as possible – and the conductor and orchestra received it only 30 minutes before the curtain was due to rise.

## SHORTEST AND LONGEST

The 20th-century French composer Erik Satie probably holds the record for a composition that is the shortest – and the longest – in the world. His piece for piano called *Vexations* lasts for just under a minute. However, Satie states in the score that it should be played 840 times in succession – a non-stop playing time of 14 hours.

## SEEN BUT NOT HEARD

Ludwig van Beethoven began to lose his hearing in 1796 when he was only 26, and by 1824 – when his *Ninth Symphony*, the 'Choral', received its premiere in Vienna – he was completely deaf. However, this did not stop him from helping the conductor, Michael Umlauf, to direct the work.

Beethoven stood before the orchestra during the performance and indicated the tempo at the beginning of each of the four movements. At the end of the symphony the audience rose and applauded vigorously. Feet were stamped, hands clapped above heads and there were loud cries of 'Bravo'. But Beethoven was unaware of all this. He had to be turned around by one of the soloists to see the ovation he could no longer hear.

## SOUNDS OF SILENCE

The quietest piece of music ever written is *4'33"* by the American experimental composer John Cage. It is usually performed by a pianist, who sits at his instrument for 4 minutes and 33 seconds indicating by gestures that the work is in three movements, but playing nothing. The score, 'composed' in 1952, is blank and can be played on any instrument or group of instruments. The music consists of any sound from inside or outside the hall that the audience can hear.

## Woodwind instruments

Woodwind instruments are either blown through a mouth-hole, as with the flute or recorder, or played by means of a vibrating reed, as with the oboe or clarinet. The bigger the instrument, the lower its notes, their pitch being varied by opening and closing the holes in the body.

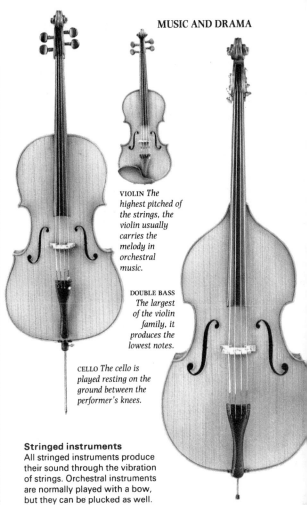

VIOLIN *The highest pitched of the strings, the violin usually carries the melody in orchestral music.*

DOUBLE BASS *The largest of the violin family, it produces the lowest notes.*

CELLO *The cello is played resting on the ground between the performer's knees.*

RECORDER *It is widely used by children and for ancient music.*

PICCOLO *The baby of the woodwinds, this small flute has a very high pitch.*

FLUTE *The standard concert flute, with its elaborate keys, can cope with even the fastest passages of music.*

CLARINET *The clarinet is fitted only with a single reed and produces a smooth warm sound.*

OBOE *The oboe's double reed produces its characteristically plaintive tone.*

## Stringed instruments

All stringed instruments produce their sound through the vibration of strings. Orchestral instruments are normally played with a bow, but they can be plucked as well.

### LOUD AND SOFT

The pianoforte, or piano, gets its name from the Italian words for 'soft' and 'loud', still commonly used in music. It was introduced by its inventor – the Florentine harpsichord-maker Bartolomeo di Francesco Cristofori – in 1709, who described it as a *gravicembalo col piano e forte* (harpsichord with soft and loud).

Gradations of tone can be produced on a piano, because the strings are struck by felt-covered hammers. The harder the keys are hit, the harder the hammers strike and the louder the notes. A harpsichord, on the other hand, in which the strings are plucked mechanically by plectra, keeps a constant volume of tone.

### BAKED IN A PIE

The English nursery rhyme *Sing a song of sixpence*, which goes on to describe 'Four and twenty blackbirds baked in a pie', may be a memory of a medieval banquet in France.

In 1454 members of the Order of the Golden Fleece – an order of knighthood founded by Philip the Good, Duke of Burgundy, in France – held a sumptuous feast at which there was an enormous baked pie. Inside the pie were more than 20 musicians who emerged to serenade the guests.

### FROM RUSSIA WITH LOVE

Irving Berlin, the songwriter who composed the unofficial national anthem of the United States, *God Bless America*, was born in Russia. Berlin, whose real name was Israel Baline, was born in Temun, Siberia, in 1888. At the age of four, he and his family emigrated to the USA and settled in New York.

### KILLED BY A TORTOISE

The Greek dramatist Aeschylus (525–456 BC) was once told by a prophet that he would die of 'a blow from heaven'. The prophet's words came true when – according to a popular story – an eagle dropped a tortoise on the playwright's bald head, mistaking it for a stone, and killed him outright. Aeschylus was buried in an austere tomb at Gela, in Sicily, which made no mention of his dramatic works. The inscription simply stated that he had been a soldier at the battle of Marathon in 490 BC, when the Greeks repelled the invading Persians.

Of Aeschylus's 90 plays, only seven have survived – including *Seven Against Thebes*, *The Suppliant Women* and the trilogy known as the *Oresteia* (458 BC), a grim tale of guilt and vengeance. Aeschylus changed the form of Greek drama by adding a second actor to the customary solo actor and chorus – and thus invented dramatic dialogue.

### PASSION AND THE PLAYWRIGHT

The world's most prolific playwright was the Spaniard Lope de Vega (1562–1635) who wrote almost 2500 plays and religious dramas (*auto sacramentales*). Of his work, 426 plays and 42 *autos* have survived. His best-known drama, *Fuenteovejuna* (*The Well of Ovejuna*) – based on a true story about rape and revenge in a village community – is still staged. After a series of passionate love affairs, de Vega became a priest in 1614. But this did not prevent him from embarking on yet another affair with a married woman. In later life he suffered greatly from guilt, and the walls of his monastic cell were splashed with blood from his weekly self-scourgings.

## SUICIDE OF A STOIC

The Roman playwright and philosopher Seneca (about 4 BC – AD 65) was as calm about his own death as he had been about life. Seneca spent much of his early career instructing the emperor Nero in the art of politics and in Stoic philosophy – which held that people should control their emotions and calmly accept everything that happened to them as part of the natural order. When Nero came to power in AD 54, Seneca was his most trusted confidant and adviser.

Eight years later, however, he fell out of favour with the emperor for reasons now unknown, and retired from court politics.

In AD 65 he was involved in an unsuccessful conspiracy to assassinate Nero and was commanded by the emperor to kill himself. Seneca accepted the verdict of his former pupil stoically. He had his veins opened and slowly bled to death.

During his time in Rome the Spanish-born dramatist wrote nine tragedies, of which the most sensational was *Thyestes*. In it a father unknowingly has his children served to him as the main course in a banquet. By 1581 all of Seneca's plays had been translated into English, and their themes of horror and revenge fascinated the early English dramatists. They were imitated by, amongst others, the young William Shakespeare in his play *Titus Andronicus*.

## BIRDS IN THE LAND

The English playwright William Shakespeare (1564 – 1616) is indirectly responsible for the presence of starlings and sparrows in North America. Neither species existed there until, in the 1890s, a wealthy New Yorker named Eugene Scheifflin (1827 – 1906) released flocks of the birds in the city's Central Park as part of a project to bring to the USA all the birds mentioned in Shakespeare's works.

## THE DEADLY DUEL

Ben Jonson (1572 – 1637), a former London bricklayer turned clergyman who became England's first poet laureate, was once jailed for murder. It happened in 1598 when Jonson, who was appearing on the London stage, quarrelled with a fellow actor named Gabriel Spencer. In the rapier duel that followed, Spencer was fatally wounded.

Jonson was arrested. He pleaded guilty to a charge of murder, but escaped the gallows by claiming 'benefit of clergy' – that is, that as a clergyman he could not be hanged. He did, however, lose all his property and, as a convicted murderer, was branded on his left thumb with a capital 'T' – standing for Tyburn, the gallows near London's Hyde Park.

Jonson was jailed for a second time in 1605 for making fun of James I's fellow Scotsmen in a court entertainment which he had helped to write. He and his two co-authors were sentenced to have their ears and noses cut off, but they secured their release unharmed through the help of some powerful friends.

Jonson regained the king's favour when his comic play *Volpone, or the Fox* was produced in 1606 – and in 1616 he was made poet laureate.

## THE STORY OF RECORDED SOUND

*Emile Berliner's early gramophone*

**1877** Thomas Alva Edison in America invents the phonograph, which reproduces recorded sound on paraffin-soaked strips of paper using a steel stylus.

**1878** Edison markets his phonograph with the paper strips replaced by thin sheets of tinfoil.

**1886** Wax cylinder, replacing tinfoil, introduced in USA.

**1888** First flat gramophone record – 125mm (5in) in diameter – introduced in the USA by Emile Berliner, a German-born immigrant.

**1892** Berliner develops the 'master disc' from which several copies of a record could be made on vulcanised rubber. Before then, singers had to repeat a song for each copy of a recording.

**1895** Shellac discs replace those made of rubber.

**1925** Microphone developed by Joseph Maxfield and researchers at Bell Telephone Laboratories in USA. The first electrically produced disc is released by the US Victor Talking Machine Company.

**1948** First plastic, long-playing disc marketed in USA.

**1958** First practical stereo records marketed in Britain and USA.

**1971** Quadraphonic sound, with four separate sound signals, introduced in Britain and USA.

**1980** First videodisc – combining pictures and sound – marketed in USA.

**1983** First Compact Disc (CD) – 120mm (4.7in) across, made of aluminium and largely unaffected by static, scratches or dust – marketed in Britain and USA. The disc is played with a special laser stylus which does not touch the surface.

## STOLEN THUNDER

The English playwright and critic John Dennis (1657 – 1734) devised a new means of producing the sound of stage thunder – and gave a new phrase to the English language. Stage thunder in the early 18th century was created by rolling iron balls around inside large bowls. Dennis was able to generate a more realistic sound by rolling the balls down long wooden troughs instead. He first used the troughs, or 'thunder runs', when his play *Appius and Virginia* (1709) was produced at London's Drury Lane theatre. However, the thunder effects were the production's only success; the play itself was taken off after only a few nights.

Not long afterwards, Dennis visited Drury Lane to see a production of Shakespeare's *Macbeth*. From his seat at the front of the pit he realised that his thunder runs were being employed. He jumped up, turned to the audience and shouted: 'The villains! That's *my* thunder they're using. They won't play my play, but they will steal my thunder!'

# Poetry and prose

## BLIND BARD

The earliest known European poems are the *Iliad* and its sequel the *Odyssey*, thought to have been compiled around 800 BC. These Greek epics – the first dealing with the events of the Trojan war, the second with the eventful journey home of Odysseus from the war – are thought to have been written by Homer, a blind bard from either Smyrna (in present-day Turkey) or the Aegean island of Chios.

Some scholars, however, assert that the epics are the work of a number of poets over many years, and that they were memorised and added to by wandering bards long before they were written down. Homer, in other words, may merely have been the last in a chain of authors. One expert – the 20th-century author and poet Robert Graves – even thought that the *Odyssey* was written by a woman.

## FARMER POET

The first European poet for whom there is indisputable documentary evidence is Hesiod, a Greek farmer who lived in Ascra, on the slopes of Helicon, in the 8th century BC. He wrote *Works and Days*, which contains a poetical treatment of the ages of man and an account of a year in the life of a farmer.

## MAN WHO SAVED THE *AENEID*

The first Roman emperor Augustus (63 BC – AD 14), who founded the empire in 27 BC, became a dedicated patron of the arts, giving financial help to the poet Virgil, among many others. When Virgil died in 19 BC, leaving instructions that his unfinished epic on the founding of Rome, the *Aeneid*, should be destroyed because it was incomplete, Augustus stepped in to save it. He overruled the dead poet and insisted that the poem should be published – establishing Virgil's reputation ever since as the most important poet of classical Rome.

## INSPIRED BY A GIRL HE NEVER MET

The Italian poet Dante was inspired to write two of his finest works – *The Divine Comedy* and *The New Life* – by a fair-haired, blue-eyed maiden whom he never spoke to and saw only twice. The girl, whom he called simply Beatrice, was Beatrice Portinori, who died in

BENNET*
killed b
a drink*

BROOKI*
buried
in Gree*

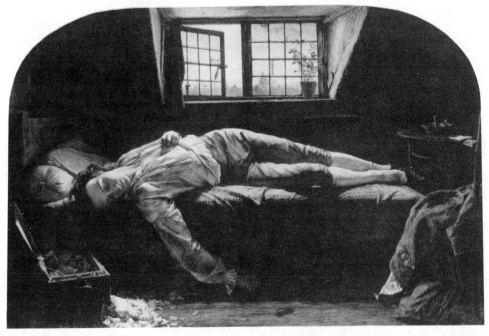

DEATH IN A GARRET *One of the most remarkable literary forgeries of all time – the poems of an imaginary 15th-century monk called Thomas Rowley – was perpetrated by a 16-year-old lawyer's apprentice, Thomas Chatterton. From childhood, Chatterton – who was born in Bristol in 1752 – was obsessed with medieval documents. He formed his own antique vocabulary and spelling, and sent one of his fabricated poems,* The Ryse of Peyncteynge yn Englande (The Rise of Painting in England), *to the author Horace Walpole in London. At first, Walpole believed the poem to be genuine and praised it highly. Chatterton moved to London, where he took lodgings in a garret off Holborn, hoping to make a living as a journalist and poet in his own right. But his Rowley poems were openly denounced as frauds by the poet Thomas Gray and Chatterton soon found himself without work, penniless and starving. On the evening of August 24, 1770, when he was still 17 years old, he proudly refused his landlady's offer of a meal and locked himself in his room. There he drank some arsenic he had acquired and died during the night in agonising convulsions. His death, and the promise shown in his poems, led the poet William Wordsworth – who was four months old when Chatterton committed suicide – to write of him later as '. . . the marvellous boy/The sleepless soul, that perished in his pride'. This picture of the dead poet, sprawled across his bed as dawn breaks over the hazy dome of St Paul's Cathedral, was painted by the English artist Henry Wallis in 1855–6.*

337

1290 at the age of 24. Dante first saw her at a party at her parents' home in Florence in 1274, when he was only nine and she was eight. He spotted her again nine years later in a street, and after her death he wrote *The New Life* (*La Vita Nuova*), in which he describes his ideal love.

**BYRON:** *'mad, dangerous to know'.*

Beatrice also appears in *The Divine Comedy* (*La Divina Commedia*), an epic poem in three sections, as the symbol of faith who guides Dante through the final section, *Paradise*. The first two sections, in which she does not appear, are *The Inferno* and *Purgatory*. The *Divine Comedy* was completed in 1321, the year of Dante's death in Ravenna.

● The most familiar quotation from Dante's *The Divine Comedy* is: 'Abandon hope, all ye who enter here.' But it is inaccurate. The correct version of the quotation – part of the inscription above the gates of Hell in the first section of the poem, *The Inferno* – is: 'Abandon all hope, you who enter.'

**CARROLL:** *inspiration in a boat.*

## MURDERER, THIEF AND POET

The poem that made François Villon famous – his 2000-line *Le Grand Testament* – is a revealing portrait of the poet as vagabond, beggar and thief. A brilliant student, Villon – who was born in Paris in 1431 – was involved in a series of drunken brawls which ended with him killing a priest with his sword. He was banished from Paris for his crime in 1455, but the following year he gained a royal pardon.

**CERVANTES:** *jailed for debt.*

Villon returned to Paris and to his life of debauchery. He was constantly in and out of prison for theft and fighting, and was finally sentenced to death after being involved in another street brawl in which someone was killed. While awaiting the noose, he wrote a poem saying that his neck would soon find out how much his body weighed. However, his friends succeeded in having his sentence reduced to one of ten years' exile. Villon – whose poetry gives an unrivalled picture of criminal life in medieval France – left Paris in 1463 and was not heard of again.

It is thought that he may have died of the effects of alcoholism, or that he may have been murdered in yet another tavern quarrel. But despite his dissipated ways, Villon was capable of lines of the highest poetic beauty – such as the haunting: '*Mais où sont les neiges d'antan?*' ('But where are the snows of yesteryear?')

**CICERO:** *hunted down.*

## THE POEM THAT WAS SHIPWRECKED

The 16th-century Portuguese poet Luiz de Camões, author of the epic *Os Lusíadas* (*The Lusiads*), hung onto only one possession when he was shipwrecked in 1558: the manuscript of his poem.

Camões – a former soldier who lost his right eye fighting the Moors in Morocco – wounded a royal official in a street fight in Lisbon in 1553. He spent some months in prison and was released on condition that he joined an expedition to India.

**DANTE:** *inspired by a girl.*

He was away for 17 years in India, China and the Portuguese colony of Macau. The shipwreck happened off the Southeast Asian coast while he was on his way from Macau to Goa in India. He lost everything he owned in the disaster, except the manuscript of his poem – which he clutched as he swam to shore.

*Os Lusíadas* relates the history of the Lusians, or Portuguese people, and concentrates on the exploits of the explorer Vasco da Gama, who discovered the sea route to India in 1497 – 9.

**DEFOE:** *changed his name.*

## MAD, BAD AND DANGEROUS TO KNOW

'I awoke one morning and found myself famous,' wrote Lord Byron shortly after the publication in 1812 of the first two cantos, or sections, of his epic narrative poem *Childe Harold's Pilgrimage*. Byron was

**DOSTOEVSKY:** *condemned to death.*

the first English poet to achieve worldwide fame in his own lifetime – and *Childe Harold* was a portrait of himself as a melancholy, romantic hero travelling alone through Europe, fleeing from a life of dissipation and idle pleasure.

One of his mistresses, Lady Caroline Lamb, called him 'mad, bad and dangerous to know'. And Byron spent much of his short life in living up to the description – and in trying to live it down. His unfinished satirical masterpiece *Don Juan* (1819 – 24) includes long digressions giving Byron's views on society, money, power, poetry and the state of England.

In 1823 Byron joined the Greek revolutionary committee for the liberation of Greece from the Turks. He arrived at the Greek town of Missolonghi in January 1824 and attempted to resolve quarrels between the Greek patriot leaders. Three months later he caught marsh fever and died there at the age of 36.

## FAMILY PROBLEMS

No poet came from a more eccentric family than Alfred, Lord Tennyson, the poet laureate of Victorian Britain. His father, a Lincolnshire parson, was a violent drunkard who terrified the neighbourhood and was once only just restrained from murdering his son Frederick with a gun and a knife. Of his 12 children, two were insane, one was a drug addict, one was an alcoholic, one was subject to outbursts of rage almost as bad as his father's – and all were subject to fits of depression and to various forms of religious mania.

Despite this background, Tennyson – who was made a peer in 1883 – produced some of the most popular poems of the 19th century. They included *The Charge of the Light Brigade* and *The Idylls of the King*, which was based on the legend of King Arthur. His masterpiece, *In Memoriam*, was written after the death of his fellow poet Arthur Hallam, who had been engaged to Tennyson's sister Emily.

## POEMS THAT WERE BURIED WITH LOVE

One night in February 1862 the London-born poet and painter Dante Gabriel Rossetti returned home to find his wife Lizzie dying of an overdose of laudanum, a tincture of opium. She had suffered from consumption for years and it appeared that she had decided to end her life.

Overcome with grief, Rossetti later placed the only manuscript of his lyrical poems in Lizzie's coffin. 'I have often been working at these poems when she was ill and suffering and I might have been attending to her,' he told two friends, 'and now they shall go!'

He had been married to Lizzie for less than two years, but she had long been his model and inspiration. Then, seven years after her death, Rossetti claimed that her spirit came to visit him in the form of a chaffinch. She told him to reclaim his poems. On the night of October 4, 1869, Rossetti had her remains dug up and the poems retrieved.

The *Poems* were published in 1870. The first edition sold out within two weeks, and by the end of the year six more editions had appeared – bringing Rossetti royalties of more than £800.

## AN AFFAIR OF VIOLENCE

An explosive friendship between two 19th-century French poets, Paul Verlaine and Arthur Rimbaud, culminated in Verlaine shooting Rimbaud in 1873 and being jailed for two years. The couple met in 1871 when the 17-year-old Rimbaud arrived in Paris from the provinces. Verlaine – who was ten years the senior – deserted his wife and travelled with the budding young genius to England and Belgium. But the couple indulged in fierce, drunken quarrels. After the

# FAMOUS PEN-NAMES

Many authors have published some or all of their works under a pseudonym, or *nom de plume* (pen-name). The pen-name signatures of five of the authors listed here – Charlotte Brontë, Charles Dickens, Samuel Clemens, Charles Dodgson and Charles Lamb – appear below.

**Pen-name, *Real name***
Acton Bell, *Anne Brontë (1820–49)*
Currer Bell, *Charlotte Brontë (1816–55)*
Ellis Bell, *Emily Brontë (1818–48)*
Nicholas Blake, *Cecil Day Lewis (1904–72)*
Boz, *Charles Dickens (1812–70)*
Lewis Carroll, *Charles Lutwidge Dodgson (1832–98)*
Elia, *Charles Lamb (1775–1834)*
George Eliot, *Mary Ann Evans (1819–80)*
Maxim Gorky, *Alexey Peshkov (1868–1936)*
O. Henry, *William Sydney Porter (1862–1910)*
John le Carré, *David Cornwell (1931– )*
George Orwell, *Eric Blair (1903–50)*
Ellery Queen, *Used by the co-authors Frederic Dannay (1905–82) and his cousin Manfred B. Lee (1905–71)*
Saki, *Hector Hugh Munro (1870–1916)*
George Sand, *Amandine Dupin (1804–76)*
Stendhal, *Marie Henri Beyle (1783–1842)*
Mark Twain, *Samuel Langhorne Clemens (1835–1910)*
Voltaire, *François-Marie Arouet (1694–1778)*
Mary Westmacott, *Agatha Christie (1890–1975)*

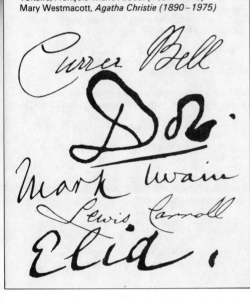

officer, but he never arrived there. He became ill in April 1915 after being bitten by a mosquito. Acute blood poisoning set in and Brooke – never a strong person – died on April 23, 1915, at the age of 27. He was buried in his own 'corner of a foreign field' in an olive grove on the Greek island of Skyros.

## FATAL KISS

According to ancient Chinese historians, one Chinese poet, Li Po (AD 705–62), died because of his dedication to his twin poetic themes of wine and love. He is said to have drowned after leaning out of a boat in a drunken attempt to kiss the reflection of the moon.

## FACING THE FIRING SQUAD

The Russian novelist Feodor Dostoevsky wrote his best works after facing his own execution. On the morning of December 22, 1849, Dostoevsky was one of 20 political prisoners marched out to face a firing squad in Semenovsky Square, St Petersburg (now Leningrad). The first three condemned men were blindfolded and tied to posts. And the second group of three – which included Dostoevsky – was moved forward. The execution squad took aim, but at the last moment an officer rode forward with a white flag and announced that the death sentences had been commuted to imprisonment in Siberia. The reprieve came too late for the well-being of one of the three men bound to the posts. The man, an officer of the Guards, had gone out of his mind.

Dostoevsky (1821–81) had been condemned to death for allegedly plotting against the tsar and for setting up a secret printing press for socialist propaganda. The writer served four years' hard labour in a camp at Omsk, and after his release wrote about his prison experiences in *The House of the Dead* (1861). Dostoevsky's views on the criminal mind are set out in his most famous book, *Crime and Punishment*, published in 1866.

## MARK MY WORDS

The US writer Mark Twain was born in 1835, the year of Halley's comet. Twain – author of *The Adventures of Tom Sawyer* and *The Adventures of Huckleberry Finn* – remarked that as he had come into the world with the comet, so he would pass from the world with it. Halley's comet returned in May 1910 and Twain died in April that year, aged 74.

Twain's real name was Samuel Clemens. He took his pen-name from a cry of Mississippi boatmen, with whom he worked for a time as a river pilot. 'Mark twain' was the call, from a sailor sounding the shallows, for a depth of two fathoms (12ft or 3.6m).

## FLOWERS ON THE PILLORY

Daniel Defoe, the author of *Robinson Crusoe*, was once put in a London pillory for libelling the Church. But instead of being abused and pelted with filth and rotten fruit (which was what normally happened to someone in the pillory), he was protected by his supporters. They formed a guard to shelter him, covered the wooden framework with flowers, and defiantly drank his health. At the same time, copies of a poem hastily written by Defoe, *Hymn to the Pillory*, were sold among the crowd.

Defoe (1660–1731) was imprisoned, fined and sentenced to three spells in the pillory in 1702 after the publication of his satirical pamphlet, *The Shortest Way with Dissenters*. In the pamphlet, he ironically suggested that all Nonconformist preachers should be hanged. Himself the son of a Dissenter (a member of a religious body which did not conform with the Church of England), Defoe meant to satirise ecclesiastical

JOHNSON: *writing for mother*

PUSHKIN *shot in a duel.*

RIMBAUD *poet and gun-runner*

FACTS ABOUT THE ARTS & ENTERTAINMENT

shooting incident, the wounded Rimbaud completed his prose poem *A Season in Hell* (*Une Saison en Enfer*), what he called a 'spiritual autobiography', at the age of 19. He then renounced literature and spent the rest of his life travelling the world. He became involved with the slave trade in North Africa and ended up as a gun-runner. In May 1891 he had his right leg amputated – because of a tumour – in Marseilles, and he died later that year.

Verlaine died in 1896 in the lodgings of one of his mistresses in Paris's Latin Quarter.

## FOR EVER ENGLAND . . .

'If I should die, think only this of me/That there's some corner of a foreign field/That is for ever England.' These lines from *The Soldier* were written by the young English poet Rupert Brooke in 1914. In the following year he sailed for the Dardanelles as a naval

intolerance. But the words of his pamphlet were taken literally – hence his punishment.

Defoe had been born plain Daniel Foe. But in 1700, in an attempt to improve his image and his debit-ridden finances, he changed it to the more aristocratic-sounding Defoe. The change was of limited value. Despite a prolific literary output, which included the bawdy novel *Moll Flanders*, he died in poverty, in cheap lodgings in the East End of London, at the age of 71.

ROSSETTI: poems from a grave.

## MUCH REJECTED
British author John Creasey (1908 – 73), who had 564 mystery novels published under his own name and 13 pseudonyms, received 743 rejection slips before his first book was published.

## BIBLICAL BANKRUPTCY
The Gutenberg Bible, the first work to be printed in Europe with movable type, made its creator, the German printer Johann Gutenberg, bankrupt. To exploit his new type, Gutenberg had joined forces with Johann Fust, a lawyer and goldsmith, from whom he borrowed money. But in 1455, the year in which the Bible appeared, Gutenberg was unable to repay the loan and the partnership was dissolved.

RUSSELL: pacifist in prison.

Fust took over the press and its types, and set up a successful business with his son-in-law, Peter Schoeffer, who was also a printer. Gutenberg himself died destitute and forgotten in Mainz in 1468, at the age of about 70. Some 48 copies of his Bible survive from the original printing of about 200. Today a Gutenberg Bible can be worth as much as £1 million.

STEVENSON: dreamt of horror.

## DEADLY GLASS OF WATER
The English novelist Arnold Bennett (1867 – 1931) died because of an act of bravado that went wrong. The 63-year-old writer defiantly drank water from a carafe in the restaurant of a small Paris hotel, in an attempt to show that the city's water was perfectly safe to drink. Bennett caught typhoid, and died two months later in London on March 27.

## A NIGHTMARE OF A BOOK
Robert Louis Stevenson (1850 – 94) threw the first version of his macabre masterpiece, *The Strange Case of Dr Jekyll and Mr Hyde*, on the fire and burnt it. This followed a quarrel with his American wife, Fanny, who violently disliked the work.

The idea for the novel came to the Scottish writer in a nightmare on a winter's night in 1885. His cries of terror frightened Fanny, who woke her husband up, only to be told: 'Why did you wake me? I was dreaming a fine bogey tale!'

TENNYSON: eccentric family.

The next morning Stevenson set to work on the story. He wrote non-stop, in bed at his home in the English seaside resort of Bournemouth, for three days and nights. He then read his tale to Fanny and, in the row that followed, destroyed the manuscript. However, he soon regretted his hasty action – and spent a further three days rewriting the 30,000-word book. This time Fanny made no objections, even though the story was virtually the same, and *Dr Jekyll and Mr Hyde* was published as a 'Shilling shocker' in 1886.

TWAIN: born under a comet.

## WET WONDERLAND
The story of *Alice in Wonderland* was first told by the English writer and mathematician Lewis Carroll (1832 – 98) to a group of four friends while rowing up the Thames from Oxford to Godstow for a midsummer picnic. One of the party was nine-year-old Alice Liddell (the model for the fictional Alice), and she and her companions remembered what Carroll called the 'gol-

den afternoon' for the rest of their lives. But meteorological records show that the day in question, July 4, 1862, was not particularly golden at all. Far from being a day of cloudless sunshine, the weather for the Oxford area was cool and somewhat wet.

## DUEL IN THE SNOW
The Russian poet Alexander Pushkin (1799 – 1837) anticipated his own death – in a duel which took place in the snow – in his novel in verse form, *Eugene Onegin*, published in 1831. In the book, the shallow and cynical Onegin, tired of social life in St Petersburg (now Leningrad), visits a country estate, where he rejects the advances of a teenage girl who falls in love with him. Bored and seeking excitement, he challenges a romantic young poet named Lenski (closely modelled on Pushkin) to a duel – and kills him. The

---

# FIGURES OF SPEECH

**Alliteration** Use of two or more words with the same initial letters: *I sing of brooks, of blossoms, birds, and bowers* (Robert Herrick, *Argument of his Book*).

**Antithesis** Placing together of sharply contrasting ideas: *They died that we might live.*

**Aphorism** Terse, witty, pointed statement on a general principle: *Anybody who hates children and dogs can't be all bad* (W. C. Fields).

**Bathos** Sudden descent into the ridiculous, often for comic effect: *He's a gentleman: look at his boots* (George Bernard Shaw).

**Climax** Series of statements in rising order of intensity: *I came. I saw. I conquered* (Julius Caesar).

**Euphemism** Polite or inoffensive way of saying something unpleasant: *Euphemisms such as 'slumber room' . . . abound in the funeral business* (Jessica Mitford).

**Hyperbole** Exaggerated statement used for emphasis: *A horse! A horse! My kingdom for a horse!* (Shakespeare, *Richard III*).

**Innuendo** Indirect or subtle implication, usually unpleasant: *I'll be delighted to attend his funeral.*

**Irony** Saying one thing but meaning the opposite: *For Brutus is an honourable man* (Shakespeare, *Julius Caesar*).

**Litotes** An ironical understatement in which an affirmative is expressed by the negative of its opposite: *This is no small problem.*

**Metaphor** Figure of speech in which something, or someone, is said to be that which it only resembles: *When it comes to fighting, he is a tiger!*

**Oxymoron** Figure of speech in which opposites are combined for effect: *Faith unfaithful kept him falsely true* (Tennyson).

**Simile** Figure of speech in which one thing is compared to another, usually with the word 'like' or 'as': *When the evening is spread out against the sky/ Like a patient etherised upon a table* (T. S. Eliot, *The Love Song of J. Alfred Prufrock*).

**Zeugma** Using the same word, in different senses, to govern two or more other words: *He took his leave and my umbrella.*

fictional situation echoed Pushkin's own life. In 1831 he married a frivolous 17-year-old, Natalia, who became infatuated with a guards officer, Baron Georges d'Anthes. Beside himself with jealousy, Pushkin insulted the officer and his family – and this led to a pistol duel in January 1837, in which Pushkin was mortally wounded by the baron.

## WINGS OF FAME
The literary fame of the Russian-born American writer Vladimir Nabokov (1899 – 1977) rests on his satirical novel *Lolita*, published in 1955. But Nabokov – a keen lepidopterist, or butterfly collector – considered his greatest achievement to be the discovery of several species of butterfly which now bear his name. His own favourite was Nabokov's Pug (*Eupithecia nabokovi*), which he discovered in Utah, USA, one night in 1943.

## MYSTERY OF THE MOVING WOUND
Dr Watson, colleague of the fictional Baker Street detective Sherlock Holmes, was given a bullet wound by their creator, the Scottish novelist Sir Arthur Conan Doyle (1859 – 1930). But Sir Arthur does not seem to have been able to make up his mind where the wound should be.

In the first book about the pair's adventures – *A Study in Scarlet*, published in 1882 – Watson has the wound in his shoulder, and it is said to be a result of his military service in India. But in *The Sign of Four*, published eight years later, Watson's wound has mysteriously moved to his leg.

## NAILED TO THE ROSTRUM
The verbal brilliance of the Roman orator Cicero (106 – 43 BC) resulted in his head and right hand being cut off and nailed to the public rostrum from which he had made some of his greatest speeches. At the age of 62, Cicero was rash enough to challenge the supremacy of his former friend, the soldier and political leader Mark Antony, who was in control of Rome after the assassination of Julius Caesar.

Cicero attacked Antony in a series of speeches known as the *Philippics* – from the speeches of the Greek orator Demosthenes against Philip of Macedon in the 4th century BC.

In response, Antony declared Cicero an outlaw and, when the orator tried to escape to Greece, he was captured and killed by a gang of bounty hunters. On Antony's orders, Cicero's head and hand were brought back to Rome and displayed on the rostrum of the Forum – a grisly reminder of the head which had thought and spoken against Antony, and the hand which had written against him.

## LORD JOZEF
The novelist Joseph Conrad (1857 – 1924), now recognised as a master of English for his books such as *Lord Jim* and *Nostromo*, did not speak a word of the language until he was 19 years old. He was born in Poland and his real name was Teodor Jozef Konrad Walecz Korzeniowksi. He learnt English after becoming a mariner aboard British merchant ships in the 1870s, and published his first novel, *Almayer's Folly*, in 1895 when he was 38 years old.

## FUNERAL COSTS
Dr Samuel Johnson (1709 – 84), the creator of the first modern English dictionary, wrote his only novel in order to pay for his sick mother's medical expenses. Mrs Johnson became ill in January 1759 at the age of 90, and her son – who was short of cash – wrote the book, *Rasselas, Prince of Abyssinia*, in the course of just seven nights. Mrs Johnson died soon after the book's completion, so the £100 Johnson earned from it went to pay her debts and the cost of her funeral. The 40,000-word book tells how the innocent young prince leaves his home in the Happy Valley to explore the world outside.

*Rasselas* was published in 1759, and three years later Dr Johnson's financial troubles were solved when he was awarded a state pension of £300 a year.

## WORDS AND SENTENCES
Some of the world's most enduring literary works – including fiction, autobiography, poetry and philosophy – were written or begun while their authors were in prison.

● The Spanish novelist and dramatist Miguel de Cervantes (1547 – 1616) began his comic novel *Don Quixote* (published in 1605) in Seville prison after he was jailed for debt in 1597.

● The English courtier, explorer, poet and historian Sir Walter Raleigh (about 1552 – 1618) was sentenced to death in 1603 on a trumped-up charge of treason against the new king, James I. He was reprieved, but not pardoned, at the last moment. Imprisoned in the Tower of London, he wrote his *History of the World*. The unfinished work appeared in 1614 – while Raleigh was still in prison. He was released on parole in 1616 to lead an expedition to find gold in South America. But he was forced to turn back empty-handed after his men clashed with Spanish troops. On his return to England, he was arrested again on the earlier treason charge, and executed in 1618.

● The English writer and preacher John Bunyan (1628 – 88) was jailed in 1675 for his Nonconformist religious teachings. During his six months in Bedford County Jail he wrote much of his religious allegory, *Pilgrim's Progress*, which was published in two parts in 1678 and 1684.

● The English writer John Cleland (1709 – 89) was put in Newgate prison in London for debt in 1749. While in jail, he was offered 20 guineas by a publisher named Drybutter to write a licentious novel. The result was *Fanny Hill, or the Memoirs of a Woman of Pleasure* (1750), and the money Cleland received for it secured his release.

● The French satirist Voltaire (1694 – 1778) was jailed in 1717 for writing poems which ridiculed France's dissolute regent, the Duke of Orleans. During his 11 months in the Bastille, Paris, Voltaire started work on his epic poem *La Henriade* (1723), an attack on religious fanaticism and political intrigue.

● The American short story writer O. Henry (1862 – 1910) served three years and three months in the federal penitentiary in Columbus, Ohio, for embezzling funds while he had been a teller with the First National Bank. He wrote some of his best stories in his cell – including the collection he published in 1908 under the title *The Gentle Grafter*.

● The British philosopher and mathematician Bertrand Russell (1872 – 1970) was jailed for six months in London during the First World War for his pacifist writings. During his confinement, he wrote *An Introduction to Mathematical Philosophy* (published in 1919). In the book he gave a simplified account of his classic work *Principia Mathematica* (1910 – 13), which had been written with the British mathematician A. E. Whitehead.

● The Nazi leader Adolf Hitler (1889 – 1945) wrote the first part of his autobiography, *Mein Kampf* (*My Struggle*), in jail. After the Munich Beer Hall *putsch*, an unsuccessful bid to seize power in 1923, he was jailed for nine months in Landsberg fortress, and while there dictated the first part of the autobiography to his disciple Rudolf Hess.

VERLAINE shot his friend.

VILLON: killed a priest.

VOLTAIRE jailed by a duke

# Newspapers and advertising

## COMIC CUTS

The word cartoon originally meant a full-sized working drawing for a painting or tapestry. But in 1841 the English satirical magazine *Punch* published its own entries for a competition for murals in the newly built Houses of Parliament in London. The magazine's drawings, which caricatured the genuine entries, were labelled 'Punch's Cartoons', and so the word came to be used first for pictorial jokes about politics, and later for any comic drawing.

## THE FIRST ADVERTISING AGENCY

The world's first advertising agency was founded by a British businessman named William Tayler in London in 1786. The first American agency was established in Philadelphia 55 years later by an Englishman called Volney B. Palmer. One of Palmer's more eccentric practices was to demand from newspapers a 25 per cent commission for any advertising placed by anyone who was – or had ever been in the past – his client. Astonishingly, it seems that he got it.

FRONT-PAGE NEWS *The Avisa-Relation oder Zeitung (left) was one of the world's first two newspapers. Both were weekly journals first published in Germany in January 1609, and both folded in the 1620s. Since then, news styles – and the speed at which news is flashed around the world – have changed radically. The Times of London, for instance, trumpeted Nelson's victory at Trafalgar on November 7, 1805 – 2½ weeks after the battle took place. But pictures taken on the Moon by the Apollo 11 astronauts Neil Armstrong and Buzz Aldrin were on the front pages of newspapers all over the world within hours of being released.*

## FLIGHT OF FACT

Reuter's, now one of the world's biggest news agencies, began in 1850 – with pigeons. German bankers needed a fast service of Paris stock-exchange prices, but the French telegraph system went only to the Belgian capital, Brussels, and the German one only from Berlin to Aachen.

Paul Julius Reuter (1816 – 99), a German bank clerk, organised a pigeon-post service to bridge the gap of 160km (100 miles). His birds beat the fastest mail train, which took up to nine hours, by seven hours. In 1851, using new submarine cable between Dover and Calais, he extended his stock prices service to London. He became a British citizen, and soon started supplying news as well as prices. Today, the network he founded flashes changing stock and commodity prices all over the world electronically within minutes or even seconds of the event.

## PARTY LINE

The leading daily newspaper in the Soviet Union, *Pravda*, has a circulation of about 7 million. It is the official organ of the Communist Party, and so has more influence than the Moscow paper *Izvestia (News)*, although *Izvestia*'s circulation is about a million higher. *Pravda* is the Russian word for 'truth'.

## EAGER READERS

More than 8000 daily and weekly newspapers are published around the world, about a quarter of them in the United States. But readership levels vary widely in different countries. According to international statistics published in 1983, the country with the most eager readers was Bulgaria. Some 624 copies of its daily newspapers were sold each day for every 1000 people in the country.

In Britain, the daily figure for sales of newspapers was 410 copies per 1000 people; in Australia, it was 336, and in New Zealand 310. The US figure was 282. The countries with the lowest circulation figures – less than 2 copies per 1000 people – were Benin, Chad, Sudan and Upper Volta.

## PRIZE JOURNALIST

Joseph Pulitzer (1847 – 1911), the Hungarian-born American who established the Pulitzer Prizes, originally had a burning ambition to be a soldier. He went to the United States in 1864 only because he had been rejected by the Austrian, French and British armies owing to his poor physique and weak eyesight. In America, however, his skill on horseback gained him a place as a cavalryman in the Union Army towards the end of the Civil War. After the war he settled in the USA and became a journalist. By the 1880s he had made a fortune with the St Louis *Post-Dispatch*, and the New York *World*. In his will he left $2 million to Columbia University to set up a school of journalism, and part of the money went to establishing the Pulitzer Prizes. The prizes have been awarded annually since 1917 to outstanding US journalists, literary writers and musical composers. There are 18 categories, each with a $1000 prize. Pulitzer prize-winners include playwright Tennessee Williams, and Carl Bernstein and Robert Woodward of the *Washington Post* for their reporting on the Watergate scandal.

## BIRTH OF THE BAFFLERS

The first newspaper crossword puzzle was published in 1913, in a Sunday supplement to the New York *World*. Compiled by an Englishman, Arthur Wynne, it contained 32 clues, which were mainly simple word definitions. Since then, other types of crossword have been developed, among them the cryptic crossword, in which the solution is hidden in an obliquely worded clue. Three of the more baffling clues, whose authorship is unknown, are:

    1 Gegs (9,4).
    2        (8).
    3 HIJKLMNO (5).

The answers? 1 Scrambled eggs ('gegs' is an anagram). 2 Clueless. 3 Water (H to O, $H_2O$).

## THE TESTIMONIALS BUSINESS

The practice of paying celebrities to endorse products began in the late 1870s when the actress Lillie Langtry allowed her name to be used in soap advertisements. However, not all celebrities were regular users of the products they endorsed and some never used them at all. Fake testimonials were finally discredited in the 1950s by the film star Grace Kelly, who later became Princess Grace of Monaco. At the time, she was appearing in Lux soap commercials, and the advertisers attributed her delicate complexion to the use of their product. However, when she was asked by a Chicago reporter how any soap could achieve her dewy freshness, she replied briskly: 'Soap of any kind, Lux or otherwise, never touches my face.'

FACE AND FORTUNE *Actress Lillie Langtry, renowned for her beauty and her friendship with Edward VII, endorsed a soap brand in the 1870s – and founded an advertising technique which is still in use.*

# WHO SPENDS WHAT

A survey of 85 non-Communist countries carried out by the International Advertising Association and published in 1983 showed that, in 1981, the countries spent a total of US$118,441 million on advertising. The United States and Canada accounted for $64,849 million, Europe for $28,802 million, Asia $13,251 million, Latin America $6940 million, Australasia $2672 million, and the Middle East and Africa $1924 million.

The major individual spenders were the United States, with an advertising budget of $61,320 million – or 52 per cent of the world's total – Japan with $11,120 million, Britain with $5925 million, West Germany with $5536 million and France with $4484 million. By contrast poorer countries spent much less – Nepal's total amounted to $1.1 million.

The amount of money spent on advertising per head also varied enormously. The average figure for each person on Earth was $43.68. But at one end of the scale, advertisers in the United States spent $266 per person, and at the other, in Nepal, the figure was the equivalent of just 7 US cents.

Expenditure on Press advertising far exceeded that spent on other sorts of advertising. On average, the countries spent almost twice as much on advertising in newspapers, magazines, catalogues and handbills as they did on television commercials – and seven times as much as they did on radio ads.

Despite inflation, the proportions spent by each country are likely to be much the same today.

BILL STICKERS *The first known printed advertisement was distributed in Strasbourg, then in Germany, in 1466. By the 1840s, when this London street scene was painted, posters and handbills were almost everywhere.*

# Cinema and television

## HOW OSCAR GOT HIS NAME

The Academy of Motion Picture Arts and Sciences, the body which awards the annual Oscars, was born on May 4, 1927. It was then that more than 30 leading figures in the US film industry met to establish a non-profit-making organisation to improve the artistic quality of the medium. The group included stars like Mary Pickford and Douglas Fairbanks, and art director Cedric Gibbons who, on a tablecloth at a banquet in Hollywood's Biltmore Hotel, sketched the design for a golden statuette. His design became the model for the academy's trophies and the first were presented in May 1929.

At first, the trophy was known simply as The Statuette. It was not until four years after the inaugural banquet that Oscar was christened. In 1931 Margaret Herrick, then the academy's librarian, spotted a copy of the statuette on an executive's desk. 'Why,' she exclaimed, 'he looks just like my Uncle Oscar!' Her off-the-cuff remark was repeated around the academy – and the name stuck.

## MOVIE MILESTONES

● The first practical motion-picture camera was invented by a French scientist, Étienne Jules Marey, in 1882. His device recorded a sequence of pictures around the edge of a sensitised glass disc. When the pictures were looked at in rapid succession, they created the illusion of movement.

The disc meant, however, that only very short sequences could be shown at a time. So in 1887, Marey replaced the discs with rolls of film – a year before roll film was introduced for still pictures in George Eastman's Kodak camera. In 1893, Marey patented a film projector, enabling his films to be seen on a screen.

● The first commercial showing of a film was in the converted basement of the Grand-Café in Paris on December 28, 1895. The films, of everyday life in the French capital, were made by the brothers Louis and Auguste Lumiére. Each reel of film lasted about a minute.

● The first motion pictures in colour were shown in a London theatre in 1909. But the films showed only two-colour pictures, and it was not until 1930 that a full-colour film was developed by the American firm Technicolor. The new process was first used in Walt Disney cartoon shorts.

● The first commercial sound-on-film production was *Der Brandstifter* (*The Arsonist*), a German film made in 1922. But 'talkies' did not supersede silent films until after the release and enormous success in 1927 of *The Jazz Singer*, starring Al Jolson.

## FLIGHT INTO THE FUTURE

The first film which realistically portrayed space travel – and also featured the first use of the countdown to zero which marks a rocket launch – was *Die Frau Im Mond* (*The Woman in the Moon*), made in Germany in 1928 by director Fritz Lang. One of his technical advisers was an engineer named Hermann Oberth, who in the late 1930s and early 1940s helped to design the 'flying bombs' – the V1 and V2 – that brought death and destruction to London. The shape of the rocket in Lang's film so much resembled the German rocket bombs that Nazi leader Adolf Hitler later demanded that all prints of the film be seized as a threat to military security.

Lang successfully predicted the future of space flight by showing his rocket ship as having several stages which fired in succession – just like the Saturn rockets which took man to the Moon. And the scene in which the craft is trundled on tracks out of a hangar in the direction of the launching pad heralded the real-life activities at Cape Canaveral a generation later.

## BIRTH OF THE 'TALKIES'

The film industry changed from 'silents' to 'talkies' in the late 1920s, after the success in 1927 of *The Jazz Singer*, starring Al Jolson. Overnight, films without

MOVIE MASTER *The Russian director Sergei Eisenstein (1898–1948) was an undisputed master of film. His films include:* October *(right);* Ivan the Terrible *(lower right); and* Alexander Nevsky *(below).*

spoken dialogue were converted into those with speech. And one of the first directors to make the change was Alfred Hitchcock – whose *Blackmail*, in 1929, became the first British 'talkie'. The film had originally been made as a 'silent', but Hitchcock – who had shrewdly kept most of the sets intact – reshot it entirely with dialogue.

His greatest problem concerned his leading lady, Anny Ondra, a Czech whose fractured English was impossible to understand. Her voice had to be dubbed.

Later that year the silent version was released for those cinemas not yet converted to sound.

*The Times* of London was in no doubt about which of the two versions was better. In a leading article on August 14, 1929, the paper declared: 'The comparison is much in favour of the silent version.' The paper was also in no doubt about the future of films with dialogue. 'The talkie is an unsuitable marriage of two dramatic forms,' it declared in the same article. 'We cannot believe that it will endure.'

## SHOOTING ACCIDENTS

Despite persistent legends about the lethal chariot scene in *Ben Hur*, the only deaths that occurred during either version of the film – made in 1925 and 1959 – involved horses, not people.

Three horsemen did die, however, during the shooting of a cavalry charge in the 1941 American film *They Died With Their Boots On*. One of the three, an actor named Bill Mead, was riding beside the film's star, Errol Flynn, when his horse stumbled. As the horse went down, Mead hurled his sword forwards in an attempt to avoid falling on it. But the sword stuck in the ground hilt down, and Mead impaled himself on the blade.

## THE SECOND JAMES STEWART

The real name of the British actor Stewart Granger (1913– ) was James Stewart. He changed it in the mid-1930s to avoid confusion with the US Hollywood star James Stewart (1908– ). The American's name was his real one.

## CINEMA CENSORSHIP

Belgium is the only Western country never to have imposed censorship of films for adults. Denmark, known for its liberal outlook, banished censorship for adult audiences in 1969, followed by Austria and Portugal in the 1970s. Film censorship was abolished in Russia by the short-lived Kerensky government in March 1917. However, the Bolsheviks brought it back in 1922 – and, under Stalin, Soviet film censorship became the strictest in the world. At the end of the First World War, Germany also abolished censorship. But the subsequent torrent of silent sex films brought the return of the censor soon afterwards in 1920.

## PAID AUDIENCES

The first cinema audiences in Hong Kong had to be paid to watch the films. Chinese people were frightened of the potential evil power of the 'moving spirits' on the screen in the first cinema for Chinese inhabitants, and refused to enter. For three weeks in the

---

# CINEMA RECORD-HOLDERS

● The world's most prolific film industry is no longer in Hollywood, but in Bombay. In 1979 – a boom year for the Indian cinema – 714 feature films were produced, each lasting at least an hour. In that same year, Japan produced 335 films, France 234, Turkey 195, the Philippines 170, and the United States 167. Only 38 films were made in Britain.

● The world's most perennially popular author among film-makers is William Shakespeare. There have been almost 300 film productions of his major plays, with 41 versions of *Hamlet* alone.

● Sherlock Holmes has been portrayed on screen more often than any other fictional character. Sir Arthur Conan Doyle's detective has been played by 62 actors in 177 films. The next most portrayed character is Count Dracula, with 133 film appearances, followed by Frankenstein's monster (91 films), Tarzan (83), Hopalong Cassidy (66) and Zorro (66).

● The longest commercially made talking film seen at one screening is *Lawrence of Arabia*. It was made by the British director David Lean in 1962 and stars Peter O'Toole. It runs for 3 hours 42 minutes – two minutes longer than *Gone With the Wind*.

● The longest film ever made was a British underground movie called *The Longest Most Meaningless Movie in the World*. In its original version, which was premiered at a Paris cinema in October 1970, it ran for 48 hours.

● The world's most expensive film was *War and Peace*, made by the Russian director Sergei Bondarchuk between 1963 and 1967. The eight-hour-long film – which is screened over three to four evenings – is reported to have cost more than £65 million. It was shot on 168 different locations – the biggest total for any film – and included a cast of 120,000 extras from the Red Army.

● The first film to be shown to airline passengers in flight was a silent version of Sir Arthur Conan Doyle's *The Lost World*. It was screened during an Imperial Airways flight from London in April 1925.

● The largest make-up budget for any film was $1 million for the 1968 American production *Planet of the Apes*; the sum took up 17 per cent of the film's total production costs. The longest make-up job was the 'tattooing' used on Rod Steiger in the 1969 film *The Illustrated Man*. It took nine men about 20 hours to apply the 'tattoos' all over his body.

● The most financially disastrous film ever made was United Artists' *Heaven's Gate*, a western. It cost an estimated $40 million and on its opening day in New York and Toronto, in November 1980, it did such poor business that it was withdrawn immediately. The film was re-edited from 219 minutes to 153, and released throughout North America in April 1981. By the autumn of 1982 it had earned less than 5 per cent of its outlay and caused the downfall of United Artists, sold to MGM for $380 million. At one stage during filming, the director, Michael Cimino, insisted that the set of an entire western town be shifted back 900mm (3ft) – at a cost of $1 million.

---

**HOLLYWOOD STARS** Groucho, Chico and Harpo Marx (right); and King Kong (below).

early days of the 'silents' the English owner hired audiences by the day, paying them for their attendance until their superstitions were shown to be without foundation. His policy paid off and by 1913 he had ten cinemas in the colony.

## TOP DOG

Rin Tin Tin, the German Shepherd Dog who became the world's most popular animal film star, was discovered as a shell-shocked puppy in a German trench in 1916 by a US serviceman, Captain Lee Duncan. He took the dog to Los Angeles with him and trained him for a film career. For several years Rin Tin Tin provided his studio, Warner Brothers, with its main source of income, and he was duly given top billing above that of his human co-stars.

At the time of his death in 1932 his fan mail was running at about 2000 letters a week – the same as that of Douglas Fairbanks senior.

## MOUSE WITH A MILLION FANS

Walt Disney's most popular cartoon figure Mickey Mouse made his debut in November 1928 in *Steamboat Willie*. Disney (1901 – 66), a former commercial artist, used his own voice for Mickey's high-pitched tones. Within a year, Mickey Mouse clubs had sprouted across the United States and by 1931 they had a million members. In London, Madame Tussaud's immortalised Mickey in wax. In 1933, according to Disney, Mickey received 800,000 fan letters – an average of more than 2000 a day and a total which still stands as a record for movie fan mail.

## A JOLLY EXPERIENCE

The first person to be interviewed on television anywhere in the world was the Irish actress Peggy O'Neil. On April 29, 1930, she appeared on a televisor, as the sets were then known, at Britain's Ideal Home Exhibition in Southampton wearing a 'Baird Television' sweater. 'Television is certainly very fascinating,' she enthused. 'This is the first time I have been interviewed by television and it's rather a jolly experience . . . to say the least, it's very wonderful. And what a top-hole present a televisor would make – there's a new idea!'

## THE FAR-SEEING GERMANS

In 1935 Germany became the first country to have a regular television service – named *Fernseh*, meaning 'far-seeing'. Broadcast from Berlin, the filmed programmes were shown three days a week at a definition of 180 lines, and the German actress Ursula Patzschke became the world's first television announcer.

In 1936 live pictures of the Berlin Olympics were transmitted, but with only partial success. Broadcasting continued until the transmitter was hit during an Allied bombing raid in 1943.

## JUNIOR WATCHERS

By the time US children reach the age of 18, it is estimated that, on average, each has watched more than 17,000 hours of television – a record total of 710 continuous days and nights of viewing. In that time each will have seen almost 360,000 commercials and witnessed more than 15,000 screen murders.

## STARS WHO CHANGED THEIR NAMES

| Screen name | Real name |
| --- | --- |
| Fred Astaire | *Frederick Austerlitz* |
| Theda Bara | *Theodosia Goodman* |
| Dirk Bogarde | *Derek Julius Gaspard Ulric Niven van den Bogaerde* |
| Michael Caine | *Maurice Micklewhite* |
| Cyd Charisse | *Tula Finklea* |
| Joan Crawford | *Lucille Le Sueur* |
| Tony Curtis | *Bernard Schwarz* |
| Doris Day | *Doris Kappelhof* |
| Diana Dors | *Diana Fluck* |
| Judy Garland | *Frances Gumm* |
| Cary Grant | *Archibald Leach* |
| Laurence Harvey | *Larushka Mischa Skikne* |
| Rita Hayworth | *Margarita Carmen Cansino* |
| Boris Karloff | *William Pratt* |
| Danny Kaye | *David Daniel Kaminsky* |
| Herbert Lom | *Herbert Charles Angelo Kuchacewich ze Schluderpacheru* |
| Dean Martin | *Dino Crocetti* |
| Walter Matthau | *Walter Matasschanskayasky* |
| Marilyn Monroe | *Norma Jean Baker* |
| Mickey Rooney | *Joe Yule* |
| Rudolph Valentino | *Rodolpho Alfonso di Valentina d'Antonguolla* |
| John Wayne | *Marion Morrison* |

CORONATION FEAT *The 1953 Coronation of Queen Elizabeth was the first major international TV transmission. It was seen live in France, Holland and West Germany, as well as Britain.*

MOON MARATHON *Station GTV-9 in Melbourne, Australia, broadcast the world's longest continuous programme in July 1969. Covering the entire Apollo 11 moon landing flight, it lasted for 163 hours 18 minutes.*

# HOW TELEVISION WAS INVENTED

**1897** The cathode-ray tube – the component that displays television pictures – was invented by the German physicist Ferdinand Braun. But it was a Russian professor named Boris Rosing who first realised that the bright spot of light the ray threw onto the screen could be made to form a picture. He experimented with this idea in St Petersburg (now Leningrad) between 1907 – 11, and managed to produce crude reproductions of simple shapes.

**1908** A Scottish electrical engineer named Alan Campbell Swinton put forward the idea of a completely electronic television system. In an article in the scientific journal *Nature* he proposed that the cathode-ray tube should be used not only as a receiver – it could also be used to transmit pictures.

**1923** The first electronic camera tube was developed by Vladimir Zworykin – who had studied electrical engineering under Professor Rosing. By the end of 1923 he had produced a cathode-ray tube which could display a crude television picture. Later he developed his camera tube – which he called the iconoscope.

**1926** The world's first public demonstration of television was given in January by the Scottish inventor John Logie Baird in his laboratory in Soho, London. He had been working on his own largely mechanical system – with electronic amplification – and his invited audience included members of the prestigious scientific organisation, the Royal Institution. Overnight Baird became a national figure.

He had beaten his rivals by successfully televising a ventriloquist's dummy. And the previous October he had also put the first human being on his 'box' – a 15-year-old office boy called Bill Taynton, who was paid half-a-crown (12½p) for his services.

**1929** Although Baird had experimented with colour television as early as 1925, it was in 1929 that an American team led by a Bell laboratories' engineer, Herbert Ives, demonstrated the first fully engineered colour system. It transmitted three separate pictures in red, green and blue – thereby using three transmission channels – and needed clumsy receivers to combine them into a single image. This drawback was not overcome until the 1950s.

**1929** Baird opened the world's first television studio in London's Long Acre. The crude, jerky pictures were made up of only 30 scanning lines on the screen – and because they contained so little visual information they could be broadcast from an ordinary medium-wave radio transmitter.

**1931 – 6** Between 1931 and 1936 television advanced dramatically. First of all Vladimir Zworykin in America produced the first practical version of his iconoscope electronic camera – and in England a similar tube, the emitron, was developed by a research team at EMI headed by Isaac Shoenberg.

The EMI team progressed from mechanical scanning to an entirely electronic system, and in 1935 they worked in conjunction with the Marconi company – formed by Guglielmo Marconi, the inventor of radio – to produce a high-definition service.

In November 1936 the BBC started a high-definition service from Alexandra Palace in North London. For three months both Baird's system and that of Marconi-EMI were used alternately in competition with each other. Baird had improved the definition of his early 30-line pictures to 240 lines, but he did not have a satisfactory electronic camera and the programmes had to be filmed. In addition, Baird's camera had to be bolted to the floor to damp down vibrations caused by the speed at which the machinery turned – and gallons of water were needed to prevent it overheating. The Marconi-EMI system provided a better picture with 405 lines. The electronic camera was also mobile and silent – and so it was finally chosen over Baird's mechanical system in January 1937.

**1939** The USA's first fully electronic service was started by the NBC company on April 30.

**1950** A meeting of European broadcasters advocated the use of a common picture standard of 625 lines. This was adopted in all but two countries: Britain, which was using its pre-war 405-line service; and France, which had already opted for 819 lines. Britain and France did not adopt 625 lines until the 1960s. Today, most of the world's nations use the 625-line standard – with the exception of the USA, Japan and a few others, who have adopted the American 525-line standard.

The colour television camera was perfected in the USA in the early 1950s with two key inventions. By using a coding system, studios became able to broadcast a colour TV signal on the same transmission channel as had previously served for black and white. And the RCA company's 'shadow mask' – a colour separation process – enabled a single cathode tube to show a colour picture.

**1956** The first practical videotape recorder was made in Redwood, California, by the Ampex Corporation. It was originally meant for use by broadcasters so that they could record programmes for later transmission without loss of quality. But the machines were large, complex and expensive – and it took some 25 years before the size and price of videotape recorders had shrunk so that viewers could tape programmes in their homes.

**1960** Transistors made it possible to construct very small television sets. The Japanese firm of Sony developed the first all-transistor portable television in 1960. The mini-television had a 200mm (8in) screen. TV screens are measured diagonally.

**1962** Until the introduction of satellite communications there were no intercontinental television links. Then, in 1962, the Telstar satellite began relaying transatlantic programmes. The first official programme exchange was on July 23, when the US transmission began with a baseball game in Chicago. Later that night US viewers saw a special Eurovision programme introduced from London by Richard Dimbleby. It opened with a shot of Big Ben. Today, programmes can be relayed from almost anywhere in the world via orbiting satellites, and TV companies plan to use satellites to transmit programmes directly to viewers – eliminating the need for expensive transmitter masts.

**1979 – 83** The Japanese firm of Matsushita took out in 1979 the first patent for a flat-screen pocket television set – with a liquid crystal display as a screen. In 1983, another Japanese company, Sony, introduced a black-and-white cathode-tube model about the size of a paperback book and costing around £250. Later that year, a British company, Sinclair Research, demonstrated a set that would cost less than £100 and use less battery power. Eventually, TV engineers predict, flat-screen sets will be no larger than a pocket calculator and will be in full colour.

FACTS ABOUT THE

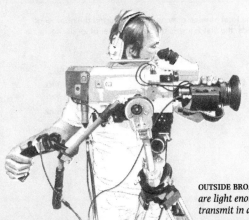

OUTSIDE BROADCAST *Modern TV cameras are light enough to be carried and can transmit in almost any conditions.*

THE TIMELESS TEST THAT NOBODY WON The longest Test match in the history of cricket – played at Durban, South Africa, in March 1939 – lasted for 11 exhausting days and the players spent a total of 43 hours 16 minutes on the pitch. The Test was arranged at the end of a tour by an English MCC team.

Because the tourists had won one match, and three matches had been drawn, it was agreed that the fifth and final international would have no set time limit.

In all, 5070 balls were bowled during the match and 1981 runs were scored – the highest total ever recorded. The total included one double and five single centuries. Among the famous names in the England team were captain Wally Hammond, Len Hutton, Paul Gibb, Les Ames, Bill Edrich, Hedley Verity and Doug Wright. The South African team included Alan Melville, Eric Rowan, Bruce Mitchell, Dudley Nourse and Ken Viljoen. In the end, the weather was the only winner. The MCC were just 42 runs short of victory with five wickets in hand when the rain came down. The match had to be abandoned to allow the English team to catch their ship home.

AMAZING GRACE The bearded Dr W. G. Grace (1848 – 1915), one of the most outstanding cricketers in the game's history, first turned out for a West Gloucestershire team at the age of nine. He was captain of England up to the age of 50 and went on playing for Gloucestershire until he was 61.

In his first-class career, he scored 54,896 runs, took 2876 wickets and held 877 catches. He was also the first cricketer to score 1000 runs and take 100 wickets in a single season (1874). His initials, the most famous in cricket, stand for William Gilbert.

MYTH OF THE ASHES The cricketing battles for the Ashes, between England and Australia, started as a contest for a trophy which did not exist. After Aus-

---

# CRICKET

## WORLD RECORDS IN FIRST-CLASS CRICKET (to May 1, 1984)

| | Holder | Record | Date |
|---|---|---|---|
| **Batting** | | | |
| Highest individual innings | H. Mohammed, Pakistan | 499 runs | Jan 8 – 11, 1959 |
| Highest individual Test innings | G. S. Sobers, West Indies | 365 runs | Feb 27 – March 1, 1958 |
| Longest innings | H. Mohammed, Pakistan | 16hr 10min | Jan 20 – 23, 1958 |
| Career record for batting | J. Hobbs, England | 61,237 runs | 1905 – 34 |
| Test match record aggregate | Sunil Gavaskar, India | 8394 runs | 1971 – 84 |
| Season record for batting | D. Compton, England | 3816 runs | 1947 |
| Most centuries (career) | J. Hobbs, England | 197 | 1905 – 34 |
| Most centuries (season) | D. Compton, England | 18 | 1947 |
| Most centuries (Tests) | Sunil Gavaskar, India | 30 | 1971 – 84 |
| Highest career batting average | D. Bradman, Australia | 28,067 runs in 338 innings (95.14 average) | 1927 – 49 |
| **Bowling** | | | |
| Most wickets taken (career) | W. Rhodes, England | 4187 | 1898 – 1930 |
| Most wickets taken (Tests) | Dennis Lillee, Australia | 355 | 1971 – 84 |
| Most wickets taken (season) | A. P. Freeman, England | 304 | 1928 |
| Lowest average (season) | A. Shaw, England | 177 wickets for 1525 runs (8.61 average) | 1880 |
| **Fielding** | | | |
| Most catches (career) | F. Woolley, England | 1018 | 1906 – 38 |
| Most catches (match) | W. Hammond, England | 10 | 1928 |

## TEST MATCHES 1877 – June 1, 1984

Reading across in this summary of results, the first figure is the total number of wins and the second the number of drawn matches against a given opponent. Reading downwards, the first figure is the total number of losses against a given opponent.

| | England | Australia | South Africa | West Indies | New Zealand | India | Pakistan | Sri Lanka |
|---|---|---|---|---|---|---|---|---|
| England | – | 83/73 | 46/38 | 21/34 | 30/27 | 28/31 | 13/23 | 1/0 |
| Australia | 95/73 | – | 29/11 | 26/15* | 8/5 | 20/11 | 18/9 | 1/0 |
| South Africa | 18/38 | 11/13 | – | None | 9/6 | None | None | None |
| West Indies | 25/34 | 16/15* | None | – | 5/9 | 22/27 | 7/8 | None |
| New Zealand | 3/27 | 2/5 | 2/6 | 3/9 | – | 4/11 | 1/12 | 4/1 |
| India | 8/31 | 8/11 | None | 5/27 | 10/11 | – | 4/23 | 0/1 |
| Pakistan | 3/23 | 8/9 | None | 4/8 | 8/12 | 6/23 | – | 2/1 |
| Sri Lanka | 0/0 | 0/0 | None | None | 0/1 | 0/1 | 0/1 | – |

* including one tie

tralia won a one-game Test at the Oval, London, in 1882, a mock obituary lamenting the death of English cricket appeared in a newspaper *The Sporting Times*. It concluded:'The body will be cremated and the ashes taken to Australia.'

The joke caught on and when an English team led by Ivo Bligh went to Australia later in the same year, a woman in Sydney burned a stump used in the third Test and presented the ashes to the England captain in an urn. The urn was bequeathed to the Marylebone Cricket Club, the MCC, by Bligh on his death in 1927. It now stands in the Memorial Gallery at Lord's cricket ground, home of the MCC, along with the 1882 match scorecard.

It remains in the gallery even when Australia wins a Test series against England.

---

*Table tennis was first played with balls made from champagne corks and bats made from cigar-box lids. It was invented in the late 1880s by James Gibb, an English runner and engineer, as a diversion for wet weekends and was first marketed, with celluloid balls replacing the corks, under the name Gossima. Its popularity soared in 1901 after the British manufacturer of the equipment, John Jacques, renamed the game Ping Pong.*

---

COO, FANCY THAT! The fastest sporting animal is the racing pigeon. With a following wind, pigeons have been clocked at speeds of up to 177km/h (110mph) in races ranging from 161km (100 miles) to 1610km (1000 miles). The most famous pigeon fancier is Britain's Queen Elizabeth, who keeps a loft of about 150 birds near her Sandringham home.

BEATEN TO BASE The all-American game of baseball – usually said to have been adapted from an old children's game by a New Yorker named Abner Doubleday in 1839 – could be English in origin. A Kent vicar wrote disparagingly in 1700 about baseball being played on Sundays.

The English author Jane Austen refers to 'base ball' in her novel *Northanger Abbey*, published in 1798. And the diamond-shaped pitch and the rule which says that a batter is out if he misses the ball three times are similar to those set out in a boy's book which was published in England in 1829 and reprinted in the United States soon afterwards.

DOCTOR'S BRAINWAVE Modern basketball was invented in 1891 by a Canadian-born teacher, Dr James Naismith, at a school in the US state of Massachusetts. In four years it had swept across the USA and it is now played in 150 countries by 100 million people. Early players had to wait after a score while the ball was retrieved by ladder from the peach baskets then used – until an unknown genius had the simple idea of cutting off the basket bottoms.

MILLIONAIRES' OBSESSION The most expensive and rule-ridden sporting event in the world must be the America's Cup yacht race. The event was inspired by the yacht *America* which won a British trophy called the Hundred Guinea Cup for a race round the Isle of Wight in 1851. Six years later the cup was given to the New York Yacht Club, whose members

beat off 24 challenges – the first in 1870 – by a succession of millionaire racers.

In 1983, however, *Australia II* won the trophy series off Rhode Island with a finned keel which the Americans tried for a time to ban as illegal. The challenge cost the boat's Australian owner Alan Bond £3.5 million, but at least he did not have to put up with one rule that had handicapped earlier challengers. Until 1958 competitors' boats had to cross the ocean to the United States under their own sail.

TOP BAT *Sir Garfield Sobers, who was knighted in 1975, led the West Indian cricket team between 1965 and 1974. He still holds the world record for a Test innings: 365 not out. In 1968, he also became the only batsman ever to hit six sixes in a single six-ball over.*

# Sport

## CYCLING

### TOUR DE FRANCE WINNERS

| Date | Name | Nationality |
|------|------|-------------|
| 1922 | Firmin Lambot | Belgium |
| 1923 | Henri Pelissier | France |
| 1924 | Ottavio Bottecchia | Italy |
| 1925 | Ottavio Bottecchia | Italy |
| 1926 | Lucien Buysse | Belgium |
| 1927 | Nicholas Frantz | Luxembourg |
| 1928 | Nicholas Frantz | Luxembourg |
| 1929 | Maurice Dewaele | Belgium |
| 1930 | André Leducq | France |
| 1931 | Antonin Magne | France |
| 1932 | André Leducq | France |
| 1933 | Georges Speicher | France |
| 1934 | Antonin Magne | France |
| 1935 | Romain Maes | Belgium |
| 1936 | Sylvere Maes | Belgium |
| 1937 | Roger Lapebie | France |
| 1938 | Gino Bartali | Italy |
| 1939 | Sylvere Maes | Belgium |
| 1947 | Jean Robic | France |
| 1948 | Gino Bartali | Italy |
| 1949 | Fausto Coppi | Italy |
| 1950 | Ferdinand Kuber | Switzerland |
| 1951 | Hugo Koblet | Switzerland |
| 1952 | Fausto Coppi | Italy |
| 1953 | Louison Bobet | France |
| 1954 | Louison Bobet | France |
| 1955 | Louison Bobet | France |
| 1956 | Roger Walkowiak | France |
| 1957 | Jacques Anquetil | France |
| 1958 | Charly Gaul | Luxembourg |
| 1959 | Federico Bahamontes | Spain |
| 1960 | Gastone Nencini | Italy |
| 1961 | Jacques Anquetil | France |
| 1962 | Jacques Anquetil | France |
| 1963 | Jacques Anquetil | France |
| 1964 | Jacques Anquetil | France |
| 1965 | Felice Gimondi | Italy |
| 1966 | Lucien Aimar | France |
| 1967 | Roger Pingeon | France |
| 1968 | Jan Janssen | Netherlands |
| 1969 | Eddy Merckx | Belgium |
| 1970 | Eddy Merckx | Belgium |
| 1971 | Eddy Merckx | Belgium |
| 1972 | Eddy Merckx | Belgium |
| 1973 | Luis Ocana | Spain |
| 1974 | Eddy Merckx | Belgium |
| 1975 | Bernard Thevenet | France |
| 1976 | Lucien van Impe | Belgium |
| 1977 | Bernard Thevenet | France |
| 1978 | Bernard Hinault | France |
| 1979 | Bernard Hinault | France |
| 1980 | Joop Zoetemelk | Netherlands |
| 1981 | Bernard Hinault | France |
| 1982 | Bernard Hinault | France |
| 1983 | Laurent Fignon | France |
| 1984 | Laurent Fignon | France |

LIGHTNING RETURN  The Mexican-born US golfer Lee Trevino, former British and US Open champion, is one of the few people in the world to have been struck by lightning, and survive. A bolt lifted him bodily nearly half a metre (18in) into the air, knocked him out and scorched his left shoulder at Chicago during the 1975 Western Open tournament. Trevino and two others were taken to hospital after the strike, but none was seriously hurt.

However, Trevino has suffered from back trouble ever since, and in 1980 was awarded a special trophy for not allowing the injury to interfere with his game.

ROUGH JUSTICE  Golf, the game traditionally given to the world by Scotland, was banned several times in that country in the 15th century – as a military precaution. The game was so popular that it was distract-

**THE GOLDEN BEAR** *Jack Nicklaus is golf's highest earner. He has won more than $4 million.*

ing men from archery practice at a time when England was embroiled in the Wars of the Roses (1455–85) and it seemed that the fighting could spill over the border. The game's earliest mention was in the first of these Scottish laws, passed in 1457, which decreed that 'goff be utterly cryit doune and not usit'. The ban did not last for long, however. By the early 1500s, the game was back in favour and even Scottish kings – including James VI, who as James I introduced the game to England – are known to have taken it up.

FIDDLER ON THE WHEELS The first known pair of roller skates was constructed by a Belgian musician named Joseph Merlin who wanted to impress guests at a masked ball held in London in 1760. Merlin made his entry on the skates playing a violin – with shattering effect. Unable to stop or change direction, he shot across the ballroom and crashed into an ornate full-length mirror, breaking the mirror and the violin and badly injuring himself.

Roller skating became more widely popular after 1823, when a London fruit-seller, Robert Tyers, demonstrated a pair of five-wheeled skates and a public rink was opened in the city. The modern, four-wheeled skate design was patented in 1863 by a New

Yorker named James L. Plimpton. Ball-bearing wheels were introduced in 1884, and plastic wheels – which give a faster, smoother and safer ride – were first marketed in the USA in the late 1970s.

BONESHAKER MARATHON The first town-to-town bicycle race – a forerunner of the Tour de France – was won by an Englishman. The race, organised by a French magazine, took place in the early summer of 1868. About 100 competitors, all riding 'boneshaker' bicycles with iron rims (pneumatic tyres were not invented until 1888), set out on the 123km (76 miles) course from Paris to Rouen. The race was won by an English doctor, James Moore, who covered the distance in 10 hours 45 minutes – at an average speed of just 11km/h (7mph).

The Tour de France, now a 23-day test of speed and endurance over a course of more than 4000km (2500 miles), was first staged in 1903.

*US sprinter Jesse Owens (1913–80) was christened James Cleveland Owens. He became known as Jesse simply from the sound of his initials: J. C.*

# GOLF

## BRITISH OPEN WINNERS

| Date | Name | Nationality |
|---|---|---|
| 1953 | Ben Hogan | USA |
| 1954 | Peter Thomson | Australia |
| 1955 | Peter Thomson | Australia |
| 1956 | Peter Thomson | Australia |
| 1957 | Bobby Locke | South Africa |
| 1958 | Peter Thomson | Australia |
| 1959 | Gary Player | South Africa |
| 1960 | Kel Nagle | Australia |
| 1961 | Arnold Palmer | USA |
| 1962 | Arnold Palmer | USA |
| 1963 | Bob Charles | New Zealand |
| 1964 | Tony Lema | USA |
| 1965 | Peter Thomson | Australia |
| 1966 | Jack Nicklaus | USA |
| 1967 | Roberto de Vicenzo | Argentina |
| 1968 | Gary Player | South Africa |
| 1969 | Tony Jacklin | UK |
| 1970 | Jack Nicklaus | USA |
| 1971 | Lee Trevino | USA |
| 1972 | Lee Trevino | USA |
| 1973 | Tom Weiskopf | USA |
| 1974 | Gary Player | South Africa |
| 1975 | Tom Watson | USA |
| 1976 | Johnny Miller | USA |
| 1977 | Tom Watson | USA |
| 1978 | Jack Nicklaus | USA |
| 1979 | Severiano Ballesteros | Spain |
| 1980 | Tom Watson | USA |
| 1981 | Bill Rogers | USA |
| 1982 | Tom Watson | USA |
| 1983 | Tom Watson | USA |
| 1984 | Severiano Ballesteros | Spain |

## US OPEN WINNERS

| Date | Name | Nationality |
|---|---|---|
| 1953 | Ben Hogan | USA |
| 1954 | Ed Furgol | USA |
| 1955 | Jack Fleck | USA |
| 1956 | Cary Middlecoff | USA |
| 1957 | Dick Mayer | USA |
| 1958 | Tommy Bolt | USA |
| 1959 | Billy Casper | USA |
| 1960 | Arnold Palmer | USA |
| 1961 | Gene Littler | USA |
| 1962 | Jack Nicklaus | USA |
| 1963 | Julius Boros | USA |
| 1964 | Ken Venturi | USA |
| 1965 | Gary Player | South Africa |
| 1966 | Billy Casper | USA |
| 1967 | Jack Nicklaus | USA |
| 1968 | Lee Trevino | USA |
| 1969 | Orville Moody | USA |
| 1970 | Tony Jacklin | UK |
| 1971 | Lee Trevino | USA |
| 1972 | Jack Nicklaus | USA |
| 1973 | Johnny Miller | USA |
| 1974 | Hale Irwin | USA |
| 1975 | Lou Graham | USA |
| 1976 | Jerry Pate | USA |
| 1977 | Hubert Green | USA |
| 1978 | Andy North | USA |
| 1979 | Hale Irwin | USA |
| 1980 | Jack Nicklaus | USA |
| 1981 | David Graham | Australia |
| 1982 | Tom Watson | USA |
| 1983 | Larry Nelson | USA |
| 1984 | Fuzzy Zoeller | USA |

FACTS ABOUT THE
ARTS & ENTERTAINMENT

# Sport

RUGBY RIDDLE The story that a 15-year-old boy at England's Rugby School invented the game of rugby in November 1823, by picking up an ordinary football during a game and running with it, rests on the testimony of only one person.

Writing in the school magazine in 1880 – 57 years later – one of the school's former pupils, Matthew Bloxham, recorded for the first time his eyewitness account of the incident. Bloxham's version has never been challenged. But it has never been corroborated, either – not even by the boy who was said to have picked up the ball, William Webb Ellis. Ellis, who became a vicar, died in 1872 without ever laying claim to be rugby's inventor.

TRY FOR A KICK A 'try' in rugby once referred to a conversion, not a touchdown. Under the early rules of the game, in the 1840s, each side had 20 players. Points were scored only by kicks at goal, and to qualify for a kick a player had to cross the goal-line with the ball and touch it down. Supporters would then shout 'a try, a try' – meaning that their team should now attempt to kick a goal.

*Two teams from a British regiment stationed at Jubbulpore, India, took part in the longest known tug of war. The battle – between H company and E company of a battalion of Sherwood Foresters – took place in 1889 and lasted for 2 hours 41 minutes. H company won.*

HOW SOCCER GOT ITS NAME Although the first official set of rules for soccer was drawn up in 1848, Association Football – as soccer was originally called – continued for most of the 19th century to be a rough-and-tumble affair. Most matches took place without referees, and tripping, hacking, elbowing and shirt-pulling were all regarded as acceptable ways of getting or keeping the ball.

The name soccer was coined by an Oxford footballer named Charles Wreford Brown in 1863, at a time when Oxford students had a habit of turning colloquial words such as 'swots' (for bookworms) and 'togs' (for clothes) into 'swotters' and 'toggers'. Wreford Brown stretched part of the word Association in the same way to create 'soccer' as a neat but distinctive counterpart to 'rugger'.

PETRIE'S LUCKY 13 Scottish footballer John Petrie's record still stands 100 years after he set it. In 1885, in what was perhaps the most one-sided match in first-class soccer, he scored 13 goals for Arbroath against an Aberdeen club called Bon Accord.

The final score was Arbroath 36, Bon Accord 0. The Arbroath goalkeeper never touched the ball; he spent most of the match sheltering from the rain under an umbrella.

TERRACE TROUBLE Soccer hooliganism is no new phenomenon. Sports fans were misbehaving in the 1st century AD, when the Roman historian Tacitus reported battles in Pompeii's amphitheatre between locals and visitors from neighbouring Nuceria. Abuse was followed by stone-throwing and fighting with weapons. Such was the carnage that the Emperor Nero forbade similar gatherings for ten years.

THE KING'S MARATHON The distance of the modern marathon – 26 miles and 385 yards – was arranged for the benefit of a British monarch. Although the race has been included in the Olympics since the modern Games were founded by the Frenchman Baron de Coubertin in 1896, the length of the course varied at first.

Then, in the London Games of 1908, the organisers originally planned for the race to be over 26 miles, from Windsor Castle to the White City stadium. The extra 385 yards were added so that the race could finish directly in front of Edward VII's royal box – and the distance, whose metric equivalent is 42.195km, was adopted as the international standard in 1924.

In the 1908 race, an Italian, Dorando Pietri, reached the stadium well ahead of the field but reeling from heat exhaustion. He fell three times and had to be helped to his feet. Finally he was helped across the line – and was disqualified for receiving aid. Pietri spent two days in hospital after the race, and the gold medal went to a US runner, Johnny Hayes.

*The modern Olympic custom of carrying a flaming torch from Athens to the site of the Games was started by Nazi leader Adolf Hitler. An international team of runners carried a torch 3200km (2000 miles) across Europe to Berlin for the opening ceremony of the 1936 Games.*

# RUGBY UNION

## INTERNATIONAL MATCHES 1871 – APRIL 1984

Reading across in this summary of results, the first figure is the total number of wins and the second the number of drawn matches against a given opponent. Reading down, the first figure is the total number of lost matches.

| | England | Scotland | Ireland | Wales | British Isles | South Africa | New Zealand | Australia | France |
|---|---|---|---|---|---|---|---|---|---|
| England | – | 47/16 | 54/8 | 35/12 | – | 2/1 | 3/0 | 4/0 | 32/6 |
| Scotland | 37/16 | – | 47/4 | 37/2 | – | 3/0 | 0/2 | 6/0 | 26/2 |
| Ireland | 34/8 | 43/4 | – | 28/5 | – | 1/1 | 0/1 | 6/0 | 25/4 |
| Wales | 42/12 | 49/2 | 53/5 | – | – | 0/1 | 3/0 | 7/0 | 36/3 |
| British Isles | – | – | – | – | – | 14/6 | 5/3 | 12/0 | – |
| South Africa | 4/1 | 5/0 | 8/1 | 6/1 | 20/6 | – | 20/2 | 21/0 | 12/4 |
| New Zealand | 10/0 | 10/2 | 8/1 | 8/0 | 24/3 | 15/2 | – | 52/4 | 14/0 |
| Australia | 6/0 | 3/0 | 3/0 | 3/0 | 2/0 | 7/0 | 18/4 | – | 4/2 |
| France | 21/6 | 26/2 | 28/4 | 18/3 | – | 3/4 | 4/0 | 9/2 | – |

**MAN WHO STARTED THE MARATHON** The modern marathon was inspired by a professional courier named Pheidippides, who is said to have carried the news of the Athenians' victory over the Persians at Marathon in 490 BC from the battlefield to Athens. He ran the 35km (22 miles) without stopping. On arriving in the city he gasped: 'Rejoice, we conquer!' – and dropped dead, possibly of heat strain.

Earlier, when the Persian army first landed at Marathon, Pheidippides completed an even longer run. He was sent from Athens to ask Sparta for help against the invaders, and he covered the 240km (150 miles) between the cities in an astonishing two days. However, the Spartans were celebrating a religious festival and refused to leave until it was over. By the time they and Pheidippides arrived at Marathon, the Persians had been routed without their help – and Pheidippides was sent off on the run that killed him.

**THE COMPANIONSHIP OF THE LONG-DISTANCE RUNNER** Top men Olympic runners can cover the marathon distance in less than 2 hours 10 minutes. And the world's best women athletes – who competed for the first time in an Olympic marathon in 1984 – can get round in less than 2 hours 30 minutes.

But interest in marathons has also spread far beyond the experts. Tens of thousands of part-time runners have pounded around marathon courses all over the world, and many of their achievements have nothing to do with speed. Bucky Cox, of Texas, recorded a time of 5 hours 29 minutes for a US marathon in 1978 . . . at the age of five. And in 1976, a Greek runner named Dimitriou Yordanidis covered the route from Marathon to Athens in 7 hours 33 minutes . . . at the age of 98.

**FIRST PAST THE POST** Winning a victor's crown in the ancient Olympics had more in common with an election than with a modern-style athletics competition. There was no timekeeping system, and crossing the finishing line first was no guarantee of victory. Rhythm, style and grace were considered to be at least as important as beating the opposition. After each event, judges would deliberate, often for several minutes. Then each would cast a secret vote, and the winner was decided on the results.

---

*The only time that the Olympic flame has ever gone out during the Games was at Montreal, Canada, on July 27, 1976. It was doused by a cloudburst during a rest day when the only people in the stadium were workmen. It was rekindled a minute or two later by a plumber named Pierre Bouchard with a cigarette lighter and a rolled-up newspaper.*

---

**OWENS VERSUS THE NAZIS** Jesse Owens, the son of a black Alabama cotton-picker, upstaged Adolf Hitler at the 1936 Olympic Games. Nazi leaders had dismissed Owens and the nine other blacks in the US team contemptuously as 'auxiliaries', but the ten beat the cream of Nazi youth to collect a total of seven gold, three silver and three bronze medals.

Owens alone picked up four golds, in the 100 and 200m sprints, in the long jump and in the 4 × 100m relay – a feat that was repeated in the 1984 Los Angeles Games by US athlete Carl Lewis.

## SOCCER

### WORLD CUP WINNERS

| Year | Championship final | Host |
|------|--------------------|------|
| 1938 | Italy 4, Hungary 2 | France |
| 1950 | Uruguay 2, Brazil 1 | Brazil |
| 1954 | West Germany 3, Hungary 2 | Switzerland |
| 1958 | Brazil 5, Sweden 2 | Sweden |
| 1962 | Brazil 3, Czechoslovakia 1 | Chile |
| 1966 | England 4, West Germany 2 | England |
| 1970 | Brazil 4, Italy 1 | Mexico |
| 1974 | West Germany 2, Netherlands 1 | W Germany |
| 1978 | Argentina 3, Netherlands 1 | Argentina |
| 1982 | Italy 3, West Germany 1 | Spain |

**SHARP SHOOTER** *Brazilian soccer star Edson Arantes do Nascimento got his nickname of Pelé from his skill at* pelada, *an informal version of football that he played in the streets as a child. In a career total of 1363 matches, he scored 1281 goals.*

# Sport

WIVES KEEP OUT  Married women were not allowed even to watch, let alone compete in, the ancient Olympics – on pain of death. The Greeks believed that the presence of wives at Olympia would defile Greece's oldest religious shrine there, although young girls were allowed in.

Ironically, the shrine the men were protecting was dedicated to a woman, the fertility goddess Rhea, who was the mother of the supreme god Zeus.

The penalty for women who broke the rule was to be thrown from a nearby cliff. Only once is a woman known to have watched the Games and lived. She was a widow named Callipateira, who dressed up as one of the judges in order to watch her son, Pisodorus, compete. When he won, she was so overjoyed that she threw off her man's clothes. She was not condemned to death, for her father, brothers and sons had

all participated gloriously in successive Olympics. Instead a new law was passed requiring all judges to appear like at least some of the athletes: naked.

HOOK, LINE AND STINKER  An international championship was abandoned in 1970 because it was thought to be too dangerous for anyone except Swedes. The championship grew out of impromptu eating contests which had been held for generations at the northern Swedish town of Örnsköldsvik, on the Gulf of Bothnia. The trouble was what the competitors had to eat: rotten herrings.

Since medieval times, fishermen in the area have preserved their summer catch by sealing the fish inside

# TENNIS

**WIMBLEDON: men's singles**

| Date | Name | Nationality |
|------|------|-------------|
| 1954 | Jaroslav Drobny | Egypt |
| 1955 | Tony Trabert | USA |
| 1956 | Lew Hoad | Australia |
| 1957 | Lew Hoad | Australia |
| 1958 | Ashley Cooper | Australia |
| 1959 | Alex Olmedo | Peru |
| 1960 | Neale Fraser | Australia |
| 1961 | Rod Laver | Australia |
| 1962 | Rod Laver | Australia |
| 1963 | Chuck McKinley | USA |
| 1964 | Roy Emerson | Australia |
| 1965 | Roy Emerson | Australia |
| 1966 | Manuelo Santana | Spain |
| 1967 | John Newcombe | Australia |
| 1968 | Rod Laver | Australia |
| 1969 | Rod Laver | Australia |
| 1970 | John Newcombe | Australia |
| 1971 | John Newcombe | Australia |
| 1972 | Stan Smith | USA |
| 1973 | Jan Kodes | Czechoslovakia |
| 1974 | Jimmy Connors | USA |
| 1975 | Arthur Ashe | USA |
| 1976 | Bjorn Borg | Sweden |
| 1977 | Bjorn Borg | Sweden |
| 1978 | Bjorn Borg | Sweden |
| 1979 | Bjorn Borg | Sweden |
| 1980 | Bjorn Borg | Sweden |
| 1981 | John McEnroe | USA |
| 1982 | Jimmy Connors | USA |
| 1983 | John McEnroe | USA |
| 1984 | John McEnroe | USA |

**WIMBLEDON: women's singles**

| Date | Name | Nationality |
|------|------|-------------|
| 1954 | Maureen Connolly | USA |
| 1955 | Louise Brough | USA |
| 1956 | Shirley Fry | USA |
| 1957 | Althea Gibson | USA |
| 1958 | Althea Gibson | USA |
| 1959 | Maria Bueno | Brazil |
| 1960 | Maria Bueno | Brazil |
| 1961 | Angela Mortimer | UK |
| 1962 | Karen Susman | USA |
| 1963 | Margaret Smith | Australia |
| 1964 | Maria Bueno | Brazil |
| 1965 | Margaret Smith | Australia |
| 1966 | Billie Jean King | USA |
| 1967 | Billie Jean King | USA |
| 1968 | Billie Jean King | USA |
| 1969 | Ann Jones | UK |
| 1970 | Margaret Court | Australia |
| 1971 | Evonne Goolagong | Australia |
| 1972 | Billie Jean King | USA |
| 1973 | Billie Jean King | USA |
| 1974 | Chris Evert | USA |
| 1975 | Billie Jean King | USA |
| 1976 | Chris Evert | USA |
| 1977 | Virginia Wade | UK |
| 1978 | Martina Navratilova | Czechoslovakia |
| 1979 | Martina Navratilova | Czechoslovakia |
| 1980 | Evonne Cawley | Australia |
| 1981 | Chris Lloyd | USA |
| 1982 | Martina Navratilova | USA |
| 1983 | Martina Navratilova | USA |
| 1984 | Martina Navratilova | USA |

containers – once barrels, now large tin cans. As the fish decay, they ferment as well, giving off gases which make the tins swell into the shape of footballs. The result, when the bulging tins are opened, is a dish which is said to taste delicious but to smell more pungent than an over-ripe Gorgonzola cheese. The tins are so highly pressurised by the gas that they cannot be exported by air because the lower pressure in a plane could make them explode. And officials in some other countries, including nearby West Germany, regard the contents with deep suspicion. In 1983, for example, a German court decided that a woman who had eaten the herring in her apartment was guilty of such a grave breach of the health laws that she should be evicted.

Örnsköldsvik's feasting festival, held every year in late August, was turned into an organised world championship as a way of attracting more tourists to the area. But the organisers hurriedly dropped the idea after some foreign contestants became very ill and had to spend several weeks in hospital. Today, the locals still challenge each other to informal contests. But though foreigners are welcome as spectators, they are not encouraged to take part. In 1984, the world record for eating the herrings was 53 complete fish in one hour. The record was set in 1964 by a trencherman named Bo Sjöström – who is Swedish.

> *Ten-pin bowling was invented as a ruse to evade the law. An ancient German version of the game, using nine pins, was taken to the USA by Dutch settlers in the 17th century, but it was banned by a number of state legislatures in the 1840s because bowling alleys had become the focus of widespread betting and attracted criminals. Promoters added the tenth pin to get round the ban.*

DRY RUN  The Henley-on-Todd Festival, which is held every year near Alice Springs in Australia's Northern Territory, is named after the elegant rowing regatta at Henley-on-Thames in England. But there the resemblance ends. Since the Australian event is held when the River Todd is dry, the competitors use boats without oars, seats – or bottoms.

However, teamwork and muscle power count just as much as they do in England. The crews have to hold their 'boats' around them and run along the dusty riverbed to the finish.

PRESENT WITH A FUTURE  *Bjorn Borg, the Swede who won the Wimbledon singles championship five times in a row, might never have played tennis but for a childhood gift. After winning a table tennis tournament at the age of nine, Bjorn was allowed to choose a prize by his father. Bjorn asked for a tennis racket, and the gift prompted him to lose interest in what had been until then his favourite sport: ice hockey.*

PIES IN THE SKY  The plastic flying saucers now known as Frisbees get their name from a US pie-maker. William Russell Frisbie opened the Frisbie Pie Company in Connecticut in 1871 near the US university of Yale.

Yale students who bought Frisbie's products invented the game, though whether it was the pie tins that they threw to each other, or the pies themselves, is not clear. Plastic versions of the saucer shape copied from the tins were first made in the 1940s by Walter Frederick Morrison and sold under the name of Morrison's Flyin' Saucer – later changed to Frisbee, after the pieman.

NOBLE TRADITION  Boxing with gloves, fixed rules and in a roped-off ring started in 1743, the heyday of bare-knuckle contests.

They were introduced by British fighter Jack Broughton, who was known as the Father of Boxing and who reigned as English champion for 21 years. The gloves – called 'feather bedders' – were issued after aristocratic boxing fans in England demanded a

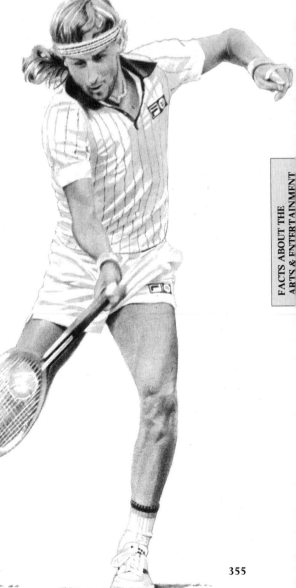

# Sport

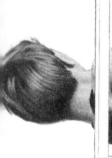

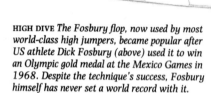

HIGH DIVE *The Fosbury flop, now used by most world-class high jumpers, became popular after US athlete Dick Fosbury (above) used it to win an Olympic gold medal at the Mexico Games in 1968. Despite the technique's success, Fosbury himself has never set a world record with it.*

## BOXING

### WORLD HEAVYWEIGHT CHAMPIONS

| Champion | Reign |
|---|---|
| Jack Johnson | 1908–15 |
| Jess Willard | 1915–19 |
| Jack Dempsey | 1919–26 |
| Gene Tunney | 1926–8 |
| Max Schmeling | 1930–2 |
| Jack Sharkey | 1932–3 |
| Primo Carnera | 1933–4 |
| Max Baer | 1934–5 |
| Jim Braddock | 1935–7 |
| Joe Louis | 1937–49 |
| Ezzard Charles | 1949–51 |
| Jersey Joe Walcott | 1951–2 |
| Rocky Marciano | 1952–6 |
| Floyd Patterson | 1956–8 |
| Ingemar Johannson | 1959–60 |
| Floyd Patterson | 1960–2 |
| Sonny Liston | 1962–4 |
| Cassius Clay | 1964–7 |
| Jimmy Ellis | 1968–70 |
| Joe Frazier | 1970–3 |
| George Foreman | 1973–4 |
| Muhammad Ali (Cassius Clay) | 1974–8 |
| Leon Spinks | 1978 |

### World Boxing Association

| | |
|---|---|
| Muhammad Ali | 1978–9 |
| John Tate | 1979–80 |
| Mike Weaver | 1980–2 |
| Mike Dokes | 1982–3 |
| Gerrie Coetzee | 1983– |

### World Boxing Council

| | |
|---|---|
| Ken Norton | 1978 |
| Larry Holmes | 1978–83 |
| Tim Witherspoon | 1984– |

chance to spar with famous professional boxers, and insisted on gloves to minimise the risk of damage to noble noses and eyes.

*The Marquess of Queensberry rules, which form the basis of modern boxing regulations, were not devised by him alone. The rules – which made the marquess's name a byword for fair play – were drawn up in 1866 by a committee which included at least two other men. The marquess (1844–1900) gave his name to them only because he was nominally the group's chairman.*

BOX ON . . . AND ON AND ON The longest gloved fight – between two American fighters, Andy Bowen and Jack Burke – lasted for more than seven hours. After 110 rounds, the fight, in New Orleans in 1893, was declared a draw because the contestants were too exhausted to continue.

THE REAL McCOY The real McCoy was not really named McCoy at all. His original name was Norman Selby. Born in Indiana, USA, in 1873, he changed his name to Charles 'Kid' McCoy in 1891 when he began a boxing career that took him to the title of world welterweight champion in 1896. He made the change because Irish boxers were popular in the USA, and he wanted to boost his appeal by sounding Irish too.

The phrase 'the real McCoy', meaning the genuine article, was in use before McCoy adopted it at the

## ATHLETICS – THE RECORD-BREAKERS/1

World records in athletics, as in other sports, have tumbled during the 20th century as diet, training methods and equipment have improved. As standards of performance have risen, though, so it has become more difficult for new generations of athletes to achieve still greater heights. In some events, such as sprinting, records are being broken by smaller and smaller margins – suggesting that, in these events at least, athletes may be reaching the limits of human endeavour. The tables here and on page 359 list world records since 1979 in major track and field events. They show the record, the athlete's name and nationality, and the year the record was set. For comparison, they also list earlier records set by some of the century's most outstanding athletes.

### MEN

**High jump**

| | | | |
|---|---|---|---|
| 2.03m (6ft 8¼in) | Harold Osborn | USA | 1924 |
| 2.15m (7ft 0½in) | Charles Dumas | USA | 1956 |
| 2.28m (7ft 5¾in) | Valeriy Brumel | USSR | 1963 |
| 2.34m (7ft 8in) | Vladimir Yaschenko | USSR | 1978 |
| 2.35m (7ft 8½in) | Jacek Wszola | Poland | 1980 |
| 2.36m (7ft 9in) | Gerd Wessing | E Germany | 1980 |
| 2.37m (7ft 9¼in) | Zhu Jianhua | China | 1983 |
| 2.38m (7ft 9¾in) | Zhu Jianhua | China | 1983 |
| 2.39m (7ft 10in) | Zhu Jianhua | China | 1983 |

**Long jump**

| | | | |
|---|---|---|---|
| 8.13m (26ft 8¼in) | Jesse Owens | USA | 1935 |
| 8.35m (27ft 5in) | Ralph Boston | USA | 1965 |
| 8.9m (29ft 2½in) | Bob Beamon | USA | 1968 |

**Shot**

| | | | |
|---|---|---|---|
| 17.4m (57ft 1in) | Jack Torrance | USA | 1934 |
| 19.3m (63ft 4in) | Parry O'Brien | USA | 1959 |
| 20.68m (67ft 10in) | Dallas Long | USA | 1964 |
| 21.78m (71ft 5½in) | Randy Matson | USA | 1967 |
| 22.15m (72ft 8in) | Udo Beyer | E Germany | 1978 |
| 22.22m (72ft 11in) | Udo Beyer | E Germany | 1983 |

**Javelin**

| | | | |
|---|---|---|---|
| 77.23m (253ft 4in) | Matti Järvinen | Finland | 1936 |
| 85.71m (281ft 2in) | Egil Danielsen | Norway | 1956 |
| 91.72m (300ft 11in) | Terje Pedersen | Norway | 1964 |
| 93.8m (307ft 9in) | Jānis Lūsis | USSR | 1972 |
| 96.72m (317ft 4in) | Ferenc Paragi | Hungary | 1980 |
| 99.72m (327ft 2in) | Tom Petranoff | USA | 1983 |

### WOMEN

**High jump**

| | | | |
|---|---|---|---|
| 1.71m (5ft 7¼in) | Fanny Blankers-Koen | Holland | 1943 |
| 1.91m (6ft 3¼in) | Iolanda Balaş | Romania | 1961 |
| 2.01m (6ft 7¼in) | Sara Simeoni | Italy | 1978 |
| 2.02m (6ft 7½in) | Ulrike Meyfarth | W Germany | 1982 |
| 2.03m (6ft 8¼in) | Tamara Bykova | USSR | 1983 |
| 2.04m (6ft 8½in) | Tamara Bykova | USSR | 1983 |
| 2.05m (6ft 9in) | Tamara Bykova | USSR | 1984 |

**Long jump**

| | | | |
|---|---|---|---|
| 6.76m (22ft 2¼in) | Mary Rand | UK | 1964 |
| 7.09m (23ft 3in) | Vilma Bardauskiene | USSR | 1978 |
| 7.15m (23ft 5½in) | Anisoara Cusmir | Romania | 1982 |
| 7.2m (23ft 7½in) | Vali Ionescu | Romania | 1982 |
| 7.21m (23ft 7¾in) | Anisoara Cusmir | Romania | 1983 |
| 7.27m (23ft 10¼in) | Anisoara Cusmir | Romania | 1983 |
| 7.43m (24ft 4½in) | Anisoara Cusmir | Romania | 1983 |

**Shot**

| | | | |
|---|---|---|---|
| 16.76m (55ft) | Galina Zybina | USSR | 1956 |
| 18.59m (61ft) | Tamara Press | USSR | 1965 |
| 21.2m (69ft 6¾in) | Nadyezhda Chizhova | USSR | 1973 |
| 22.32m (73ft 3in) | Helena Fibingerová | Czecho-slovakia | 1977 |
| 22.36m (73ft 4¼in) | Ilona Slupianek | E Germany | 1980 |
| 22.45m (73ft 7¾in) | Ilona Slupianek | E Germany | 1980 |

**Javelin**

| | | | |
|---|---|---|---|
| 59.78m (196ft 1in) | Elvira Ozolina | USSR | 1963 |
| 69.52m (228ft 1in) | Ruth Fuchs | E Germany | 1979 |
| 69.96m (229ft 6in) | Ruth Fuchs | E Germany | 1979 |
| 70.08m (229ft 11in) | Tatayana Biryulina | USSR | 1980 |
| 71.88m (235ft 10in) | Antoaneta Todorova | Bulgaria | 1981 |
| 72.4m (237ft 6in) | Tiina Lillak | Finland | 1982 |
| 74.2m (243ft 5in) | Sofia Sakorafa | Greece | 1982 |
| 74.76m (245ft 3in) | Tiina Lillak | Finland | 1983 |

# Sport

height of his boxing success to distinguish himself from another fighter named Al McCoy. It was a US adaptation of a Scottish phrase, 'the real McKay', which was applied in Scotland to a brand of top-grade whisky. When the whisky was exported to the United States, the phrase went with it. McCoy the boxer went on to become a film actor and to marry nine times – including one woman whom he married twice. He committed suicide in April 1940.

*The old question of whether a wrestler can beat a boxer has been solved three times – in favour of the wrestler. John L. Sullivan (in 1887), Bob Fitzsimmons (in about 1892) and Kingfish Levinsky (in 1936) were three boxers all defeated by wrestlers. The winners were William Muldoon, Ernest Roeber and Ray Steele.*

ALIAS SUGAR RAY  The US boxer Sugar Ray Robinson – five times world middleweight champion between 1951 and 1960 – acquired his ring name by accident. He took part in his first amateur flyweight bout as a stand-in for another boxer and, since he had no official registration card of his own at the time, he used the card of a retired fighter named Ray Robinson. He won the bout, and never bothered to acquire a card in his own name of Walker Smith. American sportswriter Jack Case added the nickname Sugar after he heard a lady at the ringside yell it during a fight. It was appropriate, said Case, because Robinson was such 'a sweet mover' in the ring.

## MOTOR RACING

### GRAND PRIX CHAMPIONS

| Date | Name | Nationality |
| --- | --- | --- |
| 1960 | Jack Brabham | Australia |
| 1961 | Phil Hill | USA |
| 1962 | Graham Hill | Britain |
| 1963 | Jim Clark | Britain |
| 1964 | John Surtees | Britain |
| 1965 | Jim Clark | Britain |
| 1966 | Jack Brabham | Australia |
| 1967 | Denis Hulme | New Zealand |
| 1968 | Graham Hill | Britain |
| 1969 | Jackie Stewart | Britain |
| 1970 | Jochen Rindt | Austria |
| 1971 | Jackie Stewart | Britain |
| 1972 | Emerson Fittipaldi | Brazil |
| 1973 | Jackie Stewart | Britain |
| 1974 | Emerson Fittipaldi | Brazil |
| 1975 | Niki Lauda | Austria |
| 1976 | James Hunt | Britain |
| 1977 | Niki Lauda | Austria |
| 1978 | Mario Andretti | USA |
| 1979 | Jodi Scheckter | South Africa |
| 1980 | Alan Jones | Australia |
| 1981 | Nelson Piquet | Brazil |
| 1982 | Keke Rosberg | Finland |
| 1983 | Nelson Piquet | Brazil |

FRONT RUNNER *Calvin Smith (left) became in 1983 the world's fastest sprinter. Then 22 years old, the American set a world record for the 100 metres of 9.93 seconds.*

## ATHLETICS – THE RECORD-BREAKERS/2

### MEN

#### 100 metres

| | | | |
|---|---|---|---|
| 10.4 | Charles Paddock | USA | 1921 |
| 10.2 | Jesse Owens | USA | 1936 |
| 10.2 | Armin Hary | W Germany | 1960 |
| 10.03 | Bob Hayes | USA | 1964 |
| 9.95 | Jim Hines | USA | 1968 |
| 9.93 | Calvin Smith | USA | 1983 |

#### 200 metres

| | | | |
|---|---|---|---|
| 20.75 | Bobby Morrow | USA | 1956 |
| 20.5 | Livio Berruti | Italy | 1960 |
| 20.2 | Henry Carr | USA | 1964 |
| 19.83 | Tommie Smith | USA | 1968 |
| 19.72 | Pietro Mennea | Italy | 1979 |

#### 400 metres

| | | | |
|---|---|---|---|
| 46.2 | Bill Carr | USA | 1932 |
| 45.9 | Herb McKenley | Jamaica | 1948 |
| 45.07 | Otis Davis | USA | 1960 |
| 43.86 | Lee Evans | USA | 1968 |

#### 800 metres

| | | | |
|---|---|---|---|
| 1:49.8 | Tom Hampson | UK | 1932 |
| 1:46.6 | Rudolf Harbig | Germany | 1939 |
| 1:44.3 | Peter Snell | New Zealand | 1962 |
| 1:42.33 | Sebastian Coe | UK | 1979 |
| 1:41.73 | Sebastian Coe | UK | 1981 |

#### 1500 metres

| | | | |
|---|---|---|---|
| 3:32.1 | Sebastian Coe | UK | 1979 |
| 3:32.1 | Steve Ovett | UK | 1980 |
| 3:31.36 | Steve Ovett | UK | 1980 |
| 3:31.24 | Sydney Maree | USA | 1983 |
| 3:30.77 | Steve Ovett | UK | 1983 |

#### 1 mile

| | | | |
|---|---|---|---|
| 4:10.4 | Paavo Nurmi | Finland | 1923 |
| 4:06.4 | Sydney Wooderson | UK | 1937 |
| 4:01.4 | Gunder Hägg | Sweden | 1945 |
| 3:59.4 | Roger Bannister | UK | 1954 |
| 3:58 | John Landy | Australia | 1954 |
| 3:57.2 | Derek Ibbotson | UK | 1957 |
| 3:54.5 | Herb Elliott | Australia | 1958 |
| 3:54.1 | Peter Snell | New Zealand | 1964 |
| 3:51.1 | Jim Ryun | USA | 1967 |
| 3:51 | Filbert Bayi | Tanzania | 1975 |
| 3:49.4 | John Walker | New Zealand | 1975 |
| 3:49 | Sebastian Coe | UK | 1979 |
| 3:48.8 | Steve Ovett | UK | 1980 |
| 3:48.53 | Sebastian Coe | UK | 1981 |
| 3:48 | Steve Ovett | UK | 1981 |
| 3:47.33 | Sebastian Coe | UK | 1981 |

#### 5000 metres

| | | | |
|---|---|---|---|
| 14:28.2 | Paavo Nurmi | Finland | 1924 |
| 13:58.2 | Gunder Hägg | Sweden | 1942 |
| 13:57.2 | Emil Zátopek | Czecho-slovakia | 1954 |
| 13:51.6 | Chris Chataway | UK | 1954 |
| 13:36.8 | Gordon Pirie | UK | 1956 |
| 13:35 | Vladimir Kuts | USSR | 1957 |
| 13:24.2 | Kipchoge Keino | Kenya | 1965 |
| 13:16.6 | Ron Clarke | Australia | 1966 |
| 13:16.4 | Lasse Viren | Finland | 1972 |
| 13:08.4 | Henry Rono | Kenya | 1978 |
| 13:06.2 | Henry Rono | Kenya | 1981 |
| 13:00.42 | David Moorcroft | UK | 1982 |

#### 10,000 metres

| | | | |
|---|---|---|---|
| 27:39.89 | Ron Clarke | Australia | 1965 |
| 27:38.35 | Lasse Viren | Finland | 1972 |
| 27:30.8 | David Bedford | UK | 1973 |
| 27:22.5 | Henry Rono | Kenya | 1978 |

#### 400 metres hurdles

| | | | |
|---|---|---|---|
| 50.6 | Glenn Hardin | USA | 1934 |
| 48.12 | David Hemery | UK | 1968 |
| 47.13 | Edwin Moses | USA | 1980 |
| 47.02 | Edwin Moses | USA | 1983 |

### WOMEN

#### 100 metres

| | | | |
|---|---|---|---|
| 11.5 | Fanny Blankers-Koen | Holland | 1948 |
| 11.08 | Wyomia Tyus | USA | 1968 |
| 10.88 | Marlies Oelsner | E Germany | 1977 |
| 10.81 | Marlies Göhr (Oelsner) | E Germany | 1983 |
| 10.79 | Evelyn Ashford | USA | 1983 |
| 10.76 | Evelyn Ashford | USA | 1984 |

#### 200 metres

| | | | |
|---|---|---|---|
| 23.59 | Marjorie Jackson | Australia | 1952 |
| 23.2 | Betty Cuthbert | Australia | 1960 |
| 22.21 | Irena Szewińska | Poland | 1974 |
| 22.02 | Marita Koch | E Germany | 1979 |
| 21.71 | Marita Koch | E Germany | 1979 |

#### 400 metres

| | | | |
|---|---|---|---|
| 51.02 | Marilyn Neufville | Jamaica | 1970 |
| 49.29 | Irena Szewińska | Poland | 1976 |
| 49.19 | Marita Koch | E Germany | 1978 |
| 49.03 | Marita Koch | E Germany | 1978 |
| 48.94 | Marita Koch | E Germany | 1978 |
| 48.89 | Marita Koch | E Germany | 1979 |
| 48.60 | Marita Koch | E Germany | 1979 |
| 48.16 | Marita Koch | E Germany | 1982 |
| 47.99 | Jarmila Kratochvilova | Czecho-slovakia | 1983 |

#### 800 metres

| | | | |
|---|---|---|---|
| 2:01.1 | Ann Packer | UK | 1964 |
| 1:58.45 | Hildegard Falck | W Germany | 1971 |
| 1:54.94 | Tatyana Kazankina | USSR | 1976 |
| 1:53.43 | Nadezhda Olizarenko | USSR | 1980 |
| 1:53.28 | Jarmila Kratochvilova | Czecho-slovakia | 1983 |

#### 1500 metres

| | | | |
|---|---|---|---|
| 3:56 | Tatyana Kazankina | USSR | 1976 |
| 3:55 | Tatyana Kazankina | USSR | 1980 |
| 3:52.47 | Tatyana Kazankina | USSR | 1980 |

#### 1 mile

| | | | |
|---|---|---|---|
| 4:37 | Anne Smith | UK | 1967 |
| 4:22.1 | Natalia Marasescu | Romania | 1979 |
| 4:21.68 | Mary Decker | USA | 1980 |
| 4:20.89 | Ludmilla Veselkova | USSR | 1981 |
| 4:18.08 | Mary Decker | USA | 1982 |
| 4:17.44 | Maricica Puica | Romania | 1982 |

#### 400 metres hurdles

| | | | |
|---|---|---|---|
| 54.78 | Marina Makeyeva | USSR | 1979 |
| 54.28 | Karin Rossley | E Germany | 1980 |
| 54.02 | Anna Ambraziene | USSR | 1983 |
| 53.58 | Margarita Ponomaryeva | USSR | 1984 |

# Games and gaming

## GAMBLER'S GUIDE

The first practical guide for gamblers was written more than 400 years ago by an Italian doctor and mathematician named Geronimo Cardano (1501–76) in his *Book of Games and Chance*.

Cardano worked out the laws of chance governing games of cards and dice, and explained in his book the most profitable strategies to adopt at each stage of the games. Cardano's calculations still hold good. For example, he worked out correctly the likelihood of throwing any particular number with one, two or three dice.

## THE CINCINNATI KILL

The United States World Series baseball championship in 1919–between the champions, the Cincinnati Reds, and the Chicago White Sox – left a riddle which has still not been solved. Was the game fixed?

Though Cincinnati won comfortably, so did a New York gambler called Arnold Rothstein, who made a $350,000 killing on the game. When it became known that Rothstein had handed over a total of $100,000 to ten Chicago players before the game, there was uproar.

Rothstein was arrested and charged with conspiracy over what became known as the Black Sox scandal. But the court could not decide whether he had bribed the players or merely lent them the money. As a result, Rothstein walked free with his winnings – and what happened to his $100,000 'investment' in the losing team has never been revealed.

## WINNER WHO LOST

A winning bet on a 15th-century sporting contest cost a Mexican Indian chief his life. The story of the contest–involving a ball game called *tlachtli*, which was played rather like the modern sport of volleyball – is told in a chronicle written by an Indian historian named Ixtlilxochitl.

According to the account, the Aztec emperor Axayacatl (1469–81) led a team of players against the ruler of the neighbouring city of Xochimilco. Axayacatl bet the marketplace of his capital Tenochtitlan (on the site of present-day Mexico City) against one of the ruler's gardens – and lost.

But Axayacatl was a poor loser. The next day, his soldiers arrived at the palace of Xochimilco, ostensibly to salute the victor. In fact, the chronicle records, 'while they saluted him and made him presents they threw a garland of flowers about his neck with a thong hidden in it, and so killed him'.

## THE MAN WHO BROKE THE BANK

Charles de Ville Wells, the gambler whose exploits were celebrated in the song *The man who broke the bank at Monte Carlo*, emptied the Monaco casino's cash reserves not once, but six times over three days, during an extraordinary run of luck in July 1891. Playing roulette and using a version of the Martingale system, in which the gambler doubles his stake every time he loses a bet, the 50-year-old London businessman turned his initial £400 into £40,000. Later that year, he won another £10,000 at the same casino.

Wells was later jailed, however, for false pretences over his English business ventures and lost his fortune and his reputation. He died penniless in 1926.

## HELLO, DOLLIES

During the 1920s, the Dolly sisters, Jennie and Rose, two Hungarian-born American cabaret artistes, had unlimited credit at the fashionable Deauville and Le Touquet casinos in France. The reason: Jennie was being courted by Gordon Selfridge–the wealthy owner of one of London's largest department stores. Selfridge bought a sizable interest in both casinos so that the twin sisters could gamble his money away–and he could collect most of it back again through the casinos' takings.

## DEAD MAN'S HAND

A poker hand consisting of the two black aces, the two black eights and the Queen of Hearts is known to professional poker players as a 'Dead Man's Hand'. The hand got its name after the murder of the US frontier marshal and gunfighter Wild Bill Hickok (1837–76). Hickok was holding the five cards when he was shot in the back during a poker game at Deadwood, South Dakota, in August 1876.

He was the last of four players to be seated and it was the only time that he had been known to sit with his back to a door. He asked his fellow gamblers to change places with him, but they refused to do so in case this spoilt their luck. Hickok's killer was an old enemy of his named Jack McCall, who the previous day had lost $500 playing poker to Wild Bill.

## BIRTHDAY BETTING

The laws of chance worked out by the 17th-century French mathematician Blaise Pascal have a number of curious and apparently implausible consequences. One of them concerns birthdays–the chances of at least two people in a random group of six having birthdays in the same month. On the face of it, this seems to be an evens bet, because there are six people and 12 months.

But the odds in fact turn out to be far better, because the chances of three, four, five or all six people having birthdays in the same month need to be added in as well. The result is that the chance of all six having birthdays in *different* months works out at just over 1 in 5–which means that the odds of at least two sharing a month are nearly 4 to 1 on.

## CHALLENGE OF THE CHAMBER OF HORRORS

For over a century people have been trying to take up a wager that never existed. The mythical challenge originated during the 1850s when the English novelist Charles Dickens, writing in the magazine *All the Year Round*, remarked how much courage would be needed to enter the Chamber of Horrors at Madame Tussaud's wax museum in London. The remark snowballed until many believed that a fortune awaited anyone who spent a night there–and, although Tussaud's have never issued a challenge and never intend to, they still receive letters from would-be challengers. The volunteers usually expect to win £100, but some have expected £5000 for lasting the night.

## WINNING DOUBLE

Millionaire Australian racehorse owner Durrell Davis pulled off one of racing's biggest gambling coups in 1930. Davis was the owner of Phar Lap, an outstandingly successful two-year-old New Zealand racehorse

*SPORT OF AN EMPIRE From highest to lowest, the ancient Romans were fascinated by games of chance and skill. Dice travelled with the legions across the empire, while the emperor Nero was addicted to an early form of backgammon.*

## PASCAL'S TRIANGLE

The laws of probability that govern all random events, including those on which bets are made, were first worked out systematically by the French mathematician Blaise Pascal (1623–62). He realised that while individual random events could not be predicted, it was possible to predict their pattern statistically if the events were repeated a large number of times. Thus, although one throw of a dice cannot be predicted accurately, it is possible to predict that, in a large number of throws, each number will appear on average once in six throws.

### Working out the odds

This number triangle gives the probabilities of each outcome when several coins are tossed together. The first and last number in each row is 1. Each other number is the sum of the two above. If six coins are tossed, consult the '6 coins' row. The sum of the numbers in that row, 64, is the total number of possible outcomes. In one case, there are six heads and no tails. The probability of this is 1 in 64. In six cases there are five heads and one tail; the probability is 6 in 64. Similarly, there are 15 chances in 64 of four heads and two tails, and so on.

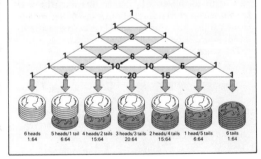

| 6 heads 1:64 | 5 heads/1 tail 6:64 | 4 heads/2 tails 15:64 | 3 heads/3 tails 20:64 | 2 heads/4 tails 15:64 | 1 head/5 tails 6:64 | 6 tails 1:64 |

that, together with another horse named Amounis, was dominating Australian races.

Davis and his friends plunged heavily on a double bet: that Amounis would win the Caufield Cup (Australia's second biggest race) and that Phar Lap would win the Melbourne Cup (the country's biggest race). Once the bets were on – and at good odds since many bookmakers had calculated that Phar Lap would beat Amounis in the Caufield Cup – Davis withdrew Phar Lap from the Caufield Cup on the grounds of illness, leaving Amounis with an easy win.

Alarmed by the size of the potential payout if Davis's double came off, some bookmakers tried to force the withdrawal of Phar Lap from the Melbourne Cup. The horse's trainer and jockey were threatened. Then unknown gunmen tried to shoot Phar Lap during a training gallop.

They missed, and Phar Lap went into hiding, until he was delivered to the Melbourne racecourse just minutes before the start of the race. Phar Lap won comfortably, clinching the double – and Davis and his friends collected an estimated £200,000.

### TINY TIPSTER

US punters can now buy a hand-held computer which gives horse-racing tips. The device works out the likely results on the basis of the horses' past performances, speed ratings and current earnings. On its first outing – in 1980 at Belmont Park, a racecourse near New York – the computer was fed information about the runners in the first three races, and asked to tip the winners. Its first two tips – both favourites – won, and its tip in the third race came in second. In the third race, however, it also successfully predicted that a 35 – 1 outsider would come in the first three.

### RAKE'S LOTTERY

The first successful French state lottery was set up by an Italian. He was history's most famous rake, Giovanni Giacomo Casanova. The lottery was started after Casanova, then 33, promised a French government minister that he would help to raise money for a new military academy – without costing the impoverished French crown a single franc. In the system he used, which was then very popular in Italy, customers bought a share in one or more of 90 numbers. In each draw five numbers were picked as winners and the prize money for each number was split between the winning ticket holders.

As an extra twist – perhaps to make the lottery seem more charitable in its aims – Casanova gave each number the name of a deserving young girl, and the five winning girls were each given a bonus prize of 200 francs.

At the first draw in April 1758, 2 million francs were raised, of which the government took 600,000, Casanova kept 20,000, and the rest were distributed in prizes. By the end of 1759, there had been 14 more draws, establishing the lottery as a fashionable amusement and making Casanova a wealthy man.

Casanova later retired to Bohemia and became a librarian for a wealthy friend. He died there in 1798 at the age of 73 – in bed . . . alone.

## FIRST BOARD GAMES

The earliest game boards and pieces that can be positively identified were discovered during excavations at the ancient Mesopotamian city of Ur by the British archaeologist Sir Leonard Woolley in 1926–7. They date from about 3000–2500 BC.

It is not known for certain how these games were played, but the evidence suggests that they were race games with rules not unlike those of Ludo. Boards and their pieces have also been found in Egyptian tombs and depicted on wall paintings, mostly dating from about 2000 BC onwards.

## NERO'S GAME

Backgammon has always been a favourite game of gamblers – the Roman emperor Nero is said to have played a very similar game for extremely high stakes. The origin of backgammon is unknown. The game probably evolved from early race games played in Egypt and the Middle East long before the Christian era. It is probably the oldest dice game still played.

## UPS AND DOWNS

The anonymous inventor of Snakes and Ladders – the earliest known board dates from 1892 – is thought to have been inspired by a Hindu religious game that was used as a teaching aid in India.

In it, the virtues (ladders) were rewarded and the vices (snakes) punished.

## MONOPOLY: MAKING A MINT

In 1975 twice as much Monopoly money was printed in the USA as real money. And in most years the Monopoly output – on face value – comfortably beats the US Treasury's. The commercial success of the board game is unrivalled, with sales averaging 2 million sets a year since its invention. By 1983, sales had topped 80 million. An out-of-work heating engineer, Charles Darrow of Philadelphia, invented Monopoly in the early 1930s and it made him a millionaire, though not immediately. Darrow first tried to sell his idea to Parker Brothers, a Massachusetts firm that was America's leading games manufacturer. But the firm turned it down on the ground that it was too complicated. Parker Brothers changed its mind only in 1935 after Darrow had 5000 sets made privately and proved, by selling them, that the game had wide appeal.

## WORD PERFECT

The highest known scores using a Scrabble set are 1961 points for a single play (Ron Jerome, England, 1974) and for a complete game 4454 points (Jeff Grant, New Zealand, 1981). Both these scores were worked out, however, with the letters face up so that the most advantageous combinations could be constructed. In competitive games, the highest known score for a single play – achieved in Britain in 1982 by Dr Saladin Khoshnaw – is 392 for 'caziques', a word meaning Indian chiefs. For a player's game total, the world record is 792; it was set by Diane Dennis of Britain in March 1984.

## CASH AND CARDS

The first mention of European playing cards was in 14th-century Italy. They were probably adapted from cards used by the Mameluke sultans who ruled Egypt for some 300 years from the middle of the 13th century. The Arabs, in turn, may have been inspired by Chinese playing cards. The Chinese cards are thought to have been based on paper money issued during the Tang dynasty (AD 618–907).

The design of the standard 52-card pack of the West is originally French. The spades replaced the French pikes (piques) and the club suit gets its shape from the French trefoil symbol.

The joker in a pack of cards is derived from the Fool, one of the cards in a tarot pack – now used for fortune-telling. The tarot pack was originally invented as a game in medieval Italy. It had 78 cards: 22 face cards and 56 numbered cards. The 52-card modern deck developed from the numbered cards.

## THREE FOR THE POT

The origin of billiards is not known, but the first known reference to it was in France in 1429 – and the French king Louis XI, who ruled France from 1461 to 1483, is said to have had a billiard table.

The game has been known in Britain since 1591.

ORIENTAL KING Indian cards, the earliest of which date from around 1527, are circular, hand-painted and lacquered. The Mir of Surkk (King of Sun) is one of only two court cards in the 98-card pack.

JACK The model for the Jack of Spades is thought to be Ogier the Dane, a fictional hero of French medieval literature. This card is 18th century.

QUEEN Britain's Queen Anne is depicted in all her regal splendour in a 1707 version of the Queen of Clubs.

# BATTLE IN BLACK AND WHITE

Chess is derived from Chaturanga, an Indian war game that dates from before the 6th century AD. The earliest known reference to it is in a 6th-century Persian document, but in 1972 two ivory figurines – thought to be chessmen and possibly dating from AD 200 – were found in Russia.

The game passed by way of Persia to the Arabs and reached Europe in about the 10th century. Its English name comes from the Persian title *shah*, meaning 'king' or 'ruler'. Chess is now international, but several Eastern countries retain their own versions of the game. In China it is known as Xiang-qi, and in Japan it is called Shogi.

● The term checkmate comes from the Persian *shah mat*, meaning 'The king is dead'.

● In Japanese chess, captured pieces change sides and are dropped back on the board in positions chosen by the player.

● The name rook, for the piece sometimes known as the castle, is a corruption of the Persian word *rukh*, meaning 'chariot'. Later the chariot came to be replaced by a piece resembling a howdah, or platform, on an elephant's back – and the rook's modern shape is derived from the howdah.

● One of the earliest sets of European chess pieces in existence was found in a sandbank on the Isle of Lewis in the Outer Hebrides in 1831. They date from the 12th century and are carved in walrus ivory. Now known as the Lewis chessmen, they are probably of Icelandic or Norwegian origin.

● In 12th-century Japan, a type of chess known as *Tai-Shogi* had a board with 625 squares and 354 pieces.

● In the Middle Ages, chess was thought by some to be too easy, so more complicated versions of the game were introduced. Tamerlane's chess, played at the court of the 14th-century Tartar conqueror, used a board of 110 squares, the pieces including camels and giraffes.

Only three balls are used: two white cue balls, one for each player; and a red. Points are scored by potting either of the other balls with the cue ball (though it is considered bad form to pot your opponent's cue ball); by going 'in off' – that is, potting the cue ball off one of the other balls, or by 'cannoning' the cue ball into both the other balls. Unlike snooker, there is theoretically no limit to the size of a break, and scores of more than 40,000 have been recorded. A pocketless variation of the game on an oval table, in which cannons are the only scoring shots, is still played in France.

## BORED WITH BILLIARDS

Snooker was invented in 1875 by British Army officers at Ootacamund, southern India, who were bored with playing billiards. The name was probably taken from the term Snookers, applied to first-year cadets at the Royal Military Academy, London. The game is played with a white cue ball and 21 coloured balls on a billiard table. The game, or 'frame', ends when all the coloured balls are potted. A sequence of successful strokes is called a 'break'. The highest possible score for clearing all the balls in one break is 147.

## SQUARING UP

Though games experts have worked out complex strategies for most games, one of the simplest of all – the children's game of Boxes – is governed by pure skill, and no satisfactory strategy has ever been devised for it. The game is played by drawing a grid of dots on a sheet of paper. Each player in turn joins two adjacent dots with a line, with the aim of completing as many boxes as possible.

## SQUOPPING THE WINK

Tiddlywinks has a language all its own. The aim of the game, which is played internationally, is to flick small counters, known as winks, into a central pot. But in the early part of the game, players also try to cover an opponent's wink with their own to prevent it being played – a technique known as squopping.

Players flick the winks by pressing down on the counter's edge with a larger counter called a squidger, and keen players have their own squidgers specially made to their personal design.

GUILLOTINED Court cards were discarded in the French Revolution. The Jack of Hearts (left) became a gardener, the Queen of Spades a symbol of Press freedom.

TELLING A MORAL Many playing cards have carried moral, educational or political messages. This card – one of a British set made for the 'Amusement of Youth' – dates from 1788.

# Collectors' items

## CHERRY TREE TIME

Clocks with movements carved from cherry wood and oak were made in the United States in the mid-18th century because brass was then both expensive and difficult to obtain in North America. The wooden clocks were invented by two brothers, Benjamin and Timothy Cheyney, clockmakers from East Hartford, Connecticut. In 1806, another clockmaker named Eli Terry, of Plymouth, Connecticut, made 4000 wooden clocks by fitting standard parts together on an assembly line. In 1836, cheaper brass spelt the end of wooden time, and few clocks now survive. They were not very accurate and the parts wore quickly. Working wooden clocks could fetch up to about £100.

## A SILVERSMITH TO REVERE

History remembers Paul Revere for his midnight ride in 1775 from Boston, Massachusetts, to Lexington to warn the armed American patriots, the Minutemen, that British troops were on the march. But he had already assured himself a lasting reputation for his skill as a silversmith, and his finely engraved work still raises high bids in the world's auction rooms. Revere also cast bells and cannons, built America's first mill for rolling sheet copper and engraved the printing plates for the first paper money in Massachusetts. Revere was the son of a French Huguenot refugee, Apollos Rivoire. Apollos changed his name to Revere, 'so that the bumpkins could pronounce it easier'.

## CONVICT'S CREATION

German alchemist Johann Böttger (1682–1719) was imprisoned in Albrechtsburg fortress in 1703 by Augustus the Strong, Elector of Saxony, because he had failed in his promise to make gold. He won his freedom by promising to make porcelain instead. At that time porcelain had to be imported at great cost – only the Chinese knew the secret of its manufacture. Böttger succeeded in 1710, and began producing high-quality, marketable porcelain at Meissen, near Dresden. The town, now in East Germany, remains to this day a centre for the production of porcelain. The most valuable Meissen pieces, dating from the early years of production, now fetch up to £35,000.

## WILLOW OF THE WEST

The popular Chinese-style willow pattern china came from Staffordshire – in England, not China. It probably started with Thomas Minton (1765–1836), who invented a simple design of a Chinese scene with willow trees in the 1780s. The standard willow pattern started to appear in the first decade of the 19th century – and is still produced. An early willow pattern plate can now be worth between £15 and £250.

The legend that the willow picture tells of a lovely Chinese girl running away with her father's impoverished secretary, pursued by the angry father, has nothing to do with China either. It was invented in England some time in the 19th century.

## THE CRAFTSMEN'S GUIDE

Sheraton furniture is known for its elegant design, yet Thomas Sheraton – the man after whom it is named – may never have made a stick of it himself. Sheraton, born in Stockton-on-Tees in 1751, was the son of a cabinetmaker. He spent the early part of his life travelling the country in his father's trade. He arrived in London in about 1790 where he became a shopkeeper, author and drawing master. His elegant designs were published in *The Cabinet-Maker's and*

---

## HOW COINS ARE GRADED

Coin collectors have a language of their own. They use, for instance, a series of precise definitions to describe the condition of coins and medals.

'Fair' means that a coin can just about be identified. 'Good' means very worn, but the outline of the design is still visible. 'Very good' means the design shows clearly, but the detail is worn away. 'Fine' shows signs of wear.

'Very fine' shows slight wear. 'Extra fine' is almost perfect. 'Uncirculated' is in mint condition, apart from marks caused by coins rubbing together. 'Proof' coins, the highest grade of all, have a mirror-like finish and are struck especially for collectors from polished dies. As a rough guide, the condition of contemporary coins is usually 'extra fine' but any coin from more than 50 years ago is generally no better than 'fine'.

---

PORCELAIN PAIR *This Harlequin typifies Meissen's products. The Columbine (right) is from Nymphenberg.*

KING OVER THE WATER *Eighteenth-century Jacobite loyalists pledged allegiance to the exiled Stuarts in glasses decorated with portraits of Bonnie Prince Charlie.*

PENCE TO POUNDS *Staffordshire pottery figures were sold at Victorian fairs – hence their name of fairings – for pennies. Some now fetch up to £300.*

*Upholsterer's Drawing Book* (published in four volumes in 1791–4) and the *Cabinet Directory* (1803), and were copied by scores of enthusiastic cabinetmakers. But there is no evidence that Sheraton ever had a workshop in London or made any of the beautiful pieces of furniture that he designed. He died, poverty-stricken, in 1806. In the early 1980s, a set of six 19th-century chairs which followed the original Sheraton designs fetched £8000.

## A POTTED PORTRAIT

The common Toby jug is thought to immortalise a Yorkshire drinker, Harry Elwes, who was said to have downed 9000 litres (16,000 pints) of beer without eating in between. An unlikely tale, perhaps, but when Elwes died in 1761, Staffordshire potter Ralph Wood began making portrait jugs. He named the jugs Toby Fillpot, said to have been Elwes's nickname. The true Toby jug was a fat old man seated on a chair with a pint pot in his hand. Now there are hundreds of varieties with differing portraits of famous people, such as Admiral Nelson, Winston Churchill and Benjamin Franklin.

## CRYSTAL-CLEAR SECRET

The secret of clear crystal glass was locked up for most of the 16th century on the island of Murano in Venice. But money talks, and by the early 17th century renegade Venetians had sold the secret–the use of manganese and skilled blowing to produce colourless glass–abroad. Other countries, especially Bohemia, started setting up rival glass-making industries, and soon they were outstripping the Venetians with better techniques. By the 18th century the Venetian industry had fallen so far behind that in 1730 a Venetian named Briati disguised himself and worked for three years in a Bohemian glassworks to learn again the secrets his city had lost. Today a Venetian glass goblet of the 17th century in good condition might fetch between £800 and £1200.

## ONE FOR THE POT

Tea was so expensive when it was first brought to Europe in the early 17th century that it was kept in locked wooden boxes. These were called caddies from the Asian word *catty*–a unit of weight, usually about 600g (1.3lb). Veneered wood, silver and even papier-mâché were used to make caddies, which today sometimes fetch more than £100 at auction.

## A BAG OF GOLD

Two disappointed sailors in the English port of Plymouth walked one day in 1863 into a small stamp shop owned by Stanley Gibbons (1840–1913), founder of the world-famous stamp dealers, and dumped on the counter a bag containing thousands of triangular stamps issued in the Cape of Good Hope between 1853 and 1863.

They explained disgustedly that they had won the stamps in a raffle in a South African pub and just wanted to get rid of them. They were delighted when Gibbons gave them £5 for the bag. Gibbons went on to sell the stamps at between 8d and 10d a dozen, making a profit of £500. Today the stamps are valued at from £40 to £13,000 each.

## WALL FURNITURE

The beautiful, simple furniture made by the Shaker religious sect in New England was designed so that it could be hung on pegs around the walls. Every evening the Shakers tidied it up in this way in case the night should be disturbed suddenly by the Second Coming of the Lord. Only the larger pieces of furniture such as chests and tables were left on the floor.

## FACE OF FORTUNE

The vanity of a king helped to make his stamps a favourite target of collectors. Ferdinand II (1810–59), the ruler of Sicily, was so vain that when postal officials suggested Sicily should issue its own postage stamps he agreed only on condition that his portrait was never to be disfigured by a franking mark. Anyone who disobeyed, he decreed, would be guilty of treason. To placate the king–who became known as King Bomba after he ordered an artillery bombardment of rebellious subjects in Palermo and Messina in the late 1840s–fearful officials designed a special franking mark that fitted as a frame around his head.

Today, the franked stamps can be worth several hundred pounds apiece, partly because of their curiosity value, but mainly because of their rarity. Largely as a result of delays caused by the king, the new stamps were not issued until January 1, 1859–and their issue was halted less than five months later, on Ferdinand's death.

## THE ONE AND ONLY

The world's most valuable stamp is a 1 cent black-on-magenta British Guiana (now Guyana) printed in the capital, Georgetown, in 1856, when supplies from Britain failed to arrive. Yet the young colonial collector who found the only known copy among some old stamps in 1873, sold it for the equivalent of 30p because he thought it was dull and uninteresting. In 1934, it fetched £7500 and in 1979 it was valued at £350,000.

The stamp is now thought to be unique; but there is a story that while it was in the possession of

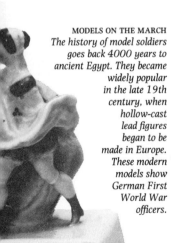

MODELS ON THE MARCH
*The history of model soldiers goes back 4000 years to ancient Egypt. They became widely popular in the late 19th century, when hollow-cast lead figures began to be made in Europe. These modern models show German First World War officers.*

British-born American millionaire Arthur Hind, in the early years of the 20th century, a British merchant seaman called on him with another genuine black-on-magenta. Hind is said to have paid the seaman a huge sum for the second stamp – and then burnt it, telling friends as he did so: 'Now there is still only one.'

## ANONYMOUS FAME
The world's first stick-on, prepaid stamps were introduced in Britain on May 6, 1840. Only two denominations were issued: the penny black and the two-penny blue. Since they were not intended for overseas use, neither stamp carried the name of the country on them and the tradition remains to this day.

## DYING FOR A STAMP
A Paraguayan stamp printed in 1932 helped to start a war. The stamp showed a map in which the Chaco territory between Bolivia and Paraguay, claimed by both sides, was labelled Chaco Paraguayo. In addition the stamp bore the provocative legend *Ha sido, es, y será* (Has been, is, and will be). On June 15, 1932, Bolivian troops attacked Paraguay. The war dragged on until June 12, 1935, by which time 100,000 men had died. In the end, the two countries signed a peace treaty in 1938 under which Paraguay gained 90 per cent of the disputed territory.

## LITTLE PERFORATIONS
The world's smallest stamps were issued in Bolivia between 1863 and 1866. They measured a mere 8 × 9.5mm (0.31 × 0.37in).

## AN EMPRESS'S CURRENCY
The autocratic head of Maria Theresa, empress of the Austrian empire from 1740 to 1780, still appears on the Austrian 1 thaler coin – a silver coin which is no longer used in Austria. During Maria Theresa's reign, the coin became so respected in countries bordering the Red Sea that traders would often accept no other coins. After the empress died, the coin continued to be minted in several European countries and it is still used in parts of the Middle East. Such coins are all dated 1780 whichever year they were minted. In 1983 each coin was worth about £7.

## TOGGLE ARTISTRY
Some of the smallest items valued by collectors are *netsuke* (pronounced 'net-ski'). These button-sized toggles were used by the Japanese to hold the drawstrings on the purses which they hung from their belts as part

of their traditional dress. *Netsuke* were made for hundreds of years, and reached their peak as an art form between the 17th and 19th centuries. Usually made of wood or ivory, they were carved in a great many shapes, the one proviso being that they should not have any sharp points to catch on clothing. More than 2000 artists made signed *netsuke*, and there are many more unsigned ones. Since the mid-19th century, fake *netsuke* have also been made. But genuine articles can now be worth up to £30,000.

# ENGLISH FURNITURE

### SAXON AND NORMAN (before 1272)
The Saxon period was the era of the oak chest. Even for the well-to-do, this was usually the most important piece of furniture in the home. Most chests had leather hinges, but more valuable ones had clasps and swirling decorations of wrought iron. Food was stored in chests perforated with air holes.

Trestle tables and benches that could be stacked away were the main items of furniture in the Norman hall. Chests had elaborate decorations and were put to a variety of uses, in addition to storage. Because such chests were portable, they could double up as chairs, tables and even beds when required. They were the ancestors of modern pieces of furniture, such as cupboards and chests of drawers. Chairs were heavy, box-like in design, square and simply carved – and only for the head of the household or important visitors. Serfs and retainers sat on benches or stools.

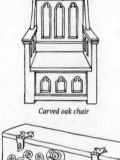

*Carved oak chair*

*Oak strongbox*

### MEDIEVAL (1272–1553)
By medieval times, the chest, now raised off the floor on short, strong legs, had become an early cupboard. Chairs were still box-like, but their carving was more delicate and elaborate.

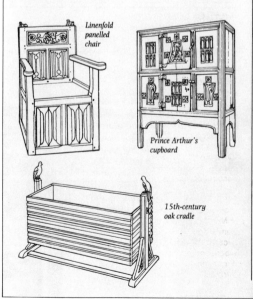

*Linenfold panelled chair*

*Prince Arthur's cupboard*

*15th-century oak cradle*

*JAPANESE CURIO Raiden, the thunder god, is caught by Uzume, the mirth goddess, in her bath on this netsuke.*

## TWO BITS OF TREASURE

The nickname 'two bits' for a US quarter dollar comes from the days of the pirates on the Spanish Main – and from their favourite coins, known as pieces of eight. Spanish silver dollars, mostly minted in Spain's silver-rich Mexican empire, were called *pesos de ocho* (meaning 'pieces of eight') because each was worth eight *reales*. The dollars were cut into wedge-shaped portions, like a cake. An eighth portion or 'bit' was worth one *real*; a half portion or 'four bits' was worth four *reales*; and a piece worth two *reales* was a quarter portion, or 'two bits'.

## LICK THAT

The most worthless stamp ever issued – taking only face value into account – was a 3000 pengö stamp issued in Hungary on February 5, 1946. At the time of issue, one British penny would have bought 50,000 million stamps.

---

## ELIZABETHAN AND JACOBEAN (1553–1660)

Round legs, turned on a lathe, transformed the previously square-cut lines of cupboards and chairs in Elizabethan times. Trestle tables were replaced by the solid oak refectory style with chunky, carved legs. Rich merchants began to use different rooms for different functions and it was no longer necessary to stack tables away between meals. Beds were heavy and draped to keep out draughts, and the chest on legs had become a carved oak cupboard.

*Jacobean carved oak bedstead*

*Turned 17th-century chair*

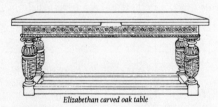

*Elizabethan carved oak table*

## RESTORATION (1660–1714)

Royalist nobles returning with Charles II from exile in France brought with them a taste for continental elegance – high-backed chairs with curved legs and serpentine stretchers. Cupboards were decorated with veneers and marquetry, while the diarist Samuel Pepys chronicled the construction of the first known bookshelves in 1666. The 12 surviving shelves, or 'presses', are at Magdalene College, Cambridge. Walnut became the fashionable wood, ending the dominance of oak furniture.

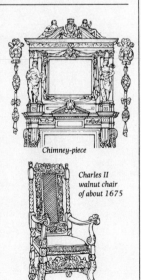

*Chimney-piece*

*Charles II walnut chair of about 1675*

## GEORGIAN AND REGENCY (1714–1837)

This was the classic age of English furniture. Walls were panelled or draped with velvet. The designer Thomas Chippendale (1718–79) set new styles in mahogany with ladderback chairs, claw-and-ball feet and tripod table stands. Robert Adam (1728–92), architect and interior designer, decorated furniture with classical medallions and brightly painted panels. George Hepplewhite, who died in 1786, perched chairs on slender sabre legs with scrolled arms and shield backs. Chests and cupboards were given elegant bow-fronted and serpentine sweeps, with polished inlays.

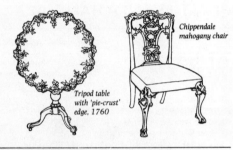

*Chippendale mahogany chair*

*Tripod table with 'pie-crust' edge, 1760*

## VICTORIAN (1837–1901)

Mahogany was still the popular wood, but design became heavy and ornate. Chunky chests of drawers were topped with swirling, carved or moulded flowers and leaves, and large mirrors. Chairs and settees were padded with horsehair and covered with leather or buttoned upholstery in rich colours.

*Balloon-back dining chair*

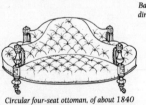

*Circular four-seat ottoman, of about 1840*

## MODERN (1901 – present day)

Today's furniture has been influenced by new materials as well as by demands for convenience and economy. Chrome-covered steel legs and glass-topped tables, moulded plywood or plastic chair seats and synthetic covers have helped to produce an enormous variety of styles.

*Plywood and leather chair*

*Tubular steel and oak office desk, 1931*

# WHAT HALLMARKS MEAN

Hallmarking is the stamping of gold and silver objects with symbols which indicate their purity, the place at which they were assayed (valued), the date of manufacture and the manufacturer. There are four recognised British assay office marks: the leopard's head of Goldsmiths' Hall, London (the 'hall' from which hallmarking gets its name); the castle that is the town mark of Edinburgh; the anchor of Birmingham; and the Tudor rose of Sheffield.

### International mark
Gold and silver are assayed by chemical analysis. Once, all imported gold and silver had to be revalued according to the standards of individual countries, but since June 1976 Britain, Austria, Finland, Sweden, Switzerland and Norway have agreed to recognise each other's marks. These countries now stamp their exports with a 'Convention mark', immediately recognised and accepted among them. The practice is not universal, however. Australia, Canada and South Africa, for instance, have never had an official system of hallmarking, though South Africa has unsuccessfully tried to devise one. Articles made entirely in Canada carry a National mark – a maple leaf surrounded by a 'C' – as well as the maker's trade

mark. Hallmarking in England began in 1300, in the reign of Edward I. Wardens toured goldsmiths' shops and confiscated gold of inferior quality on behalf of the king. Goldsmiths outside London were required by law to have their goldware brought to London 'to be ascertained of their Touch'. From 1363, master goldsmiths were required to have their own mark, to be stamped on their work after it had been assayed. Silver objects had to be stamped in the same way. These marks were usually part of their trade signs, and included such everyday objects as a jug, a fish or a bow and arrow. From about 1590, as literacy spread, the symbols were gradually replaced by the maker's initials.

### Four stamps
English gold and silver objects usually carry four stamps: a lion stamp guaranteeing its purity; the stamp of the assay office where it was tested; the maker's mark; and a date stamp. Objects dating from between 1784 and 1890 almost always carry a fifth stamp as well – the monarch's head, showing that the tax which was levied on gold and silver during that period has been paid. The lion stamp has been used on English silver since 1544; its presence guarantees that the piece is 92.5 per cent silver.

# HOW TO READ A HALLMARK DATE

The date of British gold and silver objects is denoted by a stamp showing a letter inside a distinctive shield. Together, the letter and the shield show the year in which the object was assayed. When the alphabet is completed, the design of the shield and the letter are changed, and the cycle begins again at A. The assay offices used to go through the alphabet at different rates. But in 1975 they all adopted the same sequence – shown here in the London list. Only four assay offices are currently in operation – London, Birmingham, Edinburgh and Sheffield.

### London marks since 1558
Letters 'A' to 'U' used excluding 'J'

| | | | |
|---|---|---|---|
| 1558–1577 | | 1796–1815 | |
| 1578–1597 | | 1816–1835 | |
| 1598–1617 | | 1836–1855 | |
| 1618–1637 | | 1856–1875 | |
| 1638–1657 | | 1658–1677 | 1876, shield changed for rest of series 1877–1895 |
| 1678–1696 no 'u' in this series | | | |
| 1696–1715 | | 1896–1915 | |
| 1716–1735 | | 1916–1935 | |
| 1736–1755 | | 1936–1955 | |
| 1756–1775 | | 1956–1974 | |
| 1776–1795 | | 1975– | |

### Birmingham marks
The whole alphabet is used, only excluding 'J'

| | |
|---|---|
| | 1773–1797 shields differ |
| | 1798–1823 'j' used |
| | 1824–1848 in different style |
| | 1849–1874 'J' used in this series |
| | 1875–1899 |
| | 1900–1924 |
| | 1925–1949 'J' used in this series instead of 'I' |
| | 1950–1974 |

### Dublin marks since 1773
Whole alphabet used, with exception of 'J' and 'V'

| | |
|---|---|
| | 1773–1796 |
| | 1797–1820 |
| | 1821–1845 'V' used in this series, italic 'e' alternative, and shields vary |
| | 1846–1870 'j' used instead of 'i', and 'v' used. Double 'f' 'g' and 'h' |
| | 1871–1895 'V' used in this series |
| | 1896–1915 ends at 'U' |
| | 1916–1941 'V' included in this series |
| | 1942–1967 this series used 'J' and 'V' |

### Edinburgh marks since 1780
Whole alphabet used, with exception of 'J'

| | |
|---|---|
| | 1780–1805 'I' and 'J' used in conjunction; double 'N', double 'O' and double 'R', shields differ |
| | 1806–1831 'j' used |
| | 1832–1856 |
| | 1857–1881 |
| | 1882–1905 no 'v' in this series |
| | 1906–1930 |
| | 1931–1955 |
| | 1956–1974 |

### Glasgow marks since 1819
Whole alphabet used

| | |
|---|---|
| | 1819–1844 |
| | 1845–1870 |
| | 1871–1896 |
| | 1897–1922 |
| | 1923–1948 |
| | 1949–1972 'J' and 'K' missing in this series |

Sheffield and Chester date marks are too irregular to list in chart form, but handbooks are available giving date marks for each separate year.

# THE EARTH

# The structure of the Earth

## ROCK UNSTEADY

When the German meteorologist Alfred Lothar Wegener (1880–1930) put forward in 1915 the idea that the continents move over the face of the Earth – the theory of continental drift – he was largely ignored by other scientists. The idea that anything as large as an entire continent was less than rock-steady seemed to many to be ludicrous. But Wegener was right. Not until some 40 years later – and more than 25 years after he died during an expedition to Greenland – did his theory win widespread acceptance.

Wegener formed his theory to explain several geological puzzles. He knew from fossil evidence, for instance, that tropical plants once grew in icy regions such as Alaska. Rock formations, he knew, also indicated that glaciers once covered parts of tropical Africa. And the English scientist Francis Bacon (1561–1626) had pointed out as early as 1620 the jigsaw-like fit between the west coast of Africa and the east coast of South America.

The clinching evidence for Wegener's theory, however, emerged only in the 1950s and '60s, from the study of magnetism in rocks. Scientists found that magnetic deposits in rocks formed at different times in a single continent were lined up in different directions, as though the North Pole had once been near the Equator and had moved over the ages to its present position. Since scientists knew that the Poles had always been roughly aligned with the Earth's axis of rotation, the only explanation was that the rocks themselves had moved after they were formed – and that the continents had moved with them.

PLANET EARTH *Clouds swirl across the Southern Ocean below the tip of Africa in a photograph taken from 145,000km (90,000 miles) up. The picture was snapped by US astronauts on their way back from the Moon aboard* Apollo XVII *in December 1972.*

## SUPER-CONTINENT

An astronaut looking down on the Earth 200 million years ago would have seen a single giant landmass. Geologists today call it Pangaea (from the Greek words for 'all earth'). The vast ocean that covered the rest of the Earth they have named Panthalassa (from the Greek words for 'all sea'). Between 180 and 200 million years ago Pangaea began to split into two sections: Laurasia, which consisted of present-day North America, Europe and Asia; and Gondwanaland, which consisted of Africa, South America, India, Antarctica and Australia.

As these continents drifted they continued to split up. The resulting parts – each on a giant raft-like 'plate' of rock – slowly took up their present positions. The two Americas linked. Arabia separated from Africa and became part of Asia. And India ploughed into southern Asia, producing enough pressure to throw up the giant Himalayan mountain chain.

## PARTING OF THE WORLDS

Every year the New World moves about 40mm (1.5in) farther away from the Old – pushed apart by the widening bed of the Atlantic Ocean. A chain of underwater mountains, known as the Mid-Atlantic Ridge, runs down the centre of the Atlantic. Along its length molten rock constantly wells up and cools, forming new crust and driving apart the continent-bearing plates on either side. Iceland, which sits astride the ridge, is, as a result of the movement, getting bigger every year. In a million years the Atlantic will be wider by about 40km (25 miles).

## BACK TO THE MELTING POT

Where one plate's edge dips below another, in what scientists call subduction zones, deep ocean trenches are formed. Among them is the lowest spot on the Earth's surface, the Marianas Trench, which drops to 10,914m (35,808ft) below sea level.

Some scientists have suggested that these trenches could be used in the future as a way of getting rid of long-lived nuclear waste. Dropped into a trench, the waste would eventually be swallowed up and its radioactive elements returned to the melting pot from which they originally came.

## MAN OVER MATTER

Man may soon be able to control earthquakes – with water. Water pumped into the ground in unstable areas, accidentally or deliberately, is known to be able to trigger earthquakes. It acts by lubricating the rocks beneath, allowing them to slip more freely past each other. Geologists are working on plans to release tension in unstable zones by pumping water into the ground deliberately and thereby causing a series of small, controlled quakes in place of a single large one.

## POLE REVERSAL

The Earth's magnetic field sometimes flips, reversing polarity so that north becomes south. The change happens in a relatively short span of geological time – sometimes less than 10,000 years. Then the poles remain in position until the next reversal. During the changeover, the Earth's magnetic field gradually reduces in strength until it is very weak. It then re-establishes itself the other way round. A compass

SHARP SHOOTING *Geologists, who once used to prospect for minerals on foot with little more equipment than a rock hammer, can now use satellite photographs to help track down mineral deposits anywhere in the world. This sparklingly clear picture, whose colours have been enhanced by a computer to make analysis easier, was taken from a height of 915km (580 miles) over South America. It shows a slice of northern Chile more than 160km (100 miles) long. The grey area in the lower centre is a salt flat known as the Salar de Atacama, in the Atacama Desert. The flat lies in a barren Andean basin, in a region which has been mined for centuries for its silver and copper. Sapphire-blue lakes glisten in the upper right of the picture, northeast of the salt flat, behind a row of snow-capped volcanic peaks which mark the Bolivian border.*

needle that once pointed north then points south. Evidence for this switch comes from rocks. Many record the direction of the Earth's magnetism at the time they were formed, because they contain traces of iron which reacts to magnetism. For the same reason, ordinary bricks record the magnetic field prevailing at the time they were baked. The last known reversal, which took place about 30,000 years ago, was dated through the remains of a clay fireplace built by Australian Aborigines. But the reason for the switching of the poles remains unknown.

## SHORT WAY ROUND
Britain's Transglobe expedition, which in 1982 became the first to go round the Earth via both Poles, took the short way round, though not the easy one. Because the Earth is slightly flattened at the Poles, a direct-line journey round the planet through the Poles is about 68km (42 miles) shorter than the same journey along the Equator.

## CHANGE OF BIRTHDAY
In 1656, Archbishop James Ussher of Armagh (1581–1656) announced that the world had been created at precisely 10am on October 26, 4004 BC. He calculated the date by working back through the generations and the ages of the Biblical patriarchs listed in the Old Testament. Today scientists believe, from calculating the ages of rocks, that the Earth came into being some 4500 million years ago.

## ROCK OF AGES
The oldest known rocks on the Earth's surface are about 3800 million years old – about 700 million years younger than the planet itself. The missing rocks are thought to have been lost through erosion or by being pushed back into the molten interior by the shifting of the continents.

The oldest known rocks, found in Greenland in the 1960s, were dated by measuring the decay of radioactive elements they contained.

## THE RINGING EARTH
Major earthquakes can set the whole Earth ringing like a giant bell. The frequencies are too low for the human ear to detect, but they can be measured by sensitive seismographs (instruments used for measuring earthquakes). After a Chilean earthquake in May 1960 – which had a magnitude of 8.7 on the Richter scale and an intensity of 11 on the Mercalli scale – the Earth reverberated for a month.

## HOT SPOTS IN THE DARK
In the endless blackness of the ocean deeps, far from the warmth of the Sun, some forms of life flourish thanks to the heat of the Earth alone. Temperatures at the bottom of the oceans' abysses are usually near freezing and support very little life. Where there are cracks in the Earth's crust, though, the heat from the interior escapes to warm the water.

One such hot spot was discovered by explorers aboard the scientific submarine *Alvin* in 1977. About 800km (500 miles) west of Ecuador – and about 2400m (8000ft) down – they found a densely populated colony of Earth-heated life forms, including bacteria, worms 3m (10ft) long, crabs, clams and fish.

## TERRESTRIAL FURNACE
The molten core of the Earth is as hot as the surface of the Sun. Its temperature is estimated to be 5000°C (9000°F). The temperature at the core of the Sun, however, is far higher: around 15,000,000°C (27,000,000°F).

## PROTECTIVE POISON
The atmosphere does not just provide air to breathe – it also provides vital protection. Without it, ultraviolet radiation from the Sun would destroy life on Earth. The deadly rays are largely absorbed by a poisonous form of oxygen called ozone, which is most abundant in the atmospheric layer known as the stratosphere, between 15 and 50km (9 – 30 miles) up. The radiation which does pierce the stratosphere and reach the ground is responsible for suntans and sunburn.

Only a small proportion of ozone is needed to lower the ultraviolet radiation to a safe level. If all the ozone were collected at sea level, it would form a layer no more than 4mm (0.16in) thick.

## HIGH-LIFE WEIGHT LOSS
The quickest way to lose weight is to move to a mountaintop on the Equator – and run eastwards. Because the force of gravity diminishes the farther you are away from the centre of the Earth, you weigh less standing on a mountaintop than you would at sea level. Similarly, you weigh less at the Equator than you would at either Pole because the Earth bulges at the Equator and the Poles are slightly flattened.

The running helps because the Earth's rotation sets up a mild centrifugal force which counteracts the

# THE SHIFTING SURFACE OF THE GLOBE

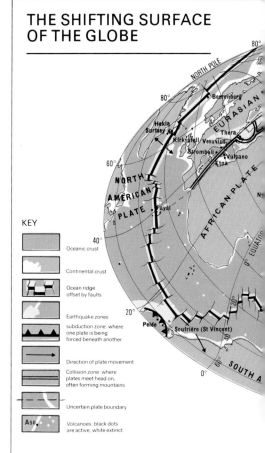

KEY

| | |
|---|---|
| | Oceanic crust |
| | Continental crust |
| | Ocean ridge offset by faults |
| | Earthquake zones |
| | subduction zone: where one plate is being forced beneath another |
| | Direction of plate movement |
| | Collision zone: where plates meet head on, often forming mountains |
| | Uncertain plate boundary |
| Aso. | Volcanoes: black dots are active, white extinct |

The Earth's surface – the land and the beds of the oceans – is made up of a patchwork of giant plates. The plates float like vast rafts on a sea of molten rock called the asthenosphere, which forms part of the planet's mantle. Below mountains such as the Himalayas, the plates can be as much as 80km (50 miles) thick, but beneath the oceans they have an average thickness of only about 5km (3 miles). Where the plates meet, massive forces are released in the effect of gravity, just as water will stay in a bucket which is swung around on a rope. Running eastwards, in the direction of the planet's spin, increases the centrifugal effect, so you weigh fractionally less than you would standing still. Running westwards, however, against the spin, you would weigh slightly more. The faster you run, the greater the difference.

In a large object, such as a ship, the difference in weight can be considerable. A 20,000 tonne ship, for instance, steaming east at 20 knots along the Equator (where the centrifugal effect is greatest) weighs about 3 tonnes less than it would if it reversed its course and headed west.

## THE WATERY SOUTH

Only 29 per cent of the Earth's surface is dry land. The Southern Hemisphere is especially watery. There the proportion of water to land is approximately 4:1, compared with 3:2 in the Northern Hemisphere.

## LAND TIDES

The seas are not alone in being subject to the tidal pull of the Sun and Moon. The solid land is affected as well. Twice daily, as the surface of the Earth's oceans rises and falls, the continents rise and fall as well, sometimes by as much as 150mm (6in) when the Moon is directly overhead.

## THE PLANET'S HEART

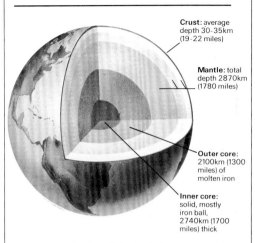

**Crust**: average depth 30-35km (19-22 miles)

**Mantle**: total depth 2870km (1780 miles)

**Outer core**: 2100km (1300 miles) of molten iron

**Inner core**: solid, mostly iron ball, 2740km (1700 miles) thick

HOW BIG IT IS *Diameter at Poles: 12,713km (7900 miles). Diameter at Equator: 12,756km (7926 miles). Surface area: 510,066,000km² (196,885,000 square miles). Land area: 148,429,000km² (57,294,000 square miles). Sea area: 361,637,000km² (139,591,000 square miles).*

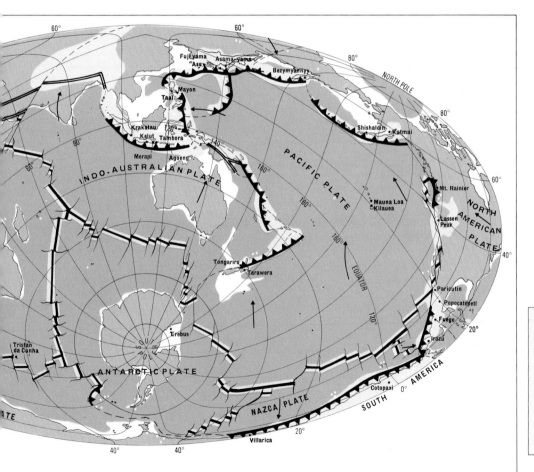

form of volcanoes and earthquakes. The theory of plate movement, known as plate tectonics from a Greek word meaning 'structure', was devised by a number of scientists in Europe and North America in the 1960s. One of the leading theorists was a Canadian scientist named J. Tuzo Wilson, who coined the term 'plate' for the rafts in 1965.

The diagram above shows the major plates on the Earth's surface. In places – along the Mid-Atlantic Ridge, for example – the plates are moving apart. As a result, the

Americas are moving away from Europe and Africa at the rate of about 40mm (1.5in) a year. Molten rock constantly wells up through the cracks between the plates and cools to form new crust. Elsewhere equal amounts of crust are being destroyed since, overall, the Earth remains the same size. In the Pacific, sections of seabed plates are being gradually forced beneath the edges of neighbouring plates and returned to the molten interior. As a result, South America is getting closer to New Zealand.

# Riches from the Earth

## THE WORLD'S MOST VALUABLE GEMS

For thousands of years men and women have worn precious stones for decoration and as talismans to protect them from ill health and misfortune. The early Egyptians were probably the first people to cut and polish gems to increase their beauty – and the stones are treasured for their colour, translucency, durability and monetary value. The four most prized gems today are diamonds, sapphires, rubies and emeralds.

**DIAMOND** The hardest and most lustrous gem, it retains its brilliance and polish for generations. It is said to make people lucky in love as well as strong and courageous.

Diamonds are a form of carbon which has been crystallised under great pressure and in enormous heat. Namibia and Australia are two major sources of the gems.

**SAPPHIRE** After diamond, it is the hardest stone. It is commonly blue, but purple, green, white, pink, gold and orange sapphires are also found. Its supposed mystical qualities include the promotion of peace and the purification of the mind.

The stone is formed from a variety of the aluminium oxide, corundum. Sri Lanka is a notable source of all the colours of sapphire.

**EMERALD** A brittle gem, it tends to chip and is rarely flawless. Its rich green is caused by chromium – a hard white metal – in the stone. In ancient times, powdered emerald was believed to cure fever and the plague.

The stone is formed from a combination of three main minerals: silicon (the chief constituent of sand and quartz); aluminium; and beryllium. Colombia is the source of the finest emeralds, which are mined from veins in shale.

**RUBY** The rarest of the gems. Its prized 'pigeon's blood' red is also the result of chromium. It was thought to promote good health and to keep people looking young. In addition, it was said to guard fruit trees from disease.

Some of the world's highest-quality rubies are quarried from gem gravels in Burma.

### BILLION-DOLLAR LOSER

The man who discovered South Africa's vast Witwatersrand gold deposits sold his claim for £10. In an affidavit to Pretoria's Mines Department in July 1886, a prospector named George Harrison reported that he had found a 'payable gold field'. This simple statement launched one of the world's biggest gold rushes.

Fortune-seekers from around the globe converged on the bleak, wind-swept patch of land in the southern African interior. By 1889, 630,500 ounces of gold had been dug from the reef. And Johannesburg, then a three-year-old shanty town of tents and wood-and-iron shacks, was on its way to becoming one of Africa's most important cities.

The Witwatersrand (Ridge of White Waters), an 80km (50 miles) long rocky outcrop, provided the bulk of the world's gold output for the next few decades. Since then, six other huge fields, stretching in a 483km (300 mile) arc from the eastern Transvaal to the Orange Free State, have been discovered. Together, they produce almost 800 tonnes of refined gold a year, 71 per cent of the world's supply.

Of George Harrison, the billion-dollar loser, there is no further trace. After collecting his £10, he became just another prospector who had sold out too cheaply and too soon.

### FOOL'S GOLD

Many early prospectors mistook iron pyrites – a gold-coloured iron ore – for gold. The ore became known as fool's gold and was considered worthless. Today, however, it does have a real value. It is used in the large-scale production of sulphuric acid.

### GOLD-PLATED COFFINS

The ancient Egyptians often plated their coffins and monuments with gold hand-beaten to a thickness of 1/2000th of a millimetre (1/50,000th of an inch), a fraction of the thickness of rice paper.

Modern techniques can do even better. Gold is so malleable that in its finest form (24 carat) an ingot measuring $50 \times 25 \times 25$mm (2 cubic inches), about the size of a matchbox, can be beaten or rolled out into enough gold leaf to cover a tennis court. Such a leaf would be less than 1/10,000th of a millimetre (1/250,000th of an inch) thick.

ALUMINA MINERALS
*Ruby and sapphire are gem varieties of corundum, a natural aluminium oxide. Aluminium is the most abundant metal in the Earth's crust, but it does not occur in its free state – only as compounds with other elements.*

CORUNDUM *After diamond, it is the hardest mineral. It is mixed with magnetite and other minerals to form emery.*

SAPPHIRE *Corundum gemstones of any colour except red are classified as sapphires. These are Sri Lankan gems.*

RUBY *Large rubies are among the most precious of jewels. The 'pigeon's blood' red stones here are from Burma.*

## ALL THE WORLD'S GOLD
The total amount of gold produced since the Stone Age is estimated to be about 100,000 tonnes, and about half of this has been mined since 1850. All of it would form a cube measuring about 18m (60ft) on all sides. It would occupy little more than the area of a tennis court.

## DOWN-UNDER GOLD-DIGGERS
The Australian gold rush of 1851 gave the Australians their nickname: 'diggers'. In 1852, 370,000 immigrants, mostly from Britain, arrived in Australia. The population of Victoria more than doubled. The colony's capital, Melbourne, emptied of adult men. Business halted, schools closed and ships lay idle in the bay, deserted by their gold-hungry crews.

The rush had been started by an Australian miner, Edward Hammond Hargraves, who was convinced by his experiences in California during the gold rush of 1848 – 9 that he could find gold in his own country. In February 1851 he panned out gold from a creek near Bathurst, New South Wales, and found more gold in another river. Hargraves received a reward of £10,000 and a life pension for his finds.

## RICHER THAN FORT KNOX
The world's largest hoard of gold is not at Fort Knox, Kentucky, USA. It is in the vaults of the Federal Reserve Bank of New York, parts of which are 26m (85ft) beneath the streets of Manhattan.

Fort Knox contains the bulk of the USA's gold reserves, which in the late 1970s amounted to around 10,000 tonnes, worth in excess of $11,000 million. But the vaults of the Federal Reserve Bank of New York hold more than 40,000 tonnes.

The gold belongs to more than 70 nations, who choose to leave part of their wealth in New York rather than in their own central banks.

Four men working in two shifts transfer gold from one nation's vaults to another's to keep pace with international dealings.

## BEANS MEANS GOLD
The term 'carat' – in which the purity of gold is measured – comes from the Greek word *keration*, meaning 'carob bean'. The beans were once used in Greece as weights. Pure gold, for instance, is 24 carats. Less valuable gold is often mixed with other metals to produce a desired colour. For example, 18-carat gold consists of 18 parts of gold mixed with six parts of another metal, usually copper or silver.

In diamonds and other gemstones, the carat is used directly as a measure of weight. Five carats are equal to 1g (0.035oz). So a stone weighing 28.3g (1oz) would contain 142 carats.

## WHY DIAMONDS MAY NOT BE FOREVER
The soft grey graphite used in pencil lead, and sometimes as a lubricant, consists of the same substance as diamond, the hardest natural substance. Both are forms of carbon. The reason for the differences between them lies in the way the atoms fit together.

If the carbon atoms are linked in flat planes, the result is graphite, because the planes slide readily over each other. But if the atoms form a rigid three-dimen-

### BERYLLIUM MINERALS
*Beryllium is used in alloys with copper, nickel and aluminium because it is light and strong, and resists corrosion. It is also used in X-ray tubes, and in nuclear reactors. The element is extracted commercially from beryl; aquamarine and emerald are gemstone varieties.*

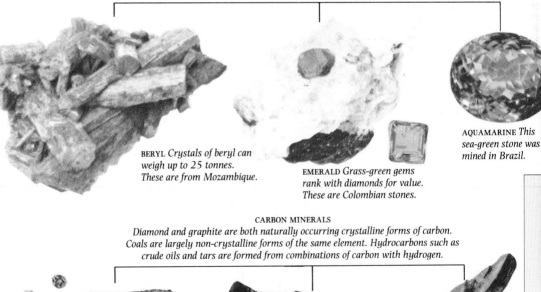

BERYL *Crystals of beryl can weigh up to 25 tonnes. These are from Mozambique.*

EMERALD *Grass-green gems rank with diamonds for value. These are Colombian stones.*

AQUAMARINE *This sea-green stone was mined in Brazil.*

### CARBON MINERALS
*Diamond and graphite are both naturally occurring crystalline forms of carbon. Coals are largely non-crystalline forms of the same element. Hydrocarbons such as crude oils and tars are formed from combinations of carbon with hydrogen.*

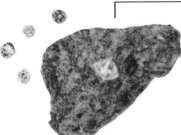

DIAMOND *Most stones are found in kimberlite, a grey rock named after Kimberley, South Africa.*

COAL *As well as being a fuel, coal is a source of coal gas, tar and ammonia. This bituminous type is mined in Britain.*

GRAPHITE *The 'lead' in lead pencils is made of graphite. This piece was mined in South Korea.*

sional network, the result is a diamond. Some scientists argue that, one day, all the diamonds that man has taken from the earth could turn into flaky graphite. The scientists claim that diamonds are inherently unstable because, once brought to the surface, they are no longer subject to the enormous pressures that created them. As a result, the scientists believe, diamonds will revert slowly to the low-density form of carbon: graphite. The reversion process is extremely slow, however, and could take many thousands of millions of years.

The diamonds-to-graphite theory is not universally supported, though. Other scientists assert that diamonds revert to graphite only if they are heated.

### FOR LOVE OF MARY

The first diamond engagement ring was made in 1477 for 18-year-old Archduke Maximilian, son of the Hapsburg Holy Roman Emperor, Frederick III. Maximilian was engaged to marry Mary, daughter of Charles the Bold, Duke of Burgundy – and to mark the coming wedding the people of Germany showered Maximilian with silver and gold.

Counsellors at Frederick's court advised Maximilian to have some of the gold made into a ring – and to set it with diamonds in the shape of the letter 'M'. Maxi-

milian did so and gave the ring to Mary at her home in Ghent. By marrying her, he gained the vast Burgundian estates in the Netherlands – and the giving of a diamond engagement ring from a man to his future wife became a tradition.

### BRILLIANT DISPLAY

The French statesman Cardinal Jules Mazarin invented in about 1650 the shape known as a 'brilliant' – in which a diamond or other gem is cut in precisely angled facets. He had 12 large diamonds cut in this shape to display their glitter and brilliance. And the brilliant – which both reflects and splits light – is still the best cut for showing off a precious stone's fire.

### LUCKY STRIKE

In 1903, blacksmith Fred La Rose, of Cobalt, Ontario, in Canada, threw his hammer at a marauding fox, missed – and struck silver. The hammer landed on what turned out to be the world's richest vein of silver. La Rose sold his claim for $30,000 – and by 1913 the vein had yielded silver worth $300 million.

### BURYING MANHATTAN

In most modern gold mines, miners have to dig tonnes of rock to find ounces of gold, and they generate mountains of waste rock in the process. If the 50 million tonnes of waste from just one gold mine, the Randfontein, near Johannesburg, South Africa, was spread out evenly, it would bury the whole of New York's Manhattan Island, an area of 57km² (22 square miles), to a depth of 2.4m (8ft).

### CRADLE OF INDUSTRY

Coalbrookdale, in the heart of England, was uniquely equipped by nature to become in the 18th and 19th centuries the iron cradle of the world's first industrial revolution. The town is built on an unusual sequence of rocks that includes layers of clay (used for making pottery and bricks for furnaces), coal, ironstone and limestone. Limestone, ironstone and coke (a high-carbon fuel made from coal) were the essential ingredients for making iron.

Percolating through part of the rocks was a strange treacly material – natural bitumen – that, in the 18th century, was burnt or used to make oils for lubricating machines and wheel axles. It, too, came to have an industrial role – to seal the wooden boats used to transport the iron.

### MINI-MINERS

Microbes are now being used throughout the world to leach minerals from rocks. One of the most widely used microbes is *Thiobacillus*, which has successfully

---

## THE SCRATCH TEST

One of the ways in which geologists identify and classify minerals – including gemstones – is by testing their hardness. The scale they use was devised by a 19th-century German mineralogist, Friedrich Mohs. Known as the Mohs scale of hardness, it has ten grades, each represented by a standard mineral. Minerals at each grade will scratch all those of lower grades, and will be scratched by all higher grades.

The ten grades and minerals, in order of increasing hardness, are: 1 talc; 2 gypsum (rock salt); 3 calcite; 4 fluorite; 5 apatite; 6 orthoclase feldspar; 7 quartz; 8 topaz; 9 corundum; and 10 diamond.

On the same scale, most gold ores have a hardness of 2.5–3, depending on what they are mixed with. Silver is 2–3, platinum 4–4.5, sapphires and rubies 9, and emeralds and aquamarine 7.5–8.

Other familiar ornamental stones have the following hardness ratings: amber 2–2.5; amethyst 7; garnet 6.5–7.5; jadeite (a type of jade) 6.5–7; lapis lazuli 5.5; malachite 3.5–4; moonstone 6; opal 5.5–6.5; tiger's eye 4; tourmaline 7–7.5; turquoise 6. By contrast, graphite – the 'lead' in pencils – has a hardness of only 1–2.

---

GOLD *Man has used gold – one of the few metals which is found in pure form – since the Stone Age. This nugget is South African.*

PLATINUM *Platinum is usually found with related metals such as palladium. These pieces come from Russia. Palladium and platinum are used as chemical catalysts as well as in jewellery.*

SILVER *Most of the world's silver goes to make photographic films. Silver deposits are often mixed with ores of lead, zinc and copper. But, like this Mexican nugget, they may also contain white quartz.*

extracted sulphur, copper and nickel. The microbes, placed in a bath of crushed rock and liquid, trigger a series of complex reactions which result in the metal being dissolved in the liquid. It can thus be extracted from the solution by traditional chemical processes.

A similar technique has been applied to recover uranium from ores in Portugal, Canada, France, Sweden and South Africa.

At present, the mini-miners are used only to work low-grade ores, or ores that are inaccessible, or unworkable or uneconomic to recover by conventional means. But it seems likely that their use will grow as biologists find more and better ways of putting them to work.

## BAMBOO OIL DRILLS
Crude oil was being drilled for in ancient China. The Chinese philosopher Confucius recorded in the 6th century BC that his countrymen drove hollow bamboo rods into the ground in search of brine to provide salt for cattle. In the process, they also came across natural gas and flammable petroleum, which they used themselves or sold for fuel.

## SEND FOR 'RED' ADAIR
The American troubleshooter Paul Neal ('Red') Adair was called in to combat the world's biggest gas fire, which raged at Gassi Touil in the Algerian Sahara from November 1961 to April 1962. The column of flame reached 137m (450ft) and the smoke rose to 182m (600ft). Adair – from Houston, Texas – used about 250kg (550lb) of dynamite to extinguish the blaze. His reported fee for the job was $1 million.

## THE FIRST GUSHER
The first oil well in modern times was drilled to 21m (69ft) by Colonel E. L. Drake near Titusville, Pennsylvania, in August 1859. It sparked off an oil rush similar to the California gold rush a decade earlier.

Crowds of adventurers began boring and cities rose like mushrooms. Immense fortunes were made by those who struck oil, while others lost their chance of riches when their wells ran dry as suddenly as they had begun to flow.

The oil was mostly used for lighting, and by the 1880s was also being distilled to make paraffin.

## OIL FROM THE OCEAN
The amount of steel used in production platforms in the giant North Sea oil fields would construct more than 170 Eiffel Towers. The first North Sea oil was discovered in 1966 in Danish waters, but the find was too small to be of commercial value.

Later that year the oil company British Petroleum discovered three large oil fields – Hewell, Leman Bank and Indefatigable – off the coast of Norfolk, and the oil boom was on. The fields, which lie in British and Norwegian waters, now produce a total of about 145 million tonnes of crude oil a year – about 3.2 million barrels of oil every day.

## ISLAND IN THE STORM
Since the discovery of North Sea oil in the late 1960s, drilling rigs have sprouted like a chain of concrete and metal islands from the storm-tossed waters between Britain and Norway. The largest rig is the jointly owned Statfjord B, about halfway between the two countries, which weighs 816,000 tonnes. Built at a cost of about £1100 million, it is the largest structure ever moved by man, and the storage tanks in its base can hold 1.9 million barrels of crude oil.

The rig was towed into position by a flotilla of powerful tugs, then its legs were flooded to set it on the seabed some 150m (500ft) below the waves. The rig, which went into production in November 1982, is so massive that to bring it to a halt from its towing speed of about 2 knots took more than 30km (about 20 miles).

**URANIUM MINERALS**
*All nuclear power stations – and atomic bombs – are based on uranium. In nature, the element occurs as chemical compounds in more than 150 minerals.*

PITCHBLENDE *Uranium and radium are both extracted from pitchblende.*

TORBERNITE *Copper, uranium and phosphorus combine to form green crystals of torbernite.*

**COPPER MINERALS**
*Gold and copper – the first metals used by man – occur naturally in fairly pure form, and both are easy to work. Copper, now used widely in electronics and in alloys such as bronze and brass, is found in more than 160 minerals.*

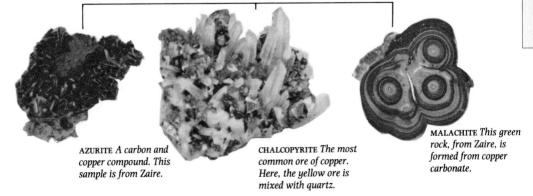

AZURITE *A carbon and copper compound. This sample is from Zaire.*

CHALCOPYRITE *The most common ore of copper. Here, the yellow ore is mixed with quartz.*

MALACHITE *This green rock, from Zaire, is formed from copper carbonate.*

# Alternative energy

## POWER SOURCE

Nearly all the world's energy comes, directly or indirectly, from the Sun. Even the winds are largely driven by the Sun's heat. And the energy contained in oil and coal was originally collected by plants from sunlight millions of years ago. The exceptions are geothermal energy (heat from the Earth's interior) and tidal power, which is caused mainly by the Moon. The Sun's total energy output is the equivalent of 3800 million million million megawatts of electricity (and 1 megawatt equals 1 million watts). But the Earth intercepts only about 1/2,000,000,000th of this energy – about 1.9 million million megawatts. As little as 1 per cent of this fraction – about 19,000 million megawatts – would be enough to supply all mankind's energy needs.

## SUN, WIND AND TIDE: THE TRIPLE CHOICE

The appeal of what are known as 'alternative' energy sources is that – unlike oil, gas, coal and nuclear power – they are inexhaustible and free of pollution. The technology for harnessing them effectively, however, is still in its infancy and, as yet, relatively expensive. Three major energy sources are being explored by scientists around the world: the Sun; the wind; and the tides.

### SUN

A huge amount of solar energy reaches the outer atmosphere – far more than the entire amount of electrical and other sorts of power which is generated and used by man. However, despite its abundance, solar energy is thinly spread and collecting it is difficult and expensive. Even so, some houses in Britain, the USA and elsewhere are now partially heated – by means of rooftop solar panels – by the Sun. The first solar cells, which turn sun power directly into electricity, were made at the Bell Laboratories in the USA in 1954. Similar cells are now used to provide spacecraft with lightweight and reliable power sources.

### WIND

The wind was being used as a power source 1300 years ago in Persia, when the first windmill drove a wheel which turned the upper of two millstones. Modern windmills are often designed to spin at high speeds so that they can generate electricity. One type – known as a Darrieus after the French scientist G. J. Darrieus who designed it in the 1920s – has a vertical axis, like the earliest Persian windmills. The advantage of this arrangement is that it needs no second set of bearings to swivel the vanes towards the wind. It works equally well regardless of the wind direction. Other types look like enormous propellers.

### TIDE

Water mills have used the power of the tides for about 1000 years. Incoming tides are trapped behind a dam across a bay or estuary, then the water is allowed to flow out past water wheels as the tide ebbs. In the 20th century more efficient turbines have been developed which can make use of water flowing in either direction to generate electricity. Despite the potential of tidal power, only one large tidal power station has so far been built: on the estuary of the River Rance in Brittany, France. It was completed in 1968 with a dam nearly 760m (2500ft) long. The dam channels the water to 24 turbines, each capable of generating 10 megawatts, or enough power to light a town of about 40,000 people. Tidal power stations are most effective where the rise and fall in the tide is substantial: 6m (20ft) or more. There are, however, relatively few such places in the world, which makes it unlikely that tidal power will be a major contributor to world energy supplies for the forseeable future.

## GETTING MORE OUT OF MUCK

Cow dung can be used to produce a substitute for fuel oil. One experimental plant, near Munich in West Germany, has shown that it is possible to turn the dung from 1000 cows into the equivalent of 2000 litres (440 gallons) of fuel oil every day. The dung is sealed inside giant fermenters and, as it decomposes, it gives off the inflammable gas methane, which can be used to replace the fuel oil in boilers and generators. In addition, the residue left behind after the gas has been collected makes a rich and odour-free fertiliser.

The system could make large farms self-sufficient in energy. But so far the high cost of the fermenters has discouraged most farmers from using them.

## STICKY END

Not all the schemes that have been tried for turning organic material into fuel have been successful. In 1982, for instance, a Kenyan company abandoned a £50 million project designed to turn molasses (made from sugar cane) into an alcohol-based fuel when it became clear that the process consumed more energy than it produced.

## COLLECTION POINT

The trouble with much renewable energy – such as the heat of the Sun or the power of the wind – is that it arrives in relatively small amounts spread over large areas. So before it can be used on a large scale, it has to be collected and concentrated. But to concentrate, say, enough power to equal the output of a medium-size 2000 megawatt power station requires an array of solar cells covering 70km² (27 square miles), or 1000 giant windmill generators covering 800km² (310 square miles).

Since few countries have this much spare land available – and since such large arrays would be enormously expensive – most researchers believe that wind and solar power are better used on a small scale, to help power individual homes rather than towns.

Another trouble with renewable energies such as solar, wind and wave power is that they cannot be switched on and off when they are needed. By contrast the energy contained in a car's petrol tank is available at the turn of the ignition switch. Nobody yet knows, for instance, how to store electricity efficiently (batteries are inefficient because they are very heavy for the amount of power they contain). It has to be generated as it is used.

One answer is to convert electricity into potential energy: the energy contained in any object at height. In Britain, engineers in 1975 began hollowing out a Welsh mountain near Llanberis to build a giant 'pumped-storage' station. The power station, known as Dinorwig, went into operation in the early 1980s. It consists of two lakes at different heights linked by huge tunnels. The tunnels guide water to turbines set in a vast artificial cavern which is as large as a soccer pitch and high enough to hold a 16-storey building. When other power stations generate too much electricity, the Llanberis station uses the surplus to pump water up the tunnels to the upper lake. When a sudden burst of power is needed, the water is allowed to run back down through the turbines, returning electricity to the national grid.

## FIRST SOLAR PANEL

The simplest way to tap the Sun's power is to collect its heat. In the 18th century, the Swiss scientist Horace-Bénédict de Saussure (1740–99) designed the first solar heating panel. The panel – a simple wooden box with a glass top and a black base – worked on the principle that sunlight penetrating glass will be absorbed by a dark surface on the other side, and trapped as heat. This is the reason why greenhouses become so much hotter than the air outside on a sunny day. De Saussure's panel reached temperatures of up to 88°C (190°F) – a full 30°C (54°F) hotter than the world record open-air temperature.

## FIVE-MINUTE EGGS

Another way to collect solar energy is to build 'solar ponds'. At their simplest, these are lakes of salty water, which gradually collect the Sun's heat in the deepest, most salty layers.

In a freshwater pond, convection currents keep lifting the warm water so that it mixes with cooler water and loses its heat. But in a saltwater pond, the saltiest layers are the densest, so they sink to the bottom and stay there, counteracting the process of convection. Insulated in this way by the cooler upper layers, the bottom layers of the pond go on absorbing heat from the Sun, and their temperature can reach boiling point.

To prove it, researchers in New Mexico, USA, have boiled eggs in five minutes by suspending them in a solar pond. Israel already generates some electricity from the heat that solar ponds accumulate. And by the year 2000, Israel plans to generate 20 per cent of its electricity in this way.

## THE FIRES BELOW

Some countries are trying to tap the heat of the Earth – what scientists call geothermal energy. In most parts of the world, the temperature of the Earth's crust rises only 25°C (45°F) with each kilometre in depth, which means that only very deep holes can tap high temperatures. In some volcanic areas such as Iceland, however, temperatures as high as 360°C (680°F) exist close to the surface, where they can be tapped relatively easily.

In Denmark and Iceland, engineers use this heat by piping hot water from underground to warm nearby homes, offices and factories. An outdoor swimming pool in the Icelandic capital of Reykjavik is heated so efficiently by this method that it remains open and in use all year round.

## SOLAR TREK

On December 19, 1982, a solar-powered car – *The Quiet Achiever* – set out on the 4130km (2566 miles) journey from the western Australian city of Perth to Sydney. The car, with an average cruising speed of about 25km/h (15mph), had a fibreglass body, bicycle racing brakes and tyres, an electric motor, batteries, chain drive – and a flat roof containing 720 solar cells.

The car was co-driven by two Australians: Larry Perkins, a racing-car driver who, with his brother Gary, designed and built the machine; and Hans Tholstrup, whose idea it was. *The Quiet Achiever* coasted into Sydney on January 7, 1983, 20 days after starting off – becoming the first machine to cross a continent on sunshine alone.

SOAKING UP THE SUN *Scores of giant mirrors swivel to follow the Sun each day at Adrano in Sicily – site of the world's first solar power station connected to a national grid. Opened in 1981, the plant, known as Eurelios, uses the mirrors to focus the Sun's rays onto a boiler. Steam from the boiler drives a conventional turbine and generator. The plant can generate up to 1 million watts (1 megawatt) – enough to power 1000 single-bar electric fires.*

## WHY THE WINDS BLOW

Weather is caused by differences in temperature on the surface of the Earth. The moving force behind the weather is the Sun. At the Equator the Sun is never far from being directly overhead, and its heat is concentrated. Near the Poles, however, the Sun's rays strike obliquely and its heat is spread more thinly. It is these unequal air temperatures that cause the winds.

Near the Equator, where the Sun's rays are hottest, warmed air expands, rises, and billows out at high altitudes. As it cools, most of it subsides back to the surface just beyond the tropics, about 30°N and 30°S. Its weight creates regions of high pressure. Surface winds blow from there, back into the low-pressure zone around the Equator. The Earth's rotation deflects these winds so that they blow from the northeast in the Northern Hemisphere and the southeast in the Southern Hemisphere. These are the great trade winds, named by the merchant sailors whose ships made use of them.

In the polar regions, air chilled by the cold ground sinks, creating a high-pressure zone from which the winds at ground level blow outwards to warmer latitudes.

### Where cold air meets warm

Between the tropical and polar winds in each hemisphere are the winds of the temperate latitudes. Here cold polar air meets warm tropical air, creating low-pressure eddies, known as cyclones, that bring rain, winds and gales.

The pattern of these major air currents is complicated by the presence of large areas of land. Because land surfaces heat up and cool down more quickly than water, the continents are hotter than the sea in summer, cooler in winter. In India and other parts of the tropics, air rising from the hot land creates low-pressure areas, which suck in the monsoon winds in summer. The same effect causes daily sea breezes in coastal areas during hot weather. In the afternoon, breezes blow shorewards as cooler air from the sea replaces rising hot air above the land. During the night and early morning, breezes blow seawards from the cooler land to the warmer sea.

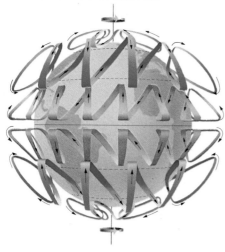

THE WINDS OF THE WORLD *Each hemisphere has three major wind systems: the trade winds; the westerlies; and the polar winds. In the Southern Hemisphere, the westerlies blow most strongly at latitudes around 40°S, where there is little land to interrupt the air flow. This is the region sailors call the Roaring Forties. Along the Equator, by contrast, sailing ships can be becalmed in the windless doldrums.*

HOT DOG DAYS The warmest days of summer, usually from about July 3 until August 15 in temperate latitudes of the Northern Hemisphere, were named the dog days by the Romans. The brightest star in the sky at that time was Sirius the Dog, and the Romans associated weather patterns with the stars.

RED FOR ALL CLEAR Countrymen are more often right than wrong when they repeat the weather rhyme: 'Red sky at night, shepherd's delight: red sky in the morning, shepherd's warning.' When the Sun is low in the sky, morning or evening, it tends to glow red anyway – whatever the weather conditions. Whether we see it or not, though, depends on whether there are clouds in the way. So if the redness is visible in the evening, in a relatively cloud-free sky, it means that the air to the west – the direction from which most of the weather comes in temperate latitudes – is fairly cloudless and dry. So the following day should be clear and fine. If, on the other hand, the redness is visible in the morning, it means that the clear weather is to the east – and less favourable weather is probably on the way.

Sayings about red skies are among the oldest of all weather lore, dating back at least to Biblical times. St Matthew's Gospel (chapter 16, verses 2 and 3) expresses the idea in these words: 'When it is evening, ye say, It will be fair weather: for the sky is red. And in the morning, It will be foul weather today: for the sky is red and lowring.'

*Blue moons do occasionally occur – when there are dust particles in the air of a critical size which scatter light at the red end of the rainbow spectrum more than light at the blue end. When this happens, the red light vanishes against the blackness of the night sky. But the unscattered light shining through makes the Moon itself look blue. One of the most recent examples was on September 26, 1950 – when dust was lifted into the Earth's upper air by violent forest fires in Canada. The moon also appeared blue after a huge volcanic explosion on the Indonesian island of Krakatoa in 1883.*

ACID RAIN Rain is slightly acidic even in unpolluted air – because carbon dioxide in the atmosphere and other naturally produced acid gases dissolve in the water. But, in parts of Europe and North America, rainwater is sometimes more acidic than lemon juice, because of man. Acid rain has been blamed for the increasing acidity of Canadian and Scandinavian lakes, and for damage to forests, especially in Germany. Other factors, however, may have contributed to forest damage, including drought. The extra, man-made acidity seems to be largely caused by the burning of fossil fuels such as oil and coal at power stations, in industry and in the home.

The main product of the burning is carbon dioxide – the same gas that all animals, including humans, breathe out. But many fuels also contain small amounts of nitrogen and sulphur dioxide ($SO_2$). When the sulphur compounds dissolve in rain in the atmosphere, they form a weak solution of sulphuric acid ($H_2SO_4$). Nitrogen oxides dissolve similarly, to form nitric acid ($HNO_3$).

THE CHILL FACTOR Air temperature is not the only factor that makes the weather feel cold. The wind plays a powerful role, too. Even in temperate latitudes, this wind chill factor is capable of making the air feel significantly colder than the thermometer alone would indicate.

As the temperature drops, the chilling effect of the wind becomes more pronounced. But as a rule of thumb, subtract 1°C from the temperature for every 3km/h of wind speed (1°F for every 1mph). So a strong breeze of 48km/h (30mph) in an air temperature of about 15°C (60°F) will feel as cold as if there were no wind and the temperature was about −1°C (30°F).

WHIRLPOOL IN THE SKY *A spiral of clouds, hundreds of kilometres across, wheels across the Earth over the northern Pacific. The anticlockwise spiral is typical of a Northern Hemisphere cyclone: a low-pressure system bringing rain and stormy winds to the surface below. A Southern Hemisphere cyclone would spin in the opposite direction.*

# Weather patterns

SITTING OUT A STORM   It is safer than houses to be in a motor car during a thunderstorm. If lightning does strike, it flashes over the outside of the car – which is virtually a metal cage – and runs to earth through the tyres. Although tyres are made of rubber they contain enough other materials to make them conductors of electricity.

HUMAN HAILSTONES   Thermal upcurrents in large clouds, which reach speeds of 100km/h (60mph), can be killers. In 1930, five glider pilots baled out into a thundercloud over the Rohn mountains in Germany.

Only one survived the drop. The others, held aloft by thermals, became entombed in ice like giant hailstones before the cloud finally released them.

On September 26, 1982, an Australian parachutist, Rick Collins, was trapped for 28 minutes in a thunder-cloud over Brisbane. He jumped from 1800m (6000ft), opened his parachute – and was buffeted by thermals up to 3800m (12,500ft). Battered by hailstones and in danger of passing out from lack of oxygen, he escaped by releasing his parachute, falling free through the cloud to 450m (1500ft), then landing with a reserve parachute.

## UNDERSTANDING A SATELLITE PHOTOGRAPH

Since the 1960s, satellites have helped to keep a weather eye on the climate and make meteorological prediction more precise.

Remote-controlled cameras on the satellites take sequences of photographs which are radioed back to Earth receiving stations at regular intervals. Placed together, they show the pattern of weather across the globe. Patterns of cloud, photographed by the satellite, can be related to weather charts drawn up by meteorologists. The commonest symbols on those charts are isobars, contours joining places of equal atmospheric pressure.

At the centre of a high-pressure region, the weather is commonly dry; at the centre of a low-pressure region, it is generally rainy. Wind direction is usually marked by arrows on the isobars. The closer the isobars are together, the stronger will be the winds around centres of pressure. Boundaries between warm and cool air are called fronts. A warm front (marked on a weather chart by rounded humps) brings a period of fairly steady rain and is where warm air is replacing cold air at the Earth's surface. A cold front (marked by spiky humps) usually brings showers with sunny intervals: it forms where cold air is replacing warm air.

OUTLOOK COOL *Satellite photography has revolutionised meteorology by revealing the global sweep of weather patterns – patterns that had been impossible to observe directly from the ground. Here meteorological symbols have been superimposed on a satellite shot taken on a chilly October morning. The outline of Britain can be seen right of centre. Numbers on the chart represent millibars of atmospheric pressure. Arrows show wind direction.*

*People who say they can feel the weather in their bones may be telling the truth. Even so, what their bones tell them is not the future state of the weather, but present conditions (which may indicate the future pattern). Why the ability exists is not known. But some people, for instance, find they get headaches when the air is damp or charged with static electricity, as it often is ahead of a thunderstorm. Others find that an aching bone or a corn twinges more when the barometer falls abruptly; and falling air pressure usually indicates approaching bad weather.*

KILLER WINDS   The great storms of the tropics, with winds of between 120 and 300km/h (75 – 190mph) are called typhoons in the north Pacific, hurricanes in the Atlantic and cyclones in the Indian Ocean and Australia. All are tight, deep low-pressure zones spawned over the sea near the Equator.

Most storms collapse within about ten days, becoming ordinary rain-bearing depressions. But while they last their power is awesome. A hurricane releases as much energy as an H-bomb every minute.

*The first person to give names to hurricanes was a 19th-century Australian weatherman called Clement L. Wragge. He had a taste for Biblical names such as Rakem, Sacar, Talmon and Uphaz.*

BIG BREEZE LOUISE   A whistling US radio operator started the 20th-century system of naming hurricanes and typhoons. He was overheard whistling a popular song, *Every little breeze seems to whisper Louise*, as news of a storm was being broadcast to a US aircraft during the Second World War. The storm was instantly named Louise, and the custom caught on.

Female names were used until 1975 when the Australian weather forecasting service began to allocate male and female names equally. The World Meteorological Organisation followed suit in 1978.

TERROR OF THE TORNADO   Tornadoes are spinning funnels of cloud, usually only 25 – 50m (80 – 160ft) across, which descend from the main base of storm clouds. If the funnel touches ground it causes considerable damage – both because of the raging winds it contains and because the winds suck air out of the funnel's core, leaving the air pressure inside drastically lower. The most destructive and most frequent tornadoes occur in the prairies of North America. The drastically lower air pressure inside a tornado has some bizarre effects. Several chickens were plucked alive by a tornado in Britain at Linslade, Bedfordshire, on May 21, 1950 – and survived. As the tornado passed over the coop, the normal air pressure inside the birds' quills was suddenly much higher than the pressure outside, so that the feathers exploded from their skins. For the same reason, houses in the path of a tornado can explode, and official US tornado advice is to open all doors and windows on the side away from the approaching storm to help equalise the air pressure inside and out.

---

*The whirling winds, which can reach speeds of more than 320km/h (200mph), can twist the tops off trees as easily as a person can twist the stalk from an apple. On the storm's fringes, by contrast, the winds can be astonishingly gentle. On September 4, 1981, a tornado which struck the Italian port of Ancona lifted a baby in its pram 15m (50ft) into the air and set it down again safely 90m (300ft) away. The baby didn't even wake up.*

---

HIGH-SPEED FLASH  Lightning travels at speeds of between 160 and 1600 kilometres per second (100 – 1000 miles per second) on its downward track to ground. But it can reach a speed of 140,000km/sec (87,000mps) on the return stroke.

The enormous spark heats the surrounding air explosively, creating the sonic boom we hear as thunder. In rare cases, the spark can generate a temperature of 30,000°C (54,000°F) – about six times hotter than the surface of the Sun.

---

*At any given moment, there are about 1800 thunderstorms raging around the world, generating between them about 6000 flashes of lightning every minute.*

---

THE BISHOP OF RAIN  Meddling English monks are to blame for the old legend that if it rains on St Swithin's Day, July 15, it will rain for the next 40 days. Swithin, Bishop of Winchester, died in AD 862, and asked to be buried 'in a vile and unworthy place, under the drip of the eaves, where the sweet rain of heaven may fall upon my grave'. When he was

TERRIBLE TWINS *Rare twin hurricanes whirl together across the Atlantic. The storms get their name from Huracan, a West Indian god of storms. Winds immediately around a hurricane's 'eye', which is usually about 32km (20 miles) across, reach more than 300km/h (190mph). But in the eye itself – seen here as a dark spot at the centre of each spiral – the weather is clear and calm.*

# Weather patterns

canonised in 971, the monks at Winchester decided to move his body to a more fitting place in the cathedral choir. They moved his body on July 15, and it rained for the next 40 days – the saint's protest, so legend has it, against the move.

There is no scientific basis for the prediction, and at least one gaping hole in the story. It was based on the Julian calendar, which Britain scrapped in 1752 and replaced with the modern Gregorian calendar. The Julian July 15 would now fall in early August.

WHY OZONE IS BAD FOR YOU  Ozone, far from being the source of the bracing air of the seaside, is poisonous. Ordinarily, oxygen exists as a molecule containing two oxygen atoms. Ozone, however, contains three oxygen atoms: an ordinary oxygen molecule plus a highly reactive single oxygen atom.

Ozone is formed naturally in the upper atmosphere and has the valuable ability to block most of the Sun's ultraviolet rays and other harmful high-energy radiation, preventing it from reaching the Earth's surface. Ozone is also formed when an electric charge – such as lightning or sparks from an electric motor – passes through the air.

If ozone is breathed in, however, in concentrated form, the spare oxygen atom is capable of reacting with living tissue, damaging it in much the same way as ordinary oxygen damages iron by turning it to rust. The effect of the damage is to alter the tissues of the lungs so that oxygen can no longer reach the bloodstream. As a result, the victim dies, paradoxically, from a lack of oxygen.

The bracing smell of the seaside? That is usually derived from rotting seaweed.

*In many of the world's towns and cities, the western end tends to be more fashionable and property more expensive than on the eastern side of town. The reason: the wind. In the temperate latitudes of both hemispheres, the prevailing winds are westerlies, bringing fresh air to the western edges of towns and carrying smoke and other types of pollution to the eastern side. As a result, in those cities and towns where there is no local reason – such as a sea view – to live anywhere else, the more prosperous families tend to settle to the west of the centre.*

RISING DAMP *Like the blast from a nuclear explosion, a vast thundercloud mushrooms upwards above the Amazon basin of South America, carrying with it thousands of tonnes of water which it will shed as rain. Scientists have learnt how to encourage clouds to unload their water by 'seeding' them with chemicals. But nobody yet knows how to make rain to order unless the right sorts of cloud are in the right place to start with.*

## THE MESSAGE IN THE CLOUDS

Clouds are the handwriting of the weather. They are formed when cooling causes some of the water vapour present in the air to condense into visible water droplets or ice crystals. In most cases the cooling is the result of the air rising.

If cloud is deep enough and lasts long enough, some water droplets or ice crystals grow to produce raindrops and snowflakes large enough to overcome the rising air currents and fall out of the cloud as rain or snow. In temperate latitudes, much of the rain starts life as snow and melts during its fall to the ground. In very deep convective clouds, hail (frozen rain) may form instead.

Cloud and rain are generally associated with low-pressure systems. This is because low-pressure systems occur in areas where a lot of air is rising – and cooling as it does so. In regions of high pressure, by contrast, the air is sinking towards the ground – warming as it falls. As a result, water droplets in the air evaporate into invisible water vapour, and the clouds formed from the droplets break up and disappear.

There are ten main types of cloud, and each carries its own message about the weather to come.

CIRRUS *High-level ice-crystal cloud – it is often a sign of bad weather to come.* ▼

CIRROCUMULUS *High-level rippling cloud – it often forms on the edge of unsettled weather.* ▼

CIRROSTRATUS *High milky cloud – it often brings showers or rain within 12 hours.* ▼

ALTOCUMULUS *Mid-level banded masses – they usually break up to give sunny periods.* ▼

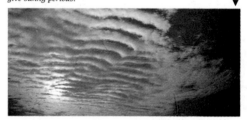

ALTOSTRATUS *Mid-level thin, blue or grey sheet – it can develop into rain clouds.* ▼

NIMBOSTRATUS *A solid mass of low cloud – it means that rain is imminent.* ▼

STRATOCUMULUS *Low rolls of cloud – they are usually associated with dry, but dull weather.* ▼

STRATUS *Low shapeless foggy cloud which often blankets hills – it commonly brings drizzle.* ▼

CUMULUS *Fluffy cauliflowers of low cloud – they are associated with sunny spells.* ▼

CUMULONIMBUS *Tall, often anvil-shaped clouds – they usually bring showers and thunder.* ▼

# Natural disasters

## DOUBLE DISASTER

Most of the 99,000 people who perished in a massive earthquake that struck the Japanese capital of Tokyo in 1923 died not in the quake itself, but in firestorms that raged through the city immediately after the first shock. The earthquake set off several fires as it brought down power cables and shattered gas mains. But hundreds of other fires were also started when family cooking stoves were tossed to the ground, igniting the wood and paper from which most of the houses were built. Almost half the city was destroyed in the quake, about 95 per cent of the damage being caused by fire.

## THE RICHTER SCALE

The Richter scale measures the total energy released during an earthquake. The scale is open-ended and is a logarithmic progression. An increase of one point on the scale indicates that the force of the earthquake is ten times greater than the number below. So an earthquake of magnitude 5 is ten times more powerful than a quake of magnitude 4, 100 times more powerful than one of magnitude 3, and 1000 times more powerful than a quake of magnitude 2.

The largest earthquakes ever recorded – such as the Lisbon earthquake of November 1755 – have measured about 8.9 on the scale.

More than 300,000 shocks with magnitudes between 2 and 2.9 occur every year. Jolts of less than 1 can be detected only on a seismograph; and humans only begin to feel shocks with a magnitude of 2 or more – although animals can detect smaller tremors. Earthquakes over 5 cause minor damage, and those over 8 can produce almost total destruction.

The scale, devised in 1935, is named after its inventor: a Californian seismologist, Charles Richter.

## THE MERCALLI SCALE

The severity of an earthquake is also measured by scientists using a scale first devised in 1902 by an Italian seismologist, Giuseppe Mercalli.

The scale, known as the Modified Mercalli, is used to assess the effects of a quake at a particular place, rather than to measure the quake's overall power.

**Intensity 0** Registered only by seismographs.
**Intensity 1** Not felt, except under 'ideal' conditions.
**Intensity 2** Felt by a few at rest. Delicately suspended objects swing.
**Intensity 3** Felt noticeably indoors. Standing cars may rock.
**Intensity 4** Felt generally indoors. People awakened. Windows rattled.
**Intensity 5** Felt generally. Some falling plaster. Dishes, windows broken.
**Intensity 6** Felt by all. Chimneys damaged. Furniture moved. Difficult to walk.
**Intensity 7** Everyone runs outdoors. Felt in moving cars. Moderate damage.
**Intensity 8** General alarm. Damage to weak structures. Monuments and walls fall down.
**Intensity 9** Panic. Total destruction of weak structures. Ground fissured.
**Intensity 10** Panic. Only strongest buildings survive. Ground badly cracked. Rails bent.
**Intensity 11** Panic. Few buildings survive. Broad fissures. Underground pipes broken.
**Intensity 12** Total destruction. Ground waves seen. Uncontrollable panic.

## LIFE-SAVING SENTENCE

A prisoner in a stone jail – a stevedore named August Cyparis, who had been jailed for brawling – was one of only three survivors of one of the world's worst volcanic eruptions. The jail was the sole building in the city of St Pierre – on the Caribbean island of Martinique – which completely withstood the volcanic blast and the fire that followed.

St Pierre was wiped out in three minutes when Mont Pelée, which loomed over the city, erupted on May 8, 1902, releasing a cloud of red-hot gas and rock dust which raced down the volcano's flanks. The eruption killed the entire population of 28,000 bar three: the man in the cell; and two people, a priest and a man driving a pony and trap, on the city outskirts.

## UNWELCOME DIVERSION

An attempt to divert a lava flow after an eruption on Mt Etna in Sicily in 1669 caused a local war. The citizens of nearby Catania tried to save their city from the lava by forcing it to flow in a different direction. However, they were attacked by the inhabitants of Paterno, a village threatened by the lava's new course. The Catanians were routed and the lava quickly flowed back on its original course, eventually destroying the western half of the city.

## BURIED ALIVE

In 1556 an earthquake devastated China's densely populated Shanxi province, killing an estimated 830,000 people in the worst quake disaster ever recorded. Many of the victims were buried alive when their cave homes collapsed, and others perished from the famine and disease that followed. Another severe earthquake struck China's Tianjin (Tientsin) region in 1976, killing some 242,000 people.

## TERROR OF THE TSUNAMIS

Tsunamis (often called tidal waves, though they have nothing to do with tides) start out as barely noticeable deep-water ripples caused by underwater earthquakes or volcanic eruptions. But they build up in shallow water into crests that can be more than 60m (200ft) high. At sea, they race through the water at speeds of up to 790km (490mph). As they approach the land, they suck back the sea, beaching ships in harbour. The giant waves then crash onto the shore, causing enormous destruction.

The largest known tsunami – an estimated 85m (278ft) high – roared past Ishigaki Island, in the Ryukyu chain in the West Pacific, in April 1971. But it is not known to have caused any damage; instead it dissipated its power in the open sea.

Tsunamis are mostly confined to the Pacific Ocean, whose basin is ringed by volcanoes. The term comes from Japanese words meaning 'overflowing waves'.

Astonishingly, the largest known wave was not a tsunami. It was caused in 1958 when a rockslide sent some 90 million tonnes of rock crashing into remote Lituya Bay in Alaska. The slide produced a single immense crest which swamped the hills on the opposite side of the bay to a height of nearly 520m (1700ft).

FUNNEL OF DEATH *A whirling tornado, hanging below the storm clouds that power it, sweeps across a prairie in the US state of Nebraska. Tornadoes generate the world's highest known wind speeds: the record is 450km/h (280mph), measured in a tornado which roared over Wichita Falls, Texas, on April 2, 1958. The most destructive tornado on record tore across Annapolis, Missouri, on March 18, 1925. It cut a 300m (1000ft) wide swath through the town, tearing up massive oak trees, splitting open stone buildings, sweeping cars over rooftops and hurling aside passenger trains. In minutes it was gone . . . leaving 823 people killed and 2990 injured.*

Then the monster surge bounced back into the bay and, as a 60m (200ft) high wave, raced harmlessly out to sea.

### THE ISLAND THAT BLEW UP

Some 36,000 people were killed by the tsunamis that followed a violent eruption on the volcanic island of Krakatoa (Krakatau) on August 27, 1883. But even

though the entire northern part of the island collapsed into the sea, no one died in the eruption itself – which was heard up to 4800km (3000 miles) away. Volcanic dust spread throughout the world, causing vivid sunsets, and the shock was felt in California, 14,500km (9000 miles) away from Krakatoa – which is in the Sunda Strait between the Indonesian islands of Java and Sumatra. The killer tsunamis raced along the coasts of Java and Sumatra, crashing up to 16km (10 miles) inland and smashing trees and houses.

Since 1883, volcanic vents on and around Krakatoa have erupted more than 30 times, the last occasion being in October 1981. However, the eruptions were minor ones and caused no known deaths. One of the vents – known as Anak Krakatau, meaning 'Child of Krakatoa' – has grown into a separate island more than 150m (490ft) high.

## LONG-DISTANCE DESTRUCTION
Homes and cars were swallowed up when the streets of Anchorage, Alaska, were buckled and cracked by a violent earthquake whose epicentre was 160km (100 miles) away. The earthquake took place on Good Friday 1964 and registered 8.6 on the Richter scale. Its seismic waves swept through the countryside, making the land rise and visibly fall over an area estimated at 207,200km² (80,000 square miles).

The earthquake was followed by a 7.5m (25ft) tsunami which destroyed the waterfront at Valdez in southern Alaska. A few hours later another and slightly smaller tsunami caused by the earthquake struck the shore at Crescent City, California, about 2900km (1800 miles) away, killing 12 people.

## DUST OVER EUROPE
In 1783 Iceland's Laki volcano erupted, killing one in five of the island's inhabitants and covering Europe with a pall of dust that took months to disperse. The world's largest volcanic eruption, the blast opened up a fissure 28km (18 miles) long, from which lava spread over an area of 570km² (221 square miles).

Dust and poisonous gas was also belched out in vast quantities by the eruption – causing disease and famine which killed more than 10,500 people and three-quarters of Iceland's livestock.

## THE DESTRUCTION OF POMPEII
The earliest recorded scientific account of a volcanic eruption was given in AD 79 by the Roman writer Pliny the Younger (about AD 62 – about 113), who witnessed the eruption of Vesuvius and the resulting destruction of the cities of Pompeii and Herculaneum. The initial explosion came on August 24 and produced a thick ash cloud which, wrote Pliny, spread over 'the earth like a flood'.

He observed the disaster from a spot 32km (20 miles) away and described how the 'black and dreadful cloud . . . burst open in twisted and quivering gusts to reveal long flames resembling large flashes of lightning'. Strong shocks caused buildings to sway as 'if they had been torn from their foundations'.

The next day Pliny went to the coast and found that earth tremors had caused the sea to 'roll back on itself', revealing the seabed. Later in the day black ash enveloped Pliny's vantage point, producing a darkness so thick that he felt he was 'in a sealed room without light'. Several hours later the cloud dispersed and a landscape 'covered by a thick layer of ash that resembled snow' emerged.

About 20,000 people died in the disaster. Pompeii disappeared beneath ash and Herculaneum was engulfed by a boiling mud flow. After some initial looting the cities were abandoned and were not rediscovered until 1748 by an engineer named Alcubierre, who was working for the king of Naples.

## POMPEII OF THE NORTH
In 1973 a fishing port on the island of Heimaey off Iceland was partially buried by a volcanic eruption – the first time this had happened to a town since Pompeii and Herculaneum were buried by the erup-

tion of Vesuvius in southern Italy in AD 79. But, thanks to an efficient evacuation operation, only one person died beneath the thick lava flow from the Icelandic volcano: a man looking for alcohol who was asphyxiated in a gas-filled cellar.

The town has since been completely rebuilt and the population has returned. Curiously, the eruption did bring the town's fishermen one major benefit. Part of the lava stream flowed into the harbour – and formed a perfect natural breakwater across the entrance.

## VOLCANIC FLAK
Only some skilful flying by the pilot of an Australian airliner on January 21, 1951, prevented the plane from being shot down by flak – from a volcano. The incident occurred when the aircraft – belonging to the Australian airline Qantas – was passing over Mt Lamington in Papua-New Guinea. The mountain – which was, unknown to scientists, a dormant volcano – suddenly erupted, spouting ash and pumice 11,000m (36,000ft) into the air. Bits of pumice stone pounded against the airliner's wings and fuselage, but the pilot kept control and flew the aircraft out of the danger zone.

The people living near Mt Lamington were not so fortunate. Almost 3000 of them died in incandescent ash clouds that raced across the countryside in the wake of the blast.

## CHRISTMAS EVE CATASTROPHE
In December 1953 a Coronation Tour of New Zealand by Queen Elizabeth coincided with one of the country's worst natural disasters. On Christmas Eve, a huge mud flow composed of some 2700 million litres (600 million gallons) of hot acidic water and debris broke from the crater lake of Mt Ruapehu volcano on the North Island.

The mud flow raced down the Whangaehu river, demolishing the Tangiwai Bridge which carried the main Auckland-to-Wellington railway line. Five minutes after the bridge collapsed, a night express train plunged into the ravine and was swept away by the mud flow, killing 151 passengers.

## THE TOWN THAT JUMPED UP AND DOWN
The strongest earthquake in Britain occurred on the morning of April 22, 1884, when a major tremor – centred on the town of Colchester in Essex – shook almost the whole of England. The earthquake lasted for less than a minute and damaged some 1200 buildings in Colchester. Three people died in the disaster, which was said to have made the town 'jump up and down'.

Although Britain lies well outside the world's earthquake zones, it is not completely free from their effects. The earliest known earthquake occurred in AD 103 in Somerset, where an entire town was said to have been swallowed up – name and all. Since then, about 40 other earthquakes strong enough to be felt by people sitting in chairs have taken place.

## BOULDER BOMBS
Large boulders exploded like bombs during an earthquake which struck the mountains of northern Assam, India, in August 1950. According to an eyewitness, a British naturalist named F. Kingdon-Ward, the shock's vibrations blurred the surrounding trees and ridges and long fissures appeared in the ground.

Despite the earthquake's violence, the naturalist escaped unharmed with only a spilt glass of water in his tent to show for the shock. Elsewhere in the region between 1500 and 2000 people died as a result of the earthquake and subsequent floods.

# THE WORLD'S WORST NATURAL DISASTERS

| Deaths | Date | Cause | Place |
|---|---|---|---|
| About 75,000,000 | Mid-14th century | Bubonic plague (Black Death) | Europe and Asia |
| About 22,000,000 | 1918 | Influenza | Worldwide |
| About 20,000,000 | 1969–71 | Famine | Northern China |
| 1,500,000 | 1943–4 | Famine | Bengal, India |
| 1,000,000 | 1939 | Flood | Henan, China |
| 900,000 | 1887 | Flood | Henan, China |
| 830,000 | 1556 | Earthquake | Shanxi, China |
| 500,000 | 1970 | Typhoon/flood | Bangladesh |
| 300,000 | 1737 | Earthquake | Calcutta, India |
| 300,000 | 1881 | Typhoon | Haiphong, Vietnam |
| 300,000 | 1642 | Flood | Huanghe River, China |
| 250,000 | 526 BC | Earthquake | Antioch, Syria |
| 242,000 | 1976 | Earthquake | Tianjin, China |
| 215,000 | 1876 | Tsunami | Bay of Bengal, India |
| 200,000 | 1703 | Earthquake | Tokyo, Japan |
| 180,000 | 1920 | Earthquake | Gansu, China |
| 137,000 | 1730 | Earthquake | Japan |
| 100,000 | 1228 | Flood | Friesland, Holland |
| 100,000 | 1290 | Earthquake | Hebei, China |
| 100,000 | 1731 | Earthquake | Beijing, China |
| 100,000 | 1911 | Flood | Changjiang River, China |
| 99,000 | 1923 | Earthquake | Tokyo, Japan |
| 60,000 | 1693 | Earthquake | Catania, Italy |
| 60,000 | 1755 | Earthquake | Lisbon, Portugal |

SON OF KRAKATOA *A jet of ash bursts from Anak Krakatau (left), a volcano that appeared off the Indonesian coast in 1952. It thunders on the site of Krakatoa, which exploded cataclysmically in 1883, and its name means 'Child of Krakatoa'. Now more than 150m (490ft) high, it is still active.*

EARTHQUAKE ISLAND *Sicilians, many of whom live near Mt Etna, have lived for centuries with quakes as well as the volcano. This town was shattered by one in 1969.*

QUALM BEFORE THE STORM *Ominous clouds darken the waterfront of Hong Kong as a typhoon sweeps in from the South China Sea. Winds in a typhoon – a Pacific hurricane – can reach 300km/h (190mph).*

# Time and the calendar

## WHY MINUTES HAVE 60 SECONDS
Hours and degrees of longitude are divided into 60 minutes and minutes into 60 seconds because 60 was the number base used by the Sumerians in Mesopotamia, the first people known to have written down a workable counting system 5000 years ago.

## DAYS OF THE GODS

English and the related Germanic languages, such as German, Dutch, Danish and Swedish, derive most of their names for the days of the week from Germanic and Norse mythology. French and other Romance languages such as Italian and Spanish derive theirs from Latin and classical mythology.

| ENGLISH | FRENCH |
|---|---|
| Sunday (Sun day) | Dimanche (*Dies Dominica*, Lord's Day) |
| Monday (Moon day) | Lundi (*Lunae dies*, Moon day) |
| Tuesday (Tiw's day, Germanic god identified with Mars) | Mardi (*Martis dies*, Mars's day) |
| Wednesday (Woden's or Odin's day) | Mercredi (*Mercurii dies*, Mercury's day) |
| Thursday (Thor's day) | Jeudi (*Jovis dies*, Jove's day) |
| Friday (Frigg's or Freya's day) | Vendredi (*Veneris dies*, Venus's day) |
| Saturday (Saturn's day) | Samedi (*Sabbati dies*, Sabbath day) |

## HOW THE MONTHS WERE NAMED

All the English names for the months of the year have Roman origins. The last four get their names from the Latin numbers seven to ten, because the early Romans began their year in March. January was named after Janus, the god of gateways, because the god's festival happened to fall at that time of year. When in about 150 BC the Romans moved the date for taking up official office (and hence the start of a new year) from March to January, the choice, years before, of Janus's name for the month must have seemed specially appropriate.

| MONTH | ORIGIN |
|---|---|
| January | Janus, god of gateways |
| February | Februa, festival of purification |
| March | Mars, god of war |
| April | *aperire*, the Latin 'to open', because of the unfolding of buds and blossom in spring |
| May | Maia, goddess of fertility |
| June | Juno, goddess of the Moon |
| July | Julius Caesar |
| August | Augustus, the first Roman emperor |
| September | *septem*, the Latin 'seven' |
| October | *octo*, the Latin 'eight' |
| November | *novem*, the Latin 'nine' |
| December | *decem*, the Latin 'ten' |

## WHY DAYS HAVE 24 HOURS
The custom of dividing each day into 24 periods seems to have originated with the ancient Egyptians in about 3500 BC. They divided daylight and darkness into periods of 12 hours each. But this meant that the length of each hour changed during the year as the nights lengthened and shortened. It was Babylonian astronomers who, in about 3000 BC, adopted the now universal practice of making all 24 hours equal in length, regardless of when the Sun rose and set.

In Europe, however, equal hours did not become standard until about AD 1350 – some 70 years after the introduction of mechanical clocks.

## THE LONGEST YEAR
The citizens of Rome must have wondered whether the year 46 BC would ever end. It went on . . . and on . . . and on . . . for 445 days. The long wait for 45 BC came about as the Roman general and statesman Julius Caesar restructured the calendar.

The calendar in use until then – the Roman republican calendar – had become hopelessly out of step with the seasons. The spring equinox, which should have coincided with the end of March, was arriving in the middle of May. The calendar, devised some time between the 5th and 1st centuries BC, was based on lunar months of $29\frac{1}{2}$ days. It consisted of 12 months and originally began on March 1, the start of the farmers' year and the time when Roman officials took up office. There were 355 days, $10\frac{1}{4}$ days short of the solar year. In an attempt to prevent a slip in the seasons – so that midsummer would always fall in June, for example – an extra, short month was added every other year. But this resulted in an average year of $366\frac{1}{4}$ days, one more than the solar year.

In 46 BC, Caesar commissioned Sosigenes, a Greek astronomer, to devise a new calendar. Sosigenes recommended a calendar based on the solar year, with a 365-day year and an extra day every fourth year – the first leap year. But before the new, Julian, system could be put into effect, the discrepancy between seasons and date had to be corrected.

An extra 23 days were due anyway in February of 46 BC; Caesar added another 67 days in the form of two extra months between November and December, so that 46 BC lasted a total of 445 days. It became known as the Year of Confusion. But by its end January fell where March had been, and the spring equinox was back around the end of March.

## IMPERIAL JEALOUSY
The month of August lasts 31 days because of an emperor's jealousy. In 8 BC August was named after Augustus, the first Roman emperor. Before, it had been called Sextilis (then the sixth month) from the time when the Roman year began on March 1. Sextilis, however, had only 30 days – one fewer than July, named after Julius Caesar – and Augustus could not bear to be outdone. So he had August extended to 31 days to match July, and he reduced February to 28 days, making it the year's shortest month.

## THE DAYS ARE DRAWING OUT
Each day is longer than the one it follows – by 0.00000002 seconds – because the Earth's spin is gradually slowing down. Too small to notice, the delay

adds up, in time, to a measurable effect. One century ago, the day was shorter by 0.00073 seconds. Over a full century – 36,525 days – the delays add up to 13 seconds. The slowing is caused by tidal friction due to the Moon's gravitational influence on shallow seas.

## THE INACCURATE EARTH

Until atomic clocks were invented in the 1940s and 1950s, all clocks were inaccurate because they were based on the Earth's rotation – which is itself irregular. As well as slowing fractionally each day because of the dragging effect of the tides, the Earth also spins at slightly different speeds from day to day because of the complex net of gravitational forces acting on its orbit.

In 1967, an international agreement finally broke the link between the measurement of time and the Earth's spin. Previously, the second had been defined as 1/86,400th of a day. The agreement replaced that definition with another: the time taken for an atom of the metal caesium to vibrate 9,192,631,770 times.

## JUST A SECOND

Clocks around the world were put back by one second at midnight Greenwich Mean Time on July 1, 1983 – the 11th such leap second to be introduced to the calendar since 1972.

The purpose of the adjustments is to keep clock time in line with astronomical time.

## COUNTDOWN TO DISASTER

Although navigators have known for centuries how to measure latitude – how far north or south they are – by taking sightings of the stars, until the 18th century they had no reliable way of working out longitude – how far east or west they were. To do that the exact time has to be known. As the Earth spins, the Sun reaches its highest point in the sky at different times – an hour later for every 1/24th of the Earth's circumference. By comparing midday locally with the time at a known point, therefore, navigators can work out how far they are east or west of that point.

Until the 18th century, most navigators made do with dead reckoning – working out their position by calculating how fast their ships had been sailing for how long and in what direction. But this method was extremely inaccurate because there was no way of allowing for the effects of ocean currents – and in 1707 it contributed to a British naval disaster. On October 22, 1707, three ships, including the *Association*, flagship of the English admiral Sir Cloudesley Shovell, were wrecked off the Scilly Isles. More than 2000 men, including the admiral, died. The tragedy helped to spur the British Admiralty to set up a Board of Longitude which offered a reward of £20,000 to anyone who could devise a means of measuring longitude at sea to within half a degree, or about

FIRST DATE *A total eclipse of the Sun – like this one photographed from India on February 16, 1980 – once blacked out the sky over Mesopotamia during a savage battle between Lydians, from present-day Turkey, and Medes, from what is now Iran. Terrified by what they took to be an omen, the armies downed weapons and made peace on the spot. Modern astronomers, tracking back eclipses, which are now known to fall at predictable intervals, have pinpointed the day as May 28, 585 BC – making the battle the earliest historical event whose date is precisely known.*

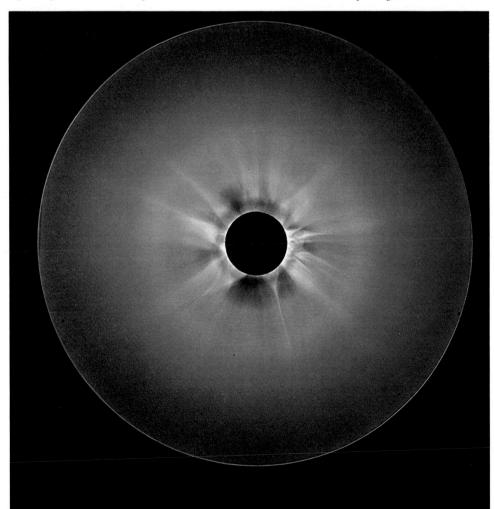

50km (30 miles). The solution – an accurate clock – was invented by a Yorkshire carpenter named John Harrison. The chronometer he made, after 40 years of work, was tested by the navy in 1761 and found to be only 5 seconds out after 81 days at sea – an accuracy precise enough to enable a ship to work out its longitude to within about 3km (2 miles).

But Harrison did not get the full reward because the navy claimed that the achievement was a fluke. After another trial in 1764, the board grudgingly handed over half the reward: £10,000. But it refused to hand over the rest on the grounds that the clock was too complicated and difficult to manufacture. After lobbying Parliament and George III, Harrison was given another £8750 in 1773. He died three years later at the age of 82, still £1250 short.

# DIVIDING UP THE YEAR

From primitive times, societies have based their calendars on the movements of the Sun and Moon. Most Western nations now use the Gregorian calendar, revised in 1582 from Julius Caesar's calendar. It is based on the Sun and the 365.242 days the Earth takes to circle it. The Hebrew and Muslim calendars are based on the Moon. The ancient Chinese calendar, based on the Sun and the Moon, is banned in China, but is still used in some other Asian countries. The Hebrew calendar periodically includes an extra month, known as First Adar, and the Chinese calendar does so occasionally. In the Muslim calendar, an extra day is added to the last month in some years to ensure that the first day of the new year coincides with the new Moon.

The Hebrew calendar is dated from 3761 BC, the supposed year of the creation of the world. The Muslim calendar is dated from AD 622, the year in which Muhammad moved from Mecca to Medina.

| GREGORIAN | HEBREW | MUSLIM | CHINESE |
|---|---|---|---|
| A widely used calendar matching the seasons, with a 365.242-day year. | The year 5746 coincides with September 16, 1985 – October 3, 1986. | The year 1406 coincides with September 16, 1985 – September 5, 1986. | The ancient Chinese agricultural calendar has 24 seasonal segments, each of about a fortnight. The Gregorian dates given are approximate. |
| *Month*    *days* | *Month*    *days* | *Month*    *days* | *Fortnight*    *Gregorian dates* |
| January ......... 31 | Tishri ........... 30 (Sept – Oct) | Muharram .......... 30 | Li Chun (Spring Begins) ..... February 5 – 19 <br> Yu Shui (Rain Water) February 19 – March 5 |
| February ......... 28 (in leap year ...... 29) | Heshvan ........... 29 (Oct – Nov) (in some years ... 30) | Safar ........... 29 | Jing Zhe (Excited Insects) ...... March 5 – 20 <br> Chun Fen (Vernal Equinox) ....... March 20 – April 4/5 |
| March ........... 31 | Kislev ........... 29 (Nov – Dec) (in some years ... 30) | Rabī I ........... 30 | Qing Ming (Clear and Bright) April 4/5 – 20 <br> Gu Yu (Grain Rains) ......... April 20 – May 5 |
| April ........... 30 | Tevet ........... 29 (Dec – Jan) | Rabī II ........... 29 | Li Xia (Summer Begins) ............. May 5 – 21 <br> Xiao Man (Grain Fills) ....... May 21 – June 5 |
| May ........... 31 | Shevat ........... 30 (January – February) | Jumādā I ........... 30 | Mang Zhong (Grain in Ear) ........ June 5 – 21 <br> Xia Zhi (Summer Solstice) June 21 – July 7 |
| June ........... 30 | Adar ........... 29 (February – March) (in leap year ....... 30) | Jumādā II ........... 29 | Xiao Shu (Slight Heat) .............. July 7 – 23 <br> Da Shu (Great Heat) ...... July 23 – August 7 |
| July ........... 31 | Nisan ........... 30 (March – April) | Rajab ........... 30 | Li Qiu (Autumn Begins) ........ August 7 – 23 <br> Chu Shu (Limit of Heat) .................... August 23 – September 7 |
| August ........... 31 | Iyar ........... 29 (April – May) | Sha'ban ........... 29 | Bai Lu (White Dew) ......... September 7 – 23 <br> Qui Fen (Autumn Equinox) ......... September 23 – October 8 |
| September ........... 30 | Sivan ........... 30 (May – June) | Ramadān ........... 30 | Han Lu (Cold Dew) ............. October 8 – 23 <br> Shuang Jiang (Frost Descends) ..... October 23 – November 7 |
| October ........... 31 | Tammuz ........... 29 (June – July) | Shawwāl ........... 29 | Li Dong (Winter Begins) .. November 7 – 22 <br> Xiao Xue (Little Snow) ................ November 22 – December 7 |
| November ........... 30 | Av ........... 30 (July – August) | Dhū al-Qa'dah .... 30 | Da Xue (Heavy Snow) ....... December 7 – 22 <br> Dong Zhi (Winter Solstice) ......... December 22 – January 6 |
| December ........... 31 | Elul ........... 29 (August – Sept) | Dhū al-Hijjah .. 29 or 30 | Xiao Han (Little Cold) .......... January 6 – 21 <br> Da Han (Severe Cold) ............. January 21 – February 5 |

# THE UNIVERSE

# Early astronomers

## HOW TO MEASURE THE WORLD

The distance around the Earth was first accurately measured by the Greek astronomer Eratosthenes (about 276–194 BC). His calculations were based on the fact that at midday on midsummer day the Sun was directly above Aswan in Egypt – where it shone down a well without casting a shadow. On the same day he measured the angle of the Sun at midday in Alexandria – where he was the Director of the Library – and compared it with that at Aswan, about 800km (500 miles) due south.

He found that there was a difference in angle of one-fiftieth of a circle – about 7 degrees – between the two cities. So he deduced that the distance between Alexandria and Aswan was about one-fiftieth of the Earth's total circumference. His figure of about 40,000km (25,000 miles) almost matched the modern measurement of 40,007km (24,859 miles) for the Earth's circumference through the Poles.

## THE GENIUS WAS A FRAUD

Many of the findings of the Greek astronomer Ptolemy (about AD 120–80) were based upon lies. That is the conclusion of a 20th-century American astronomer, Robert Russell Newton, who accuses Ptolemy of inventing bogus observations to support his theories, and of altering, for the same reason, genuine observations made by earlier astronomers. Ptolemy, who lived and worked in Alexandria, Egypt, recorded his astronomical views in a 13-volume treatise, now known by its Arabic title as the *Almagest*, meaning 'The Greatest'. Newton bases his attack on close analysis of the treatise's contents.

On one occasion, asserts Newton in his book *The Crime of Claudius Ptolemy*, published in 1978, Ptolemy reported an impossible observation. He gave the time of a lunar eclipse that took place on September 22, 200 BC, as the equivalent of 6.30pm.

Yet the time could not have been observed directly because the Moon did not rise until half an hour later on that date. To give the bogus observation credibility, Ptolemy attributed it to an earlier and widely respected Greek astronomer, Hipparchus, whose own records have long since vanished. And, since Hipparchus was thought by his contemporaries to be a man above suspicion, Newton is in no doubt about who did the faking. Far from being a genius, he insists, Ptolemy was a fraud.

## THE MAN WITH THE GOLDEN NOSE

The wealthy Danish astronomer Tycho Brahe (1546–1601) had a large part of his nose sliced off during a sword fight and ordered a replacement made of gold, silver and wax. He had the nosepiece painted the colour of flesh, glued it in place and wore it until his death more than 30 years later at the age of 54. He had fought a duel with a young nobleman over who was the better mathematician. Six years before the duel, at the age of 14, Tycho had intended to become a lawyer. But after witnessing a partial eclipse of the Sun on August 21, 1560, he determined to become an astronomer.

His career took off in November 1572 when he observed a brilliant supernova – an exploding star – which was subsequently named Tycho's Star. It was the brightest known supernova seen for 1000 years, and Tycho's description of it disproved the belief, dating back to the Greeks, that the heavens were unchanging.

## HERESY THROUGH A TELESCOPE

Although the Italian astronomer Galileo Galilei (1564–1642) was the first person to train a telescope on the skies, he did not, it seems, invent the device himself. It is thought to have been invented by accident in 1608 by the children of a Dutch spectacle-maker, Hans Lippershey.

The children are said to have been playing one day in their father's workshop in the town of Middelburg and put together a concave spectacle lens and a short-focus convex lens. Lippershey used the telescope, as he called it, to observe a distant weather vane, which looked larger and nearer.

The following year Galileo heard of the telescope and made a more powerful model for himself in his studio in Padua. His observations, which led him to support Copernicus's revolutionary theories, were regarded as heresy by the Roman Catholic Church and Galileo was later put on trial for his life. He was found guilty, but was spared after he recanted his heretical views.

Galileo spent the last eight years of his life in exile near Florence. But although, to save his life, Galileo had denied his findings in public, he never recanted in private. And on his deathbed in 1642 he stated defiantly: 'Yet still it (the Earth) moves!'

## THREE VIEWS OF THE SOLAR SYSTEM

In the history of astronomy there have been three major theories about the workings of the solar system – those of the Greek astronomer Claudius Ptolemy, the Polish astronomer Nikolaus Copernicus and the Danish astronomer Tycho Brahe. With modifications, Copernicus's theory is the one now accepted by scientists.

**Ptolemy** In the Ptolemaic theory, the Sun and planets were thought to orbit the stationary Earth in epicycles – that is, small circles whose centres moved around the circumference of larger circles. Ptolemy evolved a complex and clumsy system to explain the irregular orbits of the planets.

**Copernicus** The Ptolemaic system was challenged by Copernicus in the 16th century. He believed, correctly, that the Earth orbited the Sun. But he also believed – mistakenly – that the Sun was the centre of the entire Universe, that the planets were all of the same size, and that they moved in perfect circles. The German astronomer Johannes Kepler (1571–1630), a student of Tycho Brahe, established in the early 17th century that the planets in fact move in ellipses (ovals).

**Brahe** Tycho Brahe attempted to reconcile the theory of Ptolemy with that of Copernicus. He felt that Ptolemy's theory did not explain the movements of the planets, and he believed Copernicus's theory to be heretical. So he suggested that the planets revolved around the Sun, and that the Sun and Moon, in turn, revolved around the Earth.

## THE EARTH GOES AROUND AND AROUND

The first person to assert that the Earth spins on its axis and revolves around the Sun was not Copernicus but the Greek astronomer Aristarchus of Samos (about 310–250 BC). He anticipated later astronomers by declaring that the Earth's rotation causes daylight and darkness, that the inclination of its axis causes the seasonal changes each year, and that the Sun is larger than the Earth.

Aristarchus also tried to measure the sizes and relative distances of the Sun and the Moon by using observation and calculation. But although his method was theoretically sound, he could not obtain accurate observations. So he calculated that the Sun was 18–20 times more distant than the Moon, whereas the correct figure is about 390 times.

His heliocentric, or 'Sun-centred', theory was reviled in his lifetime – and he was threatened with prosecution for his alleged impiety. But his views were vindicated by Copernicus 1800 years later.

## THE STARS DO NOT FORETELL

Astrology, the age-old 'science' of predicting people's futures by casting their horoscopes based on the positions of the stars, the planets and the moon, is a lot of moonshine. That is the conclusion of two 20th-century French researchers, Michel Gauquelin and his wife Françoise, who spent 20 years investigating the subject. They examined the birth data of more than 40,000 people throughout Europe to try to find correlations between birth signs, jobs and personalities.

Their computerised findings were published in 1983, and their rejection of astrology was total. There was not one piece of evidence, they concluded, to show that it was anything but a sham – despite the efforts of astrologers to prove otherwise. 'It is now quite certain,' stated the Gauquelins, 'that the signs in the sky which preside over our births have no power whatsoever to decide our fates, to affect our heredity or characteristics, or to play any part, however humble, in our lives.'

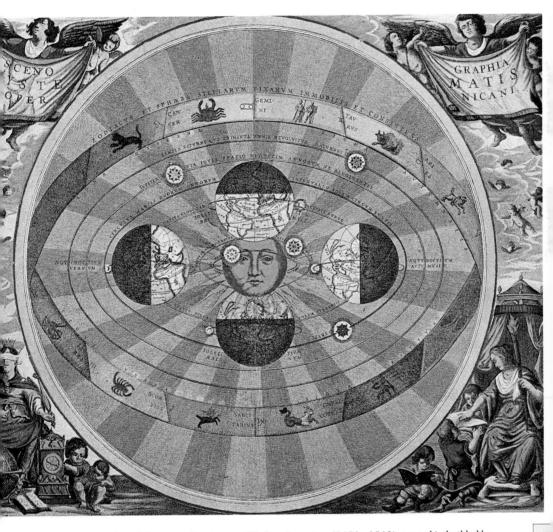

DEATHBED READING *The Polish priest and astronomer Nikolaus Copernicus (1473–1543) was on his deathbed by the time he saw the first printed copy of his book,* Concerning the Revolutions of the Celestial Bodies. *It put forward his belief – shown here in a 17th-century diagram – that the Earth was not the fixed centre of the Universe, merely a planet spinning around the Sun. He had been convinced of this since about 1510, but had been too frightened of the Roman Catholic Church to publish his findings earlier. The Vatican later condemned the book and did not remove it from the Index of prohibited books until 1822. By that time, the Copernican theory – which forms the basis of modern astronomy – had become generally accepted.*

FACTS ABOUT THE

# Modern astronomers

## RIDDLE OF THE APPLE

The story that the English astronomer Sir Isaac Newton (1642–1727) worked out his law of gravity after watching the fall of an apple is probably true. But nobody can ever know for sure. What makes some scholars doubt the story is that most of Newton's early biographers made no mention of it – an extraordinary omission considering the importance of the discovery the apple is said to have inspired.

There are only two sources for the tale and neither was an eyewitness. One is a clergyman, the Reverend William Stukely, who reported in his biography of Newton – written in the 18th century but not published until the 20th century – that the scientist told him of the incident one afternoon when they were having tea together in the apple orchard at Newton's home. The other is Newton's niece, Catherine Barton Conduitt, who looked after Newton during his latter years. Mrs Conduitt was the source of the first published account of the incident.

Her report appeared in *Elements of Newtonian Philosophy* by the French author and philosopher Voltaire. The book was published in 1738, eleven years after Newton's death and more than 70 years after the apple was said to have fallen.

## GIANTS OF MODERN ASTRONOMY

**SIR ISAAC NEWTON** (1642–1727) English physicist and mathematician who discovered the law of gravity. He published his findings in *Principia Mathematica* (1687). Newton built the first reflecting telescope in 1668, and was the first to use a prism to split white light (sunlight) into its coloured spectrum. Spectrum analysis is now the chief means by which astronomers analyse the chemical composition of the stars.

**SIR WILLIAM HERSCHEL** (1738–1822) German-born British astronomer who discovered the planet Uranus in 1781. He catalogued some 800 double stars and 2500 nebulae, and found that the stars in our Galaxy are distributed in a disc shape. Herschel also made the largest telescope of his day – 12.2m (40ft) long and with a mirror 1.2m (4ft) across.

**EDWIN POWELL HUBBLE** (1889–1953) American astronomer who proved the existence of separate galaxies and discovered that the Universe is expanding, with the more distant galaxies receding from the Earth faster than the closer ones. The ratio of the speed of recession to distance is known as Hubble's Constant. Hubble's discovery led to the Big Bang theory, which states that the Universe was created by a huge explosion about 15,000 million years ago.

**HARLOW SHAPLEY** (1885–1972) American astronomer who gave the first accurate picture of the size of our Galaxy and the Sun's position in it. In 1917 he calculated that the Galaxy was approximately 100,000 light years across, with the Sun positioned some 30,000 light years from the centre – not in the centre as had been previously thought. Shapley's figures are still widely accepted.

## PIPPED AT THE PUBLISHER

The German astronomer Friedrich Bessel (1784–1846) is officially credited with being the first person to measure the distance from Earth to a star. In fact, he was merely the first person to announce his results. An English astronomer, Thomas Henderson (1799–1844), had taken all the measurements necessary to work out a star distance about six years earlier – but had not got around to turning his observations into a distance. Both men made their calculations by trigonometry, taking two bearings on their chosen stars at intervals of six months. In this way, they got two angles – one from each side of the Earth's orbit – and since they knew the size of the orbit, they were able to work out the distance to the star.

Bessel announced his findings in 1838. He reported that the distance to a star called 61 Cygni, in the Northern Hemisphere constellation Cygnus, was 10.3 light years (near to the presently accepted figure of 11.08 light years). The following year Henderson finally came up with his long-delayed figure of 3 light years for the distance to Alpha Centauri, in the Southern Hemisphere constellation Centaurus.

Henderson had made his observations in 1832–3, while he was director of the Cape Observatory in South Africa. Alpha Centauri, now known to be 4.35 light years from the Earth, is the closest star visible to the naked eye, apart from the Sun.

## KARL'S SPARKS

Radio astronomy began in 1932 when the American engineer Karl Jansky (1905–50) intercepted radio waves from the Milky Way – by accident. Jansky was using an improvised aerial built partly from a dismantled Ford car. He made his discovery while investigating static on long-distance radio communications for the Bell Telephone Company. Jansky never followed up his breakthrough, however, because when he published his findings they aroused little interest.

After 1937, Jansky's discovery was investigated by the US radio amateur Grote Reber (1911–    ), whose work inspired the growth of radio astronomy after the Second World War.

## TOMB WITH A VIEW

The telescope at California's Lick Observatory also serves as a tomb. The 900mm (36in) refracting telescope is mounted on a pillar that contains the remains of James Lick (1796–1876), a wealthy philanthropist and landowner who financed the observatory's construction and after whom it is named.

## ACCIDENTAL OVERLOAD

The Van Allen belts (radiation-charged zones that girdle the Earth) were discovered by accident. In 1958, the USA launched its first satellite, Explorer 1. It was designed to measure the intensity of cosmic radiation from space. But as the satellite soared out beyond the atmosphere, the radiation count suddenly dropped to zero. Or seemed to.

Scientists on the ground were baffled until the US astrophysicist James Van Allen (1914–    ) realised that the satellite's meters had simply been overloaded, and so had broken down. The radiation belts now named after him lie between 650 and 65,000km (400–40,000 miles) above the Earth.

# WINDOWS ON THE UNIVERSE

Modern astronomers use three different types of telescope to look into the depths of space.

**REFRACTING** First developed early in the 17th century, refracting telescopes collect and magnify light through glass lenses. Their chief drawback is that the lenses can be supported only around their edges. As a result, very large lenses tend to sag under their own weight, producing distortions and setting a limit on their useful size. The world's largest refracting telescope, built in 1897, is at Yerkes Observatory, near Chicago in the USA. Its largest lens is 1.01m (40in) across.

**REFLECTING** First built by the English physicist and mathematician Sir Isaac Newton in about 1668, a reflecting telescope – which uses a concave mirror to collect the light from stars – can be larger than a refracting telescope because the mirror can be supported across its entire width. The largest reflecting telescope is a Russian one built in the 1970s near Zelenchukskaya in the Caucasus Mountains. Its largest mirror, which weighs 70 tonnes, is 6m (236in) across. The telescope is powerful enough to spot the light from a single candle 24,000km (15,000 miles) away.

**RADIO** The first true radio telescope was built by the US astronomer Grote Reber in 1937. Radio telescopes collect radio waves from space on a dish-shaped reflector in much the same way that a reflecting telescope collects light waves on a dish-shaped mirror. The world's largest single-dish radio telescope is slung like a hammock between the hills at Arecibo, in Puerto Rico. Completed in 1963, it has a dish 305m (1000ft) across. Near Socorro, New Mexico, US astronomers have used computers to link together 27 smaller mobile dishes spread in the shape of a huge Y. Completed in 1980, the array gives a radio view of the sky equivalent to that of a single dish 27km (17 miles) across.

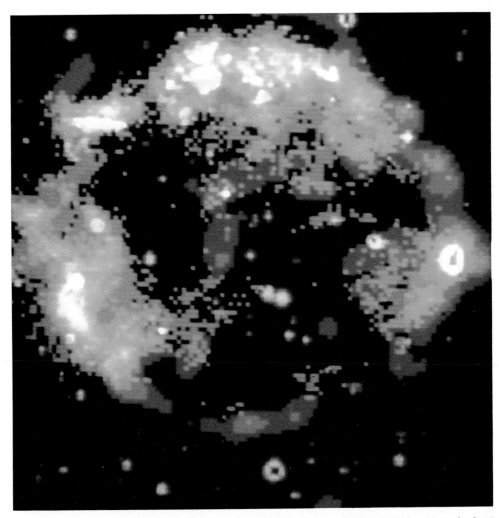

THREE IN ONE *Tycho's Star, named after the Danish astronomer Tycho Brahe, exploded in 1572, becoming so bright for a few weeks that it was visible to the naked eye even in broad daylight. Then it faded again. It was rediscovered in 1948 in the Northern Hemisphere constellation of Cassiopeia. Through an ordinary telescope, little evidence of the blast remains. Its awesome scale becomes apparent only when other views are superimposed, as in this modern triple composite put together by US astronomer John Dickel. The yellow and red patches are visible through an optical telescope; the blue areas show up on a radio telescope; and the green regions emerge on film sensitive to X-rays.*

FACTS ABOUT THE

# Origins of the Universe

## FAR HORIZONS

Space is so vast that astronomers have had to devise special units to keep their figures manageable. Their basic unit of distance is the light year – the distance light travels in one year, or 9.461 million million kilometres (about 6 million million miles). But they also use an even larger unit known as the parsec, which is equivalent to 3.26 light years.

## PIGEON PUZZLE

The strongest piece of evidence in favour of the Big Bang theory – that a vast explosion brought the Universe into being – was disregarded for a time. This was because the evidence was thought to be caused by pigeon droppings on radio antennae. Technicians working for the US Bell Telephone Company blamed the birds when, in 1965, their equipment picked up radiation from space on a wavelength of 3.2cm. They were wrong. The radiation was real, and its existence helped to confirm the Big Bang theory, first propounded in 1927 by the Belgian astronomer Georges Lemaître (1894 – 1966). Unknown to the technicians, US astronomer Robert Dicke had calculated in 1964 that precisely this sort of radiation should exist, on that wavelength, as an 'afterglow' of the Big Bang.

## FIRST MOMENTS

Scientists have been able to construct a 'history' of the Universe back to a tiny fraction of a second after the Big Bang took place. At that moment, it is reckoned, there occurred the first comprehensible event of the creation: gravity broke free from the single unifying force that had hitherto existed.

What happened before this is still a mystery. But scientists estimate that gravity broke free $10^{-43}$ seconds after the Big Bang – or a decimal point followed by 42 zeros and a 1.

COSMIC BLAST-OFF *The fan-shaped Orion Nebula, which glows in Orion's Sword (inset), 1600 light years away from the Earth, consists of a cloud of hot gases and dust spread out over at least 30 light years of space. Yet the material it contains is so rarefied that a core sample taken from it, 25mm (1in) across and 30 light years long, would weigh less than a British 1p coin or a US dime. Nebulae are the parents of stars, which form – frequently in clusters – as the result of the tug of gravity within the clouds. Here, the nebula is illuminated by the hot, newly born stars in its centre.*

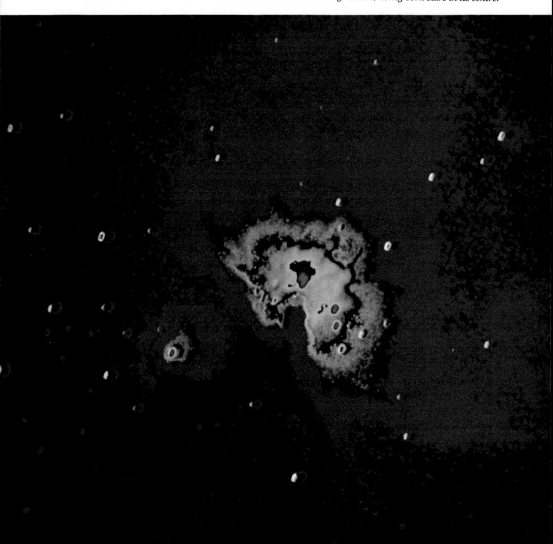

## CREATION'S CRUCIBLE

The figures involved in the concept of the Universe's origin are, in every sense, astronomical. A fraction of a second after creation, the temperature of the Universe is calculated to have been more than 100,000 million degrees Centigrade. Only 60 seconds later it had fallen to 10,000 million degrees.

Today the Universe's average temperature is −270°C (−454°F), just 3°C (5°F) above absolute zero, the lowest possible temperature.

## ARE WE ALIENS?

Life may have originated in space and been brought to Earth aboard a comet, according to a theory published in 1978 by the English astronomer Sir Fred Hoyle and the Sri Lankan astronomer Chandra Wickramasinghe. The creation of living material involves too many coincidences for it to have occurred on Earth, they say; it required all the resources of space.

They argue that life probably formed elsewhere, then was deposited here by accident and thrived in the favourable conditions.

## WHISKY GALORE

Some of the molecules associated with life have already been found in outer space. One of them is alcohol. Astronomers estimate that a huge cloud in the constellation of Sagittarius contains enough ethyl alcohol to make $10^{28}$ (10,000 million million million million) bottles of whisky.

## RIDDLE OF THE NEUTRINO

Among the most mysterious components of the Universe are neutrinos. They are unimaginably tiny sub-atomic particles. Yet some scientists suspect that they may form 90 per cent of the mass of the Universe, providing enough gravitational pull to slow and eventually reverse the headlong flight of the galaxies.

Despite their possibly central role as the Universe's glue, neutrinos are so difficult to study that their nature remains elusive. The particles, which travel at the speed of light, carry no electrical charge and can pass right through the Earth without even slowing down. Millions will pass through this page – and through you – in the time it takes to read it.

## FINAL MYSTERY

The theory of how the Universe began may now be generally agreed, but the way in which it will end is not. Everything depends on the average density of the Universe's matter. If the density exceeds a certain critical point, there will be enough gravitational pull to draw the galaxies back together and possibly cause a new Big Bang. But if the density is below this point then the galaxies will go on flying endlessly apart.

At present, there does not seem to be enough mass to hold the Universe back from endless expansion. But there is evidence of considerable hidden mass, perhaps concealed in invisible black holes. So a new explosion of colliding galaxies could still occur thousands of millions of years from now.

ORION

Orion Nebula

# BEGINNING WITH A BANG

Most astronomers now believe that the Universe started with a gigantic explosion – the Big Bang – about 15,000 million years ago. According to the theory, a 'minute cosmic egg' of immeasurable energy exploded. Matter, gravity and electromagnetism were created in the unimaginable blast, galaxies formed and the Universe began to expand at enormous speed, as it is still doing today.

Two other theories have also been proposed to explain the birth of the Universe: the Oscillating Universe theory; and the Steady State theory.

### Oscillating Universe

The Big Bang idea is taken a step further by the Oscillating Universe theory. The present expansion, it says, will be followed by a contraction, due to the force of gravity. The outward-speeding galaxies will slow and stop, like balls tossed straight up in the air, then fall back towards the centre. Finally, they will collide, triggering a new Big Bang. The theory holds that the cycle is repeated about once every 80,000 million years.

### Steady State

In the 1940s, the idea of the Big Bang was challenged by the Steady State theory. It was put forward by a series of scientists, among them Britain's Sir Fred Hoyle. They propounded a Steady State Universe, with no explosive start and an eternal life. Galaxies passing out of observable space, the theory holds, are replaced by new matter created from nothing and below the level of detectability. But the theory was progressively discarded, notably after astronomers at Cambridge, England, under Sir Martin Ryle, discovered that remote radiowave sources did not fit into the distribution pattern it demanded.

Present astronomical knowledge tends to support the Big Bang theory. But nothing is yet known about the instant of the primeval explosion, nor about why the Big Bang happened in the first place.

FACTS ABOUT THE

# The race into space

### BLOW-LAMP BLAST-OFF

In March 1926 the American physicist Robert Goddard (1882–1945) conducted the world's first tests with liquid-propelled rockets – in a field on his Aunt Effie's farm in Auburn, Massachusetts. His first rocket was fired from the back of a truck and ignited by means of a blow-lamp. At first, his rockets were only about 1.2m (4ft) tall. But in 1929 he fired a far bigger rocket which carried a small camera, barometer and thermometer. The rocket made so much noise that Goddard's neighbours complained to the police.

Goddard's work received no official backing and he and his colleagues frequently ran out of money. They got into further trouble with the police for illegally launching rockets from bits of wasteland – and their test models were often seized by the authorities or by angry farmers in whose fields the rockets had landed. However, with the aid of a $50,000 grant from the philanthropist David Guggenheim, Goddard set up an experimental rocket station in the New Mexico desert. There he built rockets which reached heights of up to 2.5km (1.5 miles) and speeds of more than 800km/h (500mph).

In 1935 Goddard became the first person to fire a liquid-propelled rocket that travelled faster than the speed of sound – in the air at sea level this is about 1200km/h (740mph). Altogether, he took out more than 200 rocketry patents, including one for a multi-stage rocket, the basis of modern three-stage booster rockets.

### ONE SMALL SLIP FOR A MAN

When Neil Armstrong – commander of the *Apollo 11* mission – became the first man to step on the surface of the Moon on July 21, 1969, he made a small slip in the words he spoke. He meant to say: 'That's one small step for a man, one giant leap for mankind.' Those are the words that have gone into the history books. In fact, the sentence lost its meaning because he actually said 'man', not 'a man'.

### BLEEP . . . BLEEP . . . BLEEP

The first space vehicle to go into orbit around the Earth was launched on October 4, 1957 – the 40th anniversary of the Communist seizure of power in the Russian Revolution. It was the Soviet *Sputnik I*, which weighed only 84kg (185lb) and was launched by means of a multi-stage rocket. *Sputnik I* – which travelled at 28,000km/h (17,500mph), then the highest speed achieved by any man-made object – transmitted a radio bleep that was picked up around the world.

### THE BIG BOOSTER

The total power developed by all three stages of the American *Saturn V* booster rocket – used for all the Apollo moonshots – is almost 4,082,000kg (9,000,000lb) of thrust. This is equivalent to the power of 50 Boeing 747 jumbo jets.

### CHEAP SHUTTLE

The price of a brand-new Space Shuttle – about $600 million – would buy just nine hours of peak advertising time on US television. The cost of the Shuttle programme as a whole – $9000 million – is the equivalent of slightly more than £1 for every man, woman and child in the world.

### THROW-AWAY FUEL TANK

The 47m (154ft) long main fuel tank on the US Space Shuttle holds 2 million litres of chilled liquid fuel, which it uses at the rate of almost 4000 litres a second. Eight minutes after blast-off, when the tank is empty, it is discarded and goes into orbit until it eventually falls back into the Earth's atmosphere to disintegrate. Astronauts have called the tank 'the world's largest throw-away cold drink can'.

### LARGEST, SLOWEST, SAFEST

The Crawler, the huge transporter which takes the Space Shuttle to its launch pad, is the world's largest and slowest vehicle. It weighs 3000 tonnes and its top speed is 3km/h (2mph). Nevertheless, in the interests of safety, the driver is ordered to wear a seat belt.

### PRECIOUS STONES

The 12 Apollo astronauts who landed on the Moon between 1969 and 1972, when the US lunar landing programme ended, brought back to Earth a total of 382kg (842lb) of lunar rocks and dust. Divided into the total cost of the Apollo programme, estimated at $40,000 million by the end of the project, the Moon samples therefore cost around $100,000 per gram ($3 million per ounce). At that rate, they are worth thousands of times their own weight in gold.

The astronauts left behind them the remains of six lunar landers, three lunar rover vehicles and more than 50 tonnes of litter – scientific equipment, empty containers, and other rubbish – probably the most expensive waste materials in history.

### MISSING THE MOON

The Apollo landings proved a great stimulus to computer engineers, mainly because of the guidance-computers the spacecraft needed. These navigational computers had to be hundreds of times more accurate than previous models.

An error of only 1.6km/h (1mph) in the spacecraft's top speed would have resulted in it missing the Moon by about 1600km (1000 miles).

### A YEAR IN SPACE

The world's most travelled man is the Soviet cosmonaut Valery Ryumin. In October 1980 he returned to Earth from his second long-duration stay aboard the space station *Salyut 6*, bringing his total time in space to 362 days – almost a full year.

During his space trips he went around the world 5750 times, covering 241 million km (150 million miles) – more than the distance to Mars and back.

### CALLING EARTH . . . QUIETLY

The radio transmitters which beam information back to Earth from space shots are usually less powerful than the ones used in walkie-talkies or CB radios. The unmanned US *Voyager* probes launched in 1977, for example, sent back spectacular pictures of Saturn and reams of scientific data across 1200 million km (800 million miles) of space – using transmitters which consumed only 28 watts. This is about half the power used by an ordinary lightbulb. Weight is so important on a space mission that it is cheaper to have very sensitive receivers on the ground than to carry more powerful – but also heavier – transmitters into space.

## SIGNAL SENSITIVITY

The radio antennae at US tracking stations which monitor the transmissions from space shots are so sensitive that they can detect incoming signals with a strength of only one hundredth of a million million millionth ($10^{-20}$) of a watt.

This is so weak that if a signal of such strength were collected for the entire 4600-million-year history of the solar system, the total accumulated energy would be enough to light a 7.5 watt Christmas-tree bulb for a mere 1/5000 of a second.

## HIGHER FLIERS

Astronauts can be temporarily 50mm (2in) taller at the end of a space flight. The reason is that, without the pressure of gravity, cartilage discs in the spine expand like sponges – increasing the body's total length. For the same reason, people are fractionally taller in the morning – because the discs have expanded during the night.

## FLYING DEBRIS

By 1989 there will be some 7000 pieces of space debris – ranging from pebble-size to objects as large as buses – orbiting the Earth. This is the forecast of satellite tracker Russell Eberst of the Royal Observatory in Edinburgh, Scotland. Each year, he states, the number of such pieces increases by up to 400 – starting with the 2100 'space items' tracked by defence radars in 1970. Ten years later the number had risen to 4400, and by the summer of 1983 it was up to more than 4900.

Of the objects currently in orbit, only about 1000 are actually satellites. The rest are discarded rocket stages and fragments of rockets and satellites that have broken up.

## SIX-MILLION-DOLLAR CLEANING BILL

Although most space debris is burnt up by friction when it enters the atmosphere, there are costly and potentially dangerous exceptions. On January 24, 1978, for instance, a Soviet nuclear-powered satellite, *Cosmos 954*, crashed over northwestern Canada, spilling radioactive debris. The Canadian government presented the Soviet Union with a $6 million bill for the clean-up operation – of which, after protracted wrangling, the Russians paid half.

Later that year, two French farmers were narrowly missed by a 20kg (44lb) lump of a re-entering Russian rocket which landed in a potato field. And in July 1979 the 75 tonne American space station *Skylab* fell in red-hot fragments across parts of Western Australia. This had its compensation for one young Australian, who flew to California with charred pieces of *Skylab* to collect a $10,000 reward offered by a San Francisco newspaper.

So far, there are two such instances of 'space damage' on record in Britain – both of them in the south of England. The first occurred in 1968, when a piece of a re-entering Russian rocket broke a house window in Southend-on-Sea, in Essex. The second was in February 1979, when part of a disintegrating Soviet satellite made an extra hole in the golf course at the seaside resort of Eastbourne, in Sussex.

*SOVIET CHALLENGE Salyut 6, one of a series of space stations to be launched by the Soviet Union, lifted off from its launching pad on October 11, 1980 (right). The first Salyut – the name means 'Salute' – was launched by the Russians in April 1971; its larger American rival, Skylab, followed it into space two years later.*

## DOG THAT DIED IN SPACE

The first animal in space was a dog called Laika, which was launched in a spacecraft by the Soviet Union in November 1957. The capsule was not designed to return to Earth and about a week later Laika died of asphyxiation when the oxygen ran out – provoking a worldwide outcry from animal-lovers. Three years later, in August 1960, the Soviet Union sent two more dogs – Strelka and Belka – on a 24 hour space flight. This time the capsule was parachuted safely back to Earth, and the animals were said to be none the worse for their experience.

## DEATH OF AN ASTRONAUT

On April 12, 1961, the Russian astronaut Yuri Gagarin (1934 – 68) became the first man to be rocketed into space. His 5 tonne vehicle, the *Vostok* (meaning 'East'), circled the Earth once and its flight lasted for just over 89 minutes. It returned safely after reaching a maximum altitude of 315km (195 miles). Ironically, having survived this pioneering flight, Gagarin was killed during a routine one. A jet he was flying seven years later crashed during a training flight. His ashes were given a place of honour in the Kremlin wall in Moscow.

## REQUIEM FOR A COW

In November 1960 an American rocket launched from Cape Canaveral, Florida, went off course and crashed in Cuba, killing a cow. The Cuban government gave the cow an official funeral as the victim of 'imperialist aggression'.

## LIVING AND WORKING IN SPACE

The first space station – *Salyut*, meaning 'Salute' – was launched by the Soviet Union in April 1971. It was designed to test the long-term capabilities of man to live and work in space; and to allow experimental work to be done in the fields of solar power, industrial processes and medicine.

The Americans launched their first space station, *Skylab*, in May 1973. It was larger than *Salyut* – about 6m (20ft) long and 6.4m (21ft) wide – and had two main compartments: a workshop and living quarters. There was a lavatory, a shower, solar-powered electric ovens and hot-plates, and sleeping bags attached vertically to the walls. There was also an exercise bicycle for the astronauts. Three teams of astronauts manned *Skylab* for a total of 172 days. Then the last astronauts returned to Earth and the space station was left empty in orbit. In July 1979 it re-entered the atmosphere and broke up as it fell to Earth.

By then, the Russians had launched a series of *Salyut* stations – each about one-third the size of *Skylab*. The last of these, *Salyut 7*, was launched in April 1982 and in late 1984 was still in orbit.

## CRADLE OF THE MIND

Although space travel is very much a 20th-century phenomenon, the idea of exploring space has fascinated mankind for centuries. The French dramatist and novelist Cyrano de Bergerac (1619 – 55) – model for Edmond de Rostand's 1897 play of the same name – predicted that one day people would travel to the Moon by rocket. The possibility of putting an artificial satellite in orbit was proposed in 1687 by the English mathematician and physicist Sir Isaac Newton. And in the 1890s a Russian scientist, Konstantin Tsiolovsky (1857 – 1935), also advocated rockets as the ideal way of travelling into outer space. 'The Earth is the cradle of the mind,' he stated, 'and man will not stay in the cradle for ever!'

# MAN IN SPACE

Manned spaceflight programmes have so far been confined to the USA and the USSR. Initially the target was the Moon. On May 25, 1961, President John Kennedy committed the USA to putting a man on the Moon before the end of the decade. The mission was successful; the first lunar astronauts stepped onto the surface on July 21, 1969. But now effort is being concentrated on the development of reusable spacecraft and orbiting space stations. The key dates in the history of man's voyages into space, along with the names of the astronauts involved and the spacecraft they flew in, are listed here.

**April 12, 1961 (USSR)** First manned spaceflight, Yuri Gagarin, *Vostok 1*.

**May 5, 1961 (USA)** First US manned spaceflight (sub-orbital), Alan Shepard, *Liberty Bell 7*.

**February 20, 1962 (USA)** First US orbital spaceflight, John Glenn, *Friendship 7*.

**August 11 – 15, 1962 (USSR)** First simultaneous spaceflights, Andrian Nikolayev, *Vostok 3*, and Pavel Popovich, *Vostok 4*.

**June 16, 1963 (USSR)** First woman in space, Valentina Tereshkova, *Vostok 6*.

**March 18, 1965 (USSR)** First spacewalk, Alexei Leonov, *Voskhod 2*.

**June 3, 1965 (USA)** First US spacewalk, Edward White, *Gemini 4*.

**January 27, 1967 (USA)** Virgil Grissom, Edward White and Roger Chaffee died during a practice countdown for *Apollo 1* when the cockpit caught fire. Apollo programme delayed for 18 months.

**December 21 – 27, 1968 (USA)** First manned flight round the Moon, Frank Borman, James Lovell, William Anders, *Apollo 8*.

**January 16, 1969 (USSR)** First transfer of crew members from one spacecraft to another. Yevgeny Khrunov and Alexei Yeliseyev spacewalked from *Soyuz 5* to *Soyuz 4*.

**July 21, 1969 (USA)** First men walk on the Moon, Neil Armstrong followed by Buzz Aldrin, *Apollo 11* (Michael Collins stayed behind in the Command Module orbiting the Moon).

**April 19, 1971 (USSR)** First space station launched, *Salyut 1*. It was manned for 23 days (June 6 – 30) by Georgi Dobrovolsky, Victor Patseyev and Vladislav Volkov, but all three men were killed on the return flight in *Soyuz 11*.

**December 11, 1972 (USA)** Last Apollo Moon mission touches down on Moon, Eugene Cernan, Jack Schmitt, *Apollo 17*.

**May 15, 1973 (USA)** First US space station launched, *Skylab*. Last crew splashed down February 8, 1974.

**July 16 – 18, 1975 (USSR/USA)** First international space-docking, *Soyuz 19* (Alexei Leonov and Valery Kubasov) and *Apollo 18* (Thomas Stafford, Deke Slayton and Vance Brand).

**April 12 – 14, 1981 (USA)** First flight of reusable space vehicle, John Young, Robert Crippen, Space Shuttle *Columbia*.

**June 18, 1983 (USA)** First US woman in space, Sally Ride, Space Shuttle *Challenger*.

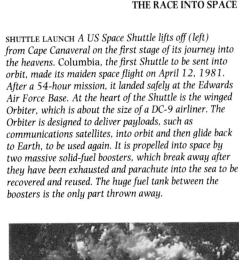

SHUTTLE LAUNCH *A US Space Shuttle lifts off (left) from Cape Canaveral on the first stage of its journey into the heavens. Columbia, the first Shuttle to be sent into orbit, made its maiden space flight on April 12, 1981. After a 54-hour mission, it landed safely at the Edwards Air Force Base. At the heart of the Shuttle is the winged Orbiter, which is about the size of a DC-9 airliner. The Orbiter is designed to deliver payloads, such as communications satellites, into orbit and then glide back to Earth, to be used again. It is propelled into space by two massive solid-fuel boosters, which break away after they have been exhausted and parachute into the sea to be recovered and reused. The huge fuel tank between the boosters is the only part thrown away.*

SHUTTLE IN SPACE *In the photograph above, the Orbiter* Challenger *is seen with the Earth behind it during the seventh Shuttle mission, launched in June 1983. Among the Shuttle's crew was Sally Ride, the first American woman to fly in space. In common with all advanced technology, the programme has had its problems: the ceramic 'tiles' fitted to the outer hull to protect the Shuttle from the heat of re-entry have proved fragile at times, and in 1984 a mission was aborted by computer seconds before lift-off because of a fuel problem.*

FACTS ABOUT THE

# Space

MOON THAT TURNS ITSELF INSIDE OUT  The most volcanically active body known is Io, the third largest of Jupiter's moons with a diameter of 3600km (2200 miles) – slightly more than that of the Earth's Moon. The *Voyager 1* space probe in 1979 photographed eight volcanoes erupting simultaneously on Io; hundreds of other volcanic vents were also visible. By comparison, it is rare for more than one volcano on Earth to erupt at the same time.

The volcanoes of Io spit out not lava but molten sulphur, giving Io a blotchy red and orange appearance. Geologists estimate that the volcanoes throw out enough material every 10,000 years to cover the entire surface with a layer about 1m (3ft) thick. So Io is continually turning itself inside out.

THE SHAPE OF RINGS TO COME  Two more planets will eventually acquire rings almost as spectacular as those of Saturn. Neptune's gravitational pull is forcing the planet's main moon, Triton, to spiral slowly closer – and astronomers expect the pull to break the moon up into a disc of debris between 10 million and

100 million years from now. Phobos, the closer of the two moons of Mars, is expected to form similar rings around Mars at about the same time.

Curiously, it is the moons' size which will cause them to form rings. Small objects like meteors, caught by a planet's gravity, usually spiral in towards the surface more or less intact – at least until they land. But the moons are so big that, as they move closer, the planets' gravity will tug far more strongly at their nearer side than at their farther edge. And the difference will be enough to rip the moons apart. A milder version of the same effect causes the tides on Earth.

IS THERE ANYONE OUT THERE?  The American space probes *Pioneer 10* and *11* that provided the first close-ups of Jupiter and Saturn are on trajectories that will take them away from our solar system for ever. On June 13, 1983, *Pioneer 10* became the first probe to move farther from the Sun than any known planet.

Both spacecraft carry metal plaques intended for any alien beings that might intercept the probes as they drift among the stars of the Galaxy millions of

years in the future. Each plaque shows a map of the solar system, the location of our Sun, and sketches of two human beings.

The probes *Voyager 1* and *2*, launched to examine the outer planets, are following *Pioneer 10* into the depths of space. They each carry long-playing records containing electronically encoded pictures of Earth as well as spoken greetings, sound effects and a selection of music from around the world.

The *Pioneer* and *Voyager* probes are travelling at about 50,000km/h (30,000mph) – faster than any man-made objects before them. But even if they were aimed at the nearest star, Alpha Centauri – and they are not – they would still take the best part of 100,000 years to get there.

THE MEN WHO 'LOST' NEPTUNE  After the discovery of Uranus in 1781, astronomers noticed that it was not keeping to its predicted path in the sky. One possible explanation was that it was being tugged off course by another, as yet unknown, planet, the eighth in the solar system. In 1846 the French astronomer Urbain Le Verrier calculated where this eighth planet might lie, and wrote to the Berlin observatory to ask astronomers there to look for it. The letter arrived on September 23, the birthday of the observatory's director, Johann Encke. Since Encke was taking the evening off to attend his birthday party, he passed the information on to his assistant, Johann Galle, who, together with Heinrich d'Arrest, sighted the new planet that evening. So, simply because it was his birthday, Encke lost the distinction of discovering the planet now called Neptune.

Le Verrier was not the only person to predict the position of Neptune. In England, John Couch Adams had made a similar prediction the year before, in 1845. He sent his results to the Astronomer Royal, George Biddell Airy, who for some time took no action. Only when Airy heard of Le Verrier's calculations did he order a search, which was undertaken at Cambridge by Professor James Challis.

One night in 1846, Challis saw an object that he thought might be the planet, but decided to wait until the following night to check it further. The next evening he delayed his arrival at the observatory to drink tea after dinner with a colleague, and by the time the two men reached the observatory, the sky had clouded over.

By the time the weather cleared, it was too late; Neptune had already been discovered by Galle at Berlin. So Challis was denied a credit in the discovery of Neptune – by a cup of tea.

---

*Along the Equator on Earth, the dawn arrives at a speed of about 1600km/h (1000mph) – faster than a jet plane. But along the Moon's equator, it comes at only 16km/h (10mph) – slowly enough for a man on a bicycle to keep up with it.*

---

THE LONGEST DAY  The combination of spin and orbit can create bizarre calendars on some bodies in the solar system.

Jupiter, for instance, spins through a 'day' in about ten hours and takes almost 12 Earth years to complete its orbit round the Sun. So a Jupiter 'year' is almost 10,400 Jupiter 'days' long.

Our own Moon is even odder. It spins on its own axis in exactly the same time – just under 28 days – as it takes to get round the Earth. Which is why we only ever see one side of it. If the Moon were a planet and the Earth its sun, the result would be that though the Moon's 'year' would be only about 28 Earth days long, its 'day' would last for ever.

The slow spin and fast orbit of Mercury, the planet closest to the Sun, have a similar reversing effect on its calendar. To an astronaut on Mercury's surface, a 'year' would last for a mere 88 Earth days. But a 'day' would last twice as long.

---

GAS GIANT *Whirling bands of gas shroud perpetually the surface of Jupiter, the solar system's largest planet. In this photograph, taken by the US space probe* Voyager 1 *in 1979, two of Jupiter's 16 known moons are visible: Europa, the ice-white ball on the extreme right; and Io, the orange ball near the planet's right-hand edge. The planet is huge. Io is bigger than the Earth's Moon; and the planet's Great Red Spot (visible in the lower left) is large enough to swallow the entire Earth.*

# Space

## THE SOLAR SYSTEM

The Earth is one of nine planets orbiting the Sun that together make up the solar system. The planets, in order of their distance from the Sun, are:

**Mercury** 4900km (3000 miles) in diameter and 58 million km (36 million miles) from the Sun; no moons; rotates once in 59 Earth days; orbits Sun once in 88 Earth days.

**Venus** 12,100km (7500 miles) in diameter and 108 million km (67 million miles) from the Sun; no moons; rotates once in 243–4 days; orbits Sun once in 225 days.

**Earth** 12,756km (7926 miles) in diameter at the Equator and 150 million km (93 million miles) from the Sun; one moon; rotates once in 24 hours; orbits Sun once in $365\frac{1}{4}$ days.

**Mars** 6800km (4200 miles) in diameter at its equator and 228 million km (142 million miles) from the Sun; two moons; rotates once in 25 hours; orbits Sun once in 687 days.

**Jupiter** 143,000km (89,400 miles) in diameter at its equator and 778 million km (480 million miles) from the Sun; 16 known moons; rotates once in ten hours; orbits Sun once in 11.86 years.

**Saturn** 120,000km (75,000 miles) in diameter at its equator and 1427 million km (886 million miles) from the Sun; 17 known moons; rotates once in $10\frac{1}{4}$ hours; orbits Sun once in 29.46 years.

**Uranus** 52,000km (32,300 miles) in diameter at its equator and 2870 million km (1783 million miles) from the Sun; five known moons; rotates once in about 16–28 hours; orbits Sun once in 84 years.

**Neptune** 48,000km (30,000 miles) in diameter at its equator and 4500 million km (2800 million miles) from the Sun; three known moons; rotates once in about 18–20 hours; orbits Sun once in 165 years.

**Pluto** Approximately 3000km (1900 miles) in diameter and averages 5970 million km (3700 million miles) from the Sun; one moon; rotates once in 6.4 days; orbits Sun once in 248 years.

**MOST DEADLY PLANET** An astronaut unlucky enough to crash-land on Venus would be simultaneously suffocated, crushed and roasted by the lethal atmosphere. The planet's atmosphere consists mostly of suffocating carbon dioxide. The gas bears down with a crushing pressure 90 times that of the Earth's atmosphere, and it traps heat like a very efficient greenhouse, raising the surface temperature to an oven-hot 475°C.

What little was left of the body would be eaten away by acid in the air. The acid – far more corrosive than the acid in a car battery – comes from clouds of sulphuric acid which surround Venus.

**AT THE EDGE OF THE SOLAR SYSTEM** In 1929 a major photographic search for new planets began at Lowell Observatory in Arizona, USA. As a result of the search, the ninth planet, Pluto, was discovered by the US astronomer Clyde Tombaugh on February 18, 1930.

Pluto turned out to be much smaller than expected, and to have a wayward orbit that sometimes brings it closer to the Sun than Neptune – as happens between January 1979 and March 1999. For that period, therefore, Neptune is the outermost planet of the solar system.

Curiously, Pluto was found only 6 degrees from the position calculated for it by the US astronomer Percival Lowell in 1915.

Lowell's calculations were based on perturbations in the motion of Uranus, but it turned out that Pluto was far too small to have produced them. There are still irregularities in the motions of the outer planets which are not fully accounted for, but which cannot be the result of Pluto's gravitational pull.

What they may be due to is a combination of slight inaccuracies in man's knowledge of the orbits of the outer planets, plus the gravitational effect of a belt of comets that some astronomers believe may exist at the edge of the solar system.

# The planets

**UP AND AWAY** Deimos, the second moon of Mars, is an irregularly shaped lump of rock no more than 15km (9 miles) across. Because of its size, its gravitational pull is so feeble that an astronaut could launch himself into space from it simply by jogging at about 11km/h (7mph) . . . and jumping into the air.

**THICK AND THIN** Saturn's rings are extraordinarily thin in relation to their 270,000km (170,000 miles) diameter. *Voyager* observations show that the rings are no more than 100m (300ft) thick. On the same ratio of thickness to diameter, a gramophone record would be 5km (3 miles) across.

**PLANET THAT SPINS BACKWARDS** Unlike the other planets in the solar system, Venus spins not from west to east, but from east to west. It also takes longer to spin on its axis than it does to orbit the Sun, making a Venusian 'day' longer than a Venusian 'year'. The reason for the reverse rotation is unknown. Until 1980, many scientists believed that the infant planet was set off on its backward spin when it collided with another embryonic planet or moon during the formation of the solar system about 4600 million years ago. But a mathematical analysis of Venus's movement has shown that theory to be incorrect and, so far, no satisfactory new theory has been devised.

**THE RED PLANET** *The sinking sun reveals the inhospitable landscape of Mars, captured by the* Viking *space probes between June and August 1977. The probes confirmed that Mars consists mainly of dusty plains, craters, mountains, valleys and canyons. Although dried-up stream beds in some valleys suggest that there was once water on the planet, organic soil tests showed that life was extremely unlikely to exist. The intelligent war-like Martians of British novelist H. G. Wells's* The War of the Worlds *remain fiction, not fact.*

**VOLCANO AND THE VALLEY** The largest volcano in the solar system is on Mars. Olympus Mons, 600km (370 miles) wide and 24,000m (79,000ft) high, is nearly three times higher than Mt Everest, and the 60km (40 mile) wide crater at its summit is large enough to swallow the whole of Greater London. Mars also has a massive rift valley called the Mariner Valley, 4000km (2500 miles) long, 75km (47 miles) wide and up to 7km (4 miles) deep. The valley would stretch across the whole of the USA.

**RINGS AROUND THE PLANETS** Saturn is not the only planet in the solar system to have rings. Smaller but similar belts of debris, which are invisible from the surface of Earth, have been discovered around both Uranus and Jupiter. The Uranus rings – there are at least nine – were detected in 1977 with the help of a telescope aboard a flying US observatory.

The single ring around Jupiter was discovered by the *Voyager 1* space probe in 1979.

**THE FASTEST MOON** A new and tiny moon of Jupiter, discovered by the *Voyager* spacecraft and officially known as 1979 J3, whips round the planet in just over seven hours – making it the fastest moon in the solar system. The speed of the moon, which is only about 40km (25 miles) across, is estimated to be about 113,300km/h (70,400mph) – fast enough to get round the Earth in little more than 20 minutes.

**THE ROLLING PLANET** Uranus is tilted on its axis more than any other planet. While most planets spin along their orbits like wandering tops (Earth, for instance, is tilted at only 23½°), Uranus is tilted at about 98° – more or less on its side. Since at times one or other of its poles is pointing at the Sun, Uranus actually rolls along its path through space. The tilt also creates the solar system's longest seasons: winters and summers that are 21 Earth years long. In winter, temperatures are estimated to drop to −219°C (−362°F), only about 50°C above absolute zero.

# Space

INSPIRATION EXPRESS  The modern theory of why the stars, including the Sun, shine was worked out by a scientist doodling on a piece of paper during a railway journey. In 1938 the German-born US physicist Hans Bethe (1906– ) was returning to Cornell University by train after attending a conference in Washington. Musing on the nature of the furnace at the heart of any star, he started scribbling on a sheet of paper – and before the end of the journey he had worked out the nuclear reaction which makes a star shine. Hydrogen deep in the core, he realised, was converted to helium, using carbon and nitrogen as catalysts. Bethe's rail-trip calculations helped to win him the Nobel prize for physics in 1967.

SPOTTING THE SUNSPOTS  The 11-year cycle of sunspots – giant magnetic disturbances which affect the weather and radio transmissions on Earth – was discovered accidentally by a German pharmacist and amateur astronomer. Heinrich Schwabe (1789–1875) began studying the Sun because he was searching for a planet that was thought to lie within the orbit of Mercury. Schwabe hoped to spot the planet as it passed across the Sun. But while watching fruitlessly for the planet (now known to be non-existent), he became interested in the dark spots which appear and disappear periodically on the Sun's brilliant surface. He began sketching the spots and kept on doing it every sunny day for 17 years.

By 1843 he had worked out their pattern: the number of spots reached a maximum about every 11 years, coinciding exactly with the periods when the aurora borealis and the aurora australis (the Northern and Southern lights) were most often visible. Other effects, such as weather patterns and radio interference, have since been shown to follow the same 11-year cycle. The last sunspot peak was in 1980 and the next is due in 1991.

BRIGHTER THAN WHITE  The solar storms known as sunspots, which can be several times larger than the entire Earth, appear to be darker than the rest of the Sun's surface only because their temperatures, at about 4000°C (7200°F), are at least 1000°C (1800°F) lower than that of the surrounding surface, or 'photosphere'. If a sunspot could be seen shining on its own, its surface brightness would be greater than that of a nearby arc-lamp.

LINES OF GENIUS  Joseph von Fraunhofer (1787–1826), the German optician who made it possible for scientists to discover the composition of the stars, owed his success to a disaster: the collapse of the building where he lived. The son of a poor but talented lens-maker, Fraunhofer was orphaned as a child and apprenticed to an apothecary in Munich, the capital of Bavaria. His employer treated him terribly, making his life a misery of semi-starvation and overwork.

Fraunhofer was only 14 when the rickety tenement he lived in collapsed. During the rescue operation, the Elector of Bavaria, Charles Theodore, came to watch. Fraunhofer was the only survivor and, moved by his plight, the Elector provided enough money to buy him out of the apprenticeship and put him through school. Later, Fraunhofer joined the staff of the Munich Optical Institute.

It was while testing a prism in 1814 that Fraunhofer became fascinated by the spectral lines now known as Fraunhofer lines after him. When sunlight is broken up into the familiar colours of the rainbow, the spectrum also contains a number of dark lines. These lines had been spotted in 1802 by an English scientist, William Wollaston. But Wollaston had thought they were merely boundaries between the bands of colour and so had ignored them. Fraunhofer realised that the lines were permanent, and significant, though he did not know why: he went on to plot more than 574 of them. There are now known to be about 25,000 lines in the Sun's spectrum, and similar lines appear in the spectra of other stars.

The significance of the lines was worked out after Fraunhofer's death by two other German scientists, Gustav Kirchhoff (1824–87) and Robert Bunsen (1811–99), inventor of the Bunsen burner. They solved the problem in 1860 when they found that the position of the lines in the spectrum corresponded exactly to the position of lines in the spectra created by heating certain elements to incandescence in the laboratory. The lines thus gave a direct indication of which elements were present, and so enabled Kirchhoff, Bunsen and later scientists to analyse the chemical composition of the Sun and the stars.

---

*The temperature at the centre of the Sun is about 15,000,000°C (27,000,000°F). The American physicist George Gamow (1904–68) once calculated that if a pinhead could be brought to the same temperature as the material at the core of the Sun it would set light to everything for 100km (60 miles) around.*

---

FLIGHT OF FANCY  The 19th-century French astronomer Jules Janssen risked his life to see an eclipse of the Sun. From the Earth, the Sun's outer atmosphere, known as the corona, can be seen well only during a total eclipse. Janssen knew that such an eclipse was due to pass across Oran in Algeria during 1870. But he was trapped in Paris by the besieging German army at the height of the Franco-Prussian War. Determined to get to Oran, he made a daring escape from the city by balloon, floating across the German lines and then hurrying south.

In the end, however, his journey was wasted. The eclipse happened on schedule, and Janssen was in the perfect position to see it. Unfortunately, the sky was solidly overcast – and he saw nothing at all.

RADIO SUNSHINE  The Sun, like most other stars, broadcasts radio waves as well as light. The Sun's transmissions were discovered in 1942 during the Second World War by a team of British scientists under John Hey.

When the scientists first picked up the crackling noise on their receivers they did not realise that the interference was from the Sun; they put it down to deliberate jamming by the Germans.

SIZE MEANS SURVIVAL  If our Sun were much larger or smaller than it is, life could not exist on the Earth today. Because larger stars burn their fuel more quickly, the Sun would have burnt out already had it been, say, only twice its size. Were it much smaller, it would give out so little heat that the Earth would be locked in a permanent ice age – far too cold for any form of life to survive.

# The Sun

**LITTLE AND LARGE** Towards the end of its life, some 5000 million years from now, the Sun will swell up into a red giant which will engulf the planets, including Earth, as far out as Mars. Most of its bulk will then be a glowing ball of gas containing about half of its total mass. The remaining half will be a much denser and much smaller core. If the red giant Sun were the size of an ordinary living room, its energy-generating core would, on the same scale, be no larger than the full stop at the end of this sentence.

**INSIDE THE SUN** *By isolating light given off at different wavelengths, scientists can study the Sun's ordinarily invisible atmosphere in detail. This colour-coded picture – taken from Skylab at ultraviolet wavelengths – reveals how gas clouds (shown as red) clump together in the atmosphere's lower layers. The solar flare at the top juts some 500,000km (300,000 miles); the Earth (right at the same scale) would fit into its length nearly 40 times.*

# Space

LIGHT OF THE PARTY  The first supernova (exploding star) to be discovered outside our own Galaxy was spotted in August 1885 – during a party in Hungary.

The supernova was seen through a small telescope which the party's hostess, a Hungarian named Baroness de Podmaniczky, set up on her lawn and turned towards an object then known as the Andromeda Nebula (now known to be an external galaxy).

The baroness – one of several independent observers to discover the supernova within a few days of each other – noted that there seemed to be a 'little star' in the nebula and this was confirmed by one of her guests, a professional astronomer called de Kövesligethy.

Some 2 million light years from the Earth, S Andromedae (the official designation of the supernova) was, at its peak, at least 15 million times more luminous than the Sun. Then it faded again. In apparent magnitude, however (its brilliance as it appeared in the sky), it remains the brightest supernova ever to have been seen in an outer galaxy.

THE BLIND OBSERVATORY  Astronomers in the world's oddest observatory cannot see the sky at all, and do not need to. The observatory is about 1600m (1 mile) underground in an old mine in the western United States, and its 'telescope' consists only of a huge tank of cleaning fluid. Yet it can 'see' into the core of the Sun better than any visual observatory in existence. The reason has to do with a sub-atomic particle called a neutrino.

Neutrinos have no electrical charge and virtually no mass. As a result, they can pass through most forms of matter unchecked – a property which makes them extremely difficult to detect. Most of the radiation generated at the Sun's core is absorbed by the Sun's surface layers. Neutrinos, however, once created, are unaffected by the outer layers and so provide a direct indication of the activity in the core.

Neutrinos are also largely unaffected by the Earth, so most pass straight through without even slowing down. But they can sometimes react with atoms of chlorine – hence the tank of cleaning fluid which is rich in chlorine. By monitoring the reactions in the tank, scientists can gauge the number of neutrinos reaching the Earth, and thus the number being produced by the Sun. The tank has to be so far underground in order to block cosmic rays which would otherwise swamp the neutrinos' effects.

LIGHTHOUSES IN THE SKY  The smallest stars known are neutron stars, so called because their electrons and protons have been crushed together to form the sub-atomic particles called neutrons. A typical neutron star is only about 25km (15 miles) across, yet it may contain as much mass as a star the size of the Sun. As a result, a pinhead of neutron star material would weigh about 1 million tonnes – as much as two of the world's largest supertanker ships put together.

Neutron stars are believed to be the remnants of large stars which have erupted as supernovae at the end of their lives. Their intense gravity has the effect of concentrating the powerful radiation they give off into beams. Since many neutron stars also spin, the radiation sweeps across space like the beam from a lighthouse. As the beams flash past Earth, the star seems to pulse with energy – which is why rotating neutron stars are known as pulsars.

The first pulsar was discovered by radio astro-

## STAR BILLING

Astronomers classify stars in two main ways: by their surface temperature; and by their brightness.

### Temperature
The system for classifying stars into types by their surface temperatures was devised by the US astronomer Edward Pickering (1846–1919). He listed the types alphabetically, starting with A for the hottest. But later discoveries forced modifications, so that the list became alphabetically chaotic.

In its modern form, the list contains seven categories – in order they are O, B, A, F, G, K and M. O-type stars are the hottest. Generally stars of types O, A and B are white or bluish; F-type stars are slightly yellow; G-type stars are yellow; K are orange; and M are orange-red. The Sun is a G-type star.

### Brightness
The brightness of a celestial object is measured in terms of its magnitude: either its *apparent* magnitude (its brilliance as it appears in the sky); or its *absolute* magnitude (as it would appear at a fixed distance).

The first scale of magnitudes was drawn up by the Greek astronomer Hipparchus (about 190–125 BC), who divided the stars into six groups, ranging from the faintest he could see (sixth magnitude) to the brightest (first magnitude). Modern astronomers have adjusted the scale so that a first-magnitude star is exactly 100 times as bright as a sixth-magnitude star. Objects fainter than magnitude six, which are visible only through telescopes, are given larger magnitude values. The faintest objects detectable are about magnitude +25. Objects brighter than magnitude 0 are given negative values. The Sun, the brightest object in the sky, has an apparent magnitude of −26.8.

The scale of absolute magnitude is used to compare the actual light output of stars, allowing for their different distances from Earth. An object's absolute magnitude, which can be estimated from its spectrum, is the brightness it would have if it were 32.6 light years from Earth. At this distance, the Sun would be very faint, with a magnitude of only +4.79. By contrast, the brightest star would be Eta Carinae, in the Southern Hemisphere constellation of Carina. Some 6 million times brighter than the Sun, Eta Carinae has an absolute magnitude of −9.

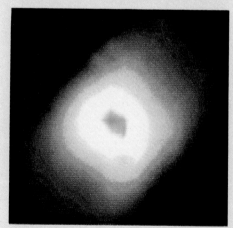

STAR BRIGHT *Eta Carinae, seen here in an infrared photograph with the hottest parts shown as blue, is the brightest known star. Ageing fast because of its ferocious energy output, it will explode as a supernova in a few thousand years.*

nomers at Cambridge, England, in 1967. Hundreds of others have been mapped since then. The first pulsar to be identified optically as well as from its radio waves was the small, faint star at the core of the Crab Nebula. Spotted in 1968, the star spins 30 times a second. Since then, other pulsars have been spotted which spin thousands of times a second.

HELLO . . . HELLO  One of the largest stars known is Betelgeuse, a red supergiant which marks the right shoulder of Orion. If Betelgeuse were positioned where the Sun is now, it would engulf the orbits of Mercury, Venus, Earth and Mars.

If it were possible to make a telephone call from one side to the other, your voice, travelling at the speed of light, would take half an hour to reach the other end of the line – even if the call were routed straight through the star's centre. If the call were routed around the surface of the star, your voice would take an hour and a half to get through.

Some astronomers believe that a mysterious and invisible object in the stellar group known as Epsilon Aurigae may be still larger. The object has not been seen directly but every so often it seems to cause a partial eclipse of its visible neighbour – for a staggering two years at a time.

By observing these effects, some astronomers calculate that, if the object is a star, it may be more than 3000 million km (2000 million miles) across – large enough, if it were in our solar system, to engulf all the planets out to Saturn.

THE GREATER BEAR  The group of stars known as the Plough or Big Dipper (part of the constellation called the Great Bear) has eight stars, not seven. One of the seven stars visible with the naked eye, Mizar – the second star from the handle end – is actually two stars. They are known as Mizar A, the brighter of the pair, and Mizar B. With the naked eye, they appear as one star; Mizar B becomes separately visible only with a small telescope.

Many stars are, like Mizar, grouped in stellar families. One of the most numerous families is known collectively as Castor, in the constellation Gemini. Castor consists of a total of six stars orbiting each other in three pairs.

CALLING EARTH  The 20th-century US astronomer Carl Sagan has estimated that there may be as many as one million advanced alien civilisations in existence on planets around the stars in our Galaxy alone. In 1960 the American radio astronomer Frank Drake made the first deliberate attempt to pick up possible incoming messages from beings around other stars. He turned the 26m (85ft) diameter radio telescope of the National Radio Astronomy Observatory, Green Bank, West Virginia, towards two nearby stars, called Tau Ceti and Epsilon Eridani. Despite listening for two months, however, Drake heard nothing.

Since then, other astronomers have searched for alien radio messages from approximately 1000 stars without success. But since there are over 100,000 million stars in our own Galaxy, and – if Sagan is right – only a million with advanced life, we will need to listen to at least 100,000 stars before we can expect statistically to pick up a signal.

Despite the odds, astronomers around the world are continuing the search, which may take until the end of the century to complete.

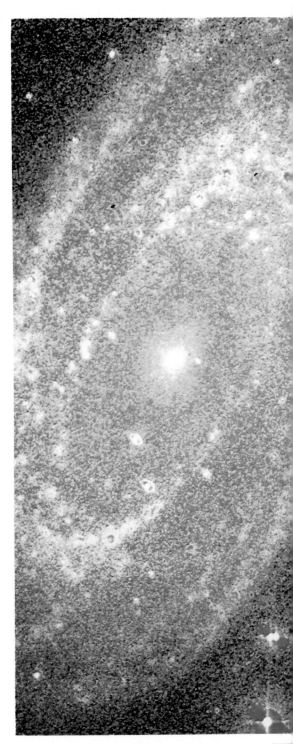

HEAVENLY TWIN *The galaxy known as M81 – in the Northern Hemisphere constellation of Ursa Major (the Great Bear) – is a twin of our own. Like the Milky Way, it is a spiral galaxy about 100,000 light years across. Older stars, mostly concentrated towards the galaxy's centre, show up as yellow or red. Younger stars, which show up as blue, mostly lie along the slender arms.*

411

# Space

The paths of dozens of comets are now known to astronomers. Some pass the Earth only once, but others, on elliptical orbits, reappear at regular intervals. The more important of these 'periodical' comets are listed here. Unlike solar and lunar eclipses, comets can be seen from all parts of the globe. Halley's Comet is the only major periodical comet visible to the naked eye.

| Name | Orbital period (years) | Date when next visible |
|---|---|---|
| Schwassmann-Wachmann | 15 | Visible throughout orbit with a telescope |
| Halley | 76.1 | 1985–6 |
| D'Arrest | 6.2 | 1986 |
| Encke | 3.3 | 1987 |
| Borrelly | 6.8 | 1987 |
| Pons-Winnecke | 6.3 | 1988 |
| Finlay | 6.9 | 1988 |
| Faye | 7.4 | 1990 |
| Tuttle | 13.8 | 1994 |
| Crommelin | 27.9 | 2011 |

PASSING STRANGER *Comet Ikeya-Seki soars above Table Mountain, South Africa, in a shot taken in November 1965. Astronomers do not expect it to return, if at all, for 880 years. Comet tails – streams of gas and dust boiled off from the nucleus by the Sun's heat and blown by a hurricane of charged solar particles – always point away from the Sun, so that a comet travels tail first as it heads back out to the edge of the solar system.*

CONSTANT BOMBARDMENT   Each day, about three or four fist-sized meteorites – each weighing a few kilograms – fall into the Earth's atmosphere. Most of them burn up before they reach the Earth's surface. The very few meteorites that do reach the Earth are usually large ones. On average, a large meteorite – weighing as much as 50,000 tonnes, or about the size of a modern passenger liner – hits the Earth once every 100,000 years.

SUPER CRATERS   One of the largest known meteorite craters is the Canyon Diablo Crater in the USA near Winslow, Arizona. It is 1km (0.7 miles) across and 174m (570ft) deep. Other large craters exist at Odessa, Texas, and at Wolf Creek and Henbury in Australia. It has been suggested, but not proven, that meteorites caused such major features as the almost circular Caribbean Sea and Hudson Bay in Canada.

> *The Earth increases in weight by about 25 tonnes each day. The extra material is composed of space dust – micro-meteors which are too small to see.*

IT'S A DOG'S LIFE   The only living creature known to have been killed by an extraterrestrial object was a dog – struck dead by a small meteorite at Nakhla, Egypt, in 1911.

BLOW FROM THE BLUE   The only person known to have been hit by a meteorite is an American, Mrs Hewlett Hodges, of Sylacauga, Alabama. On November 30, 1954, a 4kg (9lb) meteorite crashed through her roof, bounced off a radio and struck her on the hip, causing massive bruises but no permanent injury.

DIMINISHING RETURNS   Comets get smaller every time they go round the Sun. They are normally like enormous dirty snowballs – bits of rocky debris held together by frozen gases and water in outer space. But each time they approach the Sun, some of the ice is evaporated and some of the gases are boiled away by the Sun's heat, leaving the comets smaller than before.

Some of the comets that used to be seen regularly in the 19th century have now vanished, disintegrated by the Sun. Others have died more spectacularly by plunging straight into the Sun.

In 1846 one comet, Biela's Comet, which used to appear at intervals of 6.75 years, surprised astronomers by breaking in half. The two halves came round again for the last time in 1852. The comet's only legacy was a diminishing shower of hundreds of thousands of meteors formed from the remaining fragments that pepper the Earth's atmosphere every November. By the 1980s, however, the shower had petered away almost to nothing.

BAD OMEN, GOOD OMEN   Halley's Comet, which orbits the Sun about once every 76 years and is due to return in late 1985, was an object of dread for centuries. Its appearance in 1066, for instance, is recorded on the Bayeux tapestry, which shows it blazing above terrified Saxons before the Battle of Hastings. For the Norman invader, William the Conqueror, on the other hand, it was an omen of good fortune – his battle cry at Hastings was: 'A new star, a new king.' During a later appearance in 1456, when Christians and Turks were at war, Pope Calixtus III officially condemned

# Comets, meteorites and asteroids

the comet as an agent of the Devil. Despite his verdict, it seemed to be on the side of the Christians. At the Battle of Belgrade in the same year, its tail, shaped like a drawn sword, was seen pointing towards the Turks. The Christian armies, apparently encouraged by the omen, won the battle.

The comet, which is named after Edmund Halley (1656–1742), the English astronomer who first calculated its orbit in 1705, should be visible at times to the naked eye from November or December 1985 until April 1986. This time round it will not be as spectacular as on some earlier appearances, because it will swing round the far side of the Sun rather than passing between the Sun and the Earth. Nevertheless man will get his closest view ever of the visitor – thanks to an internationally planned series of space flights. Five space probes – two from Japan, two from Russia and one from the European Space Agency – will monitor the comet in March 1986.

IRON SUPPLIES FROM SPACE   Eskimos in Greenland used iron tools for centuries – even though they had no idea how to smelt iron. They mined the metal in almost pure form from three large meteorites that had fallen on Greenland in ancient times. The US explorer Robert Peary shipped the largest of the three, which weighed 34 tonnes, to New York in 1897. It is now in the city's Museum of Natural History.

## SHOWERS FROM SPACE

Meteor showers happen when the Earth passes through a swarm of space debris thought to come from comets. As the meteors collide with the Earth's atmosphere, they burn up and disintegrate through friction to produce a spectacular array of shooting stars. Although the sprays seem to radiate from a single point in space, this is an illusion of perspective because the meteors actually travel in parallel paths. The list here gives the names of the major showers, with the dates they appear each year and the constellations from which they seem to radiate.

| Name | Date | Apparent origin |
| --- | --- | --- |
| Quadrantids | 1–6 Jan | Boötes |
| Lyrids | 19–24 Apr | Lyra |
| Eta Aquarids | 1–8 May | Aquarius |
| Perseids | 25 July–18 Aug | Perseus |
| Orionids | 16–26 Oct | Orion |
| Taurids | 20 Oct–30 Nov | Taurus |
| Leonids | mid Nov | Leo |
| Phoenicids | 4–5 Dec | Phoenix |
| Geminids | 7–15 Dec | Gemini |
| Ursids | 17–24 Dec | Ursa Minor |

ROCKS FROM THE SKY *Scientists divide the rocks that bombard the Earth every day into two main, but unrelated, types – meteors and meteorites. Meteors are formed by the trails of debris from comets – most of them are no larger than pinheads – and they do not reach the Earth's surface intact, but as a fine dust. About 100 million of them hurtle into the atmosphere each day at speeds of up to about 70km/sec (45mps). They burn up and disintegrate more than 80km (50 miles) up, producing the streaks of light known as shooting stars (above). Meteorites, some of which do reach the Earth intact, are much larger chunks of debris thought to come from asteroids, whirling rocks which lie in a belt between Mars and Jupiter. Most meteorites burn up in the atmosphere before they can reach the Earth's surface. The largest surviving meteorite, weighing some 60 tonnes, was found near Grootfontein, South Africa, in 1920.*

413

# The limits of space

## DISTANT NEIGHBOURS

The nearest stars to us beyond the Sun are those of the Alpha Centauri system, which are more than four light years away. If it were possible to drive through space at a steady 88km/h (55mph), the legal speed limit for cars in the USA, you could reach the Sun in 193 years. But at the same speed it would take 52 million years to reach Alpha Centauri.

## ASTRONOMICAL ERRORS

Man's concept of the Universe was vastly inaccurate until the 20th century. The size of the Sun, for instance, was grotesquely underestimated. In the 6th century BC, the Greek philosopher Heraclitus estimated the diameter of the Sun at about one-third of a metre (1 ft). In fact it is nearly 1.4 million km (870,000 miles) across.

In about AD 150, the Greek astronomer Ptolemy calculated the distance from the Earth to the Sun at 8 million km (5 million miles). The first reasonably close estimate of the distance was not made until 1672 by the Italian-born French astronomer Giovanni Domenico Cassini (1625 – 1712). The distance is now known to be 149,597,000km (92,959,000 miles) – nearly 20 times greater than Ptolemy thought.

The size of the Universe as a whole did not become clear until the 1920s. Before then, astronomers had thought that the Milky Way encompassed the entire Universe. But in the early 1920s, an American astronomer, Edwin Hubble (1889 – 1953), confirmed for the first time the existence of galaxies beyond our own.

## HIGH-SPEED WORLD

The Earth, like everything else in the Universe, is rushing headlong through space. Every point on the Equator is moving at about 1600km/h (1000mph) as the Earth spins on its own axis; nearer the Poles, the speed is less. On its annual journey round the Sun, the Earth as a whole moves at about 107,000km/h (67,000mph). As our Galaxy – the Milky Way – spins around its own centre, completing one revolution

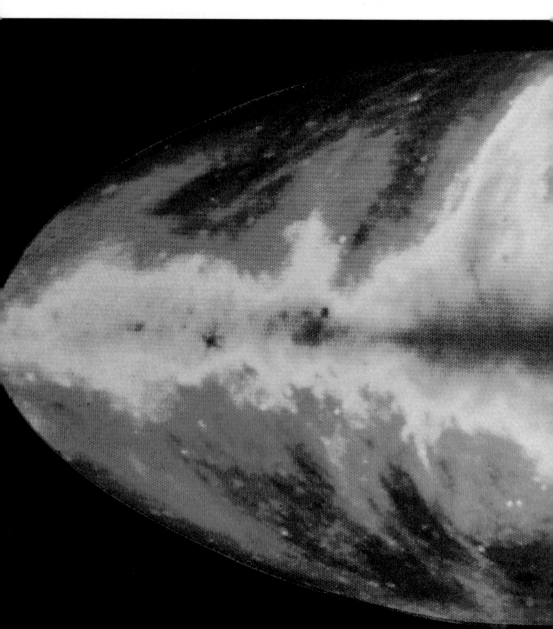

every 230 million years, the whole solar system moves with it, travelling at about 792,000km/h (492,000mph).

Finally, the most distant galaxies are rushing away from our own at speeds close to that of light – which means in turn that, from their point of view, the Milky Way is rushing in the opposite direction at nearly 300,000km (186,000 miles) per second.

## IS ANYBODY THERE?

Since 1974, a radio message to the stars has been racing outwards from Earth at the speed of light. It was broadcast from the Arecibo radio telescope in Puerto Rico, the world's largest single radio astronomy dish. The dish, which is 305m (1000ft) across, is set in a natural hollow between hills and scans the sky overhead as the Earth spins. It is so powerful that it could communicate with an identical twin of itself anywhere in the galaxy. The message, transmitted on November 16, 1974, was beamed towards a cluster of 300,000 stars called M13 in the constellation of Hercules. It consisted of 1679 on-off pulses which can be arranged to form a picture that shows the biochemistry of life on Earth, a figure of a human and a map of the solar system. The number was chosen to avoid ambiguity; 1679 pulses can be formed into a rectangular pattern only as a grid of 23 pulses by 73.

The message was the strongest radio transmission ever to leave the Earth. But even if there are any aliens at home in M13 to answer the interstellar call, the cluster is so far away that no reply will arrive until about the year AD 50,000.

## WEIGHED DOWN

Black holes – the collapsed remnants of giant stars – are so dense that not even light can escape their awesome gravitational pull. If a telephone directory weighing no more than 1kg (2.2lb) were brought to within 6m (20ft) of a black hole, it would weigh a million million tonnes.

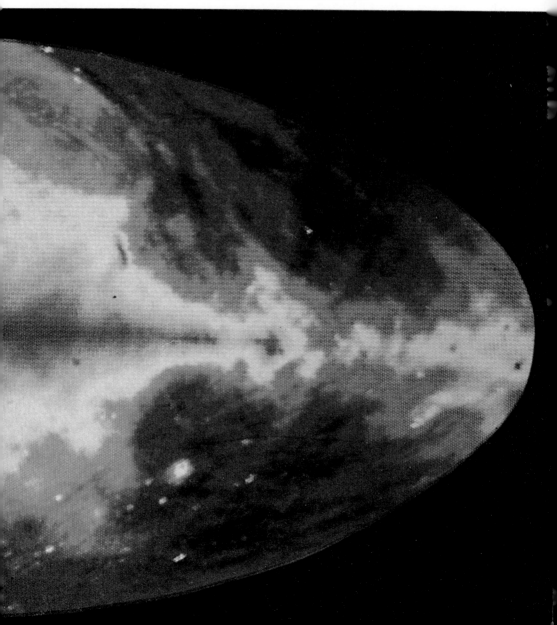

THE SKIES AT NIGHT *Three telescopes, in Britain, West Germany and Australia, worked together for 12 years to produce this radio map of the entire sky – Northern and Southern Hemispheres. Colour-coded so that the brightest areas show up red, fading through yellow, green and blue to black, the map shows how the sky is dominated by the Milky Way, which is seen edge on from Earth. An ordinary observer sees the Milky Way as an evenly powdered band because cosmic dust clouds block much of the light where the stars are thickest. But radio wavelengths cut through the dust so that the Galaxy's heart (in the centre) gleams here with its true brilliance.*

DISTANT HEART *Our Milky Way Galaxy, and the Local Group of galaxies to which it belongs, are just part of what astronomers call the Local Supercluster of galaxies. At the centre of the supercluster and some 50 million light years from Earth is the Virgo Cluster, containing about 1000 galaxies. The galaxy known as M87 (above) is the brightest in the Virgo Cluster. It glitters at the heart of the spinning cluster, making it the core of the whole supercluster. A mysterious jet of radiation streams out from M87's centre some 5000 light years into space. The brightest point on the jet's length (visible to the right of the galaxy's centre) shines with the strength of 40 million Suns.*

## EDUCATING ALBERT

For many years children have taken comfort in the belief that even Albert Einstein (1879–1955) was a failure at school. But the school records of the German-born physicist who devised the theory of relativity show that in fact Einstein was exceptionally gifted. He excelled particularly in physics, mathematics and music.

The misunderstanding may have arisen because during Einstein's last year at school in Aargau, Switzerland, in 1896, the school's system of marking was reversed. Grade 6, which had been the lowest mark, became the highest and Grade 1, which had been the highest, became the lowest. To anyone who did not know of the change, it could have appeared that Einstein's marks had plummeted.

Einstein did fail entrance exams for the Federal Technical Institute in Zurich, but this may have been because of his one area of great weakness: French. It may also have been because he took the exams at the age of 16 – two years younger than normal. Instead Einstein was sent to Aargau and went on to the Zurich institute two years later.

## DEPTH OF VISION

The farthest object clearly visible to the naked eye is a spiral galaxy named M31 in the constellation of Andromeda. On a clear night, it appears as a small hazy patch. The Andromeda galaxy is 2.2 million light years away, which means that the light we now see from it began its journey when man's ape-like ancestors were still roaming the plains of Africa.

## CHEMICAL TWINS

Carbon atoms often link with others in such a way that two molecules can have the same number of atoms and the same structure – and yet be different because the twins are mirror-images of each other. Like a pair of gloves, the twins are not interchangeable, and in living organisms only one of them is likely to be useful.

Amino acids, the building blocks for proteins, mostly occur as one type of these pairs, while their mirror-image molecules are not capable of being used to make protein. No convincing explanation (other than pure chance) has been found of why life on Earth has developed on one side of this twin relationship and not the other.

Scientists have speculated that life elsewhere might be based on similar molecules but with the opposite sets to those on Earth. A visitor from such a planet would starve to death on Earth because he would be unable to digest the proteins in earthly food.

## THE EDGES OF SPACE

Most modern astronomers believe that man may already be able to see nearly as much of the Universe as will ever be possible. The belief rests on a discovery made by the American astronomer Edwin Hubble. In 1929, he found that the more distant a galaxy was from our own, the faster it was moving away. Hubble made his discovery by analysing the light from distant galaxies.

In 1912 a US astronomer, Vesto Slipher (1875–1969), had discovered that this light was shifted towards the red end of the spectrum. Hubble worked out why – that it happened for the same reason that the pitch of a police siren drops as the police car moves away from the hearer. The galaxies were moving away from the Earth. The farther galaxies had more pronounced red shifts than nearer galaxies, and the amount of the shift gave a clue to the speed of the galaxy. The relationship between this speed and the galaxy's distance is known as Hubble's Constant. In its modern form, the constant suggests that for every 1000 million light years between any two galaxies, their relative speed of separation is slightly less than 10 per cent of the speed of light.

If Hubble's Constant holds good to the most extreme distances, there will finally come a point where galaxies are receding from us at the full speed of light. As a result, their light – along with any other radiation they emit – will never reach us and no human observer will ever be able to detect them.

This critical distance for the boundary of the observable Universe – though not necessarily the boundary of the Universe itself – is believed to be about 15,000 million light years from Earth.

## THE FARTHEST GALAXY

The most distant objects known are quasars – named from the phrase 'quasi-stellar radio source'. They are enormously powerful starlike objects, some of which are as bright as 100 galaxies combined. The most distant known quasar was discovered in 1982 by a team of international astronomers working in Aus-tralia. Known as PKS 2000-330, it is racing away from our Galaxy at about 273,000km/sec (170,000mps) – 91 per cent of the speed of light.

Its distance is estimated to be at least 13,000 million light years, putting it close to the boundary of the observable Universe.

In addition, because the quasar's light has taken 13,000 million years to reach Earth, astronomers are seeing what it was like that long ago. And since the Universe itself is thought to be about 15,000 million years old, observations of such distant galaxies enable astronomers to see the Universe as it was soon (in astronomical terms) after its birth.

# REMARKABLE RELATIVITY

The theory of relativity – published in two parts in 1905 and 1915 by the German-born physicist Albert Einstein – rests on a remarkable realisation: that at very high speeds, commonsense assumptions break down.

Commonsense dictates, for example, that two cars travelling towards each other at a relative speed of 200km/h. So they do. But if one of the cars is replaced by a beam of light, the ordinary assumption does not work. No matter how fast the remaining car travels towards or away from the beam, the light will always hit it at exactly the same speed: approximately 300,000km/sec (186,000mps).

**Einstein's starting point**

From this starting point, which had been established by experiment in the 1880s, Einstein came to the realisation that the speed of light was the Universe's only constant, and that size, mass and even time were all relative; measurements of any of them depend on the position and relative speed of the observer.

Einstein also deduced that mass and energy are interchangeable, and related by the equation $E = mc^2$, where $E$ is the energy and $m$ the mass of a particle, and $c$ is the speed of light.

Modern experiments have confirmed the existence of many of the effects predicted by Einstein's theory. In 1972, for instance, sensitive atomic clocks carried on spacecraft and then compared with identical clocks on the ground after the flight were found to have slowed down – meaning that time itself had passed more slowly aboard the spacecraft.

Particle accelerators, used in the study of sub-atomic particles, have to be specially designed to take account of the increased mass of particles boosted to significant proportions of light speed. And $E = mc^2$, which shows that a small amount of mass can be converted into a huge amount of energy; has been put to work in nuclear reactors and atomic bombs.

**How time slows down**

As the speed of any object increases, its properties, as measured by an observer at rest, change. Its mass increases, its length in the direction of travel decreases and time slows down. At ordinary Earth-bound speeds, even those of a jet plane, the changes are infinitesimal.

At very high speeds, however, the changes become extremely important. An astronaut travelling at 90 per cent of the speed of light, for instance, would not feel any different from his twin on Earth. But the mass of his spacecraft would be more than double, its length would be less than half and a clock on board would take an hour to record 26 minutes because time had slowed – and he would therefore be ageing at less than half the speed of his brother.

At the speed of light, the mass of his spacecraft would become infinite, its length would shrink to nothing and time aboard it would slow to a complete stop. Since this is impossible, nothing can travel faster than light.

# INDEX

Page numbers in **bold** type indicate a major treatment of a subject. Page numbers in *italic* indicate that the subject is illustrated.

# D

# N

# O

# P

# S

# PICTURE CREDITS

**FACTS ABOUT PEOPLE**
11 *l* Peter Jones © National Geographic Society; *r* National Museums of Kenya. 15 *c* Hans Hinz, Switzerland; *b* Jean Vertut. 17 *l* Michael Holford; *r* Lee Boltin/Anthony Blake Picture Library. 18 by courtesy of the Trustees of the British Museum. 19 Eric Lessing/Magnum/John Hillelson Agency. 20 Robert Harding Picture Library. 21 both courtesy of the Cultural Relics Bureau, Beijing and The Metropolitan Museum of Art. 22 Michael Holford. 22–23 by courtesy of the Trustees of the British Museum. 24 by permission of the Museum of Folk Culture, Chiba. 25 Rainbird/Robert Harding Picture Library. 26 Michael Holford. 27 The Metropolitan Museum of Art, Rogers Fund, 1912. 28 Ronald Sheridan Photo Library. 29 The Metropolitan Museum of Art, Rogers Fund, 1912. 30 Leonard von Matt. 31 all by courtesy of the Trustees of the British Museum. 32 *t* Michael Holford; *b* The Metropolitan Museum of Art, Gift and Bequest of Alice K. Bache, 1974 and 1977. 33 Museum of the American Indian, Heye Foundation, New York. 34 *t* Museum of the American Indian, Heye Foundation, New York; *bl* National Museum of Anthropology, Mexico City; *br* Kodansha, Japan. 35 all Kodansha, Japan. 36 Leonard von Matt. 37 *c* Mansell Collection; *b* Leonard von Matt. 38 *t* by courtesy of the Trustees of the British Museum; *b* Ashmolean Museum of Art and Archaeology, Oxford. 39 E. T. Archive Ltd. 40 Mary Evans Picture Library. 41 E. T. Archive Ltd. 42 *t* National Army Museum; *c* Mansell Collection; *b* Mary Evans Picture Library. 43 *t* Mary Evans Picture Library; *b* Imperial War Museum. 44 cartoon by Zec © Daily Mirror. 45 *t* E. T. Archive Ltd; *b* Associated Newspaper Group PLC. 46 *l* Michael Holford; *r* Mansell Collection; *b* William MacQuitty International Collection. 47 *t* by courtesy of the Trustees of the Pierpont Morgan Library, New York; *b* by courtesy of the Trustees of the British Museum. 48 *t* Ann Ronan Picture Library; *c* Mansell Collection; *b* Bibliothèque publique et universitaire, Genève. 49 *t* Bancroft Library, University of California; *b* BBC Hulton Picture Library. 50 *t* by courtesy of the Trustees of the British Museum; *b* Eric Lessing/Magnum/John Hillelson Agency. 51 *Michael Freeman.* 52 *t* Mansell Collection; *b* Mary Evans Picture Library. 53 Reader's Digest. 54 *t* Wellcome Institute Library, London; others Ann Ronan Picture Library. 55 NASA. 56 Konrad Helbig/ZEFA. 57 *t* British Tourist Authority; *b* Copyright reserved. Reproduced by gracious permission of Her Majesty the Queen. 58 Michael Holford. 59 Mary Evans Picture Library. 60

Leon Bakst © SPADEM, 1984. 61 *t* National Film Institute, Archive; *b* Zoe Dominic. 63 Museum of London. 64 *l* by courtesy of the Trustees of the Victoria and Albert Museum; *r* Copyright reserved. Reproduced by gracious permission of Her Majesty the Queen. 65 *l* Musées de la Ville, Strasbourg Château des Rohan; *r* Popperfoto; *b* E. T. Archive Ltd. 66 *t* Popperfoto; *b* Michael Holford. 67 *t* Mansell Collection; *b* Mary Evans Picture Library. 68 courtesy, the Henry Francis du Pont Winterthur Museum. 69 Eisenhower Library/Johns Hopkins University, Baltimore. 70 BBC Hulton Picture Library. 71–72 Mansell Collection. 73 both Western Americana Picture Library. 74 Mary Evans Picture Library. 75 *t* to *b* Abilene Reflector Chronicle, New York Herald Tribune, Daily News (New York), all from John Frost Historical Collection. 77 Mansell Collection. 78 Reader's Digest. 79 *t* Mansell Collection. 80 Mansell Collection. 80–81 *l* to *r* Mansell Collection. Mansell Collection. Mary Evans Picture Library. 83 *t* cartoon by Vicki, Associated Newspaper Group PLC; *b* National Portrait Gallery, London. 84 BBC Hulton Picture Library. 86 cartoon by J. W. Bengough. 88 BBC Hulton Picture Library. 89 Popperfoto. 90 Mansell Collection. 93 *l* and *tr* Mary Evans Picture Library; *c* David Jones. 94 *l* to *r* BBC Hulton Picture Library. BBC Hulton Picture Library. Popperfoto. The Photo Source. BBC Hulton Picture Library. BBC Hulton Picture Library. 95 *l* Popperfoto; *r* John Topham Picture Library. 97 Reader's Digest. 98 Mansell Collection. 99 Illustrated London News Picture Library. 100–1 Illustrated London News Picture Library. 101 Mansell Collection. 104–5 *l* by courtesy of the Trustees of the British Museum; others Mansell Collection. 106–9 Michael Holford. 110–11 artist *Andrew Aloof.* 113 Mansell Collection. 114 *bl* Mary Evans Picture Library; others from 'Of Graves and Epitaphs', Kenneth Lindley, Hutchinson, 1965. 116 Michael Holford. 117 The Warburg Institute, University of London. 118 Michael Holford. 119 Photographie Giraudon. 120 Michael Holford. 121–3 Mansell Collection. 124 Michael Holford. 125–8 Mansell Collection. 129 Mary Evans Picture Library. 130 *bl* Mansell Collection; *tr* Mary Evans Picture Library. 131 all Mary Evans Picture Library. 132 E. T. Archive Ltd. 135 BBC Hulton Picture Library. 136 Det Kongelige Bibliotek, Copenhagen. 137 Michael Holford. 139 Mary Evans Picture Library. 140 William MacQuitty International Collection. 140–1 Michael Holford. 143 by courtesy of the Trustees of the British Museum. 144 Mary Evans Picture Library.

**FACTS ABOUT PLACES**
148–9 S. Sassoon/Robert Harding Picture Library. 149 Popperfoto. 150 Media Productions Ltd, Gaborone. 151 *l* L. Nelson/Hutchison Camera Pix; *r* B. Norman/Ronald Sheridan Picture Library. 153 *The* Bridgeman Art Library/Joseph and Earle Vanderkar, London. 155 *l* The Bridgeman Art Library/Victoria and Albert Museum; *r* by courtesy of the Trustees of the British Museum. 157 by courtesy of the Trustees of the British Museum. 158 J. Pate/Hutchison Camera Pix. 159 Hutchison Camera Pix. 161 Michael Holford. 162 Ronald Sheridan Picture Library. 163 by courtesy of the Trustees of the Victoria and Albert Museum. 164 *l* Walters Art Gallery, Baltimore; *r* Ashmolean Museum of Art and Archaeology, Oxford. 165 Werner Forman Archive. 168 Howard Sochurek/John Hillelson Agency. 170 Mary Evans Picture Library. 171–2 BBC Hulton Picture Library. 173 Vivien Fifield. 175 BBC Hulton Picture Library. 177 Vivien Fifield. 182 Mary Evans Picture Library. 183 John Cleare, Mountain Camera. 184–5 D. Goulston/Bruce Coleman Ltd. 185–6 Mary Evans Picture Library. 187 *t* George Rodger/Magnum/John Hillelson Agency; *b* Tony and Marion

Morrison, South American Pictures. 188 Bruno Barbey/Magnum/John Hillelson Agency. 189 Mary Evans Picture Library. 190–1 Georg Gerster/John Hillelson Agency. 191–2 Mary Evans Picture Library. 193 *t* Mary Evans Picture Library; *b* Georg Gerster/John Hillelson Agency. 194 artist *Bob Larkin, Artright Artists.* 194–5 M. Macintyre/Hutchison Camera Pix. 197 Sonia Halliday and Laura Lushington. 199 Eliot Elisofon/Life © Time Inc., 1968. 200–1 Michael Freeman. 202–3 John Cleare, Mountain Camera. 204–5 A. Howarth/Susan Griggs Agency. 207 Franz Lazi, Stuttgart.

**FACTS ABOUT SCIENCE & TECHNOLOGY**
211 Copyright reserved. Reproduced by gracious permission of Her Majesty the Queen. 212–13 all Biophoto Associates. 215 Neils A. Lassen, MD, Bispebierg Hospital, Denmark. 216 both Bibliothèque Nationale, Paris. 217 Mary Evans Picture Library/Sigmund Freud Copyrights. 218 *l* by permission of the Trustees of the Science Museum. Copyright reserved; *r* Wellcome Institute Library, London. 219 Hirmer Fotoarchiv, Munich. 220 *l* to *r* Wellcome Institute Library, London. Federico Arborio Mella, Milan. Reader's Digest. Wellcome Institute Library, London. 221 Mansell Collection. 222 *t* Wellcome Institute Library, London; *b* by permission of the Trustees of the Science Museum. Copyright reserved. 223 *l* to *r* Wellcome Institute Library, London. Photo Deutsches Museum, Munich. Bayer AG. 225 Public Record Office, London. 227 Leonard von Matt. 228 by permission of the Trustees of the Science Museum. 229 *cr* The Metropolitan Museum of Art, Purchase, Mr and Mrs Charles Wrightsman Gift, 1977; *bl Eileen Tweedy,* object Science Museum; *br* by permission of the Trustees of the Science Museum. 233 by permission of the Trustees of the Science Museum. 234 by permission of US Army Signal Corps. 235 *t* by permission of the Trustees of the Science Museum; *b* Imperial War Museum. 237 Public Record Office, London. 239 British Aerospace. 241 *tl* Bodleian Library, Oxford; *tr* George A. Plimpton Collection, Rare Book and Manuscript Library, Columbia University; *cl* The British Library; *cr* and *bl* New York Public Library, Rare Book Division; *br* David Eugene Smith Collection, Rare Book and Manuscript Library, Columbia University. 245 both by permission of the Trustees of the Science Museum 246 Scientific American. 247 *l* Intel Corp. Inc; *r* Paul Brierly. 249 Reader's Digest. 250 *l* British Telecom International; *r Patrick Thurston.* 252 Mansell Collection. 255 artist *Hayward and Martin.* The Photo Source. 257 Nigel Press Ass. Ltd. 259 artists *Gross Thurston.* 260–1 artist *Robert Micklewright.* 263 artists *Edward Williams Arts.* 265 National Maritime Museum. 266–7 artist *Malcolm McGregor.* 268–9 all by permission of the Trustees of the Science Museum. 270–1 artist *Lancelot Jones.* 272 P. Marlow/Sygma/John Hillelson Agency.

**FACTS ABOUT ANIMALS AND PLANTS**
275 Science Photo Library. 279 *r* , 281, 283 *r*, 285 and 287 *r* Reader's Digest, from the Linnean Society. 308–9 artist *Charles Pickard.* 311 W. Williams/Planet Earth Pictures. 313 *tl* E. Lindgren/Ardea, London; *bl* Heather Angel; *r* M. Fogden/OSFPL. 314 both Heather Angel. 315 A. Bannister/NHPA. 317 S. Trevor/Bruce Coleman Ltd. 318–19 J. Foott/Bruce Coleman Ltd.

**FACTS ABOUT THE ARTS & ENTERTAINMENT**
323 A. Woolfitt/Susan Griggs Agency. 326 The Bridgeman Art Library/Mauritshuis. 327 *l* The Bridgeman Art Library/Mauritshuis; *r* The Bridgeman Art Library/Kenwood House. 328 both The Bridgeman Art Library/Private Collection. 329 Tate Gallery, London. 330–1 all Leon Bakst © SPADEM, 1984. 333 Historisches Museum der Stadt Wien (Vienna). 336 Mary Evans

Picture Library. 337 *c* Tate Gallery, London; others National Portrait Gallery, London. 338 *t* to *b* National Portrait Gallery, London. Mary Evans Picture Library. Mary Evans Picture Library. Mary Evans Picture Library. National Portrait Gallery, London. Mary Evans Picture Library. 339 *l* all BBC Hulton Picture Library; *r, t* to *b* National Portrait Gallery, London. Mary Evans Picture Library. Mary Evans Picture Library. 340 *b* Mary Evans Picture Library; others National Portrait Gallery, London. 341 all Mary Evans Picture Library. 342 *l* Niedersächsische Landesbibliothek, Hanover; *c* BBC Hulton Picture Library; *r* The News, Adelaide/John Frost Historical Collection. 343 *t* A. and F. Pears Ltd; *b* Alfred Dunhill Ltd. 344 *tl* National Film Institute Archive; others Kobal Collection. 345 *t* National Film Institute

Archive; *b* RKO Radio USA. 346 both Popperfoto. 347–58 artist *Andrew Aloof.* 361 *Michael Freeman.* 362–3 *l* to *r* Michael Holford. BBC Hulton Picture Library. BBC Hulton Picture Library. Mary Evans Picture Library. Mary Evans Picture Library. The Bridgeman Art Library, British Museum. 364–5 *l* to *r* Michael Holford. The Bridgeman Art Library/Cecil Higgins Art Gallery. The Bridgeman Art Library/Private Collection. Michael Holford. 366 Michael Holford.

**FACTS ABOUT THE EARTH**
370 NASA/Colorific! 371 Geopic/Earth Satellite Corporation. 374–7 Reader's Digest. 379 A. Vergani/Image Bank. 380–1 Science Photo Library. 384 NASA/Science Photo Library. 385 all Professor R. Scorer. 387 J. Allan Cash Photo Library. 389 *l* A. Compost/ Bruce Coleman Ltd; *tr* B. Moser/Hutchison

Camera Pix; *br* G. Morrison/Hutchison Camera Pix. 391 Dr J. Durst/Science Photo Library.

**FACTS ABOUT THE UNIVERSE**
395 Mary Evans Picture Library. 397 Dr J. Dickel/Science Photo Library. 398–9 Dr F. Espanak/Science Photo Library. 401 Novosti Press Agency. 403 *l* Spinelli/Susan Griggs Agency; *r* NASA/Science Photo Library. 404–5 NASA/Woodmansterne. 406 artist *Hayward and Martin.* 406–9 NASA/Science Photo Library. 410 R. Gehrz/Science Photo Library. 411 Dr J. Lorre/Science Photo Library. 412 Daily Telegraph Colour Library/ SF. 413 artist M. Paternostro/Science Photo Library. 414–15 Max Planck Institute for Radio Astronomy/Science Photo Library. 416 S. Gull/Science Photo Library.

# ACKNOWLEDGMENTS

A number of organisations and individuals gave assistance during the preparation of this book, and the publishers would like to thank them.

They include: The Advertising Association, London; Agricultural Research Council; BP Solar Systems, Aylesbury; British Red Cross; The Buddhist Centre, London; Catholic Information Office; Central Electricity Generating Board; Department of Energy, London; Executive Compensation Service, Brussels; Prudence Grice; Institut der deutschen Wirtschaft, Cologne; Institute of Criminology, University of Cape Town, South Africa; Institute of Jewish Affairs; International Advertising Association; London Zoo; Muslim Educational Trust; National Electronics Council; Norwegian Oil Industry Information Bureau; Panama Canal Commission; The Paul Press; Sikh Cultural Society; Starch INRA Hooper, New York; Union des Industries Metallurgiques et Minières, Paris; UN Information Centre, London; World Wildlife Fund.


Numerous embassies, legations, consulates and high commissions also provided help, and the publishers are grateful to them all.


The publishers also acknowledge their indebtedness to the following books and journals, which were consulted for reference:

*Abraham Lincoln: The Prairie Years and the War Years,* Carl Sandburg, Harcourt Brace; *The Achievement of the Airship: A History of the Development of Rigid, Semi-Rigid and Non-Rigid Airships,* Guy Hartcup, David & Charles; *Acupuncture,* Marc Duke, Constable; *Advertising in Britain: A History,* Dr T. R. Nevett, London; *African Occasions,* Leslie Blackwell, Hutchinson; *Airship: The Story of R34 and the First East-West Crossing of the Atlantic by Air,* Patrick Abbott, Adams & Dant; *The Airship: A History,* Basil Collier, Hart-Davis; *Airshipwreck,* Len Deighton &

Arnold Schwartzman, Cape; *Alexander the Great,* Frank Lipsius, Weidenfeld & Nicolson; *All the Best People . . . The Pick of Peterborough,* George Allen & Unwin; *Almost in Confidence,* Arthur Barlow, Juta, Capetown; *America in Legend,* Richard Dorson, Pantheon; *American Folklore,* Richard Dorson, University of Chicago; *The Americans: A Social History of the United States 1587/1914,* J. C. Furnas, Longman;

*Bach,* Eva & Sydney Grew, Dent; *Background to the 'Long Search',* Smart, BBC; *Balzac,* V. S. Pritchett, Chatto, London; *Banda,* Philip Short, Routledge & Kegan Paul; *Beethoven,* Marion M. Scott, Dent; *Before Civilisation,* Colin Renfrew, Jonathan Cape; *The Bible as History: Archaeology Confirms the Book of Books,* Werner Keller, Hodder & Stoughton; *The Big Umbrella: History of the Parachute,* John Lucas, Elm Tree Books; *A Biographical Dictionary of Scientists,* T. I. Williams, Black; *Bumblebees,* D. V. Alford, Davis-Poynter; *Burke's Royal Families of the World,* Hugh Montgomery-Massingberd, Burke's Peerage; *Butterflies and Moths in Britain and Europe,* D. Carter, Pan; *But Who On Earth Was . . . ?,* Eileen Hellicar, David & Charles;

*Chemistry,* L. & P. Pauling, W. H. Freeman & Co.; *The Chemistry of Life,* Steven Rose, Penguin; *China,* Sarah Allan & Cherry Barnett, Cassell; *A Chinese View of China,* John Gittings, BBC; *Christopher Columbus,* Ernle Bradford, Michael Joseph; *The Churches of Rome,* Roloff Beny & Peter Gunn, Weidenfeld & Nicolson; *The City in History,* Lewis Mumford, Secker; *Classic Descriptions of Disease with Biographical Sketches of the Authors,* Ralph H. Major, Charles Thomas; *Companion Guide to the Ile de France,* Ian Dunlop, Collins; *Complete Guide to Windsurfing,* Jeremy Evans, Evans; *Complete Handbook of Poultry Keeping,* S. Banks, Ward Lock; *Computer Appreciation,* T. F. Fry, Butterworth; *The Computer Book,* Peter Laurie, BBC; *Computer Dictionary and Handbook,* ed. Sippl & Sippl, Howard Sams; *Concise Encyclopaedia of Archaeology,* ed. Leonard Cottrell, Hutchinson; *Concise Encyclopaedia of Living Faiths,* ed. R. C. Zaehner, Hutchinson; *Concise Encyclopaedia of The Arts,* T. Rowland-Entwistle & Cooke, Purnell;

*David Livingstone: His Triumph, Decline and Fall,* C. Northcott, Lutterworth Press; *Death on the Road: A Study in Social Violence,* F. Whitlock, Tavistock Publications; *The Decline and Fall of the Roman Empire,* Edward Gibbon, Dent; *Dermatology in Internal Medicine,* S. Shuster, OUP; *The Desert,* J. L. Cloudsley-Thompson, Orbis; *Design of Cities,* Edmund N. Bacon, Thames & Hudson; *The Destruction of the Zulu Kingdom,* Jeff Guy, Longman; *Development of Transportation in*

*Modern England,* W. Jackman, Cass; *Diabetes, Coronary Thrombosis and the Saccharine Disease,* T. L. Cleave, G. D. Campbell & N. S. Painter, Wright; *Dictionary of Antiques,* George Savage, Barrie & Jenkins; *Dictionary of Art and Artists,* P. & L. Murray, Penguin; *A Dictionary of Biographical Quotation,* Justin Wintle & Richard Kenin, Routledge & Kegan Paul; *A Dictionary of Comparative Religions,* ed. S. G. F. Brandon, Weidenfeld & Nicolson;

*Encyclopaedia of Espionage,* Ronald Seth, N.E.L.; *Encyclopaedia of Military History,* Dupuy, Macdonald; *Encyclopaedia of Mountaineering,* Walter Unsworth, Robert Hale; *Encyclopaedia of Myths and Legends of All Nations,* H. S. Robinson & K. Wilson, Kaye & Ward Ltd; *Encyclopaedia of Philosophy,* ed. Paul Edwards, Collier-MacMillan; *The Encyclopaedia of Space Travel and Astronomy,* ed. John Man, Octopus; *Encyclopaedia of the Plant Kingdom,* ed. A. Huxley, Salamander Books; *Encyclopaedia of Religion and Ethics,* ed. J. Hastings, T. & T. Clark; *Encyclopaedia of Southern Africa,* Eric Rosenthal, Warne; *Encyclopaedia of Superstitions,* E. & M. Radford, Arrow; *Encyclopaedia of Witchcraft and Magic,* Venetia Newall, Hamlyn; *Everyman's Scientific Facts and Feats,* Magnus Pike & Patrick Moore, Dent;

*A Field Guide to the Sea Birds of Southern Africa and the World,* J. Tuck & H. Heinzel, Collins; *Field Guide to the Butterflies of Britain and Europe,* L. G. Higgins & N. D. Riley, Collins; *A Field Guide to the Insects of Britain and Europe,* Michael Chinery, Collins; *Field Guide to the Reptiles and Amphibians of Britain and Europe,* E. N. Arnold & J. A. Burton, Collins; *The Fire Came By,* John Baxter & Thomas Atkins, Macdonald; *First Across!,* Richard K. Smith, US Naval Ins. Press; *The First Cities,* Ruth Whitehouse, Phaidon; *The First Emperor of China,* Arthur Cotterell, Macmillan; *First Flight: The Untold Story of the Wright Brothers,* J. E. Walsh, Allen & Unwin; *The First Great Civilisations,* Jacquetta Hawkes, Hutchinson; *Fishes of the World,* Alan Cooper, Hamlyn; *Five Elizabethan Tragedies,* ed. A. K. McIlwraith, Greenwood Press; *Five Hundred Years of Printing,* A. H. Steinberg, Penguin; *Flags and Arms Across the World,* Whitney Smith, Cassell; *Flags of the World,* ed. E. M. C. Barraclough, Warne;

*The Garden of Japan,* Masao Hayakawa, Weatherhill; *The General Armory of England, Scotland, Ireland and Wales,* Sir Bernard Burke, Burke's Peerage; *General Louis Botha,* F. V. Eugelenberg, Harrap; *The Genius of China,* William Watson, Barron's Education Series; *George IV as Prince of Wales,* Christopher Hibbert, Longman; *George Stephenson,* Hunter Davies, Weidenfeld & Nicolson; *Georg Philipp Telemann,* Richard Petzoldt, Benn; *Giants in the Sky,* M. J. H.

431

Taylor & David Mondey, Jane's; *Giving Up the Gun: Japan's Reversion to the Sword, 1543–1879*, Noel Perrin, Shambhala; *The Glory That Was Greece*, J. C. Stobart, Sidgwick & Jackson; *The Golden Bough*, Sir James Frazer, Macmillan; *Gossamer Odyssey*, M. Grosser, Michael Joseph; *The Grandeur That Was Rome*, J. C. Stobart, Sidgwick & Jackson;

*Habits: Why You Do What You Do*, John Nicholson, Pan; *Haiti: Black Peasants and Their Religion*, Alfred Métraux, Harrap; *Halliwell's Filmgoer's Companion*, Granada; *Hall of Fame*, A. P. Cartwright, CNA; *Haydn*, Rosemary Hughes, Dent; *Hear That Lonesome Whistle Blow*, Dee Brown, Chatto & Windus; *Heaven, Hell & Hara Kiri: The Rise and Fall of the Japanese Superstate*, James Kirkup, Ángus & Robertson; *The Helicopter*, H. F. Gregory, Yoseloff; *The Helicopter: History, Piloting and How It Flies*, John Fay, David & Charles; *Helicopters and Autogyros of the World*, Paul Lambermont & Anthony Pirie, Cassell; *Helicopters and Other Rotorcraft Since 1907*, Kenneth Munson, Blandford; *Hell and Hazard; Or William Crockford versus The Gentlemen of England*, Henry Blyth, Weidenfeld; *Henry the Eighth*, Francis Hackett, Cape; *Henry VIII*, J. C. Scarisbrick, Eyre Methuen; *Heritage of Persia*, Richard N. Frye, Weidenfeld; *History of Medicine*, Fielding H. Garrison, W. B. Saunders; *A History of Playing Cards*, Catherine Hargrave, Dover; *A History of Polar Exploration*, David Mountfield, Hamlyn; *A History of Railways in Britain*, Frank Ferneyhough, Osprey; *A History of Scotland*, Plantagenet & Fiona Somerset Fry, Routledge & Kegan Paul; *History of Technology*, ed. Charles Singer, OUP; *History of the Ancient Olympic Games*, Lynn & Gray Poole, Obolensky;

*Ice*, Fred Hoyle, Hutchinson; *I. K. Brunel, A Biography*, L. T. C. Rolt, Penguin; *Illustrated Atlas of the Bible Lands*, T. Rowland-Entwistle, Longman; *Illustrated Atlas of the World's Great Buildings*, ed. P. Bagenal & J. Meades, Salamander Books; *An Illustrated Encyclopaedia of Traditional Symbols*, J. C. Cooper, Thames & Hudson; *The Illustrated History of Seaplanes and Flying Boats*, Louis S. Casey & John Batchelor, Hamlyn; *Illustrating Computers*, Colin Day & Donald Alcock, Pan; *IMM's General Textbook of Entomology*, ed. O. W. Richards & R. G. Davies, Chapman & Hall; *Incendiary Weapons*, S.I.P.R.I., Stockholm; *Indian Asia*, Philip Rawson, Elsevier-Phaidon; *Industrial Biography: Ironworkers and Tool Makers*, Samuel Smiles & John Murray, Kelley; *Infantry Weapons of the World*, Foss & Gander, I. Allan; *In Flanders Fields*, Wolff, Penguin; *Insect Life: The World You Never See*, T. Rowland-Entwistle, Hamlyn; *Insect Life*, Tweedie, Collins;

*Jamaican Song and Story*, Walter Jekyll, Dover; *Jan Smuts*, F. S. Crafford, Doubleday; *Jane's World Railways 1982–3*, ed. G. F. Allen, Jane's Pub. Co.; *Japan*, Pat Barr, Batsford; *Japan, A Travel Survival Kit*, Ian McQueen, Lonely Planet Publications; *Japan Behind the Fan*, James Kirkup, Dent; *Japanese Culture: A Short History*, H. Paul Varley, Faber; *Jerusalem*, Colin Thubron, Time-Life;

*K.G.B.: Secret Work of Soviet Secret Agents*, John Barron, Hodder; *K.G.B.: The Eyes of Russia*, Harry Rositzke, Sidgwick; *King George V*, Harold Nicolson, Constable; *Kings Over the Water: The Saga of the Stuart Pretenders*, Theo Aronson, Cassell; *Kino: History of the Russian and Soviet Film*, Jay Leyda, Allen & Unwin;

*Leader of the Skies*, Michael Donne, Frederick Muller; *Learning*, Sarnoff A. Mednick, Prentice-Hall; *The Legacy of China*, Raymond Dawson, Clarendon Press; *Legends of the World*, ed. Richard Cavendish, Orbis; *Lempriere's Classical Dictionary*, Routledge & Kegan Paul; *Lenten Fare and Food for Fridays*, Constance Cruikshank, Faber; *Lewis and Clark and the Crossing of North America*, David Holloway, Weidenfeld; *Lexicon of Musical Invective: Critical Assaults on Composers since Beethoven's Time*, Nicholas Slonimsky, University of Washington Press; *The Life and Times of George I*, Joyce Marlow, Weidenfeld & Nicolson; *The Life and Times of Henry VIII*, Robert Lacey, Weidenfeld & Nicolson; *The Life and Times of Joe McCarthy*, Thomas C. Reves, Blond & Briggs; *The Life and Times of Tycho Brahe*, John Allyne Gode, Greenwood Press; *Life of Marsupials*, H. Tyndale-Briscoe, E. Arnold; *The Life of*

*Reptiles*, Angus Bellairs, Weidenfeld & Nicolson; *Life on Earth*, David Attenborough, Collins;

*Man, Myth and Magic*, IPC; *Man the Tool-maker*, Kenneth P. Oakley, British Museum; *Marine Mammals*, R. J. Harrison & J. E. King, Hutchinson; *Mathematics and Mathematicians*, P. Dedron & J. Itard, Open UP; *Mathematics in Western Culture*, Morris Kline, Penguin; *The Mating Game*, Robert Burton, Elsevier; *A Matter of Trust: MI5 1945–72*, Nigel West, Weidenfeld; *Maya: The Riddle and Rediscovery of a Lost Civilisation*, Charles Gallenkamp, Penguin; *The Medieval Machine: Industrial Revolution of the Middle Ages*, Jean Gimpel, Futura; *Men of Ideas*, ed. Bryan Magee, BBC; *Mermaids and Mastodons*, Richard Carrington, Chatto; *Meteorites and Their Origins*, G. J. McCall, David & Charles; *Methods in Clinical Pharmacology*, ed. J. B. L. Howell & A. E. Tattersfield, Macmillan; *MI5: British Security Service Operations 1909–45*, Nigel West, Bodley Head; *MI6: British Secret Intelligence Service Operations 1909–45*, Nigel West, Weidenfeld; *Milestones in Medicine*, George Bankoff, Museum; *Mimicry in Plants and Animals*, Wolfgang Wickler, Weidenfeld; *Miracle of Flight*, S. Dalton, S. Low; *Model Girl*, Charles Castle, David & Charles; *Model Soldiers*, Henry Harris, Weidenfeld & Nicolson; *Monarchs in Waiting*, J. P. Walter Curley, Hutchinson; *The Monkey Puzzle: A Family Tree*, John Gribbin & Jeremy Cherfas, Bodley Head;

*National Electronics Review*; National Geographic World Magazine; *Naturalised Animals of the British Isles*, Christopher Lever, Paladin; *Nature, Mother of Invention: Engineering of Plant Life*, F. R. Paturi, Penguin; *The Netherlands in Brief*, Ministry of Foreign Affairs, The Hague; *The New Columbia Encyclopaedia*; *The New English Bible*, CUP; *The New Shell Guide to England*, Michael Joseph; *The New Solar System*, Beatty, O'Leary and Chaikin, CUP; *New York*, Carole Chester, Batsford; *Non-verbal Communication*, ed. R. A. Hinde, CUP; *North-South: A Programme for Survival*, Brandt, Pan Books; *Norway*, Ronald Popperwell, Benn; *No. 10 Downing Street: A House in History*, R. J. Minney, Cassell; *The Nuclear Barons*, Pringle & Spigelman, Michael Joseph;

*The Origin and Diversification of Language*, M. Swadesh, Routledge; *Origin of Japanese Architecture*, Kenze Tange; *The Origin of the Species*, C. Darwin; *Origins*, Richard E. Leakey & Roger Lewin, Macdonald & Jane's; *The Oscar Movies From A to Z*, Roy Pickard, Muller; *Out of the Darkness: Planet Pluto*, Clyde Tombaugh, Lutterworth Press; *Owls: Their Natural and Unnatural History*, Sparks & Soper, David & Charles; *Oxford Book of Invertebrates*, David Nichols & John A. L. Cooke, OUP; *Oxford Book of Literary Anecdotes*, ed. Sutherland, OUP; *Oxford Book of Vertebrates*, Nixon & Whiteley, OUP; *Oxford Classical Dictionary*, ed. Hammond & Scullard, OUP; *Oxford Companion to American Literature*, James D. Hart, OUP;

*Pompeii, Naples and Southern Italy*, Anthony Pereira, Batsford; *The Popes*, Friedrich Gontard, Barrie; *Popular Encyclopaedia of Plants*, V. H. Heywood & S. R. Chant, CUP; *Porcelain Through The Ages*, George Savage, Penguin; *Portugal, A Book of Folk Ways*, Rodney Gallop, Cambridge; *Practical Pilotage*, Jeremy Howard-Williams, Adlard Coles; *Pregnancy*, Gordon Bourne, Cassell; *Prehistoric Animals*, Barry Cox, Hamlyn; *Prehistoric England*, Grahame Clark, Batsford; *The Prime Ministers*, George M. Thomson, Secker & Warburg; *The Prime Ministers*, ed. Herbert Van Thal, Allen & Unwin; *Prime Ministers of Britain From Walpole to Callaghan*, Eileen Hellicar, David & Charles; *Principles of Insect Physiology*, V. B. Wigglesworth, Methuen; *Prodigal Genius – The Life of Nikola Tesla*, John O'Neill, Panther; *Prolegomena to the Study of Greek Religion*, Jane Ellen Harrison, Merlin Press; *Purnell's Encyclopaedia of Sport*, N. Barrett, Purnell Books; *Purnell's Pictorial Encyclopaedia of Nature*, ed. T. Entwistle & Cooke, Purnell; *P. W. Botha 40 Jaar*, Jan J. Van Rooyen, Kaaplandse Nasionale Party Keepstad;

*The Queens of England*, Barbara Softly, David & Charles; *Queen Victoria: Her Life and Times*, Cecil Woodham-Smith, Hamish Hamilton; *Queen Victoria*, Lytton Strachey, Chatto;

*Recent Advances in Endocrinology and Metabolism*, ed. J. L. H. O'Riordan, Churchill Livingstone; *Renaissance Florence*, Gene Brucker, John Wiley; *Reptiles and Amphibians*, John Stidworthy, Macdonald; *Republic of South Africa Parliamentary Debates*, Hansard; *Respiratory Physiology – The Essentials*, J. B. West, Blackwell; *Restless Earth*, Nigel Calder, BBC; *Rise and Fall of the Third Reich*, Shirer, Secker & Warburg; *The Rise of Big Business*, C. Northcote Parkinson, Weidenfeld and Nicolson; *The Rise of Man*, Sampson Low; *The Road to Sarajevo*, Vladimir Dedijer, MacGibbon & Kee; *Rodents: Their Lives and Habits*, P. W. Hanney, David & Charles; *Roger Moore*, Paul Donovan, W. H. Allen; *Roman Art and Architecture*, Sir Mortimer Wheeler, Thames & Hudson;

*Secrets of the Great Pyramid*, Peter Tompkins, Harper; *Semantics: A New Outline*, F. R. Palmer, CUP; *The Shadows Lengthen*, P. Van Der Byl, Timmins; *Shell Book of Firsts*, Patrick Robertson, Michael Joseph; *The Shogun Inheritance*, Michael MacIntyre, Collins; *A Short History of Buddhism*, Dr Edward Conze, Allen & Unwin; *A Short History of China*, Hilda Hookham, Longman; *A Short History of Technology from the Earliest Times to A.D. 1900*, T. K. Derry and Trevor I. Williams, OUP; *A Short Textbook of Clinical Physiology*, P. F. Binnion, Lloyd-Luke; *A Short Textbook of Medical Microbiology*, D. C. Turk & I. A. Porter, Hodder; *Sketches of Great Pianists and Great Violinists*, George T. Ferris, Wm. Reeves; *The Sky is Falling*, Arthur Weingarten, Hodder; *The Skyscraper*, Paul Goldberger, A. Lane; *Smuts*, S. G. Millin, Faber; *Snakes of the World*, John Stidworthy, Hamlyn;

*Tacitus, Annals*; *La Terra In Piazza: An Interpretation of the Palio of Siena*, Alessandro Falassi & Alan Dundes, University of California Press; *Texas, A Bicentennial History*, Joe B. Frantz, Norton; *A Textbook of Clinical Pharmacology*, H. J. Rogers, Hodder & Stoughton; *Textbook of Endocrinology*, ed. R. H. Williams, W. B. Saunders; *Textbook of Medical Physiology*, A. C. Guyton, W. B. Saunders; *Textbook of Surgery*, Frederick Christopher, W. B. Saunders; *The Plants*, F. W. Went, Life Nature Library, Time-Life International; *They Called It Passchendaele*, Lynn Macdonald, Michael Joseph; *This is Japan*, Colin Simpson, Angus; *Thoracic Medicine*, ed. P. Emerson, Butterworths; *A Million and One Nights: A History of the Motion Picture*, Terry Ramsaye, Cass;

*Underwater Medicine*, S. Miles & D. E. MacKay, Adlard Coles Ltd; *Unfinished History of the World*, Hugh Thomas, Hamish Hamilton; *Uniforms and Weapons of the Zulu War*, Christopher Wilkinson-Latham, Batsford; *Union of South Africa Parliamentary Debates*, Hansard; *The United Nations*, Victoria Schofield, Wayland; *The United Nations: First Twenty Five Years*, Edwin Tetlow, Peter Owen; *United States*, ed. S. Birnbaum, Penguin;

*The Vanishing Hitchhiker: American Urban Legends and their Meanings*, Jan H. Brunvand, Norton; *Verdi*, Dynely Hussey, Dent; *Vertebrate Palaeontology*, Alfred Romer, University of Chicago Press; *Victoria R.I.*, Elizabeth Longford, Weidenfeld; *Violin-making, As It Was, And Is*, Edward Heron-Allen, Ward Lock; *Voodoo In Haiti*, Alfred Métraux, Deutsch;

*Webster's New Geographical Dictionary*, Merriam; *Wedgwood Ware*, W. B. Honey, Faber; *West Indian Folk Tales*, Philip Sherlock, OUP; *What World Religions Teach*, E. G. Parrinder, Harrap; *Whitaker's Almanack 1983*, Whitaker; *Who Played Who In The Movies*, Roy Pickard, Muller; *Who Was Who in America 1974–76*, Marquis Who's Who Inc; *Who's Who In The Ancient World*, ed. Betty Radice, Penguin; *Wicked Uncles In Love*, Morris Marples, Michael Joseph; *Wisden Book of First Class Cricket Records*, ed. Frindall, Queen Anne Press; *Wisden Cricketers' Almanack*, Queen Anne Press; *The Witch Figure: Essays In Honour of Katherine M. Briggs*, ed. Venetia Newall, Routledge;

*The Yachtsman's Pocket Almanac*, ed. N. Dent, Mitchell Beazley; *Your Guide to Lebanon*, Nina Nelson, Redman;

*The Zulu War 1879*, Alan Lloyd, Hart-Davis.

TYPESETTING, SPRINT PRODUCTIONS LTD. BECKENHAM; PRINTING, AMBASSADOR PRESS LTD, ST ALBANS;

SEPARATIONS, GRAFASCAN LTD, DUBLIN: PAPER, TOWNSEND HOOK & CO. LTD, SNODLAND; DE FORENEDE PAPIR, DENMARK:

BINDING, HAZELL WATSON AND VINEY LTD, AYLESBURY